Vector Identities

$$\mathbf{A} = A_x\hat{\mathbf{e}}_x + A_y\hat{\mathbf{e}}_y + A_z\hat{\mathbf{e}}_z, \quad A^2 = A_x^2 + A_y^2 + A_z^2, \quad \mathbf{A} \cdot \mathbf{B} = A_xB_x + A_yB_y + A_zB_z$$

$$\mathbf{A} \times \mathbf{B} = \begin{vmatrix} A_y & A_z \\ B_y & B_z \end{vmatrix}\hat{\mathbf{e}}_x + \begin{vmatrix} A_z & A_x \\ B_z & B_x \end{vmatrix}\hat{\mathbf{e}}_y + \begin{vmatrix} A_x & A_y \\ B_x & B_y \end{vmatrix}\hat{\mathbf{e}}_z$$

$$\mathbf{A} \cdot (\mathbf{B} \times \mathbf{C}) = \begin{vmatrix} A_x & A_y & A_z \\ B_x & B_y & B_z \\ C_x & C_y & C_z \end{vmatrix} = A_x\begin{vmatrix} B_y & B_z \\ C_y & C_z \end{vmatrix}\hat{\mathbf{e}}_x + A_y\begin{vmatrix} B_z & B_x \\ C_z & C_x \end{vmatrix}\hat{\mathbf{e}}_y + A_z\begin{vmatrix} B_x & B_y \\ C_x & C_y \end{vmatrix}\hat{\mathbf{e}}_z$$

$$\mathbf{A} \times (\mathbf{B} \times \mathbf{C}) = \mathbf{B}(\mathbf{A} \cdot \mathbf{C}) - \mathbf{C}(\mathbf{A} \cdot \mathbf{B}), \qquad \sum_k \varepsilon_{ijk}\varepsilon_{pqk} = \delta_{ip}\delta_{jq} - \delta_{iq}\delta_{jp}$$

Vector Calculus

$$\mathbf{F} = -\boldsymbol{\nabla}V(r) = -\frac{\mathbf{r}}{r}\frac{dV}{dr} = -\hat{\mathbf{r}}\frac{dV}{dr}, \qquad \boldsymbol{\nabla} \cdot [\mathbf{r}f(r)] = 3f(r) + r\frac{df}{dr},$$

$$\boldsymbol{\nabla} \cdot (r^n\hat{\mathbf{r}}) = (n+2)r^{n-1}$$

$$\boldsymbol{\nabla}(\mathbf{A} \cdot \mathbf{B}) = (\mathbf{A} \cdot \boldsymbol{\nabla})\mathbf{B} + (\mathbf{B} \cdot \boldsymbol{\nabla})\mathbf{A} + \mathbf{A} \times (\boldsymbol{\nabla} \times \mathbf{B}) + \mathbf{B} \times (\boldsymbol{\nabla} \times \mathbf{A})$$

$$\boldsymbol{\nabla} \cdot (S\mathbf{A}) = \boldsymbol{\nabla}S \cdot \mathbf{A} + S\boldsymbol{\nabla} \cdot \mathbf{A}, \qquad \boldsymbol{\nabla} \times (S\mathbf{A}) = \boldsymbol{\nabla}S \times \mathbf{A} + S\boldsymbol{\nabla} \times \mathbf{A}$$

$$\boldsymbol{\nabla} \cdot (\mathbf{A} \times \mathbf{B}) = \mathbf{B} \cdot (\boldsymbol{\nabla} \times \mathbf{A}) - \mathbf{A} \cdot (\boldsymbol{\nabla} \times \mathbf{B})$$

$$\boldsymbol{\nabla} \times (\mathbf{A} \times \mathbf{B}) = \mathbf{A}\boldsymbol{\nabla} \cdot \mathbf{B} - \mathbf{B}\boldsymbol{\nabla} \cdot \mathbf{A} + (\mathbf{B} \cdot \boldsymbol{\nabla})\mathbf{A} - (\mathbf{A} \cdot \boldsymbol{\nabla})\mathbf{B},$$

$$\boldsymbol{\nabla} \cdot (\boldsymbol{\nabla} \times \mathbf{A}) = 0, \quad \boldsymbol{\nabla} \times \boldsymbol{\nabla}S = 0, \quad \boldsymbol{\nabla} \times \mathbf{r} = 0, \quad \boldsymbol{\nabla} \times [\mathbf{r}f(r)] = 0$$

$$\nabla^2 \frac{1}{r} = -4\pi\,\delta(\mathbf{r}), \qquad \boldsymbol{\nabla} \times (\boldsymbol{\nabla} \times \mathbf{A}) = \boldsymbol{\nabla}(\boldsymbol{\nabla} \cdot \mathbf{A}) - \nabla^2\mathbf{A}$$

$$\int_V \boldsymbol{\nabla} \cdot \mathbf{B}\, d^3r = \int_S \mathbf{B} \cdot d\boldsymbol{\sigma}, \quad \text{(Gauss)}$$

$$\int_S (\boldsymbol{\nabla} \times \mathbf{A}) \cdot d\boldsymbol{\sigma} = \oint \mathbf{A} \cdot d\mathbf{r}, \quad \text{(Stokes)}$$

$$\int_V (\varphi\nabla^2\psi - \psi\nabla^2\varphi)d^3r = \int_S (\varphi\boldsymbol{\nabla}\psi - \psi\boldsymbol{\nabla}\varphi) \cdot d\boldsymbol{\sigma}, \quad \text{(Green)}$$

$$\delta(ax) = \frac{1}{|a|}\,\delta(x), \quad \delta(f(x)) = \sum_{\substack{i,f(x_i)=0 \\ f'(x_i)\neq 0}} \frac{\delta(x-x_i)}{|f'(x_i)|},$$

$$\delta(t-x) = \frac{1}{2\pi}\int_{-\infty}^{\infty} e^{i\omega(t-x)}d\omega = \sum_{n=0}^{\infty} \varphi_n^*(t)\varphi_n(x)$$

D1447907

General Orthogonal Coordinates

Cartesian Coordinates

$q_1 = x$, $\quad q_2 = y$, $\quad q_3 = z$; $\quad h_1 = h_2 = h_3 = 1$, $\quad \mathbf{r} = x\,\hat{\mathbf{x}} + y\,\hat{\mathbf{y}} + z\,\hat{\mathbf{z}}$

Cylindrical Coordinates

$q_1 = \rho$, $\quad q_2 = \varphi$, $\quad q_3 = z$; $\quad h_1 = h_\rho = 1$, $\quad h_2 = h_\varphi = \rho$, $\quad h_3 = h_z = 1$,

$\mathbf{r} = \rho \cos\varphi\,\hat{\mathbf{x}} + \rho \sin\varphi\,\hat{\mathbf{y}} + z\,\hat{\mathbf{z}}$

Spherical Polar Coordinates

$q_1 = r$, $\quad q_2 = \theta$, $\quad q_3 = \varphi$; $\quad h_1 = h_r = 1$, $\quad h_2 = h_\theta = r$, $\quad h_3 = h_\varphi = r \sin\theta$,

$\mathbf{r} = r \sin\theta \cos\varphi\,\hat{\mathbf{x}} + r \sin\theta \sin\varphi\,\hat{\mathbf{y}} + r \cos\theta\,\hat{\mathbf{z}}$

$$d\mathbf{r} = \sum_i h_i dq_i\,\hat{\mathbf{q}}_i\,, \qquad \mathbf{A} = \sum_i A_i\,\hat{\mathbf{q}}_i\,, \qquad \mathbf{A}\cdot\mathbf{B} = \sum_i A_i B_i\,, \qquad \mathbf{A}\times\mathbf{B} = \begin{vmatrix} \hat{\mathbf{q}}_1 & \hat{\mathbf{q}}_2 & \hat{\mathbf{q}}_3 \\ A_1 & A_2 & A_3 \\ B_1 & B_2 & B_3 \end{vmatrix}$$

$$\int_V f\,d^3r = f(q_1, q_2, q_3) h_1 h_2 h_3\,dq_1 dq_2 dq_3\,, \qquad \int_L \mathbf{F}\cdot d\mathbf{r} = \sum_i \int_i F_i h_i\,dq_i\,,$$

$$\int_S \mathbf{B}\cdot d\boldsymbol{\sigma} = \int B_1 h_2 h_3\,dq_2 dq_3 + \int B_2 h_3 h_1\,dq_3 dq_1 + \int B_3 h_1 h_2\,dq_1 dq_2\,,$$

$$\boldsymbol{\nabla} V = \sum_i \frac{1}{h_i} \frac{\partial V}{\partial q_i}\,\hat{\mathbf{q}}_i$$

$$\boldsymbol{\nabla}\cdot\mathbf{F} = \frac{1}{h_1 h_2 h_3} \left[\frac{\partial}{\partial q_1}(F_1 h_2 h_3) + \frac{\partial}{\partial q_2}(F_2 h_3 h_1) + \frac{\partial}{\partial q_3}(F_3 h_1 h_2) \right]$$

$$\boldsymbol{\nabla}^2 V = \frac{1}{h_1 h_2 h_3} \left[\frac{\partial}{\partial q_1}\left(\frac{h_2 h_3}{h_1} \frac{\partial V}{\partial q_1} \right) + \frac{\partial}{\partial q_2}\left(\frac{h_3 h_1}{h_2} \frac{\partial V}{\partial q_2} \right) + \frac{\partial}{\partial q_3}\left(\frac{h_1 h_2}{h_3} \frac{\partial V}{\partial q_3} \right) \right]$$

$$\boldsymbol{\nabla}\times\mathbf{F} = \frac{1}{h_1 h_2 h_3} \begin{vmatrix} h_1\,\hat{\mathbf{q}}_1 & h_2\,\hat{\mathbf{q}}_2 & h_3\,\hat{\mathbf{q}}_3 \\ \partial/\partial q_1 & \partial/\partial q_2 & \partial/\partial q_3 \\ h_1 F_1 & h_2 F_2 & h_3 F_3 \end{vmatrix}$$

Euler-Mascheroni Constant

$$\gamma = \lim_{n\to\infty} \left[1 + \frac{1}{2} + \frac{1}{3} + \cdots + \frac{1}{n} - \ln(n+1) \right] = 0.57721\ 56649\ 01533$$

Bernoulli Numbers

$$B_0 = 1, \quad B_1 = -\frac{1}{2}, \quad B_2 = \frac{1}{6}, \quad B_4 = -\frac{1}{30}, \quad B_6 = \frac{1}{42}, \quad B_8 = -\frac{1}{30}, \quad \cdots$$

MATHEMATICAL METHODS FOR PHYSICISTS

SEVENTH EDITION

MATHEMATICAL METHODS FOR PHYSICISTS

A Comprehensive Guide

SEVENTH EDITION

George B. Arfken
Miami University
Oxford, OH

Hans J. Weber
University of Virginia
Charlottesville, VA

Frank E. Harris
University of Utah, Salt Lake City, UT
and
University of Florida, Gainesville, FL

AMSTERDAM • BOSTON • HEIDELBERG • LONDON
NEW DELHI • NEW YORK • OXFORD • PARIS • SAN DIEGO
SAN FRANCISCO • SINGAPORE • SYDNEY • TOKYO
Academic Press is an imprint of Elsevier

ELSEVIER

ELSEVIER

RELX India Pvt. Ltd.
Registered Office: 818, Indraprakash Building, 8th Floor, 21, Barakhamba Road, New Delhi-110001
Corporate Office: 14th Floor, Building No. 10B, DLF Cyber City, Phase II, Gurgaon-122 002, Haryana, India

Mathematical Methods for Physicists, 7/e, George B. Arfken, Hans J. Weber and Frank E. Harris

Copyright © 2013 Elsevier Inc.

All rights reserved, including those for text and data mining, AI training, and similar technologies.

ISBN: 978-0-12-384654-9

This reprint of Mathematical Methods for Physicists, 7/e by George B. Arfken, Hans J. Weber and Frank E. Harris was undertaken by RELX India Private Limited and is published by arrangement with Elsevier Inc.

Copyright © 2024 by RELX India Private Limited.

Indian Reprint ISBN: 978-93-81269-55-8

First Printed in India 2005
Reprinted 2011, 2012 (thrice), 2013, 2015, 2016 (twice), 2017 (four times), 2018, 2021, 2022, 2024

All rights reserved. No part of this publication may be reproduced or transmitted in any form or by any means, electronic or mechanical, including photocopying, recording, or any information storage and retrieval system, without permission in writing from the publisher. Details on how to seek permission, further information about the Publisher's permissions policies and our arrangements with organizations such as the Copyright Clearance Center and the Copyright Licensing Agency, can be found at our website: www.elsevier.com/permissions.

This book and the individual contributions contained in it are protected under copyright by the Publisher (other than as may be noted herein).

Notice

Practitioners and researchers must always rely on their own experience and knowledge in evaluating and using any information, methods, compounds or experiments described herein. Because of rapid advances in the medical sciences, in particular, independent verification of diagnoses and drug dosages should be made. To the fullest extent of the law, no responsibility is assumed by Elsevier, authors, editors or contributors in relation to the adaptation or for any injury and/or damage to persons or property as a matter of products liability, negligence or otherwise, or from any use or operation of any methods, products, instructions, or ideas contained in the material herein.

This publication is licensed for sale in India, Bangladesh, Bhutan, Maldives, Nepal, Pakistan and Sri Lanka only. Circulation of this version outside these territories is unauthorized and illegal.

Printed in India by Rajkamal Electric Press, Kundli, Haryana.

CONTENTS

Preface   **xi**

1 Mathematical Preliminaries   **1**
   1.1   *Infinite Series* 1
   1.2   *Series of Functions* 21
   1.3   *Binomial Theorem* 33
   1.4   *Mathematical Induction* 40
   1.5   *Operations on Series Expansions of Functions* 41
   1.6   *Some Important Series* 45
   1.7   *Vectors* 46
   1.8   *Complex Numbers and Functions* 53
   1.9   *Derivatives and Extrema* 62
   1.10   *Evaluation of Integrals* 65
   1.11   *Dirac Delta Function* 75
        Additional Readings 82

2 Determinants and Matrices   **83**
   2.1   *Determinants* 83
   2.2   *Matrices* 95
        Additional Readings 121

3 Vector Analysis   **123**
   3.1   *Review of Basic Properties* 124
   3.2   *Vectors in 3-D Space* 126
   3.3   *Coordinate Transformations* 133

	3.4	*Rotations in $\mathbb{R}^3$*	139
	3.5	*Differential Vector Operators*	143
	3.6	*Differential Vector Operators: Further Properties*	153
	3.7	*Vector Integration*	159
	3.8	*Integral Theorems*	164
	3.9	*Potential Theory*	170
	3.10	*Curvilinear Coordinates*	182
		Additional Readings	203
4		**Tensors and Differential Forms**	**205**
	4.1	*Tensor Analysis*	205
	4.2	*Pseudotensors, Dual Tensors*	215
	4.3	*Tensors in General Coordinates*	218
	4.4	*Jacobians*	227
	4.5	*Differential Forms*	232
	4.6	*Differentiating Forms*	238
	4.7	*Integrating Forms*	243
		Additional Readings	249
5		**Vector Spaces**	**251**
	5.1	*Vectors in Function Spaces*	251
	5.2	*Gram-Schmidt Orthogonalization*	269
	5.3	*Operators*	275
	5.4	*Self-Adjoint Operators*	283
	5.5	*Unitary Operators*	287
	5.6	*Transformations of Operators*	292
	5.7	*Invariants*	294
	5.8	*Summary—Vector Space Notation*	296
		Additional Readings	297
6		**Eigenvalue Problems**	**299**
	6.1	*Eigenvalue Equations*	299
	6.2	*Matrix Eigenvalue Problems*	301
	6.3	*Hermitian Eigenvalue Problems*	310
	6.4	*Hermitian Matrix Diagonalization*	311
	6.5	*Normal Matrices*	319
		Additional Readings	328
7		**Ordinary Differential Equations**	**329**
	7.1	*Introduction*	329
	7.2	*First-Order Equations*	331
	7.3	*ODEs with Constant Coefficients*	342
	7.4	*Second-Order Linear ODEs*	343
	7.5	*Series Solutions—Frobenius' Method*	346
	7.6	*Other Solutions*	358

7.7   *Inhomogeneous Linear ODEs* 375
7.8   *Nonlinear Differential Equations* 377
    Additional Readings 380

8   Sturm-Liouville Theory   **381**
8.1   *Introduction* 381
8.2   *Hermitian Operators* 384
8.3   *ODE Eigenvalue Problems* 389
8.4   *Variation Method* 395
8.5   *Summary, Eigenvalue Problems* 398
    Additional Readings 399

9   Partial Differential Equations   **401**
9.1   *Introduction* 401
9.2   *First-Order Equations* 403
9.3   *Second-Order Equations* 409
9.4   *Separation of Variables* 414
9.5   *Laplace and Poisson Equations* 433
9.6   *Wave Equation* 435
9.7   *Heat-Flow, or Diffusion PDE* 437
9.8   *Summary* 444
    Additional Readings 445

10 Green's Functions   **447**
10.1 *One-Dimensional Problems* 448
10.2 *Problems in Two and Three Dimensions* 459
    Additional Readings 467

11 Complex Variable Theory   **469**
11.1 *Complex Variables and Functions* 470
11.2 *Cauchy-Riemann Conditions* 471
11.3 *Cauchy's Integral Theorem* 477
11.4 *Cauchy's Integral Formula* 486
11.5 *Laurent Expansion* 492
11.6 *Singularities* 497
11.7 *Calculus of Residues* 509
11.8 *Evaluation of Definite Integrals* 522
11.9 *Evaluation of Sums* 544
11.10 *Miscellaneous Topics* 547
    Additional Readings 550

12 Further Topics in Analysis   **551**
12.1 *Orthogonal Polynomials* 551
12.2 *Bernoulli Numbers* 560
12.3 *Euler-Maclaurin Integration Formula* 567

12.4	*Dirichlet Series*	571
12.5	*Infinite Products*	574
12.6	*Asymptotic Series*	577
12.7	*Method of Steepest Descents*	585
12.8	*Dispersion Relations*	591
	Additional Readings	598

13 Gamma Function   **599**
13.1	*Definitions, Properties*	599
13.2	*Digamma and Polygamma Functions*	610
13.3	*The Beta Function*	617
13.4	*Stirling's Series*	622
13.5	*Riemann Zeta Function*	626
13.6	*Other Related Functions*	633
	Additional Readings	641

14 Bessel Functions   **643**
14.1	*Bessel Functions of the First Kind, $J_\nu(x)$*	643
14.2	*Orthogonality*	661
14.3	*Neumann Functions, Bessel Functions of the Second Kind*	667
14.4	*Hankel Functions*	674
14.5	*Modified Bessel Functions, $I_\nu(x)$ and $K_\nu(x)$*	680
14.6	*Asymptotic Expansions*	688
14.7	*Spherical Bessel Functions*	698
	Additional Readings	713

15 Legendre Functions   **715**
15.1	*Legendre Polynomials*	716
15.2	*Orthogonality*	724
15.3	*Physical Interpretation of Generating Function*	736
15.4	*Associated Legendre Equation*	741
15.5	*Spherical Harmonics*	756
15.6	*Legendre Functions of the Second Kind*	766
	Additional Readings	771

16 Angular Momentum   **773**
16.1	*Angular Momentum Operators*	774
16.2	*Angular Momentum Coupling*	784
16.3	*Spherical Tensors*	796
16.4	*Vector Spherical Harmonics*	809
	Additional Readings	814

17 Group Theory   **815**
17.1	*Introduction to Group Theory*	815
17.2	*Representation of Groups*	821
17.3	*Symmetry and Physics*	826

17.4   *Discrete Groups*   830
17.5   *Direct Products*   837
17.6   *Symmetric Group*   840
17.7   *Continuous Groups*   845
17.8   *Lorentz Group*   862
17.9   *Lorentz Covariance of Maxwell's Equations*   866
17.10   *Space Groups*   869
        Additional Readings   870

18 More Special Functions   **871**
18.1   *Hermite Functions*   871
18.2   *Applications of Hermite Functions*   878
18.3   *Laguerre Functions*   889
18.4   *Chebyshev Polynomials*   899
18.5   *Hypergeometric Functions*   911
18.6   *Confluent Hypergeometric Functions*   917
18.7   *Dilogarithm*   923
18.8   *Elliptic Integrals*   927
        Additional Readings   932

19 Fourier Series   **935**
19.1   *General Properties*   935
19.2   *Applications of Fourier Series*   949
19.3   *Gibbs Phenomenon*   957
        Additional Readings   962

20 Integral Transforms   **963**
20.1   *Introduction*   963
20.2   *Fourier Transform*   966
20.3   *Properties of Fourier Transforms*   980
20.4   *Fourier Convolution Theorem*   985
20.5   *Signal-Processing Applications*   997
20.6   *Discrete Fourier Transform*   1002
20.7   *Laplace Transforms*   1008
20.8   *Properties of Laplace Transforms*   1016
20.9   *Laplace Convolution Theorem*   1034
20.10   *Inverse Laplace Transform*   1038
        Additional Readings   1045

21 Integral Equations   **1047**
21.1   *Introduction*   1047
21.2   *Some Special Methods*   1053
21.3   *Neumann Series*   1064
21.4   *Hilbert-Schmidt Theory*   1069
        Additional Readings   1079

22 Calculus of Variations   **1081**

22.1   *Euler Equation* 1081

22.2   *More General Variations* 1096

22.3   *Constrained Minima/Maxima* 1107

22.4   *Variation with Constraints* 1111

       Additional Readings 1124

23 Probability and Statistics   **1125**

23.1   *Probability: Definitions, Simple Properties* 1126

23.2   *Random Variables* 1134

23.3   *Binomial Distribution* 1148

23.4   *Poisson Distribution* 1151

23.5   *Gauss' Normal Distribution* 1155

23.6   *Transformations of Random Variables* 1159

23.7   *Statistics* 1165

       Additional Readings 1179

Index   **1181**

PREFACE

This, the seventh edition of *Mathematical Methods for Physicists*, maintains the tradition set by the six previous editions and continues to have as its objective the presentation of all the mathematical methods that aspiring scientists and engineers are likely to encounter as students and beginning researchers. While the organization of this edition differs in some respects from that of its predecessors, the presentation style remains the same: Proofs are sketched for almost all the mathematical relations introduced in the book, and they are accompanied by examples that illustrate how the mathematics applies to real-world physics problems. Large numbers of exercises provide opportunities for the student to develop skill in the use of the mathematical concepts and also show a wide variety of contexts in which the mathematics is of practical use in physics.

As in the previous editions, the mathematical proofs are not what a mathematician would consider rigorous, but they nevertheless convey the essence of the ideas involved, and also provide some understanding of the conditions and limitations associated with the relationships under study. No attempt has been made to maximize generality or minimize the conditions necessary to establish the mathematical formulas, but in general the reader is warned of limitations that are likely to be relevant to use of the mathematics in physics contexts.

TO THE STUDENT

The mathematics presented in this book is of no use if it cannot be applied with some skill, and the development of that skill cannot be acquired passively, e.g., by simply reading the text and understanding what is written, or even by listening attentively to presentations by your instructor. Your passive understanding needs to be supplemented by experience in using the concepts, in deciding how to convert expressions into useful forms, and in developing strategies for solving problems. A considerable body of background knowledge needs to be built up so as to have relevant mathematical tools at hand and to gain experience in their use. This can only happen through the solving of problems, and it is for this reason that the text includes nearly 1400 exercises, many with answers (but not methods of solution). If you are using this book for self-study, or if your instructor does not assign a considerable number of problems, you would be well advised to work on the exercises until you are able to solve a reasonable fraction of them.

This book can help you to learn about mathematical methods that are important in physics, as well as serve as a reference throughout and beyond your time as a student. It has been updated to make it relevant for many years to come.

WHAT'S NEW

This seventh edition is a substantial and detailed revision of its predecessor; every word of the text has been examined and its appropriacy and that of its placement has been considered. The main features of the revision are: (1) An improved order of topics so as to reduce the need to use concepts before they have been presented and discussed. (2) An introductory chapter containing material that well-prepared students might be presumed to know and which will be relied on (without much comment) in later chapters, thereby reducing redundancy in the text; this organizational feature also permits students with weaker backgrounds to get themselves ready for the rest of the book. (3) A strengthened presentation of topics whose importance and relevance has increased in recent years; in this category are the chapters on vector spaces, Green's functions, and angular momentum, and the inclusion of the dilogarithm among the special functions treated. (4) More detailed discussion of complex integration to enable the development of increased skill in using this extremely important tool. (5) Improvement in the correlation of exercises with the exposition in the text, and the addition of 271 new exercises where they were deemed needed. (6) Addition of a few steps to derivations that students found difficult to follow. We do not subscribe to the precept that "advanced" means "compressed" or "difficult." Wherever the need has been recognized, material has been rewritten to enhance clarity and ease of understanding.

In order to accommodate new and expanded features, it was necessary to remove or reduce in emphasis some topics with significant constituencies. For the most part, the material thereby deleted remains available to instructors and their students by virtue of its inclusion in the on-line supplementary material for this text. On-line only are chapters on Mathieu functions, on nonlinear methods and chaos, and a new chapter on periodic systems. These are complete and newly revised chapters, with examples and exercises, and are fully ready for use by students and their instuctors. Because there seems to be a significant population of instructors who wish to use material on infinite series in much the same organizational pattern as in the sixth edition, that material (largely the same as in the print edition, but not all in one place) has been collected into an on-line infinite series chapter that provides this material in a single unit. The on-line material can be accessed at www.elsevierdirect.com.

PATHWAYS THROUGH THE MATERIAL

This book contains more material than an instructor can expect to cover, even in a two-semester course. The material not used for instruction remains available for reference purposes or when needed for specific projects. For use with less fully prepared students, a typical semester course might use Chapters 1 to 3, maybe part of Chapter 4, certainly Chapters 5 to 7, and at least part of Chapter 11. A standard graduate one-semester course might have the material in Chapters 1 to 3 as prerequisite, would cover at least part of Chapter 4, all of Chapters 5 through 9, Chapter 11, and as much of Chapters 12 through 16 and/or 18 as time permits. A full-year course at the graduate level might supplement the foregoing with several additional chapters, almost certainly including Chapter 20 (and Chapter 19 if not already familiar to the students), with the actual choice dependent on the institution's overall graduate curriculum. Once Chapters 1 to 3, 5 to 9, and 11 have been covered or their contents are known to the students, most selections from the remaining chapters should be reasonably accessible to students. It would be wise, however, to include Chapters 15 and 16 if Chapter 17 is selected.

ACKNOWLEDGMENTS

This seventh edition has benefited from the advice and help of many people; valuable advice was provided both by anonymous reviewers and from interaction with students at the University of Utah. At Elsevier, we received substantial assistance from our Acquisitions Editor Patricia Osborn and from Editorial Project Manager Kathryn Morrissey; production was overseen skillfully by Publishing Services Manager Jeff Freeland. FEH gratefully acknowledges the support and encouragement of his friend and partner Sharon Carlson. Without her, he might not have had the energy and sense of purpose needed to help bring this project to a timely fruition.

CHAPTER 1

MATHEMATICAL PRELIMINARIES

This introductory chapter surveys a number of mathematical techniques that are needed throughout the book. Some of the topics (e.g., complex variables) are treated in more detail in later chapters, and the short survey of special functions in this chapter is supplemented by extensive later discussion of those of particular importance in physics (e.g., Bessel functions). A later chapter on miscellaneous mathematical topics deals with material requiring more background than is assumed at this point. The reader may note that the Additional Readings at the end of this chapter include a number of general references on mathematical methods, some of which are more advanced or comprehensive than the material to be found in this book.

1.1 INFINITE SERIES

Perhaps the most widely used technique in the physicist's toolbox is the use of **infinite series** (i.e., sums consisting formally of an infinite number of terms) to represent functions, to bring them to forms facilitating further analysis, or even as a prelude to numerical evaluation. The acquisition of skill in creating and manipulating series expansions is therefore an absolutely essential part of the training of one who seeks competence in the mathematical methods of physics, and it is therefore the first topic in this text. An important part of this skill set is the ability to recognize the functions represented by commonly encountered expansions, and it is also of importance to understand issues related to the convergence of infinite series.

1

Fundamental Concepts

The usual way of assigning a meaning to the sum of an infinite number of terms is by introducing the notion of partial sums. If we have an infinite sequence of terms $u_1, u_2, u_3, u_4, u_5, \ldots$, we define the ith partial sum as

$$s_i = \sum_{n=1}^{i} u_n. \tag{1.1}$$

This is a finite summation and offers no difficulties. If the partial sums s_i converge to a finite limit as $i \to \infty$,

$$\lim_{i \to \infty} s_i = S, \tag{1.2}$$

the infinite series $\sum_{n=1}^{\infty} u_n$ is said to be **convergent** and to have the value S. Note that we **define** the infinite series as equal to S and that a necessary condition for convergence to a limit is that $\lim_{n \to \infty} u_n = 0$. This condition, however, is not sufficient to guarantee convergence.

Sometimes it is convenient to apply the condition in Eq. (1.2) in a form called the **Cauchy criterion**, namely that for each $\varepsilon > 0$ there is a fixed number N such that $|s_j - s_i| < \varepsilon$ for all i and j greater than N. This means that the partial sums must cluster together as we move far out in the sequence.

Some series **diverge**, meaning that the sequence of partial sums approaches $\pm\infty$; others may have partial sums that oscillate between two values, as for example,

$$\sum_{n=1}^{\infty} u_n = 1 - 1 + 1 - 1 + 1 - \cdots - (-1)^n + \cdots.$$

This series does not converge to a limit, and can be called **oscillatory**. Often the term *divergent* is extended to include oscillatory series as well. It is important to be able to determine whether, or under what conditions, a series we would like to use is convergent.

Example 1.1.1   THE GEOMETRIC SERIES

The geometric series, starting with $u_0 = 1$ and with a ratio of successive terms $r = u_{n+1}/u_n$, has the form

$$1 + r + r^2 + r^3 + \cdots + r^{n-1} + \cdots.$$

Its nth partial sum s_n (that of the first n terms) is[1]

$$s_n = \frac{1 - r^n}{1 - r}. \tag{1.3}$$

Restricting attention to $|r| < 1$, so that for large n, r^n approaches zero, and s_n possesses the limit

$$\lim_{n \to \infty} s_n = \frac{1}{1 - r}, \tag{1.4}$$

---

[1] Multiply and divide $s_n = \sum_{m=0}^{n-1} r^m$ by $1 - r$.

showing that for $|r| < 1$, the geometric series converges. It clearly diverges (or is oscillatory) for $|r| \geq 1$, as the individual terms do not then approach zero at large n. ∎

Example 1.1.2   THE HARMONIC SERIES

As a second and more involved example, we consider the harmonic series

$$\sum_{n=1}^{\infty} \frac{1}{n} = 1 + \frac{1}{2} + \frac{1}{3} + \frac{1}{4} + \cdots + \frac{1}{n} + \cdots . \qquad (1.5)$$

The terms approach zero for large n, i.e., $\lim_{n\to\infty} 1/n = 0$, but this is not sufficient to guarantee convergence. If we group the terms (without changing their order) as

$$1 + \frac{1}{2} + \left(\frac{1}{3} + \frac{1}{4}\right) + \left(\frac{1}{5} + \frac{1}{6} + \frac{1}{7} + \frac{1}{8}\right) + \left(\frac{1}{9} + \cdots + \frac{1}{16}\right) + \cdots ,$$

each pair of parentheses encloses p terms of the form

$$\frac{1}{p+1} + \frac{1}{p+2} + \cdots + \frac{1}{p+p} > \frac{p}{2p} = \frac{1}{2}.$$

Forming partial sums by adding the parenthetical groups one by one, we obtain

$$s_1 = 1, \quad s_2 = \frac{3}{2}, \quad s_3 > \frac{4}{2}, \quad s_4 > \frac{5}{2}, \ldots, \quad s_n > \frac{n+1}{2},$$

and we are forced to the conclusion that the harmonic series diverges.

Although the harmonic series diverges, its partial sums have relevance among other places in number theory, where $H_n = \sum_{m=1}^{n} m^{-1}$ are sometimes referred to as **harmonic numbers**. ∎

We now turn to a more detailed study of the convergence and divergence of series, considering here series of positive terms. Series with terms of both signs are treated later.

Comparison Test

If term by term a series of terms u_n satisfies $0 \leq u_n \leq a_n$, where the a_n form a convergent series, then the series $\sum_n u_n$ is also convergent. Letting s_i and s_j be partial sums of the u series, with $j > i$, the difference $s_j - s_i$ is $\sum_{n=i+1}^{j} u_n$, and this is smaller than the corresponding quantity for the a series, thereby proving convergence. A similar argument shows that if term by term a series of terms v_n satisfies $0 \leq b_n \leq v_n$, where the b_n form a divergent series, then $\sum_n v_n$ is also divergent.

For the convergent series a_n we already have the geometric series, whereas the harmonic series will serve as the divergent comparison series b_n. As other series are identified as either convergent or divergent, they may also be used as the known series for comparison tests.

Example 1.1.3   A DIVERGENT SERIES

Test $\sum_{n=1}^{\infty} n^{-p}$, $p = 0.999$, for convergence. Since $n^{-0.999} > n^{-1}$ and $b_n = n^{-1}$ forms the divergent harmonic series, the comparison test shows that $\sum_n n^{-0.999}$ is divergent. Generalizing, $\sum_n n^{-p}$ is seen to be divergent for all $p \leq 1$.   ∎

Cauchy Root Test

If $(a_n)^{1/n} \leq r < 1$ for all sufficiently large n, with r independent of n, then $\sum_n a_n$ is convergent. If $(a_n)^{1/n} \geq 1$ for all sufficiently large n, then $\sum_n a_n$ is divergent.

The language of this test emphasizes an important point: The convergence or divergence of a series depends entirely on what happens for large n. Relative to convergence, it is the behavior in the large-n limit that matters.

The first part of this test is verified easily by raising $(a_n)^{1/n}$ to the nth power. We get

$$a_n \leq r^n < 1.$$

Since r^n is just the nth term in a convergent geometric series, $\sum_n a_n$ is convergent by the comparison test. Conversely, if $(a_n)^{1/n} \geq 1$, then $a_n \geq 1$ and the series must diverge. This root test is particularly useful in establishing the properties of power series (Section 1.2).

D'Alembert (or Cauchy) Ratio Test

If $a_{n+1}/a_n \leq r < 1$ for all sufficiently large n and r is independent of n, then $\sum_n a_n$ is convergent. If $a_{n+1}/a_n \geq 1$ for all sufficiently large n, then $\sum_n a_n$ is divergent.

This test is established by direct comparison with the geometric series $(1 + r + r^2 + \cdots)$. In the second part, $a_{n+1} \geq a_n$ and divergence should be reasonably obvious. Although not quite as sensitive as the Cauchy root test, this D'Alembert ratio test is one of the easiest to apply and is widely used. An alternate statement of the ratio test is in the form of a limit: If

$$\lim_{n \to \infty} \frac{a_{n+1}}{a_n} \begin{cases} < 1, & \text{convergence,} \\ > 1, & \text{divergence,} \\ = 1, & \text{indeterminate.} \end{cases} \tag{1.6}$$

Because of this final indeterminate possibility, the ratio test is likely to fail at crucial points, and more delicate, sensitive tests then become necessary. The alert reader may wonder how this indeterminacy arose. Actually it was concealed in the first statement, $a_{n+1}/a_n \leq r < 1$. We might encounter $a_{n+1}/a_n < 1$ for all **finite** n but be unable to choose an $r < 1$ **and independent of n** such that $a_{n+1}/a_n \leq r$ for all sufficiently large n. An example is provided by the harmonic series, for which

$$\frac{a_{n+1}}{a_n} = \frac{n}{n+1} < 1.$$

Since

$$\lim_{n \to \infty} \frac{a_{n+1}}{a_n} = 1,$$

no fixed ratio $r < 1$ exists and the test fails.

Example 1.1.4   D'ALEMBERT RATIO TEST

Test $\sum_n n/2^n$ for convergence. Applying the ratio test,

$$\frac{a_{n+1}}{a_n} = \frac{(n+1)/2^{n+1}}{n/2^n} = \frac{1}{2} \frac{n+1}{n}.$$

Since

$$\frac{a_{n+1}}{a_n} \le \frac{3}{4} \quad \text{for } n \ge 2,$$

we have convergence.   ∎

Cauchy (or Maclaurin) Integral Test

This is another sort of comparison test, in which we compare a series with an integral. Geometrically, we compare the area of a series of unit-width rectangles with the area under a curve.

Let $f(x)$ be a continuous, **monotonic decreasing function** in which $f(n) = a_n$. Then $\sum_n a_n$ converges if $\int_1^\infty f(x)dx$ is finite and diverges if the integral is infinite. The ith partial sum is

$$s_i = \sum_{n=1}^i a_n = \sum_{n=1}^i f(n).$$

But, because $f(x)$ is monotonic decreasing, see Fig. 1.1(a),

$$s_i \ge \int_1^{i+1} f(x)dx.$$

On the other hand, as shown in Fig. 1.1(b),

$$s_i - a_1 \le \int_1^i f(x)dx.$$

Taking the limit as $i \to \infty$, we have

$$\int_1^\infty f(x)dx \le \sum_{n=1}^\infty a_n \le \int_1^\infty f(x)dx + a_1. \tag{1.7}$$

Hence the infinite series converges or diverges as the corresponding integral converges or diverges.

This integral test is particularly useful in setting upper and lower bounds on the remainder of a series after some number of initial terms have been summed. That is,

$$\sum_{n=1}^\infty a_n = \sum_{n=1}^N a_n + \sum_{n=N+1}^\infty a_n, \tag{1.8}$$

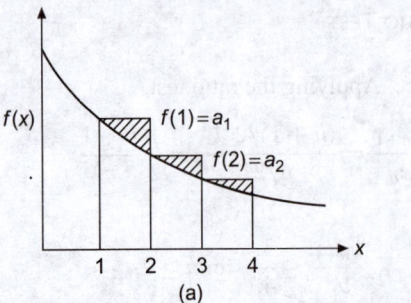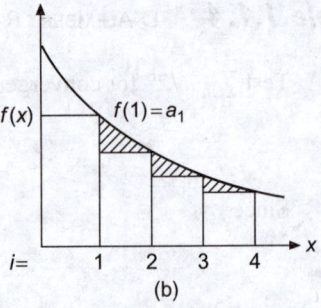

FIGURE 1.1   (a) Comparison of integral and sum-blocks leading. (b) Comparison of integral and sum-blocks lagging.

and

$$\int_{N+1}^{\infty} f(x)\,dx \le \sum_{n=N+1}^{\infty} a_n \le \int_{N+1}^{\infty} f(x)\,dx + a_{N+1}. \tag{1.9}$$

To free the integral test from the quite restrictive requirement that the interpolating function $f(x)$ be positive and monotonic, we shall show that for any function $f(x)$ with a continuous derivative, the infinite series is exactly represented as a sum of two integrals:

$$\sum_{n=N1+1}^{N_2} f(n) = \int_{N_1}^{N_2} f(x)\,dx + \int_{N_1}^{N_2} (x-[x])\,f'(x)\,dx. \tag{1.10}$$

Here $[x]$ is the integral part of x, i.e., the largest integer $\le x$, so $x-[x]$ varies sawtoothlike between 0 and 1. Equation (1.10) is useful because if both integrals in Eq. (1.10) converge, the infinite series also converges, while if one integral converges and the other does not, the infinite series diverges. If both integrals diverge, the test fails unless it can be shown whether the divergences of the integrals cancel against each other.

We need now to establish Eq. (1.10). We manipulate the contributions to the second integral as follows:

1. Using integration by parts, we observe that

$$\int_{N_1}^{N_2} x f'(x)\,dx = N_2 f(N_2) - N_1 f(N_1) - \int_{N_1}^{N_2} f(x)\,dx.$$

2. We evaluate

$$\int_{N_1}^{N_2} [x]\,f'(x)\,dx = \sum_{n=N_1}^{N_2-1} n \int_{n}^{n+1} f'(x)\,dx = \sum_{n=N_1}^{N_2-1} n\Big[f(n+1) - f(n)\Big]$$

$$= -\sum_{n=N_1+1}^{N_2} f(n) - N_1 f(N_1) + N_2 f(N_2).$$

Subtracting the second of these equations from the first, we arrive at Eq. (1.10).

An alternative to Eq. (1.10) in which the second integral has its sawtooth shifted to be symmetrical about zero (and therefore perhaps smaller) can be derived by methods similar to those used above. The resulting formula is

$$\sum_{n=N_1+1}^{N_2} f(n) = \int_{N_1}^{N_2} f(x)dx + \int_{N_1}^{N_2} (x - [x] - \tfrac{1}{2})f'(x)dx$$

$$+ \tfrac{1}{2}\Big[f(N_2) - f(N_1)\Big].$$

(1.11)

Because they do not use a monotonicity requirement, Eqs. (1.10) and (1.11) can be applied to alternating series, and even those with irregular sign sequences.

Example 1.1.5   RIEMANN ZETA FUNCTION

The Riemann zeta function is defined by

$$\zeta(p) = \sum_{n=1}^{\infty} n^{-p},$$

(1.12)

providing the series converges. We may take $f(x) = x^{-p}$, and then

$$\int_1^{\infty} x^{-p}\, dx = \frac{x^{-p+1}}{-p+1}\Big|_{x=1}^{\infty}, \quad p \neq 1,$$

$$= \ln x\Big|_{x=1}^{\infty}, \quad p = 1.$$

The integral and therefore the series are divergent for $p \leq 1$, and convergent for $p > 1$. Hence Eq. (1.12) should carry the condition $p > 1$. This, incidentally, is an independent proof that the harmonic series ($p = 1$) diverges logarithmically. The sum of the first million terms $\sum_{n=1}^{1,000,000} n^{-1}$ is only $14.392\,726\cdots$. ∎

While the harmonic series diverges, the combination

$$\gamma = \lim_{n\to\infty} \left(\sum_{m=1}^{n} m^{-1} - \ln n\right)$$

(1.13)

converges, approaching a limit known as the **Euler-Mascheroni constant**.

Example 1.1.6   A SLOWLY DIVERGING SERIES

Consider now the series

$$S = \sum_{n=2}^{\infty} \frac{1}{n \ln n}.$$

We form the integral

$$\int\limits_{2}^{\infty} \frac{1}{x \ln x}\, dx = \int\limits_{x=2}^{\infty} \frac{d \ln x}{\ln x} = \ln \ln x \Big|_{x=2}^{\infty},$$

which diverges, indicating that S is divergent. Note that the lower limit of the integral is in fact unimportant so long as it does not introduce any spurious singularities, as it is the large-x behavior that determines the convergence. Because $n \ln n > n$, the divergence is slower than that of the harmonic series. But because $\ln n$ increases more slowly than n^{ε}, where ε can have an arbitrarily small positive value, we have divergence even though the series $\sum_n n^{-(1+\varepsilon)}$ converges. ∎

More Sensitive Tests

Several tests more sensitive than those already examined are consequences of a theorem by Kummer. Kummer's theorem, which deals with two series of finite positive terms, u_n and a_n, states:

1. The series $\sum_n u_n$ converges if

$$\lim_{n \to \infty} \left(a_n \frac{u_n}{u_{n+1}} - a_{n+1} \right) \geq C > 0, \tag{1.14}$$

where C is a constant. This statement is equivalent to a simple comparison test if the series $\sum_n a_n^{-1}$ converges, and imparts new information only if that sum diverges. The more weakly $\sum_n a_n^{-1}$ diverges, the more powerful the Kummer test will be.

2. If $\sum_n a_n^{-1}$ diverges and

$$\lim_{n \to \infty} \left(a_n \frac{u_n}{u_{n+1}} - a_{n+1} \right) \leq 0, \tag{1.15}$$

then $\sum_n u_n$ diverges.

The proof of this powerful test is remarkably simple. Part 2 follows immediately from the comparison test. To prove Part 1, write cases of Eq. (1.14) for $n = N + 1$ through any larger n, in the following form:

$$u_{N+1} \leq (a_N u_N - a_{N+1} u_{N+1})/C,$$

$$u_{N+2} \leq (a_{N+1} u_{N+1} - a_{N+2} u_{N+2})/C,$$

$$\cdots \leq \cdots\cdots\cdots\cdots\cdots\cdots,$$

$$u_n \leq (a_{n-1} u_{n-1} - a_n u_n)/C.$$

Adding, we get

$$\sum_{i=N+1}^{n} u_i \le \frac{a_N u_N}{C} - \frac{a_n u_n}{C} \tag{1.16}$$

$$< \frac{a_N u_N}{C}. \tag{1.17}$$

This shows that the tail of the series $\sum_n u_n$ is bounded, and that series is therefore proved convergent when Eq. (1.14) is satisfied for all sufficiently large n.

Gauss' test is an application of Kummer's theorem to series $u_n > 0$ when the ratios of successive u_n approach unity and the tests previously discussed yield indeterminate results. If for large n

$$\frac{u_n}{u_{n+1}} = 1 + \frac{h}{n} + \frac{B(n)}{n^2}, \tag{1.18}$$

where $B(n)$ is bounded for n sufficiently large, then the Gauss test states that $\sum_n u_n$ converges for $h > 1$ and diverges for $h \le 1$: There is no indeterminate case here.

The Gauss test is extremely sensitive, and will work for all troublesome series the physicist is likely to encounter. To confirm it using Kummer's theorem, we take $a_n = n \ln n$. The series $\sum_n a_n^{-1}$ is weakly divergent, as already established in Example 1.1.6.

Taking the limit on the left side of Eq. (1.14), we have

$$\lim_{n \to \infty} \left[n \ln n \left(1 + \frac{h}{n} + \frac{B(n)}{n^2} \right) - (n+1) \ln(n+1) \right]$$

$$= \lim_{n \to \infty} \left[(n+1) \ln n + (h-1) \ln n + \frac{B(n) \ln n}{n} - (n+1) \ln(n+1) \right]$$

$$= \lim_{n \to \infty} \left[-(n+1) \ln \left(\frac{n+1}{n} \right) + (h-1) \ln n \right]. \tag{1.19}$$

For $h < 1$, both terms of Eq. (1.19) are negative, thereby signaling a divergent case of Kummer's theorem; for $h > 1$, the second term of Eq. (1.19) dominates the first and is positive, indicating convergence. At $h = 1$, the second term vanishes, and the first is inherently negative, thereby indicating divergence.

Example 1.1.7   LEGENDRE SERIES

The series solution for the Legendre equation (encountered in Chapter 7) has successive terms whose ratio under certain conditions is

$$\frac{a_{2j+2}}{a_{2j}} = \frac{2j(2j+1) - \lambda}{(2j+1)(2j+2)}.$$

To place this in the form now being used, we define $u_j = a_{2j}$ and write

$$\frac{u_j}{u_{j+1}} = \frac{(2j+1)(2j+2)}{2j(2j+1) - \lambda}.$$

In the limit of large j, the constant λ becomes negligible (in the language of the Gauss test, it contributes to an extent $B(j)/j^2$, where $B(j)$ is bounded). We therefore have

$$\frac{u_j}{u_{j+1}} \to \frac{2j+2}{2j} + \frac{B(j)}{j^2} = 1 + \frac{1}{j} + \frac{B(j)}{j^2}. \tag{1.20}$$

The Gauss test tells us that this series is divergent. ∎

Exercises

1.1.1 (a) Prove that if $\lim_{n\to\infty} n^p u_n = A < \infty$, $p > 1$, the series $\sum_{n=1}^{\infty} u_n$ converges.

(b) Prove that if $\lim_{n\to\infty} n u_n = A > 0$, the series diverges. (The test fails for $A = 0$.) These two tests, known as **limit tests**, are often convenient for establishing the convergence of a series. They may be treated as comparison tests, comparing with

$$\sum_n n^{-q}, \quad 1 \le q < p.$$

1.1.2 If $\lim_{n\to\infty} \frac{b_n}{a_n} = K$, a constant with $0 < K < \infty$, show that $\Sigma_n b_n$ converges or diverges with Σa_n.

Hint. If Σa_n converges, rescale b_n to $b_n' = \dfrac{b_n}{2K}$. If $\Sigma_n a_n$ diverges, rescale to $b_n'' = \dfrac{2b_n}{K}$.

1.1.3 (a) Show that the series $\sum_{n=2}^{\infty} \frac{1}{n(\ln n)^2}$ converges.

(b) By direct addition $\sum_{n=2}^{100,000} [n(\ln n)^2]^{-1} = 2.02288$. Use Eq. (1.9) to make a five-significant-figure estimate of the sum of this series.

1.1.4 Gauss' test is often given in the form of a test of the ratio

$$\frac{u_n}{u_{n+1}} = \frac{n^2 + a_1 n + a_0}{n^2 + b_1 n + b_0}.$$

For what values of the parameters a_1 and b_1 is there convergence? divergence?

> *ANS.* Convergent for $a_1 - b_1 > 1$,
> divergent for $a_1 - b_1 \le 1$.

1.1.5 Test for convergence

(a) $\displaystyle\sum_{n=2}^{\infty} (\ln n)^{-1}$

(b) $\displaystyle\sum_{n=1}^{\infty} \frac{n!}{10^n}$

(c) $\displaystyle\sum_{n=1}^{\infty} \frac{1}{2n(2n+1)}$

(d) $\displaystyle\sum_{n=1}^{\infty} [n(n+1)]^{-1/2}$

(e) $\displaystyle\sum_{n=0}^{\infty} \frac{1}{2n+1}$

1.1.6   Test for convergence

(a) $\displaystyle\sum_{n=1}^{\infty} \frac{1}{n(n+1)}$ (d) $\displaystyle\sum_{n=1}^{\infty} \ln\left(1 + \frac{1}{n}\right)$

(b) $\displaystyle\sum_{n=2}^{\infty} \frac{1}{n \ln n}$ (e) $\displaystyle\sum_{n=1}^{\infty} \frac{1}{n \cdot n^{1/n}}$

(c) $\displaystyle\sum_{n=1}^{\infty} \frac{1}{n 2^n}$

1.1.7   For what values of p and q will $\sum_{n=2}^{\infty} \frac{1}{n^p (\ln n)^q}$ converge?

ANS.   Convergent for $\begin{cases} p > 1, & \text{all } q, \\ p = 1, & q > 1, \end{cases}$ divergent for $\begin{cases} p < 1, & \text{all } q, \\ p = 1, & q \le 1. \end{cases}$

1.1.8   Given $\sum_{n=1}^{1,000} n^{-1} = 7.485\,470\ldots$ set upper and lower bounds on the Euler-Mascheroni constant.

ANS. $0.5767 < \gamma < 0.5778$.

1.1.9   (From **Olbers' paradox**.) Assume a static universe in which the stars are uniformly distributed. Divide all space into shells of constant thickness; the stars in any one shell by themselves subtend a solid angle of ω_0. **Allowing for the blocking out of distant stars by nearer stars**, show that the total net solid angle subtended by all stars, shells extending to infinity, is **exactly** 4π. [Therefore the night sky should be ablaze with light. For more details, see E. Harrison, *Darkness at Night: A Riddle of the Universe*. Cambridge, MA: Harvard University Press (1987).]

1.1.10   Test for convergence

$$\sum_{n=1}^{\infty} \left[\frac{1 \cdot 3 \cdot 5 \cdots (2n-1)}{2 \cdot 4 \cdot 6 \cdots (2n)} \right]^2 = \frac{1}{4} + \frac{9}{64} + \frac{25}{256} + \cdots .$$

Alternating Series

In previous subsections we limited ourselves to series of positive terms. Now, in contrast, we consider infinite series in which the signs alternate. The partial cancellation due to alternating signs makes convergence more rapid and much easier to identify. We shall prove the Leibniz criterion, a general condition for the convergence of an alternating series. For series with more irregular sign changes, the integral test of Eq. (1.10) is often helpful.

The **Leibniz criterion** applies to series of the form $\sum_{n=1}^{\infty} (-1)^{n+1} a_n$ with $a_n > 0$, and states that if a_n is *monotonically decreasing* (for sufficiently large n) and $\lim_{n\to\infty} a_n = 0$, then the series converges. To prove this theorem, note that the remainder R_{2n} of the series beyond s_{2n}, the partial sum after $2n$ terms, can be written in two alternate ways:

$$R_{2n} = (a_{2n+1} - a_{2n+2}) + (a_{2n+3} - a_{2n+4}) + \cdots$$

$$= a_{2n+1} - (a_{2n+2} - a_{2n+3}) - (a_{2n+4} - a_{2n+5}) - \cdots .$$

Since the a_n are decreasing, the first of these equations implies $R_{2n} > 0$, while the second implies $R_{2n} < a_{2n+1}$, so

$$0 < R_{2n} < a_{2n+1}.$$

Thus, R_{2n} is positive but bounded, and the bound can be made arbitrarily small by taking larger values of n. This demonstration also shows that the error from truncating an alternating series after a_{2n} results in an error that is negative (the omitted terms were shown to combine to a positive result) and bounded in magnitude by a_{2n+1}. An argument similar to that made above for the remainder after an odd number of terms, R_{2n+1}, would show that the error from truncation after a_{2n+1} is positive and bounded by a_{2n+2}. Thus, it is generally true that the error in truncating an alternating series with monotonically decreasing terms is of the same sign as the last term kept and smaller than the first term dropped.

The Leibniz criterion depends for its applicability on the presence of strict sign alternation. Less regular sign changes present more challenging problems for convergence determination.

Example 1.1.8   SERIES WITH IRREGULAR SIGN CHANGES

For $0 < x < 2\pi$, the series

$$S = \sum_{n=1}^{\infty} \frac{\cos(nx)}{n} = -\ln\left(2\sin\frac{x}{2}\right) \tag{1.21}$$

converges, having coefficients that change sign often, but not so that the Leibniz criterion applies easily. To verify the convergence, we apply the integral test of Eq. (1.10), inserting the explicit form for the derivative of $\cos(nx)/n$ (with respect to n) in the second integral:

$$S = \int_{1}^{\infty} \frac{\cos(nx)}{n}\, dn + \int_{1}^{\infty} \left(n - [n]\right)\left[-\frac{x}{n}\sin(nx) - \frac{\cos(nx)}{n^2}\right] dn. \tag{1.22}$$

Using integration by parts, the first integral in Eq. (1.22) is rearranged to

$$\int_{1}^{\infty} \frac{\cos(nx)}{n}\, dn = \left[\frac{\sin(nx)}{nx}\right]_{1}^{\infty} + \frac{1}{x}\int_{1}^{\infty} \frac{\sin(nx)}{n^2}\, dn,$$

and this integral converges because

$$\left|\int_{1}^{\infty} \frac{\sin(nx)}{n^2}\, dn\right| < \int_{1}^{\infty} \frac{dn}{n^2} = 1.$$

Looking now at the second integral in Eq. (1.22), we note that its term $\cos(nx)/n^2$ also leads to a convergent integral, so we need only to examine the convergence of

$$\int_{1}^{\infty} \left(n - [n]\right)\frac{\sin(nx)}{n}\, dn.$$

Next, setting $(n - [n]) \sin(nx) = g'(n)$, which is equivalent to defining $g(N) = \int_1^N (n - [n]) \sin(nx) \, dn$, we write

$$\int_1^\infty \left(n - [n]\right) \frac{\sin(nx)}{n} \, dn = \int_1^\infty \frac{g'(n)}{n} \, dn = \left[\frac{g(n)}{n}\right]_{n=1}^\infty + \int_1^\infty \frac{g(n)}{n^2} \, dn,$$

where the last equality was obtained using once again an integration by parts. We do not have an explicit expression for $g(n)$, but we do know that it is bounded because $\sin x$ oscillates with a period incommensurate with that of the sawtooth periodicity of $(n - [n])$. This boundedness enables us to determine that the second integral in Eq. (1.22) converges, thus establishing the convergence of S. ∎

Absolute and Conditional Convergence

An infinite series is **absolutely** convergent if the absolute values of its terms form a convergent series. If it converges, but not absolutely, it is termed **conditionally** convergent. An example of a conditionally convergent series is the alternating harmonic series,

$$\sum_{n=1}^\infty (-1)^{n-1} n^{-1} = 1 - \frac{1}{2} + \frac{1}{3} - \frac{1}{4} + \cdots + \frac{(-1)^{n-1}}{n} + \cdots . \tag{1.23}$$

This series is convergent, based on the Leibniz criterion. It is clearly not absolutely convergent; if all terms are taken with + signs, we have the harmonic series, which we already know to be divergent. The tests described earlier in this section for series of positive terms are, then, tests for absolute convergence.

Exercises

1.1.11   Determine whether each of these series is convergent, and if so, whether it is absolutely convergent:

(a) $\dfrac{\ln 2}{2} - \dfrac{\ln 3}{3} + \dfrac{\ln 4}{4} - \dfrac{\ln 5}{5} + \dfrac{\ln 6}{6} - \cdots ,$

(b) $\dfrac{1}{1} + \dfrac{1}{2} - \dfrac{1}{3} - \dfrac{1}{4} + \dfrac{1}{5} + \dfrac{1}{6} - \dfrac{1}{7} - \dfrac{1}{8} + \cdots ,$

(c) $1 - \dfrac{1}{2} - \dfrac{1}{3} + \dfrac{1}{4} + \dfrac{1}{5} + \dfrac{1}{6} - \dfrac{1}{7} - \dfrac{1}{8} - \dfrac{1}{9} - \dfrac{1}{10} + \dfrac{1}{11} \cdots + \dfrac{1}{15} - \dfrac{1}{16} \cdots - \dfrac{1}{21} + \cdots .$

1.1.12   **Catalan's constant** $\beta(2)$ is defined by

$$\beta(2) = \sum_{k=0}^\infty (-1)^k (2k + 1)^{-2} = \frac{1}{1^2} - \frac{1}{3^2} + \frac{1}{5^2} \cdots .$$

Calculate $\beta(2)$ to six-digit accuracy.

Hint. The rate of convergence is enhanced by pairing the terms,

$$(4k - 1)^{-2} - (4k + 1)^{-2} = \frac{16k}{(16k^2 - 1)^2}.$$

If you have carried enough digits in your summation, $\sum_{1 \leq k \leq N} 16k/(16k^2 - 1)^2$, additional significant figures may be obtained by setting upper and lower bounds on the tail of the series, $\sum_{k=N+1}^{\infty}$. These bounds may be set by comparison with integrals, as in the Maclaurin integral test.

$$ANS. \quad \beta(2) = 0.9159\ 6559\ 4177 \cdots .$$

Operations on Series

We now investigate the operations that may be performed on infinite series. In this connection the establishment of absolute convergence is important, because it can be proved that the terms of an absolutely convergent series may be reordered according to the familiar rules of algebra or arithmetic:

- If an infinite series is absolutely convergent, the series sum is independent of the order in which the terms are added.

- An absolutely convergent series may be added termwise to, or subtracted termwise from, or multiplied termwise with another absolutely convergent series, and the resulting series will also be absolutely convergent.

- The series (as a whole) may be multiplied with another absolutely convergent series. The limit of the product will be the product of the individual series limits. The product series, a double series, will also converge absolutely.

No such guarantees can be given for conditionally convergent series, though some of the above properties remain true if only one of the series to be combined is conditionally convergent.

Example 1.1.9   REARRANGEMENT OF ALTERNATING HARMONIC SERIES

Writing the alternating harmonic series as

$$1 - \frac{1}{2} + \frac{1}{3} - \frac{1}{4} + \cdots = 1 - \left(\frac{1}{2} - \frac{1}{3} \right) - \left(\frac{1}{4} - \frac{1}{5} \right) - \cdots , \tag{1.24}$$

it is clear that $\sum_{n=1}^{\infty} (-1)^{n-1} n^{-1} < 1$. However, if we rearrange the order of the terms, we can make this series converge to $\frac{3}{2}$. We regroup the terms of Eq. (1.24), as

$$\left(1 + \frac{1}{3} + \frac{1}{5} \right) - \left(\frac{1}{2} \right) + \left(\frac{1}{7} + \frac{1}{9} + \frac{1}{11} + \frac{1}{13} + \frac{1}{15} \right)$$

$$- \left(\frac{1}{4} \right) + \left(\frac{1}{17} + \cdots + \frac{1}{25} \right) - \left(\frac{1}{6} \right) + \left(\frac{1}{27} + \cdots + \frac{1}{35} \right) - \left(\frac{1}{8} \right) + \cdots . \tag{1.25}$$

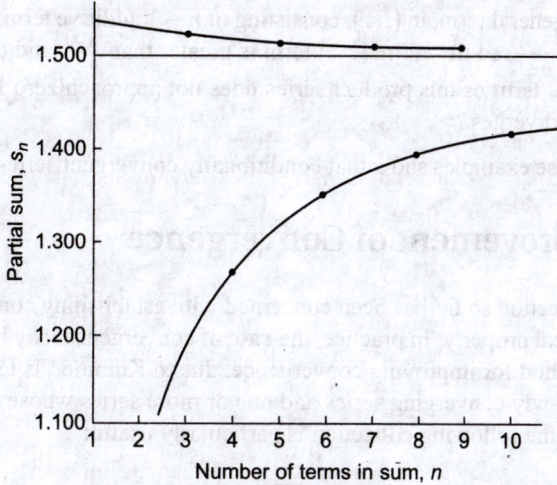

FIGURE 1.2   Alternating harmonic series. Terms are rearranged to give convergence to 1.5.

Treating the terms grouped in parentheses as single terms for convenience, we obtain the partial sums

$$
\begin{array}{ll}
s_1 = 1.5333 & s_2 = 1.0333 \\
s_3 = 1.5218 & s_4 = 1.2718 \\
s_5 = 1.5143 & s_6 = 1.3476 \\
s_7 = 1.5103 & s_8 = 1.3853 \\
s_9 = 1.5078 & s_{10} = 1.4078.
\end{array}
$$

From this tabulation of s_n and the plot of s_n versus n in Fig. 1.2, the convergence to $\frac{3}{2}$ is fairly clear. Our rearrangement was to take positive terms until the partial sum was equal to or greater than $\frac{3}{2}$ and then to add negative terms until the partial sum just fell below $\frac{3}{2}$ and so on. As the series extends to infinity, all original terms will eventually appear, but the partial sums of this rearranged alternating harmonic series converge to $\frac{3}{2}$. ∎

As the example shows, by a suitable rearrangement of terms, a conditionally convergent series may be made to converge to any desired value or even to diverge. This statement is sometimes called **Riemann's theorem**.

Another example shows the danger of multiplying conditionally convergent series.

Example 1.1.10   SQUARE OF A CONDITIONALLY CONVERGENT SERIES MAY DIVERGE

The series $\sum_{n=1}^{\infty} \frac{(-1)^{n-1}}{\sqrt{n}}$ converges by the Leibniz criterion. Its square,

$$
\left[\sum_{n=1}^{\infty} \frac{(-1)^{n-1}}{\sqrt{n}} \right]^2 = \sum_n (-1)^n \left[\frac{1}{\sqrt{1}} \frac{1}{\sqrt{n-1}} + \frac{1}{\sqrt{2}} \frac{1}{\sqrt{n-2}} + \cdots + \frac{1}{\sqrt{n-1}} \frac{1}{\sqrt{1}} \right],
$$

has a general term, in [...], consisting of $n-1$ additive terms, each of which is bigger than $\frac{1}{\sqrt{n-1}\sqrt{n-1}}$, so the entire [...] term is greater than $\frac{n-1}{n-1}$ and does not go to zero. Hence the general term of this product series does not approach zero in the limit of large n and the series diverges. ∎

These examples show that conditionally convergent series must be treated with caution.

Improvement of Convergence

This section so far has been concerned with establishing convergence as an abstract mathematical property. In practice, the **rate** of convergence may be of considerable importance. A method for improving convergence, due to Kummer, is to form a linear combination of our slowly converging series and one or more series whose sum is known. For the known series the following collection is particularly useful:

$$\alpha_1 = \sum_{n=1}^{\infty} \frac{1}{n(n+1)} = 1,$$

$$\alpha_2 = \sum_{n=1}^{\infty} \frac{1}{n(n+1)(n+2)} = \frac{1}{4},$$

$$\alpha_3 = \sum_{n=1}^{\infty} \frac{1}{n(n+1)(n+2)(n+3)} = \frac{1}{18},$$

$$\cdots\cdots\cdots\cdots\cdots\cdots\cdots$$

$$\alpha_p = \sum_{n=1}^{\infty} \frac{1}{n(n+1)\cdots(n+p)} = \frac{1}{p\,p!}. \tag{1.26}$$

These sums can be evaluated via partial fraction expansions, and are the subject of Exercise 1.5.3.

The series we wish to sum and one or more known series (multiplied by coefficients) are combined term by term. The coefficients in the linear combination are chosen to cancel the most slowly converging terms.

Example 1.1.11   RIEMANN ZETA FUNCTION $\zeta(3)$

From the definition in Eq. (1.12), we identify $\zeta(3)$ as $\sum_{n=1}^{\infty} n^{-3}$. Noting that α_2 of Eq. (1.26) has a large-n dependence $\sim n^{-3}$, we consider the linear combination

$$\sum_{n=1}^{\infty} n^{-3} + a\alpha_2 = \zeta(3) + \frac{a}{4}. \tag{1.27}$$

We did not use α_1 because it converges more slowly than $\zeta(3)$. Combining the two series on the left-hand side termwise, we obtain

$$\sum_{n=1}^{\infty} \left[\frac{1}{n^3} + \frac{a}{n(n+1)(n+2)} \right] = \sum_{n=1}^{\infty} \frac{n^2(1+a) + 3n + 2}{n^3(n+1)(n+2)}.$$

Table 1.1   Riemann Zeta Function

s	$\zeta(s)$
2	1.64493 40668
3	1.20205 69032
4	1.08232 32337
5	1.03692 77551
6	1.01734 30620
7	1.00834 92774
8	1.00407 73562
9	1.00200 83928
10	1.00099 45751

If we choose $a = -1$, we remove the leading term from the numerator; then, setting this equal to the right-hand side of Eq. (1.27) and solving for $\zeta(3)$,

$$\zeta(3) = \frac{1}{4} + \sum_{n=1}^{\infty} \frac{3n+2}{n^3(n+1)(n+2)}. \tag{1.28}$$

The resulting series may not be beautiful but it does converge as n^{-4}, faster than n^{-3}. A more convenient form with even faster convergence is introduced in Exercise 1.1.16. There, the symmetry leads to convergence as n^{-5}. ∎

Sometimes it is helpful to use the Riemann zeta function in a way similar to that illustrated for the α_p in the foregoing example. That approach is practical because the zeta function has been tabulated (see Table 1.1).

Example 1.1.12   CONVERGENCE IMPROVEMENT

The problem is to evaluate the series $\sum_{n=1}^{\infty} 1/(1+n^2)$. Expanding $(1+n^2)^{-1} = n^{-2}(1 + n^{-2})^{-1}$ by direct division, we have

$$(1+n^2)^{-1} = n^{-2}\left(1 - n^{-2} + n^{-4} - \frac{n^{-6}}{1+n^{-2}}\right)$$

$$= \frac{1}{n^2} - \frac{1}{n^4} + \frac{1}{n^6} - \frac{1}{n^8 + n^6}.$$

Therefore

$$\sum_{n=1}^{\infty} \frac{1}{1+n^2} = \zeta(2) - \zeta(4) + \zeta(6) - \sum_{n=1}^{\infty} \frac{1}{n^8 + n^6}.$$

The remainder series converges as n^{-8}. Clearly, the process can be continued as desired. You make a choice between how much algebra you will do and how much arithmetic the computer will do. ∎

Rearrangement of Double Series

An absolutely convergent double series (one whose terms are identified by two summation indices) presents interesting rearrangement opportunities. Consider

$$S = \sum_{m=0}^{\infty} \sum_{n=0}^{\infty} a_{n,m}. \tag{1.29}$$

In addition to the obvious possibility of reversing the order of summation (i.e., doing the m sum first), we can make rearrangements that are more innovative. One reason for doing this is that we may be able to reduce the double sum to a single summation, or even evaluate the entire double sum in closed form.

As an example, suppose we make the following index substitutions in our double series: $m = q, n = p - q$. Then we will cover all $n \geq 0$, $m \geq 0$ by assigning p the range $(0, \infty)$, and q the range $(0, p)$, so our double series can be written

$$S = \sum_{p=0}^{\infty} \sum_{q=0}^{p} a_{p-q,q}. \tag{1.30}$$

In the nm plane our region of summation is the entire quadrant $m \geq 0$, $n \geq 0$; in the pq plane our summation is over the triangular region sketched in Fig. 1.3. This same pq region can be covered when the summations are carried out in the reverse order, but with limits

$$S = \sum_{q=0}^{\infty} \sum_{p=q}^{\infty} a_{p-q,q}.$$

The important thing to note here is that these schemes all have in common that, by allowing the indices to run over their designated ranges, every $a_{n,m}$ is eventually encountered, and is encountered exactly once.

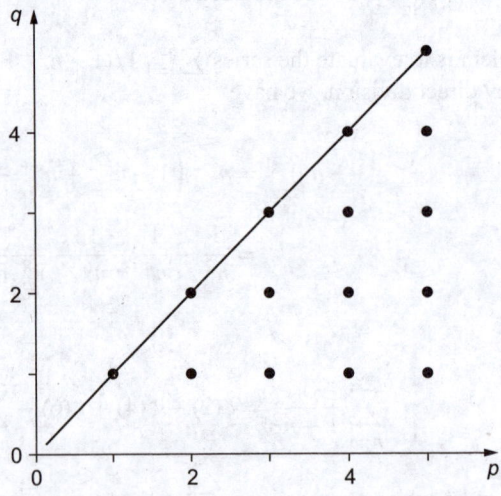

FIGURE 1.3   The pq index space.

Another possible index substitution is to set $n = s$, $m = r - 2s$. If we sum over s first, its range must be $(0, [r/2])$, where $[r/2]$ is the integer part of $r/2$, i.e., $[r/2] = r/2$ for r even and $(r - 1)/2$ for r odd. The range of r is $(0, \infty)$. This situation corresponds to

$$S = \sum_{r=0}^{\infty} \sum_{s=0}^{[r/2]} a_{s,r-2s}. \tag{1.31}$$

The sketches in Figs. 1.4 to 1.6 show the order in which the $a_{n,m}$ are summed when using the forms given in Eqs. (1.29), (1.30), and (1.31), respectively.

If the double series introduced originally as Eq. (1.29) is absolutely convergent, then all these rearrangements will give the same ultimate result.

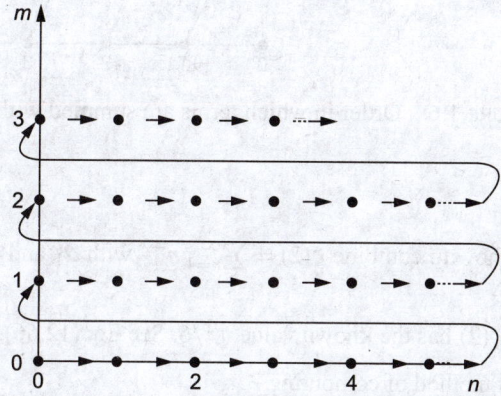

FIGURE 1.4   Order in which terms are summed with m, n index set, Eq. (1.29).

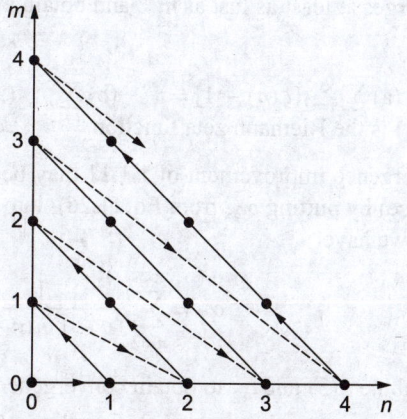

FIGURE 1.5   Order in which terms are summed with p, q index set, Eq. (1.30).

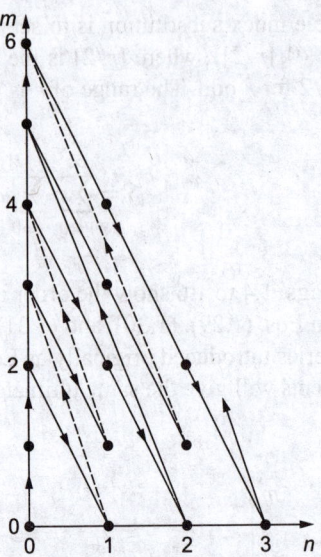

FIGURE 1.6 Order in which terms are summed with r, s index set, Eq. (1.31).

Exercises

1.1.13 Show how to combine $\zeta(2) = \sum_{n=1}^{\infty} n^{-2}$ with α_1 and α_2 to obtain a series converging as n^{-4}.

Note. $\zeta(2)$ has the known value $\pi^2/6$. See Eq. (12.66).

1.1.14 Give a method of computing

$$\lambda(3) = \sum_{n=0}^{\infty} \frac{1}{(2n+1)^3}$$

that converges at least as fast as n^{-8} and obtain a result good to six decimal places.

ANS. $\lambda(3) = 1.051800$.

1.1.15 Show that (a) $\sum_{n=2}^{\infty} [\zeta(n) - 1] = 1$,   (b) $\sum_{n=2}^{\infty} (-1)^n [\zeta(n) - 1] = \frac{1}{2}$, where $\zeta(n)$ is the Riemann zeta function.

1.1.16 The convergence improvement of 1.1.11 may be carried out more expediently (in this special case) by putting α_2, from Eq. (1.26), into a more symmetric form: Replacing n by $n - 1$, we have

$$\alpha_2' = \sum_{n=2}^{\infty} \frac{1}{(n-1)n(n+1)} = \frac{1}{4}.$$

(a) Combine $\zeta(3)$ and α_2' to obtain convergence as n^{-5}.

(b) Let α_4' be α_4 with $n \to n - 2$. Combine $\zeta(3)$, α_2', and α_4' to obtain convergence as n^{-7}.

(c)   If $\zeta(3)$ is to be calculated to six-decimal place accuracy (error 5×10^{-7}), how many terms are required for $\zeta(3)$ alone? combined as in part (a)? combined as in part (b)?

Note. The error may be estimated using the corresponding integral.

$$ANS. \quad (a) \quad \zeta(3) = \frac{5}{4} - \sum_{n=2}^{\infty} \frac{1}{n^3(n^2 - 1)}.$$

1.2   SERIES OF FUNCTIONS

We extend our concept of infinite series to include the possibility that each term u_n may be a function of some variable, $u_n = u_n(x)$. The partial sums become functions of the variable x,

$$s_n(x) = u_1(x) + u_2(x) + \cdots + u_n(x), \tag{1.32}$$

as does the series sum, defined as the limit of the partial sums:

$$\sum_{n=1}^{\infty} u_n(x) = S(x) = \lim_{n \to \infty} s_n(x). \tag{1.33}$$

So far we have concerned ourselves with the behavior of the partial sums as a function of n. Now we consider how the foregoing quantities depend on x. The key concept here is that of uniform convergence.

Uniform Convergence

If for any small $\varepsilon > 0$ there exists a number N, **independent of x** in the interval $[a, b]$ (that is, $a \le x \le b$) such that

$$|S(x) - s_n(x)| < \varepsilon, \quad \text{for all } n \ge N, \tag{1.34}$$

then the series is said to be **uniformly convergent** in the interval $[a, b]$. This says that for our series to be uniformly convergent, it must be possible to find a finite N so that the absolute value of the tail of the infinite series, $\left| \sum_{i=N+1}^{\infty} u_i(x) \right|$, will be less than an arbitrary small ε for all x in the given interval, including the endpoints.

Example 1.2.1   NONUNIFORM CONVERGENCE

Consider on the interval [0, 1] the series

$$S(x) = \sum_{n=0}^{\infty} (1 - x)x^n.$$

For $0 \leq x < 1$, the geometric series $\sum_n x^n$ is convergent, with value $1/(1-x)$, so $S(x) = 1$ for these x values. But at $x = 1$, every term of the series will be zero, and therefore $S(1) = 0$. That is,

$$\sum_{n=0}^{\infty} (1-x)x^n = 1, \quad 0 \leq x < 1,$$

$$= 0, \quad x = 1. \tag{1.35}$$

So $S(x)$ is convergent for the entire interval $[0, 1]$, and because each term is nonnegative, it is also absolutely convergent. If $x \neq 0$, this is a series for which the partial sum s_N is $1 - x^N$, as can be seen by comparison with Eq. (1.3). Since $S(x) = 1$, the uniform convergence criterion is

$$\left| 1 - (1 - x^N) \right| = x^N < \varepsilon.$$

No matter what the values of N and a sufficiently small ε may be, there will be an x value (close to 1) where this criterion is violated. The underlying problem is that $x = 1$ is the convergence limit of the geometric series, and it is not possible to have a convergence rate that is bounded independently of x in a range that includes $x = 1$.

We note also from this example that absolute and uniform convergence are independent concepts. The series in this example has absolute, but not uniform convergence. We will shortly present examples of series that are uniformly, but only conditionally convergent. And there are series that have neither or both of these properties. ∎

Weierstrass M (Majorant) Test

The most commonly encountered test for uniform convergence is the Weierstrass M test. If we can construct a series of numbers $\sum_{i=1}^{\infty} M_i$, in which $M_i \geq |u_i(x)|$ for all x in the interval $[a, b]$ and $\sum_{i=1}^{\infty} M_i$ is convergent, our series $u_i(x)$ will be **uniformly** convergent in $[a, b]$.

The proof of this Weierstrass M test is direct and simple. Since $\sum_i M_i$ converges, some number N exists such that for $n + 1 \geq N$,

$$\sum_{i=n+1}^{\infty} M_i < \varepsilon.$$

This follows from our definition of convergence. Then, with $|u_i(x)| \leq M_i$ for all x in the interval $a \leq x \leq b$,

$$\sum_{i=n+1}^{\infty} u_i(x) < \varepsilon.$$

Hence $S(x) = \sum_{n=1}^{\infty} u_i(x)$ satisfies

$$|S(x) - s_n(x)| = \left| \sum_{i=n+1}^{\infty} u_i(x) \right| < \varepsilon, \tag{1.36}$$

we see that $\sum_{n=1}^{\infty} u_i(x)$ is uniformly convergent in $[a, b]$. Since we have specified absolute values in the statement of the Weierstrass M test, the series $\sum_{n=1}^{\infty} u_i(x)$ is also seen to be absolutely convergent. As we have already observed in Example 1.2.1, absolute and uniform convergence are different concepts, and one of the limitations of the Weierstrass M test is that it can only establish uniform convergence for series that are also absolutely convergent.

To further underscore the difference between absolute and uniform convergence, we provide another example.

Example 1.2.2   UNIFORMLY CONVERGENT ALTERNATING SERIES

Consider the series

$$S(x) = \sum_{n=1}^{\infty} \frac{(-1)^n}{n + x^2}, \quad -\infty < x < \infty. \tag{1.37}$$

Applying the Leibniz criterion, this series is easily proven convergent for the entire interval $-\infty < x < \infty$, but it is **not** absolutely convergent, as the absolute values of its terms approach for large n those of the divergent harmonic series. The divergence of the absolute value series is obvious at $x = 0$, where we then exactly have the harmonic series. Nevertheless, this series is uniformly convergent on $-\infty < x < \infty$, as its convergence is for all x at least as fast as it is for $x = 0$. More formally,

$$|S(x) - s_n(x)| < |u_{n+1}(x)| \le |u_{n+1}(0)|.$$

Since $u_{n+1}(0)$ is independent of x, uniform convergence is confirmed.   ∎

Abel's Test

A somewhat more delicate test for uniform convergence has been given by Abel. If $u_n(x)$ can be written in the form $a_n f_n(x)$, and

1. The a_n form a convergent series, $\sum_n a_n = A$,
2. For all x in $[a, b]$ the functions $f_n(x)$ are monotonically decreasing in n, i.e., $f_{n+1}(x) \le f_n(x)$,
3. For all x in $[a, b]$ all the $f(n)$ are bounded in the range $0 \le f_n(x) \le M$, where M is independent of x,

then $\sum_n u_n(x)$ converges uniformly in $[a, b]$.

This test is especially useful in analyzing the convergence of power series. Details of the proof of Abel's test and other tests for uniform convergence are given in the works by Knopp and by Whittaker and Watson (see Additional Readings listed at the end of this chapter).

Properties of Uniformly Convergent Series

Uniformly convergent series have three particularly useful properties. If a series $\sum_n u_n(x)$ is uniformly convergent in $[a, b]$ and the individual terms $u_n(x)$ are continuous,

1. The series sum $S(x) = \sum_{n=1}^{\infty} u_n(x)$ is also continuous.
2. The series may be integrated term by term. The sum of the integrals is equal to the integral of the sum:

$$\int_a^b S(x)\, dx = \sum_{n=1}^{\infty} \int_a^b u_n(x)\, dx. \tag{1.38}$$

3. The derivative of the series sum $S(x)$ equals the sum of the individual-term derivatives:

$$\frac{d}{dx} S(x) = \sum_{n=1}^{\infty} \frac{d}{dx} u_n(x), \tag{1.39}$$

provided the following additional conditions are satisfied:

$$\frac{du_n(x)}{dx} \text{ is continuous in } [a, b],$$

$$\sum_{n=1}^{\infty} \frac{du_n(x)}{dx} \text{ is uniformly convergent in } [a, b].$$

Term-by-term integration of a uniformly convergent series requires only continuity of the individual terms. This condition is almost always satisfied in physical applications. Term-by-term differentiation of a series is often not valid because more restrictive conditions must be satisfied.

Exercises

1.2.1   Find the range of **uniform** convergence of the series

(a) $\eta(x) = \sum_{n=1}^{\infty} \frac{(-1)^{n-1}}{n^x}$,   (b) $\zeta(x) = \sum_{n=1}^{\infty} \frac{1}{n^x}$.

ANS.   (a) $0 < s \le x < \infty$.
     (b) $1 < s \le x < \infty$.

1.2.2   For what range of x is the geometric series $\sum_{n=0}^{\infty} x^n$ uniformly convergent?

ANS. $-1 < -s \le x \le s < 1$.

1.2.3   For what range of positive values of x is $\sum_{n=0}^{\infty} 1/(1 + x^n)$

(a) convergent?   (b) uniformly convergent?

1.2.4   If the series of the coefficients $\sum a_n$ and $\sum b_n$ are absolutely convergent, show that the Fourier series

$$\sum (a_n \cos nx + b_n \sin nx)$$

is **uniformly** convergent for $-\infty < x < \infty$.

1.2.5   The Legendre series $\sum_{j \text{ even}} u_j(x)$ satisfies the recurrence relations

$$u_{j+2}(x) = \frac{(j+1)(j+2) - l(l+1)}{(j+2)(j+3)} x^2 u_j(x),$$

in which the index j is even and l is some constant (but, in this problem, **not** a non-negative odd integer). Find the range of values of x for which this Legendre series is convergent. Test the endpoints.

ANS. $-1 < x < 1$.

1.2.6   A series solution of the Chebyshev equation leads to successive terms having the ratio

$$\frac{u_{j+2}(x)}{u_j(x)} = \frac{(k+j)^2 - n^2}{(k+j+1)(k+j+2)} x^2,$$

with $k = 0$ and $k = 1$. Test for convergence at $x = \pm 1$.

ANS.   Convergent.

1.2.7   A series solution for the ultraspherical (Gegenbauer) function $C_n^\alpha(x)$ leads to the recurrence

$$a_{j+2} = a_j \frac{(k+j)(k+j+2\alpha) - n(n+2\alpha)}{(k+j+1)(k+j+2)}.$$

Investigate the convergence of each of these series at $x = \pm 1$ as a function of the parameter α.

ANS.   Convergent for $\alpha < 1$,
divergent for $\alpha \geq 1$.

Taylor's Expansion

Taylor's expansion is a powerful tool for the generation of power series representations of functions. The derivation presented here provides not only the possibility of an expansion into a finite number of terms plus a remainder that may or may not be easy to evaluate, but also the possibility of the expression of a function as an infinite series of powers.

We assume that our function $f(x)$ has a continuous nth derivative[2] in the interval $a \leq x \leq b$. We integrate this nth derivative n times; the first three integrations yield

$$\int_a^x f^{(n)}(x_1)dx_1 = f^{(n-1)}(x_1)\Big|_a^x = f^{(n-1)}(x) - f^{(n-1)}(a),$$

$$\int_a^x dx_2 \int_a^{x_2} f^{(n)}(x_1)dx_1 = \int_a^x dx_2 \left[f^{(n-1)}(x_2) - f^{(n-1)}(a) \right]$$

$$= f^{(n-2)}(x) - f^{(n-2)}(a) - (x - a)f^{(n-1)}(a),$$

$$\int_a^x dx_3 \int_a^{x_3} dx_2 \int_a^{x_2} f^{(n)}(x_1)dx_1 = f^{(n-3)}(x) - f^{(n-3)}(a)$$

$$- (x - a)f^{(n-2)}(a) - \frac{(x-a)^2}{2!} f^{(n-1)}(a).$$

Finally, after integrating for the nth time,

$$\int_a^x dx_n \cdots \int_a^{x_2} f^{(n)}(x_1)dx_1 = f(x) - f(a) - (x-a)f'(a) - \frac{(x-a)^2}{2!} f''(a)$$

$$- \cdots - \frac{(x-a)^{n-1}}{(n-1)!} f^{n-1}(a).$$

Note that this expression is exact. No terms have been dropped, no approximations made. Now, solving for $f(x)$, we have

$$f(x) = f(a) + (x - a) f'(a)$$

$$+ \frac{(x-a)^2}{2!} f''(a) + \cdots + \frac{(x-a)^{n-1}}{(n-1)!} f^{(n-1)}(a) + R_n, \tag{1.40}$$

where the remainder, R_n, is given by the n-fold integral

$$R_n = \int_a^x dx_n \cdots \int_a^{x_2} dx_1 \, f^{(n)}(x_1). \tag{1.41}$$

We may convert R_n into a perhaps more practical form by using the **mean value theorem** of integral calculus:

$$\int_a^x g(x) \, dx = (x - a) \, g(\xi), \tag{1.42}$$

---

[2]Taylor's expansion may be derived under slightly less restrictive conditions; compare H. Jeffreys and B. S. Jeffreys, in the Additional Readings, Section 1.133.

with $a \leq \xi \leq x$. By integrating n times we get the Lagrangian form[3] of the remainder:

$$R_n = \frac{(x-a)^n}{n!} f^{(n)}(\xi). \qquad (1.43)$$

With Taylor's expansion in this form there are no questions of infinite series convergence. The series contains a finite number of terms, and the only questions concern the magnitude of the remainder.

When the function $f(x)$ is such that $\lim_{n \to \infty} R_n = 0$, Eq. (1.40) becomes Taylor's series:

$$f(x) = f(a) + (x-a) f'(a) + \frac{(x-a)^2}{2!} f''(a) + \cdots$$

$$= \sum_{n=0}^{\infty} \frac{(x-a)^n}{n!} f^{(n)}(a). \qquad (1.44)$$

Here we encounter for the first time $n!$ with $n = 0$. Note that we define $0! = 1$.

Our Taylor series specifies the value of a function at one point, x, in terms of the value of the function and its derivatives at a reference point a. It is an expansion in powers of the **change** in the variable, namely $x - a$. This idea can be emphasized by writing Taylor's series in an alternate form in which we replace x by $x + h$ and a by x:

$$f(x+h) = \sum_{n=0}^{\infty} \frac{h^n}{n!} f^{(n)}(x). \qquad (1.45)$$

Power Series

Taylor series are often used in situations where the reference point, a, is assigned the value zero. In that case the expansion is referred to as a **Maclaurin series**, and Eq. (1.40) becomes

$$f(x) = f(0) + xf'(0) + \frac{x^2}{2!} f''(0) + \cdots = \sum_{n=0}^{\infty} \frac{x^n}{n!} f^{(n)}(0). \qquad (1.46)$$

An immediate application of the Maclaurin series is in the expansion of various transcendental functions into infinite (power) series.

Example 1.2.3   EXPONENTIAL FUNCTION

Let $f(x) = e^x$. Differentiating, then setting $x = 0$, we have

$$f^{(n)}(0) = 1$$

for all n, $n = 1,\ 2,\ 3,\ \ldots$. Then, with Eq. (1.46), we have

$$e^x = 1 + x + \frac{x^2}{2!} + \frac{x^3}{3!} + \cdots = \sum_{n=0}^{\infty} \frac{x^n}{n!}. \qquad (1.47)$$

---

[3] An alternate form derived by Cauchy is $R_n = \frac{(x-\xi)^{n-1}(x-a)}{(n-1)!} f^{(n)}(\xi)$.

This is the series expansion of the exponential function. Some authors use this series to define the exponential function.

Although this series is clearly convergent for all x, as may be verified using the d'Alembert ratio test, it is instructive to check the remainder term, R_n. By Eq. (1.43) we have

$$R_n = \frac{x^n}{n!} f^{(n)}(\xi) = \frac{x^n}{n!} e^{\xi},$$

where ξ is between 0 and x. Irrespective of the sign of x,

$$|R_n| \leq \frac{|x|^n e^{|x|}}{n!}.$$

No matter how large $|x|$ may be, a sufficient increase in n will cause the denominator of this form for R_n to dominate over the numerator, and $\lim_{n \to \infty} R_n = 0$. Thus, the Maclaurin expansion of e^x converges absolutely over the entire range $-\infty < x < \infty$. ∎

Now that we have an expansion for $\exp(x)$, we can return to Eq. (1.45), and rewrite that equation in a form that focuses on its differential operator characteristics. Defining D as the **operator** d/dx, we have

$$f(x+h) = \sum_{n=0}^{\infty} \frac{h^n D^n}{n!} f(x) = e^{hD} f(x). \tag{1.48}$$

Example 1.2.4   LOGARITHM

For a second Maclaurin expansion, let $f(x) = \ln(1 + x)$. By differentiating, we obtain

$$f'(x) = (1+x)^{-1},$$

$$f^{(n)}(x) = (-1)^{n-1} (n-1)! (1+x)^{-n}. \tag{1.49}$$

Equation (1.46) yields

$$\ln(1+x) = x - \frac{x^2}{2} + \frac{x^3}{3} - \frac{x^4}{4} + \cdots + R_n$$

$$= \sum_{p=1}^{n} (-1)^{p-1} \frac{x^p}{p} + R_n. \tag{1.50}$$

In this case, for $x > 0$ our remainder is given by

$$R_n = \frac{x^n}{n!} f^{(n)}(\xi), \quad 0 \leq \xi \leq x$$

$$\leq \frac{x^n}{n}, \quad 0 \leq \xi \leq x \leq 1. \tag{1.51}$$

This result shows that the remainder approaches zero as n is increased indefinitely, providing that $0 \leq x \leq 1$. For $x < 0$, the mean value theorem is too crude a tool to establish a meaningful limit for R_n. As an infinite series,

$$\ln(1+x) = \sum_{n=1}^{\infty} (-1)^{n-1} \frac{x^n}{n} \qquad (1.52)$$

converges for $-1 < x \le 1$. The range $-1 < x < 1$ is easily established by the d'Alembert ratio test. Convergence at $x = 1$ follows by the Leibniz criterion. In particular, at $x = 1$ we have the conditionally convergent alternating harmonic series, to which we can now put a value:

$$\ln 2 = 1 - \frac{1}{2} + \frac{1}{3} - \frac{1}{4} + \frac{1}{5} - \cdots = \sum_{n=1}^{\infty} (-1)^{n-1} n^{-1}. \qquad (1.53)$$

At $x = -1$, the expansion becomes the harmonic series, which we well know to be divergent. ∎

Properties of Power Series

The power series is a special and extremely useful type of infinite series, and as illustrated in the preceding subsection, may be constructed by the Maclaurin formula, Eq. (1.44). However obtained, it will be of the general form

$$f(x) = a_0 + a_1 x + a_2 x^2 + a_3 x^3 + \cdots = \sum_{n=0}^{\infty} a_n x^n, \qquad (1.54)$$

where the coefficients a_i are constants, independent of x.

Equation (1.54) may readily be tested for convergence either by the Cauchy root test or the d'Alembert ratio test. If

$$\lim_{n \to \infty} \left| \frac{a_{n+1}}{a_n} \right| = R^{-1},$$

the series converges for $-R < x < R$. This is the interval or **radius** of convergence. Since the root and ratio tests fail when x is at the limit points $\pm R$, these points require special attention.

For instance, if $a_n = n^{-1}$, then $R = 1$ and from Section 1.1 we can conclude that the series converges for $x = -1$ but diverges for $x = +1$. If $a_n = n!$, then $R = 0$ and the series diverges for all $x \ne 0$.

Suppose our power series has been found convergent for $-R < x < R$; then it will be uniformly and absolutely convergent in any **interior** interval $-S \le x \le S$, where $0 < S < R$. This may be proved directly by the Weierstrass M test.

Since each of the terms $u_n(x) = a_n x^n$ is a continuous function of x and $f(x) = \sum a_n x^n$ converges uniformly for $-S \le x \le S$, $f(x)$ must be a continuous function in the interval of uniform convergence. This behavior is to be contrasted with the strikingly different behavior of series in trigonometric functions, which are used frequently to represent discontinuous functions such as sawtooth and square waves.

With $u_n(x)$ continuous and $\sum a_n x^n$ uniformly convergent, we find that term by term differentiation or integration of a power series will yield a new power series with continuous functions and the same radius of convergence as the original series. The new factors introduced by differentiation or integration do not affect either the root or the ratio test. Therefore our power series may be differentiated or integrated as often as desired within the interval of uniform convergence (Exercise 1.2.16). In view of the rather severe restriction placed on differentiation of infinite series in general, this is a remarkable and valuable result.

Uniqueness Theorem

We have already used the Maclaurin series to expand e^x and $\ln(1 + x)$ into power series. Throughout this book, we will encounter many situations in which functions are represented, or even defined by power series. We now establish that the power-series representation is unique.

We proceed by assuming we have two expansions of the same function whose intervals of convergence overlap in a region that includes the origin:

$$f(x) = \sum_{n=0}^{\infty} a_n x^n, \quad -R_a < x < R_a$$

$$= \sum_{n=0}^{\infty} b_n x^n, \quad -R_b < x < R_b. \tag{1.55}$$

What we need to prove is that $a_n = b_n$ for all n.

Starting from

$$\sum_{n=0}^{\infty} a_n x^n = \sum_{n=0}^{\infty} b_n x^n, \quad -R < x < R, \tag{1.56}$$

where R is the smaller of R_a and R_b, we set $x = 0$ to eliminate all but the constant term of each series, obtaining

$$a_0 = b_0.$$

Now, exploiting the differentiability of our power series, we differentiate Eq. (1.56), getting

$$\sum_{n=1}^{\infty} n a_n x^{n-1} = \sum_{n=1}^{\infty} n b_n x^{n-1}. \tag{1.57}$$

We again set $x = 0$, to isolate the new constant terms, and find

$$a_1 = b_1.$$

By repeating this process n times, we get

$$a_n = b_n,$$

which shows that the two series coincide. Therefore our power series representation is unique.

This theorem will be a crucial point in our study of differential equations, in which we develop power series solutions. The uniqueness of power series appears frequently in theoretical physics. The establishment of perturbation theory in quantum mechanics is one example.

Indeterminate Forms

The power-series representation of functions is often useful in evaluating indeterminate forms, and is the basis of **l'Hôpital's rule**, which states that if the ratio of two differentiable functions $f(x)$ and $g(x)$ becomes indeterminate, of the form 0/0, at $x = x_0$, then

$$\lim_{x \to x_0} \frac{f(x)}{g(x)} = \lim_{x \to x_0} \frac{f'(x)}{g'(x)}. \tag{1.58}$$

Proof of Eq. (1.58) is the subject of Exercise 1.2.12.

Sometimes it is easier just to introduce power-series expansions than to evaluate the derivatives that enter l'Hôpital's rule. For examples of this strategy, see the following Example and Exercise 1.2.15.

Example 1.2.5   ALTERNATIVE TO L'HÔPITAL'S RULE

Evaluate

$$\lim_{x \to 0} \frac{1 - \cos x}{x^2}. \tag{1.59}$$

Replacing $\cos x$ by its Maclaurin-series expansion, Exercise 1.2.8, we obtain

$$\frac{1 - \cos x}{x^2} = \frac{1 - (1 - \frac{1}{2!}x^2 + \frac{1}{4!}x^4 - \cdots)}{x^2} = \frac{1}{2!} - \frac{x^2}{4!} + \cdots.$$

Letting $x \to 0$, we have

$$\lim_{x \to 0} \frac{1 - \cos x}{x^2} = \frac{1}{2}. \tag{1.60}$$

∎

The uniqueness of power series means that the coefficients a_n may be identified with the derivatives in a Maclaurin series. From

$$f(x) = \sum_{n=0}^{\infty} a_n x^n = \sum_{m=0}^{\infty} \frac{1}{n!} f^{(n)}(0) x^n,$$

we have

$$a_n = \frac{1}{n!} f^{(n)}(0).$$

Inversion of Power Series

Suppose we are given a series

$$y - y_0 = a_1(x - x_0) + a_2(x - x_0)^2 + \cdots = \sum_{n=1}^{\infty} a_n (x - x_0)^n. \qquad (1.61)$$

This gives $(y - y_0)$ in terms of $(x - x_0)$. However, it may be desirable to have an explicit expression for $(x - x_0)$ in terms of $(y - y_0)$. That is, we want an expression of the form

$$x - x_0 = \sum_{n=1}^{\infty} b_n (y - y_0)^n, \qquad (1.62)$$

with the b_n to be determined in terms of the assumed known a_n. A brute-force approach, which is perfectly adequate for the first few coefficients, is simply to substitute Eq. (1.61) into Eq. (1.62). By equating coefficients of $(x - x_0)^n$ on both sides of Eq. (1.62), and using the fact that the power series is unique, we find

$$b_1 = \frac{1}{a_1},$$

$$b_2 = -\frac{a_2}{a_1^3},$$

$$b_3 = \frac{1}{a_1^5} \left(2a_2^2 - a_1 a_3 \right), \qquad (1.63)$$

$$b_4 = \frac{1}{a_1^7} \left(5a_1 a_2 a_3 - a_1^2 a_4 - 5a_2^3 \right), \text{ and so on.}$$

Some of the higher coefficients are listed by Dwight.[4] A more general and much more elegant approach is developed by the use of complex variables in the first and second editions of *Mathematical Methods for Physicists*.

Exercises

1.2.8   Show that

(a) $\sin x = \sum_{n=0}^{\infty} (-1)^n \frac{x^{2n+1}}{(2n + 1)!},$

(b) $\cos x = \sum_{n=0}^{\infty} (-1)^n \frac{x^{2n}}{(2n)!}.$

---

[4]H. B. Dwight, *Tables of Integrals and Other Mathematical Data*, 4th ed. New York: Macmillan (1961). (Compare formula no. 50.)

1.2.9   Derive a series expansion of $\cot x$ in increasing powers of x by dividing the power series for $\cos x$ by that for $\sin x$.

Note. The resultant series that starts with $1/x$ is known as a **Laurent series** ($\cot x$ does not have a Taylor expansion about $x = 0$, although $\cot(x) - x^{-1}$ does). Although the two series for $\sin x$ and $\cos x$ were valid for all x, the convergence of the series for $\cot x$ is limited by the zeros of the denominator, $\sin x$.

1.2.10   Show by series expansion that

$$\frac{1}{2} \ln \frac{\eta_0 + 1}{\eta_0 - 1} = \coth^{-1} \eta_0, \quad |\eta_0| > 1.$$

This identity may be used to obtain a second solution for Legendre's equation.

1.2.11   Show that $f(x) = x^{1/2}$ (a) has no Maclaurin expansion but (b) has a Taylor expansion about any point $x_0 \neq 0$. Find the range of convergence of the Taylor expansion about $x = x_0$.

1.2.12   Prove l'Hôpital's rule, Eq. (1.58).

1.2.13   With $n > 1$, show that

(a) $\dfrac{1}{n} - \ln\left(\dfrac{n}{n-1}\right) < 0,$ (b) $\dfrac{1}{n} - \ln\left(\dfrac{n+1}{n}\right) > 0.$

Use these inequalities to show that the limit defining the Euler-Mascheroni constant, Eq. (1.13), is finite.

1.2.14   In numerical analysis it is often convenient to approximate $d^2\psi(x)/dx^2$ by

$$\frac{d^2}{dx^2}\psi(x) \approx \frac{1}{h^2}[\psi(x+h) - 2\psi(x) + \psi(x-h)].$$

Find the error in this approximation.

ANS. $\text{Error} = \dfrac{h^2}{12}\psi^{(4)}(x).$

1.2.15   Evaluate $\displaystyle \lim_{x \to 0}\left[\frac{\sin(\tan x) - \tan(\sin x)}{x^7}\right].$

ANS. $-\dfrac{1}{30}.$

1.2.16   A power series converges for $-R < x < R$. Show that the differentiated series and the integrated series have the same interval of convergence. (Do not bother about the endpoints $x = \pm R$.)

1.3   BINOMIAL THEOREM

An extremely important application of the Maclaurin expansion is the derivation of the binomial theorem.

Let $f(x) = (1 + x)^m$, in which m may be either positive or negative and is not limited to integral values. Direct application of Eq. (1.46) gives

$$(1 + x)^m = 1 + mx + \frac{m(m-1)}{2!} x^2 + \cdots + R_n. \tag{1.64}$$

For this function the remainder is

$$R_n = \frac{x^n}{n!} (1 + \xi)^{m-n} m(m-1) \cdots (m-n+1), \tag{1.65}$$

with ξ between 0 and x. Restricting attention for now to $x \geq 0$, we note that for $n > m$, $(1 + \xi)^{m-n}$ is a maximum for $\xi = 0$, so for positive x,

$$|R_n| \leq \frac{x^n}{n!} |m(m-1) \cdots (m-n+1)|, \tag{1.66}$$

with $\lim_{n \to \infty} R_n = 0$ when $0 \leq x < 1$. Because the radius of convergence of a power series is the same for positive and for negative x, the binomial series converges for $-1 < x < 1$. Convergence at the limit points ± 1 is not addressed by the present analysis, and depends on m.

Summarizing, we have established the **binomial expansion**,

$$(1 + x)^m = 1 + mx + \frac{m(m-1)}{2!} x^2 + \frac{m(m-1)(m-2)}{3!} x^3 + \cdots, \tag{1.67}$$

convergent for $-1 < x < 1$. It is important to note that Eq. (1.67) applies whether or not m is integral, and for both positive and negative m. If m is a nonnegative integer, R_n for $n > m$ vanishes for all x, corresponding to the fact that under those conditions $(1 + x)^m$ is a finite sum.

Because the binomial expansion is of frequent occurrence, the coefficients appearing in it, which are called **binomial coefficients**, are given the special symbol

$$\binom{m}{n} = \frac{m(m-1) \cdots (m-n+1)}{n!}, \tag{1.68}$$

and the binomial expansion assumes the general form

$$(1 + x)^m = \sum_{n=0}^{\infty} \binom{m}{n} x^n. \tag{1.69}$$

In evaluating Eq. (1.68), note that when $n = 0$, the product in its numerator is empty (starting from m and **descending** to $m + 1$); in that case the convention is to assign the product the value unity. We also remind the reader that 0! is defined to be unity.

In the special case that m is a positive integer, we may write our binomial coefficient in terms of factorials:

$$\binom{m}{n} = \frac{m!}{n! (m-n)!}. \tag{1.70}$$

Since $n!$ is undefined for negative integer n, the binomial expansion for positive integer m is understood to end with the term $n = m$, and will correspond to the coefficients in the polynomial resulting from the (finite) expansion of $(1 + x)^m$.

For positive integer m, the $\binom{m}{n}$ also arise in combinatorial theory, being the number of different ways n out of m objects can be selected. That, of course, is consistent with the coefficient set if $(1+x)^m$ is expanded. The term containing x^n has a coefficient that corresponds to the number of ways one can choose the "x" from n of the factors $(1+x)$ and the 1 from the $m-n$ other $(1+x)$ factors.

For negative integer m, we can still use the special notation for binomial coefficients, but their evaluation is more easily accomplished if we set $m = -p$, with p a positive integer, and write

$$\binom{-p}{n} = (-1)^n \frac{p(p+1)\cdots(p+n-1)}{n!} = \frac{(-1)^n (p+n-1)!}{n!\,(p-1)!}. \tag{1.71}$$

For nonintegral m, it is convenient to use the **Pochhammer symbol**, defined for general a and nonnegative integer n and given the notation $(a)_n$, as

$$(a)_0 = 1, \quad (a)_1 = a, \quad (a)_{n+1} = a(a+1)\cdots(a+n), \quad (n \ge 1). \tag{1.72}$$

For both integral and nonintegral m, the binomial coefficient formula can be written

$$\binom{m}{n} = \frac{(m-n+1)_n}{n!}. \tag{1.73}$$

There is a rich literature on binomial coefficients and relationships between them and on summations involving them. We mention here only one such formula that arises if we evaluate $1/\sqrt{1+x}$, i.e., $(1+x)^{-1/2}$. The binomial coefficient

$$\binom{-\frac{1}{2}}{n} = \frac{1}{n!}\left(-\frac{1}{2}\right)\left(-\frac{3}{2}\right)\cdots\left(-\frac{2n-1}{2}\right)$$

$$= (-1)^n \frac{1 \cdot 3 \cdots (2n-1)}{2^n\, n!} = (-1)^n \frac{(2n-1)!!}{(2n)!!}, \tag{1.74}$$

where the "double factorial" notation indicates products of even or odd positive integers as follows:

$$1 \cdot 3 \cdot 5 \cdots (2n-1) = (2n-1)!!$$
$$2 \cdot 4 \cdot 6 \cdots (2n) = (2n)!!. \tag{1.75}$$

These are related to the regular factorials by

$$(2n)!! = 2^n\, n! \quad \text{and} \quad (2n-1)!! = \frac{(2n)!}{2^n\, n!}. \tag{1.76}$$

Note that these relations include the special cases $0!! = (-1)!! = 1$.

Example 1.3.1   RELATIVISTIC ENERGY

The total relativistic energy of a particle of mass m and velocity v is

$$E = mc^2 \left(1 - \frac{v^2}{c^2}\right)^{-1/2}, \tag{1.77}$$

where c is the velocity of light. Using Eq. (1.69) with $m = -1/2$ and $x = -v^2/c^2$, and evaluating the binomial coefficients using Eq. (1.74), we have

$$E = mc^2 \left[1 - \frac{1}{2} \left(-\frac{v^2}{c^2} \right) + \frac{3}{8} \left(-\frac{v^2}{c^2} \right)^2 - \frac{5}{16} \left(-\frac{v^2}{c^2} \right)^3 + \cdots \right]$$

$$= mc^2 + \frac{1}{2} mv^2 + \frac{3}{8} mv^2 \left(\frac{v^2}{c^2} \right) + \frac{5}{16} mv^2 \left(-\frac{v^2}{c^2} \right)^2 + \cdots. \tag{1.78}$$

The first term, mc^2, is identified as the rest-mass energy. Then

$$E_{\text{kinetic}} = \frac{1}{2} mv^2 \left[1 + \frac{3}{4} \frac{v^2}{c^2} + \frac{5}{8} \left(-\frac{v^2}{c^2} \right)^2 + \cdots \right]. \tag{1.79}$$

For particle velocity $v \ll c$, the expression in the brackets reduces to unity and we see that the kinetic portion of the total relativistic energy agrees with the classical result.   ■

The binomial expansion can be generalized for positive integer n to polynomials:

$$(a_1 + a_2 + \cdots + a_m)^n = \sum \frac{n!}{n_1! n_2! \cdots n_m!} a_1^{n_1} a_2^{n_2} \cdots a_m^{n_m}, \tag{1.80}$$

where the summation includes all different combinations of nonnegative integers $n_1, n_2, \ldots, n_m$ with $\sum_{i=1}^{m} n_i = n$. This generalization finds considerable use in statistical mechanics.

In everyday analysis, the combinatorial properties of the binomial coefficients make them appear often. For example, Leibniz's formula for the nth derivative of a product of two functions, $u(x) v(x)$, can be written

$$\left(\frac{d}{dx} \right)^n \left(u(x) \, v(x) \right) = \sum_{i=0}^{n} \binom{n}{i} \left(\frac{d^i u(x)}{dx^i} \right) \left(\frac{d^{n-i} v(x)}{dx^{n-i}} \right). \tag{1.81}$$

Exercises

1.3.1   The classical Langevin theory of paramagnetism leads to an expression for the magnetic polarization,

$$P(x) = c \left(\frac{\cosh x}{\sinh x} - \frac{1}{x} \right).$$

Expand $P(x)$ as a power series for small x (low fields, high temperature).

1.3.2   Given that

$$\int_0^1 \frac{dx}{1 + x^2} = \tan^{-1} x \Big|_0^1 = \frac{\pi}{4},$$

expand the integrand into a series and integrate term by term obtaining[5]

$$\frac{\pi}{4} = 1 - \frac{1}{3} + \frac{1}{5} - \frac{1}{7} + \frac{1}{9} - \cdots + (-1)^n \frac{1}{2n+1} + \cdots,$$

which is Leibniz's formula for π. Compare the convergence of the integrand series and the integrated series at $x = 1$. Leibniz's formula converges so slowly that it is quite useless for numerical work.

1.3.3 Expand the incomplete gamma function $\gamma(n+1, x) \equiv \int_0^x e^{-t} t^n dt$ in a series of powers of x. What is the range of convergence of the resulting series?

$$\text{ANS.} \quad \int_0^x e^{-t} t^n dt = x^{n+1} \left[\frac{1}{n+1} - \frac{x}{n+2} + \frac{x^2}{2!(n+3)} \right.$$
$$\left. - \cdots \frac{(-1)^p x^p}{p!(n+p+1)} + \cdots \right].$$

1.3.4 Develop a series expansion of $y = \sinh^{-1} x$ (that is, $\sinh y = x$) in powers of x by

(a) inversion of the series for $\sinh y$,

(b) a direct Maclaurin expansion.

1.3.5 Show that for integral $n \geq 0$, $\quad \dfrac{1}{(1-x)^{n+1}} = \sum\limits_{m=n}^{\infty} \binom{m}{n} x^{m-n}$.

1.3.6 Show that $(1+x)^{-m/2} = \sum\limits_{n=0}^{\infty} (-1)^n \dfrac{(m+2n-2)!!}{2^n n! (m-2)!!} x^n$, for $m = 1, 2, 3, \ldots$.

1.3.7 Using binomial expansions, compare the three Doppler shift formulas:

(a) $\quad \nu' = \nu \left(1 \mp \dfrac{v}{c}\right)^{-1}$ $\qquad$ moving source;

(b) $\quad \nu' = \nu \left(1 \pm \dfrac{v}{c}\right)$ $\qquad$ moving observer;

(c) $\quad \nu' = \nu \left(1 \pm \dfrac{v}{c}\right) \left(1 - \dfrac{v^2}{c^2}\right)^{-1/2}$ $\quad$ relativistic.

Note. The relativistic formula agrees with the classical formulas if terms of order v^2/c^2 can be neglected.

1.3.8 In the theory of general relativity there are various ways of relating (defining) a velocity of recession of a galaxy to its red shift, δ. Milne's model (kinematic relativity) gives

---

[5]The series expansion of $\tan^{-1} x$ (upper limit 1 replaced by x) was discovered by James Gregory in 1671, 3 years before Leibniz. See Peter Beckmann's entertaining book, *A History of Pi*, 2nd ed., Boulder, CO: Golem Press (1971), and L. Berggren, J. Borwein, and P. Borwein, *Pi: A Source Book*, New York: Springer (1997).

(a) $v_1 = c\delta \left(1 + \dfrac{1}{2}\delta\right),$

(b) $v_2 = c\delta \left(1 + \dfrac{1}{2}\delta\right)(1+\delta)^{-2},$

(c) $1 + \delta = \left[\dfrac{1 + v_3/c}{1 - v_3/c}\right]^{1/2}.$

1.   Show that for $\delta \ll 1$ (and $v_3/c \ll 1$), all three formulas reduce to $v = c\delta$.
2.   Compare the three velocities through terms of order δ^2.

Note. In special relativity (with δ replaced by z), the ratio of observed wavelength λ to emitted wavelength λ_0 is given by

$$\frac{\lambda}{\lambda_0} = 1 + z = \left(\frac{c+v}{c-v}\right)^{1/2}.$$

1.3.9   The relativistic sum w of two velocities u and v in the same direction is given by

$$\frac{w}{c} = \frac{u/c + v/c}{1 + uv/c^2}.$$

If

$$\frac{v}{c} = \frac{u}{c} = 1 - \alpha,$$

where $0 \leq \alpha \leq 1$, find w/c in powers of α through terms in α^3.

1.3.10   The displacement x of a particle of rest mass m_0, resulting from a constant force $m_0 g$ along the x-axis, is

$$x = \frac{c^2}{g} \left\{ \left[1 + \left(g\frac{t}{c}\right)^2\right]^{1/2} - 1 \right\},$$

including relativistic effects. Find the displacement x as a power series in time t. Compare with the classical result,

$$x = \frac{1}{2}gt^2.$$

1.3.11   By use of Dirac's relativistic theory, the fine structure formula of atomic spectroscopy is given by

$$E = mc^2 \left[1 + \frac{\gamma^2}{(s + n - |k|)^2}\right]^{-1/2},$$

where

$$s = (|k|^2 - \gamma^2)^{1/2}, \quad k = \pm 1, \pm 2, \pm 3, \ldots.$$

Expand in powers of γ^2 through order γ^4 ($\gamma^2 = Ze^2/4\pi\epsilon_0\hbar c$, with Z the atomic number). This expansion is useful in comparing the predictions of the Dirac electron theory with those of a relativistic Schrödinger electron theory. Experimental results support the Dirac theory.

1.3.12   In a head-on proton-proton collision, the ratio of the kinetic energy in the center of mass system to the incident kinetic energy is

$$R = [\sqrt{2mc^2(E_k + 2mc^2)} - 2mc^2]/E_k.$$

Find the value of this ratio of kinetic energies for

(a) $E_k \ll mc^2$ (nonrelativistic),

(b) $E_k \gg mc^2$ (extreme-relativistic).

> *ANS.*   (a) $\frac{1}{2}$,   (b)   0. The latter answer is a sort of law of diminishing returns for high-energy particle accelerators (with stationary targets).

1.3.13   With binomial expansions

$$\frac{x}{1-x} = \sum_{n=1}^{\infty} x^n, \qquad \frac{x}{x-1} = \frac{1}{1-x^{-1}} = \sum_{n=0}^{\infty} x^{-n}.$$

Adding these two series yields $\sum_{n=-\infty}^{\infty} x^n = 0$.
Hopefully, we can agree that this is nonsense, but what has gone wrong?

1.3.14   (a)   Planck's theory of quantized oscillators leads to an average energy

$$\langle \varepsilon \rangle = \frac{\displaystyle\sum_{n=1}^{\infty} n\varepsilon_0 \exp(-n\varepsilon_0/kT)}{\displaystyle\sum_{n=0}^{\infty} \exp(-n\varepsilon_0/kT)},$$

where ε_0 is a fixed energy. Identify the numerator and denominator as binomial expansions and show that the ratio is

$$\langle \varepsilon \rangle = \frac{\varepsilon_0}{\exp(\varepsilon_0/kT) - 1}.$$

(b)   Show that the $\langle \varepsilon \rangle$ of part (a) reduces to kT, the classical result, for $kT \gg \varepsilon_0$.

1.3.15   Expand by the binomial theorem and integrate term by term to obtain the Gregory series for $y = \tan^{-1} x$ (note $\tan y = x$):

$$\tan^{-1} x = \int_0^x \frac{dt}{1+t^2} = \int_0^x \{1 - t^2 + t^4 - t^6 + \cdots\}\, dt$$

$$= \sum_{n=0}^{\infty} (-1)^n \frac{x^{2n+1}}{2n+1}, \qquad -1 \le x \le 1.$$

1.3.16   The Klein-Nishina formula for the scattering of photons by electrons contains a term of the form

$$f(\varepsilon) = \frac{(1+\varepsilon)}{\varepsilon^2} \left[\frac{2+2\varepsilon}{1+2\varepsilon} - \frac{\ln(1+2\varepsilon)}{\varepsilon} \right].$$

Here $\varepsilon = h\nu/mc^2$, the ratio of the photon energy to the electron rest mass energy. Find $\lim_{\varepsilon \to 0} f(\varepsilon)$.

$$ANS. \quad \frac{4}{3}.$$

1.3.17   The behavior of a neutron losing energy by colliding elastically with nuclei of mass A is described by a parameter ξ_1,

$$\xi_1 = 1 + \frac{(A-1)^2}{2A} \ln \frac{A-1}{A+1}.$$

An approximation, good for large A, is

$$\xi_2 = \frac{2}{A + \frac{2}{3}}.$$

Expand ξ_1 and ξ_2 in powers of A^{-1}. Show that ξ_2 agrees with ξ_1 through $(A^{-1})^2$. Find the difference in the coefficients of the $(A^{-1})^3$ term.

1.3.18   Show that each of these two integrals equals Catalan's constant:

$$(a) \quad \int_0^1 \arctan t \, \frac{dt}{t}, \quad (b) \quad -\int_0^1 \ln x \frac{dx}{1+x^2}.$$

Note. The definition and numerical computation of Catalan's constant was addressed in Exercise 1.1.12.

1.4   MATHEMATICAL INDUCTION

We are occasionally faced with the need to establish a relation which is valid for a set of integer values, in situations where it may not initially be obvious how to proceed. However, it may be possible to show that if the relation is valid for an arbitrary value of some index n, then it is also valid if n is replaced by $n + 1$. If we can also show that the relation is unconditionally satisfied for some initial value n_0, we may then conclude (unconditionally) that the relation is also satisfied for $n_0 + 1, n_0 + 2, \ldots$. This method of proof is known as **mathematical induction**. It is ordinarily most useful when we know (or suspect) the validity of a relation, but lack a more direct method of proof.

Example 1.4.1   SUM OF INTEGERS

The sum of the integers from 1 through n, here denoted $S(n)$, is given by the formula $S(n) = n(n+1)/2$. An inductive proof of this formula proceeds as follows:

1.   Given the formula for $S(n)$, we calculate

$$S(n+1) = S(n) + (n+1) = \frac{n(n+1)}{2} + (n+1) = \left[\frac{n}{2} + 1\right](n+1) = \frac{(n+1)(n+2)}{2}.$$

Thus, given $S(n)$, we can establish the validity of $S(n+1)$.

2. It is obvious that $S(1) = 1(2)/2 = 1$, so our formula for $S(n)$ is valid for $n = 1$.
3. The formula for $S(n)$ is therefore valid for all integers $n \geq 1$.   ∎

Exercises

1.4.1   Show that $\displaystyle\sum_{j=1}^{n} j^4 = \frac{n}{30}(2n+1)(n+1)(3n^2 + 3n - 1)$.

1.4.2   Prove the Leibniz formula for the repeated differentiation of a product:

$$\left(\frac{d}{dx}\right)^n \left[f(x)g(x)\right] = \sum_{j=0}^{n} \binom{n}{j} \left[\left(\frac{d}{dx}\right)^j f(x)\right]\left[\left(\frac{d}{dx}\right)^{n-j} g(x)\right].$$

1.5   OPERATIONS ON SERIES EXPANSIONS OF FUNCTIONS

There are a number of manipulations (tricks) that can be used to obtain series that represent a function or to manipulate such series to improve convergence. In addition to the procedures introduced in Section 1.1, there are others that to varying degrees make use of the fact that the expansion depends on a variable. A simple example of this is the expansion of $f(x) = \ln(1+x)$, which we obtained in 1.2.4 by direct use of the Maclaurin expansion and evaluation of the derivatives of $f(x)$. An even easier way to obtain this series would have been to integrate the power series for $1/(1+x)$ term by term from 0 to x:

$$\frac{1}{1+x} = 1 - x + x^2 - x^3 + \cdots \quad \Longrightarrow$$

$$\ln(1+x) = x - \frac{x^2}{2} + \frac{x^3}{3} - \frac{x^4}{4} + \cdots.$$

A problem requiring somewhat more deviousness is given by the following example, in which we use the binomial theorem on a series that represents the derivative of the function whose expansion is sought.

Example 1.5.1   APPLICATION OF BINOMIAL EXPANSION

Sometimes the binomial expansion provides a convenient indirect route to the Maclaurin series when direct methods are difficult. We consider here the power series expansion

$$\sin^{-1} x = \sum_{n=0}^{\infty} \frac{(2n-1)!!}{(2n)!!} \frac{x^{2n+1}}{(2n+1)} = x + \frac{x^3}{6} + \frac{3x^5}{40} + \cdots. \tag{1.82}$$

Starting from $\sin y = x$, we find $dy/dx = 1/\sqrt{1 - x^2}$, and write the integral

$$\sin^{-1} x = y = \int_0^x \frac{dt}{(1 - t^2)^{1/2}}.$$

We now introduce the binomial expansion of $(1 - t^2)^{-1/2}$ and integrate term by term. The result is Eq. (1.82). ∎

Another way of improving the convergence of a series is to multiply it by a polynomial in the variable, choosing the polynomial's coefficients to remove the least rapidly convergent part of the resulting series. Here is a simple example of this.

Example 1.5.2   MULTIPLY SERIES BY POLYNOMIAL

Returning to the series for $\ln(1 + x)$, we form

$$(1 + a_1 x) \ln(1 + x) = \sum_{n=1}^{\infty} (-1)^{n-1} \frac{x^n}{n} + a_1 \sum_{n=1}^{\infty} (-1)^{n-1} \frac{x^{n+1}}{n}$$

$$= x + \sum_{n=2}^{\infty} (-1)^{n-1} \left(\frac{1}{n} - \frac{a_1}{n-1} \right) x^n$$

$$= x + \sum_{n=2}^{\infty} (-1)^{n-1} \frac{n(1 - a_1) - 1}{n(n-1)} x^n.$$

If we take $a_1 = 1$, the n in the numerator disappears and our combined series converges as n^{-2}; the resulting series for $\ln(1 + x)$ is

$$\ln(1 + x) = \left(\frac{x}{1 + x} \right) \left(1 - \sum_{n=1}^{\infty} \frac{(-1)^n}{n(n+1)} x^n \right).$$

∎

Another useful trick is to employ **partial fraction expansions**, which may convert a seemingly difficult series into others about which more may be known.

If $g(x)$ and $h(x)$ are polynomials in x, with $g(x)$ of lower degree than $h(x)$, and $h(x)$ has the factorization $h(x) = (x - a_1)(x - a_2) \ldots (x - a_n)$, in the case that the factors of $h(x)$ are distinct (i.e., h has no multiple roots), then $g(x)/h(x)$ can be written in the form

$$\frac{g(x)}{h(x)} = \frac{c_1}{x - a_1} + \frac{c_2}{x - a_2} + \cdots + \frac{c_n}{x - a_n}. \tag{1.83}$$

If we wish to leave one or more quadratic factors in $h(x)$, perhaps to avoid the introduction of imaginary quantities, the corresponding partial-fraction term will be of the form

$$\frac{ax + b}{x^2 + px + q}.$$

If $h(x)$ has repeated linear factors, such as $(x - a_1)^m$, the partial fraction expansion for this power of $x - a_1$ takes the form

$$\frac{c_{1,m}}{(x - a_1)^m} + \frac{c_{1,m-1}}{(x - a_1)^{m-1}} + \cdots + \frac{c_{1,1}}{x - a_1}.$$

The coefficients in partial fraction expansions are usually found easily; sometimes it is useful to express them as limits, such as

$$c_i = \lim_{x \to a_i} (x - a_i)g(x)/h(x). \tag{1.84}$$

Example 1.5.3   PARTIAL FRACTION EXPANSION

Let

$$f(x) = \frac{k^2}{x(x^2 + k^2)} = \frac{c}{x} + \frac{ax + b}{x^2 + k^2}.$$

We have written the form of the partial fraction expansion, but have not yet determined the values of a, b, and c. Putting the right side of the equation over a common denominator, we have

$$\frac{k^2}{x(x^2 + k^2)} = \frac{c(x^2 + k^2) + x(ax + b)}{x(x^2 + k^2)}.$$

Expanding the right-side numerator and equating it to the left-side numerator, we get

$$0(x^2) + 0(x) + k^2 = (c + a)x^2 + bx + ck^2,$$

which we solve by requiring the coefficient of each power of x to have the same value on both sides of this equation. We get $b = 0$, $c = 1$, and then $a = -1$. The final result is therefore

$$f(x) = \frac{1}{x} - \frac{x}{x^2 + k^2}. \tag{1.85}$$

∎

Still more cleverness is illustrated by the following procedure, due to Euler, for changing the expansion variable so as to improve the range over which an expansion converges. Euler's transformation, the proof of which (with hints) is deferred to Exercise 1.5.4, makes the conversion:

$$f(x) = \sum_{n=0}^{\infty} (-1)^n c_n x^n \tag{1.86}$$

$$= \frac{1}{1+x} \sum_{n=0}^{\infty} (-1)^n a_n \left(\frac{x}{1+x}\right)^n. \tag{1.87}$$

The coefficients a_n are repeated differences of the c_n:

$$a_0 = c_0, \quad a_1 = c_1 - c_0, \quad a_2 = c_2 - 2c_1 + c_0, \quad a_3 = c_3 - 3c_2 + 3c_1 - c_0, \ldots;$$

their general formula is

$$a_n = \sum_{j=0}^{n} (-1)^j \binom{n}{j} c_{n-j}. \tag{1.88}$$

The series to which the Euler transformation is applied need not be alternating. The coefficients c_n can have a sign factor which cancels that in the definition.

Example 1.5.4   EULER TRANSFORMATION

The Maclaurin series for $\ln(1+x)$ converges extremely slowly, with convergence only for $|x| < 1$. We consider the Euler transformation on the related series

$$\frac{\ln(1+x)}{x} = 1 - \frac{x}{2} + \frac{x^2}{3} - \cdots, \tag{1.89}$$

so, in Eq. (1.86), $c_n = 1/(n+1)$. The first few a_n are: $a_0 = 1$, $a_1 = \frac{1}{2} - 1 = -\frac{1}{2}$, $a_2 = \frac{1}{3} - 2\left(\frac{1}{2}\right) + 1 = \frac{1}{3}$, $a_3 = \frac{1}{4} - 3\left(\frac{1}{3}\right) + 3\left(\frac{1}{2}\right) - 1 = -\frac{1}{4}$, or in general

$$a_n = \frac{(-1)^n}{n+1}.$$

The converted series is then

$$\frac{\ln(1+x)}{x} = \frac{1}{1+x}\left[1 + \frac{1}{2}\left(\frac{x}{1+x}\right) + \frac{1}{3}\left(\frac{x}{1+x}\right)^2 + \cdots\right],$$

which rearranges to

$$\ln(1+x) = \left(\frac{x}{1+x}\right) + \frac{1}{2}\left(\frac{x}{1+x}\right)^2 + \frac{1}{3}\left(\frac{x}{1+x}\right)^3 + \cdots. \tag{1.90}$$

This new series converges nicely at $x = 1$, and in fact is convergent for all $x < \infty$. ∎

Exercises

1.5.1   Using a partial fraction expansion, show that for $0 < x < 1$,

$$\int_{-x}^{x} \frac{dt}{1 - t^2} = \ln\left(\frac{1+x}{1-x}\right).$$

1.5.2   Prove the partial fraction expansion

$$\frac{1}{n(n+1)\cdots(n+p)}$$
$$= \frac{1}{p!}\left[\binom{p}{0}\frac{1}{n} - \binom{p}{1}\frac{1}{n+1} + \binom{p}{2}\frac{1}{n+2} - \cdots + (-1)^p\binom{p}{p}\frac{1}{n+p}\right],$$

where p is a positive integer.

Hint. Use mathematical induction. Two binomial coefficient formulas of use here are

$$\frac{p+1}{p+1-j}\binom{p}{j} = \binom{p+1}{j}, \qquad \sum_{j=1}^{p+1}(-1)^{j-1}\binom{p+1}{j} = 1.$$

1.5.3   The formula for α_p, Eq. (1.26), is a summation of the form $\sum_{n=1}^{\infty} u_n(p)$, with

$$u_n(p) = \frac{1}{n(n+1)\cdots(n+p)}.$$

Applying a partial fraction decomposition to the first and last factors of the denominator, i.e.,

$$\frac{1}{n(n+p)} = \frac{1}{p}\left[\frac{1}{n} - \frac{1}{n+p}\right],$$

show that $u_n(p) = \frac{u_n(p-1) - u_{n+1}(p-1)}{p}$ and that $\sum_{n=1}^{\infty} u_n(p) = \frac{1}{p\,p!}$.

Hint. It is useful to note that $u_1(p-1) = 1/p!$.

1.5.4   Proof of Euler transformation: By substituting Eq. (1.88) into Eq. (1.87), verify that Eq. (1.86) is recovered.

Hint. It may help to rearrange the resultant double series so that both indices are summed on the range $(0, \infty)$. Then the summation not containing the coefficients c_j can be recognized as a binomial expansion.

1.5.5   Carry out the Euler transformation on the series for $\arctan(x)$:

$$\arctan(x) = x - \frac{x^3}{3} + \frac{x^5}{5} - \frac{x^7}{7} + \frac{x^9}{9} - \cdots.$$

Check your work by computing $\arctan(1) = \pi/4$ and $\arctan(3^{-1/2}) = \pi/6$.

1.6 SOME IMPORTANT SERIES

There are a few series that arise so often that all physicists should recognize them. Here is a short list that is worth committing to memory.

$$\exp(x) = \sum_{n=0}^{\infty} \frac{x^n}{n!} = 1 + x + \frac{x^2}{2!} + \frac{x^3}{3!} + \frac{x^4}{4!} + \cdots, \qquad -\infty < x < \infty, \qquad (1.91)$$

$$\sin(x) = \sum_{n=0}^{\infty} \frac{(-1)^n x^{2n+1}}{(2n+1)!} = x - \frac{x^3}{3!} + \frac{x^5}{5!} - \frac{x^7}{7!} + \cdots, \qquad -\infty < x < \infty, \qquad (1.92)$$

$$\cos(x) = \sum_{n=0}^{\infty} \frac{(-1)^n x^{2n}}{(2n)!} = 1 - \frac{x^2}{2!} + \frac{x^4}{4!} - \frac{x^6}{6!} + \cdots, \qquad -\infty < x < \infty, \qquad (1.93)$$

$$\sinh(x) = \sum_{n=0}^{\infty} \frac{x^{2n+1}}{(2n+1)!} = x + \frac{x^3}{3!} + \frac{x^5}{5!} + \frac{x^7}{7!} + \cdots, \qquad -\infty < x < \infty, \qquad (1.94)$$

$$\cosh(x) = \sum_{n=0}^{\infty} \frac{x^{2n}}{(2n)!} = 1 + \frac{x^2}{2!} + \frac{x^4}{4!} + \frac{x^6}{6!} + \cdots, \qquad -\infty < x < \infty, \qquad (1.95)$$

$$\frac{1}{1-x} = \sum_{n=0}^{\infty} x^n = 1 + x + x^2 + x^3 + x^4 + \cdots, \qquad -1 \le x < 1, \qquad (1.96)$$

$$\ln(1+x) = \sum_{n=1}^{\infty} \frac{(-1)^{n-1} x^n}{n} = x - \frac{x^2}{2} + \frac{x^3}{3} - \frac{x^4}{4} + \cdots, \quad -1 < x \le 1, \qquad (1.97)$$

$$(1+x)^p = \sum_{n=0}^{\infty} \binom{p}{n} x^n = \sum_{n=0}^{\infty} \frac{(p-n+1)_n}{n!} x^n, \qquad -1 < x < 1. \qquad (1.98)$$

Reminder. The notation $(a)_n$ is the Pochhammer symbol: $(a)_0 = 1$, $(a)_1 = a$, and for integers $n > 1$, $(a)_n = a(a+1)\cdots(a+n-1)$. It is not required that a, or p in Eq. (1.98), be positive or integral.

Exercises

1.6.1   Show that $\ln\left(\dfrac{1+x}{1-x}\right) = 2\left(x + \dfrac{x^3}{3} + \dfrac{x^5}{5} + \cdots\right)$, $\quad -1 < x < 1$.

1.7 VECTORS

In science and engineering we frequently encounter quantities that have algebraic magnitude only (i.e., magnitude and possibly a sign): mass, time, and temperature. These we label **scalar** quantities, which remain the same no matter what coordinates we may use. In contrast, many interesting physical quantities have magnitude and, in addition, an associated direction. This second group includes displacement, velocity, acceleration, force, momentum, and angular momentum. Quantities with magnitude and direction are labeled **vector** quantities. To distinguish vectors from scalars, we usually identify vector quantities with boldface type, as in **V** or **x**.

This section deals only with properties of vectors that are not specific to three-dimensional (3-D) space (thereby excluding the notion of the vector cross product and the use of vectors to describe rotational motion). We also restrict the present discussion to vectors that describe a physical quantity at a single point, in contrast to the situation where a vector is defined over an extended region, with its magnitude and/or direction a function of the position with which it is associated. Vectors defined over a region are called **vector fields**; a familiar example is the electric field, which describes the direction and magnitude of the electrical force on a test charge throughout a region of space. We return to these important topics in a later chapter.

The key items of the present discussion are (1) geometric and algebraic descriptions of vectors; (2) linear combinations of vectors; and (3) the dot product of two vectors and its use in determining the angle between their directions and the decomposition of a vector into contributions in the coordinate directions.

Basic Properties

We define a **vector** in a way that makes it correspond to an arrow from a starting point to another point in two-dimensional (2-D) or 3-D space, with **vector addition** identified as the result of placing the tail (starting point) of a second vector at the head (endpoint) of the first vector, as shown in Fig. 1.7. As seen in the figure, the result of addition is the same if the vectors are added in either order; vector addition is a **commutative** operation. Vector addition is also **associative**; if we add three vectors, the result is independent of the order in which the additions take place. Formally, this means

$$(\mathbf{A} + \mathbf{B}) + \mathbf{C} = \mathbf{A} + (\mathbf{B} + \mathbf{C}).$$

It is also useful to define an operation in which a vector **A** is multiplied by an ordinary number k (a **scalar**). The result will be a vector that is still in the original direction, but with its length multiplied by k. If k is negative, the vector's length is multiplied by $|k|$ but its direction is reversed. This means we can interpret **subtraction** as illustrated here:

$$\mathbf{A} - \mathbf{B} \equiv \mathbf{A} + (-1)\mathbf{B},$$

and we can form polynomials such as $\mathbf{A} + 2\mathbf{B} - 3\mathbf{C}$.

Up to this point we are describing our vectors as quantities that do not depend on any coordinate system that we may wish to use, and we are focusing on their **geometric** properties. For example, consider the principle of mechanics that an object will remain in static equilibrium if the vector sum of the forces on it is zero. The net force at the point O of Fig. 1.8 will be the vector sum of the forces labeled $\mathbf{F}_1$, $\mathbf{F}_2$, and $\mathbf{F}_3$. The sum of the forces at static equilibrium is illustrated in the right-hand panel of the figure.

It is also important to develop an **algebraic** description for vectors. We can do so by placing a vector **A** so that its tail is at the origin of a Cartesian coordinate system and by noting the coordinates of its head. Giving these coordinates (in 3-D space) the names A_x, A_y, A_z, we have a **component** description of **A**. From these components we can use the Pythagorean theorem to compute the length or **magnitude** of **A**, denoted A or $|\mathbf{A}|$, as

$$A = (A_x^2 + A_y^2 + A_z^2)^{1/2}. \tag{1.99}$$

The components A_x, ... are also useful for computing the result when vectors are added or multiplied by scalars. From the geometry in Cartesian coordinates, it is obvious that if $\mathbf{C} = k\mathbf{A} + k'\mathbf{B}$, then **C** will have components

$$C_x = kA_x + k'B_x, \quad C_y = kA_y + k'B_y, \quad C_z = kA_z + k'B_z.$$

At this stage it is convenient to introduce vectors of unit length (called **unit vectors**) in the directions of the coordinate axes. Letting $\hat{\mathbf{e}}_x$ be a unit vector in the x direction, we can

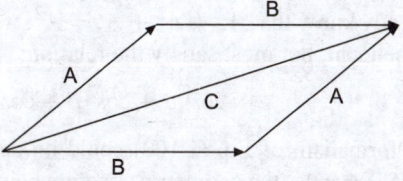

FIGURE 1.7   Addition of two vectors.

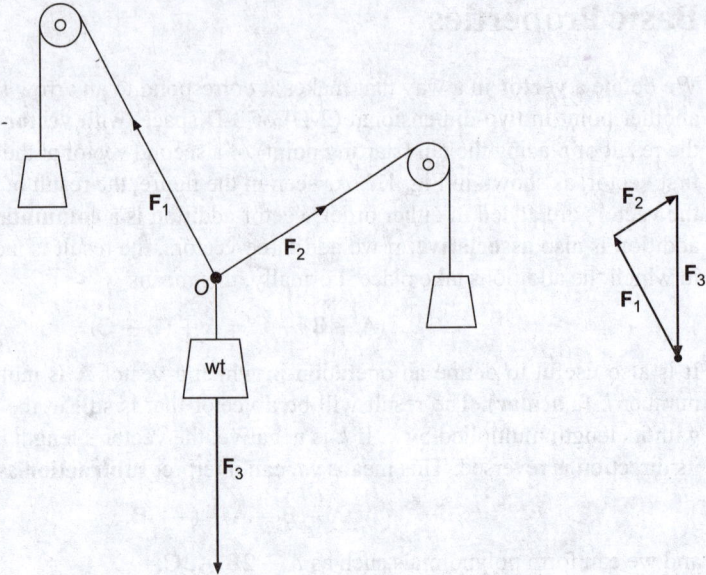

FIGURE 1.8   Equilibrium of forces at the point O.

now identify $A_x \hat{\mathbf{e}}_x$ as a vector of signed magnitude A_x in the x direction, and we see that $\mathbf{A}$ can be represented as the vector sum

$$\mathbf{A} = A_x \hat{\mathbf{e}}_x + A_y \hat{\mathbf{e}}_y + A_z \hat{\mathbf{e}}_z. \tag{1.100}$$

If $\mathbf{A}$ is itself the displacement from the origin to the point (x, y, z), we denote it by the special symbol $\mathbf{r}$ (sometimes called the **radius vector**), and Eq. (1.100) becomes

$$\mathbf{r} = x \hat{\mathbf{e}}_x + y \hat{\mathbf{e}}_y + z \hat{\mathbf{e}}_z. \tag{1.101}$$

The unit vectors are said to **span** the space in which our vectors reside, or to form a **basis** for the space. Either of these statements means that any vector in the space can be constructed as a linear combination of the basis vectors. Since a vector $\mathbf{A}$ has specific values of A_x, A_y, and A_z, this linear combination will be unique.

Sometimes a vector will be specified by its magnitude A and by the angles it makes with the Cartesian coordinate axes. Letting α, β, γ be the respective angles our vector makes with the x, y, and z axes, the components of $\mathbf{A}$ are given by

$$A_x = A \cos \alpha, \quad A_y = A \cos \beta, \quad A_z = A \cos \gamma. \tag{1.102}$$

The quantities $\cos \alpha$, $\cos \beta$, $\cos \gamma$ (see Fig. 1.9) are known as the **direction cosines** of $\mathbf{A}$. Since we already know that $A_x^2 + A_y^2 + A_z^2 = A^2$, we see that the direction cosines are not entirely independent, but must satisfy the relation

$$\cos^2 \alpha + \cos^2 \beta + \cos^2 \gamma = 1. \tag{1.103}$$

While the formalism of Eq. (1.100) could be developed with complex values for the components A_x, A_y, A_z, the geometric situation being described makes it natural to restrict these coefficients to real values; the space with all possible real values of two coordinates

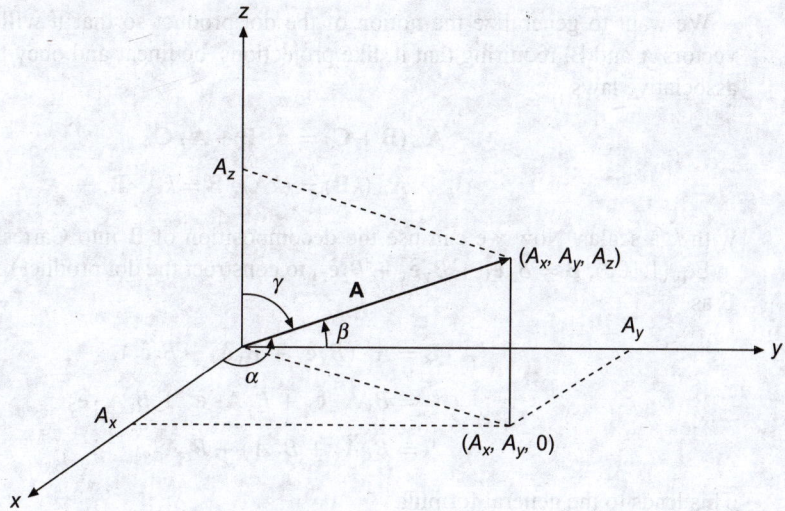

FIGURE 1.9   Cartesian components and direction cosines of **A**.

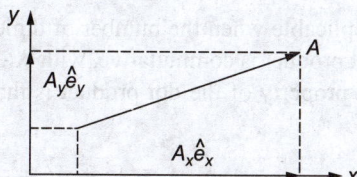

FIGURE 1.10   Projections of **A** on the x and y axes.

is denoted by mathematicians (and occasionally by us) $\mathbb{R}^2$; the complete 3-D space is named $\mathbb{R}^3$.

Dot (Scalar) Product

When we write a vector in terms of its component vectors in the coordinate directions, as in

$$\mathbf{A} = A_x \hat{\mathbf{e}}_x + A_y \hat{\mathbf{e}}_y + A_z \hat{\mathbf{e}}_z,$$

we can think of $A_x \hat{\mathbf{e}}_x$ as its **projection** in the x direction. Stated another way, it is the portion of **A** that is in the subspace spanned by $\hat{\mathbf{e}}_x$ alone. The term **projection** corresponds to the idea that it is the result of collapsing (projecting) a vector onto one of the coordinate axes. See Fig. 1.10.

It is useful to define a quantity known as the **dot product**, with the property that it produces the coefficients, e.g., A_x, in projections onto the coordinate axes according to

$$\mathbf{A} \cdot \hat{\mathbf{e}}_x = A_x = A \cos\alpha, \quad \mathbf{A} \cdot \hat{\mathbf{e}}_y = A_y = A \cos\beta, \quad \mathbf{A} \cdot \hat{\mathbf{e}}_z = A_z = A \cos\gamma, \quad (1.104)$$

where $\cos\alpha$, $\cos\beta$, $\cos\gamma$ are the direction cosines of **A**.

We want to generalize the notion of the dot product so that it will apply to arbitrary vectors **A** and **B**, requiring that it, like projections, be linear and obey the distributive and associative laws

$$\mathbf{A} \cdot (\mathbf{B} + \mathbf{C}) = \mathbf{A} \cdot \mathbf{B} + \mathbf{A} \cdot \mathbf{C}, \tag{1.105}$$

$$\mathbf{A} \cdot (k\mathbf{B}) = (k\mathbf{A}) \cdot \mathbf{B} = k\mathbf{A} \cdot \mathbf{B}, \tag{1.106}$$

with k a scalar. Now we can use the decomposition of **B** into Cartesian components as in Eq. (1.100), $\mathbf{B} = B_x \hat{\mathbf{e}}_x + B_y \hat{\mathbf{e}}_y + B_z \hat{\mathbf{e}}_z$, to construct the dot product of the vectors **A** and **B** as

$$\begin{aligned}
\mathbf{A} \cdot \mathbf{B} &= \mathbf{A} \cdot (B_x \hat{\mathbf{e}}_x + B_y \hat{\mathbf{e}}_y + B_z \hat{\mathbf{e}}_z) \\
&= B_x \mathbf{A} \cdot \hat{\mathbf{e}}_x + B_y \mathbf{A} \cdot \hat{\mathbf{e}}_y + B_z \mathbf{A} \cdot \hat{\mathbf{e}}_z \\
&= B_x A_x + B_y A_y + B_z A_z. \tag{1.107}
\end{aligned}$$

This leads to the general formula

$$\mathbf{A} \cdot \mathbf{B} = \sum_i B_i A_i = \sum_i A_i B_i = \mathbf{B} \cdot \mathbf{A}, \tag{1.108}$$

which is also applicable when the number of dimensions in the space is other than three. Note that the dot product is commutative, with $\mathbf{A} \cdot \mathbf{B} = \mathbf{B} \cdot \mathbf{A}$.

An important property of the dot product is that $\mathbf{A} \cdot \mathbf{A}$ is the square of the magnitude of **A**:

$$\mathbf{A} \cdot \mathbf{A} = A_x^2 + A_y^2 + \cdots = |\mathbf{A}|^2. \tag{1.109}$$

Applying this observation to $\mathbf{C} = \mathbf{A} + \mathbf{B}$, we have

$$|\mathbf{C}|^2 = \mathbf{C} \cdot \mathbf{C} = (\mathbf{A} + \mathbf{B}) \cdot (\mathbf{A} + \mathbf{B}) = \mathbf{A} \cdot \mathbf{A} + \mathbf{B} \cdot \mathbf{B} + 2\mathbf{A} \cdot \mathbf{B},$$

which can be rearranged to

$$\mathbf{A} \cdot \mathbf{B} = \frac{1}{2}\Big[\, |\mathbf{C}|^2 - |\mathbf{A}|^2 - |\mathbf{B}|^2 \Big]. \tag{1.110}$$

From the geometry of the vector sum $\mathbf{C} = \mathbf{A} + \mathbf{B}$, as shown in Fig. 1.11, and recalling the law of cosines and its similarity to Eq. (1.110), we obtain the well-known formula

$$\mathbf{A} \cdot \mathbf{B} = |\mathbf{A}|\,|\mathbf{B}| \cos\theta, \tag{1.111}$$

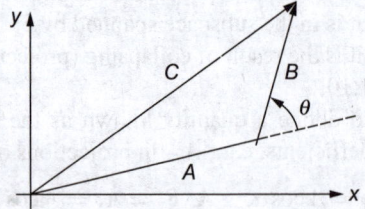

FIGURE 1.11   Vector sum, $\mathbf{C} = \mathbf{A} + \mathbf{B}$.

where θ is the angle between the directions of **A** and **B**. In contrast with the **algebraic** formula Eq. (1.108), Eq. (1.111) is a **geometric** formula for the dot product, and shows clearly that it depends only on the relative directions of **A** and **B** and is therefore independent of the coordinate system. For that reason the dot product is sometimes also identified as a **scalar product**.

Equation (1.111) also permits an interpretation in terms of the projection of a vector **A** in the direction of **B** or the reverse. If $\hat{\mathbf{b}}$ is a unit vector in the direction of **B**, the projection of A in that direction is given by

$$A_b \hat{\mathbf{b}} = (\hat{\mathbf{b}} \cdot \mathbf{A})\hat{\mathbf{b}} = (A\cos\theta)\hat{\mathbf{b}}, \tag{1.112}$$

where θ is the angle between **A** and **B**. Moreover, the dot product **A** · **B** can then be identified as $|\mathbf{B}|$ times the magnitude of the projection of **A** in the **B** direction, so $\mathbf{A} \cdot \mathbf{B} = A_b B$. Equivalently, **A** · **B** is equal to $|\mathbf{A}|$ times the magnitude of the projection of **B** in the **A** direction, so we also have $\mathbf{A} \cdot \mathbf{B} = B_a A$.

Finally, we observe that since $|\cos\theta| \leq 1$, Eq. (1.111) leads to the inequality

$$|\mathbf{A} \cdot \mathbf{B}| \leq |\mathbf{A}|\,|\mathbf{B}|. \tag{1.113}$$

The equality in Eq. (1.113) holds only if **A** and **B** are collinear (in either the same or opposite directions). This is the specialization to physical space of the **Schwarz inequality**, which we will later develop in a more general context.

Orthogonality

Equation (1.111) shows that **A** · **B** becomes zero when $\cos\theta = 0$, which occurs at $\theta = \pm\pi/2$ (i.e., at $\theta = \pm90°$). These values of θ correspond to **A** and **B** being perpendicular, the technical term for which is **orthogonal**. Thus,

A *and* **B** *are orthogonal if and only if* **A** · **B** $= 0$.

Checking this result for two dimensions, we note that **A** and **B** are perpendicular if the slope of **B**, B_y/B_x, is the negative of the reciprocal of A_y/A_x, or

$$\frac{B_y}{B_x} = -\frac{A_x}{A_y}.$$

This result expands to $A_x B_x + A_y B_y = 0$, the condition that **A** and **B** be orthogonal.

In terms of projections, **A** · **B** $= 0$ means that the projection of **A** in the **B** direction vanishes (and vice versa). That is of course just another way of saying that **A** and **B** are orthogonal.

The fact that the Cartesian unit vectors are mutually orthogonal makes it possible to simplify many dot product computations. Because

$$\hat{\mathbf{e}}_x \cdot \hat{\mathbf{e}}_y = \hat{\mathbf{e}}_x \cdot \hat{\mathbf{e}}_z = \hat{\mathbf{e}}_y \cdot \hat{\mathbf{e}}_z = 0, \quad \hat{\mathbf{e}}_x \cdot \hat{\mathbf{e}}_x = \hat{\mathbf{e}}_y \cdot \hat{\mathbf{e}}_y = \hat{\mathbf{e}}_z \cdot \hat{\mathbf{e}}_z = 1, \tag{1.114}$$

we can evaluate $\mathbf{A} \cdot \mathbf{B}$ as

$$(A_x\hat{\mathbf{e}}_x + A_y\hat{\mathbf{e}}_y + A_z\hat{\mathbf{e}}_z) \cdot (B_x\hat{\mathbf{e}}_x + B_y\hat{\mathbf{e}}_y + B_z\hat{\mathbf{e}}_z) = A_xB_x\hat{\mathbf{e}}_x \cdot \hat{\mathbf{e}}_x + A_yB_y\hat{\mathbf{e}}_y \cdot \hat{\mathbf{e}}_y + A_zB_z\hat{\mathbf{e}}_z \cdot \hat{\mathbf{e}}_z$$
$$+ (A_xB_y + A_yB_x)\hat{\mathbf{e}}_x \cdot \hat{\mathbf{e}}_y + (A_xB_z + A_zB_x)\hat{\mathbf{e}}_x \cdot \hat{\mathbf{e}}_z + (A_yB_z + A_zB_y)\hat{\mathbf{e}}_y \cdot \hat{\mathbf{e}}_z$$
$$= A_xB_x + A_yB_y + A_zB_z.$$

See Chapter 3: Vector Analysis, Section 3.2: Vectors in 3-D Space for an introduction of the cross product of vectors, needed early in Chapter 2.

Exercises

1.7.1   The vector $\mathbf{A}$ whose magnitude is 1.732 units makes equal angles with the coordinate axes. Find A_x, A_y, and A_z.

1.7.2   A triangle is defined by the vertices of three vectors $\mathbf{A}, \mathbf{B}$ and $\mathbf{C}$ that extend from the origin. In terms of $\mathbf{A}$, $\mathbf{B}$, and $\mathbf{C}$ show that the **vector** sum of the successive sides of the triangle $(AB + BC + CA)$ is zero, where the side AB is from A to B, etc.

1.7.3   A sphere of radius a is centered at a point $\mathbf{r}_1$.

(a)   Write out the algebraic equation for the sphere.

(b)   Write out a **vector** equation for the sphere.

> ANS.   (a) $(x - x_1)^2 + (y - y_1)^2 + (z - z_1)^2 = a^2$.
>
> (b) $\mathbf{r} = \mathbf{r}_1 + \mathbf{a}$, where $\mathbf{a}$ takes on all directions but has a fixed magnitude a.

1.7.4   **Hubble's law.** Hubble found that distant galaxies are receding with a velocity proportional to their distance from where we are on Earth. For the ith galaxy,

$$\mathbf{v}_i = H_0\mathbf{r}_i$$

with us at the origin. Show that this recession of the galaxies from us does **not** imply that we are at the center of the universe. Specifically, take the galaxy at $\mathbf{r}_1$ as a new origin and show that Hubble's law is still obeyed.

1.7.5   Find the diagonal vectors of a unit cube with one corner at the origin and its three sides lying along Cartesian coordinates axes. Show that there are four diagonals with length $\sqrt{3}$. Representing these as vectors, what are their components? Show that the diagonals of the cube's faces have length $\sqrt{2}$ and determine their components.

1.7.6   The vector $\mathbf{r}$, starting at the origin, terminates at and specifies the point in space (x, y, z). Find the surface swept out by the tip of $\mathbf{r}$ if

(a) $(\mathbf{r} - \mathbf{a}) \cdot \mathbf{a} = 0$. Characterize $\mathbf{a}$ geometrically.

(b) $(\mathbf{r} - \mathbf{a}) \cdot \mathbf{r} = 0$. Describe the geometric role of $\mathbf{a}$.

The vector $\mathbf{a}$ is constant (in magnitude and direction).

1.7.7 A pipe comes diagonally down the south wall of a building, making an angle of 45° with the horizontal. Coming into a corner, the pipe turns and continues diagonally down a west-facing wall, still making an angle of 45° with the horizontal. What is the angle between the south-wall and west-wall sections of the pipe?

ANS. 120°.

1.7.8 Find the shortest distance of an observer at the point $(2, 1, 3)$ from a rocket in free flight with velocity $(1, 2, 3)$ km/s. The rocket was launched at time $t = 0$ from $(1, 1, 1)$. Lengths are in kilometers.

1.7.9 Show that the medians of a triangle intersect in the center which is 2/3 of the median's length from each vertex. Construct a numerical example and plot it.

1.7.10 Prove the law of cosines starting from $\mathbf{A}^2 = (\mathbf{B} - \mathbf{C})^2$.

1.7.11 Given the three vectors,

$$\mathbf{P} = 3\hat{\mathbf{e}}_x + 2\hat{\mathbf{e}}_y - \hat{\mathbf{e}}_z,$$

$$\mathbf{Q} = -6\hat{\mathbf{e}}_x - 4\hat{\mathbf{e}}_y + 2\hat{\mathbf{e}}_z,$$

$$\mathbf{R} = \hat{\mathbf{e}}_x - 2\hat{\mathbf{e}}_y - \hat{\mathbf{e}}_z,$$

find two that are perpendicular and two that are parallel or antiparallel.

1.8 COMPLEX NUMBERS AND FUNCTIONS

Complex numbers and analysis based on complex variable theory have become extremely important and valuable tools for the mathematical analysis of physical theory. Though the results of the measurement of physical quantities must, we firmly believe, ultimately be described by real numbers, there is ample evidence that successful theories predicting the results of those measurements require the use of complex numbers and analysis. In a later chapter we explore the fundamentals of complex variable theory. Here we introduce complex numbers and identify some of their more elementary properties.

Basic Properties

A complex number is nothing more than an ordered pair of two real numbers, (a, b). Similarly, a complex variable is an ordered pair of two real variables,

$$z \equiv (x, y). \tag{1.115}$$

The ordering is significant. In general (a, b) is not equal to (b, a) and (x, y) is not equal to (y, x). As usual, we continue writing a real number $(x, 0)$ simply as x, and we call $i \equiv (0, 1)$ the imaginary unit. All of complex analysis can be developed in terms of ordered pairs of numbers, variables, and functions $(u(x, y), v(x, y))$.

We now define **addition** of complex numbers in terms of their Cartesian components as

$$z_1 + z_2 = (x_1, y_1) + (x_2, y_2) = (x_1 + x_2, y_1 + y_2). \tag{1.116}$$

Multiplication of complex numbers is defined as

$$z_1 z_2 = (x_1, y_1) \cdot (x_2, y_2) = (x_1 x_2 - y_1 y_2, x_1 y_2 + x_2 y_1). \tag{1.117}$$

It is obvious that multiplication is not just the multiplication of corresponding components. Using Eq. (1.117) we verify that $i^2 = (0, 1) \cdot (0, 1) = (-1, 0) = -1$, so we can also identify $i = \sqrt{-1}$ as usual, and further rewrite Eq. (1.115) as

$$z = (x, y) = (x, 0) + (0, y) = x + (0, 1) \cdot (y, 0) = x + iy. \tag{1.118}$$

Clearly, introduction of the symbol i is not necessary here, but it is convenient, in large part because the addition and multiplication rules for complex numbers are consistent with those for ordinary arithmetic with the additional property that $i^2 = -1$:

$$(x_1 + iy_1)(x_2 + iy_2) = x_1 x_2 + i^2 y_1 y_2 + i(x_1 y_2 + y_1 x_2) = (x_1 x_2 - y_1 y_2) + i(x_1 y_2 + y_1 x_2),$$

in agreement with Eq. (1.117). For historical reasons, i and its multiples are known as **imaginary numbers**.

The space of complex numbers, sometimes denoted $\mathcal{Z}$ by mathematicians, has the following formal properties:

- It is closed under addition and multiplication, meaning that if two complex numbers are added or multiplied, the result is also a complex number.

- It has a unique zero number, which when added to any complex number leaves it unchanged and which, when multiplied with any complex number yields zero.

- It has a unique unit number, 1, which when multiplied with any complex number leaves it unchanged.

- Every complex number z has an inverse under addition (known as $-z$), and every nonzero z has an inverse under multiplication, denoted z^{-1} or $1/z$.

- It is closed under exponentiation: if u and v are complex numbers u^v is also a complex number.

From a rigorous mathematical viewpoint, the last statement above is somewhat loose, as it does not really define exponentiation, but we will find it adequate for our purposes.

Some additional definitions and properties include the following:

Complex conjugation: Like all complex numbers, i has an inverse under addition, denoted $-i$, in two-component form, $(0, -1)$. Given a complex number $z = x + iy$, it is useful to define another complex number, $z^* = x - iy$, which we call the **complex conjugate** of z.[6] Forming

$$zz^* = (x + iy)(x - iy) = x^2 + y^2, \tag{1.119}$$

we see that zz^* is real; we define the absolute value of z, denoted $|z|$, as $\sqrt{zz^*}$.

---

[6]The complex conjugate of z is often denoted $\bar{z}$ in the mathematical literature.

Division: Consider now the division of two complex numbers: z'/z. We need to manipulate this quantity to bring it to the complex number form $u + iv$ (with u and v real). We may do so as follows:

$$\frac{z'}{z} = \frac{z'z^*}{zz^*} = \frac{(x' + iy')(x - iy)}{x^2 + y^2},$$

or

$$\frac{x' + iy'}{x + iy} = \frac{xx' + yy'}{x^2 + y^2} + i\,\frac{xy' - x'y}{x^2 + y^2}. \tag{1.120}$$

Functions in the Complex Domain

Since the fundamental operations in the complex domain obey the same rules as those for arithmetic in the space of real numbers, it is natural to define functions so that their real and complex incarnations are similar, and specifically so that the complex and real definitions agree when both are applicable. This means, among other things, that if a function is represented by a power series, we should, within the region of convergence of the power series, be able to use such series with complex values of the expansion variable. This notion is called **permanence of the algebraic form**.

Applying this concept to the exponential, we define

$$e^z = 1 + z + \frac{1}{2!}z^2 + \frac{1}{3!}z^3 + \frac{1}{4!}z^4 + \cdots. \tag{1.121}$$

Now, replacing z by iz, we have

$$e^{iz} = 1 + iz + \frac{1}{2!}(iz)^2 + \frac{1}{3!}(iz)^3 + \frac{1}{4!}(iz)^4 + \cdots$$

$$= \left[1 - \frac{1}{2!}z^2 + \frac{1}{4!}z^4 - \cdots\right] + i\left[z - \frac{1}{3!}z^3 + \frac{1}{5!}z^5 - \cdots\right]. \tag{1.122}$$

It was permissible to regroup the terms in the series of Eq. (1.122) because that series is absolutely convergent for all z; the d'Alembert ratio test succeeds for all z, real or complex. If we now identify the bracketed expansions in the last line of Eq. (1.122) as $\cos z$ and $\sin z$, we have the extremely valuable result

$$e^{iz} = \cos z + i \sin z. \tag{1.123}$$

This result is valid for all z, real, imaginary, or complex, but is particularly useful when z is real.

Any function $w(z)$ of a complex variable $z = x + iy$ can in principle be divided into its real and imaginary parts, just as we did when we added, multiplied, or divided complex numbers. That is, we can write

$$w(z) = u(x, y) + iv(x, y), \tag{1.124}$$

in which the separate functions $u(x, y)$ and $v(x, y)$ are pure real. For example, if $f(z) = z^2$, we have

$$f(z) = (z + iy)^2 = (x^2 - y^2) + i(2xy).$$

The **real part** of a function $f(z)$ will be labeled $\Re\, f(z)$, whereas the **imaginary part** will be labeled $\Im\, f(z)$. In Eq. (1.124),

$$\Re\, w(z) = u(x, y), \quad \Im\, w(z) = v(x, y).$$

The complex conjugate of our function $w(z)$ is $u(x, y) - iv(x, y)$, and depending on w, may or may not be equal to $w(z^*)$.

Polar Representation

We may visualize complex numbers by assigning them locations on a planar graph, called an **Argand diagram** or, more colloquially, the **complex plane**. Traditionally the real component is plotted horizontally, on what is called the **real axis**, with the **imaginary axis** in the vertical direction. See Fig. 1.12. An alternative to identifying points by their Cartesian coordinates (x, y) is to use polar coordinates (r, θ), with

$$x = r\cos\theta, \quad y = r\sin\theta, \quad \text{or} \quad r = \sqrt{x^2 + y^2}, \ \theta = \tan^{-1} y/x. \tag{1.125}$$

The arctan function $\tan^{-1}(y/x)$ is multiple valued; the correct location on an Argand diagram needs to be consistent with the individual values of x and y.

The Cartesian and polar representations of a complex number can also be related by writing

$$x + iy = r(\cos\theta + i\sin\theta) = re^{i\theta}, \tag{1.126}$$

where we have used Eq. (1.123) to introduce the complex exponential. Note that r is also $|z|$, so the magnitude of z is given by its distance from the origin in an Argand diagram. In complex variable theory, r is also called the **modulus** of z and θ is termed the **argument** or the **phase** of z.

If we have two complex numbers, z and z', in polar form, their product zz' can be written

$$zz' = (re^{i\theta})(r'e^{i\theta'}) = (rr')e^{i(\theta+\theta')}, \tag{1.127}$$

showing that the location of the product in an Argand diagram will have argument (polar angle) at the sum of the polar angles of the factors, and with a magnitude that is the product

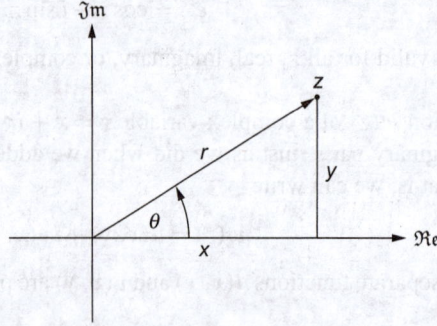

FIGURE 1.12   Argand diagram, showing location of $z = x + iy = re^{i\theta}$.

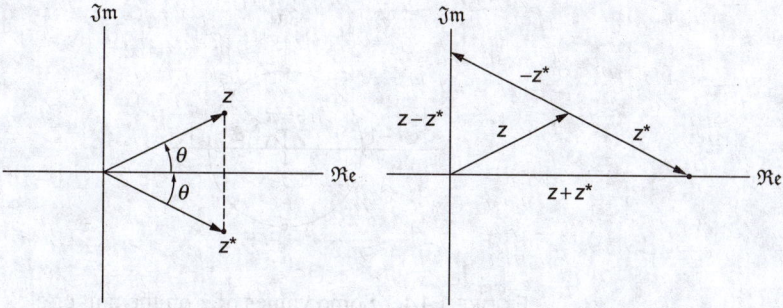

FIGURE 1.13   Left: Relation of z and z^*. Right: $z + z^*$ and $z - z^*$.

of their magnitudes. Conversely, the quotient z/z' will have magnitude r/r' and argument $\theta - \theta'$. These relationships should aid in getting a qualitative understanding of complex multiplication and division. This discussion also shows that multiplication and division are easier in the polar representation, whereas addition and subtraction have simpler forms in Cartesian coordinates.

The plotting of complex numbers on an Argand diagram makes obvious some other properties. Since addition on an Argand diagram is analogous to 2-D vector addition, it can be seen that

$$\left| |z| - |z'| \right| \leq |z \pm z'| \leq |z| + |z'|. \tag{1.128}$$

Also, since $z^* = re^{-i\theta}$ has the same magnitude as z but an argument that differs only in sign, $z + z^*$ will be real and equal to $2\,\mathfrak{Re}\,z$, while $z - z^*$ will be pure imaginary and equal to $2i\,\mathfrak{Im}\,z$. See Fig. 1.13 for an illustration of this discussion.

We can use an Argand diagram to plot values of a function $w(z)$ as well as just z itself, in which case we could label the axes u and v, referring to the real and imaginary parts of w. In that case, we can think of the function $w(z)$ as providing a **mapping** from the xy plane to the uv plane, with the effect that any curve in the xy (sometimes called z) plane is mapped into a corresponding curve in the uv ($=w$) plane. In addition, the statements of the preceding paragraph can be extended to functions:

$$\left| |w(z)| - |w'(z)| \right| \leq |w(z) \pm w'(z)| \leq |w(z)| + |w'(z)|,$$

$$\mathfrak{Re}\,w(z) = \frac{w(z) + [w(z)]^*}{2}, \quad \mathfrak{Im}\,w(z) = \frac{w(z) - [w(z)]^*}{2}. \tag{1.129}$$

Complex Numbers of Unit Magnitude

Complex numbers of the form

$$e^{i\theta} = \cos\theta + i\sin\theta, \tag{1.130}$$

where we have given the variable the name θ to emphasize the fact that we plan to restrict it to real values, correspond on an Argand diagram to points for which $x = \cos\theta$, $y = \sin\theta$,

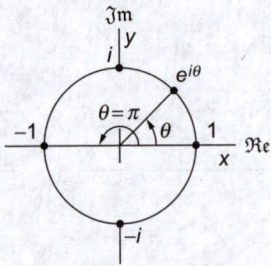

FIGURE 1.14   Some values of z on the unit circle.

and whose magnitude is therefore $\cos^2\theta + \sin^2\theta = 1$. The points $\exp(i\theta)$ therefore lie on the unit circle, at polar angle θ. This observation makes obvious a number of relations that could in principle also be deduced from Eq. (1.130). For example, if θ has the special values $\pi/2$, π, or $3\pi/2$, we have the interesting relationships

$$e^{i\pi/2} = i, \quad e^{i\pi} = -1, \quad e^{3i\pi/2} = -i. \tag{1.131}$$

We also see that $\exp(i\theta)$ is periodic, with period 2π, so

$$e^{2i\pi} = e^{4i\pi} = \cdots = 1, \quad e^{3i\pi/2} = e^{-i\pi/2} = -i, \text{ etc.} \tag{1.132}$$

A few relevant values of z on the unit circle are illustrated in Fig. 1.14. These relationships cause the real part of $\exp(i\omega t)$ to describe oscillation at angular frequency ω, with $\exp(i[\omega t + \delta])$ describing an oscillation displaced from that first mentioned by a phase difference δ.

Circular and Hyperbolic Functions

The relationship encapsulated in Eq. (1.130) enables us to obtain convenient formulas for the sine and cosine. Taking the sum and difference of $\exp(+i\theta)$ and $\exp(-i\theta)$, we have

$$\cos\theta = \frac{e^{i\theta} + e^{-i\theta}}{2}, \quad \sin\theta = \frac{e^{i\theta} - e^{-i\theta}}{2i}. \tag{1.133}$$

These formulas place the definitions of the hyperbolic functions in perspective:

$$\cosh\theta = \frac{e^{\theta} + e^{-\theta}}{2}, \quad \sinh\theta = \frac{e^{\theta} - e^{-\theta}}{2}. \tag{1.134}$$

Comparing these two sets of equations, it is possible to establish the formulas

$$\cosh iz = \cos z, \quad \sinh iz = i\sin z. \tag{1.135}$$

Proof is left to Exercise 1.8.5.

The fact that $\exp(in\theta)$ can be written in the two equivalent forms

$$\cos n\theta + i\sin n\theta = (\cos\theta + i\sin\theta)^n \tag{1.136}$$

establishes a relationship known as de Moivre's Theorem. By expanding the right member of Eq. (1.136), we easily obtain trigonometric multiple-angle formulas, of which the simplest examples are the well-known results

$$\sin(2\theta) = 2\sin\theta\cos\theta, \quad \cos(2\theta) = \cos^2\theta - \sin^2\theta.$$

If we solve the $\sin\theta$ formula of Eq. (1.133) for $\exp(i\theta)$, we get (choosing the plus sign for the radical)

$$e^{i\theta} = i\sin\theta + \sqrt{1 - \sin^2\theta}.$$

Setting $\sin\theta = z$ and $\theta = \sin^{-1}(z)$, and taking the logarithm of both sides of the above equation, we express the inverse trigonometric function in terms of logarithms.

$$\sin^{-1}(z) = -i\ln\left[iz + \sqrt{1 - z^2}\right].$$

The set of formulas that can be generated in this way includes:

$$\sin^{-1}(z) = -i\ln\left[iz + \sqrt{1 - z^2}\right], \quad \tan^{-1}(z) = \frac{i}{2}\left[\ln(1 - iz) - \ln(1 + iz)\right],$$

$$\sinh^{-1}(z) = \ln\left[z + \sqrt{1 + z^2}\right], \quad \tanh^{-1}(z) = \frac{1}{2}\left[\ln(1 + z) - \ln(1 - z)\right]. \quad (1.137)$$

Powers and Roots

The polar form is very convenient for expressing powers and roots of complex numbers. For integer powers, the result is obvious and unique:

$$z = re^{i\varphi}, \quad z^n = r^n e^{in\varphi}.$$

For roots (fractional powers), we also have

$$z = re^{i\varphi}, \quad z^{1/n} = r^{1/n} e^{i\varphi/n},$$

but the result is not unique. If we write z in the alternate but equivalent form

$$z = re^{i(\varphi + 2m\pi)},$$

where m is an integer, we now get additional values for the root:

$$z^{1/n} = r^{1/n} e^{i(\varphi + 2m\pi)/n}, \quad \text{(any integer } m\text{)}.$$

If $n = 2$ (corresponding to the square root), different choices of m will lead to two distinct values of $z^{1/2}$, both of the same modulus but differing in argument by π. This corresponds to the well-known result that the square root is double-valued and can be written with either sign.

In general, $z^{1/n}$ is n-valued, with successive values having arguments that differ by $2\pi/n$. Figure 1.15 illustrates the multiple values of $1^{1/3}$, $i^{1/3}$, and $(-1)^{1/3}$.

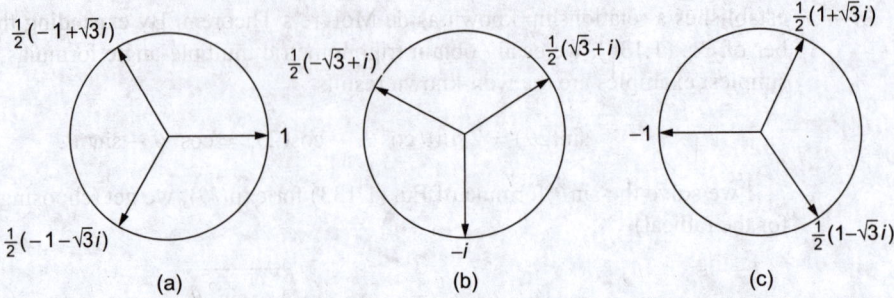

FIGURE 1.15 Cube roots: (a) $1^{1/3}$; (b) $i^{1/3}$; (c) $(-1)^{1/3}$.

Logarithm

Another multivalued complex function is the logarithm, which in the polar representation takes the form

$$\ln z = \ln(re^{i\theta}) = \ln r + i\theta.$$

However, it is also true that

$$\ln z = \ln\left(re^{i(\theta+2n\pi)}\right) = \ln r + i(\theta + 2n\pi), \tag{1.138}$$

for **any** positive or negative integer n. Thus, $\ln z$ has, for a given z, the infinite number of values corresponding to all possible choices of n in Eq. (1.138).

Exercises

1.8.1 Find the reciprocal of $x + iy$, working in polar form but expressing the final result in Cartesian form.

1.8.2 Show that complex numbers have square roots and that the square roots are contained in the complex plane. What are the square roots of i?

1.8.3 Show that

(a) $\cos n\theta = \cos^n \theta - \binom{n}{2} \cos^{n-2}\theta \sin^2\theta + \binom{n}{4} \cos^{n-4}\theta \sin^4\theta - \cdots,$

(b) $\sin n\theta = \binom{n}{1} \cos^{n-1}\theta \sin\theta - \binom{n}{3} \cos^{n-3}\theta \sin^3\theta + \cdots.$

1.8.4 Prove that

(a) $\displaystyle\sum_{n=0}^{N-1} \cos nx = \frac{\sin(Nx/2)}{\sin x/2} \cos(N-1)\frac{x}{2},$

(b) $\displaystyle\sum_{n=0}^{N-1} \sin nx = \frac{\sin(Nx/2)}{\sin x/2} \sin(N-1)\frac{x}{2}.$

These series occur in the analysis of the multiple-slit diffraction pattern.

1.8.5   Assume that the trigonometric functions and the hyperbolic functions are defined for complex argument by the appropriate power series. Show that

$$i \sin z = \sinh i z, \quad \sin i z = i \sinh z,$$

$$\cos z = \cosh i z, \quad \cos i z = \cosh z.$$

1.8.6   Using the identities

$$\cos z = \frac{e^{iz} + e^{-iz}}{2}, \quad \sin z = \frac{e^{iz} - e^{-iz}}{2i},$$

established from comparison of power series, show that

(a) $\sin(x + iy) = \sin x \cosh y + i \cos x \sinh y$,

   $\cos(x + iy) = \cos x \cosh y - i \sin x \sinh y$,

(b) $|\sin z|^2 = \sin^2 x + \sinh^2 y$, $|\cos z|^2 = \cos^2 x + \sinh^2 y$.

This demonstrates that we may have $|\sin z|, |\cos z| > 1$ in the complex plane.

1.8.7   From the identities in Exercises 1.8.5 and 1.8.6 show that

(a) $\sinh(x + iy) = \sinh x \cos y + i \cosh x \sin y$,

   $\cosh(x + iy) = \cosh x \cos y + i \sinh x \sin y$,

(b) $|\sinh z|^2 = \sinh^2 x + \sin^2 y$, $|\cosh z|^2 = \cosh^2 x + \sin^2 y$.

1.8.8   Show that

(a) $\tanh \dfrac{z}{2} = \dfrac{\sinh x + i \sin y}{\cosh x + \cos y}$,   (b) $\coth \dfrac{z}{2} = \dfrac{\sinh x - i \sin y}{\cosh x - \cos y}$.

1.8.9   By comparing series expansions, show that $\tan^{-1} x = \dfrac{i}{2} \ln \left(\dfrac{1 - ix}{1 + ix} \right)$.

1.8.10   Find the Cartesian form for **all values** of

(a) $(-8)^{1/3}$,

(b) $i^{1/4}$,

(c) $e^{i\pi/4}$.

1.8.11   Find the polar form for **all values** of

(a) $(1 + i)^3$,

(b) $(-1)^{1/5}$.

1.9 DERIVATIVES AND EXTREMA

We recall the familiar limit identified as the derivative, $df(x)/dx$, of a function $f(x)$ at a point x:

$$\frac{df(x)}{dx} = \lim_{\varepsilon=0} \frac{f(x+\varepsilon) - f(x)}{\varepsilon} ; \qquad (1.139)$$

the derivative is only defined if the limit exists and is independent of the direction from which ε approaches zero. The **variation** or **differential** of $f(x)$ associated with a change dx in its independent variable from the reference value x assumes the form

$$df = f(x+dx) - f(x) = \frac{df}{dx} \, dx, \qquad (1.140)$$

in the limit that dx is small enough that terms dependent on dx^2 and higher powers of dx become negligible. The mean value theorem (based on the continuity of f) tells us that here, df/dx is evaluated at some point ξ between x and $x + dx$, but as $dx \to 0$, $\xi \to x$.

When a quantity of interest is a function of two or more independent variables, the generalization of Eq. (1.140) is (illustrating for the physically important three-variable case):

$$
\begin{aligned}
df &= \Big[f(x+dx, y+dy, z+dz) - f(x, y+dy, z+dz) \Big] \\
&\quad + \Big[(f(x, y+dy, z+dz) - f(x, y, z+dz) \Big] \\
&\quad + \Big[f(x, y, z+dz) - f(x, y, z) \Big] \\
&= \frac{\partial f}{\partial x} \, dx + \frac{\partial f}{\partial y} \, dy + \frac{\partial f}{\partial z} \, dz, \qquad (1.141)
\end{aligned}
$$

where the **partial derivatives** indicate differentiation in which the independent variables not being differentiated are kept fixed. The fact that $\partial f/\partial x$ is evaluated at $y + dy$ and $z + dz$ instead of at y and z alters the derivative by amounts that are of order dy and dz, and therefore the change becomes negligible in the limit of small variations. It is thus consistent to interpret Eq. (1.141) as involving partial derivatives that are all evaluated at the reference point x, y, z.

Further analysis of the same sort as led to Eq. (1.141) can be used to define higher derivatives and to establish the useful result that **cross derivatives** (e.g., $\partial^2/\partial x \partial y$) are independent of the order in which the differentiations are performed:

$$\frac{\partial}{\partial y} \left(\frac{\partial f}{\partial x} \right) \equiv \frac{\partial^2 f}{\partial y \partial x} = \frac{\partial^2 f}{\partial x \partial y}. \qquad (1.142)$$

Sometimes it is not clear from the context which variables other than that being differentiated are independent, and it is then advisable to attach subscripts to the derivative notation to avoid ambiguity. For example, if x, y, and z have been defined in a problem, but only two of them are independent, one might write

$$\left(\frac{\partial f}{\partial x} \right)_y \quad \text{or} \quad \left(\frac{\partial f}{\partial x} \right)_z,$$

whichever is actually meant.

For working with functions of several variables, we note two useful formulas that follow from Eq. (1.141):

1. The **chain rule**,

$$\frac{df}{ds} = \frac{\partial f}{\partial x}\frac{dx}{ds} + \frac{\partial f}{\partial y}\frac{dy}{ds} + \frac{\partial f}{\partial z}\frac{dz}{ds}, \tag{1.143}$$

which applies when x, y, and z are functions of another variable, s,

2. A formula obtained by setting $df = 0$ (here shown for the case where there are only two independent variables and the dz term of Eq. (1.141) is absent):

$$\left(\frac{\partial y}{\partial x}\right)_f = -\frac{\left(\dfrac{\partial f}{\partial x}\right)_y}{\left(\dfrac{\partial f}{\partial y}\right)_x}. \tag{1.144}$$

In Lagrangian mechanics, one occasionally encounters expressions such as[7]

$$\frac{d}{dt} L(x, \dot{x}, t) = \left[\frac{\partial L}{\partial x}\dot{x} + \frac{\partial L}{\partial \dot{x}}\ddot{x} + \frac{\partial L}{\partial t}\right],$$

an example of use of the chain rule. Here it is necessary to distinguish between the formal dependence of L on its three arguments and the overall dependence of L on time. Note the use of the ordinary (d/dt) and partial $(\partial/\partial t)$ derivative notation.

Stationary Points

Whether or not a set of independent variables (e.g., x, y, z of our previous discussion) represents directions in space, one can ask how a function f changes if we move in various directions in the space of the independent variables; the answer is provided by Eq. (1.143), where the "direction" is defined by the values of dx/ds, dy/ds, etc.

It is often desired to find the minimum of a function f of n variables x_i, $i = 1, \ldots, n$, and a necessary but not sufficient condition on its position is that

$$\frac{df}{ds} = 0 \quad \text{for all directions of } ds.$$

This is equivalent to requiring

$$\frac{\partial f}{\partial x_i} = 0, \quad i = 1, \ldots, n. \tag{1.145}$$

All points in the $\{x_i\}$ space that satisfy Eq. (1.145) are termed **stationary**; for a stationary point of f to be a minimum, it is also necessary that the second derivatives $d^2 f/ds^2$ be positive for all directions of s. Conversely, if the second derivatives in all directions are negative, the stationary point is a maximum. If neither of these conditions are satisfied, the stationary point is neither a maximum nor a minimum, and is often called a **saddle point** because of the appearance of the surface of f when there are two independent variables

---

[7]Here dots indicate time derivatives.

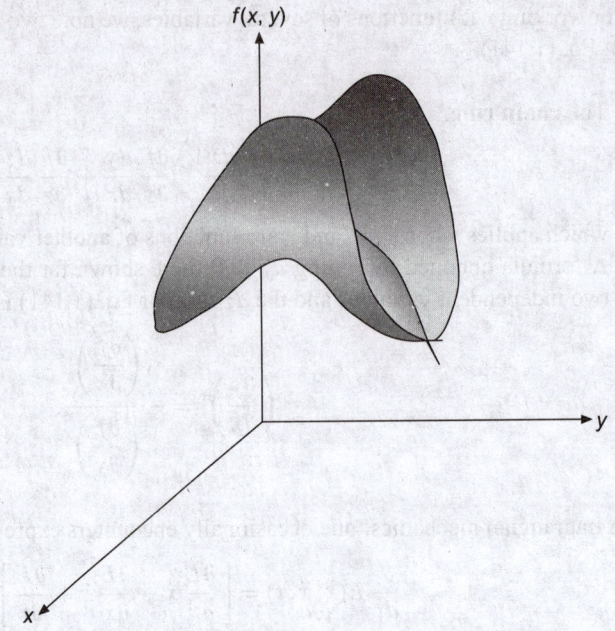

FIGURE 1.16   A stationary point that is neither a maximum nor minimum (a saddle point).

(see Fig. 1.16). It is often obvious whether a stationary point is a minimum or maximum, but a complete discussion of the issue is nontrivial.

Exercises

1.9.1   Derive the following formula for the Maclaurin expansion of a function of two variables:

$$f(x, y) = f(0, 0) + x\frac{\partial f}{\partial x} + y\frac{\partial f}{\partial y}$$

$$+ \frac{1}{2!}\left[\binom{2}{0}x^2\frac{\partial^2 f}{\partial x^2} + \binom{2}{1}xy\frac{\partial^2 f}{\partial x \partial y} + \binom{2}{2}y^2\frac{\partial^2 f}{\partial y^2}\right]$$

$$+ \frac{1}{3!}\left[\binom{3}{0}x^3\frac{\partial^3 f}{\partial x^3} + \binom{3}{1}x^2 y\frac{\partial^3 f}{\partial x^2 \partial y} + \binom{3}{2}xy^2\frac{\partial^3 f}{\partial x \partial y^2} + \binom{3}{3}y^3\frac{\partial^3 f}{\partial y^3}\right] + \cdots,$$

where all the partial derivatives are to be evaluated at the point $(0, 0)$.

1.9.2   The result in Exercise 1.9.1 can be generalized to larger numbers of independent variables. Prove that for an m-variable system, the Maclaurin expansion can be written in the symbolic form

$$f(x_1, \ldots, x_m) = \sum_{n=0}^{\infty} \frac{t^n}{n!} \left(\sum_{i=1}^{m} \alpha_i \frac{\partial}{\partial x_i} \right)^n f(0, \ldots, 0),$$

where in the right-hand side we have made the substitutions $x_j = \alpha_j t$.

1.10 EVALUATION OF INTEGRALS

Proficiency in the evaluation of integrals involves a mixture of experience, skill in pattern recognition, and a few tricks. The most familiar include the technique of integration by parts, and the strategy of changing the variable of integration. We review here some methods for integrals in one and multiple dimensions.

Integration by Parts

The technique of integration by parts is part of every elementary calculus course, but its use is so frequent and ubiquitous that it bears inclusion here. It is based on the obvious relation, for u and v arbitrary functions of x,

$$d(uv) = u \, dv + v \, du.$$

Integrating both sides of this equation over an interval (a, b), we reach

$$uv \Big|_a^b = \int_a^b u \, dv + \int_a^b v \, du,$$

which is usually rearranged to the well-known form

$$\int_a^b u \, dv = uv \Big|_a^b - \int_a^b v \, du. \tag{1.146}$$

Example 1.10.1 INTEGRATION BY PARTS

Consider the integral $\int_a^b x \sin x \, dx$. We identify $u = x$ and $dv = \sin x \, dx$. Differentiating and integrating, we find $du = dx$ and $v = -\cos x$, so Eq. (1.146) becomes

$$\int_a^b x \sin x \, dx = (x)(-\cos x) \Big|_a^b - \int_a^b (-\cos x) \, dx = a \cos a - b \cos b + \sin b - \sin a.$$

∎

The key to the effective use of this technique is to see how to partition an integrand into u and dv in a way that makes it easy to form du and v and also to integrate $\int v \, du$.

Special Functions

A number of special functions have become important in physics because they arise in frequently encountered situations. Identifying a one-dimensional (1-D) integral as one yielding a special function is almost as good as a straight-out evaluation, in part because it prevents the waste of time that otherwise might be spent trying to carry out the integration. But of perhaps more importance, it connects the integral to the full body of knowledge regarding its properties and evaluation. It is not necessary for every physicist to know everything about all known special functions, but it is desirable to have an overview permitting the recognition of special functions which can then be studied in more detail if necessary.

It is common for a special function to be defined in terms of an integral over the range for which that integral converges, but to have its definition extended to a larger domain

Table 1.2   Special Functions of Importance in Physics

Gamma function	$\Gamma(x) = \displaystyle\int_0^\infty t^{x-1} e^{-t}\, dt$	See Chap. 13.
Factorial (n integral)	$n! = \displaystyle\int_0^\infty t^n e^{-t}\, dt$	$n! = \Gamma(n+1)$
Riemann zeta function	$\zeta(x) = \dfrac{1}{\Gamma(x)} \displaystyle\int_0^\infty \dfrac{t^{x-1}\, dt}{e^t - 1}$	See Chaps. 1 and 12.
Exponential integrals	$E_n(x) = \displaystyle\int_1^\infty t^{-n} e^{-t}\, dt$	$E_1(x) \equiv -\mathrm{Ei}(-x)$
Sine integral	$\mathrm{si}(x) = -\displaystyle\int_x^\infty \dfrac{\sin t}{t}\, dt$	
Cosine integral	$\mathrm{Ci}(x) = -\displaystyle\int_x^\infty \dfrac{\cos t}{t}\, dt$	
Error functions	$\mathrm{erf}(x) = \dfrac{2}{\sqrt{\pi}} \displaystyle\int_0^x e^{-t^2}\, dt$	$\mathrm{erf}(\infty) = 1$
	$\mathrm{erfc}(x) = \dfrac{2}{\sqrt{\pi}} \displaystyle\int_x^\infty e^{-t^2}\, dt$	$\mathrm{erfc}(x) = 1 - \mathrm{erf}(x)$
Dilogarithm	$\mathrm{Li}_2(x) = -\displaystyle\int_0^x \dfrac{\ln(1-t)}{t}\, dt$	

by analytic continuation in the complex plane (cf. Chapter 11) or by the establishment of suitable functional relations. We present in Table 1.2 only the most useful integral representations of a few functions of frequent occurrence. More detail is provided by a variety of on-line sources and in material listed under Additional Readings at the end of this chapter, particularly the compilations by Abramowitz and Stegun and by Gradshteyn and Ryzhik.

A conspicuous omission from the list in Table 1.2 is the extensive family of Bessel functions. A short table cannot suffice to summarize their numerous integral representations; a survey of this topic is in Chapter 14. Other important functions in more than one variable or with indices in addition to arguments have also been omitted from the table.

Other Methods

An extremely powerful method for the evaluation of definite integrals is that of contour integration in the complex plane. This method is presented in Chapter 11 and will not be discussed here.

Integrals can often be evaluated by methods that involve integration or differentiation with respect to parameters, thereby obtaining relations between known integrals and those whose values are being sought.

Example 1.10.2   DIFFERENTIATE PARAMETER

We wish to evaluate the integral

$$I = \int\limits_0^\infty \frac{e^{-x^2}}{x^2 + a^2}\, dx.$$

We introduce a parameter, t, to facilitate further manipulations, and consider the related integral

$$J(t) = \int\limits_0^\infty \frac{e^{-t(x^2+a^2)}}{x^2 + a^2}\, dx\,;$$

we note that $I = e^{a^2} J(1)$.

We now differentiate $J(t)$ with respect to t and evaluate the resulting integral, which is a scaled version of Eq. (1.148):

$$\frac{d\,J(t)}{dt} = -\int\limits_0^\infty e^{-t(x^2+a^2)}\, dx = -e^{-ta^2} \int\limits_0^\infty e^{-tx^2}\, dx = -\frac{1}{2}\sqrt{\frac{\pi}{t}}\, e^{-ta^2}. \tag{1.147}$$

To recover $J(t)$ we integrate Eq. (1.147) between t and ∞, making use of the fact that $J(\infty) = 0$. To carry out the integration it is convenient to make the substitution $u^2 = a^2 t$, so we get

$$J(t) = \frac{\sqrt{\pi}}{2} \int\limits_{t}^{\infty} \frac{e^{-ta^2}}{t^{1/2}} \, dt = \frac{\sqrt{\pi}}{a} \int\limits_{at^{1/2}}^{\infty} e^{-u^2} \, du,$$

which we now recognize as $J(t) = (\pi/2a)\mathrm{erfc}(at^{1/2})$. Thus, our final result is

$$I = \frac{\pi}{2a} e^{a^2} \, \mathrm{erfc}(a).$$

∎

Many integrals can be evaluated by first converting them into infinite series, then manipulating the resulting series, and finally either evaluating the series or recognizing it as a special function.

Example 1.10.3   EXPAND, THEN INTEGRATE

Consider $I = \int_0^1 \frac{dx}{x} \ln\left(\frac{1+x}{1-x}\right)$. Using Eq. (1.120) for the logarithm,

$$I = \int\limits_0^1 dx \, 2\left[1 + \frac{x^2}{3} + \frac{x^4}{5} + \cdots\right] = 2\left[1 + \frac{1}{3^2} + \frac{1}{5^2} + \cdots\right].$$

Noting that

$$\frac{1}{2^2}\zeta(2) = \frac{1}{2^2} + \frac{1}{4^2} + \frac{1}{6^2} + \cdots,$$

we see that

$$\zeta(2) - \frac{1}{4}\zeta(2) = 1 + \frac{1}{3^2} + \frac{1}{5^2} + \cdots,$$

so $I = \frac{3}{2}\zeta(2)$.

∎

Simply using complex numbers aids in the evaluation of some integrals. Take, for example, the elementary integral

$$I = \int \frac{dx}{1+x^2}.$$

Making a partial fraction decomposition of $(1+x^2)^{-1}$ and integrating, we easily get

$$I = \int \frac{1}{2}\left[\frac{1}{1+ix} + \frac{1}{1-ix}\right]dx = \frac{i}{2}\left[\ln(1-ix) - \ln(1+ix)\right].$$

From Eq. (1.137), we recognize this as $\tan^{-1}(x)$.

The complex exponential forms of the trigonometric functions provide interesting approaches to the evaluation of certain integrals. Here is an example.

Example 1.10.4   A TRIGONOMETRIC INTEGRAL

Consider $I = \int\limits_0^\infty e^{-at} \cos bt \, dt,$

where a and b are real and positive. Because $\cos bt = \Re\, e^{ibt}$, we note that

$$I = \Re \int\limits_0^\infty e^{(-a+ib)t} \, dt.$$

The integral is now just that of an exponential, and is easily evaluated, leading to

$$I = \Re \frac{1}{a-ib} = \Re \frac{a+ib}{a^2+b^2},$$

which yields $I = a/(a^2+b^2)$. As a bonus, the imaginary part of the same integral gives us

$$\int\limits_0^\infty e^{-at} \sin bt \, dt = \frac{b}{a^2+b^2}.$$

∎

Recursive methods are often useful in obtaining formulas for a set of related integrals.

Example 1.10.5   RECURSION

Consider

$$I_n = \int\limits_0^1 t^n \sin \pi t \, dt$$

for positive integer n.

Integrating I_n by parts twice, taking $u = t^n$ and $dv = \sin \pi t \, dt$, we have

$$I_n = \frac{1}{\pi} - \frac{n(n-1)}{\pi^2} I_{n-2},$$

with starting values $I_0 = 2/\pi$ and $I_1 = 1/\pi$.

There is often no practical need to obtain a general, nonrecursive formula, as repeated application of the recursion is frequently more efficient that a closed formula, even when one can be found.   ∎

Multiple Integrals

An expression that corresponds to integration in two variables, say x and y, may be written with two integral signs, as in

$$\iint f(x, y)\, dx dy \quad \text{or} \quad \int_{x_1}^{x_2} dx \int_{y_1(x)}^{y_2(x)} dy\, f(x, y),$$

where the right-hand form can be more specific as to the integration limits, and also gives an explicit indication that the y integration is to be performed first, or with a single integral sign, as in

$$\int_S f(x, y)\, dA,$$

where S (if explicitly shown) is a 2-D integration region and dA is an element of "area" (in Cartesian coordinates, equal to $dx dy$). In this form we are leaving open both the choice of coordinate system to be used for evaluating the integral, and the order in which the variables are to be integrated. In three dimensions, we may either use three integral signs or a single integral with a symbol $d\tau$ indicating a 3-D "volume" element in an unspecified coordinate system.

In addition to the techniques available for integration in a single variable, multiple integrals provide further opportunities for evaluation based on changes in the order of integration and in the coordinate system used in the integral. Sometimes simply reversing the order of integration may be helpful. If, before the reversal, the range of the inner integral depends on the outer integration variable, care must be exercised in determining the integration ranges after reversal. It may be helpful to draw a diagram identifying the range of integration.

Example 1.10.6   REVERSING INTEGRATION ORDER

Consider

$$\int_0^\infty e^{-r}\, dr \int_r^\infty \frac{e^{-s}}{s}\, ds,$$

in which the inner integral can be identified as an exponential integral, suggesting difficulty if the integration is approached in a straightforward manner. Suppose we proceed by reversing the order of integration. To identify the proper coordinate ranges, we draw on a (r, s) plane, as in Fig. 1.17, the region $s > r \geq 0$, which is covered in the original integration order as a succession of vertical strips, for each r extending from $s = r$ to $s = \infty$. See the left-hand panel of the figure. If the outer integration is changed from r to s, this same region is covered by taking, for each s, a horizontal range of r that runs from $r = 0$ to $r = s$. See the right-hand panel of the figure. The transformed double integral then assumes

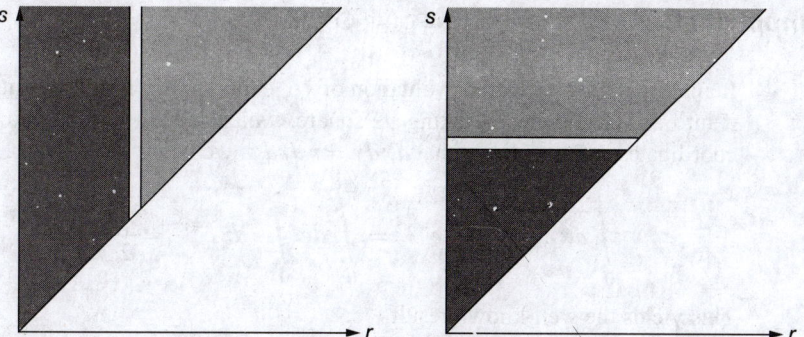

FIGURE 1.17   2-D integration region for Example 1.10.6. Left panel: inner integration over s; right panel: inner integration over r.

the form

$$\int_0^\infty \frac{e^{-s}}{s}\, ds \int_0^s e^{-r}\, dr,$$

where the inner integral over r is now elementary, evaluating to $1 - e^{-s}$. This leaves us with a 1-D integral,

$$\int_0^\infty \frac{e^{-s}}{s}(1 - e^{-s})\, ds.$$

Introducing a power series expansion for $1 - e^{-s}$, this integral becomes

$$\int_0^\infty \frac{e^{-s}}{s}\sum_{n=1}^\infty \frac{(-1)^{n-1}s^n}{n!} = \sum_{n=1}^\infty \frac{(-1)^{n-1}}{n!}\int_0^\infty s^{n-1}e^{-s}\, ds = \sum_{n=1}^\infty \frac{(-1)^{n-1}}{n!}\,(n-1)!,$$

where in the last step we have identified the s integral (cf. Table 1.2) as $(n-1)!$. We complete the evaluation by noting that $(n-1)!/n! = 1/n$, so that the summation can be recognized as $\ln 2$, thereby giving the final result

$$\int_0^\infty e^{-r}\, dr \int_r^\infty \frac{e^{-s}}{s}\, ds = \ln 2.$$

∎

A significant change in the form of 2-D or 3-D integrals can sometimes be accomplished by changing between Cartesian and polar coordinate systems.

Example 1.10.7   EVALUATION IN POLAR COORDINATES

In many calculus texts, the evaluation of $\int_0^\infty \exp(-x^2)dx$ is carried out by first converting it into a 2-D integral by taking its square, which is then written and evaluated in polar coordinates. Using the fact that $dxdy = r\,dr\,d\varphi$, we have

$$\int\limits_0^\infty dx\,e^{-x^2} \int\limits_0^\infty dy\,e^{-y^2} = \int\limits_0^{\pi/2} d\varphi \int\limits_0^\infty r\,dr\,e^{-r^2} = \frac{\pi}{2} \int\limits_0^\infty \tfrac{1}{2} du\,e^{-u} = \frac{\pi}{4}.$$

This yields the well-known result

$$\int\limits_0^\infty e^{-x^2} dx = \tfrac{1}{2}\sqrt{\pi}. \tag{1.148}$$

Example 1.10.8   ATOMIC INTERACTION INTEGRAL

For study of the interaction of a small atom with an electromagnetic field, one of the integrals that arises in a simple approximate treatment using Gaussian-type orbitals is (in dimensionless Cartesian coordinates)

$$I = \int d\tau \frac{z^2}{(x^2+y^2+z^2)^{3/2}} e^{-(x^2+y^2+z^2)},$$

where the range of the integration is the entire 3-D physical space ($\mathbb{R}^3$). Of course, this is a problem better addressed in spherical polar coordinates (r, θ, φ), where r is the distance from the origin of the coordinate system, θ is the polar angle (for the Earth, known as *colatitude*), and φ is the azimuthal angle (*longitude*). The relevant conversion formulas are: $x^2 + y^2 + z^2 = r^2$ and $z/r = \cos\theta$. The volume element is $d\tau = r^2 \sin\theta\,dr\,d\theta\,d\varphi$, and the ranges of the new coordinates are $0 \le r < \infty$, $0 \le \theta \le \pi$, and $0 \le \varphi < 2\pi$. In the spherical coordinates, our integral becomes

$$I = \int d\tau \frac{\cos^2\theta}{r} e^{-r^2} = \int\limits_0^\infty dr\,r\,e^{-r^2} \int\limits_0^\pi d\theta\,\cos^2\theta\,\sin\theta \int\limits_0^{2\pi} d\varphi$$

$$= \left(\frac{1}{2}\right)\left(\frac{2}{3}\right)(2\pi) = \frac{2\pi}{3}.$$

Remarks: Changes of Integration Variables

In a 1-D integration, a change in the integration variable from, say, x to $y = y(x)$ involves two adjustments: (1) the differential dx must be replaced by $(dx/dy)dy$, and (2) the integration limits must be changed from x_1, x_2 to $y(x_1), y(x_2)$. If $y(x)$ is not single-valued over the entire range (x_1, x_2), the process becomes more complicated and we do not consider it further at this point.

For multiple integrals, the situation is considerably more complicated and demands some discussion. Illustrating for a double integral, initially in variables x, y, but transformed to an integration in variables u, v, the differential $dx\,dy$ must be transformed to $J\,du\,dv$, where J, called the **Jacobian** of the transformation and sometimes symbolically represented as

$$J = \frac{\partial(x, y)}{\partial(u, v)}$$

may depend on the variables. For example, the conversion from 2-D Cartesian coordinates x, y to plane polar coordinates r, θ involves the Jacobian

$$J = \frac{\partial(x, y)}{\partial(r, \theta)} = r, \quad \text{so} \quad dx\,dy = r\,dr\,d\theta.$$

For some coordinate transformations the Jacobian is simple and of a well-known form, as in the foregoing example. We can confirm the value assigned to J by noticing that the area (in xy space) enclosed by boundaries at $r, r + dr, \theta$, and $\theta + d\theta$ is an infinitesimally distorted rectangle with two sides of length dr and two of length $rd\theta$. See Fig. 1.18. For other transformations we may need general methods for obtaining Jacobians. Computation of Jacobians will be treated in detail in Section 4.4.

Of interest here is the determination of the transformed region of integration. In principle this issue is straightforward, but all too frequently one encounters situations (both in other texts and in research articles) where misleading and potentially incorrect arguments are presented. The confusion normally arises in cases for which at least a part of the boundary is at infinity. We illustrate with the conversion from 2-D Cartesian to plane polar coordinates. Figure 1.19 shows that if one integrates for $0 \leq \theta < 2\pi$ and $0 \leq r < a$, there are regions in the corners of a square (of side $2a$) that are not included. If the integral is to be evaluated in the limit $a \to \infty$, it is both incorrect and meaningless to advance arguments about the "neglect" of contributions from these corner regions, as every point in these corners is ultimately included as a is increased.

A similar, but slightly less obvious situation arises if we transform an integration over Cartesian coordinates $0 \leq x < \infty$, $0 \leq y < \infty$, into one involving coordinates $u = x + y$,

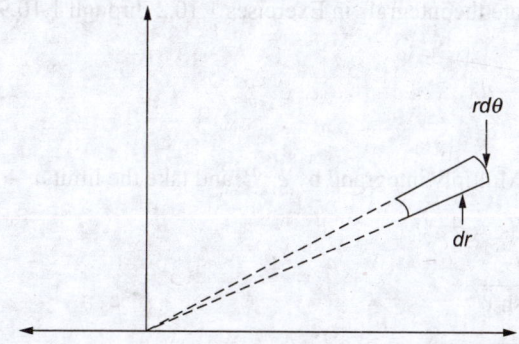

FIGURE 1.18   Element of area in plane polar coordinates.

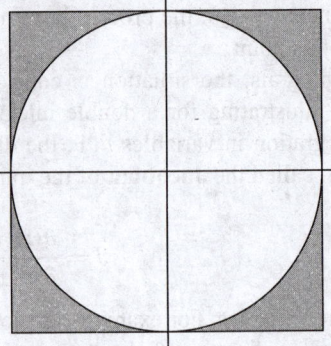

FIGURE 1.19   2-D integration, Cartesian and plane polar coordinates.

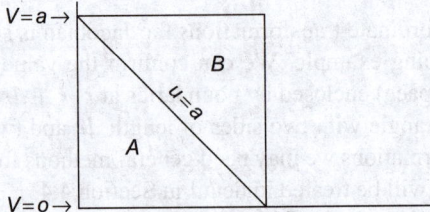

FIGURE 1.20   Integral in transformed coordinates.

$v = y$, with integration limits $0 \leq u < \infty$, $0 \leq v \leq u$. See Fig. 1.20. Again it is incorrect and meaningless to make arguments justifying the "neglect" of the outer triangle (labeled B in the figure). The relevant observation here is that ultimately, as the value of u is increased, any arbitrary point in the quarter-plane becomes included in the region being integrated.

Exercises

1.10.1   Use a recursive method to show that, for all positive integers n, $\Gamma(n) = (n - 1)!$.
Evaluate the integrals in Exercises 1.10.2 through 1.10.9.

1.10.2 $\displaystyle\int_0^\infty \frac{\sin x}{x}\, dx.$

Hint. Multiply integrand by e^{-ax} and take the limit $a \to 0$.

1.10.3 $\displaystyle\int_0^\infty \frac{dx}{\cosh x}.$

Hint. Expand the denominator is a way that converges for all relevant x.

1.10.4 $\displaystyle\int_0^\infty \frac{dx}{e^{ax}+1}$, for $a > 0$.

1.10.5 $\displaystyle\int_\pi^\infty \frac{\sin x}{x^2}\,dx$.

1.10.6 $\displaystyle\int_0^\infty \frac{e^{-x}\sin x}{x}\,dx$.

1.10.7 $\displaystyle\int_0^x \mathrm{erf}(t)\,dt$.

The result can be expressed in terms of special functions in Table 1.2.

1.10.8 $\displaystyle\int_1^x E_1(t)\,dt$.

Obtain a result in which the only special function is E_1.

1.10.9 $\displaystyle\int_0^\infty \frac{e^{-x}}{x+1}\,dx$.

1.10.10 Show that $\displaystyle\int_0^\infty \left(\frac{\tan^{-1}x}{x}\right)^2 dx = \pi\ln 2$.

Hint. Integrate by parts, to linearize in $\tan^{-1}$. Then replace $\tan^{-1}x$ by $\tan^{-1}ax$ and evaluate for $a = 1$.

1.10.11 By direct integration in Cartesian coordinates, find the area of the ellipse defined by

$$\frac{x^2}{a^2} + \frac{y^2}{b^2} = 1.$$

1.10.12 A unit circle is divided into two pieces by a straight line whose distance of closest approach to the center is $1/2$ unit. By evaluating a suitable integral, find the area of the smaller piece thereby produced. Then use simple geometric considerations to verify your answer.

1.11 DIRAC DELTA FUNCTION

Frequently we are faced with the problem of describing a quantity that is zero everywhere except at a single point, while at that point it is infinite in such a way that its integral over any interval containing that point has a finite value. For this purpose it is useful to introduce the **Dirac delta function**, which is **defined** to have the properties

$$\delta(x) = 0, \quad x \neq 0, \tag{1.149}$$

$$f(0) = \int_a^b f(x)\,\delta(x)\,dx, \tag{1.150}$$

where $f(x)$ is any well-behaved function and the integration includes the origin. As a special case of Eq. (1.150),

$$\int_{-\infty}^{\infty} \delta(x)\,dx = 1. \tag{1.151}$$

From Eq. (1.150), $\delta(x)$ must be an infinitely high, thin spike at $x = 0$, as in the description of an impulsive force or the charge density for a point charge. The problem is that **no such function exists**, in the usual sense of function. However, the crucial property in Eq. (1.150) can be developed rigorously as the limit of a **sequence** of functions, a distribution. For example, the delta function may be approximated by any of the sequences of functions, Eqs. (1.152) to (1.155) and Figs. 1.21 and 1.22:

$$\delta_n(x) = \begin{cases} 0, & x < -\frac{1}{2n} \\ n, & -\frac{1}{2n} < x < \frac{1}{2n} \\ 0, & x > \frac{1}{2n}, \end{cases} \tag{1.152}$$

$$\delta_n(x) = \frac{n}{\sqrt{\pi}}\,\exp(-n^2 x^2), \tag{1.153}$$

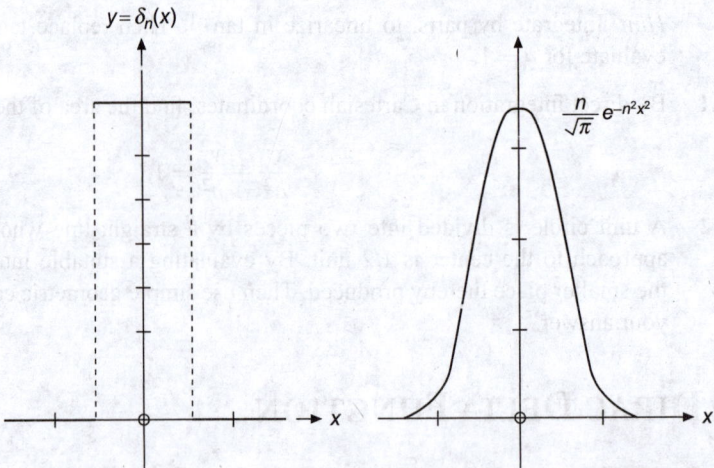

FIGURE 1.21 δ-Sequence function: left, Eq. (1.152); right, Eq. (1.153).

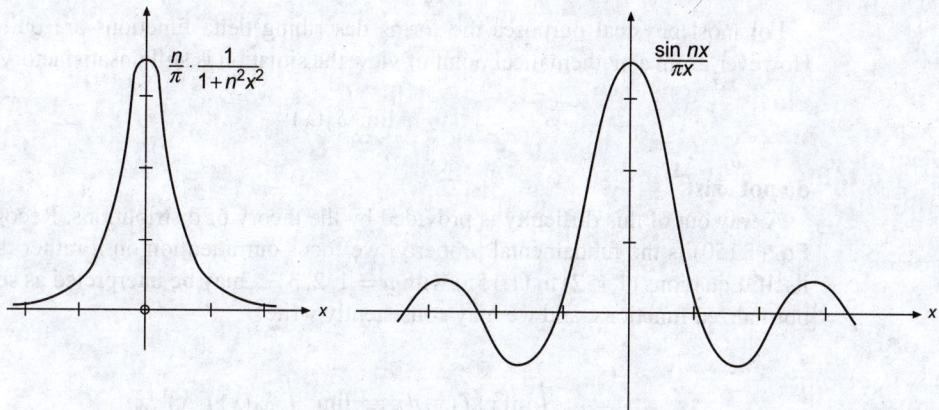

FIGURE 1.22 δ-Sequence function: left, Eq. (1.154); right, Eq. (1.155).

$$\delta_n(x) = \frac{n}{\pi} \frac{1}{1+n^2x^2}, \tag{1.154}$$

$$\delta_n(x) = \frac{\sin nx}{\pi x} = \frac{1}{2\pi} \int_{-n}^{n} e^{ixt}\, dt. \tag{1.155}$$

While all these sequences (and others) cause $\delta(x)$ to have the same properties, they differ somewhat in ease of use for various purposes. Equation (1.152) is useful in providing a simple derivation of the integral property, Eq. (1.150). Equation (1.153) is convenient to differentiate. Its derivatives lead to the Hermite polynomials. Equation (1.155) is particularly useful in Fourier analysis and in applications to quantum mechanics. In the theory of Fourier series, Eq. (1.155) often appears (modified) as the **Dirichlet kernel**:

$$\delta_n(x) = \frac{1}{2\pi} \frac{\sin[(n+\frac{1}{2})x]}{\sin\left(\frac{1}{2}x\right)}. \tag{1.156}$$

In using these approximations in Eq. (1.150) and elsewhere, we assume that $f(x)$ is well behaved—that it offers no problems at large x.

The forms for $\delta_n(x)$ given in Eqs. (1.152) to (1.155) all obviously peak strongly for large n at $x = 0$. They must also be scaled in agreement with Eq. (1.151). For the forms in Eqs. (1.152) and (1.154), verification of the scale is the topic of Exercises 1.11.1 and 1.11.2. To check the scales of Eqs. (1.153) and (1.155), we need values of the integrals

$$\int_{-\infty}^{\infty} e^{-n^2x^2}\, dx = \sqrt{\frac{\pi}{n}} \quad \text{and} \quad \int_{-\infty}^{\infty} \frac{\sin nx}{x}\, dx = \pi.$$

These results are respectively trivial extensions of Eqs. (1.148) and (11.107) (the latter of which we derive later).

For most physical purposes the forms describing delta functions are quite adequate. However, from a mathematical point of view the situation is still unsatisfactory. The limits

$$\lim_{n \to \infty} \delta_n(x)$$

do not exist.

A way out of this difficulty is provided by the theory of distributions. Recognizing that Eq. (1.150) is the fundamental property, we focus our attention on it rather than on $\delta(x)$ itself. Equations (1.152) to (1.155) with $n = 1, 2, 3 \ldots$ may be interpreted as **sequences** of normalized functions, and we may consistently write

$$\int\limits_{-\infty}^{\infty} \delta(x) f(x) \, dx \equiv \lim_{n \to \infty} \int \delta_n(x) f(x) \, dx. \tag{1.157}$$

Thus, $\delta(x)$ is labeled a **distribution** (not a function) and is regarded as defined by Eq. (1.157). We might emphasize that the integral on the left-hand side of Eq. (1.157) is not a Riemann integral.[8]

Properties of $\delta(x)$

- From any of Eqs. (1.152) through (1.155) we see that Dirac's delta function must be even in x, $\delta(-x) = \delta(x)$.

- If $a > 0$,

$$\delta(ax) = \frac{1}{a} \delta(x), \quad a > 0. \tag{1.158}$$

Equation (1.158) can be proved by making the substitution $x = y/a$:

$$\int\limits_{-\infty}^{\infty} f(x) \delta(ax) \, dx = \frac{1}{a} \int\limits_{-\infty}^{\infty} f(y/a) \delta(y) \, dy = \frac{1}{a} f(0).$$

If $a < 0$, Eq. (1.158) becomes $\delta(ax) = \delta(x)/|a|$.

- Shift of origin:

$$\int\limits_{-\infty}^{\infty} \delta(x - x_0) f(x) \, dx = f(x_0), \tag{1.159}$$

which can be proved by making the substitution $y = x - x_0$ and noting that when $y = 0$, $x = x_0$.

---

[8]It can be treated as a Stieltjes integral if desired; $\delta(x) \, dx$ is replaced by $du(x)$, where $u(x)$ is the Heaviside step function (compare Exercise 1.11.9).

- If the argument of $\delta(x)$ is a function $g(x)$ with simple zeros at points a_i on the real axis (and therefore $g'(a_i) \neq 0$),

$$\delta\big(g(x)\big) = \sum_i \frac{\delta(x - a_i)}{|g'(a_i)|}. \tag{1.160}$$

To prove Eq. (1.160), we write

$$\int_{-\infty}^{\infty} f(x)\delta(x)\,dx = \sum_i \int_{a_i-\varepsilon}^{a_i+\varepsilon} f(x)\delta\big((x - a_i)g'(a_i)\big)\,dx,$$

where we have decomposed the original integral into a sum of integrals over small intervals containing the zeros of $g(x)$. In these intervals, we replaced $g(x)$ by the leading term in its Taylor series. Applying Eqs. (1.158) and (1.159) to each term of the sum, we confirm Eq. (1.160).

- Derivative of delta function:

$$\int_{-\infty}^{\infty} f(x)\delta'(x - x_0)\,dx = -\int_{-\infty}^{\infty} f'(x)\delta(x - x_0)\,dx = -f'(x_0). \tag{1.161}$$

Equation (1.161) can be taken as **defining** the derivative $\delta'(x)$; it is evaluated by performing an integration by parts on any of the sequences defining the delta function.

- In three dimensions, the delta function $\delta(\mathbf{r})$ is interpreted as $\delta(x)\delta(y)\delta(z)$, so it describes a function localized at the origin and with unit integrated weight, irrespective of the coordinate system in use. Thus, in spherical polar coordinates,

$$\iiint f(\mathbf{r}_2)\delta(\mathbf{r}_2 - \mathbf{r}_1)r_2^2\,dr_2\sin\theta_2\,d\theta_2\,d\phi_2 = f(\mathbf{r}_1). \tag{1.162}$$

- Equation (1.155) corresponds in the limit to

$$\delta(t - x) = \frac{1}{2\pi}\int_{-\infty}^{\infty} \exp\big(i\omega(t - x)\big)\,d\omega, \tag{1.163}$$

with the understanding that this has meaning only when under an integral sign. In that context it is extremely useful for the simplification of Fourier integrals (Chapter 20).

- Expansions of $\delta(x)$ are addressed in Chapter 5. See Example 5.1.7.

Kronecker Delta

It is sometimes useful to have a symbol that is the discrete analog of the Dirac delta function, with the property that it is unity when the discrete variable has a certain value, and zero otherwise. A quantity with these properties is known as the **Kronecker delta**, defined for indices i and j as

$$\delta_{ij} = \begin{cases} 1, & i = j, \\ 0, & i \neq j. \end{cases} \tag{1.164}$$

Frequent uses of this symbol are to select a special term from a summation, or to have one functional form for all nonzero values of an index, but a different form when the index is zero. Examples:

$$\sum_{ij} f_{ij}\,\delta_{ij} = \sum_{i} f_{ii}, \quad C_n = \frac{1}{1+\delta_{n0}}\frac{2\pi}{L}.$$

Exercises

1.11.1   Let

$$\delta_n(x) = \begin{cases} 0, & x < -\dfrac{1}{2n}, \\[2mm] n, & -\dfrac{1}{2n} < x < \dfrac{1}{2n}, \\[2mm] 0, & \dfrac{1}{2n} < x. \end{cases}$$

Show that

$$\lim_{n\to\infty} \int_{-\infty}^{\infty} f(x)\delta_n(x)\,dx = f(0),$$

assuming that $f(x)$ is continuous at $x = 0$.

1.11.2   For

$$\delta_n(x) = \frac{n}{\pi}\frac{1}{1+n^2x^2},$$

show that

$$\int_{-\infty}^{\infty} \delta_n(x)\,dx = 1.$$

1.11.3   Fejer's method of summing series is associated with the function

$$\delta_n(t) = \frac{1}{2\pi n}\left[\frac{\sin(nt/2)}{\sin(t/2)}\right]^2.$$

Show that $\delta_n(t)$ is a delta distribution, in the sense that

$$\lim_{n\to\infty} \frac{1}{2\pi n} \int_{-\infty}^{\infty} f(t)\left[\frac{\sin(nt/2)}{\sin(t/2)}\right]^2 dt = f(0).$$

1.11.4   Prove that

$$\delta[a(x-x_1)] = \frac{1}{a}\delta(x-x_1).$$

Note. If $\delta[a(x-x_1)]$ is considered even, relative to x_1, the relation holds for negative a and $1/a$ may be replaced by $1/|a|$.

1.11.5   Show that

$$\delta[(x-x_1)(x-x_2)] = [\delta(x-x_1) + \delta(x-x_2)]/|x_1-x_2|.$$

Hint. Try using Exercise 1.11.4.

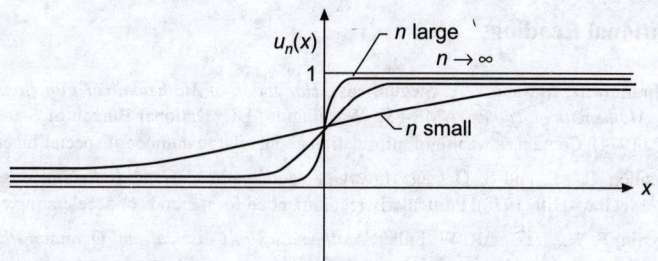

FIGURE 1.23   Heaviside unit step function.

1.11.6   Using the Gauss error curve delta sequence $\delta_n = \dfrac{n}{\sqrt{\pi}} e^{-n^2 x^2}$, show that

$$x \frac{d}{dx} \delta(x) = -\delta(x),$$

treating $\delta(x)$ and its derivative as in Eq. (1.157).

1.11.7   Show that

$$\int_{-\infty}^{\infty} \delta'(x) f(x)\, dx = -f'(0).$$

Here we assume that $f'(x)$ is continuous at $x = 0$.

1.11.8   Prove that

$$\delta(f(x)) = \left| \frac{df(x)}{dx} \right|_{x=x_0}^{-1} \delta(x - x_0),$$

where x_0 is chosen so that $f(x_0) = 0$.

Hint. Note that $\delta(f)\, df = \delta(x)\, dx$.

1.11.9   (a)   If we define a sequence $\delta_n(x) = n/(2\cosh^2 nx)$, show that

$$\int_{-\infty}^{\infty} \delta_n(x)\, dx = 1, \quad \text{independent of } n.$$

(b)   Continuing this analysis, show that[9]

$$\int_{-\infty}^{x} \delta_n(x)\, dx = \frac{1}{2}\left[1 + \tanh nx\right] \equiv u_n(x)$$

and

$$\lim_{n \to \infty} u_n(x) = \begin{cases} 0, & x < 0, \\ 1, & x > 0. \end{cases}$$

This is the Heaviside unit step function (Fig. 1.23).

---

[9]Many other symbols are used for this function. This is the AMS-55 notation (in Additional Readings, see Abramowitz and Stegun): u for unit.

Additional Readings

Abramowitz, M., and I. A. Stegun, eds., *Handbook of Mathematical Functions with Formulas, Graphs, and Mathematical Tables* (AMS-55). Washington, DC: National Bureau of Standards (1972), reprinted, Dover (1974). Contains a wealth of information about a large number of special functions.

Bender, C. M., and S. Orszag, *Advanced Mathematical Methods for Scientists and Engineers*. New York: McGraw-Hill (1978). Particularly recommended for methods of accelerating convergence.

Byron, F. W., Jr., and R. W. Fuller, *Mathematics of Classical and Quantum Physics*. Reading, MA: Addison-Wesley (1969), reprinted, Dover (1992). This is an advanced text that presupposes moderate knowledge of mathematical physics.

Courant, R., and D. Hilbert, *Methods of Mathematical Physics*, Vol. 1 (1st English ed.). New York: Wiley (Interscience) (1953). As a reference book for mathematical physics, it is particularly valuable for existence theorems and discussion of areas such as eigenvalue problems, integral equations, and calculus of variations.

Galambos, J., *Representations of Real Numbers by Infinite Series*. Berlin: Springer (1976).

Gradshteyn, I. S., and I. M. Ryzhik, *Table of Integrals, Series, and Products*. Corrected and enlarged 7th ed., edited by A. Jeffrey and D. Zwillinger. New York: Academic Press (2007).

Hansen, E., *A Table of Series and Products*. Englewood Cliffs, NJ: Prentice-Hall (1975). A tremendous compilation of series and products.

Hardy, G. H., *Divergent Series*. Oxford: Clarendon Press (1956), 2nd ed., Chelsea (1992). The standard, comprehensive work on methods of treating divergent series. Hardy includes instructive accounts of the gradual development of the concepts of convergence and divergence.

Jeffrey, A., *Handbook of Mathematical Formulas and Integrals*. San Diego: Academic Press (1995).

Jeffreys, H. S., and B. S. Jeffreys, *Methods of Mathematical Physics*, 3rd ed. Cambridge, UK: Cambridge University Press (1972). This is a scholarly treatment of a wide range of mathematical analysis, in which considerable attention is paid to mathematical rigor. Applications are to classical physics and geophysics.

Knopp, K., *Theory and Application of Infinite Series*. London: Blackie and Son, 2nd ed. New York: Hafner (1971), reprinted A. K. Peters Classics (1997). This is a thorough, comprehensive, and authoritative work that covers infinite series and products. Proofs of almost all the statements about series not proved in this chapter will be found in this book.

Mangulis, V., *Handbook of Series for Scientists and Engineers*. New York: Academic Press (1965). A most convenient and useful collection of series. Includes algebraic functions, Fourier series, and series of the special functions: Bessel, Legendre, and others.

Morse, P. M., and H. Feshbach, *Methods of Theoretical Physics*, 2 vols. New York: McGraw-Hill (1953). This work presents the mathematics of much of theoretical physics in detail but at a rather advanced level. It is recommended as the outstanding source of information for supplementary reading and advanced study.

Rainville, E. D., *Infinite Series*. New York: Macmillan (1967). A readable and useful account of series constants and functions.

Sokolnikoff, I. S., and R. M. Redheffer, *Mathematics of Physics and Modern Engineering*, 2nd ed. New York: McGraw-Hill (1966). A long chapter 2 (101 pages) presents infinite series in a thorough but very readable form. Extensions to the solutions of differential equations, to complex series, and to Fourier series are included.

Spiegel, M. R., *Complex Variables*, in *Schaum's Outline Series*. New York: McGraw-Hill (1964, reprinted 1995). Clear, to the point, and with very large numbers of examples, many solved step by step. Answers are provided for all others. Highly recommended.

Whittaker, E. T., and G. N. Watson, *A Course of Modern Analysis*, 4th ed. Cambridge, UK: Cambridge University Press (1962), paperback. Although this is the oldest of the general references (original edition 1902), it still is the classic reference. It leans strongly towards pure mathematics, as of 1902, with full mathematical rigor.

CHAPTER 2

DETERMINANTS AND MATRICES

2.1 DETERMINANTS

We begin the study of matrices by solving linear equations that will lead us to determinants and matrices. The concept of **determinant** and the notation were introduced by the renowned German mathematician and philosopher Gottfried Wilhelm von Leibniz.

Homogeneous Linear Equations

One of the major applications of determinants is in the establishment of a condition for the existence of a nontrivial solution for a set of linear homogeneous algebraic equations. Suppose we have three unknowns x_1, x_2, x_3 (or n equations with n unknowns):

$$a_1 x_1 + a_2 x_2 + a_3 x_3 = 0,$$
$$b_1 x_1 + b_2 x_2 + b_3 x_3 = 0, \qquad (2.1)$$
$$c_1 x_1 + c_2 x_2 + c_3 x_3 = 0.$$

The problem is to determine under what conditions there is any solution, apart from the trivial one $x_1 = 0, x_2 = 0, x_3 = 0$. If we use vector notation $\mathbf{x} = (x_1, x_2, x_3)$ for the solution and three rows $\mathbf{a} = (a_1, a_2, a_3), \mathbf{b} = (b_1, b_2, b_3), \mathbf{c} = (c_1, c_2, c_3)$ of coefficients, then the three equations, Eqs. (2.1), become

$$\mathbf{a} \cdot \mathbf{x} = 0, \quad \mathbf{b} \cdot \mathbf{x} = 0, \quad \mathbf{c} \cdot \mathbf{x} = 0. \qquad (2.2)$$

These three vector equations have the **geometrical** interpretation that $\mathbf{x}$ is orthogonal to $\mathbf{a}, \mathbf{b}$, and $\mathbf{c}$. If the volume spanned by $\mathbf{a}, \mathbf{b}, \mathbf{c}$ given by the determinant (or triple scalar product, see Eq. (3.12) of Section 3.2)

$$D_3 = (\mathbf{a} \times \mathbf{b}) \cdot \mathbf{c} = \det(\mathbf{a}, \mathbf{b}, \mathbf{c}) = \begin{vmatrix} a_1 & a_2 & a_3 \\ b_1 & b_2 & b_3 \\ c_1 & c_2 & c_3 \end{vmatrix} \tag{2.3}$$

is not zero, then there is only the trivial solution $\mathbf{x} = 0$. For an introduction to the cross product of vectors, see Chapter 3: Vector Analysis, Section 3.2: Vectors in 3-D Space.

Conversely, if the aforementioned determinant of coefficients vanishes, then one of the row vectors is a linear combination of the other two. Let us assume that $\mathbf{c}$ lies in the plane spanned by $\mathbf{a}$ and $\mathbf{b}$, that is, that the third equation is a linear combination of the first two and not independent. Then $\mathbf{x}$ is orthogonal to that plane so that $\mathbf{x} \sim \mathbf{a} \times \mathbf{b}$. Since homogeneous equations can be multiplied by arbitrary numbers, only ratios of the x_i are relevant, for which we then obtain ratios of 2×2 determinants

$$\frac{x_1}{x_3} = \frac{a_2 b_3 - a_3 b_2}{a_1 b_2 - a_2 b_1}, \quad \frac{x_2}{x_3} = -\frac{a_1 b_3 - a_3 b_1}{a_1 b_2 - a_2 b_1} \tag{2.4}$$

from the components of the cross product $\mathbf{a} \times \mathbf{b}$, provided $x_3 \sim a_1 b_2 - a_2 b_1 \neq 0$. This is **Cramer's rule** for three homogeneous linear equations.

Inhomogeneous Linear Equations

The simplest case of two equations with two unknowns,

$$a_1 x_1 + a_2 x_2 = a_3, \quad b_1 x_1 + b_2 x_2 = b_3, \tag{2.5}$$

can be reduced to the previous case by imbedding it in three-dimensional (3-D) space with a solution vector $\mathbf{x} = (x_1, x_2, -1)$ and row vectors $\mathbf{a} = (a_1, a_2, a_3)$, $\mathbf{b} = (b_1, b_2, b_3)$. As before, Eqs. (2.5) in vector notation, $\mathbf{a} \cdot \mathbf{x} = 0$ and $\mathbf{b} \cdot \mathbf{x} = 0$, imply that $\mathbf{x} \sim \mathbf{a} \times \mathbf{b}$, so the analog of Eq. (2.4) holds. For this to apply, though, the third component of $\mathbf{a} \times \mathbf{b}$ must not be zero, that is, $a_1 b_2 - a_2 b_1 \neq 0$, because the third component of $\mathbf{x}$ is $-1 \neq 0$. This yields the x_i as

$$x_1 = \frac{a_3 b_2 - b_3 a_2}{a_1 b_2 - a_2 b_1} = \frac{\begin{vmatrix} a_3 & a_2 \\ b_3 & b_2 \end{vmatrix}}{\begin{vmatrix} a_1 & a_2 \\ b_1 & b_2 \end{vmatrix}}, \tag{2.6}$$

$$x_2 = \frac{a_1 b_3 - a_3 b_1}{a_1 b_2 - a_2 b_1} = \frac{\begin{vmatrix} a_1 & a_3 \\ b_1 & b_3 \end{vmatrix}}{\begin{vmatrix} a_1 & a_2 \\ b_1 & b_2 \end{vmatrix}}. \tag{2.7}$$

The determinant in the numerator of x_1 (x_2) is obtained from the determinant of the coefficients $\begin{vmatrix} a_1 & a_2 \\ b_1 & b_2 \end{vmatrix}$ by replacing the first (second) column vector by the vector $\begin{pmatrix} a_3 \\ b_3 \end{pmatrix}$ of the inhomogeneous side of Eq. (2.5). This is **Cramer's rule** for a set of two inhomogeneous linear equations with two unknowns.

A full understanding of the above exposition requires now that we introduce a formal definition of the determinant and show how it relates to the foregoing.

Definitions

Before defining a determinant, we need to introduce some related concepts and definitions.

- When we write two-dimensional (2-D) arrays of.items, we identify the item in the nth horizontal row and the mth vertical column by the index set n, m; note that the row index is conventionally written first.

- Starting from a set of n objects in some reference order (e.g., the number sequence $1, 2, 3, \ldots, n$), we can make a **permutation** of them to some other order; the total number of distinct permutations that are possible is $n!$ (choose the first object n ways, then choose the second in $n - 1$ ways, etc.).

- Every permutation of n objects can be reached from the reference order by a succession of pairwise interchanges (e.g., $1234 \rightarrow 4132$ can be reached by the successive steps $1234 \rightarrow 1432 \rightarrow 4132$). Although the number of pairwise interchanges needed for a given permutation depends on the path (compare the above example with $1234 \rightarrow 1243 \rightarrow 1423 \rightarrow 4123 \rightarrow 4132$), for a given permutation the number of interchanges will always either be **even** or **odd**. Thus a permutation can be identified as having either even or odd **parity**.

- It is convenient to introduce the **Levi-Civita symbol**, which for an n-object system is denoted by $\varepsilon_{ij\ldots}$, where ε has n subscripts, each of which identifies one of the objects. This Levi-Civita symbol is defined to be $+1$ if $ij \ldots$ represents an even permutation of the objects from a reference order; it is defined to be -1 if $ij \ldots$ represents an odd permutation of the objects, and zero if $ij \ldots$ does not represent a permutation of the objects (i.e., contains an entry duplication). Since this is an important definition, we set it out in a display format:

$$\varepsilon_{ij\ldots} = +1, \quad ij \ldots \text{ an even permutation,}$$
$$= -1, \quad ij \ldots \text{ an odd permutation,}$$
$$= 0, \quad ij \ldots \text{ not a permutation.} \tag{2.8}$$

We now define a determinant of **order** n to be an $n \times n$ square array of numbers (or functions), with the array conventionally written within vertical bars (not parentheses, braces, or any other type of brackets), as follows:

$$D_n = \begin{vmatrix} a_{11} & a_{12} & \ldots & a_{1n} \\ a_{21} & a_{22} & \ldots & a_{2n} \\ a_{31} & a_{32} & \ldots & a_{3n} \\ \ldots & \ldots & \ldots & \ldots \\ a_{n1} & a_{n2} & \ldots & a_{nn} \end{vmatrix}. \tag{2.9}$$

The determinant D_n has a value that is obtained by

1. Forming all $n!$ products that can be formed by choosing one entry from each row in such a way that one entry comes from each column,
2. Assigning each product a sign that corresponds to the parity of the sequence in which the columns were used (assuming the rows were used in an ascending sequence),
3. Adding (with the assigned signs) the products.

More formally, the determinant in Eq. (2.9) is defined to have the value

$$D_n = \sum_{ij\ldots} \varepsilon_{ij\ldots} a_{1i} a_{2j} \cdots.$$ (2.10)

The summations in Eq. (2.10) need not be restricted to permutations, but can be assumed to range independently from 1 through n; the presence of the Levi-Civita symbol will cause only the index combinations corresponding to permutations to actually contribute to the sum.

Example 2.1.1   DETERMINANTS OF ORDERS 2 AND 3

To make the definition more concrete, we illustrate first with a determinant of order 2. The Levi-Civita symbols needed for this determinant are $\varepsilon_{12} = +1$ and $\varepsilon_{21} = -1$ (note that $\varepsilon_{11} = \varepsilon_{22} = 0$), leading to

$$D_2 = \begin{vmatrix} a_{11} & a_{12} \\ a_{21} & a_{22} \end{vmatrix} = \varepsilon_{12} a_{11} a_{22} + \varepsilon_{21} a_{12} a_{21} = a_{11} a_{22} - a_{12} a_{21}.$$

We see that this determinant expands into $2! = 2$ terms. A specific example of a determinant of order 2 is

$$\begin{vmatrix} a_1 & a_2 \\ b_1 & b_2 \end{vmatrix} = a_1 b_2 - b_1 a_2.$$

Determinants of order 3 expand into $3! = 6$ terms. The relevant Levi-Civita symbols are $\varepsilon_{123} = \varepsilon_{231} = \varepsilon_{312} = +1$, $\varepsilon_{213} = \varepsilon_{321} = \varepsilon_{132} = -1$; all other index combinations have $\varepsilon_{ijk} = 0$, so

$$D_3 = \begin{vmatrix} a_{11} & a_{12} & a_{13} \\ a_{21} & a_{22} & a_{23} \\ a_{31} & a_{32} & a_{33} \end{vmatrix} = \sum_{ijk} \varepsilon_{ijk} a_{1i} a_{2j} a_{3k}$$

$$= a_{11} a_{22} a_{33} - a_{11} a_{23} a_{32} - a_{13} a_{22} a_{31} - a_{12} a_{21} a_{33} + a_{12} a_{23} a_{31} + a_{13} a_{21} a_{32}.$$

The expression in Eq. (2.3) is the determinant of order 3

$$\begin{vmatrix} a_1 & a_2 & a_3 \\ b_1 & b_2 & b_3 \\ c_1 & c_2 & c_3 \end{vmatrix} = a_1 b_2 c_3 - a_1 b_3 c_2 - a_2 b_1 c_3 + a_2 b_3 c_1 + a_3 b_1 c_2 - a_3 b_2 c_1.$$

Note that half of the terms in the expansion of a determinant bear negative signs. It is quite possible that a determinant of large elements will have a very small value. Here is one example:

$$\begin{vmatrix} 8 & 11 & 7 \\ 9 & 11 & 5 \\ 8 & 12 & 9 \end{vmatrix} = 1.$$

∎

Properties of Determinants

The symmetry properties of the Levi-Civita symbol translate into a number of symmetries exhibited by determinants. For simplicity, we illustrate with determinants of order 3. The interchange of two columns of a determinant causes the Levi-Civita symbol multiplying each term of the expansion to change sign; the same is true if two rows are interchanged. Moreover, the roles of rows and columns may be interchanged; if a determinant with elements a_{ij} is replaced by one with elements $b_{ij} = a_{ji}$, we call the b_{ij} determinant the **transpose** of the a_{ij} determinant. Both these determinants have the same value. Summarizing:

> *Interchanging two rows (or two columns) changes the sign of the value of a determinant. Transposition does not alter its value.*

Thus,

$$\begin{vmatrix} a_{11} & a_{12} & a_{13} \\ a_{21} & a_{22} & a_{23} \\ a_{31} & a_{32} & a_{33} \end{vmatrix} = - \begin{vmatrix} a_{12} & a_{11} & a_{13} \\ a_{22} & a_{21} & a_{23} \\ a_{32} & a_{31} & a_{33} \end{vmatrix} = \begin{vmatrix} a_{11} & a_{21} & a_{31} \\ a_{12} & a_{22} & a_{32} \\ a_{13} & a_{23} & a_{33} \end{vmatrix}. \tag{2.11}$$

Further consequences of the definition in Eq. (2.10) are:

> *(1) Multiplication of all members of a single column (or a single row) by a constant k causes the value of the determinant to be multiplied by k,*

> *(2) If the elements of a column (or row) are actually sums of two quantities, the determinant can be decomposed into a sum of two determinants.*

Thus,

$$k \begin{vmatrix} a_{11} & a_{12} & a_{13} \\ a_{21} & a_{22} & a_{23} \\ a_{31} & a_{32} & a_{33} \end{vmatrix} = \begin{vmatrix} ka_{11} & a_{12} & a_{13} \\ ka_{21} & a_{22} & a_{23} \\ ka_{31} & a_{32} & a_{33} \end{vmatrix} = \begin{vmatrix} ka_{11} & ka_{12} & ka_{13} \\ a_{21} & a_{22} & a_{23} \\ a_{31} & a_{32} & a_{33} \end{vmatrix}, \tag{2.12}$$

$$\begin{vmatrix} a_{11} + b_1 & a_{12} & a_{13} \\ a_{21} + b_2 & a_{22} & a_{23} \\ a_{31} + b_3 & a_{32} & a_{33} \end{vmatrix} = \begin{vmatrix} a_{11} & a_{12} & a_{13} \\ a_{21} & a_{22} & a_{23} \\ a_{31} & a_{32} & a_{33} \end{vmatrix} + \begin{vmatrix} b_1 & a_{12} & a_{13} \\ b_2 & a_{22} & a_{23} \\ b_3 & a_{32} & a_{33} \end{vmatrix}. \tag{2.13}$$

These basic properties and/or the basic definition mean that

- Any determinant with two rows equal, or two columns equal, has the value zero. To prove this, interchange the two identical rows or columns; the determinant both remains the same and changes sign, and therefore must have the value zero.

- An extension of the above is that if two rows (or columns) are proportional, the determinant is zero.

- The value of a determinant is unchanged if a multiple of one row is added (column by column) to another row or if a multiple of one column is added (row by row) to another column. Applying Eq. (2.13), the addition does not contribute to the value of the determinant.

- If each element in a row or each element in a column is zero, the determinant has the value zero.

Laplacian Development by Minors

The fact that a determinant of order n expands into $n!$ terms means that it is important to identify efficient means for determinant evaluation. One approach is to expand in terms of **minors**. The minor corresponding to a_{ij}, denoted M_{ij}, or $M_{ij}(a)$ if we need to identify M as coming from the a_{ij}, is the determinant (of order $n-1$) produced by striking out row i and column j of the original determinant. When we expand into minors, the quantities to be used are the **cofactors** of the (ij) elements, defined as $(-1)^{i+j}M_{ij}$. The expansion can be made for any row or column of the original determinant. If, for example, we expand the determinant of Eq. (2.9) using row i, we have

$$D_n = \sum_{j=1}^{n} a_{ij}(-1)^{i+j}M_{ij}. \tag{2.14}$$

This expansion reduces the work involved in evaluation if the row or column selected for the expansion contains zeros, as the corresponding minors need not be evaluated.

Example 2.1.2   EXPANSION IN MINORS

Consider the determinant (arising in Dirac's relativistic electron theory)

$$D \equiv \begin{vmatrix} a_{11} & a_{12} & a_{13} & a_{14} \\ a_{21} & a_{22} & a_{23} & a_{24} \\ a_{31} & a_{32} & a_{33} & a_{34} \\ a_{41} & a_{42} & a_{43} & a_{44} \end{vmatrix} = \begin{vmatrix} 0 & 1 & 0 & 0 \\ -1 & 0 & 0 & 0 \\ 0 & 0 & 0 & 1 \\ 0 & 0 & -1 & 0 \end{vmatrix}.$$

Expanding across the top row, only one 3×3 matrix survives:

$$D = (-1)^{1+2}a_{12}M_{12}(a) = (-1) \cdot (1) \begin{vmatrix} -1 & 0 & 0 \\ 0 & 0 & 1 \\ 0 & -1 & 0 \end{vmatrix} \equiv (-1) \begin{vmatrix} b_{11} & b_{12} & b_{13} \\ b_{21} & b_{22} & b_{23} \\ b_{31} & b_{32} & b_{33} \end{vmatrix}.$$

Expanding now across the second row, we get

$$D = (-1)(-1)^{2+3}b_{23}M_{23}(b) = \begin{vmatrix} -1 & 0 \\ 0 & -1 \end{vmatrix} = 1.$$

When we finally reached a 2×2 determinant, it was simple to evaluate it without further expansion. ∎

Linear Equation Systems

We are now ready to apply our knowledge of determinants to the solution of systems of linear equations. Suppose we have the simultaneous equations

$$a_1x_1 + a_2x_2 + a_3x_3 = h_1,$$

$$b_1x_1 + b_2x_2 + b_3x_3 = h_2,$$

$$c_1x_1 + c_2x_2 + c_3x_3 = h_3. \tag{2.15}$$

To use determinants to help solve this equation system, we define

$$D = \begin{vmatrix} a_1 & a_2 & a_3 \\ b_1 & b_2 & b_3 \\ c_1 & c_2 & c_3 \end{vmatrix}. \tag{2.16}$$

Starting from $x_1 D$, we manipulate it by (1) moving x_1 to multiply the entries of the first column of D, then (2) adding to the first column x_2 times the second column and x_3 times the third column (neither of these operations change the value). We then reach the second line of Eq. (2.17) by substituting the right-hand sides of Eqs. (2.15). These operations are illustrated here:

$$x_1 D = \begin{vmatrix} a_1 x_1 & a_2 & a_3 \\ b_1 x_1 & b_2 & b_3 \\ c_1 x_1 & c_2 & c_3 \end{vmatrix} = \begin{vmatrix} a_1 x_1 + a_2 x_2 + a_3 x_3 & a_2 & a_3 \\ b_1 x_1 + b_2 x_2 + b_3 x_3 & b_2 & b_3 \\ c_1 x_1 + c_2 x_2 + c_3 x_3 & c_2 & c_3 \end{vmatrix}$$

$$= \begin{vmatrix} h_1 & a_2 & a_3 \\ h_2 & b_2 & b_3 \\ h_3 & c_2 & c_3 \end{vmatrix}. \tag{2.17}$$

If $D \neq 0$, Eq. (2.17) may now be solved for x_1:

$$x_1 = \frac{1}{D} \begin{vmatrix} h_1 & a_2 & a_3 \\ h_2 & b_2 & b_3 \\ h_3 & c_2 & c_3 \end{vmatrix}. \tag{2.18}$$

Analogous procedures starting from $x_2 D$ and $x_3 D$ give the parallel results

$$x_2 = \frac{1}{D} \begin{vmatrix} a_1 & h_1 & a_3 \\ b_1 & h_2 & b_3 \\ c_1 & h_3 & c_3 \end{vmatrix}, \quad x_3 = \frac{1}{D} \begin{vmatrix} a_1 & a_2 & h_2 \\ b_1 & b_2 & h_2 \\ c_1 & c_2 & h_3 \end{vmatrix}.$$

We see that the solution for x_i is $1/D$ times a numerator obtained by replacing the ith column of D by the right-hand-side coefficients, a result that can be generalized to an arbitrary number n of simultaneous equations. This scheme for the solution of linear equation systems is known as **Cramer's rule**.

If D is nonzero, the above construction of the x_i is definitive and unique, so that there will be exactly one solution to the equation set. If $D \neq 0$ and the equations are homogeneous (i.e., all the h_i are zero), then the unique solution is that all the x_i are zero.

Determinants and Linear Dependence

The preceding subsections go a long way toward identifying the role of the determinant with respect to linear dependence. If n linear equations in n variables, written as in Eq. (2.15), have coefficients that form a nonzero determinant, the variables are uniquely determined, meaning that the forms constituting the left-hand sides of the equations must in fact be linearly independent. However, we would still like to prove the property illustrated in the introduction to this chapter, namely that if a set of forms is linearly dependent, the determinant of their coefficients will be zero. But this result is nearly immediate. The existence of linear dependence means that there exists one equation whose coefficients are linear combinations of the coefficients of the other equations, and we may use that fact to reduce to zero the row of the determinant corresponding to that equation.

In summary, we have therefore established the following important result:

> *If the coefficients of* n *linear forms in* n *variables form a nonzero determinant, the forms are linearly independent; if the determinant of the coefficients is zero, the forms exhibit linear dependence.*

Linearly Dependent Equations

If a set of linear forms is linearly dependent, we can distinguish three distinct situations when we consider equation systems based on these forms. First, and of most importance for physics, is the case in which all the equations are **homogeneous**, meaning that the right-hand side quantities h_i in equations of the type Eq. (2.15) are all zero. Then, one or more of the equations in the set will be equivalent to linear combinations of others, and we will have less than n equations in our n variables. We can then assign one (or in some cases, more than one) variable an arbitrary value, obtaining the others as functions of the assigned variables. We thus have a **manifold** (i.e., a parameterized set) of solutions to our equation system.

Combining the above analysis with our earlier observation that if a set of homogeneous linear equations has a nonvanishing determinant it has the unique solution that all the x_i are zero, we have the following important result:

> *A system of n homogeneous linear equations in n unknowns has solutions that are not identically zero only if the determinant of its coefficients vanishes. If that determinant vanishes, there will be one or more solutions that are not identically zero and are arbitrary as to scale.*

A second case is where we have (or combine equations so that we have) the same linear form in two equations, but with different values of the right-hand quantities h_i. In that case the equations are mutually inconsistent, and the equation system has no solution.

A third, related case, is where we have a duplicated linear form, but with a common value of h_i. This also leads to a solution manifold.

Example 2.1.3   LINEARLY DEPENDENT HOMOGENEOUS EQUATIONS

Consider the equation set

$$x_1 + x_2 + x_3 = 0,$$
$$x_1 + 3x_2 + 5x_3 = 0,$$
$$x_1 + 2x_2 + 3x_3 = 0.$$

Here

$$D = \begin{vmatrix} 1 & 1 & 1 \\ 1 & 3 & 5 \\ 1 & 2 & 3 \end{vmatrix} = 1(3)(3) - 1(5)(2) - 1(3)(1) - 1(1)(3) + 1(5)(1) + 1(1)(2) = 0.$$

The third equation is half the sum of the other two, so we drop it. Then,

second equation minus first: $2x_2 + 4x_3 = 0 \longrightarrow x_2 = -2x_3,$

($3\times$ first equation) minus second: $2x_1 - 2x_3 = 0 \longrightarrow x_1 = x_3.$

Since x_3 can have any value, there is an infinite number of solutions, all of the form $(x_1, x_2, x_3) = \text{constant} \times (1, -2, 1)$.

Our solution illustrates an important property of homogeneous linear equations, namely that any multiple of a solution is also a solution. The solution only becomes less arbitrary if we impose a scale condition. For example, in the present case we could require the squares of the x_i to add to unity. Even then, the solution would still be arbitrary as to overall sign. ∎

Numerical Evaluation

There is extensive literature on determinant evaluation. Computer codes and many references are given, for example, by Press *et al.*[1] We present here a straightforward method due to Gauss that illustrates the principles involved in all the modern evaluation methods. **Gauss elimination** is a versatile procedure that can be used for evaluating determinants, for solving linear equation systems, and (as we will see later) even for matrix inversion.

Example 2.1.4   GAUSS ELIMINATION

Our example, a 3×3 linear equation system, can easily be done in other ways, but it is used here to provide an understanding of the Gauss elimination procedure. We wish to solve

$$3x + 2y + z = 11$$
$$2x + 3y + z = 13$$
$$x + y + 4z = 12. \tag{2.19}$$

For convenience and for the optimum numerical accuracy, the equations are rearranged so that, to the extent possible, the largest coefficients run along the main diagonal (upper left to lower right).

The Gauss technique is to use the first equation to eliminate the first unknown, x, from the remaining equations. Then the (new) second equation is used to eliminate y from the last equation. In general, we work down through the set of equations, and then, with one unknown determined, we work back up to solve for each of the other unknowns in succession.

[1] W. H. Press, B. P. Flannery, S. A. Teukolsky, and W. T. Vetterling, *Numerical Recipes*, 2nd ed. Cambridge, UK: Cambridge University Press (1992), Chapter 2.

It is convenient to start by dividing each row by its initial coefficient, converting Eq. (2.19) to

$$x + \frac{2}{3}y + \frac{1}{3}z = \frac{11}{3}$$

$$x + \frac{3}{2}y + \frac{1}{2}z = \frac{13}{2}$$

$$x + y + 4z = 12. \tag{2.20}$$

Now, using the first equation, we eliminate x from the second and third equations by subtracting the first equation from each of the others:

$$x + \frac{2}{3}y + \frac{1}{3}z = \frac{11}{3}$$

$$\frac{5}{6}y + \frac{1}{6}z = \frac{17}{6}$$

$$\frac{1}{3}y + \frac{11}{3}z = \frac{25}{3}. \tag{2.21}$$

Then we divide the second and third rows by their initial coefficients:

$$x + \frac{2}{3}y + \frac{1}{3}z = \frac{11}{3}$$

$$y + \frac{1}{5}z = \frac{17}{5}$$

$$y + 11z = 25. \tag{2.22}$$

Repeating the technique, we use the new second equation to eliminate y from the third equation, which can then be solved for z:

$$x + \frac{2}{3}y + \frac{1}{3}z = \frac{11}{3}$$

$$y + \frac{1}{5}z = \frac{17}{5}$$

$$\frac{54}{5}z = \frac{108}{5} \quad \longrightarrow \quad z = 2. \tag{2.23}$$

Now that z has been determined, we can return to the second equation, finding

$$y + \frac{1}{5} \times 2 = \frac{17}{5} \quad \longrightarrow \quad y = 3,$$

and finally, continuing to the first equation,

$$x + \frac{2}{3} \times 3 + \frac{1}{3} \times 2 = \frac{11}{3} \quad \longrightarrow \quad x = 1.$$

The technique may not seem as elegant as the use of Cramer's rule, but it is well adapted to computers and is far faster than the time spent with determinants.

If we had not kept the right-hand sides of the equation system, the Gauss elimination process would have simply brought the original determinant into triangular form (but note that our processes for making the leading coefficients unity cause corresponding changes in the value of the determinant). In the present problem, the original determinant

$$D = \begin{vmatrix} 3 & 2 & 1 \\ 2 & 3 & 1 \\ 1 & 1 & 4 \end{vmatrix}$$

was divided by 3 and by 2 going from Eq. (2.19) to (2.20), and multiplied by 6/5 and by 3 going from Eq. (2.21) to (2.22), so that D and the determinant represented by the left-hand side of Eq. (2.23) are related by

$$D = (3)(2)\left(\frac{5}{6}\right)\left(\frac{1}{3}\right)\begin{vmatrix} 1 & \dfrac{2}{3} & \dfrac{1}{3} \\ 0 & 1 & \dfrac{1}{5} \\ 0 & 0 & \dfrac{54}{5} \end{vmatrix} = \frac{5}{3}\frac{54}{5} = 18. \tag{2.24}$$

Because all the entries in the lower triangle of the determinant explicitly shown in Eq. (2.24) are zero, the only term that contributes to it is the product of the diagonal elements: To get a nonzero term, we must use the first element of the first row, then the second element of the second row, etc. It is easy to verify that the final result obtained in Eq. (2.24) agrees with the result of evaluating the original form of D. ∎

Exercises

2.1.1 Evaluate the following determinants:

(a) $\begin{vmatrix} 1 & 0 & 1 \\ 0 & 1 & 0 \\ 1 & 0 & 0 \end{vmatrix}$, (b) $\begin{vmatrix} 1 & 2 & 0 \\ 3 & 1 & 2 \\ 0 & 3 & 1 \end{vmatrix}$, (c) $\dfrac{1}{\sqrt{2}}\begin{vmatrix} 0 & \sqrt{3} & 0 & 0 \\ \sqrt{3} & 0 & 2 & 0 \\ 0 & 2 & 0 & \sqrt{3} \\ 0 & 0 & \sqrt{3} & 0 \end{vmatrix}$.

2.1.2 Test the set of linear homogeneous equations

$$x + 3y + 3z = 0, \quad x - y + z = 0, \quad 2x + y + 3z = 0$$

to see if it possesses a nontrivial solution. In any case, find a solution to this equation set.

2.1.3 Given the pair of equations

$$x + 2y = 3, \quad 2x + 4y = 6,$$

(a) Show that the determinant of the coefficients vanishes.

(b) Show that the numerator determinants, see Eq. (2.18), also vanish.

(c) Find at least two solutions.

2.1.4 If C_{ij} is the cofactor of element a_{ij}, formed by striking out the ith row and jth column and including a sign $(-1)^{i+j}$, show that

(a) $\sum_i a_{ij} C_{ij} = \sum_i a_{ji} C_{ji} = |A|$, where $|A|$ is the determinant with the elements a_{ij},

(b) $\sum_i a_{ij} C_{ik} = \sum_i a_{ji} C_{ki} = 0, j \neq k$.

2.1.5   A determinant with all elements of order unity may be surprisingly small. The Hilbert determinant $H_{ij} = (i + j - 1)^{-1}, i, j = 1, 2, \ldots, n$ is notorious for its small values.

(a)   Calculate the value of the Hilbert determinants of order n for $n = 1, 2$, and 3.

(b)   If an appropriate subroutine is available, find the Hilbert determinants of order n for $n = 4, 5$, and 6.

ANS.	n	$\text{Det}(H_n)$
	1	1.
	2	8.33333×10^{-2}
	3	4.62963×10^{-4}
	4	1.65344×10^{-7}
	5	3.74930×10^{-12}
	6	5.36730×10^{-18}.

2.1.6   Prove that the determinant consisting of the coefficients from a set of linearly dependent forms has the value zero.

2.1.7   Solve the following set of linear simultaneous equations. Give the results to five decimal places.

$$1.0x_1 + 0.9x_2 + 0.8x_3 + 0.4x_4 + 0.1x_5 = 1.0$$

$$0.9x_1 + 1.0x_2 + 0.8x_3 + 0.5x_4 + 0.2x_5 + 0.1x_6 = 0.9$$

$$0.8x_1 + 0.8x_2 + 1.0x_3 + 0.7x_4 + 0.4x_5 + 0.2x_6 = 0.8$$

$$0.4x_1 + 0.5x_2 + 0.7x_3 + 1.0x_4 + 0.6x_5 + 0.3x_6 = 0.7$$

$$0.1x_1 + 0.2x_2 + 0.4x_3 + 0.6x_4 + 1.0x_5 + 0.5x_6 = 0.6$$

$$0.1x_2 + 0.2x_3 + 0.3x_4 + 0.5x_5 + 1.0x_6 = 0.5.$$

Note. These equations may also be solved by matrix inversion, as discussed in Section 2.2.

2.1.8   Show that (in 3-D space)

(a) $\sum_i \delta_{ii} = 3$,

(b) $\sum_{ij} \delta_{ij} \varepsilon_{ijk} = 0$,

(c) $\sum_{pq} \varepsilon_{ipq} \varepsilon_{jpq} = 2\delta_{ij}$,

(d) $\sum_{ijk} \varepsilon_{ijk} \varepsilon_{ijk} = 6$.

Note. The symbol δ_{ij} is the Kronecker delta, defined in Eq. (1.164), and ε_{ijk} is the Levi-Civita symbol, Eq. (2.8).

2.1.9 Show that (in 3-D space)

$$\sum_k \varepsilon_{ijk}\varepsilon_{pqk} = \delta_{ip}\delta_{jq} - \delta_{iq}\delta_{jp}.$$

Note. See Exercise 2.1.8 for definitions of δ_{ij} and ε_{ijk}.

2.2 MATRICES

Matrices are 2-D arrays of numbers or functions that obey the laws that define **matrix algebra**. The subject is important for physics because it facilitates the description of linear transformations such as changes of coordinate systems, provides a useful formulation of quantum mechanics, and facilitates a variety of analyses in classical and relativistic mechanics, particle theory, and other areas. Note also that the development of a mathematics of two-dimensionally ordered arrays is a natural and logical extension of concepts involving ordered pairs of numbers (complex numbers) or ordinary vectors (one-dimensional arrays).

The most distinctive feature of matrix algebra is the rule for the multiplication of matrices. As we will see in more detail later, the algebra is defined so that a set of linear equations such as

$$a_1 x_1 + a_2 x_2 = h_1$$
$$b_1 x_1 + b_2 x_2 = h_2$$

can be written as a single matrix equation of the form

$$\begin{pmatrix} a_1 & a_2 \\ b_1 & b_2 \end{pmatrix} \begin{pmatrix} x_1 \\ x_2 \end{pmatrix} = \begin{pmatrix} h_1 \\ h_2 \end{pmatrix}.$$

In order for this equation to be valid, the multiplication indicated by writing the two matrices next to each other on the left-hand side has to produce the result

$$\begin{pmatrix} a_1 x_1 + a_2 x_2 \\ b_1 x_1 + b_2 x_2 \end{pmatrix}$$

and the statement of equality in the equation has to mean element-by-element agreement of its left-hand and right-hand sides. Let's move now to a more formal and precise description of matrix algebra.

Basic Definitions

A **matrix** is a set of numbers or functions in a 2-D square or rectangular array. There are no inherent limitations on the number of rows or columns. A matrix with m (horizontal) rows and n (vertical) columns is known as an $m \times n$ matrix, and the element of a matrix A in row i and column j is known as its i, j element, often labeled a_{ij}. As already observed

$$\begin{pmatrix} u_1 \\ u_2 \\ u_3 \\ u_4 \end{pmatrix} \quad \begin{pmatrix} 4 & 2 \\ -1 & 3 \\ 0 & 1 \end{pmatrix} \quad \begin{pmatrix} 6 & 7 & 0 \\ 1 & 4 & 3 \end{pmatrix} \quad \begin{pmatrix} 0 & 1 \\ 1 & 0 \end{pmatrix} \quad \begin{pmatrix} a_{11} & a_{12} \end{pmatrix}$$

FIGURE 2.1   From left to right, matrices of dimension 4×1 (column vector),
$3 \times 2, 2 \times 3, 2 \times 2$ (square), 1×2 (row vector).

when we introduced determinants, when row and column indices or dimensions are mentioned together, it is customary to write the row indicator first. Note also that order matters, in general the i, j and j, i elements of a matrix are different, and (if $m \neq n$) $n \times m$ and $m \times n$ matrices even have different shapes. A matrix for which $n = m$ is termed **square**; one consisting of a single column (an $m \times 1$ matrix) is often called a **column vector**, while a matrix with only one row (therefore $1 \times n$) is a **row vector**. We will find that identifying these matrices as vectors is consistent with the properties identified for vectors in Section 1.7.

The arrays constituting matrices are conventionally enclosed in parentheses (not vertical lines, which indicate determinants, or square brackets). A few examples of matrices are shown in Fig. 2.1. We will usually write the symbols denoting matrices as upper-case letters in a sans-serif font (as we did when introducing A); when a matrix is known to be a column vector we often denote it by a lower-case boldface letter in a Roman font (e.g., **x**).

Perhaps the most important fact to note is that the elements of a matrix are not combined with one another. A matrix is not a determinant. It is an ordered array of numbers, not a single number. To refer to the determinant whose elements are those of a square matrix A (more simply, "the determinant of A"), we can write det(A).

Matrices, so far just arrays of numbers, have the properties we assign to them. These properties must be specified to complete the definition of matrix algebra.

Equality

If A and B are matrices, A = B only if $a_{ij} = b_{ij}$ for all values of i and j. A necessary but not sufficient condition for equality is that both matrices have the same dimensions.

Addition, Subtraction

Addition and subtraction are defined only for matrices A and B of the same dimensions, in which case A $\pm$ B = C, with $c_{ij} = a_{ij} \pm b_{ij}$ for all values of i and j, the elements combining according to the law of ordinary algebra (or arithmetic if they are simple numbers). This means that C will be a matrix of the same dimensions as A and B. Moreover, we see that addition is **commutative**: A + B = B + A. It is also **associative**, meaning that (A + B) + C = A + (B + C). A matrix with all elements zero, called a **null matrix** or **zero matrix**, can either be written as O or as a simple zero, with its matrix character and dimensions determined from the context. Thus, for all A,

$$A + 0 = 0 + A = A. \tag{2.25}$$

Multiplication (by a Scalar)

Here what we mean by a scalar is an ordinary number or function (not another matrix). The multiplication of matrix A by the scalar quantity α produces $B = \alpha A$, with $b_{ij} = \alpha \, a_{ij}$ for all values of i and j. This operation is commutative, with $\alpha A = A\alpha$.

Note that the definition of multiplication by a scalar causes **each** element of matrix A to be multiplied by the scalar factor. This is in striking contrast to the behavior of determinants in which $\alpha \det(A)$ is a determinant in which the factor α multiplies only one column or one row of $\det(A)$ and not every element of the entire determinant. If A is an $n \times n$ square matrix, then

$$\det(\alpha A) = \alpha^n \det(A).$$

Matrix Multiplication (Inner Product)

Matrix multiplication is not an element-by-element operation like addition or multiplication by a scalar. Instead, it is a more complicated operation in which each element of the product is formed by combining elements of a row of the first operand with corresponding elements of a column of the second operand. This mode of combination proves to be that which is needed for many purposes, and gives matrix algebra its power for solving important problems. This **inner product** of matrices A and B is defined as

$$AB = C, \quad \text{with} \quad c_{ij} = \sum_k a_{ik} b_{kj}. \tag{2.26}$$

This definition causes the ij element of C to be formed from the entire ith row of **A** and the entire jth column of **B**. Obviously this definition requires that A have the same number of columns (n) as B has rows. Note that the product will have the same number of rows as A and the same number of columns as B. Matrix multiplication is defined only if these conditions are met. The summation in Eq. (2.26) is over the range of k from 1 to n, and, more explicitly, corresponds to

$$c_{ij} = a_{i1} b_{1j} + a_{i2} b_{2j} + \cdots + a_{1n} b_{nj}.$$

This combination rule is of a form similar to that of the dot product of the vectors $(a_{i1}, a_{i2}, \ldots, a_{in})$ and $(b_{1j}, b_{2j}, \ldots, b_{nj})$. Because the roles of the two operands in a matrix multiplication are different (the first is processed by rows, the second by columns), the operation is in general not commutative, that is, $AB \neq BA$. In fact, AB may even have a different shape than BA. If A and B are square, it is useful to define the **commutator** of A and B,

$$[A, B] = AB - BA, \tag{2.27}$$

which, as stated above, will in many cases be nonzero.

Matrix multiplication is **associative**, meaning that $(AB)C = A(BC)$. Proof of this statement is the topic of Exercise 2.2.26.

Example 2.2.1   MULTIPLICATION, PAULI MATRICES

These three 2×2 matrices, which occurred in early work in quantum mechanics by Pauli, are encountered frequently in physics contexts, so a familiarity with them is highly advisable. They are

$$\sigma_1 = \begin{pmatrix} 0 & 1 \\ 1 & 0 \end{pmatrix}, \quad \sigma_2 = \begin{pmatrix} 0 & -i \\ i & 0 \end{pmatrix}, \quad \sigma_3 = \begin{pmatrix} 1 & 0 \\ 0 & -1 \end{pmatrix}. \tag{2.28}$$

Let's form $\sigma_1\sigma_2$. The 1, 1 element of the product involves the first **row** of σ_1 and the first **column** of σ_2; these are shaded and lead to the indicated computation:

$$\begin{pmatrix} 0 & 1 \\ 1 & 0 \end{pmatrix} \begin{pmatrix} 0 & -i \\ i & 0 \end{pmatrix} \quad \rightarrow \quad 0(0) + 1(i) = i.$$

Continuing, we have

$$\sigma_1\sigma_2 = \begin{pmatrix} 0(0) + 1(i) & 0(-i) + 1(0) \\ 1(0) + 0(i) & 1(-i) + 0(0) \end{pmatrix} = \begin{pmatrix} i & 0 \\ 0 & -i \end{pmatrix}. \tag{2.29}$$

In a similar fashion, we can compute

$$\sigma_2\sigma_1 = \begin{pmatrix} 0 & -i \\ i & 0 \end{pmatrix} \begin{pmatrix} 0 & 1 \\ 1 & 0 \end{pmatrix} = \begin{pmatrix} -i & 0 \\ 0 & i \end{pmatrix}. \tag{2.30}$$

It is clear that σ_1 and σ_2 do not commute. We can construct their commutator:

$$[\sigma_1, \sigma_2] = \sigma_1\sigma_2 - \sigma_2\sigma_1 = \begin{pmatrix} i & 0 \\ 0 & -i \end{pmatrix} - \begin{pmatrix} -i & 0 \\ 0 & i \end{pmatrix}$$

$$= 2i \begin{pmatrix} 1 & 0 \\ 0 & -1 \end{pmatrix} = 2i\sigma_3. \tag{2.31}$$

Note that not only have we verified that σ_1 and σ_2 do not commute, we have even evaluated and simplified their commutator. ∎

Example 2.2.2   MULTIPLICATION, ROW AND COLUMN MATRICES

As a second example, consider

$$A = \begin{pmatrix} 1 \\ 2 \\ 3 \end{pmatrix}, \quad B = (4 \quad 5 \quad 6).$$

Let us form AB and BA:

$$AB = \begin{pmatrix} 4 & 5 & 6 \\ 8 & 10 & 12 \\ 12 & 15 & 18 \end{pmatrix}, \quad BA = (4 \times 1 + 5 \times 2 + 6 \times 3) = (32).$$

The results speak for themselves. Often when a matrix operation leads to a 1×1 matrix, the parentheses are dropped and the result is treated as an ordinary number or function. ∎

Unit Matrix

By direct matrix multiplication, it is possible to show that a square matrix with elements of value unity on its **principal diagonal** (the elements (i, j) with $i = j$), and zeros everywhere else, will leave unchanged any matrix with which it can be multiplied. For example, the 3×3 unit matrix has the form

$$\begin{pmatrix} 1 & 0 & 0 \\ 0 & 1 & 0 \\ 0 & 0 & 1 \end{pmatrix};$$

note that it is **not** a matrix all of whose elements are unity. Giving such a matrix the name **1**,

$$\mathbf{1}A = A\mathbf{1} = A. \tag{2.32}$$

In interpreting this equation, we must keep in mind that unit matrices, which are square and therefore of dimensions $n \times n$, exist for all n; the n values for use in Eq. (2.32) must be those consistent with the applicable dimension of A. So if A is $m \times n$, the unit matrix in $\mathbf{1}A$ must be $m \times m$, while that in $A\mathbf{1}$ must be $n \times n$.

The previously introduced null matrices have only zero elements, so it is also obvious that for all A,

$$OA = AO = O. \tag{2.33}$$

Diagonal Matrices

If a matrix D has nonzero elements d_{ij} only for $i = j$, it is said to be **diagonal**; a 3×3 example is

$$D = \begin{pmatrix} 1 & 0 & 0 \\ 0 & 2 & 0 \\ 0 & 0 & 3 \end{pmatrix}.$$

The rules of matrix multiplication cause all diagonal matrices (of the same size) to commute with each other. However, unless proportional to a unit matrix, diagonal matrices will not commute with nondiagonal matrices containing arbitrary elements.

Matrix Inverse

It will often be the case that given a square matrix A, there will be a square matrix B such that $AB = BA = \mathbf{1}$. A matrix B with this property is called the **inverse** of A and is given the name A^{-1}. If A^{-1} exists, it must be unique. The proof of this statement is simple: If B and C are both inverses of A, then

$$AB = BA = AC = CA = \mathbf{1}.$$

We now look at

$$CAB = (CA)B = B, \quad \text{but also} \quad CAB = C(AB) = C.$$

This shows that $B = C$.

Every nonzero real (or complex) number α has a nonzero multiplicative inverse, often written $1/\alpha$. But the corresponding property does not hold for matrices; there exist nonzero matrices that do not have inverses. To demonstrate this, consider the following:

$$A = \begin{pmatrix} 1 & 1 \\ 0 & 0 \end{pmatrix}, \quad B = \begin{pmatrix} 1 & 0 \\ -1 & 0 \end{pmatrix}, \quad \text{so} \quad AB = \begin{pmatrix} 0 & 0 \\ 0 & 0 \end{pmatrix}.$$

If A has an inverse, we can multiply the equation $AB = O$ **on the left** by A^{-1}, thereby obtaining

$$AB = O \quad \longrightarrow \quad A^{-1}AB = A^{-1}O \quad \longrightarrow \quad B = O.$$

Since we started with a matrix B that was nonzero, this is an inconsistency, and we are forced to conclude that A^{-1} does not exist. A matrix without an inverse is said to be **singular**, so our conclusion is that A is singular. Note that in our derivation, we had to be careful to multiply both members of $AB = O$ from the left, because multiplication is noncommutative. Alternatively, assuming B^{-1} to exist, we could multiply this equation **on the right** by B^{-1}, obtaining

$$AB = O \quad \longrightarrow \quad ABB^{-1} = OB^{-1} \quad \longrightarrow \quad A = O.$$

This is inconsistent with the nonzero A with which we started; we conclude that B is also singular. Summarizing, there are nonzero matrices that do not have inverses and are identified as singular.

The algebraic properties of real and complex numbers (including the existence of inverses for all nonzero numbers) define what mathematicians call a **field**. The properties we have identified for matrices are different; they form what is called a **ring**.

The numerical inversion of matrices is another topic that has been given much attention, and computer programs for matrix inversion are widely available. A closed, but cumbersome formula for the inverse of a matrix exists; it expresses the elements of A^{-1} in terms of the determinants that are the minors of $\det(A)$; recall that minors were defined in the paragraph immediately before Eq. (2.14). That formula, the derivation of which is in several of the Additional Readings, is

$$(A^{-1})_{ij} = \frac{(-1)^{i+j} M_{ji}}{\det(A)}. \tag{2.34}$$

We describe here a well-known method that is computationally more efficient than Eq. (2.34), namely the Gauss-Jordan procedure.

Example 2.2.3   GAUSS-JORDAN MATRIX INVERSION

The Gauss-Jordan method is based on the fact that there exist matrices M_L such that the product $M_L A$ will leave an arbitrary matrix A unchanged, except with

(a)   one row multiplied by a constant, or

(b)   one row replaced by the original row minus a multiple of another row, or

(c)   the interchange of two rows.

The actual matrices M_L that carry out these transformations are the subject of Exercise 2.2.21.

By using these transformations, the rows of a matrix can be altered (by matrix multiplication) in the same ways we were able to change the elements of determinants, so we can proceed in ways similar to those employed for the reduction of determinants by Gauss elimination. If A is nonsingular, the application of a succession of M_L, i.e., $M = (\dots M_L'' M_L' M_L)$, can reduce A to a unit matrix:

$$M A = 1, \quad \text{or} \quad M = A^{-1}.$$

Thus, what we need to do is apply successive transformations to A until these transformations have reduced A to **1**, keeping track of the product of these transformations. The way in which we keep track is to successively apply the transformations to a unit matrix.

Here is a concrete example. We want to invert the matrix

$$A = \begin{pmatrix} 3 & 2 & 1 \\ 2 & 3 & 1 \\ 1 & 1 & 4 \end{pmatrix}.$$

Our strategy will be to write, side by side, the matrix A and a unit matrix of the same size, and to perform the same operations on each until A has been converted to a unit matrix, which means that the unit matrix will have been changed to A^{-1}. We start with

$$\begin{pmatrix} 3 & 2 & 1 \\ 2 & 3 & 1 \\ 1 & 1 & 4 \end{pmatrix} \quad \text{and} \quad \begin{pmatrix} 1 & 0 & 0 \\ 0 & 1 & 0 \\ 0 & 0 & 1 \end{pmatrix}.$$

We multiply the rows as necessary to set to unity all elements of the first column of the left matrix:

$$\begin{pmatrix} 1 & \dfrac{2}{3} & \dfrac{1}{3} \\ 1 & \dfrac{3}{2} & \dfrac{1}{2} \\ 1 & 1 & 4 \end{pmatrix} \quad \text{and} \quad \begin{pmatrix} \dfrac{1}{3} & 0 & 0 \\ 0 & \dfrac{1}{2} & 0 \\ 0 & 0 & 1 \end{pmatrix}.$$

Subtracting the first row from the second and third rows, we obtain

$$\begin{pmatrix} 1 & \dfrac{2}{3} & \dfrac{1}{3} \\ 0 & \dfrac{5}{6} & \dfrac{1}{6} \\ 0 & \dfrac{1}{3} & \dfrac{11}{3} \end{pmatrix} \quad \text{and} \quad \begin{pmatrix} \dfrac{1}{3} & 0 & 0 \\ -\dfrac{1}{3} & \dfrac{1}{2} & 0 \\ -\dfrac{1}{3} & 0 & 1 \end{pmatrix}.$$

Then we divide the second row (of **both** matrices) by $\frac{5}{6}$ and subtract $\frac{2}{3}$ times it from the first row and $\frac{1}{3}$ times it from the third row. The results for both matrices are

$$
\begin{pmatrix} 1 & 0 & \dfrac{1}{5} \\ 0 & 1 & \dfrac{1}{5} \\ 0 & 0 & \dfrac{18}{5} \end{pmatrix} \quad \text{and} \quad \begin{pmatrix} \dfrac{3}{5} & -\dfrac{2}{5} & 0 \\ -\dfrac{2}{5} & \dfrac{3}{5} & 0 \\ -\dfrac{1}{5} & -\dfrac{1}{5} & 1 \end{pmatrix}.
$$

We divide the third row (of **both** matrices) by $\frac{18}{5}$. Then as the last step, $\frac{1}{5}$ times the third row is subtracted from each of the first two rows (of both matrices). Our final pair is

$$
\begin{pmatrix} 1 & 0 & 0 \\ 0 & 1 & 0 \\ 0 & 0 & 1 \end{pmatrix} \quad \text{and} \quad A^{-1} = \begin{pmatrix} \dfrac{11}{18} & -\dfrac{7}{18} & -\dfrac{1}{18} \\ -\dfrac{7}{18} & \dfrac{11}{18} & -\dfrac{1}{18} \\ -\dfrac{1}{18} & -\dfrac{1}{18} & \dfrac{5}{18} \end{pmatrix}.
$$

We can check our work by multiplying the original A by the calculated A^{-1} to see if we really do get the unit matrix **1**.   ■

Derivatives of Determinants

The formula giving the inverse of a matrix in terms of its minors enables us to write a compact formula for the derivative of a determinant det(A) where the matrix A has elements that depend on some variable x. To carry out the differentiation with respect to the x dependence of its element a_{ij}, we write det(A) as its expansion in minors M_{ij} about the elements of row i, as in Eq. (2.14), so, appealing also to Eq. (2.34), we have

$$
\frac{\partial \det(A)}{\partial a_{ij}} = (-1)^{i+j} M_{ij} = (A^{-1})_{ji} \det(A).
$$

Applying now the chain rule to allow for the x dependence of all elements of A, we get

$$
\frac{d \det(A)}{dx} = \det(A) \sum_{ij} (A^{-1})_{ji} \frac{da_{ij}}{dx}. \tag{2.35}
$$

Systems of Linear Equations

Using the matrix inverse, we can write down formal solutions to linear equation systems. To start, we note that if A is a $n \times n$ square matrix, and $\mathbf{x}$ and $\mathbf{h}$ are $n \times 1$ column vectors, the matrix equation $A\mathbf{x} = \mathbf{h}$ is, by the rule for matrix multiplication,

$$
A\mathbf{x} = \begin{pmatrix} a_{11}x_1 + a_{12}x_2 + \cdots + a_{1n}x_n \\ a_{21}x_1 + a_{22}x_2 + \cdots + a_{2n}x_n \\ \cdots\cdots\cdots\cdots \\ a_{n1}x_1 + a_{n2}x_2 + \cdots + a_{nn}x_n \end{pmatrix} = \mathbf{h} = \begin{pmatrix} h_1 \\ h_2 \\ \cdots \\ h_n \end{pmatrix},
$$

which is entirely equivalent to a system of n linear equations with the elements of A as coefficients. If A is nonsingular, we can multiply $Ax = h$ on the left by A^{-1}, obtaining the result $x = A^{-1}h$.

This result tells us two things: (1) that if we can evaluate A^{-1}, we can compute the solution x; and (2) that the existence of A^{-1} means that this equation system has a unique solution. In our study of determinants we found that a linear equation system had a unique solution if and only if the determinant of its coefficients was nonzero. We therefore see that the condition that A^{-1} exists, i.e., that A is nonsingular, is the same as the condition that the determinant of A, which we write det(A), be nonzero. This result is important enough to be emphasized:

$$A \text{ square matrix A is singular if and only if } \det(A) = 0. \tag{2.36}$$

Determinant Product Theorem

The connection between matrices and their determinants can be made deeper by establishing a **product theorem** which states that the determinant of a product of two $n \times n$ matrices A and B is equal to the products of the determinants of the individual matrices:

$$\det(AB) = \det(A)\det(B). \tag{2.37}$$

As an initial step toward proving this theorem, let us look at det(AB) with the elements of the matrix product written out. Showing the first two columns explicitly, we have

$$\det(AB) = \begin{vmatrix} a_{11}b_{11} + a_{12}b_{21} + \cdots + a_{1n}b_{n1} & a_{11}b_{12} + a_{12}b_{22} + \cdots + a_{1n}b_{n2} & \cdots \\ a_{21}b_{11} + a_{22}b_{21} + \cdots + a_{2n}b_{n1} & a_{21}b_{12} + a_{22}b_{22} + \cdots + a_{2n}b_{n2} & \cdots \\ \cdots & \cdots & \cdots \\ \cdots & \cdots & \cdots \\ a_{n1}b_{11} + a_{n2}b_{21} + \cdots + a_{nn}b_{n1} & a_{n1}b_{12} + a_{n2}b_{22} + \cdots + a_{nn}b_{n2} & \cdots \end{vmatrix}.$$

Introducing the notation

$$\mathbf{a}_j = \begin{pmatrix} a_{1j} \\ a_{2j} \\ \cdots \\ a_{nj} \end{pmatrix}, \quad \text{this becomes} \quad \det(AB) = \begin{vmatrix} \sum_{j_1} \mathbf{a}_{j_1} b_{j_1,1} & \sum_{j_2} \mathbf{a}_{j_2} b_{j_2,2} & \cdots \end{vmatrix},$$

where the summations over $j_1, j_2, \ldots, j_n$ run independently from 1 though n. Now, calling upon Eqs. (2.12) and (2.13), we can move the summations and the factors b outside the determinant, reaching

$$\det(AB) = \sum_{j_1} \sum_{j_2} \cdots \sum_{j_n} b_{j_1,1} b_{j_2,2} \cdots b_{j_n,n} \det(\mathbf{a}_{j_1} \mathbf{a}_{j_2} \cdots \mathbf{a}_{j_n}). \tag{2.38}$$

The determinant on the right-hand side of Eq. (2.38) will vanish if any of the indices j_μ are equal; if all are unequal, that determinant will be $\pm \det(A)$, with the sign corresponding to the parity of the column permutation needed to put the $\mathbf{a}_j$ in numerical order. Both of these conditions are met by writing $\det(\mathbf{a}_{j_1}\mathbf{a}_{j_2}\cdots\mathbf{a}_{j_n}) = \varepsilon_{j_1\ldots j_n}\det(A)$, where ε is the Levi-Civita symbol defined in Eq. (2.8). The above manipulations bring us to

$$\det(AB) = \det(A) \sum_{j_1\ldots j_n} \varepsilon_{j_1\ldots j_n} b_{j_1,1} b_{j_2,2}\cdots b_{j_n,n} = \det(A)\det(B),$$

where the final step was to invoke the definition of the determinant, Eq. (2.10). This result proves the determinant product theorem.

From the determinant product theorem, we can gain additional insight regarding singular matrices. Noting first that a special case of the theorem is that

$$\det(AA^{-1}) = \det(\mathbf{1}) = 1 = \det(A)\det(A^{-1}),$$

we see that

$$\det(A^{-1}) = \frac{1}{\det(A)}. \tag{2.39}$$

It is now obvious that if $\det(A) = 0$, then $\det(A^{-1})$ cannot exist, meaning that A^{-1} cannot exist either. This is a direct proof that a matrix is singular if and only if it has a vanishing determinant.

Rank of a Matrix

The concept of matrix singularity can be refined by introducing the notion of the **rank** of a matrix. If the elements of a matrix are viewed as the coefficients of a set of linear forms, as in Eq. (2.1) and its generalization to n variables, a square matrix is assigned a rank equal to the number of linearly independent forms that its elements describe. Thus, a nonsingular $n \times n$ matrix will have rank n, while a $n \times n$ singular matrix will have a rank r less than n. The rank provides a measure of the extent of the singularity; if $r = n - 1$, the matrix describes one linear form that is dependent on the others; $r = n - 2$ describes a situation in which there are two forms that are linearly dependent on the others, etc. We will in Chapter 6 take up methods for systematically determining the rank of a matrix.

Transpose, Adjoint, Trace

In addition to the operations we have already discussed, there are further operations that depend on the fact that matrices are arrays. One such operation is transposition. The **transpose** of a matrix is the matrix that results from interchanging its row and column indices. This operation corresponds to subjecting the array to reflection about its principal diagonal. If a matrix is not square, its transpose will not even have the same shape as the original matrix. The transpose of A, denoted $\tilde{A}$ or sometimes A^T, thus has elements

$$(\tilde{A})_{ij} = a_{ji}. \tag{2.40}$$

Note that transposition will convert a column vector into a row vector, so

$$\text{if} \quad \mathbf{x} = \begin{pmatrix} x_1 \\ x_2 \\ \cdots \\ x_n \end{pmatrix}, \quad \text{then} \quad \tilde{\mathbf{x}} = (x_1 \ x_2 \ \ldots \ x_n).$$

A matrix that is unchanged by transposition (i.e., $\tilde{A} = A$) is called **symmetric**.

For matrices that may have complex elements, the **complex conjugate** of a matrix is defined as the matrix resulting if all elements of the original matrix are complex conjugated. Note that this does not change the shape or move any elements to new positions. The notation for the complex conjugate of A is A^*.

The **adjoint** of a matrix A, denoted $A^\dagger$, is obtained by both complex conjugating and transposing it (the same result is obtained if these operations are performed in either order). Thus,

$$(A^\dagger)_{ij} = a_{ji}^*. \tag{2.41}$$

The **trace**, a quantity defined for square matrices, is the sum of the elements on the principal diagonal. Thus, for an $n \times n$ matrix A,

$$\text{trace}(A) = \sum_{i=1}^{n} a_{ii}. \tag{2.42}$$

From the rule for matrix addition, is is obvious that

$$\text{trace}(A + B) = \text{trace}(A) + \text{trace}(B). \tag{2.43}$$

Another property of the trace is that its value for a product of two matrices A and B is independent of the order of multiplication:

$$\text{trace}(AB) = \sum_i (AB)_{ii} = \sum_i \sum_j a_{ij} b_{ji} = \sum_j \sum_i b_{ji} a_{ij}$$

$$= \sum_j (BA)_{jj} = \text{trace}(BA). \tag{2.44}$$

This holds even if $AB \neq BA$. Equation (2.44) means that the trace of any commutator $[A, B] = AB - BA$ is zero. Considering now the trace of the matrix product ABC, if we group the factors as A(BC), we easily see that

$$\text{trace}(ABC) = \text{trace}(BCA).$$

Repeating this process, we also find trace(ABC) = trace(CAB). Note, however, that we cannot equate any of these quantities to trace(CBA) or to the trace of any other noncyclic permutation of these matrices.

Operations on Matrix Products

We have already seen that the determinant and the trace satisfy the relations

$$\det(AB) = \det(A)\det(B) = \det(BA), \quad \text{trace}(AB) = \text{trace}(BA),$$

whether or not A and B commute. We also found that $\text{trace}(A + B) = \text{trace}(A) + \text{trace}(B)$ and can easily show that $\text{trace}(\alpha A) = \alpha \text{trace}(A)$, establishing that the trace is a linear operator (as defined in Chapter 5). Since similar relations do not exist for the determinant, it is **not** a linear operator.

We consider now the effect of other operations on matrix products. The transpose of a product, $(AB)^T$, can be shown to satisfy

$$(AB)^T = \tilde{B}\tilde{A}, \tag{2.45}$$

showing that a product is transposed by taking, in reverse order, the transposes of its factors. Note that if the respective dimensions of A and B are such as to make AB defined, it will also be true that $\tilde{B}\tilde{A}$ is defined.

Since complex conjugation of a product simply amounts to conjugation of its individual factors, the formula for the adjoint of a matrix product follows a rule similar to Eq. (2.45):

$$(AB)^\dagger = B^\dagger A^\dagger. \tag{2.46}$$

Finally, consider $(AB)^{-1}$. In order for AB to be nonsingular, neither A nor B can be singular (to see this, consider their determinants). Assuming this nonsingularity, we have

$$(AB)^{-1} = B^{-1}A^{-1}. \tag{2.47}$$

The validity of Eq. (2.47) can be demonstrated by substituting it into the obvious equation $(AB)(AB)^{-1} = 1$.

Matrix Representation of Vectors

The reader may have already noted that the operations of addition and multiplication by a scalar are defined in identical ways for vectors (Section 1.7) and the matrices we are calling column vectors. We can also use the matrix formalism to generate scalar products, but in order to do so we must convert one of the column vectors into a row vector. The operation of transposition provides a way to do this. Thus, letting **a** and **b** stand for vectors in $\mathbb{R}^3$,

$$\mathbf{a} \cdot \mathbf{b} \quad \longrightarrow \quad (a_1 \ a_2 \ a_3) \begin{pmatrix} b_1 \\ b_2 \\ b_3 \end{pmatrix} = a_1 b_1 + a_2 b_2 + a_3 b_3.$$

If in a matrix context we regard **a** and **b** as column vectors, the above equation assumes the form

$$\mathbf{a} \cdot \mathbf{b} \quad \longrightarrow \quad \mathbf{a}^T \mathbf{b}. \tag{2.48}$$

This notation does not really lead to significant ambiguity if we note that when dealing with matrices, we are using lower-case boldface symbols to denote **column vectors**. Note also that because $\mathbf{a}^T \mathbf{b}$ is a 1×1 matrix, it is synonymous with its transpose, which is $\mathbf{b}^T \mathbf{a}$. The matrix notation preserves the symmetry of the dot product. As in Section 1.7, the square of the magnitude of the vector corresponding to $\mathbf{a}$ will be $\mathbf{a}^T \mathbf{a}$.

If the elements of our column vectors $\mathbf{a}$ and $\mathbf{b}$ are real, then an alternate way of writing $\mathbf{a}^T \mathbf{b}$ is $\mathbf{a}^\dagger \mathbf{b}$. But these quantities are not equal if the vectors have complex elements, as will be the case in some situations in which the column vectors do not represent displacements in physical space. In that situation, the dagger notation is the more useful because then $\mathbf{a}^\dagger \mathbf{a}$ will be real and can play the role of a magnitude squared.

Orthogonal Matrices

A real matrix (one whose elements are real) is termed **orthogonal** if its transpose is equal to its inverse. Thus, if S is orthogonal, we may write

$$S^{-1} = S^T, \quad \text{or} \quad SS^T = \mathbf{1} \quad \text{(S orthogonal)}. \tag{2.49}$$

Since, for S orthogonal, $\det(SS^T) = \det(S)\det(S^T) = [\det(S)]^2 = 1$, we see that

$$\det(S) = \pm 1 \quad \text{(S orthogonal)}. \tag{2.50}$$

It is easy to prove that if S and S' are each orthogonal, then so also are SS' and S'S.

Unitary Matrices

Another important class of matrices consists of matrices U with the property that $U^\dagger = U^{-1}$, i.e., matrices for which the adjoint is also the inverse. Such matrices are identified as **unitary**. One way of expressing this relationship is

$$U\, U^\dagger = U^\dagger U = \mathbf{1} \quad \text{(U unitary)}. \tag{2.51}$$

If all the elements of a unitary matrix are real, the matrix is also orthogonal.

Since for any matrix $\det(A^T) = \det(A)$, and therefore $\det(A^\dagger) = \det(A)^*$, application of the determinant product theorem to a unitary matrix U leads to

$$\det(U)\det(U^\dagger) = |\det(U)|^2 = 1, \tag{2.52}$$

showing that $\det(U)$ is a possibly complex number of magnitude unity. Since such numbers can be written in the form $\exp(i\theta)$, with θ real, the determinants of U and $U^\dagger$ will, for some θ, satisfy

$$\det(U) = e^{i\theta}, \quad \det(U^\dagger) = e^{-i\theta}.$$

Part of the significance of the term *unitary* is associated with the fact that the determinant has unit magnitude. A special case of this relationship is our earlier observation that if U is real, and therefore also an orthogonal matrix, its determinant must be either $+1$ or -1.

Finally, we observe that if U and V are both unitary, then UV and VU will be unitary as well. This is a generalization of our earlier result that the matrix product of two orthogonal matrices is also orthogonal.

Hermitian Matrices

There are additional classes of matrices with useful characteristics. A matrix is identified as **Hermitian**, or, synonymously, **self-adjoint**, if it is equal to its adjoint. To be self-adjoint, a matrix H must be square, and in addition, its elements must satisfy

$$(H^\dagger)_{ij} = (H)_{ij} \quad \longrightarrow \quad h^*_{ji} = h_{ij} \quad \text{(H is Hermitian).} \tag{2.53}$$

This condition means that the array of elements in a self-adjoint matrix exhibits a reflection symmetry about the principal diagonal: elements whose positions are connected by reflection must be complex conjugates. As a corollary to this observation, or by direct reference to Eq. (2.53), we see that the diagonal elements of a self-adjoint matrix must be real.

If all the elements of a self-adjoint matrix are real, then the condition of self-adjointness will cause the matrix also to be symmetric, so all real, symmetric matrices are self-adjoint (Hermitian).

Note that if two matrices A and B are Hermitian, it is not necessarily true that AB or BA is Hermitian; however, AB + BA, if nonzero, will be Hermitian, and AB − BA, if nonzero, will be **anti-Hermitian**, meaning that $(AB - BA)^\dagger = -(AB - BA)$.

Extraction of a Row or Column

It is useful to define column vectors $\hat{\mathbf{e}}_i$ which are zero except for the $(i, 1)$ element, which is unity; examples are

$$\hat{\mathbf{e}}_1 = \begin{pmatrix} 1 \\ 0 \\ 0 \\ \cdots \\ 0 \end{pmatrix}, \quad \hat{\mathbf{e}}_2 = \begin{pmatrix} 0 \\ 1 \\ 0 \\ \cdots \\ 0 \end{pmatrix}, \quad \text{etc.} \tag{2.54}$$

One use of these vectors is to extract a single column from a matrix. For example, if A is a 3×3 matrix, then

$$A\hat{\mathbf{e}}_2 = \begin{pmatrix} a_{11} & a_{12} & a_{13} \\ a_{21} & a_{22} & a_{23} \\ a_{31} & a_{32} & a_{33} \end{pmatrix} \begin{pmatrix} 0 \\ 1 \\ 0 \end{pmatrix} = \begin{pmatrix} a_{12} \\ a_{22} \\ a_{32} \end{pmatrix}.$$

The row vector $\hat{\mathbf{e}}_i^T$ can be used in a similar fashion to extract a row from an arbitrary matrix, as in

$$\hat{\mathbf{e}}_i^T A = (a_{i1} \ \ a_{i2} \ \ a_{i3}).$$

These **unit vectors** will also have many uses in other contexts.

Direct Product

A second procedure for multiplying matrices, known as the **direct** tensor or Kronecker **product**, combines a $m \times n$ matrix A and a $m' \times n'$ matrix B to make the direct product matrix $C = A \otimes B$, which is of dimension $mm' \times nn'$ and has elements

$$C_{\alpha\beta} = A_{ij} B_{kl}, \tag{2.55}$$

with $\alpha = m'(i - 1) + k$, $\beta = n'(j - 1) + l$. The direct product matrix uses the indices of the first factor as major and those of the second factor as minor; it is therefore a noncommutative process. It is, however, associative.

Example 2.2.4 DIRECT PRODUCTS

We give some specific examples. If A and B are both 2×2 matrices, we may write, first in a somewhat symbolic and then in a completely expanded form,

$$A \otimes B = \begin{pmatrix} a_{11}B & a_{12}B \\ a_{21}B & a_{22}B \end{pmatrix} = \begin{pmatrix} a_{11}b_{11} & a_{11}b_{12} & a_{12}b_{11} & a_{12}b_{12} \\ a_{11}b_{21} & a_{11}b_{22} & a_{12}b_{21} & a_{12}b_{22} \\ a_{21}b_{11} & a_{21}b_{12} & a_{22}b_{11} & a_{22}b_{12} \\ a_{21}b_{21} & a_{21}b_{22} & a_{22}b_{21} & a_{22}b_{22} \end{pmatrix}.$$

Another example is the direct product of two two-element column vectors, **x** and **y**. Again writing first in symbolic, and then expanded form,

$$\begin{pmatrix} x_1 \\ x_2 \end{pmatrix} \otimes \begin{pmatrix} y_1 \\ y_2 \end{pmatrix} = \begin{pmatrix} x_1\mathbf{y} \\ x_2\mathbf{y} \end{pmatrix} = \begin{pmatrix} x_1 y_1 \\ x_1 y_2 \\ x_2 y_1 \\ x_2 y_2 \end{pmatrix}.$$

A third example is the quantity AB from Example 2.2.2. It is an instance of the special case (column vector times row vector) in which the direct and inner products coincide: $AB = A \otimes B$. ∎

If C and C' are direct products of the respective forms

$$C = A \otimes B \quad \text{and} \quad C' = A' \otimes B', \tag{2.56}$$

and these matrices are of dimensions such that the matrix inner products AA' and BB' are defined, then

$$CC' = (AA') \otimes (BB'). \tag{2.57}$$

Moreover, if matrices A and B are of the same dimensions, then

$$C \otimes (A + B) = C \otimes A + C \otimes B \quad \text{and} \quad (A + B) \otimes C = A \otimes C + B \otimes C. \tag{2.58}$$

Example 2.2.5 DIRAC MATRICES

In the original, nonrelativistic formulation of quantum mechanics, agreement between theory and experiment for electronic systems required the introduction of the concept of electron spin (intrinsic angular momentum), both to provide a doubling in the number of available states and to explain phenomena involving the electron's magnetic moment. The concept was introduced in a relatively *ad hoc* fashion; the electron needed to be given spin quantum number 1/2, and that could be done by assigning it a two-component wave function, with the spin-related properties described using the Pauli matrices, which were introduced in Example 2.2.1:

$$\sigma_1 = \begin{pmatrix} 0 & 1 \\ 1 & 0 \end{pmatrix}, \quad \sigma_2 = \begin{pmatrix} 0 & -i \\ i & 0 \end{pmatrix}, \quad \sigma_3 = \begin{pmatrix} 1 & 0 \\ 0 & -1 \end{pmatrix}.$$

Of relevance here is the fact that these matrices anticommute and have squares that are unit matrices:

$$\sigma_i^2 = 1_2, \quad \text{and} \quad \sigma_i \sigma_j + \sigma_j \sigma_i = 0, \quad i \neq j. \tag{2.59}$$

In 1927, P. A. M. Dirac developed a relativistic formulation of quantum mechanics applicable to spin-1/2 particles. To do this it was necessary to place the spatial and time variables on an equal footing, and Dirac proceeded by converting the relativistic expression for the kinetic energy to an expression that was first order in both the energy and the momentum (parallel quantities in relativistic mechanics). He started from the relativistic equation for the energy of a free particle,

$$E^2 = (p_1^2 + p_2^2 + p_3^2)c^2 + m^2c^4 = \mathbf{p}^2c^2 + m^2c^4, \tag{2.60}$$

where p_i are the components of the momentum in the coordinate directions, m is the particle mass, and c is the velocity of light. In the passage to quantum mechanics, the quantities p_i are to be replaced by the differential operators $-i\hbar\partial/\partial x_i$, and the entire equation is applied to a wave function.

It was desirable to have a formulation that would yield a two-component wave function in the nonrelativistic limit and therefore might be expected to contain the σ_i. Dirac made the observation that a key to the solution of his problem was to exploit the fact that the Pauli matrices, taken together as a vector

$$\boldsymbol{\sigma} = \sigma_1 \hat{\mathbf{e}}_1 + \sigma_2 \hat{\mathbf{e}}_2 + \sigma_3 \hat{\mathbf{e}}_3, \tag{2.61}$$

could be combined with the vector $\mathbf{p}$ to yield the identity

$$(\boldsymbol{\sigma} \cdot \mathbf{p})^2 = \mathbf{p}^2 1_2, \tag{2.62}$$

where 1_2 denotes a 2×2 unit matrix. The importance of Eq. (2.62) is that, at the price of going to 2×2 matrices, we can linearize the quadratic occurrences of E and $\mathbf{p}$ in Eq. (2.60) as follows. We first write

$$E^2 1_2 - c^2 (\boldsymbol{\sigma} \cdot \mathbf{p})^2 = m^2 c^4 1_2. \tag{2.63}$$

We then factor the left-hand side of Eq. (2.63) and apply both sides of the resulting equation (which is a 2×2 matrix equation) to a two-component wave function that we will call ψ_1:

$$(E1_2 + c\boldsymbol{\sigma} \cdot \mathbf{p})(E1_2 - c\boldsymbol{\sigma} \cdot \mathbf{p})\psi_1 = m^2 c^4 \psi_1. \tag{2.64}$$

The meaning of this equation becomes clearer if we make the additional definition

$$(E1_2 - c\boldsymbol{\sigma} \cdot \mathbf{p})\psi_1 = mc^2 \psi_2. \tag{2.65}$$

Substituting Eq. (2.65) into Eq. (2.64), we can then write the modified Eq. (2.64) and the (unchanged) Eq. (2.65) as the equation set

$$(E\mathbf{1}_2 + c\boldsymbol{\sigma} \cdot \mathbf{p})\psi_2 = mc^2\psi_1,$$
$$(E\mathbf{1}_2 - c\boldsymbol{\sigma} \cdot \mathbf{p})\psi_1 = mc^2\psi_2; \tag{2.66}$$

both these equations will need to be satisfied simultaneously.

To bring Eqs. (2.66) to the form actually used by Dirac, we now make the substitution $\psi_1 = \psi_A + \psi_B$, $\psi_2 = \psi_A - \psi_B$, and then add and subtract the two equations from each other, reaching a set of coupled equations in ψ_A and ψ_B:

$$E\psi_A - c\boldsymbol{\sigma} \cdot \mathbf{p}\psi_B = mc^2\psi_A,$$
$$c\boldsymbol{\sigma} \cdot \mathbf{p}\psi_A - E\psi_B = mc^2\psi_B.$$

In anticipation of what we will do next, we write these equations in the matrix form

$$\left[\begin{pmatrix} E\mathbf{1}_2 & 0 \\ 0 & -E\mathbf{1}_2 \end{pmatrix} - \begin{pmatrix} 0 & c\boldsymbol{\sigma} \cdot \mathbf{p} \\ -c\boldsymbol{\sigma} \cdot \mathbf{p} & 0 \end{pmatrix}\right]\begin{pmatrix} \psi_A \\ \psi_B \end{pmatrix} = mc^2 \begin{pmatrix} \psi_A \\ \psi_B \end{pmatrix}. \tag{2.67}$$

We can now use the direct product notation to condense Eq. (2.67) into the simpler form

$$[(\sigma_3 \otimes \mathbf{1}_2)E - \gamma \otimes c(\boldsymbol{\sigma} \cdot \mathbf{p})]\,\Psi = mc^2\Psi, \tag{2.68}$$

where Ψ is the **four-component** wave function built from the two-component wave functions:

$$\Psi = \begin{pmatrix} \psi_A \\ \psi_B \end{pmatrix},$$

and the terms on the left-hand side have the indicated structure because

$$\sigma_3 = \begin{pmatrix} 1 & 0 \\ 0 & -1 \end{pmatrix} \quad \text{and we define} \quad \gamma = \begin{pmatrix} 0 & 1 \\ -1 & 0 \end{pmatrix}. \tag{2.69}$$

It has become customary to identify the matrices in Eq. (2.68) as γ^μ and to refer to them as **Dirac matrices**, with

$$\gamma^0 = \sigma_3 \otimes \mathbf{1}_2 = \begin{pmatrix} \mathbf{1}_2 & 0 \\ 0 & -\mathbf{1}_2 \end{pmatrix} = \begin{pmatrix} 1 & 0 & 0 & 0 \\ 0 & 1 & 0 & 0 \\ 0 & 0 & -1 & 0 \\ 0 & 0 & 0 & -1 \end{pmatrix}. \tag{2.70}$$

The matrices resulting from the individual components of $\boldsymbol{\sigma}$ in Eq. (2.68) are (for $i = 1, 2, 3$)

$$\gamma^i = \gamma \otimes \sigma_i = \begin{pmatrix} 0 & \sigma_i \\ -\sigma_i & 0 \end{pmatrix}. \tag{2.71}$$

Expanding Eq. (2.71), we have

$$\gamma^1 = \begin{pmatrix} 0 & 0 & 0 & 1 \\ 0 & 0 & 1 & 0 \\ 0 & -1 & 0 & 0 \\ -1 & 0 & 0 & 0 \end{pmatrix}, \quad \gamma^2 = \begin{pmatrix} 0 & 0 & 0 & -i \\ 0 & 0 & i & 0 \\ 0 & i & 0 & 0 \\ -i & 0 & 0 & 0 \end{pmatrix},$$

$$\gamma^3 = \begin{pmatrix} 0 & 0 & 1 & 0 \\ 0 & 0 & 0 & -1 \\ -1 & 0 & 0 & 0 \\ 0 & 1 & 0 & 0 \end{pmatrix}. \tag{2.72}$$

Now that the γ^μ have been defined, we can rewrite Eq. (2.68), expanding $\boldsymbol{\sigma} \cdot \mathbf{p}$ into components:

$$\left[\gamma^0 E - c(\gamma^1 p_1 + \gamma^2 p_2 + \gamma^3 p_3) \right] \Psi = mc^2 \Psi.$$

To put this matrix equation into the specific form known as the **Dirac equation** we multiply both sides of it (on the left) by γ^0. Noting that $(\gamma^0)^2 = \mathbf{1}$ and giving $\gamma^0 \gamma^i$ the new name α_i, we reach

$$\left[\gamma^0 mc^2 + c(\alpha_1 p_1 + \alpha_2 p_2 + \alpha_3 p_3) \right] \Psi = E\Psi. \tag{2.73}$$

Equation (2.73) is in the notation used by Dirac with the exception that he used β as the name for the matrix here called γ^0.

The Dirac gamma matrices have an algebra that is a generalization of that exhibited by the Pauli matrices, where we found that the $\sigma_i^2 = 1$ and that if $i \neq j$, then σ_i and σ_j anticommute. Either by further analysis or by direct evaluation, it is found that, for $\mu = 0, 1, 2, 3$ and $i = 1, 2, 3$,

$$(\gamma^0)^2 = 1, \quad (\gamma^i)^2 = -1. \tag{2.74}$$

$$\gamma^\mu \gamma^i + \gamma^i \gamma^\mu = 0, \quad \mu \neq i. \tag{2.75}$$

In the nonrelativistic limit, the four-component Dirac equation for an electron reduces to a two-component equation in which each component satisfies the Schrödinger equation, with the Pauli and Dirac matrices having completely disappeared. See Exercise 2.2.48. In this limit, the Pauli matrices reappear if we add to the Schrödinger equation an additional term arising from the intrinsic magnetic moment of the electron. The passage to the nonrelativistic limit provides justification for the seemingly arbitrary introduction of a two-component wavefunction and use of the Pauli matrices for discussions of spin angular momentum.

The Pauli matrices (and the unit matrix $\mathbf{1}_2$) form what is known as a **Clifford algebra**,[2] with the properties shown in Eq. (2.59). Since the algebra is based on 2×2 matrices, it can have only four members (the number of linearly independent such matrices), and is said to be of dimension 4. The Dirac matrices are members of a Clifford algebra of dimension 16. A complete basis for this Clifford algebra with convenient Lorentz transformation

---

[2]D. Hestenes, *Am. J. Phys.* **39**: 1013 (1971); and *J. Math. Phys.* **16**: 556 (1975).

properties consists of the 16 matrices

$$\mathbf{1}_4, \quad \boldsymbol{\gamma}^5 = i\boldsymbol{\gamma}^0\boldsymbol{\gamma}^1\boldsymbol{\gamma}^2\boldsymbol{\gamma}^3 = \begin{pmatrix} 0 & \mathbf{1}_2 \\ \mathbf{1}_2 & 0 \end{pmatrix}, \quad \boldsymbol{\gamma}^\mu \quad (\mu = 0, 1, 2, 3),$$

$$\boldsymbol{\gamma}^5\boldsymbol{\gamma}^\mu \quad (\mu = 0, 1, 2, 3), \quad \sigma^{\mu\nu} = i\boldsymbol{\gamma}^\mu\boldsymbol{\gamma}^\nu \quad (0 \le \mu < \nu \le 3). \tag{2.76}$$

∎

Functions of Matrices

Polynomials with one or more matrix arguments are well defined and occur often. Power series of a matrix may also be defined, provided the series converges for each matrix element. For example, if A is any $n \times n$ matrix, then the power series

$$\exp(\mathsf{A}) = \sum_{j=0}^{\infty} \frac{1}{j!} \mathsf{A}^j, \tag{2.77}$$

$$\sin(\mathsf{A}) = \sum_{j=0}^{\infty} \frac{(-1)^j}{(2j+1)!} \mathsf{A}^{2j+1}, \tag{2.78}$$

$$\cos(\mathsf{A}) = \sum_{j=0}^{\infty} \frac{(-1)^j}{(2j)!} \mathsf{A}^{2j} \tag{2.79}$$

are well-defined $n \times n$ matrices. For the Pauli matrices σ_k, the **Euler identity** for real θ and $k = 1$, 2, or 3,

$$\exp(i\sigma_k\theta) = \mathbf{1}_2\cos\theta + i\sigma_k\sin\theta, \tag{2.80}$$

follows from collecting all even and odd powers of θ in separate series using $\sigma_k^2 = 1$. For the 4×4 Dirac matrices $\sigma^{\mu\nu}$, defined in Eq. (2.76), we have for $1 \le \mu < \nu \le 3$,

$$\exp(i\sigma^{\mu\nu}\theta) = \mathbf{1}_4\cos\theta + i\sigma^{\mu\nu}\sin\theta, \tag{2.81}$$

while

$$\exp(i\sigma^{0k}\zeta) = \mathbf{1}_4\cosh\zeta + i\sigma^{0k}\sinh\zeta \tag{2.82}$$

holds for real ζ because $(i\sigma^{0k})^2 = 1$ for $k = 1$, 2, or 3.

Hermitian and unitary matrices are related in that U, given as

$$\mathsf{U} = \exp(i\mathsf{H}), \tag{2.83}$$

is unitary if H is Hermitian. To see this, just take the adjoint: $\mathsf{U}^\dagger = \exp(-i\mathsf{H}^\dagger) = \exp(-i\mathsf{H}) = [\exp(i\mathsf{H})]^{-1} = \mathsf{U}^{-1}$.

Another result which is important to identify here is that any Hermitian matrix H satisfies a relation known as the **trace formula**,

$$\det(\exp(\mathsf{H})) = \exp(\operatorname{trace}(\mathsf{H})). \tag{2.84}$$

This formula is derived at Eq. (6.27).

Finally, we note that the multiplication of two diagonal matrices produces a matrix that is also diagonal, with elements that are the products of the corresponding elements of the multiplicands. This result implies that an arbitrary function of a diagonal matrix will also be diagonal, with diagonal elements that are that function of the diagonal elements of the original matrix.

Example 2.2.6   EXPONENTIAL OF A DIAGONAL MATRIX

If a matrix A is diagonal, then its nth power is also diagonal, with the original diagonal matrix elements raised to the nth power. For example, given

$$\sigma_3 = \begin{pmatrix} 1 & 0 \\ 0 & -1 \end{pmatrix},$$

then

$$(\sigma_3)^n = \begin{pmatrix} 1 & 0 \\ 0 & (-1)^n \end{pmatrix}.$$

We can now compute

$$e^{\sigma_3} = \begin{pmatrix} \displaystyle\sum_{n=0}^{\infty} \frac{1}{n!} & 0 \\ 0 & \displaystyle\sum_{n=0}^{\infty} \frac{(-1)^n}{n!} \end{pmatrix} = \begin{pmatrix} e & 0 \\ 0 & e^{-1} \end{pmatrix}.$$

■

A final and important result is the **Baker-Hausdorff formula**, which, among other places is used in the coupled-cluster expansions that yield highly accurate electronic structure calculations on atoms and molecules[3]:

$$\exp(-T)A\exp(T) = A + [A,T] + \frac{1}{2!}[[A,T],T] + \frac{1}{3!}[[[A,T],T],T] + \cdots. \qquad (2.85)$$

Exercises

2.2.1   Show that matrix multiplication is associative, $(AB)C = A(BC)$.

2.2.2   Show that

$$(A+B)(A-B) = A^2 - B^2$$

if and only if A and B commute,

$$[A, B] = 0.$$

---

[3]F. E. Harris, H. J. Monkhorst, and D. L. Freeman, *Algebraic and Diagrammatic Methods in Many-Fermion Theory*. New York: Oxford University Press (1992).

2.2.3   (a) Complex numbers, $a + ib$, with a and b real, may be represented by (or are iso-morphic with) 2×2 matrices:

$$a + ib \longleftrightarrow \begin{pmatrix} a & b \\ -b & a \end{pmatrix}.$$

Show that this matrix representation is valid for (i) addition and (ii) multiplication.

(b) Find the matrix corresponding to $(a + ib)^{-1}$.

2.2.4   If A is an $n \times n$ matrix, show that

$$\det(-A) = (-1)^n \det A.$$

2.2.5   (a) The matrix equation $A^2 = 0$ does not imply $A = 0$. Show that the most general 2×2 matrix whose square is zero may be written as

$$\begin{pmatrix} ab & b^2 \\ -a^2 & -ab \end{pmatrix},$$

where a and b are real or complex numbers.

(b) If $C = A + B$, in general

$$\det C \neq \det A + \det B.$$

Construct a specific numerical example to illustrate this inequality.

2.2.6   Given

$$K = \begin{pmatrix} 0 & 0 & i \\ -i & 0 & 0 \\ 0 & -1 & 0 \end{pmatrix},$$

show that

$$K^n = KKK \cdots (n \text{ factors}) = 1$$

(with the proper choice of n, $n \neq 0$).

2.2.7   Verify the **Jacobi identity**,

$$[A, [B, C]] = [B, [A, C]] - [C, [A, B]].$$

2.2.8   Show that the matrices

$$A = \begin{pmatrix} 0 & 1 & 0 \\ 0 & 0 & 0 \\ 0 & 0 & 0 \end{pmatrix}, \quad B = \begin{pmatrix} 0 & 0 & 0 \\ 0 & 0 & 1 \\ 0 & 0 & 0 \end{pmatrix}, \quad C = \begin{pmatrix} 0 & 0 & 1 \\ 0 & 0 & 0 \\ 0 & 0 & 0 \end{pmatrix}$$

satisfy the commutation relations

$$[A, B] = C, \quad [A, C] = 0, \quad \text{and} \quad [B, C] = 0.$$

2.2.9   Let

$$i = \begin{pmatrix} 0 & 1 & 0 & 0 \\ -1 & 0 & 0 & 0 \\ 0 & 0 & 0 & 1 \\ 0 & 0 & -1 & 0 \end{pmatrix}, \quad j = \begin{pmatrix} 0 & 0 & 0 & -1 \\ 0 & 0 & -1 & 0 \\ 0 & 1 & 0 & 0 \\ 1 & 0 & 0 & 0 \end{pmatrix},$$

and

$$k = \begin{pmatrix} 0 & 0 & -1 & 0 \\ 0 & 0 & 0 & 1 \\ 1 & 0 & 0 & 0 \\ 0 & -1 & 0 & 0 \end{pmatrix}.$$

Show that

(a) $i^2 = j^2 = k^2 = -1$, where 1 is the unit matrix.

(b) $ij = -ji = k$,
      $jk = -kj = i$,
      $ki = -ik = j$.

These three matrices (i, j, and k) plus the unit matrix 1 form a basis for **quaternions**. An alternate basis is provided by the four 2×2 matrices, $i\sigma_1, i\sigma_2, -i\sigma_3$, and 1, where the σ_i are the Pauli spin matrices of Example 2.2.1.

2.2.10   A matrix with elements $a_{ij} = 0$ for $j < i$ may be called upper right triangular. The elements in the lower left (below and to the left of the main diagonal) vanish. Show that the product of two upper right triangular matrices is an upper right triangular matrix.

2.2.11   The three Pauli spin matrices are

$$\sigma_1 = \begin{pmatrix} 0 & 1 \\ 1 & 0 \end{pmatrix}, \quad \sigma_2 = \begin{pmatrix} 0 & -i \\ i & 0 \end{pmatrix}, \quad \text{and} \quad \sigma_3 = \begin{pmatrix} 1 & 0 \\ 0 & -1 \end{pmatrix}.$$

Show that

(a) $(\sigma_i)^2 = 1_2$,

(b) $\sigma_i \sigma_j = i\sigma_k$, $(i, j, k) = (1, 2, 3)$ or a cyclic permutation thereof,

(c) $\sigma_i \sigma_j + \sigma_j \sigma_i = 2\delta_{ij} 1_2$; 1_2 is the 2×2 unit matrix.

2.2.12   One description of spin-1 particles uses the matrices

$$M_x = \frac{1}{\sqrt{2}} \begin{pmatrix} 0 & 1 & 0 \\ 1 & 0 & 1 \\ 0 & 1 & 0 \end{pmatrix}, \quad M_y = \frac{1}{\sqrt{2}} \begin{pmatrix} 0 & -i & 0 \\ i & 0 & -i \\ 0 & i & 0 \end{pmatrix},$$

and

$$M_z = \begin{pmatrix} 1 & 0 & 0 \\ 0 & 0 & 0 \\ 0 & 0 & -1 \end{pmatrix}.$$

Show that

(a) $[M_x, M_y] = iM_z$, and so on (cyclic permutation of indices). Using the Levi-Civita symbol, we may write

$$[M_i, M_j] = i \sum_k \varepsilon_{ijk} M_k.$$

(b) $M^2 \equiv M_x^2 + M_y^2 + M_z^2 = 2\,\mathbf{1}_3$, where $\mathbf{1}_3$ is the 3×3 unit matrix.

(c) $[M^2, M_i] = 0$,
$[M_z, L^+] = L^+$,
$[L^+, L^-] = 2M_z$,
where $L^+ \equiv M_x + iM_y$ and $L^- \equiv M_x - iM_y$.

2.2.13 Repeat Exercise 2.2.12, using the matrices for a spin of $3/2$,

$$M_x = \frac{1}{2}\begin{pmatrix} 0 & \sqrt{3} & 0 & 0 \\ \sqrt{3} & 0 & 2 & 0 \\ 0 & 2 & 0 & \sqrt{3} \\ 0 & 0 & \sqrt{3} & 0 \end{pmatrix}, \quad M_y = \frac{i}{2}\begin{pmatrix} 0 & -\sqrt{3} & 0 & 0 \\ \sqrt{3} & 0 & -2 & 0 \\ 0 & 2 & 0 & -\sqrt{3} \\ 0 & 0 & \sqrt{3} & 0 \end{pmatrix},$$

and

$$M_z = \frac{1}{2}\begin{pmatrix} 3 & 0 & 0 & 0 \\ 0 & 1 & 0 & 0 \\ 0 & 0 & -1 & 0 \\ 0 & 0 & 0 & -3 \end{pmatrix}.$$

2.2.14 If A is a diagonal matrix, with all diagonal elements different, and A and B commute, show that B is diagonal.

2.2.15 If A and B are diagonal, show that A and B commute.

2.2.16 Show that trace(ABC) = trace(CBA) if any two of the three matrices commute.

2.2.17 Angular momentum matrices satisfy a commutation relation

$$[M_j, M_k] = iM_l, \quad j, k, l \text{ cyclic.}$$

Show that the trace of each angular momentum matrix vanishes.

2.2.18 A and B anticommute: AB = −BA. Also, $A^2 = 1$, $B^2 = 1$. Show that trace(A) = trace(B) = 0.
Note. The Pauli and Dirac matrices are specific examples.

2.2.19 (a) If two nonsingular matrices anticommute, show that the trace of each one is zero. (Nonsingular means that the determinant of the matrix is nonzero.)

(b) For the conditions of part (a) to hold, A and B must be $n \times n$ matrices with n **even**. Show that if n is **odd**, a contradiction results.

2.2.20 If A^{-1} has elements

$$(A^{-1})_{ij} = a_{ij}^{(-1)} = \frac{C_{ji}}{|A|},$$

where C_{ji} is the jith cofactor of $|A|$, show that

$$A^{-1}A = 1.$$

Hence A^{-1} is the inverse of A (if $|A| \neq 0$).

2.2.21   Find the matrices M_L such that the product $M_L A$ will be A but with:

(a)   The ith row multiplied by a constant k ($a_{ij} \rightarrow ka_{ij}$, $j = 1, 2, 3, \ldots$);

(b)   The ith row replaced by the original ith row minus a multiple of the mth row ($a_{ij} \rightarrow a_{ij} - Ka_{mj}$, $i = 1, 2, 3, \ldots$);

(c)   The ith and mth rows interchanged ($a_{ij} \rightarrow a_{mj}$, $a_{mj} \rightarrow a_{ij}$, $j = 1, 2, 3, \ldots$).

2.2.22   Find the matrices M_R such that the product AM_R will be A but with:

(a)   The ith column multiplied by a constant k ($a_{ji} \rightarrow ka_{ji}$, $j = 1, 2, 3, \ldots$);

(b)   The ith column replaced by the original ith column minus a multiple of the mth column ($a_{ji} \rightarrow a_{ji} - ka_{jm}$, $j = 1, 2, 3, \ldots$);

(c)   The ith and mth columns interchanged ($a_{ji} \rightarrow a_{jm}$, $a_{jm} \rightarrow a_{ji}$, $j = 1, 2, 3, \ldots$).

2.2.23   Find the inverse of

$$A = \begin{pmatrix} 3 & 2 & 1 \\ 2 & 2 & 1 \\ 1 & 1 & 4 \end{pmatrix}.$$

2.2.24   Matrices are far too useful to remain the exclusive property of physicists. They may appear wherever there are linear relations. For instance, in a study of population movement the initial fraction of a fixed population in each of n areas (or industries or religions, etc.) is represented by an n-component column vector **P**. The movement of people from one area to another in a given time is described by an $n \times n$ (stochastic) matrix T. Here T_{ij} is the fraction of the population in the jth area that moves to the ith area. (Those not moving are covered by $i = j$.) With **P** describing the initial population distribution, the final population distribution is given by the matrix equation $TP = Q$. From its definition, $\sum_{i=1}^{n} P_i = 1$.

(a)   Show that conservation of people requires that

$$\sum_{i=1}^{n} T_{ij} = 1, \quad j = 1, 2, \ldots, n.$$

(b)   Prove that

$$\sum_{i=1}^{n} Q_i = 1$$

continues the conservation of people.

2.2.25   Given a 6×6 matrix A with elements $a_{ij} = 0.5^{|i-j|}$, $i, j = 0, 1, 2, \ldots, 5$, find A^{-1}.

$$ANS. \quad A^{-1} = \frac{1}{3} \begin{pmatrix} 4 & -2 & 0 & 0 & 0 & 0 \\ -2 & 5 & -2 & 0 & 0 & 0 \\ 0 & -2 & 5 & -2 & 0 & 0 \\ 0 & 0 & -2 & 5 & -2 & 0 \\ 0 & 0 & 0 & -2 & 5 & -2 \\ 0 & 0 & 0 & 0 & -2 & 4 \end{pmatrix}.$$

2.2.26   Show that the product of two orthogonal matrices is orthogonal.

2.2.27   If A is orthogonal, show that its determinant $= \pm 1$.

2.2.28   Show that the trace of the product of a symmetric and an antisymmetric matrix is zero.

2.2.29   A is 2×2 and orthogonal. Find the most general form of

$$A = \begin{pmatrix} a & b \\ c & d \end{pmatrix}.$$

2.2.30   Show that

$$\det(A^*) = (\det A)^* = \det(A^\dagger).$$

2.2.31   Three angular momentum matrices satisfy the basic commutation relation

$$[J_x, J_y] = i J_z$$

(and cyclic permutation of indices). If two of the matrices have real elements, show that the elements of the third must be pure imaginary.

2.2.32   Show that $(AB)^\dagger = B^\dagger A^\dagger$.

2.2.33   A matrix $C = S^\dagger S$. Show that the trace is positive definite unless S is the null matrix, in which case trace $(C) = 0$.

2.2.34   If A and B are Hermitian matrices, show that $(AB + BA)$ and $i(AB - BA)$ are also Hermitian.

2.2.35   The matrix C is **not** Hermitian. Show that then $C + C^\dagger$ and $i(C - C^\dagger)$ are Hermitian. This means that a non-Hermitian matrix may be resolved into two Hermitian parts,

$$C = \frac{1}{2}(C + C^\dagger) + \frac{1}{2i}i(C - C^\dagger).$$

This decomposition of a matrix into two Hermitian matrix parts parallels the decomposition of a complex number z into $x + iy$, where $x = (z + z^*)/2$ and $y = (z - z^*)/2i$.

2.2.36   A and B are two noncommuting Hermitian matrices:

$$AB - BA = iC.$$

Prove that C is Hermitian.

2.2.37   Two matrices A and B are each Hermitian. Find a necessary and sufficient condition for their product AB to be Hermitian.

$$ANS. \quad [A, B] = 0.$$

2.2.38   Show that the reciprocal (that is, inverse) of a unitary matrix is unitary.

2.2.39   Prove that the direct product of two unitary matrices is unitary.

2.2.40   If $\boldsymbol{\sigma}$ is the vector with the σ_i as components given in Eq. (2.61), and $\mathbf{p}$ is an ordinary vector, show that

$$(\boldsymbol{\sigma} \cdot \mathbf{p})^2 = \mathbf{p}^2 \mathbf{1}_2,$$

where $\mathbf{1}_2$ is a 2×2 unit matrix.

2.2.41   Use the equations for the properties of direct products, Eqs. (2.57) and (2.58), to show that the four matrices γ^μ, $\mu = 0, 1, 2, 3$, satisfy the conditions listed in Eqs. (2.74) and (2.75).

2.2.42   Show that $\boldsymbol{\gamma}^5$, Eq. (2.76), anticommutes with all four γ^μ.

2.2.43   In this problem, the summations are over $\mu = 0, 1, 2, 3$. Define $g_{\mu\nu} = g^{\mu\nu}$ by the relations

$$g_{00} = 1; \quad g_{kk} = -1, \quad k = 1, 2, 3; \quad g_{\mu\nu} = 0, \quad \mu \neq \nu;$$

and define γ_μ as $\sum g_{\nu\mu} \gamma^\mu$. Using these definitions, show that

(a) $\sum \gamma_\mu \gamma^\alpha \gamma^\mu = -2\gamma^\alpha$,

(b) $\sum \gamma_\mu \gamma^\alpha \gamma^\beta \gamma^\mu = 4 g^{\alpha\beta}$,

(c) $\sum \gamma_\mu \gamma^\alpha \gamma^\beta \gamma^\nu \gamma^\mu = -2\gamma^\nu \gamma^\beta \gamma^\alpha$.

2.2.44   If $\mathsf{M} = \frac{1}{2}(1 + \boldsymbol{\gamma}^5)$, where $\boldsymbol{\gamma}^5$ is given in Eq. (2.76), show that

$$\mathsf{M}^2 = \mathsf{M}.$$

Note that this equation is still satisfied if $\boldsymbol{\gamma}$ is replaced by any other Dirac matrix listed in Eq. (2.76).

2.2.45   Prove that the 16 Dirac matrices form a linearly independent set.

2.2.46   If we assume that a given 4×4 matrix A (with constant elements) can be written as a linear combination of the 16 Dirac matrices (which we denote here as Γ_i)

$$\mathsf{A} = \sum_{i=1}^{16} c_i \Gamma_i,$$

show that

$$c_i \sim \text{trace}(\mathsf{A}\Gamma_i).$$

2.2.47   The matrix $\mathsf{C} = i\boldsymbol{\gamma}^2\boldsymbol{\gamma}^0$ is sometimes called the charge conjugation matrix. Show that $\mathsf{C}\boldsymbol{\gamma}^\mu\mathsf{C}^{-1} = -(\boldsymbol{\gamma}^\mu)^T$.

2.2.48   (a)   Show that, by substitution of the definitions of the γ^μ matrices from Eqs. (2.70) and (2.72), that the Dirac equation, Eq. (2.73), takes the following form when written as 2×2 blocks (with ψ_L and ψ_S column vectors of dimension 2). Here

L and S stand, respectively, for "large" and "small" because of their relative size in the nonrelativistic limit):

$$\begin{pmatrix} mc^2 - E & c(\sigma_1 p_1 + \sigma_2 p_2 + \sigma_3 p_3) \\ -c(\sigma_1 p_1 + \sigma_2 p_2 + \sigma_3 p_3) & -mc^2 - E \end{pmatrix} \begin{pmatrix} \psi_L \\ \psi_S \end{pmatrix} = 0.$$

(b) To reach the nonrelativistic limit, make the substitution $E = mc^2 + \varepsilon$ and approximate $-2mc^2 - \varepsilon$ by $-2mc^2$. Then write the matrix equation as two simultaneous two-component equations and show that they can be rearranged to yield

$$\frac{1}{2m} \left(p_1^2 + p_2^2 + p_3^2 \right) \psi_L = \varepsilon \psi_L,$$

which is just the Schrödinger equation for a free particle.

(c) Explain why is it reasonable to call ψ_L and ψ_S "large" and "small."

2.2.49   Show that it is consistent with the requirements that they must satisfy to take the Dirac gamma matrices to be (in 2×2 block form)

$$\gamma^0 = \begin{pmatrix} 0 & \mathbf{1}_2 \\ \mathbf{1}_2 & 0 \end{pmatrix}, \quad \gamma^i = \begin{pmatrix} 0 & \sigma_i \\ -\sigma_i & 0 \end{pmatrix}, \quad (i = 1, 2, 3).$$

This choice for the gamma matrices is called the **Weyl representation**.

2.2.50   Show that the Dirac equation separates into independent 2×2 blocks in the Weyl representation (see Exercise 2.2.49) in the limit that the mass m approaches zero. This observation is important in the ultra relativistic regime where the rest mass is inconsequential, or for particles of negligible mass (e.g., neutrinos).

2.2.51   (a) Given $\mathbf{r}' = \mathsf{U}\mathbf{r}$, with U a unitary matrix and $\mathbf{r}$ a (column) vector with complex elements, show that the magnitude of $\mathbf{r}$ is invariant under this operation.

(b) The matrix U transforms any column vector $\mathbf{r}$ with complex elements into $\mathbf{r}'$, leaving the magnitude invariant: $\mathbf{r}^\dagger \mathbf{r} = \mathbf{r}'^\dagger \mathbf{r}'$. Show that U is unitary.

Additional Readings

Aitken, A. C., *Determinants and Matrices*. New York: Interscience (1956), reprinted, Greenwood (1983). A readable introduction to determinants and matrices.

Barnett, S., *Matrices: Methods and Applications*. Oxford: Clarendon Press (1990).

Bickley, W. G., and R. S. H. G. Thompson, *Matrices—Their Meaning and Manipulation*. Princeton, NJ: Van Nostrand (1964). A comprehensive account of matrices in physical problems, their analytic properties, and numerical techniques.

Brown, W. C., *Matrices and Vector Spaces*. New York: Dekker (1991).

Gilbert, J., and L. Gilbert, *Linear Algebra and Matrix Theory*. San Diego: Academic Press (1995).

Golub, G. H., and C. F. Van Loan, *Matrix Computations*, 3rd ed. Baltimore: JHU Press (1996). Detailed mathematical background and algorithms for the production of numerical software, including methods for parallel computation. A classic computer science text.

Heading, J., *Matrix Theory for Physicists*. London: Longmans, Green and Co. (1958). A readable introduction to determinants and matrices, with applications to mechanics, electromagnetism, special relativity, and quantum mechanics.

Vein, R., and P. Dale, *Determinants and Their Applications in Mathematical Physics*. Berlin: Springer (1998).

Watkins, D.S., *Fundamentals of Matrix Computations*. New York: Wiley (1991).

CHAPTER 3

VECTOR ANALYSIS

The introductory section on vectors, Section 1.7, identified some basic properties that are universal, in the sense that they occur in a similar fashion in spaces of different dimension. In summary, these properties are (1) vectors can be represented as linear forms, with operations that include addition and multiplication by a scalar, (2) vectors have a commutative and distributive dot product operation that associates a scalar with a pair of vectors and depends on their relative orientations and hence is independent of the coordinate system, and (3) vectors can be decomposed into components that can be identified as projections onto the coordinate directions. In Section 2.2 we found that the components of vectors could be identified as the elements of a **column vector** and that the scalar product of two vectors corresponded to the matrix multiplication of the transpose of one (the transposition makes it a **row vector**) with the column vector of the other.

The current chapter builds on these ideas, mainly in ways that are specific to three-dimensional (3-D) physical space, by (1) introducing a quantity called a **vector cross product** to permit the use of vectors to represent rotational phenomena and volumes in 3-D space, (2) studying the transformational properties of vectors when the coordinate system used to describe them is rotated or subjected to a reflection operation, (3) developing mathematical methods for treating vectors that are defined over a spatial region (vector **fields**), with particular attention to quantities that depend on the spatial variation of the vector field, including vector differential operators and integrals of vector quantities, and (4) extending vector concepts to curvilinear coordinate systems, which are very useful when the symmetry of the coordinate system corresponds to a symmetry of the problem under study (an example is the use of spherical polar coordinates for systems with spherical symmetry).

A key idea of the present chapter is that a quantity that is properly called a **vector** must have the transformation properties that preserve its essential features under coordinate transformation; there exist quantities with direction and magnitude that do not transform appropriately and hence are not vectors. This study of transformation properties will, in a subsequent chapter, ultimately enable us to generalize to related quantities such as tensors.

Finally, we note that the methods developed in this chapter have direct application in electromagnetic theory as well as in mechanics, and these connections are explored through the study of examples.

3.1   REVIEW OF BASIC PROPERTIES

In Section 1.7 we established the following properties of vectors:

1. Vectors satisfy an addition law that corresponds to successive displacements that can be represented by arrows in the underlying space. Vector addition is commutative and associative: $\mathbf{A} + \mathbf{B} = \mathbf{B} + \mathbf{A}$ and $(\mathbf{A} + \mathbf{B}) + \mathbf{C} = \mathbf{A} + (\mathbf{B} + \mathbf{C})$.

2. A vector $\mathbf{A}$ can be multiplied by a scalar k; if $k > 0$ the result will be a vector in the direction of $\mathbf{A}$ but with its length multiplied by k; if $k < 0$ the result will be in the direction opposite to $\mathbf{A}$ but with its length mutiplied by $|k|$.

3. The vector $\mathbf{A} - \mathbf{B}$ is interpreted as $\mathbf{A} + (-1)\mathbf{B}$, so vector polynomials, e.g., $\mathbf{A} - 2\mathbf{B} + 3\mathbf{C}$, are well-defined.

4. A vector of unit length in the coordinate direction x_i is denoted $\hat{\mathbf{e}}_i$. An arbitrary vector $\mathbf{A}$ can be written as a sum of vectors along the coordinate directions, as

$$\mathbf{A} = A_1 \hat{\mathbf{e}}_1 + A_2 \hat{\mathbf{e}}_2 + \cdots .$$

The A_i are called the components of A, and the operations in Properties 1 to 3 correspond to the component formulas

$$\mathbf{G} = \mathbf{A} - 2\mathbf{B} + 3\mathbf{C} \implies G_i = A_i - 2B_i + 3C_i, \quad \text{(each i)}.$$

5. The magnitude or length of a vector $\mathbf{A}$, denoted $|\mathbf{A}|$ or A, is given in terms of its components as

$$|\mathbf{A}| = \left(A_1^2 + A_2^2 + \cdots \right)^{1/2}.$$

6. The dot product of two vectors is given by the formula

$$\mathbf{A} \cdot \mathbf{B} = A_1 B_1 + A_2 B_2 + \cdots ;$$

consequences are

$$|\mathbf{A}|^2 = \mathbf{A} \cdot \mathbf{A}, \quad \mathbf{A} \cdot \mathbf{B} = |\mathbf{A}|\,|\mathbf{B}| \cos\theta,$$

where θ is the angle between $\mathbf{A}$ and $\mathbf{B}$.

7. If two vectors are perpendicular to each other, their dot product vanishes and they are termed **orthogonal**. The unit vectors of a Cartesian coordinate system are orthogonal:

$$\hat{\mathbf{e}}_i \cdot \hat{\mathbf{e}}_j = \delta_{ij}, \tag{3.1}$$

where δ_{ij} is the Kronecker delta, Eq. (1.164).

8. The projection of a vector in any direction has an algebraic magnitude given by its dot product with a unit vector in that direction. In particular, the projection of $\mathbf{A}$ on the $\hat{\mathbf{e}}_i$ direction is $A_i \hat{\mathbf{e}}_i$, with

$$A_i = \hat{\mathbf{e}}_i \cdot \mathbf{A}.$$

9. The components of **A** in $\mathbb{R}^3$ are related to its direction cosines (cosines of the angles that **A** makes with the coordinate axes) by the formulas

$$A_x = A\cos\alpha, \quad A_y = A\cos\beta, \quad A_z = A\cos\gamma,$$

and $\cos^2\alpha + \cos^2\beta + \cos^2\gamma = 1$.

In Section 2.2 we noted that matrices consisting of a single column could be used to represent vectors. In particular, we found, illustrating for the 3-D space $\mathbb{R}^3$, the following properties.

10. A vector **A** can be represented by a single-column matrix **a** whose elements are the components of **A**, as in

$$\mathbf{A} \implies \mathbf{a} = \begin{pmatrix} A_1 \\ A_2 \\ A_3 \end{pmatrix}.$$

The rows (i.e., individual elements A_i) of **a** are the coefficients of the individual members of the **basis** used to represent **A**, so the element A_i is associated with the basis unit vector $\hat{\mathbf{e}}_i$.

11. The vector operations of addition and multiplication by a scalar correspond exactly to the operations of the same names applied to the single-column matrices representing the vectors, as illustrated here:

$$\mathbf{G} = \mathbf{A} - 2\mathbf{B} + 3\mathbf{C} \implies \begin{pmatrix} G_1 \\ G_2 \\ G_3 \end{pmatrix} = \begin{pmatrix} A_1 \\ A_2 \\ A_3 \end{pmatrix} - 2\begin{pmatrix} B_1 \\ B_2 \\ B_3 \end{pmatrix} + 3\begin{pmatrix} C_1 \\ C_2 \\ C_3 \end{pmatrix}$$

$$= \begin{pmatrix} A_1 - 2B_1 + 3C_1 \\ A_2 - 2B_2 + 3C_2 \\ A_3 - 2B_3 + 3C_3 \end{pmatrix}, \quad \text{or } \mathbf{g} = \mathbf{a} - 2\mathbf{b} + 3\mathbf{c}.$$

It is therefore appropriate to call these single-column matrices **column vectors**.

12. The transpose of the matrix representing a vector **A** is a single-row matrix, called a **row vector**:

$$\mathbf{a}^T = (A_1 \ \ A_2 \ \ A_3).$$

The operations illustrated in Property 11 also apply to row vectors.

13. The dot product $\mathbf{A} \cdot \mathbf{B}$ can be evaluated as $\mathbf{a}^T \mathbf{b}$, or alternatively, because **a** and **b** are real, as $\mathbf{a}^\dagger \mathbf{b}$. Moreover, $\mathbf{a}^T \mathbf{b} = \mathbf{b}^T \mathbf{a}$.

$$\mathbf{A} \cdot \mathbf{B} = \mathbf{a}^T \mathbf{b} = (A_1 \ \ A_2 \ \ A_3)\begin{pmatrix} B_1 \\ B_2 \\ B_3 \end{pmatrix} = A_1 B_1 + A_2 B_2 + A_3 B_3.$$

3.2 VECTORS IN 3-D SPACE

We now proceed to develop additional properties for vectors, most of which are applicable only for vectors in 3-D space.

Vector or Cross Product

A number of quantities in physics are related to angular motion or the torque required to cause angular acceleration. For example, **angular momentum** about a point is defined as having a magnitude equal to the distance r from the point times the component of the linear momentum **p** perpendicular to **r**—the component of **p** causing angular motion (see Fig. 3.1). The direction assigned to the angular momentum is that perpendicular to both **r** and **p**, and corresponds to the axis about which angular motion is taking place. The mathematical construction needed to describe angular momentum is the **cross product**, defined as

$$C = A \times B = (AB \sin\theta)\hat{e}_c. \tag{3.2}$$

Note that **C**, the result of the cross product, is stated to be a vector, with a magnitude that is the product of the magnitudes of **A**, **B** and the sine of the angle $\theta \le \pi$ between **A** and **B**. The direction of **C**, i.e., that of $\hat{e}_c$, is perpendicular to the plane of **A** and **B**, such that **A**, **B**, and **C** form a right-handed system.[1] This causes **C** to be aligned with the rotational axis, with a sign that indicates the sense of the rotation.

From Fig. 3.2, we also see that $A \times B$ has a magnitude equal to the area of the parallelogram formed by **A** and **B**, and with a direction **normal** to the parallelogram.

Other places the cross product is encountered include the formulas

$$v = \omega \times r \quad \text{and} \quad F_M = qv \times B.$$

The first of these equations is the relation between linear velocity **v** and and angular velocity ω, and the second equation gives the force F_M on a particle of charge q and velocity **v** in the magnetic induction field **B** (in SI units).

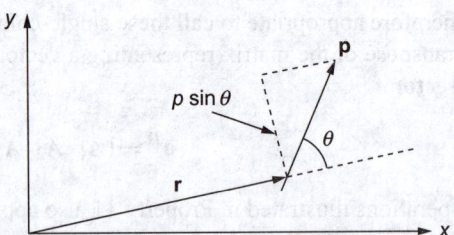

FIGURE 3.1   Angular momentum about the origin, $L = r \times p$.
L has magnitude $rp \sin\theta$ and is directed out of the plane of the paper.

---

[1] The inherent ambiguity in this statement can be resolved by the following anthropomorphic prescription: Point the right hand in the direction **A**, and then bend the fingers through the **smaller** of the two angles that can cause the fingers to point in the direction **B**; the thumb will then point in the direction of **C**.

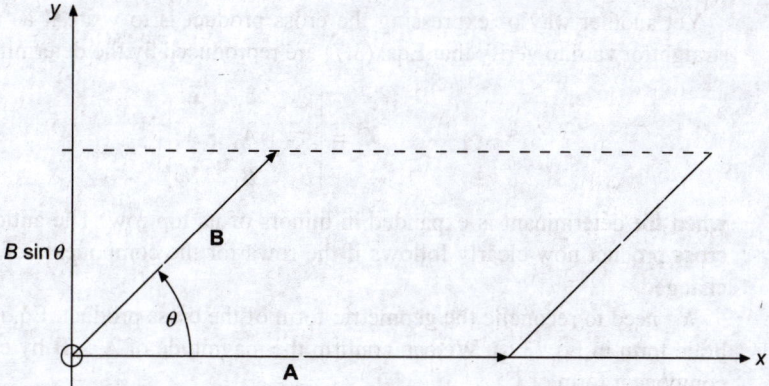

FIGURE 3.2   Parallelogram of $\mathbf{A} \times \mathbf{B}$.

We can get our right hands out of the analysis by compiling some algebraic properties of the cross product. If the roles of $\mathbf{A}$ and $\mathbf{B}$ are reversed, the cross product changes sign, so

$$\mathbf{B} \times \mathbf{A} = -\mathbf{A} \times \mathbf{B} \quad \text{(anticommutation)}. \tag{3.3}$$

The cross product also obeys the distributive laws

$$\mathbf{A} \times (\mathbf{B} + \mathbf{C}) = \mathbf{A} \times \mathbf{B} + \mathbf{A} \times \mathbf{C}, \quad k(\mathbf{A} \times \mathbf{B}) = (k\mathbf{A}) \times \mathbf{B}, \tag{3.4}$$

and when applied to unit vectors in the coordinate directions, we get

$$\hat{\mathbf{e}}_i \times \hat{\mathbf{e}}_j = \sum_k \varepsilon_{ijk} \hat{\mathbf{e}}_k. \tag{3.5}$$

Here ε_{ijk} is the Levi-Civita symbol defined in Eq. (2.8); Eq. (3.5) therefore indicates, for example, that $\hat{\mathbf{e}}_x \times \hat{\mathbf{e}}_x = 0$, $\hat{\mathbf{e}}_x \times \hat{\mathbf{e}}_y = \hat{\mathbf{e}}_z$, but $\hat{\mathbf{e}}_y \times \hat{\mathbf{e}}_x = -\hat{\mathbf{e}}_z$.

Using Eq. (3.5) and writing $\mathbf{A}$ and $\mathbf{B}$ in component form, we can expand $\mathbf{A} \times \mathbf{B}$ to obtain

$$\mathbf{C} = \mathbf{A} \times \mathbf{B} = (A_x \hat{\mathbf{e}}_x + A_y \hat{\mathbf{e}}_y + A_z \hat{\mathbf{e}}_z) \times (B_x \hat{\mathbf{e}}_x + B_y \hat{\mathbf{e}}_y + B_z \hat{\mathbf{e}}_z)$$

$$= (A_x B_y - A_y B_x)(\hat{\mathbf{e}}_x \times \hat{\mathbf{e}}_y) + (A_x B_z - A_z B_x)(\hat{\mathbf{e}}_x \times \hat{\mathbf{e}}_z)$$

$$+ (A_y B_z - A_z B_y)(\hat{\mathbf{e}}_y \times \hat{\mathbf{e}}_z)$$

$$= (A_x B_y - A_y B_x)\hat{\mathbf{e}}_z + (A_x B_z - A_z B_x)(-\hat{\mathbf{e}}_y) + (A_y B_z - A_z B_y)\hat{\mathbf{e}}_x. \tag{3.6}$$

The components of $\mathbf{C}$ are important enough to be displayed prominently:

$$C_x = A_y B_z - A_z B_y, \quad C_y = A_z B_x - A_x B_z, \quad C_z = A_x B_y - A_y B_x, \tag{3.7}$$

equivalent to

$$C_i = \sum_{jk} \varepsilon_{ijk} A_j B_k. \tag{3.8}$$

Yet another way of expressing the cross product is to write it as a determinant. It is straightforward to verify that Eqs. (3.7) are reproduced by the determinantal equation

$$\mathbf{C} = \begin{vmatrix} \hat{\mathbf{e}}_x & \hat{\mathbf{e}}_y & \hat{\mathbf{e}}_z \\ A_x & A_y & A_z \\ B_x & B_y & B_z \end{vmatrix}. \tag{3.9}$$

when the determinant is expanded in minors of its top row. The anticommutation of the cross product now clearly follows if the rows for the components of $\mathbf{A}$ and $\mathbf{B}$ are interchanged.

We need to reconcile the geometric form of the cross product, Eq. (3.2), with the algebraic form in Eq. (3.6). We can confirm the magnitude of $\mathbf{A} \times \mathbf{B}$ by evaluating (from the component form of $\mathbf{C}$)

$$(\mathbf{A} \times \mathbf{B}) \cdot (\mathbf{A} \times \mathbf{B}) = A^2 B^2 - (\mathbf{A} \cdot \mathbf{B})^2 = A^2 B^2 - A^2 B^2 \cos^2 \theta$$

$$= A^2 B^2 \sin_1^2 \theta. \tag{3.10}$$

The first step in Eq. (3.10) can be verified by expanding its left-hand side in component form, then collecting the result into the terms constituting the central member of the first line of the equation.

To confirm the direction of $\mathbf{C} = \mathbf{A} \times \mathbf{B}$, we can check that $\mathbf{A} \cdot \mathbf{C} = \mathbf{B} \cdot \mathbf{C} = 0$, showing that $\mathbf{C}$ (in component form) is perpendicular to both $\mathbf{A}$ and $\mathbf{B}$. We illustrate for $\mathbf{A} \cdot \mathbf{C}$:

$$\mathbf{A} \cdot \mathbf{C} = A_x(A_y B_z - A_z B_y) + A_y(A_z B_x - A_x B_z) + A_z(A_x B_y - A_y B_x) = 0. \tag{3.11}$$

To verify the sign of $\mathbf{C}$, it suffices to check special cases (e.g., $\mathbf{A} = \hat{\mathbf{e}}_x$, $\mathbf{B} = \hat{\mathbf{e}}_y$, or $A_x = B_y = 1$, all other components zero).

Next, we observe that it is obvious from Eq. (3.2) that if $\mathbf{C} = \mathbf{A} \times \mathbf{B}$ in a given coordinate system, then that equation will also be satisfied if we rotate the coordinates, even though the individual components of all three vectors will thereby be changed. In other words, the cross product, like the dot product, is a rotationally invariant relationship.

Finally, note that the cross product is a quantity specifically defined for 3-D space. It is possible to make analogous definitions for spaces of other dimensionality, but they do not share the interpretation or utility of the cross product in $\mathbb{R}^3$.

Scalar Triple Product

While the various vector operations can be combined in many ways, there are two combinations involving three operands that are of particular importance. We call attention first to the **scalar triple product**, of the form $\mathbf{A} \cdot (\mathbf{B} \times \mathbf{C})$. Taking $(\mathbf{B} \times \mathbf{C})$ in the determinantal form, Eq. (3.9), one can see that taking the dot product with $\mathbf{A}$ will cause the unit vector $\hat{\mathbf{e}}_x$ to be replaced by A_x, with corresponding replacements to $\hat{\mathbf{e}}_y$ and $\hat{\mathbf{e}}_z$. The overall result is

$$\mathbf{A} \cdot (\mathbf{B} \times \mathbf{C}) = \begin{vmatrix} A_x & A_y & A_z \\ B_x & B_y & B_z \\ C_x & C_y & C_z \end{vmatrix}. \tag{3.12}$$

We can draw a number of conclusions from this highly symmetric determinantal form. To start, we see that the determinant contains no vector quantities, so it must evaluate

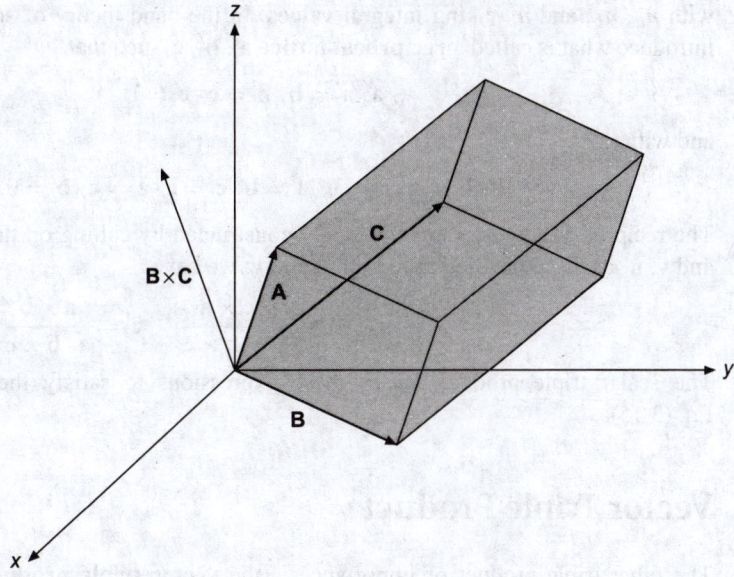

FIGURE 3.3 $\mathbf{A} \cdot (\mathbf{B} \times \mathbf{C})$ parallelepiped.

to an ordinary number. Because the left-hand side of Eq. (3.12) is a rotational invariant, the number represented by the determinant must also be rotationally invariant, and can therefore be identified as a scalar. Since we can permute the rows of the determinant (with a sign change for an odd permutation, and with no sign change for an even permutation), we can permute the vectors $\mathbf{A}$, $\mathbf{B}$, and $\mathbf{C}$ to obtain

$$\mathbf{A} \cdot \mathbf{B} \times \mathbf{C} = \mathbf{B} \cdot \mathbf{C} \times \mathbf{A} = \mathbf{C} \cdot \mathbf{A} \times \mathbf{B} = -\mathbf{A} \cdot \mathbf{C} \times \mathbf{B}, \text{ etc.} \tag{3.13}$$

Here we have followed common practice and dropped the parentheses surrounding the cross product, on the basis that they must be understood to be present in order for the expressions to have meaning. Finally, noting that $\mathbf{B} \times \mathbf{C}$ has a magnitude equal to the area of the $\mathbf{BC}$ parallelogram and a direction perpendicular to it, and that the dot product with $\mathbf{A}$ will multiply that area by the projection of $\mathbf{A}$ on $\mathbf{B} \times \mathbf{C}$, we see that the scalar triple product gives us ($\pm$) the volume of the parallelepiped defined by $\mathbf{A}$, $\mathbf{B}$, and $\mathbf{C}$; see Fig. 3.3.

Example 3.2.1   RECIPROCAL LATTICE

Let $\mathbf{a}$, $\mathbf{b}$, and $\mathbf{c}$ (not necessarily mutually perpendicular) represent the vectors that define a crystal lattice. The displacements from one lattice point to another may then be written

$$\mathbf{R} = n_a \mathbf{a} + n_b \mathbf{b} + n_c \mathbf{c}, \tag{3.14}$$

with n_a, n_b, and n_c taking integral values. In the band theory of solids,[2] it is useful to introduce what is called a **reciprocal lattice** $\mathbf{a}'$, $\mathbf{b}'$, $\mathbf{c}'$ such that

$$\mathbf{a} \cdot \mathbf{a}' = \mathbf{b} \cdot \mathbf{b}' = \mathbf{c} \cdot \mathbf{c}' = 1, \tag{3.15}$$

and with

$$\mathbf{a} \cdot \mathbf{b}' = \mathbf{a} \cdot \mathbf{c}' = \mathbf{b} \cdot \mathbf{a}' = \mathbf{b} \cdot \mathbf{c}' = \mathbf{c} \cdot \mathbf{a}' = \mathbf{c} \cdot \mathbf{b}' = 0. \tag{3.16}$$

The reciprocal-lattice vectors are easily constructed by calling on the fact that for any $\mathbf{u}$ and $\mathbf{v}$, $\mathbf{u} \times \mathbf{v}$ is perpendicular to both $\mathbf{u}$ and $\mathbf{v}$; we have

$$\mathbf{a}' = \frac{\mathbf{b} \times \mathbf{c}}{\mathbf{a} \cdot \mathbf{b} \times \mathbf{c}}, \quad \mathbf{b}' = \frac{\mathbf{c} \times \mathbf{a}}{\mathbf{a} \cdot \mathbf{b} \times \mathbf{c}}, \quad \mathbf{c}' = \frac{\mathbf{a} \times \mathbf{b}}{\mathbf{a} \cdot \mathbf{b} \times \mathbf{c}}. \tag{3.17}$$

The scalar triple product causes these expressions to satisfy the scale condition of Eq. (3.15). ∎

Vector Triple Product

The other triple product of importance is the **vector triple product**, of the form $\mathbf{A} \times (\mathbf{B} \times \mathbf{C})$. Here the parentheses are essential since, for example, $(\hat{\mathbf{e}}_x \times \hat{\mathbf{e}}_x) \times \hat{\mathbf{e}}_y = 0$, while $\hat{\mathbf{e}}_x \times (\hat{\mathbf{e}}_x \times \hat{\mathbf{e}}_y) = \hat{\mathbf{e}}_x \times \hat{\mathbf{e}}_z = -\hat{\mathbf{e}}_y$. Our interest is in reducing this triple product to a simpler form; the result we seek is

$$\mathbf{A} \times (\mathbf{B} \times \mathbf{C}) = \mathbf{B}(\mathbf{A} \cdot \mathbf{C}) - \mathbf{C}(\mathbf{A} \cdot \mathbf{B}). \tag{3.18}$$

Equation (3.18), which for convenience we will sometimes refer to as the BAC–CAB rule, can be proved by inserting components for all vectors and evaluating all the products, but it is instructive to proceed in a more elegant fashion. Using the formula for the cross product in terms of the Levi-Civita symbol, Eq. (3.8), we write

$$\mathbf{A} \times (\mathbf{B} \times \mathbf{C}) = \sum_i \hat{\mathbf{e}}_i \sum_{jk} \varepsilon_{ijk} A_j \left(\sum_{pq} \varepsilon_{kpq} B_p C_q \right)$$

$$= \sum_{ij} \sum_{pq} \hat{\mathbf{e}}_i A_j B_p C_q \sum_k \varepsilon_{ijk} \varepsilon_{kpq}. \tag{3.19}$$

The summation over k of the product of Levi-Civita symbols reduces, as shown in Exercise 2.1.9, to $\delta_{ip}\delta_{jq} - \delta_{iq}\delta_{jp}$; we are left with

$$\mathbf{A} \times (\mathbf{B} \times \mathbf{C}) = \sum_{ij} \hat{\mathbf{e}}_i A_j (B_i C_j - B_j C_i) = \sum_i \hat{\mathbf{e}}_i \left(B_i \sum_j A_j C_j - C_i \sum_j A_j B_j \right),$$

which is equivalent to Eq. (3.18).

---

[2] It is often chosen to require $\mathbf{a} \cdot \mathbf{a}'$, etc. to be 2π rather than unity, because when Bloch states for a crystal (labeled by $\mathbf{k}$) are set up, a constituent atomic function in cell $\mathbf{R}$ enters with coefficient $\exp(i\mathbf{k} \cdot \mathbf{R})$, and if $\mathbf{k}$ is changed by a reciprocal lattice step (in, say, the $\mathbf{a}'$ direction), the coefficient becomes $\exp(i[\mathbf{k} + \mathbf{a}'] \cdot \mathbf{R})$, which reduces to $\exp(2\pi i n_a) \exp(i\mathbf{k} \cdot \mathbf{R})$ and therefore, because $\exp(2\pi i n_a) = 1$, to its original value. Thus, the reciprocal lattice identifies the periodicity in $\mathbf{k}$. The unit cell of the $\mathbf{k}$ vectors is called the **Brillouin zone**

Exercises

3.2.1 If $\mathbf{P} = \hat{\mathbf{e}}_x P_x + \hat{\mathbf{e}}_y P_y$ and $\mathbf{Q} = \hat{\mathbf{e}}_x Q_x + \hat{\mathbf{e}}_y Q_y$ are any two nonparallel (also nonantiparallel) vectors in the xy-plane, show that $\mathbf{P} \times \mathbf{Q}$ is in the z-direction.

3.2.2 Prove that $(\mathbf{A} \times \mathbf{B}) \cdot (\mathbf{A} \times \mathbf{B}) = (AB)^2 - (\mathbf{A} \cdot \mathbf{B})^2$.

3.2.3 Using the vectors

$$\mathbf{P} = \hat{\mathbf{e}}_x \cos\theta + \hat{\mathbf{e}}_y \sin\theta,$$

$$\mathbf{Q} = \hat{\mathbf{e}}_x \cos\varphi - \hat{\mathbf{e}}_y \sin\varphi,$$

$$\mathbf{R} = \hat{\mathbf{e}}_x \cos\varphi + \hat{\mathbf{e}}_y \sin\varphi,$$

prove the familiar trigonometric identities

$$\sin(\theta + \varphi) = \sin\theta \cos\varphi + \cos\theta \sin\varphi,$$

$$\cos(\theta + \varphi) = \cos\theta \cos\varphi - \sin\theta \sin\varphi.$$

3.2.4 (a) Find a vector $\mathbf{A}$ that is perpendicular to

$$\mathbf{U} = 2\hat{\mathbf{e}}_x + \hat{\mathbf{e}}_y - \hat{\mathbf{e}}_z,$$

$$\mathbf{V} = \hat{\mathbf{e}}_x - \hat{\mathbf{e}}_y + \hat{\mathbf{e}}_z.$$

(b) What is $\mathbf{A}$ if, in addition to this requirement, we demand that it have unit magnitude?

3.2.5 If four vectors $\mathbf{a}$, $\mathbf{b}$, $\mathbf{c}$, and $\mathbf{d}$ all lie in the same plane, show that

$$(\mathbf{a} \times \mathbf{b}) \times (\mathbf{c} \times \mathbf{d}) = 0.$$

Hint. Consider the directions of the cross-product vectors.

3.2.6 Derive the law of sines (see Fig. 3.4):

$$\frac{\sin\alpha}{|\mathbf{A}|} = \frac{\sin\beta}{|\mathbf{B}|} = \frac{\sin\gamma}{|\mathbf{C}|}.$$

3.2.7 The magnetic induction $\mathbf{B}$ is **defined** by the Lorentz force equation,

$$\mathbf{F} = q(\mathbf{v} \times \mathbf{B}).$$

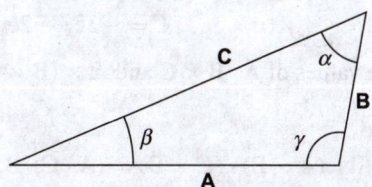

FIGURE 3.4   Plane triangle.

Carrying out three experiments, we find that if

$$\mathbf{v} = \hat{\mathbf{e}}_x, \quad \frac{\mathbf{F}}{q} = 2\hat{\mathbf{e}}_z - 4\hat{\mathbf{e}}_y,$$

$$\mathbf{v} = \hat{\mathbf{e}}_y, \quad \frac{\mathbf{F}}{q} = 4\hat{\mathbf{e}}_x - \hat{\mathbf{e}}_z,$$

$$\mathbf{v} = \hat{\mathbf{e}}_z, \quad \frac{\mathbf{F}}{q} = \hat{\mathbf{e}}_y - 2\hat{\mathbf{e}}_x.$$

From the results of these three separate experiments calculate the magnetic induction **B**.

3.2.8   You are given the three vectors **A**, **B**, and **C**,

$$\mathbf{A} = \hat{\mathbf{e}}_x + \hat{\mathbf{e}}_y,$$

$$\mathbf{B} = \hat{\mathbf{e}}_y + \hat{\mathbf{e}}_z,$$

$$\mathbf{C} = \hat{\mathbf{e}}_x - \hat{\mathbf{e}}_z.$$

(a) Compute the scalar triple product, $\mathbf{A} \cdot \mathbf{B} \times \mathbf{C}$. Noting that $\mathbf{A} = \mathbf{B} + \mathbf{C}$, give a geometric interpretation of your result for the scalar triple product.

(b) Compute $\mathbf{A} \times (\mathbf{B} \times \mathbf{C})$.

3.2.9   Prove Jacobi's identity for vector products:

$$\mathbf{a} \times (\mathbf{b} \times \mathbf{c}) + \mathbf{b} \times (\mathbf{c} \times \mathbf{a}) + \mathbf{c} \times (\mathbf{a} \times \mathbf{b}) = 0.$$

3.2.10   A vector **A** is decomposed into a radial vector $\mathbf{A}_r$ and a tangential vector $\mathbf{A}_t$. If $\hat{\mathbf{r}}$ is a unit vector in the radial direction, show that

(a) $\mathbf{A}_r = \hat{\mathbf{r}}(\mathbf{A} \cdot \hat{\mathbf{r}})$ and

(b) $\mathbf{A}_t = -\hat{\mathbf{r}} \times (\hat{\mathbf{r}} \times \mathbf{A})$.

3.2.11   Prove that a necessary and sufficient condition for the three (nonvanishing) vectors **A**, **B**, and **C** to be coplanar is the vanishing of the scalar triple product

$$\mathbf{A} \cdot \mathbf{B} \times \mathbf{C} = 0.$$

3.2.12   Three vectors **A**, **B**, and **C** are given by

$$\mathbf{A} = 3\hat{\mathbf{e}}_x - 2\hat{\mathbf{e}}_y + 2\hat{\mathbf{z}},$$

$$\mathbf{B} = 6\hat{\mathbf{e}}_x + 4\hat{\mathbf{e}}_y - 2\hat{\mathbf{z}},$$

$$\mathbf{C} = -3\hat{\mathbf{e}}_x - 2\hat{\mathbf{e}}_y - 4\hat{\mathbf{z}}.$$

Compute the values of $\mathbf{A} \cdot \mathbf{B} \times \mathbf{C}$ and $\mathbf{A} \times (\mathbf{B} \times \mathbf{C})$, $\mathbf{C} \times (\mathbf{A} \times \mathbf{B})$ and $\mathbf{B} \times (\mathbf{C} \times \mathbf{A})$.

3.2.13   Show that

$$(\mathbf{A} \times \mathbf{B}) \cdot (\mathbf{C} \times \mathbf{D}) = (\mathbf{A} \cdot \mathbf{C})(\mathbf{B} \cdot \mathbf{D}) - (\mathbf{A} \cdot \mathbf{D})(\mathbf{B} \cdot \mathbf{C}).$$

3.2.14   Show that

$$(\mathbf{A} \times \mathbf{B}) \times (\mathbf{C} \times \mathbf{D}) = (\mathbf{A} \cdot \mathbf{B} \times \mathbf{D})\mathbf{C} - (\mathbf{A} \cdot \mathbf{B} \times \mathbf{C})\mathbf{D}.$$

3.2.15   An electric charge q_1 moving with velocity $\mathbf{v}_1$ produces a magnetic induction $\mathbf{B}$ given by

$$\mathbf{B} = \frac{\mu_0}{4\pi} q_1 \frac{\mathbf{v}_1 \times \hat{\mathbf{r}}}{r^2} \quad \text{(mks units)},$$

where $\hat{\mathbf{r}}$ is a unit vector that points from q_1 to the point at which $\mathbf{B}$ is measured (Biot and Savart law).

(a) Show that the magnetic force exerted by q_1 on a second charge q_2, velocity $\mathbf{v}_2$, is given by the vector triple product

$$\mathbf{F}_2 = \frac{\mu_0}{4\pi} \frac{q_1 q_2}{r^2} \mathbf{v}_2 \times (\mathbf{v}_1 \times \hat{\mathbf{r}}).$$

(b) Write out the corresponding magnetic force $\mathbf{F}_1$ that q_2 exerts on q_1. Define your unit radial vector. How do $\mathbf{F}_1$ and $\mathbf{F}_2$ compare?

(c) Calculate $\mathbf{F}_1$ and $\mathbf{F}_2$ for the case of q_1 and q_2 moving along parallel trajectories side by side.

ANS.

(b) $\mathbf{F}_1 = -\dfrac{\mu_0}{4\pi} \dfrac{q_1 q_2}{r^2} \mathbf{v}_1 \times (\mathbf{v}_2 \times \hat{\mathbf{r}}).$

In general, there is no simple relation between $\mathbf{F}_1$ and $\mathbf{F}_2$. Specifically, Newton's third law, $\mathbf{F}_1 = -\mathbf{F}_2$, does not hold.

(c) $\mathbf{F}_1 = \dfrac{\mu_0}{4\pi} \dfrac{q_1 q_2}{r^2} v^2 \hat{\mathbf{r}} = -\mathbf{F}_2.$

Mutual attraction.

3.3   COORDINATE TRANSFORMATIONS

As indicated in the chapter introduction, an object classified as a vector must have specific transformation properties under rotation of the coordinate system; in particular, the components of a vector must transform in a way that describes the same object in the rotated system.

Rotations

Considering initially $\mathbb{R}^2$, and a rotation of the coordinate axes as shown in Fig. 3.5, we wish to find how the components A_x and A_y of a vector $\mathbf{A}$ in the unrotated system are related to A'_x and A'_y, its components in the rotated coordinate system. Perhaps the easiest way to answer this question is by first asking how the unit vectors $\hat{\mathbf{e}}_x$ and $\hat{\mathbf{e}}_y$ are represented in the new coordinates, after which we can perform vector addition on the new incarnations of $A_x \hat{\mathbf{e}}_x$ and $A_y \hat{\mathbf{e}}_y$.

From the right-hand part of Fig. 3.5, we see that

$$\hat{\mathbf{e}}_x = \cos\varphi \, \hat{\mathbf{e}}'_x - \sin\varphi \, \hat{\mathbf{e}}'_y, \quad \text{and} \quad \hat{\mathbf{e}}_y = \sin\varphi \, \hat{\mathbf{e}}'_x + \cos\varphi \, \hat{\mathbf{e}}'_y, \tag{3.20}$$

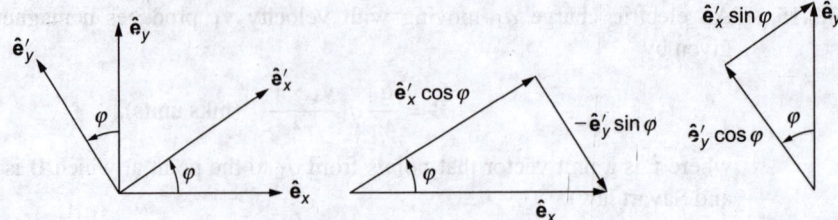

FIGURE 3.5   Left: Rotation of two-dimensional (2-D) coordinate axes through angle φ. Center and right: Decomposition of $\hat{\mathbf{e}}_x$ and $\hat{\mathbf{e}}_y$ into their components in the rotated system.

so the **unchanged** vector **A** now takes the **changed** form

$$\mathbf{A} = A_x\hat{\mathbf{e}}_x + A_y\hat{\mathbf{e}}_y = A_x(\cos\varphi\,\hat{\mathbf{e}}'_x - \sin\varphi\,\hat{\mathbf{e}}'_y) + A_y(\sin\varphi\,\hat{\mathbf{e}}'_x + \cos\varphi\,\hat{\mathbf{e}}'_y)$$

$$= (A_x\cos\varphi + A_y\sin\varphi)\hat{\mathbf{e}}'_x + (-A_x\sin\varphi + A_y\cos\varphi)\hat{\mathbf{e}}'_y. \tag{3.21}$$

If we write the vector **A** in the rotated (primed) coordinate system as

$$\mathbf{A} = A'_x\hat{\mathbf{e}}'_x + A'_y\hat{\mathbf{e}}'_y,$$

we then have

$$A'_x = A_x\cos\varphi + A_y\sin\varphi, \quad A'_y = -A_x\sin\varphi + A_y\cos\varphi, \tag{3.22}$$

which is equivalent to the matrix equation

$$\mathbf{A}' = \begin{pmatrix} A'_x \\ A'_y \end{pmatrix} = \begin{pmatrix} \cos\varphi & \sin\varphi \\ -\sin\varphi & \cos\varphi \end{pmatrix}\begin{pmatrix} A_x \\ A_y \end{pmatrix}. \tag{3.23}$$

Suppose now that we start from **A** as given by its components in the rotated system, (A'_x, A'_y), and rotate the coordinate system back to its original orientation. This will entail a rotaton in the amount $-\varphi$, and corresponds to the matrix equation

$$\begin{pmatrix} A_x \\ A_y \end{pmatrix} = \begin{pmatrix} \cos(-\varphi) & \sin(-\varphi) \\ -\sin(-\varphi) & \cos(-\varphi) \end{pmatrix}\begin{pmatrix} A'_x \\ A'_y \end{pmatrix} = \begin{pmatrix} \cos\varphi & -\sin\varphi \\ \sin\varphi & \cos\varphi \end{pmatrix}\begin{pmatrix} A'_x \\ A'_y \end{pmatrix}. \tag{3.24}$$

Assigning the 2×2 matrices in Eqs. (3.23) and (3.24) the respective names S and S′, we see that these two equations are equivalent to $\mathbf{A}' = S\mathbf{A}$ and $\mathbf{A} = S'\mathbf{A}'$, with

$$S = \begin{pmatrix} \cos\varphi & \sin\varphi \\ -\sin\varphi & \cos\varphi \end{pmatrix} \quad \text{and} \quad S' = \begin{pmatrix} \cos\varphi & -\sin\varphi \\ \sin\varphi & \cos\varphi \end{pmatrix}. \tag{3.25}$$

Now, applying S to **A** and then S′ to S**A** (corresponding to first rotating the coordinate system an amount $+\varphi$ and then an amount $-\varphi$), we recover **A**, or

$$\mathbf{A} = S'S\mathbf{A}.$$

Since this result must be valid for any **A**, we conclude that $S' = S^{-1}$. We also see that $S' = S^T$. We can check that $SS' = \mathbf{1}$ by matrix multiplication:

$$SS' = \begin{pmatrix} \cos\varphi & \sin\varphi \\ -\sin\varphi & \cos\varphi \end{pmatrix}\begin{pmatrix} \cos\varphi & -\sin\varphi \\ \sin\varphi & \cos\varphi \end{pmatrix} = \begin{pmatrix} 1 & 0 \\ 0 & 1 \end{pmatrix}.$$

Since S is real, the fact that $S^{-1} = S^T$ means that it is **orthogonal**. In summary, we have found that the transformation connecting $\mathbf{A}$ and $\mathbf{A}'$ (the same vector, but represented in the rotated coordinate system) is

$$\mathbf{A}' = SA, \tag{3.26}$$

with S an orthogonal matrix.

Orthogonal Transformations

It was no accident that the transformation describing a rotation in $\mathbb{R}^2$ was **orthogonal**, by which we mean that the matrix effecting the transformation was an orthogonal matrix.

An instructive way of writing the transformation S is, returning to Eq. (3.20), to rewrite those equations as

$$\hat{\mathbf{e}}_x = (\hat{\mathbf{e}}'_x \cdot \hat{\mathbf{e}}_x)\hat{\mathbf{e}}'_x + (\hat{\mathbf{e}}'_y \cdot \hat{\mathbf{e}}_x)\hat{\mathbf{e}}'_y, \quad \hat{\mathbf{e}}_y = (\hat{\mathbf{e}}'_x \cdot \hat{\mathbf{e}}_y)\hat{\mathbf{e}}'_x + (\hat{\mathbf{e}}'_y \cdot \hat{\mathbf{e}}_y)\hat{\mathbf{e}}'_y. \tag{3.27}$$

This corresponds to writing $\hat{\mathbf{e}}_x$ and $\hat{\mathbf{e}}_y$ as the sum of their projections on the orthogonal vectors $\hat{\mathbf{e}}'_x$ and $\hat{\mathbf{e}}'_y$. Now we can rewrite S as

$$S = \begin{pmatrix} \hat{\mathbf{e}}'_x \cdot \hat{\mathbf{e}}_x & \hat{\mathbf{e}}'_x \cdot \hat{\mathbf{e}}_y \\ \hat{\mathbf{e}}'_y \cdot \hat{\mathbf{e}}_x & \hat{\mathbf{e}}'_y \cdot \hat{\mathbf{e}}_y \end{pmatrix}. \tag{3.28}$$

This means that each row of S contains the components (in the unprimed coordinates) of a unit vector (either $\hat{\mathbf{e}}'_x$ or $\hat{\mathbf{e}}'_y$) that is orthogonal to the vector whose components are in the other row. In turn, this means that the dot products of different row vectors will be zero, while the dot product of any row vector with itself (because it is a unit vector) will be unity. That is the deeper significance of an **orthogonal** matrix S; the $\mu\nu$ element of SS^T is the dot product formed from the μth row of S and the νth column of S^T (which is the same as the νth row of S). Since these row vectors are orthogonal, we will get zero if $\mu \neq \nu$, and because they are unit vectors, we will get unity if $\mu = \nu$. In other words, SS^T will be a unit matrix.

Before leaving Eq. (3.28), note that its columns also have a simple interpretation: Each contains the components (in the primed coordinates) of one of the unit vectors of the unprimed set. Thus the dot product formed from two different **columns** of S will vanish, while the dot product of any column with itself will be unity. This corresponds to the fact that, for an orthogonal matrix, we also have $S^T S = \mathbf{1}$.

Summarizing part of the above,

> *The transformation from one orthogonal Cartesian coordinate system to another Cartesian system is described by an* **orthogonal** *matrix.*

In Chapter 2 we found that an orthogonal matrix must have a determinant that is real and of magnitude unity, i.e., ± 1. However, for rotations in ordinary space the value of the determinant will always be $+1$. One way to understand this is to consider the fact that any rotation can be built up from a large number of small rotations, and that the determinant must vary continuously as the amount of rotation is changed. The identity rotation (i.e., no rotation at all) has determinant $+1$. Since no value close to $+1$ except $+1$ itself is a permitted value for the determinant, rotations cannot change the value of the determinant.

Reflections

Another possibility for changing a coordinate system is to subject it to a reflection operation. For simplicity, consider first the **inversion** operation, in which the sign of each coordinate is reversed. In $\mathbb{R}^3$, the transformation matrix S will be the 3×3 analog of Eq. (3.28), and the transformation under discussion is to set $\hat{\mathbf{e}}'_\mu = -\hat{\mathbf{e}}_\mu$, with $\mu = x$, y, and z. This will lead to

$$S = \begin{pmatrix} -1 & 0 & 0 \\ 0 & -1 & 0 \\ 0 & 0 & -1 \end{pmatrix},$$

which clearly results in $\det S = -1$. The change in sign of the determinant corresponds to the change from a right-handed to a left-handed coordinate system (which obviously cannot be accomplished by a rotation). Reflection about a plane (as in the image produced by a plane mirror) also changes the sign of the determinant and the handedness of the coordinate system; for example, reflection in the xy-plane changes the sign of $\hat{\mathbf{e}}_z$, leaving the other two unit vectors unchanged; the transformation matrix S for this transformation is

$$S = \begin{pmatrix} 1 & 0 & 0 \\ 0 & 1 & 0 \\ 0 & 0 & -1 \end{pmatrix}.$$

Its determinant is also -1.

The formulas for vector addition, multiplication by a scalar, and the dot product are unaffected by a reflection transformation of the coordinates, but this is not true of the cross product. To see this, look at the formula for any one of the components of $\mathbf{A} \times \mathbf{B}$, and how it would change under inversion (where the same, unchanged vectors in physical space now have sign changes to all their components):

$$C_x: \quad A_y B_z - A_z B_y \quad \longrightarrow \quad (-A_y)(-B_z) - (-A_z)(-B_y) = A_y B_z - A_z B_y.$$

Note that this formula says that the sign of C_x should not change, even though it must in order to describe the unchanged physical situation. The conclusion is that our transformation law fails for the result of a cross-product operation. However, the mathematics can be salvaged if we classify $\mathbf{B} \times \mathbf{C}$ as a different type of quantity than $\mathbf{B}$ and $\mathbf{C}$. Many texts on vector analysis call vectors whose components change sign under coordinate reflection **polar vectors**, and those whose components do not then change sign **axial vectors**. The term **axial** doubtless arises from the fact that cross products frequently describe phenomena associated with rotation about the axis defined by the axial vector. Nowadays, it is becoming more usual to call **polar vectors** just **vectors**, because we want that term to describe objects that obey for all S the transformation law

$$\mathbf{A}' = S\mathbf{A} \quad \text{(vectors)}, \tag{3.29}$$

(and specifically without a restriction to S whose determinants are $+1$). Axial vectors, for which the vector transformation law fails for coordinate reflections, are then referred to as **pseudovectors**, and their transformation law can be expressed in the somewhat more complicated form

$$\mathbf{C}' = \det(S)\, S\mathbf{C} \quad \text{(pseudovectors)}. \tag{3.30}$$

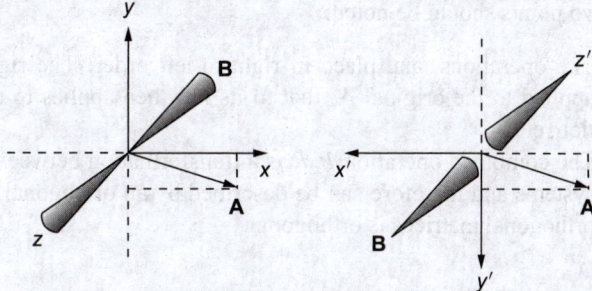

FIGURE 3.6   Inversion (right) of original coordinates (left) and the effect
on a vector **A** and a pseudovector **B**.

The effect of an inversion operation on a coordinate system and on a vector and a pseudovector are shown in Fig. 3.6.

Since vectors and pseudovectors have different transformation laws, it is in general without physical meaning to add them together.[3] It is also usually meaningless to equate quantities of different transformational properties: in $\mathbf{A} = \mathbf{B}$, both quantities must be either vectors or pseudovectors.

Pseudovectors, of course, enter into more complicated expressions, of which an example is the scalar triple product $\mathbf{A} \cdot \mathbf{B} \times \mathbf{C}$. Under coordinate reflection, the components of $\mathbf{B} \times \mathbf{C}$ do not change (as observed earlier), but those of $\mathbf{A}$ are reversed, with the result that $\mathbf{A} \cdot \mathbf{B} \times \mathbf{C}$ changes sign. We therefore need to reclassify it as a **pseudoscalar**. On the other hand, the vector triple product, $\mathbf{A} \times (\mathbf{B} \times \mathbf{C})$, which contains two cross products, evaluates, as shown in Eq. (3.18), to an expression containing only legitimate scalars and (polar) vectors. It is therefore proper to identify $\mathbf{A} \times (\mathbf{B} \times \mathbf{C})$ as a vector. These cases illustrate the general principle that a product with an odd number of pseudo quantities is "pseudo," while those with even numbers of pseudo quantities are not.

Successive Operations

One can carry out a succession of coordinate rotations and/or reflections by applying the relevant orthogonal transformations. In fact, we already did this in our introductory discussion for $\mathbb{R}^2$ where we applied a rotation and then its inverse. In general, if R and R' refer to such operations, the application to $\mathbf{A}$ of R followed by the application of R' corresponds to

$$\mathbf{A}' = \mathsf{S}(R')\mathsf{S}(R)\mathbf{A}, \tag{3.31}$$

and the overall result of the two transformations can be identified as a single transformation whose matrix $\mathsf{S}(R'R)$ is the matrix product $\mathsf{S}(R')\mathsf{S}(R)$.

---

[3]The big exception to this is in beta-decay weak interactions. Here the universe distinguishes between right- and left-handed systems, and we add polar and axial vector interactions.

Two points should be noted:

1. The operations take place in right-to-left order: The rightmost operator is the one applied to the original **A**; that to its left then applies to the result of the first operation, etc.
2. The combined operation $R'R$ is a transformation between two orthogonal coordinate systems and therefore can be described by an orthogonal matrix: The product of two orthogonal matrices is orthogonal.

Exercises

3.3.1   A rotation $\varphi_1 + \varphi_2$ about the z-axis is carried out as two successive rotations φ_1 and φ_2, each about the z-axis. Use the matrix representation of the rotations to derive the trigonometric identities

$$\cos(\varphi_1 + \varphi_2) = \cos\varphi_1 \cos\varphi_2 - \sin\varphi_1 \sin\varphi_2,$$

$$\sin(\varphi_1 + \varphi_2) = \sin\varphi_1 \cos\varphi_2 + \cos\varphi_1 \sin\varphi_2.$$

3.3.2   A corner reflector is formed by three mutually perpendicular reflecting surfaces. Show that a ray of light incident upon the corner reflector (striking all three surfaces) is reflected back along a line parallel to the line of incidence.

Hint. Consider the effect of a reflection on the components of a vector describing the direction of the light ray.

3.3.3   Let **x** and **y** be column vectors. Under an orthogonal transformation S, they become $\mathbf{x}' = \mathbf{Sx}$ and $\mathbf{y}' = \mathbf{Sy}$. Show that $(\mathbf{x}')^T \mathbf{y}' = \mathbf{x}^T \mathbf{y}$, a result equivalent to the invariance of the dot product under a rotational transformation.

3.3.4   Given the orthogonal transformation matrix S and vectors **a** and **b**,

$$S = \begin{pmatrix} 0.80 & 0.60 & 0.00 \\ -0.48 & 0.64 & 0.60 \\ 0.36 & -0.48 & 0.80 \end{pmatrix}, \quad \mathbf{a} = \begin{pmatrix} 1 \\ 0 \\ 1 \end{pmatrix}, \quad \mathbf{b} = \begin{pmatrix} 0 \\ 2 \\ -1 \end{pmatrix},$$

(a) Calculate det(S).

(b) Verify that $\mathbf{a} \cdot \mathbf{b}$ is invariant under application of S to **a** and **b**.

(c) Determine what happens to $\mathbf{a} \times \mathbf{b}$ under application of S to **a** and **b**. Is this what is expected?

3.3.5   Using **a** and **b** as defined in Exercise 3.3.4, but with

$$S = \begin{pmatrix} 0.60 & 0.00 & 0.80 \\ -0.64 & -0.60 & 0.48 \\ -0.48 & 0.80 & 0.36 \end{pmatrix} \quad \text{and} \quad \mathbf{c} = \begin{pmatrix} 2 \\ 1 \\ 3 \end{pmatrix},$$

(a) Calculate det(S).

Apply S to **a**, **b**, and **c**, and determine what happens to

(b) $\mathbf{a} \times \mathbf{b}$,

(c) $(\mathbf{a} \times \mathbf{b}) \cdot \mathbf{c}$,

(d) $\mathbf{a} \times (\mathbf{b} \times \mathbf{c})$.

(e) Classify the expressions in (b) through (d) as scalar, vector, pseudovector, or pseudoscalar.

3.4 ROTATIONS IN $\mathbb{R}^3$

Because of its practical importance, we discuss now in some detail the treatment of rotations in $\mathbb{R}^3$. An obvious starting point, based on our experience in $\mathbb{R}^2$, would be to write the 3×3 matrix S of Eq. (3.28), with rows that describe the orientations of a rotated (primed) set of unit vectors in terms of the original (unprimed) unit vectors:

$$\mathsf{S} = \begin{pmatrix} \hat{\mathbf{e}}_1' \cdot \hat{\mathbf{e}}_1 & \hat{\mathbf{e}}_1' \cdot \hat{\mathbf{e}}_2 & \hat{\mathbf{e}}_1' \cdot \hat{\mathbf{e}}_3 \\ \hat{\mathbf{e}}_2' \cdot \hat{\mathbf{e}}_1 & \hat{\mathbf{e}}_2' \cdot \hat{\mathbf{e}}_2 & \hat{\mathbf{e}}_2' \cdot \hat{\mathbf{e}}_3 \\ \hat{\mathbf{e}}_3' \cdot \hat{\mathbf{e}}_1 & \hat{\mathbf{e}}_3' \cdot \hat{\mathbf{e}}_2 & \hat{\mathbf{e}}_3' \cdot \hat{\mathbf{e}}_3 \end{pmatrix} \tag{3.32}$$

We have switched the coordinate labels from x, y, z to $1, 2, 3$ for convenience in some of the formulas that use Eq. (3.32). It is useful to make one observation about the elements of S, namely $s_{\mu\nu} = \hat{\mathbf{e}}_\mu' \cdot \hat{\mathbf{e}}_\nu$. This dot product is the projection of $\hat{\mathbf{e}}_\mu'$ onto the $\hat{\mathbf{e}}_\nu$ direction, and is therefore the change in x_ν that is produced by a unit change in x_μ'. Since the relation between the coordinates is linear, we can identify $\hat{\mathbf{e}}_\mu' \cdot \hat{\mathbf{e}}_\nu$ as $\partial x_\nu / \partial x_\mu'$, so our transformation matrix S can be written in the alternate form

$$\mathsf{S} = \begin{pmatrix} \partial x_1/\partial x_1' & \partial x_2/\partial x_1' & \partial x_3/\partial x_1' \\ \partial x_1/\partial x_2' & \partial x_2/\partial x_2' & \partial x_3/\partial x_2' \\ \partial x_1/\partial x_3' & \partial x_2/\partial x_3' & \partial x_3/\partial x_3' \end{pmatrix}. \tag{3.33}$$

The argument we made to evaluate $\hat{\mathbf{e}}_\mu' \cdot \hat{\mathbf{e}}_\nu$ could as easily have been made with the roles of the two unit vectors reversed, yielding instead of $\partial x_\nu / \partial x_\mu'$ the derivative $\partial x_\mu' / \partial x_\nu$. We then have what at first may seem to be a surprising result:

$$\frac{\partial x_\nu}{\partial x_\mu'} = \frac{\partial x_\mu'}{\partial x_\nu}. \tag{3.34}$$

A superficial look at this equation suggests that its two sides would be reciprocals. The problem is that we have not been notationally careful enough to avoid ambiguity: the derivative on the left-hand side is to be taken with the other x' coordinates fixed, while that on the right-hand side is with the other unprimed coordinates fixed. In fact, the equality in Eq. (3.34) is needed to make S an orthogonal matrix.

We note in passing that the observation that the coordinates are related linearly restricts the current discussion to Cartesian coordinate systems. Curvilinear coordinates are treated later.

Neither Eq. (3.32) nor Eq. (3.33) makes obvious the possibility of relations among the elements of S. In $\mathbb{R}^2$, we found that all the elements of S depended on a single variable, the rotation angle. In $\mathbb{R}^3$, the number of independent variables needed to specify a general rotation is three: Two parameters (usually angles) are needed to specify the direction of $\hat{\mathbf{e}}_3'$; then one angle is needed to specify the direction of $\hat{\mathbf{e}}_1'$ in the plane perpendicular to $\hat{\mathbf{e}}_3'$;

at this point the orientation of $\hat{\mathbf{e}}_2'$ is completely determined. Therefore, of the nine elements of S, only three are in fact independent. The usual parameters used to specify $\mathbb{R}^3$ rotations are the **Euler angles**.[4] It is useful to have S given explicitly in terms of them, as the Lagrangian formulation of mechanics requires the use of a set of *independent* variables.

The Euler angles describe an $\mathbb{R}^3$ rotation in three steps, the first two of which have the effect of fixing the orientation of the new $\hat{\mathbf{e}}_3$ axis (the polar direction in spherical coordinates), while the third Euler angle indicates the amount of subsequent rotation about that axis. The first two steps do more than identify a new polar direction; they describe rotations that cause the realignment. As a result, we can obtain the matrix representations of these (and the third rotation), and apply them sequentially (i.e., as a matrix product) to obtain the overall effect of the rotation.

The three steps describing rotation of the coordinate axes are the following (also illustrated in Fig. 3.7):

1. The coordinates are rotated about the $\hat{\mathbf{e}}_3$ axis counterclockwise (as viewed from positive $\hat{\mathbf{e}}_3$) through an angle α in the range $0 \leq \alpha < 2\pi$, into new axes denoted $\hat{\mathbf{e}}_1', \hat{\mathbf{e}}_2', \hat{\mathbf{e}}_3'$. (The polar direction is not changed; the $\hat{\mathbf{e}}_3$ and $\hat{\mathbf{e}}_3'$ axes coincide.)

2. The coordinates are rotated about the $\hat{\mathbf{e}}_2'$ axis counterclockwise (as viewed from positive $\hat{\mathbf{e}}_2'$) through an angle β in the range $0 \leq \beta \leq \pi$, into new axes denoted $\hat{\mathbf{e}}_1'', \hat{\mathbf{e}}_2'', \hat{\mathbf{e}}_3''$. (This tilts the polar direction toward the $\hat{\mathbf{e}}_1'$ direction, but leaves $\hat{\mathbf{e}}_2'$ unchanged.)

3. The coordinates are now rotated about the $\hat{\mathbf{e}}_3''$ axis counterclockwise (as viewed from positive $\hat{\mathbf{e}}_3''$) through an angle γ in the range $0 \leq \gamma < 2\pi$, into the final axes, denoted $\hat{\mathbf{e}}_1''', \hat{\mathbf{e}}_2''', \hat{\mathbf{e}}_3'''$. (This rotation leaves the polar direction, $\hat{\mathbf{e}}_3''$, unchanged.)

In terms of the usual spherical polar coordinates (r, θ, φ), the final polar axis is at the orientation $\theta = \beta$, $\varphi = \alpha$. The final orientations of the other axes depend on all three Euler angles.

We now need the transformation matrices. The first rotation causes $\hat{\mathbf{e}}_1'$ and $\hat{\mathbf{e}}_2'$ to remain in the xy-plane, and has in its first two rows and columns exactly the same form

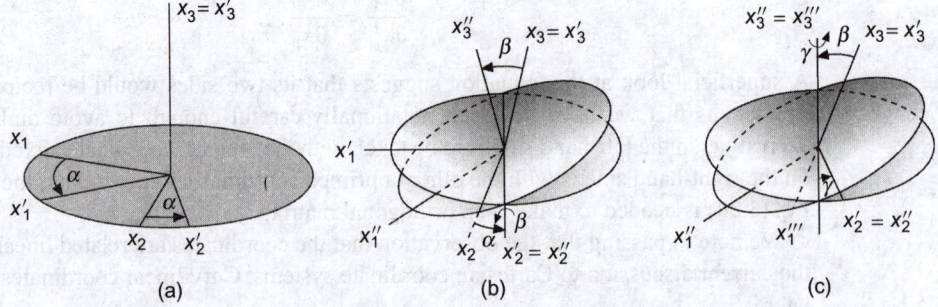

FIGURE 3.7   Euler angle rotations: (a) about $\hat{\mathbf{e}}_3$ through angle α; (b) about $\hat{\mathbf{e}}_2'$ through angle β; (c) about $\hat{\mathbf{e}}_3''$ through angle γ.

[4]There are almost as many definitions of the Euler angles as there are authors. Here we follow the choice generally made by workers in the area of group theory and the quantum theory of angular momentum.

as S in Eq. (3.25):

$$S_1(\alpha) = \begin{pmatrix} \cos\alpha & \sin\alpha & 0 \\ -\sin\alpha & \cos\alpha & 0 \\ 0 & 0 & 1 \end{pmatrix}. \tag{3.35}$$

The third row and column of S_1 indicate that this rotation leaves unchanged the $\hat{\mathbf{e}}_3$ component of any vector on which it operates. The second rotation (applied to the coordinate system as it exists **after** the first rotation) is in the $\hat{\mathbf{e}}_3'\hat{\mathbf{e}}_1'$ plane; note that the signs of $\sin\beta$ have to be consistent with a cyclic permutation of the axis numbering:

$$S_2(\beta) = \begin{pmatrix} \cos\beta & 0 & -\sin\beta \\ 0 & 1 & 0 \\ \sin\beta & 0 & \cos\beta \end{pmatrix}.$$

The third rotation is like the first, but with rotation amount γ:

$$S_3(\gamma) = \begin{pmatrix} \cos\gamma & \sin\gamma & 0 \\ -\sin\gamma & \cos\gamma & 0 \\ 0 & 0 & 1 \end{pmatrix}.$$

The total rotation is described by the triple matrix product

$$S(\alpha, \beta, \gamma) = S_3(\gamma)S_2(\beta)S_1(\alpha). \tag{3.36}$$

Note the order: $S_1(\alpha)$ operates first, then $S_2(\beta)$, and finally $S_3(\gamma)$. Direct multiplication gives

$$S(\alpha, \beta, \gamma) =$$

$$\begin{pmatrix} \cos\gamma\cos\beta\cos\alpha - \sin\gamma\sin\alpha & \cos\gamma\cos\beta\sin\alpha + \sin\gamma\cos\alpha & -\cos\gamma\sin\beta \\ -\sin\gamma\cos\beta\cos\alpha - \cos\gamma\sin\alpha & -\sin\gamma\cos\beta\sin\alpha + \cos\gamma\cos\alpha & \sin\gamma\sin\beta \\ \sin\beta\cos\alpha & \sin\beta\sin\alpha & \cos\beta \end{pmatrix}.$$

$$\tag{3.37}$$

In case they are wanted, note that the elements s_{ij} in Eq. (3.37) give the explicit forms of the dot products $\hat{\mathbf{e}}_i''' \cdot \hat{\mathbf{e}}_j$ (and therefore also the partial derivatives $\partial x_i/\partial x_j'''$).

Note that each of S_1, S_2, and S_3 are orthogonal, with determinant $+1$, so that the overall S will also be orthogonal with determinant $+1$.

Example 3.4.1   AN $\mathbb{R}^3$ ROTATION

Consider a vector originally with components $(2, -1, 3)$. We want its components in a coordinate system reached by Euler angle rotations $\alpha = \beta = \gamma = \pi/2$. Evaluating $S(\alpha, \beta, \gamma)$:

$$S(\alpha, \beta, \gamma) = \begin{pmatrix} -1 & 0 & 0 \\ 0 & 0 & 1 \\ 0 & 1 & 0 \end{pmatrix}.$$

A partial check on this value of S is obtained by verifying that $\det(S) = +1$.

Then, in the new coordinates, our vector has components

$$\begin{pmatrix} -1 & 0 & 0 \\ 0 & 0 & 1 \\ 0 & 1 & 0 \end{pmatrix} \begin{pmatrix} 2 \\ -1 \\ 3 \end{pmatrix} = \begin{pmatrix} -2 \\ 3 \\ -1 \end{pmatrix}.$$

The reader should check this result by visualizing the rotations involved. ∎

Exercises

3.4.1   Another set of Euler rotations in common use is

(1)   a rotation about the x_3-axis through an angle φ, counterclockwise,
(2)   a rotation about the x_1'-axis through an angle θ, counterclockwise,
(3)   a rotation about the x_3''-axis through an angle ψ, counterclockwise.

If

$$\begin{array}{lll} \alpha = \varphi - \pi/2 & & \varphi = \alpha + \pi/2 \\ \beta = \theta & \text{or} & \theta = \beta \\ \gamma = \psi + \pi/2 & & \psi = \gamma - \pi/2, \end{array}$$

show that the final systems are identical.

3.4.2   Suppose the Earth is moved (rotated) so that the north pole goes to 30° north, 20° west (original latitude and longitude system) and the 10° west meridian points due south (also in the original system).

(a)   What are the Euler angles describing this rotation?
(b)   Find the corresponding direction cosines.

$$ANS. \quad (b) \quad S = \begin{pmatrix} 0.9551 & -0.2552 & -0.1504 \\ 0.0052 & 0.5221 & -0.8529 \\ 0.2962 & 0.8138 & 0.5000 \end{pmatrix}$$

3.4.3   Verify that the Euler angle rotation matrix, Eq. (3.37), is invariant under the transformation

$$\alpha \to \alpha + \pi, \quad \beta \to -\beta, \quad \gamma \to \gamma - \pi.$$

3.4.4   Show that the Euler angle rotation matrix $S(\alpha, \beta, \gamma)$ satisfies the following relations:

(a) $S^{-1}(\alpha, \beta, \gamma) = \tilde{S}(\alpha, \beta, \gamma)$,
(b) $S^{-1}(\alpha, \beta, \gamma) = S(-\gamma, -\beta, -\alpha)$.

3.4.5   The coordinate system (x, y, z) is rotated through an angle Φ counterclockwise about an axis defined by the unit vector $\hat{\mathbf{n}}$ into system (x', y', z'). In terms of the new coordinates the radius vector becomes

$$\mathbf{r}' = \mathbf{r}\cos\Phi + \mathbf{r}\times\mathbf{n}\sin\Phi + \hat{\mathbf{n}}(\hat{\mathbf{n}}\cdot\mathbf{r})(1-\cos\Phi).$$

(a)   Derive this expression from geometric considerations.

(b)   Show that it reduces as expected for $\hat{\mathbf{n}} = \hat{\mathbf{e}}_z$. The answer, in matrix form, appears in Eq. (3.35).

(c)   Verify that $r'^2 = r^2$.

3.5   DIFFERENTIAL VECTOR OPERATORS

We move now to the important situation in which a vector is associated with each point in space, and therefore has a value (its set of components) that depends on the coordinates specifying its position. A typical example in physics is the electric field $\mathbf{E}(x, y, z)$, which describes the direction and magnitude of the electric force if a unit "test charge" was placed at x, y, z. The term **field** refers to a quantity that has values at all points of a region; if the quantity is a vector, its distribution is described as a **vector field**. While we already have a standard name for a simple algebraic quantity which is assigned a value at all points of a spatial region (it is called a **function**), in physics contexts it may also be referred to as a **scalar field**.

Physicists need to be able to characterize the rate at which the values of vectors (and also scalars) change with position, and this is most effectively done by introducing differential vector operator concepts. It turns out that there are a large number of relations between these differential operators, and it is our current objective to identify such relations and learn how to use them.

Gradient, ∇

Our first differential operator is that known as the **gradient**, which characterizes the change of a scalar quantity, here φ, with position. Working in $\mathbb{R}^3$, and labeling the coordinates x_1, x_2, x_3, we write $\varphi(\mathbf{r})$ as the value of φ at the point $\mathbf{r} = x_1\hat{\mathbf{e}}_1 + x_2\hat{\mathbf{e}}_2 + x_3\hat{\mathbf{e}}_3$, and consider the effect of small changes dx_1, dx_2, dx_3, respectively, in x_1, x_2, and x_3. This situation corresponds to that discussed in Section 1.9, where we introduced **partial derivatives** to describe how a function of several variables (there x, y, and z) changes its value when these variables are changed by respective amounts dx, dy, and dz. The equation governing this process is Eq. (1.141).

To first order in the differentials dx_i, φ in our present problem changes by an amount

$$d\varphi = \left(\frac{\partial\varphi}{\partial x_1}\right)dx_1 + \left(\frac{\partial\varphi}{\partial x_2}\right)dx_2 + \left(\frac{\partial\varphi}{\partial x_3}\right)dx_3, \tag{3.38}$$

which is of the form corresponding to the dot product of

$$\nabla\varphi = \begin{pmatrix} \partial\varphi/\partial x_1 \\ \partial\varphi/\partial x_2 \\ \partial\varphi/\partial x_3 \end{pmatrix} \quad \text{and} \quad d\mathbf{r} = \begin{pmatrix} dx_1 \\ dx_2 \\ dx_3 \end{pmatrix}.$$

These quantities can also be written

$$\nabla \varphi = \left(\frac{\partial \varphi}{\partial x_1}\right)\hat{\mathbf{e}}_1 + \left(\frac{\partial \varphi}{\partial x_2}\right)\hat{\mathbf{e}}_2 + \left(\frac{\partial \varphi}{\partial x_3}\right)\hat{\mathbf{e}}_3, \tag{3.39}$$

$$d\mathbf{r} = dx_1\hat{\mathbf{e}}_1 + dx_2\hat{\mathbf{e}}_2 + dx_3\hat{\mathbf{e}}_3, \tag{3.40}$$

in terms of which we have

$$d\varphi = (\nabla\varphi)\cdot d\mathbf{r}. \tag{3.41}$$

We have given the 3×1 matrix of derivatives the name $\nabla\varphi$ (often referred to in speech as "del phi" or "grad phi"); we give the differential of position its customary name $d\mathbf{r}$.

The notation of Eqs. (3.39) and (3.41) is really only appropriate if $\nabla\varphi$ is actually a vector, because the utility of the present approach depends on our ability to use it in coordinate systems of arbitrary orientation. To prove that $\nabla\varphi$ is a vector, we must show that it transforms under rotation of the coordinate system according to

$$(\nabla\varphi)' = \mathsf{S}(\nabla\varphi). \tag{3.42}$$

Taking S in the form given in Eq. (3.33), we examine $\mathsf{S}(\nabla\varphi)$. We have

$$\mathsf{S}(\nabla\varphi) = \begin{pmatrix} \partial x_1/\partial x_1' & \partial x_2/\partial x_1' & \partial x_3/\partial x_1' \\ \partial x_1/\partial x_2' & \partial x_2/\partial x_2' & \partial x_3/\partial x_2' \\ \partial x_1/\partial x_3' & \partial x_2/\partial x_3' & \partial x_3/\partial x_3' \end{pmatrix} \begin{pmatrix} \partial\varphi/\partial x_1 \\ \partial\varphi/\partial x_2 \\ \partial\varphi/\partial x_3 \end{pmatrix}$$

$$= \begin{pmatrix} \displaystyle\sum_{\nu=1}^{3} \frac{\partial x_\nu}{\partial x_1'}\frac{\partial\varphi}{\partial x_\nu} \\ \displaystyle\sum_{\nu=1}^{3} \frac{\partial x_\nu}{\partial x_2'}\frac{\partial\varphi}{\partial x_\nu} \\ \displaystyle\sum_{\nu=1}^{3} \frac{\partial x_\nu}{\partial x_3'}\frac{\partial\varphi}{\partial x_\nu} \end{pmatrix}. \tag{3.43}$$

Each of the elements in the final expression in Eq. (3.43) is a chain-rule expression for $\partial\varphi/\partial x_\mu'$, $\mu = 1, 2, 3$, showing that the transformation did produce $(\nabla\varphi)'$, the representation of $\nabla\varphi$ in the rotated coordinates.

Having now established the legitimacy of the form $\nabla\varphi$, we proceed to give ∇ a life of its own. We therefore define (calling the coordinates x, y, z)

$$\nabla = \hat{\mathbf{e}}_x\frac{\partial}{\partial x} + \hat{\mathbf{e}}_y\frac{\partial}{\partial y} + \hat{\mathbf{e}}_z\frac{\partial}{\partial z}. \tag{3.44}$$

We note that ∇ is a **vector differential operator**, capable of operating on a scalar (such as φ) to produce a vector as the result of the operation. Because a differential operator only operates on what is to its right, we have to be careful to maintain the correct order in expressions involving ∇, and we have to use parentheses when necessary to avoid ambiguity as to what is to be differentiated.

The gradient of a scalar is extremely important in physics and engineering, as it expresses the relation between a force field $\mathbf{F}(\mathbf{r})$ experienced by an object at $\mathbf{r}$ and the related potential $V(\mathbf{r})$,

$$\mathbf{F}(\mathbf{r}) = -\nabla V(\mathbf{r}). \tag{3.45}$$

The minus sign in Eq. (3.45) is important; it causes the force exerted by the field to be in a direction that lowers the potential. We consider later (in Section 3.9) the conditions that must be satisfied if a potential corresponding to a given force can exit.

The gradient has a simple geometric interpretation. From Eq. (3.41), we see that, if $d\mathbf{r}$ is constrained to have a fixed magnitude, the direction of $d\mathbf{r}$ that maximizes $d\varphi$ will be when $\nabla\varphi$ and $d\mathbf{r}$ are collinear. So, the direction of most rapid increase in φ is the gradient direction, and the magnitude of the gradient is the directional derivative of φ in that direction. We now see that $-\nabla V$, in Eq. (3.45), is the direction of most rapid *decrease* in V, and is the direction of the force associated with the potential V.

Example 3.5.1   GRADIENT OF r^n

As a first step toward computation of ∇r^n, let's look at the even simpler ∇r. We begin by writing $r = (x^2 + y^2 + z^2)^{1/2}$, from which we get

$$\frac{\partial r}{\partial x} = \frac{x}{(x^2 + y^2 + z^2)^{1/2}} = \frac{x}{r}, \quad \frac{\partial r}{\partial y} = \frac{y}{r}, \quad \frac{\partial r}{\partial z} = \frac{z}{r}. \tag{3.46}$$

From these formulas we construct

$$\nabla r = \frac{x}{r}\hat{\mathbf{e}}_x + \frac{y}{r}\hat{\mathbf{e}}_y + \frac{z}{r}\hat{\mathbf{e}}_z = \frac{1}{r}(x\hat{\mathbf{e}}_x + y\hat{\mathbf{e}}_y + z\hat{\mathbf{e}}_z) = \frac{\mathbf{r}}{r}. \tag{3.47}$$

The result is a unit vector in the direction of $\mathbf{r}$, denoted $\hat{\mathbf{r}}$. For future reference, we note that

$$\hat{\mathbf{r}} = \frac{x}{r}\hat{\mathbf{e}}_x + \frac{y}{r}\hat{\mathbf{e}}_y + \frac{z}{r}\hat{\mathbf{e}}_z \tag{3.48}$$

and that Eq. (3.47) takes the form

$$\nabla r = \hat{\mathbf{r}}. \tag{3.49}$$

The geometry of $\mathbf{r}$ and $\hat{\mathbf{r}}$ is illustrated in Fig. 3.8.

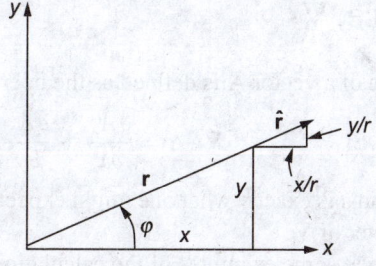

FIGURE 3.8   Unit vector $\hat{\mathbf{r}}$ (in xy-plane).

Continuing now to ∇r^n, we have

$$\frac{\partial r^n}{\partial x} = nr^{n-1}\frac{\partial r}{\partial x},$$

with corresponding results for the y and z derivatives. We get

$$\nabla r^n = nr^{n-1}\nabla r = nr^{n-1}\hat{\mathbf{r}}. \tag{3.50}$$

■

Example 3.5.2   COULOMB'S LAW

In electrostatics, it is well known that a point charge produces a potential proportional to $1/r$, where r is the distance from the charge. To check that this is consistent with the Coulomb force law, we compute

$$\mathbf{F} = -\nabla\left(\frac{1}{r}\right).$$

This is a case of Eq. (3.50) with $n = -1$, and we get the expected result

$$\mathbf{F} = \frac{1}{r^2}\hat{\mathbf{r}}.$$

■

Example 3.5.3   GENERAL RADIAL POTENTIAL

Another situation of frequent occurrence is that the potential may be a function only of the radial distance from the origin, i.e., $\varphi = f(r)$. We then calculate

$$\frac{\partial \varphi}{\partial x} = \frac{df(r)}{dr}\frac{\partial r}{\partial x}, \quad \text{etc.,}$$

which leads, invoking Eq. (3.49), to

$$\nabla\varphi = \frac{df(r)}{dr}\nabla\mathbf{r} = \frac{df(r)}{dr}\hat{\mathbf{r}}. \tag{3.51}$$

This result is in accord with intuition; the direction of maximum increase in φ must be radial, and numerically equal to $d\varphi/dr$.

■

Divergence, $\nabla\cdot$

The **divergence** of a vector $\mathbf{A}$ is defined as the operation

$$\nabla\cdot\mathbf{A} = \frac{\partial A_x}{\partial x} + \frac{\partial A_y}{\partial y} + \frac{\partial A_z}{\partial z}. \tag{3.52}$$

The above formula is exactly what one might expect given both the vector and differential-operator character of ∇.

After looking at some examples of the calculation of the divergence, we will discuss its physical significance.

Example 3.5.4   DIVERGENCE OF COORDINATE VECTOR

Calculate $\nabla \cdot \mathbf{r}$:

$$\nabla \cdot \mathbf{r} = \left(\hat{\mathbf{e}}_x \frac{\partial}{\partial x} + \hat{\mathbf{e}}_y \frac{\partial}{\partial y} + \hat{\mathbf{e}}_z \frac{\partial}{\partial z} \right) \cdot \left(\hat{\mathbf{e}}_x x + \hat{\mathbf{e}}_y y + \hat{\mathbf{e}}_z z \right)$$

$$= \frac{\partial x}{\partial x} + \frac{\partial y}{\partial y} + \frac{\partial z}{\partial z},$$

which reduces to $\nabla \cdot \mathbf{r} = 3$. ∎

Example 3.5.5   DIVERGENCE OF CENTRAL FORCE FIELD

Consider next $\nabla \cdot f(r)\hat{\mathbf{r}}$. Using Eq. (3.48), we write

$$\nabla \cdot f(r)\hat{\mathbf{r}} = \left(\hat{\mathbf{e}}_x \frac{\partial}{\partial x} + \hat{\mathbf{e}}_y \frac{\partial}{\partial y} + \hat{\mathbf{e}}_z \frac{\partial}{\partial z} \right) \cdot \left(\frac{xf(r)}{r} \hat{\mathbf{e}}_x + \frac{yf(r)}{r} \hat{\mathbf{e}}_y + \frac{zf(r)}{r} \hat{\mathbf{e}}_z \right).$$

$$= \frac{\partial}{\partial x} \left(\frac{xf(r)}{r} \right) + \frac{\partial}{\partial y} \left(\frac{yf(r)}{r} \right) + \frac{\partial}{\partial z} \left(\frac{zf(r)}{r} \right).$$

Using

$$\frac{\partial}{\partial x} \left(\frac{xf(r)}{r} \right) = \frac{f(r)}{r} - \frac{xf(r)}{r^2} \frac{\partial r}{\partial x} + \frac{x}{r} \frac{df(r)}{dr} \frac{\partial r}{\partial x} = f(r) \left[\frac{1}{r} - \frac{x^2}{r^3} \right] + \frac{x^2}{r^2} \frac{df(r)}{dr}$$

and corresponding formulas for the y and z derivatives, we obtain after simplification

$$\nabla \cdot f(r)\hat{\mathbf{r}} = 2\frac{f(r)}{r} + \frac{df(r)}{dr}. \tag{3.53}$$

In the special case $f(r) = r^n$, Eq. (3.53) reduces to

$$\nabla \cdot r^n \hat{\mathbf{r}} = (n+2)r^{n-1}. \tag{3.54}$$

For $n = 1$, this reduces to the result of Example 3.5.4. For $n = -2$, corresponding to the Coulomb field, the divergence vanishes, except at $r = 0$, where the differentiations we performed are not defined. ∎

If a vector field represents the flow of some quantity that is distributed in space, its divergence provides information as to the accumulation or depletion of that quantity at the point at which the divergence is evaluated. To gain a clearer picture of the concept, let us suppose that a vector field $\mathbf{v}(\mathbf{r})$ represents the velocity of a fluid[5] at the spatial points $\mathbf{r}$, and that $\rho(\mathbf{r})$ represents the fluid density at $\mathbf{r}$ at a given time t. Then the direction and magnitude of the flow rate at any point will be given by the product $\rho(\mathbf{r})\mathbf{v}(\mathbf{r})$.

Our objective is to calculate the net rate of change of the fluid density in a volume element at the point $\mathbf{r}$. To do so, we set up a parallelepiped of dimensions dx, dy, dz centered at $\mathbf{r}$ and with sides parallel to the xy, xz, and yz planes. See Fig. 3.9. To first order (infinitesimal $d\mathbf{r}$ and dt), the density of fluid exiting the parallelepiped per unit time

---

[5] It may be helpful to think of the fluid as a collection of molecules, so the number per unit volume (the density) at any point is affected by the flow in and out of a volume element at the point.

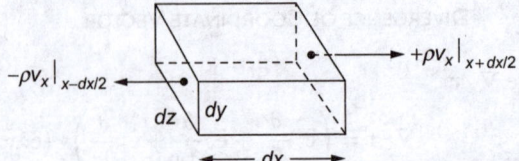

FIGURE 3.9   Outward flow of $\rho\mathbf{v}$ from a volume element in the $\pm x$ directions. The quantities $\pm\rho v_x$ must be multiplied by $dy\,dz$ to represent the total flux through the bounding surfaces at $x \pm dx/2$.

through the yz face located at $x - (dx/2)$ will be

$$\text{Flow out, face at } x - \frac{dx}{2}: \quad -(\rho v_x)\Big|_{(x-dx/2,y,z)} dy\,dz.$$

Note that only the velocity component v_x is relevant here. The other components of $\mathbf{v}$ will not cause motion through a yz face of the parallelepiped. Also, note the following: $dy\,dz$ is the area of the yz face; the average of ρv_x over the face is to first order its value at $(x-dx/2, y, z)$, as indicated, and the amount of fluid leaving per unit time can be identified as that in a column of area $dy\,dz$ and height v_x. Finally, keep in mind that **outward** flow corresponds to that in the $-x$ direction, explaining the presence of the minus sign.

We next compute the outward flow through the yz planar face at $x + dx/2$. The result is

$$\text{Flow out, face at } x + \frac{dx}{2}: \quad +(\rho v_x)\Big|_{(x+dx/2,y,z)} dy\,dz.$$

Combining these, we have for both yz faces

$$\left(-(\rho v_x)\Big|_{x-dx/2} + (\rho v_x)\Big|_{x+dx/2}\right) dy\,dz = \left(\frac{\partial(\rho v_x)}{\partial x}\right) dx\,dy\,dz.$$

Note that in combining terms at $x - dx/2$ and $x + dx/2$ we used the partial derivative notation, because all the quantities appearing here are also functions of y and z. Finally, adding corresponding contributions from the other four faces of the parallelepiped, we reach

$$\begin{aligned}\text{Net flow out} \atop \text{per unit time} &= \left[\frac{\partial}{\partial x}(\rho v_x) + \frac{\partial}{\partial y}(\rho v_y) + \frac{\partial}{\partial z}(\rho v_z)\right] dx\,dy\,dz \\ &= \nabla \cdot (\rho\mathbf{v})\,dx\,dy\,dz. \end{aligned} \tag{3.55}$$

We now see that the name **divergence** is aptly chosen. As shown in Eq. (3.55), the divergence of the vector $\rho\mathbf{v}$ represents the net outflow per unit volume, per unit time. If the physical problem being described is one in which fluid (molecules) are neither created or destroyed, we will also have an **equation of continuity**, of the form

$$\frac{\partial\rho}{\partial t} + \nabla \cdot (\rho\mathbf{v}) = 0. \tag{3.56}$$

This equation quantifies the obvious statement that a net outflow from a volume element results in a smaller density inside the volume.

When a vector quantity is divergenceless (has zero divergence) in a spatial region, we can interpret it as describing a steady-state "fluid-conserving" flow (**flux**) within that region

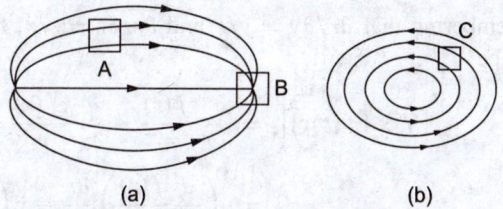

FIGURE 3.10   Flow diagrams: (a) with source and sink; (b) solenoidal. The divergence
vanishes at volume elements A and C, but is negative at B.

(even if the vector field does not represent material that is moving). This is a situation that
arises frequently in physics, applying in general to the magnetic field, and, in charge-free
regions, also to the electric field. If we draw a diagram with lines that follow the flow paths,
the lines (depending on the context) may be called **stream lines** or **lines of force**. Within a
region of zero divergence, these lines must exit any volume element they enter; they cannot
terminate there. However, lines will begin at points of positive divergence (sources) and
end at points where the divergence is negative (sinks). Possible patterns for a vector field
are shown in Fig. 3.10.

If the divergence of a vector field is zero everywhere, its lines of force will consist
entirely of closed loops, as in Fig. 3.10(b); such vector fields are termed **solenoidal**. For
emphasis, we write

$$\nabla \cdot \mathbf{B} = 0 \text{ everywhere } \longrightarrow \quad \mathbf{B} \text{ is solenoidal.} \tag{3.57}$$

Curl, $\nabla \times$

Another possible operation with the vector operator ∇ is to take its cross product with a
vector. Using the established formula for the cross product, and being careful to write the
derivatives to the left of the vector on which they are to act, we obtain

$$\nabla \times \mathbf{V} = \hat{\mathbf{e}}_x \left(\frac{\partial}{\partial y} V_z - \frac{\partial}{\partial z} V_y \right) + \hat{\mathbf{e}}_y \left(\frac{\partial}{\partial z} V_x - \frac{\partial}{\partial x} V_z \right) + \hat{\mathbf{e}}_z \left(\frac{\partial}{\partial x} V_y - \frac{\partial}{\partial y} V_x \right)$$

$$= \begin{vmatrix} \hat{\mathbf{e}}_x & \hat{\mathbf{e}}_y & \hat{\mathbf{e}}_z \\ \partial/\partial x & \partial/\partial y & \partial/\partial z \\ V_x & V_y & V_z \end{vmatrix}. \tag{3.58}$$

This vector operation is called the **curl** of $\mathbf{V}$. Note that when the determinant in Eq. (3.58)
is evaluated, it must be expanded in a way that causes the derivatives in the second row to
be applied to the functions in the third row (and not to anything in the top row); we will
encounter this situation repeatedly, and will identify the evaluation as being **from the top
down**.

Example 3.5.6   CURL OF A CENTRAL FORCE FIELD

Calculate $\nabla \times [f(r)\hat{\mathbf{r}}]$. Writing

$$\hat{\mathbf{r}} = \frac{x}{r} \hat{\mathbf{e}}_x + \frac{y}{r} \hat{\mathbf{e}}_y + \frac{z}{r} \hat{\mathbf{e}}_z,$$

and remembering that $\partial r/\partial y = y/r$ and $\partial r/\partial z = z/r$, the x-component of the result is found to be

$$\left[\nabla \times [f(r)\hat{\mathbf{r}}]\right]_x = \frac{\partial}{\partial y}\frac{zf(r)}{r} - \frac{\partial}{\partial z}\frac{yf(r)}{r}$$

$$= z\left(\frac{d}{dr}\frac{f(r)}{r}\right)\frac{\partial r}{\partial y} - y\left(\frac{d}{dr}\frac{f(r)}{r}\right)\frac{\partial r}{\partial z}$$

$$= z\left(\frac{d}{dr}\frac{f(r)}{r}\right)\frac{y}{r} - y\left(\frac{d}{dr}\frac{f(r)}{r}\right)\frac{z}{r} = 0.$$

By symmetry, the other components are also zero, yielding the final result

$$\nabla \times [f(r)\hat{\mathbf{r}}] = 0. \tag{3.59}$$

∎

Example 3.5.7 A NONZERO CURL

Calculate $\mathbf{F} = \nabla \times (-y\hat{\mathbf{e}}_x + x\hat{\mathbf{e}}_y)$, which is of the form $\nabla \times \mathbf{b}$, where $b_x = -y$, $b_y = x$, $b_z = 0$. We have

$$F_x = \frac{\partial b_z}{\partial y} - \frac{\partial b_y}{\partial z} = 0, \quad F_y = \frac{\partial b_x}{\partial z} - \frac{\partial v_z}{\partial x} = 0, \quad F_z = \frac{\partial b_y}{\partial x} - \frac{\partial b_x}{\partial y} = 2,$$

so $\mathbf{F} = 2\hat{\mathbf{e}}_z$.

∎

The results of these two examples can be better understood from a geometric interpretation of the curl operator. We proceed as follows: Given a vector field $\mathbf{B}$, consider the line integral $\oint \mathbf{B} \cdot d\mathbf{s}$ for a small closed path. The circle through the integral sign is a signal that the path is closed. For simplicity in the computations, we take a rectangular path in the xy-plane, centered at a point (x_0, y_0), of dimensions $\Delta x \times \Delta y$, as shown in Fig. 3.11. We will traverse this path in the counterclockwise direction, passing through the four segments labeled 1 through 4 in the figure. Since everywhere in this discussion $z = 0$, we do not show it explicitly.

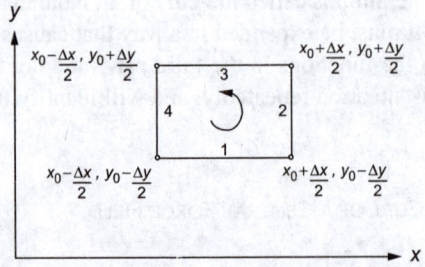

FIGURE 3.11   Path for computing circulation at (x_0, y_0).

Segment 1 of the path contributes to the integral

$$\text{Segment 1} = \int_{x_0-\Delta x/2}^{x_0+\Delta x/2} B_x(x, y_0 - \Delta y/2)\, dx \approx B_x(x_0, y_0 - \Delta y/2)\Delta x,$$

where the approximation, replacing B_x by its value at the middle of the segment, is good to first order. In a similar fashion, we have

$$\text{Segment 2} = \int_{y_0-\Delta y/2}^{y_0+\Delta y/2} B_y(x_0 + \Delta x/2, y)\, dy \approx B_y(x_0 + \Delta x/2, y_0)\Delta y,$$

$$\text{Segment 3} = \int_{x_0+\Delta x/2}^{x_0-\Delta x/2} B_x(x, y_0 + \Delta y/2)\, dx \approx -B_x(x_0, y_0 + \Delta y/2)\Delta x,$$

$$\text{Segment 4} = \int_{y_0+\Delta y/2}^{y_0-\Delta y/2} B_y(x_0 - \Delta x/2, y)\, dy \approx -B_y(x_0 - \Delta x/2, y_0)\Delta y.$$

Note that because the paths of segments 3 and 4 are in the direction of decrease in the value of the integration variable, we obtain minus signs in the contributions of these segments. Combining the contributions of Segments 1 and 3, and those of Segments 2 and 4, we have

$$\text{Segments } 1+3 = \left(B_x(x_0, y_0 - \Delta y/2) - B_x(x_0, y_0 + \Delta y/2)\right)\Delta x \approx -\frac{\partial B_x}{\partial y}\Delta y\Delta x,$$

$$\text{Segments } 2+4 = \left(B_y(x_0 + \Delta x/2, y_0) - B_y(x_0 - \Delta x/2, y_0)\right)\Delta y \approx +\frac{\partial B_y}{\partial x}\Delta x\, \Delta y.$$

Combining these contributions to obtain the value of the entire line integral, we have

$$\oint \mathbf{B} \cdot d\mathbf{s} \approx \left(\frac{\partial B_y}{\partial x} - \frac{\partial B_x}{\partial y}\right)\Delta x\Delta y \approx [\nabla \times \mathbf{B}]_z \Delta x\Delta y. \tag{3.60}$$

The thing to note is that a nonzero closed-loop line integral of $\mathbf{B}$ corresponds to a nonzero value of the component of $\nabla \times \mathbf{B}$ normal to the loop. In the limit of a small loop, the line integral will have a value proportional to the loop area; the value of the line integral per unit area is called the **circulation** (in fluid dynamics, it is also known as the **vorticity**). A nonzero circulation corresponds to a pattern of stream lines that form closed loops. Obviously, to form a closed loop, a stream line must curl; hence the name of the $\nabla \times$ operator.

Returning now to Example 3.5.6, we have a situation in which the lines of force must be entirely radial; there is no possibility to form closed loops. Accordingly, we found this example to have a zero curl. But, looking next at Example 3.5.7, we have a situation in which the stream lines of $-y\hat{\mathbf{e}}_x + x\hat{\mathbf{e}}_y$ form counterclockwise circles about the origin, and the curl is nonzero.

We close the discussion by noting that a vector whose curl is zero everywhere is termed **irrotational**. This property is in a sense the opposite of solenoidal, and deserves a parallel degree of emphasis:

$$\nabla \times \mathbf{B} = 0 \text{ everywhere} \quad \longrightarrow \quad \mathbf{B} \text{ is irrotational.} \tag{3.61}$$

Exercises

3.5.1 If $S(x, y, z) = (x^2 + y^2 + z^2)^{-3/2}$, find

    (a) ∇S at the point $(1, 2, 3)$,
    (b) the magnitude of the gradient of S, $|\nabla S|$ at $(1, 2, 3)$, and
    (c) the direction cosines of ∇S at $(1, 2, 3)$.

3.5.2 (a) Find a unit vector perpendicular to the surface

$$x^2 + y^2 + z^2 = 3$$

        at the point $(1, 1, 1)$.
    (b) Derive the equation of the plane tangent to the surface at $(1, 1, 1)$.

$$\textit{ANS.} \quad \text{(a)} \quad (\hat{\mathbf{e}}_x + \hat{\mathbf{e}}_y + \hat{\mathbf{e}}_z)/\sqrt{3}, \quad \text{(b)} \quad x + y + z = 3.$$

3.5.3 Given a vector $\mathbf{r}_{12} = \hat{\mathbf{e}}_x(x_1 - x_2) + \hat{\mathbf{e}}_y(y_1 - y_2) + \hat{\mathbf{e}}_z(z_1 - z_2)$, show that $\nabla_1 r_{12}$ (gradient with respect to x_1, y_1, and z_1 of the magnitude r_{12}) is a unit vector in the direction of $\mathbf{r}_{12}$.

3.5.4 If a vector function $\mathbf{F}$ depends on both space coordinates (x, y, z) and time t, show that

$$d\mathbf{F} = (d\mathbf{r} \cdot \nabla)\mathbf{F} + \frac{\partial \mathbf{F}}{\partial t}\, dt.$$

3.5.5 Show that $\nabla(uv) = v\nabla u + u\nabla v$, where u and v are differentiable scalar functions of x, y, and z.

3.5.6 For a particle moving in a circular orbit $\mathbf{r} = \hat{\mathbf{e}}_x r \cos \omega t + \hat{\mathbf{e}}_y r \sin \omega t$:

    (a) Evaluate $\mathbf{r} \times \dot{\mathbf{r}}$, with $\dot{\mathbf{r}} = d\mathbf{r}/dt = \mathbf{v}$.
    (b) Show that $\ddot{\mathbf{r}} + \omega^2 \mathbf{r} = 0$ with $\ddot{\mathbf{r}} = d\mathbf{v}/dt$.

Hint. The radius r and the angular velocity ω are constant.

$$\textit{ANS.} \quad \text{(a)} \quad \hat{\mathbf{e}}_z \omega r^2.$$

3.5.7 Vector $\mathbf{A}$ satisfies the vector transformation law, Eq. (3.26). Show directly that its time derivative $d\mathbf{A}/dt$ also satisfies Eq. (3.26) and is therefore a vector.

3.5.8 Show, by differentiating components, that

    (a) $\dfrac{d}{dt}(\mathbf{A} \cdot \mathbf{B}) = \dfrac{d\mathbf{A}}{dt} \cdot \mathbf{B} + \mathbf{A} \cdot \dfrac{d\mathbf{B}}{dt}$,

(b) $\dfrac{d}{dt}(\mathbf{A} \times \mathbf{B}) = \dfrac{d\mathbf{A}}{dt} \times \mathbf{B} + \mathbf{A} \times \dfrac{d\mathbf{B}}{dt}$,

just like the derivative of the product of two algebraic functions.

3.5.9 Prove $\nabla \cdot (\mathbf{a} \times \mathbf{b}) = \mathbf{b} \cdot (\nabla \times \mathbf{a}) - \mathbf{a} \cdot (\nabla \times \mathbf{b})$.

Hint. Treat as a scalar triple product.

3.5.10 Classically, orbital angular momentum is given by $\mathbf{L} = \mathbf{r} \times \mathbf{p}$, where $\mathbf{p}$ is the linear momentum. To go from classical mechanics to quantum mechanics, $\mathbf{p}$ is replaced (in units with $\hbar = 1$) by the operator $-i\nabla$. Show that the quantum mechanical angular momentum operator has Cartesian components

$$L_x = -i\left(y\dfrac{\partial}{\partial z} - z\dfrac{\partial}{\partial y}\right),$$

$$L_y = -i\left(z\dfrac{\partial}{\partial x} - x\dfrac{\partial}{\partial z}\right),$$

$$L_z = -i\left(x\dfrac{\partial}{\partial y} - y\dfrac{\partial}{\partial x}\right).$$

3.5.11 Using the angular momentum operators previously given, show that they satisfy commutation relations of the form

$$[L_x, L_y] \equiv L_x L_y - L_y L_x = i L_z$$

and hence

$$\mathbf{L} \times \mathbf{L} = i\mathbf{L}.$$

These commutation relations will be taken later as the defining relations of an angular momentum operator.

3.5.12 With the aid of the results of Exercise 3.5.11, show that if two vectors $\mathbf{a}$ and $\mathbf{b}$ commute with each other and with $\mathbf{L}$, that is, $[\mathbf{a}, \mathbf{b}] = [\mathbf{a}, \mathbf{L}] = [\mathbf{b}, \mathbf{L}] = 0$, show that

$$[\mathbf{a} \cdot \mathbf{L}, \mathbf{b} \cdot \mathbf{L}] = i(\mathbf{a} \times \mathbf{b}) \cdot \mathbf{L}.$$

3.5.13 Prove that the stream lines of $\mathbf{b}$ in of Example 3.5.7 are counterclockwise circles.

3.6 DIFFERENTIAL VECTOR OPERATORS: FURTHER PROPERTIES

Successive Applications of ∇

Interesting results are obtained when we operate with ∇ on the differential vector operator forms we have already introduced. The possible results include the following:

(a) $\nabla \cdot \nabla \varphi$ (b) $\nabla \times \nabla \varphi$ (c) $\nabla(\nabla \cdot \mathbf{V})$
(d) $\nabla \cdot (\nabla \times \mathbf{V})$ (e) $\nabla \times (\nabla \times \mathbf{V})$.

All five of these expressions involve second derivatives, and all five appear in the second-order differential equations of mathematical physics, particularly in electromagnetic theory.

Laplacian

The first of these expressions, $\nabla \cdot \nabla\varphi$, the divergence of the gradient, is named the Laplacian of φ. We have

$$\nabla \cdot \nabla\varphi = \left(\hat{\mathbf{e}}_x \frac{\partial}{\partial x} + \hat{\mathbf{e}}_y \frac{\partial}{\partial y} + \hat{\mathbf{e}}_z \frac{\partial}{\partial z} \right) \cdot \left(\hat{\mathbf{e}}_x \frac{\partial \varphi}{\partial x} + \hat{\mathbf{e}}_y \frac{\partial \varphi}{\partial y} + \hat{\mathbf{e}}_z \frac{\partial \varphi}{\partial z} \right)$$

$$= \frac{\partial^2 \varphi}{\partial x^2} + \frac{\partial^2 \varphi}{\partial y^2} + \frac{\partial^2 \varphi}{\partial z^2}. \tag{3.62}$$

When φ is the electrostatic potential, we have

$$\nabla \cdot \nabla\varphi = 0 \tag{3.63}$$

at points where the charge density vanishes, which is Laplace's equation of electrostatics. Often the combination $\nabla \cdot \nabla$ is written ∇^2, or Δ in the older European literature.

Example 3.6.1   LAPLACIAN OF A CENTRAL FIELD POTENTIAL

Calculate $\nabla^2\varphi(r)$. Using Eq. (3.51) to evaluate $\nabla\varphi$ and then Eq. (3.53) for the divergence, we have

$$\nabla^2\varphi(r) = \nabla \cdot \nabla\varphi(r) = \nabla \cdot \frac{d\varphi(r)}{dr}\hat{\mathbf{e}}_r = \frac{2}{r}\frac{d\varphi(r)}{dr} + \frac{d^2\varphi(r)}{dr^2}.$$

We get a term in addition to $d^2\varphi/dr^2$ because $\hat{\mathbf{e}}_r$ has a direction that depends on $\mathbf{r}$.

In the special case $\varphi(r) = r^n$, this reduces to

$$\nabla^2 r^n = n(n+1)r^{n-2}.$$

This vanishes for $n = 0$ (φ =constant) and for $n = -1$ (Coulomb potential). For $n = -1$, our derivation fails for $\mathbf{r} = 0$, where the derivatives are undefined.   ∎

Irrotational and Solenoidal Vector Fields

Expression (b), the second of our five forms involving two ∇ operators, may be written as a determinant:

$$\nabla \times \nabla\varphi = \begin{vmatrix} \hat{\mathbf{e}}_x & \hat{\mathbf{e}}_y & \hat{\mathbf{e}}_z \\ \partial/\partial x & \partial/\partial y & \partial/\partial z \\ \partial\varphi/\partial x & \partial\varphi/\partial y & \partial\varphi/\partial z \end{vmatrix} = \begin{vmatrix} \hat{\mathbf{e}}_x & \hat{\mathbf{e}}_y & \hat{\mathbf{e}}_z \\ \partial/\partial x & \partial/\partial y & \partial/\partial z \\ \partial/\partial x & \partial/\partial y & \partial/\partial z \end{vmatrix}\varphi = 0.$$

Because the determinant is to be evaluated from the top down, it is meaningful to move φ outside and to its right, leaving a determinant with two identical rows and yielding the indicated value of zero. We are thereby actually assuming that the order of the partial differentiations can be reversed, which is true so long as these second derivatives of φ are continuous.

Expression (d) is a scalar triple product that may be written

$$\nabla \cdot (\nabla \times \mathbf{V}) = \begin{vmatrix} \partial/\partial x & \partial/\partial y & \partial/\partial z \\ \partial/\partial x & \partial/\partial y & \partial/\partial z \\ V_x & V_y & V_z \end{vmatrix} = 0.$$

This determinant also has two identical rows and yields zero if $\mathbf{V}$ has sufficient continuity.

These two vanishing results tell us that any gradient has a vanishing curl and is therefore **irrotational**, and that any curl has a vanishing divergence, and is therefore **solenoidal**. These properties are of such importance that we set them out here in display form:

$$\nabla \times \nabla \varphi = 0, \quad \text{all } \varphi, \tag{3.64}$$

$$\nabla \cdot (\nabla \times \mathbf{V}) = 0, \quad \text{all } \mathbf{V}. \tag{3.65}$$

Maxwell's Equations

The unification of electric and magnetic phenomena that is encapsulated in Maxwell's equations provides an excellent example of the use of differential vector operators. In SI units, these equations take the form

$$\nabla \cdot \mathbf{B} = 0, \tag{3.66}$$

$$\nabla \cdot \mathbf{E} = \frac{\rho}{\varepsilon_0}, \tag{3.67}$$

$$\nabla \times \mathbf{B} = \varepsilon_0 \mu_0 \frac{\partial \mathbf{E}}{\partial t} + \mu_0 \mathbf{J}, \tag{3.68}$$

$$\nabla \times \mathbf{E} = -\frac{\partial \mathbf{B}}{\partial t}. \tag{3.69}$$

Here $\mathbf{E}$ is the electric field, $\mathbf{B}$ is the magnetic induction field, ρ is the charge density, $\mathbf{J}$ is the current density, ε_0 is the electric permittivity, and μ_0 is the magnetic permeability, so $\varepsilon_0 \mu_0 = 1/c^2$, where c is the velocity of light.

Vector Laplacian

Expressions (c) and (e) in the list at the beginning of this section satisfy the relation

$$\nabla \times (\nabla \times \mathbf{V}) = \nabla(\nabla \cdot \mathbf{V}) - \nabla \cdot \nabla \mathbf{V}. \tag{3.70}$$

The term $\nabla \cdot \nabla \mathbf{V}$, which is called the **vector Laplacian** and sometimes written $\nabla^2 \mathbf{V}$, has prior to this point not been defined; Eq. (3.70) (solved for $\nabla^2 \mathbf{V}$) can be taken to be its definition. In Cartesian coordinates, $\nabla^2 \mathbf{V}$ is a vector whose i component is $\nabla^2 V_i$, and that fact can be confirmed either by direct component expansion or by applying the BAC–CAB rule, Eq. (3.18), with care always to place $\mathbf{V}$ so that the differential operators act on it. While Eq. (3.70) is general, $\nabla^2 \mathbf{V}$ separates into Laplacians for the components of $\mathbf{V}$ only in Cartesian coordinates.

Example 3.6.2 ELECTROMAGNETIC WAVE EQUATION

Even in vacuum, Maxwell's equations can describe electromagnetic waves. To derive an electromagnetic wave equation, we start by taking the time derivative of Eq. (3.68) for the case $\mathbf{J} = 0$, and the curl of Eq. (3.69). We then have

$$\frac{\partial}{\partial t} \nabla \times \mathbf{B} = \epsilon_0 \mu_0 \frac{\partial^2 \mathbf{E}}{\partial t^2},$$

$$\nabla \times (\nabla \times \mathbf{E}) = -\frac{\partial}{\partial t} \nabla \times \mathbf{B} = -\epsilon_0 \mu_0 \frac{\partial^2 \mathbf{E}}{\partial t^2}.$$

We now have an equation that involves only $\mathbf{E}$; it can be brought to a more convenient form by applying Eq. (3.70), dropping the first term on the right of that equation because, in vacuum, $\nabla \cdot \mathbf{E} = 0$. The result is the vector electromagnetic wave equation for $\mathbf{E}$,

$$\nabla^2 \mathbf{E} = \epsilon_0 \mu_0 \frac{\partial^2 \mathbf{E}}{\partial t^2} = \frac{1}{c^2} \frac{\partial^2 \mathbf{E}}{\partial t^2}. \tag{3.71}$$

Equation (3.71) separates into three scalar wave equations, each involving the (scalar) Laplacian. There is a separate equation for each Cartesian component of $\mathbf{E}$. ∎

Miscellaneous Vector Identities

Our introduction of differential vector operators is now formally complete, but we present two further examples to illustrate how the relationships between these operators can be manipulated to obtain useful vector identities.

Example 3.6.3 DIVERGENCE AND CURL OF A PRODUCT

First, simplify $\nabla \cdot (f\mathbf{V})$, where f and $\mathbf{V}$ are, respectively, scalar and vector functions. Working with the components,

$$\nabla \cdot (f\mathbf{V}) = \frac{\partial}{\partial x}(fV_x) + \frac{\partial}{\partial y}(fV_y) + \frac{\partial}{\partial z}(fV_z)$$

$$= \frac{\partial f}{\partial x}V_x + f\frac{\partial V_x}{\partial x} + \frac{\partial f}{\partial y}V_y + f\frac{\partial V_y}{\partial y} + \frac{\partial f}{\partial z}V_z + f\frac{\partial V_z}{\partial z}$$

$$= (\nabla f) \cdot \mathbf{V} + f\nabla \cdot \mathbf{V}. \tag{3.72}$$

Now simplify $\nabla \times (f\mathbf{V})$. Consider the x-component:

$$\frac{\partial}{\partial y}(fV_z) - \frac{\partial}{\partial z}(fV_y) = f\left[\frac{\partial V_z}{\partial y} - \frac{\partial V_y}{\partial z}\right] + \left[\frac{\partial f}{\partial y}V_z - \frac{\partial f}{\partial z}V_y\right].$$

This is the x-component of $f(\nabla \times \mathbf{V}) + (\nabla f) \times \mathbf{V}$, so we have

$$\nabla \times (f\mathbf{V}) = f(\nabla \times \mathbf{V}) + (\nabla f) \times \mathbf{V}. \tag{3.73}$$

∎

Example 3.6.4   GRADIENT OF A DOT PRODUCT

Verify that

$$\nabla(\mathbf{A} \cdot \mathbf{B}) = (\mathbf{B} \cdot \nabla)\mathbf{A} + (\mathbf{A} \cdot \nabla)\mathbf{B} + \mathbf{B} \times (\nabla \times \mathbf{A}) + \mathbf{A} \times (\nabla \times \mathbf{B}). \tag{3.74}$$

This problem is easier to solve if we recognize that $\nabla(\mathbf{A} \cdot \mathbf{B})$ is a type of term that appears in the BAC–CAB expansion of a vector triple product, Eq. (3.18). From that equation, we have

$$\mathbf{A} \times (\nabla \times \mathbf{B}) = \nabla_B(\mathbf{A} \cdot \mathbf{B}) - (\mathbf{A} \cdot \nabla)\mathbf{B},$$

where we placed $\mathbf{B}$ at the end of the final term because ∇ must act on it. We write ∇_B to indicate an operation our notation is not really equipped to handle. In this term, ∇ acts only on $\mathbf{B}$, because $\mathbf{A}$ appeared to its left on the left-hand side of the equation. Interchanging the roles of $\mathbf{A}$ and $\mathbf{B}$, we also have

$$\mathbf{B} \times (\nabla \times \mathbf{A}) = \nabla_A(\mathbf{A} \cdot \mathbf{B}) - (\mathbf{B} \cdot \nabla)\mathbf{A},$$

where ∇_A acts only on $\mathbf{A}$. Adding these two equations together, noting that $\nabla_B + \nabla_A$ is simply an unrestricted ∇, we recover Eq. (3.74). ∎

Exercises

3.6.1   Show that $\mathbf{u} \times \mathbf{v}$ is solenoidal if $\mathbf{u}$ and $\mathbf{v}$ are each irrotational.

3.6.2   If $\mathbf{A}$ is irrotational, show that $\mathbf{A} \times \mathbf{r}$ is solenoidal.

3.6.3   A rigid body is rotating with constant angular velocity $\boldsymbol{\omega}$. Show that the linear velocity $\mathbf{v}$ is solenoidal.

3.6.4   If a vector function $\mathbf{V}(x, y, z)$ is not irrotational, show that if there exists a scalar function $g(x, y, z)$ such that $g\mathbf{V}$ is irrotational, then

$$\mathbf{V} \cdot \nabla \times \mathbf{V} = 0.$$

3.6.5   Verify the vector identity

$$\nabla \times (\mathbf{A} \times \mathbf{B}) = (\mathbf{B} \cdot \nabla)\mathbf{A} - (\mathbf{A} \cdot \nabla)\mathbf{B} - \mathbf{B}(\nabla \cdot \mathbf{A}) + \mathbf{A}(\nabla \cdot \mathbf{B}).$$

3.6.6   As an alternative to the vector identity of Example 3.6.4 show that

$$\nabla(\mathbf{A} \cdot \mathbf{B}) = (\mathbf{A} \times \nabla) \times \mathbf{B} + (\mathbf{B} \times \nabla) \times \mathbf{A} + \mathbf{A}(\nabla \cdot \mathbf{B}) + \mathbf{B}(\nabla \cdot \mathbf{A}).$$

3.6.7   Verify the identity

$$\mathbf{A} \times (\nabla \times \mathbf{A}) = \frac{1}{2}\nabla(A^2) - (\mathbf{A} \cdot \nabla)\mathbf{A}.$$

3.6.8   If $\mathbf{A}$ and $\mathbf{B}$ are constant vectors, show that

$$\nabla(\mathbf{A} \cdot \mathbf{B} \times \mathbf{r}) = \mathbf{A} \times \mathbf{B}.$$

3.6.9   Verify Eq. (3.70),

$$\nabla \times (\nabla \times \mathbf{V}) = \nabla(\nabla \cdot \mathbf{V}) - \nabla \cdot \nabla \mathbf{V},$$

by direct expansion in Cartesian coordinates.

3.6.10   Prove that $\nabla \times (\varphi \nabla \varphi) = 0$.

3.6.11   You are given that the curl of $\mathbf{F}$ equals the curl of $\mathbf{G}$. Show that $\mathbf{F}$ and $\mathbf{G}$ may differ by
(a)   a constant and   (b)   a gradient of a scalar function.

3.6.12   The Navier-Stokes equation of hydrodynamics contains a nonlinear term of the form $(\mathbf{v} \cdot \nabla)\mathbf{v}$. Show that the curl of this term may be written as $-\nabla \times [\mathbf{v} \times (\nabla \times \mathbf{v})]$.

3.6.13   Prove that $(\nabla u) \times (\nabla v)$ is solenoidal, where u and v are differentiable scalar functions.

3.6.14   The function φ is a scalar satisfying Laplace's equation, $\nabla^2\varphi = 0$. Show that $\nabla\varphi$ is **both** solenoidal and irrotational.

3.6.15   Show that any solution of the equation

$$\nabla \times (\nabla \times \mathbf{A}) - k^2\mathbf{A} = 0$$

automatically satisfies the vector Helmholtz equation

$$\nabla^2\mathbf{A} + k^2\mathbf{A} = 0$$

and the solenoidal condition

$$\nabla \cdot \mathbf{A} = 0.$$

Hint. Let $\nabla \cdot$ operate on the first equation.

3.6.16   The theory of heat conduction leads to an equation

$$\nabla^2\Psi = k\,|\nabla\Phi|^2,$$

where Φ is a potential satisfying Laplace's equation: $\nabla^2\Phi = 0$. Show that a solution of this equation is $\Psi = k\Phi^2/2$.

3.6.17   Given the three matrices

$$M_x = \begin{pmatrix} 0 & 0 & 0 \\ 0 & 0 & -i \\ 0 & i & 0 \end{pmatrix}, \quad M_y = \begin{pmatrix} 0 & 0 & i \\ 0 & 0 & 0 \\ -i & 0 & 0 \end{pmatrix},$$

and

$$M_z = \begin{pmatrix} 0 & -i & 0 \\ i & 0 & 0 \\ 0 & 0 & 0 \end{pmatrix},$$

show that the matrix-vector equation

$$\left(\mathbf{M} \cdot \nabla + \mathbf{1}_3 \frac{1}{c} \frac{\partial}{\partial t} \right) \boldsymbol{\psi} = 0$$

reproduces Maxwell's equations in vacuum. Here $\boldsymbol{\psi}$ is a column vector with components $\psi_j = B_j - iE_j/c$, $j = x, y, z$. Note that $\varepsilon_0\mu_0 = 1/c^2$ and that $\mathbf{1}_3$ is the 3×3 unit matrix.

3.6.18   Using the Pauli matrices $\boldsymbol{\sigma}_i$ of Eq. (2.28), show that

$$(\boldsymbol{\sigma} \cdot \mathbf{a})(\boldsymbol{\sigma} \cdot \mathbf{b}) = (\mathbf{a} \cdot \mathbf{b})\mathbf{1}_2 + i\boldsymbol{\sigma} \cdot (\mathbf{a} \times \mathbf{b}).$$

Here

$$\boldsymbol{\sigma} \equiv \hat{\mathbf{e}}_x\sigma_1 + \hat{\mathbf{e}}_y\sigma_2 + \hat{\mathbf{e}}_z\sigma_3,$$

a and **b** are ordinary vectors, and $\mathbf{1}_2$ is the 2×2 unit matrix.

3.7 VECTOR INTEGRATION

In physics, vectors occur in line, surface, and volume integrals. At least in principle, these integrals can be decomposed into scalar integrals involving the vector components; there are some useful general observations to make at this time.

Line Integrals

Possible forms for line integrals include the following:

$$\int_C \varphi\,d\mathbf{r}, \quad \int_C \mathbf{F} \cdot d\mathbf{r}, \quad \int_C \mathbf{V} \times d\mathbf{r}. \tag{3.75}$$

In each of these the integral is over some path C that may be open (with starting and endpoints distinct) or closed (forming a loop). Inserting the form of $d\mathbf{r}$, the first of these integrals reduces immediately to

$$\int_C \varphi\,d\mathbf{r} = \hat{\mathbf{e}}_x \int_C \varphi(x, y, z)\,dx + \hat{\mathbf{e}}_y \int_C \varphi(x, y, z)\,dy + \hat{\mathbf{e}}_z \int_C \varphi(x, y, z)\,dz. \tag{3.76}$$

The unit vectors need not remain within the integral beause they are constant in both magnitude and direction.

The integrals in Eq. (3.76) are one-dimensional scalar integrals. Note, however, that the integral over x cannot be evaluated unless y and z are known in terms of x; similar observations apply for the integrals over y and z. This means that the path C must be specified. Unless φ has special properties, the value of the integral will depend on the path.

The other integrals in Eq. (3.75) can be handled similarly. For the second integral, which is of common occurrence, being that which evaluates the work associated with displacement on the path C, we have:

$$W = \int_C \mathbf{F} \cdot d\mathbf{r} = \int_C F_x(x, y, z)\,dx + \int_C F_y(x, y, z)\,dy + \int_C F_z(x, y, z)\,dz. \tag{3.77}$$

Example 3.7.1   LINE INTEGRALS

We consider two integrals in 2-D space:

$$I_C = \int_C \varphi(x, y)d\mathbf{r}, \quad \text{with } \varphi(x, y) = 1,$$

$$J_C = \int_C \mathbf{F}(x, y) \cdot d\mathbf{r}, \quad \text{with } \mathbf{F}(x, y) = -y\hat{\mathbf{e}}_x + x\hat{\mathbf{e}}_y.$$

We perform integrations in the xy-plane from (0,0) to (1,1) by the two different paths shown in Fig. 3.12:

Path C_1 is $(0, 0) \rightarrow (1, 0) \rightarrow (1, 1)$,
Path C_2 is the straight line $(0, 0) \rightarrow (1, 1)$.

For the first segment of C_1, x ranges from 0 to 1 while y is fixed at zero. For the second segment, y ranges from 0 to 1 while $x = 1$. Thus,

$$I_{C_1} = \hat{\mathbf{e}}_x \int_0^1 dx\varphi(x, 0) + \hat{\mathbf{e}}_y \int_0^1 dy\varphi(1, y) = \hat{\mathbf{e}}_x \int_0^1 dx + \hat{\mathbf{e}}_y \int_0^1 dy = \hat{\mathbf{e}}_x + \hat{\mathbf{e}}_y,$$

$$J_{C_1} = \int_0^1 dx\, F_x(x, 0) + \int_0^1 dy\, F_y(1, y) = \int_0^1 = \int_0^1 dx(0) + \int_0^1 dy(1) = 1.$$

On Path 2, both dx and dy range from 0 to 1, with $x = y$ at all points of the path. Thus,

$$I_{C_2} = \hat{\mathbf{e}}_x \int_0^1 dx\, \varphi(x, x) + \hat{\mathbf{e}}_y \int_0^1 dy\, \varphi(y, y) = \hat{\mathbf{e}}_x + \hat{\mathbf{e}}_y,$$

$$J_{C_2} = \int_0^1 dx\, F_x(x, x) + \int_0^1 dy\, F_y(y, y) = \int_0^1 dx(-x) + \int_0^1 dy(y) = -\frac{1}{2} + \frac{1}{2} = 0.$$

We see that integral I is independent of the path from (0,0) to (1,1), a nearly trivial special case, while the integral J is not.   ∎

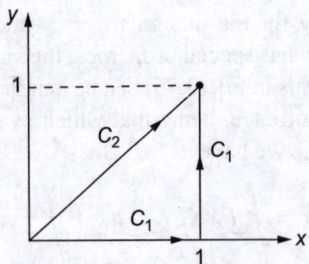

FIGURE 3.12   Line integration paths.

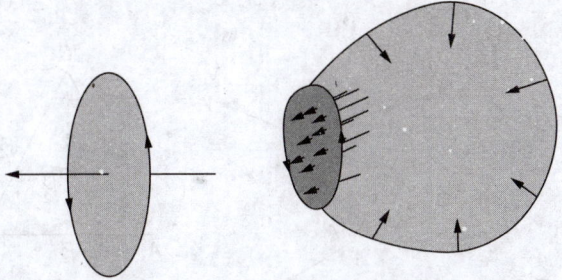

FIGURE 3.13   Positive normal directions: left, disk; right, spherical surface with hole.

Surface Integrals

Surface integrals appear in the same forms as line integrals, the element of area being a vector, $d\boldsymbol{\sigma}$, normal to the surface:

$$\int \varphi \, d\boldsymbol{\sigma}, \quad \int \mathbf{V} \cdot d\boldsymbol{\sigma}, \quad \int \mathbf{V} \times d\boldsymbol{\sigma}.$$

Often $d\boldsymbol{\sigma}$ is written $\hat{\mathbf{n}} \, dA$, where $\hat{\mathbf{n}}$ is a unit vector indicating the normal direction. There are two conventions for choosing the positive direction. First, if the surface is closed (has no boundary), we agree to take the outward normal as positive. Second, for an open surface, the positive normal depends on the direction in which the perimeter of the surface is traversed. Starting from an arbitrary point on the perimeter, we define a vector $\mathbf{u}$ to be in the direction of travel along the perimeter, and define a second vector $\mathbf{v}$ at our perimeter point but tangent to and lying on the surface. We then take $\mathbf{u} \times \mathbf{v}$ as the positive normal direction. This corresponds to a right-hand rule, and is illustrated in Fig. 3.13. It is necessary to define the orientation carefully so as to deal with cases such as that of Fig. 3.13, right.

The dot-product form is by far the most commonly encountered surface integral, as it corresponds to a flow or flux through the given surface.

Example 3.7.2   A Surface Integral

Consider a surface integral of the form $I = \int_S \mathbf{B} \cdot d\boldsymbol{\sigma}$ over the surface of a tetrahedron whose vertices are at the origin and at the points (1,0,0), (0,1,0), and (0,0,1), with $\mathbf{B} = (x+1)\hat{\mathbf{e}}_x + y\hat{\mathbf{e}}_y - z\hat{\mathbf{e}}_z$. See Fig. 3.14.

The surface consists of four triangles, which can be identified and their contributions evaluated, as follows:

1. On the xy-plane ($z = 0$), vertices at $(x, y) = (0,0)$, (1,0), and (0,1); direction of outward normal is $-\hat{\mathbf{e}}_z$, so $d\boldsymbol{\sigma} = -\hat{\mathbf{e}}_z \, dA$ ($dA =$ element of area on this triangle). Here, $\mathbf{B} = (x+1)\hat{\mathbf{e}}_x + y\hat{\mathbf{e}}_y$, and $\mathbf{B} \cdot d\boldsymbol{\sigma} = 0$. So there is no contribution to I.

2. On the xz plane ($y = 0$), vertices at $(x, z) = (0,0)$, (1,0), and (0,1); direction of outward normal is $-\hat{\mathbf{e}}_y$, so $d\boldsymbol{\sigma} = -\hat{\mathbf{e}}_y \, dA$. On this triangle, $\mathbf{B} = (x+1)\hat{\mathbf{e}}_x - z\hat{\mathbf{e}}_z$, Again, $\mathbf{B} \cdot d\boldsymbol{\sigma} = 0$. There is no contribution to I.

3. On the yz plane ($x = 0$), vertices at $(y, z) = (0,0)$, (1,0), and (0,1); direction of outward normal is $-\hat{\mathbf{e}}_x$, so $d\boldsymbol{\sigma} = -\hat{\mathbf{e}}_x \, dA$. Here, $\mathbf{B} = \hat{\mathbf{e}}_x + y\hat{\mathbf{e}}_y - z\hat{\mathbf{e}}_z$, and

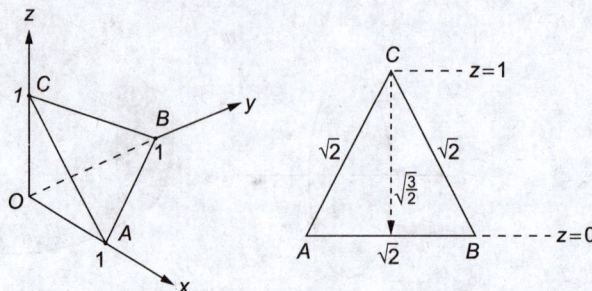

FIGURE 3.14   Tetrahedron, and detail of the oblique face.

$\mathbf{B} \cdot d\boldsymbol{\sigma} = (-1)dA$; the contribution to I is -1 times the area of the triangle ($=1/2$), or $I_3 = -1/2$.

4. Obliquely oriented, vertices at $(x, y, z) = (1,0,0)$, $(0,1,0)$, $(0,0,1)$; direction of outward normal is $\hat{\mathbf{n}} = (\hat{\mathbf{e}}_x + \hat{\mathbf{e}}_y + \hat{\mathbf{e}}_z)/\sqrt{3}$, and $d\boldsymbol{\sigma} = \hat{\mathbf{n}}dA$. Using also $\mathbf{B} = (x+1)\hat{\mathbf{e}}_x + y\hat{\mathbf{e}}_y - z\hat{\mathbf{e}}_z$, this contribution to I becomes

$$I_4 = \int\limits_{\Delta_4} \frac{x+1+y-z}{\sqrt{3}} dA = \int\limits_{\Delta_4} \frac{2(1-z)}{\sqrt{3}} dA,$$

where we have used the fact that on this triangle, $x + y + z = 1$.

To complete the evaluation, we note that the geometry of the triangle is as shown in Fig. 3.14, that the width of the triangle at height z is $\sqrt{2}(1-z)$, and a change dz in z produces a displacement $\sqrt{3/2}dz$ on the triangle. I_4 therefore can be written

$$I_4 = \int\limits_0^1 2(1-z)^2 dz = \frac{2}{3}.$$

Combining the nonzero contributions I_3 and I_4, we obtain the final result

$$I = -\frac{1}{2} + \frac{2}{3} = \frac{1}{6}.$$

∎

Volume Integrals

Volume integrals are somewhat simpler, because the volume element $d\tau$ is a scalar quantity. Sometimes $d\tau$ is written d^3r, or d^3x when the coordinates were designated (x_1, x_2, x_3). In the literature, the form $d\mathbf{r}$ is frequently encountered, but in contexts that usually reveal that it is a synonym for $d\tau$, and not a vector quantity. The volume integrals under consideration here are of the form

$$\int \mathbf{V} \, d\tau = \hat{\mathbf{e}}_x \int V_x \, d\tau + \hat{\mathbf{e}}_y \int V_y \, d\tau + \hat{\mathbf{e}}_z \int V_z \, d\tau.$$

The integral reduces to a vector sum of scalar integrals.

Some volume integrals contain vector quantities in combinations that are actually scalar. Often these can be rearranged by applying techniques such as integration by parts.

Example 3.7.3   INTEGRATION BY PARTS

Consider an integral over all space of the form $\int \mathbf{A}(\mathbf{r})\nabla \cdot f(\mathbf{r})d^3r$ in the frequently occurring special case in which either f or $\mathbf{A}$ vanish sufficiently strongly at infinity. Expanding the integrand into components,

$$\int \mathbf{A}(\mathbf{r}) \cdot \nabla f(\mathbf{r})d^3r = \iint dy\,dz \left[A_x f \Big|_{x=-\infty}^{\infty} - \int f \frac{\partial A_x}{\partial x} dx \right] + \cdots$$

$$= -\iiint f \frac{\partial A_x}{\partial x} dx\,dy\,dz - \iiint f \frac{\partial A_y}{\partial y} dx\,dy\,dz - \iiint f \frac{\partial A_z}{\partial z} dx\,dy\,dz$$

$$= -\int f(r)\nabla \cdot \mathbf{A}(\mathbf{r})d^3r. \tag{3.78}$$

For example, if $\mathbf{A} = e^{ikz}\hat{\mathbf{p}}$ describes a photon with a constant polarization vector in the direction $\hat{\mathbf{p}}$ and $\psi(\mathbf{r})$ is a bound-state wave function (so it vanishes at infinity), then

$$\int e^{ikz}\hat{\mathbf{p}} \cdot \nabla \psi(\mathbf{r})d^3r = -(\hat{\mathbf{p}} \cdot \hat{\mathbf{e}}_z)\int \psi(\mathbf{r})\frac{de^{ikz}}{dz}d^3r = -ik(\hat{\mathbf{p}} \cdot \hat{\mathbf{e}}_z)\int \psi(\mathbf{r})e^{ikz}d^3r.$$

Only the z-component of the gradient contributes to the integral.

Analogous rearrangements (assuming the integrated terms vanish at infinity) include

$$\int f(\mathbf{r})\nabla \cdot \mathbf{A}(\mathbf{r})d^3r = -\int \mathbf{A}(\mathbf{r}) \cdot \nabla f(\mathbf{r})d^3r, \tag{3.79}$$

$$\int \mathbf{C}(\mathbf{r}) \cdot (\nabla \times \mathbf{A}(\mathbf{r})d^3r = \int \mathbf{A}(\mathbf{r}) \cdot (\nabla \times \mathbf{C}(\mathbf{r}))d^3r. \tag{3.80}$$

In the cross-product example, the sign change from the integration by parts combines with the signs from the cross product to give the result shown.   ∎

Exercises

3.7.1   The origin and the three vectors $\mathbf{A}$, $\mathbf{B}$, and $\mathbf{C}$ (all of which start at the origin) define a tetrahedron. Taking the outward direction as positive, calculate the total vector area of the four tetrahedral surfaces.

3.7.2   Find the work $\oint \mathbf{F} \cdot d\mathbf{r}$ done moving on a unit circle in the xy-plane, doing work **against** a force field given by

$$\mathbf{F} = \frac{-\hat{\mathbf{e}}_x y}{x^2 + y^2} + \frac{\hat{\mathbf{e}}_y x}{x^2 + y^2}:$$

(a) Counterclockwise from 0 to π,
(b) Clockwise from 0 to $-\pi$.

Note that the work done depends on the path.

3.7.3 Calculate the work you do in going from point $(1, 1)$ tc point $(3, 3)$. The force **you exert** is given by

$$\mathbf{F} = \hat{\mathbf{e}}_x(x - y) + \hat{\mathbf{e}}_y(x + y).$$

Specify clearly the path you choose. Note that this force field is nonconservative.

3.7.4 Evaluate $\oint \mathbf{r} \cdot d\mathbf{r}$ for a closed path of your choosing.

3.7.5 Evaluate

$$\frac{1}{3} \int_s \mathbf{r} \cdot d\boldsymbol{\sigma}.$$

over the unit cube defined by the point $(0, 0, 0)$ and the unit intercepts on the positive x-, y-, and z-axes. Note that $\mathbf{r} \cdot d\boldsymbol{\sigma}$ is zero for three of the surfaces and that each of the three remaining surfaces contributes the same amount to the integral.

3.8 INTEGRAL THEOREMS

The formulas in this section relate a volume integration to a surface integral on its boundary (Gauss' theorem), or relate a surface integral to the line defining its perimeter (Stokes' theorem). These formulas are important tools in vector analysis, particularly when the functions involved are known to vanish on the boundary surface or perimeter.

Gauss' Theorem

Here we derive a useful relation between a surface integral of a vector and the volume integral of the divergence of that vector. Let us assume that a vector $\mathbf{A}$ and its first derivatives are continuous over a **simply connected** region of $\mathbb{R}^3$ (regions that contain holes, like a donut, are not simply connected). Then Gauss' theorem states that

$$\oint_{\partial V} \mathbf{A} \cdot d\boldsymbol{\sigma} = \int_V \nabla \cdot \mathbf{A} \, d\tau. \tag{3.81}$$

Here the notations V and ∂V respectively denote a volume of interest and the closed surface that bounds it. The circle on the surface integral is an additional indication that the surface is closed.

To prove the theorem, consider the volume V to be subdivided into an arbitrary large number of tiny (differential) parallelepipeds, and look at the behavior of $\nabla \cdot \mathbf{A}$ for each. See Fig. 3.15. For any given parallelepiped, this quantity is a measure of the net outward flow (of whatever $\mathbf{A}$ describes) through its boundary. If that boundary is interior (i.e., is shared by another parallelepiped), outflow from one parallelepiped is inflow to its neighbor; in a summation of all the outflows, all the contributions of interior boundaries cancel. Thus, the sum of all the outflows in the volume will just be the sum of those through the exterior boundary. In the limit of infinite subdivision, these sums become integrals: The left-hand side of Eq. (3.81) becomes the total outflow to the exterior, while its right-hand side is the sum of the outflows of the differential elements (the parallelepipeds).

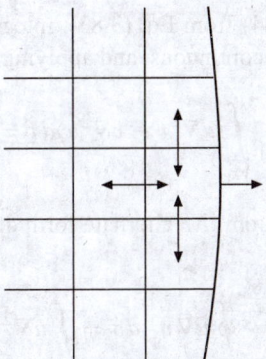

FIGURE 3.15   Subdivision for Gauss' theorem.

A simple alternate explanation of Gauss' theorem is that the volume integral sums the outflows $\nabla \cdot \mathbf{A}$ from all elements of the volume; the surface integral computes the same thing, by directly summing the flow through all elements of the boundary.

If the region of interest is the complete $\mathbb{R}^3$, and the volume integral converges, the surface integral in Eq. (3.81) must vanish, giving the useful result

$$\int \nabla \cdot \mathbf{A} \, d\tau = 0, \quad \text{integration over } \mathbb{R}^3 \text{ and convergent.} \tag{3.82}$$

Example 3.8.1   TETRAHEDRON

We check Gauss' theorem for a vector $\mathbf{B} = (x+1)\hat{\mathbf{e}}_x + y\hat{\mathbf{e}}_y - z\hat{\mathbf{e}}_z$, comparing

$$\int_V \nabla \cdot \mathbf{B} \, d\tau \quad \text{vs.} \quad \int_{\partial V} \mathbf{B} \cdot d\boldsymbol{\sigma},$$

where V is the tetrahedron of Example 3.7.2. In that example we computed the surface integral needed here, obtaining the value $1/6$. For the integral over V, we take the divergence, obtaining $\nabla \cdot \mathbf{B} = 1$. The volume integral therefore reduces to the volume of the tetrahedron that, with base of area $1/2$ and height 1, has volume $1/3 \times 1/2 \times 1 = 1/6$. This instance of Gauss' theorem is confirmed. ∎

Green's Theorem

A frequently useful corollary of Gauss' theorem is a relation known as Green's theorem. If u and v are two scalar functions, we have the identities

$$\nabla \cdot (u \nabla v) = u \nabla^2 v + (\nabla u) \cdot (\nabla v), \tag{3.83}$$

$$\nabla \cdot (u \nabla v) = u \nabla^2 v + (\nabla u) \cdot (\nabla v). \tag{3.84}$$

Subtracting Eq. (3.84) from Eq. (3.83), integrating over a volume V on which u, v, and their derivatives are continuous, and applying Gauss' theorem, Eq. (3.81), we obtain

$$\int_V (u\nabla^2 v - v\nabla^2 u)d\tau = \oint_{\partial V} (u\nabla v - v\nabla u) \cdot d\boldsymbol{\sigma}. \tag{3.85}$$

This is Green's theorem. An alternate form of Green's theorem, obtained from Eq. (3.83) alone, is

$$\oint_{\partial V} u\nabla v \cdot d\boldsymbol{\sigma} = \int_V u\nabla^2 v\, d\tau + \int_V \nabla_u \cdot \nabla v\, d\tau. \tag{3.86}$$

While the results already obtained are by far the most important forms of Gauss' theorem, volume integrals involving the gradient or the curl may also appear. To derive these, we consider a vector of the form

$$\mathbf{B}(x, y, z) = B(x, y, z)\mathbf{a}, \tag{3.87}$$

in which $\mathbf{a}$ is a vector with constant magnitude and constant but arbitrary direction. Then Eq. (3.81) becomes, applying Eq. (3.72),

$$\mathbf{a} \cdot \oint_{\partial V} B\, d\boldsymbol{\sigma} = \int_V \nabla \cdot (B\mathbf{a})d\tau = \mathbf{a}\int_V \nabla B\, d\tau.$$

This may be rewritten

$$\mathbf{a} \cdot \left[\oint_{\partial V} B\, d\boldsymbol{\sigma} - \int_V \nabla B\, d\tau \right] = 0. \tag{3.88}$$

Since the direction of $\mathbf{a}$ is arbitrary, Eq. (3.88) cannot always be satisfied unless the quantity in the square brackets evaluates to zero.[6] The result is

$$\oint_{\partial V} B\, d\boldsymbol{\sigma} = \int_V \nabla B\, d\tau. \tag{3.89}$$

In a similar manner, using $\mathbf{B} = \mathbf{a} \times \mathbf{P}$ in which $\mathbf{a}$ is a constant vector, we may show

$$\oint_{\partial V} d\boldsymbol{\sigma} \times \mathbf{P} = \int_V \nabla \times \mathbf{P}\, d\tau. \tag{3.90}$$

These last two forms of Gauss' theorem are used in the vector form of Kirchoff diffraction theory.

---

[6]This exploitation of the **arbitrary** nature of a part of a problem is a valuable and widely used technique.

Stokes' Theorem

Stokes' theorem is the analog of Gauss' theorem that relates a surface integral of a derivative of a function to the line integral of the function, with the path of integration being the perimeter bounding the surface.

Let us take the surface and subdivide it into a network of arbitrarily small rectangles. In Eq. (3.60) we saw that the circulation of a vector $\mathbf{B}$ about such a differential rectangles (in the xy-plane) is $\nabla \times \mathbf{B}\big|_z \hat{\mathbf{e}}_z \, dx \, dy$. Identifying $dx \, dy \, \hat{\mathbf{e}}_z$ as the element of area $d\boldsymbol{\sigma}$, Eq. (3.60) generalizes to

$$\sum_{\text{four sides}} \mathbf{B} \cdot d\mathbf{r} = \nabla \times \mathbf{B} \cdot d\boldsymbol{\sigma}. \tag{3.91}$$

We now sum over all the little rectangles; the surface contributions, from the right-hand side of Eq. (3.91), are added together. The line integrals (left-hand side) of all **interior** line segments cancel identically. See Fig. 3.16. Only the line integral around the perimeter survives. Taking the limit as the number of rectangles approaches infinity, we have

$$\oint_{\partial S} \mathbf{B} \cdot d\mathbf{r} = \int_S \nabla \times \mathbf{B} \cdot d\boldsymbol{\sigma}. \tag{3.92}$$

Here ∂S is the perimeter of S. This is Stokes' theorem. Note that both the sign of the line integral and the direction of $d\boldsymbol{\sigma}$ depend on the direction the perimeter is traversed, so consistent results will always be obtained. For the area and the line-integral direction shown in Fig. 3.16, the direction of $\boldsymbol{\sigma}$ for the shaded rectangle will be **out** of the plane of the paper.

Finally, consider what happens if we apply Stokes' theorem to a closed surface. Since it has no perimeter, the line integral vanishes, so

$$\int_S \nabla \times B \cdot d\boldsymbol{\sigma} = 0, \quad \text{for } S \text{ a closed surface.} \tag{3.93}$$

As with Gauss' theorem, we can derive additional relations connecting surface integrals with line integrals on their perimeter. Using the arbitrary-vector technique employed to

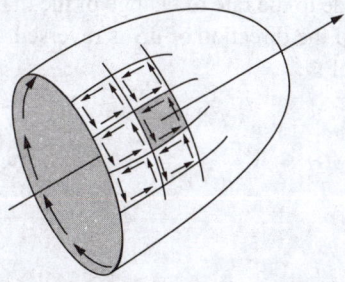

FIGURE 3.16 Direction of normal for the shaded rectangle when perimeter of the surface is traversed as indicated.

reach Eqs. (3.89) and (3.90), we can obtain

$$\int_S d\boldsymbol{\sigma} \times \nabla\varphi = \oint_{\partial S} \varphi d\mathbf{r}, \tag{3.94}$$

$$\int_S (d\boldsymbol{\sigma} \times \nabla) \times \mathbf{P} = \oint_{\partial S} d\mathbf{r} \times \mathbf{P}. \tag{3.95}$$

Example 3.8.2 OERSTED'S AND FARADAY'S LAWS

Consider the magnetic field generated by a long wire that carries a time-independent current I (meaning that $\partial\mathbf{E}/\partial t = \partial\mathbf{B}/\partial t = 0$). The relevant Maxwell equation, Eq. (3.68), then takes the form $\nabla \times \mathbf{B} = \mu_0 \mathbf{J}$. Integrating this equation over a disk S perpendicular to and surrounding the wire (see Fig. 3.17), we have

$$I = \int_S \mathbf{J} \cdot d\boldsymbol{\sigma} = \frac{1}{\mu_0} \int_S (\nabla \times \mathbf{B}) \cdot d\boldsymbol{\sigma}.$$

Now we apply Stokes' theorem, obtaining the result $I = (1/\mu_0)\oint_{\partial S} \mathbf{B} \cdot d\mathbf{r}$, which is Oersted's law.

Similarly, we can integrate Maxwell's equation for $\nabla \times \mathbf{E}$, Eq. (3.69). Imagine moving a closed loop (∂S) of wire (of area S) across a magnetic induction field B. We have

$$\int_S (\nabla \times \mathbf{E}) \cdot d\boldsymbol{\sigma} = -\frac{d}{dt} \int_S \mathbf{B} \cdot d\boldsymbol{\sigma} = -\frac{d\Phi}{dt},$$

where Φ is the magnetic flux through the area S. By Stokes' theorem, we have

$$\int_{\partial S} \mathbf{E} \cdot d\mathbf{r} = -\frac{d\Phi}{dt}.$$

This is Faraday's law. The line integral represents the voltage induced in the wire loop; it is equal in magnitude to the rate of change of the magnetic flux through the loop. There is no sign ambiguity; if the direction of ∂S is reversed, that causes a reversal of the direction of $d\boldsymbol{\sigma}$ and thereby of Φ. ∎

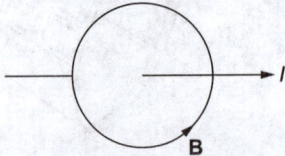

FIGURE 3.17   Direction of **B** given by Oersted's law.

Exercises

3.8.1   Using Gauss' theorem, prove that

$$\oint_S d\boldsymbol{\sigma} = 0$$

if $S = \partial V$ is a closed surface.

3.8.2   Show that

$$\frac{1}{3} \oint_S \mathbf{r} \cdot d\boldsymbol{\sigma} = V,$$

where V is the volume enclosed by the closed surface $S = \partial V$.
Note. This is a generalization of Exercise 3.7.5.

3.8.3   If $\mathbf{B} = \nabla \times \mathbf{A}$, show that

$$\oint_S \mathbf{B} \cdot d\boldsymbol{\sigma} = \mathbf{0}$$

for any closed surface S.

3.8.4   From Eq. (3.72), with $\mathbf{V}$ the electric field $\mathbf{E}$ and f the electrostatic potential φ, show that, for integration over all space,

$$\int \rho \varphi d\tau = \varepsilon_0 \int E^2 d\tau.$$

This corresponds to a 3-D integration by parts.
Hint. $\mathbf{E} = -\nabla \varphi$, $\nabla \cdot \mathbf{E} = \rho / \varepsilon_0$. You may assume that φ vanishes at large r at least as fast as r^{-1}.

3.8.5   A particular steady-state electric current distribution is localized in space. Choosing a bounding surface far enough out so that the current density $\mathbf{J}$ is zero everywhere on the surface, show that

$$\int \mathbf{J} d\tau = 0.$$

Hint. Take one component of $\mathbf{J}$ at a time. With $\nabla \cdot \mathbf{J} = 0$, show that $\mathbf{J}_i = \nabla \cdot (x_i \mathbf{J})$ and apply Gauss' theorem.

3.8.6   Given a vector $\mathbf{t} = -\hat{\mathbf{e}}_x y + \hat{\mathbf{e}}_y x$, show, with the help of Stokes' theorem, that the integral of $\mathbf{t}$ around a continuous closed curve in the xy-plane satisfies

$$\frac{1}{2} \oint \mathbf{t} \cdot d\boldsymbol{\lambda} = \frac{1}{2} \oint (x \, dy - y \, dx) = A,$$

where A is the area enclosed by the curve.

3.8.7   The calculation of the magnetic moment of a current loop leads to the line integral

$$\oint \mathbf{r} \times d\mathbf{r}.$$

(a)   Integrate around the perimeter of a current loop (in the xy-plane) and show that the scalar magnitude of this line integral is twice the area of the enclosed surface.

(b)   The perimeter of an ellipse is described by $\mathbf{r} = \hat{\mathbf{e}}_x a \cos\theta + \hat{\mathbf{e}}_y b \sin\theta$. From part (a) show that the area of the ellipse is πab.

3.8.8   Evaluate $\oint \mathbf{r} \times d\mathbf{r}$ by using the alternate form of Stokes' theorem given by Eq. (3.95):

$$\int_S (d\boldsymbol{\sigma} \times \nabla) \times \mathbf{P} = \oint d\boldsymbol{\lambda} \times \mathbf{P}.$$

Take the loop to be entirely in the xy-plane.

3.8.9   Prove that

$$\oint u \nabla v \cdot d\boldsymbol{\lambda} = -\oint v \nabla u \cdot d\boldsymbol{\lambda}.$$

3.8.10   Prove that

$$\oint u \nabla v \cdot d\boldsymbol{\lambda} = \int_S (\nabla u) \times (\nabla v) \cdot d\boldsymbol{\sigma}.$$

3.8.11   Prove that

$$\oint_{\partial V} d\boldsymbol{\sigma} \times \mathbf{P} = \int_V \nabla \times \mathbf{P} d\tau.$$

3.8.12   Prove that

$$\int_S d\boldsymbol{\sigma} \times \nabla\varphi = \oint_{\partial S} \varphi d\mathbf{r}.$$

3.8.13   Prove that

$$\int_S (d\boldsymbol{\sigma} \times \nabla) \times \mathbf{P} = \oint_{\partial S} d\mathbf{r} \times \mathbf{P}.$$

3.9   POTENTIAL THEORY

Much of physics, particularly electromagnetic theory, can be treated more simply by introducing **potentials** from which forces can be derived. This section deals with the definition and use of such potentials.

Scalar Potential

If, over a given simply connected region of space (one with no holes), a force can be expressed as the negative gradient of a scalar function φ,

$$\mathbf{F} = -\nabla\varphi, \qquad (3.96)$$

we call φ a **scalar potential**, and we benefit from the feature that the force can be described in terms of one function instead of three. Since the force is a derivative of the scalar potential, the potential is only determined up to an additive constant, which can be used to adjust its value at infinity (usually zero) or at some other reference point. We want to know what conditions $\mathbf{F}$ must satisfy in order for a scalar potential to exist.

First, consider the result of computing the work done against a force given by $-\nabla\varphi$ when an object subject to the force is moved from a point A to a point B. This is a line integral of the form

$$-\int_A^B \mathbf{F} \cdot d\mathbf{r} = \int_A^B \nabla\varphi \cdot d\mathbf{r}. \qquad (3.97)$$

But, as pointed out in Eq. (3.41), $\nabla\varphi \cdot d\mathbf{r} = d\varphi$, so the integral is in fact independent of the path, depending only on the endpoints A and B. So we have

$$-\int_A^B \mathbf{F} \cdot d\mathbf{r} = \varphi(\mathbf{r}_B) - \varphi(\mathbf{r}_A), \qquad (3.98)$$

which also means that if A and B are the same point, forming a closed loop,

$$\oint \mathbf{F} \cdot d\mathbf{r} = 0. \qquad (3.99)$$

We conclude that a force (on an object) described by a scalar potential is a **conservative force**, meaning that the work needed to move the object between any two points is independent of the path taken, and that $\varphi(\mathbf{r})$ is the work needed to move to the point $\mathbf{r}$ from a reference point where the potential has been assigned the value zero.

Another property of a force given by a scalar potential is that

$$\nabla \times \mathbf{F} = -\nabla \times \nabla\varphi = 0 \qquad (3.100)$$

as prescribed by Eq. (3.64). This observation is consistent with the notion that the lines of force of a conservative $\mathbf{F}$ cannot form closed loops.

The three conditions, Eqs. (3.96), (3.99), and (3.100), are all equivalent. If we take Eq. (3.99) for a differential loop, its left side and that of Eq. (3.100) must, according to Stokes' theorem, be equal. We already showed both these equations followed from Eq. (3.96). To complete the establishment of full equivalence, we need only to derive Eq. (3.96) from Eq. (3.99). Going backward to Eq. (3.97), we rewrite it as

$$\int_A^B (\mathbf{F} + \nabla\varphi) \cdot d\mathbf{r} = 0,$$

which must be satisfied for all A and B. This means its integrand must be identically zero, thereby recovering Eq. (3.96).

Example 3.9.1   GRAVITATIONAL POTENTIAL

We have previously, in Example 3.5.2, illustrated the generation of a force from a scalar potential. To perform the reverse process, we must integrate. Let us find the scalar potential for the gravitational force

$$\mathbf{F}_G = -\frac{Gm_1m_2\hat{\mathbf{r}}}{r^2} = -\frac{k\hat{\mathbf{r}}}{r^2},$$

radially **inward**. Setting the zero of scalar potential at infinity, we obtain by integrating (radially) from infinity to position $\mathbf{r}$,

$$\varphi_G(r) - \varphi_G(\infty) = -\int_\infty^r \mathbf{F}_G \cdot d\mathbf{r} = +\int_r^\infty \mathbf{F}_G \cdot d\mathbf{r}.$$

The minus sign in the central member of this equation arises because we are calculating the work done **against** the gravitational force. Evaluating the integral,

$$\varphi_G(r) = -\int_r^\infty \frac{kdr}{r^2} = -\frac{k}{r} = -\frac{Gm_1m_2}{r}.$$

The final negative sign corresponds to the fact that gravity is an attractive force.   ∎

Vector Potential

In some branches of physics, especially electrodynamics, it is convenient to introduce a **vector potential A** such that a (force) field **B** is given by

$$\mathbf{B} = \nabla \times \mathbf{A}. \tag{3.101}$$

An obvious reason for introducing **A** is that it causes **B** to be solenoidal; if **B** is the magnetic induction field, this property is required by Maxwell's equations. Here we want to develop a converse, namely to show that when **B** is solenoidal, a vector potential **A** exists. We demonstrate the existence of **A** by actually writing it.

Our construction is

$$\mathbf{A} = \hat{\mathbf{e}}_y \int_{x_0}^x B_z(x, y, z)\, dx + \hat{\mathbf{e}}_z \left[\int_{y_0}^y B_x(x_0, y, z)\, dy - \int_{x_0}^x B_y(x, y, z)\, dx \right]. \tag{3.102}$$

Checking the y- and z-components of $\nabla \times \mathbf{A}$ first, noting that $A_x = 0$,

$$(\nabla \times \mathbf{A})_y = -\frac{\partial A_z}{\partial x} = +\frac{\partial}{\partial x} \int_{x_0}^{x} B_y(x, y, z)\, dx = B_y,$$

$$(\nabla \times \mathbf{A})_z = +\frac{\partial A_y}{\partial x} == \frac{\partial}{\partial x} \int_{x_0}^{x} B_z(x, y, z)\, dx = B_z.$$

The x-component of $\nabla \times \mathbf{A}$ is a bit more complicated. We have

$$(\nabla \times \mathbf{A})_x = \frac{\partial A_z}{\partial y} - \frac{\partial A_y}{\partial z}$$

$$= \frac{\partial}{\partial y} \left[\int_{y_0}^{y} B_x(x_0, y, z)\, dy - \int_{x_0}^{x} B_y(x, y, z)\, dx \right] - \frac{\partial}{\partial z} \int_{x_0}^{x} B_z(x, y, z)\, dx$$

$$= B_x(x_0, y, z) - \int_{x_0}^{x} \left[\frac{\partial B_y(x, y, z)}{\partial y} + \frac{\partial B_z(x, y, z)}{\partial z} \right] dx.$$

To go further, we must use the fact that $\mathbf{B}$ is solenoidal, which means $\nabla \cdot \mathbf{B} = 0$. We can therefore make the replacement

$$\frac{\partial B_y(x, y, z)}{\partial y} + \frac{\partial B_z(x, y, z)}{\partial z} = -\frac{\partial B_x(x, y, z)}{\partial x},$$

after which the x integration becomes trivial, yielding

$$+ \int_{x_0}^{x} \frac{\partial B_x(x, y, z)}{\partial x}\, dx = B_x(x, y, z) - B_x(x_0, y, z),$$

leading to the desired final result $(\nabla \times \mathbf{A})_x = B_x$.

While we have shown that there exists a vector potential $\mathbf{A}$ such that $\nabla \times \mathbf{A} = \mathbf{B}$ subject only to the condition that $\mathbf{B}$ be solenoidal, we have in no way established that $\mathbf{A}$ is unique. In fact, $\mathbf{A}$ is far from unique, as we can add to it not only an arbitrary constant, but also the gradient of **any** scalar function, $\nabla \varphi$, without affecting $\mathbf{B}$ at all. Moreover, our verification of $\mathbf{A}$ was independent of the values of x_0 and y_0, so these can be assigned arbitrarily without affecting $\mathbf{B}$. In addition, we can derive another formula for $\mathbf{A}$ in which the roles of x and y are interchanged:

$$\mathbf{A} = -\hat{\mathbf{e}}_x \int_{y_0}^{y} B_z(x, y, z)\, dy - \hat{\mathbf{e}}_z \left[\int_{x_0}^{x} B_y(x, y_0, z)\, dx - \int_{y_0}^{y} B_x(x, y, z)\, dy \right]. \qquad (3.103)$$

Example 3.9.2   MAGNETIC VECTOR POTENTIAL

We consider the construction of the vector potential for a constant magnetic induction field

$$\mathbf{B} = B_z \hat{\mathbf{e}}_z. \tag{3.104}$$

Using Eq. (3.102), we have (choosing the arbitrary value of x_0 to be zero)

$$\mathbf{A} = \hat{\mathbf{e}}_y \int_0^x B_z \, dx = \hat{\mathbf{e}}_y x B_z. \tag{3.105}$$

Alternatively, we could use Eq. (3.103) for $\mathbf{A}$, leading to

$$\mathbf{A}' = -\hat{\mathbf{e}}_x y B_z. \tag{3.106}$$

Neither of these is the form for $\mathbf{A}$ found in many elementary texts, which for $\mathbf{B}$ from Eq. (3.104) is

$$\mathbf{A}'' = \frac{1}{2}(\mathbf{B} \times \mathbf{r}) = \frac{B_z}{2}(x\hat{\mathbf{e}}_y - y\hat{\mathbf{e}}_x). \tag{3.107}$$

These disparate forms can be reconciled if we use the freedom to add to $\mathbf{A}$ any expression of the form $\nabla\varphi$. Taking $\varphi = Cxy$, the quantity that can be added to $\mathbf{A}$ will be of the form

$$\nabla\varphi = C(y\hat{\mathbf{e}}_x + x\hat{\mathbf{e}}_y).$$

We now see that

$$\mathbf{A} - \frac{B_z}{2}(y\hat{\mathbf{e}}_x + x\hat{\mathbf{e}}_y) = \mathbf{A}' + \frac{B_z}{2}(y\hat{\mathbf{e}}_x + x\hat{\mathbf{e}}_y) = \mathbf{A}'',$$

showing that all these formulas predict the same value of $\mathbf{B}$. ∎

Example 3.9.3   POTENTIALS IN ELECTROMAGNETISM

If we introduce suitably defined scalar and vector potentials φ and $\mathbf{A}$ into Maxwell's equations, we can obtain equations giving these potentials in terms of the sources of the electromagnetic field (charges and currents). We start with $\mathbf{B} = \nabla \times \mathbf{A}$, thereby assuring satisfaction of the Maxwell's equation $\nabla \cdot \mathbf{B} = 0$. Substitution into the equation for $\nabla \times \mathbf{E}$ yields

$$\nabla \times \mathbf{E} = -\nabla \times \frac{\partial \mathbf{A}}{\partial t} \quad \longrightarrow \quad \nabla \times \left(\mathbf{E} + \frac{\partial \mathbf{A}}{\partial t}\right) = 0,$$

showing that $\mathbf{E} + \partial \mathbf{A}/\partial t$ is a gradient and can be written as $-\nabla\varphi$, thereby defining φ. This preserves the notion of an electrostatic potential in the absence of time dependence, and means that $\mathbf{A}$ and φ have now been defined to give

$$\mathbf{B} = \nabla \times \mathbf{A}, \quad \mathbf{E} = -\nabla\varphi - \frac{\partial \mathbf{A}}{\partial t}. \tag{3.108}$$

At this point $\mathbf{A}$ is still arbitrary to the extent of adding any gradient, which is equivalent to making an arbitrary choice of $\nabla \cdot \mathbf{A}$. A convenient choice is to require

$$\frac{1}{c^2}\frac{\partial \varphi}{\partial t} + \nabla \cdot \mathbf{A} = 0. \tag{3.109}$$

This **gauge condition** is called the **Lorentz gauge**, and transformations of $\mathbf{A}$ and φ to satisfy it or any other legitimate gauge condition are called **gauge transformations**. The invariance of electromagnetic theory under gauge transformation is an important precursor of contemporary directions in fundamental physical theory.

From Maxwell's equation for $\nabla \cdot \mathbf{E}$ and the Lorentz gauge condition, we get

$$\frac{\rho}{\varepsilon_0} = \nabla \cdot \mathbf{E} = -\nabla^2 \mathbf{E} - \frac{\partial}{\partial t} \nabla \cdot \mathbf{A} = -\nabla^2 \varphi + \frac{1}{c^2} \frac{\partial^2 \varphi}{\partial t^2}, \tag{3.110}$$

showing that the Lorentz gauge permitted us to decouple $\mathbf{A}$ and φ to the extent that we have an equation for φ in terms only of the charge density ρ; neither $\mathbf{A}$ nor the current density $\mathbf{J}$ enters this equation.

Finally, from the equation for $\nabla \times \mathbf{B}$, we obtain

$$\frac{1}{c^2} \frac{\partial^2 \mathbf{A}}{\partial t^2} - \nabla^2 \mathbf{A} = \mu_0 \mathbf{J}. \tag{3.111}$$

Proof of this formula is the subject of Exercise 3.9.11.   ∎

Gauss' Law

Consider a point charge q at the origin of our coordinate system. It produces an electric field $\mathbf{E}$, given by

$$\mathbf{E} = \frac{q\hat{\mathbf{r}}}{4\pi \varepsilon_0 r^2}. \tag{3.112}$$

Gauss' law states that for an arbitrary volume V,

$$\oint_{\partial V} \mathbf{E} \cdot d\boldsymbol{\sigma} = \begin{cases} \dfrac{q}{\varepsilon_0} & \text{if } \partial V \text{ encloses } q, \\ 0 & \text{if } \partial V \text{ does not enclose } q. \end{cases} \tag{3.113}$$

The case that ∂V does not enclose q is easily handled. From Eq. (3.54), the r^{-2} central force $\mathbf{E}$ is divergenceless everywhere except at $r = 0$, and for this case, throughout the entire volume V. Thus, we have, invoking Gauss' theorem, Eq. (3.81),

$$\int_V \nabla \cdot \mathbf{E} = 0 \quad \longrightarrow \quad \mathbf{E} \cdot d\boldsymbol{\sigma} = 0.$$

If q is within the volume V, we must be more devious. We surround $r = 0$ by a small spherical hole (of radius δ), with a surface we designate S', and connect the hole with the boundary of V via a small tube, thereby creating a simply connected region V' to which Gauss' theorem will apply. See Fig. 3.18. We now consider $\oint \mathbf{E} \cdot d\boldsymbol{\sigma}$ on the surface of this modified volume. The contribution from the connecting tube will become negligible in the limit that it shrinks toward zero cross section, as $\mathbf{E}$ is finite everywhere on the tube's surface. The integral over the modified ∂V will thus be that of the original ∂V (over the outer boundary, which we designate S), plus that of the inner spherical surface (S').

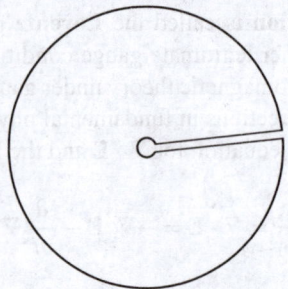

FIGURE 3.18   Making a multiply connected region simply connected.

But note that the "outward" direction for S' is toward smaller r, so $d\boldsymbol{\sigma}' = -\hat{\mathbf{r}}\,dA$. Because the modified volume contains no charge, we have

$$\oint_{\partial V'} \mathbf{E}\cdot d\boldsymbol{\sigma} = \oint_{S} \mathbf{E}\cdot d\boldsymbol{\sigma} + \frac{q}{4\pi\varepsilon_0}\oint_{S'} \frac{\hat{\mathbf{r}}\cdot d\boldsymbol{\sigma}'}{\delta^2} = 0, \tag{3.114}$$

where we have inserted the explicit form of $\mathbf{E}$ in the S' integral. Because S' is a sphere of radius δ, this integral can be evaluated. Writing $d\Omega$ as the element of solid angle, so $dA = \delta^2 d\Omega$,

$$\oint_{S'} \frac{\hat{\mathbf{r}}\cdot d\boldsymbol{\sigma}'}{\delta^2} = \int \frac{\hat{\mathbf{r}}}{\delta^2}\cdot(-\hat{\mathbf{r}}\,\delta^2\,d\Omega) = -\int d\Omega = -4\pi,$$

independent of the value of δ. Returning now to Eq. (3.114), it can be rearranged into

$$\oint_{S} \mathbf{E}\cdot d\boldsymbol{\sigma} = -\frac{q}{4\pi\varepsilon_0}(-4\pi) = +\frac{q}{\varepsilon_0},$$

the result needed to confirm the second case of Gauss' law, Eq. (3.113).

Because the equations of electrostatics are linear, Gauss' law can be extended to collections of charges, or even to continuous charge distributions. In that case, q can be replaced by $\int_V \rho\,d\tau$, and Gauss' law becomes

$$\int_{\partial V} \mathbf{E}\cdot d\boldsymbol{\sigma} = \int_V \frac{\rho}{\varepsilon_0}\,d\tau. \tag{3.115}$$

If we apply Gauss' theorem to the left side of Eq. (3.115), we have

$$\int_V \nabla\cdot\mathbf{E}\,d\tau = \int_V \frac{\rho}{\varepsilon_0}\,d\tau.$$

Since our volume is completely arbitrary, the integrands of this equation must be equal, so

$$\nabla\cdot\mathbf{E} = \frac{\rho}{\varepsilon_0}. \tag{3.116}$$

We thus see that Gauss' law is the integral form of one of Maxwell's equations.

Poisson's Equation

If we return to Eq. (3.116) and, assuming a situation independent of time, write $\mathbf{E} = -\nabla\varphi$, we obtain

$$\nabla^2\varphi = -\frac{\rho}{\varepsilon_0}. \tag{3.117}$$

This equation, applicable to electrostatics,[7] is called Poisson's equation. If, in addition, $\rho = 0$, we have an even more famous equation,

$$\nabla^2\varphi = 0, \tag{3.118}$$

Laplace's equation.

To make Poisson's equation apply to a point charge q, we need to replace ρ by a concentration of charge that is localized at a point and adds up to q. The Dirac delta function is what we need for this purpose. Thus, for a point charge q at the origin, we write

$$\nabla^2\varphi = -\frac{q}{\varepsilon_0}\delta(\mathbf{r}), \qquad (\text{charge } q \text{ at } \mathbf{r} = 0). \tag{3.119}$$

If we rewrite this equation, inserting the point-charge potential for φ, we have

$$\frac{q}{4\pi\varepsilon_0}\nabla^2\left(\frac{1}{r}\right) = -\frac{q}{\varepsilon_0}\delta(\mathbf{r}),$$

which reduces to

$$\nabla^2\left(\frac{1}{r}\right) = -4\pi\,\delta(\mathbf{r}). \tag{3.120}$$

This equation circumvents the problem that the derivatives of $1/r$ do not exist at $\mathbf{r} = 0$, and gives appropriate and correct results for systems containing point charges. Like the definition of the delta function itself, Eq. (3.120) is only meaningful when inserted into an integral. It is an important result that is used repeatedly in physics, often in the form

$$\nabla_1^2\left(\frac{1}{r_{12}}\right) = -4\pi\,\delta(\mathbf{r}_1 - \mathbf{r}_2). \tag{3.121}$$

Here $r_{12} = |\mathbf{r}_1 - \mathbf{r}_2|$, and the subscript in ∇_1 indicates that the derivatives apply to $\mathbf{r}_1$.

Helmholtz's Theorem

We now turn to two theorems that are of great formal importance, in that they establish conditions for the existence and uniqueness of solutions to time-independent problems in electromagnetic theory. The first of these theorems is:

A vector field is uniquely specified by giving its divergence and its curl within a simply connected region and its normal component on the boundary.

---

[7] For general time dependence, see Eq. (3.110).

Note that both for this theorem and the next (Helmholtz's theorem), even if there are points in the simply connected region where the divergence or the curl is only defined in terms of delta functions, these points are not to be removed from the region.

Let $\mathbf{P}$ be a vector field satisfying the conditions

$$\nabla \cdot \mathbf{P} = s, \qquad \nabla \times \mathbf{P} = \mathbf{c}, \tag{3.122}$$

where s may be interpreted as a given source (charge) density and $\mathbf{c}$ as a given circulation (current) density. Assuming that the normal component P_n on the boundary is also given, we want to show that $\mathbf{P}$ is unique.

We proceed by assuming the existence of a second vector, $\mathbf{P}'$, which satisfies Eq. (3.122) and has the same value of P_n. We form $\mathbf{Q} = \mathbf{P} - \mathbf{P}'$, which must have $\nabla \cdot \mathbf{Q}$, $\nabla \times \mathbf{Q}$, and Q_n all identically zero. Because $\mathbf{Q}$ is irrotational, there must exist a potential φ such that $\mathbf{Q} = -\nabla \varphi$, and because $\nabla \cdot \mathbf{Q} = 0$, we also have

$$\nabla^2 \varphi = 0.$$

Now we draw on Green's theorem in the form given in Eq. (3.86), letting u and v each equal φ. Because $Q_n = 0$ on the boundary, Green's theorem reduces to

$$\int_V (\nabla \varphi) \cdot (\nabla \varphi)\, d\tau = \int_V \mathbf{Q} \cdot \mathbf{Q}\, d\tau = 0.$$

This equation can only be satisfied if $\mathbf{Q}$ is identically zero, showing that $\mathbf{P}' = \mathbf{P}$, thereby proving the theorem.

The second theorem we shall prove, Helmholtz's theorem, is

A vector $\mathbf{P}$ with both source and circulation densities vanishing at infinity may be written as the sum of two parts, one of which is irrotational, the other of which is solenoidal.

Helmholtz's theorem will clearly be satisfied if $\mathbf{P}$ can be written in the form

$$\mathbf{P} = -\nabla \varphi + \nabla \times \mathbf{A}, \tag{3.123}$$

since $-\nabla \varphi$ is irrotational, while $\nabla \times \mathbf{A}$ is solenoidal. Because $\mathbf{P}$ is known, so are also s and $\mathbf{c}$, defined as

$$s = \nabla \cdot \mathbf{P}, \quad \mathbf{c} = \nabla \times \mathbf{P}.$$

We proceed by exhibiting expressions for φ and $\mathbf{A}$ that enable the recovery of s and $\mathbf{c}$. Because the region here under study is simply connected and the vector involved vanishes at infinity (so that the first theorem of this subsection applies), having the correct s and $\mathbf{c}$ guarantees that we have properly reproduced $\mathbf{P}$.

The formulas proposed for φ and $\mathbf{A}$ are the following, written in terms of the spatial variable $\mathbf{r}_1$:

$$\varphi(\mathbf{r}_1) = \frac{1}{4\pi} \int \frac{s(\mathbf{r}_2)}{r_{12}} d\tau_2, \tag{3.124}$$

$$\mathbf{A}(\mathbf{r}_1) = \frac{1}{4\pi} \int \frac{\mathbf{c}(\mathbf{r}_2)}{r_{12}} d\tau_2. \tag{3.125}$$

Here $r_{12} = |\mathbf{r}_1 - \mathbf{r}_2|$.

If Eq. (3.123) is to be satisfied with the proposed values of φ and $\mathbf{A}$, it is necessary that

$$\nabla \cdot \mathbf{P} = -\nabla \cdot \nabla\varphi + \nabla \cdot (\nabla \times \mathbf{A}) = -\nabla^2\varphi = s,$$

$$\nabla \times \mathbf{P} = -\nabla \times \nabla\varphi + \nabla \times (\nabla \times \mathbf{A}) = \nabla \times (\nabla \times \mathbf{A}) = \mathbf{c}.$$

To check that $-\nabla^2\varphi = s$, we examine

$$-\nabla_1^2\varphi(\mathbf{r}_1) = -\frac{1}{4\pi} \int \nabla_1^2\left(\frac{1}{r_{12}}\right) s(\mathbf{r}_2) d\tau_2$$

$$= -\frac{1}{4\pi} \int \left[-4\pi\delta(\mathbf{r}_1 - \mathbf{r}_2)\right] s(\mathbf{r}_2) d\tau_2 = s(\mathbf{r}_1). \tag{3.126}$$

We have written ∇_1 to make clear that it operates on $\mathbf{r}_1$ and not $\mathbf{r}_2$, and we have used the delta-function property given in Eq. (3.121). So s has been recovered.

We now check that $\nabla \times (\nabla \times \mathbf{A}) = \mathbf{c}$. We start by using Eq. (3.70) to convert this condition to a more easily utilized form:

$$\nabla \times (\nabla \times \mathbf{A}) = \nabla(\nabla \cdot \mathbf{A}) - \nabla^2\mathbf{A} = \mathbf{c}.$$

Taking $\mathbf{r}_1$ as the free variable, we look first at

$$\nabla_1\big(\nabla_1 \cdot \mathbf{A}(\mathbf{r}_1)\big) = \frac{1}{4\pi}\nabla_1 \int \nabla_1 \cdot \left(\frac{\mathbf{c}(\mathbf{r}_2)}{r_{12}}\right) d\tau_2$$

$$= \frac{1}{4\pi}\nabla_1 \int \mathbf{c}(\mathbf{r}_2) \cdot \nabla_1\left(\frac{1}{r_{12}}\right) d\tau_2$$

$$= \frac{1}{4\pi}\nabla_1 \int \mathbf{c}(\mathbf{r}_2) \cdot \left[-\nabla_2\left(\frac{1}{r_{12}}\right)\right] d\tau_2.$$

To reach the second line of this equation, we used Eq. (3.72) for the special case that the vector in that equation is not a function of the variable being differentiated. Then, to obtain the third line, we note that because the ∇_1 within the integral acts on a function of $\mathbf{r}_1 - \mathbf{r}_2$, we can change ∇_1 into ∇_2 and introduce a sign change.

Now we integrate by parts, as in Example 3.7.3, reaching

$$\nabla_1\big[\nabla_1 \cdot \mathbf{A}(\mathbf{r}_1)\big] = \frac{1}{4\pi}\nabla_1 \int \big(\nabla_2 \cdot \mathbf{c}(\mathbf{r}_2)\big)\left(\frac{1}{r_{12}}\right) d\tau_2.$$

At last we have the result we need: $\nabla_2 \cdot \mathbf{c}(\mathbf{r}_2)$ vanishes, because $\mathbf{c}$ is a curl, so the entire $\nabla(\nabla \cdot \mathbf{A})$ term is zero and may be dropped. This reduces the condition we are checking to $-\nabla^2\mathbf{A} = \mathbf{c}$.

The quantity $-\nabla^2\mathbf{A}$ is a vector Laplacian and we may individually evaluate its Cartesian components. For component j,

$$-\nabla_1^2 A_j(\mathbf{r}_1) = -\frac{1}{4\pi} \int c_j(\mathbf{r}_2) \nabla_1^2\left(\frac{1}{r_{12}}\right) d\tau_2$$

$$= -\frac{1}{4\pi} \int c_j(\mathbf{r}_2)\big[-4\pi\delta(\mathbf{r}_1 - \mathbf{r}_2)\big] d\tau_2 = c_j(\mathbf{r}_1).$$

This completes the proof of Helmholtz's theorem.

Helmholtz's theorem legitimizes the division of the quantities appearing in electromagnetic theory into an irrotational vector field $\mathbf{E}$ and a solenoidal vector field $\mathbf{B}$, together with their respective representations using scalar and vector potentials. As we have seen in numerous examples, the source s is identified as the charge density (divided by ε_0) and the circulation $\mathbf{c}$ is the current density (multiplied by μ_0).

Exercises

3.9.1   If a force $\mathbf{F}$ is given by

$$\mathbf{F} = (x^2 + y^2 + z^2)^n (\hat{\mathbf{e}}_x x + \hat{\mathbf{e}}_y y + \hat{\mathbf{e}}_z z),$$

find

(a) $\nabla \cdot \mathbf{F}$.
(b) $\nabla \times \mathbf{F}$.
(c)   A scalar potential $\varphi(x, y, z)$ so that $\mathbf{F} = -\nabla \varphi$.
(d)   For what value of the exponent n does the scalar potential diverge at both the origin and infinity?

ANS.   (a) $(2n + 3)r^{2n}$ (b) 0
         (c) $-r^{2n+2}/(2n + 2)$, $n \neq -1$ (d) $n = -1$, $\varphi = -\ln r$.

3.9.2   A sphere of radius a is uniformly charged (throughout its volume). Construct the electrostatic potential $\varphi(r)$ for $0 \leq r < \infty$.

3.9.3   The origin of the Cartesian coordinates is at the Earth's center. The moon is on the z-axis, a fixed distance R away (center-to-center distance). The tidal force exerted by the moon on a particle at the Earth's surface (point x, y, z) is given by

$$F_x = -GMm\frac{x}{R^3}, \quad F_y = -GMm\frac{y}{R^3}, \quad F_z = +2GMm\frac{z}{R^3}.$$

Find the potential that yields this tidal force.

ANS. $-\dfrac{GMm}{R^3}\left(z^2 - \dfrac{1}{2}x^2 - \dfrac{1}{2}y^2\right).$

3.9.4   A long, straight wire carrying a current I produces a magnetic induction $\mathbf{B}$ with components

$$\mathbf{B} = \frac{\mu_0 I}{2\pi}\left(-\frac{y}{x^2 + y^2}, \frac{x}{x^2 + y^2}, 0\right).$$

Find a magnetic vector potential $\mathbf{A}$.

ANS. $\mathbf{A} = -\hat{\mathbf{z}}(\mu_0 I/4\pi)\ln(x^2 + y^2)$. (This solution is not unique.)

3.9.5   If

$$\mathbf{B} = \frac{\hat{\mathbf{r}}}{r^2} = \left(\frac{x}{r^3}, \frac{y}{r^3}, \frac{z}{r^3}\right),$$

find a vector $\mathbf{A}$ such that $\nabla \times \mathbf{A} = \mathbf{B}$.

ANS.   One possible solution is $\mathbf{A} = \dfrac{\hat{\mathbf{e}}_x yz}{r(x^2 + y^2)} - \dfrac{\hat{\mathbf{e}}_y xz}{r(x^2 + y^2)}.$

3.9.6   Show that the pair of equations

$$A = \frac{1}{2}(B \times r), \quad B = \nabla \times A,$$

is satisfied by any constant magnetic induction **B**.

3.9.7   Vector **B** is formed by the product of two gradients

$$B = (\nabla u) \times (\nabla v),$$

where u and v are scalar functions.

(a)   Show that **B** is solenoidal.

(b)   Show that

$$A = \frac{1}{2}(u \nabla v - v \nabla u)$$

is a vector potential for **B**, in that

$$B = \nabla \times A.$$

3.9.8   The magnetic induction **B** is related to the magnetic vector potential **A** by $B = \nabla \times A$. By Stokes' theorem

$$\int B \cdot d\sigma = \oint A \cdot dr.$$

Show that each side of this equation is invariant under the **gauge transformation**, $A \rightarrow A + \nabla \varphi$.
Note. Take the function φ to be single-valued.

3.9.9   Show that the value of the electrostatic potential φ at any point P is equal to the average of the potential over any spherical surface centered on P, provided that there are no electric charges on or within the sphere.
Hint. Use Green's theorem, Eq. (3.85), with $u = r^{-1}$, the distance from P, and $v = \varphi$. Equation (3.120) will also be useful.

3.9.10   Using Maxwell's equations, show that for a system (steady current) the magnetic vector potential **A** satisfies a vector Poisson equation,

$$\nabla^2 A = -\mu J,$$

provided we require $\nabla \cdot A = 0$.

3.9.11   Derive, assuming the Lorentz gauge, Eq. (3.109):

$$\frac{1}{c^2} \frac{\partial^2 A}{\partial t^2} - \nabla^2 A = \mu_0 J.$$

Hint. Eq. (3.70) will be helpful.

3.9.12   Prove that an arbitrary solenoidal vector $\mathbf{B}$ can be described as $\mathbf{B} = \nabla \times \mathbf{A}$, with

$$\mathbf{A} = -\hat{\mathbf{e}}_x \int_{y_0}^{y} B_z(x, y, z)\, dy - \hat{\mathbf{e}}_z \left[\int_{x_0}^{x} B_y(x, y_0, z)\, dx - \int_{y_0}^{y} B_x(x, y, z)\, dy \right].$$

3.10   CURVILINEAR COORDINATES

Up to this point we have treated vectors essentially entirely in Cartesian coordinates; when $\mathbf{r}$ or a function of it was encountered, we wrote $\mathbf{r}$ as $\sqrt{x^2 + y^2 + z^2}$, so that Cartesian coordinates could continue to be used. Such an approach ignores the simplifications that can result if one uses a coordinate system that is appropriate to the symmetry of a problem. Central force problems are frequently easiest to deal with in spherical polar coordinates. Problems involving geometrical elements such as straight wires may be best handled in cylindrical coordinates. Yet other coordinate systems (of use too infrequent to be described here) may be appropriate for other problems.

Naturally, there is a price that must be paid for the use of a non-Cartesian coordinate system. Vector operators become different in form, and their specific forms may be position-dependent. We proceed here to examine these questions and derive the necessary formulas.

Orthogonal Coordinates in $\mathbb{R}^3$

In Cartesian coordinates the point (x_0, y_0, z_0) can be identified as the intersection of three planes: (1) the plane $x = x_0$ (a surface of constant x), (2) the plane $y = y_0$ (constant y), and (3) the plane $z = z_0$ (constant z). A change in x corresponds to a displacement **normal** to the surface of constant x; similar remarks apply to changes in y or z. The planes of constant coordinate value are mutually perpendicular, and have the obvious feature that the normal to any given one of them is in the same direction, no matter where on the plane it is constructed (a plane of constant x has a normal that is, of course, everywhere in the direction of $\hat{\mathbf{e}}_x$).

Consider now, as an example of a curvilinear coordinate system, spherical polar coordinates (see Fig. 3.19). A point $\mathbf{r}$ is identified by r (distance from the origin), θ (angle of $\mathbf{r}$ relative to the polar axis, which is conventionally in the z direction), and φ (dihedral angle between the zx plane and the plane containing $\hat{\mathbf{e}}_z$ and $\mathbf{r}$). The point $\mathbf{r}$ is therefore at the intersection of (1) a sphere of radius r, (2) a cone of opening angle θ, and (3) a half-plane through equatorial angle φ. This example provides several observations: (1) general

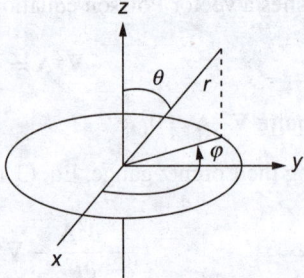

FIGURE 3.19   Spherical polar coordinates.

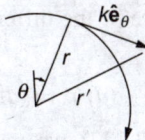

FIGURE 3.20   Effect of a "large" displacement in the direction $\hat{\mathbf{e}}_\theta$. Note that $r' \neq r$.

coordinates need not be lengths, (2) a surface of constant coordinate value may have a normal whose direction depends on position, (3) surfaces with different constant values of the same coordinate need not be parallel, and therefore also (4) changes in the value of a coordinate may move $\mathbf{r}$ in both an amount and a direction that depends on position.

It is convenient to define unit vectors $\hat{\mathbf{e}}_r$, $\hat{\mathbf{e}}_\theta$, $\hat{\mathbf{e}}_\varphi$ in the directions of the normals to the surfaces, respectively, of constant r, θ, and φ. The spherical polar coordinate system has the feature that these unit vectors are mutually perpendicular, meaning that, for example, $\hat{\mathbf{e}}_\theta$ will be tangent to both the constant-r and constant-φ surfaces, so that a small displacement in the $\hat{\mathbf{e}}_\theta$ direction will not change the values of either the r or the φ coordinate. The reason for the restriction to "small" displacements is that the directions of the normals are position-dependent; a "large" displacement in the $\hat{\mathbf{e}}_\theta$ direction would change r (see Fig. 3.20). If the coordinate unit vectors are mutually perpendicular, the coordinate system is said to be **orthogonal**.

If we have a vector field $\mathbf{V}$ (so we associate a value of $\mathbf{V}$ with each point in a region of $\mathbb{R}^3$), we can write $\mathbf{V}(\mathbf{r})$ in terms of the orthogonal set of unit vectors that are defined for the point $\mathbf{r}$; symbolically, the result is

$$\mathbf{V}(\mathbf{r}) = V_r\,\hat{\mathbf{e}}_r + V_\theta\,\hat{\mathbf{e}}_\theta + V_\varphi\,\hat{\mathbf{e}}_\varphi.$$

It is important to realize that the unit vectors $\hat{\mathbf{e}}_i$ have directions that depend on the value of $\mathbf{r}$. If we have another vector field $\mathbf{W}(\mathbf{r})$ for the **same** point $\mathbf{r}$, we can perform **algebraic** processes[8] on $\mathbf{V}$ and $\mathbf{W}$ by the same rules as for Cartesian coordinates. For example, **at the point r**,

$$\mathbf{V} \cdot \mathbf{W} = V_r W_r + V_\theta W_\theta + V_\varphi W_\varphi.$$

However, if $\mathbf{V}$ and $\mathbf{W}$ are not associated with the same $\mathbf{r}$, we cannot carry out such operations in this way, and it is important to realize that

$$\mathbf{r} \neq r\hat{\mathbf{e}}_r + \theta\hat{\mathbf{e}}_\theta + \varphi\hat{\mathbf{e}}_\varphi.$$

Summarizing, the component formulas for $\mathbf{V}$ or $\mathbf{W}$ describe component decompositions applicable to the point at which the vector is specified; an attempt to decompose $\mathbf{r}$ as illustrated above is incorrect because it uses fixed unit-vector orientations where they do not apply.

Dealing for the moment with an arbitrary curvilinear system, with coordinates labeled (q_1, q_2, q_3), we consider how changes in the q_i are related to changes in the Cartesian coordinates. Since x can be thought of as a function of the q_i, namely $x(q_1, q_2, q_3)$, we have

$$dx = \frac{\partial x}{\partial q_1}dq_1 + \frac{\partial x}{\partial q_2}dq_2 + \frac{\partial x}{\partial q_3}\,dq_3, \tag{3.127}$$

with similar formulas for dy and dz.

---

[8]Addition, multiplication by a scalar, dot and cross products (but not application of differential or integral operators).

We next form a measure of the differential displacement, $d\mathbf{r}$, associated with changes dq_i. We actually examine

$$(dr)^2 = (dx)^2 + (dy)^2 + (dz)^2.$$

Taking the square of Eq. (3.127), we get

$$(dx)^2 = \sum_{ij} \frac{\partial x}{\partial q_i} \frac{\partial x}{\partial q_j} dq_i dq_j$$

and similar expressions for $(dy)^2$ and $(dz)^2$. Combining these and collecting terms with the same $dq_i dq_j$, we reach the result

$$(dr)^2 = \sum_{ij} g_{ij} dq_i dq_j, \tag{3.128}$$

where

$$g_{ij}(q_1, q_2, q_3) = \frac{\partial x}{\partial q_i} \frac{\partial x}{\partial q_j} + \frac{\partial y}{\partial q_i} \frac{\partial y}{\partial q_j} + \frac{\partial z}{\partial q_i} \frac{\partial z}{\partial q_j}. \tag{3.129}$$

Spaces with a measure of distance given by Eq. (3.128) are called **metric** or **Riemannian**.

Equation (3.129) can be interpreted as the dot product of a vector in the dq_i direction, of components $(\partial x/\partial q_i, \partial y/\partial q_i, \partial z/\partial q_i)$, with a similar vector in the dq_j direction. If the q_i coordinates are perpendicular, the coefficients g_{ij} will vanish when $i \neq j$.

Since it is our objective to discuss orthogonal coordinate systems, we specialize Eqs. (3.128) and (3.129) to

$$(dr)^2 = (h_1 dq_1)^2 + (h_2 dq_2)^2 + (h_3 dq_3)^2, \tag{3.130}$$

$$h_i^2 = \left(\frac{\partial x}{\partial q_i}\right)^2 + \left(\frac{\partial y}{\partial q_i}\right)^2 + \left(\frac{\partial y}{\partial q_i}\right)^2. \tag{3.131}$$

If we consider Eq. (3.130) for a case $dq_2 = dq_3 = 0$, we see that we can identify $h_1 dq_1$ as dr_1, meaning that the element of displacement in the q_1 direction is $h_1 dq_1$. Thus, in general,

$$dr_i = h_i dq_i, \quad \text{or} \quad \frac{\partial \mathbf{r}}{\partial q_i} = h_i \hat{\mathbf{e}}_i. \tag{3.132}$$

Here $\hat{\mathbf{e}}_i$ is a unit vector in the q_i direction, and the overall $d\mathbf{r}$ takes the form

$$d\mathbf{r} = h_1 dq_1 \hat{\mathbf{e}}_1 + h_2 dq_2 \hat{\mathbf{e}}_2 + h_3 dq_3 \hat{\mathbf{e}}_3. \tag{3.133}$$

Note that h_i may be position-dependent and must have the dimension needed to cause $h_i dq_i$ to be a length.

Integrals in Curvilinear Coordinates

Given the scale factors h_i for a set of coordinates, either because they have been tabulated or because we have evaluated them via Eq. (3.131), we can use them to set up formulas for integration in the curvilinear coordinates. Line integrals will take the form

$$\int_C \mathbf{V} \cdot d\mathbf{r} = \sum_i \int_C V_i h_i dq_i. \tag{3.134}$$

Surface integrals take the same form as in Cartesian coordinates, with the exception that instead of expressions like $dx\, dy$ we have $(h_1 dq_1)(h_2 dq_2) = h_1 h_2\, dq_1\, dq_2$ etc. This means that

$$\int_S \mathbf{V} \cdot d\boldsymbol{\sigma} = \int_S V_1 h_2 h_3\, dq_2 dq_3 + \int_S V_2 h_3 h_1\, dq_3 dq_1 + \int_S V_3 h_1 h_2\, dq_1 dq_2. \qquad (3.135)$$

The element of volume in orthogonal curvilinear coordinates is

$$d\tau = h_1 h_2 h_3\, dq_1 dq_2 dq_3, \qquad (3.136)$$

so volume integrals take the form

$$\int_V \varphi(q_1, q_2, q_3) h_1 h_2 h_3 dq_1 dq_2 dq_3, \qquad (3.137)$$

or the analogous expression with φ replaced by a vector $\mathbf{V}(q_1, q_2, q_3)$.

Differential Operators in Curvilinear Coordinates

We continue with a restriction to orthogonal coordinate systems.

Gradient—Because our curvilinear coordinates are orthogonal, the gradient takes the same form as for Cartesian coordinates, providing we use the differential displacements $dr_i = h_i\, dq_i$ in the formula. Thus, we have

$$\nabla \varphi(q_1, q_2, q_3) = \hat{\mathbf{e}}_1 \frac{1}{h_1} \frac{\partial \varphi}{\partial q_1} + \hat{\mathbf{e}}_2 \frac{1}{h_2} \frac{\partial \varphi}{\partial q_2} + \hat{\mathbf{e}}_3 \frac{1}{h_3} \frac{\partial \varphi}{\partial q_3}, \qquad (3.138)$$

this corresponds to writing ∇ as

$$\nabla = \hat{\mathbf{e}}_1 \frac{1}{h_1} \frac{\partial}{\partial q_1} + \hat{\mathbf{e}}_2 \frac{1}{h_2} \frac{\partial}{\partial q_2} + \hat{\mathbf{e}}_3 \frac{1}{h_3} \frac{\partial}{\partial q_3}. \qquad (3.139)$$

Divergence—This operator must have the same meaning as in Cartesian coordinates, so $\nabla \cdot \mathbf{V}$ must give the net outward flux of $\mathbf{V}$ per unit volume at the point of evaluation. The key difference from the Cartesian case is that an element of volume will no longer be a parallelepiped, as the scale factors h_i are in general functions of position. See Fig. 3.21. To compute the net outflow of $\mathbf{V}$ in the q_1 direction from a volume element defined by

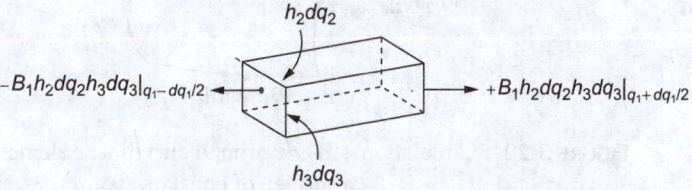

FIGURE 3.21   Outflow of B_1 in the q_1 direction from a curvilinear volume element.

dq_1, dq_2, dq_3 and centered at (q_1, q_2, q_3), we must form

$$\text{Net } q_1 \text{ outflow} = -V_1 h_2 h_3 \, dq_2 dq_3 \Big|_{q_1 - dq_1/2, q_2, q_3} + V_1 h_2 h_3 \, dq_2 dq_3 \Big|_{q_1 + dq_1/2, q_2, q_3}.$$

(3.140)

Note that not only V_1, but also $h_2 h_3$ must be evaluated at the displaced values of q_1; this product may have different values at $q_1 + dq_1/2$ and $q_1 - dq_1/2$. Rewriting Eq. (3.140) in terms of a derivative with respect to q_1, we have

$$\text{Net } q_1 \text{ outflow} = \frac{\partial}{\partial q_1}(V_1 h_2 h_3) dq_1 dq_2 dq_3.$$

Combining this with the q_2 and q_3 outflows and dividing by the differential volume $h_1 h_2 h_3 \, dq_1 dq_2 dq_3$, we get the formula

$$\nabla \cdot \mathbf{V}(q_1, q_2, q_3) = \frac{1}{h_1 h_2 h_3} \left[\frac{\partial}{\partial q_1}(V_1 h_2 h_3) + \frac{\partial}{\partial q_2}(V_2 h_3 h_1) + \frac{\partial}{\partial q_3}(V_3 h_1 h_2) \right]. \quad (3.141)$$

Laplacian—From the formulas for the gradient and divergence, we can form the Laplacian in curvilinear coordinates:

$$\nabla^2 \varphi(q_1, q_2, q_3) = \nabla \cdot \nabla \varphi =$$
$$\frac{1}{h_1 h_2 h_3} \left[\frac{\partial}{\partial q_1}\left(\frac{h_2 h_3}{h_1} \frac{\partial \varphi}{\partial q_1} \right) + \frac{\partial}{\partial q_2}\left(\frac{h_3 h_1}{h_2} \frac{\partial \varphi}{\partial q_2} \right) + \frac{\partial}{\partial q_3}\left(\frac{h_1 h_2}{h_3} \frac{\partial \varphi}{\partial q_3} \right) \right]. \quad (3.142)$$

Note that the Laplacian contains no cross derivatives, such as $\partial^2/\partial q_1 \partial q_2$. They do not appear because the coordinate system is orthogonal.

Curl—In the same spirit as our treatment of the divergence, we calculate the circulation around an element of area in the $q_1 q_2$ plane, and therefore associated with a vector in the q_3 direction. Referring to Fig. 3.22, the line integral $\oint \mathbf{B} \cdot d\mathbf{r}$ consists of four segment

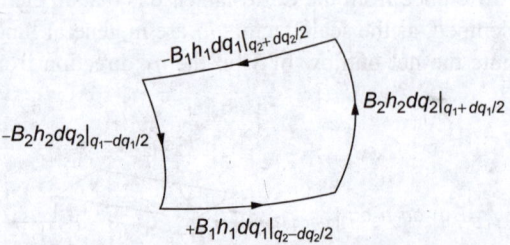

FIGURE 3.22   Circulation $\oint \mathbf{B} \cdot d\mathbf{r}$ around curvilinear element of area on a surface of constant q_3.

contributions, which to first order are

$$\text{Segment 1} = (h_1 B_1)\Big|_{q_1, q_2 - dq_2/2, q_3} dq_1,$$

$$\text{Segment 2} = (h_2 B_2)\Big|_{q_1 + dq_1/2, q_2, q_3} dq_2,$$

$$\text{Segment 3} = -(h_1 B_1)\Big|_{q_1, q_2 + dq_2/2, q_3} dq_1,$$

$$\text{Segment 4} = -(h_2 B_2)\Big|_{q_1 - dq_1/2, q_2, q_3} dq_2.$$

Keeping in mind that the h_i are functions of position, and that the loop has area $h_1 h_2 \, dq_1 dq_2$, these contributions combine into a circulation per unit area

$$(\nabla \times \mathbf{B})_3 = \frac{1}{h_1 h_2}\left[-\frac{\partial}{\partial q_2}(h_1 B_1) + \frac{\partial}{\partial q_1}(h_2 B_2)\right].$$

The generalization of this result to arbitrary orientation of the circulation loop can be brought to the determinantal form

$$\nabla \times \mathbf{B} = \frac{1}{h_1 h_2 h_3}\begin{vmatrix} \hat{\mathbf{e}}_1 h_1 & \hat{\mathbf{e}}_2 h_2 & \hat{\mathbf{e}}_3 h_3 \\ \dfrac{\partial}{\partial q_1} & \dfrac{\partial}{\partial q_2} & \dfrac{\partial}{\partial q_3} \\ h_1 B_1 & h_2 B_2 & h_3 B_3 \end{vmatrix}. \tag{3.143}$$

Just as for Cartesian coordinates, this determinant is to be evaluated from the top down, so that the derivatives will act on its bottom row.

Circular Cylindrical Coordinates

Although there are at least 11 coordinate systems that are appropriate for use in solving physics problems, the evolution of computers and efficient programming techniques have greatly reduced the need for most of these coordinate systems, with the result that the discussion in this book is limited to (1) Cartesian coordinates, (2) spherical polar coordinates (treated in the next subsection), and (3) circular cylindrical coordinates, which we discuss here. Specifications and details of other coordinate systems will be found in the first two editions of this work and in Additional Readings at the end of this chapter (Morse and Feshbach, Margenau and Murphy).

In the circular cylindrical coordinate system the three curvilinear coordinates are labeled (ρ, φ, z). We use ρ for the perpendicular distance from the z-axis because we reserve r for the distance from the origin. The ranges of ρ, φ, and z are

$$0 \le \rho < \infty, \quad 0 \le \varphi < 2\pi, \quad -\infty < z < \infty.$$

For $\rho = 0$, φ is not well defined. The coordinate surfaces, shown in Fig. 3.23, follow:

1. Right circular cylinders having the z-axis as a common axis,

$$\rho = \left(x^2 + y^2\right)^{1/2} = \text{constant}.$$

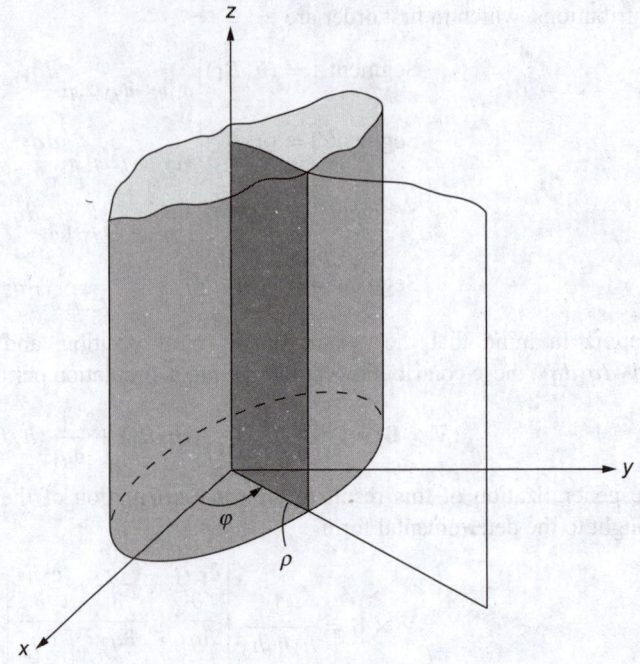

FIGURE 3.23   Cylindrical coordinates ρ, φ, z.

2. Half-planes through the z-axis, at an angle φ measured from the x direction,

$$\varphi = \tan^{-1}\left(\frac{y}{x}\right) = \text{constant}.$$

The arctangent is double valued on the range of φ, and the correct value of φ must be determined by the individual signs of x and y.

3. Planes parallel to the xy-plane, as in the Cartesian system,

$$z = \text{constant}.$$

Inverting the preceding equations, we can obtain

$$x = \rho \cos\varphi, \quad y = \rho \sin\varphi, \quad z = z. \tag{3.144}$$

This is essentially a 2-D curvilinear system with a Cartesian z-axis added on to form a 3-D system.

The coordinate vector $\mathbf{r}$ and a general vector $\mathbf{V}$ are expressed as

$$\mathbf{r} = \rho\,\hat{\mathbf{e}}_\rho + z\,\hat{\mathbf{e}}_z, \quad \mathbf{V} = V_\rho\,\hat{\mathbf{e}}_\rho + V_\varphi\,\hat{\mathbf{e}}_\varphi + V_z\,\hat{\mathbf{e}}_z.$$

From Eq. (3.131), the scale factors for these coordinates are

$$h_\rho = 1, \quad h_\varphi = \rho, \quad h_z = 1, \tag{3.145}$$

so the elements of displacement, area, and volume are

$$d\mathbf{r} = \hat{\mathbf{e}}_\rho \, d\rho + \rho \, \hat{\mathbf{e}}_\varphi \, d\varphi + \hat{\mathbf{e}}_z \, dz,$$

$$d\boldsymbol{\sigma} = \rho \, \hat{\mathbf{e}}_\rho \, d\varphi \, dz + \hat{\mathbf{e}}_\varphi d\rho \, dz + \rho \, \hat{\mathbf{e}}_z \, d\rho \, d\varphi, \qquad (3.146)$$

$$d\tau = \rho \, d\rho \, d\varphi \, dz.$$

It is perhaps worth emphasizing that the unit vectors $\hat{\mathbf{e}}_\rho$ and $\hat{\mathbf{e}}_\varphi$ have directions that vary with φ; if expressions containing these unit vectors are differentiated with respect to φ, the derivatives of these unit vectors must be included in the computations.

Example 3.10.1   KEPLER'S AREA LAW FOR PLANETARY MOTION

One of Kepler's laws states that the radius vector of a planet, relative to an origin at the sun, sweeps out equal areas in equal time. It is instructive to derive this relationship using cylindrical coordinates. For simplicity we consider a planet of unit mass and motion in the plane $z = 0$.

The gravitational force $\mathbf{F}$ is of the form $f(r) \, \hat{\mathbf{e}}_r$, and hence the torque about the origin, $\mathbf{r} \times \mathbf{F}$, vanishes, so angular momentum $\mathbf{L} = \mathbf{r} \times d\mathbf{r}/dt$ is conserved. To evaluate $d\mathbf{r}/dt$, we start from $d\mathbf{r}$ as given in Eq. (3.146), writing

$$\frac{d\mathbf{r}}{dt} = \hat{\mathbf{e}}_\rho \dot{\rho} + \hat{\mathbf{e}}_\varphi \rho \dot{\varphi},$$

where we have used the dot notation (invented by Newton) to indicate time derivatives. We now form

$$\mathbf{L} = \rho \, \hat{\mathbf{e}}_\rho \times \left(\hat{\mathbf{e}}_\rho \dot{\rho} + \hat{\mathbf{e}}_\varphi \rho \dot{\varphi} \right) = \rho^2 \dot{\varphi} \hat{\mathbf{e}}_z.$$

We conclude that $\rho^2 \dot{\varphi}$ is constant. Making the identification $\rho^2 \dot{\varphi} = 2 \, dA/dt$, where A is the area swept out, we confirm Kepler's law. ∎

Continuing now to the vector differential operators, using Eqs. (3.138), (3.141), (3.142), and (3.143), we have

$$\boldsymbol{\nabla}\psi(\rho,\varphi,z) = \hat{\mathbf{e}}_\rho \frac{\partial \psi}{\partial b\rho} + \hat{\mathbf{e}}_\varphi \frac{1}{\rho}\frac{\partial \psi}{\partial \varphi} + \hat{\mathbf{e}}_z \frac{\partial \psi}{\partial z}, \qquad (3.147)$$

$$\boldsymbol{\nabla} \cdot \mathbf{V} = \frac{1}{\rho}\frac{\partial}{\partial \rho}(\rho V_\rho) + \frac{1}{\rho}\frac{\partial V_\varphi}{\partial \varphi} + \frac{\partial V_z}{\partial z}, \qquad (3.148)$$

$$\nabla^2 \psi = \frac{1}{\rho}\frac{\partial}{\partial \rho}\left(\rho \frac{\partial \psi}{\partial \rho} \right) + \frac{1}{\rho^2}\frac{\partial^2 \psi}{\partial \varphi^2} + \frac{\partial^2 \psi}{\partial z^2}, \qquad (3.149)$$

$$\boldsymbol{\nabla} \times V = \frac{1}{\rho}\begin{vmatrix} \hat{\mathbf{e}}_\rho & \rho\hat{\mathbf{e}}_\varphi & \hat{\mathbf{e}}_z \\ \dfrac{\partial}{\partial \rho} & \dfrac{\partial}{\partial \varphi} & \dfrac{\partial}{\partial z} \\ V_\rho & \rho V_\varphi & V_z \end{vmatrix}. \qquad (3.150)$$

Finally, for problems such as circular wave guides and cylindrical cavity resonators, one needs the vector Laplacian $\nabla^2\mathbf{V}$. From Eq. (3.70), its components in cylindrical coordinates can be shown to be

$$
\begin{aligned}
\nabla^2\mathbf{V}\big|_\rho &= \nabla^2 V_\rho - \frac{1}{\rho^2}V_\rho - \frac{2}{\rho^2}\frac{\partial V_\varphi}{\partial\varphi},\\[6pt]
\nabla^2\mathbf{V}\big|_\varphi &= \nabla^2 V_\varphi - \frac{1}{\rho^2}V_\varphi + \frac{2}{\rho^2}\frac{\partial V_\rho}{\partial\varphi},\\[6pt]
\nabla^2\mathbf{V}\big|_z &= \nabla^2 V_z.
\end{aligned}
\tag{3.151}
$$

Example 3.10.2   A NAVIER-STOKES TERM

The Navier-Stokes equations of hydrodynamics contain a nonlinear term

$$\nabla \times \left[\mathbf{v} \times (\nabla \times \mathbf{v})\right],$$

where $\mathbf{v}$ is the fluid velocity. For fluid flowing through a cylindrical pipe in the z direction,

$$\mathbf{v} = \hat{\mathbf{e}}_z v(\rho).$$

From Eq. (3.150),

$$
\nabla \times \mathbf{v} = \frac{1}{\rho}
\begin{vmatrix}
\hat{\mathbf{e}}_\rho & \rho\hat{\mathbf{e}}_\varphi & \hat{\mathbf{e}}_z \\
\dfrac{\partial}{\partial\rho} & \dfrac{\partial}{\partial\varphi} & \dfrac{\partial}{\partial z} \\
0 & 0 & v(\rho)
\end{vmatrix}
= -\hat{\mathbf{e}}_\varphi\frac{\partial v}{\partial\rho},
$$

$$
\mathbf{v} \times (\nabla \times \mathbf{v}) =
\begin{vmatrix}
\hat{\mathbf{e}}_\rho & \hat{\mathbf{e}}_\varphi & \hat{\mathbf{e}}_z \\
0 & 0 & v \\
0 & -\dfrac{\partial v}{\partial\rho} & 0
\end{vmatrix}
= \hat{\mathbf{e}}_\rho\, v(\rho)\,\frac{\partial v}{\partial\rho}.
$$

Finally,

$$
\nabla \times \left(\mathbf{v} \times (\nabla \times \mathbf{v})\right) = \frac{1}{\rho}
\begin{vmatrix}
\hat{\mathbf{e}}_\rho & \rho\hat{\mathbf{e}}_\varphi & \hat{\mathbf{e}}_z \\
\dfrac{\partial}{\partial\rho} & \dfrac{\partial}{\partial\varphi} & \dfrac{\partial}{\partial z} \\
v\dfrac{\partial v}{\partial\rho} & 0 & 0
\end{vmatrix}
= 0.
$$

For this particular case, the nonlinear term vanishes.   ∎

Spherical Polar Coordinates

Spherical polar coordinates were introduced as an initial example of a curvilinear coordinate system, and were illustrated in Fig. 3.19. We reiterate: The coordinates are labeled (r, θ, φ). Their ranges are

$$0 \le r < \infty, \quad 0 \le \theta \le \pi, \quad 0 \le \varphi < 2\pi.$$

For $r = 0$, neither θ nor φ is well defined. Additionally, φ is ill-defined for $\theta = 0$ and $\theta = \pi$. The coordinate surfaces follow:

1. Concentric spheres centered at the origin,

$$r = \left(x^2 + y^2 + z^2\right)^{1/2} = \text{constant}.$$

2. Right circular cones centered on the z (polar) axis with vertices at the origin,

$$\theta = \arccos \frac{z}{r} = \text{constant}.$$

3. Half-planes through the z (polar) axis, at an angle φ measured from the x direction,

$$\varphi = \arctan \frac{y}{x} = \text{constant}.$$

The arctangent is double valued on the range of φ, and the correct value of φ must be determined by the individual signs of x and y.

Inverting the preceding equations, we can obtain

$$x = r \sin\theta \cos\varphi, \quad y = r \sin\theta \sin\varphi, \quad z = r \cos\theta. \tag{3.152}$$

The coordinate vector $\mathbf{r}$ and a general vector $\mathbf{V}$ are expressed as

$$\mathbf{r} = r\,\hat{\mathbf{e}}_r, \quad \mathbf{V} = V_r\,\hat{\mathbf{e}}_r + V_\theta\,\hat{\mathbf{e}}_\theta + V_\varphi\,\hat{\mathbf{e}}_\varphi.$$

From Eq. (3.131), the scale factors for these coordinates are

$$h_r = 1, \quad h_\theta = r, \quad h_\varphi = r \sin\theta, \tag{3.153}$$

so the elements of displacement, area, and volume are

$$d\mathbf{r} = \hat{\mathbf{e}}_r\, dr + r\,\hat{\mathbf{e}}_\theta\, d\theta + r \sin\theta\,\hat{\mathbf{e}}_\varphi\, d\varphi,$$
$$d\boldsymbol{\sigma} = r^2 \sin\theta\,\hat{\mathbf{e}}_r\, d\theta\, d\varphi + r \sin\theta\,\hat{\mathbf{e}}_\theta\, dr\, d\varphi + r\,\hat{\mathbf{e}}_\varphi\, dr\, d\theta, \tag{3.154}$$
$$d\tau = r^2 \sin\theta\, d\rho\, d\theta\, d\varphi.$$

Frequently one encounters a need to perform a surface integration over the angles, in which case the angular dependence of $d\boldsymbol{\sigma}$ reduces to

$$d\Omega = \sin\theta\, d\theta\, d\varphi, \tag{3.155}$$

where $d\Omega$ is called an element of solid angle, and has the property that its integral over all angles has the value

$$\int d\Omega = 4\pi.$$

Note that for spherical polar coordinates, all three of the unit vectors have directions that depend on position, and this fact must be taken into account when expressions containing the unit vectors are differentiated.

The vector differential operators may now be evaluated, using Eqs. (3.138), (3.141), (3.142), and (3.143):

$$\nabla \psi (r, \theta, \varphi) = \hat{\mathbf{e}}_r \frac{\partial \psi}{\partial r} + \hat{\mathbf{e}}_\theta \frac{1}{r} \frac{\partial \psi}{\partial \theta} + \hat{\mathbf{e}}_\varphi \frac{1}{r \sin \theta} \frac{\partial \psi}{\partial \varphi}, \tag{3.156}$$

$$\nabla \cdot \mathbf{V} = \frac{1}{r^2 \sin \theta} \left[\sin \theta \frac{\partial}{\partial r} (r^2 V_r) + r \frac{\partial}{\partial \theta} (\sin \theta \, V_\theta) + r \frac{\partial V_\varphi}{\partial \varphi} \right], \tag{3.157}$$

$$\nabla^2 \psi = \frac{1}{r^2 \sin \theta} \left[\sin \theta \frac{\partial}{\partial r} \left(r^2 \frac{\partial \psi}{\partial r} \right) + \frac{\partial}{\partial \theta} \left(\sin \theta \frac{\partial \psi}{\partial \theta} \right) + \frac{1}{\sin \theta} \frac{\partial^2 \psi}{\partial \varphi^2} \right], \tag{3.158}$$

$$\nabla \times V = \frac{1}{r^2 \sin \theta} \begin{vmatrix} \hat{\mathbf{e}}_r & r \hat{\mathbf{e}}_\theta & r \sin \theta \, \hat{\mathbf{e}}_\varphi \\ \frac{\partial}{\partial r} & \frac{\partial}{\partial \theta} & \frac{\partial}{\partial \varphi} \\ V_r & r V_\theta & r \sin \theta V_\varphi \end{vmatrix}. \tag{3.159}$$

Finally, again using Eq. (3.70), the components of the vector Laplacian $\nabla^2 \mathbf{V}$ in spherical polar coordinates can be shown to be

$$\nabla^2 \mathbf{V} \Big|_r = \nabla^2 V_r - \frac{2}{r^2} V_r - \frac{2}{r^2} \cot \theta V_\theta - \frac{2}{r^2} \frac{\partial V_\theta}{\partial \theta} - \frac{2}{r^2 \sin \theta} \frac{\partial V_\varphi}{\partial \varphi},$$

$$\nabla^2 \mathbf{V} \Big|_\theta = \nabla^2 V_\theta - \frac{1}{r^2 \sin^2 \theta} V_\theta + \frac{2}{r^2} \frac{\partial V_r}{\partial \theta} - \frac{2 \cos \theta}{r^2 \sin^2 \theta} \frac{\partial V_\varphi}{\partial \varphi}, \tag{3.160}$$

$$\nabla^2 \mathbf{V} \Big|_\varphi = \nabla^2 V_\varphi - \frac{1}{r^2 \sin^2 \theta} V_\varphi + \frac{2}{r^2 \sin \theta} \frac{\partial V_r}{\partial \varphi} + \frac{2 \cos \theta}{r^2 \sin^2 \theta} \frac{\partial V_\varphi}{\partial \varphi}.$$

Example 3.10.3 $\nabla, \nabla \cdot, \nabla \times$ FOR A CENTRAL FORCE

We can now easily derive some of the results previously obtained more laboriously in Cartesian coordinates:

From Eq. (3.156),

$$\nabla f(r) = \hat{\mathbf{e}}_r \frac{df}{dr}, \quad \nabla r^n = \hat{\mathbf{e}}_r n r^{n-1}. \tag{3.161}$$

Specializing to the Coulomb potential of a point charge at the origin, $V = Ze/(4\pi \varepsilon_0 r)$, so the electric field has the expected value $\mathbf{E} = -\nabla V = (Ze/4\pi \varepsilon_0 r^2) \hat{\mathbf{e}}_r$.

Taking next the divergence of a radial function, we have from Eq. (3.157),

$$\nabla \cdot \left(\hat{\mathbf{e}}_r f(r) \right) = \frac{2}{r} f(r) + \frac{df}{dr}, \quad \nabla \cdot (\hat{\mathbf{e}}_r r^n) = (n+2) r^{n-1}. \tag{3.162}$$

Specializing the above to the Coulomb force ($n = -2$), we have (except for $r = 0$) $\nabla \cdot r^{-2} = 0$, which is consistent with Gauss' law.

Continuing now to the Laplacian, from Eq. (3.158) we have

$$\nabla^2 f(r) = \frac{2}{r} \frac{df}{dr} + \frac{d^2 f}{dr^2}, \quad \nabla^2 r^n = n(n+1) r^{n-2}, \tag{3.163}$$

in contrast to the ordinary second derivative of r^n involving $n - 1$.

Finally, from Eq. (3.159),

$$\nabla \times \left(\hat{\mathbf{e}}_r f(r)\right) = 0, \tag{3.164}$$

which confirms that central forces are irrotational. ∎

Example 3.10.4 MAGNETIC VECTOR POTENTIAL

A single current loop in the xy-plane has a vector potential $\mathbf{A}$ that is a function only of r and θ, is entirely in the $\hat{\mathbf{e}}_\varphi$ direction and is related to the current density $\mathbf{J}$ by the equation

$$\mu_0 \mathbf{J} = \nabla \times \mathbf{B} = \nabla \times \left[\nabla \times \hat{\mathbf{e}}_\varphi A_\varphi(r, \theta)\right].$$

In spherical polar coordinates this reduces to

$$\mu_0 \mathbf{J} = \nabla \times \frac{1}{r^2 \sin\theta} \begin{vmatrix} \hat{\mathbf{e}}_r & r\hat{\mathbf{e}}_\theta & r\sin\theta\,\hat{\mathbf{e}}_\varphi \\ \dfrac{\partial}{\partial r} & \dfrac{\partial}{\partial \theta} & \dfrac{\partial}{\partial \varphi} \\ 0 & 0 & r\sin\theta A_\varphi \end{vmatrix}$$

$$= \nabla \times \frac{1}{r^2 \sin\theta}\left[\hat{\mathbf{e}}_r \frac{\partial}{\partial\theta}(r\sin\theta A_\varphi) - r\hat{\mathbf{e}}_\theta \frac{\partial}{\partial r}(r\sin\theta A_\varphi)\right].$$

Taking the curl a second time, we obtain

$$\mu_0 \mathbf{J} = \frac{1}{r^2 \sin\theta} \begin{vmatrix} \hat{\mathbf{e}}_r & r\hat{\mathbf{e}}_\theta & r\sin\theta\,\hat{\mathbf{e}}_\varphi \\ \dfrac{\partial}{\partial r} & \dfrac{\partial}{\partial \theta} & \dfrac{\partial}{\partial \varphi} \\ \dfrac{1}{r\sin\theta}\dfrac{\partial}{\partial\theta}(\sin\theta A_\varphi) & -\dfrac{1}{r}\dfrac{\partial}{\partial r}(rA_\varphi) & 0 \end{vmatrix}.$$

Expanding this determinant from the top down, we reach

$$\mu_0 \mathbf{J} = -\hat{\mathbf{e}}_\varphi \left[\frac{\partial^2 A_\varphi}{\partial r^2} + \frac{2}{r}\frac{\partial A_\varphi}{\partial r} + \frac{1}{r^2 \sin\theta}\frac{\partial}{\partial\theta}\left(\sin\theta \frac{\partial A_\varphi}{\partial\theta}\right) - \frac{1}{r^2 \sin^2\theta}A_\varphi\right]. \tag{3.165}$$

Note that we get, in addition to $\nabla^2 A_\varphi$, one more term: $-A_\varphi/r^2 \sin^2\theta$. ∎

Example 3.10.5 STOKES' THEOREM

As a final example, let's compute $\oint \mathbf{B} \cdot d\mathbf{r}$ for a closed loop, comparing the result with integrals $\int (\nabla \times \mathbf{B}) \cdot d\boldsymbol{\sigma}$ for two different surfaces having the same perimeter. We use spherical polar coordinates, taking $\mathbf{B} = e^{-r}\hat{\mathbf{e}}_\varphi$.

The loop will be a unit circle about the origin in the xy-plane; the line integral about it will be taken in a counterclockwise sense as viewed from positive z, so the normal to the surfaces it bounds will pass through the xy-plane in the direction of positive z. The surfaces we consider are (1) a circular disk bounded by the loop, and (3) a hemisphere bounded by the loop, with its surface in the region $z < 0$. See Fig. 3.24.

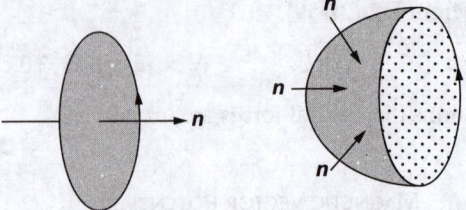

FIGURE 3.24   Surfaces for Example 3.10.5: (left) S_1, disk; (right) S_2, hemisphere.

For the line integral, $d\mathbf{r} = r\sin\theta\,\hat{\mathbf{e}}_\varphi\,d\varphi$, which reduces to $d\mathbf{r} = \hat{\mathbf{e}}_\varphi\,d\varphi$ since $\theta = \pi/2$ and $r = 1$ on the entire loop. We then have

$$\oint \mathbf{B}\cdot d\mathbf{r} = \int\limits_{\varphi=0}^{2\pi} e^{-1}\hat{\mathbf{e}}_\varphi\cdot\hat{\mathbf{e}}_\varphi\,d\varphi = \frac{2\pi}{e}.$$

For the surface integrals, we need $\nabla\times\mathbf{B}$:

$$\nabla\times\mathbf{B} = \frac{1}{r^2\sin\theta}\left[\frac{\partial}{\partial\theta}(r\sin\theta\,e^{-r})\hat{\mathbf{e}}_r - r\frac{\partial}{\partial r}(r\sin\theta\,e^{-r})\hat{\mathbf{e}}_\theta\right]$$

$$= \frac{e^{-r}\cos\theta}{r\sin\theta}\,\hat{\mathbf{e}}_r - (1-r)e^{-r}\hat{\mathbf{e}}_\theta.$$

Taking first the disk, at all points of which $\theta = \pi/2$, with integration range $0 \le r \le 1$, and $0 \le \varphi < 2\pi$, we note that $d\boldsymbol{\sigma} = -\hat{\mathbf{e}}_\theta\,r\sin\theta\,dr\,d\varphi = -\hat{\mathbf{e}}_\theta\,r\,dr\,d\varphi$. The minus sign arises because the positive normal is in the direction of **decreasing** θ. Then,

$$\int\limits_{S_1} -(\nabla\times\mathbf{B})\cdot\hat{\mathbf{e}}_\theta\,r\,dr\,d\varphi = \int\limits_0^{2\pi} d\varphi\int\limits_0^1 dr\,(1-r)\,e^{-r} = \frac{2\pi}{e}.$$

For the hemisphere, defined by $r = 1$, $\pi/2 \le \theta < \pi$, and $0 \le \varphi < 2\pi$, we have $d\boldsymbol{\sigma} = -\hat{\mathbf{e}}_r\,r^2\sin\theta\,d\theta\,d\varphi = -\hat{\mathbf{e}}_r\sin\theta\,d\theta\,d\varphi$ (the normal is in the direction of decreasing r), and

$$\int\limits_{S_2} -(\nabla\times\mathbf{B})\cdot\hat{\mathbf{e}}_r\,\sin\theta\,d\theta\,d\varphi = -\int\limits_{\pi/2}^{\pi} d\theta e^{-1}\cos\theta\int\limits_0^{2\pi} d\varphi = \frac{2\pi}{e}.$$

The results for both surfaces agree with that from the line integral of their common perimeter. Because $\nabla\times\mathbf{B}$ is solenoidal, all the flux that passes through the disk in the xy-plane must continue through the hemispherical surface, and for that matter, through **any** surface with the same perimeter. That is why Stokes' theorem is indifferent to features of the surface other than its perimeter. ∎

Rotation and Reflection in Spherical Coordinates

It is infrequent that rotational coordinate transformations need be applied in curvilinear coordinate systems, and they usually arise only in contexts that are compatible with the symmetry of the coordinate system. We limit the current discussion to rotations (and reflections) in spherical polar coordinates.

Rotation—Suppose a coordinate rotation identified by Euler angles (α, β, γ) converts the coordinates of a point from (r, θ, φ) to (r, θ', φ'). It is obvious that r retains its original value. Two questions arise: (1) How are θ' and φ' related to θ and φ? and (2) How do the components of a vector $\mathbf{A}$, namely $(A_r, A_\theta, A_\varphi)$, transform?

It is simplest to proceed, as we did for Cartesian coordinates, by analyzing the three consecutive rotations implied by the Euler angles. The first rotation, by an angle α about the z-axis, leaves θ unchanged, and converts φ into $\varphi - \alpha$. However, it causes no change in any of the components of $\mathbf{A}$.

The second rotation, which inclines the polar direction by an angle β toward the (new) x-axis, does change the values of both θ and φ and, in addition, changes the directions of $\hat{\mathbf{e}}_\theta$ and $\hat{\mathbf{e}}_\varphi$. Referring to Fig. 3.25, we see that these two unit vectors are subjected to a rotation χ in the plane tangent to the sphere of constant r, thereby yielding new unit vectors $\hat{\mathbf{e}}_\theta'$ and $\hat{\mathbf{e}}_\varphi'$ such that

$$\hat{\mathbf{e}}_\theta = \cos \chi \, \hat{\mathbf{e}}_\theta' - \sin \chi \, \hat{\mathbf{e}}_\varphi', \quad \hat{\mathbf{e}}_\varphi = \sin \chi \, \hat{\mathbf{e}}_\theta' + \cos \chi \, \hat{\mathbf{e}}_\varphi'.$$

This transformation corresponds to

$$S_2 = \begin{pmatrix} \cos \chi & \sin \chi \\ -\sin \chi & \cos \chi \end{pmatrix}.$$

Carrying out the spherical trigonometry corresponding to Fig. 3.25, we have the new coordinates

$$\cos \theta' = \cos\beta \cos \theta + \sin \beta \sin \theta \cos(\varphi - \alpha), \quad \cos \varphi' = \frac{\cos \beta \cos \theta' - \cos \theta}{\sin \beta \sin \theta'}, \quad (3.166)$$

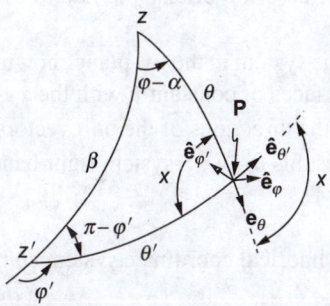

FIGURE 3.25 Rotation and unit vectors in spherical polar coordinates, shown on a sphere of radius r. The original polar direction is marked z; it is moved to the direction z', at an inclination given by the Euler angle β. The unit vectors $\hat{\mathbf{e}}_\theta$ and $\hat{\mathbf{e}}_\varphi$ at the point $\mathbf{P}$ are thereby rotated through the angle χ.

and

$$\cos\chi = \frac{\cos\beta - \cos\theta\cos\theta'}{\sin\theta\sin\theta'}. \tag{3.167}$$

The third rotation, by an angle γ about the new z-axis, leaves the components of $\mathbf{A}$ unchanged but requires the replacement of φ' by $\varphi' - \gamma$.

Summarizing,

$$\begin{pmatrix} A_r' \\ A_\theta' \\ A_\varphi' \end{pmatrix} = \begin{pmatrix} 1 & 0 & 0 \\ 0 & \cos\chi & \sin\chi \\ 0 & -\sin\chi & \cos\chi \end{pmatrix} \begin{pmatrix} A_r \\ A_\theta \\ A_\varphi \end{pmatrix}. \tag{3.168}$$

This equation specifies the components of $\mathbf{A}$ in the rotated coordinates at the point $(r, \theta', \varphi' - \gamma)$ in terms of the original components at the same physical point, (r, θ, φ).

Reflection—Inversion of the coordinate system reverses the sign of each Cartesian coordinate. Taking the angle φ as that which moves the new $+x$ coordinate toward the new $+y$ coordinate, the system (which was originally right-handed) now becomes left-handed. The coordinates (r, θ, φ) of a (fixed) point become, in the new system, $(r, \pi - \theta, \pi + \varphi)$. The unit vectors $\hat{\mathbf{e}}_r$ and $\hat{\mathbf{e}}_\varphi$ are invariant under inversion, but $\hat{\mathbf{e}}_\theta$ changes sign, so

$$\begin{pmatrix} A_r' \\ A_\theta' \\ A_\varphi' \end{pmatrix} = \begin{pmatrix} A_r \\ -A_\theta \\ A_\varphi \end{pmatrix}, \qquad \text{coordinate inversion.} \tag{3.169}$$

Exercises

3.10.1   The u-, v-, z-coordinate system frequently used in electrostatics and in hydrodynamics is defined by

$$xy = u, \quad x^2 - y^2 = v, \quad z = z.$$

This u-, v-, z-system is orthogonal.

(a) In words, describe briefly the nature of each of the three families of coordinate surfaces.

(b) Sketch the system in the xy-plane showing the intersections of surfaces of constant u and surfaces of constant v with the xy-plane.

(c) Indicate the directions of the unit vectors $\hat{\mathbf{e}}_u$ and $\hat{\mathbf{e}}_v$ in all four quadrants.

(d) Finally, is this u-, v-, z-system right-handed ($\hat{\mathbf{e}}_u \times \hat{\mathbf{e}}_v = +\hat{\mathbf{e}}_z$) or left-handed ($\hat{\mathbf{e}}_u \times \hat{\mathbf{e}}_v = -\hat{\mathbf{e}}_z$)?

3.10.2   The elliptic cylindrical coordinate system consists of three families of surfaces:

$$(1) \ \ \frac{x^2}{a^2\cosh^2 u} + \frac{y^2}{a^2\sinh^2 u} = 1; \quad (2) \ \ \frac{x^2}{a^2\cos^2 v} - \frac{y^2}{a^2\sin^2 v} = 1; \quad (3) \ \ z = z.$$

Sketch the coordinate surfaces $u = $ constant and $v = $ constant as they intersect the first quadrant of the xy-plane. Show the unit vectors $\hat{\mathbf{e}}_u$ and $\hat{\mathbf{e}}_v$. The range of u is $0 \le u < \infty$. The range of v is $0 \le v \le 2\pi$.

3.10.3   Develop arguments to show that dot and cross products (not involving ∇) in orthogonal curvilinear coordinates in $\mathbb{R}^3$ proceed, as in Cartesian coordinates, **with no involvement of scale factors**.

3.10.4   With $\hat{\mathbf{e}}_1$ a unit vector in the direction of increasing q_1, show that

(a) $\nabla \cdot \hat{\mathbf{e}}_1 = \dfrac{1}{h_1 h_2 h_3} \dfrac{\partial (h_2 h_3)}{\partial q_1}$

(b) $\nabla \times \hat{\mathbf{e}}_1 = \dfrac{1}{h_1} \left[\hat{\mathbf{e}}_2 \dfrac{1}{h_3} \dfrac{\partial h_1}{\partial q_3} - \hat{\mathbf{e}}_3 \dfrac{1}{h_2} \dfrac{\partial h_1}{\partial q_2} \right].$

Note that even though $\hat{\mathbf{e}}_1$ is a unit vector, its divergence and curl **do not necessarily vanish**.

3.10.5   Show that a set of orthogonal unit vectors $\hat{\mathbf{e}}_i$ may be defined by

$$\hat{\mathbf{e}}_i = \frac{1}{h_i} \frac{\partial \mathbf{r}}{\partial q_i}.$$

In particular, show that $\hat{\mathbf{e}}_i \cdot \hat{\mathbf{e}}_i = 1$ leads to an expression for h_i in agreement with Eq. (3.131).
The above equation for $\hat{\mathbf{e}}_i$ may be taken as a starting point for deriving

$$\frac{\partial \hat{\mathbf{e}}_i}{\partial q_j} = \hat{\mathbf{e}}_j \frac{1}{h_i} \frac{\partial h_j}{\partial q_i}, \quad i \neq j$$

and

$$\frac{\partial \hat{\mathbf{e}}_i}{\partial q_i} = -\sum_{j \neq i} \hat{\mathbf{e}}_j \frac{1}{h_j} \frac{\partial h_i}{\partial q_j}.$$

3.10.6   Resolve the circular cylindrical unit vectors into their Cartesian components (see Fig. 3.23).

$$ANS. \quad \begin{aligned} \hat{\mathbf{e}}_\rho &= \hat{\mathbf{e}}_x \cos \varphi + \hat{\mathbf{e}}_y \sin \varphi, \\ \hat{\mathbf{e}}_\varphi &= -\hat{\mathbf{e}}_x \sin \varphi + \hat{\mathbf{e}}_y \cos \varphi, \\ \hat{\mathbf{e}}_z &= \hat{\mathbf{e}}_z. \end{aligned}$$

3.10.7   Resolve the Cartesian unit vectors into their circular cylindrical components (see Fig. 3.23).

$$ANS. \quad \begin{aligned} \hat{\mathbf{e}}_x &= \hat{\mathbf{e}}_\rho \cos \varphi - \hat{\mathbf{e}}_\varphi \sin \varphi, \\ \hat{\mathbf{e}}_y &= \hat{\mathbf{e}}_\rho \sin \varphi + \hat{\mathbf{e}}_\varphi \cos \varphi, \\ \hat{\mathbf{e}}_z &= \hat{\mathbf{e}}_z. \end{aligned}$$

3.10.8   From the results of Exercise 3.10.6, show that

$$\frac{\partial \hat{\mathbf{e}}_\rho}{\partial \varphi} = \hat{\mathbf{e}}_\varphi, \quad \frac{\partial \hat{\mathbf{e}}_\varphi}{\partial \varphi} = -\hat{\mathbf{e}}_\rho$$

and that all other first derivatives of the circular cylindrical unit vectors with respect to the circular cylindrical coordinates vanish.

3.10.9   Compare $\nabla \cdot \mathbf{V}$ as given for cylindrical coordinates in Eq. (3.148) with the result of its computation by applying to $\mathbf{V}$ the operator

$$\nabla = \hat{\mathbf{e}}_\rho \frac{\partial}{\partial \rho} + \hat{\mathbf{e}}_\varphi \frac{1}{\rho} \frac{\partial}{\partial \varphi} + \hat{\mathbf{e}}_z \frac{\partial}{\partial z}$$

Note that ∇ acts both on the unit vectors and on the components of $\mathbf{V}$.

3.10.10   (a)   Show that $\mathbf{r} = \hat{\mathbf{e}}_\rho \rho + \hat{\mathbf{e}}_z z$.

(b)   Working entirely in circular cylindrical coordinates, show that

$$\nabla \cdot \mathbf{r} = 3 \quad \text{and} \quad \nabla \times \mathbf{r} = 0.$$

3.10.11   (a)   Show that the parity operation (reflection through the origin) on a point (ρ, φ, z) relative to **fixed** x-, y-, z-axes consists of the transformation

$$\rho \to \rho, \quad \varphi \to \varphi \pm \pi, \quad z \to -z.$$

(b)   Show that $\hat{\mathbf{e}}_\rho$ and $\hat{\mathbf{e}}_\varphi$ have odd parity (reversal of direction) and that $\hat{\mathbf{e}}_z$ has even parity.
Note. The Cartesian unit vectors $\hat{\mathbf{e}}_x$, $\hat{\mathbf{e}}_y$, and $\hat{\mathbf{e}}_z$ remain constant.

3.10.12   A rigid body is rotating about a fixed axis with a constant angular velocity $\boldsymbol{\omega}$. Take $\boldsymbol{\omega}$ to lie along the z-axis. Express the position vector $\mathbf{r}$ in circular cylindrical coordinates and using circular cylindrical coordinates,

(a)   calculate $\mathbf{v} = \boldsymbol{\omega} \times \mathbf{r}$,

(b)   calculate $\nabla \times \mathbf{v}$.

$$\begin{aligned} ANS. \quad &(a) \quad \mathbf{v} = \hat{\mathbf{e}}_\varphi \omega \rho \\ &(b) \quad \nabla \times \mathbf{v} = 2\boldsymbol{\omega}. \end{aligned}$$

3.10.13   Find the circular cylindrical components of the velocity and acceleration of a moving particle,

$$\begin{aligned} v_\rho &= \dot{\rho}, & a_\rho &= \ddot{\rho} - \rho \dot{\varphi}^2, \\ v_\varphi &= \rho \dot{\varphi}, & a_\varphi &= \rho \ddot{\varphi} + 2\dot{\rho} \dot{\varphi}, \\ v_z &= \dot{z}, & a_z &= \ddot{z}. \end{aligned}$$

Hint. $\quad \mathbf{r}(t) = \hat{\mathbf{e}}_\rho(t) \rho(t) + \hat{\mathbf{e}}_z z(t)$

$\qquad\qquad = [\hat{\mathbf{e}}_x \cos \varphi(t) + \hat{\mathbf{e}}_y \sin \varphi(t)] \rho(t) + \hat{\mathbf{e}}_z z(t).$

Note. $\dot{\rho} = d\rho/dt$, $\ddot{\rho} = d^2\rho/dt^2$, and so on.

3.10.14   In right circular cylindrical coordinates, a particular vector function is given by

$$\mathbf{V}(\rho, \varphi) = \hat{\mathbf{e}}_\rho V_\rho(\rho, \varphi) + \hat{\mathbf{e}}_\varphi V_\varphi(\rho, \varphi).$$

Show that $\nabla \times \mathbf{V}$ has only a z-component. Note that this result will hold for any vector confined to a surface $q_3 = $ constant as long as the products $h_1 V_1$ and $h_2 V_2$ are each independent of q_3.

3.10.15 A conducting wire along the z-axis carries a current I. The resulting magnetic vector potential is given by

$$\mathbf{A} = \hat{\mathbf{e}}_z \frac{\mu I}{2\pi} \ln\left(\frac{1}{\rho}\right).$$

Show that the magnetic induction $\mathbf{B}$ is given by

$$\mathbf{B} = \hat{\mathbf{e}}_\varphi \frac{\mu I}{2\pi\rho}.$$

3.10.16 A force is described by

$$\mathbf{F} = -\hat{\mathbf{e}}_x \frac{y}{x^2 + y^2} + \hat{\mathbf{e}}_y \frac{x}{x^2 + y^2}.$$

(a) Express $\mathbf{F}$ in circular cylindrical coordinates.
Operating entirely in circular cylindrical coordinates for (b) and (c),
(b) Calculate the curl of $\mathbf{F}$ and
(c) Calculate the work done by $\mathbf{F}$ in encircling the unit circle once counter-clockwise.
(d) How do you reconcile the results of (b) and (c)?

3.10.17 A calculation of the magnetohydrodynamic pinch effect involves the evaluation of $(\mathbf{B} \cdot \nabla)\mathbf{B}$. If the magnetic induction $\mathbf{B}$ is taken to be $\mathbf{B} = \hat{\mathbf{e}}_\varphi B_\varphi(\rho)$, show that

$$(\mathbf{B} \cdot \nabla)\mathbf{B} = -\hat{\mathbf{e}}_\rho B_\varphi^2 / \rho.$$

3.10.18 Express the spherical polar unit vectors in terms of Cartesian unit vectors.

$$\begin{aligned} ANS. \quad \hat{\mathbf{e}}_r &= \hat{\mathbf{e}}_x \sin\theta \cos\varphi + \hat{\mathbf{e}}_y \sin\theta \sin\varphi + \hat{\mathbf{e}}_z \cos\theta, \\ \hat{\mathbf{e}}_\theta &= \hat{\mathbf{e}}_x \cos\theta \cos\varphi + \hat{\mathbf{e}}_y \cos\theta \sin\varphi - \hat{\mathbf{e}}_z \sin\theta, \\ \hat{\mathbf{e}}_\varphi &= -\hat{\mathbf{e}}_x \sin\varphi + \hat{\mathbf{e}}_y \cos\varphi. \end{aligned}$$

3.10.19 Resolve the Cartesian unit vectors into their spherical polar components:

$$\hat{\mathbf{e}}_x = \hat{\mathbf{e}}_r \sin\theta \cos\varphi + \hat{\mathbf{e}}_\theta \cos\theta \cos\varphi - \hat{\mathbf{e}}_\varphi \sin\varphi,$$

$$\hat{\mathbf{e}}_y = \hat{\mathbf{e}}_r \sin\theta \sin\varphi + \hat{\mathbf{e}}_\theta \cos\theta \sin\varphi + \hat{\mathbf{e}}_\varphi \cos\varphi,$$

$$\hat{\mathbf{e}}_z = \hat{\mathbf{e}}_r \cos\theta - \hat{\mathbf{e}}_\theta \sin\theta.$$

3.10.20 (a) Explain why it is not possible to relate a column vector $\mathbf{r}$ (with components x, y, z) to another column vector $\mathbf{r}'$ (with components r, θ, φ), via a matrix equation of the form $\mathbf{r}' = \mathsf{B}\mathbf{r}$.

(b) One can write a matrix equation relating the Cartesian components of a vector to its components in spherical polar coordinates. Find the transformation matrix and determine whether it is orthogonal.

3.10.21 Find the transformation matrix that converts the components of a vector in spherical polar coordinates into its components in circular cylindrical coordinates. Then find the matrix of the inverse transformation.

3.10.22 (a) From the results of Exercise 3.10.18, calculate the partial derivatives of $\hat{\mathbf{e}}_r$, $\hat{\mathbf{e}}_\theta$, and $\hat{\mathbf{e}}_\varphi$ with respect to r, θ, and φ.

(b)   With $\boldsymbol{\nabla}$ given by

$$\hat{\mathbf{e}}_r \frac{\partial}{\partial r} + \hat{\mathbf{e}}_\theta \frac{1}{r} \frac{\partial}{\partial \theta} + \hat{\mathbf{e}}_\varphi \frac{1}{r \sin \theta} \frac{\partial}{\partial \varphi}$$

(greatest space rate of change), use the results of part (a) to calculate $\boldsymbol{\nabla} \cdot \boldsymbol{\nabla} \psi$. This is an alternate derivation of the Laplacian.

Note. The derivatives of the left-hand $\boldsymbol{\nabla}$ operate on the unit vectors of the right-hand $\boldsymbol{\nabla}$ **before** the dot product is evaluated.

3.10.23   A rigid body is rotating about a fixed axis with a constant angular velocity $\boldsymbol{\omega}$. Take $\boldsymbol{\omega}$ to be along the z-axis. Using spherical polar coordinates,

(a)   calculate $\mathbf{v} = \boldsymbol{\omega} \times \mathbf{r}$.
(b)   calculate $\boldsymbol{\nabla} \times \mathbf{v}$.

> *ANS.*   (a) $\mathbf{v} = \hat{\mathbf{e}}_\varphi \omega r \sin \theta$.
> (b) $\boldsymbol{\nabla} \times \mathbf{v} = 2 \boldsymbol{\omega}$.

3.10.24   A certain vector $\mathbf{V}$ has no radial component. Its curl has no tangential components. What does this imply about the radial dependence of the tangential components of $\mathbf{V}$?

3.10.25   Modern physics lays great stress on the property of parity (whether a quantity remains invariant or changes sign under an inversion of the coordinate system). In Cartesian coordinates this means $x \to -x$, $y \to -y$, and $z \to -z$.

(a)   Show that the inversion (reflection through the origin) of a point (r, θ, φ) relative to **fixed** x-, y-, z-axes consists of the transformation

$$r \to r, \quad \theta \to \pi - \theta, \quad \varphi \to \varphi \pm \pi.$$

(b)   Show that $\hat{\mathbf{e}}_r$ and $\hat{\mathbf{e}}_\varphi$ have odd parity (reversal of direction) and that $\hat{\mathbf{e}}_\theta$ has even parity.

3.10.26   With $\mathbf{A}$ any vector,

$$\mathbf{A} \cdot \boldsymbol{\nabla} \mathbf{r} = \mathbf{A}.$$

(a)   Verify this result in Cartesian coordinates.
(b)   Verify this result using spherical polar coordinates. Equation (3.156) provides $\boldsymbol{\nabla}$.

3.10.27   Find the spherical coordinate components of the velocity and acceleration of a moving particle:

$$v_r = \dot{r}, \qquad a_r = \ddot{r} - r \dot{\theta}^2 - r \sin^2 \theta \dot{\varphi}^2,$$

$$v_\theta = r \dot{\theta}, \qquad a_\theta = r \ddot{\theta} + 2 \dot{r} \dot{\theta} - r \sin \theta \cos \theta \dot{\varphi}^2,$$

$$v_\varphi = r \sin \theta \dot{\varphi}, \quad a_\varphi = r \sin \theta \ddot{\varphi} + 2 \dot{r} \sin \theta \dot{\varphi} + 2 r \cos \theta \dot{\theta} \dot{\varphi}.$$

Hint. $\mathbf{r}(t) = \hat{\mathbf{e}}_r(t) r(t)$

$$= [\hat{\mathbf{e}}_x \sin\theta(t)\cos\varphi(t) + \hat{\mathbf{e}}_y \sin\theta(t)\sin\varphi(t) + \hat{\mathbf{e}}_z \cos\theta(t)]r(t).$$

Note. The dot in $\dot{r}, \dot{\theta}, \dot{\varphi}$ means time derivative: $\dot{r} = dr/dt, \dot{\theta} = d\theta/dt,$ $\dot{\varphi} = d\varphi/dt.$

3.10.28   Express $\partial/\partial x$, $\partial/\partial y$, $\partial/\partial z$ in spherical polar coordinates.

$$ANS.\quad \frac{\partial}{\partial x} = \sin\theta\cos\varphi\frac{\partial}{\partial r} + \cos\theta\cos\varphi\frac{1}{r}\frac{\partial}{\partial\theta} - \frac{\sin\varphi}{r\sin\theta}\frac{\partial}{\partial\varphi},$$

$$\frac{\partial}{\partial y} = \sin\theta\sin\varphi\frac{\partial}{\partial r} + \cos\theta\sin\varphi\frac{1}{r}\frac{\partial}{\partial\theta} + \frac{\cos\varphi}{r\sin\theta}\frac{\partial}{\partial\varphi},$$

$$\frac{\partial}{\partial z} = \cos\theta\frac{\partial}{\partial r} - \sin\theta\frac{1}{r}\frac{\partial}{\partial\theta}.$$

Hint. Equate ∇_{xyz} and $\nabla_{r\theta\varphi}$.

3.10.29   Using results from Exercise 3.10.28, show that

$$-i\left(x\frac{\partial}{\partial y} - y\frac{\partial}{\partial x}\right) = -i\frac{\partial}{\partial\varphi}.$$

This is the quantum mechanical operator corresponding to the z-component of orbital angular momentum.

3.10.30   With the quantum mechanical orbital angular momentum operator defined as $\mathbf{L} = -i(\mathbf{r} \times \nabla)$, show that

(a) $L_x + iL_y = e^{i\varphi}\left(\dfrac{\partial}{\partial\theta} + i\cot\theta\dfrac{\partial}{\partial\varphi}\right),$

(b) $L_x - iL_y = -e^{-i\varphi}\left(\dfrac{\partial}{\partial\theta} - i\cot\theta\dfrac{\partial}{\partial\varphi}\right).$

3.10.31   Verify that $\mathbf{L} \times \mathbf{L} = i\mathbf{L}$ in spherical polar coordinates. $\mathbf{L} = -i(\mathbf{r} \times \nabla)$, the quantum mechanical orbital angular momentum operator.
Written in component form, this relation is

$$L_yL_z - L_zL_y = iL_x, \quad L_zL_x - L_xL_z = -L_y, \quad L_xL_y - L_yL_x = iL_z.$$

Using the commutator notation, $[A, B] = AB - BA$, and the definition of the Levi-Civita symbol ε_{ijk}, the above can also be written

$$[L_i, L_j] = i\,\varepsilon_{ijk}\,L_k,$$

where i, j, k are x, y, z in any order.
Hint. Use spherical polar coordinates for $\mathbf{L}$ but Cartesian components for the cross product.

3.10.32 (a) Using Eq. (3.156) show that

$$\mathbf{L} = -i\,(\mathbf{r} \times \nabla) = i\left(\hat{\mathbf{e}}_\theta \frac{1}{\sin\theta}\frac{\partial}{\partial\varphi} - \hat{\mathbf{e}}_\varphi \frac{\partial}{\partial\theta}\right).$$

(b) Resolving $\hat{\mathbf{e}}_\theta$ and $\hat{\mathbf{e}}_\varphi$ into Cartesian components, determine L_x, L_y, and L_z in terms of θ, φ, and their derivatives.

(c) From $L^2 = L_x^2 + L_y^2 + L_z^2$ show that

$$L^2 = -\frac{1}{\sin\theta}\frac{\partial}{\partial\theta}\left(\sin\theta\frac{\partial}{\partial\theta}\right) - \frac{1}{\sin^2\theta}\frac{\partial^2}{\partial\varphi^2}$$

$$= -r^2\nabla^2 + \frac{\partial}{\partial r}\left(r^2\frac{\partial}{\partial r}\right).$$

3.10.33 With $\mathbf{L} = -i\,\mathbf{r} \times \nabla$, verify the operator identities

(a) $\nabla = \hat{\mathbf{e}}_r \dfrac{\partial}{\partial r} - i\dfrac{\mathbf{r} \times \mathbf{L}}{r^2},$

(b) $\mathbf{r}\nabla^2 - \nabla\left(1 + r\dfrac{\partial}{\partial r}\right) = i\nabla \times \mathbf{L}.$

3.10.34 Show that the following three forms (spherical coordinates) of $\nabla^2\psi(r)$ are equivalent:

(a) $\dfrac{1}{r^2}\dfrac{d}{dr}\left[r^2\dfrac{d\psi(r)}{dr}\right];$ (b) $\dfrac{1}{r}\dfrac{d^2}{dr^2}[r\psi(r)];$ (c) $\dfrac{d^2\psi(r)}{dr^2} + \dfrac{2}{r}\dfrac{d\psi(r)}{dr}.$

The second form is particularly convenient in establishing a correspondence between spherical polar and Cartesian descriptions of a problem.

3.10.35 A certain force field is given in spherical polar coordinates by

$$\mathbf{F} = \hat{\mathbf{e}}_r \frac{2P\cos\theta}{r^3} + \hat{\mathbf{e}}_\theta \frac{P}{r^3}\sin\theta, \quad r \geq P/2.$$

(a) Examine $\nabla \times \mathbf{F}$ to see if a potential exists.

(b) Calculate $\oint \mathbf{F} \cdot d\mathbf{r}$ for a unit circle in the plane $\theta = \pi/2$. What does this indicate about the force being conservative or nonconservative?

(c) If you believe that $\mathbf{F}$ may be described by $\mathbf{F} = -\nabla\psi$, find ψ. Otherwise simply state that no acceptable potential exists.

3.10.36 (a) Show that $\mathbf{A} = -\hat{\mathbf{e}}_\varphi \cot\theta/r$ is a solution of $\nabla \times \mathbf{A} = \hat{\mathbf{e}}_r/r^2$.

(b) Show that this spherical polar coordinate solution agrees with the solution given for Exercise 3.9.5:

$$\mathbf{A} = \hat{\mathbf{e}}_x \frac{yz}{r(x^2 + y^2)} - \hat{\mathbf{e}}_y \frac{xz}{r(x^2 + y^2)}.$$

Note that the solution diverges for $\theta = 0$, π corresponding to x, $y = 0$.

(c) Finally, show that $\mathbf{A} = -\hat{\mathbf{e}}_\theta\varphi\sin\theta/r$ is a solution. Note that although this solution does not diverge $(r \neq 0)$, it is no longer single-valued for all possible azimuth angles.

3.10.37   An electric dipole of moment **p** is located at the origin. The dipole creates an electric potential at **r** given by

$$\psi(\mathbf{r}) = \frac{\mathbf{p} \cdot \mathbf{r}}{4\pi\varepsilon_0 r^3}.$$

Find the electric field, $\mathbf{E} = -\nabla\psi$ at **r**.

Additional Readings

Borisenko, A. I., and I. E. Tarpov, *Vector and Tensor Analysis with Applications*. Englewood Cliffs, NJ: Prentice-Hall (1968), reprinting, Dover (1980).

Davis, H. F., and A. D. Snider, *Introduction to Vector Analysis*, 7th ed. Boston: Allyn & Bacon (1995).

Kellogg, O. D., *Foundations of Potential Theory*. Berlin: Springer (1929), reprinted, Dover (1953). The classic text on potential theory.

Lewis, P. E., and J. P. Ward, *Vector Analysis for Engineers and Scientists*. Reading, MA: Addison-Wesley (1989).

Margenau, H., and G. M. Murphy, *The Mathematics of Physics and Chemistry*, 2nd ed. Princeton NJ: Van Nostrand (1956). Chapter 5 covers curvilinear coordinates and 13 specific coordinate systems.

Marion, J. B., *Principles of Vector Analysis*. New York: Academic Press (1965). A moderately advanced presentation of vector analysis oriented toward tensor analysis. Rotations and other transformations are described with the appropriate matrices.

Morse, P. M., and H. Feshbach, *Methods of Theoretical Physics*. New York: McGraw-Hill (1953). Chapter 5 includes a description of several different coordinate systems. Note that Morse and Feshbach are not above using left-handed coordinate systems even for Cartesian coordinates. Elsewhere in this excellent (and difficult) book there are many examples of the use of the various coordinate systems in solving physical problems. Eleven additional fascinating but seldom-encountered orthogonal coordinate systems are discussed in the second (1970) edition of *Mathematical Methods for Physicists*.

Spiegel, M. R., *Vector Analysis*. New York: McGraw-Hill (1989).

Tai, C.-T., *Generalized Vector and Dyadic Analysis*. Oxford: Oxford University Press (1966).

Wrede, R. C., *Introduction to Vector and Tensor Analysis*. New York: Wiley (1963), reprinting, Dover (1972). Fine historical introduction. Excellent discussion of differentiation of vectors and applications to mechanics.

CHAPTER 4

TENSORS AND DIFFERENTIAL FORMS

4.1 TENSOR ANALYSIS

Introduction, Properties

Tensors are important in many areas of physics, ranging from topics such as general relativity and electrodynamics to descriptions of the properties of bulk matter such as stress (the pattern of force applied to a sample) and strain (its response to the force), or the moment of inertia (the relation between a torsional force applied to an object and its resultant angular acceleration). Tensors constitute a generalization of quantities previously introduced: scalars and vectors. We identified a **scalar** as an quantity that remained invariant under rotations of the coordinate system and which could be specified by the value of a single real number. **Vectors** were identified as quantities that had a number of real components equal to the dimension of the coordinate system, with the components transforming like the coordinates of a fixed point when a coordinate system is rotated. Calling scalars **tensors of rank** 0 and vectors **tensors of rank** 1, we identify a tensor of rank n in a d-dimensional space as an object with the following properties:

- It has components labeled by n indices, with each index assigned values from 1 through d, and therefore having a total of d^n components;
- The components transform in a specified manner under coordinate transformations.

The behavior under coordinate transformation is of central importance for tensor analysis and conforms both with the way in which mathematicians define linear spaces and with the physicist's notion that physical observables must not depend on the choice of coordinate frames.

Covariant and Contravariant Tensors

In Chapter 3, we considered the rotational transformation of a vector $\mathbf{A} = A_1\hat{\mathbf{e}}_1 + A_2\hat{\mathbf{e}}_2 + A_3\hat{\mathbf{e}}_3$ from the Cartesian system defined by $\hat{\mathbf{e}}_i$ $(i = 1, 2, 3)$ into a rotated coordinate system defined by $\hat{\mathbf{e}}'_i$, with the same vector $\mathbf{A}$ then represented as $\mathbf{A}' = A'_1\hat{\mathbf{e}}'_1 + A'_2\hat{\mathbf{e}}'_2 + A'_3\mathbf{e}'_3$. The components of $\mathbf{A}$ and $\mathbf{A}'$ are related by

$$A'_i = \sum_j (\hat{\mathbf{e}}'_i \cdot \hat{\mathbf{e}}_j) A_j, \tag{4.1}$$

where the coefficients $(\hat{\mathbf{e}}'_i \cdot \hat{\mathbf{e}}_j)$ are the projections of $\hat{\mathbf{e}}'_i$ in the $\hat{\mathbf{e}}_j$ directions. Because the $\hat{\mathbf{e}}_i$ and the $\hat{\mathbf{e}}_j$ are linearly related, we can also write

$$A'_i = \sum_j \frac{\partial x'_i}{\partial x_j} A_j. \tag{4.2}$$

The formula of Eq. (4.2) corresponds to the application of the chain rule to convert the set A_j into the set A'_i, and is valid for A_j and A'_i of arbitrary magnitude because both vectors depend linearly on their components.

We have also previously noted that the gradient of a scalar φ has in the unrotated Cartesian coordinates the components $(\boldsymbol{\nabla}\varphi)_j = (\partial\varphi/\partial x_j)\hat{\mathbf{e}}_j$, meaning that in a rotated system we would have

$$(\boldsymbol{\nabla}\varphi)'_i \equiv \frac{\partial\varphi}{\partial x'_i} = \sum_j \frac{\partial x_j}{\partial x'_i} \frac{\partial\varphi}{\partial x_j}, \tag{4.3}$$

showing that the gradient has a transformation law that differs from that of Eq. (4.2) in that $\partial x'_i/\partial x_j$ has been replaced by $\partial x_j/\partial x'_i$. Remembering that these two expressions, if written in detail, correspond, respectively, to $(\partial x'_i/\partial x_j)_{x_k}$ and $(\partial x_j/\partial x'_i)_{x'_k}$, where k runs over the index values other than that already in the denominator, and also noting that (in Cartesian coordinates) they are two different ways of computing the same quantity (the magnitude and sign of the projection of one of these unit vectors upon the other), we see that it was legitimate to identify both $\mathbf{A}$ and $\boldsymbol{\nabla}\varphi$ as *vectors*, as we did in Chapter 3.

However, as the alert reader may note from the repeated insertion of the word "Cartesian," the partial derivatives in Eqs. (4.2) and (4.3) are only guaranteed to be equal in Cartesian coordinate systems, and since there is sometimes a need to use non-Cartesian systems it becomes necessary to distinguish these two different transformation rules. Quantities transforming according to Eq. (4.2) are called **contravariant** vectors, while those transforming according to Eq. (4.3) are termed **covariant**. When non-Cartesian systems may be in play, it is therefore customary to distinguish these transformation properties by writing the index of a contravariant vector as a superscript and that of a covariant vector as a subscript. This means, among other things, that the components of the position vector $\mathbf{r}$, which is contravariant, must now be written (x^1, x^2, x^3). Thus, summarizing,

$$(A')^i = \sum_j \frac{\partial (x')^i}{\partial x^j} A^j \quad \mathbf{A}, \text{ a contravariant vector,} \tag{4.4}$$

$$A'_i = \sum_j \frac{\partial x^j}{\partial (x')^i} A_j \quad \mathbf{A}, \text{ a covariant vector.} \tag{4.5}$$

It is useful to note that the occurrence of subscripts and superscripts is systematic; the **free** (i.e., unsummed) index i occurs as a superscript on both sides of Eq. (4.4), while it appears as a subscript on both sides of Eq. (4.5), if we interpret an upper index in the denominator as equivalent to a lower index. The summed index occurs once as upper and once as lower (again treating an upper index in the denominator as a lower index). A frequently used shorthand (the **Einstein convention**) is to omit the summation sign in formulas like Eqs. (4.4) and (4.5) and to understand that when the same symbol occurs both as an upper and a lower index in the same expression, it is to be summed. We will gradually back into the use of the Einstein convention, giving the reader warnings as we start to do so.

Tensors of Rank 2

Now we proceed to define **contravariant, mixed, and covariant tensors of rank 2** by the following equations for their components under coordinate transformations:

$$(A')^{ij} = \sum_{kl} \frac{\partial (x')^i}{\partial x^k} \frac{\partial (x')^j}{\partial x^l} A^{kl},$$

$$(B')^i_j = \sum_{kl} \frac{\partial (x')^i}{\partial x^k} \frac{\partial x^l}{\partial (x')^j} B^k_l, \tag{4.6}$$

$$(C')_{ij} = \sum_{kl} \frac{\partial x^k}{\partial (x')^i} \frac{\partial x^l}{\partial (x')^j} C_{kl}.$$

Clearly, the rank goes as the number of partial derivatives (or direction cosines) in the definition: 0 for a scalar, 1 for a vector, 2 for a second-rank tensor, and so on. Each index (subscript or superscript) ranges over the number of dimensions of the space. The number of indices (equal to the rank of tensor) is not limited by the dimensionality of the space. We see that A^{kl} is contravariant with respect to both indices, C_{kl} is covariant with respect to both indices, and B^k_l transforms contravariantly with respect to the index k but covariantly with respect to the index l. Once again, if we are using Cartesian coordinates, all three forms of the tensors of second rank, contravariant, mixed, and covariant are the same.

As with the components of a vector, the transformation laws for the components of a tensor, Eq. (4.6), cause its physically relevant properties to be independent of the choice of reference frame. This is what makes tensor analysis important in physics. The independence relative to reference frame (invariance) is ideal for expressing and investigating universal physical laws.

The second-rank tensor A (with components A^{kl}) may be conveniently represented by writing out its components in a square array (3×3 if we are in three-dimensional (3-D) space):

$$A = \begin{pmatrix} A^{11} & A^{12} & A^{13} \\ A^{21} & A^{22} & A^{23} \\ A^{31} & A^{32} & A^{33} \end{pmatrix}. \tag{4.7}$$

This does not mean that any square array of numbers or functions forms a tensor. The essential condition is that the components transform according to Eq. (4.6).

We can view each of Eq. (4.6) as a matrix equation. For A, it takes the form

$$(A')^{ij} = \sum_{kl} S_{ik} A^{ki} (S^T)_{lj}, \quad \text{or} \quad A' = SAS^T, \tag{4.8}$$

a construction that is known as a **similarity transformation** and is discussed in Section 5.6.

> In summary, tensors are systems of components organized by one or more indices that transform according to specific rules under a set of transformations. The number of indices is called the rank of the tensor.

Addition and Subtraction of Tensors

The addition and subtraction of tensors is defined in terms of the individual elements, just as for vectors. If

$$A + B = C, \tag{4.9}$$

then, taking as an example A, B, and C to be contravariant tensors of rank 2,

$$A^{ij} + B^{ij} = C^{ij}. \tag{4.10}$$

In general, of course, A and B must be tensors of the same rank (of both contra- and co-variance) and in the same space.

Symmetry

The order in which the indices appear in our description of a tensor is important. In general, A^{mn} is independent of A^{nm}, but there are some cases of special interest. If, for all m and n,

$$A^{mn} = A^{nm}, \quad \text{A is symmetric}. \tag{4.11}$$

If, on the other hand,

$$A^{mn} = -A^{nm}, \quad \text{A is antisymmetric}. \tag{4.12}$$

Clearly, every (second-rank) tensor can be resolved into symmetric and antisymmetric parts by the identity

$$A^{mn} = \frac{1}{2}(A^{mn} + A^{nm}) + \frac{1}{2}(A^{mn} - A^{nm}), \tag{4.13}$$

the first term on the right being a symmetric tensor, the second, an antisymmetric tensor.

Isotropic Tensors

To illustrate some of the techniques of tensor analysis, let us show that the now-familiar Kronecker delta, δ_{kl}, is really a mixed tensor of rank 2, δ_l^k.[1] The question is: Does δ_l^k transform according to Eq. (4.6)? This is our criterion for calling it a tensor. If δ_l^k is the mixed tensor corresponding to this notation, it must satisfy (using the summation convention, meaning that the indices k and l are to be summed)

$$(\delta')^i_j = \frac{\partial (x')^i}{\partial x^k} \frac{\partial x^l}{\partial (x')^j} \delta_l^k = \frac{\partial (x')^i}{\partial x^k} \frac{\partial x^k}{\partial (x')^j},$$

where we have performed the l sum and used the definition of the Kronecker delta. Next,

$$\frac{\partial (x')^i}{\partial x^k} \frac{\partial x^k}{\partial (x')^j} = \frac{\partial (x')^i}{\partial (x')^j},$$

where we have identified the k summation on the left-hand side as an instance of the chain rule for differentiation. However, $(x')^i$ and $(x')^j$ are independent coordinates, and therefore the variation of one with respect to the other must be zero if they are different, unity if they coincide; that is,

$$\frac{\partial (x')^i}{\partial (x')^j} = (\delta')^i_j. \tag{4.14}$$

Hence

$$(\delta')^i_j = \frac{\partial (x')^i}{\partial x^k} \frac{\partial x^l}{\partial (x')^j} \delta_l^k, \tag{4.15}$$

showing that the δ_l^k are indeed the components of a mixed second-rank tensor. Note that this result is independent of the number of dimensions of our space.

The Kronecker delta has one further interesting property. It has the same components in all of our rotated coordinate systems and is therefore called **isotropic**. In Section 4.2 and Exercise 4.2.4 we shall meet a third-rank isotropic tensor and three fourth-rank isotropic tensors. No isotropic first-rank tensor (vector) exists.

Contraction

When dealing with vectors, we formed a scalar product by summing products of corresponding components:

$$\mathbf{A} \cdot \mathbf{B} = \sum_i A_i B_i.$$

The generalization of this expression in tensor analysis is a process known as contraction. Two indices, one covariant and the other contravariant, are set equal to each other, and then (as implied by the summation convention) we sum over this repeated index. For example,

---

[1] It is common practice to refer to a tensor A by specifying a typical component, such as A_{ij}, thereby also conveying information as to its covariant vs. contravariant nature. As long as you refrain from writing nonsense such as $A = A_{ij}$, no harm is done.

let us contract the second-rank mixed tensor B^i_j by setting j to i, then summing over i. To see what happens, let's look at the transformation formula that converts B into B'. Using the summation convention,

$$(B')^i_i = \frac{\partial (x')^i}{\partial x^k} \frac{\partial x^l}{\partial (x')^i} B^k_l = \frac{\partial x^l}{\partial x^k} B^k_l,$$

where we recognized the i summation as an instance of the chain rule for differentiation. Then, because the x^i are independent, we may use Eq. (4.14) to reach

$$(B')^i_i = \delta^l_k B^k_l = B^k_k. \qquad (4.16)$$

Remembering that the repeated index (i or k) is summed, we see that the contracted B is invariant under transformation and is therefore a scalar.[2] In general, the operation of contraction reduces the rank of a tensor by 2.

Direct Product

The components of two tensors (of any ranks and covariant/contravariant characters) can be multiplied, component by component, to make an object with all the indices of both factors. The new quantity, termed the **direct product** of the two tensors, can be shown to be a tensor whose rank is the sum of the ranks of the factors, and with covariant/contravariant character that is the sum of those of the factors. We illustrate:

$$C^{ij}_{klm} = A^i_k B^j_{lm}, \quad F^{ij}_{kl} = A^j B^i_{lk}.$$

Note that the index order in the direct product can be defined as desired, but the covariance/contravariance of the factors must be maintained in the direct product.

Example 4.1.1   DIRECT PRODUCT OF TWO VECTORS

Let's form the direct product of a covariant vector a_i (rank-1 tensor) and a contravariant vector b^j (also a rank-1 tensor) to form a mixed tensor of rank 2, with components $C^j_i = a_i b^j$. To verify that C^j_i is a tensor, we consider what happens to it under transformation:

$$(C')^j_i = (a')_i (b')^j = \frac{\partial x^k}{\partial (x')_i} a_k \frac{\partial (x')^j}{\partial x^l} b_l = \frac{\partial x^k}{\partial (x')_i} \frac{\partial (x')^j}{\partial x^l} C^l_k, \qquad (4.17)$$

confirming that C^j_i is the mixed tensor indicated by its notation.

If we now form the contraction C^i_i (remember that i is summed), we obtain the scalar product $a_i b^i$. From Eq. (4.17) it is easy to see that $a_i b^i = (a')_i (b')^i$, indicating the invariance required of a scalar product. ∎

Note that the direct product concept gives a meaning to quantities such as $\nabla \mathbf{E}$, which was not defined within the framework of vector analysis. However, this and other tensor-like quantities involving differential operators must be used with caution, because their

---

[2] In matrix analysis this scalar is the **trace** of the matrix whose elements are the B^i_j.

transformation rules are simple only in Cartesian coordinate systems. In non-Cartesian systems, operators $\partial/\partial x^i$ act also on the partial derivatives in the transformation expressions and alter the tensor transformation rules.

We summarize the key idea of this subsection:

The direct product is a technique for creating new, higher-rank tensors.

Inverse Transformation

If we have a contravariant vector A^i, which must have the transformation rule (using summation convention)

$$(A')^j = \frac{\partial (x')^j}{\partial x^i} A^i,$$

the inverse transformation (which can be obtained simply by interchanging the roles of the primed and unprimed quantities) is

$$A^i = \frac{\partial x^i}{\partial (x')^j} (A')^j, \tag{4.18}$$

as may also be verified by applying $\partial (x')^k/\partial x^i$ (and summing i) to A^i as given by Eq. (4.18):

$$\frac{\partial (x')^k}{\partial x^i} A^i = \frac{\partial (x')^k}{\partial x^i} \frac{\partial x^i}{\partial (x')^j} (A')^j = \delta_j^k (A')^j = (A')^k. \tag{4.19}$$

We see that $(A')^k$ is recovered. Incidentally, note that

$$\frac{\partial x^i}{\partial (x')^j} \neq \left[\frac{\partial (x')^j}{\partial x^i} \right]^{-1};$$

as we have previously pointed out, these derivatives have different other variables held fixed. The cancellation in Eq. (4.19) only occurs because the product of derivatives is summed. In Cartesian systems, we do have

$$\frac{\partial x^i}{\partial (x')^j} = \frac{\partial (x')^j}{\partial x^i},$$

both equal to the direction cosine connecting the x^i and $(x')^j$ axes, but this equality does not extend to non-Cartesian systems.

Quotient Rule

If, for example, A_{ij} and B_{kl} are tensors, we have already observed that their direct product, $A_{ij}B_{kl}$, is also a tensor. Here we are concerned with the inverse problem, illustrated by equations such as

$$K_i A^i = B,$$

$$K_i^j A_j = B_i,$$

$$K_i^j A_{jk} = B_{ik}, \tag{4.20}$$

$$K_{ijkl} A^{ij} = B_{kl},$$

$$K^{ij} A_k = B^{ijk}.$$

In each of these expressions A and B are known tensors of ranks indicated by the number of indices, A is arbitrary, and the summation convention is in use. In each case K is an unknown quantity. We wish to establish the transformation properties of K. The quotient rule asserts:

> *If the equation of interest holds in all transformed coordinate systems, then K is a tensor of the indicated rank and covariant/contravariant character.*

Part of the importance of this rule in physical theory is that it can establish the tensor nature of quantities. For example, the equation giving the dipole moment **m** induced in an anisotropic medium by an electric field **E** is

$$m_i = P_{ij} E^j.$$

Since presumably we know that **m** and **E** are vectors, the general validity of this equation tells us that the **polarization matrix** P is a tensor of rank 2.

Let's prove the quotient rule for a typical case, which we choose to be the second of Eqs. (4.20). If we apply a transformation to that equation, we have

$$K_i^j A_j = B_i \quad \longrightarrow \quad (K')_i^j A'_j = B'_i. \tag{4.21}$$

We now evaluate B'_i, reaching the last member of the equation below by using Eq. (4.18) to convert A_j into components of A′ (note that this is the **inverse** of the transformation to the primed quantities):

$$B'_i = \frac{\partial x^m}{\partial (x')^i} B_m = \frac{\partial x^m}{\partial (x')^i} K_m^j A_j = \frac{\partial x^m}{\partial (x')^i} K_m^j \frac{\partial (x')^n}{\partial x^j} A'_n. \tag{4.22}$$

It may lessen possible confusion if we rename the dummy indices in Eq. (4.22), so we interchange n and j, causing that equation to then read

$$B'_i = \frac{\partial x^m}{\partial (x')^i} \frac{\partial (x')^j}{\partial x^n} K_m^n A'_j. \tag{4.23}$$

It has now become clear that if we subtract the expression for B'_i in Eq. (4.23) from that in Eq. (4.21) we will get

$$\left[(K')_i^j - \frac{\partial x^m}{\partial (x')^i} \frac{\partial (x')^j}{\partial x^n} K_m^n \right] A'_j = 0. \tag{4.24}$$

Since A′ is arbitrary, the coefficient of A'_j in Eq. (4.24) must vanish, showing that K has the transformation properties of the tensor corresponding to its index configuration.

Other cases may be treated similarly. One minor pitfall should be noted: The quotient rule does not necessarily apply if B is zero. The transformation properties of zero are indeterminate.

Example 4.1.2   EQUATIONS OF MOTION AND FIELD EQUATIONS

In classical mechanics, Newton's equations of motion $m\dot{\mathbf{v}} = \mathbf{F}$ tell us on the basis of the quotient rule that, if the mass is a scalar and the force a vector, then the acceleration $\mathbf{a} \equiv \dot{\mathbf{v}}$ is a vector. In other words, the vector character of the force as the driving term imposes its vector character on the acceleration, provided the scale factor m is scalar.

The wave equation of electrodynamics can be written in relativistic four-vector form as

$$\left[\frac{1}{c^2}\frac{\partial^2}{\partial t^2} - \mathbf{\nabla}^2\right] A^\mu = J^\mu,$$

where J^μ is the external charge/current density (a four-vector) and A^μ is the four-component vector potential. The second-derivative expression in square brackets can be shown to be a scalar. From the quotient rule, we may then infer that A^μ must be a tensor of rank 1, i.e., also a four-vector. ∎

The quotient rule is a substitute for the illegal division of tensors.

Spinors

It was once thought that the system of scalars, vectors, tensors (second-rank), and so on formed a complete mathematical system, one that is adequate for describing a physics independent of the choice of reference frame. But the universe and mathematical physics are not that simple. In the realm of elementary particles, for example, spin-zero particles[3] (π mesons, α particles) may be described with scalars, spin 1 particles (deuterons) by vectors, and spin 2 particles (gravitons) by tensors. This listing omits the most common particles: electrons, protons, and neutrons, all with spin $\frac{1}{2}$. These particles are properly described by **spinors**. A spinor does not have the properties under rotation consistent with being a scalar, vector, or tensor of any rank. A brief introduction to spinors in the context of group theory appears in Chapter 17.

Exercises

4.1.1   Show that if all the components of any tensor of any rank vanish in one particular coordinate system, they vanish in all coordinate systems.
Note. This point takes on special importance in the four-dimensional (4-D) curved space of general relativity. If a quantity, expressed as a tensor, exists in one coordinate system, it exists in all coordinate systems and is not just a consequence of a **choice** of a coordinate system (as are centrifugal and Coriolis forces in Newtonian mechanics).

---

[3]The particle spin is intrinsic angular momentum (in units of $\hbar$). It is distinct from classical (often called **orbital**) angular momentum that arises from the motion of the particle.

4.1.2   The components of tensor A are equal to the corresponding components of tensor B in one particular coordinate system denoted, by the superscript 0; that is,

$$A_{ij}^0 = B_{ij}^0.$$

Show that tensor A is equal to tensor B, $A_{ij} = B_{ij}$, in all coordinate systems.

4.1.3   The last three components of a 4-D vector vanish in each of two reference frames. If the second reference frame is not merely a rotation of the first about the x_0 axis, meaning that at least one of the coefficients $\partial(x')^i/\partial x^0$ ($i = 1, 2, 3$) is nonzero, show that the zeroth component vanishes in all reference frames. Translated into relativistic mechanics, this means that if momentum is conserved in two Lorentz frames, then energy is conserved in all Lorentz frames.

4.1.4   From an analysis of the behavior of a general second-rank tensor under 90° and 180° rotations about the coordinate axes, show that an isotropic second-rank tensor in 3-D space must be a multiple of δ_j^i.

4.1.5   The 4-D fourth-rank Riemann-Christoffel curvature tensor of general relativity, R_{iklm}, satisfies the symmetry relations

$$R_{iklm} = -R_{ikml} = -R_{kilm}.$$

With the indices running from 0 to 3, show that the number of independent components is reduced from 256 to 36 and that the condition

$$R_{iklm} = R_{lmik}$$

further reduces the number of independent components to 21. Finally, if the components satisfy an identity $R_{iklm} + R_{ilmk} + R_{imkl} = 0$, show that the number of independent components is reduced to 20.

Note. The final three-term identity furnishes new information only if all four indices are different.

4.1.6 T_{iklm} is antisymmetric with respect to all pairs of indices. How many independent components has it (in 3-D space)?

4.1.7   If $T_{...i}$ is a tensor of rank n, show that $\partial T_{...i}/\partial x^j$ is a tensor of rank $n + 1$ (Cartesian coordinates).

Note. In non-Cartesian coordinate systems the coefficients a_{ij} are, in general, functions of the coordinates, and the derivatives the components of a tensor of rank n do not form a tensor except in the special case $n = 0$. In this case the derivative does yield a covariant vector (tensor of rank 1).

4.1.8   If $T_{ijk...}$ is a tensor of rank n, show that $\sum_j \partial T_{ijk...}/\partial x^j$ is a tensor of rank $n - 1$ (Cartesian coordinates).

4.1.9   The operator

$$\nabla^2 - \frac{1}{c^2}\frac{\partial^2}{\partial t^2}$$

may be written as

$$\sum_{i=1}^{4} \frac{\partial^2}{\partial x_i^2},$$

using $x_4 = ict$. This is the 4-D Laplacian, sometimes called the d'Alembertian and denoted by $\square^2$. Show that it is a **scalar** operator, that is, invariant under Lorentz transformations, i.e., under rotations in the space of vectors (x^1, x^2, x^3, x^4).

4.1.10   The double summation $K_{ij} A^i B^j$ is invariant for any two vectors A^i and B^j. Prove that K_{ij} is a second-rank tensor.

Note. In the form ds^2 (invariant) $= g_{ij} \, dx^i \, dx^j$, this result shows that the matrix g_{ij} is a tensor.

4.1.11   The equation $K_{ij} A^{jk} = B_i^k$ holds for all orientations of the coordinate system. If A and B are arbitrary second-rank tensors, show that K is a second-rank tensor also.

4.2   PSEUDOTENSORS, DUAL TENSORS

The topics of this section will be treated for tensors restricted for practical reasons to Cartesian coordinate systems. This restriction is not conceptually necessary but simplifies the discussion and makes the essential points easy to identify.

Pseudotensors

So far the coordinate transformations in this chapter have been restricted to **passive rotations**, by which we mean rotation of the coordinate system, keeping vectors and tensors at fixed orientations. We now consider the effect of reflections or inversions of the coordinate system (sometimes also called **improper rotations**).

In Section 3.3, where attention was restricted to orthogonal systems of Cartesian coordinates, we saw that the effect of a coordinate rotation on a fixed vector could be described by a transformation of its components according to the formula

$$A' = SA, \tag{4.25}$$

where S was an orthogonal matrix with determinant $+1$. If the coordinate transformation included a reflection (or inversion), the transformation matrix was still orthogonal, but had determinant -1. While the transformation rule of Eq. (4.25) was obeyed by vectors describing quantities such as position in space or velocity, it produced the wrong sign when vectors describing angular velocity, torque, and angular momentum were subject to improper rotations. These quantities, called **axial vectors**, or nowadays **pseudovectors**, obeyed the transformation rule

$$A' = \det(S)SA \quad \text{(pseudovector)}. \tag{4.26}$$

The extension of this concept to tensors is straightforward. We insist that the designation *tensor* refer to objects that transform as in Eq. (4.6) and its generalization to arbitrary rank, but we also accommodate the possibility of having, at arbitrary rank, objects whose transformation requires an additional sign factor to adjust for the effect associated with improper rotations. These objects are called **pseudotensors**, and constitute a generalization of the objects already identified as pseudoscalars and pseudovectors.

If we form a tensor or pseudotensor as a direct product or identify one via the quotient rule, we can determine its pseudo status by what amounts to a sign rule. Letting T be a tensor and P a pseudotensor, then, symbolically,

$$T \otimes T = P \otimes P = T, \quad T \otimes P = P \otimes T = P. \tag{4.27}$$

Example 4.2.1   LEVI-CIVITA SYMBOL

The three-index version of the Levi-Civita symbol, introduced in Eq. (2.8), has the values

$$\varepsilon_{123} = \varepsilon_{231} = \varepsilon_{312} = +1,$$

$$\varepsilon_{132} = \varepsilon_{213} = \varepsilon_{321} = -1, \tag{4.28}$$

$$\text{all other } \varepsilon_{ijk} = 0.$$

Suppose now that we have a rank-3 pseudotensor η_{ijk}, which in one particular Cartesian coordinate system is equal to ε_{ijk}. Then, letting A stand for the matrix of coefficients in an orthogonal transformation of $\mathbb{R}^3$, we have in the transformed coordinate system

$$\eta'_{ijk} = \det(A) \sum_{pqr} a_{ip} a_{jq} a_{kr} \varepsilon_{pqr}, \tag{4.29}$$

by definition of pseudotensor. All terms of the pqr sum will vanish except those where pqr is a permutation of 123, and when pqr is such a permutation the sum will correspond to the determinant of A except that its rows will have been permuted from 123 to ijk. This means that the pqr sum will have the value $\varepsilon_{ijk} \det(A)$, and

$$\eta'_{ijk} = \varepsilon_{ijk} [\det(A)]^2 = \varepsilon_{ijk}, \tag{4.30}$$

where the final result depends on the fact that $|\det(A)| = 1$. If the reader is uncomfortable with the above analysis, the result can be checked by enumeration of the contributions of the six permutations that correspond to nonzero values of η'_{ijk}.

Equation (4.30) not only shows that ε is a rank-3 pseudotensor, but that it is also isotropic. In other words, it has the same components in all rotated Cartesian coordinate systems, and -1 times those component values in all Cartesian systems that are reached by improper rotations. ∎

Dual Tensors

With any **antisymmetric** second-rank tensor C (in 3-D space) we may associate a pseudovector **C** with components defined by

$$C_i = \tfrac{1}{2} \varepsilon_{ijk} C^{jk}. \tag{4.31}$$

In matrix form the antisymmetric C may be written

$$C = \begin{pmatrix} 0 & C^{12} & -C^{31} \\ -C^{12} & 0 & C^{23} \\ C^{31} & -C^{23} & 0 \end{pmatrix}. \tag{4.32}$$

We know that C_i must transform as a vector under rotations because it was obtained from the double contraction of $\varepsilon_{ijk}C^{jk}$, but that it is really a pseudovector because of the pseudo nature of ε_{ijk}. Specifically, the components of **C** are given by

$$(C_1, C_2, C_3) = (C^{23}, C^{31}, C^{12}). \tag{4.33}$$

Note the cyclic order of the indices that comes from the cyclic order of the components of ε_{ijk}.

We identify the pseudovector of Eq. (4.33) and the antisymmetric tensor of Eq. (4.32) as **dual tensors**; they are simply different representations of the same information. Which of the dual pair we choose to use is a matter of convenience.

Here is another example of duality. If we take three vectors **A**, **B**, and **C**, we may define the direct product

$$V^{ijk} = A^i B^j C^k. \tag{4.34}$$

V^{ijk} is evidently a rank-3 tensor. The dual quantity

$$V = \varepsilon_{ijk} V^{ijk} \tag{4.35}$$

is clearly a pseudoscalar. By expansion it is seen that

$$V = \begin{vmatrix} A^1 & B^1 & C^1 \\ A^2 & B^2 & C^2 \\ A^3 & B^3 & C^3 \end{vmatrix} \tag{4.36}$$

is our familiar scalar triple product.

Exercises

4.2.1   An antisymmetric square array is given by

$$\begin{pmatrix} 0 & C_3 & -C_2 \\ -C_3 & 0 & C_1 \\ C_2 & -C_1 & 0 \end{pmatrix} = \begin{pmatrix} 0 & C^{12} & C^{13} \\ -C^{12} & 0 & C^{23} \\ -C^{13} & -C^{23} & 0 \end{pmatrix},$$

where (C_1, C_2, C_3) form a pseudovector. Assuming that the relation

$$C_i = \frac{1}{2!} \varepsilon_{ijk} C^{jk}$$

holds in all coordinate systems, prove that C^{jk} is a tensor. (This is another form of the quotient theorem.)

4.2.2   Show that the vector product is unique to 3-D space, that is, only in three dimensions can we establish a one-to-one correspondence between the components of an antisymmetric tensor (second-rank) and the components of a vector.

4.2.3   Write $\nabla \cdot \nabla \times \mathbf{A}$ and $\nabla \times \nabla \varphi$ in tensor (index) notation in $I\!R^3$ so that it becomes obvious that each expression vanishes.

$$ANS. \quad \nabla \cdot \nabla \times \mathbf{A} = \varepsilon_{ijk} \frac{\partial}{\partial x^i} \frac{\partial}{\partial x^j} A^k$$

$$(\nabla \times \nabla \varphi)_i = \varepsilon_{ijk} \frac{\partial}{\partial x^j} \frac{\partial}{\partial x^k} \varphi.$$

4.2.4   Verify that each of the following fourth-rank tensors is isotropic, that is, that it has the same form independent of any rotation of the coordinate systems.

(a) $A^{ik}_{jl} = \delta^i_j \delta^k_l,$

(b) $B^{ij}_{kl} = \delta^i_k \delta^j_l + \delta^i_l \delta^j_k,$

(c) $C^{ij}_{kl} = \delta^i_k \delta^j_l - \delta^i_l \delta^j_k.$

4.2.5   Show that the two-index Levi-Civita symbol ε_{ij} is a second-rank pseudotensor (in two-dimensional [2-D] space). Does this contradict the uniqueness of δ^i_j (Exercise 4.1.4)?

4.2.6   Represent ε_{ij} by a 2×2 matrix, and using the 2×2 rotation matrix of Eq. (3.23), show that ε_{ij} is invariant under orthogonal similarity transformations.

4.2.7   Given $A_k = \frac{1}{2} \varepsilon_{ijk} B^{ij}$ with $B^{ij} = -B^{ji}$, antisymmetric, show that

$$B^{mn} = \varepsilon^{mnk} A_k.$$

4.3   TENSORS IN GENERAL COORDINATES

Metric Tensor

The distinction between contravariant and covariant transformations was established in Section 4.1, where we also observed that it only became meaningful when working with coordinate systems that are not Cartesian. We now want to examine relationships that can systematize the use of more general **metric spaces** (also called **Riemannian spaces**). Our initial illustrations will be for spaces with three dimensions.

Letting q^i denote coordinates in a general coordinate system, writing the index as a superscript to reflect the fact that coordinates transform contravariantly, we define **covariant basis vectors** $\boldsymbol{\varepsilon}_i$ that describe the displacement (in Euclidean space) per unit change in q^i, keeping the other q^j constant. For the situations of interest here, both the direction and magnitude of $\boldsymbol{\varepsilon}_i$ may be functions of position, so it is defined as the derivative

$$\boldsymbol{\varepsilon}_i = \frac{\partial x}{\partial q^i} \hat{\mathbf{e}}_x + \frac{\partial y}{\partial q^i} \hat{\mathbf{e}}_y + \frac{\partial z}{\partial q^i} \hat{\mathbf{e}}_z. \tag{4.37}$$

An arbitrary vector $\mathbf{A}$ can now be formed as a linear combination of the basis vectors, multiplied by coefficients:

$$\mathbf{A} = A^1 \boldsymbol{\varepsilon}_1 + A^2 \boldsymbol{\varepsilon}_2 + A^3 \boldsymbol{\varepsilon}_3. \tag{4.38}$$

At this point we have a linguistic ambiguity: $\mathbf{A}$ is a fixed object (usually called a vector) that may be described in various coordinate systems. But it is also customary to call the collection of coefficients A^i a vector (more specifically, a **contravariant vector**), while we have already called $\boldsymbol{\varepsilon}_i$ a covariant basis vector. The important thing to observe here is that $\mathbf{A}$ is a fixed object that is not changed by our transformations, while its representation (the A^i) and the basis used for the representation (the $\boldsymbol{\varepsilon}_i$) change in mutually inverse ways (as the coordinate system is changed) so as to keep $\mathbf{A}$ fixed.

Given our basis vectors, we can compute the displacement (change in position) associated with changes in the q^i. Because the basis vectors depend on position, our computation needs to be for small (infinitesimal) displacements ds. We have

$$(ds)^2 = \sum_{ij} (\boldsymbol{\varepsilon}_i \, dq^i) \cdot (\boldsymbol{\varepsilon}_j \, dq^j),$$

which, using the summation convention, can be written

$$(ds)^2 = g_{ij} dq^i dq^j, \tag{4.39}$$

with

$$g_{ij} = \boldsymbol{\varepsilon}_i \cdot \boldsymbol{\varepsilon}_j. \tag{4.40}$$

Since $(ds)^2$ is an invariant under rotational (and reflection) transformations, it is a scalar, and the quotient rule permits us to identify g_{ij} as a covariant tensor. Because of its role in defining displacement, g_{ij} is called the **covariant metric tensor**.

Note that the basis vectors can be defined by their Cartesian components, but they are, in general, neither unit vectors nor mutually orthogonal. Because they are often **not** unit vectors we have identified them by the symbol $\boldsymbol{\varepsilon}$, not $\hat{\mathbf{e}}$. The lack of both a normalization and an orthogonality requirement means that g_{ij}, though manifestly symmetric, is not required to be diagonal, and its elements (including those on the diagonal) may be of either sign.

It is convenient to define a **contravariant** metric tensor that satisfies

$$g^{ik} g_{kj} = g_{jk} g^{ki} = \delta^i_j, \tag{4.41}$$

and is therefore the inverse of the covariant metric tensor. We will use g_{ij} and g^{ij} to make conversions between contravariant and covariant vectors that we then regard as related. Thus, we write

$$g_{ij} F^j = F_i \quad \text{and} \quad g^{ij} F_j = F^i. \tag{4.42}$$

Returning now to Eq. (4.38), we can manipulate it as follows:

$$\mathbf{A} = A^i \boldsymbol{\varepsilon}_i = A^i \delta^k_i \boldsymbol{\varepsilon}_k = \left(A^i g_{ij} \right) \left(g^{jk} \boldsymbol{\varepsilon}_k \right) = A_j \boldsymbol{\varepsilon}^j, \tag{4.43}$$

showing that the same vector can be represented either by contravariant or covariant components, with the two sets of components related by the transformation in Eq. (4.42).

Covariant and Contravariant Bases

We now define the **contravariant basis vectors**

$$\boldsymbol{\varepsilon}^i = \frac{\partial q^i}{\partial x}\,\hat{\mathbf{e}}_x + \frac{\partial q^i}{\partial y}\,\hat{\mathbf{e}}_y + \frac{\partial q^i}{\partial z}\,\hat{\mathbf{e}}_z, \tag{4.44}$$

giving them this name in anticipation of the fact that we can prove them to be the contravariant versions of the $\boldsymbol{\varepsilon}_i$. Our first step in this direction is to verify that

$$\boldsymbol{\varepsilon}^i \cdot \boldsymbol{\varepsilon}_j = \frac{\partial q^i}{\partial x}\frac{\partial x}{\partial q^j} + \frac{\partial q^i}{\partial y}\frac{\partial y}{\partial q^j} + \frac{\partial q^i}{\partial z}\frac{\partial z}{\partial q^j} = \delta^i_j, \tag{4.45}$$

a consequence of the chain rule and the fact that q^i and q^j are independent variables.
    We next note that

$$(\boldsymbol{\varepsilon}^i \cdot \boldsymbol{\varepsilon}^j)(\boldsymbol{\varepsilon}_j \cdot \boldsymbol{\varepsilon}_k) = \delta^i_k, \tag{4.46}$$

also proved using the chain rule; the terms can be collected so that groups of them correspond to the identities in Eq. (4.45). Equation (4.46) shows that

$$g^{ij} = \boldsymbol{\varepsilon}^i \cdot \boldsymbol{\varepsilon}^j. \tag{4.47}$$

Multiplying both sides of Eq. (4.47) on the right by $\boldsymbol{\varepsilon}_j$ and performing the implied summation, the left-hand side of that equation, $g^{ij}\boldsymbol{\varepsilon}_j$, becomes the formula for $\boldsymbol{\varepsilon}^i$, while the right-hand side simplifies to the expression in Eq. (4.44), thereby proving that the contravariant vector in that equation was appropriately named.
    We illustrate now some typical metric tensors and basis vectors in both covariant and contravariant form.

Example 4.3.1   SOME METRIC TENSORS

In spherical polar coordinates, $(q^1, q^2, q^3) \equiv (r, \theta, \varphi)$, and $x = r\sin\theta\cos\varphi$, $y = r\sin\theta\sin\varphi$, $z = r\cos\theta$. The covariant basis vectors are

$$\boldsymbol{\varepsilon}_r = \sin\theta\cos\varphi\,\hat{\mathbf{e}}_x + \sin\theta\sin\varphi\,\hat{\mathbf{e}}_y + \cos\theta\,\hat{\mathbf{e}}_z,$$

$$\boldsymbol{\varepsilon}_\theta = r\cos\theta\cos\varphi\,\hat{\mathbf{e}}_x + r\cos\theta\sin\varphi\,\hat{\mathbf{e}}_y - r\sin\theta\,\hat{\mathbf{e}}_z,$$

$$\boldsymbol{\varepsilon}_\varphi = -r\sin\theta\sin\varphi\,\hat{\mathbf{e}}_x + r\sin\theta\cos\varphi\,\hat{\mathbf{e}}_y,$$

and the contravariant basis vectors, which can be obtained in many ways, one of which is to start from $r^2 = x^2 + y^2 + z^2$, $\cos\theta = z/r$, $\tan\varphi = y/x$, are

$$\boldsymbol{\varepsilon}^r = \sin\theta\cos\varphi\,\hat{\mathbf{e}}_x + \sin\theta\sin\varphi\,\hat{\mathbf{e}}_y + \cos\theta\,\hat{\mathbf{e}}_z,$$

$$\boldsymbol{\varepsilon}^\theta = r^{-1}\cos\theta\cos\varphi\,\hat{\mathbf{e}}_x + r^{-1}\cos\theta\sin\varphi\,\hat{\mathbf{e}}_y - r^{-1}\sin\theta\,\hat{\mathbf{e}}_z,$$

$$\boldsymbol{\varepsilon}^\varphi = -\frac{\sin\varphi}{r\sin\theta}\,\hat{\mathbf{e}}_x + \frac{\cos\varphi}{r\sin\theta}\,\hat{\mathbf{e}}_y,$$

leading to

$$g_{11} = \boldsymbol{\varepsilon}_r \cdot \boldsymbol{\varepsilon}_r = 1,$$

$$g_{22} = \boldsymbol{\varepsilon}_\theta \cdot \boldsymbol{\varepsilon}_\theta = r^2,$$

$$g_{33} = \boldsymbol{\varepsilon}_\varphi \cdot \boldsymbol{\varepsilon}_\varphi = r^2 \sin^2 \theta;$$

all other g_{ij} vanish. Combining these to make g_{ij} and taking the inverse (to make g^{ij}), we have

$$(g_{ij}) = \begin{pmatrix} 1 & 0 & 0 \\ 0 & r^2 & 0 \\ 0 & 0 & r^2 \sin^2 \theta \end{pmatrix}, \quad (g^{ij}) = \begin{pmatrix} 1 & 0 & 0 \\ 0 & r^{-2} & 0 \\ 0 & 0 & (r \sin \theta)^{-2} \end{pmatrix}.$$

We can check that we have inverted g_{ij} correctly by comparing the expression given for g^{ij} from that built directly from $\boldsymbol{\varepsilon}^i \cdot \boldsymbol{\varepsilon}^j$. This check is left for the reader.

The Minkowski metric of special relativity has the form

$$(g_{ij}) = (g^{ij}) = \begin{pmatrix} 1 & 0 & 0 & 0 \\ 0 & -1 & 0 & 0 \\ 0 & 0 & -1 & 0 \\ 0 & 0 & 0 & -1 \end{pmatrix}.$$

The motivation for including it in this example is to emphasize that for some metrics important in physics, distances ds^2 need not be positive (meaning that ds can be imaginary). ∎

The relation between the covariant and contravariant basis vectors is useful for writing relationships between vectors. Let **A** and **B** be vectors with contravariant representations (A^i) and (B^i). We may convert the representation of **B** to $B_i = g_{ij} B^j$, after which the scalar product $\mathbf{A} \cdot \mathbf{B}$ takes the form

$$\mathbf{A} \cdot \mathbf{B} = (A^i \, \boldsymbol{\varepsilon}_i) \cdot (B_j \, \boldsymbol{\varepsilon}^j) = A^i B_j (\boldsymbol{\varepsilon}_i \cdot \boldsymbol{\varepsilon}^j) = A^i B_i. \tag{4.48}$$

Another application is in writing the gradient in general coordinates. If a function ψ is given in a general coordinate system (q^i), its gradient $\nabla \psi$ is a vector with Cartesian components

$$(\nabla \psi)_j = \frac{\partial \psi}{\partial q^i} \frac{\partial q^i}{\partial x^j}. \tag{4.49}$$

In vector notation, Eq. (4.49) becomes

$$\nabla \psi = \frac{\partial \psi}{\partial q^i} \boldsymbol{\varepsilon}^i, \tag{4.50}$$

showing that the covariant representation of $\nabla \psi$ is the set of derivatives $\partial \psi / \partial q^i$. If we have reason to use a contravariant representation of the gradient, we can convert its components using Eq. (4.42).

Covariant Derivatives

Moving on to the derivatives of a vector, we find that the situation is much more complicated because the basis vectors $\boldsymbol{\varepsilon}_i$ are in general not constant, and the derivative will not be a tensor whose components are the derivatives of the vector components.

Starting from the transformation rule for a contravariant vector,

$$(V')^i = \frac{\partial x^i}{\partial q_k} V^k,$$

and differentiating with respect to q^j, we get (for each i)

$$\frac{\partial (V')^i}{\partial q^j} = \frac{\partial x^i}{\partial q_k} \frac{\partial V^k}{\partial q^j} + \frac{\partial^2 x^i}{\partial q^j \partial q^k} V^k, \tag{4.51}$$

which appears to differ from the transformation law for a second-rank tensor because it contains a second derivative.

To see what to do next, let's write Eq. (4.51) as a single vector equation in the x_i coordinates, which we take to be Cartesian. The result is

$$\frac{\partial \mathbf{V}'}{\partial q^j} = \frac{\partial V^k}{\partial q^j} \boldsymbol{\varepsilon}_k + V^k \frac{\partial \boldsymbol{\varepsilon}_k}{\partial q^j}. \tag{4.52}$$

We now recognize that $\partial \boldsymbol{\varepsilon}_k / \partial q^j$ must be some vector in the space spanned by the set of all $\boldsymbol{\varepsilon}_i$ and we therefore write

$$\frac{\partial \boldsymbol{\varepsilon}_k}{\partial q^j} = \Gamma^\mu_{jk} \boldsymbol{\varepsilon}_\mu. \tag{4.53}$$

The quantities Γ^μ_{jk} are known as **Christoffel symbols of the second kind** (those of the first kind will be encountered shortly). Using the orthogonality property of the $\boldsymbol{\varepsilon}$, Eq. (4.45), we can solve Eq. (4.53) by taking its dot product with any $\boldsymbol{\varepsilon}^m$, reaching

$$\Gamma^m_{jk} = \boldsymbol{\varepsilon}^m \cdot \frac{\partial \boldsymbol{\varepsilon}_k}{\partial q^j}. \tag{4.54}$$

Moreover, we note that $\Gamma^m_{kj} = \Gamma^m_{jk}$, which can be demonstrated by writing out the components of $\partial \boldsymbol{\varepsilon}_k / \partial q^j$.

Returning now to Eq. (4.52) and inserting Eq. (4.53), we initially get

$$\frac{\partial \mathbf{V}'}{\partial q^j} = \frac{\partial V^k}{\partial q^j} \boldsymbol{\varepsilon}_k + V^k \Gamma^\mu_{jk} \boldsymbol{\varepsilon}_\mu. \tag{4.55}$$

Interchanging the dummy indices k and μ in the last term of Eq. (4.55), we get the final result

$$\frac{\partial \mathbf{V}'}{\partial q^j} = \left(\frac{\partial V^k}{\partial q^j} + V^\mu \Gamma^k_{j\mu} \right) \boldsymbol{\varepsilon}_k. \tag{4.56}$$

The parenthesized quantity in Eq. (4.56) is known as the **covariant derivative** of V, and it has (unfortunately) become standard to identify it by the awkward notation

$$V^k_{;j} = \frac{\partial V^k}{\partial q^j} + V^\mu \Gamma^k_{j\mu}, \quad \text{so} \quad \frac{\partial \mathbf{V}'}{\partial q^j} = V^k_{;j} \boldsymbol{\varepsilon}_k. \tag{4.57}$$

If we rewrite Eq. (4.56) in the form

$$d\mathbf{V}' = \left[V^k_{;j}\, dq^j \right] \boldsymbol{\varepsilon}_k,$$

and take note that dq^j is a contravariant vector, while $\boldsymbol{\varepsilon}_k$ is covariant, we see that the covariant derivative, $V^k_{;j}$ is a mixed second-rank tensor.[4] However, it is important to realize that although they bristle with indices, **neither** $\partial V^k/\partial q^j$ **nor** Γ^k_{jv} have individually the correct transformation properties to be tensors. It is only the combination in Eq. (4.57) that has the requisite transformational attributes.

It can be shown (see Exercise 4.3.6) that the covariant derivative of a **covariant** vector V_i is given by

$$V_{i;j} = \frac{\partial V_i}{\partial q^j} - V_k \Gamma^k_{ij}. \tag{4.58}$$

Like $V^i_{;j}$, $V_{i;j}$ is a second-rank tensor.

The physical importance of the covariant derivative is that it includes the changes in the basis vectors pursuant to a general dq^i, and is therefore more appropriate for describing physical phenomena than a formulation that considers only the changes in the coefficients multiplying the basis vectors.

Evaluating Christoffel Symbols

It may be more convenient to evaluate the Christoffel symbols by relating them to the metric tensor than simply to use Eq. (4.54). As an initial step in this direction, we define the Christoffel symbol of the **first kind** $[ij, k]$ by

$$[ij, k] \equiv g_{mk} \Gamma^m_{ij}, \tag{4.59}$$

from which the symmetry $[ij, k] = [ji, k]$ follows. Again, this $[ij, k]$ is not a third-rank tensor. Inserting Eq. (4.54) and applying the index-lowering transformation, Eq. (4.42), we have

$$[ij, k] = g_{mk}\, \boldsymbol{\varepsilon}^m \cdot \frac{\partial \boldsymbol{\varepsilon}_i}{\partial q^j}$$

$$= \boldsymbol{\varepsilon}_k \cdot \frac{\partial \boldsymbol{\varepsilon}_i}{\partial q^j}. \tag{4.60}$$

Next, we write $g_{ij} = \boldsymbol{\varepsilon}_i \cdot \boldsymbol{\varepsilon}_j$ as in Eq. (4.40) and differentiate it, identifying the result with the aid of Eq. (4.60):

$$\frac{\partial g_{ij}}{\partial q^k} = \frac{\partial \boldsymbol{\varepsilon}_i}{\partial q^k} \cdot \boldsymbol{\varepsilon}_j + \boldsymbol{\varepsilon}_i \cdot \frac{\partial \boldsymbol{\varepsilon}_j}{\partial q^k}$$

$$= [ik, j] + [jk, i].$$

---

[4]$\mathbf{V}'$ does not contribute to the covariant/contravariant character of the equation as its implicit index labels the Cartesian coordinates, as is also the case for $\boldsymbol{\varepsilon}_k$.

We then note that we can combine three of these derivatives with different index sets, with a result that simplifies to give

$$\frac{1}{2}\left[\frac{\partial g_{ik}}{\partial q^j} + \frac{\partial g_{jk}}{\partial q^i} - \frac{\partial g_{ij}}{\partial q^k}\right] = [ij, k]. \tag{4.61}$$

We now return to Eq. (4.59), which we solve for Γ_{ij}^m by multiplying both sides by g^{nk}, summing over k, and using the fact that $(g_{\mu\nu})$ and $(g^{\mu\nu})$ are mutually inverse, see Eq. (4.41):

$$\Gamma_{ij}^n = \sum_k g^{nk}[ij, k]. \tag{4.62}$$

Finally, substituting for $[ij, k]$ from Eq. (4.61), and once again using the summation convention, we get:

$$\Gamma_{ij}^n = g^{nk}[ij, k] = \frac{1}{2}g^{nk}\left[\frac{\partial g_{ik}}{\partial q^j} + \frac{\partial g_{jk}}{\partial q^i} - \frac{\partial g_{ij}}{\partial q^k}\right]. \tag{4.63}$$

The apparatus of this subsection becomes unnecessary in Cartesian coordinates, because the basis vectors have vanishing derivatives, and the covariant and ordinary partial derivatives then coincide.

Tensor Derivative Operators

With covariant differentiation now available, we are ready to derive the vector differential operators in general tensor form.

Gradient—We have already discussed it, with the result from Eq. (4.50):

$$\nabla\psi = \frac{\partial\psi}{\partial q^i}\boldsymbol{\varepsilon}^i. \tag{4.64}$$

Divergence—A vector $\mathbf{V}$ whose contravariant representation is $V^i\boldsymbol{\varepsilon}_i$ has divergence

$$\nabla\cdot\mathbf{V} = \boldsymbol{\varepsilon}^j\cdot\frac{\partial(V^i\boldsymbol{\varepsilon}_i)}{\partial q^j} = \boldsymbol{\varepsilon}^j\cdot\left(\frac{\partial V^i}{\partial q^j} + V^k\Gamma_{jk}^i\right)\boldsymbol{\varepsilon}_i = \frac{\partial V^i}{\partial q^i} + V^k\Gamma_{ik}^i. \tag{4.65}$$

Note that the covariant derivative has appeared here. Expressing Γ_{ik}^i by Eq. (4.63), we have

$$\Gamma_{ik}^i = \frac{1}{2}g^{im}\left[\frac{\partial g_{im}}{\partial q^k} + \frac{\partial g_{km}}{\partial q^i} - \frac{\partial g_{ik}}{\partial q^m}\right] = \frac{1}{2}g^{im}\frac{\partial g_{im}}{\partial q^k}, \tag{4.66}$$

where we have recognized that the last two terms in the bracket will cancel because by changing the names of their dummy indices they can be identified as identical except in sign.

Because (g^{im}) is the matrix inverse to (g_{im}), we note that the combination of matrix elements on the right-hand side of Eq. (4.66) is similar to those in the formula for the derivative of a determinant, Eq. (2.35); remember that g is symmetric: $g^{im} = g^{mi}$. In the present notation, the relevant formula is

$$\frac{d\det(g)}{dq^k} = \det(g)\,g^{im}\frac{\partial g_{im}}{\partial q^k}, \tag{4.67}$$

where $\det(g)$ is the determinant of the **covariant** metric tensor $(g_{\mu\nu})$. Using Eq. (4.67), Eq. (4.66) becomes

$$\Gamma^i_{ik} = \frac{1}{2\det(g)} \frac{d\det(g)}{dq^k} = \frac{1}{[\det(g)]^{1/2}} \frac{\partial[\det(g)]^{1/2}}{\partial q^k}. \tag{4.68}$$

Combining the result in Eq. (4.68) with Eq. (4.65), we obtain a maximally compact formula for the divergence of a contravariant vector **V**:

$$\nabla \cdot \mathbf{V} = V^i_{;i} = \frac{1}{[\det(g)]^{1/2}} \frac{\partial}{\partial q^k} \left([\det(g)]^{1/2} V^k \right). \tag{4.69}$$

To compare this result with that for an orthogonal coordinate system, Eq. (3.141), note that $\det(g) = (h_1 h_2 h_3)^2$ and that the k component of the vector represented by **V** in Eq. (3.141) is, in the present notation, equal to $V^k |\boldsymbol{\varepsilon}_k| = h_k V^k$ (no summation).

Laplacian—We can form the Laplacian $\nabla^2 \psi$ by inserting an expression for the gradient $\nabla\psi$ into the formula for the divergence, Eq. (4.69). However, that equation uses the contravariant coefficients V^k, so we must describe the gradient in its contravariant representation. Since Eq. (4.64) shows that the covariant coefficients of the gradient are the derivatives $\partial\psi/\partial q^i$, its contravariant coefficients have to be

$$g^{ki} \frac{\partial\psi}{\partial q^i}.$$

Insertion into Eq. (4.69) then yields

$$\nabla^2 \psi = \frac{1}{[\det(g)]^{1/2}} \frac{\partial}{\partial q^k} \left([\det(g)]^{1/2} g^{ki} \frac{\partial\psi}{\partial q^i} \right). \tag{4.70}$$

For **orthogonal** systems the metric tensor is diagonal and the contravariant $g^{ii} = (h_i)^{-2}$ (no summation). Equation (4.70) then reduces to

$$\nabla \cdot \nabla \psi = \frac{1}{h_1 h_2 h_3} \frac{\partial}{\partial q^i} \left(\frac{h_1 h_2 h_3}{h_i^2} \frac{\partial\psi}{\partial q^i} \right),$$

in agreement with Eq. (3.142).

Curl—The difference of derivatives that appears in the curl has components that can be written

$$\frac{\partial V_i}{\partial q^j} - \frac{\partial V_j}{\partial q^i} = \frac{\partial V_i}{\partial q^j} - V_k \Gamma^k_{ij} - \frac{\partial V_j}{\partial q^i} + V_k \Gamma^k_{ji} = V_{i;j} - V_{j;i}, \tag{4.71}$$

where we used the symmetry of the Christoffel symbols to obtain a cancellation. The reason for the manipulation in Eq. (4.71) is to bring all the terms on its right-hand side to tensor form. In using Eq. (4.71), it is necessary to remember that the quantities V_i are coefficients of the possibly nonunit $\boldsymbol{\varepsilon}^i$ and are therefore **not** components of **V** in the orthonormal basis $\hat{\mathbf{e}}_i$.

Exercises

4.3.1   For the special case of 3-D space (ε_1, ε_2, ε_3 defining a right-handed coordinate system, not necessarily orthogonal), show that

$$\varepsilon^i = \frac{\varepsilon_j \times \varepsilon_k}{\varepsilon_j \times \varepsilon_k \cdot \varepsilon_i}, \quad i, j, k = 1, 2, 3 \text{ and cyclic permutations.}$$

Note. These contravariant basis vectors ε^i define the reciprocal lattice space of Example 3.2.1.

4.3.2   If the covariant vectors ε_i are orthogonal, show that

(a) g_{ij} is diagonal,

(b) $g^{ii} = 1/g_{ii}$ (no summation),

(c) $|\varepsilon^i| = 1/|\varepsilon_i|$.

4.3.3   Prove that $(\varepsilon^i \cdot \varepsilon^j)(\varepsilon_j \cdot \varepsilon_k) = \delta^i_k$.

4.3.4   Show that $\Gamma^m_{jk} = \Gamma^m_{kj}$.

4.3.5   Derive the covariant and contravariant metric tensors for circular cylindrical coordinates.

4.3.6   Show that the covariant derivative of a covariant vector is given by

$$V_{i;j} \equiv \frac{\partial V_i}{\partial q^j} - V_k \Gamma^k_{ij}.$$

Hint. Differentiate

$$\varepsilon^i \cdot \varepsilon_j = \delta^i_j.$$

4.3.7   Verify that $V_{i;j} = g_{ik} V^k_{;j}$ by showing that

$$\frac{\partial V_i}{\partial q^j} - V_k \Gamma^k_{ij} = g_{ik}\left[\frac{\partial V^k}{\partial q^j} + V^m \Gamma^k_{mj}\right].$$

4.3.8   From the circular cylindrical metric tensor g_{ij}, calculate the Γ^k_{ij} for circular cylindrical coordinates.

Note. There are only three nonvanishing Γ.

4.3.9   Using the Γ^k_{ij} from Exercise 4.3.8, write out the covariant derivatives $V^i_{;j}$ of a vector $\mathbf{V}$ in circular cylindrical coordinates.

4.3.10   Show that for the metric tensor $g_{ij;k} = g^{ij}_{;k} = 0$.

4.3.11   Starting with the divergence in tensor notation, Eq. (4.70), develop the divergence of a vector in spherical polar coordinates, Eq. (3.157).

4.3.12   The covariant vector A_i is the gradient of a scalar. Show that the difference of covariant derivatives $A_{i;j} - A_{j;i}$ vanishes.

4.4 JACOBIANS

In the preceding chapters we have considered the use of curvilinear coordinates, but have not placed much focus on transformations between coordinate systems, and in particular on the way in which multidimensional integrals must transform when the coordinate system is changed. To provide formulas that will be useful in spaces with arbitrary numbers of dimensions, and with transformations involving coordinate systems that are not orthogonal, we now return to the notion of the **Jacobian**, introduced but not fully developed in Chapter 1.

As already mentioned in Chapter 1, changes of variables in multiple integrations, say from variables x_1, $x_2, \ldots$ to u_1, $u_2, \ldots$ requires that we replace the differential $dx_1 dx_2 \ldots$ with $J \, du_1 du_2 \ldots$, where J, called the Jacobian, is the quantity (usually dependent on the variables) needed to make these expressions mutually consistent. More specifically, we identify $d\tau = J \, du_1 du_2 \ldots$ as the "volume" of a region of width du_1 in u_1, du_2 in $u_2, \ldots$, where the "volume" is to be computed in the x_1, $x_2, \ldots$ space, treated as Cartesian coordinates.

To obtain a formula for J we start by identifying the displacement (in the Cartesian system defined by the x_i) that corresponds to a change in each variable u_i. Letting $d\mathbf{s}(u_i)$ be that displacement (which is a vector), we can decompose it into Cartesian components as follows:

$$d\mathbf{s}(u_1) = \left[\left(\frac{\partial x_1}{\partial u_1} \right) \hat{\mathbf{e}}_1 + \left(\frac{\partial x_2}{\partial u_1} \right) \hat{\mathbf{e}}_2 + \cdots \right] du_1,$$

$$d\mathbf{s}(u_2) = \left[\left(\frac{\partial x_1}{\partial u_2} \right) \hat{\mathbf{e}}_1 + \left(\frac{\partial x_2}{\partial u_2} \right) \hat{\mathbf{e}}_2 + \cdots \right] du_2, \tag{4.72}$$

$$d\mathbf{s}(u_3) = \left[\left(\frac{\partial x_1}{\partial u_3} \right) \hat{\mathbf{e}}_1 + \left(\frac{\partial x_2}{\partial u_3} \right) \hat{\mathbf{e}}_2 + \cdots \right] du_3,$$

$$\ldots \ldots = \ldots \ldots \ldots$$

The partial derivatives $(\partial x_i / \partial u_j)$ in Eq. (4.72) must be understood to be evaluated with the other u_k held constant. It would clutter the formula an unreasonable amount to indicate this explicitly.

If we had only two variables, u_1 and u_2, the differential area would simply be $|d\mathbf{s}(u_1)|$ times the component of $d\mathbf{s}(u_2)$ that is perpendicular to $d\mathbf{s}(u_1)$. If there were a third variable, u_3, we would further multiply by the component of $d\mathbf{s}(u_3)$ that was perpendicular to both $d\mathbf{s}(u_1)$ and $d\mathbf{s}(u_2)$. Extension to arbitrary numbers of dimensions is obvious.

What is less obvious is an explicit formula for the "volume" for an arbitrary number of dimensions. Let's start by writing Eq. (4.72) in matrix form:

$$
\begin{pmatrix} \dfrac{d\mathbf{s}(u_1)}{du_1} \\[2mm] \dfrac{d\mathbf{s}(u_2)}{du_2} \\[2mm] \dfrac{d\mathbf{s}(u_3)}{du_3} \\[2mm] \cdots \end{pmatrix}
=
\begin{pmatrix} \dfrac{\partial x_1}{\partial u_1} & \dfrac{\partial x_2}{\partial u_1} & \dfrac{\partial x_3}{\partial u_1} & \cdots \\[2mm] \dfrac{\partial x_1}{\partial u_2} & \dfrac{\partial x_2}{\partial u_2} & \dfrac{\partial x_3}{\partial u_2} & \cdots \\[2mm] \dfrac{\partial x_1}{\partial u_3} & \dfrac{\partial x_2}{\partial u_3} & \dfrac{\partial x_3}{\partial u_3} & \cdots \\[2mm] \cdots & \cdots & \cdots & \cdots \end{pmatrix}
\begin{pmatrix} \hat{\mathbf{e}}_1 \\[2mm] \hat{\mathbf{e}}_2 \\[2mm] \hat{\mathbf{e}}_3 \\[2mm] \cdots \end{pmatrix}.
\tag{4.73}
$$

We now proceed to make changes to the second and succeeding rows of the square matrix in Eq. (4.73) that may destroy the relation to the $d\mathbf{s}(u_i)/du_i$, but which will leave the "volume" unchanged. In particular, we subtract from the second row of the derivative matrix that multiple of the first row which will cause the first element of the modified second row to vanish. This will not change the "volume" because it modifies $d\mathbf{s}(u_2)/du_2$ by adding or subtracting a vector in the $d\mathbf{s}(u_1)/du_1$ direction, and therefore does not affect the component of $d\mathbf{s}(u_2)/du_2$ perpendicular to $d\mathbf{s}(u_1)/du_1$. See Fig. 4.1.

The alert reader will recall that this modification of the second row of our matrix is an operation that was used when evaluating determinants, and was there justified because it did not change the value of the determinant. We have a similar situation here; the operation will not change the value of the differential "volume" because we are changing only the component of $d\mathbf{s}(u_2)/du_2$ that is in the $d\mathbf{s}(u_1)/du_1$ direction. In a similar fashion, we can carry out further operations of the same kind that will lead to a matrix in which all the elements below the principal diagonal have been reduced to zero. The situation at this point is indicated schematically for an 4-D space as the transition from the first to the second matrix in Fig. 4.2. These modified $d\mathbf{s}(u_i)/du_i$ will lead to the same differential volume as the original $d\mathbf{s}(u_i)/du_i$. This modified matrix will no longer provide a faithful representation of the differential region in the u_i space, but that is irrelevant since our only objective is to evaluate the differential "volume."

We next take the final (nth) row of our modified matrix, which will be entirely zero except for its last element, and subtract a suitable multiple of it from all the other rows to introduce zeros in the last element of every row above the principal diagonal. These operations correspond to changes in which we modify only the components of the other $d\mathbf{s}(u_i)/du_i$ that are in the direction of $d\mathbf{s}(u_n)$, and therefore will not change the differential "volume." Then, using the next-to-last row (which now has only a diagonal element), we can in a similar fashion introduce zeros in the next-to-last column of all the preceding rows. Continuing this process, we will ultimately have a set of modified $d\mathbf{s}(u_i)/du_i$ that will have the structure shown as the last matrix in Fig. 4.2. Because our modified matrix is diagonal, with each nonzero element associated with a single different $\hat{\mathbf{e}}_i$, the "volume" is

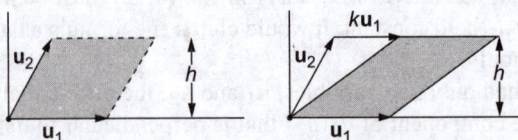

FIGURE 4.1   Area remains unchanged when vector proportional to $\mathbf{u}_1$ is added to $\mathbf{u}_2$.

$$
\begin{pmatrix} a_{11} & a_{12} & a_{13} & a_{14} \\ a_{21} & a_{22} & a_{23} & a_{24} \\ a_{31} & a_{32} & a_{33} & a_{34} \\ a_{41} & a_{42} & a_{43} & a_{44} \end{pmatrix} \rightarrow \begin{pmatrix} a_{11} & a_{12} & a_{13} & a_{14} \\ 0 & b_{22} & b_{23} & b_{24} \\ 0 & 0 & b_{33} & b_{34} \\ 0 & 0 & 0 & b_{44} \end{pmatrix} \rightarrow \begin{pmatrix} a_{11} & 0 & 0 & 0 \\ 0 & b_{22} & 0 & 0 \\ 0 & 0 & b_{33} & 0 \\ 0 & 0 & 0 & b_{44} \end{pmatrix}
$$

FIGURE 4.2   Manipulation of Jacobian matrix. Here $a_{ij} = (\partial x_j/\partial u_i)$, and b_{ij} are formed by combining rows (see text).

then easily computed as the product of the diagonal elements. This product of the diagonal elements of a diagonal matrix is an evaluation of its determinant.

Reviewing what we have done, we see that we have identified the differential "volume" as a quantity which is equal to the determinant of the original derivative set. This must be so, because we obtained our final result by carrying out operations each of which leaves a determinant unchanged. The final result can be expressed as the well-known formula for the Jacobian:

$$d\tau = J\, du_1 du_2 \ldots, \quad J = \begin{vmatrix} \dfrac{\partial x_1}{\partial u_1} & \dfrac{\partial x_2}{\partial u_1} & \dfrac{\partial x_3}{\partial u_1} & \cdots \\[2mm] \dfrac{\partial x_1}{\partial u_2} & \dfrac{\partial x_2}{\partial u_2} & \dfrac{\partial x_3}{\partial u_2} & \cdots \\[2mm] \dfrac{\partial x_1}{\partial u_3} & \dfrac{\partial x_2}{\partial u_3} & \dfrac{\partial x_3}{\partial u_3} & \cdots \\[2mm] \cdots & \cdots & \cdots & \cdots \end{vmatrix} \equiv \frac{\partial(x_1, x_2, \ldots)}{\partial(u_1, u_2, \ldots)}. \tag{4.74}$$

The standard notation for the Jacobian, shown as the last member of Eq. (4.74), is a convenient reminder of the way in which the partial derivatives appear in it. Note also that when the standard notation for J is inserted in the expression for $d\tau$, the overall expression has $du_1 du_2 \ldots$ in the numerator, while $\partial(u_1, u_2, \ldots)$ appears in the denominator. This feature can help the user to make a proper identification of the Jacobian.

A few words about nomenclature: The matrix in Eq. (4.73) is sometimes called the **Jacobian matrix**, with the determinant in Eq. (4.74) then distinguished by calling it the **Jacobian determinant**. Unless within a discussion in which both these quantities appear and need to be separately identified, most authors simply call J, the determinant in Eq. (4.74), **the Jacobian**. That is the usage we follow in this book.

We close with one final observation. Since J is a determinant, it will have a sign that depends on the order in which the x_i and u_i are specified. This ambiguity corresponds to our freedom to choose either right- or left-handed coordinates. In typical applications involving a Jacobian, it is usual to take its absolute value and to choose the ranges of the individual u_i integrals in a way that gives the correct sign for the overall integral.

Example 4.4.1   2-D and 3-D JACOBIANS

In two dimensions, with Cartesian coordinates x, y and transformed coordinates u, v, the element of area dA has, following Eq. (4.74), the form

$$dA = du\, dv \left[\left(\frac{\partial x}{\partial u} \right) \left(\frac{\partial y}{\partial v} \right) - \left(\frac{\partial x}{\partial v} \right) \left(\frac{\partial y}{\partial u} \right) \right].$$

This is the expected result, as the quantity in square brackets is the formula for the z component of the cross product of the two vectors

$$\left(\frac{\partial x}{\partial u} \right) \hat{\mathbf{e}}_x + \left(\frac{\partial y}{\partial u} \right) \hat{\mathbf{e}}_y \quad \text{and} \quad \left(\frac{\partial x}{\partial v} \right) \hat{\mathbf{e}}_x + \left(\frac{\partial y}{\partial v} \right) \hat{\mathbf{e}}_y,$$

and it is well known that the magnitude of the cross product of two vectors is a measure of the area of the parallelogram with sides formed by the vectors.

In three dimensions, the determinant in the Jacobian corresponds exactly with the formula for the scalar triple product, Eq. (3.12). Letting A_x, A_y, A_z in that formula refer to the derivatives $(\partial x/\partial u)$, $(\partial y/\partial u)$, $(\partial z/\partial u)$, with the components of **B** and **C** similarly related to derivatives with respect to v and w, we recover the formula for the volume within the parallelepiped defined by three vectors.   ∎

Inverse of Jacobian

Since the x_i and the u_i are arbitrary sets of coordinates, we could have carried out the entire analysis of the preceding subsection regarding the u_i as the fundamental coordinate system, with the x_i as coordinates reached by a change of variables. In that case, our Jacobian (which we choose to label J^{-1}), would be

$$J^{-1} = \frac{\partial(u_1, u_2, \ldots)}{\partial(x_1, x_2, \ldots)}. \tag{4.75}$$

It is clear that if $dx_1 dx_2 \ldots = J\, du_1 du_2 \ldots$, then it must also be true that $du_1 du_2 \ldots = (1/J)\, dx_1 dx_2 \ldots$. Let's verify that the quantity we have called J^{-1} is in fact $1/J$.

Let's represent the two Jacobian **matrices** involved here as

$$A = \begin{pmatrix} \dfrac{\partial x_1}{\partial u_1} & \dfrac{\partial x_2}{\partial u_1} & \dfrac{\partial x_3}{\partial u_1} & \cdots \\[2mm] \dfrac{\partial x_1}{\partial u_2} & \dfrac{\partial x_2}{\partial u_2} & \dfrac{\partial x_3}{\partial u_2} & \cdots \\[2mm] \dfrac{\partial x_1}{\partial u_3} & \dfrac{\partial x_2}{\partial u_3} & \dfrac{\partial x_3}{\partial u_3} & \cdots \\[1mm] \cdots & \cdots & \cdots & \cdots \end{pmatrix}, \quad B = \begin{pmatrix} \dfrac{\partial u_1}{\partial x_1} & \dfrac{\partial u_2}{\partial x_1} & \dfrac{\partial u_3}{\partial x_1} & \cdots \\[2mm] \dfrac{\partial u_1}{\partial x_2} & \dfrac{\partial u_2}{\partial x_2} & \dfrac{\partial u_3}{\partial x_2} & \cdots \\[2mm] \dfrac{\partial u_1}{\partial x_3} & \dfrac{\partial u_2}{\partial x_3} & \dfrac{\partial u_3}{\partial x_3} & \cdots \\[1mm] \cdots & \cdots & \cdots & \cdots \end{pmatrix}.$$

We then have $J = \det(A)$ and $J^{-1} = \det(B)$. We would like to show that $J J^{-1} = \det(A)\det(B) = 1$. The proof is fairly simple if we use the determinant product theorem. Thus, we write

$$\det(A)\det(B) = \det(AB),$$

and now all we need show is that the matrix product AB is a unit matrix. Carrying out the matrix multiplication, we find, as a result of the chain rule,

$$(AB)_{ij} = \sum_k \left(\frac{\partial x_k}{\partial u_i}\right)\left(\frac{\partial u_j}{\partial x_k}\right) = \left(\frac{\partial u_j}{\partial u_i}\right) = \delta_{ij}, \tag{4.76}$$

verifying that AB is indeed a unit matrix.

The relation between the Jacobian and its inverse is of practical interest. It may turn out that the derivatives $\partial u_i/\partial x_j$ are easier to compute than $\partial x_i/\partial u_j$, making it convenient to obtain J by first constructing and evaluating the determinant for J^{-1}.

Example 4.4.2   DIRECT AND INVERSE APPROACHES TO JACOBIAN

Suppose we need the Jacobian $\dfrac{\partial(r,\theta,\varphi)}{\partial(x,y,z)}$, where x, y, and z are Cartesian coordinates and r, θ, φ are spherical polar coordinates. Using Eq. (4.74) and the relations

$$r = \sqrt{x^2+y^2+z^2}, \quad \theta = \cos^{-1}\left(\frac{z}{\sqrt{x^2+y^2+z^2}}\right), \quad \varphi = \tan^{-1}\left(\frac{y}{x}\right),$$

we find after significant effort (letting $\rho^2 = x^2+y^2$),

$$J = \frac{\partial(r,\theta,\varphi)}{\partial(x,y,z)} = \begin{vmatrix} \dfrac{x}{r} & \dfrac{y}{r} & \dfrac{z}{r} \\ \dfrac{xz}{r^2\rho} & \dfrac{yz}{r^2\rho} & -\dfrac{\rho}{r^2} \\ -\dfrac{y}{\rho^2} & \dfrac{x}{\rho^2} & 0 \end{vmatrix} = \frac{1}{r\rho} = \frac{1}{r^2\sin\theta}.$$

It is much less effort to use the relations

$$x = r\sin\theta\cos\varphi, \quad y = r\sin\theta\sin\varphi, \quad z = r\cos\theta,$$

and then to evaluate (easily),

$$J^{-1} = \frac{\partial(x,y,z)}{\partial(r,\theta,\varphi)} = \begin{vmatrix} \sin\theta\cos\varphi & \sin\theta\sin\varphi & \cos\theta \\ r\cos\theta\cos\varphi & r\cos\theta\sin\varphi & -r\sin\theta \\ -r\sin\theta\sin\varphi & r\sin\theta\cos\varphi & 0 \end{vmatrix} = r^2\sin\theta.$$

We finish by writing $J = 1/J^{-1} = 1/r^2\sin\theta$. ∎

Exercises

4.4.1   Assuming the functions u and v to be differentiable,

(a) Show that a necessary and sufficient condition that $u(x,y,z)$ and $v(x,y,z)$ are related by some function $f(u,v) = 0$ is that $(\nabla u)\times(\nabla v) = 0$;

(b) If $u = u(x,y)$ and $v = v(x,y)$, show that the condition $(\nabla u)\times(\nabla v) = 0$ leads to the 2-D Jacobian

$$J = \frac{\partial(u,v)}{\partial(x,y)} = \begin{vmatrix} \dfrac{\partial u}{\partial x} & \dfrac{\partial u}{\partial y} \\ \dfrac{\partial v}{\partial x} & \dfrac{\partial v}{\partial y} \end{vmatrix} = 0.$$

4.4.2   A 2-D orthogonal system is described by the coordinates q_1 and q_2. Show that the Jacobian J satisfies the equation

$$J \equiv \frac{\partial(x,y)}{\partial(q_1,q_2)} \equiv \frac{\partial x}{\partial q_1}\frac{\partial y}{\partial q_2} - \frac{\partial x}{\partial q_2}\frac{\partial y}{\partial q_1} = h_1 h_2.$$

Hint. It's easier to work with the square of each side of this equation.

4.4.3   For the transformation $u = x + y$, $v = x/y$, with $x \geq 0$ and $y \geq 0$, find the Jacobian
$$\frac{\partial(x, y)}{\partial(u, v)}$$

(a) By direct computation,

(b) By first computing J^{-1}.

4.5   DIFFERENTIAL FORMS

Our study of tensors has indicated that significant complications arise when we leave Cartesian coordinate systems, even in traditional contexts such as the introduction of spherical or cylindrical coordinates. Much of the difficulty arises from the fact that the metric (as expressed in a coordinate system) becomes position-dependent, and that the lines or surfaces of constant coordinate values become curved. Many of the most vexing problems can be avoided if we work in a geometry that deals with infinitesimal displacements, because the situations of most importance in physics then become locally similar to the simpler and more familiar conditions based on Cartesian coordinates.

The calculus of differential forms, of which the leading developer was Elie Cartan, has become recognized as a natural and very powerful tool for the treatment of curved coordinates, both in classical settings and in contemporary studies of curved space-time. Cartan's calculus leads to a remarkable unification of concepts and theorems of vector analysis that is worth pursuing, with the result that in differential geometry and in theoretical physics the use of differential forms is now widespread.

Differential forms provide an important entry to the role of geometry in physics, and the connectivity of the spaces under discussion (technically, referred to as their **topology**) has physical implications. Illustrations are provided already by situations as simple as the fact that a coordinate defined on a circle cannot be single-valued and continuous at all angles. More sophisticated consequences of topology in physics, largely beyond the scope of the present text, include gauge transformations, flux quantization, the Bohm-Aharanov effect, emerging theories of elementary particles, and phenomena of general relativity.

Introduction

For simplicity we begin our discussion of differential forms in a notation appropriate for ordinary 3-D space, though the real power of the methods under study is that they are not limited either by the dimensionality of the space or by its metric properties (and are therefore also relevant to the curved space-time of general relativity). The basic quantities under consideration are the **differentials** dx, dy, dz (identified with linearly independent directions in the space), linear combinations thereof, and more complicated quantities built from these by combination rules we will shortly discuss in detail. Taking for example dx, it is essential to understand that in our current context it is not just an infinitesimal number describing a change in the x coordinate, but is to be viewed as a mathematical object with certain operational properties (which, admittedly, may include its eventual use in contexts such as the evaluation of line, surface, or volume integrals). The rules by which dx and related quantities can be manipulated have been designed to permit expressions such as

$$\omega = A(x, y, z)\, dx + B(x, y, z)\, dy + C(x, y, z)\, dz, \tag{4.77}$$

which are called **1-forms**, to be related to quantities that occur as the integrands of line integrals, to permit expressions of the type

$$\omega = F(x, y, z)\, dx \wedge dy + G(x, y, z)\, dx \wedge dz + H(x, y, z)\, dy \wedge dz, \tag{4.78}$$

which are called **2-forms**, to be related to the integrands of surface integrals, and to permit expressions like

$$\omega = K(x, y, z)\, dx \wedge dy \wedge dz, \tag{4.79}$$

known as **3-forms**, to be related to the integrands of volume integrals.

The $\wedge$ symbol (called "wedge") indicates that the individual differentials are to be combined to form more complicated objects using the rules of **exterior algebra** (sometimes called **Grassmann algebra**), so more is being implied by Eqs. (4.77) to (4.79) than the somewhat similar formulas that might appear in the conventional notation for various kinds of integrals. To maintain contact with other presentations on differential forms, we note that some authors omit the wedge symbol, thereby assuming that the reader knows that the differentials are to be combined according to the rules of exterior algebra. In order to minimize potential confusion, we will continue to write the wedge symbol for these combinations of differentials (which are called **exterior**, or **wedge** products).

To write differential forms in ways that do not presuppose the dimension of the underlying space, we sometimes write the differentials as dx_i, designating a form as a p-**form** if it contains p factors dx_i. Ordinary functions (containing no dx_i) can be identified as **0-forms**.

The mathematics of differential forms was developed with the aim of systematizing the application of calculus to **differentiable manifolds**, loosely defined as sets of points that can be identified by coordinates that locally vary "smoothly" (meaning that they are differentiable to whatever degree is needed for analysis).[5] We are presently focusing attention on the differentials that appear in the forms; one could also consider the behavior of the coefficients. For example, when we write the 1-form

$$\omega = A_x\, dx + A_y\, dy + A_z\, dz,$$

A_x, A_y, A_z will behave under a coordinate transformation like the components of a vector, and in the older differential-forms literature the differentials and the coefficients were referred to as contravariant and covariant vector components, since these two sets of quantities must transform in mutually inverse ways under rotations of the coordinate system. What is relevant for us at this point is that relationships we develop for differential forms can be translated into related relationships for their vector coefficients, yielding not only various well-known formulas of vector analysis but also showing how they can be generalized to spaces of higher dimension.

---

[5]A manifold defined on a circle or sphere must have a coordinate that cannot be globally smooth (in the usual coordinate systems it will jump somewhere by 2π). This and related issues connect topology and physics, and are for the most part outside the scope of this text.

Exterior Algebra

The central idea in exterior algebra is that the operations are designed to create permutational antisymmetry. Assuming the basis 1-forms are dx_i, that ω_j are arbitrary p-forms (of respective orders p_j), and that a and b are ordinary numbers or functions, the wedge product is defined to have the properties

$$(a\omega_1 + b\omega_2) \wedge \omega_3 = a\,\omega_1 \wedge \omega_3 + b\,\omega_2 \wedge \omega_3 \quad (p_1 = p_2),$$

$$(\omega_1 \wedge \omega_2) \wedge \omega_3 = \omega_1 \wedge (\omega_2 \wedge \omega_3), \quad a(\omega_1 \wedge \omega_2) = (a\omega_1) \wedge \omega_2, \tag{4.80}$$

$$dx_i \wedge dx_j = -dx_j \wedge dx_i.$$

We thus have the usual associative and distributive laws, and each term of an arbitrary differential form can be reduced to a coefficient multiplying a dx_i or a wedge product of the generic form

$$dx_i \wedge dx_j \wedge \cdots \wedge dx_p.$$

Moreover, the properties in Eq. (4.80) permit all the coefficient functions to be collected at the beginning of a form. For example,

$$a\,dx_1 \wedge b\,dx_2 = -a(b\,dx_2 \wedge dx_1) = -ab(dx_2 \wedge dx_1) = ab(dx_1 \wedge dx_2).$$

We therefore generally do not need parentheses to indicate the order in which products are to be carried out.

We can use the last of Eqs. (4.80) to bring the index set into any desired order. If any two of the dx_i are the same, the expression will vanish because $dx_i \wedge dx_i = -dx_i \wedge dx_i = 0$; otherwise, the ordered-index form will have a sign determined by the parity of the index permutation needed to obtain the ordering. It is **not** a coincidence that this is the sign rule for the terms of a determinant, compare Eq. (2.10). Letting ε_P stand for the Levi-Civita symbol for the permutation to ascending index order, an arbitrary wedge product of dx_i can, for example, be brought to the form

$$\varepsilon_P\,dx_{h_1} \wedge dx_{h_2} \wedge \cdots \wedge dx_{h_p}, \quad 1 \leq h_1 < h_2 < \cdots < h_p.$$

If any of the dx_i in a differential form is linearly dependent on the others, then its expansion into linearly independent terms will produce a duplicated dx_j and cause the form to vanish. Since the number of linearly independent dx_j cannot be larger than the dimension of the underlying space, we see that in a space of dimension d we only need to consider p-forms with $p \leq d$. Thus, in 3-D space, only up through 3-forms are relevant; for Minkowski space (ct, x, y, z), we will also have 4-forms.

Example 4.5.1 SIMPLIFYING DIFFERENTIAL FORMS

Consider the wedge product

$$\omega = (3dx + 4dy - dz) \wedge (dx - dy + 2dz) = 3\,dx \wedge dx - 3\,dx \wedge dy + 6\,dx \wedge dz$$

$$+ 4\,dy \wedge dx - 4\,dy \wedge dy + 8\,dy \wedge dz - dz \wedge dx + dz \wedge dy - 2\,dz \wedge dz.$$

The terms with duplicate differentials, e.g., $dx \wedge dx$, vanish, and products that differ only in the order of the 1-forms can be combined, changing the sign of the product when we interchange its factors. We get

$$\omega = -7\,dx \wedge dy + 7\,dx \wedge dz + 7\,dy \wedge dz = 7(dy \wedge dz - dz \wedge dx - dx \wedge dy).$$

We will shortly see that in three dimensions there are some advantages to bringing the 1-forms into cyclic order (rather than ascending or descending order) in the wedge products, and we did so in the final simplification of ω. ■

The antisymmetry built into the exterior algebra has an important purpose: It causes p-forms to depend on the differentials in ways appropriate (in three dimensions) for the description of elements of length, area, and volume, in part because the fact that $dx_i \wedge dx_i = 0$ prevents the appearance of duplicated differentials. In particular, 1-forms can be associated with elements of length, 2-forms with area, and 3-forms with volume. This feature carries forward to spaces of arbitrary dimensionality, thereby resolving potentially difficult questions that would otherwise have to be handled on a case-by-case basis. In fact, one of the virtues of the differential-forms approach is that there now exists a considerable body of general mathematical results that is pretty much completely absent from tensor analysis. For example, we will shortly find that the rules for differentiation in the exterior algebra cause the derivative of a p-form to be a $(p + 1)$-form, thereby avoiding a pitfall that arises in tensor calculus: When the transformation coefficients are position-dependent, simply differentiating the coefficients representing a tensor of rank p does **not** yield another tensor. As we have seen, this dilemma is resolved in tensor analysis by introducing the notion of **covariant derivative**. Another consequence of the antisymmetry is that lengths, areas, volumes, and (at higher dimensionality) hypervolumes are **oriented** (meaning that they have signs that depend on the way the p-forms defining them are written), and the orientation must be taken into account when making computations based on differential forms.

Complementary Differential Forms

Associated with each differential form is a complementary (or **dual**) form that contains the differentials **not** included in the original form. Thus, if our underlying space has dimension d, the form dual to a p-form will be a $(d - p)$-form. In three dimensions, the complement to a 1-form will be a 2-form (and vice versa), while the complement to a 3-form will be a 0-form (a scalar). It is useful to work with these complementary forms, and this is done by introducing an operator known as the **Hodge operator**; it is usually designated notationally as an asterisk (preceding the quantity to which it is applied, not as a superscript), and is therefore also referred to either as the **Hodge star operator** or simply as the **star operator**. Formally, its definition requires the introduction of a metric and the selection of an **orientation** (chosen by specifying the standard order of the differentials comprising the 1-form basis), and if the 1-form basis is not orthogonal there result complications we shall not discuss. For orthogonal bases, the dual forms depend on the index positions of the factors and on the metric tensor.[6]

---

[6]In the current discussion, restricted to Euclidean and Minkowski metrics, the metric tensor is diagonal, with diagonal elements ± 1, and the relevant quantities are the signs of the diagonal elements.

To find $*\omega$, where ω is a p-form, we start by writing the wedge product ω' of all members of the 1-form basis not represented in ω, with the sign corresponding to the permutation that is needed to bring the index set

$$\text{(indices of } \omega\text{) followed by (indices of } \omega')$$

to standard order. Then $*\omega$ consists of ω' (with the sign we just found), but also multiplied by $(-1)^\mu$, where μ is the number of differentials in ω' whose metric-tensor diagonal element is -1. For $\mathbb{R}^3$, ordinary 3-D space, the metric tensor is a unit matrix, so this final multiplication can be omitted, but it becomes relevant for our other case of current interest, the Minkowski metric.

For Euclidean 3-D space, we have

$$*1 = dx_1 \wedge dx_2 \wedge dx_3,$$

$$*dx_1 = dx_2 \wedge dx_3, \quad *dx_2 = dx_3 \wedge dx_1, \quad *dx_3 = dx_1 \wedge dx_2,$$

$$*(dx_1 \wedge dx_2) = dx_3, \quad *(dx_3 \wedge dx_1) = dx_2, \quad *(dx_2 \wedge dx_3) = dx_1,$$

$$*(dx_1 \wedge dx_2 \wedge dx_3) = 1.$$

$$(4.81)$$

Cases not shown above are linearly dependent on those that were shown and can be obtained by permuting the differentials in the above formulas and taking the resulting sign changes into account.

At this point, two observations are in order. First, note that by writing the indices 1, 2, 3 in cyclic order, we have caused all the starred quantities to have positive signs. This choice makes the symmetry more evident. Second, it can be seen that all the formulas in Eq. (4.81) are consistent with $*(*\omega) = \omega$. However, this is not universally true; compare with the formulas for Minkowski space, which are in the example we next consider. See also Exercise 4.5.1.

Example 4.5.2   HODGE OPERATOR IN MINKOWSKI SPACE

Taking the oriented 1-form basis (dt, dx_1, dx_2, dx_3), and the metric tensor

$$\begin{pmatrix} 1 & 0 & 0 & 0 \\ 0 & -1 & 0 & 0 \\ 0 & 0 & -1 & 0 \\ 0 & 0 & 0 & -1 \end{pmatrix},$$

let's determine the effect of the Hodge operator on the various possible differential forms. Consider initially $*1$, for which the complementary form contains $dt \wedge dx_1 \wedge dx_2 \wedge dx_3$. Since we took these differentials in the basis order, they are assigned a plus sign. Since $\omega = 1$ contains no differentials, its number μ of negative metric-tensor diagonal elements is zero, so $(-1)^\mu = (-1)^0 = 1$ and there is no sign change arising from the metric. Therefore,

$$*1 = dt \wedge dx_1 \wedge dx_2 \wedge dx_3.$$

Next, take $*(dt \wedge dx_1 \wedge dx_2 \wedge dx_3)$. The complementary form is just unity, with no sign change due to the index ordering, as the differentials are already in standard order.

However, this time we have three entries in the quantity being starred with negative metric-tensor diagonal elements; this generates $(-1)^3 = -1$, so

$$*(dt \wedge dx_1 \wedge dx_2 \wedge dx_3) = -1.$$

Moving next to $*dx_1$, the complementary form is $dt \wedge dx_2 \wedge dx_3$, and the index ordering (based on dx_1, dt, dx_2, dx_3) requires one pair interchange to reach the standard order (thereby yielding a minus sign). But the quantity being starred contains one differential that generates a minus sign, namely dx_1, so

$$*dx_1 = dt \wedge dx_2 \wedge dx_3.$$

Looking explicitly at one more case, consider $*(dt \wedge dx_1)$, for which the complementary form is $dx_2 \wedge dx_3$. This time the indices are in standard order, but the dx_1 being starred generates a minus sign, so

$$*(dt \wedge dx_1) = -dx_2 \wedge dx_3.$$

Development of the remaining possibilities is left to Exercise 4.5.1; the results are summarized below, where i, j, k denotes any cyclic permutation of 1,2,3.

$$*1 = dt \wedge dx_1 \wedge dx_2 \wedge dx_3,$$

$$*dx_i = dt \wedge dx_j \wedge dx_k, \quad *dt = dx_1 \wedge dx_2 \wedge dx_3,$$

$$*(dx_j \wedge dx_k) = dt \wedge dx_i, \quad *(dt \wedge dx_i) = -dx_j \wedge dx_k, \qquad (4.82)$$

$$*(dx_1 \wedge dx_2 \wedge dx_3) = dt, \quad *(dt \wedge dx_i \wedge dx_j) = dx_k,$$

$$*(dt \wedge dx_1 \wedge dx_2 \wedge dx_3) = -1.$$

Note that all the starred forms in Eq. (4.82) with an even number of differentials have the property that $*(*\omega) = -\omega$, confirming our earlier statement that complementing twice does not always restore the original form with its original sign. ∎

We now consider some examples illustrating the utility of the star operator.

Example 4.5.3   MISCELLANEOUS DIFFERENTIAL FORMS

In the Euclidean space $\mathbb{R}^3$, consider the wedge product $A \wedge B$ of the two 1-forms $A = A_x \, dx + A_y \, dy + A_z \, dz$ and $B = B_x \, dx + B_y \, dy + B_z \, dz$. Simplifying using the rules for exterior products,

$$A \wedge B = (A_y B_z - A_z B_y) \, dy \wedge dz + (A_z B_x - A_x B_z) \, dz \wedge dx + (A_x B_y - A_y B_x) \, dx \wedge dy.$$

If we now apply the star operator and use the formulas in Eq. (4.81) we get

$$*(A \wedge B) = (A_y B_z - A_z B_y) \, dx + (A_z B_x - A_x B_z) \, dy + (A_x B_y - A_y B_x) \, dz,$$

showing that in $\mathbb{R}^3$, $*(A \wedge B)$ forms an expression that is analogous to the cross product $\mathbf{A} \times \mathbf{B}$ of vectors $A_x \hat{\mathbf{e}}_x + A_y \hat{\mathbf{e}}_y + A_z \hat{\mathbf{e}}_z$ and $B_x \hat{\mathbf{e}}_x + B_y \hat{\mathbf{e}}_y + B_z \hat{\mathbf{e}}_z$. In fact, we can write

$$*(A \wedge B) = (\mathbf{A} \times \mathbf{B})_x \, dx + (\mathbf{A} \times \mathbf{B})_y \, dy + (\mathbf{A} \times \mathbf{B})_z \, dz. \qquad (4.83)$$

Note that the sign of $*(A \wedge B)$ is determined by our implicit choice that the standard ordering of the basis differentials is (dx, dy, dz).

Next, consider the exterior product $A \wedge B \wedge C$, where C is a 1-form with coefficients C_x, C_y, C_z. Applying the evaluation rules, we find that every surviving term in the product is proportional to $dx \wedge dy \wedge dz$, and we obtain

$$
\begin{aligned}
A \wedge B \wedge C = (A_x B_y C_z - A_x B_z C_y - A_y B_x C_z \\
+ A_y B_z C_x + A_z B_x C_y - A_z B_y C_x)\, dx \wedge dy \wedge dz,
\end{aligned}
$$

which we recognize can be written in the form

$$
A \wedge B \wedge C = \begin{vmatrix} A_x & A_y & A_z \\ B_x & B_y & B_z \\ C_x & C_y & C_z \end{vmatrix} dx \wedge dy \wedge dz.
$$

Applying now the star operator, we reach

$$
*(A \wedge B \wedge C) = \begin{vmatrix} A_x & A_y & A_z \\ B_x & B_y & B_z \\ C_x & C_y & C_z \end{vmatrix} = \mathbf{A} \cdot (\mathbf{B} \times \mathbf{C}). \tag{4.84}
$$

Not only were the results in Eqs. (4.83) and (4.84) easily obtained, they also generalize nicely to spaces of arbitrary dimension and metric, while the traditional vector notation, which uses the cross product, is applicable only to $\mathbb{R}^3$. ∎

Exercises

4.5.1   Using the rules for the application of the Hodge star operator, verify the results given in Eq. (4.82) for its application to all linearly independent differential forms in Minkowski space.

4.5.2   If the force field is constant and moving a particle from the origin to $(3, 0, 0)$ requires a units of work, from $(-1, -1, 0)$ to $(-1, 1, 0)$ takes b units of work, and from $(0, 0, 4)$ to $(0, 0, 5)$ c units of work, find the 1-form of the work.

4.6   DIFFERENTIATING FORMS

Exterior Derivatives

Having introduced differential forms and their exterior algebra, we next develop their properties under differentiation. To accomplish this, we define the **exterior derivative**, which we consider to be an **operator** identified by the traditional symbol d. We have, in fact, already introduced that operator when we wrote dx_i, stating at the time that we intended to interpret dx_i as a mathematical object with specified properties and not just as a small change in x_i. We are now refining that statement to interpret dx_i as the result of applying the operator d to the quantity x_i. We complete our definition of the operator d by requiring it to have the following properties, where ω is a p-form, ω' is a p'-form, and f is an ordinary function (a 0-form):

$$d(\omega + \omega') = d\omega + d\omega' \quad (p = p'),$$
$$d(f\,\omega) = (df) \wedge \omega + f\,d\omega,$$
$$d(\omega \wedge \omega') = d\omega \wedge \omega' + (-1)^p\,\omega \wedge d\omega', \tag{4.85}$$
$$d(d\omega) = 0,$$
$$df = \sum_j \frac{\partial f}{\partial x_j}\,dx_j,$$

where the sum over j spans the underlying space. The formula for the derivative of the wedge product is sometime called by mathematicians an **antiderivation**, referring to the fact that when applied to the right-hand factor an antisymmetry-motivated minus sign appears.

Example 4.6.1   EXTERIOR DERIVATIVE

Equations (4.85) are *axioms*, so they are not subject to proof, though they **are** required to be consistent. It is of interest to verify that the sign for the derivative of the second term in a wedge product is needed. Taking ω and ω' to be monomials, we first bring their coefficients to the left and then apply the differentiation operator (which, irrespective of the choice of sign, gives zero when applied to any of the differentials). Thus,

$$d(\omega \wedge \omega') = d(AB)\Big[dx_1 \wedge \cdots \wedge dx_p\Big] \wedge \Big[dx_1 \wedge \cdots \wedge dx_{p'}\Big]$$
$$= \sum_\mu \left[\frac{\partial A}{\partial x_\mu}B + A\frac{\partial B}{\partial x_\mu}\right]dx_\mu \wedge \Big[dx_1 \wedge \cdots \wedge dx_p\Big] \wedge \Big[dx_1 \wedge \cdots \wedge dx_{p'}\Big].$$

On expanding the sum, the first term is clearly $d\omega \wedge \omega'$; to make the second term look like $\omega \wedge d\omega'$, it is necessary to permute dx_μ through the p differentials in ω, yielding the sign factor $(-1)^p$. Extension to general polynomial forms is trivial.

One might also ask whether the fourth of the above axioms, $d(d\omega) = 0$, sometimes referred to as **Poincaré's lemma**, is necessary or consistent with the others. First, it provides new information, as otherwise we have no way of reducing $d(dx_i)$. Next, to see why the axiom set is consistent, we illustrate by examining (in $\mathbb{R}^2$)

$$df = \frac{\partial f}{\partial x}\,dx + \frac{\partial f}{\partial y}\,dy,$$

from which we form

$$d(df) = \frac{\partial}{\partial x}\left(\frac{\partial f}{\partial x}\right) dx \wedge dx + \frac{\partial}{\partial y}\left(\frac{\partial f}{\partial x}\right) dy \wedge dx$$

$$+ \frac{\partial}{\partial x}\left(\frac{\partial f}{\partial y}\right) dx \wedge dy + \frac{\partial}{\partial y}\left(\frac{\partial f}{\partial y}\right) dy \wedge dy = 0.$$

We obtain the zero result because of the antisymmetry of the wedge product and because the mixed second derivatives are equal. We see that the central reason for the validity of Poincaré's lemma is that the mixed derivatives of a sufficiently differentiable function are invariant with respect to the order in which the differentiations are carried out.   ∎

To catalog the possibilities for the action of the d operator in ordinary 3-D space, we first note that the derivative of an ordinary function (a 0-form) is

$$df = \frac{\partial f}{\partial x} dx + \frac{\partial f}{\partial y} dy + \frac{\partial f}{\partial z} dz = (\nabla f)_x dx + (\nabla f)_y dy + (\nabla f)_z dz. \tag{4.86}$$

We next differentiate the 1-form $\omega = A_x dx + A_y dy + A_z dz$. After simplification,

$$d\omega = \left[\frac{\partial A_z}{\partial y} - \frac{\partial A_y}{\partial z}\right] dy \wedge dz + \left[\frac{\partial A_x}{\partial z} - \frac{\partial A_z}{\partial x}\right] dz \wedge dx + \left[\frac{\partial A_y}{\partial x} - \frac{\partial A_x}{\partial y}\right] dx \wedge dy.$$

We recognize this as

$$d(A_x dx + A_y dy + A_z dz) =$$

$$(\nabla \times \mathbf{A})_x dy \wedge dz + (\nabla \times \mathbf{A})_y dz \wedge dx + (\nabla \times \mathbf{A})_z dx \wedge dy, \tag{4.87}$$

which is equivalent to

$$*d\left(A_x dx + A_y dy + A_z dz\right) = (\nabla \times \mathbf{A})_x dx + (\nabla \times \mathbf{A})_y dy + (\nabla \times \mathbf{A})_z dz. \tag{4.88}$$

Finally we differentiate the 2-form $B_x dy \wedge dz + B_y dz \wedge dx + B_z dx \wedge dy$, obtaining the three-form

$$d\left(B_x dy \wedge dz + B_y dz \wedge dx + B_z dx \wedge dy\right) = \left[\frac{\partial B_x}{\partial x} + \frac{\partial B_y}{\partial y} + \frac{\partial B_z}{\partial z}\right] dx \wedge dy \wedge dz,$$

equivalent to

$$d\left(B_x dy \wedge dz + B_y dz \wedge dx + B_z dx \wedge dy\right) = (\nabla \cdot \mathbf{B}) dx \wedge dy \wedge dz \tag{4.89}$$

and

$$*d\left(B_x dy \wedge dz + B_y dz \wedge dx + B_z dx \wedge dy\right) = \nabla \cdot \mathbf{B}. \tag{4.90}$$

We see that application of the d operator directly generates all the differential operators of traditional vector analysis.

If now we return to Eq. (4.87) and take the 1-form on its left-hand side to be df, so that $\mathbf{A} = \nabla f$, we have, inserting Eq. (4.86),

$$d(df) = \left(\nabla \times (\nabla f)\right)_x dy \wedge dz + \left(\nabla \times (\nabla f)\right)_y dz \wedge dx + \left(\nabla \times (\nabla f)\right)_z dx \wedge dy = 0.$$
(4.91)

We have invoked Poincaré's lemma to set this expression to zero. The result is equivalent to the well-known identity $\nabla \times (\nabla f) = 0$.

Another identity is obtained if we start from Eq. (4.89) and take the 2-form on its left-hand side to be $d(A_x\, dx + A_y\, dy + A_z\, dz)$. Then, with the aid of Eq. (4.88), we have

$$d\left(d(A_x\, dx + A_y\, dy + A_z\, dz)\right) = \nabla \cdot (\nabla \times \mathbf{A})\, dx \wedge dy \wedge dz = 0,$$
(4.92)

where once again the zero result follows from Poincaré's lemma and we have established the well-known formula $\nabla \cdot (\nabla \times \mathbf{A}) = 0$. Part of the importance of the derivation of these formulas using differential-forms methods is that these are merely the first members of hierarchies of identities that can be derived for spaces with higher numbers of dimensions and with different metric properties.

Example 4.6.2 MAXWELL'S EQUATIONS

Maxwell's equations of electromagnetic theory can be written in an extremely compact and elegant way using differential forms notation. In that notation, the independent elements of the electromagnetic field tensor can be written as the coefficients of a 2-form in Minkowski space with oriented basis (dt, dx, dy, dz):

$$F = -E_x\, dt \wedge dx - E_y\, dt \wedge dy - E_z\, dt \wedge dz$$
$$+ B_x\, dy \wedge dz + B_y\, dz \wedge dx + B_z\, dx \wedge dy.$$
(4.93)

Here $\mathbf{E}$ and $\mathbf{B}$ are respectively the electric field and the magnetic induction. The sources of the field, namely the charge density ρ and the components of the current density $\mathbf{J}$, become the coefficients of the 3-form

$$J = \rho\, dx \wedge dy \wedge dz - J_x\, dt \wedge dy \wedge dz - J_y\, dt \wedge dz \wedge dx - J_z\, dt \wedge dx \wedge dy.$$
(4.94)

For simplicity we work in units with the permitivity, magnetic permeability, and velocity of light all set to unity ($\varepsilon = \mu = c = 1$). Note that it is natural that the charge and current densities occur in a 3-form; although they have together the number of components needed to constitute a four-vector, they are of dimension inverse volume. Note also that some of the signs in the formulas of this example depend on the details of the metric, and are chosen to be correct for the Minkowski metric as given in Example 4.5.2. This Minkowski metric has **signature** (1,3), meaning that it has one positive and three negative diagonal elements. Some workers define the Minkowski metric to have signature (3,1), reversing all its signs. Either choice will give correct results to problems of physics if used consistently; trouble only arises if material from inconsistent sources is combined.

The two homogeneous Maxwell equations are obtained from the simple formula $dF = 0$. This equation is not a mathematical requirement on F; it is a statement of the physical properties of electric and magnetic fields. To relate our new formula to the more usual vector equations, we simply apply the d operator to F:

$$dF = -\left[\frac{\partial E_x}{\partial y}\,dy + \frac{\partial E_x}{\partial z}\,dz\right] \wedge dt \wedge dx - \left[\frac{\partial E_y}{\partial x}\,dx + \frac{\partial E_y}{\partial z}\,dz\right] \wedge dt \wedge dy$$

$$-\left[\frac{\partial E_z}{\partial x}\,dx + \frac{\partial E_z}{\partial y}\,dy\right] \wedge dt \wedge dz + \left[\frac{\partial B_x}{\partial t}\,dt + \frac{\partial B_x}{\partial x}\,dx\right] \wedge dy \wedge dz$$

$$+\left[\frac{\partial B_y}{\partial t}\,dt + \frac{\partial B_y}{\partial y}\,dy\right] \wedge dz \wedge dx + \left[\frac{\partial B_z}{\partial t}\,dt + \frac{\partial B_z}{\partial z}\,dz\right] \wedge dx \wedge dy = 0. \quad (4.95)$$

Equation (4.95) is easily simplified to

$$dF = \left[\frac{\partial E_z}{\partial y} - \frac{\partial E_y}{\partial z} + \frac{\partial B_x}{\partial t}\right] dt \wedge dy \wedge dz + \left[\frac{\partial E_x}{\partial z} - \frac{\partial E_z}{\partial x} + \frac{\partial B_y}{\partial t}\right] dt \wedge dz \wedge dx$$

$$+\left[\frac{\partial E_y}{\partial x} - \frac{\partial E_x}{\partial y} + \frac{\partial B_z}{\partial t}\right] dt \wedge dx \wedge dy + \left[\frac{\partial B_x}{\partial x} + \frac{\partial B_y}{\partial y} + \frac{\partial B_z}{\partial z}\right] dx \wedge dy \wedge dz = 0.$$

$$(4.96)$$

Since the coefficient of each 3-form monomial must individually vanish, we obtain from Eq. (4.96) the vector equations

$$\nabla \times \mathbf{E} + \frac{\partial \mathbf{B}}{\partial t} = 0 \quad \text{and} \quad \nabla \cdot \mathbf{B} = 0.$$

We now go on to obtain the two inhomogeneous Maxwell equations from the almost equally simple formula $d(*F) = J$. To verify this, we first form $*F$, evaluating the starred quantities using the formulas in Eqs. (4.82):

$$*F = E_x\,dy \wedge dz + E_y\,dz \wedge dx + E_z\,dx \wedge dy + B_x\,dt \wedge dx + B_y\,dt \wedge dy + B_z\,dt \wedge dz.$$

We now apply the d operator, reaching after steps similar to those taken while obtaining Eq. (4.96):

$$d(*F) = \nabla \cdot \mathbf{E}\,dx \wedge dy \wedge dz + \left[\frac{\partial E_x}{\partial t} - (\nabla \times \mathbf{B}_x)\right] dt \wedge dy \wedge dz$$

$$+\left[\frac{\partial E_y}{\partial t} - (\nabla \times \mathbf{B}_y)\right] dt \wedge dz \wedge dx + \left[\frac{\partial E_z}{\partial t} - (\nabla \times \mathbf{B}_z)\right] dt \wedge dx \wedge dy. \quad (4.97)$$

Setting $d(*F)$ from Eq. (4.97) equal to J as given in Eq. (4.94), we obtain the remaining Maxwell equations

$$\nabla \cdot \mathbf{E} = \rho \quad \text{and} \quad \nabla \times \mathbf{B} - \frac{\partial \mathbf{E}}{\partial t} = \mathbf{J}.$$

We close this example by applying the d operator to J. The result must vanish because $dJ = d(d(*F))$. We get, starting from Eq. (4.94),

$$dJ = \left[\frac{\partial \rho}{\partial t} + \frac{\partial J_x}{\partial x} + \frac{\partial J_y}{\partial y} + \frac{\partial J_z}{\partial z}\right] dt \wedge dx \wedge dy \wedge dz = 0,$$

showing that

$$\frac{\partial \rho}{\partial t} + \nabla \cdot \mathbf{J} = 0. \tag{4.98}$$

Summarizing, the differential-forms approach has reduced Maxwell's equations to the two simple formulas

$$dF = 0 \quad \text{and} \quad d(*F) = J, \tag{4.99}$$

and we have also shown that $\mathbf{J}$ must satisfy an equation of continuity. ∎

Exercises

4.6.1 Given the two 1-forms $\omega_1 = x\,dy + y\,dx$ and $\omega_2 = x\,dy - y\,dx$, calculate

(a) $d\omega_1$,

(b) $d\omega_2$.

(c) For each of your answers to (a) or (b) that is nonzero, apply the operator d a second time and verify that $d(d\omega_i) = 0$.

4.6.2 Apply the operator d twice to $\omega_3 = xy\,dz + xz\,dy - yz\,dx$. Verify that the second application of d yields a zero result.

4.6.3 For ω_2 and ω_3 the 1-forms with these names in Exercises 4.6.1 and 4.6.2, evaluate $d(\omega_2 \wedge \omega_3)$:

(a) By forming the exterior product and then differentiating, and

(b) Using the formula for differentiating a product of two forms.

Verify that both approaches give the same result.

4.7 INTEGRATING FORMS

It is natural to define the integrals of differential forms in a way that preserves our usual notions of integration. The integrals with which we are concerned are over regions of the manifolds on which our differential forms are defined; this fact and the antisymmetry of the wedge product need to be taken into account in developing definitions and properties of integrals. For convenience, we illustrate in two or three dimensions; the notions extend to spaces of arbitrary dimensionality.

Consider first the integral of a 1-form ω in 2-D space, integrated over a curve C from a start-point P to an endpoint Q:

$$\int_C \omega = \int_C \left[A_x\,dx + A_y\,dy \right].$$

We interpret the integration as a conventional line integral. If the curve is described parametrically by $x(t)$, $y(t)$ as t increases monotonically from t_P to t_Q, our integral takes the elementary form

$$\int_C \omega = \int_{t_P}^{t_Q} \left[A_x(t)\frac{dx}{dt} + A_y(t)\frac{dy}{dt} \right] dt,$$

and (at least in principle) the integral can be evaluated by the usual methods.

Sometimes the integral will have a value that will be independent of the path from P to Q; in physics this situation arises when a 1-form with coefficients $\mathbf{A} = (A_x, A_y)$ describes what is known as a **conservative force** (i.e., one that can be written as the gradient of a potential). In our present language, we then call ω **exact**, meaning that there exists some function f such that

$$\omega = df(x, y) \tag{4.100}$$

for a region that includes the points P, Q, and all other points through which the path may pass.

To check the significance of Eq. (4.100), note that it implies

$$\omega = \frac{\partial f}{\partial x} dx + \frac{\partial f}{\partial y} dy,$$

showing that ω has as coefficients the components of the gradient of f. Given Eq. (4.100), we also see that

$$\text{if } \omega = df, \quad \int_P^Q \omega = f(Q) - f(P). \tag{4.101}$$

This admittedly obvious result is independent of the dimension of the space, and is of importance to the remainder of this section.

Looking next at 2-forms, we have (in 2-D space) integrals such as

$$\int_S \omega = \int_S B(x, y)\, dx \wedge dy. \tag{4.102}$$

We interpret $dx \wedge dy$ as the element of area corresponding to displacements dx and dy in mutually orthogonal directions, so in the usual notation of integral calculus we would write $dx\, dy$.

Let's now return to the wedge product notation and consider what happens if we make a change of variables from x, y to u, v, with $x = au + bv$, $y = eu + fv$. Then $dx = a\, du + b\, dv$, $dy = e\, du + f\, dv$, and

$$dx \wedge dy = (a\, du + b\, dv) \wedge (e\, du + f\, dv) = (af - be)\, du \wedge dv. \tag{4.103}$$

We note that the coefficient of $du \wedge dv$ is just the Jacobian of the transformation from x, y to u, v, which becomes clear if we write $a = \partial x/\partial u$, etc., after which we have

$$af - be = \begin{vmatrix} \dfrac{\partial x}{\partial u} & \dfrac{\partial x}{\partial v} \\ \dfrac{\partial y}{\partial u} & \dfrac{\partial y}{\partial v} \end{vmatrix} = \begin{vmatrix} a & b \\ e & f \end{vmatrix}. \tag{4.104}$$

We now see a fundamental reason why the wedge product has been introduced; it has the algebraic properties needed to generate in a natural fashion the relations between elements of area (or its higher-dimension analogs) in different coordinate systems. To emphasize that observation, note that the Jacobian occurred as a natural consequence of the transformation; we did not have to take additional steps to insert it, and it was generated simply by evaluating the relevant differential forms. In addition, the present formulation has one new feature: because $dx \wedge dy$ and $dy \wedge dx$ are opposite in sign, areas must be assigned algebraic signs, and it is necessary to retain the sign of the Jacobian if we make a change of variables. We therefore take as the element of area corresponding to $dx \wedge dy$ the ordinary product $\pm dx dy$, with a choice of sign known as the **orientation** of the area. Then, Eq. (4.102) becomes

$$\int_S \omega = \int_S B(x, y)(\pm dx dy), \tag{4.105}$$

and if elsewhere in the same computation we had $dy \wedge dx$, we must convert it to $dx dy$ using the sign opposite to that used for $dx \wedge dy$.

For p-forms with $p > 2$, a corresponding analysis applies: If we transform from $(x, y, \dots)$ to $(u, v, \dots)$, the wedge product $dx \wedge dy \wedge \cdots$ becomes $J \, du \wedge dv \wedge \cdots$, where J is the (signed) Jacobian of the transformation. Since the p-space volumes are *oriented*, the sign of the Jacobian is relevant and must be retained. Exercise 4.7.1 shows that the change of variables from the 3-form $dx \wedge dy \wedge dz$ to $du \wedge dv \wedge dw$ yields the determinant which is the (signed) Jacobian of the transformation.

Stokes' Theorem

A key result regarding the integration of differential forms is a formula known as **Stokes' theorem**, a restricted form of which we encountered in our study of vector analysis in Chapter 3. Stokes' theorem, in its simplest form, states that if

- R is a simply-connected region (i.e., one with no holes) of a p-dimensional differentiable manifold in a n-dimensional space ($n \geq p$);

- R has a boundary denoted ∂R, of dimension $p - 1$;

- ω is a $(p - 1)$-form defined on R and its boundary, with derivative $d\omega$;

then

$$\int_R d\omega = \int_{\partial R} \omega. \tag{4.106}$$

This is the generalization, to p dimensions, of Eq. (4.101). Note that because $d\omega$ results from applying the d operator to ω, the differentials in $d\omega$ consist of all those in ω, in the same order, but preceded by that produced by the differentiation. This observation is relevant for identifying the signs to be associated with the integrations.

A rigorous proof of Stokes' theorem is somewhat complicated, but an indication of its validity is not too involved. It is sufficient to consider the case that ω is a monomial:

$$\omega = A(x_1, \ldots, x_p) \, dx_2 \wedge \cdots dx_p, \quad d\omega = \frac{\partial A}{\partial x_1} \, dx_1 \wedge dx_2 \cdots dx_p. \quad (4.107)$$

We start by approximating the portion of R adjacent to the boundary by a set of small p-dimensional parallelepipeds whose thickness in the x_1 direction is δ, with δ having for each parallelepiped the sign that makes $x_1 \to x_1 - \delta$ in the interior of R. For each such parallelepiped (symbolically denoted Δ, with faces of constant x_1 denoted $\partial \Delta$), we integrate $d\omega$ in x_1 from $x_1 - \delta$ to x_1 and over the full range of the other x_i, obtaining

$$\int_\Delta d\omega = \int_{\partial \Delta} \int_{x_1 - \delta}^{x_1} \left(\frac{\partial A}{\partial x_1} \right) dx_1 \wedge dx_2 \wedge \cdots dx_p$$

$$= \int_{\partial \Delta} A(x_1, x_2, \ldots) \, dx_2 \wedge \cdots dx_p - \int_{\partial \Delta} A(x_1 - \delta, x_2, \ldots) \, dx_2 \wedge \cdots dx_p. \quad (4.108)$$

Equation (4.108) indicates the validity of Stokes' theorem for a laminar region whose exterior boundary is ∂R; if we perform the same process repeatedly, we can collapse the inner boundary to a region of zero volume, thereby reaching Eq. (4.106).

Stokes' theorem applies for manifolds of any dimension; different cases of this single theorem in two and three dimensions correspond to results originally identified as distinct theorems. Some examples follow.

Example 4.7.1   GREEN'S THEOREM IN THE PLANE

Consider in a 2-D space the 1-form ω and its derivative:

$$\omega = P(x, y) \, dx + Q(x, y) \, dy, \quad (4.109)$$

$$d\omega = \frac{\partial P}{\partial y} \, dy \wedge dx + \frac{\partial Q}{\partial x} \, dx \wedge dy = \left[\frac{\partial Q}{\partial x} - \frac{\partial P}{\partial y} \right] dx \wedge dy, \quad (4.110)$$

where we have without comment discarded terms containing $dx \wedge dx$ or $dy \wedge dy$.

We apply Stokes' theorem for this ω to a region S with boundary C, obtaining

$$\int_S \left[\frac{\partial Q}{\partial x} - \frac{\partial P}{\partial y} \right] dx \wedge dy = \int_C (P \, dx + Q \, dy).$$

With orientation such that $dx \wedge dy = dS$ (ordinary element of area), we have the formula usually identified as *Green's theorem in the plane*:

$$\int_C \left(P \, dx + Q \, dy \right) = \int_S \left[\frac{\partial Q}{\partial x} - \frac{\partial P}{\partial y} \right] dS. \quad (4.111)$$

Some cases of this theorem: taking $P = 0$, $Q = x$, we have the well-known formula

$$\int_C x \, dy = \int_S dS = A,$$

where A is the area enclosed by C with the line integral evaluated in the mathematically positive (counterclockwise) direction.

If we take $P = y$, $Q = 0$, we get instead another familiar formula:

$$\int_C y \, dx = \int_S (-1) dS = -A.$$

When working Example 4.7.1, we assumed (without comment) that the line integral on the closed curve C was to be evaluated for travel in the counterclockwise direction, and we also related area to the conversion from $dx \wedge dy$ to $+dx dy$. These are choices that were not dictated by the theory of differential forms but by our intention to make its results correspond to computation in the usual system of planar Cartesian coordinates. What is certainly true is that the differential forms calculus gives a different sign for the integral of $y \, dx$ than it gave for the integral of $x \, dy$; the user of the calculus has the responsibility to make definitions corresponding to the situation for which the results are claimed to be relevant.

Example 4.7.2   STOKES' THEOREM (USUAL 3-D CASE)

Let the vector potential $\mathbf{A}$ be represented by the differential form ω, with it and its derivative of the forms

$$\omega = A_x \, dx + A_y \, dy + A_z \, dz, \tag{4.112}$$

$$d\omega = \left[\frac{\partial A_z}{\partial y} - \frac{\partial A_y}{\partial z}\right] dy \wedge dz + \left[\frac{\partial A_x}{\partial z} - \frac{\partial A_z}{\partial x}\right] dz \wedge dx + \left[\frac{\partial A_y}{\partial x} - \frac{\partial A_x}{\partial y}\right] dx \wedge dy$$

$$= (\nabla \times \mathbf{A})_x \, dy \wedge dz + (\nabla \times \mathbf{A})_y \, dz \wedge dx + (\nabla \times \mathbf{A})_z \, dx \wedge dy. \tag{4.113}$$

Applying Stokes' theorem to a region S with boundary C and noting that if the standard order for orienting the differentials is dx, dy, dz, then $dy \wedge dz \to d\sigma_x$, $dz \wedge dz \to d\sigma_y$, $dx \wedge dy \to d\sigma_z$, and Stokes' theorem takes the familiar form

$$\int_C (A_x \, dx + A_y \, dy + A_z \, dz) = \int_C \mathbf{A} \cdot d\mathbf{r} = \int_S (\nabla \times \mathbf{A}) \cdot d\sigma. \tag{4.114}$$

Once again we have results whose interpretation depends on how we have chosen to define the quantities involved. The differential forms calculus does not know whether we intend to use a right-handed coordinate system, and that choice is implicit in our identification of the elements of area $d\sigma_j$. In fact, the mathematics does not even tell us that the quantities we identified as components of $\nabla \times \mathbf{A}$ actually correspond to anything physical in their indicated directions. So, once again, we emphasize that the mathematics of differential forms provides a structure appropriate to the physics to which we apply it, but part of what the physicist brings to the table is the correlation between mathematical objects and the physical quantities they represent.

Example 4.7.3   GAUSS' THEOREM

As a final example, consider a 3-D region V with boundary ∂V, containing an electric field given on ∂V as the 2-form ω, with

$$\omega = E_x \, dy \wedge dz + E_y \, dz \wedge dz + E_z \, dx \wedge dy, \tag{4.115}$$

$$d\omega = \left[\frac{\partial E_x}{\partial x} + \frac{\partial E_y}{\partial y} + \frac{\partial E_z}{\partial z} \right] dx \wedge dy \wedge dz = (\mathbf{\nabla} \cdot \mathbf{E}) \, dx \wedge dy \wedge dz. \tag{4.116}$$

For this case, Stokes' theorem is

$$\int_V d\omega = \int_V (\mathbf{\nabla} \cdot \mathbf{E}) \, dx \wedge dy \wedge dz = \int_V (\mathbf{\nabla} \cdot \mathbf{E}) \, d\tau = \int_{\partial V} \mathbf{E} \cdot d\boldsymbol{\sigma}, \tag{4.117}$$

where $dx \wedge dy \wedge dz \to d\tau$ and, just as in Example 4.7.2, $dy \wedge dz \to d\sigma_x$, etc. We have recovered Gauss' theorem. ∎

Exercises

4.7.1   Use differential-forms relations to transform the integral $A(x, y, z) \, dx \wedge dy \wedge dz$ to the equivalent expression in $du \wedge dv \wedge dw$, where u, v, w is a linear transformation of x, y, z, and thereby find the determinant that can be identified as the Jacobian of the transformation.

4.7.2   Write Oersted's law,

$$\int_{\partial S} \mathbf{H} \cdot d\mathbf{r} = \int_S \mathbf{\nabla} \times \mathbf{H} \cdot d\mathbf{a} \sim I,$$

in differential form notation.

4.7.3   A 1-form $A\,dx + B\,dy$ is defined as **closed** if $\dfrac{\partial A}{\partial y} = \dfrac{\partial B}{\partial x}$. It is called **exact** if there is a function f such that $\dfrac{\partial f}{\partial x} = A$ and $\dfrac{\partial f}{\partial y} = B$. Determine which of the following 1-forms are closed, or exact, and find the corresponding functions f for those that are exact:

$$y\,dx + x\,dy, \qquad \frac{y\,dx + x\,dy}{x^2 + y^2}, \qquad [\ln(xy) + 1]\,dx + \frac{x}{y}\,dy,$$

$$-\frac{y\,dx}{x^2 + y^2} + \frac{x\,dy}{x^2 + y^2}, \qquad f(z)\,dz \text{ with } z = x + iy.$$

Additional Readings

Dirac, P. A. M., *General Theory of Relativity*. Princeton, NJ: Princeton University Press (1996).

Edwards, H. M., *Advanced Calculus: A Differential Forms Approach*. Boston, MA: Birkhäuser (1994).

Flanders, H., *Differential Forms with Applications to the Physical Sciences*. New York: Dover (1989).

Hartle, J. B., *Gravity*. San Francisco: Addison-Wesley (2003). This text uses a minimum of tensor analysis.

Hassani, S., *Foundations of Mathematical Physics*. Boston, MA: Allyn and Bacon (1991).

Jeffreys, H., *Cartesian Tensors*. Cambridge: Cambridge University Press (1952). This is an excellent discussion of Cartesian tensors and their application to a wide variety of fields of classical physics.

Lawden, D. F., *An Introduction to Tensor Calculus, Relativity and Cosmology*, 3rd ed. New York: Wiley (1982).

Margenau, H., and G. M. Murphy, *The Mathematics of Physics and Chemistry*, 2nd ed. Princeton, NJ: Van Nostrand (1956). Chapter 5 covers curvilinear coordinates and 13 specific coordinate systems.

Misner, C. W., K. S. Thorne, and J. A. Wheeler, *Gravitation*. San Francisco: W. H. Freeman (1973). A leading text on general relativity and cosmology.

Moller, C., *The Theory of Relativity*. Oxford: Oxford University Press (1955), reprinting, (1972). Most texts on general relativity include a discussion of tensor analysis. Chapter 4 develops tensor calculus, including the topic of dual tensors. The extension to non-Cartesian systems, as required by general relativity, is presented in Chapter 9.

Morse, P. M., and H. Feshbach, *Methods of Theoretical Physics*. New York: McGraw-Hill (1953). Chapter 5 includes a description of several different coordinate systems. Note that Morse and Feshbach are not above using left-handed coordinate systems even for Cartesian coordinates. Elsewhere in this excellent (and difficult) book there are many examples of the use of the various coordinate systems in solving physical problems. Eleven additional fascinating but seldom encountered orthogonal coordinate systems are discussed in the second (1970) edition of *Mathematical Methods for Physicists*.

Ohanian, H. C., and R. Ruffini, *Gravitation and Spacetime*, 2nd ed. New York: Norton & Co. (1994). A well-written introduction to Riemannian geometry.

Sokolnikoff, I. S., *Tensor Analysis—Theory and Applications*, 2nd ed. New York: Wiley (1964). Particularly useful for its extension of tensor analysis to non-Euclidean geometries.

Weinberg, S., *Gravitation and Cosmology. Principles and Applications of the General Theory of Relativity*. New York: Wiley (1972). This book and the one by Misner, Thorne, and Wheeler are the two leading texts on general relativity and cosmology (with tensors in non-Cartesian space).

Young, E. C., *Vector and Tensor Analysis*, 2nd ed. New York: Dekker (1993).

CHAPTER 5

VECTOR SPACES

A large body of physical theory can be cast within the mathematical framework of vector spaces. Vector spaces are far more general than vectors in ordinary space, and the analogy may to the uninitiated seem somewhat strained. Basically, this subject deals with quantities that can be represented by expansions in a series of functions, and includes the methods by which such expansions can be generated and used for various purposes. A key aspect of the subject is the notion that a more or less arbitrary **function** can be represented by such an expansion, and that the coefficients in these expansions have transformation properties similar to those exhibited by vector components in ordinary space. Moreover, **operators** can be introduced to describe the application of various processes to a function, thereby converting it (and also the coefficients defining it) into other functions within our vector space. The concepts presented in this chapter are crucial to an understanding of quantum mechanics, to classical systems involving oscillatory motion, transport of material or energy, even to fundamental particle theory. Indeed, it is not excessive to claim that vector spaces are one of the most fundamental mathematical structures in physical theory.

5.1 VECTORS IN FUNCTION SPACES

We now seek to extend the concepts of classical vector analysis (from Chapter 3) to more general situations. Suppose that we have a two-dimensional (2-D) space in which the two coordinates, which are real (or in the most general case, complex) numbers that we will call a_1 and a_2, are, respectively, associated with the two functions $\varphi_1(s)$ and $\varphi_2(s)$. It is important at the outset to understand that our new 2-D space has nothing whatsoever to do with the physical xy space. It is a space in which the coordinate point (a_1, a_2) corresponds to the function

$$f(s) = a_1\varphi_1(s) + a_2\varphi_2(s). \tag{5.1}$$

The analogy with a physical 2-D vector space with vectors $\mathbf{A} = A_1\hat{\mathbf{e}}_1 + A_2\hat{\mathbf{e}}_2$ is that $\varphi_i(s)$ corresponds to $\hat{\mathbf{e}}_i$, while $a_i \longleftrightarrow A_i$, and $f(s) \longleftrightarrow \mathbf{A}$. In other words, the coordinate values are the **coefficients** of the $\varphi_i(s)$, so each point in the space identifies a different function $f(s)$. Both f and φ are shown above as dependent on an independent variable we call s. We choose the name s to emphasize the fact that the formulation is not restricted to the spatial variables x, y, z, but can be whatever variable, or set of variables, is needed for the problem at hand. Note further that the variable s is not a continuous analog of the discrete variables x_i of an ordinary vector space. It is a parameter reminding the reader that the φ_i that correspond to the dimensions of our vector space are usually not just numbers, but are functions of one or more variables. The variable(s) denoted by s may sometimes correspond to physical displacements, but that is not always the case. What should be clear is that s has nothing to do with the coordinates in our vector space; that is the role of the a_i.

Equation (5.1) defines a set of functions (a **function space**) that can be built from the **basis** φ_1, φ_2; we call this space a **linear vector space** because its members are linear combinations of the basis functions and the addition of its members corresponds to component (coefficient) addition. If $f(s)$ is given by Eq. (5.1) and $g(s)$ is given by another linear combination of **the same** basis functions,

$$g(s) = b_1\varphi_1(s) + b_2\varphi_2(s),$$

with b_1 and b_2 the coefficients defining $g(s)$, then

$$h(s) = f(s) + g(s) = (a_1 + b_1)\varphi_1(s) + (a_2 + b_2)\varphi_2(s) \tag{5.2}$$

defines $h(s)$, the member of our space (i.e., the function), which is the sum of the members $f(s)$ and $g(s)$. In order for our vector space to be useful, we consider only spaces in which the sum of any two members of the space is also a member.

In addition, the notion of linearity includes the requirement that if $f(s)$ is a member of our vector space, then $u(s) = k\,f(s)$, where k is a real or complex number, is also a member, and we can write

$$u(s) = k\,f(s) = ka_1\varphi_1(s) + ka_2\varphi_2(s). \tag{5.3}$$

Vector spaces for which addition of two members or multiplication of a member by scalar always produces a result that is also a member are termed **closed** under these operations.

We can summarize our findings up to this point as follows: addition of two members of our vector space causes the coefficients of the sum, $h(s)$ in Eq. (5.2), to be the sum of the coefficients of the addends, namely $f(s)$ and $g(s)$; multiplication of $f(s)$ by a ordinary number k (which, by analogy with ordinary vectors, we call a **scalar**), results in the multiplication of the coefficients by k. These are exactly the operations we would carry out to form the sum of two ordinary vectors, $\mathbf{A} + \mathbf{B}$, or the multiplication of a vector by a scalar, as in $k\mathbf{A}$. However, here we have the coefficients a_i and b_i, which combine under vector addition and multiplication by a scalar in exactly the same way that we would combine the ordinary vector components A_i and B_i.

The functions that form the basis of our vector space can be ordinary functions, and may be as simple as powers of s, or more complicated, as for example $\varphi_1 = (1 + 3s + 3s^2)e^s$, $\varphi_2 = (1 - 3s + 3s^2)e^{-s}$, or compound quantities such as the Pauli matrices σ_i, or even completely abstract quantities that are defined only by certain properties they may possess. The number of basis functions (i.e., the **dimension** of our basis) may be a small number such as 2 or 3, a larger but finite integer, or even denumerably infinite (as would arise in an untruncated power series). The main universal restriction on the form of a basis is that the basis members be linearly independent, so that any function (member) of our vector space will be described by a unique linear combination of the basis functions. We illustrate the possibilities with some simple examples.

Example 5.1.1   Some Vector Spaces

1. We consider first a vector space of dimension 3, which is **spanned by** (meaning that it has a basis that consists of) the three functions $P_0(s) = 1$, $P_1(s) = s$, $P_2(s) = \frac{3}{2}s^2 - \frac{1}{2}$. Some members of this vector space include the functions

$$s + 3 = 3P_0(s) + P_1(s), \quad s^2 = \frac{1}{3}P_0(s) + \frac{2}{3}P_2(s), \quad 4 - 3s = 4P_0(s) - 3P_1(s).$$

In fact, because we can write 1, s, and s^2 in terms of our basis, we can see that **any** quadratic form in s will be a member of our vector space, and that our space includes only functions of s that can be written in the form $c_0 + c_1 s + c_2 s^2$.

To illustrate our vector-space operations, we can form

$$s^2 - 2(s + 3) = \left[\frac{1}{3}P_0(s) + \frac{2}{3}P_2(s)\right] - 2\left[3P_0(s) + P_1(s)\right]$$

$$= \left(\frac{1}{3} - 6\right)P_0(s) - 2P_1(s) + \frac{2}{3}P_2(s).$$

This calculation involves only operations on the coefficients; we do not need to refer to the definitions of the P_n to carry it out.

Note that we are free to define our basis any way we want, so long as its members are linearly independent. We could have chosen as our basis for this same vector space $\varphi_0 = 1$, $\varphi_1 = s$, $\varphi_2 = s^2$, but we chose not to do so.

2. The set of functions $\varphi_n(s) = s^n$ ($n = 0, 1, 2, \ldots$) is a basis for a vector space whose members consist of functions that can be represented by a Maclaurin series. To avoid difficulties with this infinite-dimensional basis, we will usually need to restrict consideration to functions and ranges of s for which the Maclaurin series converges. Convergence and related issues are of great interest in pure mathematics; in physics problems we usually proceed in ways such that convergence is assured.

The members of our vector space will have representations

$$f(s) = a_0 + a_1 s + a_2 s^2 + \cdots = \sum_{n=0}^{\infty} a_n s^n,$$

and we can (at least in principle) use the rules for making power series expansions to find the coefficients that correspond to a given $f(s)$.

3. The spin space of an electron is spanned by a basis that consists of a linearly independent set of possible spin states. It is well known that an electron can have two linearly independent spin states, and they are often denoted by the symbols α and β. One possible spin state is $f = a_1 \alpha + a_2 \beta$, and another is $g = b_1 \alpha + b_2 \beta$. We do not even need

to know what α and β really stand for to discuss the 2-D vector space spanned by these functions, nor do we need to know the role of any parametric variable such as s. We can, however, state that the particular spin state corresponding to $f + ig$ must have the form

$$f + ig = (a_1 + ib_1)\alpha + (a_2 + ib_2)\beta.$$

∎

Scalar Product

To make the vector space concept useful and parallel to that of vector algebra in ordinary space, we need to introduce the concept of a scalar product in our function space. We shall write the scalar product of two members of our vector space, f and g, as $\langle f|g \rangle$. This is the notation that is almost universally used in physics; various other notations can be found in the mathematics literature; examples include $[f, g]$ and (f, g).

The scalar product has two main features, the full meaning of which may only become clear as we proceed. They are:

1. The scalar product of a member with itself, e.g., $\langle f|f \rangle$, must evaluate to a numerical value (not a function) that plays the role of the square of the magnitude of that member, corresponding to the dot product of an ordinary vector with itself, and
2. The scalar product must be linear in each of the two members.[1]

There exists an extremely wide range of possibilities for defining scalar products that meet these criteria. The situation that arises most often in physics is that the members of our vector space are ordinary functions of the variable s (as in the first vector space of Example 5.1.1), and the scalar product of the two members $f(s)$ and $g(s)$ is computed as an integral of the type

$$\langle f|g \rangle = \int_a^b f^*(s)g(s)\,w(s)\,ds, \tag{5.4}$$

with the choice of a, b, and $w(s)$ dependent on the particular definition we wish to adopt for our scalar product. In the special case $\langle f|f \rangle$, the scalar product is to be interpreted as the square of a "length," and this scalar product must therefore be positive for any f that is not itself identically zero. Since the integrand in the scalar product is then $f^*(s)f(s)w(s)$ and $f^*(s)f(s) \geq 0$ for all s (even if $f(s)$ is complex), we can see that $w(s)$ must be positive over the entire range $[a, b]$ except possibly for zeros at isolated points.

Let's review some of the implications of Eq. (5.4). It is not appropriate to interpret that equation as a continuum analog of the ordinary dot product, with the variable s thought of as the continuum limit of an index labeling vector components. The integral actually arises pursuant to a decision to compute a "squared length" as a possibly weighted average over the range of values of the parameter s. We can illustrate this point by considering the

---

[1] If the members of the vector space are complex, this statement will need adjustment; see the formal definitions in the next subsection.

other situation that arises occasionally in physics, and illustrated by the third vector space in Example 5.1.1. Here we simply **define** the scalar products of the individual $\boldsymbol{\alpha}$ and $\boldsymbol{\beta}$ to have values

$$\langle \boldsymbol{\alpha}|\boldsymbol{\alpha}\rangle = \langle \boldsymbol{\beta}|\boldsymbol{\beta}\rangle = 1, \quad \langle \boldsymbol{\alpha}|\boldsymbol{\beta}\rangle = \langle \boldsymbol{\beta}|\boldsymbol{\alpha}\rangle = 0,$$

and then, taking the simple one-electron functions

$$f = a_1\boldsymbol{\alpha} + a_2\boldsymbol{\beta}, \quad g = b_1\boldsymbol{\alpha} + b_2\boldsymbol{\beta},$$

and assuming a_i and b_i to be real, we expand $\langle f|g\rangle$ (using its linearity property) to reach

$$\langle f|g\rangle = a_1 b_1 \langle \boldsymbol{\alpha}|\boldsymbol{\alpha}\rangle + a_1 b_2 \langle \boldsymbol{\alpha}|\boldsymbol{\beta}\rangle + a_2 b_1 \langle \boldsymbol{\beta}|\boldsymbol{\alpha}\rangle + a_2 b_2 \langle \boldsymbol{\beta}|\boldsymbol{\beta}\rangle = a_1 b_1 + a_2 b_2. \quad (5.5)$$

These equations show that the introduction of an integral is not an indispensible step toward generalization of the scalar product; they also show that the final formula in Eq. (5.5), which **is** analogous to ordinary vector algebra, arises from the expansion of $\langle f|g\rangle$ in a basis whose two members, $\boldsymbol{\alpha}$ and $\boldsymbol{\beta}$, are orthogonal (i.e., have a zero scalar product). Thus, the analogy to ordinary vector algebra is that the "unit vectors" of this spin system define an orthogonal "coordinate system" and that the "dot product" then has the expected form.

Vector spaces that are closed under addition and multiplication by a scalar and which have a scalar product that exists for all pairs of its members are termed **Hilbert spaces**; these are the vector spaces of primary importance in physics.

Hilbert Space

Proceeding now somewhat more formally (but still without complete rigor), and including the possibility that our function space may require more than two basis functions, we identify a Hilbert space $\mathcal{H}$ as having the following properties:

- Elements (members) f, g, or h of $\mathcal{H}$ are subject to two operations, **addition**, and **multiplication by a scalar** (here k, k_1, or k_2). These operations produce quantities that are also members of the space.

- Addition is commutative and associative:

$$f(s) + g(s) = g(s) + f(s), \quad [f(s) + g(s)] + h(s) = f(s) + [g(s) + h(s)].$$

- Multiplication by a scalar is commutative, associative, and distributive:

$$k f(s) = f(s)k, \quad k[f(s) + g(s)] = kf(s) + kg(s),$$

$$(k_1 + k_2)f(s) = k_1 f(s) + k_2 f(s), \quad k_1[k_2 f(s)] = k_1 k_2 f(s).$$

- $\mathcal{H}$ is **spanned** by a set of basis functions φ_i, where for the purposes of this book the number of such basis functions (the range of i) can either be finite or denumerably infinite (like the positive integers). This means that every function in $\mathcal{H}$ can be represented by the linear form $f(s) = \sum_n a_n \varphi_n(s)$. This property is also known as **completeness**. We require that the basis functions be linearly independent, so that each function in the space will be a unique linear combination of the basis functions.

- For all functions $f(s)$ and $g(s)$ in $\mathcal{H}$, there exists a scalar product, denoted as $\langle f|g \rangle$, which evaluates to a finite real or complex numerical value (i.e., does not contain s) and which has the properties that

  1. $\langle f|f \rangle \geq 0$, with the equality holding only if f is identically zero.[2] The quantity $\langle f|f \rangle^{1/2}$ is called the **norm** of f and is written $\|f\|$.

  2. $\langle g|f \rangle^* = \langle f|g \rangle$, $\langle f|g + h \rangle = \langle f|g \rangle + \langle f|h \rangle$, and $\langle f|kg \rangle = k\langle f|g \rangle$.

  Consequences of these properties are that $\langle f|k_1 g + k_2 h \rangle = k_1 \langle f|g \rangle + k_2 \langle f|h \rangle$, but $\langle kf|g \rangle = k^* \langle f|g \rangle$ and $\langle k_1 f + k_2 g|h \rangle = k_1^* \langle f|h \rangle + k_2^* \langle g|h \rangle$.

Example 5.1.2   SOME SCALAR PRODUCTS

Continuing with the first vector space of Example 5.1.1, let's assume that our scalar product of any two functions $f(s)$ and $g(s)$ takes the form

$$\langle f|g \rangle = \int_{-1}^{1} f^*(s)\, g(s)\, ds, \tag{5.6}$$

i.e., the formula given as Eq. (5.4) with $a = -1$, $b = 1$, and $w(s) = 1$. Since all the members of this vector space are quadratic forms and the integral in Eq. (5.6) is over the finite range from -1 to $+1$, the scalar product will always exist and our three basis functions indeed define a Hilbert space. Before we make a few sample computations, let's note that the brackets in the left member of Eq. (5.6) do not show the detailed form of the scalar product, thereby concealing information about the integration limits, the number of variables (here we have only one, s), the nature of the space involved, the presence or absence of a weight factor $w(s)$, and even the exact operation that forms the product. All these features must be inferred from the context or by a previously provided definition.

Now let's evaluate two scalar products:

$$\langle P_0|s^2 \rangle = \int_{-1}^{1} P_0^*(s) s^2\, ds = \int_{-1}^{1} (1)(s^2) dx = \left[\frac{s^3}{3} \right]_{-1}^{1} = \frac{2}{3},$$

$$\langle P_0|P_2 \rangle = \int_{-1}^{1} (1)\left[\frac{3}{2} s^2 - \frac{1}{2} \right] ds = \left[\frac{3}{2} \frac{s^3}{3} - \frac{1}{2} s \right]_{-1}^{1} = 0. \tag{5.7}$$

Looking further at the scalar product definition of the present example, we note that it is consistent with the general requirements for a scalar product, as (1) $\langle f|f \rangle$ is formed as the integral of an inherently nonnegative integrand, and will be positive for all nonzero

---

[2] To be rigorous, the phrase "identically zero" needs to be replaced by "zero except on a set of measure zero," and other conditions need to be more tightly specified. These are niceties that are important for a precise formulation of the mathematics but are not often of practical importance to the working physicist. We note, however, that discontinuous functions do arise in applications of Fourier series, with consequences that are discussed in Chapter 19.

f; and (2) the placement of the complex-conjugate asterisk makes it obvious that $\langle g|f\rangle^* = \langle f|g\rangle$. ∎

Schwarz Inequality

Any scalar product that meets the Hilbert space conditions will satisfy the **Schwarz inequality**, which can be stated as

$$|\langle f|g\rangle|^2 \le \langle f|f\rangle\langle g|g\rangle. \tag{5.8}$$

Here there is equality only if f and g are proportional. In ordinary vector space, the equivalent result is, referring to Eq. (1.113),

$$(\mathbf{A} \cdot \mathbf{B})^2 = |\mathbf{A}|^2|\mathbf{B}|^2 \cos^2\theta \le |\mathbf{A}|^2|\mathbf{B}|^2, \tag{5.9}$$

where θ is the angle between the directions of $\mathbf{A}$ and $\mathbf{B}$. As observed previously, the equality only holds if $\mathbf{A}$ and $\mathbf{B}$ are collinear. If we also require $\mathbf{A}$ to be of unit length, we have the intuitively obvious result that the projection of $\mathbf{B}$ onto a noncollinear $\mathbf{A}$ direction will have a magnitude less than that of $\mathbf{B}$. The Schwarz inequality extends this property to functions; their norms shrink on nontrivial projection.

The Schwarz inequality can be proved by considering

$$I = \langle f - \lambda g|f - \lambda g\rangle \ge 0, \tag{5.10}$$

where λ is an as yet undetermined constant. Treating λ and λ^* as linearly independent,[3] we differentiate I with respect to λ^* (remember that the left member of the product is complex conjugated) and set the result to zero, to find the λ value for which I is a minimum:

$$-\langle g|f - \lambda g\rangle = 0 \quad \implies \quad \lambda = \frac{\langle g|f\rangle}{\langle g|g\rangle}.$$

Substituting this λ value into Eq. (5.10), we get (using properties of the scalar product)

$$\langle f|f\rangle - \frac{\langle f|g\rangle\langle g|f\rangle}{\langle g|g\rangle} \ge 0.$$

Noting that $\langle g|g\rangle$ must be positive, and rewriting $\langle g|f\rangle$ as $\langle f|g\rangle^*$, we confirm the Schwarz inequality, Eq. (5.8).

Orthogonal Expansions

With now a well-behaved scalar product in hand, we can make the definition that two functions f and g are **orthogonal** if $\langle f|g\rangle = 0$, which means that $\langle g|f\rangle$ will also vanish. An example of two functions that are orthogonal under the then-applicable definition of the scalar product are $P_0(s)$ and $P_2(s)$, where the scalar product is that defined in Eq. (5.6) and P_0, P_2 are the functions from Example 5.1.1; the orthogonality is shown by Eq. (5.7). We further define a function f as **normalized** if the scalar product $\langle f|f\rangle = 1$; this is the

---

[3] It is not obvious that one can do this, but consider $\lambda = \mu + i\nu$, $\lambda^* = \mu - i\nu$, with μ and ν real. Then $\frac{1}{2}[\partial/\partial\mu + i\partial/\partial\nu]$ is equivalent to taking $\partial/\partial\lambda^*$ keeping λ constant.

function-space equivalent of a unit vector. We will find that great convenience results if the basis functions for our function space are normalized and mutually orthogonal, corresponding to the description of a 2-D or three-dimensional (3-D) physical vector space based on orthogonal unit vectors. A set of functions that is both normalized and mutually orthogonal is called an **orthonormal** set. If a member f of an orthogonal set is not normalized, it can be made so without disturbing the orthogonality: we simply rescale it to $\overline{f} = f/\langle f|f \rangle^{1/2}$, so any orthogonal set can easily be made orthonormal if desired.

If our basis is orthonormal, the coefficients for the expansion of an arbitrary function in that basis take a simple form. We return to our 2-D example, with the assumption that the φ_i are orthonormal, and consider the result of taking the scalar product of $f(s)$, as given by Eq. (5.1), with $\varphi_1(s)$:

$$\langle \varphi_1 | f \rangle = \langle \varphi_1 | (a_1 \varphi_1 + a_2 \varphi_2) \rangle = a_1 \langle \varphi_1 | \varphi_1 \rangle + a_2 \langle \varphi_1 | \varphi_2 \rangle. \tag{5.11}$$

The orthonormality of the φ now comes into play; the scalar product multiplying a_1 is unity, while that multiplying a_2 is zero, so we have the simple and useful result $\langle \varphi_1 | f \rangle = a_1$. Thus, we have a rather mechanical means of identifying the components of f. The general result corresponding to Eq. (5.11) follows:

$$\text{If } \langle \varphi_i | \varphi_j \rangle = \delta_{ij} \quad \text{and} \quad f = \sum_{i=1}^{n} a_i \varphi_i, \quad \text{then} \quad a_i = \langle \varphi_i | f \rangle. \tag{5.12}$$

Here the **Kronecker delta**, δ_{ij}, is unity if $i = j$ and zero otherwise. Looking once again at Eq. (5.11), we consider what happens if the φ_i are orthogonal but not normalized. Then instead of Eq. (5.12) we would have:

$$\text{If the } \varphi_i \text{ are orthogonal and } f = \sum_{i=1}^{n} a_i \varphi_i, \quad \text{then} \quad a_i = \frac{\langle \varphi_i | f \rangle}{\langle \varphi_i | \varphi_i \rangle}. \tag{5.13}$$

This form of the expansion will be convenient when normalization of the basis introduces unpleasant factors.

Example 5.1.3   EXPANSION IN ORTHONORMAL FUNCTIONS

Consider the set of functions $\chi_n(x) = \sin nx$, for $n = 1, 2, \ldots$, to be used for x in the interval $0 \leq x \leq \pi$ with scalar product

$$\langle f | g \rangle = \int_0^{\pi} f^*(x) g(x) dx. \tag{5.14}$$

We wish to use these functions for the expansion of the function $x^2(\pi - x)$.

First, we check that they are orthogonal:

$$S_{nm} = \int_0^{\pi} \chi_n^*(x) \chi_m(x) dx = \int_0^{\pi} \sin nx \sin mx \, dx.$$

For $n \neq m$ this integral can be shown to vanish, either by symmetry considerations or by consulting a table of integrals. To determine normalization, we need S_{nn}; from symmetry considerations, the integrand, $\sin^2 nx = \frac{1}{2}(1 - \cos 2nx)$, can be seen to have average value $1/2$ over the range $(0, \pi)$, leading to $S_{nn} = \pi/2$ for all integer n. This means the χ_n are not normalized, but can be made so if we multiply by $\sqrt{2/\pi}$. So our orthonormal basis will be

$$\varphi_n(x) = \left(\frac{2}{\pi}\right)^{1/2} \sin nx, \quad n = 1, 2, 3, \ldots. \tag{5.15}$$

To expand $x^2(\pi - x)$, we apply Eq. (5.2), which requires the evaluation of

$$a_n = \langle \varphi_n | x^2(\pi - x) \rangle = \left(\frac{2}{\pi}\right)^{1/2} \int_0^\pi (\sin nx)\, x^2(\pi - x)\, dx, \tag{5.16}$$

for use in the expansion

$$x^2(\pi - x) = \left(\frac{2}{\pi}\right)^{1/2} \sum_{n=0}^\infty a_n \sin nx. \tag{5.17}$$

Evaluating cases of Eq. (5.16) by hand or using a computer for symbolic computation, we have for the first few a_n: $a_1 = 5.0132$, $a_2 = -1.8300$, $a_3 = 0.1857$, $a_4 = -0.2350$. The convergence is not very fast. ∎

Example 5.1.4   SPIN SPACE

A system of four spin-$\frac{1}{2}$ particles in a triplet state has the following three linearly independent spin functions:

$$\chi_1 = \alpha\beta\alpha\alpha - \beta\alpha\alpha\alpha, \quad \chi_2 = \alpha\alpha\alpha\beta - \alpha\alpha\beta\alpha, \quad \chi_3 = \alpha\alpha\alpha\beta + \alpha\alpha\beta\alpha - \alpha\beta\alpha\alpha - \beta\alpha\alpha\alpha.$$

The four symbols in each term of these expressions refer to the spin assignments of the four particles, in numerical order.

The scalar product in the spin space has the form, for monomials,

$$\langle abcd | wxyz \rangle = \delta_{aw}\delta_{bx}\delta_{cy}\delta_{dz},$$

meaning that the scalar product is unity if the two monomials are identical, and is zero if they are not. Scalar products involving polynomials can be evaluated by expanding them into sums of monomial products. It is easy to confirm that this definition meets the requirements for a valid scalar product.

Our mission will be (1) verify that the χ_i are orthogonal; (2) convert them, if necessary, to normalized form to make an orthonormal basis for the spin space; and (3) expand the following triplet spin function as a linear combination of the orthonormal spin basis functions:

$$\chi_0 = \alpha\alpha\beta\alpha - \alpha\beta\alpha\alpha.$$

The functions χ_1 and χ_2 are orthogonal, as they have no terms in common. Although χ_1 and χ_3 have two terms in common, they occur in sign combinations leading to a vanishing scalar product. The same observation applies to $\langle \chi_2 | \chi_3 \rangle$. However, none of the χ_i are normalized. We find $\langle \chi_1 | \chi_1 \rangle = \langle \chi_2 | \chi_2 \rangle = 2$, $\langle \chi_3 | \chi_3 \rangle = 4$, so an orthonormal basis would be

$$\varphi_1 = 2^{-1/2} \chi_1, \quad \varphi_2 = 2^{-1/2} \chi_2, \quad \varphi_3 = \frac{1}{2} \chi_3.$$

Finally, we obtain the coefficients for the expansion of χ_0 by forming $a_1 = \langle \varphi_1 | \chi_0 \rangle = -1/\sqrt{2}$, $a_2 = \langle \varphi_2 | \chi_0 \rangle = -1/\sqrt{2}$, and $a_3 = \langle \varphi_3 | \chi_0 \rangle = 1$. Thus, the desired expansion is

$$\chi_0 = -\frac{1}{\sqrt{2}} \varphi_1 - \frac{1}{\sqrt{2}} \varphi_2 + \varphi_3.$$

■

Expansions and Scalar Products

If we have found the expansions of two functions,

$$f = \sum_\mu a_\mu \varphi_\mu \quad \text{and} \quad g = \sum_\nu b_\nu \varphi_\nu,$$

then their scalar product can be written

$$\langle f | g \rangle = \sum_{\mu \nu} a_\mu^* b_\nu \langle \varphi_\mu | \varphi_\nu \rangle.$$

If the φ set is orthonormal, the above reduces to

$$\langle f | g \rangle = \sum_\mu a_\mu^* b_\mu. \tag{5.18}$$

In the special case $g = f$, this reduces to

$$\langle f | f \rangle = \sum_\mu |a_\mu|^2, \tag{5.19}$$

consistent with the requirement that $\langle f | f \rangle \geq 0$, with equality only if f is zero "almost everywhere."

If we regard the set of expansion coefficients a_μ as the elements of a column vector $\mathbf{a}$ representing f, with column vector $\mathbf{b}$ similarly representing g, Eqs. (5.18) and (5.19) correspond to the matrix equations

$$\langle f | g \rangle = \mathbf{a}^\dagger \mathbf{b}, \quad \langle f | f \rangle = \mathbf{a}^\dagger \mathbf{a}. \tag{5.20}$$

Note that by taking the adjoint of $\mathbf{a}$, we both complex conjugate it and convert it into a row vector, so that the matrix products in Eq. (5.20) collapse to scalars, as required.

Example 5.1.5   COEFFICIENT VECTORS

A set of functions that is orthonormal on $0 \leq x \leq \pi$ is

$$\varphi_n(x) = \sqrt{\frac{2 - \delta_{n0}}{\pi}} \cos nx, \quad n = 0, 1, 2, \ldots.$$

First, let us expand in terms of this basis the two functions

$$\psi_1 = \cos^3 x + \sin^2 x + \cos x + 1 \quad \text{and} \quad \psi_2 = \cos^2 x - \cos x.$$

We write the expansions as vectors $\mathbf{a}_1$ and $\mathbf{a}_2$ with components $n = 0, \ldots, 3$:

$$\mathbf{a}_1 = \begin{pmatrix} \langle \varphi_0 | \psi_1 \rangle \\ \langle \varphi_1 | \psi_1 \rangle \\ \langle \varphi_2 | \psi_1 \rangle \\ \langle \varphi_3 | \psi_1 \rangle \end{pmatrix}, \quad \mathbf{a}_2 = \begin{pmatrix} \langle \varphi_0 | \psi_2 \rangle \\ \langle \varphi_1 | \psi_2 \rangle \\ \langle \varphi_2 | \psi_2 \rangle \\ \langle \varphi_3 | \psi_2 \rangle \end{pmatrix}.$$

All components beyond $n = 3$ vanish and need not be shown. It is straightforward to evaluate these scalar products. Alternatively, we can rewrite the ψ_i using trigonometric identities, reaching the forms

$$\psi_1 = \frac{\cos 3x}{4} - \frac{\cos 2x}{2} + \frac{7}{4} \cos x + \frac{3}{2}, \quad \psi_2 = \frac{\cos 2x}{2} - \cos x + \frac{1}{2}.$$

These expressions are now easily recognized as equivalent to

$$\psi_1 = \sqrt{\frac{\pi}{2}} \left(\frac{\varphi_3}{4} - \frac{\varphi_2}{2} + \frac{7\varphi_1}{4} + \frac{3\sqrt{2}\,\varphi_0}{2} \right), \quad \psi_2 = \sqrt{\frac{\pi}{2}} \left(\frac{\varphi_2}{2} - \varphi_1 + \frac{\sqrt{2}\,\varphi_0}{2} \right),$$

so

$$\mathbf{a}_1 = \sqrt{\frac{\pi}{2}} \begin{pmatrix} 3\sqrt{2}/2 \\ 7/4 \\ -1/2 \\ 1/4 \end{pmatrix}, \quad \mathbf{a}_2 = \sqrt{\frac{\pi}{2}} \begin{pmatrix} \sqrt{2}/2 \\ -1 \\ 1/2 \\ 0 \end{pmatrix}.$$

We see from the above that the general formula for finding the coefficients in an orthonormal expansion, Eq. (5.12), is a systematic way of doing what sometimes can be carried out in other ways.

We can now evaluate the scalar products $\langle \psi_i | \psi_j \rangle$. Identifying these first as matrix products that we then evaluate,

$$\langle \psi_1 | \psi_1 \rangle = \mathbf{a}_1^\dagger \mathbf{a}_1 = \frac{63\pi}{16}, \quad \langle \psi_1 | \psi_2 \rangle = \mathbf{a}_1^\dagger \mathbf{a}_2 = -\frac{\pi}{4}, \quad \langle \psi_2 | \psi_2 \rangle = \mathbf{a}_2^\dagger \mathbf{a}_2 = \frac{7\pi}{8}.$$

∎

Bessel's Inequality

Given a set of basis functions and the definition of a space, it is not necessarily assured that the basis functions span the space (a property sometimes referred to as **completeness**). For example, we might have a space defined to be that containing all functions possessing a scalar product of a given definition, while the basis functions have been specified by giving their functional form. This issue is of some importance, because we need to know whether an attempt to expand a function in a given basis can be guaranteed to converge to the correct result. Totally general criteria are not available, but useful results have been obtained if the function being expanded has, at worst, a finite number of finite discontinuities, and results are accepted as "accurate" if deviations from the correct value occur only at isolated points. Power series and trigonometric series have been proved complete for the expansion of square integrable functions f (those for which $\langle f|f \rangle$ as defined in Eq. (5.7) exists; mathematicians identify such spaces by the designation $\mathcal{L}^2$). Also proved complete are the orthonormal sets of functions that arise as the solutions to Hermitian eigenvalue problems.[4]

A not too practical test for completeness is provided by **Bessel's inequality**, which states that if a function f has been expanded in an orthonormal basis as $\sum_n a_n \varphi_n$, then

$$\langle f|f \rangle \ge \sum_n |a_n|^2, \tag{5.21}$$

with the inequality occurring if the expansion of f is incomplete. The impracticality of this as a completeness test is that one needs to apply it for all f before using it to claim completeness of the space.

We establish Bessel's inequality by considering

$$I = \left\langle f - \sum_i a_i \varphi_i \,\middle|\, f - \sum_j a_j \varphi_j \right\rangle \ge 0, \tag{5.22}$$

where $I = 0$ represents what is termed **convergence in the mean**, a criterion that permits the integrand to deviate from zero at isolated points. Expanding the scalar product, and eliminating terms that vanish because the φ are orthonormal, we arrive at Eq. (5.21), with equality only resulting if the expansion converges to f. We note in passing that convergence in the mean is a less stringent requirement than **uniform convergence**, but is adequate for almost all physical applications of basis-set expansions.

Example 5.1.6   EXPANSION OF A DISCONTINUOUS FUNCTION

The functions $\cos nx$ $(n = 0, 1, 2, \dots)$ and $\sin nx$ $(n = 1, 2, \dots)$ have (together) been shown to form a complete set on the interval $-\pi < x < \pi$. Since this determination is obtained subject to convergence in the mean, there is the possibility of deviation at isolated points, thereby permitting the description of functions with isolated discontinuities.

---

[4]See R. Courant and D. Hilbert, *Methods of Mathematical Physics* (English translation), Vol. 1, New York: Interscience (1953), reprinting, Wiley (1989), chapter 6, section 3.

We illustrate with the square-wave function

$$f(x) = \begin{cases} \dfrac{h}{2}, & 0 < x < \pi \\ -\dfrac{h}{2}, & -\pi < x < 0. \end{cases} \qquad (5.23)$$

The functions $\cos nx$ and $\sin nx$ are orthogonal on the expansion interval (with unit weight in the scalar product), and the expansion of $f(x)$ takes the form

$$f(x) = a_0 + \sum_{n=1}^{\infty} (a_n \cos nx + b_n \sin nx).$$

Because $f(x)$ is an odd function of x, all the a_n vanish, and we only need to compute

$$b_n = \frac{1}{\pi} \int_{-\pi}^{\pi} f(t) \sin nt \, dt.$$

The factor $1/\pi$ preceding the integral arises because the expansion functions are not normalized.

Upon substitution of $\pm h/2$ for $f(t)$, we find

$$b_n = \frac{h}{n\pi}(1 - \cos n\pi) = \begin{cases} 0, & n \text{ even,} \\ \dfrac{2h}{n\pi}, & n \text{ odd.} \end{cases}$$

Thus, the expansion of the square wave is

$$f(x) = \frac{2h}{\pi} \sum_{n=0}^{\infty} \frac{\sin(2n+1)x}{2n+1}. \qquad (5.24)$$

To give an idea of the rate at which the series in Eq. (5.24) converges, some of its partial sums are plotted in Fig. 5.1.

■

Expansions of Dirac Delta Function

Orthogonal expansions provide opportunities to develop additional representations of the Dirac delta function. In fact, such a representation can be built from any complete set of functions $\varphi_n(x)$. For simplicity we assume the φ_n to be orthonormal with unit weight on the interval (a, b), and consider the expansion

$$\delta(x - t) = \sum_{n=0}^{\infty} c_n(t) \, \varphi_n(x), \qquad (5.25)$$

where, as indicated, the coefficients must be functions of t. From the rule for determining the coefficients, we have, for t also in the interval (a, b),

$$c_n(t) = \int_a^b \varphi_n^*(x) \, \delta(x - t) \, dx = \varphi_n^*(t), \qquad (5.26)$$

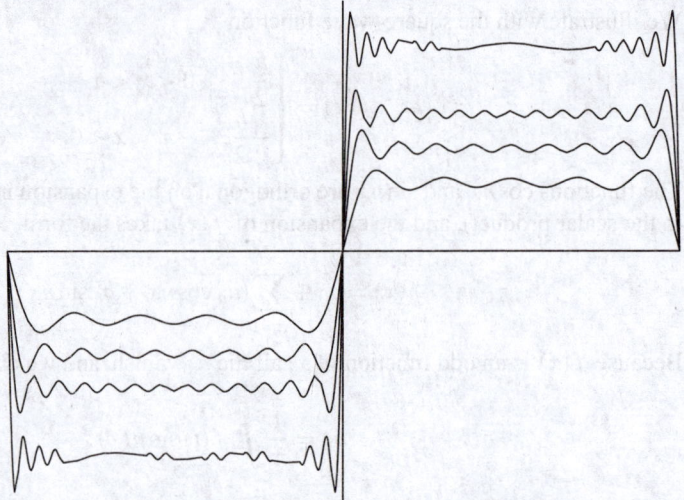

FIGURE 5.1   Expansion of square wave. Computed using Eq. (5.24) with summation
terminated after $n = 4, 8, 12$, and 20. Curves are at different vertical scales to
enhance visibility.

where the evaluation has used the defining property of the delta function. Substituting this
result back into Eq. (5.25), we have

$$\delta(x - t) = \sum_{n=0}^{\infty} \varphi_n^*(t)\, \varphi_n(x). \tag{5.27}$$

This result is clearly not uniformly convergent at $x = t$. However, remember that it is not
to be used by itself, but has meaning only when it appears as part of an integrand. Note
also that Eq. (5.27) is only valid when x and t are within the range (a, b).

Equation (5.27) is called the **closure** relation for the Dirac delta function (with respect
to the φ_n) and obviously depends on the completeness of the φ set. If we apply Eq. (5.27)
to an arbitrary function $F(t)$ that we assume to have the expansion $F(t) = \sum_p c_p \varphi_p(t)$,
we have

$$\int_a^b F(t)\, \delta(x - t)\, dt = \int_a^b dt \sum_{p=0}^{\infty} c_p \varphi_p(t) \sum_{n=0}^{\infty} \varphi_n^*(t)\, \varphi_n(x)$$

$$= \sum_{p=0}^{\infty} c_p \varphi_p(x) = F(x), \tag{5.28}$$

which is the expected result. However, if we replace the integration limits (a, b) by (t_1, t_2)
such that $a \le t_1 < t_2 \le b$, we get a more general result that reflects the fact that our

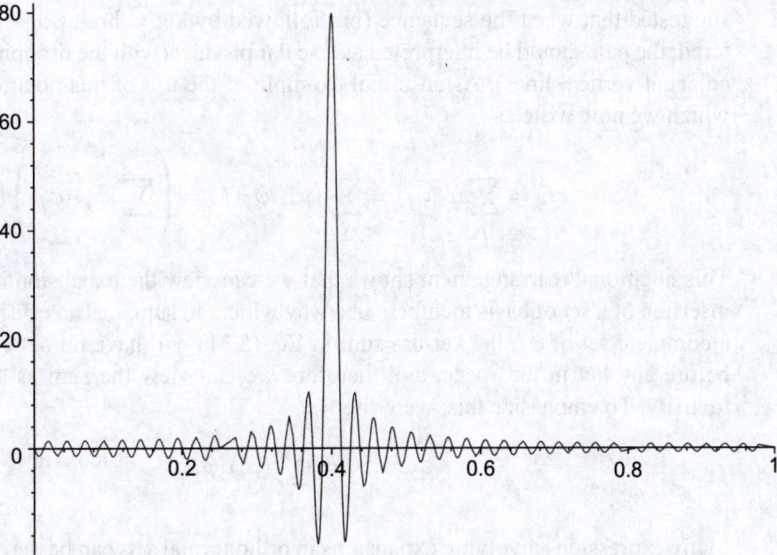

FIGURE 5.2 Approximation at $N = 80$ to $\delta(t - x)$, Eq. (5.30), for $t = 0.4$.

representation of $\delta(x - t)$ is negligible except when $x \approx t$:

$$\int_{t_1}^{t_2} F(t)\,\delta(x - t)\,dt = \begin{cases} F(x), & t_1 < x < t_2, \\ 0, & x < t_1 \text{ or } x > t_2. \end{cases} \tag{5.29}$$

Example 5.1.7   DELTA FUNCTION REPRESENTATION

To illustrate an expansion of the Dirac delta function in an orthonormal basis, take $\varphi_n(x) = \sqrt{2}\,\sin n\pi x$, which are orthonormal and complete on $x = (0, 1)$ for $n = 1, 2, \ldots$. Then the Dirac delta function has representation, valid for $0 < x < 1$, $0 < t < 1$,

$$\delta(x - t) = \lim_{N \to \infty} \sum_{n=1}^{N} 2 \sin n\pi t \sin n\pi x. \tag{5.30}$$

Plotting this with $N = 80$ for $t = 0.4$ and $0 < x < 1$ gives the result shown in Fig. 5.2.   ∎

Dirac Notation

Much of what we have discussed can be brought to a form that promotes clarity and suggests possibilities for additional analysis by using a notational device invented by P. A. M. Dirac. Dirac suggested that instead of just writing a function f, it be written enclosed in the right half of an angle-bracket pair, which he named a **ket**. Thus $f \to |f\rangle$, $\varphi_i \to |\varphi_i\rangle$, etc. Then he suggested that the complex conjugates of functions be enclosed in left half-brackets, which he named **bras**. An example of a bra is $\varphi_i^* \to \langle\varphi_i|$. Finally, he suggested that when the sequence (bra followed by ket = bra+ket ∼ bracket) is encountered, the pair should be interpreted as a scalar product (with the dropping of one of the two adjacent vertical lines). As an initial example of the use of this notation, take Eq. (5.12), which we now write as

$$|f\rangle = \sum_j a_j |\varphi_j\rangle = \sum_j |\varphi_j\rangle\langle\varphi_j|f\rangle = \left(\sum_j |\varphi_j\rangle\langle\varphi_j|\right)|f\rangle. \qquad (5.31)$$

This notational rearrangement shows that we can view the expansion in the φ basis as the insertion of a set of basis members in a way which, in sum, has no effect. If the sum is over a complete set of φ_j, the ket-bra sum in Eq. (5.31) will have no net effect when inserted before any ket in the space, and therefore we can view the sum as a **resolution of the identity**. To emphasize this, we write

$$1 = \sum_j |\varphi_j\rangle\langle\varphi_j|. \qquad (5.32)$$

Many expressions involving expansions in orthonormal sets can be derived by the insertion of resolutions of the identity.

Dirac notation can also be applied to expressions involving vectors and matrices, where it illuminates the parallelism between physical vector spaces and the function spaces here under study. If $\mathbf{a}$ and $\mathbf{b}$ are column vectors and M is a matrix, then we can write $|\mathbf{b}\rangle$ as a synonym for $\mathbf{b}$, we can write $\langle\mathbf{a}|$ to mean $\mathbf{a}^\dagger$, and then $\langle\mathbf{a}|\mathbf{b}\rangle$ is interpreted as equivalent to $\mathbf{a}^\dagger\mathbf{b}$, which (when the vectors are real) is matrix notation for the (scalar) dot product $\mathbf{a} \cdot \mathbf{b}$. Other examples are expressions such as

$$\mathbf{a} = M\mathbf{b} \leftrightarrow |\mathbf{a}\rangle = |M\mathbf{b}\rangle = M|\mathbf{b}\rangle \quad \text{or} \quad \mathbf{a}^\dagger M\mathbf{b} = (M^\dagger\mathbf{a})^\dagger\mathbf{b} \leftrightarrow \langle\mathbf{a}|M\mathbf{b}\rangle = \langle M^\dagger\mathbf{a}|\mathbf{b}\rangle.$$

Exercises

5.1.1   A function $f(x)$ is expanded in a series of orthonormal functions

$$f(x) = \sum_{n=0}^{\infty} a_n\varphi_n(x).$$

Show that the series expansion is unique for a given set of $\varphi_n(x)$. The functions $\varphi_n(x)$ are being taken here as the **basis** vectors in an infinite-dimensional Hilbert space.

5.1.2   A function $f(x)$ is represented by a finite set of basis functions $\varphi_i(x)$,

$$f(x) = \sum_{i=1}^{N} c_i\varphi_i(x).$$

Show that the components c_i are unique, that no different set c_i' exists.

Note. Your basis functions are automatically linearly independent. They are not necessarily orthogonal.

5.1.3   A function $f(x)$ is approximated by a power series $\sum_{i=0}^{n-1} c_i x^i$ over the interval $[0, 1]$. Show that minimizing the mean square error leads to a set of linear equations

$$\mathbf{Ac} = \mathbf{b},$$

where

$$A_{ij} = \int_0^1 x^{i+j}\, dx = \frac{1}{i+j+1}, \quad i, j = 0, 1, 2, \ldots, n-1$$

and

$$b_i = \int_0^1 x^i f(x)\, dx, \quad i = 0, 1, 2, \ldots, n-1.$$

Note. The A_{ij} are the elements of the Hilbert matrix of order n. The determinant of this Hilbert matrix is a rapidly decreasing function of n. For $n = 5$, $\det A = 3.7 \times 10^{-12}$ and the set of equations $\mathbf{Ac} = \mathbf{b}$ is becoming ill-conditioned and unstable.

5.1.4   In place of the expansion of a function $F(x)$ given by

$$F(x) = \sum_{n=0}^{\infty} a_n \varphi_n(x),$$

with

$$a_n = \int_a^b F(x)\varphi_n(x)w(x)\, dx,$$

take the **finite** series approximation

$$F(x) \approx \sum_{n=0}^{m} c_n \varphi_n(x).$$

Show that the mean square error

$$\int_a^b \left[F(x) - \sum_{n=0}^{m} c_n \varphi_n(x) \right]^2 w(x)\, dx$$

is minimized by taking $c_n = a_n$.

Note. The values of the coefficients are independent of the number of terms in the finite series. This independence is a consequence of orthogonality and would not hold for a least-squares fit using powers of x.

5.1.5   From Example 5.1.6,

$$f(x) = \begin{cases} \dfrac{h}{2}, & 0 < x < \pi \\[2mm] -\dfrac{h}{2}, & -\pi < x < 0 \end{cases} = \frac{2h}{\pi} \sum_{n=0}^{\infty} \frac{\sin(2n+1)x}{2n+1}.$$

(a) Show that

$$\int_{-\pi}^{\pi} \left[f(x) \right]^2 dx = \frac{\pi}{2} h^2 = \frac{4h^2}{\pi} \sum_{n=0}^{\infty} (2n+1)^{-2}.$$

For a finite upper limit this would be Bessel's inequality. For the upper limit ∞, this is Parseval's identity.

(b) Verify that

$$\frac{\pi}{2} h^2 = \frac{4h^2}{\pi} \sum_{n=0}^{\infty} (2n+1)^{-2}$$

by evaluating the series.

Hint. The series can be expressed in terms of the Riemann zeta function $\zeta(2) = \pi^2/6$.

5.1.6 Derive the Schwarz inequality from the identity

$$\left[\int_a^b f(x)g(x)\, dx \right]^2 = \int_a^b \left[f(x) \right]^2 dx \int_a^b [\left[g(x) \right]^2 dx$$

$$- \frac{1}{2} \int_a^b dx \int_a^b dy \left[f(x)g(y) - f(y)g(x) \right]^2.$$

5.1.7 Starting from $I = \left\langle f - \sum_i a_i \, \varphi_i \, \middle| \, f - \sum_j a_j \, \varphi_j \right\rangle \geq 0$,

derive Bessel's inequality, $\langle f | f \rangle \geq \sum_n |a_n|^2$.

5.1.8 Expand the function $\sin \pi x$ in a series of functions φ_i that are orthogonal (but not normalized) on the range $0 \leq x \leq 1$ when the scalar product has definition

$$\langle f | g \rangle = \int_0^1 f^*(x) g(x)\, dx.$$

Keep the first four terms of the expansion. The first four φ_i are:

$$\varphi_0 = 1, \quad \varphi_1 = 2x - 1, \quad \varphi_2 = 6x^2 - 6x + 1, \quad \varphi_3 = 20x^3 - 30x^2 + 12x - 1.$$

Note. The integrals that are needed are the subject of Example 1.10.5.

5.1.9 Expand the function e^{-x} in Laguerre polynomials $L_n(x)$, which are orthonormal on the range $0 \leq x < \infty$ with scalar product

$$\langle f | g \rangle = \int_0^\infty f^*(x) g(x) e^{-x}\, dx.$$

Keep the first four terms of the expansion. The first four $L_n(x)$ are

$$L_0 = 1, \quad L_1 = 1 - x, \quad L_2 = \frac{2 - 4x + x^2}{2}, \quad L_3 = \frac{6 - 18x + 9x^2 - x^3}{6}.$$

5.1.10 The explicit form of a function f is not known, but the coefficients a_n of its expansion in the orthonormal set φ_n are available. Assuming that the φ_n and the members of another orthonormal set, χ_n, are available, use Dirac notation to obtain a formula for the coefficients for the expansion of f in the χ_n set.

5.1.11 Using conventional vector notation, evaluate $\sum_j |\hat{\mathbf{e}}_j\rangle\langle\hat{\mathbf{e}}_j|\mathbf{a}\rangle$, where $\mathbf{a}$ is an arbitrary vector in the space spanned by the $\hat{\mathbf{e}}_j$.

5.1.12 Letting $\mathbf{a} = a_1\hat{\mathbf{e}}_1 + a_2\hat{\mathbf{e}}_2$ and $\mathbf{b} = b_1\hat{\mathbf{e}}_1 + b_2\hat{\mathbf{e}}_2$ be vectors in $\mathbb{R}^2$, for what values of k, if any, is

$$\langle\mathbf{a}|\mathbf{b}\rangle = a_1 b_1 - a_1 b_2 - a_2 b_1 + k a_2 b_2$$

a valid definition of a scalar product?

5.2 GRAM-SCHMIDT ORTHOGONALIZATION

Crucial to carrying out the expansions and transformations under discussion is the availability of useful orthonormal sets of functions. We therefore proceed to the description of a process whereby a set of functions that is neither orthogonal or normalized can be used to construct an orthonormal set that spans the same function space. There are many ways to accomplish this task. We present here the method called the **Gram-Schmidt** orthogonalization process.

The Gram-Schmidt process assumes the availability of a set of functions χ_μ and an appropriately defined scalar product $\langle f|g\rangle$. We orthonormalize **sequentially** to form the orthonormal functions φ_ν, meaning we make the first orthonormal function, φ_0, from χ_0, the next, φ_1, from χ_0 and χ_1, etc. If, for example, the χ_μ are powers x^μ, the orthonormal function φ_ν will be a polynomial of degree ν in x. Because the Gram-Schmidt process is often applied to powers, we have chosen to number both the χ and the φ sets starting from zero (rather than 1).

Thus, our first orthonormal function will simply be a normalized version of χ_0. Specifically,

$$\varphi_0 = \frac{\chi_0}{\langle\chi_0|\chi_0\rangle^{1/2}}. \tag{5.33}$$

To check that Eq. (5.33) is correct, we form

$$\langle\varphi_0|\varphi_0\rangle = \left\langle \frac{\chi_0}{\langle\chi_0|\chi_0\rangle^{1/2}} \middle| \frac{\chi_0}{\langle\chi_0|\chi_0\rangle^{1/2}} \right\rangle = 1.$$

Next, starting from φ_0 and χ_1, we form a function that is orthogonal to φ_0. We use φ_0 rather than χ_0 to be consistent with what we will do in later steps of the process. Thus, we write

$$\psi_1 = \chi_1 - a_{1,0}\varphi_0. \tag{5.34}$$

What we are doing here is the removal from χ_1 of its projection onto φ_0, leaving a remainder that will be orthogonal to φ_0. Remembering that φ_0 is normalized (of "unit length"), that projection is identified as $\langle\varphi_0|\chi_1\rangle\varphi_0$, so that

$$a_{1,0} = \langle\varphi_0|\chi_1\rangle. \tag{5.35}$$

In case Eq. (5.35) is not intuitively obvious, we can confirm it by writing the requirement that ψ_1 be orthogonal to φ_0:

$$\langle\varphi_0|\psi_1\rangle = \Big\langle\varphi_0\Big|\,\big(\chi_1 - a_{1,0}\varphi_0\big)\Big\rangle = \langle\varphi_0|\chi_1\rangle - a_{1,0}\langle\varphi_0|\varphi_0\rangle = 0,$$

which, because φ_0 is normalized, reduces to Eq. (5.35). The function ψ_1 is not in general normalized. To normalize it and thereby obtain φ_1, we form

$$\varphi_1 = \frac{\psi_1}{\langle\psi_1|\psi_1\rangle^{1/2}}. \tag{5.36}$$

To continue further, we need to make, from φ_0, φ_1, and χ_2, a function that is orthogonal to both φ_0 and φ_1. It will have the form

$$\psi_2 = \chi_2 - a_{0,2}\varphi_0 - a_{1,2}\varphi_1. \tag{5.37}$$

The last two terms of Eq. (5.37), respectively, remove from χ_2 its projections on φ_0 and φ_1; these projections are independent because φ_0 and φ_1 are orthogonal. Thus, either from our knowledge of projections or by setting to zero the scalar products $\langle\varphi_i|\psi_2\rangle$ ($i = 0$ and 1), we establish

$$a_{0,2} = \langle\varphi_0|\chi_2\rangle, \quad a_{1,2} = \langle\varphi_1|\chi_2\rangle. \tag{5.38}$$

Finally, we make $\varphi_2 = \psi_2/\langle\psi_2|\psi_2\rangle^{1/2}$.

The generalization for which the above is the first few terms is that, given the prior formation of φ_i, $i = 0, \ldots, n-1$, the orthonormal function φ_n is obtained from χ_n by the following two steps:

$$\psi_n = \chi_n - \sum_{\mu=0}^{n-1}\langle\varphi_\mu|\chi_n\rangle\varphi_\mu,$$

$$\varphi_n = \frac{\psi_n}{\langle\psi_n|\psi_n\rangle^{1/2}}. \tag{5.39}$$

Reviewing the above process, we note that different results would have been obtained if we used the same set of χ_i, but simply took them in a different order. For example, if we had started with χ_3, one of our orthonormal functions would have been a multiple of χ_3, while the set we constructed yielded φ_3 as a linear combination of χ_μ, $\mu = 0, 1, 2, 3$.

Example 5.2.1   LEGENDRE POLYNOMIALS

Let us form an orthonormal set, taking the χ_μ as x^μ, and making the definition

$$\langle f|g\rangle = \int\limits_{-1}^{1} f^*(x)g(x)dx. \tag{5.40}$$

This scalar product definition will cause the members of our set to be orthogonal, with unit weight, on the range $(-1, 1)$. Moreover, since the χ_μ are real, the complex conjugate asterisk has no operational significance here.

The first orthonormal function, φ_0, is

$$\varphi_0(x) = \frac{1}{\langle 1|1\rangle^{1/2}} = \frac{1}{\left[\int\limits_{-1}^{1} dx\right]^{1/2}} = \frac{1}{\sqrt{2}}.$$

To obtain φ_1, we first obtain ψ_1 by evaluating

$$\psi_1(x) = x - \langle \varphi_0|x\rangle \varphi_0(x) = x,$$

where the scalar product vanishes because φ_0 is an even function of x, whereas x is odd, and the range of integration is even. We then find

$$\varphi_1(x) = \frac{x}{\left[\int\limits_{-1}^{1} x^2 dx\right]^{1/2}} = \sqrt{\frac{3}{2}}\, x.$$

The next step is less trivial. We form

$$\psi_2(x) = x^2 - \langle \varphi_0|x^2\rangle \varphi_0(x) - \langle \varphi_1|x^2\rangle \varphi_1(x) = x^2 - \left\langle \frac{1}{\sqrt{2}}\Big|x^2\right\rangle\left(\frac{1}{\sqrt{2}}\right) = x^2 - \frac{1}{3},$$

where we have used symmetry to set $\langle \varphi_1|x^2\rangle$ to zero and evaluated the scalar product

$$\left\langle \frac{1}{\sqrt{2}}\Big|x^2\right\rangle = \frac{1}{\sqrt{2}}\int\limits_{-1}^{1} x^2 dx = \frac{\sqrt{2}}{3}.$$

Then,

$$\varphi_2(x) = \frac{x^2 - \frac{1}{3}}{\left[\int\limits_{-1}^{1}\left(x^2 - \frac{1}{3}\right)^2 dx\right]^{1/2}} = \sqrt{\frac{5}{2}}\left(\frac{3}{2}x^2 - \frac{1}{2}\right).$$

Continuation to one more orthonormal function yields

$$\varphi_3(x) = \sqrt{\frac{7}{2}}\left(\frac{5}{2}x^3 - \frac{3}{2}x\right).$$

Reference to Chapter 15 will show that

$$\varphi_n(x) = \sqrt{\frac{2n+1}{2}}\, P_n(x), \tag{5.41}$$

where $P_n(x)$ is the nth degree Legendre polynomial. Our Gram-Schmidt process provides a possible but very cumbersome method of generating the Legendre polynomials; other, more efficient approaches exist. ∎

Table 5.1 Orthogonal Polynomials Generated by Gram-Schmidt Orthogonalization of $u_n(x) = x^n$, $n = 0, 1, 2, \ldots$.

Polynomials	Scalar Products	Table
Legendre	$\int_{-1}^{1} P_n(x) P_m(x) dx = 2\delta_{mn}/(2n+1)$	Table 15.1
Shifted Legendre	$\int_{0}^{1} P_n^*(x) P_m^*(x) dx = \delta_{mn}/(2n+1)$	Table 15.2
Chebyshev I	$\int_{-1}^{1} T_n(x) T_m(x)\left(1 - x^2\right)^{-1/2} dx = \delta_{mn}\pi/(2 - \delta_{n0})$	Table 18.4
Shifted Chebyshev I	$\int_{0}^{1} T_n^*(x) T_m^*(x)[x(1-x)]^{-1/2} dx = \delta_{mn}\pi/(2 - \delta_{n0})$	Table 18.5
Chebyshev II	$\int_{-1}^{1} U_n(x) U_m(x)\left(1 - x^2\right)^{1/2} dx = \delta_{mn}\pi/2$	Table 18.4
Laguerre	$\int_{0}^{\infty} L_n(x) L_m(x) e^{-x} dx = \delta_{mn}$	Table 18.2
Associated Laguerre	$\int_{0}^{\infty} L_n^k(x) L_m^k(x) e^{-x} dx = \delta_{mn}(n+k)!/n!$	Table 18.3
Hermite	$\int_{-\infty}^{\infty} H_n(x) H_m(x) e^{-x^2} dx = 2^n \delta_{mn} \pi^{1/2} n!$	Table 18.1

The intervals, weights, and conventional normalization can be deduced from the forms of the scalar products. Tables of explicit formulas for the first few polynomials of each type are included in the indicated tables appearing in Chapters 15 and 18 of this book.

The Legendre polynomials are, except for sign and scale, uniquely defined by the Gram-Schmidt process, the use of successive powers of x, and the definition adopted for the scalar product. By changing the scalar product definition (different weight or range), we can generate other useful sets of orthogonal polynomials. A number of these are presented in Table 5.1. For various reasons most of these polynomial sets are not normalized to unity. The scalar product formulas in the table give the conventional normalizations, and are those of the explicit formulas referenced in the table.

Orthonormalizing Physical Vectors

The Gram-Schmidt process also works for ordinary vectors that are simply given by their components, it being understood that the scalar product is just the ordinary dot product.

Example 5.2.2   ORTHONORMALIZING A 2-D MANIFOLD

A 2-D manifold (subspace) in 3-D space is defined by the two vectors $\mathbf{a}_1 = \hat{\mathbf{e}}_1 + \hat{\mathbf{e}}_2 - 2\hat{\mathbf{e}}_3$ and $\mathbf{a}_2 = \hat{\mathbf{e}}_1 + 2\hat{\mathbf{e}}_2 - 3\hat{\mathbf{e}}_3$. In Dirac notation, these vectors (written as column matrices) are

$$|\mathbf{a}_1\rangle = \begin{pmatrix} 1 \\ 1 \\ -2 \end{pmatrix}, \quad |\mathbf{a}_2\rangle = \begin{pmatrix} 1 \\ 2 \\ -3 \end{pmatrix}.$$

Our task is to span this manifold with an orthonormal basis.

We proceed exactly as for functions: Our first orthonormal basis vector, which we call $\mathbf{b}_1$, will be a normalized version of $\mathbf{a}_1$, and therefore formed as

$$|\mathbf{b}_1\rangle = \frac{\mathbf{a}_1}{\langle \mathbf{a}_1|\mathbf{a}_1\rangle^{1/2}} = \frac{1}{6^{1/2}} |\mathbf{a}_1\rangle = \frac{1}{6^{1/2}} \begin{pmatrix} 1 \\ 1 \\ -2 \end{pmatrix}.$$

An unnormalized version of a second orthonormal function will have the form

$$|\mathbf{b}_2'\rangle = |\mathbf{a}_2\rangle - \langle \mathbf{b}_1|\mathbf{a}_2\rangle|\mathbf{b}_1\rangle = |\mathbf{a}_2\rangle - \frac{9}{6^{1/2}} |\mathbf{b}_1\rangle = \begin{pmatrix} -1/2 \\ 1/2 \\ 0 \end{pmatrix}.$$

Normalizing, we reach

$$|\mathbf{b}_2\rangle = \frac{\mathbf{b}_2'}{\langle \mathbf{b}_2'|\mathbf{b}_2'\rangle^{1/2}} = \frac{1}{\sqrt{2}} \begin{pmatrix} -1 \\ 1 \\ 0 \end{pmatrix}.$$

∎

Exercises

For the Gram-Schmidt constructions in Exercises 5.2.1 through 5.2.6, use a scalar product of the form given in Eq. (5.7) with the specified interval and weight.

5.2.1   Following the Gram-Schmidt procedure, construct a set of polynomials $P_n^*(x)$ orthogonal (unit weighting factor) over the range $[0, 1]$ from the set $[1, x, x^2, \ldots]$. Scale so that $P_n^*(1) = 1$.

$$\begin{aligned} ANS. \quad & P_n^*(x) = 1, \\ & P_1^*(x) = 2x - 1, \\ & P_2^*(x) = 6x^2 - 6x + 1, \\ & P_3^*(x) = 20x^3 - 30x^2 + 12x - 1. \end{aligned}$$

These are the first four **shifted** Legendre polynomials.

Note. The "*" is the standard notation for "shifted": $[0, 1]$ instead of $[-1, 1]$. It does **not** mean complex conjugate.

5.2.2   Apply the Gram-Schmidt procedure to form the first three Laguerre polynomials:

$$u_n(x) = x^n, \quad n = 0, 1, 2, \ldots, \quad 0 \leq x < \infty, \quad w(x) = e^{-x}.$$

The conventional normalization is

$$\int_0^\infty L_m(x)L_n(x)e^{-x}dx = \delta_{mn}.$$

ANS. $L_0 = 1$, $L_1 = (1-x)$, $L_2 = \dfrac{2-4x+x^2}{2}$.

5.2.3 You are given

(a) a set of functions $u_n(x) = x^n$, $n = 0, 1, 2, \ldots$,

(b) an interval $(0, \infty)$,

(c) a weighting function $w(x) = xe^{-x}$. Use the Gram-Schmidt procedure to construct the first **three orthonormal** functions from the set $u_n(x)$ for this interval and this weighting function.

ANS. $\varphi_0(x) = 1$, $\varphi_1(x) = (x-2)/\sqrt{2}$, $\varphi_2(x) = (x^2 - 6x + 6)/2\sqrt{3}$.

5.2.4 Using the Gram-Schmidt orthogonalization procedure, construct the lowest three Hermite polynomials:

$$u_n(x) = x^n, \quad n = 0, 1, 2, \ldots, \quad -\infty < x < \infty, \quad w(x) = e^{-x^2}.$$

For this set of polynomials the usual normalization is

$$\int_{-\infty}^\infty H_m(x)H_n(x)w(x)\,dx = \delta_{mn}2^m m!\,\pi^{1/2}.$$

ANS. $H_0 = 1$, $H_1 = 2x$, $H_2 = 4x^2 - 2$.

5.2.5 Use the Gram-Schmidt orthogonalization scheme to construct the first three Chebyshev polynomials (type I):

$$u_n(x) = x^n, \quad n = 0, 1, 2, \ldots, \quad -1 \le x \le 1, \quad w(x) = (1-x^2)^{-1/2}.$$

Take the normalization

$$\int_{-1}^1 T_m(x)T_n(x)w(x)dx = \delta_{mn} \begin{cases} \pi, & m = n = 0, \\ \dfrac{\pi}{2}, & m = n \ge 1. \end{cases}$$

Hint. The needed integrals are given in Exercise 13.3.2.

ANS. $T_0 = 1$, $T_1 = x$, $T_2 = 2x^2 - 1$, $(T_3 = 4x^3 - 3x)$.

5.2.6 Use the Gram-Schmidt orthogonalization scheme to construct the first three Chebyshev polynomials (type II):

$$u_n(x) = x^n, \quad n = 0, 1, 2, \ldots, \quad -1 \le x \le 1, \quad w(x) = (1-x^2)^{+1/2}.$$

Take the normalization to be

$$\int_{-1}^1 U_m(x)U_n(x)w(x)\,dx = \delta_{mn}\frac{\pi}{2}.$$

Hint.

$$\int_{-1}^{1} (1-x^2)^{1/2} x^{2n}\, dx = \frac{\pi}{2} \times \frac{1\cdot 3 \cdot 5 \cdots (2n-1)}{4 \cdot 6 \cdot 8 \cdots (2n+2)}, \quad n = 1, 2, 3, \ldots$$

$$= \frac{\pi}{2}, \quad n = 0.$$

ANS. $U_0 = 1, \quad U_1 = 2x, \quad U_2 = 4x^2 - 1.$

5.2.7   As a modification of Exercise 5.2.5, apply the Gram-Schmidt orthogonalization procedure to the set $u_n(x) = x^n$, $n = 0, 1, 2, \ldots$, $0 \le x < \infty$. Take $w(x)$ to be $\exp(-x^2)$. Find the first two nonvanishing polynomials. Normalize so that the coefficient of the highest power of x is unity. In Exercise 5.2.5, the interval $(-\infty, \infty)$ led to the Hermite polynomials. The functions found here are certainly not the Hermite polynomials.

ANS. $\varphi_0 = 1, \quad \varphi_1 = x - \pi^{-1/2}.$

5.2.8   Form a set of three orthonormal vectors by the Gram-Schmidt process using these input vectors in the order given:

$$\mathbf{c}_1 = \begin{pmatrix} 1 \\ 1 \\ 1 \end{pmatrix}, \quad \mathbf{c}_2 = \begin{pmatrix} 1 \\ 1 \\ 2 \end{pmatrix}, \quad \mathbf{c}_3 = \begin{pmatrix} 1 \\ 0 \\ 2 \end{pmatrix}.$$

5.3   OPERATORS

An operator is a mapping between functions in its **domain** (those to which it can be applied) and functions in its **range** (those it can produce). While the domain and the range need not be in the same space, our concern here is for operators whose domain and range are both in all or part of the same Hilbert space. To make this discussion more concrete, here are a few examples of operators:

- Multiplication by 2: Converts f into $2f$;

- For a space containing algebraic functions of a variable x, d/dx: Converts $f(x)$ into df/dx;

- An integral operator A defined by $A f(x) = \int G(x, x') f(x')\, dx'$: A special case of this is a projection operator $|\varphi_i\rangle\langle\varphi_i|$, which converts f into $\langle\varphi_i|f\rangle\varphi_i$.

In addition to the abovementioned restriction on domain and range, we also for our present purposes restrict attention to operators that are **linear**, meaning that if A and B are linear operators, f and g functions, and k a constant, then

$$(A + B)f = Af + Bf, \quad A(f + g) = Af + Ag, \quad Ak = kA.$$

For both electromagnetic theory and quantum mechanics, an important class of operators are **differential operators**, those that include differentiation of the functions to which they are applied. These operators arise when differential equations are written in operator form;

for example, the operator

$$\mathcal{L}(x) = \left(1 - x^2\right)\frac{d^2}{dx^2} - 2x\frac{d}{dx}$$

enables us to write Legendre's differential equation,

$$\left(1 - x^2\right)\frac{d^2y}{dx^2} - 2x\frac{dy}{dx} + \lambda y = 0,$$

in the form $\mathcal{L}(y)y = -\lambda y$. When no confusion thereby results, this can be shortened to $\mathcal{L}y = -\lambda y$.

Commutation of Operators

Because differential operators act on the function(s) to their right, they do not necessarily commute with other operators containing the same independent variable. This fact makes it useful to consider the **commutator** of operators A and B,

$$[A, B] = AB - BA. \tag{5.42}$$

We can often reduce $AB - BA$ to a simpler operator expression. When we write an operator equation, its meaning is that the operator on the left-hand side of the equation produces the same effect on every function in its domain as is produced by the operator on the right-hand side. Let's illustrate this point by evaluating the commutator $[x, p]$, where $p = -i\,d/dx$. The imaginary unit i and the name p appear because this operator is that corresponding in quantum mechanics to momentum (in a system of units such that $\hbar = h/2\pi = 1$). The operator x stands for multiplication by x.

To carry out the evaluation, we apply $[x, p]$ to an arbitrary function $f(x)$. Inserting the explicit form of p, we have

$$[x, p]f(x) = (xp - px)f(x) = -ix\frac{df(x)}{dx} - \left(-i\frac{d}{dx}\right)\left(x\,f(x)\right)$$

$$= -ixf'(x) + i\left(f(x) + xf'(x)\right) = i\,f(x),$$

indicating that

$$[x, p] = i. \tag{5.43}$$

As indicated before, this means $[x, p]f(x) = i\,f(x)$ for all f.

We can carry out various algebraic manipulations on commutators. In general, if A, B, C are operators and k is a constant,

$$[A, B] = -[B, A], \qquad [A, B + C] = [A, B] + [A, C], \qquad k[A, B] = [kA, B] = [A, kB]. \tag{5.44}$$

Example 5.3.1   OPERATOR MANIPULATION

Given $[x, p]$, we can simplify the commutator $[x, p^2]$. We write, being careful about the operator ordering and using Eq. (5.43),

$$[x, p^2] = xp^2 - pxp + pxp - p^2x = [x, p]p + p[x, p] = 2i\,p, \qquad (5.45)$$

a result also obtainable from

$$x\left(-\frac{d^2}{dx^2}\right)f(x) - \left(-\frac{d^2}{dx^2}\right)xf(x) = 2f'(x) = 2i\left(-i\frac{d}{dx}\right)f(x).$$

However, note that Eq. (5.45) follows solely from the validity of Eq. (5.43), and will apply to any quantities x and p that satisfy that commutation relation, whether or not we are operating with ordinary functions and their derivatives. Put another way, if x and p are operators in some abstract Hilbert space and all we know about them is Eq. (5.43), we may still conclude that Eq. (5.45) is also valid. ∎

Identity, Inverse, Adjoint

An operator that is generally available is the **identity operator**, namely one that leaves functions unchanged. Depending on the context, this operator will be denoted either I or simply **1**. Some, but not all operators will have an inverse, namely an operator that will "undo" its effect. Letting A^{-1} denote the inverse of A, if A^{-1} exists, it will have the property

$$A^{-1}A = AA^{-1} = 1. \qquad (5.46)$$

Associated with many operators will be another operator, called its **adjoint** and denoted $A^\dagger$, which will be such that for all functions f and g in the Hilbert space,

$$\langle f|Ag\rangle = \langle A^\dagger f|g\rangle. \qquad (5.47)$$

Thus, we see that $A^\dagger$ is an operator that, applied to the left member of **any** scalar product, produces the same result as is obtained if A is applied to the right member of the same scalar product. Equation (5.47) is, in essence, the defining equation for $A^\dagger$.

Depending on the specific operator A, and the definitions in use of the Hilbert space and the scalar product, $A^\dagger$ may or may not be equal to A. If $A = A^\dagger$, A is referred to as **self-adjoint**, or equivalently, **Hermitian**. If $A^\dagger = -A$, A is called **anti-Hermitian**. This definition is worth emphasis:

$$\text{If } \quad H^\dagger = H, \quad H \text{ is Hermitian.} \qquad (5.48)$$

Another situation of frequent occurrence is that the adjoint of an operator is equal to its inverse, in which case the operator is called **unitary**. A unitary operator U is therefore defined by the following statement:

$$\text{If } \quad U^\dagger = U^{-1}, \quad U \text{ is unitary.} \qquad (5.49)$$

In the special case that U is both real and unitary, it is called **orthogonal**.

The reader will doubtless note that the nomenclature for operators is similar to that previously introduced for matrices. This is not accidental; we shall shortly develop correspondences between operator and matrix expressions.

Example 5.3.2   FINDING THE ADJOINT

Consider an operator $A = x(d/dx)$ whose domain is the Hilbert space whose members f have a finite value of $\langle f|f \rangle$ when the scalar product has definition

$$\langle f|g \rangle = \int\limits_{-\infty}^{\infty} f^*(x)g(x)\,dx.$$

This space is often referred to as $\mathcal{L}^2$ on $(-\infty, \infty)$. Starting from $\langle f|A\,g \rangle$, we integrate by parts as needed to move the operator out of the right half of the scalar product. Because f and g must vanish at $\pm\infty$, the integrated terms vanish, and we get

$$\langle f|A\,g \rangle = \int\limits_{-\infty}^{\infty} f^* x \frac{dg}{dx}\,dx = \int\limits_{-\infty}^{\infty} (xf^*) \frac{dg}{dx}\,dx = -\int\limits_{-\infty}^{\infty} \frac{d(xf^*)}{dx} g\,dx$$

$$= \left\langle -\left(\frac{d}{dx}\right) xf \,\middle|\, g \right\rangle.$$

We see from the above that $A^\dagger = -(d/dx)x$, from which we can find $A^\dagger = -A - 1$. This A is clearly neither Hermitian nor unitary (with the specified definition of the scalar product). ∎

Example 5.3.3   ADJOINT DEPENDS ON SCALAR PRODUCT

For the Hilbert space and scalar product of Example 5.3.2, an integration by parts easily establishes that an operator $A = -i(d/dx)$ is self-adjoint, i.e., $A^\dagger = A$. But now let's consider the same operator A, but for the $\mathcal{L}^2$ space with $-1 \le x \le 1$ (and with a scalar product of the same form, but with integration limits ± 1). In this space, the integrated terms from the integration by parts do not vanish, but we can incorporate them into an operator on the left half of the scalar product by adding delta-function terms:

$$\left\langle f \,\middle|\, -i\frac{d}{dx} \,\middle|\, g \right\rangle = -if^*g \,\Big|_{-1}^{1} + \int\limits_{-1}^{1} \left(-i\frac{df}{dx}\right)^* g\,dx$$

$$= \int\limits_{-1}^{1} \left(\left[i\delta(x-1) - i\delta(x+1) - i\frac{d}{dx}\right] f(x)\right)^* g(x)\,dx.$$

In this truncated space the operator A is **not** self-adjoint. ∎

Basis Expansions of Operators

Because we are dealing only with linear operators, we can write the effect of an operator on an arbitrary function if we know the result of its action on all members of a basis spanning our Hilbert space. In particular, assume that the action of an operator A on member φ_μ of an orthonormal basis has the result, also expanded in that basis,

$$A\varphi_\mu = \sum_\nu a_{\nu\mu}\varphi_\nu. \tag{5.50}$$

Assuming this form for the result of operation with A is not a major restriction; all it says is that the result is in our Hilbert space. Formally, the coefficients $a_{\nu\mu}$ can be obtained by taking scalar products:

$$a_{\nu\mu} = \langle \varphi_\nu | A\varphi_\mu \rangle = \langle \varphi_\nu | A | \varphi_\mu \rangle. \tag{5.51}$$

Following common usage, we have inserted an optional (operationally meaningless) vertical line between A and φ_μ. This notation has the aesthetic effect of separating the operator from the two functions entering the scalar product, and also emphasizes the possibility that instead of evaluating the scalar product as written, we can without changing its value evaluate it using the adjoint of A, as $\langle A^\dagger \varphi_\nu | \varphi_\mu \rangle$.

We now apply Eq. (5.50) to a function ψ whose expansion in the φ basis is

$$\psi = \sum_\mu c_\mu \varphi_\mu, \quad c_\mu = \langle \varphi_\mu | \psi \rangle. \tag{5.52}$$

The result is

$$A\psi = \sum_\mu c_\mu\, A\varphi_\mu = \sum_\mu c_\mu \sum_\nu a_{\nu\mu}\varphi_\nu = \sum_\nu \left(\sum_\mu a_{\nu\mu} c_\mu \right) \varphi_\nu. \tag{5.53}$$

If we think of $A\psi$ as a function χ in our Hilbert space, with expansion

$$\chi = \sum_\nu b_\nu \varphi_\nu, \tag{5.54}$$

we then see from Eq. (5.53) that the coefficients b_ν are related to c_μ and $a_{\nu\mu}$ in a way corresponding to matrix multiplication. To make this more concrete,

- Define $\mathbf{c}$ as a column vector with elements c_i, representing the function ψ,
- Define $\mathbf{b}$ as a column vector with elements b_i, representing the function χ,
- Define A as a matrix with elements a_{ij}, representing the operator A,
- The operator equation $\chi = A\psi$ then corresponds to the matrix equation $\mathbf{b} = \mathsf{A}\mathbf{c}$.

In other words, the expansion of the result of applying A to any function ψ can be computed (by matrix multiplication) from the expansions of A and ψ. In effect, that means that the operator A can be thought of as completely defined by its **matrix elements**, while ψ and $\chi = A\psi$ are completely characterized by their coefficients.

We obtain an interesting expression if we introduce Dirac notation for all the quantities entering Eq. (5.53). We then have, moving the ket representing φ_ν to the left,

$$A\psi = \sum_{\nu\mu} |\varphi_\nu\rangle\langle\varphi_\nu|A|\varphi_\mu\rangle\langle\varphi_\mu|\psi\rangle, \qquad (5.55)$$

which leads us to identify A as

$$A = \sum_{\nu\mu} |\varphi_\nu\rangle\langle\varphi_\nu|A|\varphi_\mu\rangle\langle\varphi_\mu|, \qquad (5.56)$$

which we note is nothing other than A, multiplied on each side by a resolution of the identity, of the form given in Eq. (5.32).

Another interesting observation results if we reintroduce into Eq. (5.56) the coefficient $a_{\nu\mu}$, bringing us to

$$A = \sum_{\nu\mu} |\varphi_\nu\rangle a_{\nu\mu}\langle\varphi_\mu|. \qquad (5.57)$$

Here we have the general form for an operator A, with a specific behavior that is determined entirely by the set of coefficients $a_{\nu\mu}$. The special case $A = 1$ has already been seen to be of the form of Eq. (5.57) with $a_{\nu\mu} = \delta_{\nu\mu}$.

Example 5.3.4   MATRIX ELEMENTS OF AN OPERATOR

Consider the expansion of the operator x in a basis consisting of functions $\varphi_n(x) = C_n H_n(x)e^{-x^2/2}$, $n = 0, 1, \ldots$, where the H_n are Hermite polynomials, with scalar product

$$\langle f|g\rangle = \int\limits_{-\infty}^{\infty} f^*(x)g(x)\,dx.$$

From Table 5.1, we can see that the φ_n are orthogonal and that they will also be normalized if $C_n = (2^n n!\sqrt{\pi})^{-1/2}$. The matrix elements of x, which we denote $x_{\nu\mu}$ and are written collectively as a matrix denoted x, are given by

$$x_{\nu\mu} = \langle\varphi_\nu|x|\varphi_\mu\rangle = C_\nu C_\mu \int\limits_{-\infty}^{\infty} H_\nu(x)\, x\, H_\mu(x)e^{-x^2}\,dx.$$

The integral leading to $x_{\nu\mu}$ can be evaluated in general by using the properties of the Hermite polynomials, but our present purposes are adequately served by a straightforward case-by-case computation. From the table of Hermite polynomials in Table 18.1, we identify

$$H_0 = 1, \quad H_1 = 2x, \quad H_2 = 4x^2 - 2, \quad H_3 = 8x^3 - 12x, \quad \ldots,$$

and we take note of the integration formula

$$I_n = \int\limits_{-\infty}^{\infty} x^{2n}e^{-x^2}\,dx = \frac{(2n-1)!!\sqrt{\pi}}{2^n}.$$

Making use of the parity (even/odd symmetry) of the H_n and the fact that the matrix x is symmetric, we note that many matrix elements are either zero or equal to others. We illustrate with the explicit computation of one matrix element, x_{12}:

$$x_{12} = C_1 C_2 \int\limits_{-\infty}^{\infty} (2x)x(4x^2 - 2)e^{-x^2} \, dx = C_1 C_2 \int\limits_{-\infty}^{\infty} (8x^4 - 4x^2)e^{-x^2} \, dx$$

$$= C_1 C_2 \Big[8I_2 - 4I_1 \Big] = 1.$$

Evaluating other matrix elements, we find that x, the matrix of x, has the form

$$\mathsf{x} = \begin{pmatrix} 0 & \sqrt{2}/2 & 0 & 0 & \cdots \\ \sqrt{2}/2 & 0 & 1 & 0 & \cdots \\ 0 & 1 & 0 & \sqrt{6}/2 & \cdots \\ 0 & 0 & \sqrt{6}/2 & 0 & \cdots \\ \cdots & \cdots & \cdots & \cdots & \cdots \end{pmatrix}. \tag{5.58}$$

Basis Expansion of Adjoint

We now look at the adjoint of our operator A as an expansion in the same basis. Our starting point is the definition of the adjoint. For arbitrary functions ψ and χ,

$$\langle \psi | A | \chi \rangle = \langle A^\dagger \psi | \chi \rangle = \langle \chi | A^\dagger | \psi \rangle^*,$$

where we reached the last member of the equation by using the complex conjugation property of the scalar product. This is equivalent to

$$\langle \chi | A^\dagger | \psi \rangle = \langle \psi | A | \chi \rangle^* = \left[\langle \psi | \left(\sum_{\nu\mu} |\varphi_\nu\rangle a_{\nu\mu} \langle \varphi_\mu | \right) | \chi \rangle \right]^*$$

$$= \sum_{\nu\mu} \langle \psi | \varphi_\nu \rangle^* a_{\nu\mu}^* \langle \varphi_\mu | \chi \rangle^*$$

$$= \sum_{\nu\mu} \langle \chi | \varphi_\mu \rangle a_{\nu\mu}^* \langle \varphi_\nu | \psi \rangle, \tag{5.59}$$

where in the last line we have again used the scalar product complex conjugation property and have reordered the factors in the sum.

We are now in a position to note that Eq. (5.59) corresponds to

$$A^\dagger = \sum_{\nu\mu} |\varphi_\nu\rangle a_{\mu\nu}^* \langle \varphi_\mu |. \tag{5.60}$$

In writing Eq. (5.60) we have changed the dummy indices to make the formula as similar as possible to Eq. (5.57). It is important to note the differences: The coefficient $a_{\nu\mu}$ of Eq. (5.57) has been replaced by $a_{\mu\nu}^*$, so we see that the index order has been reversed and the complex conjugate taken. This is the general recipe for forming the basis set expansion of the adjoint of an operator. The relation between the matrix elements of A and of $A^\dagger$ is exactly that which relates a matrix A to its adjoint $A^\dagger$, showing that the similarity in nomenclature is purposeful. We thus have the important and general result:

- If A is the matrix representing an operator A, then the operator $A^\dagger$, the adjoint of A, is represented by the matrix $A^\dagger$.

Example 5.3.5   ADJOINT OF SPIN OPERATOR

Consider a spin space spanned by functions we call α and β, with a scalar product completely defined by the equations $\langle \alpha | \alpha \rangle = \langle \beta | \beta \rangle = 1$, $\langle \alpha | \beta \rangle = 0$. An operator B is such that

$$B\alpha = 0, \quad B\beta = \alpha.$$

Taking all possible linearly independent scalar products, this means that

$$\langle \alpha | B\alpha \rangle = 0, \quad \langle \beta | B\alpha \rangle = 0, \quad \langle \alpha | B\beta \rangle = 1, \quad \langle \beta | B\beta \rangle = 0.$$

It is therefore necessary that

$$\langle B^\dagger \alpha | \alpha \rangle = 0, \quad \langle B^\dagger \beta | \alpha \rangle = 0, \quad \langle B^\dagger \alpha | \beta \rangle = 1, \quad \langle B^\dagger \beta | \beta \rangle = 0,$$

which means that $B^\dagger$ is an operator such that

$$B^\dagger \alpha = \beta, \quad B^\dagger \beta = 0.$$

The above equations correspond to the matrices

$$\mathsf{B} = \begin{pmatrix} 0 & 1 \\ 0 & 0 \end{pmatrix}, \quad \mathsf{B}^\dagger = \begin{pmatrix} 0 & 0 \\ 1 & 0 \end{pmatrix}.$$

We see that $\mathsf{B}^\dagger$ is the adjoint of B, as required.   ∎

Functions of Operators

Our ability to represent operators by matrices also implies that the observations made in Chapter 3 regarding functions of matrices also apply to linear operators. Thus, we have definite meanings for quantities such as $\exp(A)$, $\sin(A)$, or $\cos(A)$, and can also apply to operators various identities involving matrix commutators. Important examples include the Jacobi identity (Exercise 2.2.7), and the Baker-Hausdorff formula, Eq. (2.85).

Exercises

5.3.1   Show (without introducing matrix representations) that the adjoint of the adjoint of an operator restores the original operator, i.e., that $(A^\dagger)^\dagger = A$.

5.3.2 U and V are two arbitrary operators. Without introducing matrix representations of these operators, show that

$$(UV)^\dagger = V^\dagger U^\dagger.$$

Note the resemblance to adjoint matrices.

5.3.3   Consider a Hilbert space spanned by the three functions $\varphi_1 = x_1$, $\varphi_2 = x_2$, $\varphi_3 = x_3$, and a scalar product defined by $\langle x_\nu | x_\mu \rangle = \delta_{\nu\mu}$.

(a)   Form the 3×3 matrix of each of the following operators:

$$A_1 = \sum_{i=1}^{3} x_i \left(\frac{\partial}{\partial x_i} \right), \quad A_2 = x_1 \left(\frac{\partial}{\partial x_2} \right) - x_2 \left(\frac{\partial}{\partial x_1} \right).$$

(b)   Form the column vector representing $\psi = x_1 - 2x_2 + 3x_3$.

(c)   Form the matrix equation corresponding to $\chi = (A_1 - A_2)\psi$ and verify that the matrix equation reproduces the result obtained by direct application of $A_1 - A_2$ to ψ.

5.3.4   (a)   Obtain the matrix representation of $A = x(d/dx)$ in a basis of Legendre polynomials, keeping terms through P_3. Use the orthonormal forms of these polynomials as given in 5.2.1 and the scalar product defined there.

(b)   Expand x^3 in the orthonormal Legendre polynomial basis.

(c)   Verify that Ax^3 is given correctly by its matrix representation.

5.4   SELF-ADJOINT OPERATORS

Operators that are self-adjoint (Hermitian) are of particular importance in quantum mechanics because observable quantities are associated with Hermitian operators. In particular, the average value of an observable A in a quantum mechanical state described by any normalized wave function ψ is given by the **expectation value** of A, defined as

$$\langle A \rangle = \langle \psi | A | \psi \rangle. \tag{5.61}$$

This, of course, only makes sense if it can be assured that $\langle A \rangle$ is real, even if ψ and/or A is complex. Using the fact that A is postulated to be Hermitian, we take the complex conjugate of $\langle A \rangle$:

$$\langle A \rangle^* = \langle \psi | A | \psi \rangle^* = \langle A\psi | \psi \rangle,$$

which reduces to $\langle A \rangle$ because A is self-adjoint.

We have already seen that if A and $A^\dagger$ are expanded in a basis, the matrix $A^\dagger$ must be the matrix adjoint of the matrix A. This means that the coefficients in its expansion must satisfy

$$a_{\nu\mu} = a_{\mu\nu}^* \quad \text{(coefficients of self-adjoint } A\text{)}.$$

Thus, we have the nearly self-evident result: A matrix representing a Hermitian operator is a Hermitian matrix. It is also obvious from Eq. (5.62) that the diagonal elements of a Hermitian matrix (which are expectation values for the basis functions) are real.

We can easily verify from basis expansions that $\langle A \rangle$ must be real. Letting **c** be the vector of expansion coefficients of ψ in the basis for which $a_{\nu\mu}$ are the matrix elements of A, then

$$\langle A \rangle = \langle \psi | A | \psi \rangle = \left\langle \sum_\nu c_\nu \varphi_\nu \left| A \right| \sum_\mu c_\mu \varphi_\mu \right\rangle = \sum_{\nu\mu} c_\nu^* \langle \varphi_\nu | A | \varphi_\mu \rangle c_\mu$$

$$= \sum_{\nu\mu} c_\nu^* a_{\nu\mu} c_\mu = \mathbf{c}^\dagger \mathbf{A} \mathbf{c},$$

which reduces, as it must, to a scalar. Because A is a self-adjoint matrix, $\mathbf{c}^\dagger \mathbf{A} \mathbf{c}$ is easily seen to be a self-adjoint 1×1 matrix, i.e., a **real** scalar (use the facts that $(\mathbf{BAC})^\dagger = \mathbf{C}^\dagger \mathbf{A}^\dagger \mathbf{B}^\dagger$ and that $\mathbf{A}^\dagger = \mathbf{A}$).

Example 5.4.1   SOME SELF-ADJOINT OPERATORS

Consider the operators x and p introduced earlier, with a scalar product of definition

$$\langle f | g \rangle = \int\limits_{-\infty}^{\infty} f^*(x) g(x)\, dx, \tag{5.63}$$

where our Hilbert space is the set of all functions f for which $\langle f | f \rangle$ exists (i.e., $\langle f | f \rangle$ is finite). This is the $\mathcal{L}^2$ space on the interval $(-\infty, \infty)$. To test whether x is self-adjoint, we compare $\langle f | xg \rangle$ and $\langle xf | g \rangle$. Writing these out as integrals, we consider

$$\int\limits_{-\infty}^{\infty} f^*(x) x\, g(x)\, dx \quad \text{vs.} \quad \int\limits_{-\infty}^{\infty} [xf(x)]^* g(x)\, dx.$$

Because the order of ordinary functions (including x) can be changed without affecting the value of an integral, and because x is inherently real, these two expressions are equal and x is self-adjoint.

Turning next to $p = -i(d/dx)$, the comparison we must make is

$$\int\limits_{-\infty}^{\infty} f^*(x) \left[-i \frac{d\,g(x)}{dx} \right] dx \quad \text{vs.} \quad \int\limits_{-\infty}^{\infty} \left[-i \frac{df(x)}{dx} \right]^* g(x)\, dx. \tag{5.64}$$

We can bring these expressions into better correspondence if we integrate the first by parts, differentiating $f^*(x)$ and integrating $dg(x)/dx$. Doing so, the first expression above becomes

$$\int\limits_{-\infty}^{\infty} f^*(x) \left[-i \frac{d\,g(x)}{dx} \right] dx = -i f^*(x) g(x) \Big|_{-\infty}^{\infty} - \int\limits_{-\infty}^{\infty} \left[\frac{df(x)}{dx} \right]^* \left[-i g(x) \right] dx.$$

The boundary terms to be evaluated at $\pm\infty$ must vanish because $\langle f|f\rangle$ and $\langle g|g\rangle$ are finite, which assures also (from the Schwarz inequality) that $\langle f|g\rangle$ is finite as well. Upon moving i within the complex conjugate in the remaining integral, we verify agreement with the second expression in Eq. (5.64). Thus both x and p are self-adjoint. Note that if p had not contained the factor i, it would **not** have been self-adjoint, as we obtained a needed sign change when i was moved within the scope of the complex conjugate.   ∎

Example 5.4.2   EXPECTATION VALUE OF p

Because p, though Hermitian, is also imaginary, consider what happens when we compute its expectation value for a wave function of the form $\psi(x) = e^{i\theta} f(x)$, where $f(x)$ is a real $\mathcal{L}^2$ wave function and θ is a real phase angle. Using the scalar product as defined in Eq. (5.63), and remembering that $p = -i(d/dx)$, we have

$$\langle p \rangle = -i \int\limits_{-\infty}^{\infty} f(x) \frac{df(x)}{dx}\, dx = -\frac{i}{2} \int\limits_{-\infty}^{\infty} \frac{d}{dx}\Big[f(x) \Big]^2 dx$$

$$= -\frac{i}{2}\Big[f(+\infty)^2 - f(-\infty)^2 \Big] = 0.$$

As shown, this integral vanishes because $f(x) = 0$ at $\pm\infty$ (this is fortunate because expectation values must be real). This result corresponds to the well-known property that wave functions that describe time-dependent phenomena (nonzero momentum) cannot either be real or real except for a constant (complex) phase factor.   ∎

The relations between operators and their adjoints provide opportunities for rearrangements of operator expressions that may facilitate their evaluation. Some examples follow.

Example 5.4.3   OPERATOR EXPRESSIONS

(a) Suppose we wish to evaluate $\langle (x^2 + p^2)\psi|\varphi \rangle$, with ψ of a complicated functional form that might be unpleasant to differentiate (as required to apply p^2), whereas φ is simple. Because x is self-adjoint, so also is x^2:

$$\langle x^2\psi|\varphi\rangle = \langle x\psi|x\varphi\rangle = \langle \psi|x^2\varphi\rangle.$$

The same is true of p^2, so $\langle (x^2 + p^2)\psi|\varphi\rangle = \langle \psi|(x^2 + p^2)\varphi\rangle$.

(b) Look next at $\langle (x+ip)\psi|(x+ip)\psi\rangle$, which is the expression to be evaluated if we want the norm of $(x+ip)\psi$. Note that $x + ip$ is **not** self-adjoint, but has adjoint $x - ip$. Our norm rearranges to

$$\langle (x+ip)\psi|(x+ip)\psi\rangle = \langle \psi|(x-ip)(x+ip)|\psi\rangle$$

$$= \langle \psi|x^2 + p^2 + i(xp - px)|\psi\rangle$$

$$= \langle \psi|x^2 + p^2 + i(i)|\psi\rangle = \langle \psi|x^2 + p^2 - 1|\psi\rangle.$$

To reach the last line of the above equation, we recognized the commutator $[x, p] = i$, as established in Eq. (5.43).

(c)   Suppose that A and B are self-adjoint. What can we say about the self-adjointness of AB? Consider

$$\langle \psi | AB | \varphi \rangle = \langle A\psi | B | \varphi \rangle = \langle BA\psi | \varphi \rangle.$$

Note that because we moved A to the left first (with no dagger needed because it is self-adjoint), it is part of what the subsequently moved B must operate on. So we see that the adjoint of AB is BA. We conclude that AB is only self-adjoint if A and B commute (so that $BA = AB$). Note that if A and B were not individually self-adjoint, their commutation would not be sufficient to make AB self-adjoint.   ∎

Exercises

5.4.1   (a) A is a non-Hermitian operator. Show that the operators $A + A^\dagger$ and $i(A - A^\dagger)$ are Hermitian.

(b)   Using the preceding result, show that every non-Hermitian operator may be written as a linear combination of two Hermitian operators.

5.4.2   Prove that the product of two Hermitian operators is Hermitian if and only if the two operators commute.

5.4.3 A and B are noncommuting quantum mechanical operators, and C is given by the formula

$$AB - BA = iC.$$

Show that C is Hermitian. Assume that appropriate boundary conditions are satisfied.

5.4.4   The operator $\mathcal{L}$ is Hermitian. Show that $\langle \mathcal{L}^2 \rangle \geq 0$, meaning that for all ψ in the space in which $\mathcal{L}$ is defined, $\langle \psi | \mathcal{L}^2 | \psi \rangle \geq 0$.

5.4.5   Consider a Hilbert space whose members are functions defined on the surface of the unit sphere, with a scalar product of the form

$$\langle f | g \rangle = \int d\Omega \, f^* g,$$

where $d\Omega$ is the element of solid angle. Note that the total solid angle of the sphere is 4π. We work here with the three functions $\varphi_1 = Cx/r$, $\varphi_2 = Cy/r$, $\varphi_3 = Cz/r$, with C assigned a value that makes the φ_i normalized.

(a)   Find C, and show that the φ_i are also mutually orthogonal.

(b)   Form the 3×3 matrices of the angular momentum operators

$$L_x = -i \left(y \frac{\partial}{\partial z} - z \frac{\partial}{\partial y} \right), \quad L_y = -i \left(z \frac{\partial}{\partial x} - x \frac{\partial}{\partial z} \right),$$

$$L_z = -i \left(x \frac{\partial}{\partial y} - y \frac{\partial}{\partial x} \right).$$

(c) Verify that the matrix representations of the components of **L** satisfy the angular momentum commutator $[L_x, L_y] = i L_z$.

5.5 UNITARY OPERATORS

One of the reasons unitary operators are important in physics is that they can be used to describe transformations between orthonormal bases. This property is the generalization to the complex domain of the rotational transformations of ordinary (physical) vectors that we analyzed in Chapter 3.

Unitary Transformations

Suppose we have a function ψ that has been expanded in the orthonormal basis φ:

$$\psi = \sum_\mu c_\mu \varphi_\mu = \left(\sum_\mu |\varphi_\mu\rangle\langle\varphi_\mu| \right) |\psi\rangle. \tag{5.65}$$

We now wish to convert this expansion to a different orthonormal basis, with functions φ'_ν. A possible starting point is to recognize that each of the original basis functions can be expanded in the primed basis. We can obtain the expansion by inserting a resolution of the identity in the primed basis:

$$\varphi_\mu = \sum_\nu u_{\nu\mu} \varphi'_\nu = \left(\sum_\nu |\varphi'_\nu\rangle\langle\varphi'_\nu| \right) |\varphi_\mu\rangle = \sum_\nu \langle\varphi'_\nu|\varphi_\mu\rangle \varphi'_\nu. \tag{5.66}$$

Comparing the second and fourth members of this equation, we identify $u_{\nu\mu}$ as the elements of a matrix U:

$$u_{\nu\mu} = \langle\varphi'_\nu|\varphi_\mu\rangle. \tag{5.67}$$

Note how the use of resolutions of the identity makes these formulas obvious, and that Eqs. (5.65) to (5.67) are only valid because the φ_μ and the φ'_ν are complete orthonormal sets.

Inserting the expansion for φ_μ from Eq. (5.66) into Eq. (5.65), we reach

$$\psi = \sum_\mu c_\mu \sum_\nu u_{\nu\mu} \varphi'_\nu = \sum_\nu \left(\sum_\mu u_{\nu\mu} c_\mu \right) \varphi'_\nu = c'_\nu \varphi'_\nu, \tag{5.68}$$

where the coefficients c'_ν of the expansion in the primed basis form a column vector $\mathbf{c}'$ that is related to the coefficient vector $\mathbf{c}$ in the unprimed basis by the matrix equation

$$\mathbf{c}' = \mathsf{U}\,\mathbf{c}, \tag{5.69}$$

with U the matrix whose elements are given in Eq. (5.67).

If we now consider the reverse transformation, **from** an expansion in the primed basis **to** one in the unprimed basis, starting from

$$\varphi'_\mu = \sum_\nu v_{\nu\mu} \varphi_\nu = \sum_\nu \langle\varphi_\nu|\varphi'_\mu\rangle \varphi_\nu, \tag{5.70}$$

we see that V, the matrix of the transformation inverse to U, has elements

$$v_{\nu\mu} = \langle \varphi_\nu | \varphi'_\mu \rangle = (U^*)_{\mu\nu} = (U^\dagger)_{\nu\mu}. \tag{5.71}$$

In other words,

$$V = U^\dagger. \tag{5.72}$$

If we now transform the expansion of ψ, given in the unprimed basis by the coefficient vector **c**, first to the primed basis and then back to the original unprimed basis, the coefficients will transform, first to **c'** and then back to **c**, according to

$$\mathbf{c} = V\,U\,\mathbf{c} = U^\dagger U\,\mathbf{c}. \tag{5.73}$$

In order for Eq. (5.73) to be consistent it is necessary that $U^\dagger U$ be a unit matrix, meaning that U must be **unitary**. We thus have the important following result:

> *The transformation that converts the expansion of a vector* **c** *in any orthonormal basis* $\{\varphi_\mu\}$ *to its expansion* **c'** *in any other orthonormal basis* $\{\varphi'_\nu\}$ *is described by the matrix equation* $\mathbf{c'} = U\mathbf{c}$, *where the transformation matrix* U *is* **unitary** *and has elements* $u_{\nu\mu} = \langle \varphi'_\nu | \varphi_\mu \rangle$. *A transformation between orthonormal bases is called a* **unitary transformation**.

Equation (5.69) is a direct generalization of the ordinary 2-D vector rotational transformation equation, Eq. (3.26),

$$\mathbf{A'} = \mathbf{S}\mathbf{A}.$$

For further emphasis, we compare the transformation matrix U introduced here (at right, below) with the matrix S (at left) from Eq. (3.28), for rotations in ordinary 2-D space:

$$\mathbf{S} = \begin{pmatrix} \hat{\mathbf{e}}'_1 \cdot \hat{\mathbf{e}}_1 & \hat{\mathbf{e}}'_1 \cdot \hat{\mathbf{e}}_2 \\ \hat{\mathbf{e}}'_2 \cdot \hat{\mathbf{e}}_1 & \hat{\mathbf{e}}'_2 \cdot \hat{\mathbf{e}}_2 \end{pmatrix} \quad \mathbf{U} = \begin{pmatrix} \langle \varphi'_1 | \varphi_1 \rangle & \langle \varphi'_1 | \varphi_2 \rangle & \cdots \\ \langle \varphi'_2 | \varphi_1 \rangle & \langle \varphi'_2 | \varphi_2 \rangle & \cdots \\ \cdots & \cdots & \cdots \end{pmatrix}.$$

The resemblance becomes even more striking if we recognize that in Dirac notation, the quantities $\hat{\mathbf{e}}'_i \cdot \hat{\mathbf{e}}_j$ assume the form $\langle \hat{\mathbf{e}}'_i | \hat{\mathbf{e}}_j \rangle$.

As for ordinary vectors (except that the quantities involved here are complex), the ith row of U contains the (complex conjugated) components (a.k.a. coefficients) of φ'_i in terms of the unprimed basis; the orthonormality of the primed φ is consistent with the fact that $UU^\dagger$ is a unit matrix. The columns of U contain the components of the φ_j in terms of the primed basis; that also is analogous to our earlier observations. The matrix S is orthogonal; U is unitary, which is the generalization to a complex space of the orthogonality condition.

Summarizing, we see that unitary transformations are analogous, in vector spaces, to the orthogonal transformations that describe rotations (or reflections) in ordinary space.

Example 5.5.1   A Unitary Transformation

A Hilbert space is spanned by five functions defined on the surface of a unit sphere and expressed in spherical polar coordinates θ, φ:

$$\chi_1 = \sqrt{\frac{15}{4\pi}} \sin\theta \cos\theta \cos\varphi, \quad \chi_2 = \sqrt{\frac{15}{4\pi}} \sin\theta \cos\theta \sin\varphi,$$

$$\chi_3 = \sqrt{\frac{15}{4\pi}} \sin^2\theta \sin\varphi \cos\varphi, \quad \chi_4 = \sqrt{\frac{15}{16\pi}} \sin^2\theta (\cos^2\varphi - \sin^2\varphi),$$

$$\chi_5 = \sqrt{\frac{5}{16\pi}} (3\cos^2\theta - 1).$$

These are orthonormal when the scalar product is defined as

$$\langle f|g \rangle = \int\limits_0^\pi \sin\theta \, d\theta \int\limits_0^{2\pi} d\varphi \, f^*(\theta, \varphi) \, g(\theta, \varphi).$$

This Hilbert space can alternatively be spanned by the orthonormal set of functions

$$\chi_1' = -\sqrt{\frac{15}{8\pi}} \sin\theta \cos\theta \, e^{i\varphi}, \quad \chi_2' = \sqrt{\frac{15}{8\pi}} \sin\theta \cos\theta \, e^{-i\varphi},$$

$$\chi_3' = \sqrt{\frac{15}{32\pi}} \sin^2\theta \, e^{2i\varphi}, \quad \chi_4' = \sqrt{\frac{15}{32\pi}} \sin^2\theta \, e^{-2i\varphi},$$

$$\chi_5' = \chi_5.$$

The matrix U describing the transformation from the unprimed to the primed basis has elements $u_{\nu\mu} = \langle \chi_\nu' | \chi_\mu \rangle$. Working out a representative matrix element,

$$u_{22} = \langle \chi_2' | \chi_2 \rangle = \frac{15}{4\pi\sqrt{2}} \int\limits_0^\pi \sin\theta \, d\theta \int\limits_0^{2\pi} d\varphi \, \sin^2\theta \cos^2\theta \, e^{+i\varphi} \sin\varphi$$

$$= \frac{15}{4\pi\sqrt{2}} \int\limits_0^\pi \sin^3\theta \cos^2\theta \, d\theta \int\limits_0^{2\pi} d\varphi \, e^{+i\varphi} \frac{e^{i\varphi} - e^{-i\varphi}}{2i}$$

$$= \frac{15}{4\pi\sqrt{2}} \left(\frac{4}{15} \right) \frac{-2\pi}{2i} = \frac{i}{\sqrt{2}}.$$

We obtained this result by using the formula $\int_0^{2\pi} e^{ni\varphi} \, d\varphi = 2\pi \, \delta_{n0}$ and by looking up a tabulated value for the θ integral. We evaluate explicitly one more matrix element:

$$u_{21} = \langle \chi_2' | \chi_1 \rangle = \frac{15}{4\pi\sqrt{2}} \int_0^\pi \sin^3 \theta \cos^2 \theta \, d\theta \int_0^{2\pi} d\varphi \, e^{+i\varphi} \frac{e^{i\varphi} + e^{-i\varphi}}{2}$$

$$= \frac{15}{4\pi\sqrt{2}} \left(\frac{4}{15}\right) \frac{2\pi}{2} = \frac{1}{\sqrt{2}}.$$

Evaluating the remaining elements of U, we reach

$$\mathsf{U} = \begin{pmatrix} -1/\sqrt{2} & -i/\sqrt{2} & 0 & 0 & 0 \\ 1/\sqrt{2} & -i/\sqrt{2} & 0 & 0 & 0 \\ 0 & 0 & i/\sqrt{2} & 1/\sqrt{2} & 0 \\ 0 & 0 & -i/\sqrt{2} & 1/\sqrt{2} & 0 \\ 0 & 0 & 0 & 0 & 1 \end{pmatrix}.$$

As a check, note that the ith column of U should yield the components of χ_i in the primed basis. For the first column, we have

$$\sqrt{\frac{15}{4\pi}} \sin\theta \cos\theta \cos\varphi = -\frac{1}{\sqrt{2}} \left(-\sqrt{\frac{15}{8\pi}} \sin\theta \cos\theta \, e^{i\varphi}\right) + \frac{1}{\sqrt{2}} \left(\sqrt{\frac{15}{8\pi}} \sin\theta \cos\theta \, e^{-i\varphi}\right),$$

which simplifies easily to an identity. Further checks are left as Exercise 5.5.1. ∎

Successive Transformations

It is possible to make two or more successive unitary transformations, each of which will convert an input orthonormal basis to an output basis that is also orthonormal. Just as for ordinary vectors, the successive transformations are applied in right-to-left order, and the product of the transformations can be viewed as a resultant unitary transformation.

Exercises

5.5.1   Show that the matrix U of Example 5.5.1 correctly transforms the vector $f(\theta, \varphi) = 3\chi_1 + 2i\chi_2 - \chi_3 + \chi_5$ to the $\{\chi_i'\}$ basis by

(a) (1) Making a column vector **c** that represents $f(\theta, \varphi)$ in the $\{\chi_i\}$ basis,

   (2) forming $\mathbf{c}' = \mathsf{U}\mathbf{c}$, and

   (3) comparing the expansion $\sum_i c_i' \chi_i'(\theta, \varphi)$ with $f(\theta, \varphi)$;

(b) Verifying that U is unitary.

5.5.2   (a) Given (in $\mathbb{R}^3$) the basis $\varphi_1 = x$, $\varphi_2 = y$, $\varphi_3 = z$, consider the basis transformation $x \to z$, $y \to y$, $z \to -x$. Find the 3×3 matrix U for this transformation.

(b) This transformation corresponds to a rotation of the coordinate axes. Identify the rotation and reconcile your transformation matrix with an appropriate matrix $S(\alpha, \beta, \gamma)$ of the form given in Eq. (3.37).

(c) Form the column vector $\mathbf{c}$ representing (in the original basis) $f = 2x - 3y + z$, find the result of applying U to $\mathbf{c}$, and show that this is consistent with the basis transformation of part (a).

Note. You do not need to be able to form scalar products to handle this exercise; a knowledge of the linear relationship between the original and transformed functions is sufficient.

5.5.3   Construct the matrix representing the inverse of the transformation in Exercise 5.5.2, and show that this matrix and the transformation matrix of that exercise are matrix inverses of each other.

5.5.4   The unitary transformation U that converts an orthonormal basis $\{\varphi_i\}$ into the basis $\{\varphi_i'\}$ and the unitary transformation V that converts the basis $\{\varphi_i'\}$ into the basis $\{\chi_i\}$ have matrix representations

$$U = \begin{pmatrix} i\sin\theta & \cos\theta & 0 \\ -\cos\theta & i\sin\theta & 0 \\ 0 & 0 & 1 \end{pmatrix}, \quad V = \begin{pmatrix} 1 & 0 & 0 \\ 0 & \cos\theta & i\sin\theta \\ 0 & \cos\theta & -i\sin\theta \end{pmatrix}.$$

Given the function $f(x) = 3\varphi_1(x) - \varphi_2(x) - 2\varphi_3(x)$,

(a) By applying U, form the vector representing $f(x)$ in the $\{\varphi_i'\}$ basis and then by applying V form the vector representing $f(x)$ in the $\{\chi_i\}$ basis. Use this result to write $f(x)$ as a linear combination of the χ_i.

(b) Form the matrix products UV and VU and then apply each to the vector representing $f(x)$ in the $\{\varphi_i\}$ basis. Verify that the results of these applications differ and that only one of them gives the result corresponding to part (a).

5.5.5   Three functions which are orthogonal with unit weight on the range $-1 \leq x \leq 1$ are $P_0 = 1$, $P_1 = x$, and $P_2 = \frac{3}{2}x^2 - \frac{1}{2}$. Another set of functions that are orthogonal and span the same space are $F_0 = x^2$, $F_1 = x$, $F_2 = 5x^2 - 3$. Although much of this exercise can be done by inspection, write down and evaluate all the integrals that lead to the results when they are obtained in terms of scalar products.

(a) Normalize each of the P_i and F_i.

(b) Find the unitary matrix U that transforms from the normalized P_i basis to the normalized F_i basis.

(c) Find the unitary matrix V that transforms from the normalized F_i basis to the normalized P_i basis.

(d) Show that U and V are unitary, and that $V = U^{-1}$.

(e) Expand $f(x) = 5x^2 - 3x + 1$ in terms of the **normalized** versions of both bases, and verify that the transformation matrix U converts the P-basis expansion of $f(x)$ into its F-basis expansion.

5.6 TRANSFORMATIONS OF OPERATORS

We have seen how unitary transformations can be used to transform the expansion of a function from one orthonormal basis set to another. We now consider the corresponding transformation for operators. Given an operator A, which when expanded in the φ basis has the form

$$A = \sum_{\mu\nu} |\varphi_\mu\rangle a_{\mu\nu} \langle\varphi_\nu|,$$

we convert it to the φ' basis by the simple expedient of inserting resolutions of the identity (written in terms of the primed basis) on both sides of the above expression. This is an excellent example of the benefits of using Dirac notation. Remembering that this does not change A (but of course does change its appearance), we get

$$A = \sum_{\mu\nu\sigma\tau} |\varphi'_\sigma\rangle \langle\varphi'_\sigma|\varphi_\mu\rangle a_{\mu\nu} \langle\varphi_\nu|\varphi'_\tau\rangle \langle\varphi'_\tau|,$$

which we simplify by identifying $\langle\varphi'_\sigma|\varphi_\mu\rangle = u_{\sigma\mu}$, as defined in Eq. (5.67), and $\langle\varphi_\nu|\varphi'_\tau\rangle = u^*_{\tau\nu}$. Thus,

$$A = \sum_{\mu\nu\sigma\tau} |\varphi'_\sigma\rangle u_{\sigma\mu} a_{\mu\nu} u^*_{\tau\nu} \langle\varphi'_\tau| = \sum_{\sigma\tau} |\varphi'_\sigma\rangle a'_{\sigma\tau} \langle\varphi'_\tau|, \tag{5.74}$$

where $a'_{\sigma\tau}$ is the $\sigma\tau$ matrix element of A in the primed basis, related to the unprimed values by

$$a'_{\sigma\tau} = \sum_{\mu\nu} u_{\sigma\mu} a_{\mu\nu} u^*_{\tau\nu}. \tag{5.75}$$

If we now note that $u^*_{\tau\nu} = (U^\dagger)_{\nu\tau}$, we can write Eq. (5.75) as the matrix equation

$$A' = UAU^\dagger = UAU^{-1}, \tag{5.76}$$

where in the final member of the equation we used the fact that U is unitary.

Another way of getting at Eq. (5.76) is to consider the operator equation $A\psi = \chi$, where initially A, ψ, and χ are all regarded as expanded in the orthonormal set φ, with A having matrix elements $a_{\mu\nu}$, and with ψ and χ having the forms $\psi = \sum_\nu c_\mu \varphi_\mu$ and $\chi = \sum_\nu b_\nu \varphi_\nu$. This state of affairs corresponds to the matrix equation

$$A\mathbf{c} = \mathbf{b}.$$

Now we simply insert $U^{-1}U$ between A and $\mathbf{c}$, and multiply both sides of the equation on the left by U. The result is

$$\left(UAU^{-1}\right)\left(U\mathbf{c}\right) = U\mathbf{b} \quad \longrightarrow \quad A'\mathbf{c}' = \mathbf{b}', \tag{5.77}$$

showing that the operator and the functions are properly related when the functions have been transformed by applying U and the operator has been transformed as required by Eq. (5.76). Since this relationship is valid for any choice of $\mathbf{c}$ and U, it confirms the transformation equation for A.

Nonunitary Transformations

It is possible to consider transformations similar to that illustrated by Eq. (5.77), but using a transformation matrix G that must be nonsingular, but is not required to be unitary. Such more general transformations occasionally appear in physics applications, are called **similarity transformations**, and lead to an equation deceptively similar to Eq. (5.77):

$$\left(\mathsf{GAG}^{-1} \right) \left(\mathsf{Gc} \right) = \mathsf{Gb}. \tag{5.78}$$

There is one important difference: Although a general similarity transformation preserves the original operator equation, corresponding items do not describe the same quantity in a different basis. Instead, they describe quantities that have been systematically (but consistently) altered by the transformation.

Sometimes we encounter a need for transformations that are not even similarity transformations. For example, we may have an operator whose matrix elements are given in a nonorthogonal basis, and we consider the transformation to an orthonormal basis generated by use of the Gram-Schmidt procedure.

Example 5.6.1   GRAM-SCHMIDT TRANSFORMATION

The Gram-Schmidt process describes the transformation from an initial function set χ_i to an orthonormal set φ_μ according to equations that can be brought to the form

$$\varphi_\mu = \sum_{i=1}^{\mu} t_{i\mu} \chi_i, \quad \mu = 1, 2, \ldots.$$

Because the Gram-Schmidt process only generates coefficients $t_{i\mu}$ with $i \leq \mu$, the transformation matrix T can be described as **upper triangular**, i.e., a square matrix with nonzero elements $t_{i\mu}$ only on and above its principal diagonal. Defining S as a matrix with elements $s_{ij} = \langle \chi_i | \chi_j \rangle$ (often called an **overlap** matrix), the orthonormality of the φ_μ is evidenced by the equation

$$\langle \varphi_\mu | \varphi_\nu \rangle = \sum_{ij} \langle t_{i\mu} \chi_i | t_{j\nu} \chi_j \rangle = \sum_{ij} t_{i\mu}^* \langle \chi_i | \chi_j \rangle t_{j\nu} = (\mathsf{T}^\dagger \mathsf{ST})_{\mu\nu} = \delta_{\mu\nu}. \tag{5.79}$$

Note that because T is upper triangular, $\mathsf{T}^\dagger$ must be **lower triangular**. In writing Eq. (5.79) we did not have to restrict the i and j summations, as the coefficients outside the contributing ranges of i and j are present, but set to zero.

From Eq. (5.79) we can obtain a representation of S:

$$\mathsf{S} = (\mathsf{T}^\dagger)^{-1} \mathsf{T}^{-1} = (\mathsf{TT}^\dagger)^{-1}. \tag{5.80}$$

Moreover, if we replace S from Eq. (5.79) by the matrix of a general operator A (in the χ_i basis), we find that in the orthonormal φ basis its representation A' is

$$\mathsf{A}' = \mathsf{T}^\dagger \mathsf{AT}. \tag{5.81}$$

In general, $\mathsf{T}^\dagger$ will not be equal to T^{-1}, so this equation does not define a similarity transformation. ∎

Exercises

5.6.1 (a) Using the two spin functions $\varphi_1 = \alpha$ and $\varphi_2 = \beta$ as an orthonormal basis (so $\langle \alpha | \alpha \rangle = \langle \beta | \beta \rangle = 1$, $\langle \alpha | \beta \rangle = 0$), and the relations

$$S_x \alpha = \frac{1}{2}\beta, \quad S_x \beta = \frac{1}{2}\alpha, \quad S_y \alpha = \frac{1}{2}i\beta, \quad S_y \beta = -\frac{1}{2}i\alpha, \quad S_z \alpha = \frac{1}{2}\alpha, \quad S_z \beta = -\frac{1}{2}\beta,$$

construct the 2×2 matrices of S_x, S_y, and S_z.

(b) Taking now the basis $\varphi_1' = C(\alpha + \beta)$, $\varphi_2' = C(\alpha - \beta)$:

(i) Verify that φ_1' and φ_2' are orthogonal,

(ii) Assign C a value that makes φ_1' and φ_2' normalized,

(iii) Find the unitary matrix for the transformation $\{\varphi_i\} \to \{\varphi_i'\}$.

(c) Find the matrices of S_x, S_y, and S_z in the $\{\varphi_i'\}$ basis.

5.6.2 For the basis $\varphi_1 = Cxe^{-r^2}$, $\varphi_2 = Cye^{-r^2}$, $\varphi_3 = Cze^{-r^2}$, where $r^2 = x^2 + y^2 + z^2$, with the scalar product defined as an unweighted integral over $\mathbb{R}^3$ and with C chosen to make the φ_i normalized:

(a) Find the 3×3 matrix of $L_x = -i\left(y\dfrac{\partial}{\partial z} - z\dfrac{\partial}{\partial y} \right)$;

(b) Using the transformation matrix $\mathsf{U} = \begin{pmatrix} 1 & 0 & 0 \\ 0 & 1/\sqrt{2} & -i/\sqrt{2} \\ 0 & 1/\sqrt{2} & i/\sqrt{2} \end{pmatrix}$, find the transformed matrix of L_x;

(c) Find the new basis functions φ_i' defined by the transformation U, and write explicitly (in terms of x, y, and z) the functional forms of $L_x \varphi_i'$, $i = 1, 2, 3$.

Hint. Use $\int e^{-r^2} d^3r = \pi^{3/2}$, $\int x^2 e^{-r^2} d^3r = \frac{1}{2}\pi^{3/2}$; the integrals are over $\mathbb{R}^3$.

5.6.3 The Gram-Schmidt process for converting an arbitrary basis χ_ν into an orthonormal set φ_ν is described in Section 5.2 in a way that introduces coefficients of the form $-\langle \varphi_\mu | \chi_\nu \rangle$. For bases consisting of three functions, convert the formulation so that φ_ν is expressed entirely in terms of the χ_μ, thereby obtaining an expression for the upper-triangular matrix T appearing in Eq. (5.81).

5.7 INVARIANTS

Just as coordinate rotations leave invariant the essential properties of physical vectors, we can expect unitary transformations to preserve essential features of our vector spaces. These invariances are most directly observed in the basis-set expansions of operators and functions.

Consider first a matrix equation of the form $\mathbf{b} = \mathsf{A}\mathbf{c}$, where all quantities have been evaluated using a particular orthonormal basis φ_i. Now suppose that we wish to use a basis χ_i which can be reached from the original basis by applying a unitary transformation such that

$$\mathbf{c}' = \mathsf{U}\,\mathbf{c} \quad \text{and} \quad \mathbf{b}' = \mathsf{U}\,\mathbf{b}.$$

In the new basis, the matrix A becomes $\mathsf{A}' = \mathsf{U}\mathsf{A}\mathsf{U}^{-1}$, and the invariance we seek corresponds to $\mathbf{b}' = \mathsf{A}'\mathbf{c}'$. In other words, all the quantities must change coherently so that their relationship is unaltered. It is easy to verify that this is the case. Substituting for the primed quantities,

$$\mathsf{U}\,\mathbf{b} = (\mathsf{U}\mathsf{A}\mathsf{U}^{-1})(\mathsf{U}\,\mathbf{c}) \quad \longrightarrow \quad \mathsf{U}\,\mathbf{b} = \mathsf{U}\mathsf{A}\mathbf{c},$$

from which we can recover $\mathbf{b} = \mathsf{A}\mathbf{c}$ by multiplying from the left by U^{-1}.

Scalar quantities should remain invariant under unitary transformation; the prime example here is the scalar product. If f and g are represented in some orthonormal basis, respectively, by $\mathbf{a}$ and $\mathbf{b}$, their scalar product is given by $\mathbf{a}^\dagger\mathbf{b}$. Under a unitary transformation whose matrix representation is U, $\mathbf{a}$ becomes $\mathbf{a}' = \mathsf{U}\,\mathbf{a}$ and $\mathbf{b}$ becomes $\mathbf{b}' = \mathsf{U}\,\mathbf{b}$, and

$$\langle f|g \rangle = (\mathbf{a}')^\dagger \mathbf{b}' = (\mathsf{U}\,\mathbf{a})^\dagger(\mathsf{U}\,\mathbf{b}) = (\mathbf{a}^\dagger \mathsf{U}^\dagger)(\mathsf{U}\,\mathbf{b}) = \mathbf{a}^\dagger\mathbf{b}. \tag{5.82}$$

The fact that $\mathsf{U}^\dagger = \mathsf{U}^{-1}$ enables us to confirm the invariance.

Another scalar that should remain invariant under basis transformation is the expectation value of an operator.

Example 5.7.1 EXPECTATION VALUE IN TRANSFORMED BASIS

Suppose that $\psi = \sum_i c_i\varphi_i$, and that we wish to compute the expectation value of A for this ψ, where A, the matrix corresponding to A, has elements $a_{\nu\mu} = \langle \varphi_\nu | A | \varphi_\mu \rangle$. We have

$$\langle A \rangle = \langle \psi | A | \psi \rangle \quad \longrightarrow \quad \mathbf{c}^\dagger \mathsf{A}\mathbf{c}.$$

If we now choose to use a basis obtained from the φ_i by a unitary transformation U, the expression for $\langle A \rangle$ becomes

$$(\mathsf{U}\,\mathbf{c})^\dagger(\mathsf{U}\mathsf{A}\mathsf{U}^{-1})(\mathsf{U}\,\mathbf{c}) = \mathbf{c}^\dagger \mathsf{U}^\dagger \mathsf{U}\mathsf{A}\mathsf{U}^{-1}\mathsf{U}\,\mathbf{c},$$

which, because U is unitary and therefore $\mathsf{U}^\dagger = \mathsf{U}^{-1}$, reduces, as it must, to the previously obtained value of $\langle A \rangle$. ∎

Vector spaces have additional useful matrix invariants. The **trace** of a matrix is invariant under unitary transformation. If $\mathsf{A}' = \mathsf{U}\mathsf{A}\mathsf{U}^{-1}$, then

$$\text{trace}(\mathsf{A}') = \sum_\nu (\mathsf{U}\mathsf{A}\mathsf{U}^{-1})_{\nu\nu} = \sum_{\nu\mu\tau} u_{\nu\mu}a_{\mu\tau}(\mathsf{U}^{-1})_{\tau\nu} = \sum_{\mu\tau}\left(\sum_\nu (\mathsf{U}^{-1})_{\tau\nu}u_{\nu\mu}\right)a_{\mu\tau}$$

$$= \sum_{\mu\tau}\delta_{\mu\tau}a_{\mu\tau} = \sum_\mu a_{\mu\mu} = \text{trace}(\mathsf{A}). \tag{5.83}$$

Here we simply used the property $\mathsf{U}^{-1}\mathsf{U} = \mathbf{1}$.

Another matrix invariant is the determinant. From the determinant product theorem, $\det(\mathsf{U}\mathsf{A}\mathsf{U}^{-1}) = \det(\mathsf{U}^{-1}\mathsf{U}\mathsf{A}) = \det(\mathsf{A})$. Further invariants will be identified when we study matrix eigenvalue problems in Chapter 6.

Exercises

5.7.1 Using the formal properties of unitary transformations, show that the commutator $[x, p] = i$ is invariant under unitary transformation of the matrices representing x and p.

5.7.2 The Pauli matrices

$$\sigma_1 = \begin{pmatrix} 0 & 1 \\ 1 & 0 \end{pmatrix}, \quad \sigma_2 = \begin{pmatrix} 0 & -i \\ i & 0 \end{pmatrix}, \quad \sigma_3 = \begin{pmatrix} 1 & 0 \\ 0 & -1 \end{pmatrix},$$

have commutator $[\sigma_1, \sigma_2] = 2i\sigma_3$. Show that this relationship continues to be valid if these matrices are transformed by

$$U = \begin{pmatrix} \cos\theta & \sin\theta \\ -\sin\theta & \cos\theta \end{pmatrix}.$$

5.7.3 (a) The operator L_x is defined as

$$L_x = -i\left(y\frac{\partial}{\partial z} - z\frac{\partial}{\partial y} \right).$$

Verify that the basis $\varphi_1 = Cxe^{-r^2}$, $\varphi_2 = Cye^{-r^2}$, $\varphi_3 = Cze^{-r^2}$, where $r^2 = x^2 + y^2 + z^2$, forms a closed set under the operation of L_x, meaning that when L_x is applied to any member of this basis the result is a function within the basis space, and construct the 3×3 matrix of L_x in this basis from the result of the application of L_x to each basis function.

(b) Verify that $L_x\left[(x + iy)e^{-r^2} \right] = -ze^{-r^2}$, and note that this result, using the $\{\varphi_i\}$ basis, can be written $L_x(\varphi_1 + i\varphi_2) = -\varphi_3$.

(c) Express the equation of part (b) in matrix form, and write the matrix equation that results when each of the quantities is transformed using the transformation matrix

$$U = \begin{pmatrix} 1 & 0 & 0 \\ 0 & 1/\sqrt{2} & -i/\sqrt{2} \\ 0 & 1/\sqrt{2} & i/\sqrt{2} \end{pmatrix}.$$

(d) Regarding the transformation U as producing a new basis $\{\varphi_i'\}$, find the explicit form (in x, y, z) of the φ_i'.

(e) Using the operator form of L_x and the explicit forms of the φ_i', verify the validity of the transformed equation found in part (c).

Hint. The results of Exercise 5.6.2 may be useful.

5.8 SUMMARY—VECTOR SPACE NOTATION

It may be useful to summarize some of the relationships found in this chapter, highlighting the essentially complete mathematical parallelism between the properties of vectors and those of basis expansions in vector spaces. We do so here, using Dirac notation wherever appropriate.

1. **Scalar product:**

$$\langle\varphi|\psi\rangle = \int_a^b \varphi^*(t)\psi(t)w(t)\,dt \iff \langle\mathbf{u}|\mathbf{v}\rangle = \mathbf{u}^\dagger\mathbf{v} = \mathbf{u}^* \cdot \mathbf{v}. \qquad (5.84)$$

The result of the scalar product operation is a scalar (i.e., a real or complex number). Here $\mathbf{u}^\dagger\mathbf{v}$ represents the product of a row and a column vector; it is equivalent to the dot-product notation also shown.

2. **Expectation value:**

$$\langle\varphi|A|\varphi\rangle = \int_a^b \varphi^*(t)A\varphi(t)w(t)\,dt \iff \langle\mathbf{u}|A|\mathbf{u}\rangle = \mathbf{u}^\dagger A\mathbf{u}. \qquad (5.85)$$

3. **Adjoint:**

$$\langle\varphi|A|\psi\rangle = \langle A^\dagger\varphi|\psi\rangle \iff \langle\mathbf{u}|A|\mathbf{v}\rangle = \langle A^\dagger\mathbf{u}|\mathbf{v}\rangle = [A^\dagger\mathbf{u}]^\dagger\mathbf{v} = \mathbf{u}^\dagger A\mathbf{v}. \qquad (5.86)$$

Note that the simplification of $[A^\dagger\mathbf{u}]^\dagger\mathbf{v}$ shows that the matrix $A^\dagger$ has the property expected of an operator adjoint.

4. **Unitary transformation:**

$$\psi = A\varphi \longrightarrow U\psi = (UAU^{-1})(U\varphi) \iff \mathbf{w} = A\mathbf{v} \longrightarrow U\mathbf{w} = (UAU^{-1})(U\mathbf{v}). \quad (5.87)$$

5. **Resolution of identity:**

$$\mathbf{1} = \sum_i |\varphi_i\rangle\langle\varphi_i| \iff \mathbf{1} = \sum_i |\hat{\mathbf{e}}_i\rangle\langle\hat{\mathbf{e}}_i|, \qquad (5.88)$$

where the φ_i are orthonormal and the $\hat{\mathbf{e}}_i$ are orthogonal unit vectors. Applying Eq. (5.88) to a function (or vector):

$$\psi = \sum_i |\varphi_i\rangle\langle\varphi_i|\psi\rangle = \sum_i a_i\varphi_i \iff \mathbf{w} = \sum_i |\hat{\mathbf{e}}_i\rangle\langle\hat{\mathbf{e}}_i|\mathbf{w}\rangle = \sum_i w_i\hat{\mathbf{e}}_i, \qquad (5.89)$$

where $a_i = \langle\varphi_i|\psi\rangle$ and $w_i = \langle\hat{\mathbf{e}}_i|\mathbf{w}\rangle = \hat{\mathbf{e}}_i \cdot \mathbf{w}$.

Additional Readings

Brown, W. A., *Matrices and Vector Spaces*. New York: M. Dekker (1991).

Byron, F. W., Jr., and R. W. Fuller, *Mathematics of Classical and Quantum Physics*. Reading, MA: Addison-Wesley (1969), reprinting, Dover (1992).

Dennery, P., and A. Krzywicki, *Mathematics for Physicists*. New York: Harper & Row, reprinting, Dover (1996).

Halmos, P. R., *Finite-Dimensional Vector Spaces*, 2nd ed. Princeton, NJ: Van Nostrand (1958), reprinting, Springer (1993).

Jain, M. C., *Vector Spaces and Matrices in Physics*, 2nd ed. Oxford: Alpha Science International (2007).

Kreyszig, E., *Advanced Engineering Mathematics*, 6th ed. New York: Wiley (1988).

Lang, S., *Linear Algebra*. Berlin: Springer (1987).

Roman, S., *Advanced Linear Algebra*, Graduate Texts in Mathematics 135, 2nd ed. Berlin: Springer (2005).

CHAPTER 6

EIGENVALUE PROBLEMS

6.1 EIGENVALUE EQUATIONS

Many important problems in physics can be cast as equations of the generic form

$$A\psi = \lambda\psi, \tag{6.1}$$

where A is a linear operator whose domain and range is a Hilbert space, ψ is a function in the space, and λ is a constant. The operator A is known, but both ψ and λ are unknown, and the task at hand is to solve Eq. (6.1). Because the solutions to an equation of this type yield functions ψ that are unchanged by the operator (except for multiplication by a scale factor λ), they are termed **eigenvalue equations**: **Eigen** is German for "[its] own." A function ψ that solves an eigenvalue equation is called an **eigenfunction**, and the value of λ that goes with an eigenfunction is called an **eigenvalue**.

The formal definition of an eigenvalue equation may not make its essential content totally apparent. The requirement that the operator A leaves ψ unchanged except for a scale factor constitutes a severe restriction upon ψ. The possibility that Eq. (6.1) has any solutions at all is in many cases not intuitively obvious.

To see why eigenvalue equations are common in physics, let's cite a few examples:

1. The resonant standing waves of a vibrating string will be those in which the restoring force on the elements of the string (represented by $A\psi$) are proportional to their displacements ψ from equilibrium.

2. The angular momentum $\mathbf{L}$ and the angular velocity $\boldsymbol{\omega}$ of a rigid body are three-dimensional (3-D) vectors that are related by the equation

$$\mathbf{L} = \mathsf{I}\,\boldsymbol{\omega},$$

where I is the 3×3 moment of inertia matrix. Here the direction of $\boldsymbol{\omega}$ defines the axis of rotation, while the direction of $\mathbf{L}$ defines the axis about which angular momentum is

299

generated. The condition that these two axes be in the same direction (thereby defining what are known as the **principal axes** of inertia) is that $\mathbf{L} = \lambda\boldsymbol{\omega}$, where λ is a proportionality constant. Combining with the formula for $\mathbf{L}$, we obtain

$$\mathsf{I}\boldsymbol{\omega} = \lambda\boldsymbol{\omega},$$

which is an eigenvalue equation in which the operator is the matrix I and the eigenfunction (then usually called an **eigenvector**) is the vector $\boldsymbol{\omega}$.

3. The time-independent Schrödinger equation in quantum mechanics is an eigenvalue equation, with A the Hamiltonian operator H, ψ a wave function and $\lambda = E$ the energy of the state represented by ψ.

Basis Expansions

A powerful approach to eigenvalue problems is to express them in terms of an orthonormal basis whose members we designate φ_i, using the formulas developed in Chapter 5. Then the operator A and the function ψ are represented by a matrix A and a vector $\mathbf{c}$ whose elements are obtained, according to Eqs. (5.51) and (5.52), as the scalar products

$$a_{ij} = \langle \varphi_i | A | \varphi_j \rangle, \quad c_i = \langle \varphi_i | \psi \rangle.$$

Our original eigenvalue equation has now been reduced to a matrix equation:

$$\mathsf{A}\mathbf{c} = \lambda\mathbf{c}. \tag{6.2}$$

When an eigenvalue equation is presented in this form, we can call it a **matrix eigenvalue equation** and call the vectors $\mathbf{c}$ that solve it **eigenvectors**. As we shall see in later sections of this chapter, there is a well-developed technology for the solution of matrix eigenvalue equations, so a route always available for solving eigenvalue equations is to cast them in matrix form. Once a matrix eigenvalue problem has been solved, we can recover the eigenfunctions of the original problem from their expansion:

$$\psi = \sum_i c_i \varphi_i.$$

Sometimes, as in the moment of inertia example mentioned above, our eigenvalue problem originates as a matrix problem. Then, of course, we do not have to begin its solution process by introducing a basis and converting it into matrix form, and our solutions will be vectors that do not need to be interpreted as expansions in a basis.

Equivalence of Operator and Matrix Forms

It is important to note that we are dealing with eigenvalue equations in which the operator involved is linear and that it operates on elements of a Hilbert space. Once these conditions are met, the operator and function involved can always be expanded in a basis, leading to a matrix eigenvalue equation that is totally equivalent to our original problem. Among other things, this means that any theorems about properties of eigenvectors or eigenvalues that are developed from basis-set expansions of an eigenvalue problem must apply also to the original problem, and that solution of the matrix eigenvalue equation provides also a solution to the original problem. These facts, plus the practical observation that we know how to solve matrix eigenvalue problems, strongly suggest that the detailed investigation of the matrix problems should be on our agenda.

When we explore matrix eigenvalue problems, we will find that certain properties of the matrix influence the nature of the solutions, and that in particular significant simplifications become available when the matrix is Hermitian. Many eigenvalue equations of interest in physics involve differential operators, so it is of importance to understand whether (or under what conditions) these operators are Hermitian. That issue is taken up in Chapter 8.

Finally, we note that the introduction of a basis-set expansion is not the only possibility for solving an eigenvalue equation. Eigenvalue equations involving differential operators can also be approached by the general methods for solving differential equations. That topic is also discussed in Chapter 8.

6.2 MATRIX EIGENVALUE PROBLEMS

While in principle the notion of an eigenvalue problem is already fully defined, we open this section with a simple example that may help to make it clearer how such problems are set up and solved.

A Preliminary Example

We consider here a simple problem of two-dimensional (2-D) motion in which a particle slides frictionlessly in an ellipsoidal basin (see Fig. 6.1). If we release the particle (initially at rest) at an arbitrary point in the basin, it will start to move downhill in the (negative) gradient direction, which in general will not aim directly at the potential minimum at the bottom of the basin. The particle's overall trajectory will then be a complicated path, as sketched in the bottom panel of Fig. 6.1. Our objective is to find the positions, if any, from which the trajectories will aim at the potential minimum, and will therefore represent simple one-dimensional oscillatory motion.

This problem is sufficiently elementary that we can analyze it without great difficulty. We take a potential of the form

$$V(x, y) = ax^2 + bxy + cy^2,$$

with parameters a, b, c in ranges that describe an ellipsoidal basin with a minimum in V at $x = y = 0$. We then calculate the x and y components of the force on our particle when at (x, y):

$$F_x = -\frac{\partial V}{\partial x} = -2ax - by, \quad F_y = -\frac{\partial V}{\partial y} = -bx - 2cy.$$

It is pretty clear that, for most values of x and y, $F_x/F_y \neq x/y$, so the force will not be directed toward the minimum at $x = y = 0$.

To search for directions in which the force is directed toward $x = y = 0$, we begin by writing the equations for the force in matrix form:

$$\begin{pmatrix} F_x \\ F_y \end{pmatrix} = \begin{pmatrix} -2a & -b \\ -b & -2c \end{pmatrix} \begin{pmatrix} x \\ y \end{pmatrix}, \quad \text{or} \quad \mathbf{f} = \mathbf{H}\mathbf{r},$$

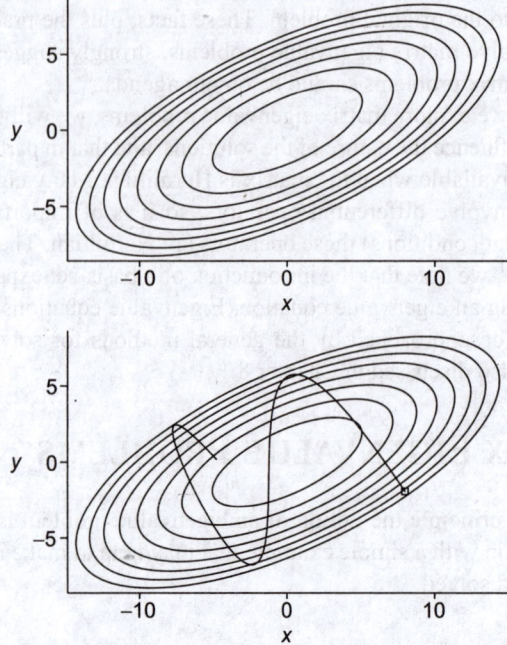

FIGURE 6.1   Top: Contour lines of basin potential $V = x^2 - \sqrt{5}xy + 3y^2$. Bottom: Trajectory of sliding particle of unit mass starting from rest at $(8.0, -1.92)$.

where $\mathbf{f}$, H, and $\mathbf{r}$ are defined as indicated. Now the condition $F_x/F_y = x/y$ is equivalent to the statement that $\mathbf{f}$ and $\mathbf{r}$ are proportional, and therefore we can write

$$\mathsf{H}\mathbf{r} = \lambda\mathbf{r}, \qquad (6.3)$$

where, as already suggested, H is a known matrix, while λ and $\mathbf{r}$ are to be determined. This is an eigenvalue equation, and the column vectors $\mathbf{r}$ that are its solutions are its eigenvectors, while the corresponding values of λ are its eigenvalues.

Equation (6.3) is a homogeneous linear equation system, as becomes more obvious if written as

$$(\mathsf{H} - \lambda\mathbf{1})\mathbf{r} = 0, \qquad (6.4)$$

and we know from Chapter 2 that it will have the unique solution $\mathbf{r} = 0$ unless $\det(\mathsf{H} - \lambda\mathbf{1}) = 0$. However, the value of λ is at our disposal, so we can search for values of λ that cause this determinant to vanish. Proceeding symbolically, we look for λ such that

$$\det(\mathsf{H} - \lambda\mathbf{1}) = \begin{vmatrix} h_{11} - \lambda & h_{12} \\ h_{21} & h_{22} - \lambda \end{vmatrix} = 0.$$

Expanding the determinant, which is sometimes called a **secular determinant** (the name arising from early applications in celestial mechanics), we have an algebraic equation, the **secular equation**,

$$(h_{11} - \lambda)(h_{22} - \lambda) - h_{12}h_{21} = 0, \qquad (6.5)$$

which can be solved for λ. The left hand side of Eq. (6.5) is also called the **characteristic polynomial** (in λ) of H, and Eq. (6.5) is for that reason also known as the **characteristic equation** of H.

Once a value of λ that solves Eq. (6.5) has been obtained, we can return to the homogeneous equation system, Eq. (6.4), and solve it for the vector $\mathbf{r}$. This can be repeated for all λ that are solutions to the secular equation, thereby giving a set of eigenvalues and the associated eigenvectors.

Example 6.2.1   2-D ELLIPSOIDAL BASIN

Let's continue with our ellipsoidal basin example, with the specific parameter values $a = 1$, $b = -\sqrt{5}$, $c = 3$. Then our matrix H has the form

$$H = \begin{pmatrix} -2 & \sqrt{5} \\ \sqrt{5} & -6 \end{pmatrix},$$

and the secular equation takes the form

$$\det(H - \lambda \mathbf{1}) = \begin{vmatrix} -2 - \lambda & \sqrt{5} \\ \sqrt{5} & -6 - \lambda \end{vmatrix} = \lambda^2 + 8\lambda + 7 = 0.$$

Since $\lambda^2 + 8\lambda + 7 = (\lambda + 1)(\lambda + 7)$, we see that the secular equation has as solutions the eigenvalues $\lambda = -1$ and $\lambda = -7$.

To get the eigenvector corresponding to $\lambda = -1$, we return to Eq. (6.4), which, written in great detail, is

$$(H - \lambda \mathbf{1})\mathbf{r} = \begin{pmatrix} -2 - (-1) & \sqrt{5} \\ \sqrt{5} & -6 - (-1) \end{pmatrix} \begin{pmatrix} x \\ y \end{pmatrix} = \begin{pmatrix} -1 & \sqrt{5} \\ \sqrt{5} & -5 \end{pmatrix} \begin{pmatrix} x \\ y \end{pmatrix} = 0,$$

which expands into a linearly dependent pair of equations:

$$-x + \sqrt{5}\, y = 0$$

$$\sqrt{5}\, x - 5y = 0.$$

This is, of course, the intention associated with the secular equation, because if these equations were linearly independent they would inexorably lead to the solution $x = y = 0$. Instead, from either equation, we have $x = \sqrt{5}\, y$, so we have the eigenvalue/eigenvector pair

$$\lambda_1 = -1, \quad \mathbf{r}_1 = C \begin{pmatrix} \sqrt{5} \\ 1 \end{pmatrix},$$

where C is a constant that can assume any value. Thus, there is an infinite number of x, y pairs that define a **direction** in the 2-D space, with the magnitude of the displacement in that direction arbitrary. The arbitrariness of scale is a natural consequence of the fact that the equation system was homogeneous; any multiple of a solution of a linear homogeneous equation set will also be a solution. This eigenvector corresponds to trajectories that start from the particle at rest anywhere on the line defined by $\mathbf{r}_1$. A trajectory of this sort is illustrated in the top panel of Fig. 6.2.

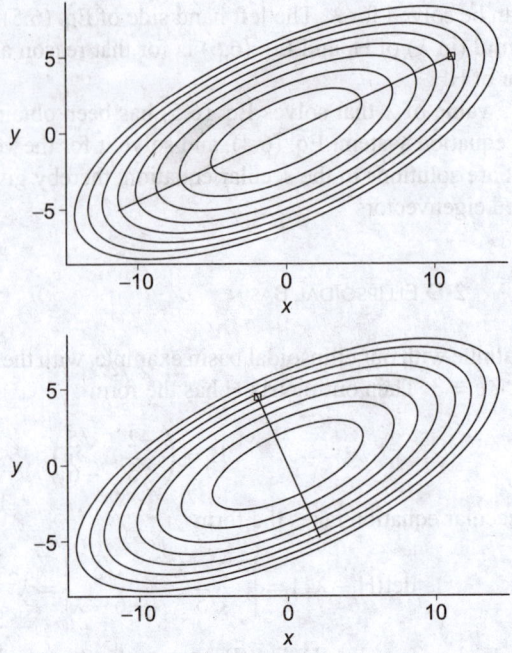

FIGURE 6.2   Trajectories starting at rest. Top: At a point on the line $x = y\sqrt{5}$.
Bottom: At a point on the line $y = -x\sqrt{5}$.

We have not yet considered the possibility that $\lambda = -7$. This leads to a different eigenvector, obtained by solving

$$(\mathbf{H} - \lambda\mathbf{1})\mathbf{r} = \begin{pmatrix} -2+7 & \sqrt{5} \\ \sqrt{5} & -6+7 \end{pmatrix} \begin{pmatrix} x \\ y \end{pmatrix} = \begin{pmatrix} 5 & \sqrt{5} \\ \sqrt{5} & 1 \end{pmatrix} \begin{pmatrix} x \\ y \end{pmatrix} = 0,$$

corresponding to $y = -x\sqrt{5}$. This defines the eigenvalue/eigenvector pair

$$\lambda_2 = -7, \quad \mathbf{r}_2 = C'\begin{pmatrix} -1 \\ \sqrt{5} \end{pmatrix}.$$

A trajectory of this sort is shown in the bottom panel of Fig. 6.2.

We thus have two directions in which the force is directed toward the minimum, and they are mutually perpendicular: the first direction has $dy/dx = 1/\sqrt{5}$; for the second, $dy/dx = -\sqrt{5}$.

We can easily check our eigenvectors and eigenvalues. For λ_1 and $\mathbf{r}_1$,

$$\mathbf{Hr}_1 = \begin{pmatrix} -2 & \sqrt{5} \\ \sqrt{5} & -6 \end{pmatrix} \begin{pmatrix} C\sqrt{5} \\ C \end{pmatrix} = C\begin{pmatrix} -\sqrt{5} \\ -1 \end{pmatrix} = (-1)\begin{pmatrix} C\sqrt{5} \\ C \end{pmatrix} = \lambda_1\mathbf{r}_1.$$

It is often useful to **normalize** eigenvectors, which we can do by choosing the constant (C or C') to make $\mathbf{r}$ of magnitude unity. In the present example,

$$\mathbf{r}_1 = \begin{pmatrix} \sqrt{5/6} \\ \sqrt{1/6} \end{pmatrix}, \quad \mathbf{r}_2 = \begin{pmatrix} -\sqrt{1/6} \\ \sqrt{5/6} \end{pmatrix}. \tag{6.6}$$

Each of these normalized eigenvectors is still arbitrary as to overall sign (or if we accept complex coefficients, as to an arbitrary complex factor of magnitude unity).

Before leaving this example, we make three further observations: (1) the number of eigenvalues was equal to the dimension of the matrix H. This is a consequence of the fundamental theorem of algebra, namely that an equation of degree n will have n roots; (2) although the secular equation was of degree 2 and quadratic equations can have complex roots, our eigenvalues were real; and (3) our two eigenvectors are orthogonal. ∎

Our 2-D example is easily understood physically. The directions in which the displacement and the force are collinear are the symmetry directions of the elliptical potential field, and they are associated with different eigenvalues (the proportionality constant between position and force) because the ellipses have axes of different lengths. We have, in fact, identified the **principal axes** of our basin. With the parameters of Example 6.2.1, the potential could have been written (using the normalized eigenvectors)

$$V = \frac{1}{2}\left(\frac{\sqrt{5}x + y}{\sqrt{6}}\right)^2 + \frac{7}{2}\left(\frac{x - \sqrt{5}y}{\sqrt{6}}\right)^2 = \tfrac{1}{2}(x')^2 + \tfrac{7}{2}(y')^2,$$

which shows that V divides into two quadratic terms, each dependent on a parenthesized quantity (a new coordinate) proportional to one of our eigenvectors. The new coordinates are related to the original x, y by a rotation with unitary transformation U:

$$\mathsf{U}\mathbf{r} = \begin{pmatrix} \sqrt{5/6} & \sqrt{1/6} \\ \sqrt{1/6} & -\sqrt{5/6} \end{pmatrix}\begin{pmatrix} x \\ y \end{pmatrix} = \begin{pmatrix} (\sqrt{5}x + y)/\sqrt{6} \\ (x - \sqrt{5}y)/\sqrt{6} \end{pmatrix} = \begin{pmatrix} x' \\ y' \end{pmatrix}.$$

Finally, we note that when we calculate the force in the primed coordinate system, we get

$$F_{x'} = -x', \quad F_{y'} = -7y',$$

corresponding to the eigenvalues we found.

Another Eigenproblem

Example 6.2.1 is not complicated enough to provide a full illustration of the matrix eigenvalue problem. Consider next the following example.

Example 6.2.2 BLOCK-DIAGONAL MATRIX

Find the eigenvalues and eigenvectors of

$$H = \begin{pmatrix} 0 & 1 & 0 \\ 1 & 0 & 0 \\ 0 & 0 & 2 \end{pmatrix}. \tag{6.7}$$

Writing the secular equation and expanding in minors using the third row, we have

$$\begin{vmatrix} -\lambda & 1 & 0 \\ 1 & -\lambda & 0 \\ 0 & 0 & 2-\lambda \end{vmatrix} = (2-\lambda)\begin{vmatrix} -\lambda & 1 \\ 1 & -\lambda \end{vmatrix} = (2-\lambda)(\lambda^2 - 1) = 0. \tag{6.8}$$

We see that the eigenvalues are 2, +1, and −1.

To obtain the eigenvector corresponding to $\lambda = 2$, we examine the equation set $[H - 2(1)]c = 0$:

$$-2c_1 + c_2 = 0,$$

$$c_1 - 2c_2 = 0,$$

$$0 = 0.$$

The first two equations of this set lead to $c_1 = c_2 = 0$. The third obviously conveys no information, and we are led to the conclusion that c_3 is arbitrary. Thus, at this point we have

$$\lambda_1 = 2, \quad c_1 = \begin{pmatrix} 0 \\ 0 \\ C \end{pmatrix}. \tag{6.9}$$

Taking next $\lambda = +1$, our matrix equation is $[H - 1(1)]c = 0$, which is equivalent to the ordinary equations

$$-c_1 + c_2 = 0,$$

$$c_1 - c_2 = 0,$$

$$c_3 = 0.$$

We clearly have $c_1 = c_2$ and $c_3 = 0$, so

$$\lambda_2 = +1, \quad c_2 = \begin{pmatrix} C \\ C \\ 0 \end{pmatrix}. \tag{6.10}$$

Similar operations for $\lambda = -1$ yield

$$\lambda_3 = -1, \quad c_3 = \begin{pmatrix} C \\ -C \\ 0 \end{pmatrix}. \tag{6.11}$$

Collecting our results, and normalizing the eigenvectors (often useful, but not in general necessary), we have

$$\lambda_1 = 2, \quad c_1 = \begin{pmatrix} 0 \\ 0 \\ 1 \end{pmatrix}, \qquad \lambda_2 = 1, \quad c_2 = \begin{pmatrix} 2^{-1/2} \\ 2^{-1/2} \\ 0 \end{pmatrix}, \qquad \lambda_3 = -1, \quad c_3 = \begin{pmatrix} 2^{-1/2} \\ -2^{-1/2} \\ 0 \end{pmatrix}.$$

Note that because H was block-diagonal, with an upper-left 2×2 block and a lower-right 1×1 block, the secular equation separated into a product of the determinants for the two blocks, and its solutions corresponded to those of an individual block, with coefficients of value zero for the other block(s). Thus, $\lambda = 2$ was a solution for the 1×1 block in row/column 3, and its eigenvector involved only the coefficient c_3. The λ values ± 1 came from the 2×2 block in rows/columns 1 and 2, with eigenvectors involving only coefficients c_1 and c_2. ∎

In the case of a 1×1 block in row/column i, we saw, for $i = 3$ in Example 6.2.2, that its only element was the eigenvalue, and that the corresponding eigenvector is proportional to $\hat{\mathbf{e}}_i$ (a unit vector whose only nonzero element is $c_i = 1$). A generalization of this observation is that if a matrix H is diagonal, its diagonal elements h_{ii} will be the eigenvalues λ_i, and that the eigenvectors $\mathbf{c}_i$ will be the unit vectors $\hat{\mathbf{e}}_i$.

Degeneracy

If the secular equation has a multiple root, the eigensystem is said to be **degenerate** or to exhibit **degeneracy**. Here is an example.

Example 6.2.3   DEGENERATE EIGENPROBLEM

Let's find the eigenvalues and eigenvectors of

$$H = \begin{pmatrix} 0 & 0 & 1 \\ 0 & 1 & 0 \\ 1 & 0 & 0 \end{pmatrix}. \tag{6.12}$$

The secular equation for this problem is

$$\begin{vmatrix} -\lambda & 0 & 1 \\ 0 & 1-\lambda & 0 \\ 1 & 0 & -\lambda \end{vmatrix} = \lambda^2(1-\lambda) - (1-\lambda) = (\lambda^2 - 1)(1-\lambda) = 0 \tag{6.13}$$

with the three roots $+1$, $+1$, and -1. Let's consider first $\lambda = -1$. Then we have

$$c_1 + c_3 = 0,$$

$$2c_2 = 0,$$

$$c_1 + c_3 = 0.$$

Thus,

$$\lambda_1 = -1, \quad \mathbf{c}_1 = C \begin{pmatrix} 1 \\ 0 \\ -1 \end{pmatrix}. \tag{6.14}$$

For the double root $\lambda = +1$,

$$-c_1 + c_3 = 0,$$

$$0 = 0,$$

$$c_1 - c_3 = 0.$$

Note that of the three equations, only one is now linearly independent; the double root signals **two** linear dependencies, and we have solutions for **any** values of c_1 and c_2, with only the condition that $c_3 = c_1$. The eigenvectors for $\lambda = +1$ thus span a 2-D **manifold** (= subspace), in contrast to the trivial one-dimensional manifold characteristic of nondegenerate solutions. The general form for these eigenvectors is

$$\lambda = +1, \quad \mathbf{c} = \begin{pmatrix} C \\ C' \\ C \end{pmatrix}. \tag{6.15}$$

It is convenient to describe the degenerate eigenspace for $\lambda = 1$ by identifying two mutually orthogonal vectors that span it. We can pick the first vector by choosing arbitrary values of C and C' (an obvious choice is to set one of these, say C', to zero). Then, using the Gram-Schmidt process (or in this case by simple inspection), we find a second eigenvector orthogonal to the first. Here, this leads to

$$\lambda_2 = \lambda_3 = +1, \quad \mathbf{c}_2 = C \begin{pmatrix} 1 \\ 0 \\ 1 \end{pmatrix}, \quad \mathbf{c}_3 = C' \begin{pmatrix} 0 \\ 1 \\ 0 \end{pmatrix}. \tag{6.16}$$

Normalizing, our eigenvalues and eigenvectors become

$$\lambda_1 = -1, \quad \mathbf{c}_1 = \begin{pmatrix} 2^{-1/2} \\ 0 \\ -2^{-1/2} \end{pmatrix}, \quad \lambda_2 = \lambda_3 = 1, \quad \mathbf{c}_2 = \begin{pmatrix} 2^{-1/2} \\ 0 \\ 2^{-1/2} \end{pmatrix}, \quad \mathbf{c}_3 = \begin{pmatrix} 0 \\ 1 \\ 0 \end{pmatrix}. \tag{$\blacksquare$}$$

The eigenvalue problems we have used as examples all led to secular equations with simple solutions; realistic applications frequently involve matrices of large dimension and secular equations of high degree. The solution of matrix eigenvalue problems has been an active field in numerical analysis and very sophisticated computer programs for this purpose are now available. Discussion of the details of such programs is outside the scope of this book, but the ability to use such programs should be part of the technology available to the working physicist.

Exercises

Find the eigenvalues and corresponding normalized eigenvectors of the matrices in Exercises 6.2.1 through 6.2.14. Orthogonalize any degenerate eigenvectors.

6.2.1 $\quad A = \begin{pmatrix} 1 & 0 & 1 \\ 0 & 1 & 0 \\ 1 & 0 & 1 \end{pmatrix}.$

ANS. $\lambda = 0, 1, 2.$

6.2.2 $\quad A = \begin{pmatrix} 1 & \sqrt{2} & 0 \\ \sqrt{2} & 0 & 0 \\ 0 & 0 & 0 \end{pmatrix}.$

ANS. $\lambda = -1, 0, 2.$

6.2.3 $\quad A = \begin{pmatrix} 1 & 1 & 0 \\ 1 & 0 & 1 \\ 0 & 1 & 1 \end{pmatrix}.$

ANS. $\lambda = -1, 1, 2.$

6.2.4 $A = \begin{pmatrix} 1 & \sqrt{8} & 0 \\ \sqrt{8} & 1 & \sqrt{8} \\ 0 & \sqrt{8} & 1 \end{pmatrix}$.

ANS. $\lambda = -3, 1, 5$.

6.2.5 $A = \begin{pmatrix} 1 & 0 & 0 \\ 0 & 1 & 1 \\ 0 & 1 & 1 \end{pmatrix}$.

ANS. $\lambda = 0, 1, 2$.

6.2.6 $A = \begin{pmatrix} 1 & 0 & 0 \\ 0 & 1 & \sqrt{2} \\ 0 & \sqrt{2} & 0 \end{pmatrix}$.

ANS. $\lambda = -1, 1, 2$.

6.2.7 $A = \begin{pmatrix} 0 & 1 & 0 \\ 1 & 0 & 1 \\ 0 & 1 & 0 \end{pmatrix}$.

ANS. $\lambda = -\sqrt{2}, 0, \sqrt{2}$.

6.2.8 $A = \begin{pmatrix} 2 & 0 & 0 \\ 0 & 1 & 1 \\ 0 & 1 & 1 \end{pmatrix}$.

ANS. $\lambda = 0, 2, 2$.

6.2.9 $A = \begin{pmatrix} 0 & 1 & 1 \\ 1 & 0 & 1 \\ 1 & 1 & 0 \end{pmatrix}$.

ANS. $\lambda = -1, -1, 2$.

6.2.10 $A = \begin{pmatrix} 1 & -1 & -1 \\ -1 & 1 & -1 \\ -1 & -1 & 1 \end{pmatrix}$.

ANS. $\lambda = -1, 2, 2$.

6.2.11 $A = \begin{pmatrix} 1 & 1 & 1 \\ 1 & 1 & 1 \\ 1 & 1 & 1 \end{pmatrix}$.

ANS. $\lambda = 0, 0, 3$.

6.2.12 $A = \begin{pmatrix} 5 & 0 & 2 \\ 0 & 1 & 0 \\ 2 & 0 & 2 \end{pmatrix}$.

ANS. $\lambda = 1, 1, 6$.

6.2.13 $A = \begin{pmatrix} 1 & 1 & 0 \\ 1 & 1 & 0 \\ 0 & 0 & 0 \end{pmatrix}$.

ANS. $\lambda = 0, 0, 2$.

6.2.14 $A = \begin{pmatrix} 5 & 0 & \sqrt{3} \\ 0 & 3 & 0 \\ \sqrt{3} & 0 & 3 \end{pmatrix}$.

ANS. $\lambda = 2, 3, 6.$

6.2.15   Describe the geometric properties of the surface

$$x^2 + 2xy + 2y^2 + 2yz + z^2 = 1.$$

How is it oriented in 3-D space? Is it a conic section? If so, which kind?

6.3   HERMITIAN EIGENVALUE PROBLEMS

All the illustrative problems we have thus far examined have turned out to have real eigenvalues; this was also true of all the exercises at the end of Section 6.2. We also found, whenever we bothered to check, that the eigenvectors corresponding to different eigenvalues were orthogonal. The purpose of the present section is to show that these properties are consequences of the fact that all the eigenvalue problems we have considered were for Hermitian matrices.

We remind the reader that the check for Hermiticity is simple: We simply verify that H is equal to its adjoint, $H^\dagger$; if a matrix is real, this condition is simply that it be symmetric. All the matrices to which we referred are clearly Hermitian.

We now proceed to characterize the eigenvalues and eigenvectors of Hermitian matrices. Let H be a Hermitian matrix, with c_i and c_j two of its eigenvectors corresponding, respectively, to the eigenvalues λ_i and λ_j. Then, using Dirac notation,

$$H|c_i\rangle = \lambda_i|c_i\rangle, \quad H|c_j\rangle = \lambda_j|c_j\rangle. \tag{6.17}$$

Multiplying on the left the first of these by $c_j^\dagger$, which in Dirac notation is $\langle c_j|$, and the second by $\langle c_i|$,

$$\langle c_j|H|c_i\rangle = \lambda_i\langle c_j|c_i\rangle, \quad \langle c_i|H|c_j\rangle = \lambda_j\langle c_i|c_j\rangle. \tag{6.18}$$

We next take the complex conjugate of the second of these equations, noting that $\langle c_i|c_j\rangle^* = \langle c_j|c_i\rangle$, that we must complex conjugate the occurrence of λ_j, and that

$$\langle c_i|Hc_j\rangle^* = \langle Hc_j|c_i\rangle = \langle c_j|H|c_i\rangle. \tag{6.19}$$

Note that the first member of Eq. (6.19) contains the scalar product of c_i with Hc_j. Complex conjugating this scalar product yields the second member of that equation. The final member of the equation follows because H is Hermitian.

The complex conjugation therefore converts Eqs. (6.18) into

$$\langle c_j|H|c_i\rangle = \lambda_i\langle c_j|c_i\rangle, \quad \langle c_j|H|c_i\rangle = \lambda_j^*\langle c_j|c_i\rangle. \tag{6.20}$$

Equations (6.20) permit us to obtain two important results: First, if $i = j$, the scalar product $\langle c_j|c_i\rangle$ becomes $\langle c_i|c_i\rangle$, which is an inherently positive quantity. This means that the two equations are only consistent if $\lambda_i = \lambda_i^*$, meaning that λ_i must be real. Thus,

The eigenvalues of a Hermitian matrix are real.

Next, if $i \neq j$, combining the two equations of Eq. (6.20), and remembering that the λ_i are real,

$$(\lambda_i - \lambda_j)\langle \mathbf{c}_j | \mathbf{c}_i \rangle = 0, \tag{6.21}$$

so that either $\lambda_i = \lambda_j$ or $\langle \mathbf{c}_j | \mathbf{c}_i \rangle = 0$. This tells us that

> *Eigenvectors of a Hermitian matrix corresponding to different eigenvalues are orthogonal.*

Note, however, that if $\lambda_i = \lambda_j$, which will occur if i and j refer to two degenerate eigenvectors, we know nothing about their orthogonality. In fact, in Example 6.2.3 we examined a pair of degenerate eigenvectors, noting that they spanned a two-dimensional manifold and were not required to be orthogonal. However, we also noted in that context that we could **choose** them to be orthogonal. Sometimes (as in Example 6.2.3), it is obvious how to choose orthogonal degenerate eigenvectors. When it is not obvious, we can start from any linearly independent set of degenerate eigenvectors and orthonormalize them by the Gram-Schmidt process.

Since the total number of eigenvectors of a Hermitian matrix is equal to its dimension, and since (whether or not there is degeneracy) we can make from them an orthonormal set of eigenvectors, we have the following important result:

> *It is possible to choose the eigenvectors of a Hermitian matrix in such a way that they form an orthonormal set that spans the space of the matrix basis. This situation is often referred to by the statement, "The eigenvectors of a Hermitian matrix form a **complete set**." This means that if the matrix is of order* n, *any vector of dimension* n *can be written as a linear combination of the orthonormal eigenvectors, with coefficients determined by the rules for orthogonal expansions.*

We close this section by reminding the reader that theorems which have been established for an arbitrary basis-set expansion of a Hermitian eigenvalue equation apply also to that eigenvalue equation in its original form. Therefore, this section has also shown that:

> *If H is a linear Hermitian operator on an arbitrary Hilbert space,*

> 1. *The eigenvalues of H are real.*
> 2. *Eigenfunctions corresponding to different eigenvalues of H are orthogonal.*
> 3. *It is possible to choose the eigenfunctions of H in a way such that they form a orthonormal basis for the Hilbert space. In general, the eigenfunctions of a Hermitian operator form a complete set (i.e., a complete basis for the Hilbert space).*

6.4   HERMITIAN MATRIX DIAGONALIZATION

In Section 6.2 we observed that if a matrix is diagonal, the diagonal elements are its eigenvalues. This observation opens an alternative approach to the matrix eigenvalue problem. Given the matrix eigenvalue equation

$$\mathsf{H}\mathbf{c} = \lambda\mathbf{c}, \tag{6.22}$$

where H is a Hermitian matrix, consider what happens if we insert unity between H and $\mathbf{c}$, as follows, with U a unitary matrix, and then left-multiply the resulting equation by U:

$$HU^{-1}U\mathbf{c} = \lambda\mathbf{c} \quad \longrightarrow \quad UHU^{-1}(U\mathbf{c}) = \lambda(U\mathbf{c}). \tag{6.23}$$

Equation (6.23) shows that our original eigenvalue equation has been converted into one in which H has been replaced by its unitary transformation (by U) and the eigenvector $\mathbf{c}$ has also been transformed by U, but the value of λ remains unchanged. We thus have the important result:

> *The eigenvalues of a matrix remain unchanged when the matrix is subjected to a unitary transformation.*

Next, suppose that we choose U in such a way that the transformed matrix UHU^{-1} is in the eigenvector basis. While we may or may not know how to construct this U, we know that such a unitary matrix exists because the eigenvectors form a complete orthogonal set, and can be specified to be normalized. If we transform with the chosen U, the matrix UHU^{-1} will be diagonal, with the eigenvalues as diagonal elements. Moreover, the eigenvector $U\mathbf{c}$ of UHU^{-1} corresponding to the eigenvalue $\lambda_i = (UHU^{-1})_{ii}$ is $\hat{\mathbf{e}}_i$ (a column vector with all elements zero except for unity in the ith row). We may find the eigenvector $\mathbf{c}_i$ of Eq. (6.22) by solving the equation $U\mathbf{c}_i = \hat{\mathbf{e}}_i$, obtaining $\mathbf{c}_i = U^{-1}\hat{\mathbf{e}}_i$.

These observations correspond to the following:

> *For any Hermitian matrix H, there exists a unitary transformation U that will cause UHU^{-1} to be diagonal, with the eigenvalues of H as its diagonal elements.*

This is an extremely important result. Another way of stating it is:

> *A Hermitian matrix can be diagonalized by a unitary transformation, with its eigenvalues as the diagonal elements.*

Looking next at the ith eigenvector $U^{-1}\hat{\mathbf{e}}_i$, we have

$$\begin{pmatrix} (U^{-1})_{11} & \cdots & (U^{-1})_{1i} & \cdots & (U^{-1})_{1n} \\ (U^{-1})_{21} & \cdots & (U^{-1})_{2i} & \cdots & (U^{-1})_{2n} \\ \cdots & \cdots & \cdots & \cdots & \cdots \\ \cdots & \cdots & \cdots & \cdots & \cdots \\ (U^{-1})_{n1} & \cdots & (U^{-1})_{ni} & \cdots & (U^{-1})_{nn} \end{pmatrix} \begin{pmatrix} 0 \\ \cdots \\ 1 \\ \cdots \\ 0 \end{pmatrix} = \begin{pmatrix} (U^{-1})_{1i} \\ (U^{-1})_{2i} \\ \cdots \\ \cdots \\ (U^{-1})_{ni} \end{pmatrix}. \tag{6.24}$$

We see that the columns of U^{-1} are the eigenvectors of H, normalized because U^{-1} is a unitary matrix. It is also clear from Eq. (6.24) that U^{-1} is not entirely unique; if its columns are permuted, all that will happen is that the order of the eigenvectors are changed, with a corresponding permutation of the diagonal elements of the diagonal matrix UHU^{-1}. Summarizing,

> *If a unitary matrix U is such that, for a Hermitian matrix H, UHU^{-1} is diagonal, the normalized eigenvector of H corresponding to the eigenvalue $(UHU^{-1})_{ii}$ will be the ith column of U^{-1}.*

If H is not degenerate, U^{-1} (and also U) will be unique except for a possible permutation of the columns of U^{-1} (and a corresponding permutation of the rows of U). However, if H is degenerate (has a repeated eigenvalue), then the columns of U^{-1} corresponding to the same eigenvalue can be transformed among themselves, thereby giving additional flexibility to U and U^{-1}.

Finally, calling on the fact that both the determinant and the trace of a matrix are unchanged when the matrix is subjected to a unitary transformation (shown in Section 5.7), we see that the determinant of a Hermitian matrix can be identified as the product of its eigenvalues, and its trace will be their sum. Apart from the individual eigenvalues themselves, these are the most useful of the invariants that a matrix has with respect to unitary transformation.

We illustrate the ideas thus far introduced in this section in the next example.

Example 6.4.1 TRANSFORMING A MATRIX TO DIAGONAL FORM

We return to the matrix H of Example 6.2.2:

$$H = \begin{pmatrix} 0 & 1 & 0 \\ 1 & 0 & 0 \\ 0 & 0 & 2 \end{pmatrix}.$$

We note that it is Hermitian, so there exists a unitary transformation U that will diagonalize it. Since we already know the eigenvectors of H, we can use them to construct U. Noting that we need **normalized** eigenvectors, and consulting Eqs. (6.9) to (6.11), we have

$$\lambda = 2, \quad \begin{pmatrix} 0 \\ 0 \\ 1 \end{pmatrix}; \quad \lambda = 1, \quad \begin{pmatrix} 1/\sqrt{2} \\ 1/\sqrt{2} \\ 0 \end{pmatrix}; \quad \lambda = -1, \quad \begin{pmatrix} 1/\sqrt{2} \\ -1/\sqrt{2} \\ 0 \end{pmatrix}.$$

Combining these as columns into U^{-1},

$$U^{-1} = \begin{pmatrix} 0 & 1/\sqrt{2} & 1/\sqrt{2} \\ 0 & 1/\sqrt{2} & -1/\sqrt{2} \\ 1 & 0 & 0 \end{pmatrix}.$$

Since $U = (U^{-1})^{\dagger}$, we easily form

$$U = \begin{pmatrix} 0 & 0 & 1 \\ 1/\sqrt{2} & 1/\sqrt{2} & 0 \\ 1/\sqrt{2} & -1/\sqrt{2} & 0 \end{pmatrix} \quad \text{and} \quad UHU^{-1} = \begin{pmatrix} 2 & 0 & 0 \\ 0 & 1 & 0 \\ 0 & 0 & -1 \end{pmatrix}.$$

The trace of H is 2, as is the sum of the eigenvalues; $\det(H)$ is -2, equal to $2 \times 1 \times (-1)$.

∎

Finding a Diagonalizing Transformation

As Example 6.4.1 shows, a knowledge of the eigenvectors of a Hermitian matrix H enables the direct construction of a unitary matrix U that transforms H into diagonal form. But we are interested in diagonalizing matrices for the purpose of **finding** their eigenvectors and eigenvalues, so the construction illustrated in Example 6.4.1 does not meet our present needs. Applied mathematicians (and even theoretical chemists!) have over many years given attention to numerical methods for diagonalizing matrices of order large enough that direct, exact solution of the secular equation is not possible, and computer programs for carrying out these methods have reached a high degree of sophistication and efficiency. In varying ways, such programs involve processes that approach diagonalization via successive approximations. That is to be expected, since explicit formulas for the solution of high-degree algebraic equations (including, of course, secular equations) do not exist. To give the reader a sense of the level that has been reached in matrix diagonalization technology, we identify a computation[1] that determined some of the eigenvalues and eigenvectors of a matrix whose dimension exceeded 10^9.

One of the older techniques for diagonalizing a matrix is due to Jacobi. It has now been supplanted by more efficient (but less transparent) methods, but we discuss it briefly here to illustrate the ideas involved. The essence of the Jacobi method is that if a Hermitian matrix H has a nonzero value of some off-diagonal h_{ij} (and thus also h_{ji}), a unitary transformation that alters only rows/columns i and j can reduce h_{ij} and h_{ji} to zero. While this transformation may cause other, previously zeroed elements to become nonzero, it can be shown that the resulting matrix is closer to being diagonal (meaning that the sum of the squared magnitudes of its off-diagonal elements has been reduced). One may therefore apply Jacobi-type transformations repeatedly to reduce individual off-diagonal elements to zero, continuing until there is no off-diagonal element larger than an acceptable tolerance. If one constructs the unitary matrix that is the product of the individual transformations, one obtains thereby the overall diagonalizing transformation. Alternatively, one can use the Jacobi method only for retrieval of the eigenvalues, after which the method presented previously can be used to obtain the eigenvectors.

Simultaneous Diagonalization

It is of interest to know whether two Hermitian matrices A and B can have a common set of eigenvectors. It turns out that this is possible if and only if they commute. The proof is simple if the eigenvectors of either A or **B** are nondegenerate.

Assume that c_i are a set of eigenvectors of both A and B with respective eigenvalues a_i and b_i. Then form, for any i,

$$BAc_i = Ba_i c_i = b_i a_i c_i,$$

$$ABc_i = Ab_i c_i = a_i b_i c_i.$$

These equations show that $BAc_i = ABc_i$ for every c_i. Since any vector **v** can be written as a linear combination of the c_i, we find that $(BA - AB)v = 0$ for all **v**, which means that $BA = AB$. We have found that the existence of a common set of eigenvectors implies commutation. It remains to prove the converse, namely that commutation permits construction of a common set of eigenvectors.

For the converse, we assume that A and B commute, that c_i is an eigenvector of A with eigenvalue a_i, and that this eigenvector of A is nondegenerate. Then we form

$$ABc_i = BAc_i = Ba_i c_i, \quad \text{or} \quad A(Bc_i) = a_i(Bc_i).$$

[1] J. Olsen, P. Jørgensen, and J. Simons, Passing the one-billion limit in full configuration-interaction calculations, *Chem. Phys. Lett.* **169**: 463 (1990).

This equation shows that $B\mathbf{c}_i$ is also an eigenvector of A with eigenvalue a_i. Since the eigenvector of A was assumed nondegenerate, $B\mathbf{c}_i$ must be proportional to $\mathbf{c}_i$, meaning that $\mathbf{c}_i$ is also an eigenvector of **B**. This completes the proof that if A and B commute, they have common eigenvectors.

The proof of this theorem can be extended to include the case in which both operators have degenerate eigenvectors. Including that extension, we summarize by stating the general result:

> *Hermitian matrices have a complete set of eigenvectors in common if and only if they commute.*

It may happen that we have three matrices A, B, and C, and that $[\Lambda, B] = 0$ and $[A, C] = 0$, but $[B, C] \neq 0$. In that case, which is actually quite common in atomic physics, we have a choice. We can insist upon a set of $\mathbf{c}_i$ that are simultaneous eigenvectors of A and B, in which case not all the $\mathbf{c}_i$ can be eigenvectors of C, or we can have simultaneous eigenvectors of A and C, but not B. In atomic physics these choices typically correspond to descriptions in which different angular momenta are required to have definite values.

Spectral Decomposition

Once the eigenvalues and eigenvectors of a Hermitian matrix H have been found, we can express H in terms of these quantities. Since mathematicians call the set of eigenvalues of H its **spectrum**, the expression we now derive for H is referred to as its **spectral decomposition**.

As previously noted, in the orthonormal eigenvector basis the matrix H will be diagonal. Then, instead of the general form for the basis expansion of an operator, H will be of the diagonal form

$$H = \sum_\mu |\mathbf{c}_\mu\rangle \lambda_\mu \langle \mathbf{c}_\mu|, \quad \text{each } \mathbf{c}_\mu \text{ satisfies } H\mathbf{c}_\mu = \lambda_\mu \mathbf{c}_\mu \text{ and } \langle \mathbf{c}_\mu | \mathbf{c}_\mu \rangle = 1. \tag{6.25}$$

This result, the **spectral decomposition** of H, is easily checked by applying it to any eigenvector $\mathbf{c}_\nu$.

Another result related to the spectral decomposition of H can be obtained if we multiply both sides of the equation $H\mathbf{c}_\mu = \lambda_\mu \mathbf{c}_\mu$ on the left by H, reaching

$$H^2 \mathbf{c}_\mu = (\lambda_\mu)^2 \mathbf{c}_\mu;$$

further applications of H show that all positive powers of H have the same eigenvectors as H, so if $f(H)$ is any function of H that has a power-series expansion, it has spectral decomposition

$$f(H) = \sum_\mu |\mathbf{c}_\mu\rangle f(\lambda_\mu)\langle \mathbf{c}_\mu|. \tag{6.26}$$

Equation (6.26) can be extended to include negative powers if H is nonsingular; to do so, multiply $H\mathbf{c}_\mu = \lambda_\mu \mathbf{c}_\mu$ on the left by H^{-1} and rearrange, to obtain

$$H^{-1}\mathbf{c}_\mu = \frac{1}{\lambda_\mu}\mathbf{c}_\mu,$$

showing that negative powers of H also have the same eigenvectors as H.

Finally, we can now easily prove the trace formula, Eq. (2.84). In the eigenvector basis,

$$\det\left(\exp(A)\right) = \prod_\mu e^{\lambda_\mu} = \exp\left(\sum_\mu \lambda_\mu\right) = \exp\left(\text{trace}(A)\right). \tag{6.27}$$

Since the determinant and trace are basis-independent, this proves the trace formula.

Expectation Values

The expectation value of a Hermitian operator H associated with the normalized function ψ was defined in Eq. (5.61) as

$$\langle H \rangle = \langle \psi | H | \psi \rangle, \tag{6.28}$$

where it was shown that if an orthonormal basis was introduced, with H then represented by a matrix H and ψ represented by a vector $\mathbf{a}$, this expectation value assumed the form

$$\langle H \rangle = \mathbf{a}^\dagger H \mathbf{a} = \langle \mathbf{a}|H|\mathbf{a}\rangle = \sum_{\nu\mu} a_\nu^* h_{\nu\mu} a_\mu. \tag{6.29}$$

If these quantities are expressed in the orthonormal eigenvector basis, Eq. (6.29) becomes

$$\langle H \rangle = \sum_\mu a_\mu^* \lambda_\mu a_\mu = \sum_\mu |a_\mu|^2 \lambda_\mu, \tag{6.30}$$

where a_μ is the coefficient of the eigenvector $\mathbf{c}_\mu$ (with eigenvalue λ_μ) in the expansion of ψ. We note that the expectation value is a weighted sum of the eigenvalues, with the weights nonnegative, and adding to unity because

$$\langle \mathbf{a}|\mathbf{a}\rangle = \sum_\mu a_\mu^* a_\mu = \sum_\mu |a_\mu|^2 = 1. \tag{6.31}$$

An obvious implication of Eq. (6.30) is that the expectation value $\langle H \rangle$ cannot be smaller than the smallest eigenvalue nor larger than the largest eigenvalue. The quantum-mechanical interpretation of this observation is that if H corresponds to a physical quantity, measurements of that quantity will yield the values λ_μ with relative probabilities given by $|a_\mu|^2$, and hence with an average value corresponding to the weighted sum, which is the expectation value.

Hermitian operators arising in physical problems often have finite smallest eigenvalues. This, in turn, means that the expectation value of the physical quantity associated with the operator has a finite lower bound. We thus have the frequently useful relation

> If the algebraically smallest eigenvalue of H is finite, then, for **any** ψ, $\langle\psi|H|\psi\rangle$ will be greater than or equal to this eigenvalue, with the equality occurring only if ψ is an eigenfunction corresponding to the smallest eigenvalue.

Positive Definite and Singular Operators

If all the eigenvalues of an operator A are positive, it is termed **positive definite**. If and only if A is positive definite, its expectation value for any nonzero ψ, namely $\langle\psi|A|\psi\rangle$, will also be positive, since (when ψ is normalized) it must be equal to or larger than the smallest eigenvalue.

Example 6.4.2   OVERLAP MATRIX

Let S be an **overlap matrix** of elements $s_{\nu\mu} = \langle\chi_\nu|\chi_\mu\rangle$, where the χ_ν are members of a linearly independent, but nonorthogonal basis. If we assume an arbitrary nonzero function ψ to be expanded in terms of the χ_ν, according to $\psi = \sum_\nu b_\nu\chi_\nu$, the scalar product $\langle\psi|\psi\rangle$ will be given by

$$\langle\psi|\psi\rangle = \sum_{\nu\mu} b_\nu^* s_{\nu\mu} b_\mu,$$

which is of the form of an expectation value for the matrix S. Since $\langle\psi|\psi\rangle$ is an inherently positive quantity, we conclude that S is positive definite. ∎

If, on the other hand, the rows (or the columns) of a square matrix represent linearly dependent forms, either as coefficients in a basis-set expansion or as the coefficients of a linear expression in a set of variables, the matrix will be singular, and that fact will be signaled by the presence of eigenvalues that are zero. The number of zero eigenvalues provides an indication of the extent of the linear dependence; if an $n \times n$ matrix has m zero eigenvalues, its rank will be $n - m$.

Exercises

6.4.1 Show that the eigenvalues of a matrix are unaltered if the matrix is transformed by a similarity transformation—a transformation that need not be unitary, but of the form given in Eq. (5.78).

This property is not limited to symmetric or Hermitian matrices. It holds for any matrix satisfying an eigenvalue equation of the type $Ax = \lambda x$. If our matrix can be brought into diagonal form by a similarity transformation, then two immediate consequences are that:

1. The trace (sum of eigenvalues) is invariant under a similarity transformation.
2. The determinant (product of eigenvalues) is invariant under a similarity transformation.

Note. The invariance of the trace and determinant are often demonstrated by using the Cayley-Hamilton theorem, which states that a matrix satisfies its own characteristic (secular) equation.

6.4.2 As a converse of the theorem that Hermitian matrices have real eigenvalues and that eigenvectors corresponding to distinct eigenvalues are orthogonal, show that if

(a) the eigenvalues of a matrix are real and

(b) the eigenvectors satisfy $\mathbf{x}_i^\dagger \mathbf{x}_j = \delta_{ij}$,

then the matrix is Hermitian.

6.4.3   Show that a real matrix that is not symmetric cannot be diagonalized by an orthogonal or unitary transformation.

Hint. Assume that the nonsymmetric real matrix can be diagonalized and develop a contradiction.

6.4.4   The matrices representing the angular momentum components L_x, L_y, and L_z are all Hermitian. Show that the eigenvalues of $\mathbf{L}^2$, where $\mathbf{L}^2 = L_x^2 + L_y^2 + L_z^2$, are real and nonnegative.

6.4.5   A has eigenvalues λ_i and corresponding eigenvectors $|\mathbf{x}_i\rangle$. Show that A^{-1} has the same eigenvectors but with eigenvalues λ_i^{-1}.

6.4.6   A square matrix with zero determinant is labeled **singular**.

(a) If A is singular, show that there is at least one nonzero column vector $\mathbf{v}$ such that

$$A|\mathbf{v}\rangle = 0.$$

(b) If there is a nonzero vector $|\mathbf{v}\rangle$ such that

$$A|\mathbf{v}\rangle = 0,$$

show that A is a singular matrix. This means that if a matrix (or operator) has zero as an eigenvalue, the matrix (or operator) has no inverse and its determinant is zero.

6.4.7   Two Hermitian matrices A and B have the same eigenvalues. Show that A and B are related by a unitary transformation.

6.4.8   Find the eigenvalues and an orthonormal set of eigenvectors for each of the matrices of Exercise 2.2.12.

6.4.9   The unit process in the iterative matrix diagonalization procedure known as the Jacobi method is a unitary transformation that operates on rows/columns i and j of a real symmetric matrix A to make $a_{ij} = a_{ji} = 0$. If this transformation (from basis functions φ_i and φ_j to φ_i' and φ_j') is written

$$\varphi_i' = \varphi_i \cos\theta - \varphi_j \sin\theta, \quad \varphi_j' = \varphi_i \sin\theta + \varphi_j \cos\theta,$$

(a) Show that a_{ij} is transformed to zero if $\tan 2\theta = \dfrac{2a_{ij}}{a_{jj} - a_{ii}}$,

(b) Show that $a_{\mu\nu}$ remains unchanged if neither μ nor ν is i or j,

(c) Find a_{ii}' and a_{jj}' and show that the trace of A is not changed by the transformation,

(d) Find $a_{i\mu}'$ and $a_{j\mu}'$ (where μ is neither i nor j) and show that the sum of the squares of the off-diagonal elements of A is reduced by the amount $2a_{ij}^2$.

6.5 NORMAL MATRICES

Thus far the discussion has been centered on Hermitian eigenvalue problems, which we showed to have real eigenvalues and orthogonal eigenvectors, and therefore capable of being diagonalized by a unitary transformation. However, the class of matrices which can be diagonalized by a unitary transformation contains, in addition to Hermitian matrices, all other matrices that commute with their adjoints; a matrix A with this property, namely

$$[\mathsf{A}, \mathsf{A}^\dagger] = 0,$$

is termed **normal**.[2] Clearly Hermitian matrices are normal, as $\mathsf{H}^\dagger = \mathsf{H}$. Unitary matrices are also normal, as U commutes with its inverse. Anti-Hermitian matrices (with $\mathsf{A}^\dagger = -\mathsf{A}$) are also normal. And there exist normal matrices that are not in any of these categories.

To show that normal matrices can be diagonalized by a unitary transformation, it suffices to prove that their eigenvectors can form an orthonormal set, which reduces to the requirement that eigenvectors of different eigenvalues be orthogonal. The proof proceeds in two steps, of which the first is to demonstrate that a normal matrix A and its adjoint have the same eigenvectors.

Assuming $|\mathbf{x}\rangle$ to be an eigenvector of A with eigenvalue λ, we have the equation

$$(\mathsf{A} - \lambda\mathbf{1})|\mathbf{x}\rangle = 0.$$

Multiplying this equation on its left by $\langle\mathbf{x}|(\mathsf{A}^\dagger - \lambda^*\mathbf{1})$, we have

$$\langle\mathbf{x}|(\mathsf{A}^\dagger - \lambda^*\mathbf{1})(\mathsf{A} - \lambda\mathbf{1})|\mathbf{x}\rangle = 0,$$

after which we use the normal property to interchange the two parenthesized quantities, bringing us to

$$\langle\mathbf{x}|(\mathsf{A} - \lambda\mathbf{1})(\mathsf{A}^\dagger - \lambda^*\mathbf{1})|\mathbf{x}\rangle = 0.$$

Moving the first parenthesized quantity into the left half-bracket, we have

$$\langle(\mathsf{A}^\dagger - \lambda^*\mathbf{1})\mathbf{x}|(\mathsf{A}^\dagger - \lambda^*\mathbf{1})|\mathbf{x}\rangle = 0,$$

which we identify as a scalar product of the form $\langle f|f\rangle$. The only way this scalar product can vanish is if

$$(\mathsf{A}^\dagger - \lambda^*\mathbf{1})|\mathbf{x}\rangle = 0,$$

showing that $|\mathbf{x}\rangle$ is an eigenvector of $\mathsf{A}^\dagger$ in addition to being an eigenvector of A. However, the eigenvalues of A and $\mathsf{A}^\dagger$ are complex conjugates; for general normal matrices λ need not be real.

A demonstration that the eigenvectors are orthogonal proceeds along the same lines are for Hermitian matrices. Letting $|\mathbf{x}_i\rangle$ and $|\mathbf{x}_j\rangle$ be two eigenvectors (of both A and $\mathsf{A}^\dagger$), we form

$$\langle\mathbf{x}_j|\mathsf{A}|\mathbf{x}_i\rangle = \lambda_i\langle\mathbf{x}_j|\mathbf{x}_i\rangle, \quad \langle\mathbf{x}_i|\mathsf{A}^\dagger|\mathbf{x}_j\rangle = \lambda_j^*\langle\mathbf{x}_i|\mathbf{x}_j\rangle. \tag{6.32}$$

---

[2]Normal matrices are the largest class of matrices that can be diagonalized by unitary transformations. For an extensive discussion of normal matrices, see P. A. Macklin, Normal matrices for physicists, *Am. J. Phys.* **52**: 513 (1984).

We now take the complex conjugate of the second of these equations, noting that $\langle x_i | x_j \rangle^* = \langle x_j | x_i \rangle$. To form the complex conjugate of $\langle x_i | A^\dagger | x_j \rangle$, we convert it first to $\langle Ax_i | x_j \rangle$ and then interchange the two half-brackets. Equations (6.32) then become

$$\langle x_j | A | x_i \rangle = \lambda_i \langle x_j | x_i \rangle, \quad \langle x_j | A | x_i \rangle = \lambda_j \langle x_j | x_i \rangle. \tag{6.33}$$

These equations indicate that if $\lambda_i \neq \lambda_j$, we must have $\langle x_j | x_i \rangle = 0$, thus proving orthogonality.

The fact that the eigenvalues of a normal matrix $A^\dagger$ are complex conjugates of the eigenvalues of A enables us to conclude that

- the eigenvalues of an anti-Hermitian matrix are pure imaginary (because $A^\dagger = -A$, $\lambda^* = -\lambda$), and

- the eigenvalues of a unitary matrix are of unit magnitude (because $\lambda^* = 1/\lambda$, equivalent to $\lambda^* \lambda = 1$).

Example 6.5.1   A NORMAL EIGENSYSTEM

Consider the unitary matrix

$$U = \begin{pmatrix} 0 & 0 & 1 \\ 1 & 0 & 0 \\ 0 & 1 & 0 \end{pmatrix}.$$

This matrix describes a rotational transformation in which $z \to x$, $x \to y$, and $y \to z$. Because it is unitary, it is also normal, and we may find its eigenvalues from the secular equation

$$\det(U - \lambda \mathbf{1}) = \begin{vmatrix} -\lambda & 0 & 1 \\ 1 & -\lambda & 0 \\ 0 & 1 & -\lambda \end{vmatrix} = -\lambda^3 + 1 = 0,$$

which has solutions $\lambda = 1$, ω, and ω^*, where $\omega = e^{2\pi i/3}$. (Note that $\omega^3 = 1$, so $\omega^* = 1/\omega = \omega^2$.) Because U is real, unitary and describes a rotation, its eigenvalues must fall on the unit circle, their sum (the trace) must be real, and their product (the determinant) must be $+1$. This means that one of the eigenvalues must be $+1$, and the remaining two may be real (both $+1$ or both -1) or form a complex conjugate pair. We see that the eigenvalues we have found satisfy these criteria. The trace of U is zero, as is the sum $1 + \omega + \omega^*$ (this may be verified graphically; see Fig. 6.3).

Proceeding to the eigenvectors, substitution into the equation

$$(U - \lambda \mathbf{1}) \mathbf{c} = 0$$

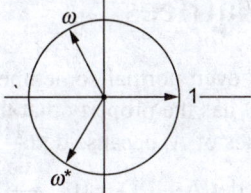

FIGURE 6.3 Eigenvalues of the matrix U, Example 6.5.1.

yields (in unnormalized form)

$$\lambda_1 = 1, \quad \mathbf{c}_1 = \begin{pmatrix} 1 \\ 1 \\ 1 \end{pmatrix}, \quad \lambda_2 = \omega, \quad \mathbf{c}_2 = \begin{pmatrix} 1 \\ \omega^* \\ \omega \end{pmatrix}, \quad \lambda_3 = \omega^2, \quad \mathbf{c}_3 = \begin{pmatrix} 1 \\ \omega \\ \omega^* \end{pmatrix}.$$

The interpretation of this result is interesting. The eigenvector $\mathbf{c}_1$ is unchanged by U (application of U multiplies it by unity), so it must lie in the direction of the axis of the rotation described by U. The other two eigenvectors are complex linear combinations of the coordinates that are invariant in "direction," but not in phase under application of U. We write "direction" in quotes, since the complex coefficients in the eigenvectors cause them not to identify directions in physical space. Nevertheless, they do form quantities that are invariant except for multiplication by the eigenvalue (which we identify as a phase, since it is of magnitude unity). The argument of ω, $2\pi/3$, identifies the amount of the rotation about the $\mathbf{c}_1$ axis. Coming back to physical reality, we note that we have found that U corresponds to a rotation of amount $2\pi/3$ about an axis in the $(1,1,1)$ direction; the reader can verify that this indeed takes x into y, y into z, and z into x.

Because U is normal, its eigenvectors must be orthogonal. Since we now have complex quantities, in order to check this we must compute the scalar product of two vectors $\mathbf{a}$ and $\mathbf{b}$ from the formula $\mathbf{a}^\dagger \mathbf{b}$. Our eigenvectors pass this test.

Finally, let's verify that U and $U^\dagger$ have the same eigenvectors, and that corresponding eigenvalues are complex conjugates. Taking the adjoint of U, we have

$$U^\dagger = \begin{pmatrix} 0 & 1 & 0 \\ 0 & 0 & 1 \\ 1 & 0 & 0 \end{pmatrix}.$$

Using the eigenvectors we have already found to form $U^\dagger \mathbf{c}_i$, the verification is easily established. We illustrate with $\mathbf{c}_2$:

$$\begin{pmatrix} 0 & 1 & 0 \\ 0 & 0 & 1 \\ 1 & 0 & 0 \end{pmatrix} \begin{pmatrix} 1 \\ \omega^* \\ \omega \end{pmatrix} = \begin{pmatrix} \omega^* \\ \omega \\ 1 \end{pmatrix} = \omega^* \begin{pmatrix} 1 \\ \omega^* \\ \omega \end{pmatrix},$$

as required.

Nonnormal Matrices

Matrices that are not even normal sometimes enter problems of importance in physics. Such a matrix, A, still has the property that the eigenvalues of $A^\dagger$ are the complex conjugates of the eigenvalues of A, because $\det(A^\dagger) = [\det(A)]^*$, so

$$\det(A - \lambda\mathbf{1}) = 0 \quad \longrightarrow \quad \det(A^\dagger - \lambda^*\mathbf{1}) = 0,$$

for the same λ, but it is no longer true that the eigenvectors are orthogonal or that A and $A^\dagger$ have common eigenvectors.

Here is an example arising from the analysis of vibrations in mechanical systems. We consider the vibrations of a classical model of the CO_2 molecule. Even though the model is classical, it is a good representation of the actual quantum-mechanical system, as to good approximation the nuclei execute small (classical) oscillations in the Hooke's-law potential generated by the electron distribution. This problem is an illustration of the application of matrix techniques to a problem that does not start as a matrix problem. It also provides an example of the eigenvalues and eigenvectors of an asymmetric real matrix.

Example 6.5.2   NORMAL MODES

Consider three masses on the x-axis joined by springs as shown in Fig. 6.4. The spring forces are assumed to be linear in the displacements from equilibrium (small displacements, Hooke's law), and the masses are constrained to stay on the x-axis.

Using a different coordinate for the displacement of each mass from its equilibrium position, Newton's second law yields the set of equations

$$\ddot{x}_1 = -\frac{k}{M}(x_1 - x_2)$$

$$\ddot{x}_2 = -\frac{k}{m}(x_2 - x_1) - \frac{k}{m}(x_2 - x_3) \qquad (6.34)$$

$$\ddot{x}_3 = -\frac{k}{M}(x_3 - x_2),$$

where $\ddot{x}$ stands for d^2x/dt^2. We seek the frequencies, ω, such that all the masses vibrate at the same frequency. These are called the **normal** modes of vibration,[3] and are solutions to Eqs. (6.34) with

$$x_i(t) = x_i \sin \omega t, \quad i = 1, 2, 3.$$

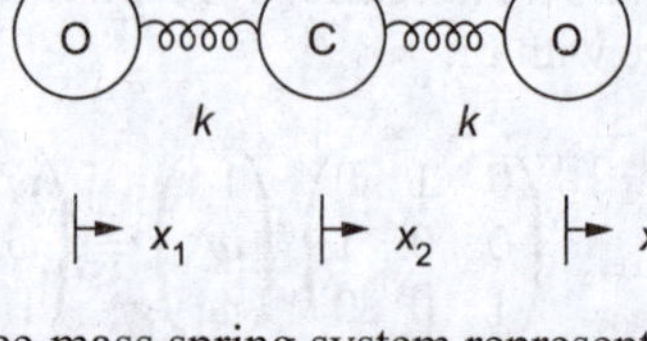

FIGURE 6.4   The three-mass spring system representing the CO_2 molecule.

[3]For detailed discussion of normal modes of vibration, see E. B. Wilson, Jr., J. C. Decius, and P. C. Cross, *Molecular Vibrations—The Theory of Infrared and Raman Vibrational Spectra.* New York: Dover (1980).

Substituting this solution set into Eqs. (6.34), these equations, after cancellation of the common factor $\sin \omega t$, become equivalent to the matrix equation

$$\mathbf{A}\mathbf{x} \equiv \begin{pmatrix} \dfrac{k}{M} & -\dfrac{k}{M} & 0 \\ -\dfrac{k}{m} & \dfrac{2k}{m} & -\dfrac{k}{m} \\ 0 & -\dfrac{k}{M} & \dfrac{k}{M} \end{pmatrix} \begin{pmatrix} x_1 \\ x_2 \\ x_3 \end{pmatrix} = +\omega^2 \begin{pmatrix} x_1 \\ x_2 \\ x_3 \end{pmatrix}. \tag{6.35}$$

We can find the eigenvalues of A by solving the secular equation

$$\begin{vmatrix} \dfrac{k}{M} - \omega^2 & -\dfrac{k}{M} & 0 \\ -\dfrac{k}{m} & \dfrac{2k}{m} - \omega^2 & -\dfrac{k}{m} \\ 0 & -\dfrac{k}{M} & \dfrac{k}{M} - \omega^2 \end{vmatrix} = 0, \tag{6.36}$$

which expands to

$$\omega^2 \left(\frac{k}{M} - \omega^2 \right) \left(\omega^2 - \frac{2k}{m} - \frac{k}{M} \right) = 0.$$

The eigenvalues are

$$\omega^2 = 0, \quad \frac{k}{M}, \quad \frac{k}{M} + \frac{2k}{m}.$$

For $\omega^2 = 0$, substitution back into Eq. (6.35) yields

$$x_1 - x_2 = 0, \quad -x_1 + 2x_2 - x_3 = 0, \quad -x_2 + x_3 = 0,$$

which corresponds to $x_1 = x_2 = x_3$. This describes pure translation with no relative motion of the masses and no vibration.

For $\omega^2 = k/M$, Eq. (6.35) yields

$$x_1 = -x_3, \quad x_2 = 0.$$

The two outer masses are moving in opposite directions. The central mass is stationary. In CO_2 this is called the **symmetric stretching** mode.

Finally, for $\omega^2 = k/M + 2k/m$, the eigenvector components are

$$x_1 = x_3, \quad x_2 = -\frac{2M}{m} x_1.$$

In this **antisymmetric stretching** mode, the two outer masses are moving, together, in a direction opposite to that of the central mass, so one CO bond stretches while the other contracts the same amount. In both of these stretching modes, the net momentum of the motion is zero.

Any displacement of the three masses along the x-axis can be described as a linear combination of these three types of motion: translation plus two forms of vibration.

The matrix A of Eq. (6.35) is not **normal**; the reader can check that $AA^\dagger \neq A^\dagger A$. As a result, the eigenvectors we have found are not orthogonal, as is obvious by examination of the unnormalized eigenvectors:

$$\omega^2 = 0, \quad \mathbf{x} = \begin{pmatrix} 1 \\ 1 \\ 1 \end{pmatrix} \qquad \omega^2 = \frac{k}{M}, \quad \mathbf{x} = \begin{pmatrix} 1 \\ 0 \\ -1 \end{pmatrix}, \qquad \omega^2 = \frac{k}{M} + \frac{2k}{m}, \quad \mathbf{x} = \begin{pmatrix} 1 \\ -2M/m \\ 1 \end{pmatrix}.$$

Using the same λ values, we can solve the simultaneous equations

$$\left(A^\dagger - \lambda^* \mathbf{1} \right) \mathbf{y} = 0.$$

The resulting eigenvectors are

$$\omega^2 = 0, \quad \mathbf{x} = \begin{pmatrix} 1 \\ m/M \\ 1 \end{pmatrix}, \qquad \omega^2 = \frac{k}{M}, \quad \mathbf{x} = \begin{pmatrix} 1 \\ 0 \\ 1 \end{pmatrix}, \qquad \omega^2 = \frac{k}{M} + \frac{2k}{m}, \quad \mathbf{x} = \begin{pmatrix} 1 \\ -2 \\ 1 \end{pmatrix}.$$

These vectors are neither orthogonal nor the same as the eigenvectors of A. ∎

Defective Matrices

If a matrix is not normal, it may not even have a full complement of eigenvectors. Such matrices are termed **defective**. By the fundamental theorem of algebra, a matrix of dimension N will have N eigenvalues (when their multiplicity is taken into account). It can also be shown that any matrix will have at least one eigenvector corresponding to each of its distinct eigenvalues. But it is **not** always true that that an eigenvalue of multiplicity $k > 1$ will have k eigenvectors. We give as a simple example a matrix with the doubly degenerate eigenvalue $\lambda = 1$:

$$\begin{pmatrix} 1 & 1 \\ 0 & 1 \end{pmatrix} \quad \text{has only the single eigenvector} \quad \begin{pmatrix} 1 \\ 0 \end{pmatrix}.$$

Exercises

6.5.1 Find the eigenvalues and corresponding eigenvectors for

$$\begin{pmatrix} 2 & 4 \\ 1 & 2 \end{pmatrix}.$$

Note that the eigenvectors are **not** orthogonal.

ANS. $\lambda_1 = 0$, $\mathbf{c}_1 = (2, -1)$;
$\lambda_2 = 4$, $\mathbf{c}_2 = (2, \ 1)$.

6.5.2 If A is a 2×2 matrix, show that its eigenvalues λ satisfy the secular equation

$$\lambda^2 - \lambda \operatorname{trace}(A) + \det(A) = 0.$$

6.5.3 Assuming a unitary matrix U to satisfy an eigenvalue equation $U\mathbf{c} = \lambda \mathbf{c}$, show that the eigenvalues of the unitary matrix have unit magnitude. This same result holds for real orthogonal matrices.

6.5.4 Since an orthogonal matrix describing a rotation in real 3-D space is a special case of a unitary matrix, such an orthogonal matrix can be diagonalized by a unitary transformation.

(a) Show that the sum of the three eigenvalues is $1 + 2\cos\varphi$, where φ is the net angle of rotation about a single fixed axis.

(b) Given that one eigenvalue is 1, show that the other two eigenvalues must be $e^{i\varphi}$ and $e^{-i\varphi}$.

Our orthogonal rotation matrix (real elements) has complex eigenvalues.

6.5.5 A is an nth-order Hermitian matrix with orthonormal eigenvectors $|\mathbf{x}_i\rangle$ and real eigenvalues $\lambda_1 \le \lambda_2 \le \lambda_3 \le \cdots \le \lambda_n$. Show that for a unit magnitude vector $|\mathbf{y}\rangle$,

$$\lambda_1 \le \langle \mathbf{y}|A|\mathbf{y}\rangle \le \lambda_n.$$

6.5.6 A particular matrix is both Hermitian and unitary. Show that its eigenvalues are all ± 1.

Note. The Pauli and Dirac matrices are specific examples.

6.5.7 For his relativistic electron theory Dirac required a set of **four** anticommuting matrices. Assume that these matrices are to be Hermitian and unitary. If these are $n \times n$ matrices, show that n must be even. With 2×2 matrices inadequate (why?), this demonstrates that the smallest possible matrices forming a set of four anticommuting, Hermitian, unitary matrices are 4×4.

6.5.8 A is a normal matrix with eigenvalues λ_n and orthonormal eigenvectors $|\mathbf{x}_n\rangle$. Show that A may be written as

$$A = \sum_n \lambda_n |\mathbf{x}_n\rangle\langle\mathbf{x}_n|.$$

Hint. Show that both this eigenvector form of A and the original A give the same result acting on an arbitrary vector $|\mathbf{y}\rangle$.

6.5.9 A has eigenvalues 1 and -1 and corresponding eigenvectors $\begin{pmatrix} 1 \\ 0 \end{pmatrix}$ and $\begin{pmatrix} 0 \\ 1 \end{pmatrix}$. Construct A.

$$\textit{ANS.} \quad A = \begin{pmatrix} 1 & 0 \\ 0 & -1 \end{pmatrix}.$$

6.5.10 A non-Hermitian matrix A has eigenvalues λ_i and corresponding eigenvectors $|\mathbf{u}_i\rangle$. The adjoint matrix $A^\dagger$ has the same set of eigenvalues but **different** corresponding eigenvectors, $|\mathbf{v}_i\rangle$. Show that the eigenvectors form a **biorthogonal** set in the sense that

$$\langle \mathbf{v}_i|\mathbf{u}_j\rangle = 0 \quad \text{for} \quad \lambda_i^* \ne \lambda_j.$$

6.5.11 You are given a pair of equations:

$$A|\mathbf{f}_n\rangle = \lambda_n|\mathbf{g}_n\rangle$$

$$\tilde{A}|\mathbf{g}_n\rangle = \lambda_n|\mathbf{f}_n\rangle \quad \text{with A real.}$$

(a) Prove that $|f_n\rangle$ is an eigenvector of $(\tilde{A}A)$ with eigenvalue λ_n^2.

(b) Prove that $|g_n\rangle$ is an eigenvector of $(A\tilde{A})$ with eigenvalue λ_n^2.

(c) State how you know that

(1) The $|f_n\rangle$ form an orthogonal set.

(2) The $|g_n\rangle$ form an orthogonal set.

(3) λ_n^2 is real.

6.5.12   Prove that A of the preceding exercise may be written as

$$A = \sum_n \lambda_n |g_n\rangle\langle f_n|,$$

with the $|g_n\rangle$ and $\langle f_n|$ normalized to unity.

Hint. Expand an arbitrary vector as a linear combination of $|f_n\rangle$.

6.5.13   Given

$$A = \frac{1}{\sqrt{5}} \begin{pmatrix} 2 & 2 \\ 1 & -4 \end{pmatrix},$$

(a) Construct the transpose $\tilde{A}$ and the symmetric forms $\tilde{A}A$ and $A\tilde{A}$.

(b) From $A\tilde{A}|g_n\rangle = \lambda_n^2 |g_n\rangle$, find λ_n and $|g_n\rangle$. Normalize the $|g_n\rangle$.

(c) From $\tilde{A}A|f_n\rangle = \lambda_n^2 |g_n\rangle$, find λ_n [same as (b)] and $|f_n\rangle$. Normalize the $|f_n\rangle$.

(d) Verify that $A|f_n\rangle = \lambda_n |g_n\rangle$ and $\tilde{A}|g_n\rangle = \lambda_n |f_n\rangle$.

(e) Verify that $A = \sum_n \lambda_n |g_n\rangle\langle f_n|$.

6.5.14   Given the eigenvalues $\lambda_1 = 1, \lambda_2 = -1$ and the corresponding eigenvectors

$$|f_1\rangle = \begin{pmatrix} 1 \\ 0 \end{pmatrix}, \quad |g_1\rangle = \frac{1}{\sqrt{2}} \begin{pmatrix} 1 \\ 1 \end{pmatrix}, \quad |f_2\rangle = \begin{pmatrix} 0 \\ 1 \end{pmatrix}, \quad \text{and}$$

$$|g_2\rangle = \frac{1}{\sqrt{2}} \begin{pmatrix} 1 \\ -1 \end{pmatrix},$$

(a) construct A;

(b) verify that $A|f_n\rangle = \lambda_n |g_n\rangle$;

(c) verify that $\tilde{A}|g_n\rangle = \lambda_n |f_n\rangle$.

$$\textit{ANS.} \quad A = \frac{1}{\sqrt{2}} \begin{pmatrix} 1 & -1 \\ 1 & 1 \end{pmatrix}.$$

6.5.15   Two matrices U and H are related by

$$U = e^{iaH},$$

with a real.

(a)   If H is Hermitian, show that U is unitary.

(b)   If U is unitary, show that H is Hermitian. (H is independent of a.)

(c)   If trace H $= 0$, show that det U $= +1$.

(d)   If det U $= +1$, show that trace H $= 0$.

Hint. H may be diagonalized by a similarity transformation. Then U is also diagonal. The corresponding eigenvalues are given by $u_j = \exp(iah_j)$.

6.5.16   An $n \times n$ matrix A has n eigenvalues A_i. If $B = e^A$, show that B has the same eigenvectors as A with the corresponding eigenvalues B_i given by $B_i = \exp(A_i)$.

6.5.17   A matrix P is a projection operator satisfying the condition

$$P^2 = P.$$

Show that the corresponding eigenvalues $(\rho^2)_\lambda$ and ρ_λ satisfy the relation

$$(\rho^2)_\lambda = (\rho_\lambda)^2 = \rho_\lambda.$$

This means that the eigenvalues of P are 0 and 1.

6.5.18   In the **matrix** eigenvector-eigenvalue equation

$$A|\mathbf{x}_i\rangle = \lambda_i |\mathbf{x}_i\rangle,$$

A is an $n \times n$ Hermitian matrix. For simplicity assume that its n real eigenvalues are distinct, λ_1 being the largest. If $|\mathbf{x}\rangle$ is an approximation to $|\mathbf{x}_1\rangle$,

$$|\mathbf{x}\rangle = |\mathbf{x}_1\rangle + \sum_{i=2}^{n} \delta_i |\mathbf{x}_i\rangle,$$

show that

$$\frac{\langle \mathbf{x}|A|\mathbf{x}\rangle}{\langle \mathbf{x}|\mathbf{x}\rangle} \leq \lambda_1$$

and that the error in λ_1 is of the order $|\delta_i|^2$. Take $|\delta_i| \ll 1$.

Hint. The n vectors $|\mathbf{x}_i\rangle$ form a **complete** orthogonal set spanning the n-dimensional (complex) space.

6.5.19   Two equal masses are connected to each other and to walls by springs as shown in Fig. 6.5. The masses are constrained to stay on a horizontal line.

(a)   Set up the Newtonian acceleration equation for each mass.

(b)   Solve the secular equation for the eigenvectors.

(c)   Determine the eigenvectors and thus the normal modes of motion.

6.5.20   Given a normal matrix A with eigenvalues λ_j, show that $A^\dagger$ has eigenvalues λ_j^*, its real part $(A + A^\dagger)/2$ has eigenvalues $\Re e(\lambda_j)$, and its imaginary part $(A - A^\dagger)/2i$ has eigenvalues $\Im m(\lambda_j)$.

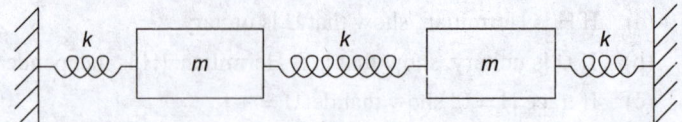

FIGURE 6.5   Triple oscillator.

6.5.21   Consider a rotation given by Euler angles $\alpha = \pi/4$, $\beta = \pi/2$, $\gamma = 5\pi/4$.

(a)   Using the formula of Eq. (3.37), construct the matrix U representing this rotation.

(b)   Find the eigenvalues and eigenvectors of U, and from them describe this rotation by specifying a single rotation axis and an angle of rotation about that axis.

Note. This technique provides a representation of rotations alternative to the Euler angles.

Additional Readings

Bickley, W. G., and R. S. H. G. Thompson, *Matrices—Their Meaning and Manipulation*. Princeton, NJ: Van Nostrand (1964). A comprehensive account of matrices in physical problems, and their analytic properties and numerical techniques.

Byron, F. W., Jr., and R. W. Fuller, *Mathematics of Classical and Quantum Physics*. Reading, MA: Addison-Wesley (1969), reprinting, Dover (1992).

Gilbert, J. and L. Gilbert, *Linear Algebra and Matrix Theory*. San Diego: Academic Press (1995).

Golub, G. H., and C. F. Van Loan, *Matrix Computations*, 3rd ed. Baltimore: JHU Press (1996). Detailed mathematical background and algorithms for the production of numerical software, including methods for parallel computation. A classic computer science text.

Halmos, P. R., *Finite-Dimensional Vector Spaces*, 2nd ed. Princeton, NJ: Van Nostrand (1958), reprinting, Springer (1993).

Hirsch, M., *Differential Equations, Dynamical Systems, and Linear Algebra*. San Diego: Academic Press (1974).

Heading, J., *Matrix Theory for Physicists*. London: Longmans, Green and Co. (1958). A readable introduction to determinants and matrices, with applications to mechanics, electromagnetism, special relativity, and quantum mechanics.

Jain, M. C., *Vector Spaces and Matrices in Physics*, 2nd ed. Oxford: Alpha Science International (2007).

Watkins, D. S., *Fundamentals of Matrix Computations*. New York: Wiley (1991).

Wilkinson, J. H., *The Algebraic Eigenvalue Problem*. London: Oxford University Press (1965), reprinting (2004). Classic treatise on numerical computation of eigenvalue problems. Perhaps the most widely read book in the field of numerical analysis.

CHAPTER 7

ORDINARY DIFFERENTIAL EQUATIONS

Much of theoretical physics is originally formulated in terms of differential equations in the three-dimensional physical space (and sometimes also time). These variables (e.g., x, y, z, t) are usually referred to as **independent variables**, while the function or functions being differentiated are referred to as **dependent variable(s)**. A differential equation involving more than one independent variable is called a **partial differential equation**, often abbreviated **PDE**. The simpler situation considered in the present chapter is that of an equation in a single independent variable, known as an **ordinary differential equation**, abbreviated **ODE**. As we shall see in a later chapter, some of the most frequently used methods for solving PDEs involve their expression in terms of the solutions to ODEs, so it is appropriate to begin our study of differential equations with ODEs.

7.1 INTRODUCTION

To start, we note that the taking of a derivative is a **linear operation**, meaning that

$$\frac{d}{dx}\big(a\varphi(x) + b\psi(x)\big) = a\frac{d\varphi}{dx} + b\frac{d\psi}{dx},$$

and the derivative operation can be viewed as defining a linear operator: $\mathcal{L} = d/dx$. Higher derivatives are also linear operators, as for example

$$\frac{d^2}{dx^2}\big(a\varphi(x) + b\psi(x)\big) = a\frac{d^2\varphi}{dx^2} + b\frac{d^2\psi}{dx^2}.$$

329

Note that the linearity under discussion is that of the **operator**. For example, if we define

$$\mathcal{L} = p(x)\frac{d}{dx} + q(x),$$

it is identified as **linear** because

$$\mathcal{L}\big(a\varphi(x) + b\psi(x)\big) = a\left(p(x)\frac{d\varphi}{dx} + q(x)\varphi\right) + b\left(p(x)\frac{d\psi}{dx} + q(x)\psi\right)$$

$$= a\mathcal{L}\varphi + b\mathcal{L}\psi.$$

We see that the linearity of $\mathcal{L}$ imposes no requirement that either $p(x)$ or $q(x)$ be a linear function of x. Linear differential operators therefore include those of the form

$$\mathcal{L} \equiv \sum_{\nu=0}^{n} p_\nu(x)\left(\frac{d^\nu}{dx^\nu}\right),$$

where the functions $p_\nu(x)$ are arbitrary.

An ODE is termed **homogeneous** if the dependent variable (here φ) occurs to the same power in all its terms, and **inhomogeneous** otherwise; it is termed **linear** if it can be written in the form

$$\mathcal{L}\varphi(x) = F(x), \tag{7.1}$$

where $\mathcal{L}$ is a linear differential operator and $F(x)$ is an algebraic function of x (i.e., not a differential operator). An important class of ODEs are those that are both linear and homogeneous, and thereby of the form $\mathcal{L}\varphi = 0$.

The solutions to ODEs are in general not unique, and if there are multiple solutions it is useful to identify those that are linearly independent (**linear dependence** is discussed in Section 2.1). Homogeneous linear ODEs have the general property that any multiple of a solution is also a solution, and that if there are multiple linearly independent solutions, any linear combination of those solutions will also solve the ODE. This statement is equivalent to noting that if $\mathcal{L}$ is linear, then, for all a and b,

$$\mathcal{L}\varphi = 0 \quad \text{and} \quad \mathcal{L}\psi = 0 \quad \longrightarrow \quad \mathcal{L}(a\varphi + b\psi) = 0.$$

The Schrödinger equation of quantum mechanics is a homogeneous linear ODE (or if in more than one dimension, a homogeneous linear PDE), and the property that any linear combination of its solutions is also a solution is the conceptual basis for the well-known **superposition principle** in electrodynamics, wave optics and quantum theory.

Notationally, it is often convenient to use the symbols x and y to refer, respectively, to independent and dependent variables, and a typical linear ODE then takes the form $\mathcal{L}y = F(x)$. It is also customary to use primes to indicate derivatives: $y' \equiv dy/dx$. In terms of this notation, the superposition property of solutions y_1 and y_2 of a homogeneous linear ODE tells us that the ODE also has as solutions $c_1 y_1$, $c_2 y_2$, and $c_1 y_1 + c_2 y_2$, with the c_i arbitrary constants.

Some physically important problems (particularly in fluid mechanics and in chaos theory) give rise to nonlinear differential equations. A well-studied example is the Bernoulli equation

$$y' = p(x)y + q(x)y^n, \quad n \neq 0, 1,$$

which cannot be written in terms of a linear operator applied to y.

Further terms used to classify ODEs include their **order** (highest derivative appearing therein), and **degree** (power to which the highest derivative appears after the ODE is rationalized if that is necessary). For many applications, the concept of **linearity** is more relevant than that of **degree**.

7.2 FIRST-ORDER EQUATIONS

Physics involves some first-order differential equations. For completeness it seems desirable to touch upon them briefly. We consider the general form

$$\frac{dy}{dx} = f(x, y) = -\frac{P(x, y)}{Q(x, y)}. \tag{7.2}$$

While there is no systematic way to solve the most general first-order ODE, there are a number of techniques that are often useful. After reviewing some of these techniques, we proceed to a more detailed treatment of linear first-order ODEs, for which systematic procedures are available.

Separable Equations

Frequently Eq. (7.2) will have the special form

$$\frac{dy}{dx} = -\frac{P(x)}{Q(y)}. \tag{7.3}$$

Then it may be rewritten as

$$P(x)dx + Q(y)dy = 0.$$

Integrating from (x_0, y_0) to (x, y) yields

$$\int_{x_0}^{x} P(x)dx + \int_{y_0}^{y} Q(y)dy = 0.$$

Since the lower limits, x_0 and y_0, contribute constants, we may ignore them and simply add a constant of integration. Note that this separation of variables technique does **not** require that the differential equation be linear.

Example 7.2.1 PARACHUTIST

We want to find the velocity of a falling parachutist as a function of time and are particularly interested in the constant limiting velocity, v_0, that comes about by air drag, taken to be quadratic, $-bv^2$, and opposing the force of the gravitational attraction, mg, of the Earth on the parachutist. We choose a coordinate system in which the positive direction is downward so that the gravitational force is positive. For simplicity we assume that the parachute opens immediately, that is, at time $t = 0$, where $v(t) = 0$, our initial condition. Newton's law applied to the falling parachutist gives

$$m\dot{v} = mg - bv^2, \tag{7.4}$$

where m includes the mass of the parachute.

The terminal velocity, v_0, can be found from the equation of motion as $t \to \infty$; when there is no acceleration, $\dot{v} = 0$, and

$$bv_0^2 = mg, \quad \text{or} \quad v_0 = \sqrt{\frac{mg}{b}}.$$

It simplifies further work to rewrite Eq. (7.4) as

$$\frac{m}{b}\dot{v} = v_0^2 - v^2.$$

This equation is separable, and we write it in the form

$$\frac{dv}{v_0^2 - v^2} = \frac{b}{m}dt. \tag{7.5}$$

Using partial fractions to write

$$\frac{1}{v_0^2 - v^2} = \frac{1}{2v_0}\left(\frac{1}{v + v_0} - \frac{1}{v - v_0}\right),$$

it is straightforward to integrate both sides of Eq. (7.5) (the left-hand side from $v = 0$ to v, the right-hand side from $t = 0$ to t), yielding

$$\frac{1}{2v_0}\ln\frac{v_0 + v}{v_0 - v} = \frac{b}{m}t.$$

Solving for the velocity, we have

$$v = \frac{e^{2t/T} - 1}{e^{2t/T} + 1}v_0 = v_0\frac{\sinh(t/T)}{\cosh(t/T)} = v_0\tanh\frac{t}{T},$$

where $T = \sqrt{m/gb}$ is the time constant governing the asymptotic approach of the velocity to its limiting value, v_0.

Inserting numerical values, $g = 9.8$ m/s^2, and taking $b = 700$ kg/m, $m = 70$ kg, gives $v_0 = \sqrt{9.8/10} \approx 1$ m/s ≈ 3.6 km/h ≈ 2.234 mi/h, the walking speed of a pedestrian at landing, and $T = \sqrt{m/bg} = 1/\sqrt{10 \cdot 9.8} \approx 0.1$ s. Thus, the constant speed v_0 is reached within a second. Finally, because **it is always important to check the solution**, we verify that our solution satisfies the original differential equation:

$$\dot{v} = \frac{\cosh(t/T)}{\cosh(t/T)}\frac{v_0}{T} - \frac{\sinh^2(t/T)}{\cosh^2(t/T)}\frac{v_0}{T} = \frac{v_0}{T} - \frac{v^2}{Tv_0} = g - \frac{b}{m}v^2.$$

A more realistic case, where the parachutist is in free fall with an initial speed $v(0) > 0$ before the parachute opens, is addressed in Exercise 7.2.16.   ∎

Exact Differentials

Again we rewrite Eq. (7.2) as

$$P(x, y)dx + Q(x, y)dy = 0. \tag{7.6}$$

This equation is said to be **exact** if we can match the left-hand side of it to a differential $d\varphi$, and thereby reach

$$d\varphi = \frac{\partial \varphi}{\partial x}dx + \frac{\partial \varphi}{\partial y}dy = 0. \tag{7.7}$$

Exactness therefore implies that there exists a function $\varphi(x, y)$ such that

$$\frac{\partial \varphi}{\partial x} = P(x, y) \quad \text{and} \quad \frac{\partial \varphi}{\partial y} = Q(x, y), \tag{7.8}$$

because then our ODE corresponds to an instance of Eq. (7.7), and its solution will be $\varphi(x, y) = $ constant.

Before seeking to find a function φ satisfying Eq. (7.8), it is useful to determine whether such a function exists. Taking the two formulas from Eq. (7.8), differentiating the first with respect to y and the second with respect to x, we find

$$\frac{\partial^2 \varphi}{\partial y \partial x} = \frac{\partial P(x, y)}{\partial y} \quad \text{and} \quad \frac{\partial^2 \varphi}{\partial x \partial y} = \frac{\partial Q(x, y)}{\partial x},$$

and these are consistent if and only if

$$\frac{\partial P(x, y)}{\partial y} = \frac{\partial Q(x, y)}{\partial x}. \tag{7.9}$$

We therefore conclude that Eq. (7.6) is exact only if Eq. (7.9) is satisfied. Once exactness has been verified, we can integrate Eqs. (7.8) to obtain φ and therewith a solution to the ODE.

The solution takes the form

$$\varphi(x, y) = \int_{x_0}^{x} P(x, y)dx + \int_{y_0}^{y} Q(x_0, y)dy = \text{constant.} \tag{7.10}$$

Proof of Eq. (7.10) is left to Exercise 7.2.7.

We note that separability and exactness are independent attributes. All separable ODEs are automatically exact, but not all exact ODEs are separable.

Example 7.2.2   A NONSEPARABLE EXACT ODE

Consider the ODE

$$y' + \left(1 + \frac{y}{x}\right) = 0.$$

Multiplying by $x\, dx$, this ODE becomes

$$(x + y)dx + x\, dy = 0,$$

which is of the form

$$P(x, y)dx + Q(x, y)dy = 0,$$

with $P(x, y) = x + y$ and $Q(x, y) = x$. The equation is not separable. To check if it is exact, we compute

$$\frac{\partial P}{\partial y} = \frac{\partial (x + y)}{\partial y} = 1, \quad \frac{\partial Q}{\partial x} = \frac{\partial x}{\partial x} = 1.$$

These partial derivatives are equal; the equation is exact, and can be written in the form

$$d\varphi = P\,dx + Q\,dy = 0.$$

The solution to the ODE will be $\varphi = C$, with φ computed according to Eq. (7.10):

$$\varphi = \int_{x_0}^{x} (x + y)dx + \int_{y_0}^{y} x_0 dy = \left(\frac{x^2}{2} + xy - \frac{x_0^2}{2} - x_0 y \right) + (x_o y - x_0 y_0)$$

$$= \frac{x^2}{2} + xy + \text{constant terms.}$$

Thus, the solution is

$$\frac{x^2}{2} + xy = C,$$

which if desired can be solved to give y as a function of x. We can also check to make sure that our solution actually solves the ODE. ∎

It may well turn out that Eq. (7.6) is not exact and that Eq. (7.9) is not satisfied. However, there always exists at least one and perhaps an infinity of **integrating factors** $\alpha(x, y)$ such that

$$\alpha(x, y)P(x, y)dx + \alpha(x, y)Q(x, y)dy = 0$$

is exact. Unfortunately, an integrating factor is not always obvious or easy to find. A systematic way to develop an integrating factor is known only when a first-order ODE is linear; this will be discussed in the subsection on linear first-order ODEs.

Equations Homogeneous in *x* and *y*

An ODE is said to be homogeneous (of order n) in x and y if the combined powers of x and y add to n in all the terms of $P(x, y)$ and $Q(x, y)$ when the ODE is written as in Eq. (7.6). Note that this use of the term "homogeneous" has a different meaning than when it was used to describe a linear ODE as given in Eq. (7.1) with the term $F(x)$ equal to zero, because it now applies to the combined power of x and y.

A first-order ODE, which is homogeneous of order n in the present sense (and not necessarily linear), can be made separable by the substitution $y = xv$, with $dy = x\,dv + v\,dx$. This substitution causes the x dependence of all the terms of the equation containing dv to be x^{n+1}, with all the terms containing dx having x-dependence x^n. The variables x and v can then be separated.

Example 7.2.3   AN ODE HOMOGENEOUS IN x AND y

Consider the ODE

$$(2x + y)dx + x\,dy = 0,$$

which is homogeneous in x and y. Making the substitution $y = xv$, with $dy = x\,dv + v\,dx$, the ODE becomes

$$(2v + 2)dx + x\,dv = 0,$$

which is separable, with solution $\ln x + \frac{1}{2}\ln(v+1) = C$, which is equivalent to $x^2(v+1) = C$. Forming $y = xv$, the solution can be rearranged into

$$y = \frac{C}{x} - x.$$

■

Isobaric Equations

A generalization of the preceding subsection is to modify the definition of homogeneity by assigning different weights to x and y (note that corresponding weights must then also be assigned to dx and dy). If assigning unit weight to each instance of x or dx and a weight m to each instance of y or dy makes the ODE homogeneous as defined here, then the substitution $y = x^m v$ will make the equation separable. We illustrate with an example.

Example 7.2.4   AN ISOBARIC ODE

Here is an isobaric ODE:

$$(x^2 - y)dx + x\,dy = 0.$$

Assigning x weight 1, and y weight m, the term $x^2 dx$ has weight 3; the other two terms have weight $1 + m$. Setting $3 = 1 + m$, we find that all terms can be assigned equal weight if we take $m = 2$. This means that we should make the substitution $y = x^2 v$. Doing so, we get

$$(1 - v)dx + x\,dv = 0,$$

which separates into

$$\frac{dx}{x} + \frac{dv}{v+1} = 0 \quad \longrightarrow \quad \ln x + \ln(v+1) = \ln C, \quad \text{or} \quad x(v+1) = C.$$

From this, we get $v = \dfrac{C}{x} - 1$. Since $y = x^2 v$, the ODE has solution $y = Cx - x^2$.   ■

Linear First-Order ODEs

While nonlinear first-order ODEs can often (but not always) be solved using the strategies already presented, the situation is different for the linear first-order ODE because procedures exist for solving the most general equation of this type, which we write in the form

$$\frac{dy}{dx} + p(x)y = q(x). \tag{7.11}$$

If our linear first-order ODE is exact, its solution is straightforward. If it is not exact, we make it exact by introducing an integrating factor $\alpha(x)$, so that the ODE becomes

$$\alpha(x)\frac{dy}{dx} + \alpha(x)p(x)y = \alpha(x)q(x). \tag{7.12}$$

The reason for multiplication by $\alpha(x)$ is to cause the left-hand side of Eq. (7.12) to become a perfect differential, so we require that $\alpha(x)$ be such that

$$\frac{d}{dx}\big[\alpha(x)y\big] = \alpha(x)\frac{dy}{dx} + \alpha(x)p(x)y. \tag{7.13}$$

Expanding the left-hand side of Eq. (7.13), that equation becomes

$$\alpha(x)\frac{dy}{dx} + \frac{d\alpha}{dx}y = \alpha(x)\frac{dy}{dx} + \alpha(x)p(x)y,$$

so α must satisfy

$$\frac{d\alpha}{dx} = \alpha(x)p(x). \tag{7.14}$$

This is a **separable** equation and therefore soluble. Separating the variables and integrating, we obtain

$$\int^{\alpha}\frac{d\alpha}{\alpha} = \int^{x} p(x)dx.$$

We need not consider the lower limits of these integrals because they combine to yield a constant that does not affect the performance of the integrating factor and can be set to zero. Completing the evaluation, we reach

$$\alpha(x) = \exp\left[\int^{x} p(x)dx\right]. \tag{7.15}$$

With α now known we proceed to integrate Eq. (7.12), which, because of Eq. (7.13), assumes the form

$$\frac{d}{dx}\big[\alpha(x)y(x)\big] = \alpha(x)q(x),$$

which can be integrated (and divided through by α) to yield

$$y(x) = \frac{1}{\alpha(x)}\left[\int^{x} \alpha(x)q(x)dx + C\right] \equiv y_2(x) + y_1(x). \tag{7.16}$$

The two terms of Eq. (7.16) have an interesting interpretation. The term $y_1 = C/\alpha(x)$ is the general solution of the homogeneous equation obtained by replacing $q(x)$ with zero. To see this, write the homogeneous equation as

$$\frac{dy}{y} = -p(x)dx,$$

which integrates to

$$\ln y = - \int^x p(x)dx + C = -\ln \alpha + C.$$

Taking the exponential of both sides and renaming e^C as C, we get just $y = C/\alpha(x)$. The other term of Eq. (7.16),

$$y_2 = \frac{1}{\alpha(x)} \int^x \alpha(x)q(x)dx \tag{7.17}$$

corresponds to the right-hand side (**source**) term $q(x)$, and is a solution of the original inhomogeneous equation (as is obvious because C can be set to zero). We thus have the general solution to the inhomogeneous equation presented as a **particular solution** (or, in ODE parlance, a **particular integral**) plus the general solution to the corresponding homogeneous equation.

The above observations illustrate the following theorem:

> *The solution of an inhomogeneous first-order linear ODE is unique except for an arbitrary multiple of the solution of the corresponding homogeneous ODE.*

To show this, suppose y_1 and y_2 both solve the inhomogeneous ODE, Eq. (7.11). Then, subtracting the equation for y_2 from that for y_1, we have

$$y_1' - y_2' + p(x)(y_1 - y_2) = 0.$$

This shows that $y_1 - y_2$ is (at some scale) a solution of the homogeneous ODE. Remember that any solution of the homogeneous ODE remains a solution when multiplied by an arbitrary constant.

We also have the theorem:

> *A first-order linear homogeneous ODE has only one linearly independent solution.*

Two functions $y_1(x)$ and $y_2(x)$ are linearly dependent if there exist two constants a and b, both nonzero, that cause $ay_1 + by_2$ to vanish for all x. In the present situation, this is equivalent to the statement that y_1 and y_2 are linearly dependent if they are proportional to each other.

To prove the theorem, assume that the homogeneous ODE has the linearly independent solutions y_1 and y_2. Then, from the homogeneous ODE, we have

$$\frac{y_1'}{y_1} = -p(x) = \frac{y_2'}{y_2}.$$

Integrating the first and last members of this equation, we obtain

$$\ln y_1 = \ln y_2 + C, \quad \text{equivalent to} \quad y_1 = Cy_2,$$

contradicting our assumption that y_1 and y_2 are linearly independent.

Example 7.2.5   RL CIRCUIT

For a resistance-inductance circuit Kirchoff's law leads to

$$L\frac{dI(t)}{dt} + RI(t) = V(t),$$

where $I(t)$ is the current, L and R are, respectively, constant values of the inductance and the resistance, and $V(t)$ is the time-dependent input voltage.

From Eq. (7.15), our integrating factor $\alpha(t)$ is

$$\alpha(t) = \exp \int^t \frac{R}{L} dt = e^{Rt/L}.$$

Then, by Eq. (7.16),

$$I(t) = e^{-Rt/L} \left[\int^t e^{Rt/L} \frac{V(t)}{L} dt + C \right],$$

with the constant C to be determined by an initial condition.

For the special case $V(t) = V_0$, a constant,

$$I(t) = e^{-Rt/L} \left[\frac{V_0}{L} \cdot \frac{L}{R} e^{Rt/L} + C \right] = \frac{V_0}{R} + Ce^{-Rt/L}.$$

If the initial condition is $I(0) = 0$, then $C = -V_0/R$ and

$$I(t) = \frac{V_0}{R} \left[1 - e^{-Rt/L} \right].$$

∎

We close this section by pointing out that the inhomogeneous linear first-order ODE can also be solved by a method called **variation of the constant**, or alternatively **variation of parameters**, as follows. First, we solve the homogeneous ODE $y' + py = 0$ by separation of variables as before, giving

$$\frac{y'}{y} = -p, \quad \ln y = -\int^x p(X)dX + \ln C, \quad y(x) = C \exp\left(-\int^x p(X)dX \right).$$

Next we allow the integration constant to become x-dependent, that is, $C \to C(x)$. This is the reason the method is called "variation of the constant." To prepare for substitution into the inhomogeneous ODE, we calculate y':

$$y' = \exp\left(-\int^x p(X)dX \right) \left[-pC(x) + C'(x) \right] = -py(x) + C'(x) \exp\left(-\int^x p(X)dX \right).$$

Making the substitution for y' into the inhomogeneous ODE $y' + py = q$, some cancellation occurs, and we are left with

$$C'(x) \exp\left(-\int^x p(X)dX \right) = q,$$

which is a separable ODE for $C(x)$ that integrates to yield

$$C(x) = \int^x \exp\left(\int^X p(Y)dY\right) q(X)dX \quad \text{and} \quad y = C(x)\exp\left(-\int^x p(X)dX\right).$$

This particular solution of the inhomogeneous ODE is in agreement with that called y_2 in Eq. (7.17).

Exercises

7.2.1   From Kirchhoff's law the current I in an RC (resistance-capacitance) circuit (Fig. 7.1) obeys the equation

$$R\frac{dI}{dt} + \frac{1}{C}I = 0.$$

(a)   Find $I(t)$.

(b)   For a capacitance of 10,000 μF charged to 100 V and discharging through a resistance of 1 MΩ, find the current I for $t = 0$ and for $t = 100$ seconds.

Note. The initial voltage is $I_0 R$ or Q/C, where $Q = \int_0^\infty I(t)dt$.

7.2.2   The Laplace transform of Bessel's equation ($n = 0$) leads to

$$(s^2 + 1)f'(s) + sf(s) = 0.$$

Solve for $f(s)$.

7.2.3   The decay of a population by catastrophic two-body collisions is described by

$$\frac{dN}{dt} = -kN^2.$$

This is a first-order, **nonlinear** differential equation. Derive the solution

$$N(t) = N_0\left(1 + \frac{t}{\tau_0}\right)^{-1},$$

where $\tau_0 = (kN_0)^{-1}$. This implies an infinite population at $t = -\tau_0$.

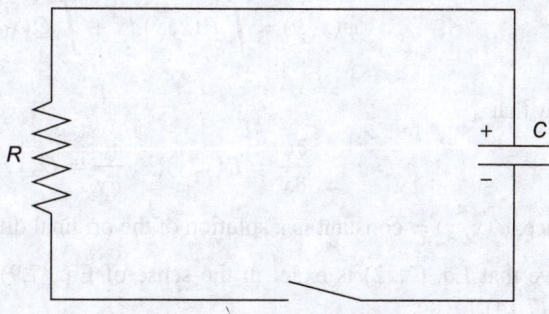

FIGURE 7.1   RC circuit.

7.2.4 The rate of a particular chemical reaction $A + B \rightarrow C$ is proportional to the concentrations of the reactants A and B:

$$\frac{dC(t)}{dt} = \alpha[A(0) - C(t)][B(0) - C(t)].$$

(a) Find $C(t)$ for $A(0) \neq B(0)$.

(b) Find $C(t)$ for $A(0) = B(0)$.

The initial condition is that $C(0) = 0$.

7.2.5 A boat, coasting through the water, experiences a resisting force proportional to v^n, v being the boat's instantaneous velocity. Newton's second law leads to

$$m\frac{dv}{dt} = -kv^n.$$

With $v(t = 0) = v_0$, $x(t = 0) = 0$, integrate to find v as a function of time and v as a function of distance.

7.2.6 In the first-order differential equation $dy/dx = f(x, y)$, the function $f(x, y)$ is a function of the ratio y/x:

$$\frac{dy}{dx} = g(y/x).$$

Show that the substitution of $u = y/x$ leads to a separable equation in u and x.

7.2.7 The differential equation

$$P(x, y)dx + Q(x, y)dy = 0$$

is **exact**. Show that its solution is of the form

$$\varphi(x, y) = \int_{x_0}^{x} P(x, y)dx + \int_{y_0}^{y} Q(x_0, y)dy = \text{constant}.$$

7.2.8 The differential equation

$$P(x, y)dx + Q(x, y)dy = 0$$

is **exact**. If

$$\varphi(x, y) = \int_{x_0}^{x} P(x, y)dx + \int_{y_0}^{y} Q(x_0, y)dy,$$

show that

$$\frac{\partial\varphi}{\partial x} = P(x, y), \quad \frac{\partial\varphi}{\partial y} = Q(x, y).$$

Hence, $\varphi(x, y) = \text{constant}$ is a solution of the original differential equation.

7.2.9 Prove that Eq. (7.12) is exact in the sense of Eq. (7.9), provided that $\alpha(x)$ satisfies Eq. (7.14).

7.2.10   A certain differential equation has the form

$$f(x)dx + g(x)h(y)dy = 0,$$

with none of the functions $f(x), g(x), h(y)$ identically zero. Show that a necessary and sufficient condition for this equation to be exact is that $g(x) = $ constant.

7.2.11   Show that

$$y(x) = \exp\left[-\int^x p(t)dt\right]\left\{\int^x \exp\left[\int^s p(t)dt\right]q(s)ds + C\right\}$$

is a solution of

$$\frac{dy}{dx} + p(x)y(x) = q(x)$$

by differentiating the expression for $y(x)$ and substituting into the differential equation.

7.2.12   The motion of a body falling in a resisting medium may be described by

$$m\frac{dv}{dt} = mg - bv$$

when the retarding force is proportional to the velocity, v. Find the velocity. Evaluate the constant of integration by demanding that $v(0) = 0$.

7.2.13   Radioactive nuclei decay according to the law

$$\frac{dN}{dt} = -\lambda N,$$

N being the concentration of a given nuclide and λ, the particular decay constant. In a radioactive series of two different nuclides, with concentrations $N_1(t)$ and $N_2(t)$, we have

$$\frac{dN_1}{dt} = -\lambda_1 N_1,$$

$$\frac{dN_2}{dt} = \lambda_1 N_1 - \lambda_2 N_2.$$

Find $N_2(t)$ for the conditions $N_1(0) = N_0$ and $N_2(0) = 0$.

7.2.14   The rate of evaporation from a particular spherical drop of liquid (constant density) is proportional to its surface area. Assuming this to be the sole mechanism of mass loss, find the radius of the drop as a function of time.

7.2.15   In the linear homogeneous differential equation

$$\frac{dv}{dt} = -av$$

the variables are separable. When the variables are separated, the equation is exact. Solve this differential equation subject to $v(0) = v_0$ by the following three methods:

(a)   Separating variables and integrating.

(b)   Treating the separated variable equation as exact.

(c) Using the result for a linear homogeneous differential equation.

$$ANS. \quad v(t) = v_0 e^{-at}.$$

7.2.16 (a) Solve Example 7.2.1, assuming that the parachute opens when the parachutist's velocity has reached $v_i = 60$ mi/h (regard this time as $t = 0$). Find $v(t)$.

(b) For a skydiver in free fall use the friction coefficient $b = 0.25$ kg/m and mass $m = 70$ kg. What is the limiting velocity in this case?

7.2.17 Solve the ODE

$$(xy^2 - y)dx + x\,dy = 0.$$

7.2.18 Solve the ODE

$$(x^2 - y^2 e^{y/x})dx + (x^2 + xy)e^{y/x}dy = 0.$$

Hint. Note that the quantity y/x in the exponents is of combined degree zero and does not affect the determination of homogeneity.

7.3   ODEs with Constant Coefficients

Before addressing second-order ODEs, the main topic of this chapter, we discuss a specialized, but frequently occurring class of ODEs that are not constrained to be of specific order, namely those that are linear and whose homogeneous terms have constant coefficients. The generic equation of this type is

$$\frac{d^n y}{dx^n} + a_{n-1}\frac{d^{n-1}y}{dx^{n-1}} + \cdots + a_1\frac{dy}{dx} + a_0 y = F(x). \tag{7.18}$$

The homogeneous equation corresponding to Eq. (7.18) has solutions of the form $y = e^{mx}$, where m is a solution of the algebraic equation

$$m^n + a_{n-1}m^{n-1} + \cdots + a_1 m + a_0 = 0,$$

as may be verified by substitution of the assumed form of the solution.

In the case that the m equation has a multiple root, the above prescription will not yield the full set of n linearly independent solutions for the original nth order ODE. If one then considers the limiting process in which two roots approach each other, it is possible to conclude that if e^{mx} is a solution, then so is $d\,e^{mx}/dm = xe^{mx}$. A triple root would have solutions $e^{mx}, xe^{mx}, x^2 e^{mx}$, etc.

Example 7.3.1   Hooke's Law Spring

A mass M attached to a Hooke's Law spring (of spring constant k) is in oscillatory motion. Letting y be the displacement of the mass from its equilibrium position, Newton's law of motion takes the form

$$M\frac{d^2 y}{dt^2} = -ky,$$

which is an ODE of the form $y'' + a_0 y = 0$, with $a_0 = +k/M$. The general solution to this ODE is of the form $C_1 e^{m_1 t} + C_2 e^{m_2 t}$, where m_1 and m_2 are the solutions of the algebraic equation $m^2 + a_0 = 0$.

The values of m_1 and m_2 are $\pm i\omega$, where $\omega = \sqrt{k/M}$, so the ODE has solution

$$y(t) = C_1 e^{+i\omega t} + C_2 e^{-i\omega t}.$$

Since the ODE is homogeneous, we may alternatively describe its general solution using arbitrary linear combinations of the above two terms. This permits us to combine them to obtain forms that are real and therefore appropriate to the current problem. Noting that

$$\frac{e^{i\omega t} + e^{-i\omega t}}{2} = \cos \omega t \quad \text{and} \quad \frac{e^{i\omega t} - e^{-i\omega t}}{2i} = \sin \omega t,$$

a convenient alternate form is

$$y(t) = C_1 \cos \omega t + C_2 \sin \omega t.$$

The solution to a specific oscillation problem will now involve fitting the coefficients C_1 and C_2 to the initial conditions, as for example $y(0)$ and $y'(0)$. ∎

Exercises

Find the general solutions to the following ODEs. Write the solutions in forms that are entirely real (i.e., that contain no complex quantities).

7.3.1 $y''' - 2y'' - y' + 2y = 0.$

7.3.2 $y''' - 2y'' + y' - 2y = 0.$

7.3.3 $y''' - 3y' + 2y = 0.$

7.3.4 $y'' + 2y' + 2y = 0.$

7.4 SECOND-ORDER LINEAR ODES

We now turn to the main topic of this chapter, second-order linear ODEs. These are of particular importance because they arise in the most frequently used methods for solving PDEs in quantum mechanics, electromagnetic theory, and other areas in physics. Unlike the first-order linear ODE, we do not have a universally applicable closed-form solution, and in general it is found advisable to use methods that produce solutions in the form of power series. As a precursor to the general discussion of series-solution methods, we begin by examining the notion of singularity as applied to ODEs.

Singular Points

The concept of singularity of an ODE is important to us for two reasons: (1) it is useful for classifying ODEs and identifying those that can be transformed into common forms (discussed later in this subsection), and (2) it bears on the feasibility of finding series solutions to the ODE. This feasibility is the topic of Fuchs' theorem (to be discussed shortly).

When a linear homogeneous second-order ODE is written in the form

$$y'' + P(x)y' + Q(x)y = 0, \tag{7.19}$$

points x_0 for which $P(x)$ and $Q(x)$ are finite are termed **ordinary points** of the ODE. However, if either $P(x)$ or $Q(x)$ diverge as $x \to x_0$, the point x_0 is called a **singular point**. Singular points are further classified as **regular** or **irregular** (the latter also sometimes called **essential singularities**):

- A singular point x_0 is **regular** if either $P(x)$ or $Q(x)$ diverges there, but $(x - x_0)P(x)$ and $(x - x_0)^2 Q(x)$ remain finite.

- A singular point x_0 is **irregular** if $P(x)$ diverges faster than $1/(x - x_0)$ so that $(x - x_0)P(x)$ goes to infinity as $x \to x_0$, or if $Q(x)$ diverges faster than $1/(x - x_0)^2$ so that $(x - x_0)^2 Q(x)$ goes to infinity as $x \to x_0$.

These definitions hold for all finite values of x_0. To analyze the behavior at $x \to \infty$, we set $x = 1/z$, substitute into the differential equation, and examine the behavior in the limit $z \to 0$. The ODE, originally in the dependent variable $y(x)$, will now be written in terms of $w(z)$, defined as $w(z) = y(z^{-1})$. Converting the derivatives,

$$y' = \frac{dy(x)}{dx} = \frac{dy(z^{-1})}{dz}\frac{dz}{dx} = \frac{dw(z)}{dz}\left(-\frac{1}{x^2}\right) = -z^2 w', \tag{7.20}$$

$$y'' = \frac{dy'}{dz}\frac{dz}{dx} = (-z^2)\frac{d}{dz}\left[-z^2 w'\right] = z^4 w'' + 2z^3 w'. \tag{7.21}$$

Using Eqs. (7.20) and (7.21), we transform Eq. (7.19) into

$$z^4 w'' + \left[2z^3 - z^2 P(z^{-1})\right]w' + Q(z^{-1})w = 0. \tag{7.22}$$

Dividing through by z^4 to place the ODE in standard form, we see that the possibility of a singularity at $z = 0$ depends on the behavior of

$$\frac{2z - P(z^{-1})}{z^2} \quad \text{and} \quad \frac{Q(z^{-1})}{z^4}.$$

If these two expressions remain finite at $z = 0$, the point $x = \infty$ is an ordinary point. If they diverge no more rapidly than $1/z$ and $1/z^2$, respectively, $x = \infty$ is a regular singular point; otherwise it is an irregular singular point (an essential singularity).

Example 7.4.1   BESSEL'S EQUATION

Bessel's equation is

$$x^2 y'' + xy' + (x^2 - n^2)y = 0.$$

Comparing it with Eq. (7.19), we have

$$P(x) = \frac{1}{x}, \quad Q(x) = 1 - \frac{n^2}{x^2},$$

which shows that the point $x = 0$ is a regular singularity. By inspection we see that there are no other singularities in the finite range. As $x \to \infty$ $(z \to 0)$, from Eq. (7.22) we have the coefficients

$$\frac{2z - z}{z^2} \quad \text{and} \quad \frac{1 - n^2 z^2}{z^4}.$$

Since the latter expression diverges as $1/z^4$, the point $x = \infty$ is an irregular, or essential, singularity. ∎

Table 7.1 lists the singular points of a number of ODEs of importance in physics. It will be seen that the first three equations in Table 7.1, the hypergeometric, Legendre, and Chebyshev, all have three regular singular points. The hypergeometric equation, with regular singularities at 0, 1, and ∞, is taken as the standard, the canonical form. The solutions of the other two may then be expressed in terms of its solutions, the hypergeometric functions. This is done in Chapter 18.

In a similar manner, the confluent hypergeometric equation is taken as the canonical form of a linear second-order differential equation with one regular and one irregular singular point.

Table 7.1 Singularities of Some Important ODEs.

Equation	Regular Singularity $x =$	Irregular Singularity $x =$
1. Hypergeometric $x(x-1)y'' + [(1 + a + b)x + c]y' + aby = 0$	$0, 1, \infty$	$\cdots$
2. Legendre[a] $(1 - x^2)y'' - 2xy' + l(l+1)y = 0$	$-1, 1, \infty$	$\cdots$
3. Chebyshev $(1 - x^2)y'' - xy' + n^2 y = 0$	$-1, 1, \infty$	$\cdots$
4. Confluent hypergeometric $xy'' + (c - x)y' - ay = 0$	0	∞
5. Bessel $x^2 y'' + xy' + (x^2 - n^2)y = 0$	0	∞
6. Laguerre[a] $xy'' + (1 - x)y' + ay = 0$	0	∞
7. Simple harmonic oscillator $y'' + \omega^2 y = 0$	$\cdots$	∞
8. Hermite $y'' - 2xy' + 2\alpha y = 0$	$\cdots$	∞

[a] The associated equations have the same singular points.

Exercises

7.4.1   Show that Legendre's equation has regular singularities at $x = -1, \ 1$, and ∞.

7.4.2   Show that Laguerre's equation, like the Bessel equation, has a regular singularity at $x = 0$ and an irregular singularity at $x = \infty$.

7.4.3   Show that Chebyshev's equation, like the Legendre equation, has regular singularities at $x = -1, \ 1$, and ∞.

7.4.4   Show that Hermite's equation has no singularity other than an irregular singularity at $x = \infty$.

7.4.5   Show that the substitution

$$x \to \frac{1-x}{2}, \quad a = -l, \quad b = l+1, \quad c = 1$$

converts the hypergeometric equation into Legendre's equation.

7.5   SERIES SOLUTIONS—FROBENIUS' METHOD

In this section we develop a method of obtaining solution(s) of the linear, second-order, homogeneous ODE. For the moment, we develop the mechanics of the method. After studying examples, we return to discuss the conditions under which we can expect these series solutions to exist.

Consider a linear, second-order, homogeneous ODE, in the form

$$\frac{d^2y}{dx^2} + P(x)\frac{dy}{dx} + Q(x)y = 0. \tag{7.23}$$

In this section we develop (at least) one solution of Eq. (7.23) by expansion about the point $x = 0$. In the next section we develop the **second, independent solution and prove that no third, independent solution exists**. Therefore the **most general solution** of Eq. (7.23) may be written in terms of the two independent solutions as

$$y(x) = c_1 y_1(x) + c_2 y_2(x). \tag{7.24}$$

Our physical problem may lead to a **nonhomogeneous**, linear, second-order ODE,

$$\frac{d^2y}{dx^2} + P(x)\frac{dy}{dx} + Q(x)y = F(x). \tag{7.25}$$

The function on the right, $F(x)$, typically represents a source (such as electrostatic charge) or a driving force (as in a driven oscillator). Methods for solving this inhomogeneous ODE are also discussed later in this chapter and, using Laplace transform techniques, in Chapter 20. Assuming a single **particular integral** (i.e., specific solution), y_p, of the inhomogeneous ODE to be available, we may add to it any solution of the corresponding homogeneous equation, Eq. (7.23), and write the **most general solution** of Eq. (7.25) as

$$y(x) = c_1 y_1(x) + c_2 y_2(x) + y_p(x). \tag{7.26}$$

In many problems, the constants c_1 and c_2 will be fixed by boundary conditions.

For the present, we assume that $F(x) = 0$, and that therefore our differential equation is homogeneous. We shall attempt to develop a solution of our linear, second-order, homogeneous differential equation, Eq. (7.23), by substituting into it a power series with undetermined coefficients. Also available as a parameter is the power of the lowest nonvanishing term of the series. To illustrate, we apply the method to two important differential equations.

First Example—Linear Oscillator

Consider the linear (classical) oscillator equation

$$\frac{d^2y}{dx^2} + \omega^2 y = 0, \qquad (7.27)$$

which we have already solved by another method in Example 7.3.1. The solutions we found there were $y = \sin \omega x$ and $\cos \omega x$.

We try

$$y(x) = x^s(a_0 + a_1 x + a_2 x^2 + a_3 x^3 + \cdots)$$

$$= \sum_{j=0}^{\infty} a_j x^{s+j}, \quad a_0 \neq 0, \qquad (7.28)$$

with the exponent s and all the coefficients a_j still undetermined. Note that s need not be an integer. By differentiating twice, we obtain

$$\frac{dy}{dx} = \sum_{j=0}^{\infty} a_j (s+j) x^{s+j-1},$$

$$\frac{d^2y}{dx^2} = \sum_{j=0}^{\infty} a_j (s+j)(s+j-1) x^{s+j-2}.$$

By substituting into Eq. (7.27), we have

$$\sum_{j=0}^{\infty} a_j (s+j)(s+j-1) x^{s+j-2} + \omega^2 \sum_{j=0}^{\infty} a_j x^{s+j} = 0. \qquad (7.29)$$

From our analysis of the uniqueness of power series (Chapter 1), we know that the coefficient of each power of x on the left-hand side of Eq. (7.29) must vanish individually, x^s being an overall factor.

The lowest power of x appearing in Eq. (7.29) is x^{s-2}, occurring only for $j=0$ in the first summation. The requirement that this coefficient vanish yields

$$a_0 s(s-1) = 0.$$

Recall that we chose a_0 as the coefficient of the lowest nonvanishing term of the series in Eq. (7.28), so that, by definition, $a_0 \neq 0$. Therefore we have

$$s(s-1) = 0. \qquad (7.30)$$

This equation, coming from the coefficient of the lowest power of x, is called the **indicial equation**. The indicial equation and its roots are of critical importance to our analysis. Clearly, in this example it informs us that either $s = 0$ or $s = 1$, so that our series solution must start either with an x^0 or an x^1 term.

Looking further at Eq. (7.29), we see that the next lowest power of x, namely x^{s-1}, also occurs uniquely (for $j = 1$ in the first summation). Setting the coefficient of x^{s-1} to zero, we have

$$a_1(s+1)s = 0.$$

This shows that if $s = 1$, we must have $a_1 = 0$. However, if $s = 0$, this equation imposes no requirement on the coefficient set.

Before considering further the two possibilities for s, we return to Eq. (7.29) and demand that the remaining net coefficients vanish. The contributions to the coefficient of x^{s+j}, $(j \geq 0)$, come from the term containing a_{j+2} in the first summation and from that with a_j in the second. Because we have already dealt with $j = 0$ and $j = 1$ in the first summation, when we have used all $j \geq 0$, we will have used all the terms of both series. For each value of j, the vanishing of the net coefficient of x^{s+j} results in

$$a_{j+2}(s+j+2)(s+j+1) + \omega^2 a_j = 0,$$

equivalent to

$$a_{j+2} = -a_j \frac{\omega^2}{(s+j+2)(s+j+1)}. \tag{7.31}$$

This is a two-term **recurrence relation**.[1] In the present problem, given a_j, Eq. (7.31) permits us to compute a_{j+2} and then a_{j+4}, a_{j+6}, and so on, continuing as far as desired. Thus, if we start with a_0, we can make the even coefficients $a_2, a_4, \ldots$, but we obtain no information about the odd coefficients $a_1, a_3, a_5, \ldots$. But because a_1 is arbitrary if $s = 0$ and necessarily zero if $s = 1$, let us set it equal to zero, and then, by Eq. (7.31),

$$a_3 = a_5 = a_7 = \cdots = 0;$$

the result is that all the odd-numbered coefficients vanish.

Returning now to Eq. (7.30), our indicial equation, we first try the solution $s = 0$. The recurrence relation, Eq. (7.31), becomes

$$a_{j+2} = -a_j \frac{\omega^2}{(j+2)(j+1)}, \tag{7.32}$$

---

[1] In some problems, the recurrence relation may involve more than two terms; its exact form will depend on the functions $P(x)$ and $Q(x)$ of the ODE.

which leads to

$$a_2 = -a_0 \frac{\omega^2}{1 \cdot 2} = -\frac{\omega^2}{2!} a_0,$$

$$a_4 = -a_2 \frac{\omega^2}{3 \cdot 4} = +\frac{\omega^4}{4!} a_0,$$

$$a_6 = -a_4 \frac{\omega^2}{5 \cdot 6} = -\frac{\omega^6}{6!} a_0, \quad \text{and so on.}$$

By inspection (and mathematical induction, see Section 1.4),

$$a_{2n} = (-1)^n \frac{\omega^{2n}}{(2n)!} a_0, \tag{7.33}$$

and our solution is

$$y(x)_{s=0} = a_0 \left[1 - \frac{(\omega x)^2}{2!} + \frac{(\omega x)^4}{4!} - \frac{(\omega x)^6}{6!} + \cdots \right] = a_0 \cos \omega x. \tag{7.34}$$

If we choose the indicial equation root $s = 1$ from Eq. (7.30), the recurrence relation of Eq. (7.31) becomes

$$a_{j+2} = -a_j \frac{\omega^2}{(j+3)(j+2)}. \tag{7.35}$$

Evaluating this successively for $j = 0, 2, 4, \ldots$, we obtain

$$a_2 = -a_0 \frac{\omega^2}{2 \cdot 3} = -\frac{\omega^2}{3!} a_0,$$

$$a_4 = -a_2 \frac{\omega^2}{4 \cdot 5} = +\frac{\omega^4}{5!} a_0,$$

$$a_6 = -a_4 \frac{\omega^2}{6 \cdot 7} = -\frac{\omega^6}{7!} a_0, \quad \text{and so on.}$$

Again, by inspection and mathematical induction,

$$a_{2n} = (-1)^n \frac{\omega^{2n}}{(2n+1)!} a_0. \tag{7.36}$$

For this choice, $s = 1$, we obtain

$$y(x)_{s=1} = a_0 x \left[1 - \frac{(\omega x)^2}{3!} + \frac{(\omega x)^4}{5!} - \frac{(\omega x)^6}{7!} + \cdots \right]$$

$$= \frac{a_0}{\omega} \left[(\omega x) - \frac{(\omega x)^3}{3!} + \frac{(\omega x)^5}{5!} - \frac{(\omega x)^7}{7!} + \cdots \right]$$

$$= \frac{a_0}{\omega} \sin \omega x. \tag{7.37}$$

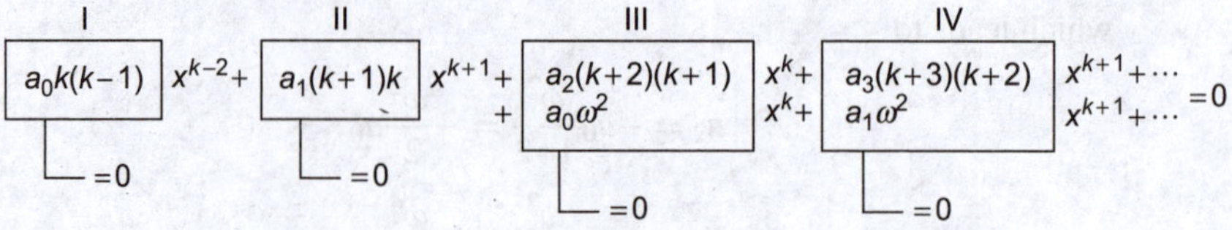

FIGURE 7.2   Schematics of series solution.

For future reference we note that the ODE solution from the indicial equation root $s = 0$ consisted only of even powers of x, while the solution from the root $s = 1$ contained only odd powers.

To summarize this approach, we may write Eq. (7.29) schematically as shown in Fig. 7.2. From the uniqueness of power series (Section 1.2), the total coefficient of each power of x *must vanish—all by itself. The requirement that the first coefficient vanish (I) leads to the indicial equation, Eq. (7.30). The second coefficient is handled by setting* $a_1 = 0$ *(II). The vanishing of the coefficients of* x^s *(and higher powers, taken one at a time) is ensured by imposing the recurrence relation, Eq. (7.31), (III), (IV).*

This expansion in power series, known as Frobenius' method, has given us two series solutions of the linear oscillator equation. However, there are two points about such series solutions that must be strongly emphasized:

1. The series solution should always be substituted back into the differential equation, to see if it works, as a precaution against algebraic and logical errors. If it works, it is a solution.
2. The acceptability of a series solution depends on its convergence (including asymptotic convergence). It is quite possible for Frobenius' method to give a series solution that satisfies the original differential equation when substituted in the equation but that does **not** converge over the region of interest. Legendre's differential equation (examined in Section 8.3) illustrates this situation.

Expansion about x_0

Equation (7.28) is an expansion about the origin, $x_0 = 0$. It is perfectly possible to replace Eq. (7.28) with

$$y(x) = \sum_{j=0}^{\infty} a_j (x - x_0)^{s+j}, \quad a_0 \neq 0. \tag{7.38}$$

Indeed, for the Legendre, Chebyshev, and hypergeometric equations, the choice $x_0 = 1$ has some advantages. The point x_0 should not be chosen at an essential singularity, or Frobenius' method will probably fail. The resultant series (x_0 an ordinary point or regular singular point) will be valid where it converges. You can expect a divergence of some sort when $|x - x_0| = |z_1 - x_0|$, where z_1 is the ODE's closest singularity to x_0 (in the complex plane).

Symmetry of Solutions

Let us note that for the classical oscillator problem we obtained one solution of even symmetry, $y_1(x) = y_1(-x)$, and one of odd symmetry, $y_2(x) = -y_2(-x)$. This is not just an accident but a direct consequence of the form of the ODE. Writing a general homogeneous ODE as

$$\mathcal{L}(x)y(x) = 0, \tag{7.39}$$

in which $\mathcal{L}(x)$ is the differential operator, we see that for the linear oscillator equation, Eq. (7.27), $\mathcal{L}(x)$ is even under parity; that is,

$$\mathcal{L}(x) = \mathcal{L}(-x).$$

Whenever the differential operator has a specific parity or symmetry, either even or odd, we may interchange $+x$ and $-x$, and Eq. (7.39) becomes

$$\pm \mathcal{L}(x)y(-x) = 0.$$

Clearly, if $y(x)$ is a solution of the differential equation, $y(-x)$ is also a solution. Then, either $y(x)$ and $y(-x)$ are linearly dependent (i.e., proportional), meaning that y is either even or odd, or they are linearly independent solutions that can be combined into a pair of solutions, one even, and one odd, by forming

$$y_{\text{even}} = y(x) + y(-x), \quad y_{\text{odd}} = y(x) - y(-x).$$

For the classical oscillator example, we obtained two solutions; our method for finding them caused one to be even, the other odd.

If we refer back to Section 7.4 we can see that Legendre, Chebyshev, Bessel, simple harmonic oscillator, and Hermite equations are all based on differential operators with even parity; that is, their $P(x)$ in Eq. (7.19) is odd and $Q(x)$ even. Solutions of all of them may be presented as series of even powers of x or separate series of odd powers of x. The Laguerre differential operator has neither even nor odd symmetry; hence its solutions cannot be expected to exhibit even or odd parity. Our emphasis on parity stems primarily from the importance of parity in quantum mechanics. We find that in many problems wave functions are either even or odd, meaning that they have a definite parity. Most interactions (beta decay is the big exception) are also even or odd, and the result is that parity is conserved.

A Second Example—Bessel's Equation

This attack on the linear oscillator was perhaps a bit too easy. By substituting the power series, Eq. (7.28), into the differential equation, Eq. (7.27), we obtained two independent solutions with no trouble at all.

To get some idea of other things that can happen, we try to solve Bessel's equation,

$$x^2 y'' + xy' + (x^2 - n^2)y = 0. \tag{7.40}$$

Again, assuming a solution of the form

$$y(x) = \sum_{j=0}^{\infty} a_j x^{s+j},$$

we differentiate and substitute into Eq. (7.40). The result is

$$\sum_{j=0}^{\infty} a_j(s+j)(s+j-1)x^{s+j} + \sum_{j=0}^{\infty} a_j(s+j)x^{s+j}$$

$$+ \sum_{j=0}^{\infty} a_j x^{s+j+2} - \sum_{j=0}^{\infty} a_j n^2 x^{s+j} = 0. \tag{7.41}$$

By setting $j = 0$, we get the coefficient of x^s, the lowest power of x appearing on the left-hand side,

$$a_0\big[s(s-1)+s-n^2\big] = 0, \tag{7.42}$$

and again $a_0 \neq 0$ by definition. Equation (7.42) therefore yields the **indicial** equation

$$s^2 - n^2 = 0, \tag{7.43}$$

with solutions $s = \pm n$.

We need also to examine the coefficient of x^{s+1}. Here we obtain

$$a_1[(s+1)s+s+1-n^2] = 0,$$

or

$$a_1(s+1-n)(s+1+n) = 0. \tag{7.44}$$

For $s = \pm n$, neither $s+1-n$ nor $s+1+n$ vanishes and we **must** require $a_1 = 0$.

Proceeding to the coefficient of x^{s+j} for $s = n$, we see that it is the term containing a_j in the first, second, and fourth terms of Eq. (7.41), but is that containing a_{j-2} in the third term. By requiring the overall coefficient of x^{s+j} to vanish, we obtain

$$a_j[(n+j)(n+j-1)+(n+j)-n^2]+a_{j-2} = 0.$$

When j is replaced by $j+2$, this can be rewritten for $j \geq 0$ as

$$a_{j+2} = -a_j \frac{1}{(j+2)(2n+j+2)}, \tag{7.45}$$

which is the desired recurrence relation. Repeated application of this recurrence relation leads to

$$a_2 = -a_0 \frac{1}{2(2n+2)} = -\frac{a_0 n!}{2^2 1!(n+1)!},$$

$$a_4 = -a_2 \frac{1}{4(2n+4)} = \frac{a_0 n!}{2^4 2!(n+2)!},$$

$$a_6 = -a_4 \frac{1}{6(2n+6)} = -\frac{a_0 n!}{2^6 3!(n+3)!}, \quad \text{and so on,}$$

and in general,

$$a_{2p} = (-1)^p \frac{a_0 n!}{2^{2p} p!(n+p)!}.$$ (7.46)

Inserting these coefficients in our assumed series solution, we have

$$y(x) = a_0 x^n \left[1 - \frac{n! x^2}{2^2 1!(n+1)!} + \frac{n! x^4}{2^4 2!(n+2)!} - \cdots \right].$$ (7.47)

In summation form,

$$y(x) = a_0 \sum_{j=0}^{\infty} (-1)^j \frac{n! x^{n+2j}}{2^{2j} j!(n+j)!}$$

$$= a_0 2^n n! \sum_{j=0}^{\infty} (-1)^j \frac{1}{j!(n+j)!} \left(\frac{x}{2}\right)^{n+2j}.$$ (7.48)

In Chapter 14 the final summation (with $a_0 = 1/2^n n!$) is identified as the Bessel function $J_n(x)$:

$$J_n(x) = \sum_{j=0}^{\infty} (-1)^j \frac{1}{j!(n+j)!} \left(\frac{x}{2}\right)^{n+2j}.$$ (7.49)

Note that this solution, $J_n(x)$, has either even or odd symmetry,[2] as might be expected from the form of Bessel's equation.

When $s = -n$ and n is not an integer, we may generate a second distinct series, to be labeled $J_{-n}(x)$. However, when $-n$ is a negative integer, trouble develops. The recurrence relation for the coefficients a_j is still given by Eq. (7.45), but with $2n$ replaced by $-2n$. Then, when $j + 2 = 2n$ or $j = 2(n-1)$, the coefficient a_{j+2} blows up and Frobenius' method does not produce a solution consistent with our assumption that the series starts with x^{-n}.

By substituting in an infinite series, we have obtained two solutions for the linear oscillator equation and one for Bessel's equation (two if n is not an integer). To the questions "Can we always do this? Will this method always work?" the answer is "No, we cannot always do this. This method of series solution will not always work."

Regular and Irregular Singularities

The success of the series substitution method depends on the roots of the indicial equation and the degree of singularity of the coefficients in the differential equation. To understand better the effect of the equation coefficients on this naive series substitution approach,

---

[2] $J_n(x)$ is an even function if n is an even integer, and an odd function if n is an odd integer. For nonintegral n, J_n has no such simple symmetry.

consider four simple equations:

$$y'' - \frac{6}{x^2}y = 0, \tag{7.50}$$

$$y'' - \frac{6}{x^3}y = 0, \tag{7.51}$$

$$y'' + \frac{1}{x}y' - \frac{b^2}{x^2}y = 0, \tag{7.52}$$

$$y'' + \frac{1}{x^2}y' - \frac{b^2}{x^2}y = 0. \tag{7.53}$$

The reader may show easily that for Eq. (7.50) the indicial equation is

$$s^2 - s - 6 = 0,$$

giving $s = 3$ and $s = -2$. Since the equation is homogeneous in x (counting d^2/dx^2 as x^{-2}), there is no recurrence relation. However, we are left with two perfectly good solutions, x^3 and x^{-2}.

Equation (7.51) differs from Eq. (7.50) by only one power of x, but this sends the indicial equation to

$$-6a_0 = 0,$$

with no solution at all, for we have agreed that $a_0 \neq 0$. Our series substitution worked for Eq. (7.50), which had only a regular singularity, but broke down at Eq. (7.51), which has an irregular singular point at the origin.

Continuing with Eq. (7.52), we have added a term y'/x. The indicial equation is

$$s^2 - b^2 = 0,$$

but again, there is no recurrence relation. The solutions are $y = x^b$ and x^{-b}, both perfectly acceptable one-term series.

When we change the power of x in the coefficient of y' from -1 to -2, in Eq. (7.53), there is a drastic change in the solution. The indicial equation (with only the y' term contributing) becomes

$$s = 0.$$

There is a recurrence relation,

$$a_{j+1} = +a_j \frac{b^2 - j(j-1)}{j+1}.$$

Unless the parameter b is selected to make the series terminate, we have

$$\lim_{j \to \infty}\left|\frac{a_{j+1}}{a_j}\right| = \lim_{j \to \infty}\frac{j(j+1)}{j+1}$$

$$= \lim_{j \to \infty}\frac{j^2}{j} = \infty.$$

Hence our series solution diverges for all $x \neq 0$. Again, our method worked for Eq. (7.52) with a regular singularity but failed when we had the irregular singularity of Eq. (7.53).

Fuchs' Theorem

The answer to the basic question as to when the method of series substitution can be expected to work is given by Fuchs' theorem, which asserts that we can always obtain at least one power-series solution, provided that we are expanding about a point which is an ordinary point or at worst a regular singular point.

If we attempt an expansion about an irregular or essential singularity, our method may fail as it did for Eqs. (7.51) and (7.53). Fortunately, the more important equations of mathematical physics, listed in Section 7.4, have no irregular singularities in the finite plane. Further discussion of Fuchs' theorem appears in Section 7.6.

From Table 7.1, Section 7.4, infinity is seen to be a singular point for all the equations considered. As a further illustration of Fuchs' theorem, Legendre's equation (with infinity as a regular singularity) has a convergent series solution in negative powers of the argument (Section 15.6). In contrast, Bessel's equation (with an irregular singularity at infinity) yields asymptotic series (Sections 12.6 and 14.6). Although only asymptotic, these solutions are nevertheless extremely useful.

Summary

If we are expanding about an ordinary point or at worst about a regular singularity, the series substitution approach will yield at least one solution (Fuchs' theorem).

Whether we get one or two distinct solutions depends on the roots of the indicial equation.

1. If the two roots of the indicial equation are equal, we can obtain only one solution by this series substitution method.
2. If the two roots differ by a nonintegral number, two independent solutions may be obtained.
3. If the two roots differ by an integer, the larger of the two will yield a solution, while the smaller may or may not give a solution, depending on the behavior of the coefficients.

The usefulness of a series solution for numerical work depends on the rapidity of convergence of the series and the availability of the coefficients. Many ODEs will not yield nice, simple recurrence relations for the coefficients. In general, the available series will probably be useful for very small $|x|$ (or $|x - x_0|$). Computers can be used to determine additional series coefficients using a symbolic language, such as Mathematica[3] or Maple.[4] Often, however, for numerical work a direct numerical integration will be preferred.

---

[3] S. Wolfram, *Mathematica: A System for Doing Mathematics by Computer*. Reading, MA. Addison Wesley (1991).
[4] A. Heck, *Introduction to Maple*. New York: Springer (1993).

Exercises

7.5.1   Uniqueness theorem. The function $y(x)$ satisfies a second-order, linear, homogeneous differential equation. At $x = x_0$, $y(x) = y_0$ and $dy/dx = y_0'$. Show that $y(x)$ is unique, in that no other solution of this differential equation passes through the points (x_0, y_0) with a slope of y_0'.

Hint. Assume a second solution satisfying these conditions and compare the Taylor series expansions.

7.5.2   A series solution of Eq. (7.23) is attempted, expanding about the point $x = x_0$. If x_0 is an ordinary point, show that the indicial equation has roots $s = 0, 1$.

7.5.3   In the development of a series solution of the simple harmonic oscillator (SHO) equation, the second series coefficient a_1 was neglected except to set it equal to zero. From the coefficient of the next-to-the-lowest power of x, x^{s-1}, develop a second-indicial type equation.

(a)   (SHO equation with $s = 0$). Show that a_1, may be assigned any finite value (including zero).

(b)   (SHO equation with $s = 1$). Show that a_1 must be set equal to zero.

7.5.4   Analyze the series solutions of the following differential equations to see when a_1 **may** be set equal to zero without irrevocably losing anything and when a_1 **must** be set equal to zero.

(a) Legendre, (b) Chebyshev, (c) Bessel, (d) Hermite.

ANS. (a)   Legendre, (b)   Chebyshev, and   (d)   Hermite: For $s = 0$, a_1 **may** be set equal to zero; for $s = 1$, a_1 **must** be set equal to zero.
(c)   Bessel: a_1 **must** be set equal to zero (except for $s = \pm n = -\frac{1}{2}$).

7.5.5   Obtain a series solution of the hypergeometric equation

$$x(x - 1)y'' + [(1 + a + b)x - c]y' + aby = 0.$$

Test your solution for convergence.

7.5.6   Obtain two series solutions of the confluent hypergeometric equation

$$xy'' + (c - x)y' - ay = 0.$$

Test your solutions for convergence.

7.5.7   A quantum mechanical analysis of the Stark effect (parabolic coordinates) leads to the differential equation

$$\frac{d}{d\xi}\left(\xi\frac{du}{d\xi}\right) + \left(\frac{1}{2}E\xi + \alpha - \frac{m^2}{4\xi} - \frac{1}{4}F\xi^2\right)u = 0.$$

Here α is a constant, E is the total energy, and F is a constant such that Fz is the potential energy added to the system by the introduction of an electric field.

Using the larger root of the indicial equation, develop a power-series solution about $\xi = 0$. Evaluate the first three coefficients in terms of a_o.

ANS.   Indicial equation $s^2 - \frac{m^2}{4} = 0$,

$$u(\xi) = a_0 \xi^{m/2} \left\{ 1 - \frac{\alpha}{m+1} \xi + \left[\frac{\alpha^2}{2(m+1)(m+2)} - \frac{E}{4(m+2)} \right] \xi^2 + \cdots \right\}.$$

Note that the perturbation F does not appear until a_3 is included.

7.5.8   For the special case of no azimuthal dependence, the quantum mechanical analysis of the hydrogen molecular ion leads to the equation

$$\frac{d}{d\eta} \left[(1 - \eta^2) \frac{du}{d\eta} \right] + \alpha u + \beta \eta^2 u = 0.$$

Develop a power-series solution for $u(\eta)$. Evaluate the first three nonvanishing coefficients in terms of a_0.

ANS.   Indicial equation $s(s - 1) = 0$,

$$u_{k=1} = a_0 \eta \left\{ 1 + \frac{2-\alpha}{6} \eta^2 + \left[\frac{(2-\alpha)(12-\alpha)}{120} - \frac{\beta}{20} \right] \eta^4 + \cdots \right\}.$$

7.5.9   To a good approximation, the interaction of two nucleons may be described by a mesonic potential

$$V = \frac{Ae^{-ax}}{x},$$

attractive for A negative. Show that the resultant Schrödinger wave equation

$$\frac{\hbar^2}{2m} \frac{d^2\psi}{dx^2} + (E - V)\psi = 0$$

has the following series solution through the first three nonvanishing coefficients:

$$\psi = a_0 \left\{ x + \frac{1}{2} A' x^2 + \frac{1}{6} \left[\frac{1}{2} A'^2 - E' - aA' \right] x^3 + \cdots \right\},$$

where the prime indicates multiplication by $2m/\hbar^2$.

7.5.10   If the parameter b^2 in Eq. (7.53) is equal to 2, Eq. (7.53) becomes

$$y'' + \frac{1}{x^2} y' - \frac{2}{x^2} y = 0.$$

From the indicial equation and the recurrence relation, **derive** a solution $y = 1 + 2x + 2x^2$. Verify that this is indeed a solution by substituting back into the differential equation.

7.5.11   The modified Bessel function $I_0(x)$ satisfies the differential equation

$$x^2 \frac{d^2}{dx^2} I_0(x) + x \frac{d}{dx} I_0(x) - x^2 I_0(x) = 0.$$

Given that the leading term in an asymptotic expansion is known to be

$$I_0(x) \sim \frac{e^x}{\sqrt{2\pi x}},$$

assume a series of the form

$$I_0(x) \sim \frac{e^x}{\sqrt{2\pi x}} \left\{ 1 + b_1 x^{-1} + b_2 x^{-2} + \cdots \right\}.$$

Determine the coefficients b_1 and b_2.

ANS. $b_1 = \frac{1}{8}, \quad b_2 = \frac{9}{128}.$

7.5.12   The even power-series solution of Legendre's equation is given by Exercise 8.3.1. Take $a_0 = 1$ and n not an even integer, say $n = 0.5$. Calculate the partial sums of the series through $x^{200}, x^{400}, x^{600}, \ldots, x^{2000}$ for $x = 0.95(0.01)1.00$. Also, write out the individual term corresponding to each of these powers.

Note. This calculation does **not** constitute proof of convergence at $x = 0.99$ or divergence at $x = 1.00$, but perhaps you can see the difference in the behavior of the sequence of partial sums for these two values of x.

7.5.13   (a)   The odd power-series solution of Hermite's equation is given by Exercise 8.3.3. Take $a_0 = 1$. Evaluate this series for $\alpha = 0, x = 1, 2, 3$. Cut off your calculation after the last term calculated has dropped below the maximum term by a factor of 10^6 or more. Set an upper bound to the error made in ignoring the remaining terms in the infinite series.

(b)   As a check on the calculation of part (a), show that the Hermite series $y_{odd}(\alpha = 0)$ corresponds to $\int_0^x \exp(x^2) dx$.

(c)   Calculate this integral for $x = 1, 2, 3$.

7.6   OTHER SOLUTIONS

In Section 7.5 a solution of a second-order homogeneous ODE was developed by substituting in a power series. By Fuchs' theorem this is possible, provided the power series is an expansion about an ordinary point or a nonessential singularity.[5] There is no guarantee that this approach will yield the two independent solutions we expect from a linear second-order ODE. In fact, we shall prove that such an ODE has at most two linearly independent solutions. Indeed, the technique gave only one solution for Bessel's equation (n an integer). In this section we also develop two methods of obtaining a second independent solution: an integral method and a power series containing a logarithmic term. First, however, we consider the question of independence of a set of functions.

---

[5]This is why the classification of singularities in Section 7.4 is of vital importance.

Linear Independence of Solutions

In Chapter 2 we introduced the concept of linear dependence for forms of the type $a_1 x_1 + a_2 x_2 + \ldots$, and identified a set of such forms as linearly dependent if any one of the forms could be written as a linear combination of others. We need now to extend the concept to a set of functions φ_λ. The criterion for linear dependence of a set of functions of a variable x is the existence of a relation of the form

$$\sum_\lambda k_\lambda \varphi_\lambda(x) = 0, \tag{7.54}$$

in which not all the coefficients k_λ are zero. The interpretation we attach to Eq. (7.54) is that it indicates linear dependence if it is satisfied for all relevant values of x. Isolated points or partial ranges of satisfaction of Eq. (7.54) do not suffice to indicate linear dependence. The essential idea being conveyed here is that if there is linear dependence, the function space spanned by the $\varphi_\lambda(x)$ can be spanned using less than all of them. On the other hand, if the only global solution of Eq. (7.54) is $k_\lambda = 0$ for all λ, the set of functions $\varphi_\lambda(x)$ is said to be linearly **independent**.

If the members of a set of functions are mutually orthogonal, then they are automatically linearly independent. To establish this, consider the evaluation of

$$S = \left\langle \sum_\lambda k_\lambda \varphi_\lambda \middle| \sum_\mu k_\mu \varphi_\mu \right\rangle$$

for a set of orthonormal φ_λ and with arbitrary values of the coefficients k_λ. Because of the orthonormality, S evaluates to $\sum_\lambda |k_\lambda|^2$, and will be nonzero (showing that $\sum_\lambda k_\lambda \varphi_\lambda \neq 0$) unless all the k_λ vanish.

We now proceed to consider the ramifications of linear dependence for solutions of ODEs, and for that purpose it is appropriate to assume that the functions $\varphi_\lambda(x)$ are differentiable as needed. Then, differentiating Eq. (7.54) repeatedly, with the assumption that it is valid for all x, we generate a set of equations

$$\sum_\lambda k_\lambda \varphi'_\lambda(x) = 0,$$

$$\sum_\lambda k_\lambda \varphi''_\lambda(x) = 0,$$

continuing until we have generated as many equations as the number of λ values. This gives us a set of homogeneous linear equations in which k_λ are the unknown quantities. By Section 2.1 there is a solution other than all $k_\lambda = 0$ only if the determinant of the coefficients of the k_λ vanishes. This means that the linear dependence we have assumed by accepting Eq. (7.54) implies that

$$\begin{vmatrix} \varphi_1 & \varphi_2 & \cdots & \varphi_n \\ \varphi'_1 & \varphi'_2 & \cdots & \varphi'_n \\ \cdots & \cdots & \cdots & \cdots \\ \varphi_1^{(n-1)} & \varphi_2^{(n-1)} & \cdots & \varphi_n^{(n-1)} \end{vmatrix} = 0. \tag{7.55}$$

This determinant is called the **Wronskian**, and the analysis leading to Eq. (7.55) shows that:

1. If the Wronskian is not equal to zero, then Eq. (7.54) has no solution other than $k_\lambda = 0$. The set of functions φ_λ is therefore linearly independent.

2. If the Wronskian vanishes at isolated values of the argument, this does not prove linear dependence. However, if the Wronskian is zero over the entire range of the variable, the functions φ_λ are linearly dependent over this range.[6]

Example 7.6.1   LINEAR INDEPENDENCE

The solutions of the linear oscillator equation, Eq. (7.27), are $\varphi_1 = \sin \omega x$, $\varphi_2 = \cos \omega x$. The Wronskian becomes

$$\begin{vmatrix} \sin \omega x & \cos \omega x \\ \omega \cos \omega x & -\omega \sin \omega x \end{vmatrix} = -\omega \neq 0.$$

These two solutions, φ_1 and φ_2, are therefore linearly independent. For just two functions this means that one is not a multiple of the other, which is obviously true here.

Incidentally, you know that

$$\sin \omega x = \pm (1 - \cos^2 \omega x)^{1/2},$$

but this is **not** a **linear** relation, of the form of Eq. (7.54). ∎

Example 7.6.2   LINEAR DEPENDENCE

For an illustration of linear dependence, consider the solutions of the ODE

$$\frac{d^2 \varphi(x)}{dx^2} = \varphi(x).$$

This equation has solutions $\varphi_1 = e^x$ and $\varphi_2 = e^{-x}$, and we add $\varphi_3 = \cosh x$, also a solution. The Wronskian is

$$\begin{vmatrix} e^x & e^{-x} & \cosh x \\ e^x & -e^{-x} & \sinh x \\ e^x & e^{-x} & \cosh x \end{vmatrix} = 0.$$

The determinant vanishes for all x because the first and third rows are identical. Hence e^x, e^{-x}, and $\cosh x$ are linearly dependent, and, indeed, we have a relation of the form of Eq. (7.54):

$$e^x + e^{-x} - 2 \cosh x = 0 \quad \text{with} \quad k_\lambda \neq 0.$$

∎

---

[6]Compare H. Lass, *Elements of Pure and Applied Mathematics*, New York: McGraw-Hill (1957), p. 187, for proof of this assertion. It is assumed that the functions have continuous derivatives and that at least one of the minors of the bottom row of Eq. (7.55) (Laplace expansion) does not vanish in $[a, b]$, the interval under consideration.

Number of Solutions

Now we are ready to prove the theorem that a second-order homogeneous ODE has two linearly independent solutions.

Suppose y_1, y_2, y_3 are three solutions of the homogeneous ODE, Eq. (7.23). Then we form the Wronskian $W_{jk} = y_j y'_k - y'_j y_k$ of any pair y_j, y_k of them and note also that

$$W'_{jk} = (y'_j y'_k + y_j y''_k) - (y''_j y_k + y'_j y'_k)$$

$$= y_j y''_k - y''_j y_k. \tag{7.56}$$

Next we divide the ODE by y and move $Q(x)$ to its right-hand side (where it becomes $-Q(x)$), so, for solutions y_j and y_k:

$$\frac{y''_j}{y_j} + P(x)\frac{y'_j}{y_j} = -Q(x) = \frac{y''_k}{y_k} + P(x)\frac{y'_k}{y_k}$$

Taking now the first and third members of this equation, multiplying by $y_j y_k$ and rearranging, we find that

$$(y_j y''_k - y''_j y_k) + P(x)(y_j y'_k - y'_j y_k) = 0,$$

which simplifies for any pair of solutions to

$$W'_{jk} = -P(x)W_{jk}. \tag{7.57}$$

Finally, we evaluate the Wronskian of all three solutions, expanding it by minors along the second row and identifying each term as containing a W'_{ij} as given by Eq. (7.56):

$$W = \begin{vmatrix} y_1 & y_2 & y_3 \\ y'_1 & y'_2 & y'_3 \\ y''_1 & y''_2 & y''_3 \end{vmatrix} = -y'_1 W'_{23} + y'_2 W'_{13} - y'_3 W'_{12}.$$

We now use Eq. (7.57) to replace each W'_{ij} by $-P(x)W_{ij}$ and then reassemble the minors into a 3×3 determinant, which vanishes because it contains two identical rows:

$$W = P(x)\left(y'_1 W_{23} - y'_2 W_{13} + y'_3 W_{12}\right) = -P(x)\begin{vmatrix} y_1 & y_2 & y_3 \\ y'_1 & y'_2 & y'_3 \\ y'_1 & y'_2 & y'_3 \end{vmatrix} = 0.$$

We therefore have $W = 0$, which is just the condition for linear dependence of the solutions y_j. Thus, we have proved the following:

A linear second-order homogeneous ODE has at most two linearly independent solutions. Generalizing, a linear homogeneous nth-order ODE has at most n linearly independent solutions y_j, and its general solution will be of the form $y(x) = \sum_{j=1}^{n} c_j y_j(x)$.

Finding a Second Solution

Returning to our linear, second-order, homogeneous ODE of the general form

$$y'' + P(x)y' + Q(x)y = 0, \tag{7.58}$$

let y_1 and y_2 be two independent solutions. Then the Wronskian, by definition, is

$$W = y_1 y_2' - y_1' y_2. \tag{7.59}$$

By differentiating the Wronskian, we obtain, as already demonstrated in Eq. (7.57),

$$W' = -P(x)W. \tag{7.60}$$

In the special case that $P(x) = 0$, that is,

$$y'' + Q(x)y = 0, \tag{7.61}$$

the Wronskian

$$W = y_1 y_2' - y_1' y_2 = \text{constant}. \tag{7.62}$$

Since our original differential equation is homogeneous, we may multiply the solutions y_1 and y_2 by whatever constants we wish and arrange to have the Wronskian equal to unity (or -1). This case, $P(x) = 0$, appears more frequently than might be expected. Recall that $\nabla^2(\psi/r)$ in spherical polar coordinates contains no first radial derivative. Finally, every linear second-order differential equation can be transformed into an equation of the form of Eq. (7.61) (compare Exercise 7.6.12).

For the general case, let us now assume that we have one solution of Eq. (7.58) by a series substitution (or by guessing). We now proceed to develop a second, independent solution for which $W \neq 0$. Rewriting Eq. (7.60) as

$$\frac{dW}{W} = -P \, dx,$$

we integrate over the variable x, from a to x, to obtain

$$\ln \frac{W(x)}{W(a)} = -\int_a^x P(x_1) \, dx_1,$$

or[7]

$$W(x) = W(a) \exp \left[-\int_a^x P(x_1) \, dx_1 \right]. \tag{7.63}$$

---

[7]If $P(x)$ remains finite in the domain of interest, $W(x) \neq 0$ unless $W(a) = 0$. That is, the Wronskian of our two solutions is either identically zero or never zero. However, if $P(x)$ does not remain finite in our interval, then $W(x)$ can have isolated zeros in that domain and one must be careful to choose a so that $W(a) \neq 0$.

Now we make the observation that

$$W(x) = y_1 y_2' - y_1' y_2 = y_1^2 \frac{d}{dx}\left(\frac{y_2}{y_1}\right),$$ (7.64)

and, by combining Eqs. (7.63) and (7.64), we have

$$\frac{d}{dx}\left(\frac{y_2}{y_1}\right) = W(a)\frac{\exp[-\int_a^x P(x_1)dx_1]}{y_1^2}.$$ (7.65)

Finally, by integrating Eq. (7.65) from $x_2 = b$ to $x_2 = x$ we get

$$y_2(x) = y_1(x)W(a)\int_b^x \frac{\exp\left[-\int_a^{x_2} P(x_1)dx_1\right]}{[y_1(x_2)]^2}dx_2.$$ (7.66)

Here a and b are arbitrary constants and a term $y_1(x)y_2(b)/y_1(b)$ has been dropped, because it is a multiple of the previously found first solution y_1. Since $W(a)$, the Wronskian evaluated at $x = a$, is a constant and our solutions for the homogeneous differential equation always contain an arbitrary normalizing factor, we set $W(a) = 1$ and write

$$y_2(x) = y_1(x)\int^x \frac{\exp[-\int^{x_2} P(x_1)dx_1]}{[y_1(x_2)]^2}dx_2.$$ (7.67)

Note that the lower limits $x_1 = a$ and $x_2 = b$ have been omitted. If they are retained, they simply make a contribution equal to a constant times the known first solution, $y_1(x)$, and hence add nothing new. If we have the important special case $P(x) = 0$, Eq. (7.67) reduces to

$$y_2(x) = y_1(x)\int^x \frac{dx_2}{[y_1(x_2)]^2}.$$ (7.68)

This means that by using either Eq. (7.67) or Eq. (7.68) we can take one known solution and by integrating can generate a second, independent solution of Eq. (7.58). This technique is used in Section 15.6 to generate a second solution of Legendre's differential equation.

Example 7.6.3   A SECOND SOLUTION FOR THE LINEAR OSCILLATOR EQUATION

From $d^2y/dx^2 + y = 0$ with $P(x) = 0$ let one solution be $y_1 = \sin x$. By applying Eq. (7.68), we obtain

$$y_2(x) = \sin x \int^x \frac{dx_2}{\sin^2 x_2} = \sin x(-\cot x) = -\cos x,$$

which is clearly independent (not a linear multiple) of $\sin x$. ∎

Series Form of the Second Solution

Further insight into the nature of the second solution of our differential equation may be obtained by the following sequence of operations.

1. Express $P(x)$ and $Q(x)$ in Eq. (7.58) as

$$P(x) = \sum_{i=-1}^{\infty} p_i x^i, \quad Q(x) = \sum_{j=-2}^{\infty} q_j x^j. \tag{7.69}$$

The leading terms of the summations are selected to create the strongest possible **regular** singularity (at the origin). These conditions just satisfy Fuchs' theorem and thus help us gain a better understanding of that theorem.

2. Develop the first few terms of a power-series solution, as in Section 7.5.

3. Using this solution as y_1, obtain a second series-type solution, y_2, from Eq. (7.67), by integrating it term by term.

Proceeding with Step 1, we have

$$y'' + (p_{-1}x^{-1} + p_0 + p_1 x + \cdots)y' + (q_{-2}x^{-2} + q_{-1}x^{-1} + \cdots)y = 0, \tag{7.70}$$

where $x = 0$ is at worst a regular singular point. If $p_{-1} = q_{-1} = q_{-2} = 0$, it reduces to an ordinary point. Substituting

$$y = \sum_{\lambda=0}^{\infty} a_\lambda x^{s+\lambda}$$

(Step 2), we obtain

$$\sum_{\lambda=0}^{\infty}(s+\lambda)(s+\lambda-1)a_\lambda x^{s+\lambda-2} + \sum_{i=-1}^{\infty} p_i x^i \sum_{\lambda=0}^{\infty}(s+\lambda)a_\lambda x^{s+\lambda-1}$$

$$+ \sum_{j=-2}^{\infty} q_j x^j \sum_{\lambda=0}^{\infty} a_\lambda x^{s+\lambda} = 0. \tag{7.71}$$

Assuming that $p_{-1} \neq 0$, our indicial equation is

$$s(s-1) + p_{-1}k + q_{-2} = 0,$$

which sets the net coefficient of x^{s-2} equal to zero. This reduces to

$$s^2 + (p_{-1} - 1)s + q_{-2} = 0. \tag{7.72}$$

We denote the two roots of this indicial equation by $s = \alpha$ and $s = \alpha - n$, where n is zero or a positive integer. (If n is not an integer, we expect two independent series solutions by the methods of Section 7.5 and we are done.) Then

$$(s-\alpha)(s-\alpha+n) = 0, \tag{7.73}$$

or

$$s^2 + (n - 2\alpha)s + \alpha(\alpha - n) = 0,$$

and equating coefficients of s in Eqs. (7.72) and (7.73), we have

$$p_{-1} - 1 = n - 2\alpha. \tag{7.74}$$

The known series solution corresponding to the larger root $s = \alpha$ may be written as

$$y_1 = x^\alpha \sum_{\lambda=0}^{\infty} a_\lambda x^\lambda.$$

Substituting this series solution into Eq. (7.67) (Step 3), we are faced with

$$y_2(x) = y_1(x) \int^x \left(\frac{\exp\left(-\int_a^{x_2} \sum_{i=-1}^{\infty} p_i x_1^i \, dx_1\right)}{x_2^{2\alpha} \left(\sum_{\lambda=0}^{\infty} a_\lambda x_2^\lambda\right)^2} \right) dx_2, \tag{7.75}$$

where the solutions y_1 and y_2 have been normalized so that the Wronskian $W(a) = 1$. Tackling the exponential factor first, we have

$$\int_a^{x_2} \sum_{i=-1}^{\infty} p_i x_1^i \, dx_1 = p_{-1} \ln x_2 + \sum_{k=0}^{\infty} \frac{p_k}{k+1} x_2^{k+1} + f(a), \tag{7.76}$$

with $f(a)$ an integration constant that may depend on a. Hence,

$$\exp\left(-\int_a^{x_2} \sum_i p_i x_1^i \, dx_1\right) = \exp[-f(a)] x_2^{-p_{-1}} \exp\left(-\sum_{k=0}^{\infty} \frac{p_k}{k+1} x_2^{k+1}\right)$$

$$= \exp[-f(a)] x_2^{-p_{-1}} \left[1 - \sum_{k=0}^{\infty} \frac{p_k}{k+1} x_2^{k+1} + \frac{1}{2!}\left(-\sum_{k=0}^{\infty} \frac{p_k}{k+1} x_2^{k+1}\right)^2 + \cdots \right]. \tag{7.77}$$

This final series expansion of the exponential is certainly convergent if the original expansion of the coefficient $P(x)$ was uniformly convergent.

The denominator in Eq. (7.75) may be handled by writing

$$\left[x_2^{2\alpha} \left(\sum_{\lambda=0}^{\infty} a_\lambda x_2^\lambda\right)^2 \right]^{-1} = x_2^{-2\alpha} \left(\sum_{\lambda=0}^{\infty} a_\lambda x_2^\lambda\right)^{-2} = x_2^{-2\alpha} \sum_{\lambda=0}^{\infty} b_\lambda x_2^\lambda. \tag{7.78}$$

Neglecting constant factors, which will be picked up anyway by the requirement that $W(a) = 1$, we obtain

$$y_2(x) = y_1(x) \int^x x_2^{-p_{-1}-2\alpha} \left(\sum_{\lambda=0}^{\infty} c_\lambda x_2^\lambda\right) dx_2. \tag{7.79}$$

Applying Eq. (7.74),

$$x_2^{-p_{-1}-2\alpha} = x_2^{-n-1}, \tag{7.80}$$

and we have assumed here that n is an integer. Substituting this result into Eq. (7.79), we obtain

$$y_2(x) = y_1(x) \int^x \left(c_0 x_2^{-n-1} + c_1 x_2^{-n} + c_2 x_2^{-n+1} + \cdots + c_n x_2^{-1} + \cdots \right) dx_2. \qquad (7.81)$$

The integration indicated in Eq. (7.81) leads to a coefficient of $y_1(x)$ consisting of two parts:

1. A power series starting with x^{-n}.
2. A logarithm term from the integration of x^{-1} (when $\lambda = n$). This term always appears when n is an integer, **unless** c_n fortuitously happens to vanish.[8]

   If we choose to combine y_1 and the power series starting with x^{-n}, our second solution will assume the form

$$y_2(x) = y_1(x) \ln |x| + \sum_{j=-n}^{\infty} d_j x^{j+\alpha}. \qquad (7.82)$$

Example 7.6.4   A Second Solution of Bessel's Equation

From Bessel's equation, Eq. (7.40), divided by x^2 to agree with Eq. (7.59), we have

$$P(x) = x^{-1} \quad Q(x) = 1 \quad \text{for the case} \quad n = 0.$$

Hence $p_{-1} = 1$, $q_0 = 1$; all other p_i and q_j vanish. The Bessel indicial equation, Eq. (7.43) with $n = 0$, is

$$s^2 = 0.$$

Hence we verify Eqs. (7.72) to (7.74) with n and α set to zero.
   Our first solution is available from Eq. (7.49). It is[9]

$$y_1(x) = J_0(x) = 1 - \frac{x^2}{4} + \frac{x^4}{64} - O(x^6). \qquad (7.83)$$

Now, substituting all this into Eq. (7.67), we have the specific case corresponding to Eq. (7.75):

$$y_2(x) = J_0(x) \int^x \left(\frac{\exp\left[-\int^{x_2} x_1^{-1} dx_1 \right]}{\left[1 - \frac{x_2^2}{4} + \frac{x_2^4}{64} - \cdots \right]^2} \right) dx_2. \qquad (7.84)$$

---

[8] For parity considerations, $\ln x$ is taken to be $\ln |x|$, even.
[9] The capital O (order of) as written here means terms proportional to x^6 and possibly higher powers of x.

From the numerator of the integrand,

$$\exp\left[-\int^{x_2}\frac{dx_1}{x_1}\right] = \exp[-\ln x_2] = \frac{1}{x_2}.$$

This corresponds to the x_2^{-P-1} in Eq. (7.77). From the denominator of the integrand, using a binomial expansion, we obtain

$$\left[1 - \frac{x_2^2}{4} + \frac{x_2^4}{64}\right]^{-2} = 1 + \frac{x_2^2}{2} + \frac{5x_2^4}{32} + \cdots.$$

Corresponding to Eq. (7.79), we have

$$y_2(x) = J_0(x)\int^x \frac{1}{x_2}\left[1 + \frac{x_2^2}{2} + \frac{5x_2^4}{32} + \cdots\right]dx_2$$

$$= J_0(x)\left\{\ln x + \frac{x^2}{4} + \frac{5x^4}{128} + \cdots\right\}. \tag{7.85}$$

Let us check this result. From Eq. (14.62), which gives the standard form of the second solution, which is called a **Neumann function** and designated Y_0,

$$Y_0(x) = \frac{2}{\pi}\left[\ln x - \ln 2 + \gamma\right]J_0(x) + \frac{2}{\pi}\left\{\frac{x^2}{4} - \frac{3x^4}{128} + \cdots\right\}. \tag{7.86}$$

Two points arise: (1) Since Bessel's equation is homogeneous, we may multiply $y_2(x)$ by any constant. To match $Y_0(x)$, we multiply our $y_2(x)$ by $2/\pi$. (2) To our second solution, $(2/\pi)y_2(x)$, we may add any constant multiple of the first solution. Again, to match $Y_0(x)$ we add

$$\frac{2}{\pi}\left[-\ln 2 + \gamma\right]J_0(x),$$

where γ is the Euler-Mascheroni constant, defined in Eq. (1.13).[10] Our new, modified second solution is

$$y_2(x) = \frac{2}{\pi}\left[\ln x - \ln 2 + \gamma\right]J_0(x) + \frac{2}{\pi}J_0(x)\left\{\frac{x^2}{4} + \frac{5x^4}{128} + \cdots\right\}. \tag{7.87}$$

Now the comparison with $Y_0(x)$ requires only a simple multiplication of the series for $J_0(x)$ from Eq. (7.83) and the curly bracket of Eq. (7.87). The multiplication checks, through terms of order x^2 and x^4, which is all we carried. Our second solution from Eqs. (7.67) and (7.75) agrees with the standard second solution, the Neumann function $Y_0(x)$. ∎

The analysis that indicated the second solution of Eq. (7.58) to have the form given in Eq. (7.82) suggests the possibility of just substituting Eq. (7.82) into the original differential equation and determining the coefficients d_j. However, the process has some features different from that of Section 7.5, and is illustrated by the following example.

---

[10]The Neumann function Y_0 is defined as it is in order to achieve convenient asymptotic properties; see Sections 14.3 and 14.6.

Example 7.6.5   MORE NEUMANN FUNCTIONS

We consider here second solutions to Bessel's ODE of integer orders $n > 0$, using the expansion given in Eq. (7.82). The first solution, designated J_n and presented in Eq. (7.49), arises from the value $\alpha = n$ from the indicial equation, while the quantity called n in Eq. (7.82), the separation of the two roots of the indicial equation, has in the current context the value $2n$. Thus, Eq. (7.82) takes the form

$$y_2(x) = J_n(x) \ln |x| + \sum_{j=-2n}^{\infty} d_j x^{j+n}, \tag{7.88}$$

where y_2 must, apart from scale and a possible multiple of J_n, be the second solution Y_n of the Bessel equation. Substituting this form into Bessel's equation, carrying out the indicated differentiations and using the fact that $J_n(x)$ is a solution of our ODE, we get after combining similar terms

$$x^2 y_2'' + x y_2' + (x^2 - n^2) y_2 =$$

$$2x J_n'(x) + \sum_{j \geq -2n} j(j+2n) d_j x^{j+n} + \sum_{j \geq -2n} d_j x^{j+n+2} = 0. \tag{7.89}$$

We next insert the power-series expansion

$$2x J_n'(x) = \sum_{j \geq 0} a_j x^{j+n}, \tag{7.90}$$

where the coefficients can be obtained by differentiation of the expansion of J_n, see Eq. (7.49), and have the values (for $j \geq 0$)

$$a_{2j} = \frac{(-1)^j (n+2j)}{j!(n+j)! 2^{n+2j-1}},$$

$$a_{2j+1} = 0. \tag{7.91}$$

This, and a redefinition of the index j in the last term, bring Eq. (7.89) to the form

$$\sum_{j \geq 0} a_j x^{j+n} + \sum_{j \geq -2n} j(j+2n) d_j x^{j+n} + \sum_{j \geq -2n+2} d_{j-2} x^{j+n} = 0. \tag{7.92}$$

Considering first the coefficient of x^{-n+1} (corresponding to $j = -2n + 1$), we note that its vanishing requires that d_{-2n+1} vanish, as the only contribution comes from the middle summation. Since all a_j of odd j vanish, the vanishing of d_{-2n+1} implies that all other d_j of odd j must also vanish. We therefore only need to give further consideration to even j.

We next note that the coefficient d_0 is arbitrary, and may without loss of generality be set to zero. This is true because we may bring d_0 to any value by adding to y_2 an appropriate multiple of the solution J_n, whose expansion has an x^n leading term. We have then exhausted all freedom in specifying y_2; its scale is determined by our choice of its logarithmic term.

Now, taking the coefficient of x^n (terms with $j = 0$), and remembering that $d_0 = 0$, we have

$$d_{-2} = -a_0,$$

and we may recur **downward** in steps of 2, using formulas based on the coefficients of $x^{n-2}, x^{n-4}, \ldots$, corresponding to

$$d_{j-2} = -j(2n+j)d_j, \quad j = -2, -4, \ldots, -2n+2.$$

To obtain d_j with positive j, we recur upward, obtaining from the coefficient of x^{n+j}

$$d_j = \frac{-a_j - d_{j-2}}{j(2n+j)}, \quad j = 2, 4, \ldots,$$

again remembering that $d_0 = 0$.

Proceeding to $n = 1$ as a specific example, we have from Eq. (7.91) $a_0 = 1$, $a_2 = -3/8$, and $a_4 = 5/192$, so

$$d_{-2} = -1, \quad d_2 = -\frac{a_2}{8} = \frac{3}{64}, \quad d_4 = \frac{-a_4 - d_2}{24} = -\frac{7}{2304};$$

thus

$$y_2(x) = J_1(x)\ln|x| - \frac{1}{x} + \frac{3}{64}x^3 - \frac{7}{2304}x^5 + \cdots,$$

in agreement (except for a multiple of J_1 and a scale factor) with the standard form of the Neumann function Y_1:

$$Y_1(x) = \frac{2}{\pi}\left[\ln\left|\frac{x}{2}\right| + \gamma - \frac{1}{2}\right]J_1(x) + \frac{2}{\pi}\left[-\frac{1}{x} + \frac{3}{64}x^3 - \frac{7}{2304}x^5 + \cdots\right]. \qquad (7.93)$$

∎

As shown in the examples, the second solution will usually diverge at the origin because of the logarithmic factor and the negative powers of x in the series. For this reason $y_2(x)$ is often referred to as the **irregular solution**. The first series solution, $y_1(x)$, which usually converges at the origin, is called the **regular solution**. The question of behavior at the origin is discussed in more detail in Chapters 14 and 15, in which we take up Bessel functions, modified Bessel functions, and Legendre functions.

Summary

The two solutions of both sections (together with the exercises) provide a **complete solution** of our linear, homogeneous, second-order ODE, assuming that the point of expansion is no worse than a regular singularity. At least one solution can always be obtained by series substitution (Section 7.5). A **second, linearly independent solution** can be constructed by the **Wronskian** double integral, Eq. (7.67). This is all there are: **No third, linearly independent solution exists** (compare Exercise 7.6.10).

The **inhomogeneous**, linear, second-order ODE will have a general solution formed by adding a **particular solution** to the complete inhomogeneous equation to the general solution of the corresponding homogeneous ODE. Techniques for finding particular solutions of linear but inhomogeneous ODEs are the topic of the next section.

Exercises

7.6.1   You know that the three unit vectors $\hat{\mathbf{e}}_x$, $\hat{\mathbf{e}}_y$, and $\hat{\mathbf{e}}_z$ are mutually perpendicular (orthogonal). Show that $\hat{\mathbf{e}}_x$, $\hat{\mathbf{e}}_y$, and $\hat{\mathbf{e}}_z$ are linearly independent. Specifically, show that no relation of the form of Eq. (7.54) exists for $\hat{\mathbf{e}}_x$, $\hat{\mathbf{e}}_y$, and $\hat{\mathbf{e}}_z$.

7.6.2   The criterion for the linear **independence** of three vectors $\mathbf{A}$, $\mathbf{B}$, and $\mathbf{C}$ is that the equation

$$a\mathbf{A} + b\mathbf{B} + c\mathbf{C} = 0,$$

analogous to Eq. (7.54), has no solution other than the trivial $a = b = c = 0$. Using components $\mathbf{A} = (A_1, A_2, A_3)$, and so on, set up the determinant criterion for the existence or nonexistence of a nontrivial solution for the coefficients a, b, and c. Show that your criterion is equivalent to the scalar triple product $\mathbf{A} \cdot \mathbf{B} \times \mathbf{C} \neq 0$.

7.6.3   Using the Wronskian determinant, show that the set of functions

$$\left\{ 1, \frac{x^n}{n!}(n = 1, 2, \ldots, N) \right\}$$

is linearly independent.

7.6.4   If the Wronskian of two functions y_1 and y_2 is identically zero, show by direct integration that

$$y_1 = cy_2,$$

that is, that y_1 and y_2 are linearly dependent. Assume the functions have continuous derivatives and that at least one of the functions does not vanish in the interval under consideration.

7.6.5   The Wronskian of two functions is found to be zero at $x_0 - \varepsilon \leq x \leq x_0 + \varepsilon$ for arbitrarily small $\varepsilon > 0$. Show that this Wronskian vanishes for all x and that the functions are linearly dependent.

7.6.6   The three functions $\sin x$, e^x, and e^{-x} are linearly independent. No one function can be written as a linear combination of the other two. Show that the Wronskian of $\sin x$, e^x, and e^{-x} vanishes but only at isolated points.

$$ANS. \quad W = 4\sin x,$$
$$W = 0 \text{ for } x = \pm n\pi, \quad n = 0, 1, 2, \ldots.$$

7.6.7   Consider two functions $\varphi_1 = x$ and $\varphi_2 = |x|$. Since $\varphi_1' = 1$ and $\varphi_2' = x/|x|$, $W(\varphi_1, \varphi_2) = 0$ for any interval, including $[-1, +1]$. Does the vanishing of the Wronskian over $[-1, +1]$ prove that φ_1 and φ_2 are linearly dependent? Clearly, they are not. What is wrong?

7.6.8   Explain that **linear independence** does not mean the absence of any dependence. Illustrate your argument with $\cosh x$ and e^x.

7.6.9   Legendre's differential equation

$$(1 - x^2)y'' - 2xy' + n(n+1)y = 0$$

has a regular solution $P_n(x)$ and an irregular solution $Q_n(x)$. Show that the Wronskian of P_n and Q_n is given by

$$P_n(x)Q_n'(x) - P_n'(x)Q_n(x) = \frac{A_n}{1-x^2},$$

with A_n **independent** of x.

7.6.10   Show, by means of the Wronskian, that a linear, second-order, homogeneous ODE of the form

$$y''(x) + P(x)y'(x) + Q(x)y(x) = 0$$

cannot have three independent solutions.

Hint. Assume a third solution and show that the Wronskian vanishes for all x.

7.6.11   Show the following when the linear second-order differential equation $py'' + qy' + ry = 0$ is expressed in self-adjoint form:

(a)   The Wronskian is equal to a constant divided by p:

$$W(x) = \frac{C}{p(x)}.$$

(b)   A second solution $y_2(x)$ is obtained from a first solution $y_1(x)$ as

$$y_2(x) = Cy_1(x) \int^x \frac{dt}{p(t)[y_1(t)]^2}.$$

7.6.12   Transform our linear, second-order ODE

$$y'' + P(x)y' + Q(x)y = 0$$

by the substitution

$$y = z \exp\left[-\frac{1}{2} \int^x P(t)\,dt \right]$$

and show that the resulting differential equation for z is

$$z'' + q(x)z = 0,$$

where

$$q(x) = Q(x) - \frac{1}{2}P'(x) - \frac{1}{4}P^2(x).$$

Note. This substitution can be derived by the technique of Exercise 7.6.25.

7.6.13   Use the result of Exercise 7.6.12 to show that the replacement of $\varphi(r)$ by $r\varphi(r)$ may be expected to eliminate the first derivative from the Laplacian in spherical polar coordinates. See also Exercise 3.10.34.

7.6.14   By direct differentiation and substitution show that

$$y_2(x) = y_1(x) \int^x \frac{\exp[-\int^s P(t)dt]}{[y_1(s)]^2} ds$$

satisfies, like $y_1(x)$, the ODE

$$y_2''(x) + P(x)y_2'(x) + Q(x)y_2(x) = 0.$$

Note. The Leibniz formula for the derivative of an integral is

$$\frac{d}{d\alpha} \int_{g(\alpha)}^{h(\alpha)} f(x,\alpha)dx = \int_{g(\alpha)}^{h(\alpha)} \frac{\partial f(x,\alpha)}{\partial \alpha} dx + f[h(\alpha),\alpha]\frac{dh(\alpha)}{d\alpha} - f[g(\alpha),\alpha]\frac{dg(\alpha)}{d\alpha}.$$

7.6.15   In the equation

$$y_2(x) = y_1(x) \int^x \frac{\exp[-\int^s P(t)dt]}{[y_1(s)]^2} ds,$$

$y_1(x)$ satisfies

$$y_1'' + P(x)y_1' + Q(x)y_1 = 0.$$

The function $y_2(x)$ is a linearly **independent** second solution of the same equation. Show that the inclusion of lower limits on the two integrals leads to nothing new, that is, that it generates only an overall constant factor and a constant multiple of the known solution $y_1(x)$.

7.6.16   Given that one solution of

$$R'' + \frac{1}{r}R' - \frac{m^2}{r^2}R = 0$$

is $R = r^m$, show that Eq. (7.67) predicts a second solution, $R = r^{-m}$.

7.6.17   Using

$$y_1(x) = \sum_{n=0}^{\infty} \frac{(-1)^n}{(2n+1)!} x^{2n+1}$$

as a solution of the linear oscillator equation, follow the analysis that proceeds through Eq. (7.81) and show that in that equation $c_n = 0$, so that in this case the second solution does not contain a logarithmic term.

7.6.18   Show that when n is **not** an integer in Bessel's ODE, Eq. (7.40), the second solution of Bessel's equation, obtained from Eq. (7.67), does **not** contain a logarithmic term.

7.6.19 (a) One solution of Hermite's differential equation

$$y'' - 2xy' + 2\alpha y = 0$$

for $\alpha = 0$ is $y_1(x) = 1$. Find a second solution, $y_2(x)$, using Eq. (7.67). Show that your second solution is equivalent to y_{odd} (Exercise 8.3.3).

(b) Find a second solution for $\alpha = 1$, where $y_1(x) = x$, using Eq. (7.67). Show that your second solution is equivalent to y_{even} (Exercise 8.3.3).

7.6.20 One solution of Laguerre's differential equation

$$xy'' + (1 - x)y' + ny = 0$$

for $n = 0$ is $y_1(x) = 1$. Using Eq. (7.67), develop a second, linearly independent solution. Exhibit the logarithmic term explicitly.

7.6.21 For Laguerre's equation with $n = 0$,

$$y_2(x) = \int^x \frac{e^s}{s} ds.$$

(a) Write $y_2(x)$ as a logarithm plus a power series.

(b) Verify that the integral form of $y_2(x)$, previously given, is a solution of Laguerre's equation ($n = 0$) by direct differentiation of the integral and substitution into the differential equation.

(c) Verify that the series form of $y_2(x)$, part (a), is a solution by differentiating the series and substituting back into Laguerre's equation.

7.6.22 One solution of the Chebyshev equation

$$(1 - x^2)y'' - xy' + n^2 y = 0$$

for $n = 0$ is $y_1 = 1$.

(a) Using Eq. (7.67), develop a second, linearly independent solution.

(b) Find a second solution by direct integration of the Chebyshev equation.

Hint. Let $v = y'$ and integrate. Compare your result with the second solution given in Section 18.4.

ANS. (a) $y_2 = \sin^{-1} x$.

(b) The second solution, $V_n(x)$, is not defined for $n = 0$.

7.6.23 One solution of the Chebyshev equation

$$(1 - x^2)y'' - xy' + n^2 y = 0$$

for $n = 1$ is $y_1(x) = x$. Set up the Wronskian double integral solution and derive a second solution, $y_2(x)$.

ANS. $y_2 = -(1 - x^2)^{1/2}$.

7.6.24   The radial Schrödinger wave equation for a spherically symmetric potential can be written in the form

$$\left[-\frac{\hbar^2}{2m}\frac{d^2}{dr^2} + l(l+1)\frac{\hbar^2}{2mr^2} + V(r) \right] y(r) = E y(r).$$

The potential energy $V(r)$ may be expanded about the origin as

$$V(r) = \frac{b_{-1}}{r} + b_0 + b_1 r + \cdots .$$

(a)   Show that there is one (regular) solution $y_1(r)$ starting with r^{l+1}.

(b)   From Eq. (7.69) show that the irregular solution $y_2(r)$ diverges at the origin as r^{-l}.

7.6.25   Show that if a second solution, y_2, is assumed to be related to the first solution, y_1, according to $y_2(x) = y_1(x) f(x)$, substitution back into the original equation

$$y_2'' + P(x)y_2' + Q(x)y_2 = 0$$

leads to

$$f(x) = \int^x \frac{\exp[-\int^s P(t)dt]}{[y_1(s)]^2} ds,$$

in agreement with Eq. (7.67).

7.6.26   (a)   Show that

$$y'' + \frac{1 - \alpha^2}{4x^2} y = 0$$

has two solutions:

$$y_1(x) = a_0 x^{(1+\alpha)/2},$$
$$y_2(x) = a_0 x^{(1-\alpha)/2}.$$

(b)   For $\alpha = 0$ the two linearly independent solutions of part (a) reduce to the single solution $y_{1'} = a_0 x^{1/2}$. Using Eq. (7.68) derive a second solution,

$$y_{2'}(x) = a_0 x^{1/2} \ln x.$$

Verify that $y_{2'}$ is indeed a solution.

(c)   Show that the second solution from part (b) may be obtained as a limiting case from the two solutions of part (a):

$$y_{2'}(x) = \lim_{\alpha \to 0} \left(\frac{y_1 - y_2}{\alpha} \right).$$

7.7 INHOMOGENEOUS LINEAR ODEs

We frame the discussion in terms of second-order ODEs, although the methods can be extended to equations of higher order. We thus consider ODEs of the general form

$$y'' + P(x)y' + Q(x)y = F(x), \qquad (7.94)$$

and proceed under the assumption that the corresponding homogeneous equation, with $F(x) = 0$, has been solved, thereby obtaining two independent solutions designated $y_1(x)$ and $y_2(x)$.

Variation of Parameters

The method of variation of parameters (variation of the constant) starts by writing a particular solution of the inhomogeneous ODE, Eq. (7.94), in the form

$$y(x) = u_1(x)y_1(x) + u_2(x)y_2(x). \qquad (7.95)$$

We have specifically written $u_1(x)$ and $u_2(x)$ to emphasize that these are functions of the independent variable, and **not** constant coefficients. This, of course, means that Eq. (7.95) does not constitute a restriction to the functional form of $y(x)$. For clarity and compactness, we will usually write these functions just as u_1 and u_2.

In preparation for inserting $y(x)$, from Eq. (7.95), into the inhomogeneous ODE, we compute its derivative:

$$y' = u_1 y_1' + u_2 y_2' + (y_1 u_1' + y_2 u_2'),$$

and take advantage of the redundancy in the form assumed for y by choosing u_1 and u_2 in such a way that

$$y_1 u_1' + y_2 u_2' = 0, \qquad (7.96)$$

where Eq. (7.96) is assumed to be an identity (i.e., to apply for all x). We will shortly show that requiring Eq. (7.96) does not lead to an inconsistency.

After applying Eq. (7.96), y', and its derivative y'', are found to be

$$y' = u_1 y_1' + u_2 y_2',$$
$$y'' = u_1 y_1'' + u_2 y_2'' + u_1' y_1' + u_2' y_2',$$

and substitution into Eq. (7.94) yields

$$(u_1 y_1'' + u_2 y_2'' + u_1' y_1' + u_2' y_2') + P(x)(u_1 y_1' + u_2 y_2') + Q(x)(u_1 y_1 + u_2 y_2) = F(x),$$

which, because y_1 and y_2 are solutions of the homogeneous equation, reduces to

$$u_1' y_1' + u_2' y_2' = F(x). \qquad (7.97)$$

Equations (7.96) and (7.97) are, for each value of x, a set of two simultaneous **algebraic** equations in the variables u_1' and u_2'; to emphasize this point we repeat them here:

$$y_1 u_1' + y_2 u_2' = 0,$$
$$y_1' u_1' + y_2' u_2' = F(x). \qquad (7.98)$$

The determinant of the coefficients of these equations is

$$\begin{vmatrix} y_1 & y_2 \\ y_1' & y_2' \end{vmatrix},$$

which we recognize as the Wronskian of the linearly independent solutions to the homogeneous equation. That means this determinant is nonzero, so there will, for each x, be a unique solution to Eqs. (7.98), i.e., unique functions u_1' and u_2'. We conclude that the restriction implied by Eq. (7.96) is permissible.

Once u_1' and u_2' have been identified, each can be integrated, respectively yielding u_1 and u_2, and, via Eq. (7.95), a particular solution of our inhomogeneous ODE.

Example 7.7.1   AN INHOMOGENEOUS ODE

Consider the ODE

$$(1-x)y'' + xy' - y = (1-x)^2. \tag{7.99}$$

The corresponding homogeneous ODE has solutions $y_1 = x$ and $y_2 = e^x$. Thus, $y_1' = 1$, $y_2' = e^x$, and the simultaneous equations for u_1' and u_2' are

$$\begin{aligned} x u_1' + e^x u_2' &= 0, \\ u_1' + e^x u_2' &= F(x). \end{aligned} \tag{7.100}$$

Here $F(x)$ is the inhomogeneous term when the ODE has been written in the standard form, Eq. (7.94). This means that we must divide Eq. (7.99) through by $1-x$ (the coefficient of y''), after which we see that $F(x) = 1 - x$.

With the above choice of $F(x)$, we solve Eqs. (7.100), obtaining

$$u_1' = 1, \quad u_2' = -xe^{-x},$$

which integrate to

$$u_1 = x, \quad u_2 = (x+1)e^{-x}.$$

Now forming a particular solution to the inhomogeneous ODE, we have

$$y_p(x) = u_1 y_1 + u_2 y_2 = x(x) + \left((x+1)e^{-x}\right)e^x = x^2 + x + 1.$$

Because x is a solution to the homogeneous equation, we may remove it from the above expression, leaving the more compact formula $y_p = x^2 + 1$.

The general solution to our ODE therefore takes the final form

$$y(x) = C_1 x + C_2 e^x + x^2 + 1.$$

∎

Exercises

7.7.1   If our linear, second-order ODE is inhomogeneous, that is, of the form of Eq. (7.94), the **most general solution is**

$$y(x) = y_1(x) + y_2(x) + y_p(x),$$

where y_1 and y_2 are independent solutions of the homogeneous equation. Show that

$$y_p(x) = y_2(x) \int^x \frac{y_1(s)F(s)ds}{W\{y_1(s), y_2(s)\}} - y_1(x) \int^x \frac{y_2(s)F(s)ds}{W\{y_1(s), y_2(s)\}},$$

with $W\{y_1(x), y_2(x)\}$ the Wronskian of $y_1(s)$ and $y_2(s)$.

Find the general solutions to the following inhomogeneous ODEs:

7.7.2 $y'' + y = 1$.

7.7.3 $y'' + 4y = e^x$.

7.7.4 $y'' - 3y' + 2y = \sin x$.

7.7.5 $xy'' - (1+x)y' + y = x^2$.

7.8   NONLINEAR DIFFERENTIAL EQUATIONS

The main outlines of large parts of physical theory have been developed using mathematics in which the objects of concern possessed some sort of linearity property. As a result, linear algebra (matrix theory) and solution methods for linear differential equations were appropriate mathematical tools, and the development of these mathematical topics has progressed in the directions illustrated by most of this book. However, there is some physics that requires the use of nonlinear differential equations (NDEs). The hydrodynamics of viscous, compressible media is described by the Navier-Stokes equations, which are nonlinear. The nonlinearity evidences itself in phenomena such as turbulent flow, which cannot be described using linear equations. Nonlinear equations are also at the heart of the description of behavior known as **chaotic**, in which the evolution of a system is so sensitive to its initial conditions that it effectively becomes unpredictable.

The mathematics of nonlinear ODEs is both more difficult and less developed than that of linear ODEs, and accordingly we provide here only an extremely brief survey. Much of the recent progress in this area has been in the development of computational methods for nonlinear problems; that is also outside the scope of this text.

In this final section of the present chapter we discuss briefly some specific NDEs, the classical Bernoulli and Riccati equations.

Bernoulli and Riccati Equations

Bernoulli equations are nonlinear, having the form

$$y'(x) = p(x)y(x) + q(x)[y(x)]^n, \tag{7.101}$$

where p and q are real functions and $n \neq 0, 1$ to exclude first-order linear ODEs. However, if we substitute

$$u(x) = [y(x)]^{1-n},$$

then Eq. (7.101) becomes a first-order linear ODE,

$$u' = (1-n)y^{-n}y' = (1-n)\big[p(x)u(x) + q(x)\big], \tag{7.102}$$

which we can solve (using an integrating factor) as described in Section 7.2.

Riccati equations are quadratic in $y(x)$:

$$y' = p(x)y^2 + q(x)y + r(x), \tag{7.103}$$

where we require $p \neq 0$ to exclude linear ODEs and $r \neq 0$ to exclude Bernoulli equations. There is no known general method for solving Riccati equations. However, when a special solution $y_0(x)$ of Eq. (7.103) is known by a guess or inspection, then one can write the general solution in the form $y = y_0 + u$, with u satisfying the Bernoulli equation

$$u' = pu^2 + (2py_0 + q)u, \tag{7.104}$$

because substitution of $y = y_0 + u$ into Eq. (7.103) removes $r(x)$ from the resulting equation.

There are no general methods for obtaining exact solutions of most nonlinear ODEs. This fact makes it more important to develop methods for finding the qualitative behavior of solutions. In Section 7.5 of this chapter we mentioned that power-series solutions of ODEs exist except (possibly) at essential singularities of the ODE. The coefficients in the power-series expansions provide us with the asymptotic behavior of the solutions. By making expansions of solutions to NDEs and retaining only the linear terms, it will often be possible to understand the qualitative behavior of the solutions in the neighborhood of the expansion point.

Fixed and Movable Singularities, Special Solutions

A first step in analyzing the solutions of NDEs is to identify their singularity structures. Solutions of NDEs may have singular points that are independent of the initial or boundary conditions; these are called **fixed singularities**. But in addition they may have **spontaneous**, or **movable**, singularities that vary with the initial or boundary conditions. This feature complicates the asymptotic analysis of NDEs.

Example 7.8.1 MOVEABLE SINGULARITY

Compare the linear ODE

$$y' + \frac{y}{x-1} = 0,$$

(which has an obvious regular singularity at $x = 1$), with the NDE $y' = y^2$. Both have the same solution with initial condition $y(0) = 1$, namely $y(x) = 1/(1-x)$. But for $y(0) = 2$, the linear ODE has solution $y = 1 + 1/(1-x)$, while the NDE now has solution $y(x) = 2/(1-2x)$. The singularity in the solution of the NDE has moved to $x = 1/2$. ∎

For a linear second-order ODE we have a complete description of its solutions and their asymptotic behavior when two linearly independent solutions are known. But for NDEs there may still be **special solutions** whose asymptotic behavior is not obtainable from two independent solutions. This is another characteristic property of NDEs, which we illustrate again by an example.

Example 7.8.2 SPECIAL SOLUTION

The NDE $y'' = yy'/x$ has two linearly independent solutions that define the two-parameter family of curves

$$y(x) = 2c_1 \tan(c_1 \ln x + c_2) - 1, \tag{7.105}$$

where the c_i are integration constants. However, this NDE also has the special solution $y = c_3 = $ constant, which cannot be obtained from Eq. (7.105) by any choice of the parameters c_1, c_2.

The "general solution" in Eq. (7.105) can be obtained by making the substitution $x = e^t$, and then defining $Y(t) \equiv y(e^t)$ so that $x(dy/dx) = dY/dt$, thereby obtaining the ODE $Y'' = Y'(Y + 1)$. This ODE can be integrated once to give $Y' = \frac{1}{2}Y^2 + Y + c$ with $c = 2(c_1^2 + 1/4)$ an integration constant. The equation for Y' is separable and can be integrated again to yield Eq. (7.105). ∎

Exercises

7.8.1 Consider the Riccati equation $y' = y^2 - y - 2$. A particular solution to this equation is $y = 2$. Find a more general solution.

7.8.2 A particular solution to $y' = y^2/x^3 - y/x + 2x$ is $y = x^2$. Find a more general solution.

7.8.3 Solve the Bernoulli equation $y' + xy = xy^3$.

7.8.4 ODEs of the form $y = xy' + f(y')$ are known as Clairaut equations. The first step in solving an equation of this type is to differentiate it, yielding

$$y' = y' + xy'' + f'(y')y'', \quad \text{or} \quad y''(x + f'(y')) = 0.$$

Solutions may therefore be obtained both from $y'' = 0$ and from $f'(y') = -x$. The so-called general solution comes from $y'' = 0$.

For $f(y') = (y')^2$,

(a) Obtain the general solution (note that it contains a single constant).
(b) Obtain the so-called singular solution from $f'(y') = -x$. By substituting back into the original ODE show that this singular solution contains no adjustable constants.

Note. The singular solution is the envelope of the general solutions.

Additional Readings

Cohen, H., *Mathematics for Scientists and Engineers*. Englewood Cliffs, NJ: Prentice-Hall (1992).

Golomb, M., and M. Shanks, *Elements of Ordinary Differential Equations*. New York: McGraw-Hill (1965).

Hubbard, J., and B. H. West, *Differential Equations*. Berlin: Springer (1995).

Ince, E. L., *Ordinary Differential Equations*. New York: Dover (1956). The classic work in the theory of ordinary differential equations.

Jackson, E. A., *Perspectives of Nonlinear Dynamics*. Cambridge: Cambridge University Press (1989).

Jordan, D. W., and P. Smith, *Nonlinear Ordinary Differential Equations*, 2nd ed. Oxford: Oxford University Press (1987).

Margenau, H., and G. M. Murphy, *The Mathematics of Physics and Chemistry*, 2nd ed. Princeton, NJ: Van Nostrand (1956).

Miller, R. K., and A. N. Michel, *Ordinary Differential Equations*. New York: Academic Press (1982).

Murphy, G. M., *Ordinary Differential Equations and Their Solutions*. Princeton, NJ: Van Nostrand (1960). A thorough, relatively readable treatment of ordinary differential equations, both linear and nonlinear.

Ritger, P. D., and N. J. Rose, *Differential Equations with Applications*. New York: McGraw-Hill (1968).

Sachdev, P. L., *Nonlinear Differential Equations and their Applications*. New York: Marcel Dekker (1991).

Tenenbaum, M., and H. Pollard, *Ordinary Differential Equations*. New York: Dover (1985). Detailed and readable (over 800 pages). This is a reprint of a work originally published in 1963, and stresses formal manipulations. Its references to numerical methods are somewhat dated.

CHAPTER 8

STURM-LIOUVILLE THEORY

8.1 INTRODUCTION

Chapter 7 examined methods for solving ordinary differential equations (ODEs), with emphasis on techniques that can generate the solutions. In the present chapter we shift the focus to the general properties that solutions must have to be appropriate for specific physics problems, and to discuss the solutions using the notions of vector spaces and eigenvalue problems that were developed in Chapters 5 and 6.

A typical physics problem controlled by an ODE has two important properties: (1) Its solution must satisfy **boundary conditions**, and (2) It contains a parameter whose value must be set in a way that satisfies the boundary conditions. From a vector-space perspective, the boundary conditions (plus continuity and differentiability requirements) define the Hilbert space of our problem, while the parameter normally occurs in a way that permits the ODE to be written as an eigenvalue equation within that Hilbert space.

These ideas can be made clearer by examining a specific example. The standing waves of a vibrating string clamped at its ends are governed by the ODE

$$\frac{d^2\psi}{dx^2} + k^2\psi = 0, \tag{8.1}$$

where $\psi(x)$ is the amplitude of the transverse displacement at the point x along the string, and k is a parameter. This ODE has solutions for any value of k, but the solutions of relevance to the string problem must have $\psi(x) = 0$ for the values of x at the ends of the string.

The boundary conditions of this problem can be interpreted as defining a Hilbert space whose members are differentiable functions with zeros at the boundary values of x; the ODE itself can be written as the eigenvalue equation

$$\mathcal{L}\psi = k^2\psi, \quad \mathcal{L} = -\frac{d^2}{dx^2}. \tag{8.2}$$

For practical reasons the eigenvalue is given the name k^2. It is required to find functions $\psi(x)$ that solve Eq. (8.2) subject to the boundary conditions, i.e., to find members $\psi(x)$ of our Hilbert space that solve the eigenvalue equation.

We could now follow the procedures developed in Chapter 5, namely (1) choose a basis for our Hilbert space (a set of functions with zeros at the boundary values of x), (2) define a scalar product for our space, (3) expand $\mathcal{L}$ and ψ in terms of our basis, and (4) solve the resulting matrix equation. However, that procedure makes no use of any specific features of the current ODE, and in particular ignores the fact that it is easily solved.

Instead, we continue with the example defined by Eq. (8.1), using our ability to solve the ODE involved.

Example 8.1.1   STANDING WAVES, VIBRATING STRING

We consider a string clamped at $x = 0$ and $x = l$ and undergoing transverse vibrations. As already indicated, its standing wave amplitudes $\psi(x)$ are solutions of the differential equation

$$\frac{d^2\psi(x)}{dx^2} + k^2\psi(x) = 0, \tag{8.3}$$

where k is not initially known and $\psi(x)$ is subject to the boundary conditions that the ends of the string be fixed in position: $\psi(0) = \psi(l) = 0$. This is the eigenvalue problem defined in Eq. (8.2).

The general solution to this differential equation is $\psi(x) = A \sin kx + B \cos kx$, and in the absence of the boundary conditions solutions would exist for all values of k, A, and B. However, the boundary condition at $x = 0$ requires us to set $B = 0$, leaving $\psi(x) = A \sin kx$. We have yet to satisfy the boundary condition at $x = l$. The fact that A is as yet unspecified is not helpful for this purpose, as $A = 0$ leaves us with only the trivial solution $\psi = 0$. We must, instead, require $\sin kl = 0$, which is accomplished by setting $kl = n\pi$, where n is a nonzero integer, leading to

$$\psi_n(x) = A \sin\left(\frac{n\pi x}{l}\right), \quad k^2 = \frac{n^2\pi^2}{l^2}, \quad n = 1, 2, \ldots. \tag{8.4}$$

Because Eq. (8.3) is homogeneous, it will have solutions of arbitrary scale, so A can have any value. Since our purpose is usually to identify linearly independent solutions, we disregard changes in the sign or magnitude of A. In the vibrating string problem, these quantities control the amplitude and phase of the standing waves. Since changing the sign of n simply changes the sign of ψ, $+n$ and $-n$ in Eq. (8.4) are regarded here as equivalent, so we restricted n to positive values. The first few ψ_n are shown in Fig. 8.1. Note that the number of nodes increases with n: ψ_n has $n + 1$ nodes (including the two nodes at the ends of the string).

The fact that our problem has solutions only for discrete values of k is typical of eigenvalue problems, and in this problem the discreteness in k can be traced directly to the presence of the boundary conditions. Figure 8.2 shows what happens when k is varied in either direction from the acceptable value π/l, with the boundary condition at $x = 0$ maintained for all k. It is obvious that the eigenvalues (here k^2) lie at separated points, and

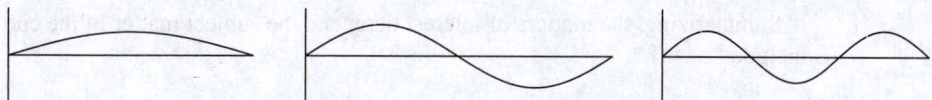

FIGURE 8.1   Standing wave patterns of a vibrating string.

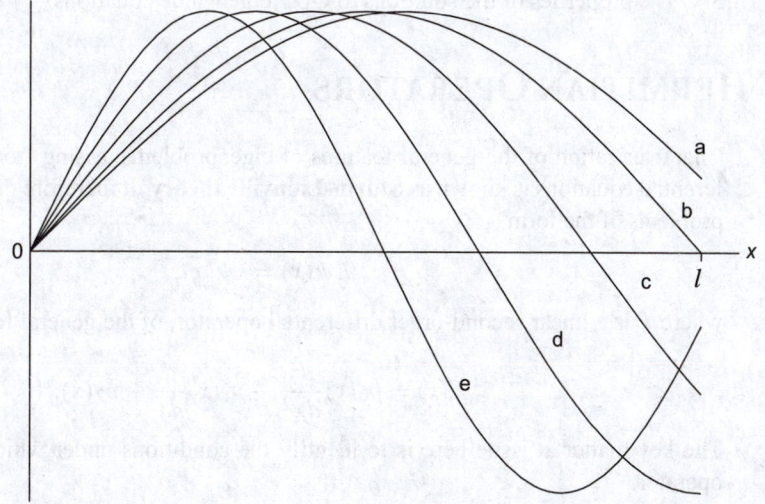

FIGURE 8.2   Solutions to Eq. (8.3) on the range $0 \leq x \leq l$ for: (a) $k = 0.9\pi/l$,
(b) $k = \pi/l$, (c) $k = 1.2\pi/l$, (d) $k = 1.5\pi/l$, (e) $k = 1.9\pi/l$.

that the boundary condition at $x = l$ cannot be satisfied for $k < \pi/l$. Moreover, the first
acceptable k value larger than π/l is clearly larger than $1.9\pi/l$ (it is actually $2\pi/l$).

As already noted, the solution to this eigenvalue problem is undetermined as to scale
because the underlying equation (together with its boundary conditions) is homogeneous.
However, if we introduce a scalar product of definition

$$\langle f|g \rangle = \int_0^l f^*(x)g(x)dx, \tag{8.5}$$

we can define solutions that are normalized; requiring $\langle \psi_n|\psi_n \rangle = 1$, we have, with arbitrary
sign,

$$\psi_n(x) = \sqrt{\frac{2}{l}} \sin\left(\frac{n\pi x}{l}\right). \tag{8.6}$$

Although we did not solve Eq. (8.2) by an expansion technique, the solutions (the eigenfunctions) will still have properties that depend on whether the operator $\mathcal{L}$ is Hermitian. As
we saw in Chapter 5, the Hermitian property depends both on $\mathcal{L}$ and the definition of the
scalar product, and a topic for discussion in the present chapter is the identification of conditions making an operator Hermitian. This issue is important because Hermiticity implies
real eigenvalues as well as orthogonality and completeness of the eigenfunctions.   ∎

Summarizing, the matters of interest here, and the subject matter of the current chapter, include:

1. The conditions under which an ODE can be written as an eigenvalue equation with a self-adjoint (Hermitian) operator,
2. Methods for the solution of ODEs subject to boundary conditions, and
3. The properties of the solutions to ODE eigenvalue equations.

8.2   HERMITIAN OPERATORS

Characterization of the general features of eigenproblems arising from second-order differential equations is known as **Sturm-Liouville theory**. It therefore deals with eigenvalue problems of the form

$$\mathcal{L}\psi(x) = \lambda\psi(x), \tag{8.7}$$

where $\mathcal{L}$ is a linear second-order differential operator, of the general form

$$\mathcal{L}(x) = p_0(x)\frac{d^2}{dx^2} + p_1(x)\frac{d}{dx} + p_2(x). \tag{8.8}$$

The key matter at issue here is to identify the conditions under which $\mathcal{L}$ is a Hermitian operator.

Self-Adjoint ODEs

$\mathcal{L}$ is known in differential equation theory as **self-adjoint** if

$$p_0'(x) = p_1(x). \tag{8.9}$$

This feature enables $\mathcal{L}(x)$ to be written

$$\mathcal{L}(x) = \frac{d}{dx}\left[p_0(x)\frac{d}{dx}\right] + p_2(x), \tag{8.10}$$

and the operation of $\mathcal{L}$ on a function $u(x)$ then takes the form

$$\mathcal{L}u = (p_0 u')' + p_2 u. \tag{8.11}$$

Inserting Eq. (8.11) into an integral of the form $\int_a^b v^*(x)\mathcal{L}u(x)dx$, we proceed by applying an integration by parts to the p_0 term (assuming that p_0 is real):

$$\int_a^b v^*(x)\mathcal{L}u(x)\,dx = \int_a^b \left[v^*\left(p_0 u'\right)' + v^* p_2 u\right]dx$$

$$= \left[v^* p_0 u'\right]_a^b + \int_a^b \left[-(v^*)' p_0 u' + v^* p_2 u\right]dx.$$

Another integration by parts leads to

$$\int_a^b v^*(x)\mathcal{L}u(x)\,dx = \Big[v^* p_0 u' - (v^*)' p_0 u \Big]_a^b + \int_a^b \Big[[p_0(v^*)']' u + v^* p_2 u \Big] dx$$

$$= \Big[v^* p_0 u' - (v^*)' p_0 u \Big]_a^b + \int_a^b (\mathcal{L}v)^* u\,dx. \tag{8.12}$$

Equation (8.12) shows that, if the boundary terms $\Big[\cdots \Big]_a^b$ vanish and the scalar product is an unweighted integral from a to b, then the operator $\mathcal{L}$ is self-adjoint, as that term was defined for operators. In passing, we observe that the notion of self-adjointness in differential equation theory is weaker than the corresponding concept for operators in our Hilbert spaces, due to the lack of a requirement on the boundary terms. We again stress that the Hilbert-space definition of self-adjoint depends not only on the form of $\mathcal{L}$ but also on the definition of the scalar product and the boundary conditions.

Looking further at the boundary terms, we see that they are surely zero if u and v both vanish at the endpoints $x = a$ and $x = b$ (a case of what are termed **Dirichlet boundary conditions**). The boundary terms are also zero if both u' and v' vanish at a and b (**Neumann boundary conditions**). Even if neither Dirichlet nor Neumann boundary conditions apply, it may happen (particularly in a periodic system, such as a crystal lattice) that the boundary terms vanish because $v^* p_0 u'\big|_a = v^* p_0 u'\big|_b$ for all u and v.

Specializing Eq. (8.12) to the case that u and v are eigenfunctions of $\mathcal{L}$ with respective real eigenvalues λ_u and λ_v, that equation reduces to

$$(\lambda_u - \lambda_v) \int_a^b v^* u\,dx = \Big[p_0(v^* u' - (v^*)' u) \Big]_a^b. \tag{8.13}$$

It is thus apparent that if the boundary terms vanish and $\lambda_u \neq \lambda_v$, then u and v must be orthogonal on the interval (a, b). This is a specific illustration of the orthogonality requirement for eigenfunctions of a Hermitian operator in a Hilbert space.

Making an ODE Self-Adjoint

Some of the differential equations that are important in physics involve operators $\mathcal{L}$ that are self-adjoint in the differential-equation sense, meaning that they satisfy Eq. (8.9); others are not. However, if an operator does not satisfy Eq. (8.9), it is known how to multiply it by a quantity that converts it into self-adjoint form. Letting such a quantity be designated $w(x)$, the Sturm-Liouville eigenvalue problem of Eq. (8.7) becomes

$$w(x)\mathcal{L}(x)\psi(x) = w(x)\lambda\psi(x), \tag{8.14}$$

an equation that has the same eigenvalues λ and eigenfunctions $\psi(x)$ as the original problem in Eq. (8.7). If now $w(x)$ is chosen to be

$$w(x) = p_0^{-1} \exp\left(\int \frac{p_1(x)}{p_0(x)}\,dx \right), \tag{8.15}$$

where p_0 and p_1 are the quantities in $\mathcal{L}$ as given in Eq. (8.8), we can by direct evaluation find that

$$w(x)\mathcal{L}(x) = \overline{p}_0\frac{d^2}{dx^2} + \overline{p}_1\frac{d}{dx} + w(x)p_2(x), \tag{8.16}$$

where

$$\overline{p}_0 = \exp\left(\int \frac{p_1(x)}{p_0(x)}\, dx\right), \quad \overline{p}_1 = \frac{p_1}{p_0}\exp\left(\int \frac{p_1(x)}{p_0(x)}\, dx\right). \tag{8.17}$$

It is then straightforward to show that $\overline{p}_0' = \overline{p}_1$, so $w\mathcal{L}$ satisfies the self-adjoint condition.

If we now apply the process represented by Eq. (8.12) to $w\mathcal{L}$, we get

$$\int\limits_a^b v^*(x)w(x)\mathcal{L}u(x)\, dx = \left[v^*\overline{p}_0u' - (v^*)'\,\overline{p}_0u\right]_a^b + \int\limits_a^b w(x)\,(\mathcal{L}v)^*\,u\, dx. \tag{8.18}$$

If the boundary terms vanish, Eq. (8.18) is equivalent to $\langle v|\mathcal{L}|u\rangle = \langle\mathcal{L}v|u\rangle$ when the scalar product is defined to be

$$\langle v|u\rangle = \int\limits_a^b v^*(x)u(x)w(x)\, dx. \tag{8.19}$$

Again considering the case that u and v are eigenfunctions of $\mathcal{L}$, with respective eigenvalues λ_u and λ_v, Eq. (8.18) reduces to

$$(\lambda_u - \lambda_v)\int\limits_a^b v^*u\, w\, dx = \left[wp_0\left(v^*u' - (v^*)'u\right)\right]_a^b, \tag{8.20}$$

where p_0 is the coefficient of y'' in the original ODE. We thus see that if the right-hand side of Eq. (8.20) vanishes, then u and v are orthogonal on (a, b) with weight factor w when $\lambda_u \neq \lambda_v$. In other words, our choice of scalar product definition and boundary conditions have made $\mathcal{L}$ a self-adjoint operator in our Hilbert space, thereby producing an eigenfunction orthogonality condition.

Summarizing, we have the useful and important result:

> *If a second-order differential operator $\mathcal{L}$ has coefficients $p_0(x)$ and $p_1(x)$ that satisfy the self-adjoint condition, Eq. (8.9), then it is Hermitian, given (a) a scalar product of uniform weight and (b) boundary conditions that remove the endpoint terms of Eq. (8.12).*
>
> *If Eq. (8.9) is not satisfied, then $\mathcal{L}$ is Hermitian if (a) the scalar product is defined to include the weight factor given in Eq. (8.15), and (b) boundary conditions cause removal of the endpoint terms in Eq. (8.18).*

Note that once the problem has been defined such that $\mathcal{L}$ is Hermitian, then the general properties proved for Hermitian problems apply: the eigenvalues are real; the eigenfunctions are (or if degenerate can be made) orthogonal, **using the relevant scalar product definition**.

Example 8.2.1   LAGUERRE FUNCTIONS

Consider the eigenvalue problem $\mathcal{L}\psi = \lambda\psi$, with

$$\mathcal{L} = x\frac{d^2}{dx^2} + (1-x)\frac{d}{dx}, \tag{8.21}$$

subject to (a) ψ nonsingular on $0 \le x < \infty$, and (b) $\lim_{x\to\infty}\psi(x) = 0$. Condition (a) is simply a requirement that we use the solution of the differential equation that is regular at $x = 0$; and condition (b) is a typical Dirichlet boundary condition.

The operator $\mathcal{L}$ is not self-adjoint, with $p_0 = x$ and $p_1 = 1 - x$. But we can form

$$w(x) = \frac{1}{x}\exp\left(\int\frac{1-x}{x}dx\right) = \frac{1}{x}e^{\ln x - x} = e^{-x}. \tag{8.22}$$

The boundary terms, for arbitrary eigenfunctions u and v, are of the form

$$\left[xe^{-x}\left(v^*u' - (v^*)'u\right)\right]_0^\infty;$$

their contributions at $x = \infty$ vanish because u and v go to zero; the common factor x causes the $x = 0$ contribution to vanish also. We therefore have a self-adjoint problem, with u and v of different eigenvalues orthogonal under the definition

$$\langle v|u\rangle = \int\limits_0^\infty v^*(x)u(x)e^{-x}dx.$$

The eigenvalue equation of this example is that whose solutions are the Laguerre polynomials; what we have shown here is that they are orthogonal on $(0, \infty)$ with weight e^{-x}. ∎

Exercises

8.2.1   Show that Laguerre's ODE, Table 7.1, may be put into self-adjoint form by multiplying by e^{-x} and that $w(x) = e^{-x}$ is the weighting function.

8.2.2   Show that the Hermite ODE, Table 7.1, may be put into self-adjoint form by multiplying by e^{-x^2} and that this gives $w(x) = e^{-x^2}$ as the appropriate weighting function.

8.2.3   Show that the Chebyshev ODE, Table 7.1, may be put into self-adjoint form by multiplying by $(1-x^2)^{-1/2}$ and that this gives $w(x) = (1-x^2)^{-1/2}$ as the appropriate weighting function.

8.2.4   The Legendre, Chebyshev, Hermite, and Laguerre equations, given in Table 7.1, have solutions that are polynomials. Show that ranges of integration that guarantee that the Hermitian operator boundary conditions will be satisfied are

(a) Legendre $[-1, 1]$,   (b) Chebyshev $[-1, 1]$,
(c) Hermite $(-\infty, \infty)$,   (d) Laguerre $[0, \infty)$.

8.2.5   The functions $u_1(x)$ and $u_2(x)$ are eigenfunctions of the same Hermitian operator but for distinct eigenvalues λ_1 and λ_2. Prove that $u_1(x)$ and $u_2(x)$ are linearly independent.

8.2.6   Given that

$$P_1(x) = x \quad \text{and} \quad Q_0(x) = \frac{1}{2}\ln\left(\frac{1+x}{1-x}\right)$$

are solutions of Legendre's differential equation (Table 7.1) corresponding to different eigenvalues:

(a)   Evaluate their orthogonality integral

$$\int_{-1}^{1} \frac{x}{2}\ln\left(\frac{1+x}{1-x}\right) dx.$$

(b)   Explain why these two functions are not orthogonal, that is, why the proof of orthogonality does not apply.

8.2.7 $T_0(x) = 1$ and $V_1(x) = (1-x^2)^{1/2}$ are solutions of the Chebyshev differential equation corresponding to different eigenvalues. Explain, in terms of the boundary conditions, why these two functions are not orthogonal on the range $(-1, 1)$ with the weighting function found in Exercise 8.2.3.

8.2.8   A set of functions $u_n(x)$ satisfies the Sturm-Liouville equation

$$\frac{d}{dx}\left[p(x)\frac{d}{dx}u_n(x)\right] + \lambda_n w(x)u_n(x) = 0.$$

The functions $u_m(x)$ and $u_n(x)$ satisfy boundary conditions that lead to orthogonality. The corresponding eigenvalues λ_m and λ_n are distinct. Prove that for appropriate boundary conditions, $u'_m(x)$ and $u'_n(x)$ are orthogonal with $p(x)$ as a weighting function.

8.2.9   Linear operator A has n distinct eigenvalues and n corresponding eigenfunctions: $A\psi_i = \lambda_i \psi_i$. Show that the n eigenfunctions are linearly independent. Do not assume A to be Hermitian.
Hint. Assume linear dependence, i.e., that $\psi_n = \sum_{i=1}^{n-1} a_i \psi_i$. Use this relation and the operator-eigenfunction equation first in one order and then in the reverse order. Show that a contradiction results.

8.2.10   The ultraspherical polynomials $C_n^{(\alpha)}(x)$ are solutions of the differential equation

$$\left\{(1-x^2)\frac{d^2}{dx^2} - (2\alpha+1)x\frac{d}{dx} + n(n+2\alpha)\right\}C_n^{(\alpha)}(x) = 0.$$

(a)   Transform this differential equation into self-adjoint form.

(b)   Find an interval of integration and weighting factor that make $C_n^{(\alpha)}(x)$ of the same α but different n orthogonal.

Note. Assume that your solutions are polynomials.

8.3   ODE Eigenvalue Problems

Now that we have identified the conditions that make a second-order ODE eigenvalue problem Hermitian, let's examine several such problems to gain further understanding of the processes involved and to illustrate techniques for finding solutions.

Example 8.3.1   Legendre Equation

The Legendre equation,

$$\mathcal{L}y(x) = -(1 - x^2)y''(x) + 2xy'(x) = \lambda y(x), \tag{8.23}$$

defines an eigenvalue problem that arises when ∇^2 is written in spherical polar coordinates, with x identified as $\cos\theta$, where θ is the polar angle of the coordinate system. The range of x in this context is $-1 \le x \le 1$, and in typical circumstances one needs solutions to Eq. (8.23) that are nonsingular on the entire range of x. It turns out that this is a nontrivial requirement, mainly because $x = \pm 1$ are singular points of the Legendre ODE. If we regard nonsingularity of y at $x = \pm 1$ as a set of boundary conditions, we shall find that this requirement is sufficient to define eigenfunctions of the Legendre operator.

This eigenvalue problem, namely Eq. (8.23) plus nonsingularity at $x = \pm 1$, is conveniently handled by the method of Frobenius. We assume solutions of the form

$$y = \sum_{j=0}^{\infty} a_j x^{s+j}, \tag{8.24}$$

with indicial equation $s(s - 1) = 0$, whose solutions are $s = 0$ and $s = 1$. For $s = 0$, we obtain the following recurrence relation for the coefficients a_j:

$$a_{j+2} = \frac{j(j+1) - \lambda}{(j+1)(j+2)}a_j. \tag{8.25}$$

We may set $a_1 = 0$, thereby causing all a_j of odd j to vanish, so (for $s = 0$) our series will contain only even powers of x. The boundary condition comes into play because Eq. (8.24) diverges at $x = \pm 1$ for all λ except those that actually cause the series to terminate after a finite number of terms.

To see how the divergence arises, note that for large j and $|x| = 1$ the ratio of successive terms of the series approaches

$$\frac{a_j x^j}{a_{j+2} x^{j+2}} \to \frac{j(j+1)}{(j+1)(j+2)} \to 1,$$

so the ratio test is indeterminate. However, application of the Gauss test shows that this series diverges, as was discussed in more detail in Example 1.1.7.

The series in Eq. (8.24) can be made to terminate after a_l for some even l by choosing $\lambda = l(l + 1)$, a value that makes $a_{l+2} = 0$. Then a_{l+4}, $a_{l+6}, \dots$ will also vanish, and our solution will be a polynomial, which is clearly nonsingular for all $|x| \le 1$. Summarizing, we have, **for even** l, solutions that are polynomials of degree l as eigenfunctions, and the corresponding eigenvalues are $l(l + 1)$.

For $s = 1$ we must set $a_1 = 0$ and the recurrence relation is

$$a_{j+2} = \frac{(j+1)(j+2) - \lambda}{(j+2)(j+3)} a_j, \tag{8.26}$$

which also leads to divergence at $|x| = 1$. However, the divergence can now be avoided by setting $\lambda = (l+1)(l+2)$ for some even value of l, thereby causing $a_{l+2}, a_{l+4}, \dots$ to vanish. The result will be a polynomial of degree $l + s$, i.e., of an odd degree $l + 1$. These solutions can be described equivalently as, for odd l, polynomials of degree l with eigenvalues $\lambda = l(l+1)$, so the overall set of eigenfunctions consists of polynomials of all integer degrees l, with respective eigenvalues $l(l+1)$. When given the conventional scaling, these polynomials are called **Legendre polynomials**. Verification of these properties of solutions to the Legendre equation is left to Exercise 8.3.1.

Before leaving the Legendre equation, note that its ODE is self-adjoint, and that the coefficient of d^2/dx^2 in the Legendre operator is $p_0 = -(1 - x^2)$, which vanishes at $x = \pm 1$. Comparing with Eq. (8.12), we see that this value of p_0 causes the vanishing of the boundary terms when we take the adjoint of $\mathcal{L}$, so the Legendre operator on the range $-1 \leq x \leq 1$ is Hermitian, and therefore has orthogonal eigenfunctions. In other words, the Legendre polynomials are orthogonal with unit weight on $(-1, 1)$. ∎

Let's examine one more ODE that leads to an interesting eigenvalue problem.

Example 8.3.2   HERMITE EQUATION

Consider the Hermite differential equation,

$$\mathcal{L}y = -y'' + 2xy' = \lambda y, \tag{8.27}$$

which we wish to regard as an eigenvalue problem on the range $-\infty < x < \infty$. To make $\mathcal{L}$ Hermitian, we define a scalar product with a weight factor as given by Eq. (8.15),

$$\langle f | g \rangle = \int_{-\infty}^{\infty} f^*(x) g(x) e^{-x^2} \, dx, \tag{8.28}$$

and demand (as a boundary condition) that our eigenfunctions y_n have finite norms using this scalar product, meaning that $\langle y_n | y_n \rangle < \infty$.

Again we obtain a solution by the method of Frobenius, as a series of the form given in Eq. (8.24). Again the indicial equation is $s(s - 1) = 0$, and for $s = 0$ we can develop a series of even powers of x with coefficients satisfying the recurrence relation

$$a_{j+2} = \frac{2j - \lambda}{(j+1)(j+2)} a_j. \tag{8.29}$$

This series converges for all x, but (assuming it does not terminate) it behaves asymptotically for large $|x|$ as e^{x^2} and therefore does not describe a function of finite norm, even with the e^{-x^2} weight factor in the scalar product. Thus, even though the series solution always converges, our boundary conditions require that we arrange to terminate the series, thereby producing polynomial solutions. From Eq. (8.29) we see that the condition for obtaining an even polynomial of degree j is that $\lambda = 2j$. Odd polynomial solutions can be obtained using the indicial equation solution $s = 1$. Details of both the solutions and the asymptotic properties are the subject of Exercise 8.3.3.

Since we have established that this is a Hermitian eigenvalue problem with the scalar product as defined in Eq. (8.28), its solutions (when scaled conventionally they are called **Hermite polynomials**) are orthogonal using that scalar product.   ∎

Some ODE eigenvalue problems can be attacked by dividing the space in which they reside into regions that are most naturally treated in different ways. The following example illustrates this situation, with a potential that is assumed nonzero only within a finite region.

Example 8.3.3   DEUTERON GROUND STATE

The deuteron is a bound state of a neutron and a proton. Due to the short range of the nuclear force, the deuteron properties do not depend much on the detailed shape of the interaction potential. Thus, this system may be modeled by a spherically symmetric square well potential with the value $V = V_0 < 0$ when the nucleons are within a distance a of each other, but with $V = 0$ when the internucleon distance is greater than a. The Schrödinger equation for the relative motion of the two nucleons assumes the form

$$-\frac{\hbar^2}{2\mu}\nabla^2\psi + V\psi = E\psi,$$

where μ is the reduced mass of the system (approximately half the mass of either particle). This eigenvalue equation must be solved subject to the boundary conditions that ψ be finite at $r = 0$ and approach zero at $r = \infty$ sufficiently rapidly to be a member of an $\mathcal{L}^2$ Hilbert space. The eigenfunctions ψ must also be continuous and differentiable for all r, including $r = a$.

It can be shown that if there is to be a bound state, E will have to have a negative value in the range $V_0 < E < 0$, and the lowest state (the **ground state**) will be described by a wave function ψ that is spherically symmetric (thereby having no angular momentum). Thus, taking $\psi = \psi(r)$ and using a result from Exercise 3.10.34 to write

$$\nabla^2\psi = \frac{1}{r}\frac{d^2u}{dr^2}, \quad \text{with } u(r) = r\psi(r),$$

the Schrödinger equation reduces to an ODE that assumes the form, for $r < a$,

$$\frac{d^2u_1}{dr^2} + k_1^2 u_1 = 0, \quad \text{with} \quad k_1^2 = \frac{2\mu}{\hbar^2}(E - V_0) > 0,$$

while, for $r > a$,

$$\frac{d^2u_2}{dr^2} - k_2^2 u_2 = 0, \quad \text{with} \quad k_2^2 = -\frac{2\mu E}{\hbar^2} > 0.$$

The solutions for these two ranges of r must connect smoothly, meaning that both u and du/dr must be continuous across $r = a$, and therefore must satisfy the **matching conditions** $u_1(a) = u_2(a)$, $u_1'(a) = u_2'(a)$. In addition, the requirement that ψ be finite at $r = 0$ dictates that $u_1(0) = 0$, and the boundary condition at $r = \infty$ requires that $\lim_{r\to\infty} u_2(r) = 0$.

For $r < a$, our Schrödinger equation has the general solution

$$u_1(r) = A \sin k_1 r + C \cos k_1 r,$$

and the boundary condition at $r = 0$ is only met if we set $C = 0$. The Schrödinger equation for $r > a$ has the general solution

$$u_2(r) = C' \exp(k_2 r) + B \exp(-k_2 r), \tag{8.30}$$

and the boundary condition at $r = \infty$ requires us to set $C' = 0$. The matching conditions at $r = a$ then take the form

$$A \sin k_1 a = B \exp(-k_2 a) \quad \text{and} \quad A k_1 \cos k_1 a = -k_2 B \exp(-k_2 a).$$

Using the second of these equations to eliminate $B \exp(-k_2 a)$ from the first, we reach

$$A \sin k_1 a = -A \frac{k_1}{k_2} \cos k_1 a, \tag{8.31}$$

showing that the overall scale of the solution (i.e., A) is arbitrary, which is of course a consequence of the fact that the Schrödinger equation is homogeneous.

Rearranging Eq. (8.31), and inserting values for k_1 and k_2, our matching conditions become

$$\tan k_1 a = -\frac{k_1}{k_2}, \quad \text{or} \quad \tan \left[\frac{2\mu a^2}{\hbar^2}(E - V_0) \right]^{1/2} = -\sqrt{\frac{E - V_0}{-E}}. \tag{8.32}$$

This is an admittedly unpleasant implicit equation for E; if it has solutions with E in the range $V_0 < E < 0$, our model predicts deuteron bound state(s).

One way to search for solutions to Eq. (8.32) is to plot its left- and right-hand sides as a function of E, identifying the E values, if any, for which they are equal. Taking $V_0 = -4.046 \times 10^{-12}$ J, $a = 2.5$ fermi,[1] $\mu = 0.835 \times 10^{-27}$ kg, and $\hbar = 1.05 \times 10^{-34}$ J-s (joule-seconds), the two sides of Eq. (8.32) are plotted in Fig. 8.3 for the range of E in which a bound state is possible. The E values have been plotted in MeV (mega electron volts), the energy unit most frequently used in nuclear physics (1 MeV $\approx 1.6 \times 10^{-13}$ J). The curves cross at only one point, indicating that the model predicts just one bound state. Its energy is at approximately $E = -2.2$ MeV.

It is instructive to see what happens if we take E values that may or may not solve Eq. (8.32), using $u(r) = A \sin k_1 r$ for $r < a$ (thereby satisfying the $r = 0$ boundary condition) but for $r > a$ using the general form of $u(r)$ as given in Eq. (8.30), with the coefficient values B and C' that are required by the matching conditions for the chosen E value. Letting E_- and E_+, respectively, denote values of E less than and greater than the eigenvalue E, we find that by forcing a smooth connection at $r = a$ we lose the required asymptotic behavior except at the eigenvalue. See Fig. 8.4.   ∎

---

[1] 1 fermi = 10^{-15} m.

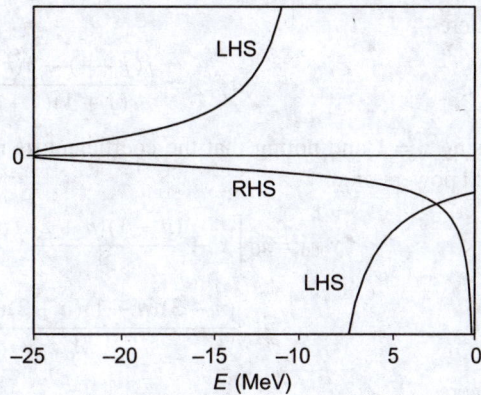

FIGURE 8.3   Left- and right-hand sides of Eq. (8.32) as a function of E for the model
parameters given in the text.

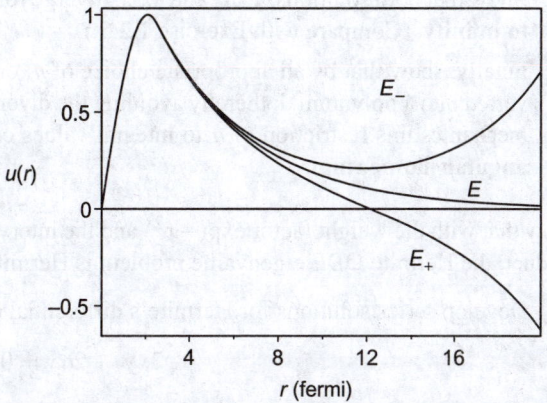

FIGURE 8.4   Wavefunctions for the deuteron problem when the energy is chosen to be
less than the eigenvalue E $(E_- < E)$ or greater than E $(E_+ > E)$.

Exercises

8.3.1   Solve the Legendre equation

$$(1 - x^2)y'' - 2xy' + n(n + 1)y = 0$$

by direct series substitution.

(a)   Verify that the indicial equation is

$$s(s - 1) = 0.$$

(b)   Using $s = 0$ and setting the coefficient $a_1 = 0$, obtain a series of even powers of x:

$$y_{even} = a_0 \left[1 - \frac{n(n + 1)}{2!}x^2 + \frac{(n - 2)n(n + 1)(n + 3)}{4!}x^4 + \cdots \right],$$

where

$$a_{j+2} = \frac{j(j+1) - n(n+1)}{(j+1)(j+2)} a_j.$$

(c) Using $s = 1$ and noting that the coefficient a_1 must be zero, develop a series of odd powers of x:

$$y_{odd} = a_0 \left[x - \frac{(n-1)(n+2)}{3!} x^3 \right.$$

$$\left. + \frac{(n-3)(n-1)(n+2)(n+4)}{5!} x^5 + \cdots \right],$$

where

$$a_{j+2} = \frac{(j+1)(j+2) - n(n+1)}{(j+2)(j+3)} a_j.$$

(d) Show that both solutions, y_{even} and y_{odd}, diverge for $x = \pm 1$ **if the series continue to infinity**. (Compare with Exercise 1.2.5.)

(e) Finally, show that by an appropriate choice of n, one series at a time may be converted into a polynomial, thereby avoiding the divergence catastrophe. In quantum mechanics this restriction of n to integral values corresponds to **quantization of angular momentum**.

8.3.2   Show that with the weight factor $\exp(-x^2)$ and the interval $-\infty < x < \infty$ for the scalar product, the Hermite ODE eigenvalue problem is Hermitian.

8.3.3   (a) Develop series solutions for Hermite's differential equation

$$y'' - 2xy' + 2\alpha y = 0.$$

$\quad$ *ANS.* $\quad s(s-1) = 0$, indicial equation.

For $s = 0$,

$$a_{j+2} = 2a_j \frac{j - \alpha}{(j+1)(j+2)} \quad (j \text{ even}),$$

$$y_{even} = a_0 \left[1 + \frac{2(-\alpha)x^2}{2!} + \frac{2^2(-\alpha)(2-\alpha)x^4}{4!} + \cdots \right].$$

For $s = 1$,

$$a_{j+2} = 2a_j \frac{j + 1 - \alpha}{(j+2)(j+3)} \quad (j \text{ even}),$$

$$y_{odd} = a_1 \left[x + \frac{2(1-\alpha)x^3}{3!} + \frac{2^2(1-\alpha)(3-\alpha)x^5}{5!} + \cdots \right].$$

(b) Show that both series solutions are convergent for all x, the ratio of successive coefficients behaving, for a large index, like the corresponding ratio in the expansion of $\exp(x^2)$.

(c) Show that by appropriate choice of α, the series solutions may be cut off and converted to finite polynomials. (These polynomials, properly normalized, become the Hermite polynomials in Section 18.1.)

8.3.4   Laguerre's ODE is

$$xL_n''(x) + (1 - x)L_n'(x) + nL_n(x) = 0.$$

Develop a series solution and select the parameter n to make your series a polynomial.

8.3.5   Solve the Chebyshev equation

$$(1 - x^2)T_n'' - xT_n' + n^2T_n = 0,$$

by series substitution. What restrictions are imposed on n if you demand that the series solution converge for $x = \pm 1$?

> *ANS.*   The infinite series does converge for $x = \pm 1$ and no restriction on n exists (compare with Exercise 1.2.6).

8.3.6   Solve

$$(1 - x^2)U_n''(x) - 3xU_n'(x) + n(n + 2)U_n(x) = 0,$$

choosing the root of the indicial equation to obtain a series of **odd** powers of x. Since the series will diverge for $x = 1$, choose n to convert it into a polynomial.

8.4   VARIATION METHOD

We saw in Chapter 6 that the expectation value of a Hermitian operator H for the normalized function ψ can be written as

$$\langle H \rangle \equiv \langle \psi | H | \psi \rangle,$$

and that the expansion of this quantity in a basis consisting of the orthonormal eigenfunctions of H had the form given in Eq. (6.30):

$$\langle H \rangle = \sum_\mu |a_\mu|^2 \lambda_\mu,$$

where a_μ is the coefficient of the μth eigenfunction of H and λ_i is the corresponding eigenvalue. As we noted when we obtained this result, one of its consequences is that $\langle H \rangle$ is a weighted average of the eigenvalues of H, and therefore is at least as large as the smallest eigenvalue, and equal to the smallest eigenvalue only if ψ is actually an eigenfunction to which that eigenvalue corresponds.

The observations of the foregoing paragraph hold true even if we do not actually make an expansion of ψ and even if we do not actually know or have available the eigenfunctions or eigenvalues of H. The knowledge that $\langle H \rangle$ is an upper limit to the smallest eigenvalue of H is sufficient to enable us to devise a method for approximating that eigenvalue and the associated eigenfunction. This eigenfunction will be the member of the Hilbert space of our problem that yields the smallest expectation value of H, and a strategy for finding it is to search for the minimum in $\langle H \rangle$ within our Hilbert space. This is the essential idea behind what is known as the **variation method** for the approximate solution of eigenvalue problems.

Since in many problems (including most that arise in quantum mechanics) it is impractical to compute $\langle H \rangle$ for all members of a Hilbert space, the actual approach is to define a portion of the Hilbert space by introducing an assumed functional form for ψ that contains parameters, and then to minimize $\langle H \rangle$ with respect to the parameters; this is the source of the name "variation method." The success of the method will depend on whether the functional form that is chosen is capable of representing functions that are "close" to the desired eigenfunction (meaning that its coefficient in the expansion is relatively large, with other coefficients much smaller). The great advantage of the variation method is that we do not need to know anything about the exact eigenfunction and we do not actually have to make an expansion; we simply choose a suitable functional form and minimize $\langle H \rangle$.

Since eigenvalue equations for energies and related quantities in quantum mechanics usually have finite smallest eigenvalues (e.g., ground energy levels), the variation method is frequently applicable. We point out that it is not a method having only academic interest; it is at the heart of some of the most powerful methods for solving the Schrödinger eigenvalue equation for complex quantum systems.

Example 8.4.1   VARIATION METHOD

Given a single-electron wave function (in three-dimensional space) of the form

$$\psi = \left(\frac{\zeta^3}{\pi} \right)^{1/2} e^{-\zeta r}, \tag{8.33}$$

where the factor $(\zeta/\pi)^{3/2}$ makes ψ normalized, it can be shown that, in units with the electron mass, its charge, and $\hbar$ (Planck's constant divided by 2π) all set to unity (so-called **Hartree atomic units**), the quantum-mechanical kinetic energy operator has expectation value $\langle \psi | T | \psi \rangle = \zeta^2/2$, and the potential energy of interaction between the electron and a fixed nucleus of charge $+Z$ has $\langle \psi | V | \psi \rangle = -Z\zeta$. For a one-electron atom with a nucleus of charge $+Z$ at $r = 0$, the total energy will be less than or equal to the expectation value of the Hamiltonian $H = T + V$, given for the ψ of Eq. (8.33) as

$$\langle H \rangle = \langle T \rangle + \langle V \rangle = \frac{\zeta^2}{2} - Z\zeta. \tag{8.34}$$

As is customary when the meaning is clear, we no longer explicitly show ψ within all the angle brackets. We can now optimize our upper bound to the lowest eigenvalue of H by minimizing the expectation value $\langle H \rangle$ with respect to the parameter ζ in ψ. To do so, we set

$$\frac{d}{d\zeta} \left[\frac{\zeta^2}{2} - Z\zeta \right] = 0,$$

leading to $\zeta - Z = 0$, or $\zeta = Z$. This tells us that the wave function yielding the energy closest to the smallest eigenvalue is that with $\zeta = Z$, and the energy expectation value for this value of ζ is $Z^2/2 - Z^2 = -Z^2/2$.

The result we have just found is exact, because, with malice aforethought and with appropriate knowledge, we chose a functional form that included the exact wave function. But now let us continue to a two-electron atom, taking a wave function of the form $\Psi = \psi(1)\psi(2)$, with both ψ of the same ζ value. For this two-electron atom, the scalar product is defined as integration over the coordinates of both electrons, and the Hamiltonian is now $H = T(1) + T(2) + V(1) + V(2) + U(1,2)$, where $T(i)$ and $V(i)$ denote the kinetic energy and the electron-nuclear potential energy for electron i; $U(1,2)$ is the electron-electron repulsion energy operator, equal in Hartree units to $1/r_{12}$, where r_{12} is the distance between the positions of the two electrons. For the wave function in use here, the electron-electron repulsion has expectation value $\langle U \rangle = 5\zeta/8$ and the expectation value $\langle H \rangle$ (for $Z = 2$, thereby representing the He atom) is

$$\langle H \rangle = \frac{\zeta^2}{2} + \frac{\zeta^2}{2} - Z\zeta - Z\zeta + \frac{5\zeta}{8} = \zeta^2 - \frac{27\zeta}{8}.$$

Minimizing $\langle H \rangle$ with respect to ζ, we obtain the optimum value $\zeta = 27/16$, and for this value of ζ we have $\langle H \rangle = -(27/16)^2 = -2.8477$ hartree. This is the best approximation available using a wave function of the form we chose. It cannot be exact, as the exact solution for this system with two interacting electrons cannot be a product of two one-electron functions. We have therefore not included in our variational search the exact ground-state eigenfunction. A highly precise value of the smallest eigenvalue for this problem can only be obtained numerically, and in fact was produced by using the variation method with a trial function containing thousands of parameters and yielding a result accurate to about 40 decimal places.[2] The value found here by very simple means is higher than the exact value, $-2.9037\cdots$ hartree, by only about 2%, and already conveys much physically relevant information. If the two electrons did not interact, they would each have had an optimum wave function with $\zeta = 2$; the fact that the optimum ζ is somewhat smaller shows that each electron partially screens the nucleus from the other electron.

From the viewpoint of the mathematical method in use here, it is desirable to note that we did not need to assume any relation between the trial wave function and the exact form of the eigenfunction; the variational optimization adjusts the trial function to give an energetically optimum fit. The quality of the final result of course depends on the degree to which the trial function can mimic the actual eigenfunction, and trial functions are ordinarily chosen in a way that balances inherent quality against convenience of use. ∎

Exercises

8.4.1   A function that is normalized on the interval $0 \le x < \infty$ with an unweighted scalar product is

$$\psi = 2\alpha^{3/2}xe^{-\alpha x}.$$

(a)   Verify the normalization.

(b)   Verify that for this ψ, $\langle x^{-1} \rangle = \alpha$.

[2]C. Schwartz, Experiment and theory in computations of the He atom ground state, *Int. J. Mod. Phys. E: Nuclear Physics* **15**: 877 (2006).

(c) Verify that for this ψ, $\langle d^2/dx^2 \rangle = -\alpha^2$.

(d) Use the variation method to find the value of α that minimizes

$$\left\langle \psi \left| -\frac{1}{2}\frac{d^2}{dx^2} - \frac{1}{x} \right| \psi \right\rangle,$$

and find the minimum value of this expectation value.

8.5 SUMMARY, EIGENVALUE PROBLEMS

Because any Hermitian operator on a Hilbert space can be expanded in a basis and is there-fore mathematically equivalent to a matrix, all the properties derived for matrix eigenvalue problems automatically apply whether or not a basis-set expansion is actually carried out. It may be helpful to summarize some of those results, along with some that were developed in the present chapter.

1. A second-order differential operator is Hermitian if it is self-adjoint in the differential-equation sense and the functions on which it operates are required to satisfy appropri-ate boundary conditions. In that event, the scalar product consistent with Hermiticity is an unweighted integral over the range between its boundaries.

2. If a second-order differential operator is not self-adjoint in the differential-equation sense, it will nevertheless be Hermitian if it satisfies appropriate boundary condi-tions and if the scalar product includes the weight function that makes the original differential equation self-adjoint.

3. A Hermitian operator on a Hilbert space has a complete set of eigenfunctions. Thus, they span the space and can be used as basis for an expansion.

4. The eigenvalues of a Hermitian operator are real.

5. The eigenfunctions of a Hermitian operator corresponding to different eigenvalues are orthogonal, using the appropriate scalar product.

6. Degenerate eigenfunctions of a Hermitian operator can be orthogonalized using the Gram-Schmidt or any other orthogonalization process.

7. Two operators have a common set of eigenfunctions if and only if they commute.

8. An algebraic function of an operator has the same eigenfunctions as the original operator, and its eigenvalues are the corresponding function of the eigenvalues of the original operator.

9. Eigenvalue problems involving a differential operator may be solved either by expressing the problem in any basis and solving the resulting matrix problem or by using relevant properties of the differential equation.

10. The matrix representation of a Hermitian operator can be brought to diagonal form by a unitary transformation. In diagonal form, the diagonal elements are the eigenvalues, and the eigenvectors are the basis functions. The orthonormal eigenvectors are the columns of the unitary matrix U^{-1} when a Hermitian matrix H is transformed to the diagonal matrix UHU^{-1}.

11. Hermitian-operator eigenvalue problems which have a finite smallest eigenvalue may have their solutions approximated by the variation method, which is based on the theorem that for all members of the relevant Hilbert space, the expectation value of the operator will be larger than its smallest eigenvalue (or equal to it only if the Hilbert space member is actually a corresponding eigenfunction).

Additional Readings

Byron, F. W., Jr., and R. W. Fuller, *Mathematics of Classical and Quantum Physics*. Reading, MA: Addison-Wesley (1969).

Dennery, P., and A. Krzywicki, *Mathematics for Physicists*. Reprinted. New York: Dover (1996).

Hirsch, M., *Differential Equations, Dynamical Systems, and Linear Algebra*. San Diego: Academic Press (1974).

Miller, K. S., *Linear Differential Equations in the Real Domain*. New York: Norton (1963).

Titchmarsh, E. C., *Eigenfunction Expansions Associated with Second-Order Differential Equations, Part 1*. 2nd ed. London: Oxford University Press (1962).

Titchmarsh, E. C., *Eigenfunction Expansions Associated with Second-Order Differential Equations. Part 2*. London: Oxford University Press (1958).

CHAPTER 9

PARTIAL DIFFERENTIAL EQUATIONS

9.1 INTRODUCTION

As mentioned in Chapter 7, partial differential equations (PDEs) involve derivatives with respect to more than one independent variable; if the independent variables are x and y, a PDE in a dependent variable $\varphi(x, y)$ will contain **partial derivatives**, with the meaning discussed in Eq. (1.141). Thus, $\partial \varphi / \partial x$ implies an x derivative with y held constant, $\partial^2 \varphi / \partial x^2$ is the second derivative with respect to x (again keeping y constant), and we may also have **mixed derivatives**

$$\frac{\partial^2 \varphi}{\partial x \partial y} = \frac{\partial}{\partial x} \left(\frac{\partial \varphi}{\partial y} \right).$$

Like ordinary derivatives, partial derivatives (of any order, including mixed derivatives) are linear operators, since they satisfy equations of the type

$$\frac{\partial [\varphi(x, y) + b\varphi(x, y)]}{\partial x} = a \frac{\partial \varphi(x, y)}{\partial x} + b \frac{\partial \varphi(x, y)}{\partial x}.$$

Similar to the situation for ODEs, general differential operators, $\mathcal{L}$, which may contain partial derivatives of any order, pure or mixed, multiplied by arbitrary functions of the independent variables, are **linear** operators, and equations of the form

$$\mathcal{L}\varphi(x, y) = F(x, y)$$

are linear PDEs. If the **source term** $F(x, y)$ vanishes, the PDE is termed **homogeneous**; if $F(x, y)$ is nonzero, it is **inhomogeneous**.

Homogeneous PDEs have the property, previously noted in other contexts, that any linear combination of solutions will also be a solution to the PDE. This is the **superposition principle** that is fundamental in electrodynamics and quantum mechanics, and which also permits us to build specific solutions by the linear combination of suitable members of the set of functions constituting the general solution to the homogeneous PDE.

Example 9.1.1   VARIOUS TYPES OF PDEs

Laplace	$\nabla^2 \psi = 0,$	linear, homogeneous
Poisson	$\nabla^2 \psi = f(\mathbf{r}),$	linear, inhomogeneous
Euler (inviscid flow)	$\dfrac{\partial \mathbf{u}}{\partial t} + \mathbf{u} \cdot \nabla \mathbf{u} = -\dfrac{\nabla P}{\rho}$	nonlinear, inhomogeneous

∎

Since the dynamics of many physical systems involve just two derivatives, for example, acceleration in classical mechanics, and the kinetic energy operator $\sim \nabla^2$ in quantum mechanics, differential equations of second order occur most frequently in physics. Even when the defining equations are first order, they may, as in Maxwell's equations, involve two coupled unknown vector functions (they are the electric and magnetic fields), and the elimination of one unknown vector yields a second-order PDE for the other (compare Example 3.6.2).

Examples of PDEs

Among the most frequently encountered PDEs are the following:

1. Laplace's equation, $\nabla^2 \psi = 0$.
   This very common and very important equation occurs in studies of

   (a) electromagnetic phenomena, including electrostatics, dielectrics, steady currents, and magnetostatics,
   (b) hydrodynamics (irrotational flow of perfect fluid and surface waves),
   (c) heat flow,
   (d) gravitation.

2. Poisson's equation, $\nabla^2 \psi = -\rho/\varepsilon_0$.
   This inhomogeneous equation describes electrostatics with a source term $-\rho/\varepsilon_0$.

3. Helmholtz and time-independent diffusion equations, $\nabla^2 \psi \pm k^2 \psi = 0$.
   These equations appear in such diverse phenomena as

   (a) elastic waves in solids, including vibrating strings, bars, membranes,
   (b) acoustics (sound waves),
   (c) electromagnetic waves,
   (d) nuclear reactors.

4. The time-dependent diffusion equation, $\nabla^2 \psi = \dfrac{1}{a^2} \dfrac{\partial \psi}{\partial t}$.

5. The time-dependent classical wave equation, $\dfrac{1}{c^2} \dfrac{\partial^2 \psi}{\partial t^2} = \nabla^2 \psi$.

6. The Klein-Gordon equation, $\partial^2 \psi = -\mu^2 \psi$, and the corresponding vector equations in which the scalar function ψ is replaced by a vector function. Other, more complicated forms are also common.

7. The time-dependent Schrödinger wave equation,

$$-\frac{\hbar^2}{2m}\nabla^2 \psi + V\psi = i\hbar \frac{\partial \psi}{\partial t}$$

and its time-independent form

$$-\frac{\hbar^2}{2m}\nabla^2 \psi + V\psi = E\psi.$$

8. The equations for elastic waves and viscous fluids and the telegraphy equation.

9. Maxwell's coupled partial differential equations for electric and magnetic fields and those of Dirac for relativistic electron wave functions.

We begin our study of PDEs by considering first-order equations, which illustrate some of the most important principles involved. We then continue to classification and properties of second-order PDEs, and a preliminary discussion of prototypical homogeneous equations of the different classes. Finally, we examine a very useful and powerful method for obtaining solutions to homogeneous PDEs, namely the method of **separation of variables**.

This chapter is mainly devoted to general properties of homogeneous PDEs; full detail on specific equations is for the most part postponed to chapters that discuss the special functions involved. Questions arising from the extension to inhomogeneous PDEs (i.e., problems involving **sources** or **driving terms**) are also deferred, mainly to later chapters on **Green's functions** and integral transforms.

Occasionally, we encounter equations of higher order. In both the theory of the slow motion of a viscous fluid and the theory of an elastic body we find the equation

$$(\nabla^2)^2 \psi = 0.$$

Fortunately, these higher-order differential equations are relatively rare and are not discussed here. Sometimes, particularly in fluid mechanics, we encounter nonlinear PDEs.

9.2 FIRST-ORDER EQUATIONS

While the most important PDEs arising in physics are linear and second order, many involving three spatial variables plus possibly a time variable, first-order PDEs do arise (e.g., the Cauchy-Riemann equations of complex variable theory). Part of the motivation for studying these easily solved equations is that the study provides insights that apply also to higher-order problems.

Characteristics

Let us start by considering the following homogeneous linear first-order equation in two independent variables x and y, with constant coefficients a and b, and with dependent variable $\varphi(x, y)$:

$$\mathcal{L}\varphi = a\frac{\partial\varphi}{\partial x} + b\frac{\partial\varphi}{\partial y} = 0. \tag{9.1}$$

This equation would be easier to solve if we could rearrange it so that it contained only one derivative; one way to do this is would be to rewrite our PDE in terms of new coordinates (s, t) such that one of them, say s, is such that $(\partial/\partial s)_t$ would expand into the linear combination of $\partial/\partial x$ and $\partial/\partial y$ in the original PDE, while the other new coordinate, t, is such that $(\partial/\partial t)_s$ does not occur in the PDE. It is easily verified that definitions of s and t consistent with these objectives for the PDE in Eq. (9.1) are $s = ax + by$ and $t = bx - ay$. To check this, write $\varphi(x, y) = \varphi(x(s, t), y(s, t)) = \hat{\varphi}(s, t)$, and we can verify that

$$\left(\frac{\partial\varphi}{\partial x}\right)_y = a\left(\frac{\partial\varphi}{\partial s}\right)_t + b\left(\frac{\partial\varphi}{\partial t}\right)_s \quad \text{and} \quad \left(\frac{\partial\varphi}{\partial y}\right)_x = b\left(\frac{\partial\varphi}{\partial s}\right)_t - a\left(\frac{\partial\varphi}{\partial t}\right)_s,$$

so

$$a\frac{\partial\varphi}{\partial x} + b\frac{\partial\varphi}{\partial y} = (a^2 + b^2)\frac{\partial\hat{\varphi}}{\partial s}.$$

We see that the PDE does not contain a derivative with respect to t. Since our PDE now has the simple form

$$(a^2 + b^2)\frac{\partial\hat{\varphi}}{\partial s} = 0,$$

it clearly has solution

$$\hat{\varphi}(s, t) = f(t), \quad \text{with } f(t) \text{ completely arbitrary.} \tag{9.2}$$

In terms of the original variables,

$$\varphi(x, y) = f(bx - ay), \tag{9.3}$$

where we again stress that $f(t)$ is an arbitrary function of its argument.

Checking our work to this point, we note that

$$\mathcal{L}\varphi = a\frac{\partial f(bx - ay)}{\partial x} + b\frac{\partial f(bx - ay)}{\partial y} = abf'(bx - ay) + b\big[-af'(bx - ay)\big] = 0.$$

Since the satisfaction of this equation does not depend on the properties of the function f, we verify that $\varphi(x, y)$ as given in Eq. (9.3) is a solution of our PDE, **irrespective of the choice of the function** f. In fact, it is the general solution of our PDE.

It is useful to visualize the significance of what we have just observed. Note that holding $t = bx - ay$ to a fixed value defines a line in the xy plane on which our solution φ is constant, with individual points on this line corresponding to different values of $s = ax + by$. In addition, we observe that the lines of constant s are orthogonal to those of constant t, and that s has the same coefficients as the derivatives in the PDE. The general solution to our PDE can thus be characterized as **independent of s and with arbitrary dependence on t.**

The curves of constant t are called **characteristic curves**, or more frequently just **characteristics** of our PDE. An alternative and insightful way of describing the characteristic curves is to observe that they are the stream lines (flow lines) of s. Put another way, they are the lines that are traced out as the value of s is changed, keeping t constant. The characteristic can also be characterized by its slope,

$$\frac{dy}{dx} = \frac{b}{a}, \quad \text{for } \mathcal{L} \text{ in Eq. (9.1).} \tag{9.4}$$

For our present first-order PDE, the solution φ is constant along each characteristic. We shall shortly see that more general PDEs can be solved using ODE methods on characteristic lines, a feature that causes it to be said that PDE solutions **propagate** along the characteristics, giving further significance to the notion that in some sense these are lines of flow. In the present problem this translates into the statement that if we know φ at any point on a characteristic, we know it on the entire characteristic line.

The characteristics have one additional (but related) property of importance. Ordinarily, if a PDE solution $\varphi(x, y)$ is specified on a curve segment (a **boundary condition**), one can deduce from it the values of the solution at nearby points that are not on the curve. If one introduces a Taylor expansion about some point (x_0, y_0) on the curve (thereby tacitly assuming that there are no singularities that invalidate the expansion), the value of φ at a nearby point (x, y) will be given by

$$\varphi(x, y) = \varphi(x_0, y_0) + \frac{\partial \varphi(x_0, y_0)}{\partial x}(x - x_0) + \frac{\partial \varphi(x_0, y_0)}{\partial y}(y - y_0) + \cdots . \tag{9.5}$$

To use Eq. (9.5), we need values of the derivatives of φ. To obtain these derivatives, note the following:

- The specification of φ on a given curve, with the curve parametrically described by $x(l)$, $y(l)$, means that the curve direction, i.e., dx/dl and dy/dl, is known, as is the derivative of φ along the curve, namely

$$\frac{d\varphi}{dl} = \frac{\partial \varphi}{\partial x}\frac{dx}{dl} + \frac{\partial \varphi}{\partial y}\frac{dy}{dl}. \tag{9.6}$$

Equation (9.6) therefore provides us with a linear equation satisfied by the two derivatives $\partial \varphi / \partial x$ and $\partial \varphi / \partial y$.

- The PDE supplies a second linear equation, in this case

$$a\frac{\partial \varphi}{\partial x} + b\frac{\partial \varphi}{\partial y} = 0. \tag{9.7}$$

- Providing that the determinant of their coefficients is not zero, we can solve Eqs. (9.6) and (9.7) for $\partial \varphi / \partial x$ and $\partial \varphi / \partial y$ at (x_0, y_0) and therefore evaluate the leading terms of the Taylor series for $\varphi(x, y)$.[1] The determinant of coefficients of Eqs. (9.6) and (9.7) takes the form

$$D = \begin{vmatrix} \dfrac{dx}{dl} & \dfrac{dy}{dl} \\ a & b \end{vmatrix} = b\frac{dx}{dl} - a\frac{dy}{dl}.$$

---

[1] The linear terms are all that are necessary; one can choose x and y close enough to (x_0, y_0) that second- and higher-order terms can be made negligible relative to those retained.

Now we make the observation that if φ was specified along a characteristic (for which $t = bx - ay =$ constant), we have

$$b\,dx - a\,dy = 0, \quad \text{or} \quad b\frac{dx}{dl} - a\frac{dy}{dl} = 0,$$

so that $D = 0$ and we cannot solve for the derivatives of φ. Our conclusions relative to characteristics, which can be extended to more general equations, are:

1. *If the dependent variable φ of the PDE in Eq. (9.1) is specified along a curve (i.e., φ has a* **boundary condition** *specified on a* **boundary curve**)*, this fixes the value of φ at a point of each characteristic that intersects the boundary curve, and hence at all points of each such characteristic;*

2. *If the boundary curve is along a characteristic, the boundary condition on it will ordinarily lead to inconsistency, and therefore, unless the boundary condition is redundant (i.e., coincidentally equal everywhere to the solution constructed from the value of φ at any one point on the characteristic), the PDE will not have a solution;*

3. *If the boundary curve has more than one intersection with the same characteristic, this will usually lead to an inconsistency, as the PDE may not have a solution that is simultaneously consistent with the values of φ at both intersections; and*

4. *Only if the boundary curve is* **not** *a characteristic can a boundary condition fix the value of φ at points not on the curve. Values of φ specified only on a characteristic of the PDE provide no information as to the value of φ at points not on that characteristic.*

In the above example, the argument t of the arbitrary function f was a linear combination of x and y, which worked because the coefficients of the derivatives in the PDE were constants. If these coefficients were more general functions of x and y, the foregoing type of analysis could still be carried out, but the form of t would have to be different. This more complicated case is illustrated in Exercises 9.2.5 and 9.2.6.

More General PDEs

Consider now a first-order PDE of a form more general than Eq. (9.1),

$$\mathcal{L}\varphi = a\frac{\partial\varphi}{\partial x} + b\frac{\partial\varphi}{\partial y} + q(x, y)\varphi = F(x, y). \tag{9.8}$$

We may identify its characteristic curves just as before, which amounts to making a transformation to new variables $s = ax + by, t = bx - ay$, in terms of which our PDE becomes, compare Eq. (9.5),

$$(a^2 + b^2)\left(\frac{\partial\varphi}{\partial s}\right) + \hat{q}(s, t)\hat{\varphi} = \hat{F}(s, t). \tag{9.9}$$

Here $\hat{q}(s, t)$ is obtained by converting $q(x, y)$ to the new coordinates:

$$\hat{q}(s, t) = q\left(\frac{as + bt}{a^2 + b^2}, \frac{bs - at}{a^2 + b^2}\right),$$

and $\hat{F}$ is related in a similar fashion to F. Equation (9.9) is really an ODE in s (containing what can be viewed as a parameter, t), and its general solution can be obtained by the usual procedures for solving ODEs.

Example 9.2.1   ANOTHER FIRST-ORDER PDE

Consider the PDE

$$\frac{\partial \varphi}{\partial x} + \frac{\partial \varphi}{\partial y} + (x+y)\varphi = 0.$$

Applying a transformation to the characteristic direction $t = x - y$ and the direction orthogonal thereto $s = x + y$, our PDE becomes

$$2\frac{\partial \varphi}{\partial s} + s\varphi = 0.$$

This equation separates into

$$2\frac{d\varphi}{\varphi} + s\,ds = 0,$$

with general solution

$$\ln \varphi = -\frac{s^2}{4} + C(t), \quad \text{or} \quad \varphi = e^{-s^2/4} f(t),$$

where $f(t)$, originally $\exp[C(t)]$, is completely arbitrary. One can simplify the result slightly by noting that $s^2/4 = t^2/4 + xy$; then $\exp(-t^2/4)$ can be absorbed into $f(t)$, leaving the compact result (in terms of x and y)

$$\varphi(x, y) = e^{-xy} f(x - y), \quad (f \text{ arbitrary}).$$

∎

More Than Two Independent Variables

It is useful to consider how the concept of characteristic can be generalized to PDEs with more than two independent variables. Given the three-dimensional (3-D) differential form

$$a\frac{\partial \varphi}{\partial x} + b\frac{\partial \varphi}{\partial y} + c\frac{\partial \varphi}{\partial z},$$

we apply a transformation to convert our PDE to the new variables $s = ax + by + cz$, $t = \alpha_1 x + \alpha_2 y + \alpha_3 z$, $u = \beta_1 x + \beta_2 y + \beta_3 z$, with α_i and β_i such that (s, t, u) form an orthogonal coordinate system. Then our 3-D differential form is found equivalent to

$$(a^2 + b^2 + c^2)\frac{\partial \varphi}{\partial s},$$

and the stream lines of s (those with t and u constant) are our characteristics, along which we can propagate a solution φ by solving an ODE. Each characteristic can be identified by its fixed values of t and u. For the 3-D analog of Eq. (9.1),

$$a \frac{\partial \varphi}{\partial x} + b \frac{\partial \varphi}{\partial y} + c \frac{\partial \varphi}{\partial z} = 0, \tag{9.10}$$

we have

$$(a^2 + b^2 + c^2) \frac{\partial \varphi}{\partial s} = 0,$$

with solution $\varphi = f(t, u)$, with f a completely arbitrary function of its two arguments.

Consider next an attempt to solve our 3-D PDE subject to a boundary condition fixing the values of the PDE solution φ on a surface. If the characteristic through a point on the surface lies **in the surface**, we have a potential inconsistency between the boundary condition and the solution propagated along the characteristic. We are then also unable to extend φ away from the boundary surface because the data on the surface is insufficient to yield values of the derivatives that are needed for a Taylor expansion. To see this, note that the derivatives $\partial \varphi / \partial x$, $\partial \varphi / \partial y$, and $\partial \varphi / \partial z$ can only be determined if we can find two directions (parametrically designated l and l') such that we can solve simultaneously Eq. (9.10) and

$$\frac{\partial \varphi}{\partial l} = \frac{\partial \varphi}{\partial x} \frac{dx}{dl} + \frac{\partial \varphi}{\partial y} \frac{dy}{dl} + \frac{\partial \varphi}{\partial z} \frac{dz}{dl},$$

$$\frac{\partial \varphi}{\partial l'} = \frac{\partial \varphi}{\partial x} \frac{dx}{dl'} + \frac{\partial \varphi}{\partial y} \frac{dy}{dl'} + \frac{\partial \varphi}{\partial z} \frac{dz}{dl'}.$$

A solution can be obtained only if

$$D = \begin{vmatrix} \dfrac{dx}{dl} & \dfrac{dy}{dl} & \dfrac{dz}{dl} \\[2mm] \dfrac{dx}{dl'} & \dfrac{dy}{dl'} & \dfrac{dz}{dl'} \\[2mm] a & b & c \end{vmatrix} \neq 0.$$

If a characteristic, with $dx/dl'' = a$, $dy/dl'' = b$, and $dz/dl'' = c$, lies in the two-dimensional (2-D) surface, there will only be one further linearly independent direction l, and D will necessarily be zero.

Summarizing, our earlier observations extend to the 3-D case:

> *A boundary condition is effective in determining a unique solution to a first-order PDE only if the boundary does not include a characteristic, and inconsistencies may arise if a characteristic intersects a boundary more than once.*

Exercises

Find the general solutions of the PDEs in Exercises 9.2.1 to 9.2.4.

9.2.1 $\quad \dfrac{\partial \psi}{\partial x} + 2 \dfrac{\partial \psi}{\partial y} + (2x - y)\psi = 0.$

9.2.2 $\quad \dfrac{\partial \psi}{\partial x} - 2 \dfrac{\partial \psi}{\partial y} + x + y = 0.$

9.2.3 $\dfrac{\partial \psi}{\partial x} + \dfrac{\partial \psi}{\partial y} = \dfrac{\partial \psi}{\partial z}.$

9.2.4 $\dfrac{\partial \psi}{\partial x} + \dfrac{\partial \psi}{\partial y} + \dfrac{\partial \psi}{\partial z} = x - y.$

9.2.5   (a)   Show that the PDE

$$y\frac{\partial \psi}{\partial x} + x\frac{\partial \psi}{\partial y} = 0$$

can be transformed into a readily soluble form by writing it in the new variables $u = xy$, $v = x^2 - y^2$, and find its general solution.

(b)   Discuss this result in terms of characteristics.

9.2.6   Find the general solution to the PDE

$$x\frac{\partial \psi}{\partial x} - y\frac{\partial \psi}{\partial y} = 0.$$

Hint. The solution to Exercise 9.2.5 may provide a suggestion as to how to proceed.

9.3   SECOND-ORDER EQUATIONS

Classes of PDEs

We consider here extending the notion of characteristics to second-order PDEs. This can sometimes be done in a useful fashion. As a preliminary example, consider the following homogeneous second-order equation

$$a^2\frac{\partial^2 \varphi(x, y)}{\partial x^2} - c^2\frac{\partial^2 \varphi(x, y)}{\partial y^2} = 0, \tag{9.11}$$

where a and c are assumed to be real. This equation can be written in the factored form

$$\left[a\frac{\partial}{\partial x} + c\frac{\partial}{\partial y}\right]\left[a\frac{\partial}{\partial x} - c\frac{\partial}{\partial y}\right]\varphi = 0, \tag{9.12}$$

and, since the two operator factors commute, we see that Eq. (9.12) will be satisfied if φ is a solution to either of the first-order equations

$$a\frac{\partial \varphi}{\partial x} + c\frac{\partial \varphi}{\partial y} = 0 \quad \text{or} \quad a\frac{\partial \varphi}{\partial x} - c\frac{\partial \varphi}{\partial y} = 0. \tag{9.13}$$

However, these first-order equations are of just the type discussed in the preceding subsection, so we can identify their respective general solutions as

$$\varphi_1(x, y) = f(cx - ay), \quad \varphi_2(x, y) = g(cx + ay), \tag{9.14}$$

where f and g are arbitrary (and totally unrelated) functions. Moreover, we can identify the stream lines of $ax + cy$ and $ax - cy$ as characteristics, with implications as to the effectiveness and possible consistency of boundary conditions. For some PDEs with second derivatives as given in Eq. (9.11), it will also be practical to propagate solutions along the characteristics.

Look next at the superficially similar equation

$$a^2 \frac{\partial^2 \varphi(x, y)}{\partial x^2} + c^2 \frac{\partial^2 \varphi(x, y)}{\partial y^2} = 0, \tag{9.15}$$

with a and c again assumed to be real. If we factor this, we get

$$\left[a \frac{\partial}{\partial x} + ic \frac{\partial}{\partial y} \right] \left[a \frac{\partial}{\partial x} - ic \frac{\partial}{\partial y} \right] \varphi = 0. \tag{9.16}$$

This factorization is of less practical value, as it leads to **complex** characteristics, which do not have an obvious relevance to boundary conditions. In addition, propagation along such characteristics does not provide a solution to the PDE for physically relevant (i.e., real) coordinate values.

It is customary to identify second-order PDEs as **hyperbolic** if they are of (or can be transformed into) the form given in Eq. (9.11), with real values of a and c. PDEs that are of (or can be transformed into) the form given in Eq. (9.15) are called **elliptic**. The designation is useful because it correlates with the existence (or nonexistence) of real characteristics, and therefore with the behavior of the PDE relative to boundary conditions, with further implications as to convenient methods for solving the PDE. The terms *elliptic* and *hyperbolic* have been introduced based on an analogy to quadratic forms, where $a^2 x^2 + c^2 y^2 = d$ is the equation of an ellipse, while $a^2 x^2 - c^2 y^2 = d$ is that of a hyperbola.

More general PDEs will have second derivatives of the differential form

$$\mathcal{L} = a \frac{\partial^2 \varphi}{\partial x^2} + 2b \frac{\partial^2 \varphi}{\partial x \partial y} + c \frac{\partial^2 \varphi}{\partial y^2}. \tag{9.17}$$

The form in Eq. (9.17) has the following factorization:

$$\mathcal{L} = \left(\frac{b + \sqrt{b^2 - ac}}{c^{1/2}} \frac{\partial}{\partial x} + c^{1/2} \frac{\partial}{\partial y} \right) \left(\frac{b - \sqrt{b^2 - ac}}{c^{1/2}} \frac{\partial}{\partial x} + c^{1/2} \frac{\partial}{\partial y} \right). \tag{9.18}$$

Equation (9.18) is easily verified by expanding the product. The equation also shows that the characteristics of Eq. (9.17) are real if and only if $b^2 - ac \geq 0$. This quantity is well known from elementary algebra, being the **discriminant** of the quadratic form $at^2 + 2bt + c$. If $b^2 - ac > 0$, the two factors identify two linearly independent real characteristics, as were found for the prototype hyperbolic PDE discussed in Eqs. (9.11) to (9.14). If $b^2 - ac < 0$, the characteristics will, as for the prototype elliptic PDE in Eqs. (9.15) and (9.16), form a complex conjugate pair. We now have, however, one new possibility: If $b^2 - ac = 0$ (a case that for quadratic forms is that of a parabola), we have a PDE that has exactly one linearly independent characteristic; such PDEs are termed **parabolic**, and the canonical form adopted for them is

$$a \frac{\partial \varphi}{\partial x} = \frac{\partial^2 \varphi}{\partial y^2}. \tag{9.19}$$

If the original PDE lacked a $\partial / \partial x$ term, it would in effect be an ODE in y that depends on x only parametrically and need not be considered further in the context of methods for PDEs.

To complete our discussion of the second-order form in Eq. (9.17), we need to show that it can be transformed into the canonical form for the PDE of its classification. For this purpose we consider the transformation to new variables ξ, η, defined as

$$\xi = c^{1/2}x - c^{-1/2}by, \quad \eta = c^{-1/2}y. \tag{9.20}$$

By systematic application of the chain rule to evaluate $\partial^2/\partial x^2$, $\partial^2/\partial x \partial y$, and $\partial^2/\partial y^2$, it can be shown that

$$\mathcal{L} = (ac - b^2)\frac{\partial^2 \varphi}{\partial \xi^2} + \frac{\partial^2 \varphi}{\partial \eta^2}. \tag{9.21}$$

Verification of Eq. (9.21) is the subject of Exercise 9.3.1.

Equation (9.21) shows that the classification of our PDE remains invariant under transformation, and is hyperbolic if $b^2 - ac > 0$, elliptic if $b^2 - ac < 0$, and parabolic if $b^2 - ac = 0$. Perhaps better seen from Eq. (9.18), we see that the stream lines of the characteristics have slope

$$\frac{dy}{dx} = \frac{c}{b \pm \sqrt{b^2 - ac}}. \tag{9.22}$$

More than Two Independent Variables

While we will not carry out a full analysis, it is important to note that many problems in physics involve more than two dimensions (often, three spatial dimensions or several spatial dimensions plus time). Often, the behavior in the multiple spatial dimensions is similar, and we apply the terms *hyperbolic*, *elliptic*, and *parabolic* in a way that relates the spatial to the time derivatives when the latter occur. Thus, these equations are classified as indicated:

Laplace equation	$\nabla^2 \psi = 0$	elliptic
Poisson equation	$\nabla^2 \psi = -\rho/\varepsilon_0$	elliptic
Wave equation	$\nabla^2 \psi = \dfrac{1}{c^2}\dfrac{\partial^2 \psi}{\partial t^2}$	hyperbolic
Diffusion equation	$a\dfrac{\partial \psi}{\partial t} = \nabla^2 \psi$	parabolic

The specific equations mentioned here are very important in physics and will be further discussed in later sections of this chapter. These examples, of course, do not represent the full range of second-order PDEs, and do not include cases where the coefficients in the differential operator are functions of the coordinates. In that case, the classification into elliptic, hyperbolic, and parabolic is only local; the class may change as the coordinates vary.

Boundary Conditions

Usually, when we know a physical system at some time and the law governing the physical process, then we are able to predict the subsequent development. Such initial values are the most common boundary conditions associated with ODEs and PDEs. Finding solutions that match given points, curves, or surfaces corresponds to boundary value problems. Solutions usually are required to satisfy certain imposed (for example, asymptotic) boundary conditions. These boundary conditions ordinarily take one of three forms:

1. **Cauchy boundary conditions**. The value of a function and normal derivative specified on the boundary. In electrostatics this would mean φ, the potential, and E_n, the normal component of the electric field.
2. **Dirichlet boundary conditions**. The value of a function specified on the boundary. In electrostatics, this would mean the potential φ.
3. **Neumann boundary conditions**. The normal derivative (normal gradient) of a function specified on the boundary. In the electrostatic case this would be E_n and therefore σ, the surface charge density.

Because the three classes of second-order PDEs have different patterns of characteristics, the boundary conditions needed to specify (in a consistent way) a unique solution will depend on the equation class. An exact analysis of the role of boundary conditions is complicated and beyond the scope of the present text. However, a summary of the relation of these three types of boundary conditions to the three classes of 2-D partial differential equations is given in Table 9.1. For a more extended discussion of these partial differential equations the reader may consult Morse and Feshbach, Chapter 6 (see Additional Readings).

Parts of Table 9.1 are simply a matter of maintaining internal consistency or of common sense. For instance, for Poisson's equation with a closed surface, Dirichlet conditions lead

Table 9.1   Relation between PDE and Boundary Conditions

Boundary Conditions	Class of Partial Differential Equation		
	Elliptic	Hyperbolic	Parabolic
	Laplace, Poisson in (x, y)	Wave equation in (x, t)	Diffusion equation in (x, t)
Cauchy			
Open surface	Unphysical results (instability)	**Unique, stable solution**	Too restrictive
Closed surface	Too restrictive	Too restrictive	Too restrictive
Dirichlet			
Open surface	Insufficient	Insufficient	**Unique, stable solution** in one direction
Closed surface	**Unique, stable solution**	Solution not unique	Too restrictive
Neumann			
Open surface	Insufficient	Insufficient	**Unique, stable solution** in one direction
Closed surface	**Unique, stable solution**	Solution not unique	Too restrictive

to a unique, stable solution. Neumann conditions, independent of the Dirichlet conditions, likewise lead to a unique stable solution independent of the Dirichlet solution. Therefore, Cauchy boundary conditions (meaning Dirichlet plus Neumann) could lead to an inconsistency.

The term **boundary conditions** includes as a special case the concept of **initial conditions**. For instance, specifying the initial position x_0 and the initial velocity v_0 in some dynamical problem would correspond to the Cauchy boundary conditions. Note, however, that an initial condition corresponds to applying the condition at only one end of the allowed range of the (time) variable.

Finally, we note that Table 9.1 oversimplifies the situation in various ways. For example, the Helmholtz PDE,

$$\nabla^2 \psi \pm k^2 \psi = 0,$$

(which could be thought of as the reduction of a parabolic time-dependent equation to its spatial part) has solution(s) for Dirichlet conditions on a closed boundary only for certain values of its parameter k. The determination of k and the characterization of these solutions is an eigenvalue problem and is important for physics.

Nonlinear PDEs

Nonlinear ODEs and PDEs are a rapidly growing and important field. We encountered earlier the simplest linear wave equation,

$$\frac{\partial \psi}{\partial t} + c \frac{\partial \psi}{\partial x} = 0,$$

as the first-order PDE of the wavefronts of the wave equation. The simplest nonlinear wave equation,

$$\frac{\partial \psi}{\partial t} + c(\psi) \frac{\partial \psi}{\partial x} = 0, \tag{9.23}$$

results if the local speed of propagation, c, is not constant but depends on the wave ψ. When a nonlinear equation has a solution of the form $\psi(x, t) = A \cos(kx - \omega t)$, where $\omega(k)$ varies with k so that $\omega''(k) \neq 0$, then it is called **dispersive**. Perhaps the best-known nonlinear dispersive equation is the **Korteweg-deVries** equation,

$$\frac{\partial \psi}{\partial t} + \psi \frac{\partial \psi}{\partial x} + \frac{\partial^3 \psi}{\partial x^3} = 0, \tag{9.24}$$

which models the lossless propagation of shallow water waves and other phenomena. It is widely known for its **soliton** solutions. A soliton is a traveling wave with the property of persisting through an interaction with another soliton: After they pass through each other, they emerge in the same shape and with the same velocity and acquire no more than a phase shift. Let $\psi(\xi = x - ct)$ be such a traveling wave. When substituted into Eq. (9.24) this yields the nonlinear ODE

$$(\psi - c) \frac{d\psi}{d\xi} + \frac{d^3 \psi}{d\xi^3} = 0, \tag{9.25}$$

which can be integrated to yield

$$\frac{d^2\psi}{d\xi^2} = c\psi - \frac{\psi^2}{2}. \tag{9.26}$$

There is no additive integration constant in Eq. (9.26), because the solution must be such that $d^2\psi/d\xi^2 \to 0$ with $\psi \to 0$ for large ξ. This causes ψ to be localized at the characteristic $\xi = 0$, or $x = ct$. Multiplying Eq. (9.26) by $d\psi/d\xi$ and integrating again yields

$$\left(\frac{d\psi}{d\xi}\right)^2 = c\psi^2 - \frac{\psi^3}{3}, \tag{9.27}$$

where $d\psi/d\xi \to 0$ for large ξ. Taking the root of Eq. (9.27) and integrating again yields the soliton solution

$$\psi(x - ct) = \frac{3c}{\cosh^2\left(\frac{1}{2}\sqrt{c}(x - ct)\right)}. \tag{9.28}$$

Exercises

9.3.1   Show that by making a change of variables to $\xi = c^{1/2}x - c^{-1/2}by$, $\eta = c^{-1/2}y$, the operator $\mathcal{L}$ of Eq. (9.18) can be brought to the form

$$\mathcal{L} = (ac - b^2)\frac{\partial^2}{\partial\xi^2} + \frac{\partial^2}{\partial\eta^2}.$$

9.4   SEPARATION OF VARIABLES

Partial differential equations are clearly important in physics, as evidenced by the PDEs listed in Section 9.1, and of equal importance is the development of methods for their solution. Our discussion of characteristics has suggested an approach that will be useful for some problems. Other general techniques for solving PDEs can be found, for example, in the books by Bateman and by Gustafson listed in the Additional Readings at the end of this chapter. However, the technique described in the present section is probably that most widely used.

The method developed in this section for solution of a PDE splits a partial differential equation of n variables into n ordinary differential equations, with the intent that an overall solution to the PDE will be a product of single-variable functions which are solutions to the individual ODEs. In problems amenable to this method, the boundary conditions are usually such that they separate at least partially into conditions that can be applied to the separate ODEs.

Further discussion of the method depends on the nature of the problem we seek to solve, so we now make the observation that PDEs occur in physics in two contexts, either as

An equation with no unknown parameters for which there is expected to be a unique solution consistent with the boundary conditions (typical example: Laplace equation for the electrostatic potential with the potential specified on the boundary), or

An eigenvalue problem which will have solutions consistent with the boundary conditions only for certain values of an embedded but initially unknown parameter (the eigenvalue).

In the first of these two cases, the unique solution is typically approached by first applying boundary conditions to the separate ODEs to specialize their solutions as much as possible. The solution is at this point normally not unique, and we have a (usually infinite) number of product solutions that satisfy the boundary conditions thus far applied. We then regard these product solutions as a basis that can be used to form an expansion that satisfies the remaining boundary condition(s). We illustrate with the first and fourth examples of this section.

In the second case identified above, we typically have homogeneous boundary conditions (solution equal to zero on the boundary), and in favorable situations can satisfy all the boundary conditions by imposing them on the separate ODEs. At this point we usually find that each product solves our PDE with a different value of its embedded parameter, so that we are obtaining eigenfunctions and eigenvalues. This process is illustrated in the second and third examples of the present section.

The method of separation of variables proceeds by dividing the PDE into pieces each of which can be set equal to a **constant of separation**. If our PDE has n independent variables, there will be $n - 1$ independent separation constants (though we often prefer a more symmetric formulation with n separation constants plus an equation connecting them). The separation constants may have values that are restricted by invoking boundary conditions.

To get a broad understanding of the method of separation of variables, it is useful to see how it is carried out in a variety of coordinate systems. Here we examine the process in Cartesian, cylindrical, and spherical polar coordinates. For application to other coordinate systems we refer the reader to the second edition of this text.

Cartesian Coordinates

In Cartesian coordinates the Helmholtz equation becomes

$$\frac{\partial^2 \psi}{\partial x^2} + \frac{\partial^2 \psi}{\partial y^2} + \frac{\partial^2 \psi}{\partial z^2} + k^2 \psi = 0, \tag{9.29}$$

using Eq. (3.62) for the Laplacian. For the present, let k^2 be a constant. As stated in the introductory paragraphs of this section, our strategy will be to split Eq. (9.29) into a set of ordinary differential equations. To do so, let

$$\psi(x, y, z) = X(x)Y(y)Z(z) \tag{9.30}$$

and substitute back into Eq. (9.29). How do we know Eq. (9.30) is valid? When the differential operators in various variables are additive in the PDE, that is, when there are no products of differential operators in different variables, the separation method has a chance to succeed. For success, it is usually also necessary that at least some of the boundary conditions separate into conditions on the separate factors. At any rate, we are proceeding in the spirit of let's try and see if it works. If our attempt succeeds, then Eq. (9.30) will be justified. If it does not succeed, we shall find out soon enough and then we can try another attack, such as Green's functions, integral transforms, or brute-force numerical analysis. With ψ assumed given by Eq. (9.30), Eq. (9.29) becomes

$$YZ\frac{d^2X}{dx^2} + XZ\frac{d^2Y}{dy^2} + XY\frac{d^2Z}{dz^2} + k^2XYZ = 0. \tag{9.31}$$

Dividing by $\psi = XYZ$ and rearranging terms, we obtain

$$\frac{1}{X}\frac{d^2X}{dx^2} = -k^2 - \frac{1}{Y}\frac{d^2Y}{dy^2} - \frac{1}{Z}\frac{d^2Z}{dz^2}. \tag{9.32}$$

Equation (9.32) exhibits one separation of variables. The left-hand side is a function of x alone, whereas the right-hand side depends only on y and z and not on x. But x, y, and z are all independent coordinates. The equality of two sides that depend on different variables can only be attained if each side must be equal to the same constant, a constant of separation. We choose[2]

$$\frac{1}{X}\frac{d^2X}{dx^2} = -l^2, \tag{9.33}$$

$$-k^2 - \frac{1}{Y}\frac{d^2Y}{dy^2} - \frac{1}{Z}\frac{d^2Z}{dz^2} = -l^2. \tag{9.34}$$

Now, turning our attention to Eq. (9.34), we obtain

$$\frac{1}{Y}\frac{d^2Y}{dy^2} = -k^2 + l^2 - \frac{1}{Z}\frac{d^2Z}{dz^2}, \tag{9.35}$$

and a second separation has been achieved. Here we have a function of y equated to a function of z. We resolve it, as before, by equating each side to another constant of separation, $-m^2$,

$$\frac{1}{Y}\frac{d^2Y}{dy^2} = -m^2, \tag{9.36}$$

$$-k^2 + l^2 - \frac{1}{Z}\frac{d^2Z}{dz^2} = -m^2. \tag{9.37}$$

The separation is now complete, but to make the formulation more symmetrical, we will set

$$\frac{1}{Z}\frac{d^2Z}{dz^2} = -n^2, \tag{9.38}$$

and then consistency with Eq. (9.37) leads to the condition

$$l^2 + m^2 + n^2 = k^2. \tag{9.39}$$

Now we have three ODEs, Eqs. (9.33), (9.36), and (9.38), to replace Eq. (9.29). Our assumption, Eq. (9.30), has succeeded in splitting the PDE; if we can also use the factored form to satisfy the boundary conditions, our solution of the PDE will be complete.

---

[2]The choice of sign for separation constants is completely arbitrary, and will be fixed in specific problems by the need to satisfy specific boundary conditions, and particularly to avoid the unnecessary introduction of complex numbers.

It is convenient to label the solution according to the choice of our constants l, m, and n; that is,

$$\psi_{lmn}(x, y, z) = X_l(x)Y_m(y)Z_n(z). \tag{9.40}$$

Subject to the boundary conditions of the problem being solved and to the condition $k^2 = l^2 + m^2 + n^2$, we may choose l, m, and n as we like, and Eq. (9.40) will still be a solution of Eq. (9.29), provided only that $X_l(x)$ is a solution of Eq. (9.33), and so on. Because our original PDE is homogeneous and linear, we may develop **the most general solution** of Eq. (9.29) by taking a **linear combination of solutions** ψ_{lmn},

$$\Psi = \sum_{l,m} a_{lm}\psi_{lmn}, \tag{9.41}$$

where it is understood that n will be given a value consistent with Eq. (9.39) and with the values of l and m.

Finally, the constant coefficients a_{lm} must be chosen to permit Ψ to satisfy the boundary conditions of the problem, leading usually to a discrete set of values l, m.

Reviewing what we have done, it can be seen that the separation into ODEs could still have been achieved if k^2 were replaced by any function that depended additively on the variables, i.e., if

$$k^2 \longrightarrow f(x) + g(y) + h(z).$$

A case of practical importance would be the choice $k^2 \longrightarrow C(x^2 + y^2 + z^2)$, leading to the problem of a 3-D quantum harmonic oscillator. Replacing the constant term k^2 by a separable function of the variables will, of course, change the ODEs we obtain in the separation process and may have implications relative to the boundary conditions.

Example 9.4.1   LAPLACE EQUATION FOR A PARALLELEPIPED

As a concrete example we take Eq. (9.29) with $k = 0$, which makes it a Laplace equation, and ask for its solution in a parallelepiped defined by the planar surfaces $x = 0$, $x = c$, $y = 0$, $y = c$, $z = 0$, $z = L$, with the Dirichlet boundary condition $\psi = 0$ on all the boundaries except that at $z = L$; on that boundary ψ is given the constant value V. See Fig. 9.1. This is a problem in which the PDE contains no unknown parameters and should have a unique solution.

We expect a solution of the generic form given by Eq. (9.41), with ψ_{lmn} given by Eq. (9.40). To proceed further, we need to develop the actual functional forms of $X(x)$, $Y(y)$, and $Z(z)$. For X and Y, the ODEs, written in conventional form, are

$$X'' = -l^2 X, \quad Y'' = -m^2 Y,$$

with general solutions

$$X = A \sin lx + B \cos lx, \quad Y = A' \sin my + B' \cos my.$$

We could have written X and Y as complex exponentials, but that choice would be less convenient when we consider the boundary conditions. To satisfy the boundary condition at $x = 0$, we set $X(0) = 0$, which can be accomplished by choosing $B = 0$; to satisfy

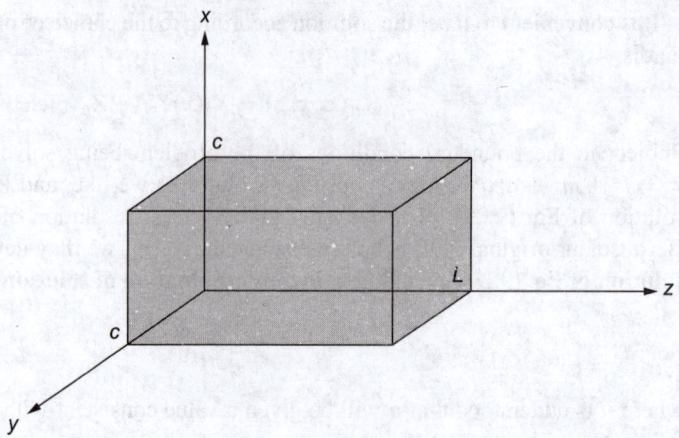

FIGURE 9.1   Parallelepiped for solution of Laplace equation.

the boundary condition at $x = c$, we set $X(c) = 0$, which causes us to choose l such that $lc = \lambda\pi$, where λ must be a nonzero integer. Without loss of generality, we can restrict λ to positive values, as $-X$ and X are linearly dependent. Moreover, we can include whatever scale factor is ultimately needed in our solution for $Z(z)$, so we may set $A = 1$. Similar remarks apply to the solution $Y(y)$, so our solutions for X and Y take the final form

$$X_\lambda(x) = \sin\left(\frac{\lambda\pi x}{c}\right), \quad Y_\mu(y) = \sin\left(\frac{\mu\pi y}{c}\right), \tag{9.42}$$

with $\lambda = 1, 2, 3, \ldots$ and $\mu = 1, 2, 3, \ldots$.

Next we consider the ODE for Z. It must be solved with a value of n^2, calculated from Eq. (9.39) with $k = 0$ as

$$n^2 = -\frac{\pi^2}{c^2}(\lambda^2 + \mu^2).$$

This equation suggests that n will be imaginary, but that is unimportant here. Returning to the ODE for Z, we now see that it becomes

$$Z'' = +\frac{\pi^2}{c^2}(\lambda^2 + \mu^2)Z,$$

and the general solution for $Z(z)$ for given λ and μ is then easily identified as

$$Z_{\lambda\mu}(z) = A\,e^{\rho_{\lambda\mu}z} + B\,e^{-\rho_{\lambda\mu}z}, \quad \text{with } \rho_{\lambda\mu} = \frac{\pi}{c}\sqrt{\lambda^2 + \mu^2}. \tag{9.43}$$

We now specialize Eq. (9.43) in a way that makes $Z_{\lambda\mu}(0) = 0$ and $Z_{\lambda\mu}(L) = V$. Noting that $\sinh(\rho_{\lambda\mu}z)$ is a linear combination of $e^{\rho_{\lambda\mu}z}$ and $e^{-\rho_{\lambda\mu}z}$, we write

$$Z_{\lambda\mu}(z) = V\frac{\sinh(\rho_{\lambda\mu}z)}{\sinh(\rho_{\lambda\mu}L)}. \tag{9.44}$$

At this point, we have made choices that cause all the boundary conditions to be satisfied except that at $z = L$, and we are now ready to select the coefficients $a_{\lambda\mu}$ as required by the remaining boundary condition, which because of Eq. (9.44) corresponds to

$$\frac{1}{V}\Psi(x, y, L) = \sum_{\lambda\mu} a_{\lambda\mu} \sin\left(\frac{\lambda\pi x}{c}\right) \sin\left(\frac{\mu\pi y}{c}\right) = 1. \tag{9.45}$$

The symmetry of this expression suggests that we write $a_{\lambda\mu} = b_\lambda b_\mu$, and find the coefficients b_λ from the equation

$$\sum_\lambda b_\lambda \sin\left(\frac{\lambda\pi x}{c}\right) = 1. \tag{9.46}$$

Because the sine functions in Eq. (9.46) are the eigenfunctions of the one-dimensional (1-D) equation for X, which is a Hermitian eigenproblem, they form an orthogonal set on the interval $(0, c)$, so the b_λ can be computed by the following formulas:

$$b_\lambda = \frac{\left\langle \sin\left(\frac{\lambda\pi x}{c}\right) \middle| 1 \right\rangle}{\left\langle \sin\left(\frac{\lambda\pi x}{c}\right) \middle| \sin\left(\frac{\lambda\pi x}{c}\right) \right\rangle} = \frac{\displaystyle\int_0^c \sin(\lambda\pi x/c)\, dx}{\displaystyle\int_0^c \sin^2(\lambda\pi x/c)\, dx}$$

$$= \frac{4}{\lambda\pi}, \quad \lambda \text{ odd},$$

$$= 0, \qquad \lambda \text{ even},$$

and our complete solution for the potential in the parallelepiped becomes

$$\Psi(x, y, z) = V \sum_{\lambda\mu} b_\lambda b_\mu \sin\left(\frac{\lambda\pi x}{c}\right) \sin\left(\frac{\mu\pi y}{c}\right) \frac{\sinh(\rho_{\lambda\mu} z)}{\sinh(\rho_{\lambda\mu} L)}. \tag{9.47}$$

∎

As briefly mentioned earlier, PDEs also occur as eigenvalue problems. Here is a simple example.

Example 9.4.2   QUANTUM PARTICLE IN A BOX

We consider a particle of mass m trapped in a box with planar faces at $x = 0$, $x = a$, $y = 0$, $y = b$, $z = 0$, $z = c$. The quantum stationary states of this system are the eigenfunctions of the Schrödinger equation

$$-\frac{1}{2}\nabla^2 \psi(x, y, z) = E\psi(x, y, z), \tag{9.48}$$

where this PDE is subject to the Dirichlet boundary condition $\psi = 0$ on the walls of the box. We identify E as the stationary-state energy (the eigenvalue), in a system of units with $m = \hbar = 1$. This is a Helmholtz equation with the new wrinkle that E is not initially known. The boundary conditions are such that this PDE has no solution except for a set of discrete values of E. We want to find both those values and the corresponding eigenfunctions.

Separating the variables in Eq. (9.48) by assuming a solution of the form Eq. (9.30), the PDE becomes

$$-\left(\frac{X''}{X} + \frac{Y''}{Y} + \frac{Z''}{Z}\right) = 2E, \tag{9.49}$$

and the separation yields

$$\frac{X''}{X} = -l^2, \quad \text{with solution } X = A \sin lx + B \cos lx.$$

After applying the boundary conditions at $x = 0$ and $x = a$ we get (scaling to $A = 1$)

$$X_\lambda = \sin\left(\frac{\lambda \pi x}{a}\right), \quad \lambda = 1, 2, 3, \ldots, \quad \text{so } l = \lambda \pi / a. \tag{9.50}$$

Because the X equation is a 1-D Hermitian eigenvalue problem, these functions $X_\lambda(x)$ are orthogonal on $0 \le x \le a$.

Similar processing of the Y and Z equations, with separation constants $-m^2$ and $-n^2$, yields

$$Y_\mu = \sin\left(\frac{\mu \pi y}{b}\right), \quad \mu = 1, 2, 3, \ldots, \quad \text{so } m = \mu \pi / b,$$

$$Z_\nu = \sin\left(\frac{\nu \pi z}{c}\right), \quad \nu = 1, 2, 3, \ldots, \quad \text{so } n = \nu \pi / c, \tag{9.51}$$

yielding two additional 1-D eigenvalue problems.

Replacing X''/X, Y''/Y, Z''/Z in Eq. (9.49), respectively, by $-l^2$, $-m^2$, $-n^2$, and then evaluating these quantities from Eqs. (9.50) and (9.51), we have

$$l^2 + m^2 + n^2 = 2E, \quad \text{or} \quad E = \frac{\pi^2}{2}\left(\frac{\lambda^2}{a^2} + \frac{\mu^2}{b^2} + \frac{\nu^2}{c^2}\right), \tag{9.52}$$

with λ, μ, and μ arbitrary positive integers. The situation is quite different from our solution, Example 9.4.1, of the Laplace equation. Instead of a unique solution we have an infinite set of solutions, corresponding to all positive integer triples (λ, μ, ν), each with its own value of E. Making the observation that the differential operator on the left-hand side of Eq. (9.47) is Hermitian in the presence of the chosen boundary conditions, we have found a complete orthogonal set of its eigenfunctions. The orthogonality is obvious, as it can be confirmed from the orthogonality of the X_λ, Y_μ, and Z_ν on their respective 1-D intervals. Because we set the coefficients of all the sine functions to unity, our overall eigenfunctions are not normalized, but we can easily normalize them if we so choose.

We close this example with the observation that this boundary-value problem will not have a solution for arbitrarily chosen values of E, as the E values must satisfy Eq. (9.52) with **integer values** of λ, μ, and ν. This will cause the E values of the problem solutions to be a discrete set; using terminology introduced in a previous chapter, our boundary-value problem can be said to have a **discrete spectrum**. ∎

Circular Cylindrical Coordinates

Curvilinear coordinate systems introduce additional nuances into the process for separating variables. Again we consider the Helmholtz equation, now in circular cylindrical coordinates. With our unknown function ψ dependent on ρ, φ, and z, that equation becomes, using Eq. (3.149) for ∇^2:

$$\nabla^2 \psi(\rho, \varphi, z) + k^2 \psi(\rho, \varphi, z) = 0, \tag{9.53}$$

or

$$\frac{1}{\rho} \frac{\partial}{\partial \rho} \left(\rho \frac{\partial \psi}{\partial \rho} \right) + \frac{1}{\rho^2} \frac{\partial^2 \psi}{\partial \varphi^2} + \frac{\partial^2 \psi}{\partial z^2} + k^2 \psi = 0. \tag{9.54}$$

As before, we assume a factored form[3] for ψ,

$$\psi(\rho, \varphi, z) = P(\rho)\Phi(\varphi)Z(z). \tag{9.55}$$

Substituting into Eq. (9.46), we have

$$\frac{\Phi Z}{\rho} \frac{d}{d\rho} \left(\rho \frac{dP}{d\rho} \right) + \frac{PZ}{\rho^2} \frac{d^2\Phi}{d\varphi^2} + P\Phi \frac{d^2Z}{dz^2} + k^2 P\Phi Z = 0. \tag{9.56}$$

All the partial derivatives have become ordinary derivatives. Dividing by $P\Phi Z$ and moving the z derivative to the right-hand side yields

$$\frac{1}{\rho P} \frac{d}{d\rho} \left(\rho \frac{dP}{d\rho} \right) + \frac{1}{\rho^2 \Phi} \frac{d^2\Phi}{d\varphi^2} + k^2 = -\frac{1}{Z} \frac{d^2Z}{dz^2}. \tag{9.57}$$

Again, a function of z on the right appears to depend on a function of ρ and φ on the left. We resolve this by setting each side of Eq. (9.57) equal to the same constant. Let us choose[4] $-l^2$. Then

$$\frac{d^2Z}{dz^2} = l^2 Z \tag{9.58}$$

and

$$\frac{1}{\rho P} \frac{d}{d\rho} \left(\rho \frac{dP}{d\rho} \right) + \frac{1}{\rho^2 \Phi} \frac{d^2\Phi}{d\varphi^2} + k^2 = -l^2. \tag{9.59}$$

Setting

$$k^2 + l^2 = n^2, \tag{9.60}$$

multiplying by ρ^2, and rearranging terms, we obtain

$$\frac{\rho}{P} \frac{d}{d\rho} \left(\rho \frac{dP}{d\rho} \right) + n^2 \rho^2 = -\frac{1}{\Phi} \frac{d^2\Phi}{d\varphi^2}. \tag{9.61}$$

---

[3] For those with limited familiarity with the Greek alphabet, we point out that the symbol P is the upper-case form of ρ.

[4] Again, the choice of sign of the separation constant is arbitrary. However, the minus sign chosen for the axial coordinate z is optimum if we expect exponential dependence on z, from Eq. (9.58). A positive sign is chosen for the azimuthal coordinate φ in expectation of a periodic dependence on φ, from Eq. (9.62).

We set the right-hand side equal to m^2, so

$$\frac{d^2\Phi}{d\varphi^2} = -m^2\Phi, \tag{9.62}$$

and the left-hand side of Eq. (9.61) rearranges into a separate equation for ρ:

$$\rho\frac{d}{d\rho}\left(\rho\frac{dP}{d\rho}\right) + (n^2\rho^2 - m^2)P = 0. \tag{9.63}$$

Typically, Eq. (9.62) will be subject to the boundary condition that Φ have periodicity 2π and will therefore have solutions

$$e^{\pm im\varphi} \text{ or, equivalently } \sin m\varphi, \cos m\varphi, \text{ with integer } m.$$

The ρ equation, Eq. (9.63), is Bessel's differential equation (in the independent variable $n\rho$), originally encountered in Chapter 7. Because of its occurrence here (and in many other places relevant to physics), it warrants extensive study and is the topic of Chapter 14. The separation of variables of Laplace's equation in parabolic coordinates also gives rise to Bessel's equation. It may be noted that the Bessel equation is notorious for the variety of disguises it may assume. For an extensive tabulation of possible forms the reader is referred to *Tables of Functions* by Jahnke and Emde.[5]

Summarizing, we have found that the original Helmholtz equation, a 3-D PDE, can be replaced by three ODEs, Eqs. (9.58), (9.62), and (9.63). Noting that the ODE for ρ contains the separation constants from the z and φ equations, the solutions we have obtained for the Helmholtz equation can be written, with labels, as

$$\psi_{lm}(\rho, \varphi, z) = P_{lm}(\rho)\Phi_m(\varphi)Z_l(z), \tag{9.64}$$

where we probably should recall that the n in Eq. (9.63) for P is a function of l (specifically, $n^2 = l^2 + k^2$). The most general solution of the Helmholtz equation can now be constructed as a linear combination of the product solutions:

$$\Psi(\rho, \varphi, z) = \sum_{l,m} a_{lm}P_{lm}(\rho)\Phi_m(\varphi)Z_l(z). \tag{9.65}$$

Reviewing what we have done, we note that the separation could still have been achieved if k^2 had been replaced by any additive function of the form

$$k^2 \quad\longrightarrow\quad f(r) + \frac{g(\varphi)}{\rho^2} + h(z).$$

Example 9.4.3   CYLINDRICAL EIGENVALUE PROBLEM

In this example we regard Eq. (9.53) as an eigenvalue problem, with Dirichlet boundary conditions $\psi = 0$ on all boundaries of a finite cylinder, with k^2 initially unknown and to be determined. Our region of interest will be a cylinder with curved boundaries at $\rho = R$ and with end caps at $z = \pm L/2$, as shown in Fig. 9.2. To emphasize that k^2 is an eigenvalue,

---

[5]E. Jahnke and F. Emde, *Tables of Functions*, 4th rev. ed., New York: Dover (1945), p. 146; also, E. Jahnke, F. Emde, and F. Lösch, *Tables of Higher Functions*, 6th ed., New York: McGraw-Hill (1960).

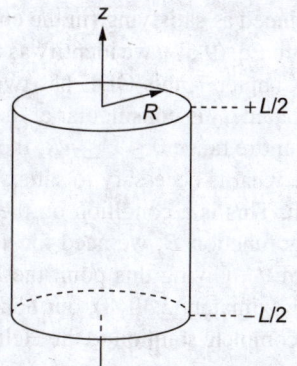

FIGURE 9.2   Cylindrical region for solution of the Helmholtz equation.

we rename it λ, and our eigenvalue equation is, symbolically,

$$-\nabla^2\psi = \lambda\psi, \tag{9.66}$$

with boundary conditions $\psi = 0$ at $\rho = R$ and at $z = \pm L/2$. Apart from constants, this is the time-independent Schrödinger equation for a particle in a cylindrical cavity. We limit the present example to the determination of the smallest eigenvalue (the **ground state**). This will be the solution to the PDE with the smallest number of oscillations, so we seek a solution without zeros (**nodes**) in the interior of the cylindrical region.

Again, we seek separated solutions of the form given in Eq. (9.55). The ODEs for Z and Φ, Eqs. (9.58) and (9.62), have the simple forms

$$Z'' = l^2 Z, \quad \Phi'' = -m^2\Phi,$$

with general solutions

$$Z = A\,e^{lz} + B\,e^{-lz}, \quad \Phi = A'\sin m\varphi + B'\cos m\varphi.$$

We now need to specialize these solutions to satisfy the boundary conditions. The condition on Φ is simply that it be periodic in φ with period 2π; this result will be obtained if m is any integer (including $m = 0$, which corresponds to the simple solution $\Phi = $ constant). Since our objective here is to obtain the least oscillatory solution, we choose that form, $\Phi = $ constant, for Φ.

Looking next at Z, we note that the arbitrary choice of sign for the separation constant l^2 has led to a form of solution that appears not to be optimum for fulfilling conditions requiring $Z = 0$ at the boundaries. But, writing $l^2 = -\omega^2$, $l = i\omega$, Z becomes a linear combination of $\sin\omega z$ and $\cos\omega z$; the least oscillatory solution with $Z(\pm L/2) = 0$ is $Z = \cos(\pi z/L)$, so $\omega = \pi/L$, and $l^2 = -\pi^2/L^2$.

The functions $Z(z)$ and $\Phi(\varphi)$ that we have found satisfy the boundary conditions in z and φ but it remains to choose $P(\rho)$ in a way that produces $P = 0$ at $\rho = R$ with the least oscillation in P. The equation governing P, Eq. (9.63), is

$$\rho^2 P'' + \rho P' + n^2\rho^2 P = 0, \tag{9.67}$$

where n was introduced as satisfying (in the current notation) $n^2 = \lambda + l^2$, see Eq. (9.60). Continuing now with Eq. (9.67), we identify as the Bessel equation of order zero in $x = n\rho$. As we learned in Chapter 7, this ODE has two linearly independent solutions, of which only the one designated J_0 is nonsingular at the origin. Since we need here a solution that is regular over the entire range $0 \leq x \leq nR$, the solution we must choose is $J_0(n\rho)$.

We can now see what is necessary to satisfy the boundary condition at $\rho = R$, namely that $J_0(nR)$ vanish. This is a condition on the parameter n. Remembering that we want the least oscillatory function P, we need for n to be such that nR will be the location of the smallest zero of J_0. Giving this point the name α (which by numerical methods can be found to be approximately 2.4048), our boundary condition takes the form $nR = \alpha$, or $n = \alpha/R$, and our complete solution to the Helmholtz equation can be written

$$\psi(\rho, \varphi, z) = J_0\left(\frac{\alpha\rho}{R}\right)\cos\left(\frac{\pi z}{L}\right). \tag{9.68}$$

To complete our analysis, we must figure out how to arrange that $n = \alpha/R$. Since the condition connecting n, l, and λ rearranges to

$$\lambda = n^2 - l^2, \tag{9.69}$$

we see that the condition on n translates into one on λ. Our PDE has a unique ground-state solution consistent with the boundary conditions, namely an *eigenfunction* whose *eigenvalue* can be computed from Eq. (9.69), yielding

$$\lambda = \frac{\alpha^2}{R^2} + \frac{\pi^2}{L^2}.$$

If we had not restricted consideration to the ground state (by choosing the least oscillatory solution), we would have (in principle) been able to obtain a complete set of eigenfunctions, each with its own eigenvalue. ∎

Spherical Polar Coordinates

As a final exercise in the separation of variables in PDEs, let us try to separate the Helmholtz equation, again with k^2 constant, in spherical polar coordinates. Using Eq. (3.158), our PDE is

$$\frac{1}{r^2 \sin\theta}\left[\sin\theta \frac{\partial}{\partial r}\left(r^2 \frac{\partial \psi}{\partial r}\right) + \frac{\partial}{\partial \theta}\left(\sin\theta \frac{\partial \psi}{\partial \theta}\right) + \frac{1}{\sin\theta}\frac{\partial^2 \psi}{\partial \varphi^2}\right] = -k^2 \psi. \tag{9.70}$$

Now, in analogy with Eq. (9.30) we try

$$\psi(r, \theta, \varphi) = R(r)\Theta(\theta)\Phi(\varphi). \tag{9.71}$$

By substituting back into Eq. (9.70) and dividing by $R\Theta\Phi$, we have

$$\frac{1}{R r^2}\frac{d}{dr}\left(r^2 \frac{dR}{dr}\right) + \frac{1}{\Theta r^2 \sin\theta}\frac{d}{d\theta}\left(\sin\theta \frac{d\Theta}{d\theta}\right) + \frac{1}{\Phi r^2 \sin^2\theta}\frac{d^2\Phi}{d\varphi^2} = -k^2. \tag{9.72}$$

Note that all derivatives are now ordinary derivatives rather than partials. By multiplying by $r^2 \sin^2 \theta$, we can isolate $(1/\Phi)(d^2\Phi/d\varphi^2)$ to obtain

$$\frac{1}{\Phi}\frac{d^2\Phi}{d\varphi^2} = r^2 \sin^2\theta \left[-k^2 - \frac{1}{Rr^2}\frac{d}{dr}\left(r^2\frac{dR}{dr}\right) - \frac{1}{\Theta r^2 \sin\theta}\frac{d}{d\theta}\left(\sin\theta\frac{d\Theta}{d\theta}\right) \right]. \quad (9.73)$$

Equation (9.73) relates a function of φ alone to a function of r and θ alone. Since r, θ, and φ are independent variables, we equate each side of Eq. (9.73) to a constant. In almost all physical problems, φ will appear as an azimuth angle. This suggests a periodic solution rather than an exponential. With this in mind, let us use $-m^2$ as the separation constant, which then must be an integer squared. Then

$$\frac{1}{\Phi}\frac{d^2\Phi(\varphi)}{d\varphi^2} = -m^2 \quad (9.74)$$

and

$$\frac{1}{Rr^2}\frac{d}{dr}\left(r^2\frac{dR}{dr}\right) + \frac{1}{\Theta r^2 \sin\theta}\frac{d}{d\theta}\left(\sin\theta\frac{d\Theta}{d\theta}\right) - \frac{m^2}{r^2 \sin^2\theta} = -k^2. \quad (9.75)$$

Multiplying Eq. (9.75) by r^2 and rearranging terms, we obtain

$$\frac{1}{R}\frac{d}{dr}\left(r^2\frac{dR}{dr}\right) + r^2 k^2 = -\frac{1}{\Theta \sin\theta}\frac{d}{d\theta}\left(\sin\theta\frac{d\Theta}{d\theta}\right) + \frac{m^2}{\sin^2\theta}. \quad (9.76)$$

Again, the variables are separated. We equate each side to a constant, λ, and finally obtain

$$\frac{1}{\sin\theta}\frac{d}{d\theta}\left(\sin\theta\frac{d\Theta}{d\theta}\right) - \frac{m^2}{\sin^2\theta}\Theta + \lambda\Theta = 0, \quad (9.77)$$

$$\frac{1}{r^2}\frac{d}{dr}\left(r^2\frac{dR}{dr}\right) + k^2 R - \frac{\lambda R}{r^2} = 0. \quad (9.78)$$

Once more we have replaced a partial differential equation of three variables by three ODEs.

The ODE for Φ is the same as that encountered in cylindrical coordinates, with solutions $\exp(\pm im\varphi)$ or $\sin m\varphi$, $\cos m\varphi$. The Θ ODE can be made less forbidding by changing the independent variable from θ to $t = \cos\theta$, after which Eq. (9.77), with $\Theta(\theta)$ now written as $P(\cos\theta) = P(t)$, becomes

$$(1 - t^2)P''(t) - 2t P'(t) - \frac{m^2}{1-t^2}P(t) + \lambda P(t) = 0. \quad (9.79)$$

This is the **associated Legendre equation** (called the **Legendre equation** if $m = 0$), and is discussed in detail in Chapter 15. We normally require solutions for $P(t)$ that do not have singularities in the region within the range of the spherical polar coordinate θ (namely that it be nonsingular for the entire range $0 \le \theta \le \pi$, equivalent to $-1 \le t \le +1$). The solutions satisfying these conditions, called **associated Legendre functions**, are traditionally denoted P_l^m, with l a nonnegative integer. In Section 8.3 we discussed the Legendre equation as a 1-D eigenvalue problem, finding that the requirement of nonsingularity at $t = \pm 1$ is a sufficient boundary condition to make its solutions well defined. We found also that its eigenfunctions are the **Legendre polynomials** and that its eigenvalues

(λ in the present notation) have the values $l(l+1)$, where l is an integer. The generalization of these findings to the associated Legendre equation (that with nonzero m) shows that λ continues to be given as $l(l+1)$, but with the additional restriction that $l \geq |m|$. Details are deferred to Chapter 15.

Before continuing to the R equation, Eq. (9.78), let us observe that in deriving the Φ and Θ equations we have assumed that k^2 was a constant. However, if k^2 was not a constant, but an additive expression of the form

$$k^2 \quad \longrightarrow \quad f(r) + \frac{g(\theta)}{r^2} + \frac{h(\varphi)}{r^2 \sin^2 \theta},$$

we could still carry out the separation of variables, but the relatively familiar Φ and Θ equations we have identified will be changed in ways that make them different, and probably less tractable. However, if the departure of k^2 from a constant value is restricted to the form $k^2 = k^2(r)$, then the angular parts of the separation will remain as presented in Eqs. (9.74) and (9.79), and we only need to deal with increased generality in the R equation.

It is worth stressing that the great importance of this separation of variables in spherical polar coordinates stems from the fact that the case $k^2 = k^2(r)$ covers a tremendous amount of physics, such as a great deal of the theories of gravitation, electrostatics and atomic, nuclear, and particle physics. Problems with $k^2 = k^2(r)$ can be characterized as **central force problems**, and the use of spherical polar coordinates is natural in such problems. From both a practical and a theoretical point of view, it is a key observation that the angular dependence is isolated in Eqs. (9.74) and (9.77), or its equivalent, Eq. (9.79), that these equations are the same for all central force problems, and that **they can be solved exactly**. A detailed discussion of the angular properties of central force problems in quantum mechanics is deferred to Chapter 16.

Returning now to the remaining separated ODE, namely the R equation, we consider in some depth two special cases: (1) The case $k^2 = 0$, corresponding to the Laplace equation, and (2) k^2 a nonzero constant, corresponding to the Helmholtz equation. For both cases we assume that the Φ and Θ equations have been solved subject to the boundary conditions already discussed, so that the separation constant λ must have the value $l(l+1)$ for some nonnegative integer l. Continuing on the assumption that k^2 is a (possibly zero) constant, Eq. (9.79) expands into

$$r^2 R'' + 2r\, R' + \left[k^2 r^2 - l(l+1) \right] R = 0. \tag{9.80}$$

Taking first the case of the Laplace equation, for which $k^2 = 0$, Eq. (9.80) is easy to solve. Either by inspection or by attempting to carry out a series solution by the method of Frobenius, it is found that the initial term of the series, $a_0 r^s$, is by itself a complete solution to Eq. (9.80). In fact, substituting the assumed solution $R = r^s$ into Eq. (9.80), that equation reduces to

$$s(s-1)r^s + 2s\, r^s - l(l+1)r^s = 0,$$

showing that $s(s+1) = l(l+1)$, which has two solutions, $s = l$ (obviously), and $s = -l - 1$. In other words, given the value l from the choice of solution to the Θ equation, we find that the R equation (for the Laplace equation) has the two solutions r^l and r^{-l-1}, so its general solution takes the form

$$R(r) = A r^l + B r^{-l-1}. \tag{9.81}$$

Combining the solutions to the separated ODEs, and summing over all choices of the separation constants, we see that the most general solution of the Laplace equation that has a nonsingular angular dependence can be written

$$\psi(r, \theta, \varphi) = \sum_{l,m} (A_{lm} r^l + B_{lm} r^{-l-1}) P_l^m (\cos\theta)(A'_{lm} \sin m\varphi + B'_{lm} \cos m\varphi). \tag{9.82}$$

If our problem now has Dirichlet or Neumann boundary conditions on a spherical surface (with the region under study either within or outside the sphere), we may be able (by methods more fully articulated in later chapters) to choose the coefficients in Eq. (9.82) so that the boundary conditions are satisfied. Note that if the region in which we are to solve the Laplace equation includes the origin, $r = 0$, then only the r^l term should be retained and we set B_{lm} to zero. If our region for the Laplace equation is, say, external to a sphere of some finite radius, then we must avoid the large-r divergence of r^l and set A_{lm} to zero, retaining only r^{-l-1}. More complicated cases, e.g., where we study the annular region between two concentric spheres, will require the retention of both A_{lm} and B_{lm} and will in general be somewhat more difficult.

We continue now to the case of nonzero but constant k^2. Equation (9.80) looks a lot like a Bessel equation, but differs therefrom by the coefficient "2" in the R' term and the factor k^2 that multiplies r^2 in the coefficient of R. Both these differences can be resolved by rewriting $R(r)$ as

$$R(r) = \frac{Z(kr)}{(kr)^{1/2}}, \tag{9.83}$$

which will then give us a differential equation for Z. Carrying out the differentiations to obtain R' and R'' in terms of Z, and changing the independent variable from r to $x = kr$, Eq. (9.83) becomes

$$x^2 Z'' + x Z' + \left[x^2 - \left(l + \tfrac{1}{2} \right)^2 \right] Z = 0, \tag{9.84}$$

showing that Z is a Bessel function, of order $l + \tfrac{1}{2}$. Returning to Eq. (9.83), we can now identify $R(r)$ in terms of quantities known as **spherical Bessel functions**, where $j_l(x)$, the spherical Bessel functions that are regular at $x = 0$, have definition

$$j_l(x) = \sqrt{\frac{\pi}{2x}} J_{l+1/2}(x).$$

Since the status of $R(r)$ as the solution to a homogeneous ODE is not affected by the scale factor in the definition of $j_l(x)$, we see that Eq. (9.83) is equivalent to the observation that Eq. (9.80) has a solution $j_l(kr)$. The spherical Bessel function that is the second solution of Eq. (9.80) is designated y_l, so that solution is $y_l(kr)$, and the general solution of Eq. (9.80) can be written

$$R(r) = A j_l(kr) + B y_l(kr). \tag{9.85}$$

We note here that the properties of spherical Bessel functions are discussed more fully in Chapter 14.

With the solutions to the radial ODE in hand, we can now write that the general solution to the Helmholtz equation in spherical polar coordinates takes the form

$$\psi(r,\theta,\varphi) = \sum_{l,m} \left[A_{lm} j_l(kr) + B_{lm} y_l(kr) \right] \times P_l^m(\cos\theta)(A'_{lm} \sin m\varphi + B'_{lm} \cos m\varphi).$$

$$(9.86)$$

The above discussion assumes that $k^2 > 0$; negative values of k^2 (and therefore imaginary values of k) simply correspond to our identifying an equation of the form $(\nabla^2 - k^2)\psi = 0$ as a somewhat peculiar case of $(\nabla^2 + k^2)\psi = 0$. For negative k^2, we can see we then get solutions that involve $j_l(kr)$ or $y_l(kr)$ with imaginary k. In order to avoid notations that unnecessarily involve imaginary quantities, it is usual to define a new set of functions $i_l(x)$ that are proportional to $j_l(ix)$, and are called **modified** spherical Bessel functions. The modified solutions parallel to $y_l(ix)$ are denoted $k_l(x)$. These functions are also discussed in Chapter 14.

The cases we have just surveyed do not, of course, cover all possibilities, and various other choices of $k^2(r)$ lead to problems that are of importance in physics. Without proceeding to a detailed analysis here, we cite a couple:

- Taking $k_2 = A/r + \lambda$ yields (with boundary condition that ψ vanish in the limit $r \to \infty$) the time-independent Schrödinger equation for the hydrogen atom; the R equation can then be identified as the associated Laguerre differential equation, discussed in Chapter 18.

- Taking $k^2 = Ar^2 + \lambda$ yields (with boundary condition at $r = \infty$) the equation for the 3-D quantum harmonic oscillator, for which the R equation can be reduced to the Hermite ODE, also discussed in Chapter 18.

Some other boundary-value problems lead to well-studied ODEs. However, sometimes the practicing physicist will encounter a radial equation that may have to be solved using the techniques presented in Chapter 7, or if all else fails, by numerical methods.

We close this subsection with an example that is a simple boundary-value problem in spherical coordinates.

Example 9.4.4   SPHERE WITH BOUNDARY CONDITION

In this example we solve the Laplace equation for the electrostatic potential $\psi(\mathbf{r})$ in a region interior to a sphere of radius a, using spherical polar coordinates (r,θ,φ) with origin at the center of the sphere. Our solution is to be subject to the Neumann boundary condition $d\psi/d\mathbf{n} = -V_0 \cos\theta$ on the spherical surface. See Fig. 9.3.

To start, we note that totally arbitrary Neumann boundary conditions will not be consistent with our assumption of a charge-free sphere, as the integral of the normal derivative on the spherical surface gives, according to Gauss' law, a measure of the total charge within.

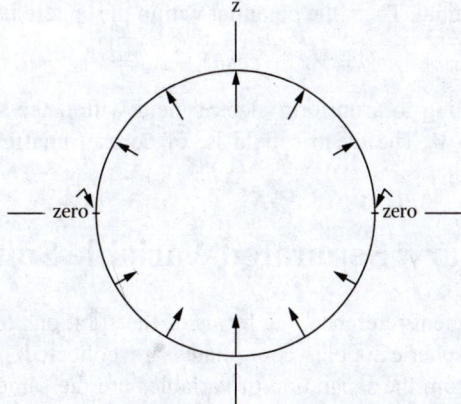

FIGURE 9.3   Arrows indicate sign and relative magnitude of the (inward) normal derivative of the electrostatic potential on a spherical surface (boundary condition for Example 9.4.4).

The present example is internally consistent, as

$$\int_S \cos\theta \, d\sigma = \int_0^\pi d\theta \int_0^{2\pi} d\varphi \cos\theta = 0.$$

Next, we need to take the general solution for the Laplace equation within a sphere, as given by Eq. (9.82), and calculate therefrom the inward normal derivative at $r = a$. Since the normal is in the $-r$ direction, we need only compute $-\partial\psi/\partial r$, evaluated at $r = a$. Noting that for the present problem $B_{lm} = 0$, our boundary condition becomes

$$-V\cos\theta = -\sum_{l,m} l \, A_{lm} a^{l-1} P_l^m(\cos\theta)(A_{lm}' \sin m\varphi + B_{lm}' \cos m\varphi).$$

Since the left-hand side of this equation is independent of φ, its right-hand side has nonzero coefficients only for $m = 0$, for which we only have the term originally containing B_{l0}', because $\sin(0) = 0$. Thus, consolidating the constants, the boundary condition becomes the simpler form

$$- V\cos\theta = -\sum_l l \, A_l a^{l-1} P_l(\cos\theta), \tag{9.87}$$

Without having made a detailed study of the properties of Legendre functions, the solution of an equation of this type might need to be deferred to Chapter 15, but this one is easy to solve because $P_1(\cos\theta) = \cos\theta$ (see Legendre polynomials in Table 15.1) Thus, from Eq. (9.87),

$$l A_l a^{l-1} = V \delta_{l1},$$

so $A_1 = V$ and all the other coefficients except A_0 vanish. The coefficient A_0 is not determined by the boundary conditions and represents an arbitrary constant that may be added to the potential. Thus, the potential within the sphere has the form

$$\psi = Vr P_1(cos\theta) + A_0 = Vr\cos\theta + A_0 = Vz + A_0,$$

corresponding to a uniform electric field within the sphere, in the $-z$ direction and of magnitude V. The electric field is, of course, unaffected by the arbitrary value of the constant A_0. ∎

Summary: Separated-Variable Solutions

For convenient reference, the forms of the solutions of Laplace's and Helmholtz's equations for spherical polar coordinates are collected in Table 9.2. Although the ODEs obtained from the separation of variables are the same irrespective of the boundary conditions, the ODE solutions to be used, and the constants of separation, do depend on the boundaries. Boundaries with less than spherical symmetry may lead to values of m and l that are not integral, and may also require use of the second solution of the Legendre equation (quantities normally denoted Q_l^m). Engineering applications frequently require solutions to PDEs for regions of low symmetry, but such problems are nowadays almost universally approached using numerical, rather than analytical methods. Consequently, Table 9.2 only contains data that are relevant for problems inside or outside a spherical boundary, or between two concentric spherical boundaries. This restriction to spherical symmetry causes the angular portion of the solutions to be uniquely of the form we have already identified.

In contrast to the unique angular solution, both linearly independent solutions to the radial ODE are relevant, with the choice of solution dependent on the geometry. Solutions within a sphere must employ only the radial functions that are regular at the origin, i.e., r^l, j_l, or i_l. Solutions external to a sphere may employ r^{-l-1}, k_l (defined so that it will decay exponentially to zero at large r), or a linear combination of j_l and y_l (both of which are oscillatory and decay as $r^{-1/2}$). Solutions between concentric spheres can use both the radial functions appropriate to the PDE.

It is also possible to summarize the forms of solution to the Laplace and Helmholtz equations in circular cylindrical coordinates, if we restrict attention to problems that have circular symmetry about the axial direction of the coordinate system. However, the situation is considerably more complicated than for spherical coordinates, as we now have two

Table 9.2 Solutions of PDEs in Spherical Polar Coordinates[a]

$$\psi = \sum_{l,m} f_l(r) P_l^m(\cos\theta) \begin{Bmatrix} a_{lm}\cos m\varphi + b_{lm}\sin m\varphi) \\ \text{or} \\ c_{lm}e^{im\varphi} \end{Bmatrix}$$

$\nabla^2\psi = 0$	$f_l(r) = r^l,\ r^{-l-1}$
$\nabla^2\psi + k^2\psi = 0$	$f_l(r) = j_l(kr),\ y_l(kr)$
$\nabla^2\psi - k^2\psi = 0$	$f_l(r) = i_l(kr),\ k_l(kr)$

[a] For i_l, j_l, k_l, y_l, see Chapter 14; for P_l^m, see Chapters 15 and 16.

Table 9.3   Solutions of PDEs in Circular Cylindrical Coordinates[a]

$$\psi = \sum_{m,\alpha} f_{m\alpha}(\rho) g_\alpha(z) \begin{Bmatrix} a_{m\alpha}\cos m\varphi + b_{m\alpha}\sin m\varphi \\ \text{or} \\ c_{m\alpha}e^{im\varphi} \end{Bmatrix}$$

$\nabla^2\psi = 0$	$f_{m\alpha}(\rho) = J_m(\alpha\rho),\, Y_m(\alpha\rho)$	$g_\alpha(z) = e^{\alpha z},\, e^{-\alpha z}$
or	$f_{m\alpha}(\rho) = I_m(\alpha\rho),\, K_m(\alpha\rho)$	$g_\alpha(z) = \sin(\alpha z),\cos(\alpha z)$ or $e^{i\alpha z}$
or	$f_{m\alpha}(\rho) = \rho^m,\, \rho^{-m}$	$g_\alpha(z) = 1$
$\nabla^2\psi + \lambda\psi = 0$	$f_{m\alpha}(\rho) = J_m(\alpha\rho),\, Y_m(\alpha\rho)$	
	if $\beta^2 = \alpha^2 - \lambda > 0$,	$g_\alpha(z) = e^{\beta z},\, e^{-\beta z}$
	if $\beta^2 = \lambda - \alpha^2 > 0$,	$g_\alpha(z) = \sin(\beta z),\cos(\beta z)$ or $e^{i\beta z}$
	if $\lambda = \alpha^2$,	$g_\alpha(z) = 1$
or	$f_{m\alpha}(\rho) = I_m(\alpha\rho),\, K_m(\alpha\rho)$	
	if $\beta^2 = -\lambda - \alpha^2 > 0$,	$g_\alpha(z) = e^{\beta z},\, e^{-\beta z}$
	if $\beta^2 = \lambda + \alpha^2 > 0$,	$g_\alpha(z) = \sin(\beta z),\cos(\beta z)$ or $e^{i\beta z}$
	if $\lambda = -\alpha^2$,	$g_\alpha(z) = 1$
or	$f_{m\alpha}(\rho) = \rho^m,\, \rho^{-m}$	
	if $\beta^2 = -\lambda > 0$,	$g_\alpha(z) = e^{\beta z},\, e^{-\beta z}$
	if $\beta^2 = \lambda > 0$,	$g_\alpha(z) = \sin(\beta z),\cos(\beta z)$ or $e^{i\beta z}$

[a] The parameter α can have any real values consistent with the boundary conditions. For I_m, J_m, K_m, Y_m, see Chapter 14.

coordinates (ρ and z) that can have a variety of boundary conditions, in contrast to the single such coordinate (r) in the spherical system. In spherical coordinates the form of the radial function is completely determined by the PDE, and specific problems differ only in the choice (or relative weight) of the two linearly independent radial solutions. But in cylindrical coordinates the forms of the ρ and z solutions, as well as their coefficients, are determined by the boundary conditions, and not entirely by the value of the constant in the Helmholtz equation. Choices of the ρ and z solutions, though coupled, can vary widely. For details, the reader is referred to Table 9.3.

Our final observations of this section deal with the functions we encountered in the course of the separations in cylindrical and spherical coordinates. For the purpose of this discussion, it is useful to think of our PDE as an operator equation subject to boundary conditions. If, in cylindrical coordinates, we restrict attention to PDEs in which the parameter k^2 is independent of φ (and with boundary conditions that do not depend upon φ), we have chosen our operator equation as one that has circular symmetry. Moreover, we will then always get the same Φ equation, with (of course) the same solutions. In these circumstances, the solutions will have symmetry properties derived from those of our overall boundary-value problem.[6] The Φ equation can also be thought of as an operator equation, and we can go further and identify the operator as $L_z^2 = -\partial^2/\partial\varphi^2$, where L_z is the z component of the angular momentum. The solutions of the Φ equation are eigenfunctions of this operator; the reason they can occur as part of the PDE solution is because

---

[6]Note that the solutions to a boundary-value problem need not have the full problem symmetry (a point that will be elaborated in great detail when we develop group-theoretical methods). An obvious example is that the Sun-Earth gravitational potential is spherically symmetric, while the most familiar solution (the Earth's orbit) is planar. The dilemma is resolved by noting that the spherical symmetry manifests itself in the possible existence of Earth orbits at all angular orientations.

L_z^2 commutes with the operator defining the PDE (clearly so, because the PDE operator does not contain φ). In other words, because L_z^2 and the PDE operator commute, they will have simultaneous eigenfunctions, and the overall solutions of the PDE can be labeled to identify the L_z^2 eigenfunction that was chosen.

Looking now at the situation in spherical polar coordinates, we note that if k^2 is independent of the angles, i.e., $k^2 = k^2(r)$, then our PDE always has the same angular solutions $\Theta_{lm}(\theta)\Phi_m(\varphi)$. Looking further at the angular terms of our PDE, we can identify them as the operator L^2, and we see that the angular solutions we have found are eigenfunctions of this operator. When the PDE operator is independent of the angles, it will commute with L^2 and the solutions to the PDE can be labeled accordingly. These symmetry features are very important and are discussed in great detail in Chapter 16.

Exercises

9.4.1 By letting the operator $\nabla^2 + k^2$ act on the general form $a_1\psi_1(x, y, z) + a_2\psi_2(x, y, z)$, show that it is linear, i.e., that $(\nabla^2 + k^2)(a_1\psi_1 + a_2\psi_2) = a_1(\nabla^2 + k^2)\psi_1 + a_2(\nabla^2 + k^2)\psi_2$.

9.4.2 Show that the Helmholtz equation,

$$\nabla^2\psi + k^2\psi = 0,$$

is still separable in circular cylindrical coordinates if k^2 is generalized to $k^2 + f(\rho) + (1/\rho^2)g(\varphi) + h(z)$.

9.4.3 Separate variables in the Helmholtz equation in spherical polar coordinates, splitting off the radial dependence **first**. Show that your separated equations have the same form as Eqs. (9.74), (9.77), and (9.78).

9.4.4 Verify that

$$\nabla^2\psi(r, \theta, \varphi) + \left[k^2 + f(r) + \frac{1}{r^2}g(\theta) + \frac{1}{r^2\sin^2\theta}h(\varphi)\right]\psi(r, \theta, \varphi) = 0$$

is separable (in spherical polar coordinates). The functions f, g, and h are functions only of the variables indicated; k^2 is a constant.

9.4.5 An atomic (quantum mechanical) particle is confined inside a rectangular box of sides a, b, and c. The particle is described by a wave function ψ that satisfies the Schrödinger wave equation

$$-\frac{\hbar^2}{2m}\nabla^2\psi = E\psi.$$

The wave function is required to vanish at each surface of the box (but not to be identically zero). This condition imposes constraints on the separation constants and therefore on the energy E. What is the smallest value of E for which such a solution can be obtained?

$$ANS. \quad E = \frac{\pi^2\hbar^2}{2m}\left(\frac{1}{a^2} + \frac{1}{b^2} + \frac{1}{c^2}\right).$$

9.4.6 The quantum mechanical angular momentum operator is given by $\mathbf{L} = -i(\mathbf{r} \times \nabla)$. Show that

$$\mathbf{L} \cdot \mathbf{L}\psi = l(l+1)\psi$$

leads to the associated Legendre equation.
Hint. Section 8.3 and Exercise 8.3.1 may be helpful.

9.4.7 The 1-D Schrödinger wave equation for a particle in a potential field $V = \frac{1}{2}kx^2$ is

$$-\frac{\hbar^2}{2m}\frac{d^2\psi}{dx^2} + \frac{1}{2}kx^2\psi = E\psi(x).$$

(a) Defining

$$a = \left(\frac{mk}{\hbar^2}\right)^{1/4}, \quad \lambda = \frac{2E}{\hbar}\left(\frac{m}{k}\right)^{1/2},$$

and setting $\xi = ax$, show that

$$\frac{d^2\psi(\xi)}{d\xi^2} + (\lambda - \xi^2)\psi(\xi) = 0.$$

(b) Substituting

$$\psi(\xi) = y(\xi)e^{-\xi^2/2},$$

show that $y(\xi)$ satisfies the Hermite differential equation.

9.5 LAPLACE AND POISSON EQUATIONS

The Laplace equation can be considered the prototypical elliptic PDE. At this point we supplement the discussion motivated by the method of separation of variables with some additional observations. The importance of Laplace's equation for electrostatics has stimulated the development of a great variety of methods for its solution in the presence of boundary conditions ranging from simple and symmetrical to complicated and convoluted. Techniques for present-day engineering problems tend to rely heavily on computational methods. The thrust of this section, however, will be on general properties of the Laplace equation and its solutions.

The basic properties of the Laplace equation are independent of the coordinate system in which it is expressed; we assume for the moment that we will use Cartesian coordinates. Then, because the PDE sets the sum of the second derivatives, $\partial^2\psi/\partial x_i^2$, to zero, it is obvious that if any of the second derivatives has a positive sign, at least one of the others must be negative. This point is illustrated in Example 9.4.1, where the x and y dependence of a solution to the Laplace equation was sinusoidal, and as a result, the z dependence was exponential (corresponding to different signs for the second derivative). Since the second derivative is a measure of curvature, we conclude that if ψ has positive curvature in any coordinate direction, it must have negative curvature in some other coordinate direction. That observation, in turn, means that all the **stationary points** of ψ (points where its first derivatives in all directions vanish) must be **saddle points**, not maxima or minima.

Since the Laplace equation describes the static electric potential in charge-free regions, we conclude that the potential cannot have an extremum at a point where there is no charge. A corollary to this observation is that the extrema of the electrostatic potential in a charge-free region must be on the boundary of the region.

A related property of the Laplace equation is that its solution, subject to Dirichlet boundary conditions for the entire closed boundary of its region, is unique. This property applies also to its inhomogeneous generalization, the Poisson equation. The proof is simple: Suppose there are two distinct solutions ψ_1 and ψ_2 for the same boundary conditions. Then, their difference $\psi = \psi_1 - \psi_2$ (for either the Laplace or Poisson equation) will be a solution to the Laplace equation with $\psi = 0$ on the boundary. Since ψ cannot have extrema within the bounded region, it must be zero everywhere, meaning that $\psi_1 = \psi_2$.

If we have a Laplace or Poisson equation subject to Neumann boundary conditions on the entire closed boundary of its region, then the difference $\psi = \psi_1 - \psi_2$ of two solutions will also be a solution to the Laplace equation with a zero Neumann boundary condition. To analyze this situation, we invoke Green's Theorem, in the form provided by Eq. (3.86), taking both u and v of that equation to be ψ. Equation (3.86) then becomes

$$\int_S \psi \frac{\partial \psi}{\partial \mathbf{n}} dS = \int_V \psi \nabla^2 \psi \, d\tau + \int_V \nabla \psi \cdot \nabla \psi \, d\tau. \tag{9.88}$$

The boundary condition causes the left-hand side of Eq. (9.88) to vanish, the first integral on the right-hand side vanishes because ψ is a solution of the Laplace equation, and the remaining integral on the right-hand side must therefore also vanish. But that integral can only vanish if $\nabla \psi$ is zero everywhere, which can only be true if ψ is constant. Thus, solutions to the Laplace equation with Neumann boundary conditions are also unique, except for an additive constant to the potential.

An oft-cited application of this uniqueness theorem is the solution of electrostatics problems by the method of images, which replaces a problem containing boundaries by one without a boundary but with additional charge added in such a way that the potential at the boundary location has the desired value. For example, a positive charge in front of a grounded boundary (one with $\psi = 0$) can be augmented by a negative charge at the mirror-image position behind the boundary. Then the two-charge system (ignoring the boundary) will yield the desired zero potential at the boundary location, and the uniqueness theorem tells us that the potential calculated for the two-charge system must be the same (within the original region) as that for the original system.

Exercises

9.5.1   Verify that the following are solutions of Laplace's equation:

(a) $\psi_1 = 1/r$, $r \neq 0$,   (b) $\psi_2 = \frac{1}{2r} \ln \frac{r+z}{r-z}$.

9.5.2   If Ψ is a solution of Laplace's equation, $\nabla^2 \Psi = 0$, show that $\partial \Psi / \partial z$ is also a solution.

9.5.3   Show that an argument based on Eq. (9.88) can be used to prove that the Laplace and Poisson equations with Dirichlet boundary conditions have unique solutions.

9.6 WAVE EQUATION

The wave equation is the prototype hyperbolic PDE. As we have seen earlier in this chapter, hyperbolic PDEs have two *characteristics*, and for the equation

$$\frac{1}{c^2}\frac{\partial^2 \psi}{\partial t^2} = \frac{\partial^2 \psi}{\partial x^2},\tag{9.89}$$

the characteristics are lines of constant $x - ct$ and those of constant $x + ct$. This means that the general solution to Eq. (9.89) takes the form

$$\psi(x,t) = f(x - ct) + g(x + ct),\tag{9.90}$$

with f and g completely arbitrary.

Viewing x as a position variable and t as the time, we can interpret $f(x - ct)$ as a wave, moving with velocity c, in the $+x$ direction. By this we mean that the entire profile of f, as a function of x at $t = 0$, will be shifted uniformly toward positive x by an amount c when $t = 1$. See Fig. 9.4. Similarly, $g(x + ct)$ describes a wave moving at velocity c in the $-x$ direction. Because f and g are arbitrary, the **traveling waves** they describe need not be sinusoidal or periodic, but may be entirely irregular; moreover, there is no requirement that f and g have any particular relationship to each other.

An obvious special case of the general situation described above is that when $f(x - ct)$ is chosen to be sinusoidal, $f = \sin(x - ct)$. For simplicity we have taken f to have unit amplitude and wavelength 2π. We also take $g(x + ct)$ to be $g = \sin(x + ct)$, a sinusoidal wave of the same wavelength and amplitude traveling in the direction opposite to f. At a point x and time t, these two waves add to produce a resultant

$$\psi(x,t) = \sin(x - ct) + \sin(x + ct),$$

which, using trigonometric identities, can be rearranged to

$$\psi(x,t) = (\sin x \cos ct - \cos x \sin ct) + (\sin x \cos ct + \cos x \sin ct) = 2\sin x \cos ct.$$

This form for ψ can be identified as a **standing wave** distribution, meaning that the time evolution of the wave's profile in x is an oscillation in amplitude, with the wave pattern not moving in either direction. An obvious point of difference from a traveling wave is that for a standing wave, the **nodes** (points where $\psi = 0$) are stationary in time, while in a traveling wave they are moving in time at velocity $\pm c$.

Our current interest in traveling vs. standing waves is their relation to solutions to the wave equation that we might find using the method of separation of variables. That method would obviously lead us to standing-wave solutions. However, it is useful to note that the totality of the solution set from the separated variables has the same content as

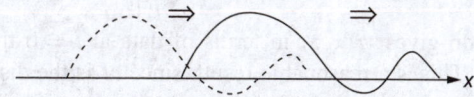

FIGURE 9.4   Traveling wave $f(x - ct)$. Dashed line is profile at $t = 0$; full line is profile at a time $t > 0$.

the traveling-wave solutions. For example, the products $\sin x \cos ct$ and $\cos x \sin ct$ are solutions we would get by separating the variables, and linear combinations of these yield $\sin(x \pm ct)$.

d'Alembert's Solution

While all ways of writing the general solution to the wave equation are mathematically equivalent, diverse forms differ in their convenience of use for various purposes. To illustrate this, we consider how we might construct a solution to the wave equation, given, as an initial condition, (1) the entire spatial distribution of the wave amplitude at $t = 0$ and (2) the time derivative of the wave amplitude at $t = 0$ for the entire spatial distribution. The solution to this problem is generally referred to as **d'Alembert's solution** of the wave equation; it was also (and slightly earlier) found by Euler.

We start by using Eq. (9.90) to write our initial conditions in terms of the presently unknown functions f and g:

$$\psi(x, 0) = f(x) + g(x), \tag{9.91}$$

$$\left. \frac{\partial \psi(x, t)}{\partial t} \right|_{t=0} = -cf'(x) + cg'(x). \tag{9.92}$$

We now integrate Eq. (9.92) between the limits $x - ct$ and $x + ct$ (and divide the result by $2c$), obtaining

$$\frac{1}{2c} \int_{x-ct}^{x+ct} \frac{\partial \psi(x, 0)}{\partial t} dx = \frac{1}{2}\left[-f(x + ct) + f(x - ct) + g(x + ct) - g(x - ct) \right]. \tag{9.93}$$

From Eq. (9.91), we also have

$$\frac{1}{2}\left[\psi(x + ct, 0) + \psi(x - ct, 0)\right] =$$

$$\frac{1}{2}\left[f(x + ct) + g(x + ct) + f(x - ct) + g(x - ct)\right]. \tag{9.94}$$

Adding together the right-hand sides of Eqs. (9.93) and (9.94), half the terms cancel, and those that survive combine to give the result

$$f(x - ct) + g(x + ct), \quad \text{which is } \psi(x, t).$$

Therefore, from the left-hand sides of Eqs. (9.93) and (9.94), we obtain the final result

$$\psi(x, t) = \frac{1}{2}\left[\psi(x + ct, 0) + \psi(x - ct, 0)\right] + \frac{1}{2c} \int_{x-ct}^{x+ct} \frac{\partial \psi(x, 0)}{\partial t} dx. \tag{9.95}$$

This equation gives $\psi(x, t)$ in terms of data at $t = 0$ that are within the distance ct of the point x. This is a reasonable result, since ct is the distance that waves in this problem can move between times $t = 0$ and $t = t$. More specifically, Eq. (9.95) contains terms that represent half the $t = 0$ amplitude at distances $\pm ct$ from x (half, because a disturbance that starts at these points is split between propagation in both directions), plus an additional integral that accumulates the effect of the initial amplitude derivative over the region of influence.

Exercises

Solve the wave equation, Eq. (9.89), subject to the indicated conditions.

9.6.1   Determine $\psi(x, t)$ given that at $t = 0$ $\psi_0(x) = \sin x$ and $\partial\psi(x)/\partial t = \cos x$.

9.6.2   Determine $\psi(x, t)$ given that at $t = 0$ $\psi_0(x) = \delta(x)$ (Dirac delta function) and the initial time derivative of ψ is zero.

9.6.3   Determine $\psi(x, t)$ given that at $t = 0$ $\psi_0(x)$ is a single square-wave pulse as defined below, and the initial time derivative of ψ is zero.

$$\psi_0(x) = 0, \quad |x| > a/2, \quad \psi_0(x) = 1/a, \quad |x| < a/2.$$

9.6.4   Determine $\psi(x, t)$ given that at $t = 0$ $\psi_0 = 0$ for all x, but $\partial\psi/\partial t = \sin(x)$.

9.7   HEAT-FLOW, OR DIFFUSION PDE

Here we return to a parabolic PDE to develop methods that adapt a special solution of a PDE to boundary conditions by introducing parameters. The methods are fairly general and apply to other second-order PDEs with constant coefficients as well. To some extent, they are complementary to the earlier basic separation method for finding solutions in a systematic way.

We consider the 3-D time-dependent diffusion PDE for an isotropic medium, using it to describe heat flow subject to given boundary conditions. Assuming isotropy actually is not much of a restriction because, in case we have different (constant) rates of diffusion in different directions, for example, in wood, our heat-flow PDE takes the form

$$\frac{\partial\psi}{\partial t} = a^2\frac{\partial^2\psi}{\partial x^2} + b^2\frac{\partial^2\psi}{\partial y^2} + c^2\frac{\partial^2\psi}{\partial z^2}, \tag{9.96}$$

if we put the coordinate axes along the principal directions of anisotropy. Now we simply rescale the coordinates using the substitutions $x = a\xi, y = b\eta, z = c\zeta$ to get back the original isotropic form of Eq. (9.96),

$$\frac{\partial\Phi}{\partial t} = \frac{\partial^2\Phi}{\partial\xi^2} + \frac{\partial^2\Phi}{\partial\eta^2} + \frac{\partial^2\Phi}{\partial\zeta^2}, \tag{9.97}$$

for the temperature distribution function $\Phi(\xi, \eta, \zeta, t) = \psi(x, y, z, t)$.

For simplicity, we first solve the time-dependent PDE for a homogeneous one-dimensional medium, a long metal rod in the x-direction, for which the PDE is

$$\frac{\partial\psi}{\partial t} = a^2\frac{\partial^2\psi}{\partial x^2}, \tag{9.98}$$

where the constant a measures the diffusivity, or heat conductivity, of the medium. We obtain solutions to this linear PDE with constant coefficients by the method of separation of variables, for which we set $\psi(x, t) = X(x)T(t)$, leading to the separate equations

$$\frac{1}{T}\frac{dT}{dt} = \beta, \quad \frac{1}{X}\frac{d^2X}{dx^2} = \frac{\beta}{a^2}.$$

These equations have, for any nonzero value of β, solutions $T = e^{\beta t}$ and $X = e^{\pm\alpha x}$, with $\alpha^2 = \beta/a^2$. We seek solutions whose time dependence decays exponentially at large t, that is, solutions with negative values of β, and therefore set $\alpha = i\omega$, $a^2 = -\omega^2$ for real ω, and have

$$\psi(x, t) = e^{i\omega x} e^{-\omega^2 a^2 t} = (\cos \omega x \pm i \sin \omega x) e^{-\omega^2 a^2 t}. \tag{9.99}$$

Note that $\beta = 0$, for which

$$\psi(x, t) = C_0' x + C_0, \tag{9.100}$$

is also included in the solution set for the PDE. If we use this solution for a rod of infinite length, we must set $C_0' = 0$ to avoid a nonphysical divergence; in any case, the value of C_0 is then the constant value that the temperature approaches at long times.

Forming real linear combinations of $\sin \omega x$ and $\cos \omega x$ with arbitrary coefficients, and keeping the $\beta = 0$ solution, we obtain from Eq. (9.99) for any choice of A, B, ω, C_0', and C_0, a solution

$$\psi(x, t) = (A \cos \omega x + B \sin \omega x) e^{-\omega^2 a^2 t} + C_0' x + C_0. \tag{9.101}$$

Solutions for different values of these parameters can now be combined as needed to form an overall solution consistent with the required boundary conditions.

If the rod we are studying is finite in length, it may be that the boundary conditions can be satisfied if we restrict ω to discrete nonzero values that are multiples of a basic value ω_0. For a rod of infinite length, it may be better to let ω assume a continuous range of values, so that $\psi(x, t)$ will have the general form

$$\psi(x, t) = \int [A(\omega) \cos \omega x + B(\omega) \sin \omega x] e^{-a^2 \omega^2 t} d\omega + C_0. \tag{9.102}$$

We call specific attention to the fact that

- Forming linear combinations of solutions by summation or integration over parameters is a powerful and standard method for generalizing specific PDE solutions in order to adapt them to boundary conditions.

Example 9.7.1   A Specific Boundary Condition

Let us solve a 1-D case explicitly, where the temperature at time $t = 0$ is $\psi_0(x) = 1 =$ constant in the interval between $x = +1$ and $x = -1$ and zero for $x > 1$ and $x < -1$. At the ends, $x = \pm 1$, the temperature is always held at zero. Note that this problem, including its initial conditions, has even parity, $\psi_0(x) = \psi_0(-x)$, so $\psi(x, t)$ must also be even.

We choose the spatial solutions of Eq. (9.98) to be of the form given in Eq. (9.101), but restricted to $C_0' = C_0 = 0$ (since the $t \to \infty$ limit of $\psi(x, t)$ is zero for the entire range $-1 \le x \le 1$), and to $\cos(l\pi x/2)$ for odd integer l, because these functions are the even-parity members of an orthonormal basis for the interval $-1 \le x \le 1$ that satisfy the boundary condition $\psi = 0$ at $x = \pm 1$. Then, at $t = 0$ our solution takes the form

$$\psi(x, 0) = \sum_{l=1}^{\infty} a_l \cos \frac{\pi l x}{2}, \quad -1 < x < 1,$$

and we need to choose the coefficients a_l so that $\psi(x, 0) = 1$.

Using the orthonormality, we compute

$$a_l = \int_{-1}^{1} 1 \cdot \cos \frac{\pi l x}{2} = \frac{2}{l\pi} \sin \frac{\pi l x}{2} \Big|_{x=-1}^{1}$$

$$= \frac{4}{\pi l} \sin \frac{l\pi}{2} = \frac{4(-1)^m}{(2m+1)\pi}, \quad l = 2m+1.$$

Including its time dependence, the full solution is given by the series

$$\psi(x,t) = \frac{4}{\pi} \sum_{m=0}^{\infty} \frac{(-1)^m}{2m+1} \cos\left[(2m+1)\frac{\pi x}{2}\right] e^{-t((2m+1)\pi a/2)^2}, \tag{9.103}$$

which converges absolutely for $t > 0$ but only conditionally at $t = 0$, as a result of the discontinuity at $x = \pm 1$. ∎

We are now ready to consider the diffusion equation in three dimensions. We start by assuming a solution of the form $\psi = f(x, y, z)T(t)$, and separate the spatial from the time dependence. As in the 1-D case, $T(t)$ will have exponentials as solutions, and we can choose the solution that decays exponentially at large t. Assigning the separation constant the value $-k^2$, so that the time dependence is $\exp(-k^2 t)$, the separated equation in the spatial coordinates takes the form

$$\frac{\partial^2 f}{\partial x^2} + \frac{\partial^2 f}{\partial y^2} + \frac{\partial^2 f}{\partial z^2} + k^2 f = 0, \tag{9.104}$$

which we recognize as the **Helmholtz** equation. Assuming that we can solve this equation for various values of k^2 by further separations of variables or by other means, we can form whatever sum or integral of individual solutions that may be needed to satisfy the boundary conditions.

Alternate Solutions

In an alternative approach to the heat flow equation, we now return to the one-dimensional PDE, Eq. (9.98), seeking solutions of a new functional form $\psi(x,t) = u(x/\sqrt{t})$, which is suggested by dimensional considerations and experimental data. Substituting $u(\xi)$, $\xi = x/\sqrt{t}$, into Eq. (9.98) using

$$\frac{\partial \psi}{\partial x} = \frac{u'}{\sqrt{t}}, \quad \frac{\partial^2 \psi}{\partial x^2} = \frac{u''}{t}, \quad \frac{\partial \psi}{\partial t} = -\frac{x}{2\sqrt{t^3}} u' \tag{9.105}$$

with the notation $u'(\xi) \equiv du/d\xi$, the PDE is reduced to the ODE

$$2a^2 u''(\xi) + \xi u'(\xi) = 0. \tag{9.106}$$

Writing this ODE as

$$\frac{u''}{u'} = -\frac{\xi}{2a^2},$$

we can integrate it once to get $\ln u' = -\xi^2/4a^2 + \ln C_1$, where C_1 is an integration constant. Exponentiating and integrating again we find the general solution

$$u(\xi) = C_1 \int_0^\xi e^{-\xi^2/4a^2} d\xi + C_2, \qquad (9.107)$$

which contains two integration constants C_i. We initialize this solution at time $t = 0$ to temperature $+1$ for $x > 0$ and -1 for $x < 0$, corresponding to $u(\infty) = +1$ and $u(-\infty) = -1$. Noting that

$$\int_0^\infty e^{-\xi^2/4a^2} d\xi = a\sqrt{\pi},$$

a case of the integral evaluated in Eq. (1.148), we obtain

$$u(\infty) = a\sqrt{\pi} C_1 + C_2 = 1, \quad u(-\infty) = -a\sqrt{\pi} C_1 + C_2 = -1,$$

which fixes the constants $C_1 = 1/a\sqrt{\pi}$, $C_2 = 0$. We therefore have the specific solution

$$\psi = \frac{1}{a\sqrt{\pi}} \int_0^{x/\sqrt{t}} e^{-\xi^2/4a^2} d\xi = \frac{2}{\sqrt{\pi}} \int_0^{x/2a\sqrt{t}} e^{-v^2} dv = \operatorname{erf}\left(\frac{x}{2a\sqrt{t}}\right), \qquad (9.108)$$

where **erf** is the standard name for Gauss' error function (one of the special functions listed in Table 1.2). We need to generalize this specific solution to adapt it to boundary conditions.

To this end we now generate **new solutions of the PDE with constant coefficients by differentiating the special solution** given in Eq. (9.108). In other words, if $\psi(x, t)$ solves the PDE in Eq. (9.98), so do $\partial\psi/\partial t$ and $\partial\psi/\partial x$, because these derivatives and the differentiations of the PDE commute; that is, the order in which they are carried out does not matter. Note carefully that this method no longer works if any coefficient of the PDE depends on t or x explicitly. However, PDEs with constant coefficients dominate in physics. Examples are Newton's equations of motion in classical mechanics, the wave equations of electrodynamics, and Poisson's and Laplace's equations in electrostatics and gravity. Even Einstein's nonlinear field equations of general relativity take on this special form in local geodesic coordinates.

Therefore, by differentiating Eq. (9.108) with respect to x, we find the simpler, more basic solution,

$$\psi_1(x, t) = \frac{1}{a\sqrt{t\pi}} e^{-x^2/4a^2 t}, \qquad (9.109)$$

and, repeating the process, another basic solution

$$\psi_2(x, t) = \frac{x}{2a^3\sqrt{t^3\pi}} e^{-x^2/4a^2 t}. \qquad (9.110)$$

Again, these solutions have to be generalized to adapt them to boundary conditions. And there is yet another method of generating new solutions of a PDE with constant coefficients: We can **translate** a given solution, for example, $\psi_1(x, t) \to \psi_1(x - \alpha, t)$, and then

integrate over the translation parameter α. Therefore,

$$\psi(x,t) = \frac{1}{2a\sqrt{t\pi}} \int_{-\infty}^{\infty} C(\alpha)e^{-(x-\alpha)^2/4a^2t}\,d\alpha \tag{9.111}$$

is again a solution, which we rewrite using the substitution

$$\xi = \frac{x-\alpha}{2a\sqrt{t}}, \quad \alpha = x - 2a\xi\sqrt{t}, \quad d\alpha = -2a\sqrt{t}d\xi. \tag{9.112}$$

These substitutions lead to

$$\psi(x,t) = \frac{1}{\sqrt{\pi}} \int_{-\infty}^{\infty} C(x - 2a\xi\sqrt{t})e^{-\xi^2}\,d\xi, \tag{9.113}$$

a solution of our PDE. Equation (9.113) is in a form permitting us to understand the significance of the weight function $C(x)$ from the translation method. If we set $t = 0$ in that equation, the function C in the integrand then becomes independent of ξ, and the integral can then be recognized as

$$\int_{-\infty}^{\infty} e^{-\xi^2}\,d\xi = \sqrt{\pi},$$

a well-known result equivalent to Eq. (1.148). Equation (9.113) then becomes the simpler form

$$\psi(x,0) = C(x), \quad \text{or} \quad C(x) = \psi_0(x),$$

where ψ_0 is the initial spatial distribution of ψ. Using this notation, we can write the solution to our PDE as

$$\psi(x,t) = \frac{1}{\sqrt{\pi}} \int_{-\infty}^{\infty} \psi_0(x - 2a\xi\sqrt{t})e^{-\xi^2}\,d\xi, \tag{9.114}$$

a form that explicitly displays the role of the boundary (initial) condition. From Eq. (9.114) we see that the initial temperature distribution, $\psi_0(x)$, spreads out over time and is damped by the Gaussian weight function.

Example 9.7.2   SPECIAL BOUNDARY CONDITION AGAIN

We consider now a problem similar to Example 9.7.1, but instead of keeping $\psi = 0$ at all times at $x = \pm 1$, we regard the system as infinite in length, with $\psi_0 = 0$ everywhere except for $|x| < 1$, where $\psi_0 = 1$. This change makes Eq. (9.114) usable, because our PDE now applies over the range $(-\infty, \infty)$, and heat will flow (and temporarily increase the temperature) at and beyond $|x| = 1$.

The range of $\psi_0(x)$ corresponds to a range of ξ with endpoints found from $x - 2a\xi\sqrt{t} = \pm 1$, so our solution becomes

$$\psi(x,t) = \frac{1}{\sqrt{\pi}} \int_{(x-1)/2a\sqrt{t}}^{(x+1)/2a\sqrt{t}} e^{-\xi^2}\,d\xi.$$

In terms of the error function, we can also write this solution as

$$\psi(x, t) = \frac{1}{2}\left[\text{erf}\left(\frac{x+1}{2a\sqrt{t}}\right) - \text{erf}\left(\frac{x-1}{2a\sqrt{t}}\right)\right]. \tag{9.115}$$

Equation (9.115) applies for all x, including $|x| > 1$.   ∎

Next we consider the problem of heat flow for an extended **spherically symmetric** medium centered at the origin, suggesting that we should use polar coordinates r, θ, φ. We expect a solution of the form $u(r, t)$. Using Eq. (3.158) for the Laplacian, we find the PDE

$$\frac{\partial u}{\partial t} = a^2\left(\frac{\partial^2 u}{\partial r^2} + \frac{2}{r}\frac{\partial u}{\partial r}\right), \tag{9.116}$$

which we transform to the 1-D heat-flow PDE by the substitution

$$u = \frac{v(r, t)}{r}, \quad \frac{\partial u}{\partial r} = \frac{1}{r}\frac{\partial v}{\partial r} - \frac{v}{r^2}, \quad \frac{\partial u}{\partial t} = \frac{1}{r}\frac{\partial v}{\partial t},$$

$$\frac{\partial^2 u}{\partial r^2} = \frac{1}{r}\frac{\partial^2 v}{\partial r^2} - \frac{2}{r^2}\frac{\partial v}{\partial r} + \frac{2v}{r^3}. \tag{9.117}$$

This yields the PDE

$$\frac{\partial v}{\partial t} = a^2\frac{\partial^2 v}{\partial r^2}. \tag{9.118}$$

Example 9.7.3   SPHERICALLY SYMMETRIC HEAT FLOW

Let us apply the 1-D heat-flow PDE to a spherically symmetric heat flow under fairly common boundary conditions, where x is replaced by the radial variable. Initially we have zero temperature everywhere. Then, at time $t = 0$, a finite amount of heat energy Q is released at the origin, spreading evenly in all directions. What is the resulting spatial and temporal temperature distribution?

Inspecting our special solution in Eq. (9.110) we see that, for $t \to 0$, the temperature

$$\frac{v(r, t)}{r} = \frac{C}{\sqrt{t^3}}e^{-r^2/4a^2 t} \tag{9.119}$$

goes to zero for all $r \neq 0$, so zero initial temperature is guaranteed. As $t \to \infty$, the temperature $v/r \to 0$ for all r including the origin, which is implicit in our boundary conditions. The constant C can be determined from energy conservation, which gives (for arbitrary t) the constraint

$$Q = \sigma\rho\int\frac{v}{r}d\tau = \frac{4\pi\sigma\rho C}{\sqrt{t^3}}\int_0^\infty r^2 e^{-r^2/4a^2 t}dr = 8\sqrt{\pi^3}\sigma\rho a^3 C, \tag{9.120}$$

where ρ is the constant density of the medium and σ is its specific heat. The final result in Eq. (9.120) is obtained by first making a change of variable from r to $\xi = r/2a\sqrt{t}$, obtaining

$$\int_0^\infty e^{-r^2/4a^2t} r^2\, dr = (2a\sqrt{t})^3 \int_0^\infty e^{-\xi^2} \xi^2\, d\xi,$$

then evaluating the ξ integral via an integration by parts:

$$\int_0^\infty e^{-\xi^2} \xi^2\, d\xi = -\frac{\xi}{2} e^{-\xi^2}\Big|_0^\infty + \frac{1}{2}\int_0^\infty e^{-\xi^2}\, d\xi = \frac{\sqrt{\pi}}{4}.$$

The temperature, as given by Eq. (9.119) at any moment, i.e., at fixed t, is a Gaussian distribution that flattens out as time increases, because its width is proportional to $\sqrt{t}$. As a function of time the temperature at any fixed point is proportional to $t^{-3/2}e^{-T/t}$, with $T \equiv r^2/4a^2$. This functional form shows that the temperature rises from zero to a maximum and then falls off to zero again for large times. To find the maximum, we set

$$\frac{d}{dt}\left(t^{-3/2}e^{-T/t}\right) = t^{-5/2}e^{-T/t}\left(\frac{T}{t} - \frac{3}{2}\right) = 0, \tag{9.121}$$

from which we find $t_{max} = 2T/3 = r^2/6a^2$. The temperature maximum arrives at later times at larger distances from the origin. ∎

In the case of **cylindrical symmetry** (in the plane $z = 0$ in plane polar coordinates $\rho = \sqrt{x^2 + y^2}, \varphi$), we look for a temperature $\psi = u(\rho, t)$ that then satisfies the ODE (using Eq. (2.35) in the diffusion equation)

$$\frac{\partial u}{\partial t} = a^2\left(\frac{\partial^2 u}{\partial \rho^2} + \frac{1}{\rho}\frac{\partial u}{\partial \rho}\right), \tag{9.122}$$

which is the planar analog of Eq. (9.118). This ODE also has solutions with the functional dependence $\rho/\sqrt{t} \equiv r$. Upon substituting

$$u = v\left(\frac{\rho}{\sqrt{t}}\right), \quad \frac{\partial u}{\partial t} = -\frac{\rho v'}{2t^{3/2}}, \quad \frac{\partial u}{\partial \rho} = \frac{v'}{\sqrt{t}}, \quad \frac{\partial^2 u}{\partial \rho^2} = \frac{v'}{t} \tag{9.123}$$

into Eq. (9.122) with the notation $v' \equiv dv/dr$, we find the ODE

$$a^2 v'' + \left(\frac{a^2}{r} + \frac{r}{2}\right)v' = 0. \tag{9.124}$$

This is a first-order ODE for v', which we can integrate when we separate the variables v and r as

$$\frac{v''}{v'} = -\left(\frac{1}{r} + \frac{r}{2a^2}\right). \tag{9.125}$$

This yields

$$v(r) = \frac{C}{r}e^{-r^2/4a^2} = C\frac{\sqrt{t}}{\rho}e^{-\rho^2/4a^2t}. \tag{9.126}$$

This special solution for cylindrical symmetry can be similarly generalized and adapted to boundary conditions, as for the spherical case. Finally, the z-dependence can be factored in, because z separates from the plane polar radial variable ρ.

Exercises

9.7.1   For a homogeneous spherical solid with constant thermal diffusivity, K, and no heat sources, the equation of heat conduction becomes

$$\frac{\partial T(r,t)}{\partial t} = K\nabla^2 T(r,t).$$

Assume a solution of the form

$$T = R(r)T(t)$$

and separate variables. Show that the radial equation may take on the standard form

$$r^2\frac{d^2 R}{dr^2} + 2r\frac{dR}{dr} + \alpha^2 r^2 R = 0,$$

and that $\sin\alpha r/r$ and $\cos\alpha r/r$ are its solutions.

9.7.2   Separate variables in the thermal diffusion equation of Exercise 9.7.1 in circular cylindrical coordinates. Assume that you can neglect end effects and take $T = T(\rho,t)$.

9.7.3   Solve the PDE

$$\frac{\partial\psi}{\partial t} = a^2\frac{\partial^2\psi}{\partial x^2},$$

to obtain $\psi(x,t)$ for a rod of infinite extent (in both the $+x$ and $-x$ directions), with a heat pulse at time $t = 0$ that corresponds to $\psi_0(x) = A\delta(x)$.

9.7.4   Solve the same PDE as in Exercise 9.7.3 for a rod of length L, with position on the rod given by the variable x, with the two ends of the rod at $x = 0$ and $x = L$ kept (at all times t) at the respective temperatures $T = 1$ and $T = 0$, and with the rod initially at $T(x) = 0$, for $0 < x \le L$.

9.8   SUMMARY

This chapter has provided an overview of methods for the solution of first- and second-order linear PDEs, with emphasis on homogeneous second-order PDEs subject to boundary conditions that either determine unique solutions or define eigenvalue problems. We found that the usual boundary conditions are identified as of Dirichlet type (solution specified on boundary), Neumann type (normal derivative of solution specified on boundary), or Cauchy type (both solution and its normal derivative specified). Applicable types of boundary conditions depend on the classification of the PDE; second-order PDEs are classified as hyperbolic (e.g., wave equation), elliptic (e.g., Laplace equation), or parabolic (e.g., heat/diffusion equation).

The method of widest applicability to the solution of PDEs is the method of separation of variables, which, when effective, reduces a PDE to a set of ODEs. The chapter has presented a very small number of complete PDE solutions to illustrate the technique. A wider variety of examples only becomes possible when we are prepared to exploit the properties of the special functions that are the solutions of various ODEs, and, as a result, fuller illustration of PDE solutions will be provided in the chapters that discuss these special functions. We point out, in particular, that general PDEs with spherical symmetry all have the same angular solutions, known as **spherical harmonics**. These, and the functions from which they are constructed (Legendre polynomials and associated Legendre functions), are the subject matter of Chapters 15 and 16. Some spherically symmetric problems have radial solutions that can be identified as **spherical Bessel functions**; these are treated in the Bessel function chapter (Chapter 14).

PDE problems with cylindrical symmetry usually involve Bessel functions, often in ways more complex than in the examples of the present chapter. Further illustrations appear in Chapter 14.

This chapter has not attempted to discuss methods for the solution of inhomogeneous PDEs. That topic deserves its own chapter, and will be developed in Chapter 10.

Finally, we repeat an earlier observation: Fourier expansions (Chapter 19) and integral transforms (Chapter 20) can also have a role in the solution of PDEs, and applications of these techniques to PDEs are included in the appropriate chapters of this book.

Additional Readings

Bateman, H., *Partial Differential Equations of Mathematical Physics*. New York: Dover (1944), 1st ed. (1932). A wealth of applications of various partial differential equations in classical physics. Excellent examples of the use of different coordinate systems, including ellipsoidal, paraboloidal, toroidal coordinates, and so on.

Cohen, H., *Mathematics for Scientists and Engineers*. Englewood Cliffs, NJ: Prentice-Hall (1992).

Folland, G. B., *Introduction to Partial Differential Equations*, 2nd ed. Princeton, NJ: Princeton University Press (1995).

Guckenheimer, J., P. Holmes, and F. John, *Nonlinear Oscillations, Dynamical Systems and Bifurcations of Vector Fields*, revised ed. New York: Springer-Verlag (1990).

Gustafson, K. E., *Partial Differential Equations and Hilbert Space Methods*, 2nd ed., New York: Wiley (1987), reprinting Dover (1998).

Margenau, H., and G. M. Murphy, *The Mathematics of Physics and Chemistry*, 2nd ed. Princeton, NJ: Van Nostrand (1956). Chapter 5 covers curvilinear coordinates and 13 specific coordinate systems.

Morse, P. M., and H. Feshbach, *Methods of Theoretical Physics*. New York: McGraw-Hill (1953). Chapter 5 includes a description of several different coordinate systems. Note that Morse and Feshbach are not above using left-handed coordinate systems even for Cartesian coordinates. Elsewhere in this excellent (and difficult) book are many examples of the use of the various coordinate systems in solving physical problems. Chapter 6 discusses characteristics in detail.

CHAPTER 10

GREEN'S FUNCTIONS

In contrast to the linear differential operators that have been our main concern when formulating problems as differential equations, we now turn to methods involving integral operators, and in particular to those known as **Green's functions**. Green's-function methods enable the solution of a differential equation containing an inhomogeneous term (often called a **source term**) to be related to an integral operator containing the source. As a preliminary and elementary example, consider the problem of determining the potential $\psi(\mathbf{r})$ generated by a charge distribution whose charge density is $\rho(\mathbf{r})$. From the Poisson equation, we know that $\psi(\mathbf{r})$ satisfies

$$-\nabla^2 \psi(\mathbf{r}) = \frac{1}{\varepsilon_0}\, \rho(\mathbf{r}). \tag{10.1}$$

We also know, applying Coulomb's law to the potential at $\mathbf{r}_1$ produced by each element of charge $\rho(\mathbf{r}_2) d^3 r_2$, and assuming the space is empty except for the charge distribution, that

$$\psi(\mathbf{r}_1) = \frac{1}{4\pi\varepsilon_0} \int d^3 r_2 \frac{\rho(\mathbf{r}_2)}{|\mathbf{r}_1 - \mathbf{r}_2|}. \tag{10.2}$$

Here the integral is over the entire region where $\rho(\mathbf{r}_2) \neq 0$. We can view the right-hand side of Eq. (10.2) as an integral operator that converts ρ into ψ, and identify the **kernel** (the function of two variables, one of which is to be integrated) as the Green's function for this problem. Thus, we write

$$G(\mathbf{r}_1, \mathbf{r}_2) = \frac{1}{4\pi\varepsilon} \frac{1}{|\mathbf{r}_1 - \mathbf{r}_2|}, \tag{10.3}$$

$$\psi(\mathbf{r}_1) = \int d^3 r_2\, G(\mathbf{r}_1, \mathbf{r}_2)\rho(\mathbf{r}_2), \tag{10.4}$$

assigning our Green's function the symbol G (for "Green").

This example is preliminary because the response of more general problems to an inhomogeneous term will depend on the boundary conditions. For example, an electrostatics problem may include conductors whose surfaces will contain charge layers with magnitudes that depend on ρ and which will also contribute to the potential at general $\mathbf{r}$. It is elementary because the form of the Green's function will also depend on the differential equation to be solved, and often it will not be possible to obtain a Green's function in a simple, closed form.

The essential feature of any Green's function is that it provides a way to describe the response of the differential-equation solution to an arbitrary source term (in the presence of the boundary conditions). In our present example, $G(\mathbf{r}_1, \mathbf{r}_2)$ gives us the contribution to ψ at the point $\mathbf{r}_1$ produced by a point source of unit magnitude (a delta function) at the point $\mathbf{r}_2$. The fact that we can determine ψ everywhere by an integration is a consequence of the fact that our differential equation is linear, so each element of the source contributes additively. In the more general context of a PDE that depends on both spatial and time coordinates, Green's functions also appear as responses of the PDE solution to impulses at given positions and times.

The aim of this chapter is to identify some general properties of Green's functions, to survey methods for finding them, and to begin building connections between differential-operator and integral-operator methods for the description of physics problems. We start by considering problems in one dimension.

10.1 ONE-DIMENSIONAL PROBLEMS

Let's consider the second-order self-adjoint inhomogeneous ODE

$$\mathcal{L}y \equiv \frac{d}{dx}\left(p(x)\frac{dy}{dx}\right) + q(x)\,y = f(x), \tag{10.5}$$

which is to be satisfied on the range $a \le x \le b$ subject to homogeneous boundary conditions at $x = a$ and $x = b$ that will cause $\mathcal{L}$ to be Hermitian.[1] Our Green's function for this problem needs to satisfy the boundary conditions and the ODE

$$\mathcal{L}G(x, t) = \delta(x - t), \tag{10.6}$$

so that $y(x)$, the solution to Eq. (10.5) with its boundary conditions, can be obtained as

$$y(x) = \int_a^b G(x, t)\, f(t)\, dt. \tag{10.7}$$

To verify Eq. (10.7), simply apply $\mathcal{L}$:

$$\mathcal{L}y(x) = \int_a^b \mathcal{L}G(x, t)\, f(t)\, dt = \int_a^b \delta(x - t)\, f(t)\, dt = f(x).$$

---

[1] A **homogeneous** boundary condition is one that continues to be satisfied if the function satisfying it is multiplied by a scale factor. Most of the more commonly encountered types of boundary conditions are homogeneous, e.g., $y = 0$, $y' = 0$, even $c_1 y + c_2 y' = 0$. However, $y = c$ with c a nonzero constant is not homogeneous.

General Properties

To gain an understanding of the properties $G(x, t)$ must have, we first consider the result of integrating Eq. (10.6) over a small range of x that includes $x = t$. We have

$$\int_{t-\varepsilon}^{t+\varepsilon} \frac{d}{dx}\left[p(x)\frac{dG(x,t)}{dx}\right]dx + \int_{t-\varepsilon}^{t+\varepsilon} q(x)\,G(x,t)\,dx = \int_{t-\varepsilon}^{t+\varepsilon} \delta(t-x)\,dx,$$

which, carrying out some of the integrations, simplifies to

$$p(x)\frac{dG(x,t)}{dx}\bigg|_{t-\varepsilon}^{t+\varepsilon} + \int_{t-\varepsilon}^{t+\varepsilon} q(x)\,G(x,t)\,dx = 1. \tag{10.8}$$

It is clear that Eq. (10.8) cannot be satisfied in the limit of small ε if $G(x,t)$ and $dG(x,t)/dx$ are both continuous (in x) at $x = t$, but we can satisfy that equation if we require $G(x,t)$ to be continuous but accept a discontinuity in $dG(x,t)/dx$ at $x = t$. In particular, continuity in G will cause the integral containing $q(x)$ to vanish in the limit $\varepsilon \to 0$, and we are left with the requirement

$$\lim_{\varepsilon \to 0+}\left[\frac{dG(x,t)}{dx}\bigg|_{x=t+\varepsilon} - \frac{dG(x,t)}{dx}\bigg|_{x=t-\varepsilon}\right] = \frac{1}{p(t)}. \tag{10.9}$$

Thus, the discontinuous impulse at $x = t$ leads to a discontinuity in the x derivative of $G(x,t)$ at that x value. Note, however, that because of the integration in Eq. (10.7), the singularity in dG/dx does not lead to a similar singularity in the overall solution $y(x)$ in the usual case that $f(x)$ is continuous.

As a next step toward reaching understanding of the properties of Green's functions, let's expand $G(x,t)$ in the eigenfunctions of our operator $\mathcal{L}$, obtained subject to the boundary conditions already identified. Since $\mathcal{L}$ is Hermitian, its eigenfunctions can be chosen to be orthonormal on (a, b), with

$$\mathcal{L}\varphi_n(x) = \lambda_n\varphi_n(x), \quad \langle\varphi_n|\varphi_m\rangle = \delta_{nm}. \tag{10.10}$$

Expanding both the x and the t dependence of $G(x,t)$ in this orthonormal set (using the complex conjugates of the φ_n for the t expansion),

$$G(x,t) = \sum_{nm} g_{nm}\varphi_n(x)\varphi_m^*(t). \tag{10.11}$$

We also expand $\delta(x - t)$ in the same orthonormal set, according to Eq. (5.27):

$$\delta(x - t) = \sum_m \varphi_m(x)\varphi_m^*(t). \tag{10.12}$$

Inserting both these expansions into Eq. (10.6), we have before any simplification

$$\mathcal{L}\sum_{nm} g_{nm}\varphi_n(x)\varphi_m^*(t) = \sum_m \varphi_m(x)\varphi_m^*(t). \tag{10.13}$$

Applying $\mathcal{L}$, which operates only on $\varphi_n(x)$, Eq. (10.13) reduces to

$$\sum_{nm} \lambda_n g_{nm} \varphi_n(x) \varphi_m^*(t) = \sum_m \varphi_m(x) \varphi_m^*(t).$$

Taking scalar products in the x and t domains, we find that $g_{nm} = \delta_{nm}/\lambda_n$, so $G(x,t)$ must have the expansion

$$G(x,t) = \sum_n \frac{\varphi_n^*(t) \varphi_n(x)}{\lambda_n}. \tag{10.14}$$

The above analysis fails in the case that any λ_n is zero, but we shall not pursue that special case further.

The importance of Eq. (10.14) does not lie in its dubious value as a computational tool, but in the fact that it reveals the symmetry of G:

$$G(x,t) = G(t,x)^*. \tag{10.15}$$

Form of Green's Function

The properties we have identified for G are sufficient to enable its more complete identification, given a Hermitian operator $\mathcal{L}$ **and its boundary conditions**. We continue with the study of problems on an interval (a,b) with one homogeneous boundary condition at each endpoint of the interval.

Given a value of t, it is necessary for x in the range $a \le x < t$ that $G(x,t)$ have an x dependence $y_1(x)$ that is a solution to the homogeneous equation $\mathcal{L} = 0$ and that also satisfies the boundary condition at $x = a$. The most general $G(x,t)$ satisfying these conditions must have the form

$$G(x,t) = y_1(x)h_1(t), \quad (x < t), \tag{10.16}$$

where $h_1(t)$ is presently unknown. Conversely, in the range $t < x \le b$, it is necessary that $G(x,t)$ have the form

$$G(x,t) = y_2(x)h_2(t), \quad (x > t), \tag{10.17}$$

where y_2 is a solution of $\mathcal{L} = 0$ that satisfies the boundary condition at $x = b$. The symmetry condition, Eq. (10.15), permits Eqs. (10.16) and (10.17) to be consistent only if $h_2^* = A\, y_1$ and $h_1^* = A\, y_2$, with A a constant that is still to be determined. Assuming that y_1 and y_2 can be chosen to be real, we are led to the conclusion that

$$G(x,t) = \begin{cases} A\, y_1(x) y_2(t), & x < t, \\ A\, y_2(x) y_1(t), & x > t, \end{cases} \tag{10.18}$$

where $\mathcal{L} y_i = 0$, with y_1 satisfying the boundary condition at $x = a$ and y_2 satisfying that at $x = b$. The value of A in Eq. (10.18) depends, of course, on the scale at which the y_i have been specified, and must be set to a value that is consistent with Eq. (10.9). As applied here, that condition reduces to

$$A\Big[y_2'(t) y_1(t) - y_1'(t) y_2(t) \Big] = \frac{1}{p(t)},$$

equivalent to

$$A = \left(p(t)\left[y_2'(t)y_1(t) - y_1'(t)y_2(t)\right]\right)^{-1}. \tag{10.19}$$

Despite its appearance, A does not depend on t. The expression involving the y_i is their Wronskian, and it has a value proportional to $1/p(t)$. See Exercise 7.6.11.

It is instructive to verify that the form for $G(x, t)$ given by Eq. (10.18) causes Eq. (10.7) to generate the desired solution to the ODE $\mathcal{L}y = f$. To this end, we obtain an explicit form for $y(x)$:

$$y(x) = A\, y_2(x) \int_a^x y_1(t) f(t)\, dt + A\, y_1(x) \int_x^b y_2(t) f(t)\, dt. \tag{10.20}$$

From Eq. (10.20) it is easy to verify that the boundary conditions on $y(x)$ are satisfied; if $x = a$ the first of the two integrals vanishes, and the second is proportional to y_1; corresponding remarks apply at $x = b$.

It remains to show that Eq. (10.20) yields $\mathcal{L}y = f$. Differentiating with respect to x, we first have

$$y'(x) = A\, y_2'(x) \int_a^x y_1(t) f(t)\, dt + A\, y_2(x)y_1(x)f(x)$$

$$+ A\, y_1'(x) \int_x^b y_2(t) f(t)\, dt - A\, y_1(x)y_2(x)f(x)$$

$$= A\, y_2'(x) \int_a^x y_1(t) f(t)\, dt + A\, y_1'(x) \int_x^b y_2(t) f(t)\, dt. \tag{10.21}$$

Proceeding to $(py')'$:

$$\left[p(x)y'(x)\right]' = A\left[p(x)y_2'(x)\right]' \int_a^x y_1(t) f(t)\, dt + A\left[p(x)y_2'(x)\right]y_1(x)f(x)$$

$$+ A\left[p(x)y_1'(x)\right]' \int_x^b y_2(t) f(t)\, dt - A\left[p(x)y_1'(x)\right]y_2(x)f(x). \tag{10.22}$$

Combining Eq. (10.22) and $q(x)$ times Eq. (10.20), many terms drop because $\mathcal{L}y_1 = \mathcal{L}y_2 = 0$, leaving

$$\mathcal{L}y(x) = A\, p(x)\left[y_2'(x)y_1(x) - y_1'(x)y_2(x)\right]f(x) = f(x), \tag{10.23}$$

where the final simplification took place using Eq. (10.19).

Example 10.1.1   SIMPLE SECOND-ORDER ODE

Consider the ODE

$$-y'' = f(x),$$

with boundary conditions $y(0) = y(1) = 0$. The corresponding homogeneous equation $-y'' = 0$ has general solution $y_0 = c_0 + c_1 x$; from these we construct the solution $y_1 = x$ that satisfies $y_1(0) = 0$ and the solution $y_2 = 1 - x$, satisfying $y_2(1) = 0$. For this ODE, the coefficient $p(x) = -1$, $y_1'(x) = 1$, $y_2'(x) = -1$, and the constant A in the Green's function is

$$A = \left[(-1)[(-1)(x) - (1)(1-x)] \right]^{-1} = 1.$$

Our Green's function is therefore

$$G(x, t) = \begin{cases} x(1-t), & 0 \le x < t, \\ t(1-x), & t < x \le 1. \end{cases}$$

Assuming we can perform the integral, we can now solve this ODE with boundary conditions for any function $f(x)$. For example, if $f(x) = \sin \pi x$, our solution would be

$$y(x) = \int_0^1 G(x, t) \sin \pi t \, dt = (1 - x) \int_0^x t \sin \pi t \, dt + x \int_x^1 (1 - t) \sin \pi t \, dt$$

$$= \frac{1}{\pi^2} \sin \pi x.$$

The correctness of this result is easily checked.

One advantage of the Green's function formalism is that we do not need to repeat most of our work if we change the function $f(x)$. If we now take $f(x) = \cos \pi x$, we get

$$y(x) = \frac{1}{\pi^2} \left(2x - 1 + \cos \pi x \right).$$

Note that our solution takes full account of the boundary conditions.   ∎

Other Boundary Conditions

Occasionally one encounters problems other than the Hermitian second-order ODEs we have been considering. Some, but not always all of the Green's-function properties we have identified, carry over to such problems.

Consider first the possibility that we may have nonhomogeneous boundary conditions, such as the problem $\mathcal{L}y = f$ with $y(a) = c_1$ and $y(b) = c_2$, with one or both c_i nonzero. This problem can be converted into one with homogeneous boundary conditions by making a change of the dependent variable from y to

$$u = y - \frac{c_1(b - x) + c_2(x - a)}{b - a}.$$

In terms of u, the boundary conditions are homogeneous: $u(a) = u(b) = 0$. A nonhomogeneous condition on the derivative, e.g., $y'(a) = c$, can be treated analogously.

Another possibility for a second-order ODE is that we may have two boundary conditions at one endpoint and none at the other; this situation corresponds to an initial-value problem, and has lost the close connection to Sturm-Liouville eigenvalue problems. The result is that Green's functions can still be constructed by invoking the condition of continuity in $G(x, t)$ at $x = t$ and the prescribed discontinuity in $\partial G/\partial x$, but they will no longer be symmetric.

Example 10.1.2 INITIAL VALUE PROBLEM

Consider

$$\mathcal{L}y = \frac{d^2 y}{dx^2} + y = f(x), \tag{10.24}$$

with the initial conditions $y(0) = 0$ and $y'(0) = 0$. This operator $\mathcal{L}$ has $p(x) = 1$.

We start by noting that the homogeneous equation $\mathcal{L}y = 0$ has the two linearly independent solutions $y_1 = \sin x$ and $y_2 = \cos x$. However, the only linear combination of these solutions that satisfies the boundary condition at $x = 0$ is the trivial solution $y = 0$, so our Green's function for $x < t$ can only be $G(x, t) = 0$. On the other hand, for the region $x > t$ there are no boundary conditions to serve as constraints, and in that region we are free to write

$$G(x, t) = C_1(t)y_1 + C_2(t)y_2, \quad \text{or} \quad G(x, t) = C_1(t)\sin x + C_2(t)\cos x, \quad x > t.$$

We now impose the requirements

$$G(t_-, t) = G(t_+, t) \longrightarrow 0 = C_1(t)\sin t + C_2(t)\cos t,$$

$$\frac{\partial G}{\partial x}(t_+, t) - \frac{\partial G}{\partial x}(t_-, t) = \frac{1}{p(t)} = 1 \longrightarrow C_1(t)\cos t - C_2(t)\sin t - (0) = 1.$$

These equations can now be solved, yielding $C_1(t) = \cos t$, $C_2(t) = -\sin t$, so for $x > t$

$$G(x, t) = \cos t \sin x - \sin t \cos x = \sin(x - t).$$

Thus, the complete specification of $G(x, t)$ is

$$G(x, t) = \begin{cases} 0, & x < t, \\ \sin(x - t), & x > t. \end{cases} \tag{10.25}$$

The lack of correspondence to a Sturm-Liouville problem is reflected in the lack of symmetry of the Green's function. Nevertheless, the Green's function can be used to construct the solution to Eq. (10.24) subject to its initial conditions:

$$y(x) = \int_0^\infty G(x,t)\,f(t)\,dt$$

$$= \int_0^x \sin(x-t)\,f(t)\,dt. \tag{10.26}$$

Note that if we regard x as a time variable, our solution at "time" x is only influenced by source contributions from times t prior to x, so Eq. (10.24) obeys causality.

We conclude this example by observing that we can verify that $y(x)$ as given by Eq. (10.26) is the correct solution to our problem. Details are left as Exercise 10.1.3. ∎

Example 10.1.3   BOUNDARY AT INFINITY

Consider

$$\left(\frac{d^2}{dx^2}+k^2\right)\psi(x) = g(x), \tag{10.27}$$

an equation essentially similar to one we have already studied several times, but now with boundary conditions that correspond (when multiplied by $e^{-i\omega t}$) to an outgoing wave.

The general solution to Eq. (10.27) with $g = 0$ is spanned by the two functions

$$y_1 = e^{-ikx} \quad \text{and} \quad y_2 = e^{+ikx}.$$

The outgoing wave boundary condition means that for large positive x we must have the solution y_2, while for large negative x the solution must be y_1. This information suffices to indicate that the Green's function for this problem must have the form

$$G(x,x') = \begin{cases} A y_1(x')y_2(x), & x > x', \\ A y_2(x')y_1(x), & x < x'. \end{cases}$$

We find the coefficient A from Eq. (10.19), in which $p(x) = 1$:

$$A = \frac{1}{y_2'(x)y_1(x) - y_1'(x)y_2(x)} = \frac{1}{ik+ik} = -\frac{i}{2k}.$$

Combining these results, we reach

$$G(x,x') = -\frac{i}{2k}\exp\left(i|x-x'|\right). \tag{10.28}$$

This result is yet another illustration that the Green's function depends on boundary conditions as well as on the differential equation.

Verification that this Green's function yields the desired problem solution is the topic of Exercise 10.1.8. ∎

Relation to Integral Equations

Consider now an eigenvalue equation of the form

$$\mathcal{L}y(x) = \lambda y(x), \tag{10.29}$$

where we assume $\mathcal{L}$ to be self-adjoint and subject to the boundary conditions $y(a) = y(b) = 0$. We can proceed formally by treating Eq. (10.29) as an inhomogeneous equation whose right-hand side is the particular function $\lambda y(x)$. To do so, we would first find the Green's function $G(x, t)$ for the operator $\mathcal{L}$ and the given boundary conditions, after which, as in Eq. (10.7), we could write

$$y(x) = \lambda \int_a^b G(x, t)\, y(t)\, dt. \tag{10.30}$$

Equation (10.30) is not a solution to our eigenvalue problem, since the unknown function $y(x)$ appears on both sides and, moreover, it does not tell us the possible values of the eigenvalue λ. What we have accomplished, however, is to convert our eigenvalue ODE and its boundary conditions into an **integral equation** which we can regard as an alternate starting point for solution of our eigenvalue problem.

Our generation of Eq. (10.30) shows that it is implied by Eq. (10.29). If we can also show that we can connect these equations in the reverse order, namely that Eq. (10.30) implies Eq. (10.29), we can then conclude that they are equivalent formulations of the same eigenvalue problem. We proceed by applying $\mathcal{L}$ to Eq. (10.30), labeling it $\mathcal{L}_x$ to make clear that it is an operator on x, not t:

$$\mathcal{L}_x y(x) = \lambda \mathcal{L}_x \int_a^b G(x, t) y(t)\, dt$$

$$= \lambda \int_a^b \mathcal{L}_x G(x, t) y(t)\, dt = \lambda \int_a^b \delta(x - t) y(t)\, dt$$

$$= \lambda y(x). \tag{10.31}$$

The above analysis shows that under rather general circumstances we will be able to convert an eigenvalue equation based on an ODE into an entirely equivalent eigenvalue equation based on an integral equation. Note that to specify completely the ODE eigenvalue equation we had to make an explicit identification of the accompanying boundary conditions, while the corresponding integral equation appears to be entirely self-contained. Of course, what has happened is that the effect of the boundary conditions has influenced the specification of the Green's function that is the **kernel** of the integral equation.

Conversion to an integral equation may be useful for two reasons, the more practical of which is that the integral equation may suggest different computational procedures for solution of our eigenvalue problem. There is also a fundamental mathematical reason why an integral-equation formulation may be preferred: It is that integral operators, such as that in Eq. (10.30), are **bounded** operators (meaning that their application to a function y of finite norm produces a result whose norm is also finite). On the other hand, differential operators are **unbounded**; their application to a function of finite norm can produce a result of unbounded norm. Stronger theorems can be developed for operators that are bounded.

We close by making the now obvious observation that Green's functions provide the link between differential-operator and integral-operator formulations of the same problem.

Example 10.1.4   DIFFERENTIAL VS. INTEGRAL FORMULATION

Here we return to an eigenvalue problem we have already treated several times in various contexts, namely

$$-y''(x) = \lambda y(x),$$

subject to boundary conditions $y(0) = y(1) = 0$. In Example 10.1.1 we found the Green's function for this problem to be

$$G(x,t) = \begin{cases} x(1-t), & 0 \le x < t, \\ t(1-x), & t < x \le 1, \end{cases}$$

and, following Eq. (10.30), our eigenvalue problem can be rewritten as

$$y(x) = \lambda \int_0^1 G(x,t)\, y(t)\, dt. \tag{10.32}$$

Methods for solution of integral equations will not be discussed until Chapter 21, but we can easily verify that the well-known solution set for this problem,

$$y = \sin n\pi x, \quad \lambda_n = n^2 \pi^2, \quad n = 1, 2, \ldots,$$

also solves Eq. (10.32). ∎

Exercises

10.1.1   Show that

$$G(x,t) = \begin{cases} x, & 0 \le x < t, \\ t, & t < x \le 1, \end{cases}$$

is the Green's function for the operator $\mathcal{L} = -d^2/dx^2$ and the boundary conditions $y(0) = 0$, $y'(1) = 0$.

10.1.2   Find the Green's function for

(a) $\mathcal{L}y(x) = \dfrac{d^2 y(x)}{dx^2} + y(x), \quad \begin{cases} y(0) = 0, \\ y'(1) = 0. \end{cases}$

(b) $\mathcal{L}y(x) = \dfrac{d^2 y(x)}{dx^2} - y(x), \quad y(x) \text{ finite for } -\infty < x < \infty.$

10.1.3 Show that the function $y(x)$ defined by Eq. (10.26) satisfies the initial-value problem defined by Eq. (10.24) and its initial conditions $y(0) = y'(0) = 0$.

10.1.4 Find the Green's function for the equation

$$-\frac{d^2y}{dx^2} - \frac{y}{4} = f(x),$$

with boundary conditions $y(0) = y(\pi) = 0$.

$$ANS. \quad G(x,t) = \begin{cases} 2\sin(x/2)\cos(t/2), & 0 \le x < t, \\ 2\cos(x/2)\sin(t/2), & t < x \le \pi. \end{cases}$$

10.1.5 Construct the Green's function for

$$x^2\frac{d^2y}{dx^2} + x\frac{dy}{dx} + (k^2x^2 - 1)y = 0,$$

subject to the boundary conditions $y(0) = 0$, $y(1) = 0$.

10.1.6 Given that

$$\mathcal{L} = (1-x^2)\frac{d^2}{dx^2} - 2x\frac{d}{dx}$$

and that $G(\pm 1, t)$ remains finite, show that no Green's function can be constructed by the techniques of this section.

Note. The solutions to $\mathcal{L} = 0$ needed for the regions $x < t$ and $x > t$ are linearly dependent.

10.1.7 Find the Green's function for

$$\frac{d^2\psi}{dt^2} + k\frac{d\psi}{dt} = f(t),$$

subject to the initial conditions $\psi(0) = \psi'(0) = 0$, and solve this ODE for $t > 0$ given $f(t) = \exp(-t)$.

10.1.8 Verify that the Green's function

$$G(x, x') = -\frac{i}{2k}\exp\left(ik|x - x'|\right)$$

yields an outgoing wave solution to the ODE

$$\left(\frac{d^2}{dx^2} + k^2\right)\psi(x) = g(x).$$

Note. Compare with Example 10.1.3.

10.1.9 Construct the 1-D Green's function for the modified Helmholtz equation,

$$\left(\frac{d^2}{dx^2} - k^2\right)\psi(x) = f(x).$$

The boundary conditions are that the Green's function must vanish for $x \to \infty$ and $x \to -\infty$.

$$ANS. \quad G(x_1, x_2) = -\frac{1}{2k} \exp\left(-k|x_1 - x_2|\right).$$

10.1.10   From the eigenfunction expansion of the Green's function show that

(a) $\quad \dfrac{2}{\pi^2} \displaystyle\sum_{n=1}^{\infty} \dfrac{\sin n\pi x \sin n\pi t}{n^2} = \begin{cases} x(1-t), & 0 \le x < t, \\ t(1-x), & t < x \le 1. \end{cases}$

(b) $\quad \dfrac{2}{\pi^2} \displaystyle\sum_{n=0}^{\infty} \dfrac{\sin(n+\frac{1}{2})\pi x \, \sin(n+\frac{1}{2})\pi t}{(n+\frac{1}{2})^2} = \begin{cases} x, & 0 \le x < t, \\ t, & t < x \le 1. \end{cases}$

10.1.11   Derive an integral equation corresponding to
$$y''(x) - y(x) = 0, \quad y(1) = 1, \quad y(-1) = 1,$$

(a)   by integrating twice.

(b)   by forming the Green's function.

$$ANS. \quad y(x) = 1 - \int_{-1}^{1} K(x,t)\, y(t)\, dt,$$

$$K(x,t) = \begin{cases} \frac{1}{2}(1-x)(t+1), & x > t, \\ \frac{1}{2}(1-t)(x+1), & x < t. \end{cases}$$

10.1.12   The general second-order linear ODE with constant coefficients is
$$y''(x) + a_1 y'(x) + a_2 y(x) = 0.$$

Given the boundary conditions $y(0) = y(1) = 0$, integrate twice and develop the integral equation
$$y(x) = \int_{0}^{1} K(x,t)\, y(t)\, dt,$$

with
$$K(x,t) = \begin{cases} a_2 t(1-x) + a_1(x-1), & t < x, \\ a_2 x(1-t) + a_1 x, & x < t. \end{cases}$$

Note that $K(x,t)$ is symmetric and continuous if $a_1 = 0$. How is this related to self-adjointness of the ODE?

10.1.13   Transform the ODE
$$\frac{d^2 y(r)}{dr^2} - k^2 y(r) + V_0 \frac{e^{-r}}{r} y(r) = 0$$

and the boundary conditions $y(0) = y(\infty) = 0$ into an integral equation of the form

$$y(r) = -V_0 \int_0^\infty G(r, t) \frac{e^{-t}}{t} y(t) \, dt.$$

The quantities V_0 and k^2 are constants. The ODE is derived from the Schrödinger wave equation with a mesonic potential:

$$G(r, t) = \begin{cases} -\dfrac{1}{k} e^{-kt} \sinh kr, & 0 \le r < t, \\[2mm] -\dfrac{1}{k} e^{-kr} \sinh kt, & t < r < \infty. \end{cases}$$

10.2 PROBLEMS IN TWO AND THREE DIMENSIONS

Basic Features

The principles, but unfortunately not all the details of our analysis of Green's functions in one dimension, extend to problems of higher dimensionality. We summarize here properties of general validity for the case where $\mathcal{L}$ is a linear second-order differential operator in two or three dimensions.

1. A homogeneous PDE $\mathcal{L}\psi(\mathbf{r}_1) = 0$ **and its boundary conditions** define a **Green's function** $G(\mathbf{r}_1, \mathbf{r}_2)$, which is the solution of the PDE

    $$\mathcal{L}G(\mathbf{r}_1, \mathbf{r}_2) = \delta(\mathbf{r}_1 - \mathbf{r}_2)$$

    subject to the relevant boundary conditions.
2. The inhomogeneous PDE $\mathcal{L}\psi(\mathbf{r}) = f(\mathbf{r})$ has, subject to the boundary conditions of Item 1, the solution

    $$\psi(\mathbf{r}_1) = \int G(\mathbf{r}_1, \mathbf{r}_2)\, f(\mathbf{r}_2)\, d^3 r_2,$$

    where the integral is over the entire space relevant to the problem.
3. When $\mathcal{L}$ and its boundary conditions define the Hermitian eigenvalue problem $\mathcal{L}\psi = \lambda\psi$ with eigenfunctions $\varphi_n(\mathbf{r})$ and corresponding eigenvalues λ_n, then

    * $G(\mathbf{r}_1, \mathbf{r}_2)$ is symmetric, in the sense that

      $$G(\mathbf{r}_1, \mathbf{r}_2) = G^*(\mathbf{r}_2, \mathbf{r}_1), \text{ and}$$

    * $G(\mathbf{r}_1, \mathbf{r}_2)$ has the eigenfunction expansion

      $$G(\mathbf{r}_1, \mathbf{r}_2) = \sum_n \frac{\varphi_n^*(\mathbf{r}_2)\varphi_n(\mathbf{r}_1)}{\lambda_n}.$$

4. $G(\mathbf{r}_1, \mathbf{r}_2)$ will be continuous and differentiable at all points such that $\mathbf{r}_1 \neq \mathbf{r}_2$. We cannot even require continuity in a strict sense at $\mathbf{r}_1 = \mathbf{r}_2$ (because our Green's function may become infinite there), but we can have the weaker condition that G remain continuous in regions that surround, but do not include $\mathbf{r}_1 = \mathbf{r}_2$. G must have more serious singularities in its first derivatives, so that the second-order derivatives in $\mathcal{L}$ will generate the delta-function singularity characteristic of G and specified in Item 1.

What does not carry over from the 1-D case are the explicit formulas we used to construct Green's functions for a variety of problems.

Self-Adjoint Problems

In more than one dimension, a second-order differential equation is self-adjoint if it has the form

$$\mathcal{L}\psi(\mathbf{r}) = \nabla \cdot \left[p(\mathbf{r})\nabla\psi(\mathbf{r}) \right] + q(\mathbf{r})\psi(\mathbf{r}) = f(\mathbf{r}), \tag{10.33}$$

with $p(\mathbf{r})$ and $q(\mathbf{r})$ real. This operator will define a Hermitian problem if its boundary conditions are such that $\langle\varphi|\mathcal{L}\psi\rangle = \langle\mathcal{L}\varphi|\psi\rangle$. See Exercise 10.2.2.

Assuming we have a Hermitian problem, consider the scalar product

$$\left\langle G(\mathbf{r}, \mathbf{r}_1) \middle| \mathcal{L}\check{G}(\mathbf{r}, \mathbf{r}_2) \right\rangle = \left\langle \mathcal{L}G(\mathbf{r}, \mathbf{r}_1) \middle| G(\mathbf{r}, \mathbf{r}_2) \right\rangle. \tag{10.34}$$

Here the scalar product and $\mathcal{L}$ both refer to the variable $\mathbf{r}$, and the Hermitian property is responsible for this equality. The points $\mathbf{r}_1$ and $\mathbf{r}_2$ are arbitrary. Noting that $\mathcal{L}G$ results in a delta function, we have, from the left-hand side of Eq. (10.34),

$$\left\langle G(\mathbf{r}, \mathbf{r}_1) \middle| \mathcal{L}G(\mathbf{r}, \mathbf{r}_2) \right\rangle = \left\langle G(\mathbf{r}, \mathbf{r}_1) \middle| \delta(\mathbf{r} - \mathbf{r}_2) \right\rangle = G^*(\mathbf{r}_2, \mathbf{r}_1). \tag{10.35}$$

But, from the right-hand side of Eq. (10.34),

$$\left\langle \mathcal{L}G(\mathbf{r}, \mathbf{r}_1) \middle| G(\mathbf{r}, \mathbf{r}_2) \right\rangle = \left\langle \delta(\mathbf{r} - \mathbf{r}_1) \middle| G(\mathbf{r}, \mathbf{r}_2) \right\rangle = G(\mathbf{r}_1, \mathbf{r}_2). \tag{10.36}$$

Substituting Eqs. (10.35) and (10.36) into Eq. (10.34), we recover the symmetry condition $G(\mathbf{r}_1, \mathbf{r}_2) = G^*(\mathbf{r}_2, \mathbf{r}_1)$.

Eigenfunction Expansions

We already saw, in 1-D Hermitian problems, that the Green's function of a Hermitian problem can be written as an eigenfunction expansion. If $\mathcal{L}$, with its boundary conditions, has normalized eigenfunctions $\varphi_n(\mathbf{r})$ and corresponding eigenvalues λ_n, our expansion took the form

$$G(\mathbf{r}_1, \mathbf{r}_2) = \sum_n \frac{\varphi_n^*(\mathbf{r}_2)\varphi_n(\mathbf{r}_1)}{\lambda_n}. \tag{10.37}$$

It turns out to be useful to consider the somewhat more general equation

$$\mathcal{L}\psi(\mathbf{r}_1) - \lambda\psi(\mathbf{r}_1) = \delta(\mathbf{r}_2 - \mathbf{r}_1), \tag{10.38}$$

where λ is a parameter (not an eigenvalue of $\mathcal{L}$). In this more general case, an expansion in the φ_n yields for the Green's function of the entire left-hand side of Eq. (10.38) the formula

$$G(\mathbf{r}_1, \mathbf{r}_2) = \sum_n \frac{\varphi_n^*(\mathbf{r}_2)\varphi_n(\mathbf{r}_1)}{\lambda_n - \lambda}. \tag{10.39}$$

Note that Eq. (10.39) will be well-defined only if the parameter λ is not equal to any of the eigenvalues of $\mathcal{L}$.

Form of Green's Functions

In spaces of more than one dimension, we cannot divide the region under consideration into two intervals, one on each side of a point (here designated $\mathbf{r}_2$), then choosing for each interval a solution to the homogeneous equation appropriate to its outer boundary. A more fruitful approach will often be to obtain a Green's function for an operator $\mathcal{L}$ subject to some particularly convenient boundary conditions, with a subsequent plan to add to it whatever solution to the homogeneous equation $\mathcal{L}\psi(\mathbf{r}) = 0$ that may be needed to adapt to the boundary conditions actually under consideration. This approach is clearly legitimate, as the addition of any solution to the homogeneous equation will not affect the (dis)continuity properties of the Green's function.

We consider first the Laplace operator in three dimensions, with the boundary condition that G vanish at infinity. We therefore seek a solution to the inhomogeneous PDE

$$\nabla_1^2 G(\mathbf{r}_1, \mathbf{r}_2) = \delta(\mathbf{r}_1 - \mathbf{r}_2) \tag{10.40}$$

with $\lim_{r_1 \to \infty} G(\mathbf{r}_1, \mathbf{r}_2) = 0$. We have added a subscript "1" to ∇ to remind the reader that it operates on $\mathbf{r}_1$ and not on $\mathbf{r}_2$. Since our boundary conditions are spherically symmetric and at an infinite distance from $\mathbf{r}_1$ and $\mathbf{r}_2$, we may make the simplifying assumption that $G(\mathbf{r}_1, \mathbf{r}_2)$ is a function only of $r_{12} = |\mathbf{r}_1 - \mathbf{r}_2|$.

Our first step in processing Eq. (10.40) is to integrate it over a spherical volume of radius a centered at $\mathbf{r}_2$:

$$\int_{r_{12} < a} \nabla_1 \cdot \nabla_1 G(\mathbf{r}_1, \mathbf{r}_2)\, d^3 r_1 = 1, \tag{10.41}$$

where we have reduced the right-hand side using the properties of the delta function and written the left-hand side in a form making it ready for the application of Gauss' theorem. We now apply that theorem to the left-hand side of Eq. (10.41), reaching

$$\int_{r_{12} = a} \nabla_1 G(\mathbf{r}_1, \mathbf{r}_2) \cdot d\boldsymbol{\sigma}_1 = 4\pi a^2 \left.\frac{dG}{dr_{12}}\right|_{r_{12}=a} = 1. \tag{10.42}$$

Since Eq. (10.42) must be satisfied for all values of a, it is necessary that

$$\frac{d}{dr_{12}} G(\mathbf{r}_1, \mathbf{r}_2) = \frac{1}{4\pi r_{12}^2},$$

which can be integrated to yield

$$G(\mathbf{r}_1, \mathbf{r}_2) = -\frac{1}{4\pi} \frac{1}{|\mathbf{r}_1 - \mathbf{r}_2|}. \tag{10.43}$$

We do not need to add a constant of integration because this form for G vanishes at infinity.

At this point it may be useful to note that the sign of $G(\mathbf{r}_1, \mathbf{r}_2)$ depends on the sign associated with the differential operator of which it is a Green's function. Some texts (including previous editions of this book) have defined G as produced by a negative delta function so that Eq. (10.43) when associated with $+\nabla^2$ would not need a minus sign. There is, of course, no ambiguity in any physical results because a change in the sign of G must be accompanied by a change in the sign of the integral in which G is combined with the inhomogeneous term of a differential equation.

The Green's function of Eq. (10.43) is only going to be appropriate for an infinite system with $G = 0$ at infinity but, as mentioned already, it can be converted into the Green's functions of another problem by addition of a suitable solution to the homogeneous equation (in this case, Laplace's equation). Since that is a reasonable starting point for a variety of problems, the form given in Eq. (10.43) is sometimes called the **fundamental** Green's function of Laplace's equation (in three dimensions).

Let's now repeat our analysis for the Laplace operator in two dimensions for a region of infinite extent, using circular coordinates $\boldsymbol{\rho} = (\rho, \varphi)$. The integral in Eq. (10.41) is then over a circular area, and the 2-D analog of Eq. (10.42) becomes

$$\int\limits_{\rho_{12}=a} \nabla_1 G(\boldsymbol{\rho}_1, \boldsymbol{\rho}_2) \cdot d\boldsymbol{\sigma}_1 = 2\pi a \left.\frac{dG}{d\rho_{12}}\right|_{\rho_{12}=a} = 1,$$

leading to

$$\frac{d}{d\rho_{12}} G(\boldsymbol{\rho}_1, \boldsymbol{\rho}_2) = \frac{1}{2\pi \rho_{12}},$$

which has the indefinite integral

$$G(\boldsymbol{\rho}_1, \boldsymbol{\rho}_2) = \frac{1}{2\pi} \ln |\boldsymbol{\rho}_1 - \boldsymbol{\rho}_2|. \tag{10.44}$$

The form given in Eq. (10.44) becomes infinite at infinity, but it nevertheless can be regarded as a fundamental 2-D Green's function. However, note that we will generally need to add to it a suitable solution to the 2-D Laplace equation to obtain the form needed for specific problems.

The above analysis indicates that the Green's function for the Laplace equation in 2-D space is rather different than the 3-D result. This observation illustrates the fact that there is a real difference between flatland (2-D) physics and actual (3-D) physics, even when the latter is applied to problems with translational symmetry in one direction.

This is also a good time to note that the symmetry in the Green's function corresponds to the notion that a source at $\mathbf{r}_2$ produces a result (a potential) at $\mathbf{r}_1$ that is the same as the potential at $\mathbf{r}_2$ from a similar source at $\mathbf{r}_1$. This property will persist in more complicated problems so long as their definition makes them Hermitian.

Table 10.1 Fundamental Green's Functions[a]

	Laplace ∇^2	Helmholtz[b] $\nabla^2 + k^2$	Modified Helmholtz[c] $\nabla^2 - k^2$
1-D	$\dfrac{1}{2}\|x_1 - x_2\|$	$-\dfrac{i}{2k}\exp(ik\|x_1 - x_2\|)$	$-\dfrac{1}{2k}\exp(-k\|x_1 - x_2\|)$
2-D	$\dfrac{1}{2\pi}\ln\|\boldsymbol{\rho}_1 - \boldsymbol{\rho}_2\|$	$-\dfrac{i}{4}H_0^{(1)}(k\|\boldsymbol{\rho}_1 - \boldsymbol{\rho}_2\|)$	$-\dfrac{1}{2\pi}K_0(k\|\boldsymbol{\rho}_1 - \boldsymbol{\rho}_2\|)$
3-D	$-\dfrac{1}{4\pi}\dfrac{1}{\|\mathbf{r}_1 - \mathbf{r}_2\|}$	$-\dfrac{\exp(ik\|\mathbf{r}_1 - \mathbf{r}_2\|)}{4\pi\|\mathbf{r}_1 - \mathbf{r}_2\|}$	$-\dfrac{\exp(-k\|\mathbf{r}_1 - \mathbf{r}_2\|)}{4\pi\|\mathbf{r}_1 - \mathbf{r}_2\|}$

[a] Boundary conditions: For the Helmholtz equation, outgoing wave; for modified Helmholtz and 3-D Laplace equations, $G \to 0$ at infinity; for 1-D and 2-D Laplace equation, arbitrary.

[b] H_0^1 is a Hankel function, Section 14.4.

[c] K_0 is a modified Bessel function, Section 14.5.

Because they occur rather frequently, it is useful to have Green's functions for the Helmholtz and modified Helmholtz equations in two and three dimensions (for one dimension these Green's functions were introduced in Example 10.1.3 and Exercise 10.1.9). For the Helmholtz equation, a convenient fundamental form results if we take boundary conditions corresponding to an outgoing wave, meaning that the asymptotic r dependence must be of the form $\exp(+ikr)$. For the modified Helmholtz equation, the most convenient boundary condition (for one, two, and three dimensions) is that G decay to zero in all directions at large r. The one-, two-, and three-dimensional (3-D) fundamental Green's functions for the Laplace, Helmholtz, and modified Helmholtz operators are listed in Table 10.1.

We shall not derive here the forms of the Green's functions for the Helmholtz equations; in fact, for two dimensions, they involve Bessel functions and are best treated in detail in a later chapter. However, for three dimensions, the Green's functions are of relatively simple form, and the verification that they return correct results is the topic of Exercises 10.2.4 and 10.2.6. The fundamental Green's function for the 1-D Laplace equation may not be instantly recognizable in comparison to the formulas we derived in Section 10.1, but consistency with our earlier analysis is the topic of Example 10.2.1.

Sometimes it is useful to represent Green's functions as expansions that take advantage of the specific properties of various coordinate systems. The so-called **spherical Green's function** is the radial part of such an expansion in spherical polar coordinates. For the Laplace operator, it takes a form developed in Eqs. (16.65) and (16.66). We write it here only to show that it exhibits the two-region character that provides a convenient representation of the discontinuity in the derivative:

$$-\frac{1}{4\pi}\frac{1}{|\mathbf{r}_1 - \mathbf{r}_2|} = \sum_{l=0}^{\infty}\frac{2l+1}{4\pi}g(r_1, r_2)P_l(\cos\chi),$$

where χ is the angle between $\mathbf{r}_1$ and $\mathbf{r}_2$, P_l is a Legendre polynomial, and the spherical Green's function $g(r_1, r_2)$ is

$$
g_l(r_1, r_2) = \begin{cases} -\dfrac{1}{2l+1}\dfrac{r_1^l}{r_2^{l+1}}, & r_1 < r_2, \\[3mm] -\dfrac{1}{2l+1}\dfrac{r_2^l}{r_1^{l+1}}, & r_1 > r_2. \end{cases}
$$

An explicit derivation of the formula for g_l is given in Example 16.3.2.

In cylindrical coordinates (ρ, φ, z) one encounters an **axial Green's function** $g_m(\rho_1, \rho_2)$, in terms of which the fundamental Green's function for the Laplace operator takes the form (also involving a continuous parameter k)

$$
G(\mathbf{r}_1, \mathbf{r}_2) = -\frac{1}{4\pi}\frac{1}{|\mathbf{r}_1 - \mathbf{r}_2|}
$$

$$
= \frac{1}{2\pi^2} \sum_{m=-\infty}^{\infty} e^{im(\varphi_1-\varphi_2)} \int_0^\infty g_m(k\rho_1, k\rho_2) \cos k(z_1 - z_2)\, dk .
$$

Here

$$
g_m(k\rho_1, k\rho_2) = -I_m(k\rho_<) K_m(k\rho_>),
$$

where $\rho_<$ and $\rho_>$ are, respectively, the smaller and larger of ρ_1 and ρ_2. The quantities I_m and K_m are modified Bessel functions, defined in Chapter 14. This expansion is discussed in more detail in Example 14.5.1. Again we note the two-region character.

Example 10.2.1   ACCOMMODATING BOUNDARY CONDITIONS

Let's use the fundamental Green's function of the 1-D Laplace equation,

$$
\frac{d^2\psi(x)}{dx^2} = 0, \quad \text{namely} \quad G(x_1, x_2) = \frac{1}{2}|x_1 - x_2|,
$$

to illustrate how we can modify it to accommodate specific boundary conditions. We return to the oft-used example with Dirichlet conditions $\psi = 0$ at $x = 0$ and $x = 1$. The continuity of G and the discontinuity in its derivative are unaffected if we add to the above G one or more terms of the form $f(x_1)g(x_2)$, where f and g are solutions of the 1-D Laplace equation, i.e., any functions of the form $ax + b$.

For the boundary conditions we have specified, the Green's function we require has the form

$$
G(x_1, x_2) = -\frac{1}{2}(x_1 + x_2) + x_1 x_2 + \frac{1}{2}|x_1 - x_2|.
$$

The continuous and differentiable terms we have added to the fundamental form bring us to the result

$$
G(x_1, x_2) = \begin{cases} -\frac{1}{2}(x_1 + x_2) + x_1 x_2 + \frac{1}{2}(x_2 - x_1) = -x_1(1 - x_2), & x_1 < x_2, \\[2mm] -\frac{1}{2}(x_1 + x_2) + x_1 x_2 + \frac{1}{2}(x_1 - x_2) = -x_2(1 - x_1), & x_2 < x_1. \end{cases}
$$

This result is consistent with what we found in Example 10.1.1.   ∎

Example 10.2.2   QUANTUM MECHANICAL SCATTERING: BORN APPROXIMATION

The quantum theory of scattering provides a nice illustration of Green's function techniques and the use of the Green's function to obtain an integral equation. Our physical picture of scattering is as follows. A beam of particles moves along the negative z-axis toward the origin. A small fraction of the particles is scattered by the potential $V(\mathbf{r})$ and goes off as an outgoing spherical wave. Our wave function $\psi(\mathbf{r})$ must satisfy the time-independent Schrödinger equation

$$-\frac{\hbar^2}{2m}\nabla^2\psi(\mathbf{r}) + V(\mathbf{r})\psi(\mathbf{r}) = E\psi(\mathbf{r}), \tag{10.45}$$

or

$$\nabla^2\psi(\mathbf{r}) + k^2\psi(\mathbf{r}) = \left[\frac{2m}{\hbar^2}V(\mathbf{r})\psi(\mathbf{r})\right], \quad k^2 = \frac{2mE}{\hbar^2}. \tag{10.46}$$

From the physical picture just presented we look for a solution having the **asymptotic** form

$$\psi(\mathbf{r}) \sim e^{i\mathbf{k}_0\cdot\mathbf{r}} + f_k(\theta,\varphi)\frac{e^{ikr}}{r}, \tag{10.47}$$

where $e^{i\mathbf{k}_0\cdot\mathbf{r}}$ is an incident plane wave[2] with the propagation vector $\mathbf{k}_0$ carrying the subscript 0 to indicate that it is in the $\theta = 0$ (z-axis) direction. The e^{ikr}/r term describes an outgoing spherical wave with an angular and energy-dependent amplitude factor $f_k(\theta,\varphi)$,[3] and its $1/r$ radial dependence causes its asymptotic total flux to be independent of r. This is a consequence of the fact that the scattering potential $V(\mathbf{r})$ becomes negligible at large r.

Equation (10.45) contains nothing describing the internal structure or possible motion of the scattering center and therefore can only represent **elastic scattering**, so the propagation vector of the incoming wave, $\mathbf{k}_0$, must have the same magnitude, k, as the scattered wave. In quantum mechanics texts it is shown that the differential probability of scattering, called the **scattering cross section**, is given by $|f_k(\theta,\varphi)|^2$.

We now need to solve Eq. (10.46) to obtain $\psi(r)$ and the scattering cross section. Our approach starts by writing the solution in terms of the Green's function for the operator on the left-hand side of Eq. (10.46), obtaining an integral equation because the inhomogeneous term of that equation has the form $(2m/\hbar^2)V(\mathbf{r})\psi(\mathbf{r})$:

$$\psi(\mathbf{r}_1) = \int \frac{2m}{\hbar^2}V(\mathbf{r}_2)\,\psi(\mathbf{r}_2)\,G(\mathbf{r}_1,\mathbf{r}_2)\,d^3r_2. \tag{10.48}$$

We intend to take the Green's function to be the fundamental form given for the Helmholtz equation in Table 10.1. We then recover the $\exp(ikr)/r$ part of the desired asymptotic form, but the incident-wave term will be absent. We therefore modify our tentative formula, Eq. (10.48), by adding to its right-hand side the term $\exp(i\mathbf{k}_0\cdot\mathbf{r})$, which is legitimate because this quantity is a solution to the homogeneous (Helmholtz) equation. That

---

[2] For simplicity we assume a continuous incident beam. In a more sophisticated and more realistic treatment, Eq. (10.47) would be one component of a wave packet.

[3] If $V(\mathbf{r})$ represents a central force, f_k will be a function of θ only, independent of the azimuthal angle φ.

approach leads us to

$$\psi(\mathbf{r}_1) = e^{i\mathbf{k}_0 \cdot \mathbf{r}_1} - \int \frac{2m}{\hbar^2} V(\mathbf{r}_2)\psi(\mathbf{r}_2) \frac{e^{ik|\mathbf{r}_1 - \mathbf{r}_2|}}{4\pi|\mathbf{r}_1 - \mathbf{r}_2|} d^3 r_2. \tag{10.49}$$

This integral equation analog of the original Schrödinger wave equation is **exact**. It is called the **Lippmann-Schwinger** equation, and is an important starting point for studies of quantum-mechanical scattering phenomena.

We will later study methods for solving integral equations such as that in Eq. (10.49). However, in the special case that the unscattered amplitude

$$\psi_0(\mathbf{r}_1) = e^{i\mathbf{k}_0 \cdot \mathbf{r}_1} \tag{10.50}$$

dominates the solution, it is a satisfactory approximation to replace $\psi(\mathbf{r}_2)$ by $\psi_0(\mathbf{r}_2)$ within the integral, obtaining

$$\psi_1(\mathbf{r}_1) = e^{i\mathbf{k}_0 \cdot \mathbf{r}_1} - \int \frac{2m}{\hbar^2} V(\mathbf{r}_2) \frac{e^{ik|\mathbf{r}_1 - \mathbf{r}_2|}}{4\pi|\mathbf{r}_1 - \mathbf{r}_2|} e^{i\mathbf{k}_0 \cdot \mathbf{r}_2} d^3 r_2. \tag{10.51}$$

This is the famous **Born approximation**. It is expected to be most accurate for weak potentials and high incident energy. ∎

Exercises

10.2.1   Show that the fundamental Green's function for the 1-D Laplace equation, $|x_1 - x_2|/2$, is consistent with the form found in Example 10.1.1.

10.2.2   Show that if

$$\mathcal{L}\psi(\mathbf{r}) \equiv \nabla \cdot \left[p(\mathbf{r})\nabla\psi(\mathbf{r}) \right] + q(\mathbf{r})\psi(\mathbf{r}),$$

then $\mathcal{L}$ is Hermitian for $p(\mathbf{r})$ and $q(\mathbf{r})$ real, assuming Dirichlet boundary conditions on the boundary of a region and that the scalar product is an integral over that region with unit weight.

10.2.3   Show that the terms $+k^2$ in the Helmholtz operator and $-k^2$ in the modified Helmholtz operator do not affect the behavior of $G(\mathbf{r}_1, \mathbf{r}_2)$ in the immediate vicinity of the singular point $\mathbf{r}_1 = \mathbf{r}_2$. Specifically, show that

$$\lim_{|\mathbf{r}_1 - \mathbf{r}_2| \to 0} \int k^2 G(\mathbf{r}_1, \mathbf{r}_2) d^3 r_2 = -1.$$

10.2.4   Show that

$$-\frac{\exp(ik|\mathbf{r}_1 - \mathbf{r}_2|)}{4\pi|\mathbf{r}_1 - \mathbf{r}_2|}$$

satisfies the appropriate criteria and therefore is a Green's function for the Helmholtz equation.

10.2.5   Find the Green's function for the 3-D Helmholtz equation, Exercise 10.2.4, when the wave is a standing wave.

10.2.6   Verify that the formula given for the 3-D Green's function of the modified Helmholtz equation in Table 10.1 is correct when the boundary conditions of the problem are that G vanish at infinity.

10.2.7   An electrostatic potential (mks units) is

$$\varphi(\mathbf{r}) = \frac{Z}{4\pi\varepsilon_0}\frac{e^{-ar}}{r}.$$

Reconstruct the electrical charge distribution that will produce this potential. Note that $\varphi(r)$ vanishes exponentially for large r, showing that the net charge is zero.

$$ANS.\quad \rho(r) = Z\delta(r) - \frac{Za^2}{4\pi}\frac{e^{-ar}}{r}.$$

Additional Readings

Byron, F. W., Jr., and R. W. Fuller, *Mathematics of Classical and Quantum Physics*. Reading, MA: Addison-Wesley (1969), reprinting, Dover (1992). This book contains nearly 100 pages on Green's functions, starting with some good introductory material.

Courant, R., and D. Hilbert, *Methods of Mathematical Physics*, Vol. 1 (English edition). New York: Interscience (1953). This is one of the classic works of mathematical physics. Originally published in German in 1924, the revised English edition is an excellent reference for a rigorous treatment of integral equations, Green's functions, and a wide variety of other topics on mathematical physics.

Jackson, J. D., *Classical Electrodynamics*, 3rd ed. New York: Wiley (1999). Contains applications to electromagnetic theory.

Morse, P. M., and H. Feshbach, *Methods of Theoretical Physics*, 2 vols. New York: McGraw-Hill (1953). Chapter 7 is a particularly detailed, complete discussion of Green's functions from the point of view of mathematical physics. Note, however, that Morse and Feshbach frequently choose a source of $4\pi\delta(\mathbf{r} - \mathbf{r}')$ in place of our $\delta(\mathbf{r} - \mathbf{r}')$. Considerable attention is devoted to bounded regions.

Stakgold, I., *Green's Functions and Boundary Value Problems*. New York: Wiley (1979).

CHAPTER 11

COMPLEX VARIABLE THEORY

The imaginary numbers are a wonderful
flight of God's spirit; they are almost an
amphibian between being and not being.

GOTTFRIED WILHELM VON LEIBNIZ, 1702

We turn now to a study of complex variable theory. In this area we develop some of the most powerful and widely useful tools in all of analysis. To indicate, at least partly, why complex variables are important, we mention briefly several areas of application.

1. In two dimensions, the electric potential, viewed as a solution of Laplace's equation, can be written as the real (or the imaginary) part of a complex-valued function, and this identification enables the use of various features of complex variable theory (specifically, conformal mapping) to obtain formal solutions to a wide variety of electrostatics problems.

2. The time-dependent Schrödinger equation of quantum mechanics contains the imaginary unit i, and its solutions are complex.

3. In Chapter 9 we saw that the second-order differential equations of interest in physics may be solved by power series. The same power series may be used in the complex plane to replace x by the complex variable z. The dependence of the solution $f(z)$ at a given z_0 on the behavior of $f(z)$ elsewhere gives us greater insight into the behavior of our solution and a powerful tool (analytic continuation) for extending the region in which the solution is valid.

4. The change of a parameter k from real to imaginary, $k \to ik$, transforms the Helmholtz equation into the time-independent diffusion equation. The same change connects the spherical and hyperbolic trigonometric functions, transforms Bessel functions into their *modified* counterparts, and provides similar connections between other superficially dissimilar functions.

5. Integrals in the complex plane have a wide variety of useful applications:

- Evaluating definite integrals and infinite series,
- Inverting power series,
- Forming infinite products,
- Obtaining solutions of differential equations for large values of the variable (asymptotic solutions),
- Investigating the stability of potentially oscillatory systems,
- Inverting integral transforms.

6. Many physical quantities that were originally real become complex as a simple physical theory is made more general. The real index of refraction of light becomes a complex quantity when absorption is included. The real energy associated with an energy level becomes complex when the finite lifetime of the level is considered.

11.1 COMPLEX VARIABLES AND FUNCTIONS

We have already seen (in Chapter 1) the definition of complex numbers $z = x + iy$ as ordered pairs of two real numbers, x and y. We reviewed there the rules for their arithmetic operations, identified the **complex conjugate** z^* of the complex number z, and discussed both the Cartesian and polar representations of complex numbers, introducing for that purpose the **Argand diagram** (complex plane). In the polar representation $z = re^{i\theta}$, we noted that r (the magnitude of the complex number) is also called its **modulus**, and the angle θ is known as its **argument**. We proved that $e^{i\theta}$ satisfies the important equation

$$e^{i\theta} = \cos\theta + i\sin\theta. \tag{11.1}$$

This equation shows that for real θ, $e^{i\theta}$ is of unit magnitude and is therefore situated on the unit circle, at an angle θ from the real axis.

Our focus in the present chapter is on functions of a complex variable and on their analytical properties. We have already noted that by defining complex functions $f(z)$ to have the same power-series expansion (in z) as the expansion (in x) of the corresponding real function $f(x)$, the real and complex definitions coincide when z is real. We also showed that by use of the polar representation, $z = re^{i\theta}$, it becomes clear how to compute powers and roots of complex quantities. In particular, we noted that roots, viewed as fractional powers, become **multivalued** functions in the complex domain, due to the fact that $\exp(2n\pi i) = 1$ for all positive and negative integers n. We thus found $z^{1/2}$ to have two values (not a surprise, since for positive real x, we have $\pm\sqrt{x}$). But we also noted that $z^{1/m}$ will have m different complex values. We also noted that the logarithm becomes multivalued when extended to complex values, with

$$\ln z = \ln(re^{i\theta}) = \ln r + i(\theta + 2n\pi), \tag{11.2}$$

with n any positive or negative integer (including zero).

If necessary, the reader should review the topics mentioned above by rereading Section 1.8.

11.2 CAUCHY-RIEMANN CONDITIONS

Having established complex functions of a complex variable, we now proceed to differentiate them. The derivative of $f(z)$, like that of a real function, is defined by

$$\lim_{\delta z \to 0} \frac{f(z + \delta z) - f(z)}{(z + \delta z) - z} = \lim_{\delta z \to 0} \frac{\delta f(z)}{\delta z} = \frac{df}{dz} = f'(z), \tag{11.3}$$

provided that the limit is **independent** of the particular approach to the point z. For real variables we require that the right-hand limit ($x \to x_0$ from above) and the left-hand limit ($x \to x_0$ from below) be equal for the derivative $df(x)/dx$ to exist at $x = x_0$. Now, with z (or z_0) some point in a plane, our requirement that the limit be independent of the direction of approach is very restrictive.

Consider increments δx and δy of the variables x and y, respectively. Then

$$\delta z = \delta x + i \delta y. \tag{11.4}$$

Also, writing $f = u + iv$,

$$\delta f = \delta u + i \delta v, \tag{11.5}$$

so that

$$\frac{\delta f}{\delta z} = \frac{\delta u + i \delta v}{\delta x + i \delta y}. \tag{11.6}$$

Let us take the limit indicated by Eq. (11.3) by two different approaches, as shown in Fig. 11.1. First, with $\delta y = 0$, we let $\delta x \to 0$. Equation (11.3) yields

$$\lim_{\delta z \to 0} \frac{\delta f}{\delta z} = \lim_{\delta x \to 0} \left(\frac{\delta u}{\delta x} + i \frac{\delta v}{\delta x} \right) = \frac{\partial u}{\partial x} + i \frac{\partial v}{\partial x}, \tag{11.7}$$

assuming that the partial derivatives exist. For a second approach, we set $\delta x = 0$ and then let $\delta y \to 0$. This leads to

$$\lim_{\delta z \to 0} \frac{\delta f}{\delta z} = \lim_{\delta y \to 0} \left(-i \frac{\delta u}{\delta y} + \frac{\delta v}{\delta y} \right) = -i \frac{\partial u}{\partial y} + \frac{\partial v}{\partial y}. \tag{11.8}$$

If we are to have a derivative df/dz, Eqs. (11.7) and (11.8) must be identical. Equating real parts to real parts and imaginary parts to imaginary parts (like components of vectors), we obtain

$$\frac{\partial u}{\partial x} = \frac{\partial v}{\partial y}, \quad \frac{\partial u}{\partial y} = -\frac{\partial v}{\partial x}. \tag{11.9}$$

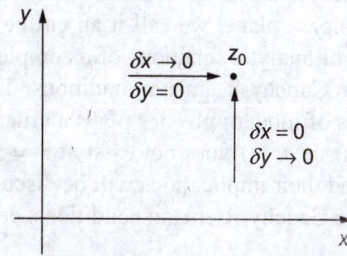

FIGURE 11.1   Alternate approaches to z_0.

These are the famous **Cauchy-Riemann** conditions. They were discovered by Cauchy and used extensively by Riemann in his development of complex variable theory. These Cauchy-Riemann conditions are necessary for the existence of a derivative of $f(z)$. That is, in order for df/dz to exist, the Cauchy-Riemann conditions must hold.

Conversely, if the Cauchy-Riemann conditions are satisfied and the partial derivatives of $u(x, y)$ and $v(x, y)$ are continuous, the derivative df/dz exists. To show this, we start by writing

$$\delta f = \left(\frac{\partial u}{\partial x} + i \frac{\partial v}{\partial x} \right) \delta x + \left(\frac{\partial u}{\partial y} + i \frac{\partial v}{\partial y} \right) \delta y, \tag{11.10}$$

where the justification for this expression depends on the continuity of the partial derivatives of u and v. Using the Cauchy-Riemann equations, Eq. (11.9), we convert Eq. (11.10) to the form

$$\delta f = \left(\frac{\partial u}{\partial x} + i \frac{\partial v}{\partial x} \right) \delta x + \left(-\frac{\partial v}{\partial x} + i \frac{\partial u}{\partial x} \right) \delta y$$

$$= \left(\frac{\partial u}{\partial x} + i \frac{\partial v}{\partial x} \right) (\delta x + i \delta y). \tag{11.11}$$

Replacing $\delta x + i \delta y$ by δz and bringing it to the left-hand side of Eq. (11.11), we reach

$$\frac{\delta f}{\delta z} = \frac{\partial u}{\partial x} + i \frac{\partial v}{\partial x}, \tag{11.12}$$

an equation whose right-hand side is independent of the direction of δz (i.e., the relative values of δx and δy). This independence of directionality meets the condition for the existence of the derivative, df/dz.

Analytic Functions

If $f(z)$ is differentiable and single-valued in a region of the complex plane, it is said to be an **analytic** function in that region.[1] Multivalued functions can also be analytic under certain restrictions that make them single-valued in specific regions; this case, which is of great importance, is taken up in detail in Section 11.6. If $f(z)$ is analytic everywhere in the (finite) complex plane, we call it an **entire** function. Our theory of complex variables here is one of analytic functions of a complex variable, which points up the crucial importance of the Cauchy-Riemann conditions. The concept of analyticity carried on in advanced theories of modern physics plays a crucial role in the dispersion theory (of elementary particles). If $f'(z)$ does not exist at $z = z_0$, then z_0 is labeled a **singular point**; singular points and their implications will be discussed shortly.

To illustrate the Cauchy-Riemann conditions, consider two very simple examples.

---

[1] Some writers use the term **holomorphic** or **regular**.

Example 11.2.1 z^2 IS ANALYTIC

Let $f(z) = z^2$. Multiplying out $(x - iy)(x - iy) = x^2 - y^2 + 2ixy$, we identify the real part of z^2 as $u(x, y) = x^2 - y^2$ and its imaginary part as $v(x, y) = 2xy$. Following Eq. (11.9),

$$\frac{\partial u}{\partial x} = 2x = \frac{\partial v}{\partial y}, \quad \frac{\partial u}{\partial y} = -2y = -\frac{\partial v}{\partial x}.$$

We see that $f(z) = z^2$ satisfies the Cauchy-Riemann conditions throughout the complex plane. Since the partial derivatives are clearly continuous, we conclude that $f(z) = z^2$ is analytic, and is an entire function. ∎

Example 11.2.2 z^* IS NOT ANALYTIC

Let $f(z) = z^*$, the complex conjugate of z. Now $u = x$ and $v = -y$. Applying the Cauchy-Riemann conditions, we obtain

$$\frac{\partial u}{\partial x} = 1 \neq \frac{\partial v}{\partial y} = -1.$$

The Cauchy-Riemann conditions are not satisfied for any values of x or y and $f(z) = z^*$ is nowhere an analytic function of z. It is interesting to note that $f(z) = z^*$ is continuous, thus providing an example of a function that is everywhere continuous but nowhere differentiable in the complex plane. ∎

The derivative of a real function of a real variable is essentially a local characteristic, in that it provides information about the function only in a local neighborhood, for instance, as a truncated Taylor expansion. The existence of a derivative of a function of a complex variable has much more far-reaching implications, one of which is that the real and imaginary parts of our analytic function must separately satisfy Laplace's equation in two dimensions, namely

$$\frac{\partial^2 \psi}{\partial x^2} + \frac{\partial^2 \psi}{\partial y^2} = 0.$$

To verify the above statement, we differentiate the first Cauchy-Riemann equation in Eq. (11.9) with respect to x and the second with respect to y, obtaining

$$\frac{\partial^2 u}{\partial x^2} = \frac{\partial^2 v}{\partial x \partial y}, \quad \frac{\partial^2 u}{\partial y^2} = -\frac{\partial^2 v}{\partial y \partial x}.$$

Combining these two equations, we easily reach

$$\frac{\partial^2 u}{\partial x^2} + \frac{\partial^2 u}{\partial y^2} = 0, \tag{11.13}$$

confirming that $u(x, y)$, the real part of a differentiable complex function, satisfies the Laplace equation. Either by recognizing that if $f(z)$ is differentiable, so is $-if(z) = v(x, y) - iu(x, y)$, or by steps similar to those leading to Eq. (11.13), we can confirm that $v(x, y)$ also satisfies the two-dimensional (2-D) Laplace equation. Sometimes u and v are referred to as **harmonic functions** (not to be confused with **spherical harmonics**, which we will later encounter as the angular solutions to central force problems).

The solutions $u(x, y)$ and $v(x, y)$ are complementary in that the curves of constant $u(x, y)$ make orthogonal intersections with the curves of constant $v(x, y)$. To confirm this, note that if (x_0, y_0) is on the curve $u(x, y) = c$, then $x_0 + dx$, $y_0 + dy$ is also on that curve if

$$\frac{\partial u}{\partial x} dx + \frac{\partial u}{\partial y} dy = 0,$$

meaning that the slope of the curve of constant u at (x_0, y_0) is

$$\left(\frac{dy}{dx}\right)_u = \frac{-\partial u/\partial x}{\partial u/\partial y}, \tag{11.14}$$

where the derivatives are to be evaluated at (x_0, y_0). Similarly, we can find that the slope of the curve of constant v at (x_0, y_0) is

$$\left(\frac{dy}{dx}\right)_v = \frac{-\partial v/\partial x}{\partial v/\partial y} = \frac{\partial u/\partial y}{\partial u/\partial x}, \tag{11.15}$$

where the last member of Eq. (11.15) was reached using the Cauchy-Riemann equations. Comparing Eqs. (11.14) and (11.15), we note that at the same point, the slopes they describe are orthogonal (to check, verify that $dx_u dx_v + dy_u dy_v = 0$).

The properties we have just examined are important for the solution of 2-D electrostatics problems (governed by the Laplace equation). If we have identified (by methods outside the scope of the present text) an appropriate analytic function, its lines of constant u will describe electrostatic equipotentials, while those of constant v will be the stream lines of the electric field.

Finally, the global nature of our analytic function is also illustrated by the fact that it has not only a first derivative, but in addition, derivatives of all higher orders, a property which is not shared by functions of a real variable. This property will be demonstrated in Section 11.4.

Derivatives of Analytic Functions

Working with the real and imaginary parts of an analytic function $f(z)$ is one way to take its derivative; an example of that approach is to use Eq. (11.12). However, it is usually easier to use the fact that complex differentiation follows the same rules as those for real variables. As a first step in establishing this correspondence, note that, **if $f(z)$ is analytic**, then, from Eq. (11.12),

$$f'(z) = \frac{\partial f}{\partial x},$$

and that

$$\left[f(z)g(z)\right]' = \left(\frac{d}{dz}\right)\left[f(z)g(z)\right] = \left(\frac{\partial}{\partial x}\right)\left[f(z)g(z)\right]$$

$$= \left(\frac{\partial f}{\partial x}\right)g(z) + f(z)\left(\frac{\partial g}{\partial x}\right) = f'(z)g(z) + f(z)g'(z),$$

the familiar rule for differentiating a product. Given also that

$$\frac{dz}{dz} = \frac{\partial z}{\partial x} = 1,$$

we can easily establish that

$$\frac{dz^2}{dz} = 2z, \quad \text{and, by induction,} \quad \frac{dz^n}{dz} = nz^{n-1}.$$

Functions defined by power series will then have differentiation rules identical to those for the real domain. Functions not ordinarily defined by power series also have the same differentiation rules as for the real domain, but that will need to be demonstrated case by case. Here is an example that illustrates the establishment of a derivative formula.

Example 11.2.3   DERIVATIVE OF LOGARITHM

We want to verify that $d \ln z / dz = 1/z$. Writing, as in Eq. (1.138),

$$\ln z = \ln r + i\theta + 2n\pi i,$$

we note that if we write $\ln z = u + iv$, we have $u = \ln r$, $v = \theta + 2n\pi$. To check whether $\ln z$ satisfies the Cauchy-Riemann equations, we evaluate

$$\frac{\partial u}{\partial x} = \frac{1}{r}\frac{\partial r}{\partial x} = \frac{x}{r^2}, \quad \frac{\partial u}{\partial y} = \frac{1}{r}\frac{\partial r}{\partial y} = \frac{y}{r^2},$$

$$\frac{\partial v}{\partial x} = \frac{\partial \theta}{\partial x} = \frac{-y}{r^2}, \quad \frac{\partial v}{\partial y} = \frac{\partial \theta}{\partial y} = \frac{x}{r^2}.$$

The derivatives of r and θ with respect to x and y are obtained from the equations connecting Cartesian and polar coordinates. Except at $r = 0$, where the derivatives are undefined, the Cauchy-Riemann equations can be confirmed.

Then, to obtain the derivative, we can simply apply Eq. (11.12),

$$\frac{d \ln z}{dz} = \frac{\partial u}{\partial x} + i\frac{\partial v}{\partial x} = \frac{x - iy}{r^2} = \frac{1}{x + iy} = \frac{1}{z}.$$

Because $\ln z$ is multivalued, it will not be analytic except under conditions restricting it to single-valuedness in a specific region. This topic will be taken up in Section 11.6.   ∎

Point at Infinity

In complex variable theory, infinity is regarded as a single point, and behavior in its neighborhood is discussed after making a change of variable from z to $w = 1/z$. This transformation has the effect that, for example, $z = -R$, with R large, lies in the w plane close to $z = +R$, thereby among other things influencing the values computed for derivatives. An elementary consequence is that entire functions, such as z or e^z, have singular points at $z = \infty$. As a trivial example, note that at infinity the behavior of z is identified as that of $1/w$ as $w \to 0$, leading to the conclusion that z is singular there.

Exercises

11.2.1 Show whether or not the function $f(z) = \Re(z) = x$ is analytic.

11.2.2 Having shown that the real part $u(x, y)$ and the imaginary part $v(x, y)$ of an analytic function $w(z)$ each satisfy Laplace's equation, show that neither $u(x, y)$ nor $v(x, y)$ **can have either a maximum or a minimum** in the interior of any region in which $w(z)$ is analytic. (They can have saddle points only.)

11.2.3 Find the analytic function

$$w(z) = u(x, y) + iv(x, y)$$

(a) if $u(x, y) = x^3 - 3xy^2$, (b) if $v(x, y) = e^{-y} \sin x$.

11.2.4 If there is some common region in which $w_1 = u(x, y) + iv(x, y)$ and $w_2 = w_1^* = u(x, y) - iv(x, y)$ are both analytic, prove that $u(x, y)$ and $v(x, y)$ are constants.

11.2.5 Starting from $f(z) = 1/(x + iy)$, show that $1/z$ is analytic in the entire finite z plane except at the point $z = 0$. This extends our discussion of the analyticity of z^n to negative integer powers n.

11.2.6 Show that given the Cauchy-Riemann equations, the derivative $f'(z)$ has the same value for $dz = a\,dx + ib\,dy$ (with neither a nor b zero) as it has for $dz = dx$.

11.2.7 Using $f(re^{i\theta}) = R(r, \theta)e^{i\Theta(r,\theta)}$, in which $R(r, \theta)$ and $\Theta(r, \theta)$ are differentiable real functions of r and θ, show that the Cauchy-Riemann conditions in polar coordinates become

(a) $\dfrac{\partial R}{\partial r} = \dfrac{R}{r}\dfrac{\partial \Theta}{\partial \theta}$, (b) $\dfrac{1}{r}\dfrac{\partial R}{\partial \theta} = -R\dfrac{\partial \Theta}{\partial r}$.

Hint. Set up the derivative first with δz radial and then with δz tangential.

11.2.8 As an extension of Exercise 11.2.7 show that $\Theta(r, \theta)$ satisfies the 2-D Laplace equation in polar coordinates,

$$\frac{\partial^2 \Theta}{\partial r^2} + \frac{1}{r}\frac{\partial \Theta}{\partial r} + \frac{1}{r^2}\frac{\partial^2 \Theta}{\partial \theta^2} = 0.$$

11.2.9 For each of the following functions $f(z)$, find $f'(z)$ and identify the maximal region within which $f(z)$ is analytic.

(a) $f(z) = \dfrac{\sin z}{z}$,

(b) $f(z) = \dfrac{1}{z^2 + 1}$,

(c) $f(z) = \dfrac{1}{z(z + 1)}$,

(d) $f(z) = e^{-1/z}$,

(e) $f(z) = z^2 - 3z + 2$,

(f) $f(z) = \tan(z)$,

(g) $f(z) = \tanh(z)$.

11.2.10   For what complex values do each of the following functions $f(z)$ have a derivative?

  (a) $f(z) = z^{3/2}$,

  (b) $f(z) = z^{-3/2}$,

  (c) $f(z) = \tan^{-1}(z)$,

  (d) $f(z) = \tanh^{-1}(z)$.

11.2.11   Two-dimensional irrotational fluid flow is conveniently described by a complex potential $f(z) = u(x, v) + iv(x, y)$. We label the real part, $u(x, y)$, the velocity potential, and the imaginary part, $v(x, y)$, the stream function. The fluid velocity $\mathbf{V}$ is given by $\mathbf{V} = \nabla u$. If $f(z)$ is analytic:

  (a)   Show that $df/dz = V_x - iV_y$.

  (b)   Show that $\nabla \cdot \mathbf{V} = 0$ (no sources or sinks).

  (c)   Show that $\nabla \times \mathbf{V} = 0$ (irrotational, nonturbulent flow).

11.2.12   The function $f(z)$ is analytic. Show that the derivative of $f(z)$ with respect to z^* does not exist unless $f(z)$ is a constant.

  Hint. Use the chain rule and take $x = (z + z^*)/2$, $y = (z - z^*)/2i$.

  Note. This result emphasizes that our analytic function $f(z)$ is not just a complex function of two real variables x and y. It is a function of the complex variable $x + iy$.

11.3   CAUCHY'S INTEGRAL THEOREM

Contour Integrals

With differentiation under control, we turn to integration. The integral of a complex variable over a path in the complex plane (known as a **contour**) may be defined in close analogy to the (Riemann) integral of a real function integrated along the real x-axis.

We divide the contour, from z_0 to z_0', designated C, into n intervals by picking $n - 1$ intermediate points $z_1, z_2, \ldots$ on the contour (Fig. 11.2). Consider the sum

$$S_n = \sum_{j=1}^{n} f(\zeta_j)(z_j - z_{j-1}),$$

where ζ_j is a point on the curve between z_j and z_{j-1}. Now let $n \to \infty$ with

$$|z_j - z_{j-1}| \to 0$$

for all j. If $\lim_{n \to \infty} S_n$ exists, then

$$\lim_{n \to \infty} \sum_{j=1}^{n} f(\zeta_j)(z_j - z_{j-1}) = \int_{z_0}^{z_0'} f(z)\, dz = \int_C f(z)\, dz. \qquad (11.16)$$

The right-hand side of Eq. (11.16) is called the contour integral of $f(z)$ (along the specified contour C from $z = z_0$ to $z = z_0'$).

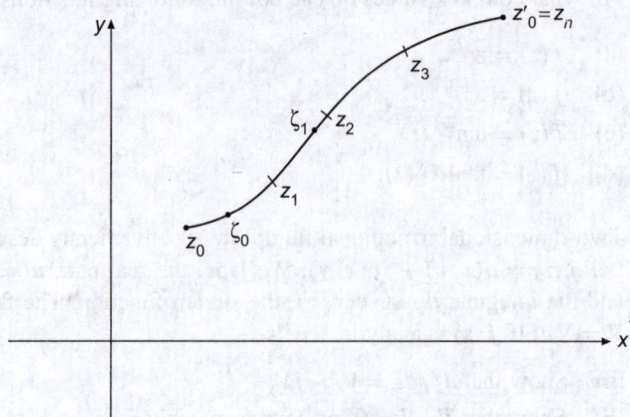

FIGURE 11.2   Integration path.

As an alternative to the above, the contour integral may be defined by

$$\int_{z_1}^{z_2} f(z)dz = \int_{x_1,y_1}^{x_2,y_2} [u(x,y) + iv(x,y)][dx + i\,dy]$$

$$= \int_{x_1,y_1}^{x_2,y_2} [u(x,y)dx - v(x,y)dy] + i \int_{x_1,y_1}^{x_2,y_2} [v(x,y)dx + u(x,y)dy], \quad (11.17)$$

with the path joining (x_1, y_1) and (x_2, y_2) specified. This reduces the complex integral to the complex sum of real integrals. It is somewhat analogous to the replacement of a vector integral by the vector sum of scalar integrals.

Often we are interested in contours that are **closed**, meaning that the start and end of the contour are at the same point, so that the contour forms a closed loop. We normally define the region enclosed by a contour as that which lies to the left when the contour is traversed in the indicated direction; thus a contour intended to surround a finite area will normally be deemed to be traversed in the counterclockwise direction. If the origin of a polar coordinate system is within the contour, this convention will cause the normal direction of travel on the contour to be that in which the polar angle θ increases.

Statement of Theorem

Cauchy's integral theorem states that:

> *If f(z) is an analytic function at all points of a simply connected region in the complex plane and if C is a closed contour within that region, then*

$$\oint_C f(z)\,dz = 0. \quad (11.18)$$

To clarify the above, we need the following definition:

- A region is **simply connected** if every closed curve within it can be shrunk continuously to a point that is within the region.

In everyday language, a simply connected region is one that has no holes. We also need to explain that the symbol $\oint$ will be used from now on to indicate an integral over a closed contour; a subscript (such as C) is attached when further specification of the contour is desired. Note also that for the theorem to apply, the contour must be "within" the region of analyticity. That means it cannot be on the boundary of the region.

Before proving Cauchy's integral theorem, we look at some examples that do (and do not) meet its conditions.

Example 11.3.1 z^n ON CIRCULAR CONTOUR

Let's examine the contour integral $\oint_C z^n dz$, where C is a circle of radius $r > 0$ around the origin $z = 0$ in the positive mathematical sense (counterclockwise). In polar coordinates, cf. Eq. (1.125), we parameterize the circle as $z = re^{i\theta}$ and $dz = ire^{i\theta} d\theta$. For $n \neq -1, n$ an integer, we then obtain

$$\oint_C z^n dz = i \, r^{n+1} \int_0^{2\pi} \exp[i(n+1)\theta] \, d\theta$$

$$= i \, r^{n+1} \left[\frac{e^{i(n+1)\theta}}{i(n+1)} \right]_0^{2\pi} = 0 \tag{11.19}$$

because 2π is a period of $e^{i(n+1)\theta}$. However, for $n = -1$

$$\oint_C \frac{dz}{z} = i \int_0^{2\pi} d\theta = 2\pi i, \tag{11.20}$$

independent of r but nonzero.

The fact that Eq. (11.19) is satisfied for all integers $n \geq 0$ is required by Cauchy's theorem, because for these n values z^n is analytic for all finite z, and certainly for all points within a circle of radius r. Cauchy's theorem does not apply for any negative integer n because, for these n, z^n is singular at $z = 0$. The theorem therefore does not prescribe any particular values for the integrals of negative n. We see that one such integral (that for $n = -1$) has a nonzero value, and that others (for integral $n \neq -1$) do vanish. ■

Example 11.3.2 z^n ON SQUARE CONTOUR

We next examine the integration of z^n for a different contour, a square with vertices at $\pm\frac{1}{2} \pm \frac{1}{2}i$. It is somewhat tedious to perform this integration for general integer n, so we illustrate only with $n = 2$ and $n = -1$.

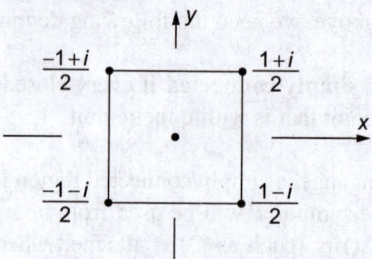

FIGURE 11.3   Square integration contour.

For $n = 2$, we have $z^2 = x^2 - y^2 + 2ixy$. Referring to Fig. 11.3, we identify the contour as consisting of four line segments. On Segment 1, $dz = dx$ ($y = -\frac{1}{2}$ and $dy = 0$); on Segment 2, $dz = i\, dy$, $x = \frac{1}{2}$, $dx = 0$; on Segment 3, $dz = dx$, $y = \frac{1}{2}$, $dy = 0$; and on Segment 4, $dz = i\, dy$, $x = -\frac{1}{2}$, $dx = 0$. Note that for Segments 3 and 4 the integration is in the direction of decreasing value of the integration variable. These segments therefore contribute as follows to the integral:

Segment 1: $\displaystyle\int_{-\frac{1}{2}}^{\frac{1}{2}} dx(x^2 - \tfrac{1}{4} - ix) = \frac{1}{3}\left[\frac{1}{8} - \left(-\frac{1}{8}\right)\right] - \frac{1}{4} - \frac{i}{2}(0) = -\frac{1}{6},$

Segment 2: $\displaystyle\int_{-\frac{1}{2}}^{\frac{1}{2}} i\, dy(\tfrac{1}{4} - y^2 + iy) = \frac{i}{4} - \frac{i}{3}\left[\frac{1}{8} - \left(-\frac{1}{8}\right)\right] - \frac{1}{2}(0) = \frac{i}{6},$

Segment 3: $\displaystyle\int_{\frac{1}{2}}^{-\frac{1}{2}} (dx)(x^2 - \tfrac{1}{4} + ix) = -\frac{1}{3}\left[\frac{1}{8} - \left(-\frac{1}{8}\right)\right] + \frac{1}{4} - \frac{i}{2}(0) = \frac{1}{6},$

Segment 4: $\displaystyle\int_{\frac{1}{2}}^{-\frac{1}{2}} (i\, dy)(\tfrac{1}{4} - y^2 - iy) = -\frac{i}{4} + \frac{i}{3}\left[\frac{1}{8} - \left(-\frac{1}{8}\right)\right] - \frac{1}{2}(0) = -\frac{i}{6}.$

We find that the integral of z^2 over the square vanishes, just as it did over the circle. This is required by Cauchy's theorem.

For $n = -1$, we have, in Cartesian coordinates,

$$z^{-1} = \frac{x - iy}{x^2 + y^2},$$

and the integral over the four segments of the square contour takes the form

$$
\int_{-\frac{1}{2}}^{\frac{1}{2}} \frac{x+i/2}{x^2+\frac{1}{4}}\,dx + \int_{-\frac{1}{2}}^{\frac{1}{2}} \frac{\frac{1}{2}-iy}{y^2+\frac{1}{4}}(i\,dy) + \int_{\frac{1}{2}}^{-\frac{1}{2}} \frac{x-i/2}{x^2+\frac{1}{4}}\,dx + \int_{\frac{1}{2}}^{-\frac{1}{2}} \frac{\frac{1}{2}+iy}{y^2+\frac{1}{4}}(i\,dy).
$$

Several of the terms vanish because they involve the integration of an odd integrand over an even interval, and others simply cancel. All that remains is

$$
\int_{\square} z^{-1}dz = i\int_{-\frac{1}{2}}^{\frac{1}{2}} \frac{dx}{x^2+\frac{1}{4}} = 2i\int_{-1}^{1} \frac{du}{u^2+1} = 2i\left[\frac{\pi}{2} - \left(-\frac{\pi}{2}\right)\right] = 2\pi i,
$$

the same result as was obtained for the integration of z^{-1} around a circle of any radius. Cauchy's theorem does not apply here, so the nonzero result is not problematic. ∎

Cauchy's Theorem: Proof

We now proceed to a proof of Cauchy's integral theorem. The proof we offer is subject to a restriction originally accepted by Cauchy but later shown unnecessary by Goursat. What we need to show is that

$$
\oint_C f(z)\,dz = 0,
$$

subject to the requirement that C is a closed contour within a simply connected region R where $f(z)$ is analytic. See Fig. 11.4. The restriction needed for Cauchy's (and the present) proof is that if we write $f(z) = u(x, y) + iv(x, y)$, the partial derivatives of u and v are continuous.

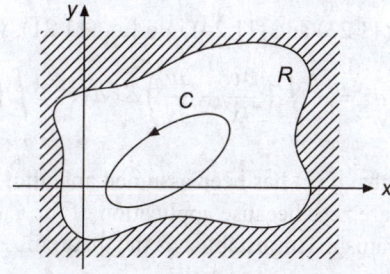

FIGURE 11.4   A closed-contour C within a simply connected region R.

We intend to prove the theorem by direct application of Stokes' theorem (Section 3.8). Writing $dz = dx + i\,dy$,

$$\oint_C f(z)\,dz = \oint_C (u + iv)(dx + i\,dy)$$

$$= \oint_C (u\,dx - v\,dy) + i \oint_C (v\,dx + u\,dy). \tag{11.21}$$

These two line integrals may be converted to surface integrals by Stokes' theorem, a procedure that is justified because we have assumed the partial derivatives to be continuous within the area enclosed by C. In applying Stokes' theorem, note that the final two integrals of Eq. (11.21) are real.

To proceed further, we note that all the integrals involved here can be identified as having integrands of the form $(V_x \hat{\mathbf{e}}_x + V_y \hat{\mathbf{e}}_y) \cdot d\mathbf{r}$, the integration is around a loop in the xy plane, and the value of the integral will be the surface integral, over the enclosed area, of the z component of $\nabla \times (V_x \hat{\mathbf{e}}_x + V_y \hat{\mathbf{e}}_y)$. Thus, Stokes' theorem says that

$$\oint_C (V_x\,dx + V_y\,dy) = \int_A \left(\frac{\partial V_y}{\partial x} - \frac{\partial V_x}{\partial y} \right) dx\,dy, \tag{11.22}$$

with A being the 2-D region enclosed by C.

For the first integral in the second line of Eq. (11.21), let $u = V_x$ and $v = -V_y$.[2] Then

$$\oint_C (u\,dx - v\,dy) = \oint_C (V_x\,dx + V_y\,dy)$$

$$= \int_A \left(\frac{\partial V_y}{\partial x} - \frac{\partial V_x}{\partial y} \right) dx\,dy = -\int_A \left(\frac{\partial v}{\partial x} + \frac{\partial u}{\partial y} \right) dx\,dy. \tag{11.23}$$

For the second integral on the right side of Eq. (11.21) we let $u = V_y$ and $v = V_x$. Using Stokes' theorem again, we obtain

$$\oint_C (v\,dx + u\,dy) = \int_A \left(\frac{\partial u}{\partial x} - \frac{\partial v}{\partial y} \right) dx\,dy. \tag{11.24}$$

Inserting Eqs. (11.23) and (11.24) into Eq. (11.21), we now have

$$\oint_C f(z)\,dz = -\int_A \left(\frac{\partial v}{\partial x} + \frac{\partial u}{\partial y} \right) dx\,dy + i \int_A \left(\frac{\partial u}{\partial x} - \frac{\partial v}{\partial y} \right) dx\,dy = 0. \tag{11.25}$$

Remembering that $f(z)$ has been assumed analytic, we find that both the surface integrals in Eq. (11.25) are zero because application of the Cauchy-Riemann equations causes their integrands to vanish. This establishes the theorem.

---

[2] For Stokes' theorem, V_x and V_y are any two functions with continuous partial derivatives, and they need not be connected by any relations stemming from complex variable theory.

Multiply Connected Regions

The original statement of Cauchy's integral theorem demanded a simply connected region of analyticity. This restriction may be relaxed by the creation of a barrier, a narrow region we choose to exclude from the region identified as analytic. The purpose of the barrier construction is to permit, within a multiply connected region, the identification of curves that can be shrunk to a point within the region, that is, construction of a subregion that is simply connected.

Consider the multiply connected region of Fig. 11.5, in which $f(z)$ is only analytic in the unshaded area labeled R. Cauchy's integral theorem is not valid for the contour C, as shown, but we can construct a contour C' for which the theorem holds. We draw a barrier from the interior forbidden region, R', to the forbidden region exterior to R and then run a new contour, C', as shown in Fig. 11.6.

The new contour, C', through $ABDEFGA$, never crosses the barrier that converts R into a simply connected region. Incidentally, the three-dimensional analog of this technique was used in Section 3.9 to prove Gauss' law. Because $f(z)$ is in fact continuous across the barrier dividing DE from GA and the line segments DE and GA can be arbitrarily close together, we have

$$\int_G^A f(z)\,dz = -\int_E^D f(z)\,dz. \qquad (11.26)$$

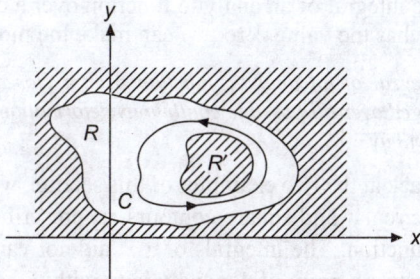

FIGURE 11.5   A closed contour C in a multiply connected region.

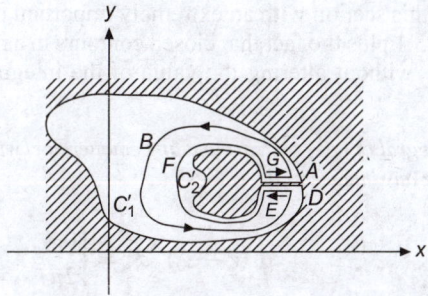

FIGURE 11.6   Conversion of a multiply connected region into a simply connected region.

Then, invoking Cauchy's integral theorem, because the contour is now within a simply connected region, and using Eq. (11.26) to cancel the contributions of the segments along the barrier,

$$\oint_{C'} f(z)\,dz = \int_{ABD} f(z)\,dz + \int_{EFG} f(z)\,dz = 0. \tag{11.27}$$

Now that we have established Eq. (11.27), we note that A and D are only infinitesimally separated and that $f(z)$ is actually continuous across the barrier. Hence, integration on the path ABD will yield the same result as a truly closed contour $ABDA$. Similar remarks apply to the path EFG, which can be replaced by $EFGE$. Renaming $ABDA$ as C_l' and $EFGE$ as $-C_2'$, we have the simple result

$$\oint_{C_1'} f(z)\,dz = \oint_{C_2'} f(z)\,dz, \tag{11.28}$$

in which C_1' and C_2' are both traversed in the same (counterclockwise, that is, positive) direction.

This result calls for some interpretation. What we have shown is that the integral of an analytic function over a closed contour surrounding an "island" of nonanalyticity can be subjected to any continuous deformation within the region of analyticity without changing the value of the integral. The notion of *continuous deformation* means that the change in contour must be able to be carried out via a series of small steps, which precludes processes whereby we "jump over" a point or region of nonanalyticity. Since we already know that the integral of an analytic function over a contour in a simply connected region of analyticity has the value zero, we can make the more general statement

> *The integral of an analytic function over a closed path has a value that remains unchanged over all possible continuous deformations of the contour within the region of analyticity.*

Looking back at the two examples of this section, we see that the integrals of z^2 vanished for both the circular and square contours, as prescribed by Cauchy's integral theorem for an analytic function. The integrals of z^{-1} did not vanish, and vanishing was not required because there was a point of nonanalyticity within the contours. However, the integrals of z^{-1} for the two contours had the same value, as either contour can be reached by continuous deformation of the other.

We close this section with an extremely important observation. By a trivial extension to Example 11.3.1 plus the fact that closed contours in a region of analyticity can be deformed continuously without altering the value of the integral, we have the valuable and useful result:

> *The integral of $(z - z_0)^n$ around any counterclockwise closed path C that encloses z_0 has, for any integer n, the values*

$$\oint_C (z - z_0)^n\,dz = \begin{cases} 0, & n \neq -1, \\ 2\pi i, & n = -1. \end{cases} \tag{11.29}$$

Exercises

11.3.1 Show that $\displaystyle\int_{z_1}^{z_2} f(z)\,dz = -\int_{z_2}^{z_1} f(z)\,dz.$

11.3.2 Prove that $\displaystyle\left| \int_C f(z)\,dz \right| \le |f|_{\max} \cdot L,$

where $|f|_{\max}$ is the maximum value of $|f(z)|$ along the contour C and L is the length of the contour.

11.3.3 Show that the integral

$$\int_{3+4i}^{4-3i} (4z^2 - 3iz)\,dz$$

has the same value on the two paths: (a) the straight line connecting the integration limits, and (b) an arc on the circle $|z| = 5$.

11.3.4 Let $\displaystyle F(z) = \int_{\pi(1+i)}^{z} \cos 2\zeta \,d\zeta.$

Show that $F(z)$ is independent of the path connecting the limits of integration, and evaluate $F(\pi i)$.

11.3.5 Evaluate $\oint_C (x^2 - iy^2)\,dz$, where the integration is (a) clockwise around the unit circle, (b) on a square with vertices at $\pm 1 \pm i$. Explain why the results of parts (a) and (b) are or are not identical.

11.3.6 Verify that

$$\int_0^{1+i} z^* dz$$

depends on the path by evaluating the integral for the two paths shown in Fig. 11.7. Recall that $f(z) = z^*$ is not an analytic function of z and that Cauchy's integral theorem therefore does not apply.

11.3.7 Show that

$$\oint_C \frac{dz}{z^2 + z} = 0,$$

in which the contour C is a circle defined by $|z| = R > 1$.

Hint. Direct use of the Cauchy integral theorem is illegal. The integral may be evaluated by expanding into partial fractions and then treating the two terms individually. This yields 0 for $R > 1$ and $2\pi i$ for $R < 1$.

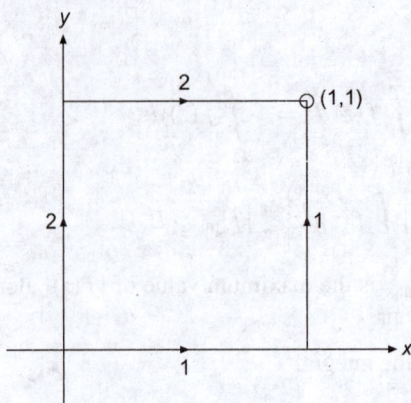

FIGURE 11.7   Contours for Exercise 11.3.6.

11.4 CAUCHY'S INTEGRAL FORMULA

As in the preceding section, we consider a function $f(z)$ that is analytic on a closed contour C and within the interior region bounded by C. This means that the contour C is to be traversed in the **counterclockwise** direction. We seek to prove the following result, known as **Cauchy's integral formula**:

$$\frac{1}{2\pi i} \oint_C \frac{f(z)}{z - z_0}\, dz = f(z_0), \tag{11.30}$$

in which z_0 is any point in the interior region bounded by C. Note that since z is on the contour C while z_0 is in the interior, $z - z_0 \neq 0$ and the integral Eq. (11.30) is well defined. Although $f(z)$ is assumed analytic, the integrand is $f(z)/(z - z_0)$ and is not analytic at $z = z_0$ unless $f(z_0) = 0$. We now deform the contour, to make it a circle of small radius r about $z = z_0$, traversed, like the original contour, in the counterclockwise direction. As shown in the preceding section, this does not change the value of the integral. We therefore write $z = z_0 + re^{i\theta}$, so $dz = ire^{i\theta}\, d\theta$, the integration is from $\theta = 0$ to $\theta = 2\pi$, and

$$\oint_C \frac{f(z)}{z - z_0}\, dz = \int_0^{2\pi} \frac{f(z_0 + re^{i\theta})}{re^{i\theta}} ire^{i\theta}\, d\theta.$$

Taking the limit $r \to 0$, we obtain

$$\oint_C \frac{f(z)}{z - z_0}\, dz = if(z_0) \int_0^{2\pi} d\theta = 2\pi i f(z_0), \tag{11.31}$$

where we have replaced $f(z)$ by its limit $f(z_0)$ because it is analytic and therefore continuous at $z = z_0$. This proves the Cauchy integral formula.

Here is a remarkable result. The value of an analytic function $f(z)$ is given at an arbitrary interior point $z = z_0$ once the values on the boundary C are specified.

It has been emphasized that z_0 is an interior point. What happens if z_0 is exterior to C? In this case the entire integrand is analytic on and within C. Cauchy's integral theorem, Section 11.3, applies and the integral vanishes. Summarizing, we have

$$\frac{1}{2\pi i} \oint_C \frac{f(z)\, dz}{z - z_0} = \begin{cases} f(z_0), & z_0 \text{ within the contour,} \\ 0, & z_0 \text{ exterior to the contour.} \end{cases}$$

Example 11.4.1   AN INTEGRAL

Consider

$$I = \oint_C \frac{dz}{z(z+2)},$$

where the integration is counterclockwise over the unit circle. The factor $1/(z+2)$ is analytic within the region enclosed by the contour, so this is a case of Cauchy's integral formula, Eq. (11.30), with $f(z) = 1/(z+2)$ and $z_0 = 0$. The result is immediate:

$$I = 2\pi i \left[\frac{1}{z+2} \right]_{z=0} = \pi i.$$

■

Example 11.4.2   INTEGRAL WITH TWO SINGULAR FACTORS

Consider now

$$I = \oint_C \frac{dz}{4z^2 - 1},$$

also integrated counterclockwise over the unit circle. The denominator factors into $4\left(z - \frac{1}{2}\right)\left(z + \frac{1}{2}\right)$, and it is apparent that the region of integration contains two singular factors. However, we may still use Cauchy's integral formula if we make the partial fraction expansion

$$\frac{1}{4z^2 - 1} = \frac{1}{4}\left(\frac{1}{z - \frac{1}{2}} - \frac{1}{z + \frac{1}{2}} \right),$$

after which we integrate the two terms individually. We have

$$I = \frac{1}{4}\left[\oint_C \frac{dz}{z - \frac{1}{2}} - \oint_C \frac{dz}{z + \frac{1}{2}} \right].$$

Each integral is a case of Cauchy's formula with $f(z) = 1$, and for both integrals the point $z_0 = \pm\frac{1}{2}$ is within the contour, so each evaluates to $2\pi i$, and their sum is zero. So $I = 0$.

■

Derivatives

Cauchy's integral formula may be used to obtain an expression for the derivative of $f(z)$. Differentiating Eq. (11.30) with respect to z_0, and interchanging the differentiation and the z integration,[3]

$$f'(z_0) = \frac{1}{2\pi i} \oint \frac{f(z)}{(z - z_0)^2} \, dz.$$ (11.32)

Differentiating again,

$$f''(z_0) = \frac{2}{2\pi i} \oint \frac{f(z) \, dz}{(z - z_0)^3}.$$

Continuing, we get[4]

$$f^{(n)}(z_0) = \frac{n!}{2\pi i} \oint \frac{f(z) \, dz}{(z - z_0)^{n+1}};$$ (11.33)

that is, the requirement that $f(z)$ be analytic guarantees not only a first derivative but derivatives of **all** orders as well! The derivatives of $f(z)$ are automatically analytic. As indicated in a footnote, this statement assumes the Goursat version of the Cauchy integral theorem. This is a reason why Goursat's contribution is so significant in the development of the theory of complex variables.

Example 11.4.3   USE OF DERIVATIVE FORMULA

Consider

$$I = \oint_C \frac{\sin^2 z \, dz}{(z - a)^4},$$

where the integral is counterclockwise on a contour that encircles the point $z = a$. This is a case of Eq. (11.33) with $n = 3$ and $f(z) = \sin^2 z$. Therefore,

$$I = \frac{2\pi i}{3!} \left[\frac{d^3}{dz^3} \sin^2 z \right]_{z=a} = \frac{\pi i}{3} \left[-8 \sin z \cos z \right]_{z=a} = -\frac{8\pi i}{3} \sin a \cos a.$$

■

---

[3] The interchange can be proved legitimate, but the proof requires that Cauchy's integral theorem not be subject to the continuous derivative restriction in Cauchy's original proof. We are therefore now depending on Goursat's proof of the integral theorem.

[4] This expression is a starting point for defining derivatives of **fractional order**. See A. Erdelyi, ed., *Tables of Integral Transforms*, Vol. 2. New York: McGraw-Hill (1954). For more recent applications to mathematical analysis, see T. J. Osler, An integral analogue of Taylor's series and its use in computing Fourier transforms, *Math. Comput.* **26**: 449 (1972), and references therein.

Morera's Theorem

A further application of Cauchy's integral formula is in the proof of Morera's **theorem**, which is the converse of Cauchy's integral theorem. The theorem states the following:

If a function $f(z)$ is continuous in a simply connected region R and $\oint_C f(z)dz = 0$ for every closed contour C within R, then $f(z)$ is analytic throughout R.

To prove the theorem, let us integrate $f(z)$ from z_1 to z_2. Since every closed-path integral of $f(z)$ vanishes, this integral is independent of path and depends only on its endpoints. We may therefore write

$$F(z_2) - F(z_1) = \int_{z_1}^{z_2} f(z)\, dz, \tag{11.34}$$

where $F(z)$, presently unknown, can be called the indefinite integral of $f(z)$. We then construct the identity

$$\frac{F(z_2) - F(z_1)}{z_2 - z_1} - f(z_1) = \frac{1}{z_2 - z_1} \int_{z_1}^{z_2} \Big[f(t) - f(z_1) \Big]\, dt, \tag{11.35}$$

where we have introduced another complex variable, t. Next, using the fact that $f(t)$ is continuous, we write, keeping only terms to first order in $t - z_1$,

$$f(t) - f(z_1) = f'(z_1)(t - z_1) + \cdots,$$

which implies that

$$\int_{z_1}^{z_2} \Big[f(t) - f(z_1) \Big]\, dt = \int_{z_1}^{z_2} \Big[f'(z_1)(t - z_1) + \cdots \Big]\, dt = \frac{f'(z_1)}{2}(z_2 - z_1)^2 + \cdots.$$

It is thus apparent that the right-hand side of Eq. (11.35) approaches zero in the limit $z_2 \to z_1$, so

$$f(z_1) = \lim_{z_2 \to z_1} \frac{F(z_2) - F(z_1)}{z_2 - z_1} = F'(z_1). \tag{11.36}$$

Equation (11.36) shows that $F(z)$, which by construction is single-valued, has a derivative at all points within R and is therefore analytic in that region. Since $F(z)$ is analytic, then so also must be its derivative, $f(z)$, thereby proving Morera's theorem.

At this point, one comment might be in order. Morera's theorem, which establishes the analyticity of $F(z)$ in a simply connected region, cannot be extended to prove that $F(z)$, as well as $f(z)$, is analytic throughout a multiply connected region via the device of introducing a barrier. It is not possible to show that $F(z)$ will have the same value on both sides of the barrier, and in fact it does not always have that property. Thus, if extended to a multiply connected region, $F(z)$ may fail to have the single-valuedness that is one of the requirements for analyticity. Put another way, a function which is analytic in a multiply connected region will have analytic derivatives of all orders in that region, but its integral is not guaranteed to be analytic in the entire multiply connected region. This issue is elaborated in Section 11.6.

The proof of Morera's theorem has given us something additional, namely that the indefinite integral of $f(z)$ is its antiderivative, showing that:

> *The rules for integration of complex functions are the same as those for real functions.*

Further Applications

An important application of Cauchy's integral formula is the following **Cauchy inequality**. If $f(z) = \sum a_n z^n$ is analytic and bounded, $|f(z)| \le M$ on a circle of radius r about the origin, then

$$|a_n| r^n \le M \quad \text{(Cauchy's inequality)} \tag{11.37}$$

gives upper bounds for the coefficients of its Taylor expansion. To prove Eq. (11.37) let us define $M(r) = \max_{|z|=r} |f(z)|$ and use the Cauchy integral for $a_n = f^{(n)}(z)/n!$,

$$|a_n| = \frac{1}{2\pi} \left| \oint_{|z|=r} \frac{f(z)}{z^{n+1}} \, dz \right| \le M(r) \frac{2\pi r}{2\pi r^{n+1}}.$$

An immediate consequence of the inequality, Eq. (11.37), is **Liouville's theorem**: If $f(z)$ is analytic and bounded in the entire complex plane it is a constant. In fact, if $|f(z)| \le M$ for all z, then Cauchy's inequality Eq. (11.37), applied for $|z| = r$, gives $|a_n| \le M r^{-n}$. If now we choose to let r approach ∞, we may conclude that for all $n > 0$, $|a_n| = 0$. Hence $f(z) = a_0$.

Conversely, the slightest deviation of an analytic function from a constant value implies that there must be at least one singularity somewhere in the infinite complex plane. Apart from the trivial constant functions then, singularities are a fact of life, and we must learn to live with them. As pointed out when introducing the concept of the point at infinity, even innocuous functions such as $f(z) = z$ have singularities at infinity; we now know that this is a property of every entire function that is not simply a constant. But we shall do more than just tolerate the existence of singularities. In the next section, we show how to expand a function in a Laurent series at a singularity, and we go on to use singularities to develop the powerful and useful calculus of residues in a later section of this chapter.

A famous application of Liouville's theorem yields the **fundamental theorem of algebra** (due to C. F. Gauss), which says that any polynomial $P(z) = \sum_{v=0}^{n} a_v z^v$ with $n > 0$ and $a_n \ne 0$ has n roots. To prove this, suppose $P(z)$ has no zero. Then $1/P(z)$ is analytic and bounded as $|z| \to \infty$, and, because of Liouville's theorem, $P(z)$ would have to be a constant. To resolve this contradiction, it must be the case that $P(z)$ has at least one root λ that we can divide out, forming $P(z)/(z-\lambda)$, a polynomial of degree $n-1$. We can repeat this process until the polynomial has been reduced to degree zero, thereby finding exactly n roots.

Exercises

Unless explicitly stated otherwise, closed contours occurring in these exercises are to be understood as traversed in the mathematically positive (counterclockwise) direction.

11.4.1 Show that

$$\frac{1}{2\pi i} \oint z^{m-n-1} dz, \quad m \text{ and } n \text{ integers}$$

(with the contour encircling the origin once), is a representation of the Kronecker δ_{mn}.

11.4.2 Evaluate

$$\oint_C \frac{dz}{z^2 - 1},$$

where C is the circle $|z - 1| = 1$.

11.4.3 Assuming that $f(z)$ is analytic on and within a closed contour C and that the point z_0 is within C, show that

$$\oint_C \frac{f'(z)}{z - z_0} dz = \oint_C \frac{f(z)}{(z - z_0)^2} dz.$$

11.4.4 You know that $f(z)$ is analytic on and within a closed contour C. You suspect that the nth derivative $f^{(n)}(z_0)$ is given by

$$f^{(n)}(z_0) = \frac{n!}{2\pi i} \oint_C \frac{f(z)}{(z - z_0)^{n+1}} dz.$$

Using mathematical induction (Section 1.4), prove that this expression is correct.

11.4.5 (a) A function $f(z)$ is analytic within a closed contour C (and continuous on C). If $f(z) \neq 0$ within C and $|f(z)| \leq M$ on C, show that

$$|f(z)| \leq M$$

for all points within C.

Hint. Consider $w(z) = 1/f(z)$.

(b) If $f(z) = 0$ within the contour C, show that the foregoing result does not hold and that it is possible to have $|f(z)| = 0$ at one or more points in the interior with $|f(z)| > 0$ over the entire bounding contour. Cite a specific example of an analytic function that behaves this way.

11.4.6 Evaluate

$$\oint_C \frac{e^{iz}}{z^3} dz,$$

for the contour a square with sides of length $a > 1$, centered at $z = 0$.

11.4.7   Evaluate

$$\oint_C \frac{\sin^2 z - z^2}{(z-a)^3} dz,$$

where the contour encircles the point $z = a$.

11.4.8   Evaluate

$$\oint_C \frac{dz}{z(2z+1)},$$

for the contour the unit circle.

11.4.9   Evaluate

$$\oint_C \frac{f(z)}{z(2z+1)^2} dz,$$

for the contour the unit circle.

Hint. Make a partial fraction expansion.

11.5   LAURENT EXPANSION

Taylor Expansion

The Cauchy integral formula of the preceding section opens up the way for another derivation of Taylor's series (Section 1.2), but this time for functions of a complex variable. Suppose we are trying to expand $f(z)$ about $z = z_0$ and we have $z = z_1$ as the nearest point on the Argand diagram for which $f(z)$ is not analytic. We construct a circle C centered at $z = z_0$ with radius less than $|z_1 - z_0|$ (Fig. 11.8). Since z_1 was assumed to be the nearest point at which $f(z)$ was not analytic, $f(z)$ is necessarily analytic on and within C.

From the Cauchy integral formula, Eq. (11.30),

$$\begin{aligned}
f(z) &= \frac{1}{2\pi i} \oint_C \frac{f(z')\,dz'}{z'-z} \\
&= \frac{1}{2\pi i} \oint_C \frac{f(z')\,dz'}{(z'-z_0) - (z-z_0)} \\
&= \frac{1}{2\pi i} \oint_C \frac{f(z')\,dz'}{(z'-z_0)[1 - (z-z_0)/(z'-z_0)]}.
\end{aligned} \tag{11.38}$$

Here z' is a point on the contour C and z is any point interior to C. It is not legal yet to expand the denominator of the integrand in Eq. (11.38) by the binomial theorem, for

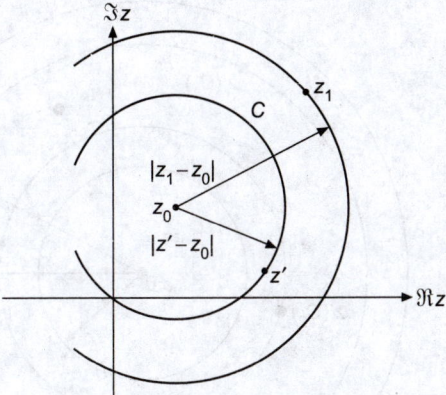

FIGURE 11.8   Circular domains for Taylor expansion.

we have not yet proved the binomial theorem for complex variables. Instead, we note the identity

$$\frac{1}{1-t} = 1 + t + t^2 + t^3 + \cdots = \sum_{n=0}^{\infty} t^n, \tag{11.39}$$

which may easily be verified by multiplying both sides by $1 - t$. The infinite series, following the methods of Section 1.2, is convergent for $|t| < 1$.

Now, for a point z interior to C, $|z - z_0| < |z' - z_0|$, and, using Eq. (11.39), Eq. (11.38) becomes

$$f(z) = \frac{1}{2\pi i} \oint_C \sum_{n=0}^{\infty} \frac{(z - z_0)^n f(z') \, dz'}{(z' - z_0)^{n+1}}. \tag{11.40}$$

Interchanging the order of integration and summation, which is valid because Eq. (11.39) is uniformly convergent for $|t| < 1 - \varepsilon$, with $0 < \varepsilon < 1$, we obtain

$$f(z) = \frac{1}{2\pi i} \sum_{n=0}^{\infty} (z - z_0)^n \oint_C \frac{f(z') \, dz'}{(z' - z_0)^{n+1}}. \tag{11.41}$$

Referring to Eq. (11.33), we get

$$f(z) = \sum_{n=0}^{\infty} \frac{f^{(n)}(z_0)}{n!} (z - z_0)^n, \tag{11.42}$$

which is our desired Taylor expansion.

It is important to note that our derivation not only produces the expansion given in Eq. (11.41); it also shows that this expansion converges when $|z - z_0| < |z_1 - z_0|$. For this reason the circle defined by $|z - z_0| = |z_1 - z_0|$ is called the **circle of convergence** of our

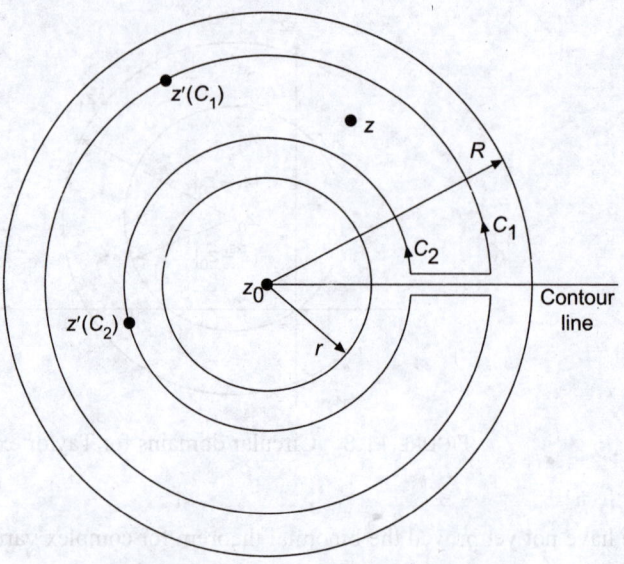

FIGURE 11.9   Annular region for Laurent series.
$$|z' - z_0|_{C_1} > |z - z_0|; \; |z' - z_0|_{C_2} < |z - z_0|.$$

Taylor series. Alternatively, the distance $|z_1 - z_0|$ is sometimes referred to as the **radius of convergence** of the Taylor series. In view of the earlier definition of z_1, we can say that:

> *The Taylor series of a function $f(z)$ about any interior point z_0 of a region in which $f(z)$ is analytic is a* **unique expansion** *that will have a radius of convergence equal to the distance from z_0 to the singularity of $f(z)$ closest to z_0, meaning that the Taylor series will converge* **within** *this circle of convergence. The Taylor series may or may not converge at individual points* **on** *the circle of convergence.*

From the Taylor expansion for $f(z)$ a binomial theorem may be derived. That task is left to Exercise 11.5.2.

Laurent Series

We frequently encounter functions that are analytic in an annular region, say, between circles of inner radius r and outer radius R about a point z_0, as shown in Fig. 11.9. We assume $f(z)$ to be such a function, with z a typical point in the annular region. Drawing an imaginary barrier to convert our region into a simply connected region, we apply Cauchy's integral formula to evaluate $f(z)$, using the contour shown in the figure. Note that the contour consists of the two circles centered at z_0, labeled C_1 and C_2 (which can be considered closed since the barrier is fictitious), plus segments on either side of the barrier whose contributions will cancel. We assign C_2 and C_1 the radii r_2 and r_1, respectively, where $r < r_2 < r_1 < R$. Then, from Cauchy's integral formula,

$$f(z) = \frac{1}{2\pi i} \oint_{C_1} \frac{f(z')\,dz'}{z' - z} - \frac{1}{2\pi i} \oint_{C_2} \frac{f(z')\,dz'}{z' - z}. \tag{11.43}$$

Note that in Eq. (11.43)) an explicit minus sign has been introduced so that the contour C_2 (like C_1) is to be traversed in the positive (counterclockwise) sense. The treatment of

Eq. (11.43) now proceeds exactly like that of Eq. (11.38) in the development of the Taylor series. Each denominator is written as $(z' - z_0) - (z - z_0)$ and expanded by the binomial theorem, which is now regarded as proven (see Exercise 11.5.2).

Noting that for C_1, $|z' - z_0| > |z - z_0|$, while for C_2, $|z' - z_0| < |z - z_0|$, we find

$$f(z) = \frac{1}{2\pi i} \sum_{n=0}^{\infty} (z - z_0)^n \oint_{C_1} \frac{f(z')\, dz'}{(z' - z_0)^{n+1}} + \frac{1}{2\pi i} \sum_{n=1}^{\infty} (z - z_0)^{-n} \oint_{C_2} (z' - z_0)^{n-1} f(z')\, dz'.$$

(11.44)

The minus sign of Eq. (11.43) has been absorbed by the binomial expansion. Labeling the first series S_1 and the second S_2 we have

$$S_1 = \frac{1}{2\pi i} \sum_{n=0}^{\infty} (z - z_0)^n \oint_{C_1} \frac{f(z')\, dz'}{(z' - z_0)^{n+1}},$$

(11.45)

which has the same form as the regular Taylor expansion, convergent for $|z - z_0| < |z' - z_0| = r_1$, that is, for all z **interior** to the larger circle, C_1. For the second series in Eq. (6.65) we have

$$S_2 = \frac{1}{2\pi i} \sum_{n=1}^{\infty} (z - z_0)^{-n} \oint_{C_2} (z' - z_0)^{n-1} f(z')\, dz',$$

(11.46)

convergent for $|z - z_0| > |z' - z_0| = r_2$, that is, for all z **exterior** to the smaller circle, C_2. Remember, C_2 now goes counterclockwise.

These two series are combined into one series,[5] known as a **Laurent series**, of the form

$$f(z) = \sum_{n=-\infty}^{\infty} a_n (z - z_0)^n,$$

(11.47)

where

$$a_n = \frac{1}{2\pi i} \oint_{C} \frac{f(z')\, dz'}{(z' - z_0)^{n+1}}.$$

(11.48)

Since convergence of a binomial expansion is not relevant to the evaluation of Eq. (11.48), C in that equation may be any contour within the annular region $r < |z - z_0| < R$ that encircles z_0 once in a counterclockwise sense. If such an annular region of analyticity does exist, then Eq. (11.47) is the Laurent series, or Laurent expansion, of $f(z)$.

The Laurent series differs from the Taylor series by the obvious feature of negative powers of $(z - z_0)$. For this reason the Laurent series will always diverge at least at $z = z_0$ and perhaps as far out as some distance r. In addition, note that Laurent series coefficients need not come from evaluation of contour integrals (which may be very intractable). Other techniques, such as ordinary series expansions, may provide the coefficients.

Numerous examples of Laurent series appear later in this book. We limit ourselves here to one simple example to illustrate the application of Eq. (11.47).

---

[5]Replace n by $-n$ in S_2 and add.

Example 11.5.1   LAURENT EXPANSION

Let $f(z) = [z(z-1)]^{-1}$. If we choose to make the Laurent expansion about $z_0 = 0$, then $r > 0$ and $R < 1$. These limitations arise because $f(z)$ diverges both at $z = 0$ and $z = 1$. A partial fraction expansion, followed by the binomial expansion of $(1-z)^{-1}$, yields the Laurent series

$$\frac{1}{z(z-1)} = -\frac{1}{1-z} \cdot \frac{1}{z} = -\frac{1}{z} - 1 - z - z^2 - z^3 - \cdots = -\sum_{n=-1}^{\infty} z^n. \qquad (11.49)$$

From Eqs. (11.49), (11.47), and (11.48), we then have

$$a_n = \frac{1}{2\pi i} \oint \frac{dz'}{(z')^{n+2}(z'-1)} = \begin{cases} -1 & \text{for } n \geq -1, \\ 0 & \text{for } n < -1, \end{cases} \qquad (11.50)$$

where the contour for Eq. (11.50) is counterclockwise in the annular region between $z' = 0$ and $|z'| = 1$.

The integrals in Eq. (11.50) can also be directly evaluated by insertion of the geometric-series expansion of $(1-z')^{-1}$:

$$a_n = \frac{-1}{2\pi i} \oint \sum_{m=0}^{\infty} (z')^m \frac{dz'}{(z')^{n+2}}. \qquad (11.51)$$

Upon interchanging the order of summation and integration (permitted because the series is uniformly convergent), we have

$$a_n = -\frac{1}{2\pi i} \sum_{m=0}^{\infty} \oint (z')^{m-n-2} \, dz'. \qquad (11.52)$$

The integral in Eq. (11.52) (including the initial factor $1/2\pi i$, but not the minus sign) was shown in Exercise 11.4.1 to be an integral representation of the Kronecker delta, and is therefore equal to $\delta_{m,n+1}$. The expression for a_n then reduces to

$$a_n = -\sum_{m=0}^{\infty} \delta_{m,n+1} = \begin{cases} -1, & n \geq -1, \\ 0, & n < -1, \end{cases}$$

in agreement with Eq. (11.50).   ∎

Exercises

11.5.1   Develop the Taylor expansion of $\ln(1+z)$.

$$ANS. \quad \sum_{n=1}^{\infty} (-1)^{n-1} \frac{z^n}{n}.$$

11.5.2   Derive the binomial expansion

$$(1+z)^m = 1 + mz + \frac{m(m-1)}{1 \cdot 2} z^2 + \cdots = \sum_{n=0}^{\infty} \binom{m}{n} z^n$$

for m, any real number. The expansion is convergent for $|z| < 1$. Why?

11.5.3   A function $f(z)$ is analytic on and within the unit circle. Also, $|f(z)| < 1$ for $|z| \leq 1$ and $f(0) = 0$. Show that $|f(z)| < |z|$ for $|z| \leq 1$.

Hint. One approach is to show that $f(z)/z$ is analytic and then to express $[f(z_0)/z_0]^n$ by the Cauchy integral formula. Finally, consider absolute magnitudes and take the nth root. This exercise is sometimes called Schwarz's theorem.

11.5.4   If $f(z)$ is a real function of the complex variable $z = x + iy$, that is, $f(x) = f^*(x)$, and the Laurent expansion about the origin, $f(z) = \sum a_n z^n$, has $a_n = 0$ for $n < -N$, show that all of the coefficients a_n are real.

Hint. Show that $z^N f(z)$ is analytic (via Morera's theorem, Section 11.4).

11.5.5   Prove that the Laurent expansion of a given function about a given point is unique; that is, if

$$f(z) = \sum_{n=-N}^{\infty} a_n (z - z_0)^n = \sum_{n=-N}^{\infty} b_n (z - z_0)^n,$$

show that $a_n = b_n$ for all n.

Hint. Use the Cauchy integral formula.

11.5.6   Obtain the Laurent expansion of e^z/z^2 about $z = 0$.

11.5.7   Obtain the Laurent expansion of $ze^z/(z-1)$ about $z = 1$.

11.5.8   Obtain the Laurent expansion of $(z-1)\,e^{1/z}$ about $z = 0$.

11.6   SINGULARITIES

Poles

We define a point z_0 as an **isolated** singular point of the function $f(z)$ if $f(z)$ is not analytic at $z = z_0$ but is analytic at all neighboring points. There will therefore be a Laurent expansion about an isolated singular point, and one of the following statements will be true:

1.   The most negative power of $z - z_0$ in the Laurent expansion of $f(z)$ about $z = z_0$ will be some finite power, $(z - z_0)^{-n}$, where n is an integer, or
2.   The Laurent expansion of $f(z)$ about $z - z_0$ will continue to negatively infinite powers of $z - z_0$.

In the first case, the singularity is called a **pole**, and is more specifically identified as a pole of **order** n. A pole of order 1 is also called a **simple pole**. The second case is not referred to as a "pole of infinite order," but is called an **essential singularity**.

One way to identify a pole of $f(z)$ without having available its Laurent expansion is to examine

$$\lim_{z \to z_0} (z - z_0)^n f(z_0)$$

for various integers n. The smallest integer n for which this limit exists (i.e., is finite) gives the order of the pole at $z = z_0$. This rule follows directly from the form of the Laurent expansion.

Essential singularities are often identified directly from their Laurent expansions. For example,

$$e^{1/z} = 1 + \frac{1}{z} + \frac{1}{2!}\left(\frac{1}{z}\right)^2 + \cdots$$

$$= \sum_{n=0}^{\infty} \frac{1}{n!}\left(\frac{1}{z}\right)^n$$

clearly has an essential singularity at $z = 0$. Essential singularities have many pathological features. For instance, we can show that in any small neighborhood of an essential singularity of $f(z)$ the function $f(z)$ comes arbitrarily close to any (and therefore every) preselected complex quantity w_0.[6] Here, the entire w-plane is mapped by f into the neighborhood of the point z_0.

The behavior of $f(z)$ as $z \to \infty$ is defined in terms of the behavior of $f(1/t)$ as $t \to 0$. Consider the function

$$\sin z = \sum_{n=0}^{\infty} \frac{(-1)^n z^{2n+1}}{(2n+1)!}. \tag{11.53}$$

As $z \to \infty$, we replace the z by $1/t$ to obtain

$$\sin\left(\frac{1}{t}\right) = \sum_{n=0}^{\infty} \frac{(-1)^n}{(2n+1)! t^{2n+1}}. \tag{11.54}$$

It is clear that $\sin(1/t)$ has an essential singularity at $t = 0$, from which we conclude that $\sin z$ has an essential singularity at $z = \infty$. Note that although the absolute value of $\sin x$ for all real x is equal to or less than unity, the absolute value of $\sin iy = i \sinh y$ increases exponentially without limit as y increases.

A function that is analytic throughout the finite complex plane except for isolated poles is called **meromorphic**. Examples are ratios of two polynomials, also $\tan z$ and $\cot z$. As previously mentioned, functions that have no singularities in the finite complex plane are called **entire** functions. Examples are $\exp z$, $\sin z$, and $\cos z$.

---

[6]This theorem is due to Picard. A proof is given by E. C. Titchmarsh, *The Theory of Functions*, 2nd ed. New York: Oxford University Press (1939).

Branch Points

In addition to the isolated singularities identified as poles or essential singularities, there are singularities uniquely associated with multivalued functions. It is useful to work with these functions in ways that to the maximum possible extent remove ambiguity as to the function values. Thus, if at a point z_0 (at which $f(z)$ has a derivative) we have chosen a specific value of the multivalued function $f(z)$, then we can assign to $f(z)$ values at nearby points in a way that causes continuity in $f(z)$. If we think of a succession of closely spaced points as in the limit of zero spacing defining a path, our current observation is that a given value of $f(z_0)$ then leads to a unique definition of the value of $f(z)$ to be assigned to each point on the path. This scheme creates no ambiguity so long as the path is entirely **open**, meaning that the path does not return to any point previously passed. But if the path returns to z_0, thereby forming a **closed loop**, our prescription might lead, upon the return, to a different one of the multiple values of $f(z_0)$.

Example 11.6.1   VALUE OF $z^{1/2}$ ON A CLOSED LOOP

We consider $f(z) = z^{1/2}$ on the path consisting of counterclockwise passage around the unit circle, starting and ending at $z = +1$. At the start point, where $z^{1/2}$ has the multiple values $+1$ and -1, let us choose $f(z) = +1$. See Fig. 11.10. Writing $f(z) = e^{i\theta/2}$, we note that this form (with $\theta = 0$) is consistent with the desired starting value of $f(z)$, $+1$. In the figure, the start point is labeled A. Next, we note that passage counterclockwise on the unit circle corresponds to an increase in θ, so that at the points marked B, C, and D in the figure, the respective values of θ are $\pi/2$, π, and $3\pi/2$. Note that because of the path we have decided to take, we cannot assign to point C the θ value $-\pi$ or to point D the θ value $-\pi/2$. Continuing further along the path, when we return to point A the value of θ has become 2π (not zero).

Now that we have identified the behavior of θ, let's examine what happens to $f(z)$. At the points B, C, and D, we have

$$f(z_B) = e^{i\theta_B/2} = e^{i\pi/4} = \frac{1+i}{\sqrt{2}},$$

$$f(z_C) = e^{i\pi/2} = +i,$$

$$f(z_D) = e^{3i\pi/4} = \frac{-1+i}{\sqrt{2}}.$$

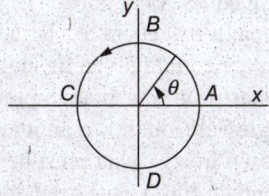

FIGURE 11.10   Path encircling $z = 0$ for evaluation of $z^{1/2}$.

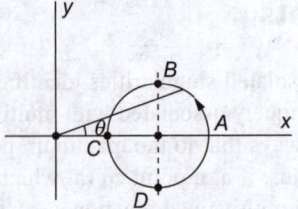

FIGURE 11.11   Path not encircling $z = 0$ for evaluation of $z^{1/2}$.

When we return to point A, we have $f(+1) = e^{i\pi} = -1$, which is the other value of the multivalued function $z^{1/2}$.

If we continue for a second counterclockwise circuit of the unit circle, the value of θ would continue to increase, from 2π to 4π (reached when we arrive at point A after the second loop). We now have $f(+1) = e^{(4\pi i)/2} = e^{2\pi i} = 1$, so a second circuit has brought us back to the original value. It should now be clear that we are only going to be able to obtain two different values of $z^{1/2}$ for the same point z.   ∎

Example 11.6.2   ANOTHER CLOSED LOOP

Let's now see what happens to the function $z^{1/2}$ as we pass counterclockwise around a circle of unit radius centered at $z = +2$, starting and ending at $z = +3$. See Fig. 11.11. At $z = 3$, the values of $f(z)$ are $+\sqrt{3}$ and $-\sqrt{3}$; let's start with $f(z_A) = +\sqrt{3}$. As we move from point A through point B to point C, note from the figure that the value of θ first increases (actually, to 30°) and then decreases again to zero; further passage from C to D and back to A causes θ first to decrease (to $-30°$) and then to return to zero at A. So in this example the closed loop does not bring us to a different value of the multivalued function $z^{1/2}$.   ∎

The essential difference between these two examples is that in the first, the path encircled $z = 0$; in the second it did not. What is special about $z = 0$ is that (from a complex-variable viewpoint) it is singular; the function $z^{1/2}$ does not have a derivative there. The lack of a well-defined derivative means that ambiguity in the function value will result from paths that circle such a singular point, which we call a **branch point**. The **order** of a branch point is defined as the number of paths around it that must be taken before the function involved returns to its original value; in the case of $z^{1/2}$, we saw that the branch point at $z = 0$ is of order 2.

We are now ready to see what must be done to cause a multivalued function to be restricted to single-valuedness on a portion of the complex plane. We simply need to prevent its evaluation on paths that encircle a branch point. We do so by drawing a line (known as a **branch line**, or more commonly, a **branch cut**) that the evaluation path cannot cross; the branch cut must start from our branch point and continue to infinity (or if consistent with maintaining single-valuedness) to another finite branch point. The precise path of a branch cut can be chosen freely; what must be chosen appropriately are its endpoints.

Once appropriate branch cut(s) have been drawn, the originally multivalued function has been restricted to being single-valued in the region bounded by the branch cut(s); we call the function as made single-valued in this way a **branch** of our original function. Since we could construct such a branch starting from any one of the values of the original function at a single arbitrary point in our region, we identify our multivalued function as having multiple branches. In the case of $z^{1/2}$, which is double-valued, the number of branches is two.

Note that a function with a branch point and a corresponding branch cut will not be continuous across the cut line. Hence line integrals in opposite directions on the two sides of the branch cut will not generally cancel each other. Branch cuts, therefore, are real boundaries to a region of analyticity, in contrast to the artificial barriers we introduced in extending Cauchy's integral theorem to multiply connected regions.

While from a fundamental viewpoint all branches of a multivalued function $f(z)$ are equally legitimate, it is often convenient to agree on the branch to be used, and such a branch is sometimes called the **principal branch**, with the value of $f(z)$ on that branch called its **principal value**. It is common to take the branch of $z^{1/2}$ which is positive for real, positive z as its principal branch.

An observation that is important for complex analysis is that by drawing appropriate branch cut(s), we have restricted a multivalued function to single-valuedness, so that it can be an analytic function within the region bounded by the branch cut(s), and we can therefore apply Cauchy's two theorems to contour integrals within the region of analyticity.

Example 11.6.3   ln z HAS AN INFINITE NUMBER OF BRANCHES

Here we examine the singularity structure of $\ln z$. As we already saw in Eq. (1.138), the logarithm is multivalued, with the polar representation

$$\ln z = \ln\left(re^{i(\theta + 2n\pi)}\right) = \ln r + i(\theta + 2n\pi), \tag{11.55}$$

where n can have **any** positive or negative integer value.

Noting that $\ln z$ is singular at $z = 0$ (it has no derivative there), we now identify $z = 0$ as a branch point. Let's consider what happens if we encircle it by a counterclockwise path on a circle of radius r, starting from the initial value $\ln r$, at $z = r = re^{i\theta}$ with $\theta = 0$. Every passage around the circle will add 2π to θ, and after n complete circuits the value we have for $\ln z$ will be $\ln r + 2n\pi i$. The branch point of $\ln z$ at $z = 0$ is of infinite order, corresponding to the infinite number of its multiple values. (By encircling $z = 0$ repeatedly in the *clockwise* direction, we can also reach all negative integer values of n.)

We can make $\ln z$ single-valued by drawing a branch cut from $z = 0$ to $z = \infty$ in **any** way (though there is ordinarily no reason to use cuts that are not straight lines). It is typical to identify the branch with $n = 0$ as the principal branch of the logarithm. Incidentally, we note that the inverse trigonometric functions, which can be written in terms of logarithms, as in Eq. (1.137), will also be infinitely multivalued, with principal values that are usually chosen on a branch that will yield real values for real z. Compare with the usual choices of the values assigned the real-variable forms of $\sin^{-1} x = \arcsin x$, etc.   ∎

Using the logarithm, we are now in a position to look at the singularity structures of expressions of the form z^p, where both z and p may be complex. To do so, we write

$$z = e^{\ln z}, \quad \text{so } z^p = e^{p \ln z}, \tag{11.56}$$

which is single-valued if p is an integer, t-valued if p is a real rational fraction (in lowest terms) of the form s/t, and infinitely multivalued otherwise.

Example 11.6.4　Multiple Branch Points

Consider the function

$$f(z) = (z^2 - 1)^{1/2} = (z+1)^{1/2}(z-1)^{1/2}.$$

The first factor on the right-hand side, $(z+1)^{1/2}$, has a branch point at $z = -1$. The second factor has a branch point at $z = +1$. At infinity $f(z)$ has a simple pole. This is best seen by substituting $z = 1/t$ and making a binomial expansion at $t = 0$:

$$(z^2 - 1)^{1/2} = \frac{1}{t}(1 - t^2)^{1/2} = \frac{1}{t} \sum_{n=0}^{\infty} \binom{1/2}{n} (-1)^n t^{2n} = \frac{1}{t} - \frac{1}{2}t - \frac{1}{8}t^3 + \cdots.$$

We want to make $f(z)$ single-valued by making appropriate branch cut(s). There are many ways to accomplish this, but one we wish to investigate is the possibility of making a branch cut from $z = -1$ to $z = +1$, as shown in Fig. 11.12.

To determine whether this branch cut makes our $f(z)$ single-valued, we need to see what happens to each of the multivalent factors in $f(z)$ as we move around on its Argand diagram. Figure 11.12 also identifies the quantities that are relevant for this purpose, namely those that relate a point P to the branch points. In particular, we have written the position relative to the branch point at $z = 1$ as $z - 1 = \rho e^{i\varphi}$, with the position relative to $z = -1$ denoted $z + 1 = r e^{i\theta}$. With these definitions, we have

$$f(z) = r^{1/2}\rho^{1/2}e^{(\theta+\varphi)/2}.$$

Our mission is to note how φ and θ change as we move along the path, so that we can use the correct value of each for evaluating $f(z)$.

We consider a closed path starting at point A in Fig. 11.13, proceeding via points B through F, then back to A. At the start point, we choose $\theta = \varphi = 0$, thereby causing the multivalued $f(z_A)$ to have the specific value $+\sqrt{3}$. As we pass **above** $z = +1$ on the way to point B, θ remains essentially zero, but φ increases from zero to π. These angles do not change as we pass from B to C, but on going to point D, θ increases to π, and then, passing **below** $z = -1$ on the way to point E, it further increases to 2π (not zero!). Meanwhile, φ remains essentially at π. Finally, returning to point A **below** $z = +1$, φ increases to 2π, so that upon the return to point A both φ and θ have become 2π. The behavior of these angles and the values of $(\theta + \varphi)/2$ (the argument of $f(z)$) are tabulated in Table 11.1.

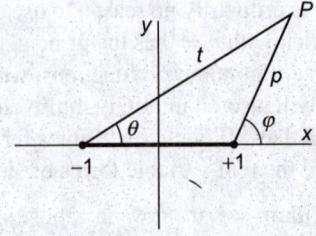

FIGURE 11.12　Possible branch cut for Example 11.6.4 and the quantities relating a point P to the branch points.

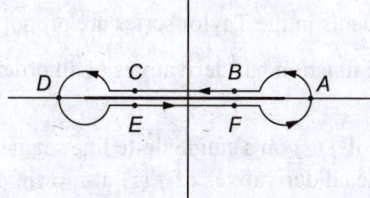

FIGURE 11.13   Path around the branch cut in Example 11.6.4.

Table 11.1   Phase Angles, Path in Fig. 11.13

Point	θ	φ	$(\theta + \varphi)/2$
A	0	0	0
B	0	π	$\pi/2$
C	0	π	$\pi/2$
D	π	π	π
E	2π	π	$\pi/2$
F	2π	π	$3\pi/2$
A	2π	2π	2π

Two features emerge from this analysis:

1. The phase of $f(z)$ at points B and C is not the same as that at points E and F. This behavior can be expected at a branch cut.
2. The phase of $f(z)$ at point A' (the return to A) exceeds that at point A by 2π, meaning that the function $f(z) = (z^2 - 1)^{1/2}$ is **single-valued** for the contour shown, encircling **both** branch points.

What actually happened is that each of the two multivalued factors contributed a sign change upon passage around the closed loop, so the two factors together restored the original sign of $f(z)$.

Another way we could have made $f(z)$ single-valued would have been to make a separate branch cut from each branch point to infinity; a reasonable way to do this would be to make cuts on the real axis for all $x > 1$ and for all $x < -1$. This alternative is explored in Exercises 11.6.2 and 11.6.4.   ∎

Analytic Continuation

We saw in Section 11.5 that a function $f(z)$ which is analytic within a region can be uniquely expanded in a Taylor series about any interior point z_0 of the region of analyticity, and that the resulting expansion will be convergent within a circle of convergence extending to the singularity of $f(z)$ closest to z_0. Since

- The coefficients in the Taylor series are proportional to the derivatives of $f(z)$,

- An analytic function has derivatives of all orders that are independent of direction, and therefore

- The values of $f(z)$ on a single finite line segment with z_0 as a interior point will suffice to determine all derivatives of $f(z)$ at $z = z_0$,

we conclude that if two apparently different analytic functions (e.g., a closed expression vs. an integral representation or a power series) have values that coincide on a range as restricted as a single finite line segment, then they are actually **the same function** within the region where both functional forms are defined.

The above conclusion will provide us with a technique for extending the definition of an analytic function beyond the range of any particular functional form initially used to define it. All we will need to do is to find another functional form whose range of definition is not entirely included in that of the initial form and which yields the same function values on at least a finite line segment within the area where both functional forms are defined.

To make the approach more concrete, consider the situation illustrated in Fig. 11.14, where a function $f(z)$ is defined by its Taylor expansion about a point z_0 with a circle of convergence C_0 defined by the singularity nearest to z_0, labeled z_s. If we now make a Taylor expansion about some point z_1 within C_0 (which we can do because $f(z)$ has known values in the neighborhood of z_1), this new expansion may have a circle of convergence C_1 that is not entirely within C_0, thereby defining a function that is analytic in the region that is the union of C_1 and C_2. Note that if we need to obtain actual values of $f(z)$ for z within the intersection of C_0 and C_1 we may use either Taylor expansion, but in the region within only one circle we must use the expansion that is valid there (the other expansion will not converge). A generalization of the above analysis leads to the beautiful and valuable result that if two analytic functions coincide in any region, or even on any finite line segment, they are the same function, and therefore defined over the entire range of both function definitions.

After Weierstrass this process of enlarging the region in which we have the specification of an analytic function is called **analytic continuation**, and the process may be carried out repeatedly to maximize the region in which the function is defined. Consider the situation pictured in Fig. 11.15, where the only singularity of $f(z)$ is at z_s and $f(z)$ is originally defined by its Taylor expansion about z_0, with circle of convergence C_0. By making analytic continuations as shown by the series of circles $C_1, \ldots,$ we can cover the entire annular region of analyticity shown in the figure, and can use the original Taylor series to generate new expansions that apply to regions within the other circles.

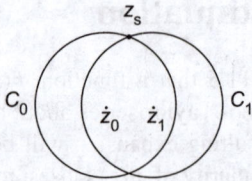

FIGURE 11.14   Analytic continuation. One step.

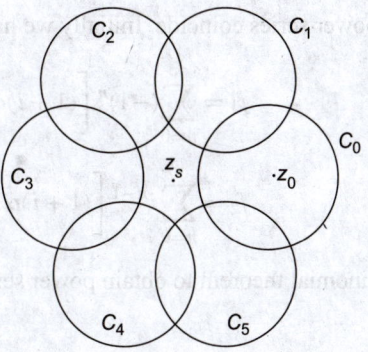

FIGURE 11.15   Analytic continuation. Many steps.

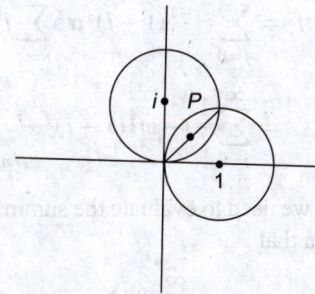

FIGURE 11.16   Radii of convergence of power-series expansions for Example 11.6.5.

Example 11.6.5   ANALYTIC CONTINUATION

Consider these two power-series expansions:

$$f_1(z) = \sum_{n=0}^{\infty} (-1)^n (z-1)^n, \tag{11.57}$$

$$f_2(z) = \sum_{n=0}^{\infty} i^{n-1} (z-i)^n. \tag{11.58}$$

Each has a unit radius of convergence; the circles of convergence overlap, as can be seen from Fig. 11.16.

To determine whether these expansions represent the same analytic function in overlapping domains, we can check to see if $f_1(z) = f_2(z)$ for at least a line segment in the region of overlap. A suitable line is the diagonal that connects the origin with $1 + i$, passing through the intermediate point $(1+i)/2$. Setting $z = (\alpha + \frac{1}{2})(1+i)$ (chosen to make $\alpha = 0$ an interior point of the overlap region), we expand f_1 and f_2 about $\alpha = 0$ to find out whether their power series coincide. Initially we have (as functions of α)

$$f_1 = \sum_{n=0}^{\infty} (-1)^n \left[(1+i)\alpha - \frac{1-i}{2} \right]^n ,$$

$$f_2 = \sum_{n=0}^{\infty} i^{n-1} \left[(1+i)\alpha + \frac{1-i}{2} \right]^n .$$

Applying the binomial theorem to obtain power series in α, and interchanging the order of the two sums,

$$f_1 = \sum_{j=0}^{\infty} (-1)^j (1+i)^j \alpha^j \sum_{n=j}^{\infty} \binom{n}{j} \left(\frac{1-i}{2} \right)^{n-j} ,$$

$$f_2 = \sum_{j=0}^{\infty} i^{j-1} (1+i)^j \alpha^j \sum_{n=j}^{\infty} i^{n-j} \binom{n}{j} \left(\frac{1-i}{2} \right)^{n-j}$$

$$= \sum_{j=0}^{\infty} \frac{1}{i} (-1)^j (1-i)^j \alpha^j \sum_{n=j}^{\infty} \binom{n}{j} \left(\frac{1+i}{2} \right)^{n-j} .$$

To proceed further we need to evaluate the summations over n. Referring to Exercise 1.3.5, where it was shown that

$$\sum_{n=j}^{\infty} \binom{n}{j} x^{n-j} = \frac{1}{(1-x)^{j+1}} ,$$

we get

$$f_1 = \sum_{j=0}^{\infty} (-1)^j (1+i)^j \alpha^j \left(\frac{2}{1+i} \right)^{j+1} = \sum_{j=0}^{\infty} \frac{(-1)^j 2^{j+1} \alpha^j}{1+i} ,$$

$$f_2 = \sum_{j=0}^{\infty} \frac{1}{i} (-1)^j (1-i)^j \alpha^j \left(\frac{2}{1-i} \right)^{j+1} = \sum_{j=0}^{\infty} \frac{(-1)^j 2^{j+1} \alpha^j}{i(1-i)} = f_1 ,$$

confirming that f_1 and f_2 are the same analytic function, now defined over the union of the two circles in Fig. 11.16.

Incidentally, both f_1 and f_2 are expansions of $1/z$ (about the respective points 1 and i), so $1/z$ could also be regarded as an analytic continuation of f_1, f_2, or both to the entire complex plane except the singular point at $z = 0$. The expansion in powers of α is also a representation of $1/z$, but its range of validity is only a circle of radius $1/\sqrt{2}$ about $(1+i)/2$ and it does not analytically continue $f(z)$ outside the union of C_1 and C_2. ∎

The use of power series is not the only mechanism for carrying out analytic continuations; an alternative and powerful method is the use of **functional relations**, which are formulas that relate values of the same analytic function $f(z)$ at different z. As an example of a functional relation, the integral representation of the gamma function, given in

Table 1.2, can be manipulated (see Chapter 13) to show that $\Gamma(z+1) = z\Gamma(z)$, consistent with the elementary result that $n! = n(n-1)!$. This functional relation can be used to analytically continue $\Gamma(z)$ to values of z for which the integral representation does not converge.

Exercises

11.6.1 As an example of an essential singularity consider $e^{1/z}$ as z approaches zero. For any complex number z_0, $z_0 \neq 0$, show that

$$e^{1/z} = z_0$$

has an infinite number of solutions.

11.6.2 Show that the function

$$w(z) = (z^2 - 1)^{1/2}$$

is single-valued if we make branch cuts on the real axis for $x > 1$ and for $x < -1$.

11.6.3 A function $f(z)$ can be represented by

$$f(z) = \frac{f_1(z)}{f_2(z)},$$

in which $f_1(z)$ and $f_2(z)$ are analytic. The denominator, $f_2(z)$, vanishes at $z = z_0$, showing that $f(z)$ has a pole at $z = z_0$. However, $f_1(z_0) \neq 0$, $f_2'(z_0) \neq 0$. Show that a_{-1}, the coefficient of $(z - z_0)^{-1}$ in a Laurent expansion of $f(z)$ at $z = z_0$, is given by

$$a_{-1} = \frac{f_1(z_0)}{f_2'(z_0)}.$$

11.6.4 Determine a unique branch for the function of Exercise 11.6.2 that will cause the value it yields for $f(i)$ to be the same as that found for $f(i)$ in Example 11.6.4. Although Exercise 11.6.2 and Example 11.6.4 describe the same multivalued function, the specific values assigned for various z will not agree everywhere, due to the difference in the location of the branch cuts. Identify the portions of the complex plane where both these descriptions do and do not agree, and characterize the differences.

11.6.5 Find all singularities of

$$z^{-1/3} + \frac{z^{-1/4}}{(z-3)^3} + (z-2)^{1/2},$$

and identify their types (e.g., second-order branch point, fifth-order pole, ...). Include any singularities at the point at infinity.

Note. A branch point is of nth order if it requires n, but no fewer, circuits around the point to restore the original value.

11.6.6 The function $F(z) = \ln(z^2 + 1)$ is made single-valued by straight-line branch cuts from $(x, y) = (0, -1)$ to $(-\infty, -1)$ and from $(0, +1)$ to $(0, +\infty)$. See Fig. 11.17. If $F(0) = -2\pi i$, find the value of $F(i - 2)$.

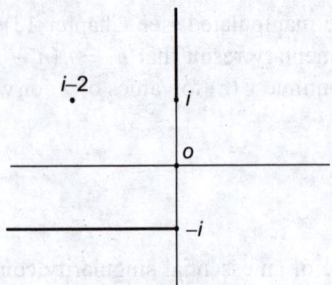

FIGURE 11.17   Branch cuts for Exercise 11.6.6.

11.6.7   Show that negative numbers have logarithms in the complex plane. In particular, find $\ln(-1)$.

ANS. $\ln(-1) = i\pi$.

11.6.8   For noninteger m, show that the binomial expansion of Exercise 11.5.2 holds only for a suitably defined branch of the function $(1 + z)^m$. Show how the z-plane is cut. Explain why $|z| < 1$ may be taken as the circle of convergence for the expansion of this branch, in light of the cut you have chosen.

11.6.9   The Taylor expansion of Exercises 11.5.2 and 11.6.8 is **not** suitable for branches other than the one suitably defined branch of the function $(1 + z)^m$ for noninteger m. (Note that other branches cannot have the same Taylor expansion since they must be distinguishable.) Using the same branch cut of the earlier exercises for all other branches, find the corresponding Taylor expansions, detailing the phase assignments and Taylor coefficients.

11.6.10   (a) Develop a Laurent expansion of $f(z) = [z(z - 1)]^{-1}$ about the point $z = 1$ valid for small values of $|z - 1|$. Specify the exact range over which your expansion holds. This is an analytic continuation of the infinite series in Eq. (11.49).

(b) Determine the Laurent expansion of $f(z)$ about $z = 1$ but for $|z - 1|$ large.

Hint. Make a partial fraction decomposition of this function and use the geometric series.

11.6.11   (a) Given $f_1(z) = \int_0^\infty e^{-zt} dt$ (with t real), show that the domain in which $f_1(z)$ exists (and is analytic) is $\mathfrak{Re}(z) > 0$.

(b) Show that $f_2(z) = 1/z$ equals $f_1(z)$ over $\mathfrak{Re}(z) > 0$ and is therefore an analytic continuation of $f_1(z)$ over the entire z-plane except for $z = 0$.

(c) Expand $1/z$ about the point $z = -i$. You will have

$$f_3(z) = \sum_{n=0}^{\infty} a_n (z + i)^n.$$

What is the domain of this formula for $f_3(z)$?

ANS. $\dfrac{1}{z} = i \sum_{n=0}^{\infty} i^{-n}(z + i)^n, \quad |z + i| < 1.$

11.7   CALCULUS OF RESIDUES

Residue Theorem

If the Laurent expansion of a function,

$$f(z) = \sum_{n=-\infty}^{\infty} a_n (z - z_0)^n,$$

is integrated term by term by using a closed contour that encircles one isolated singular point z_0 once in a counterclockwise sense, we obtain, applying Eq. (11.29),

$$a_n \oint (z - z_0)^n dz = 0, \quad n \neq -1. \tag{11.59}$$

However, for $n = -1$, Eq. (11.29) yields

$$a_{-1} \oint (z - z_0)^{-1} dz = 2\pi i a_{-1}. \tag{11.60}$$

Summarizing Eqs. (11.59) and (11.60), we have

$$\oint f(z)\, dz = 2\pi i a_{-1}. \tag{11.61}$$

The constant a_{-1}, the coefficient of $(z - z_0)^{-1}$ in the Laurent expansion, is called the **residue** of $f(z)$ at $z = z_0$.

Now consider the evaluation of the integral, over a closed contour C, of a function that has isolated singularities at points $z_1, z_2, \ldots$. We can handle this integral by deforming our contour as shown in Fig. 11.18. Cauchy's integral theorem (Section 11.3) then leads to

$$\oint_C f(z)\, dz + \oint_{C_1} f(z)\, dz + \oint_{C_2} f(z)\, dz + \cdots = 0, \tag{11.62}$$

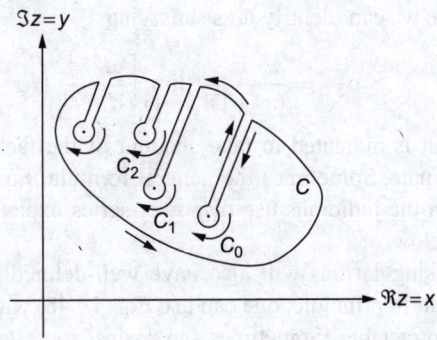

FIGURE 11.18   Excluding isolated singularities.

where C is in the positive, counterclockwise direction, but the contours $C_1, C_2, \ldots$, that, respectively, encircle $z_1, z_2, \ldots$ are all clockwise. Thus, referring to Eq. (11.61), the integrals C_i about the individual isolated singularities have the values

$$\oint_{C_i} f(z)\, dz = -2\pi i a_{-1,i}, \tag{11.63}$$

where $a_{-1,i}$ is the residue obtained from the Laurent expansion about the singular point $z = z_i$. The negative sign comes from the clockwise integration. Combining Eqs. (11.62) and (11.63), we have

$$\oint_C f(z)\, dz = 2\pi i (a_{-1,1} + a_{-1,2} + \cdots)$$

$$= 2\pi i \text{ (sum of the enclosed residues).} \tag{11.64}$$

This is the **residue theorem**. The problem of evaluating a set of contour integrals is replaced by the algebraic problem of computing residues at the enclosed singular points.

Computing Residues

It is, of course, not necessary to obtain an entire Laurent expansion of $f(z)$ about $z = z_0$ to identify a_{-1}, the coefficient of $(z - z_0)^{-1}$ in the expansion. If $f(z)$ has a simple pole at $z - z_0$, then, with a_n the coefficients in the expansion of $f(z)$,

$$(z - z_0) f(z) = a_{-1} + a_0(z - z_0) + a_1(z - z_0)^2 + \cdots, \tag{11.65}$$

and, recognizing that $(z - z_0) f(z)$ may not have a form permitting an obvious cancellation of the factor $z - z_0$, we take the limit of Eq. (11.65) as $z \to z_0$:

$$a_{-1} = \lim_{z \to z_0} \left((z - z_0) f(z) \right). \tag{11.66}$$

If there is a pole of order $n > 1$ at $z - z_0$, then $(z - z_0)^n f(z)$ must have the expansion

$$(z - z_0)^n f(z) = a_{-n} + \cdots + a_{-1}(z - z_0)^{n-1} + a_0(z - z_0)^n + \cdots. \tag{11.67}$$

We see that a_{-1} is the coefficient of $(z - z_0)^{n-1}$ in the Taylor expansion of $(z - z_0)^n f(z)$, and therefore we can identify it as satisfying

$$a_{-1} = \frac{1}{(n-1)!} \lim_{z \to z_0} \left[\frac{d^{n-1}}{dz^{n-1}} \left((z - z_0)^n f(z) \right) \right], \tag{11.68}$$

where a limit is indicated to take account of the fact that the expression involved may be indeterminate. Sometimes the general formula, Eq. (11.68), is found to be more complicated than the judicious use of power-series expansions. See items 4 and 5 in Example 11.7.1 below.

Essential singularities will also have well-defined residues, but finding them may be more difficult. In principle, one can use Eq. (11.48) with $n = -1$, but the integral involved may seem intractable. Sometimes the easiest route to the residue is by first finding the Laurent expansion.

Example 11.7.1   COMPUTING RESIDUES

Here are some examples:

1. Residue of $\frac{1}{4z+1}$ at $z = -\frac{1}{4}$ is $\lim_{z=-\frac{1}{4}} \left(\frac{z+\frac{1}{4}}{4z+1} \right) = \frac{1}{4}$,

2. Residue of $\frac{1}{\sin z}$ at $z = 0$ is $\lim_{z \to 0} \left(\frac{z}{\sin z} \right) = 1$,

3. Residue of $\frac{\ln z}{z^2+4}$ at $z = 2e^{\pi i}$ is

$$\lim_{z \to 2e^{\pi i}} \left(\frac{(z - 2e^{\pi i}) \ln z}{z^2 + 4} \right) = \frac{(\ln 2 + \pi i)}{4i} = \frac{\pi}{4} - \frac{i \ln 2}{4},$$

4. Residue of $\frac{z}{\sin^2 z}$ at $z = \pi$; the pole is second order, and the residue is given by

$$\frac{1}{1!} \lim_{z \to \pi} \left(\frac{d}{dz} \frac{z(z - \pi)}{\sin^2 z} \right).$$

However, it may be easier to make the substitution $w = z - \pi$, to note that $\sin^2 z = \sin^2 w$, and to identify the residue as the coefficient of $1/w$ in the expansion of $(w + \pi)/\sin^2 w$ about $w = 0$. This expansion can be written

$$\frac{w + \pi}{\left(w - \frac{w^3}{3!} + \cdots \right)^2} = \frac{w + \pi}{w^2 - \frac{w^4}{3} + \cdots}.$$

The denominator expands entirely into even powers of w, so the π in the numerator cannot contribute to the residue. Then, from the w in the numerator and the leading term of the denominator, we find the residue to be 1.

5. Residue of $f(z) = \frac{\cot \pi z}{z(z+2)}$ at $z = 0$.

The pole at $z = 0$ is second-order, and direct application of Eq. (11.48) leads to a complicated indeterminate expression requiring multiple applications of l'Hôpital's rule. Perhaps easier is to introduce the initial terms of the expansions about $z = 0$: $\cot \pi z = (\pi z)^{-1} + O(z)$, $1/(z+2) = \frac{1}{2}[1 - (z/2) + O(z^2)]$, reaching

$$f(z) = \frac{1}{z} \left[\frac{1}{\pi z} + O(z) \right] \left(\frac{1}{2} \right) \left[1 - \frac{z}{2} + O(z^2) \right],$$

from which we can read out the residue as the coefficient of z^{-1}, namely $-1/4\pi$.

6. Residue of $e^{-1/z}$ at $z = 0$. This is at an essential singularity; from the Taylor series of e^w with $w = -1/z$, we have

$$e^{-1/z} = 1 - \frac{1}{z} + \frac{1}{2!} \left(-\frac{1}{z} \right)^2 + \cdots,$$

from which we read out the value of the residue, -1.

■

Cauchy Principal Value

Occasionally an isolated pole will be directly on the contour of an integration, causing the integral to diverge. A simple example is provided by an attempt to evaluate the real integral

$$\int_{-a}^{b} \frac{dx}{x},$$

(11.69)

which is divergent because of the logarithmic singularity at $x = 0$; note that the indefinite integral of x^{-1} is $\ln x$. However, the integral in Eq. (11.69) can be given a meaning if we obtain a convergent form when replaced by a limit of the form

$$\lim_{\delta \to 0^{+}} \int_{-a}^{-\delta} \frac{dx}{x} + \int_{\delta}^{b} \frac{dx}{x}.$$

(11.70)

To avoid issues with the logarithm of negative values of x, we change the variable in the first integral to $y = -x$, and the two integrals are then seen to have the respective values $\ln \delta - \ln a$ and $\ln b - \ln \delta$, with sum $\ln b - \ln a$. What has happened is that the increase toward $+\infty$ as $1/x$ approaches zero from positive values of x is compensated by a decrease toward $-\infty$ as $1/x$ approaches zero from negative x. This situation is illustrated graphically in Fig. 11.19.

Note that the procedure we have described does **not** make the original integral of Eq. (11.69) convergent. In order for that integral to be convergent, it would be necessary

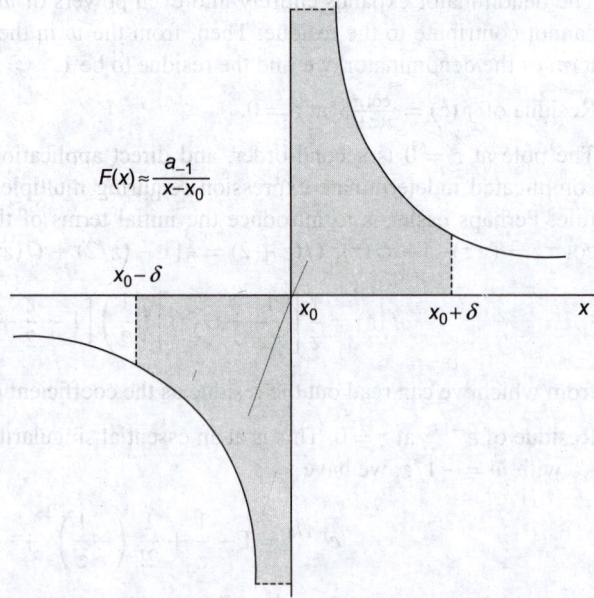

FIGURE 11.19   Cauchy principal value cancellation, integral of $1/z$.

that

$$\lim_{\delta_1, \delta_2 \to 0^+} \left[\int_{-a}^{-\delta_1} \frac{dx}{x} + \int_{\delta_2}^{b} \frac{dx}{x} \right]$$

exist (meaning that the limit has a unique value) when δ_1 and δ_2 approach zero **independently**. However, different rates of approach to zero by δ_1 and δ_2 will cause a change in value of the integral. For example, if $\delta_2 = 2\delta_1$, then an evaluation like that of Eq. (11.70) would yield the result $(\ln \delta_1 - \ln a) + (\ln b - \ln \delta_2) = \ln b - \ln a - \ln 2$. The limit then has no definite value, confirming our original statement that the integral diverges.

Generalizing from the above example, we define the **Cauchy principal value** of the real integral of a function $f(x)$ with an isolated singularity on the integration path at the point x_0 as the limit

$$\lim_{\delta \to 0^+} \int^{x_0-\delta} f(x)\,dx + \int_{x_0+\delta} f(x)\,dx. \tag{11.71}$$

The Cauchy principal value is sometimes indicated by preceding the integral sign by P or by drawing a horizontal line through the integration sign, as in

$$P \int f(x)\,dx \quad \text{or} \quad \fint f(x)\,dx.$$

This notation, of course, presumes that the location of the singularity is known.

Example 11.7.2   A Cauchy Principal Value

Consider the integral

$$I = \int_0^\infty \frac{\sin x}{x}\,dx. \tag{11.72}$$

If we substitute for $\sin x$ the equivalent formula

$$\sin x = \frac{e^{ix} - e^{-ix}}{2i},$$

we then have

$$I = \int_0^\infty \frac{e^{ix} - e^{-ix}}{2ix}\,dx. \tag{11.73}$$

We would like to separate this expression for I into two terms, but if we do so, each will become a logarithmically divergent integral. However, if we change the integration range in Eq. (11.72), originally $(0, \infty)$, to (δ, ∞), that integral remains unchanged in the limit of small δ, and the integrals in Eq. (11.73) remain convergent so long as δ is not precisely zero. Then, rewriting the second of the two integrals in Eq. (11.73), to reach

$$\int_{\delta}^{\infty} \frac{e^{-ix}}{2ix}\,dx = \int_{-\infty}^{-\delta} \frac{e^{ix}}{2ix}\,dx,$$

we see that the two integrals which together form I can be written (in the limit $\delta \to 0^+$) as the Cauchy principal value integral

$$I = \fint_{-\infty}^{\infty} \frac{e^{ix}}{2ix}\,dx. \tag{11.74}$$

■

The Cauchy principal value has implications for complex variable theory. Suppose now that, instead of having a break in the integration path from $x_0 - \delta$ to $x_0 + \delta$, we connect the two parts of the path by a circular arc passing, in the complex plane, either above or below the singularity at x_0. Let's continue the discussion in conventional complex-variable notation, denoting the singular point as z_0, so our arc will be a half circle (of radius δ) passing either counterclockwise **below** the singularity at z_0 or clockwise **above** z_0. We restrict further analysis to singularities no stronger than $1/(z - z_0)$, so we are dealing with a simple pole. Looking at the Laurent expansion of the function $f(z)$ to be integrated, it will have initial terms

$$\frac{a_{-1}}{z - z_0} + a_0 + \cdots,$$

and the integration over a semicircle of radius δ will take (in the limit $\delta \to 0^+$) one of the two forms (in the polar representation $z - z_0 = re^{i\theta}$, with $dz = ire^{i\theta}\,d\theta$ and $r = \delta$):

$$I_{\text{over}} = \int_{\pi}^{0} d\theta\, i\delta e^{i\theta} \left[\frac{a_{-1}}{\delta e^{i\theta}} + a_0 + \cdots \right] = \int_{\pi}^{0} \left(ia_{-1} + i\delta e^{i\theta} a_0 + \cdots \right) d\theta \to -i\pi a_{-1},$$

$$\tag{11.75}$$

$$I_{\text{under}} = \int_{\pi}^{2\pi} d\theta\, i\delta e^{i\theta} \left[\frac{a_{-1}}{\delta e^{i\theta}} + a_0 + \cdots \right] = \int_{\pi}^{2\pi} \left(ia_{-1} + i\delta e^{i\theta} a_0 + \cdots \right) d\theta \to i\pi a_{-1}.$$

$$\tag{11.76}$$

Note that all but the first term of each of Eqs. (11.75) and (11.76) vanishes in the limit $\delta \to 0^+$, and that each of these equations yields a result that is in magnitude half the value that would have been obtained by a full circuit around the pole. The signs associated with the semicircles correspond as expected to the direction of travel, and the two semicircular integrals average to zero.

We occasionally will want to evaluate a contour integral of a function $f(z)$ on a closed path that includes the two pieces of a Cauchy principal value integral $\fint f(z)\,dz$ with a simple pole at z_0, a semicircular arc connecting them at the singularity, and whatever other curve C is needed to close the contour (see Fig. 11.20).

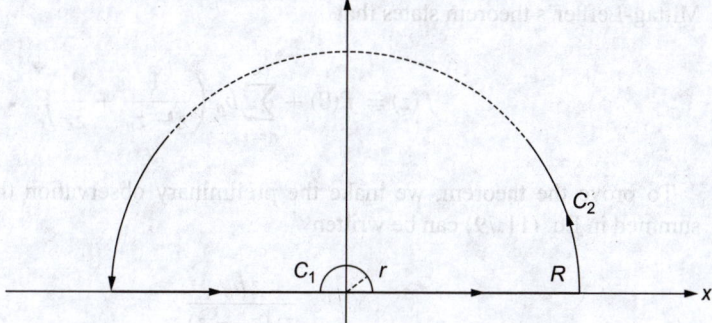

FIGURE 11.20 A contour including a Cauchy principal value integral.

These contributions combine as follows, noting that in the figure the contour passes **over** the point z_0:

$$\oint f(z)\,dz + I_{\text{over}} + \int_{C_2} f(z)\,dz = 2\pi i \sum \text{residues (other than at } z_0\text{)},$$

which rearranges to give

$$\oint f(z)\,dz = -I_{\text{over}} - \int_{C_2} f(z)\,dz + 2\pi i \sum \text{residues (other than at } z_0\text{)}. \qquad (11.77)$$

On the other hand, we could have chosen the contour to pass **under** z_0, in which case, instead of Eq. (11.77) we would get

$$\oint f(z)\,dz = -I_{\text{under}} - \int_{C_2} f(z)\,dz + 2\pi i \sum \text{residues (other than at } z_0\text{)} + 2\pi i a_{-1},$$

$$(11.78)$$

where the residue denoted a_{-1} is from the pole at z_0. Equations (11.77) and (11.78) are in agreement because $2\pi i a_{-1} - I_{\text{under}} = -I_{\text{over}}$, so for the purpose of evaluating the Cauchy principal value integral, it makes no difference whether we go below or above the singularity on the original integration path.

Pole Expansion of Meromorphic Functions

Analytic functions $f(z)$ that have only isolated poles as singularities are called **meromorphic**. Mittag-Leffler showed that, instead of making an expansion about a single regular point (a Taylor expansion) or about an isolated singular point (a Laurent expansion), it was also possible to make an expansion each of whose terms arises from a different pole of $f(z)$. Mittag-Leffler's theorem assumes that $f(z)$ is analytic at $z = 0$ and at all other points (excluding infinity) with the exception of discrete simple poles at points z_1, $z_2, \ldots$, with respective residues $b_1, b_2, \ldots$. We choose to order the poles in a way such that $0 < |z_1| \le |z_2| \le \cdots$, and we assume that in the limit of large z, $|f(z)/z| \to 0$. Then,

Mittag-Leffler's theorem states that

$$f(z) = f(0) + \sum_{n=1}^{\infty} b_n \left(\frac{1}{z - z_n} + \frac{1}{z_n} \right). \tag{11.79}$$

To prove the theorem, we make the preliminary observation that the quantity being summed in Eq. (11.79) can be written

$$\frac{z \, b_n}{z_n(z_n - z)},$$

suggesting that it might be useful to consider a contour integral of the form

$$I_N = \oint_{C_N} \frac{f(w) \, dw}{w(w - z)},$$

where w is another complex variable and C_N is a circle enclosing the first N poles of $f(z)$. Since C_N, which has a radius we denote R_N, has total arc length $2\pi R_N$, and the absolute value of the integrand asymptotically approaches $|f(R_N)|/R_N^2$, the large-z behavior of $f(z)$ guarantees that $\lim_{R_N \to \infty} I_N = 0$.

We now obtain an alternate expression for I_N using the residue theorem. Recognizing that C_N encircles simple poles at $w = 0$, $w = z$, and $w = z_n$, $n = 1 \ldots N$, that $f(w)$ is nonsingular at $w = 0$ and $w = z$, and that the residue of $f(z)/w(w - z)$ at z_n is just $b_n/z_n(z_n - z)$, we have

$$I_N = 2\pi i \, \frac{f(0)}{-z} + 2\pi i \, \frac{f(z)}{z} + \sum_{n=1}^{N} \frac{2\pi i b_n}{z_n(z_n - z)}.$$

Taking the large-N limit, in which $I_N = 0$, we recover Mittag-Leffler's theorem, Eq. (11.79). The pole expansion converges when the condition $\lim_{z \to \infty} |f(z)/z| = 0$ is satisfied.

Mittag-Leffler's theorem leads to a number of interesting pole expansions. Consider the following examples.

Example 11.7.3   POLE EXPANSION OF tan z

Writing

$$\tan z = \frac{e^{iz} - e^{-iz}}{i(e^{iz} + e^{-iz})},$$

we easily see that the only singularities of $\tan z$ are for real values of z, and they occur at the zeros of $\cos x$, namely at $\pm \pi/2, \pm 3\pi/2, \ldots$, or in general at $z_n = \pm(2n + 1)\pi/2$.

To obtain the residues at these points, we take the limit (using l'Hôpital's rule)

$$b_n = \lim_{z \to \frac{(2n+1)\pi}{2}} \frac{(z - (2n+1)\pi/2)\sin z}{\cos z}$$

$$= \left. \frac{\sin z + (z - (2n+1)\pi/2)\cos z}{-\sin z} \right|_{z = \frac{(2n+1)\pi}{2}} = -1,$$

the same value for every pole.

Noting that $\tan(0) = 0$, and that the poles within a circle of radius $(N+1)\pi$ will be those (of both signs) referred to here by n values 0 through N, Eq. (11.79) for the current case (but only through N) yields

$$\tan z = \sum_{n=0}^{N} (-1) \left(\frac{1}{z - (2n+1)\pi/2} + \frac{1}{(2n+1)\pi/2} \right)$$

$$+ \sum_{n=0}^{N} (-1) \left(\frac{1}{z + (2n+1)\pi/2} + \frac{1}{-(2n+1)\pi/2} \right)$$

$$= \sum_{n=0}^{N} (-1) \left(\frac{1}{z - (2n+1)\pi/2} + \frac{1}{z + (2n+1)\pi/2} \right).$$

Combining terms over a common denominator, and taking the limit $N \to \infty$, we reach the usual form of the expansion:

$$\tan z = 2z \left(\frac{1}{(\pi/2)^2 - z^2} + \frac{1}{(3\pi/2)^2 - z^2} + \frac{1}{(5\pi/2)^2 - z^2} + \cdots \right). \tag{11.80}$$

∎

Example 11.7.4 POLE EXPANSION OF cot z

This example proceeds much as the preceding one, except that $\cot z$ has a simple pole at $z = 0$, with residue $+1$. We therefore consider instead $\cot z - 1/z$, thereby removing the singularity. The singular points are now simple poles at $\pm n\pi$ ($n \neq 0$), with residues (again obtained via l'Hôpital's rule)

$$b_n = \lim_{z \to n\pi} (z - n\pi) \cot z = \lim_{z \to n\pi} \frac{(z - n\pi)(z \cos z - \sin z)}{z \sin z}$$

$$= \left. \frac{z \cos z - \sin z + (z - n\pi)(-z \sin z)}{\sin z + z \cos z} \right|_{z = n\pi} = +1.$$

Noting that $\cot z - 1/z$ is zero at $z = 0$ (the second term in the expansion of $\cot z$ is $-z/3$), we have

$$\cot z - \frac{1}{z} = \sum_{n=1}^{N} \left(\frac{1}{z - n\pi} + \frac{1}{n\pi} + \frac{1}{z + n\pi} + \frac{1}{-n\pi} \right),$$

which rearranges to

$$\cot z = \frac{1}{z} + 2z\left(\frac{1}{z^2 - \pi^2} + \frac{1}{z^2 - (2\pi)^2} + \frac{1}{z^2 - (3\pi)^2} + \cdots\right). \tag{11.81}$$

∎

In addition to Eqs. (11.80) and (11.81), two other pole expansions of importance are

$$\sec z = \pi\left(\frac{1}{(\pi/2)^2 - z^2} - \frac{3}{(3\pi/2)^2 - z^2} + \frac{5}{(5\pi/2)^2 - z^2} -\right), \tag{11.82}$$

$$\csc z = \frac{1}{z} - 2z\left(\frac{1}{z^2 - \pi^2} - \frac{1}{z^2 - (2\pi)^2} + \frac{1}{z^2 - (3\pi)^2} + \cdots\right). \tag{11.83}$$

Counting Poles and Zeros

It is possible to obtain information about the numbers of poles and zeros of a function $f(z)$ that is otherwise analytic within a closed region by consideration of its logarithmic derivative, namely $f'(z)/f(z)$. The starting point for this analysis is to write an expression for $f(z)$ relative to a point z_0 where there is either a zero or a pole in the form

$$f(z) = (z - z_0)^\mu g(z),$$

with $g(z)$ finite and nonzero at $z = z_0$. That requirement identifies the limiting behavior of $f(z)$ near z_0 as proportional to $(z - z_0)^\mu$, and also causes f'/f to assume near $z = z_0$ the form

$$\frac{f'(z)}{f(z)} = \frac{\mu(z - z_0)^{\mu-1}g(z) + (z - z_0)^\mu g'(z)}{(z - z_0)^\mu g(z)} = \frac{\mu}{z - z_0} + \frac{g'(z)}{g(z)}. \tag{11.84}$$

Equation (11.84) shows that, for all nonzero μ (i.e., if z_0 is either a zero or a pole), f'/f has a simple pole at $z = z_0$ with residue μ. Note that because $g(z)$ is required to be nonzero and finite, the second term of Eq. (11.84) cannot be singular.

Applying now the residue theorem to Eq. (11.84) for a closed region within which $f(z)$ is analytic except possibly at poles, we see that the integral of f'/f around a closed contour yields the result

$$\oint_C \frac{f'(z)}{f(z)} dz = 2\pi i\left(N_f - P_f\right), \tag{11.85}$$

where P_f is the number of poles of $f(z)$ within the region enclosed by C, each multiplied by its order, and N is the number of zeros of $f(z)$ enclosed by C, each multiplied by its multiplicity.

The counting of zeros is often facilitated by using **Rouché's theorem**, which states

> *If $f(z)$ and $g(z)$ are analytic in the region bounded by a curve C and $|f(z)| > |g(z)|$ on C, then $f(z)$ and $f(z) + g(z)$ have the same number of zeros in the region bounded by C.*

To prove Rouché's theorem, we first write, from Eq. (11.85),

$$\oint_C \frac{f'(z)}{f(z)}\,dz = 2\pi i N_f \quad \text{and} \quad \oint_C \frac{f'(z)+g'(z)}{f(z)+g(z)}\,dz = 2\pi i N_{f+g},$$

where N_f designates the number of zeros of f within C. Then we observe that because the indefinite integral of f'/f is $\ln f$, N_f is the number of times the argument of f cycles through 2π when C is traversed once in the counterclockwise direction. Similarly, we note that N_{f+g} is the number of times the argument of $f+g$ cycles through 2π on traversal of the contour C.

We next write

$$f + g = f\left(1 + \frac{g}{f}\right) \quad \text{and} \quad \arg(f+g) = \arg(f) + \arg\left(1 + \frac{g}{f}\right), \tag{11.86}$$

using the fact that the argument of a product is the sum of the arguments of its factors. It is then clear that the number of cycles through 2π of $\arg(f+g)$ is equal to the number of cycles of $\arg(f)$ **plus** the number of cycles of $\arg(1+g/f)$. But because $|g/f| < 1$, the real part of $1 + g/f$ never becomes negative, and its argument is therefore restricted to the range $-\pi/2 < \arg(1+g/f) < \pi/2$. Therefore $\arg(1+g/f)$ cannot cycle through 2π, the number of cycles of $\arg(f+g)$ must be equal to the number of cycles of $\arg f$, and $f+g$ and f must have the same number of zeros within C. This completes the proof of Rouché's theorem.

Example 11.7.5   Counting Zeros

Our problem is to determine the number of zeros of $F(z) = z^3 - 2z + 11$ with moduli between 1 and 3. Since $F(z)$ is analytic for all finite z, we could in principle simply apply Eq. (11.85) for the contour consisting of the circles $|z| = 1$ (clockwise) and $|z| = 3$ (counterclockwise), setting $P_F = 0$ and solving for N_F. However, that approach will in practice prove difficult. Instead, we simplify the problem by using Rouché's theorem.

We first compute the number of zeros within $|z| = 1$, writing $F(z) = f(z) + g(z)$, with $f(z) = 11$ and $g(z) = z^3 - 2z$. It is clear that $|f(z)| > |g(z)|$ when $|z| = 1$, so, by Rouché's theorem, f and $f+g$ have the same number of zeros within this circle. Since $f(z) = 11$ has no zeros, we conclude that all the zeros of $F(z)$ are outside $|z| = 1$.

Next we compute the number of zeros within $|z| = 3$, taking for this purpose $f(z) = z^3$, $g(z) = 11 - 2z$. When $|z| = 3$, we have $|f(z)| = 27 > |g(z)|$, so F and f have the same number of zeros, namely three (the three-fold zero of f at $z = 0$). Thus, the answer to our problem is that F has three zeros, all with moduli between 1 and 3. ∎

Product Expansion of Entire Functions

We remind the reader that a function $f(z)$ that is analytic for all finite z is called an **entire** function. Referring to Eq. (11.84), we see that if $f(z)$ is an entire function, then $f'(z)/f(z)$ will be meromorphic, with all its poles simple. Assuming for simplicity that the zeros of f

are simple and at points z_n, so that μ in Eq. (11.84) is 1, we can invoke the Mittag-Leffler theorem to write f'/f as the pole expansion

$$\frac{f'(z)}{f(z)} = \frac{f'(0)}{f(0)} + \sum_{n=1}^{\infty} \left[\frac{1}{z - z_n} + \frac{1}{z_n} \right]. \tag{11.87}$$

Integrating Eq. (11.87) yields

$$\int_0^z \frac{f'(z)}{f(z)} dz = \ln f(z) - \ln f(0)$$

$$= \frac{z f'(0)}{f(0)} + \sum_{n=1}^{\infty} \left[\ln(z - z_n) - \ln(-z_n) + \frac{z}{z_n} \right].$$

Exponentiating, we obtain the product expansion

$$f(z) = f(0) \exp\left(\frac{z f'(0)}{f(0)} \right) \prod_{n=1}^{\infty} \left(1 - \frac{z}{z_n} \right) e^{z/z_n}. \tag{11.88}$$

Examples are the product expansions for

$$\sin z = z \prod_{\substack{n=-\infty \\ n \neq 0}}^{\infty} \left(1 - \frac{z}{n\pi} \right) e^{z/n\pi} = z \prod_{n=1}^{\infty} \left(1 - \frac{z^2}{n^2 \pi^2} \right), \tag{11.89}$$

$$\cos z = \prod_{n=1}^{\infty} \left(1 - \frac{z^2}{(n - 1/2)^2 \pi^2} \right). \tag{11.90}$$

The expansion of $\sin z$ cannot be obtained directly from Eq. (11.88), but its derivation is the subject of Exercise 11.7.5. We also point out here that the gamma function has a product expansion, discussed in Chapter 13.

Exercises

11.7.1   Determine the nature of the singularities of each of the following functions and evaluate the residues $(a > 0)$.

(a) $\dfrac{1}{z^2 + a^2}$.

(b) $\dfrac{1}{(z^2 + a^2)^2}$.

(c) $\dfrac{z^2}{(z^2 + a^2)^2}$.

(d) $\dfrac{\sin 1/z}{z^2 + a^2}$.

(e) $\dfrac{z e^{+iz}}{z^2 + a^2}$.

(f) $\dfrac{z e^{+iz}}{z^2 - a^2}$.

(g) $\dfrac{e^{+iz}}{z^2 - a^2}$.

(h) $\dfrac{z^{-k}}{z + 1}$, $0 < k < 1$.

Hint. For the point at infinity, use the transformation $w = 1/z$ for $|z| \to 0$. For the residue, transform $f(z)dz$ into $g(w)dw$ and look at the behavior of $g(w)$.

11.7.2   Evaluate the residues at $z = 0$ and $z = -1$ of $\pi \cot \pi z / z(z + 1)$.

11.7.3   The classical definition of the exponential integral $\mathrm{Ei}(x)$ for $x > 0$ is the Cauchy principal value integral

$$\mathrm{Ei}(x) = \fint_{-\infty}^{x} \frac{e^t}{t} \, dt,$$

where the integration range is cut at $x = 0$. Show that this definition yields a convergent result for positive x.

11.7.4   Writing a Cauchy principal value integral to deal with the singularity at $x = 1$, show that, if $0 < p < 1$,

$$\fint_{0}^{\infty} \frac{x^{-p}}{x - 1} \, dx = -\pi \cot p\pi.$$

11.7.5   Explain why Eq. (11.88) is not directly applicable to the product expansion of $\sin z$. Show how the expansion, Eq. (11.89), can be obtained by expanding instead $\sin z / z$.

11.7.6   Starting from the observations

1. $f(z) = a_n z^n$ has n zeros, and

2.   for sufficiently large $|R|$, $|\sum_{m=0}^{n-1} a_m R^m| < |a_n R^n|$,

use Rouché's theorem to prove the fundamental theorem of algebra (namely that every polynomial of degree n has n roots).

11.7.7   Using Rouché's theorem, show that all the zeros of $F(z) = z^6 - 4z^3 + 10$ lie between the circles $|z| = 1$ and $|z| = 2$.

11.7.8   Derive the pole expansions of $\sec z$ and $\csc z$ given in Eqs. (11.82) and (11.83).

11.7.9   Given that $f(z) = (z^2 - 3z + 2)/z$, apply a partial fraction decomposition to f'/f and show directly that $\oint_C f'(z)/f(z) \, dz = 2\pi i (N_f - P_f)$, where N_f and P_f are, respectively, the numbers of zeros and poles encircled by C (including their multiplicities).

11.7.10   The statement that the integral halfway around a singular point is equal to one-half the integral all the way around was limited to simple poles. Show, by a specific example, that

$$\int_{\text{Semicircle}} f(z) \, dz = \frac{1}{2} \oint_{\text{Circle}} f(z) \, dz$$

does not necessarily hold if the integral encircles a pole of higher order.

Hint. Try $f(z) = z^{-2}$.

11.7.11   A function $f(z)$ is analytic along the real axis except for a third-order pole at $z = x_0$. The Laurent expansion about $z = x_0$ has the form

$$f(z) = \frac{a_{-3}}{(z - x_0)^3} + \frac{a_{-1}}{z - x_0} + g(z),$$

with $g(z)$ analytic at $z = x_0$. Show that the Cauchy principal value technique is applicable, in the sense that

(a) $\lim_{\delta \to 0} \left\{ \int_{-\infty}^{x_0 - \delta} f(x)\, dx + \int_{x_0 + \delta}^{\infty} f(x)\, dx \right\}$ is finite.

(b) $\int_{C_{x_0}} f(z)\, dz = \pm i\pi a_{-1}$,

     where C_{x_0} denotes a **small semicircle** about $z = x_0$.

11.7.12   The unit step function is defined as (compare Exercise 1.15.13)

$$u(s - a) = \begin{cases} 0, & s < a \\ 1, & s > a. \end{cases}$$

Show that $u(s)$ has the integral representations

(a) $u(s) = \lim_{\varepsilon \to 0^+} \dfrac{1}{2\pi i} \displaystyle\int_{-\infty}^{\infty} \dfrac{e^{ixs}}{x - i\varepsilon}\, dx.$

(b) $u(s) = \dfrac{1}{2} + \dfrac{1}{2\pi i} \displaystyle\int_{-\infty}^{\infty} \dfrac{e^{ixs}}{x}\, dx.$

Note. The parameter s is real.

11.8   EVALUATION OF DEFINITE INTEGRALS

Definite integrals appear repeatedly in problems of mathematical physics as well as in pure mathematics. In Chapter 1 we reviewed several methods for integral evaluation, there noting that contour integration methods were powerful and deserved detailed study. We have now reached a point where we can explore these methods, which are applicable to a wide variety of definite integrals with physically relevant integration limits. We start with applications to integrals containing trigonometric functions, which we can often convert to forms in which the variable of integration (originally an angle) is converted into a complex variable z, with the integration integral becoming a contour integral over the unit circle.

Trigonometric Integrals, Range $(0, 2\pi)$

We consider here integrals of the form

$$I = \int_0^{2\pi} f(\sin\theta, \cos\theta)\, d\theta, \tag{11.91}$$

where f is finite for all values of θ. We also require f to be a rational function of $\sin\theta$ and $\cos\theta$ so that it will be single-valued. We make a change of variable to

$$z = e^{i\theta}, \quad dz = ie^{i\theta}\,d\theta,$$

with the range in θ, namely $(0, 2\pi)$, corresponding to $e^{i\theta}$ moving counterclockwise around the unit circle to form a closed contour. Then we make the substitutions

$$d\theta = -i\frac{dz}{z}, \quad \sin\theta = \frac{z - z^{-1}}{2i}, \quad \cos\theta = \frac{z + z^{-1}}{2}, \tag{11.92}$$

where we have used Eq. (1.133) to represent $\sin\theta$ and $\cos\theta$. Our integral then becomes

$$I = -i \oint f\left(\frac{z - z^{-1}}{2i}, \frac{z + z^{-1}}{2}\right)\frac{dz}{z}, \tag{11.93}$$

with the path of integration the unit circle. By the residue theorem, Eq. (11.64),

$$I = (-i)\,2\pi i \sum \text{residues within the unit circle.} \tag{11.94}$$

Note that we must use the residues of f/z. Here are two preliminary examples.

Example 11.8.1   INTEGRAL OF cos IN DENOMINATOR

Our problem is to evaluate the definite integral

$$I = \int_0^{2\pi} \frac{d\theta}{1 + a\cos\theta}, \quad |a| < 1.$$

By Eq. (11.93) this becomes

$$I = -i \oint_{\text{unit circle}} \frac{dz}{z[1 + (a/2)(z + z^{-1})]}$$

$$= -i\frac{2}{a} \oint \frac{dz}{z^2 + (2/a)z + 1}.$$

The denominator has roots

$$z_1 = -\frac{1 + \sqrt{1 - a^2}}{a} \quad \text{and} \quad z_2 = -\frac{1 - \sqrt{1 - a^2}}{a}.$$

Noting that $z_1 z_2 = 1$, it is easy to see that z_2 is within the unit circle and z_1 is outside. Writing the integral in the form

$$\oint \frac{dz}{(z - z_1)(z - z_2)},$$

we see that the residue of the integrand at $z = z_2$ is $1/(z_2 - z_1)$, so application of the residue theorem yields

$$I = -i\frac{2}{a} \cdot 2\pi i \frac{1}{z_2 - z_1}.$$

Inserting the values of z_1 and z_2, we obtain the final result

$$\int_0^{2\pi} \frac{d\theta}{1 + a\cos\theta} = \frac{2\pi}{\sqrt{1 - a^2}}, \quad |a| < 1.$$

■

Example 11.8.2   ANOTHER TRIGONOMETRIC INTEGRAL

Consider

$$I = \int_0^{2\pi} \frac{\cos 2\theta \, d\theta}{5 - 4\cos\theta}.$$

Making the substitutions identified in Eqs. (11.92) and (11.93), the integral I assumes the form

$$I = \oint \frac{\frac{1}{2}(z^2 + z^{-2})}{5 - 2(z + z^{-1})} \left(\frac{-i\,dz}{z}\right)$$

$$= \frac{i}{4} \oint \frac{(z^4 + 1)\,dz}{z^2\left(z - \frac{1}{2}\right)(z - 2)},$$

where the integration is around the unit circle. Note that we identified $\cos 2\theta$ as $(z^2 + z^{-2})/2$, which is simpler than reducing it first to its equivalent in terms of $\sin z$ and $\cos z$. We see that the integrand has poles at $z = 0$ (of order 2), and simple poles at $z = 1/2$ and $z = 2$. Only the poles at $z = 0$ and $z = 1/2$ are within the contour.

At $z = 0$ the residue of the integrand is

$$\frac{d}{dz}\left[\frac{z^4 + 1}{\left(z - \frac{1}{2}\right)(z - 2)}\right]_{z=0} = \frac{5}{2},$$

while its residue at $z = 1/2$ is

$$\left[\frac{z^4 + 1}{z^2(z - 2)}\right]_{z=1/2} = -\frac{17}{6}.$$

Applying the residue theorem, we have

$$I = \frac{i}{4}(2\pi i)\left[\frac{5}{2} - \frac{17}{6}\right] = \frac{\pi}{6}.$$

■

We stress that integrals of the type now under consideration are evaluated after transforming them so that they can be identified as exactly equivalent to contour integrals to which we can apply the residue theorem. Further examples are in the exercises.

Integrals, Range $-\infty$ to ∞

Consider now definite integrals of the form

$$I = \int_{-\infty}^{\infty} f(x)\,dx, \tag{11.95}$$

where it is assumed that

- $f(z)$ is analytic in the upper half-plane except for a finite number of poles. For the moment will be assumed that there are no poles on the real axis. Cases not satisfying this condition will be considered later.

- In the limit $|z| \to \infty$ in the upper half-plane ($0 \leq \arg z \leq \pi$), $f(z)$ vanishes more strongly than $1/z$.

Note that there is nothing unique about the upper half-plane. The method described here can be applied, with obvious modifications, if $f(z)$ vanishes sufficiently strongly on the lower half-plane.

The second assumption stated above makes it useful to evaluate the contour integral $\oint f(z)\,dz$ on the contour shown in Fig. 11.21, because the integral I is given by the integration along the real axis, while the arc, of radius R, with $R \to \infty$, gives a negligible contribution to the contour integral. Thus,

$$I = \oint f(z)\,dz,$$

and the contour integral can be evaluated by applying the residue theorem.

Situations of this sort are of frequent occurrence, and we therefore formalize the conditions under which the integral over a large arc becomes negligible:

If $\lim_{R \to \infty} z f(z) = 0$ for all $z = Re^{i\theta}$ with θ in the range $\theta_1 \leq \theta \leq \theta_2$, then

$$\lim_{R \to \infty} \int_{C} f(z)\,dz = 0, \tag{11.96}$$

where C is the arc over the angular range θ_1 to θ_2 on a circle of radius R with center at the origin.

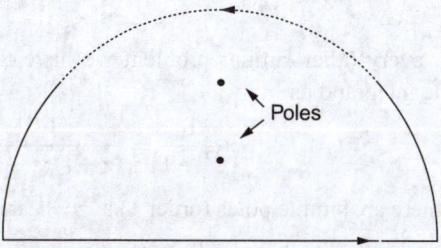

FIGURE 11.21   A contour closed by a large semicircle in the upper half-plane.

To prove Eq. (11.96), simply write the integral over C in polar form:

$$\lim_{R\to\infty}\left|\int_C f(z)\,dz\right| \le \int_{\theta_1}^{\theta_2} \lim_{R\to\infty}\left|f(Re^{i\theta})iRe^{i\theta}\right|d\theta$$

$$\le (\theta_2 - \theta_1)\lim_{R\to\infty}\left|f(Re^{i\theta})Re^{i\theta}\right| = 0.$$

Now, using the contour of Fig. 11.21, letting C denote the semicircular arc from $\theta = 0$ to $\theta = \pi$,

$$\oint f(z)\,dz = \lim_{R\to\infty}\int_{-R}^{R} f(x)\,dx + \lim_{R\to\infty}\int_C f(z)\,dz$$

$$= 2\pi i \sum \text{residues (upper half-plane)}, \tag{11.97}$$

where our second assumption has caused the vanishing of the integral over C.

Example 11.8.3   INTEGRAL OF MEROMORPHIC FUNCTION

Evaluate

$$I = \int_0^\infty \frac{dx}{1+x^2}.$$

This is not in the form we require, but it can be made so by noting that the integrand is even and we can write

$$I = \frac{1}{2}\int_{-\infty}^{\infty} \frac{dx}{1+x^2}. \tag{11.98}$$

We note that $f(z) = 1/(1+z^2)$ is meromorphic; all its singularities for finite z are poles, and it also has the property that $zf(z)$ vanishes in the limit of large $|z|$. Therefore, we may apply Eq. (11.97), so

$$\frac{1}{2}\int_{-\infty}^{\infty} \frac{dx}{1+x^2} = \frac{1}{2}(2\pi i)\sum \text{residues of } \frac{1}{1+z^2} \text{ (upper half-plane)}.$$

Here and in every other similar problem we have the question: Where are the poles? Rewriting the integrand as

$$\frac{1}{z^2+1} = \frac{1}{(z+i)(z-i)},$$

we see that there are simple poles (order 1) at $z = i$ and $z = -i$. The residues are

$$\text{at } z = i: \ \left.\frac{1}{z+i}\right|_{z=i} = \frac{1}{2i}, \quad \text{and} \quad \text{at } z = -i: \ \left.\frac{1}{z-i}\right|_{z=-i} = -\frac{1}{2i}.$$

However, only the pole at $z = +i$ is enclosed by the contour, so our result is

$$\int_0^\infty \frac{dx}{1+x^2} = \frac{1}{2}(2\pi i)\frac{1}{2i} = \frac{\pi}{2}. \tag{11.99}$$

This result is hardly a surprise, as we presumably already know that

$$\int_0^\infty \frac{dx}{1+x^2} = \tan^{-1} x \Big|_0^\infty = \arctan x \Big|_0^\infty = \frac{\pi}{2},$$

but, as shown in later examples, the techniques illustrated here are also easy to apply when more elementary methods are difficult or impossible.

Before leaving this example, note that we could equally well have closed the contour with a semicircle in the lower half-plane, as $zf(z)$ vanishes on that arc as well as that in the upper half-plane. Then, taking the contour so the real axis is traversed from $-\infty$ to $+\infty$, the path would be **clockwise** (see Fig. 11.22), so we would need to take $-2\pi i$ times the residue of the pole that is now encircled (at $z = -i$). Thus, we have $I = -\frac{1}{2}(2\pi i)(-1/2i)$, which (as it must) evaluates to the same result we obtained previously, namely $\pi/2$. ■

Integrals with Complex Exponentials

Consider the definite integral

$$I = \int_{-\infty}^\infty f(x)e^{iax}\, dx, \tag{11.100}$$

with a real and positive. (This is a Fourier transform; see Chapter 19.) We assume the following two conditions:

- $f(z)$ is analytic in the upper half-plane except for a finite number of poles.
- $\lim_{|z| \to \infty} f(z) = 0, \quad 0 \le \arg z \le \pi.$

Note that this is a less restrictive condition than the second condition imposed on $f(z)$ for our previous integration of $\int_{-\infty}^\infty f(x)\, dx$.

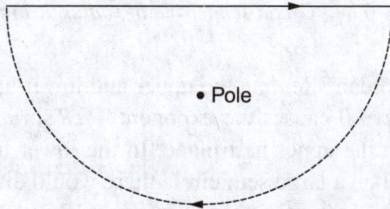

FIGURE 11.22   A contour closed by a large semicircle in the lower half-plane.

We again employ the half-circle contour shown in Fig. 11.21. The application of the calculus of residues is the same as the example just considered, but here we have to work harder to show that the integral over the (infinite) semicircle goes to zero. This integral becomes, for a semicircle of radius R,

$$I_R = \int_0^\pi f(Re^{i\theta}) e^{iaR\cos\theta - aR\sin\theta} i Re^{i\theta} \, d\theta,$$

where the θ integration is over the upper half-plane, $0 \le \theta \le \pi$. Let R be sufficiently large that $|f(z)| = |f(Re^{i\theta})| < \varepsilon$ for all θ within the integration range. Our second assumption on $f(z)$ tells us that as $R \to \infty$, $\varepsilon \to 0$. Then

$$|I_R| \le \varepsilon R \int_0^\pi e^{-aR\sin\theta} \, d\theta = 2\varepsilon R \int_0^{\pi/2} e^{-aR\sin\theta} \, d\theta. \tag{11.101}$$

We now note that in the range $[0, \pi/2]$,

$$\frac{2}{\pi}\theta \le \sin\theta,$$

as is easily seen from Fig. 11.23. Substituting this inequality into Eq. (11.101), we have

$$|I_R| \le 2\varepsilon R \int_0^{\pi/2} e^{-2aR\theta/\pi} \, d\theta = 2\varepsilon R \frac{1 - e^{-aR}}{2aR/\pi} < \frac{\pi}{a}\varepsilon,$$

showing that

$$\lim_{R\to\infty} I_R = 0.$$

This result is also important enough to commemorate; it is sometimes known as **Jordan's lemma**. Its formal statement is

If $\lim_{R=\infty} f(z) = 0$ for all $z = Re^{i\theta}$ in the range $0 \le \theta \le \pi$, then

$$\lim_{R\to\infty} \int_C e^{iaz} f(z) \, dz = 0, \tag{11.102}$$

where $a > 0$ and C is a semicircle of radius R in the upper half-plane with center at the origin.

Note that for Jordan's lemma the upper and lower half-planes are not equivalent, because the condition $a > 0$ causes the exponent $-aR\sin\theta$ only to be negative and yield a negligible result in the upper half-plane. In the lower half-plane, the exponential is positive and the integral on a large semicircle there would diverge. Of course, we could extend the theorem by considering the case $a < 0$, in which event the contour to be used would then be a semicircle in the lower half-plane.

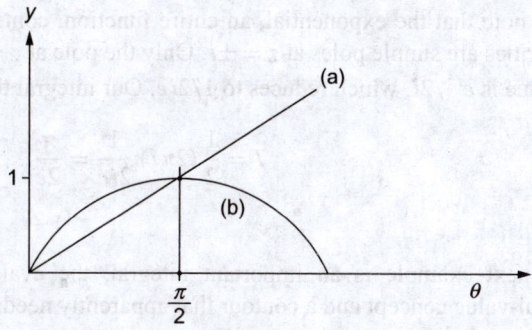

FIGURE 11.23   (a) $y = (2/\pi)\theta$, (b) $y = \sin\theta$.

Returning now to integrals of the type represented by Eq. (11.100), and using the contour shown in Fig. 11.21, application of the residue theorem yields the general result (for $a > 0$),

$$\int_{-\infty}^{\infty} f(x)e^{iax}\,dx = 2\pi i \sum \text{residues of } e^{iaz} f(z) \text{ (upper half-plane)}, \qquad (11.103)$$

where we have used Jordan's lemma to set to zero the contribution to the contour integral from the large semicircle.

Example 11.8.4   OSCILLATORY INTEGRAL

Consider

$$I = \int_{0}^{\infty} \frac{\cos x}{x^2 + 1}\,dx,$$

which we initially manipulate, introducing $\cos x = (e^{ix} + e^{-ix})/2$, as follows:

$$I = \frac{1}{2} \int_{0}^{\infty} \frac{e^{ix}\,dx}{x^2 + 1} + \frac{1}{2} \int_{0}^{\infty} \frac{e^{-ix}\,dx}{x^2 + 1}$$

$$= \frac{1}{2} \int_{0}^{\infty} \frac{e^{ix}\,dx}{x^2 + 1} + \frac{1}{2} \int_{0}^{-\infty} \frac{e^{ix}\,d(-x)}{(-x)^2 + 1} = \frac{1}{2} \int_{-\infty}^{\infty} \frac{e^{ix}\,dx}{x^2 + 1},$$

thereby bringing I to the form presently under discussion.

We now note that in this problem $f(z) = 1/(z^2 + 1)$, which certainly approaches zero for large $|z|$, and the exponential factor is of the form e^{iaz}, with $a = +1$. We may therefore evaluate the integral using Eq. (11.103), with the contour shown in Fig. 11.21.

The quantity whose residues are needed is

$$\frac{e^{iz}}{z^2 + 1} = \frac{e^{iz}}{(z + i)(z - i)},$$

and we note that the exponential, an entire function, contributes no singularities. So our singularities are simple poles at $z = \pm i$. Only the pole at $z = +i$ is within the contour, and its residue is $e^{i^2}/2i$, which reduces to $1/2ie$. Our integral therefore has the value

$$I = \frac{1}{2}(2\pi i)\frac{1}{2ie} = \frac{\pi}{2e}.$$

∎

Our next example is an important integral, the evaluation of which involves the principal-value concept and a contour that apparently needs to go through a pole.

Example 11.8.5   SINGULARITY ON CONTOUR OF INTEGRATION

We now consider the evaluation of

$$I = \int_0^\infty \frac{\sin x}{x}\,dx. \tag{11.104}$$

Writing the integrand as $(e^{iz} - e^{-iz})/2iz$, an attempt to do as we did in Example 11.8.4 leads to the problem that each of the two integrals into which I can be separated is individually divergent. This is a problem we have already encountered in discussing the Cauchy principal value of this integral. Referring to (11.74), we write I as

$$I = \fint_{-\infty}^\infty \frac{e^{ix}\,dx}{2ix}, \tag{11.105}$$

suggesting that we consider the integral of $e^{iz}/2iz$ over a suitable closed contour.

We now note that although the gap at $x = 0$ is infinitesimal, that point is a pole of $e^{iz}/2iz$, and we must draw a contour which avoids it, using a small semicircle to connect the points at $-\delta$ and $+\delta$. Compare with the discussion at Eqs. (11.75) and (11.76). Choosing the small semicircle **above** the pole, as in Fig. 11.20, we then have a contour that encloses **no** singularities.

The integral around this contour can now be identified as consisting of (1) the two semi-infinite segments constituting the principal value integral in Eq. (11.105), (2) the large semicircle C_R of radius R ($R \to \infty$), and (3) a semicircle C_r of radius r ($r \to 0$), traversed **clockwise**, so

$$\oint \frac{e^{iz}}{2iz}\,dz = I + \int_{C_r} \frac{e^{iz}}{2iz}\,dz + \int_{C_R} \frac{e^{iz}}{2iz}\,dz = 0. \tag{11.106}$$

By Jordan's lemma, the integral over C_R vanishes. As discussed at Eq. (11.75), the clockwise path C_r half-way around the pole at $z = 0$ contributes half the value of a full circuit, namely (allowing for the clockwise direction of travel) $-\pi i$ times the residue of $e^{iz}/2iz$ at $z = 0$. This residue has value $1/2i$, so $\int_{C_r} = -\pi i(1/2i) = -\pi/2$, and, solving Eq. (11.106) for I, we then obtain

$$I = \int\limits_0^\infty \frac{\sin x}{x}\, dx = \frac{\pi}{2}. \tag{11.107}$$

Note that it was necessary to close the contour in the upper half-plane. On a large circle in the lower half-plane, e^{iz} becomes infinite and Jordan's lemma cannot be applied. ∎

Another Integration Technique

Sometimes we have an integral on the real range $(0, \infty)$ that lacks the symmetry needed to extend the integration range to $(-\infty, \infty)$. However, it may be possible to identify a direction in the complex plane on which the integrand has a value identical to or conveniently related to that of the original integral, thereby permitting construction of a contour facilitating the evaluation.

Example 11.8.6   EVALUATION ON A CIRCULAR SECTOR

Our problem is to evaluate the integral

$$I = \int\limits_0^\infty \frac{dx}{x^3 + 1},$$

which we cannot convert easily into an integral on the range $(-\infty, \infty)$. However, we note that along a line with argument $\theta = 2\pi/3$, z^3 will have the same values as at corresponding points on the real line; note that $(re^{2\pi i/3})^3 = r^3 e^{2\pi i} = r^3$. We therefore consider

$$\oint \frac{dz}{z^3 + 1}$$

on the contour shown in Fig. 11.24. The part of the contour along the positive real axis, labeled A, simply yields our integral I. The integrand approaches zero sufficiently rapidly for large $|z|$ that the integral on the large circular arc, labeled C in the figure, vanishes. On

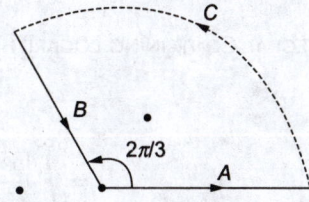

FIGURE 11.24   Contour for Example 11.8.6.

the remaining segment of the contour, labeled B, we note that $dz = e^{2\pi i/3} dr$, $z^3 = r^3$, and

$$\int_B \frac{dz}{z^3+1} = \int_\infty^0 \frac{e^{2\pi i/3} dr}{r^3+1} = -e^{2\pi i/3} \int_0^\infty \frac{dr}{r^3+1} = -e^{2\pi i/3} I.$$

Therefore,

$$\oint \frac{dz}{z^3+1} = \left(1 - e^{2\pi i/3}\right) I. \tag{11.108}$$

We now need to evaluate our complete contour integral using the residue theorem. The integrand has simple poles at the three roots of $z^3 + 1$, which are at $z_1 = e^{\pi i/3}$, $z_2 = e^{\pi i}$, and $z_3 = e^{5\pi i/3}$, as marked in Fig. 11.24. Only the pole at z_1 is enclosed by our contour. The residue at $z = z_1$ is

$$\lim_{z=z_1} \frac{z-z_1}{z^3+1} = \frac{1}{3z^2}\bigg|_{z=z_1} = \frac{1}{3e^{2\pi i/3}}.$$

Equating $2\pi i$ times this result to the value of the contour integral as given in Eq. (11.108), we have

$$\left(1 - e^{2\pi i/3}\right) I = 2\pi i \left(\frac{1}{3e^{2\pi i/3}}\right).$$

Solution for I is facilitated if we multiply through by $e^{-\pi i/3}$, obtaining initially

$$\left(e^{-\pi i/3} - e^{\pi i/3}\right) I = 2\pi i \left(-\frac{1}{3}\right),$$

which is easily rearranged to

$$I = \frac{\pi}{3\sin \pi/3} = \frac{\pi}{3\sqrt{3}/2} = \frac{2\pi}{3\sqrt{3}}.$$

∎

Avoidance of Branch Points

Sometimes we must deal with integrals whose integrands have branch points. In order to use contour integration methods for such integrals we must choose contours that avoid the branch points, enclosing only point singularities.

Example 11.8.7   INTEGRAL CONTAINING LOGARITHM

We now look at

$$I = \int_0^\infty \frac{\ln x \, dx}{x^3+1}. \tag{11.109}$$

The integrand in Eq. (11.109) is singular at $x = 0$, but the integration converges (the indefinite integral of $\ln x$ is $x \ln x - x$). However, in the complex plane this singularity manifests

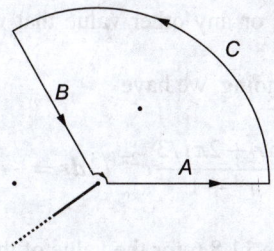

FIGURE 11.25   Contour for Example 11.8.7.

itself as a branch point, so if we are to recast this problem in a way involving a contour integral, we must avoid $z = 0$ and a branch cut from that point to $z = \infty$. It turns out to be convenient to use a contour similar to that for Example 11.8.6, except that we must make a small circular detour about $z = 0$ and then draw the branch cut in a direction that remains outside our chosen contour. Noting also that the integrand has poles at the same points as those of Example 11.8.6, we consider a contour integral

$$\oint \frac{\ln z \, dz}{z^3 + 1},$$

where the contour and the locations of the singularities of the integrand are as illustrated in Fig. 11.25.

The integral over the large circular arc, labeled C, vanishes, as the factor z^3 in the denominator dominates over the weakly divergent factor $\ln z$ in the numerator (which diverges more weakly than any positive power of z). We also get no contribution to the contour integral from the arc at small r, since we have there

$$\lim_{r \to 0} \int_0^{2\pi/3} \frac{\ln(re^{i\theta})}{1 + r^3 e^{3i\theta}} i r e^{i\theta} \, d\theta,$$

which vanishes because $r \ln r \to 0$.

The integrals over the segments labeled A and B do not vanish. To evaluate the integral over these segments, we need to make an appropriate choice of the branch of the multi-valued function $\ln z$. It is natural to choose the branch so that on the real axis we have $\ln z = \ln x$ (and not $\ln x + 2n\pi i$ with some nonzero n). Then the integral over the segment labeled A will have the value I.[7]

To compute the integral over B, we note that on this segment $z^3 = r^3$ and $dz = e^{2\pi i/3} dr$ (as in Example 11.8.6), also but note that $\ln z = \ln r + 2\pi i/3$. There is little temptation here to use a different one of the multiple values of the logarithm, but for future reference note that we **must** use the value that is reached continuously from the value we already chose on the positive real axis, moving in a way that does not cross the branch cut. Thus, we cannot reach segment A by clockwise travel from the positive real axis (thereby getting

---

[7]Because the integration converges at $x = 0$, the value is not affected by the fact that this segment terminates infinitesimally before reaching that point.

$\ln z = \ln r - 4\pi i/3$) or any other value that would require multiple circuits around the branch point $z = 0$.

Based on the foregoing, we have

$$\int_B \frac{\ln z \, dz}{z^3+1} = \int_\infty^0 \frac{\ln r + 2\pi i/3}{r^3+1} e^{2\pi i/3} \, dr = -e^{2\pi i/3} I - \frac{2\pi i}{3} e^{2\pi i/3} \int_0^\infty \frac{dr}{r^3+1}. \quad (11.110)$$

Referring to Example 11.8.6 for the value of the integral in the final term of Eq. (11.110), and combining the contributions to the overall contour integral,

$$\oint \frac{\ln z \, dz}{z^3+1} = \left(1 - e^{2\pi i/3}\right) I - \frac{2\pi i}{3} e^{2\pi i/3} \left(\frac{2\pi}{3\sqrt{3}}\right). \quad (11.111)$$

Our next step is to use the residue theorem to evaluate the contour integral. Only the pole at $z = z_1$ lies within the contour. The residue we must compute is

$$\lim_{z=z_1} \frac{(z-z_1)\ln z}{z^3+1} = \frac{\ln z}{3z^2}\bigg|_{z=z_1} = \frac{\pi i/3}{3e^{2\pi i/3}} = \frac{\pi i}{9} e^{-2\pi i/3},$$

and application of the residue theorem to Eq. (11.111) yields

$$\left(1 - e^{2\pi i/3}\right) I - \frac{2\pi i}{3} e^{2\pi i/3} \left(\frac{2\pi}{3\sqrt{3}}\right) = (2\pi i) \left(\frac{\pi i}{9}\right) e^{-2\pi i/3}. \quad (11.112)$$

Solving for I, we get

$$I = -\frac{2\pi^2}{27}. \quad (11.113)$$

Verification of the passage from Eq. (11.112) to (11.113) is left to Exercise 11.8.6. ∎

Exploiting Branch Cuts

Sometimes, rather than being an annoyance, a branch cut provides an opportunity for a creative way of evaluating difficult integrals.

Example 11.8.8   USING A BRANCH CUT

Let's evaluate

$$I = \int_0^\infty \frac{x^p \, dx}{x^2+1}, \quad 0 < p < 1.$$

Consider the contour integral

$$\oint \frac{z^p \, dz}{z^2+1},$$

where the contour is that shown in Fig. 11.26. Note that $z = 0$ is a branch point, and we have taken the cut along the positive real axis. We assign z^p its usual principal value

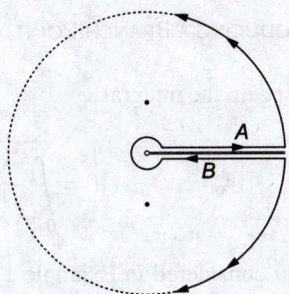

FIGURE 11.26   Contour for Example 11.8.8.

(which is x^p) just above the cut, so that the segment of the contour labeled A, which actually extends from ε to ∞, converges in the limit of small ε to the integral I. Neither the circle of radius ε nor that at $R \to \infty$ contributes to the value of the contour integral. On the remaining segment of the contour, labeled B, we have $z = re^{2\pi i}$, written this way so we can see that $z^p = r^p e^{2p\pi i}$. We use this value for z^p on segment B because we must get to B by encircling $z = 0$ in the counterclockwise, mathematically positive direction. The contribution of segment B to the contour integral is then seen to be

$$\int_{\infty}^{0} \frac{r^p e^{2p\pi i}\, dr}{r^2 + 1} = -e^{2p\pi i} I,$$

so

$$\oint \frac{z^p\, dz}{z^2 + 1} = \left(1 - e^{2p\pi i}\right) I. \tag{11.114}$$

To apply the residue theorem, we note that there are simple poles at $z_1 = i$ and $z_2 = -i$; to use these for evaluation of z^p we need to identify these as $z_1 = e^{\pi i/2}$ and $z_2 = e^{3\pi i/2}$. It would be a serious mistake to use $z_2 = e^{-\pi i/2}$ when evaluating z_2^p. We now find the residues to be:

$$\text{Residue at } z_1\colon \quad \frac{e^{p\pi i/2}}{2i}, \quad \text{Residue at } z_2\colon \quad \frac{e^{3p\pi i/2}}{-2i},$$

and we have, referring to Eq. (11.114),

$$\left(1 - e^{2p\pi i}\right) I = (2\pi i)\, \frac{1}{2i}\left(e^{p\pi i/2} - e^{3p\pi i/2}\right). \tag{11.115}$$

This equation simplifies to

$$I = \frac{\pi \sin(p\pi/2)}{\sin p\pi} = \frac{\pi}{2\cos(p\pi/2)}. \tag{11.116}$$

The details of the evaluation are left to Exercise 11.8.7.   ∎

The use of a branch cut, as illustrated in Example 11.8.8, is so helpful that sometimes it is advisable to insert a factor into a contour integral to create one that would not otherwise exist. To illustrate this, we return to an integral we evaluated earlier by another method.

Example 11.8.9   INTRODUCING A BRANCH POINT

Let's evaluate once again the integral

$$I = \int_0^\infty \frac{dx}{x^3 + 1},$$

which we previously considered in Example 11.8.6. This time, we proceed by setting up the contour integral

$$\oint \frac{\ln z \, dz}{z^3 + 1},$$

taking the contour to be that depicted in Fig. 11.26. Note that in the present problem the poles of the integrand are not those shown in Fig. 11.26, which was originally drawn to illustrate a different problem; for the locations of the poles of the present integrand, see Fig. 11.24.

The virtue of the introduction of the factor $\ln z$ is that its presence causes the integral segments above and below the positive real axis not to cancel completely, but to yield a net contribution corresponding to an integral of interest. In the present problem (using the labeling in Fig. 11.26), we again have vanishing contributions from the small and large circles, and (taking the usual principal value for the logarithm on segment A), that segment contributes to the contour integral the expected value

$$\int_A \frac{\ln z \, dz}{z^3 + 1} = \int_0^\infty \frac{\ln x \, dx}{x^3 + 1}. \tag{11.117}$$

However, segment B make the contribution

$$\int_B \frac{\ln z \, dz}{z^3 + 1} = \int_\infty^0 \frac{(\ln x + 2\pi i) \, dx}{x^3 + 1}, \tag{11.118}$$

and when Eqs. (11.117) and (11.118) are combined, the logarithmic terms cancel, and we are left with

$$\oint \frac{\ln z \, dz}{z^3 + 1} = \int_{A+B} \frac{\ln z \, dz}{z^3 + 1} = -2\pi i \int_0^\infty \frac{dx}{x^3 + 1} = -2\pi i \, I. \tag{11.119}$$

Note that what has happened is that the logarithm has disappeared (its contributions canceled), but its presence caused the integral of current interest to be proportional to the value of the contour integral we introduced.

To complete the evaluation, we need to evaluate the contour integral using the residue theorem. Note that the residues are those of the integrand, including the logarithmic factor, and this factor must be computed taking account of the branch cut. In the present problem, we identify poles at $z_1 = e^{\pi i/3}$, $z_2 = e^{\pi i}$, and $z_3 = e^{5\pi i/3}$ (**not** $e^{-\pi i/3}$). The contour now in use encircles all three poles. Their respective residues (denoted R_i) are

$$R_1 = \left(\frac{\pi i}{3}\right) \frac{1}{3\,e^{2\pi i/3}}, \quad R_2 = (\pi i)\,\frac{1}{3\,e^{6\pi i/3}}, \quad \text{and} \quad R_3 = \left(\frac{5\pi i}{3}\right) \frac{1}{3\,e^{10\pi i/3}},$$

where the first parenthesized factor of each residue comes from the logarithm.

Continuing, we have, referring to Eq. (11.119),

$$-2\pi i\,I = 2\pi i\,(R_1 + R_2 + R_3);$$

$$I = -(R_1 + R_2 + R_3) = -\frac{\pi i}{9}\left[e^{-2\pi i/3} + 3 + 5\,e^{2\pi i/3}\right] = \frac{2\pi}{3\sqrt{3}}.$$

More robust examples involving the introduction of $\ln z$ appear in the exercises. ■

Exploiting Periodicity

The periodicity of the trigonometric functions (and that, in the complex plane, of the hyperbolic functions) creates opportunities to devise contours in which multiple contributions corresponding to an integral of interest can be used to encircle singularities and enable use of the residue theorem. We illustrate with one example.

Example 11.8.10   INTEGRAND PERIODIC ON IMAGINARY AXIS

We wish to evaluate

$$I = \int_0^\infty \frac{x\,dx}{\sinh x}.$$

Taking account of the sinusoidal behavior of the hyperbolic sine in the imaginary direction, we consider

$$\oint \frac{z\,dz}{\sinh z} \tag{11.120}$$

on the contour shown in Fig. 11.27. In drawing the contour we needed to be mindful of the singularities of the integrand, which are poles associated with the zeros of $\sinh z$. Recognizing that

$$\sinh(x + iy) = \sinh x \cosh iy + \cosh x \sinh iy = \sinh x \cos y + i \cosh x \sin y, \tag{11.121}$$

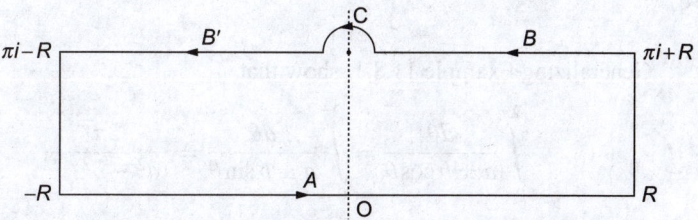

FIGURE 11.27   Contour for Example 11.8.10.

and that for all x, $\cosh x \geq 1$, we see that $\sinh z$ is zero only for $z = n\pi i$, with n an integer. Moreover, because $\lim_{z \to 0} z/\sinh z = 1$, the integrand of our present contour integral will not have a pole at $z = 0$, but will have poles at $z = n\pi i$ for all nonzero integral n. For that reason, the lower horizontal line of the contour in Fig. 11.27, marked A, continues through $z = 0$ as a straight line on the real axis, but the upper horizontal line (for which $y = \pi$), marked B and B', has an infinitesimal semicircular detour, marked C, around the pole at $z = \pi i$.

Because the integrand in Eq. (11.120) is an even function of z, the integral on segment A, which extends from $-\infty$ to $+\infty$, has the value $2I$. To evaluate the integral on segments B and B', we first note, using Eq. (11.121), that $\sinh(x + i\pi) = -\sinh x$, and that the integral on these segments is in the direction of negative x. Recognizing the integral on these segments as a Cauchy principal value, we write

$$\int_{B+B'} \frac{z\,dz}{\sinh z} = \fint_{-\infty}^{\infty} \frac{x + i\pi}{\sinh x} dx.$$

Because $x/\sinh x$ is even and nonsingular at $z = 0$, while $i\pi/\sinh x$ is odd, this integral reduces to

$$\fint_{-\infty}^{\infty} \frac{x + i\pi}{\sinh x} dx = 2I.$$

Combining what we have up to this point, invoking the residue theorem, and noting that the integrand is negligible on the vertical connections at $x = \pm\infty$. We have

$$\oint \frac{z\,dz}{\sinh z} = 4I + \int_C \frac{z\,dz}{\sinh z} = 2\pi i \text{ (residue of } z/\sinh z \text{ at } z = \pi i). \tag{11.122}$$

To complete the evaluation, we now note that the residue we need is

$$\lim_{z \to \pi i} \frac{z(z - \pi i)}{\sinh z} = \frac{\pi i}{\cosh \pi i} = -\pi i,$$

and, cf. Eqs. (11.75) and (11.76), the counterclockwise semicircle C evaluates to πi times this residue. We have then

$$4I + (\pi i)(-\pi i) = (2\pi i)(-\pi i), \quad \text{so } I = \frac{\pi^2}{4}.$$

■

Exercises

11.8.1   Generalizing Example 11.8.1, show that

$$\int_0^{2\pi} \frac{d\theta}{a \pm b\cos\theta} = \int_0^{2\pi} \frac{d\theta}{a \pm b\sin\theta} = \frac{2\pi}{(a^2 - b^2)^{1/2}}, \quad \text{for } a > |b|.$$

What happens if $|b| > |a|$?

11.8.2   Show that $\displaystyle\int_0^{\pi} \frac{d\theta}{(a + \cos\theta)^2} = \frac{\pi a}{(a^2 - 1)^{3/2}}, \quad a > 1.$

11.8.3   Show that $\displaystyle\int_0^{2\pi} \frac{d\theta}{1 - 2t\cos\theta + t^2} = \frac{2\pi}{1 - t^2}, \quad$ for $|t| < 1.$

What happens if $|t| > 1$?   What happens if $|t| = 1$?

11.8.4   Evaluate $\displaystyle\int_0^{2\pi} \frac{\cos 3\theta\, d\theta}{5 - 4\cos\theta}.$

ANS. $\pi/12.$

11.8.5   With the calculus of residues, show that

$$\int_0^{\pi} \cos^{2n}\theta\, d\theta = \pi \frac{(2n)!}{2^{2n}(n!)^2} = \pi \frac{(2n-1)!!}{(2n)!!}, \quad n = 0, 1, 2, \ldots.$$

The double factorial notation is defined in Eq. (1.76).

Hint. $\cos\theta = \frac{1}{2}(e^{i\theta} + e^{-i\theta}) = \frac{1}{2}(z + z^{-1}), \quad |z| = 1.$

11.8.6   Verify that simplification of the expression in Eq. (11.112) yields the result given in Eq. (11.113).

11.8.7   Complete the details of Example 11.8.8 by verifying that there is no contribution to the contour integral from either the small or the large circles of the contour, and that Eq. (11.115) simplifies to the result given as (11.116).

11.8.8   Evaluate $\displaystyle\int_{-\infty}^{\infty} \frac{\cos bx - \cos ax}{x^2}\, dx, \quad a > b > 0.$

ANS. $\pi(a - b).$

11.8.9   Prove that $\displaystyle\int_{-\infty}^{\infty} \frac{\sin^2 x}{x^2}\, dx = \frac{\pi}{2}.$

Hint. $\sin^2 x = \frac{1}{2}(1 - \cos 2x).$

11.8.10   Show that $\displaystyle\int_0^{\infty} \frac{x \sin x}{x^2 + 1}\, dx = \frac{\pi}{2e}.$

11.8.11   A quantum mechanical calculation of a transition probability leads to the function $f(t, \omega) = 2(1 - \cos \omega t)/\omega^2$. Show that

$$\int\limits_{-\infty}^{\infty} f(t, \omega)\, d\omega = 2\pi t.$$

11.8.12   Show that ($a > 0$):

(a) $\displaystyle \int\limits_{-\infty}^{\infty} \frac{\cos x}{x^2 + a^2}\, dx = \frac{\pi}{a} e^{-a}.$

How is the right side modified if $\cos x$ is replaced by $\cos kx$?

(b) $\displaystyle \int\limits_{-\infty}^{\infty} \frac{x \sin x}{x^2 + a^2}\, dx = \pi e^{-a}.$

How is the right side modified if $\sin x$ is replaced by $\sin kx$?

11.8.13   Use the contour shown (Fig. 11.28) with $R \to \infty$ to prove that

$$\int\limits_{-\infty}^{\infty} \frac{\sin x}{x}\, dx = \pi.$$

11.8.14   In the quantum theory of atomic collisions, we encounter the integral

$$I = \int\limits_{-\infty}^{\infty} \frac{\sin t}{t} e^{ipt}\, dt,$$

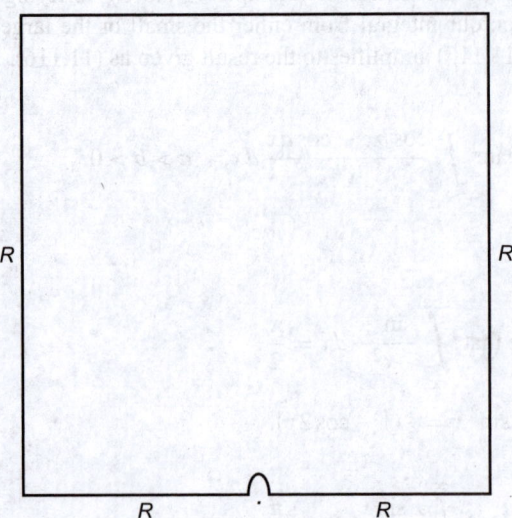

FIGURE 11.28   Contour for Exercise 11.8.13.

in which p is real. Show that

$$I = 0, \quad |p| > 1$$
$$I = \pi, \quad |p| < 1.$$

What happens if $p = \pm 1$?

11.8.15 Show that $\displaystyle\int_0^\infty \frac{dx}{(x^2 + a^2)^2} = \frac{\pi}{4a^3}, \quad a > 0.$

11.8.16 Evaluate $\displaystyle\int_{-\infty}^\infty \frac{x^2}{1 + x^4}\, dx.$

ANS. $\pi/\sqrt{2}.$

11.8.17 Evaluate $\displaystyle\int_0^\infty \frac{x^p \ln x}{x^2 + 1}\, dx, \quad 0 < p < 1.$

ANS. $\dfrac{\pi^2}{4}\dfrac{\sin(\pi p/2)}{\cos^2(\pi p/2)}.$

11.8.18 Evaluate $\displaystyle\int_0^\infty \frac{(\ln x)^2}{1 + x^2}\, dx,$

(a) by appropriate series expansion of the integrand to obtain

$$4 \sum_{n=0}^\infty (-1)^n (2n + 1)^{-3},$$

(b) and by contour integration to obtain $\dfrac{\pi^3}{8}.$

Hint. $x \to z = e^t$. Try the contour shown in Fig. 11.29, letting $R \to \infty.$

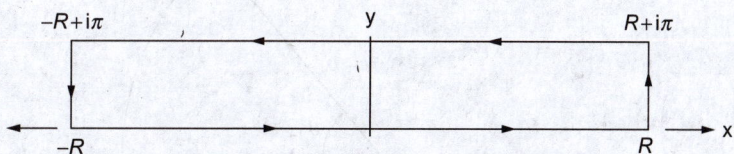

FIGURE **11.29**   Contour for Exercise 11.8.18.

11.8.19   Prove that $\displaystyle\int_0^\infty \frac{\ln(1+x^2)}{1+x^2}\,dx = \pi \ln 2.$

11.8.20   Show that

$$\int_0^\infty \frac{x^a}{(x+1)^2}\,dx = \frac{\pi a}{\sin \pi a},$$

where $-1 < a < 1$.

Hint. Use the contour shown in Fig. 11.26, noting that $z = 0$ is a branch point and the positive x-axis can be chosen to be a cut line.

11.8.21   Show that

$$\int_{-\infty}^\infty \frac{x^2\,dx}{x^4 - 2x^2 \cos 2\theta + 1} = \frac{\pi}{2 \sin \theta} = \frac{\pi}{2^{1/2}(1 - \cos 2\theta)^{1/2}}.$$

Exercise 11.8.16 is a special case of this result.

11.8.22   Show that

$$\int_0^\infty \frac{dx}{1 + x^n} = \frac{\pi/n}{\sin(\pi/n)}.$$

Hint. Try the contour shown in Fig. 11.30, with $\theta = 2\pi/n$.

11.8.23   (a)   Show that

$$f(z) = z^4 - 2z^2 \cos 2\theta + 1$$

has zeros at $e^{i\theta}, e^{-i\theta}, -e^{i\theta},$ and $-e^{-i\theta}$.

   (b)   Show that

$$\int_{-\infty}^\infty \frac{dx}{x^4 - 2x^2 \cos 2\theta + 1} = \frac{\pi}{2 \sin \theta} = \frac{\pi}{2^{1/2}(1 - \cos 2\theta)^{1/2}}.$$

Exercise 11.8.22 $(n = 4)$ is a special case of this result.

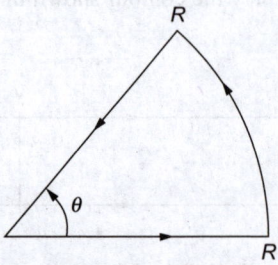

FIGURE 11.30   Sector contour.

11.8.24 Show that

$$\int_0^\infty \frac{x^{-a}}{x+1}\, dx = \frac{\pi}{\sin a\pi},$$

where $0 < a < 1$.

Hint. You have a branch point and you will need a cut line. Try the contour shown in Fig. 11.26.

11.8.25 Show that $\displaystyle\int_0^\infty \frac{\cosh bx}{\cosh x}\, dx = \frac{\pi}{2\cos(\pi b/2)},\quad |b| < 1.$

Hint. Choose a contour that encloses one pole of $\cosh z$.

11.8.26 Show that

$$\int_0^\infty \cos(t^2)\, dt = \int_0^\infty \sin(t^2)\, dt = \frac{\sqrt{\pi}}{2\sqrt{2}}.$$

Hint. Try the contour shown in Fig. 11.30, with $\theta = \pi/4$.

Note. These are the Fresnel integrals for the special case of infinity as the upper limit. For the general case of a varying upper limit, asymptotic expansions of the Fresnel integrals are the topic of Exercise 12.6.1.

11.8.27 Show that $\displaystyle\int_0^1 \frac{1}{(x^2 - x^3)^{1/3}}\, dx = 2\pi/\sqrt{3}.$

Hint. Try the contour shown in Fig. 11.31.

11.8.28 Evaluate $\displaystyle\int_{-\infty}^\infty \frac{\tan^{-1} ax\, dx}{x(x^2 + b^2)}$, for a and b positive, with $ab < 1$.

Explain why the integrand does not have a singularity at $x = 0$.

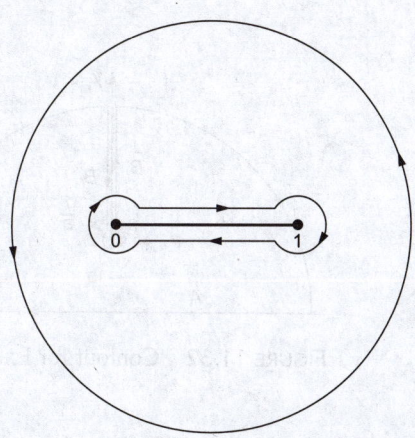

FIGURE 11.31   Contour for Exercise 11.8.27.

Hint. Try the contour shown in Fig. 11.32, and use Eq. (1.137) to represent $\tan^{-1} az$. After cancellation, the integrals on segments B and B' combine to give an elementary integral.

11.9 EVALUATION OF SUMS

The fact that the cotangent is a meromorphic function with regularly spaced poles, all with the same residue, enables us to use it to write a wide variety of infinite summations in terms of contour integrals. To start, note that $\pi \cot \pi z$ has simple poles at all integers on the real axis, each with residue

$$\lim_{z \to n} \frac{\pi \cos \pi z}{\sin \pi z} = 1.$$

Suppose that we now evaluate the integral

$$I_N = \oint_{C_N} f(z) \pi \cot \pi z \, dz,$$

where the contour is a circle about $z = 0$ of radius $N + \frac{1}{2}$ (thereby not passing close to the singularities of $\cot \pi z$). Assuming also that $f(z)$ has only isolated singularities, at points z_j other than real integers, we get by application of the residue theorem (see also Exercise 11.9.1),

$$I_N = 2\pi i \sum_{n=-N}^{N} f(n) + 2\pi i \sum_{j} (\text{residues of } f(z) \pi \cot \pi z \text{ at singularities } z_j \text{ of } f).$$

This integral over the circular contour C_N will be negligible for large $|z|$ if $zf(z) \to 0$ at large $|z|$.[8] When that condition is met, $\lim_{N \to \infty} I_N = 0$, and we have the useful result

$$\sum_{n=-\infty}^{\infty} f(n) = - \sum_{j} (\text{residues of } f(z) \pi \cot \pi z \text{ at singularities } z_j \text{ of } f). \tag{11.123}$$

The condition required of $f(z)$ will usually be satisfied if the summation of Eq. (11.123) converges.

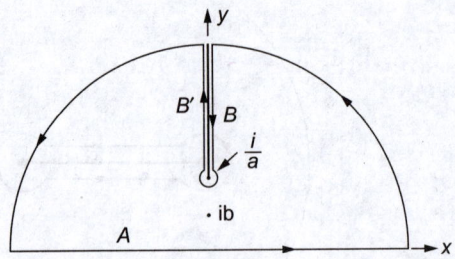

FIGURE 11.32   Contour for Exercise 11.8.28.

---

[8] See also Exercise 11.9.2.

Example 11.9.1 EVALUATING A SUM

Consider the summation

$$S = \sum_{n=1}^{\infty} \frac{1}{n^2 + a^2},$$

where, for simplicity, we assume that a is nonintegral. To bring our problem to the form we know how to treat, we note that also

$$\sum_{n=-\infty}^{-1} \frac{1}{n^2 + a^2} = S,$$

so that

$$\sum_{n=-\infty}^{\infty} \frac{1}{n^2 + a^2} = 2S + \frac{1}{a^2}, \tag{11.124}$$

where we have added on the right-hand side the contribution from $n = 0$ that was not included in S.

The summation is now identified as of the form of Eq. (11.123), with $f(z) = 1/(z^2 + a^2)$; $f(z)$ approaches zero at large z rapidly enough to make Eq. (11.123) applicable. We therefore proceed to the observation that the only singularities of $f(z)$ are simple poles at $z = \pm ia$. The residues we need are those of $\pi \cot(\pi z)/(z^2 + a^2)$; they are

$$\frac{\pi \cot i\pi a}{2ia} = \frac{-\pi \coth \pi a}{2a} \quad \text{and} \quad \frac{\pi \cot(-i\pi a)}{-2ia} = \frac{-\pi \coth(-\pi a)}{-2a}.$$

These are equal, so from Eqs. (11.123) and (11.124),

$$2S + \frac{1}{a^2} = \frac{\pi \coth \pi a}{a},$$

which we easily solve to reach $S = \dfrac{\pi \coth \pi a}{2a} - \dfrac{1}{2a^2}$. ∎

Additional types of summations can be performed if we replace $\cot \pi z$ by functions with other regularly repeating patterns of residues. For example, $\pi \csc \pi z$ has residues for integer z that alternate in sign between $+1$ and -1; $\pi \tan \pi z$ has residues that are all $+1$, but occur at the points $n + \frac{1}{2}$. And $\pi \sec \pi z$ has residues ± 1 at the half-integers with a sign alternation. For convenience, we list in Table 11.2 the contour-integral formulas for the four types of summations we have just discussed.

We close this section with another example, this time illustrating what can be done if $f(z)$ has a pole at an integer value of z.

Example 11.9.2 ANOTHER SUM

Consider now the summation

$$S = \sum_{n=1}^{\infty} \frac{1}{n(n+1)}.$$

Table 11.2   Contour-Integral-Based Formulas for Summations

Summation	Formula
$\displaystyle\sum_{n=-\infty}^{\infty} f(n)$	$-\sum$(residues of $f(z)\pi\cot\pi z$ at singularities of f).
$\displaystyle\sum_{n=-\infty}^{\infty} (-1)^n f(n)n$	$-\sum$(residues of $f(z)\pi\csc\pi z$ at singularities of f).
$\displaystyle\sum_{n=-\infty}^{\infty} f\left(n+\tfrac{1}{2}\right)$	$\sum$(residues of $f(z)\pi\tan\pi z$ at singularities of f).
$\displaystyle\sum_{n=-\infty}^{\infty} (-1)^n f\left(n+\tfrac{1}{2}\right)$	$\sum$(residues of $f(z)\pi\sec\pi z$ at singularities of f).

To extend the summation to $n=-\infty$, we note that $S = \displaystyle\sum_{n=-\infty}^{-2}\frac{1}{n(n+1)}$, so that

$$2S = \sum_{n=-\infty}^{\infty}{}'\frac{1}{n(n+1)}, \tag{11.125}$$

where the prime on the sum indicates that the terms for $n=0$ and $n=-1$ are to be omitted. The derivation of Eq. (11.123) indicates that this equation will apply if we omit the (singular) $n=0$ and $n=-1$ terms from the sum and include the points $z=0$ and $z=-1$ as points where the residues of $f(z)\pi\cot\pi z$ are to be included.

Based on that insight, we find that in the present problem,

$$2S = -(\text{sum of residues of } \pi\cot\pi z/z(z+1) \text{ at } z=0 \text{ and } z=-1).$$

The singularities at $z=0$ and $z=-1$ are second-order poles, at which the residues are most easily computed by the method illustrated in item 5 of Example 11.7.1. In Exercise 11.7.2 it is shown that the residue at each pole has value -1. Completing the problem,

$$2S = -(-1-1) = 2, \quad \text{so } S=1.$$

In this instance the result is easily verified by making the partial fraction expansion

$$\frac{1}{n(n+1)} = \frac{1}{n} - \frac{1}{n+1}.$$

When inserted in the summation S, all terms cancel except the initial term of the $1/n$ summation, yielding $S=1$. ∎

Exercises

11.9.1   Show that if $f(z)$ is analytic at $z=z_0$ and $g(z)$ has a simple pole at $z=z_0$ with residue b_0, then $f(z)g(z)$ also has a simple pole at $z=z_0$, with residue $f(z_0)b_0$.

11.9.2   Show that $\cot z$ has magnitude of order 1 for large $|z|$ when not extremely close to one of its poles and does not affect the limiting behavior of I_N.

11.9.3 Evaluate $\frac{1}{1^3} - \frac{1}{3^3} + \frac{1}{5^3} - \cdots$.

11.9.4 Evaluate $\sum_{n=1}^{\infty} \frac{1}{n(n+2)}$.

11.9.5 Evaluate $\sum_{n=-\infty}^{\infty} \frac{(-1)^n}{(n+a)^2}$, where a is real and not an integer.

11.9.6 (a) Using a method based on contour integration, evaluate $\sum_{n=0}^{\infty} \frac{1}{(2n+1)^2}$.

(b) Check your work by relating your answer to an appropriate expression involving zeta functions.

11.9.7 Show that $\frac{1}{\cosh(\pi/2)} - \frac{1}{3\cosh(3\pi/2)} + \frac{1}{5\cosh(5\pi/2)} - \cdots = \frac{\pi}{8}$.

11.9.8 For $-\pi \leq \varphi \leq +\pi$, show that $\sum_{n=1}^{\infty}(-1)^n \frac{\sin n\varphi}{n^3} = \frac{\varphi}{12}(\varphi^2 - \pi^2)$.

11.10 MISCELLANEOUS TOPICS

Schwarz Reflection Principle

Our starting point for this topic is the observation that $g(z) = (z - x_0)^n$ for integral n and real x_0 satisfies

$$g^*(z) = [(z - x_0)^n]^* = (z^* - x_0)^n = g(z^*). \tag{11.126}$$

A generalization of the result in Eq. (11.126) is the Schwarz reflection principle:

> If a function $f(z)$ is (1) analytic over some region including a portion of the real axis and (2) real when z is real, then

$$f^*(z) = f(z^*). \tag{11.127}$$

Expanding $f(z)$ about some point x_0 within the region of analyticity on the real axis,

$$f(z) = \sum_{n=0}^{\infty} (z - x_0)^n \frac{f^{(n)}(x_0)}{n!}.$$

Since $f(z)$ is analytic at $z = x_0$, this Taylor expansion exists. Since $f(z)$ is real when z is real, $f^{(n)}(x_0)$ must be real for all n. Then, invoking Eq. (11.126), the Schwarz reflection principle, Eq. (11.127), follows immediately. This completes the proof within a circle of convergence. Analytic continuation then permits the extension of this result to the entire region of analyticity.

Note that the reflection principle can also be derived by the consideration of Laurent expansions. See Exercise 11.10.2.

Mapping

An analytic function $w(z) = u(x, y) + iv(x, y)$ can be regarded as a **mapping** in which points or curves in an xy plane can be associated with the corresponding points or curves in a uv plane. As a relatively simple example, consider the transformation $w = 1/z$. From an examination of its polar form, with $z = re^{i\theta}$, $w = \rho e^{i\varphi}$, we see that $\rho = 1/r$ and $\varphi = -\theta$, leading to the conclusion that the interior of the unit circle maps into its exterior (see Fig. 11.33). Circles in other locations in the z plane are transformed by $w = 1/z$ into other circles (or straight lines, which can be thought of as circles of infinite radius). This statement is the subject of Exercise 11.10.6. The transformation of two such circles are shown in the four panels of Fig. 11.34. Compare the way in which the interiors of the circles transform in Figs. 11.33 and 11.34. Note that the transformation does not preserve lengths, as can be seen in the figure from the labeling of various points and their locations when mapped.

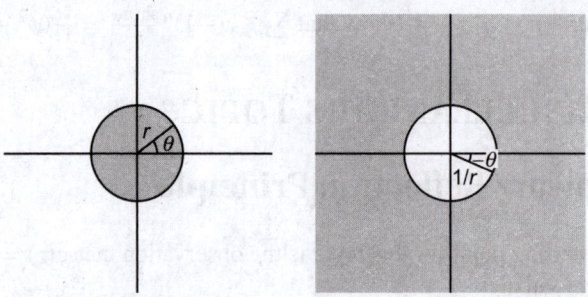

FIGURE 11.33   Mapping $w = 1/z$. The shaded areas transform into each other.

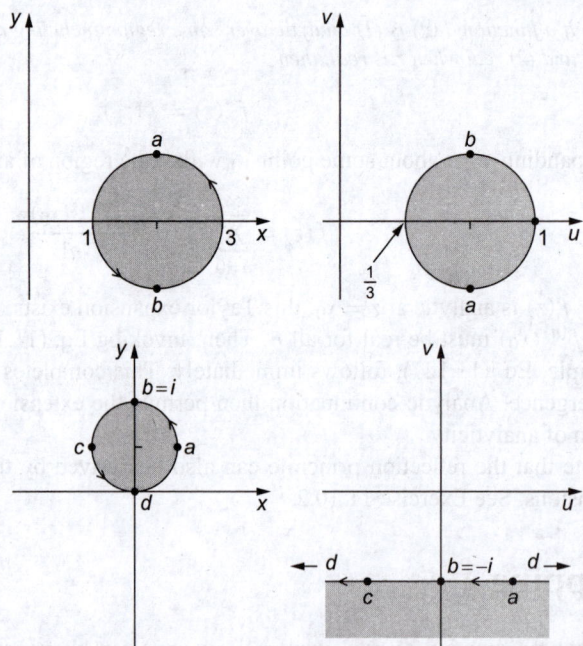

FIGURE 11.34   Left panels: circles in z plane. Right panels: their transformations in w plane under $w = 1/z$.

Historically, the notion of mapping was useful for identifying and carrying out transformations that would facilitate the solution of 2-D problems in electrostatics, fluid dynamics, and other areas of classical physics. An important aspect of such mappings is that they are **conformal**, meaning that (except at singularities of the transformation) the angles at which curves intersect remain unchanged when transformed. This feature preserves relations, e.g., between equipotentials and lines of force (stream lines). With the nearly universal use of high-speed computers, procedures based on conformal mapping are no longer central to the practical solution of most physics and engineering problems, and as a consequence will not be explored here in further detail. For problems where these techniques are still relevant, we refer the reader to earlier editions of this book and to sources identified under Additional Readings. In that connection, we call particular attention to the book by Spiegel, which contains (in chapter 8) descriptions of a large number of mappings and (in chapter 9) many applications to problems of fluid flow, electrostatics, and heat conduction.

Exercises

11.10.1 A function $f(z) = u(x, y) + iv(x, y)$ satisfies the conditions for the Schwarz reflection principle. Show that

(a) u is an even function of y.   (b) v is an odd function of y.

11.10.2 A function $f(z)$ can be expanded in a Laurent series about the origin with the coefficients a_n real. Show that the complex conjugate of this function of z is the same function of the complex conjugate of z; that is,

$$f^*(z) = f(z^*).$$

Verify this explicitly for

(a) $f(z) = z^n$, n an integer.   (b) $f(z) = \sin z$.

If $f(z) = iz(a_1 = i)$, show that the foregoing statement does not hold.

11.10.3 The function $f(z)$ is analytic in a domain that includes the real axis. When z is real $(z = x)$, $f(x)$ is pure imaginary.

(a)   Show that

$$f(z^*) = -[f(z)]^*.$$

(b)   For the specific case $f(z) = iz$, develop the Cartesian forms of $f(z)$, $f(z^*)$, and $f^*(z)$. Do not quote the general result of part (a).

11.10.4 How do circles centered on the origin in the z-plane transform for

(a) $w_1(z) = z + \dfrac{1}{z}$,   (b) $w_2(z) = z - \dfrac{1}{z}$,   for $z \neq 0$?

What happens when $|z| \to 1$?

11.10.5 What part of the z-plane corresponds to the interior of the unit circle in the w-plane if

(a) $w = \dfrac{z-1}{z+1}$?   (b) $w = \dfrac{z-i}{z+i}$?

11.10.6 (a) Writing $z = x + iy$, $w = u + iv$, show that if $w = 1/z$, the circle in the xy plane defined by $(x-a)^2 + (y-b)^2 = r^2$ transforms into $(u-A)^2 + (v-B)^2 = R^2$.

(b) Does the center of the circle in the z plane transform into the center of the corresponding circle in the w plane?

11.10.7 Assume that a curve in the xy plane passes through point z_0 in the direction $dz = e^{i\theta}ds$, where s indicates arc length on the curve. Then, if $w = f(z)$, with $f(z)$ analytic at $z = z_0$, we have $dw = (dw/dz)dz = f'(z)e^{i\theta}ds$, where dw is in the direction the mapping of the xy curve passes through $w_0 = f(z_0)$ in the w plane. Use this observation to prove that if $f'(z_0) \neq 0$, the angle at which two curves intersect in the z plane is the same (both in magnitude and direction) as the angle of intersection of their mappings in the w plane.

Additional Readings

Ahlfors, L. V., *Complex Analysis*, 3rd ed. New York: McGraw-Hill (1979). This text is detailed, thorough, rigorous, and extensive.

Churchill, R. V., J. W. Brown, and R. F. Verkey, *Complex Variables and Applications*, 5th ed. New York: McGraw-Hill (1989). This is an excellent text for both the beginning and advanced student. It is readable and quite complete. A detailed proof of the Cauchy-Goursat theorem is given in Chapter 5.

Greenleaf, F. P., *Introduction to Complex Variables*. Philadelphia: Saunders (1972). This very readable book has detailed, careful explanations.

Kurala, A., *Applied Functions of a Complex Variable*. New York: Wiley (Interscience) (1972). An intermediate-level text designed for scientists and engineers. Includes many physical applications.

Levinson, N., and R. M. Redheffer, *Complex Variables*. San Francisco: Holden-Day (1970). This text is written for scientists and engineers who are interested in applications.

Morse, P. M., and H. Feshbach, *Methods of Theoretical Physics*. New York: McGraw-Hill (1953). Chapter 4 is a presentation of portions of the theory of functions of a complex variable of interest to theoretical physicists.

Remmert, R., *Theory of Complex Functions*. New York: Springer (1991).

Sokolnikoff, I. S., and R. M. Redheffer, *Mathematics of Physics and Modern Engineering*, 2nd ed. New York: McGraw-Hill (1966). Chapter 7 covers complex variables.

Spiegel, M. R., *Complex Variables*, in *Schaum's Outline Series*. New York: McGraw-Hill (original 1964, reprinted 1995). An excellent summary of the theory of complex variables for scientists.

Titchmarsh, E. C., *The Theory of Functions*, 2nd ed. New York: Oxford University Press (1958). A classic.

Watson, G. N., *Complex Integration and Cauchy's Theorem*. New York: Hafner (original 1917, reprinted 1960). A short work containing a rigorous development of the Cauchy integral theorem and integral formula. Applications to the calculus of residues are included. *Cambridge Tracts in Mathematics, and Mathematical Physics*, No. 15.

CHAPTER 12

FURTHER TOPICS IN ANALYSIS

The broader perspective and additional tools made available through complex variable theory enable us to consider fruitfully a number of topics in analysis that have wide application in areas of relevance to physics. In this chapter we survey several such topics.

12.1 ORTHOGONAL POLYNOMIALS

Many physical problems lead to second-order differential equations corresponding to Sturm-Liouville problems, and often the solutions of interest in physics are polynomials, defined on a range and with weighting factors that make them eigenfunctions of Hermitian problems. A number of interesting features of such problems can be approached with the aid of complex variable theory.

Rodrigues Formulas

Odile Rodrigues showed that a large class of second-order Sturm-Liouville ordinary differential equations (ODEs) had polynomial solutions which could be put in a compact and useful form now generally called a Rodrigues formula. While such formulas could be presented case by case with an aura of coincidence or mystery, the approach we take here is to develop them from a general viewpoint, after which we can proceed to more detailed discussion of well-known special cases.

Consider a second-order Sturm-Liouville ODE of the general form

$$p(x)y'' + q(x)y' + \lambda y = 0, \tag{12.1}$$

with $p(x)$ and $q(x)$ restricted to the polynomial forms

$$p(x) = \alpha x^2 + \beta x + \gamma, \quad q(x) = \mu x + \nu. \tag{12.2}$$

The forms of p and q are sufficiently general to include most of the ODEs with classical sets of polynomials as solutions (the Legendre, Hermite, and Laguerre ODEs, among others). When Eq. (12.1) has as a solution a polynomial of degree n, we can write

$$y_n(x) = \sum_{j=0}^{n} g_j x^j, \tag{12.3}$$

with coefficient g_n nonzero. Setting to zero the coefficient of x^n when y_n is inserted into the ODE, we have

$$n(n-1)\alpha g_n + n\mu g_n + \lambda g_n = 0, \tag{12.4}$$

showing that the eigenvalue λ_n which corresponds to y_n must have the value

$$\lambda_n = -n(n-1)\alpha - n\mu. \tag{12.5}$$

In Chapter 7 we identified an ODE of the form of Eq. (12.1) as self-adjoint if $p'(x) = q(x)$, and also showed that if an ODE was not already self-adjoint as written, it could be converted to self-adjoint form by multiplying all its terms by a weight factor $w(x)$, which must be such that

$$(wp)' = wq, \quad \text{or} \quad w' = w\frac{q - p'}{p}. \tag{12.6}$$

As shown previously, this equation is separable and has solution

$$w(x) = p^{-1} \exp\left(\int^{x} \frac{q(x)}{p(x)} dx \right). \tag{12.7}$$

The introduction of w enables the ODE to assume the form

$$\frac{d}{dx}\left[w(x)p(x)y' \right] + \lambda w(x)y = 0, \tag{12.8}$$

which was useful for discussing orthogonality properties of its solutions.

Our current interest in $w(x)$, however, is in the observation by Rodrigues that its particular form permits the solutions $y_n(x)$ to be written in the compact and interesting form that is now called its **Rodrigues formula**:

$$y_n(x) = \frac{1}{w(x)} \left(\frac{d}{dx} \right)^n \left[wp(x)^n \right]. \tag{12.9}$$

The proof of Eq. (12.9) is both simple and ingenious. Using the defining condition for $w(x)$, Eq. (12.6), we first obtain

$$p\left[wp^n \right]' = wp^n\left[(n-1)p' + q \right]. \tag{12.10}$$

We then differentiate this equation $n + 1$ times and divide by w. Because p is only quadratic in x and q is linear, application of Leibniz's formula to the multiple differentiations leads to only three terms on the left-hand side and two on the right:

$$\frac{p}{w}\left(\frac{d}{dx}\right)^{n+2}[wp^n] + \frac{(n+1)p'}{w}\left(\frac{d}{dx}\right)^{n+1}[wp^n] + \frac{n(n+1)p''}{2w}\left(\frac{d}{dx}\right)^n[wp^n]$$

$$= \frac{(n-1)p'+q}{w}\left(\frac{d}{dx}\right)^{n+1}[wp^n] + \frac{(n+1)[(n-1)p''+q']}{w}\left(\frac{d}{dx}\right)^n[wp^n].$$

$$(12.11)$$

Our objective is to manipulate Eq. (12.11) into a form showing that y_n as given in Eq. (12.9) is a solution to the ODE of Eq. (12.1). We start by identifying the terms with y_n where that is possible, and then, combining or canceling similar terms, we reach

$$\frac{p}{w}\left(\frac{d}{dx}\right)^{n+2}[wp^n] + \frac{2p'-q}{w}\left(\frac{d}{dx}\right)^{n+1}[wp^n] - \left[\frac{n^2-n-2}{2}p'' + (n+1)q'\right]y_n = 0.$$

$$(12.12)$$

To complete our analysis we now need to move the factors $1/w$ so that only n differentiations appear to their right, enabling identification of the remaining terms of the equation with y_n or its derivatives. We note the identity

$$\frac{p}{w}\left(\frac{d}{dx}\right)^{n+2}[wp^n] = p\left[\frac{1}{w}\left(\frac{d}{dx}\right)^n[wp^n]\right]'' - 2p\left(\frac{dw^{-1}}{dx}\right)\left(\frac{d}{dx}\right)^{n+1}[wp^n]$$

$$- p\left(\frac{d^2w^{-1}}{dx^2}\right)\left(\frac{d}{dx}\right)^n[wp^n],$$

which reduces, using Eq. (12.6), to

$$\frac{p}{w}\left(\frac{d}{dx}\right)^{n+2}[wp^n] = py_n'' + \frac{2(q-p')}{w}\left(\frac{d}{dx}\right)^{n+1}[wp^n] - \left[p'' - q' - \frac{q-p'}{p}\right]y_n.$$

$$(12.13)$$

Substituting Eq. (12.13) into Eq. (12.12), some further simplification results:

$$py_n'' + \frac{q}{w}\left(\frac{d}{dx}\right)^{n+1}[wp^n] - \left[\frac{n^2-n}{2}p'' + nq' - \frac{q(q-p')}{p}\right]y_n = 0. \qquad (12.14)$$

Our final step is to use the identity

$$\frac{q}{w}\left(\frac{d}{dx}\right)^{n+1}[wp^n] = qy_n' - \frac{q(q-p')}{p}y_n, \qquad (12.15)$$

which brings us to

$$py_n'' + qy_n' - \left[\frac{n^2-n}{2}p'' + nq'\right]y_n = 0. \qquad (12.16)$$

Noting that $p'' = 2\alpha$ and $q' = \mu$, we confirm that y_n is a solution of Eq. (12.1) with the eigenvalue given in Eq. (12.5).

Finally, we need to show that Rodrigues' formula, Eq. (12.9), results in an expression that is a polynomial of degree n. We note that a typical term of that formula will involve a j-fold differentiation of w and an $(n - j)$-fold differentiation of p^n. After the differentiation of p^n, we are left with p^j times a polynomial. The differentiation of w will, applying Eq. (12.6), leave (w/p^j) times a polynomial, and the numerator and denominator factors p^j cancel. In addition, the w from the differentiation cancels against the initial factor w^{-1}, leaving each term of y_n in polynomial form. When all terms of y_n are combined, the resulting polynomial must have the degree consistent with Eq. (12.5), namely n.

Example 12.1.1   RODRIGUES FORMULA FOR HERMITE ODE

The Hermite ODE is

$$y'' - 2xy' + \lambda y = 0, \quad \text{or} \quad py'' + qy' + \lambda y = 0$$

with $p = 1, q = -2x$. We easily find

$$w = \exp\left(\int^x (-2x)dx\right) = e^{-x^2}.$$

The Rodrigues formula is therefore (with a factor $(-1)^n$ to obtain the Hermite polynomials with their conventional signs)

$$y_n(x) = \frac{(-1)^n}{w}\left(\frac{d}{dx}\right)^n [wp^n] = (-1)^n e^{x^2}\left(\frac{d}{dx}\right)^n e^{-x^2}. \tag{12.17}$$

∎

Schlaefli Integral

One of the nice features of the Rodrigues formulas is that the multiple differentiations can be converted to a convenient form by use of Cauchy's integral formula. Using Eq. (11.33), we have

$$y_n(x) = \frac{1}{w(x)}\frac{n!}{2\pi i}\oint_C \frac{w(z)[p(z)]^n}{(z - x)^{n+1}}dz, \tag{12.18}$$

where the contour C encloses the point x, and must be such that $w(z)[p(z)]^n$ is analytic everywhere on and within C. This formula is known as the **Schlaefli integral** for $y_n(x)$.

It is possible to introduce the Schlaefli integral as the definition of a set of functions y_n and, from that definition, prove that y_n is a solution to the corresponding ODE. Because we created the Schaefli integral to represent a function already known to be a solution, verification that it solves the ODE becomes redundant.

Generating Functions

Many sets of functions arising in mathematical physics can be defined in terms of generating functions. Such functions include, but are not limited to the orthogonal polynomials y_n that have been the subject of our discussion of Rodrigues formulas. For now, we make no assumptions as to the source of the functions involved.

If $f_n(x)$ is a set of functions, defined for integer values of the index n, it may be the case that the $f_n(x)$ can be described as the coefficients of the powers of an auxiliary variable, t, in the expansion of a function $g(x, t)$, which is called a **generating function**:

$$g(x, t) = \sum_n c_n f_n(x) t^n. \tag{12.19}$$

The range of n may be semi-infinite, with $n \geq 0$, thereby describing a Taylor series, or it may extend from $-\infty$ to $+\infty$, thus describing a Laurent series. The additional coefficient, c_n, permits adjustment of the function set to an agreed-upon scaling. Different choices of c_n will also lead to different generating functions $g(x, t)$ for the same set of f_n.

Applying the residue theorem, we can see that the generating function expansion is closely related to contour integral representations of the functions f_n:

$$c_n f_n(x) = \frac{1}{2\pi i} \oint \frac{g(x, t)}{t^{n+1}} dt, \tag{12.20}$$

where the contour encircles $t = 0$ but no other singularities of the integrand (with respect to t).

A generating function may be regarded as providing the definition of a function set $f_n(x)$, or alternatively it may have been obtained as the encapsulation of the f_n which were already defined in some other way (e.g., as polynomial solutions of a Sturm-Liouville ODE). We shall later take up the issue of obtaining generating functions for previously specified f_n, focusing for now only on ways in which they can be used.

It is obvious that by explicitly evaluating the implied expansion one can extract the members of a function set from its generating function. However, a more important feature of generating functions is that they can be very useful in deriving relationships between members of the set f_n. For example,

$$\frac{\partial g(x, t)}{\partial t} = \sum_n n c_n f_n(x) t^{n-1} = \sum_n (n + 1) c_{n+1} f_{n+1}(x) t^n,$$

and if we can relate g and $\partial g / \partial t$ we have a corresponding relation between f_n and f_{n+1}. Relations between the $f_n(x)$ and their derivatives $f_n'(x)$ can be deduced by differentiating $g(x, t)$ with respect to x.

Example 12.1.2   HERMITE POLYNOMIALS

A generating function formula for the Hermite polynomials $H_n(x)$ (at their conventional scaling) is

$$e^{-t^2 + 2tx} = \sum_{n=0}^{\infty} H_n(x) \frac{t^n}{n!}. \tag{12.21}$$

To develop a recurrence formula connecting H_n of contiguous index values, we compute

$$\frac{\partial}{\partial t} e^{-t^2 + 2tx} = (2x - 2t)e^{-t^2 + 2tx} = \sum_{n=0}^{\infty} n H_n(x) \frac{t^{n-1}}{n!}. \tag{12.22}$$

Expanding the exponential in the central member of Eq. (12.22) (and suppressing temporarily the argument of H_n),

$$\sum_{n=0}^{\infty} 2x H_n \frac{t^n}{n!} - \sum_{n=0}^{\infty} 2H_n \frac{t^{n+1}}{n!} = \sum_{n=0}^{\infty} n H_n \frac{t^{n-1}}{n!}.$$

Extracting the coefficient of t^n from each of these summations, we reach (for each n)

$$\frac{2x H_n}{n!} - \frac{2H_{n-1}}{(n-1)!} = \frac{(n+1)H_{n+1}}{(n+1)!},$$

which reduces to

$$2x H_n(x) - 2n H_{n-1}(x) = H_{n+1}(x). \tag{12.23}$$

Equation (12.23) is called a **recurrence formula**; it permits the construction of the entire series of H_n from starting values (typically H_0 and H_1, which are easily computed directly).

A derivative formula can be obtained by differentiating Eq. (12.21) with respect to x. We have

$$\frac{\partial}{\partial x} e^{-t^2 + 2tx} = 2t e^{-t^2 + 2tx} = \sum_{n=0}^{\infty} H_n'(x) \frac{t^n}{n!}.$$

Substituting Eq. (12.21) into the central member of this equation, we get

$$\sum_{n=0}^{\infty} 2H_n(x) \frac{t^{n+1}}{n!} = \sum_{n=0}^{\infty} H_n'(x) \frac{t^n}{n!},$$

which leads directly to

$$2n H_{n-1}(x) = H_n'(x). \tag{12.24}$$

∎

In later chapters we illustrate the application of these ideas to a variety of special functions; in the next section of this chapter we apply them to a generating function that leads to quantities known as **Bernoulli numbers**.

Finding Generating Functions

To take generating functions out of the realm of magic, we next consider how they might be obtained. For a more or less arbitrary function set, this question has been a topic of current interest in mathematical research, with methods of several sorts devised during the past century by Rainville, Weisner, Truesdell, and others. See the works by McBride and Talman in Additional Readings.

For sets of polynomials arising in Sturm-Liouville problems and described by Rodrigues formulas, we can be more explicit. Using the Schlaefli integral, Eq. (12.18), we can form

$$g(x,t) = \frac{1}{w(x)} \sum_{n=0}^{\infty} c_n t^n \frac{n!}{2\pi i} \oint_C \frac{w(z)[p(z)]^n}{(z-x)^{n+1}} dz. \tag{12.25}$$

Recall that C encloses x and that wp^n must be analytic throughout the region within the contour.

In principle Eq. (12.25) can be evaluated to obtain $g(x,t)$, for example by choosing C to be such that the summation can be brought inside the z integral and (after specifying c_n) evaluating first the sum and then the contour integral. In practice the difficulty of doing this may depend on the problem, including the choice of c_n. We provide one example of the process.

Example 12.1.3   LEGENDRE POLYNOMIALS

We use the formal process described above to obtain a generating function for the Legendre polynomials. The Legendre ODE is of the form discussed in Eq. (12.1),

$$(1 - x^2)y'' - 2xy' + \lambda y = 0,$$

implying that

$$p(x) = 1 - x^2, \quad q(x) = -2x,$$

and the equation is, as written, self-adjoint, so $w(x) = 1$. From the generating-function formula based on the Schlaefli integral, Eq. (12.25), we choose $c_n = (-1)^n / 2^n n!$, thereby reaching

$$g(x,t) = \sum_{n=0}^{\infty} \left(\frac{(-1)^n t^n}{2^n n!} \right) \frac{n!}{2\pi i} \oint_C \frac{(1-z^2)^n}{(z-x)^{n+1}} dz.$$

Interchanging the summation and integration (which we will justify later), the factors dependent on n form a geometric series, which we can sum:

$$\sum_{n=0}^{\infty} \left(\frac{(z^2-1)t}{2(z-x)} \right)^n \frac{1}{z-x} = \frac{1}{z - x - \frac{1}{2}(z^2-1)t}$$

$$= -\frac{2}{t} \left[z^2 - \frac{2z}{t} + \frac{2x-t}{t} \right]^{-1}.$$

Inserting this result into the formula for $g(x,t)$, we now have

$$g(x,t) = -\frac{2}{t} \frac{1}{2\pi i} \oint_C \left[z^2 - \frac{2z}{t} + \frac{2x-t}{t} \right]^{-1} dz$$

$$= -\frac{2}{t} \frac{1}{2\pi i} \oint_C \frac{dz}{(z-z_1)(z-z_2)}, \tag{12.26}$$

where z_1 and z_2 are the roots of the quadratic form in the first line of the equation:

$$z_1 = \frac{1}{t} - \frac{\sqrt{1 - 2xt + t^2}}{t}, \quad z_2 = \frac{1}{t} + \frac{\sqrt{1 - 2xt + t^2}}{t}.$$

In order for Eq. (12.26) to be valid, it must have been legitimate to interchange the summation and integration, which is the case only if the summation is uniformly convergent (with respect to z) for all points at which it is used (i.e., everywhere on the contour C). It is convenient to analyze the convergence for small t and x and for a contour with $|z| = 1$. Once a final formula has been obtained, its range of validity can be extended by appeal to analytic continuation.

On the assumed contour and for small x, there will be a range of $|t| \ll 1$ for which

$$\left| \frac{(z^2 - 1)t}{2(z - x)} \right| < 1,$$

guaranteeing convergence of the geometric series. We now return to the evaluation of the contour integral in Eq. (12.26). It has two poles, at $z = z_1$ and $z = z_2$. For small x and $|t|$, z_2 will be approximately $2/t$ and will be exterior to the contour, while z_1 will be close to the origin of z. Thus, only the residue of the integrand at $z = z_1$ will contribute to the contour integral, which will have the value

$$g(x, t) = -\frac{2}{t} \frac{1}{z_1 - z_2}.$$

Since

$$z_1 - z_2 = -\frac{2}{t}\sqrt{1 - 2xt + t^2},$$

we obtain the Legendre polynomial generating function as

$$g(x, t) = \frac{1}{\sqrt{1 - 2xt + t^2}}. \tag{12.27}$$

■

Summary—Orthogonal Polynomials

For five classical sets of orthogonal polynomials, we summarize in Table 12.1 their ODEs, Rodrigues formulas, and generating functions. Omitted from the list are important subsidiary polynomial sets (e.g., those connected with the associated Legendre and associated Laguerre ODEs).

Exercises

12.1.1   Starting from the Rodrigues formula in Table 12.1 for the Hermite polynomials H_n, derive the generating function for the H_n given in that table.

Table 12.1 Orthogonal Polynomials: ODEs, Rodrigues Formulas, and Generating Functions

Rodrigues Formula	Generating Function

Legendre: $(1-x^2)y'' - 2xy' + n(n+1)y = 0$

$$P_n(x) = \frac{1}{2^n n!}\left(\frac{d}{dx}\right)^n (x^2-1)^n \qquad\qquad (1-2xt+t^2)^{-1/2} = \sum_{n=0}^{\infty} P_n(x)t^n$$

Hermite: $y'' - 2xy' + 2ny = 0$

$$H_n(x) = (-1)^n e^{x^2}\left(\frac{d}{dx}\right)^n e^{-x^2} \qquad\qquad e^{-t^2+2xt} = \sum_{n=0}^{\infty} \frac{1}{n!}H_n(x)t^n$$

Laguerre: $xy'' + (1-x)y' + ny = 0$

$$L_n(x) = \frac{e^x}{n!}\left(\frac{d}{dx}\right)^n (x^n e^{-x}) \qquad\qquad \frac{e^{-xt/(1-t)}}{1-t} = \sum_{n=0}^{\infty} L_n(x)t^n$$

Chebyshev I: $(1-x^2)y'' - xy' + n^2 y = 0$

$$T_n(x) = \frac{(-1)^n(1-x^2)^{1/2}}{(2n-1)!!}\left(\frac{d}{dx}\right)^n (1-x^2)^{n-1/2} \qquad\qquad \frac{1-t^2}{1-2xt+t^2} = T_0(x) + 2\sum_{n=1}^{\infty} T_n(x)t^n$$

Chebyshev II: $(1-x^2)y'' - 3xy' + n(n+2)y = 0$

$$U_n(x) = \frac{(-1)^n(n+1)}{(2n+1)!!(1-x^2)^{1/2}}\left(\frac{d}{dx}\right)^n (1-x^2)^{n+1/2} \qquad\qquad \frac{1}{1-2xt+t^2} = \sum_{n=0}^{\infty} U_n(x)t^n$$

12.1.2 (a) Starting from the Laguerre ODE,

$$xy'' + (1-x)y' + \lambda y = 0,$$

obtain the Rodrigues formula for its polynomial solutions $L_n(x)$.

(b) From the Rodrigues formula, scaled as in Table 12.1, derive the generating function for the $L_n(x)$ given in that table.

12.1.3 Carry out in detail the steps needed to confirm that the $(n+1)$-fold differentiation of Eq. (12.10) leads to Eq. (12.12).

12.1.4 Confirm the algebraic steps that convert Eq. (12.12) into Eq. (12.16).

12.1.5 Given the following integral representations, in which the contours encircle the origin but no other singular points, derive the corresponding generating functions:

(a) Bessel functions:

$$J_n(x) = \frac{1}{2\pi i}\oint e^{(x/2)(t-1/t)}t^{-n-1}\,dt.$$

(b) Modified Bessel functions:

$$I_n(x) = \frac{1}{2\pi i}\oint e^{(x/2)(t+1/t)}t^{-n-1}\,dt.$$

12.1.6   Expand the generating function for the Legendre polynomials, $(1 - 2tz + t^2)^{-1/2}$, in powers of t. Assume that t is small. Collect the coefficients of t^0, t^1, and t^2.

$$ANS. \quad a_0 = P_0(z) = 1,$$
$$a_1 = P_1(z) = z,$$
$$a_2 = P_2(z) = \tfrac{1}{2}(3z^2 - 1).$$

12.1.7   The set of Chebyshev polynomials usually denoted $U_n(x)$ has the generating-function formula

$$\frac{1}{1 - 2xt + t^2} = \sum_{n=0}^{\infty} U_n(x)t^n.$$

Derive a recurrence formula (for integer $n \geq 0$) connecting three U_n of consecutive n.

12.2   BERNOULLI NUMBERS

A generating-function approach is a convenient way to introduce the set of numbers first used in mathematics by Jacques (James, Jacob) Bernoulli. These quantities have been defined in a number of different ways, so extreme care must be taken in combining formulas from works by different authors. Our definition corresponds to that used in the reference work *Handbook of Mathematical Functions* (AMS-55). See Additional Readings.

Since the Bernoulli numbers, denoted B_n, do not depend on a variable, their generating function depends only on a single (complex) variable, and the generating-function formula has the specific form

$$\frac{t}{e^t - 1} = \sum_{n=0}^{\infty} \frac{B_n t^n}{n!}. \tag{12.28}$$

The inclusion of the factor $1/n!$ in the definition is just one of the ways some definitions of Bernoulli numbers differ. We defer for the moment the important question as to the circle of convergence of the expansion in Eq. (12.28).

Since Eq. (12.28) is a Taylor series, we may identify the B_n as successive derivatives of the generating function:

$$B_n = \left[\frac{d^n}{dt^n} \left(\frac{t}{e^t - 1} \right) \right]_{t=0}. \tag{12.29}$$

To obtain B_0, we must take the limit of $t/(e^t - 1)$ as $t \to 0$, easily finding $B_0 = 1$. Applying Eq. (12.29), we also have

$$B_1 = \frac{d}{dt} \left(\frac{t}{e^t - 1} \right) \bigg|_{t=0} = \lim_{t \to 0} \left(\frac{1}{e^t - 1} - \frac{te^t}{(e^t - 1)^2} \right) = -\frac{1}{2}. \tag{12.30}$$

In principle we could continue to obtain further B_n, but it is more convenient to proceed in a more sophisticated fashion. Our starting point is to examine

$$\sum_{n=2}^{\infty} \frac{B_n t^n}{n!} = \frac{t}{e^t - 1} - B_0 - B_1 t = \frac{t}{e^t - 1} - 1 + \frac{t}{2}$$

$$= \frac{-t}{e^{-t} - 1} - 1 - \frac{t}{2}, \qquad (12.31)$$

where we have used the fact that

$$\frac{t}{e^t - 1} = \frac{-t}{e^{-t} - 1} - t. \qquad (12.32)$$

Equation (12.31) shows that the summation on its left-hand side is an even function of t, leading to the conclusion that all B_n of odd n (other than B_1) must vanish.

We next use the generating function to obtain a recursion relation for the Bernoulli numbers. We form

$$\frac{e^t - 1}{t} \frac{t}{e^t - 1} = 1 = \left[\sum_{m=0}^{\infty} \frac{t^m}{(m+1)!} \right] \left[1 - \frac{t}{2} + \sum_{n=1}^{\infty} B_{2n} \frac{t^{2n}}{(2n)!} \right]$$

$$= 1 + \sum_{m=1}^{\infty} t^m \left[\frac{1}{(m+1)!} - \frac{1}{2m!} \right]$$

$$+ \sum_{N=2}^{\infty} t^N \sum_{n=1}^{\leq N/2} \frac{B_{2n}}{(2n)!(N-2n+1)!}$$

$$= 1 + \sum_{N=2}^{\infty} \frac{t^N}{(N+1)!} \left[-\frac{N-1}{2} + \sum_{n=1}^{\leq N/2} \binom{N+1}{2n} B_{2n} \right]. \qquad (12.33)$$

Since the coefficient of each power of t in the final summation of Eq. (12.33) must vanish, we may set to zero for each N the expression in its square brackets. Changing N, if even, to $2N$ and if odd, to $2N - 1$, Eq. (12.33) leads to the pair of equations

$$N - \frac{1}{2} = \sum_{n=1}^{N} \binom{2N+1}{2n} B_{2n},$$

$$\qquad (12.34)$$

$$N - 1 = \sum_{n=1}^{N-1} \binom{2N}{2n} B_{2n}.$$

Either of these equations can be used to obtain the B_{2n} sequentially, starting from B_2. The first few B_n are listed in Table 12.2.

To obtain additional relations involving the Bernoulli numbers, we next consider the following representation of $\cot t$:

$$\cot t = \frac{\cos t}{\sin t} = i \left(\frac{e^{it} + e^{-it}}{e^{it} - e^{-it}} \right) = i \left(\frac{e^{2it} + 1}{e^{2it} - 1} \right) = i \left(1 + \frac{2}{e^{2it} - 1} \right).$$

Table 12.2   Bernoulli Numbers

n	B_n	B_n
0	1	1.000000000
1	$-\dfrac{1}{2}$	-0.500000000
2	$\dfrac{1}{6}$	0.166666667
4	$-\dfrac{1}{30}$	-0.033333333
6	$\dfrac{1}{42}$	0.023809524
8	$-\dfrac{1}{30}$	-0.033333333
10	$\dfrac{5}{66}$	0.075757576

Note. Further values are given in AMS-55;
see Abramowitz in Additional Readings.

Multiplying by t and rearranging slightly,

$$t \cot t = \frac{2it}{2} + \frac{2it}{e^{2it} - 1} = \sum_{n=0}^{\infty} B_{2n} \frac{(2it)^{2n}}{(2n)!}$$

$$= \sum_{n=0}^{\infty} (-1)^n B_{2n} \frac{(2t)^{2n}}{(2n)!}, \tag{12.35}$$

where the term $2it/2$ has canceled the B_1 term that would otherwise appear in the expansion.

Now that we have our Bernoulli-number expansion identified with $t \cot t$, we can see that it represents a function with singularities (poles) at $t = m\pi$, where $m = \pm 1, \pm 2, \ldots$. There is no singularity at $t = 0$ (due to the presence of the factor t), so the singularity nearest the expansion point (the origin) is at $|t| = \pi$. Since the argument in the expansion is $2t$, we conclude that the generating series for the Bernoulli numbers, Eq. (12.28), will have the radius of convergence $|2t| = 2\pi$. This observation is, of course, consistent with the fact that the zeros of $e^t - 1$ are for t at integer multiples of $2\pi i$.

To obtain another representation of the Bernoulli numbers, we write B_n using the contour-integration formula, Eq. (12.20). Noting that for use in this equation $c_n f_n(x) = B_n/n!$, we have

$$B_n = \frac{n!}{2\pi i} \oint \frac{t}{e^t - 1} \frac{dt}{t^{n+1}}, \tag{12.36}$$

where the integral is a circle within the radius of convergence of the generating series. We can, at least in principle, evaluate the integral using the residue theorem. For $n = 0$ we have a simple pole with a residue of $+1$, and

$$B_0 = \frac{0!}{2\pi i} \cdot 2\pi i (+1) = 1.$$

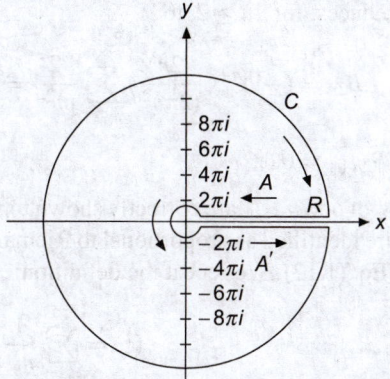

FIGURE 12.1   Contour of integration for Bernoulli numbers.

For $n = 1$ the singularity at $t = 0$ becomes a second-order pole, and the limiting process prescribed by Eq. (11.68) yields the residue $-\frac{1}{2}$, so

$$B_1 = \frac{1!}{2\pi i} \cdot 2\pi i \left(-\frac{1}{2} \right) = -\frac{1}{2},$$

consistent with our previous result. For $n \geq 2$ the poles at $t = 0$ are of increasing order and this procedure becomes rather tedious, so we resort to a different approach. We deform the contour of our integral representation as shown in Fig. 12.1, which differs from the original circular contour in that it surrounds all the poles of the integrand at $t = \pm 2\pi m i$, $m = 1, 2, \ldots$, while avoiding the inclusion of the pole at $t = 0$. In contrast to the high-order pole at $t = 0$, the other poles are all first-order, with residues that are easily evaluated.

To use the new contour, we need to identify the contributions from its constituent parts. The direction of travel around the contour causes the small circle about $t = 0$ to contribute $+2\pi i$ times the residue of the integrand at $t = 0$, i.e., the result that when multiplied by $n!/2\pi i$ is equal to B_n. The remainder of the contour makes no contribution to the integral: (1) Because the integrand is analytic along the real axis and there is no branch cut there, the segments A and A', which are in opposite directions of travel, cancel; and (2) the large circle contributes negligibly (for $n \geq 2$) because at large $|t|$ the integrand behaves asymptotically as $1/|t|^n$. Noting that the poles at nonzero t are encircled in a clockwise sense, we have the following relatively simple result (for $n \geq 2$):

$$B_n = -\frac{n!}{2\pi i} \sum 2\pi i \left(\text{residues of } \frac{t^{-n}}{e^t - 1} \text{ at poles } t \neq 0 \right). \qquad (12.37)$$

Since the residue at $t = 2\pi m i$ is simply $(2\pi m i)^{-n}$, Eq. (12.37) becomes

$$B_n = -\frac{n!}{(2\pi i)^n} \sum_{m=1}^{\infty} \left[\frac{1}{m^n} + \frac{1}{(-m)^n} \right],$$

which further reduces, for $2n \geq 2$, to

$$B_{2n} = (-1)^{n+1} \frac{(2n)!}{(2\pi)^{2n}} \sum_{m=1}^{\infty} \frac{2}{m^{2n}} = (-1)^{n+1} \frac{2(2n)!}{(2\pi)^{2n}} \zeta(2n),$$
(12.38)

$$B_{2n+1} = 0.$$

Note that the B_n of odd $n > 1$ are correctly shown to vanish, and that the Bernoulli numbers of even $n > 0$ are identified as proportional to Riemann zeta functions, which first appeared in this book at Eq. (1.12). We repeat the definition:

$$\zeta(z) = \sum_{m=1}^{\infty} \frac{1}{m^z}.$$

Equation (12.38) is an important result because we already have a straightforward way to obtain values of the B_n, via Eq. (12.34), and Eq. (12.38) can be inverted to give a closed expression for $\zeta(2n)$, which otherwise was known only as a summation. This representation of the Bernoulli numbers was discovered by Euler.

It is readily seen from Eq. (12.38) that $|B_{2n}|$ increases without limit as $n \to \infty$. Numerical values have been calculated by Glaisher.[1] Illustrating the divergent behavior of the Bernoulli numbers, we have

$$B_{20} = -5.291 \times 10^2$$

$$B_{200} = -3.647 \times 10^{215}.$$

Some authors prefer to define the Bernoulli numbers with a modified version of Eq. (12.38) by using

$$\mathcal{B}_n = \frac{2(2n)!}{(2\pi)^{2n}} \zeta(2n),$$
(12.39)

the subscript being just half of our subscript and all signs positive. Again, when using other texts or references, you must check to see exactly how the Bernoulli numbers are defined.

The Bernoulli numbers occur frequently in number theory. The von Staudt-Clausen theorem states that

$$B_{2n} = A_n - \frac{1}{p_1} - \frac{1}{p_2} - \frac{1}{p_3} - \cdots - \frac{1}{p_k},$$
(12.40)

in which A_n is an integer and $p_1, p_2, \ldots, p_k$ are all the prime numbers such that $p_i - 1$ is a divisor of $2n$. It may readily be verified that this holds for

$$B_6 \quad (A_3 = 1, \quad p = 2, 3, 7),$$

$$B_8 \quad (A_4 = 1, \quad p = 2, 3, 5),$$

$$B_{10} \quad (A_5 = 1, \quad p = 2, 3, 11),$$

and other special cases.

---

[1] J. W. L. Glaisher, table of the first 250 Bernoulli numbers (to nine figures) and their logarithms (to ten figures). *Trans. Cambridge Philos. Soc.* **12**: 390 (1871-1879).

The Bernoulli numbers appear in the summation of integral powers of the integers,

$$\sum_{j=1}^{N} j^p, \quad p \text{ integral,}$$

and in numerous series expansions of the transcendental functions, including $\tan x$, $\cot x$, $\ln|\sin x|$, $(\sin x)^{-1}$, $\ln|\cos x|$, $\ln|\tan x|$, $(\cosh x)^{-1}$, $\tanh x$, and $\coth x$. For example,

$$\tan x = x + \frac{x^3}{3} + \frac{2}{15}x^5 + \cdots + \frac{(-1)^{n-1} 2^{2n}(2^{2n}-1)B_{2n}}{(2n)!} x^{2n-1} + \cdots. \qquad (12.41)$$

The Bernoulli numbers are likely to appear in such series expansions because of the definition, Eq. (12.28), the form of Eq. (12.35), and the relation to the Riemann zeta function, Eq. (12.38).

Bernoulli Polynomials

If Eq. (12.28) is generalized slightly, we have

$$\frac{te^{ts}}{e^t - 1} = \sum_{n=0}^{\infty} B_n(s) \frac{t^n}{n!} \qquad (12.42)$$

defining the **Bernoulli polynomials**, $B_n(s)$. It is clear that $B_n(s)$ will be a polynomial of degree n, since the Taylor expansion of the generating function will contain contributions in which each instance of t may (or may not) be accompanied by a factor s. The first seven Bernoulli polynomials are given in Table 12.3.

If we set $s = 0$ in the generating function formula, Eq. (12.42), we have

$$B_n(0) = B_n, \quad n = 0, 1, 2, \ldots, \qquad (12.43)$$

showing that the Bernoulli polynomial evaluated at zero equals the corresponding Bernoulli number.

Table 12.3   Bernoulli Polynomials

$$B_0 = 1$$

$$B_1 = x - \frac{1}{2}$$

$$B_2 = x^2 - x + \frac{1}{6}$$

$$B_3 = x^3 - \frac{3}{2}x^2 + \frac{1}{2}x$$

$$B_4 = x^4 - 2x^3 + x^2 - \frac{1}{30}$$

$$B_5 = x^5 - \frac{5}{2}x^4 + \frac{5}{3}x^3 - \frac{1}{6}x$$

$$B_6 = x^6 - 3x^5 + \frac{5}{2}x^4 - \frac{1}{2}x^2 + \frac{1}{42}$$

Two other important properties of the Bernoulli polynomials follow from the defining relation, Eq. (12.42). If we differentiate both sides of that equation with respect to s, we have

$$\frac{t^2 e^{ts}}{e^t - 1} = \sum_{n=0}^{\infty} B_n'(s) \frac{t^n}{n!}$$

$$= \sum_{n=0}^{\infty} B_n(s) \frac{t^{n+1}}{n!} = \sum_{n=1}^{\infty} B_{n-1}(s) \frac{t^n}{(n-1)!}, \tag{12.44}$$

where the second line of Eq. (12.44) is obtained by rewriting its left-hand side using the generating-function formula. Equating the coefficients of equal powers of t in the two lines of Eq. (12.44), we obtain the differentiation formula

$$\frac{d}{ds} B_n(s) = n B_{n-1}(s), \quad n = 1, 2, 3, \ldots. \tag{12.45}$$

We also have a symmetry relation, which we can obtain by setting $s = 1$ in Eq. (12.42). The left-hand side of that equation then becomes

$$\frac{t e^t}{e^t - 1} = \frac{-t}{e^{-t} - 1}. \tag{12.46}$$

Thus, equating Eq. (12.42) for $s = 1$ with the Bernoulli-number expansion (in $-t$) of the right-hand side of Eq. (12.46), we reach

$$\sum_{n=0}^{\infty} B_n(1) \frac{t^n}{n!} = \sum_{n=0}^{\infty} B_n \frac{(-t)^n}{n!},$$

which is equivalent to

$$B_n(1) = (-1)^n B_n(0). \tag{12.47}$$

These relations are used in the development of the Euler-Maclaurin integration formula.

Exercises

12.2.1   Verify the identities, Eqs. (12.32) and (12.46).

12.2.2   Show that the first Bernoulli polynomials are

$$B_0(s) = 1$$
$$B_1(s) = s - \tfrac{1}{2}$$
$$B_2(s) = s^2 - s + \tfrac{1}{6}.$$

Note that $B_n(0) = B_n$, the Bernoulli number.

12.2.3   Show that

$$\tan x = \sum_{n=1}^{\infty} \frac{(-1)^{n-1}2^{2n}(2^{2n}-1)B_{2n}}{(2n)!}x^{2n-1}, \quad -\frac{\pi}{2} < x < \frac{\pi}{2}.$$

Hint. $\tan x = \cot x - 2\cot 2x$.

12.3   EULER-MACLAURIN INTEGRATION FORMULA

One use of the Bernoulli polynomials is in the derivation of the **Euler-Maclaurin integration formula**. This formula is used both to develop asymptotic expansions (treated later in this chapter) and to obtain approximate values for summations. An important application of the Euler-Maclaurin formula, presented in Chapter 13, is its use to derive **Stirling's formula**, an asymptotic expression for the gamma function.

The technique we use to develop the Euler-Maclaurin formula is repeated integration by parts, using Eq. (12.45) to create new derivatives. We start with

$$\int_0^1 f(x)dx = \int_0^1 f(x)B_0(x)dx, \tag{12.48}$$

where we have, for reasons that will shortly become apparent, inserted the redundant factor $B_0(x) = 1$. From Eq. (12.45), we note that

$$B_0(x) = B_1'(x),$$

and we substitute $B_1'(x)$ for $B_0(x)$ in Eq. (12.48), integrate by parts, and identify $B_1(1) = -B_1(0) = \frac{1}{2}$, thereby obtaining

$$\int_0^1 f(x)dx = f(1)B_1(1) - f(0)B_1(0) - \int_0^1 f'(x)B_1(x)dx$$

$$= \frac{1}{2}\big[f(1) + f(0)\big] - \int_0^1 f'(x)B_1(x)dx. \tag{12.49}$$

Again using Eq. (12.45), we have

$$B_1(x) = \frac{1}{2}B_2'(x).$$

Inserting $B_2'(x)$ and integrating by parts again, we get

$$\int_0^1 f(x)dx = \frac{1}{2}\Big[f(1) + f(0)\Big] - \frac{1}{2}\Big[f'(1)B_2(1) - f'(0)B_2(0)\Big]$$

$$+ \frac{1}{2}\int_0^1 f^{(2)}(x)B_2(x)dx. \tag{12.50}$$

Using the relation

$$B_{2n}(1) = B_{2n}(0) = B_{2n}, \quad n = 0, 1, 2, \ldots, \tag{12.51}$$

Eq. (12.50) simplifies to

$$\int_0^1 f(x)dx = \frac{1}{2}\Big[f(1) + f(0) \Big] - \frac{B_2}{2}\Big[f'(1) - f'(0) \Big] + \frac{1}{2}\int_0^1 f^{(2)}(x)B_2(x)dx. \tag{12.52}$$

Continuing, we replace $B_2(x)$ by $B_3'(x)/3$ and once again integrate by parts. Because

$$B_{2n+1}(1) = B_{2n+1}(0) = 0, \quad n = 1, 2, 3, \ldots, \tag{12.53}$$

the integration by parts produces no integrated terms, and

$$\frac{1}{2}\int_0^1 f^{(2)}(x)B_2(x)dx = \frac{1}{2\cdot 3}\int_0^1 f^{(2)}(x)B_3'(x)dx = -\frac{1}{3!}\int_0^1 f^{(3)}(x)B_3(x)dx. \tag{12.54}$$

Substituting $B_3(x) = B_4'(x)/4$ and carrying out one more partial integration, we get integrated terms containing $B_4(x)$, which simplify according to Eq. (12.51). The result is

$$-\frac{1}{3!}\int_0^1 f^{(3)}(x)B_3(x)dx = \frac{B_4}{4!}\Big[f^{(3)}(1) - f^{(3)}(0) \Big] + \frac{1}{4!}\int_0^1 f^{(4)}(x)B_4(x)dx. \tag{12.55}$$

We may continue this process, with steps that are entirely analogous to those that led to Eqs. (12.54) and (12.55). After steps leading to derivatives of f of order $2q - 1$, we have

$$\int_0^1 f(x)dx = \frac{1}{2}\Big[f(1) + f(0) \Big] - \sum_{p=1}^q \frac{1}{(2p)!} B_{2p}\Big[f^{(2p-1)}(1) - f^{(2p-1)}(0) \Big]$$

$$+ \frac{1}{(2q)!}\int_0^1 f^{(2q)}(x)B_{2q}(x)dx. \tag{12.56}$$

This is the Euler-Maclaurin integration formula. It assumes that the function $f(x)$ has the required derivatives.

The range of integration in Eq. (12.56) may be shifted from [0, 1] to [1, 2] by replacing $f(x)$ by $f(x + 1)$. Adding such results up to $[n - 1, n]$, we obtain

$$\int_0^n f(x)dx = \frac{1}{2}f(0) + f(1) + f(2) + \cdots + f(n-1) + \frac{1}{2}f(n)$$

$$- \sum_{p=1}^q \frac{1}{(2p)!} B_{2p}\left[f^{(2p-1)}(n) - f^{(2p-1)}(0) \right]$$

$$+ \frac{1}{(2q)!} \int_0^1 B_{2q}(x) \sum_{v=0}^{n-1} f^{(2q)}(x + v)dx. \tag{12.57}$$

Note that the derivative terms at the intermediate integer arguments all cancel. However, the intermediate terms $f(j)$ do not, and $\frac{1}{2}f(0) + f(1) + \cdots + \frac{1}{2}f(n)$ appear exactly as in trapezoidal integration, or quadrature, so the summation over p may be interpreted as a correction to the trapezoidal approximation. Equation (12.57) may therefore be seen as a generalization of Eq. (1.10).

In many applications of Eq. (12.57) the final integral containing $f^{(2q)}$, though small, will not approach zero as q is increased without limit, and the Euler-Maclaurin formula then has an asymptotic, rather than convergent character. Such series, and the implications regarding their use, are the topic of a later section of this chapter.

One of the most important uses of the Euler-Maclaurin formula is in summing series by converting them to integrals plus correction terms.[2] Here is an illustration of the process.

Example 12.3.1   ESTIMATION OF $\zeta(3)$

A straightforward application of Eq. (12.57) to $\zeta(3)$ proceeds as follows (noting that all derivatives of $f(x) = 1/x^3$ vanish in the limit $x \to \infty$):

$$\zeta(3) = \sum_{n=1}^{\infty} \frac{1}{n^3} = \frac{1}{2}f(1) + \int_1^{\infty} \frac{dx}{x^3} - \sum_{p=1}^{q} \frac{B_{2p}}{(2p)!} f^{(2p-1)}(1) + \text{remainder}. \tag{12.58}$$

Evaluating the integral, setting $f(1) = 1$, and inserting

$$f^{(2n-1)}(x) = -\frac{(2n+1)!}{2x^{2n+2}}$$

with $x = 1$, Eq. (12.58) becomes

$$\zeta(3) = \frac{1}{2} + \frac{1}{2} + \sum_{p=1}^{q} \frac{(2p+1)B_{2p}}{2x^{2p+2}} + \text{remainder}. \tag{12.59}$$

---

[2] See R. P. Boas and C. Stutz, Estimating sums with integrals. *Am. J. Phys.* **39**: 745 (1971), for a number of examples.

Table 12.4   Contributions to $\zeta(3)$ of Terms in Euler-Maclaurin Formula

	$n_0 = 1$	$n_0 = 2$	$n_0 = 4$
Explicit terms	0.500000	1.062500	1.169849
$\int_{n_0}^{\infty} x^{-3} dx$	0.500000	0.125000	0.031250
B_2 term	0.250000	0.015615	0.000977
B_4 term	−0.083333	−0.001302	−0.000020
B_6 term	0.083333	0.000326	0.000001
B_8 term	−0.150000	−0.000146	−0.000000
B_{10} term	0.416667	0.000102	0.000000
B_{12} term	−1.645238	−0.000100	−0.000000
B_{14} term	8.750000	0.000134	0.000000
Sum[a]	1.166667	1.201995	1.202057

[a] Sums only include data above horizontal marker.
Left column: formula applied to entire summation; central column: formula applied starting from second term; right column: formula starting from fourth term.

To assess the quality of this result, we list, in the first data column of Table 12.4, the contributions to it. The line marked "explicit terms" consists presently of only the term $\frac{1}{2} f(1)$. We note that the individual terms start to increase after the B_4 term; since it is our intention not to evaluate the remainder, the accuracy of the expansion is limited. As discussed more extensively in the section on asymptotic expansions, the best result available from these data is obtained by truncating the expansion before the terms start to increase; adding the contributions above the marker line in the table, we get the value listed as "Sum." For reference, the accurate value of $\zeta(3)$ is 1.202057.

We can improve the result available from the Euler-Maclaurin formula by explicitly calculating some initial terms and applying the formula only to those that remain. This stratagem causes the derivatives entering the formula to be smaller and diminishes the correction from the trapezoid-rule estimate. Simply starting the formula at $n = 2$ instead of $n = 1$ reduces the error markedly; see the second data column of Table 12.4. Now the "explicit terms" consist of $f(1) + \frac{1}{2} f(2)$. Starting the Euler-Maclaurin formula at $n = 4$ further improves the result, then reaching better than seven-figure accuracy.   ∎

When the Euler-Maclaurin formula is applied to sums whose summands have a finite number of nonzero derivatives, it can evaluate them exactly. See Exercise 12.3.1.

Exercises

12.3.1   The Euler-Maclaurin integration formula may be used for the evaluation of finite series:

$$\sum_{m=1}^{n} f(m) = \int_{1}^{n} f(x)dx + \frac{1}{2}f(1) + \frac{1}{2}f(n) + \frac{B_2}{2!}\left[f'(n) - f'(1) \right] + \cdots .$$

Show that

(a) $\displaystyle\sum_{m=1}^{n} m = \frac{1}{2}n(n+1)$.

(b) $\displaystyle\sum_{m=1}^{n} m^2 = \frac{1}{6}n(n+1)(2n+1)$.

(c) $\displaystyle\sum_{m=1}^{n} m^3 = \frac{1}{4}n^2(n+1)^2$.

(d) $\displaystyle\sum_{m=1}^{n} m^4 = \frac{1}{30}n(n+1)(2n+1)(3n^2+3n-1)$.

12.3.2 The Euler-Maclaurin integration formula provides a way of calculating the Euler-Mascheroni constant γ to high accuracy. Using $f(x) = 1/x$ in Eq. (12.57) (with interval $[1, n]$) and the definition of γ, Eq. (1.13), we obtain

$$\gamma = \sum_{s=1}^{n} s^{-1} - \ln n - \frac{1}{2n} + \sum_{k=1}^{N} \frac{B_{2k}}{(2k)n^{2k}}.$$

Using double-precision arithmetic, calculate γ for $N = 1, 2, \ldots$.

Note. See D. E. Knuth, Euler's constant to 1271 places. *Math. Comput.* **16**: 275 (1962).

ANS.   For $n = 1000$, $N = 2$

$\gamma = 0.5772\,1566\,4901$.

12.4 DIRICHLET SERIES

Series expansions of the general form

$$S(s) = \sum_n \frac{a_n}{n^s}$$

are known as **Dirichlet series**, and our knowledge of contour integration methods and Bernoulli numbers enables us to evaluate a variety of expressions of this type. One of the most important Dirichlet series is that of the Riemann zeta function,

$$\zeta(s) = \sum_{n=1}^{\infty} \frac{1}{n^s}. \tag{12.60}$$

We have already evaluated a sum from which $\zeta(2)$ can be extracted.

Example 12.4.1   EVALUATION OF $\zeta(2)$

From Example 11.9.1, we have

$$S(a) = \sum_{n=1}^{\infty} \frac{1}{n^2 + a^2} = \frac{\pi \coth \pi a}{2a} - \frac{1}{2a^2}.$$

Simply by taking the limit $a \to 0$, we have

$$\zeta(2) = \lim_{a \to 0} S(a) = \lim_{a \to 0} \left[\frac{\pi}{2a} \left(\frac{1}{\pi a} + \frac{\pi a}{3} + \cdots \right) - \frac{1}{2a^2} \right] = \frac{\pi^2}{6}. \tag{12.61}$$

∎

From the relation with the Bernoulli numbers, or alternatively (and perhaps less conveniently) by contour-integration methods, we find

$$\zeta(4) = \frac{\pi^4}{90}.$$

Values of $\zeta(2n)$ through $\zeta(10)$ are listed in Exercise 12.4.1. The zeta functions of odd integer argument seem unamenable to evaluation in closed form, but are easy to compute numerically (see Example 12.3.1).

Other useful Dirichlet series, in the notation of AMS-55 (see Additional Readings), include

$$\eta(s) = \sum_{n=1}^{\infty} (-1)^{n-1} n^{-s} = (1 - 2^{1-s})\zeta(s), \tag{12.62}$$

$$\lambda(s) = \sum_{n=0}^{\infty} (2n-1)^{-s} = (1 - 2^{-s})\zeta(s), \tag{12.63}$$

$$\beta(s) = \sum_{n=0}^{\infty} (-1)^n (2n+1)^{-s}. \tag{12.64}$$

Closed expressions are available (for integer $n \geq 1$) for $\zeta(2n)$, $\eta(2n)$, and $\lambda(2n)$, and for $\beta(2n-1)$. The sums with exponents of opposite parity cannot be reduced to $\zeta(2n)$ or performed by the contour-integral methods we discussed in Chapter 11. An important series that can only be evaluated numerically is that whose result is **Catalan's constant**, which is

$$\beta(2) = 1 - \frac{1}{3^2} + \frac{1}{5^2} - \cdots = 0.91596559\ldots. \tag{12.65}$$

For reference, we list a few of these summable Dirichlet series:

$$\zeta(2) = 1 + \frac{1}{2^2} + \frac{1}{3^2} + \cdots = \frac{\pi^2}{6}, \tag{12.66}$$

$$\zeta(4) = 1 + \frac{1}{2^4} + \frac{1}{3^4} + \cdots = \frac{\pi^4}{90}, \tag{12.67}$$

$$\eta(2) = 1 - \frac{1}{2^2} + \frac{1}{3^2} + \cdots = \frac{\pi^2}{12}, \tag{12.68}$$

$$\eta(4) = 1 - \frac{1}{2^4} + \frac{1}{3^4} + \cdots = \frac{7\pi^4}{720}, \tag{12.69}$$

$$\lambda(2) = 1 + \frac{1}{3^2} + \frac{1}{5^2} + \cdots = \frac{\pi^2}{8}, \tag{12.70}$$

$$\lambda(4) = 1 + \frac{1}{3^4} + \frac{1}{5^4} + \cdots = \frac{\pi^4}{96}, \tag{12.71}$$

$$\beta(1) = 1 - \frac{1}{3} + \frac{1}{5} - \cdots = \frac{\pi}{4}, \tag{12.72}$$

$$\beta(3) = 1 - \frac{1}{3^3} + \frac{1}{5^3} - \cdots = \frac{\pi^3}{32}. \tag{12.73}$$

Exercises

12.4.1   From $B_{2n} = (-1)^{n-1} \dfrac{2(2n)!}{(2\pi)^{2n}} \zeta(2n)$, show that

(a) $\zeta(2) = \dfrac{\pi^2}{6}$,   (d) $\zeta(8) = \dfrac{\pi^8}{9450}$,

(b) $\zeta(4) = \dfrac{\pi^4}{90}$,   (e) $\zeta(10) = \dfrac{\pi^{10}}{93,555}$.

(c) $\zeta(6) = \dfrac{\pi^6}{945}$,

12.4.2   The integral

$$\int_0^1 [\ln(1-x)]^2 \frac{dx}{x}$$

appears in the fourth-order correction to the magnetic moment of the electron. Show that it equals $2\zeta(3)$.

Hint. Let $1 - x = e^{-t}$.

12.4.3   (a) Show that

$$\int_0^\infty \frac{(\ln z)^2}{1+z^2} dz = 4\left(1 - \frac{1}{3^3} + \frac{1}{5^3} - \frac{1}{7^3} + \cdots\right).$$

(b) By contour integration show that this series evaluates to $\pi^3/8$.

12.4.4   Show that Catalan's constant, $\beta(2)$, may be written as

$$\beta(2) = 2\sum_{k=1}^\infty (4k-3)^{-2} - \frac{\pi^2}{8}.$$

Hint. $\pi^2 = 6\zeta(2)$.

12.4.5   Show that

(a) $\int_0^1 \frac{\ln(1+x)}{x} dx = \frac{1}{2}\zeta(2),$ (b) $\lim_{a\to 1}\int_0^a \frac{\ln(1-x)}{x} dx = \zeta(2).$

Note that the integrand in part (b) diverges for $a=1$ but that the integral is convergent.

12.4.6   (a) Show that the equation $\ln 2 = \sum_{s=1}^\infty (-1)^{s+1} s^{-1}$, Eq. (1.53), may be rewritten as

$$\ln 2 = \sum_{s=2}^n 2^{-s}\zeta(s) + \sum_{p=1}^\infty (2p)^{-n-1}\left[1 - \frac{1}{2p}\right]^{-1}.$$

Hint. Take the terms in pairs.

(b) Calculate $\ln 2$ to six significant figures.

12.4.7   (a) Show that the equation $\pi/4 = \sum_{s=1}^\infty (-1)^{s+1}(2s-1)^{-1}$, Eq. (12.72), may be rewritten as

$$\frac{\pi}{4} = 1 - 2\sum_{s=1}^n 4^{-2s}\zeta(2s) - 2\sum_{p=1}^\infty (4p)^{-2n-2}\left[1 - \frac{1}{(4p)^2}\right]^{-1}.$$

(b) Calculate $\pi/4$ to six significant figures.

12.5 INFINITE PRODUCTS

We saw in Chapter 11 that complex variable theory can be used to generate infinite-product representations of analytic functions. Here we develop some of their properties. For that purpose it is convenient to write these products in the form

$$P = \prod_{n=1}^\infty (1 + a_n).$$

The infinite product may be related to an infinite series by the obvious method of taking the logarithm:

$$\ln \prod_{n=1}^\infty (1 + a_n) = \sum_{n=1}^\infty \ln(1 + a_n). \tag{12.74}$$

The main theorem regarding convergence of infinite products is the following:

If $0 \le a_n < 1$, the infinite products $\prod_{n=1}^{\infty}(1 + a_n)$ and $\prod_{n=1}^{\infty}(1 - a_n)$ converge if $\sum_{n=1}^{\infty} a_n$ converges and diverge if $\sum_{n=1}^{\infty} a_n$ diverges.

For the infinite product $\prod(1 + a_n)$, note that

$$1 + a_n \le e^{a_n},$$

which means that the partial product consisting of the first n factors satisfies

$$p_n \le e^{s_n},$$

where s_n is the sum of the first n a_n. Letting $n \to \infty$,

$$\prod_{n=1}^{\infty}(1 + a_n) \le \exp \sum_{m=1}^{\infty} a_n, \tag{12.75}$$

thereby giving an upper bound for the infinite product.

To develop a lower bound, we note that, because all $a_i > 0$,

$$p_n = 1 + \sum_{i=1}^{n} a_i + \sum_{i=1}^{n}\sum_{j=1}^{n} a_i a_j + \cdots \ge s_n.$$

Hence

$$\prod_{n=1}^{\infty}(1 + a_n) \ge \sum_{n=1}^{\infty} a_n. \tag{12.76}$$

If the infinite sum remains finite, the infinite product will also. But if the infinite sum diverges, so will the infinite product.

The case $\prod(1 - a_n)$ is complicated by the negative signs, but a proof similar to the foregoing may be developed by noting that for $a_n < \frac{1}{2}$,

$$(1 - a_n) \le (1 + a_n)^{-1} \quad \text{and} \quad (1 - a_n) \ge (1 + 2a_n)^{-1}.$$

Example 12.5.1 CONVERGENCE OF INFINITE PRODUCTS FOR $\sin z$ AND $\cos z$

These products, developed in Eqs. (11.89) and (11.90), are

$$\sin z = z \prod_{n=1}^{\infty}\left(1 - \frac{z^2}{n^2\pi^2}\right), \quad \cos z = \prod_{n=1}^{\infty}\left(1 - \frac{z^2}{(n - 1/2)^2\pi^2}\right). \tag{12.77}$$

The product expansion of $\sin z$ converges for all z, because, writing the factors as $(1 - a_n)$,

$$\sum_{n=1}^{\infty} a_n = \frac{z^2}{\pi^2}\sum_{n=1}^{\infty} n^{-2} = \frac{z^2}{\pi^2}\zeta(2) = \frac{z^2}{6},$$

a convergent result. For the expansion of $\cos z$, we have

$$\sum_{n=1}^{\infty} a_n = \frac{4z^2}{\pi^2} \sum_{n=1}^{\infty} (2n-1)^{-2} = \frac{4z^2}{\pi^2} \lambda(2) = \frac{z^2}{2},$$

also convergent for all z. Note, however, that if z is large, many terms of the product will have to be taken before either of these series approaches convergence. In fact, the main use of these series is in establishing mathematical results rather than for precise numerical work in physics.   ∎

We close this section with one further example illustrating a technique for working with infinite products.

Example 12.5.2   An Interesting Product

We wish to evaluate the infinite product

$$P = \prod_{n=2}^{\infty} \left(1 - \frac{1}{n^2}\right).$$

We note that the product we seek is equivalent to all but the first term of the product expansion of $\sin z$ with $z = \pi$ as given in Eq. (12.77). In fact, the missing first term, which is zero, guarantees that we will get the correct result for $\sin \pi$. For general z, we move the first term (and the prefactor z) to the left-hand side of the product formula for $\sin z$, reaching

$$\frac{\sin z}{z(1 - z^2/\pi^2)} = \prod_{n=2}^{\infty} \left(1 - \frac{z^2}{n^2 \pi^2}\right).$$

We now take the limits of the two sides of this equation as $z \to \pi$, applying l'Hôpital's rule to evaluate the left-hand side and recognizing the right-hand side as P. Thus,

$$P = \lim_{z \to \pi} \frac{\sin z}{z(1 - z^2/\pi^2)} = \frac{\cos z}{1 - 3z^2/\pi^2} \bigg|_{z=\pi} = \frac{-1}{1-3} = +\frac{1}{2}.$$

                                                                      ∎

Exercises

12.5.1   Using

$$\ln \prod_{n=1}^{\infty} (1 \pm a_n) = \sum_{n=1}^{\infty} \ln(1 \pm a_n)$$

and the Maclaurin expansion of $\ln(1 \pm a_n)$, show that the infinite product $\prod_{n=1}^{\infty} (1 \pm a_n)$ converges or diverges with the infinite series $\sum_{n=1}^{\infty} a_n$.

12.5.2   An infinite product appears in the form

$$\prod_{n=1}^{\infty} \left(\frac{1+a/n}{1+b/n} \right),$$

where a and b are constants. Show that this infinite product converges only if $a = b$.

12.5.3   Show that the infinite product representations of $\sin x$ and $\cos x$ are consistent with the identity $2 \sin x \cos x = \sin 2x$.

12.5.4   Determine the limit to which $\prod_{n=2}^{\infty} \left(1 + \frac{(-1)^n}{n} \right)$ converges.

12.5.5   Show that $\prod_{n=2}^{\infty} \left[1 - \frac{2}{n(n+1)} \right] = \frac{1}{3}$.

12.5.6   Prove that $\prod_{n=2}^{\infty} \left(1 - \frac{1}{n^2} \right) = \frac{1}{2}$.

12.5.7   Verify the Euler identity $\prod_{p=1}^{\infty} (1 + z^p) = \prod_{q=1}^{\infty} (1 - z^{2q-1})^{-1}$, $|z| < 1$.

12.5.8   Show that $\prod_{r=1}^{\infty} (1 + x/r) e^{-x/r}$ converges for all finite x (except for the zeros of $1 + x/r$).

Hint. Write the nth factor as $1 + a_n$.

12.5.9   Derive the formula, valid for small x,

$$\ln \sin x = \ln x + \sum a_n x^n,$$

giving the explicit form for the coefficients a_n.

Hint. $d(\ln \sin x)/dx = \cot x$.

12.5.10   Using the infinite product representations of $\sin z$, show that

$$z \cot z = 1 - 2 \sum_{m,n=1}^{\infty} \left(\frac{z}{n\pi} \right)^{2m},$$

and hence that the Bernoulli numbers are given by the formula

$$B_{2n} = (-1)^{n-1} \frac{2(2n)!}{(2\pi)^{2n}} \zeta(2n).$$

This is an alternate route to Eq. (12.38).

Hint. The result of Exercise 12.5.9 will be helpful.

12.6   ASYMPTOTIC SERIES

Asymptotic series frequently occur in physics. In fact, one of the earliest and still important approximations of quantum mechanics, the **WKB expansion** (the initials stand for its originators, Wenzel, Kramers, and Brillouin), is an asymptotic series. In numerical computations, these series are employed for the accurate computation of a variety of functions.

We consider here two types of integrals that lead to asymptotic series: first, integrals of the form

$$I_1(x) = \int_x^\infty e^{-u} f(u)\,du,$$

where the variable x appears as the lower limit of an integral. Second, we consider the form

$$I_2(x) = \int_0^\infty e^{-u} f\left(\frac{u}{x}\right) du,$$

with the function f to be expanded as a Taylor series (binomial series). Asymptotic series often occur as solutions of differential equations; we encounter many examples in later chapters of this book.

Exponential Integral

The nature of an asymptotic series is perhaps best illustrated by a specific example. Suppose that we have the exponential integral function[3]

$$\mathrm{Ei}(x) = \int_{-\infty}^x \frac{e^u}{u}\,du, \tag{12.78}$$

which we find more convenient to write in the form

$$-\mathrm{Ei}(-x) = \int_x^\infty \frac{e^{-u}}{u}\,du = E_1(x), \tag{12.79}$$

to be evaluated for large values of x. This function has a series expansion that converges for all x, namely

$$E_1(x) = -\gamma - \ln x - \sum_{n=1}^\infty \frac{(-1)^n x^n}{nn!}, \tag{12.80}$$

which we derive in Chapter 13, but the series is totally useless for numerical evaluation when x is large. We need another approach, for which it is convenient to generalize Eq. (12.79) to

$$I(x, p) = \int_x^\infty \frac{e^{-u}}{u^p}\,du, \tag{12.81}$$

where we restrict consideration to cases in which x and p are positive. As already stated, we seek an evaluation for large values of x.

---

[3]This function occurs frequently in astrophysical problems involving gas with a Maxwell-Boltzmann energy distribution.

Integrating by parts, we obtain

$$I(x, p) = \frac{e^{-x}}{x^p} - p \int_x^\infty \frac{e^{-u}}{u^{p+1}} du = \frac{e^{-x}}{x^p} - \frac{pe^{-x}}{x^{p+1}} + p(p+1) \int_x^\infty \frac{e^{-u}}{u^{p+2}} du.$$

Continuing to integrate by parts, we develop the series

$$I(x, p) = e^{-x} \left(\frac{1}{x^p} - \frac{p}{x^{p+1}} + \frac{p(p+1)}{x^{p+2}} - \cdots + (-1)^{n-1} \frac{(p+n-2)!}{(p-1)! x^{p+n-1}} \right)$$

$$+ (-1)^n \frac{(p+n-1)!}{(p-1)!} \int_x^\infty \frac{e^{-u}}{u^{p+n}} du. \tag{12.82}$$

This is a remarkable series. Checking the convergence by the d'Alembert ratio test, we find

$$\lim_{n\to\infty} \frac{|u_{n+1}|}{|u_n|} = \lim_{n\to\infty} \frac{(p+n)!}{(p+n-1)!} \cdot \frac{1}{x} = \lim_{n\to\infty} \frac{p+n}{x} = \infty \tag{12.83}$$

for all finite values of x. Therefore our series as an infinite series diverges everywhere! Before discarding Eq. (12.83) as worthless, let us see how well a given partial sum approximates our function $I(x, p)$. Taking s_n as the partial sum of the series through n terms and R_n as the corresponding remainder,

$$I(x, p) - s_n(x, p) = (-1)^{n+1} \frac{(p+n)!}{(p-1)!} \int_x^\infty \frac{e^{-u}}{u^{p+n+1}} du = R_n(x, p).$$

In absolute value

$$|R_n(x, p)| \le \frac{(p+n)!}{(p-1)!} \int_x^\infty \frac{e^{-u}}{u^{p+n+1}} du.$$

When we substitute $u = v + x$, the integral becomes

$$\int_x^\infty \frac{e^{-u}}{u^{p+n+1}} du = e^{-x} \int_0^\infty \frac{e^{-v}}{(v+x)^{p+n+1}} dv$$

$$= \frac{e^{-x}}{x^{p+n+1}} \int_0^\infty e^{-v} \left(1 + \frac{v}{x} \right)^{-p-n-1} dv.$$

For large x the final integral approaches 1 and

$$|R_n(x, p)| \approx \frac{(p+n)!}{(p-1)!} \frac{e^{-x}}{x^{p+n+1}}. \tag{12.84}$$

This means that if we take x large enough, our partial sum s_n will be an arbitrarily good approximation to the function $I(x, p)$. Our divergent series, Eq. (12.82), therefore is perfectly good for computations of partial sums. For this reason it is sometimes called a **semiconvergent series**. Note that the power of x in the denominator of the remainder, namely $p+n+1$, is higher than the power of x in the last term included in $s_n(x, p)$, namely $p+n$.

Thus, our asymptotic series for $E_1(x)$ assumes the form

$$e^x E_1(x) = e^x \int_x^\infty \frac{e^{-u}}{u} du$$

$$\approx s_n(x) = \frac{1}{x} - \frac{1!}{x^2} + \frac{2!}{x^2} - \frac{3!}{x^4} + \cdots + (-1)^n \frac{n!}{x^{n+1}}, \tag{12.85}$$

where we must choose to terminate the series after some n.

Since the remainder $R_n(x, p)$ alternates in sign, the successive partial sums give alternately upper and lower bounds for $I(x, p)$. The behavior of the series (with $p = 1$) as a function of the number of terms included is shown in Fig. 12.2, where we have plotted partial sums of $e^x E_1(x)$ for the value $x = 5$. The optimum determination of $e^x E_1(x)$ is given by the closest approach of the upper and lower bounds, that is, for $x = 5$, between $s_6 = 0.1664$ and $s_5 = 0.1741$. Therefore

$$0.1664 \le e^x E_1(x)\Big|_{x=5} \le 0.1741. \tag{12.86}$$

Actually, from tables,

$$e^x E_1(x)\Big|_{x=5} = 0.1704, \tag{12.87}$$

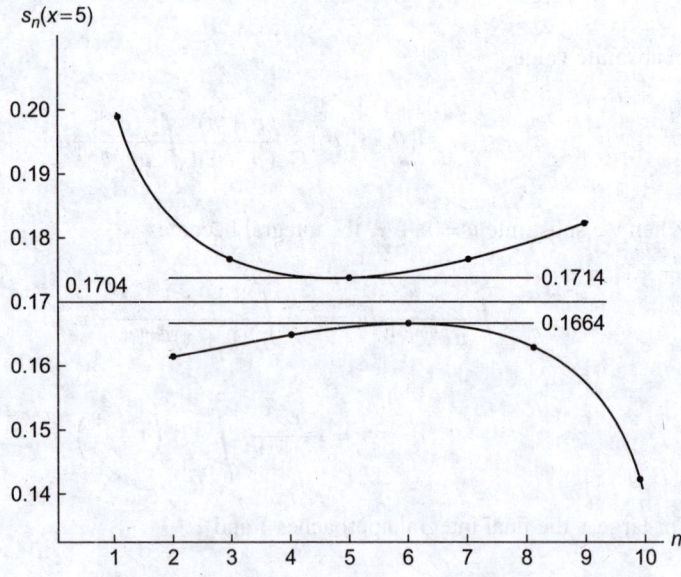

FIGURE 12.2   Partial sums of $e^x E_1(x)\,|_{x=5}$.

within the limits established by our asymptotic expansion. Note that inclusion of additional terms in the series expansion beyond the optimum point reduces the accuracy of the representation. As x is increased, the spread between the lowest upper bound and the highest lower bound will diminish. By taking x large enough, one may compute $e^x E_1(x)$ to any desired degree of accuracy. Other properties of $E_1(x)$ are derived and discussed in Section 13.6.

Cosine and Sine Integrals

Asymptotic series may also be developed from definite integrals, provided that the integrand has the required behavior. As an example, the cosine and sine integrals (in Table 1.2) are defined by

$$\text{Ci}(u) = -\int_u^\infty \frac{\cos t}{t} dt, \tag{12.88}$$

$$\text{si}(u) = -\int_u^\infty \frac{\sin t}{t} dt. \tag{12.89}$$

Combining these, using the formula for e^{it},

$$\text{Ci}(u) + i\,\text{si}(u) = -\int_u^\infty \frac{e^{-it}}{t} dt,$$

and then changing the integration variable from t to z, we reach

$$F(u) = \text{Ci}(u) + i\,\text{si}(u) = -e^{iu} \int_0^\infty \frac{e^{iz} dz}{u + z}. \tag{12.90}$$

To further process $F(u)$, we now consider the contour integral

$$-e^{iu} \oint_C \frac{e^{iz} dz}{u + z},$$

where the contour C is that shown in Fig. 12.3. Since we are interested in evaluation for large positive (and real) u, our integrand has as its only singularity a pole on the negative real axis, so the region enclosed by the contour is entirely analytic and the contour integral therefore vanishes. The exponential and the denominator cause the arc at infinity (labeled B) not to contribute to the contour integral, so the integral we seek is obtained from segment A and must be equal to the negative of the integral on segment D. Therefore, we have

$$F(u) = -e^{iu} \int_0^\infty \frac{e^{-y} i\,dy}{u + iy}, \tag{12.91}$$

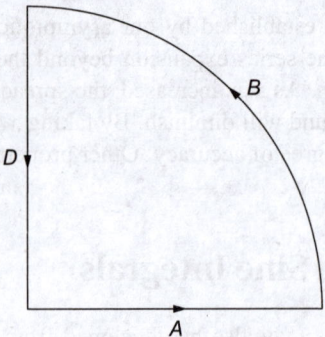

FIGURE 12.3   Contour for sine and cosine integrals.

which is already helpful since we have converted an oscillatory integral into one with a monotonically and exponentially decreasing integrand. To obtain an asymptotic expansion, we continue by expanding the denominator of the integrand using the binomial theorem, writing

$$\frac{1}{u+iy} = \frac{1}{u}\left[1 - \frac{iy}{u} + \left(\frac{iy}{u}\right)^2 - \cdots\right].$$

We plan to integrate in y from zero to infinity, and the proposed expansion will be divergent when $y > u$, but we proceed anyway, because the terms of the series will initially be decreasing and will be satisfactory as an asymptotic expansion. Formally, we take the viewpoint that we are writing $1/(u + iy)$ as a finite series plus a remainder, and we will abandon the expansion at or before the point that the remainder is a minimum.

Inserting the expansion, and integrating termwise using the formula

$$\int_0^\infty y^n e^{-y} dy = n!,$$

we get

$$F(u) \approx -\frac{ie^{iu}}{u}\left[1 - i\left(\frac{1!}{u}\right) - \left(\frac{2!}{u^2}\right) + i\left(\frac{3!}{u^3}\right) + \left(\frac{4!}{u^4}\right) - \cdots\right]. \qquad (12.92)$$

As for our earlier example, the exponential integral, this series will diverge for all u, but if u is sufficiently large the terms will initially decrease to very small values before increasing again toward divergence.

To go from the expansion of $F(u)$ to those of Ci and si, we need to separate it into real and imaginary parts. Writing $e^{iu} = \cos u + i \sin u$ and collecting terms appropriately, we get as the desired asymptotic expansions

$$\mathrm{Ci}(u) \approx \frac{\sin u}{u} \sum_{n=0}^{N} (-1)^n \frac{(2n)!}{u^{2n}} - \frac{\cos u}{u} \sum_{n=0}^{N} (-1)^n \frac{(2n+1)!}{u^{2n+1}}, \tag{12.93}$$

$$\mathrm{si}(u) \approx -\frac{\cos u}{u} \sum_{n=0}^{N} (-1)^n \frac{(2n)!}{u^{2n}} - \frac{\sin u}{u} \sum_{n=0}^{N} (-1)^n \frac{(2n+1)!}{u^{2n+1}}. \tag{12.94}$$

Definition of Asymptotic Series

Poincaré has introduced a formal definition for an asymptotic series.[4] Following Poincaré, we consider a function $f(x)$ whose asymptotic expansion is sought, the partial sums s_n in its expansion, and the corresponding remainders $R_n(x)$. Though the expansion need not be a power series, we assume that form for simplicity in the present discussion. Thus,

$$x^n R_n(x) = x^n [f(x) - s_n(x)], \tag{12.95}$$

where

$$s_n(x) = a_0 + \frac{a_1}{x} + \frac{a_2}{x^2} + \cdots + \frac{a_n}{x^n}. \tag{12.96}$$

The asymptotic expansion of $f(x)$ is defined to have the properties that

$$\lim_{x \to \infty} x^n R_n(x) = 0, \quad \text{for fixed } n, \tag{12.97}$$

and

$$\lim_{n \to \infty} x^n R_n(x) = \infty, \quad \text{for fixed } x. \tag{12.98}$$

These conditions were met for our examples, Eqs. (12.85), (12.93), and (12.94).[5]

For power series, as assumed in the form of $s_n(x)$, $R_n(x) \approx x^{-n-1}$. With the conditions of Eqs. (12.97) and (12.98) satisfied, we write

$$f(x) \sim \sum_{n=0}^{\infty} a_n x^{-n}. \tag{12.99}$$

Note the use of $\sim$ in place of $=$. The function $f(x)$ is equal to the series only in the limit as $x \to \infty$ and with the restriction to a finite number of terms in the series.

Asymptotic expansions of two functions may be multiplied together, and the result will be an asymptotic expansion of the product of the two functions. The asymptotic expansion of a given function $f(t)$ may be integrated term by term (just as in a uniformly convergent series of continuous functions) from $x \le t < \infty$, and the result will be an asymptotic

---

[4]Poincaré's definition allows (or neglects) exponentially decreasing functions. The refinement of his definition is of considerable importance for the advanced theory of asymptotic expansions, particularly for extensions into the complex plane. However, for purposes of an introductory treatment and especially for numerical computation of expansions for which the variable is real and positive, Poincaré's approach is perfectly satisfactory.

[5]Some writers feel that the requirement of Eq. (12.98), which excludes convergent series of inverse powers of x, is artificial and unnecessary.

expansion of $\int_x^\infty f(t)dt$. Term-by-term differentiation, however, is valid only under very special conditions.

Some functions do not possess an asymptotic expansion; e^x is an example of such a function. However, if a function has an asymptotic expansion of the power-series form in Eq. (12.99), it has only one. The correspondence is not one to one; many functions may have the same asymptotic expansion.

One of the most useful and powerful methods of generating asymptotic expansions, the method of steepest descents, is developed in the next section of this text.

Exercises

12.6.1 Integrating by parts, develop asymptotic expansions of the Fresnel integrals

$$\text{(a) } C(x) = \int_0^x \cos\frac{\pi u^2}{2}\,du, \quad \text{(b) } s(x) = \int_0^x \sin\frac{\pi u^2}{2}\,du.$$

These integrals appear in the analysis of a knife-edge diffraction pattern.

12.6.2 Rederive the asymptotic expansions of $\text{Ci}(x)$ and $\text{si}(x)$ by repeated integration by parts.

Hint. $\text{Ci}(x) + i\,\text{si}(x) = -\int_x^\infty \frac{e^{it}}{t}\,dt.$

12.6.3 Derive the asymptotic expansion of the Gauss error function

$$\text{erf}(x) = \frac{2}{\sqrt{\pi}}\int_0^x e^{-t^2}\,dt$$

$$\approx 1 - \frac{e^{-x^2}}{\sqrt{\pi}\,x}\left(1 - \frac{1}{2x^2} + \frac{1\cdot 3}{2^2 x^4} - \frac{1\cdot 3\cdot 5}{2^3 x^6} + \cdots + (-1)^n\frac{(2n-1)!!}{2^n x^{2n}}\right).$$

Hint. $\text{erf}(x) = 1 - \text{erfc}(x) = 1 - \dfrac{2}{\sqrt{\pi}}\displaystyle\int_x^\infty e^{-t^2}\,dt.$

Normalized so that $\text{erf}(\infty) = 1$, this function plays an important role in probability theory. It may be expressed in terms of the Fresnel integrals (Exercise 12.6.1), the incomplete gamma functions (Section 13.6), or the confluent hypergeometric functions (Section 18.5).

12.6.4 The asymptotic expressions for the various Bessel functions, Section 14.6, contain the series

$$P_\nu(z) \sim 1 + \sum_{n=1}^\infty (-1)^n \frac{\prod_{s=1}^{2n}[4\nu^2 - (2s-1)^2]}{(2n)!\,(8z)^{2n}},$$

$$Q_\nu(z) \sim \sum_{n=1}^\infty (-1)^{n+1} \frac{\prod_{s=1}^{2n-1}[4\nu^2 - (2s-1)^2]}{(2n-1)!\,(8z)^{2n-1}}.$$

Show that these two series are indeed asymptotic series.

12.6.5   For $x > 1$,

$$\frac{1}{1+x} = \sum_{n=0}^{\infty} (-1)^n \frac{1}{x^{n+1}}.$$

Test this series to see if it is an asymptotic series.

12.6.6   Derive the following Bernoulli-number asymptotic series for the Euler-Mascheroni constant, defined in Eq. (1.13):

$$\gamma \sim \sum_{s=1}^{n} s^{-1} - \ln n - \frac{1}{2n} + \sum_{k=1}^{\infty} \frac{B_{2k}}{(2k)n^{2k}}.$$

Here n plays the role of x.

Hint. Apply the Euler-Maclaurin integration formula to $f(x) = x^{-1}$ over the interval $[1, n]$ for $N = 1, 2, \ldots$.

12.6.7   Develop an asymptotic series for

$$\int_0^{\infty} \frac{e^{-xv}}{(1+v^2)^2} dv.$$

Take x to be real and positive.

$$ANS. \quad \frac{1}{x} - \frac{2!}{x^3} + \frac{4!}{x^5} - \cdots + \frac{(-1)^n (2n)!}{x^{2n+1}}.$$

12.7   METHOD OF STEEPEST DESCENTS

In this section we consider the frequently occurring situation that we require the asymptotic behavior (for large t, assumed real) of a function $f(t)$, where

- $f(t)$ is represented by an integral of the generic form

$$f(t) = \int_C F(z, t) dz,$$

with $F(z, t)$ analytic in z, but also parametrically dependent on t;

- The integration path C is, or can be deformed to be, such that for large t the dominant contribution to the integral arises from a small range of z in the neighborhood of the point z_0 where $|F(z_0, t)|$ is a maximum **on the path**;

- The integration path will pass through z_0 in the orientation that causes the most rapid decrease in $|F|$ on departure from z_0 in either direction along the path (hence the name **steepest descents**); and

- In the limit of large t the contribution to the integral from the neighborhood of z_0 asymptotically approaches the exact value of $f(t)$.

While the above conditions seem rather restrictive, they can in fact be met for many of the important special functions of mathematical physics, including, among others, the gamma function and various Bessel functions.

Saddle Points

The integration path supplied with the original definition of an integral representation defining a function $f(t)$ will not usually meet the conditions outlined above, and we need to consider the features of the integrand $F(z, t)$ that will be useful in defining a more suitable path which, even if the original formulation is entirely real, may be a more general contour in the complex plane. We already know (Exercise 11.2.2) that neither the real nor the imaginary part of an analytic function can have an extremum (either a minimum or maximum) within the region of analyticity, and the same is also true of its modulus (this result is Jensen's theorem; see Exercise 12.7.1). To better understand that, let us represent $F(z, t)$ (in a region where it is assumed nonzero) in the form

$$F(z, t) = e^{w(z,t)} = e^{u(z,t)+iv(z,t)}, \qquad (12.100)$$

where u and v are the real and imaginary parts of an analytic function w; this representation permits us to identify u as $\ln|F|$; the fact that u cannot have an extremum makes Jensen's theorem obvious.

Although u cannot have an extremum, it can have a saddle point (a point at which $w' = 0$; then also $du/ds = 0$ for all directions ds, but with higher derivatives that are positive in some directions and negative in others (see Fig. 12.4). Let us examine some general features of w and its components u and v in the neighborhood of a saddle point of u, which we designate z_0. We proceed by expanding $w(z, t)$ in a Taylor series about z_0. Because $w' = 0$ there, the first two nonzero terms of the expansion are

$$w(z, t) = w(z_0, t) + \frac{w''(z_0, t)}{2!}(z - z_0)^2 + \cdots. \qquad (12.101)$$

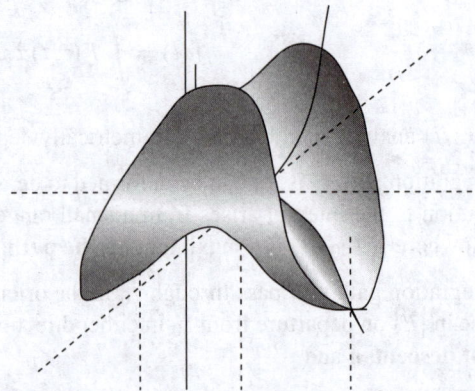

FIGURE 12.4   Saddle point of u ($= |F|$); see Eq. (12.100).

It could be that $w''(z_0, t) = 0$, but that possibility makes the analysis more complicated without changing it in a fundamental way, so we proceed under the assumption that $w''(z_0, t) \neq 0$. Using the abbreviated notations $w_0 = w(z_0, t)$, $w''(z_0, t) = w_0''$, and introducing the polar forms $w_0'' = |w_0''|e^{i\alpha}$, $z - z_0 = re^{i\theta}$, Eq. (12.101) becomes

$$w(z, t) = w_0 + \frac{1}{2}|w_0''|e^{i(\alpha+2\theta)}r^2 + \cdots \tag{12.102}$$

$$= w_0 + \frac{1}{2}|w_0''|r^2\Big[\cos(\alpha + 2\theta) + i\sin(\alpha + 2\theta)\Big] + \cdots. \tag{12.103}$$

For later reference we note that α is the **argument** of $w''(z_0, t)$. We see that, in general at a saddle point, u (the real part of w) will increase most rapidly when $\alpha + 2\theta = 2n\pi$, corresponding to the opposite directions $\theta = -\alpha/2$ and $\theta = -\alpha/2 + \pi$. On the other hand, u will decrease most rapidly when $\alpha + 2\theta = (2n + 1)\pi$, i.e., $\theta = -\alpha/2 + (\frac{1}{2}\pi$ or $\frac{3}{2}\pi)$, the two directions perpendicular to those of maximum increase. And u will (to second order) remain constant (so-called **level lines**) in the directions $\theta = -\alpha/2 + (\frac{1}{4}\pi, \frac{3}{4}\pi, \frac{5}{4}\pi, \frac{7}{4}\pi)$. See the left panel of Fig. 12.5.

The behavior of v (the imaginary part of w) will be similar to that of u, but displaced in angle by 45°. The level lines of v will be in the directions $\theta = -\alpha_s + (0, \pi/2, \pi, 3\pi/2)$, and therefore will coincide with the directions of maximum increase or decrease in u. See the right panel of Fig. 12.5.

We are now ready to identify an optimum contour for evaluating the integral representation of $f(t)$, namely one that passes through the saddle point z_0 in the directions of maximum rate of decrease in u with distance from z_0, and therefore also in $|F|$. These directions have the additional advantage that they are level lines of v, so that the factor e^{iv} will not produce changes of phase (oscillatory behavior and therefore numerical instability) in F as we leave the saddle point. If we had chosen z_0 to be a point other than a saddle point, the expansion of w would have contained a nonzero linear term in r, and it would not have been possible to construct a curve through z_0 that would cause $|F|$ to decrease in both path directions, or to keep the phase of F constant.

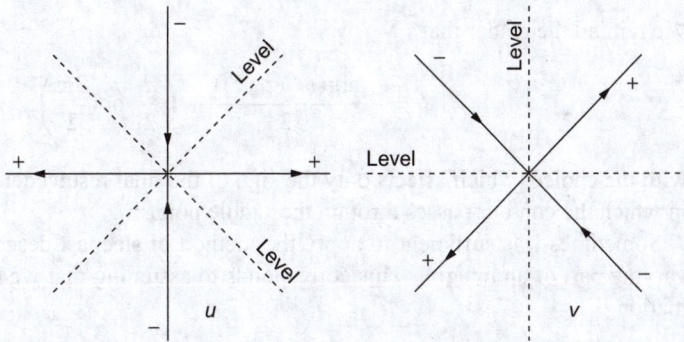

FIGURE 12.5   Near a saddle point in $w = u + iv$: When features of u are oriented as in the left panel, those of v are as shown in the right panel. Arrows indicate ascending directions.

Saddle Point Method

Now that we have identified z_0 and the directions of steepest descent in $|F(z,t)|$, we complete the specification of the method of steepest descents, also called the **saddle point method** of asymptotic approximation, by assuming that the significant contributions to the integral are from a small range of $0 \leq r \leq a$ in each of the two directions along the path. Before obtaining a final result, we must make one more observation. Looking at the way in which the contour had to be deformed to pass through z_0, we need to determine the sense of the path (i.e., we must decide whether the direction of travel is at $\theta = -\alpha/2 + \frac{1}{2}\pi$ or at $\theta = -\alpha/2 + \frac{3}{2}\pi$). Assuming that this has been decided, we can then identify, for the portion of the path in which we descend from $F(z_0)$, $dz = e^{i\theta} dr$. The contribution in which we ascend to $F(z_0)$ will have the opposite sign for dz but we can handle it simply by multiplying the descending contribution by two. Then, noting that $e^{i(\alpha+2\theta)} = -1$, our approximation to $f(t)$ is

$$f(t) \approx 2e^{w_0+i\theta} \int_0^a e^{-|w_0''|r^2/2} dr, \tag{12.104}$$

where the initial "2" causes inclusion of the ascent to z_0. We now make the key assumption of the method, namely that $|w_0''|$, the measure of the rate of decrease in $|F|$ as we leave z_0, is large enough that the bulk of the value of the integral has already been attained for small a, and that the exponential decrease in the value of the integrand enables us to replace a by infinity without making significant error. In problems where the saddle point method is applicable, this condition is met when t is sufficiently large. We complete the present analysis by remembering that $e^{w_0} = F(z_0, t)$ and by evaluating the integral for $a = \infty$, where, cf. Eq. (1.148), it has the value $\sqrt{\pi/2|w_0''|}$. We get

$$f(t) \approx F(z_0, t)e^{i\theta} \sqrt{\frac{2\pi}{|w''(z_0, t)|}}. \tag{12.105}$$

We remind the reader that

$$\theta = -\frac{\arg(w''(z_0, t))}{2} + \left(\frac{\pi}{2} \text{ or } \frac{3\pi}{2}\right), \tag{12.106}$$

with the choice (which affects only the sign of the final result) determined from the sense in which the contour passes through the saddle point z_0.

Sometimes it is sufficient to apply the method of steepest descents only to the rapidly varying part of an integral. This corresponds to assuming that we may make the approximation

$$f(t) = \int_C g(z, t)F(z, t)dz \approx g(z_0, t) \int_C F(z, t)dz, \tag{12.107}$$

after which we proceed as before. Note that this causes g not to be considered when we define w or w'', and our final formula is replaced by

$$f(t) \approx g(z_0, t) F(z_0, t) e^{i\theta} \sqrt{\frac{2\pi}{|w''(z_0, t)|}}. \tag{12.108}$$

A final note of warning: We assumed that the only significant contribution to the integral came from the immediate vicinity of the saddle point $z = z_0$. This condition must be checked for each new problem.

Example 12.7.1   ASYMPTOTIC FORM OF THE GAMMA FUNCTION

In many physical problems, particularly in the field of statistical mechanics, it is desirable to have an accurate approximation of the gamma or factorial function of very large numbers. As listed in Table 1.2, the factorial function may be defined by the Euler integral

$$t! = \Gamma(t+1) = \int_0^\infty \rho^t e^{-\rho} d\rho = t^{t+1} \int_0^\infty e^{t(\ln z - z)} dz. \tag{12.109}$$

Here we have made the substitution $\rho = zt$ in order to convert the integral to the form given in Eq. (12.108). As before, we assume that t is real and positive, from which it follows that the integrand vanishes at the limits 0 and ∞. By differentiating the exponent, which we call $w(z, t)$, we obtain

$$\frac{dw}{dz} = t \frac{d}{dz} (\ln z - z) = \frac{t}{z} - t, \quad w'' = -\frac{t}{z^2},$$

which shows that the point $z = 1$ is a saddle point and $\arg w''(1, t) = \arg(-t) = \pi$. Applying Eq. (12.106), we see that the direction of travel through the saddle point is

$$\theta = -\frac{\arg w''}{2} + \left(\frac{\pi}{2} \text{ or } \frac{3\pi}{2} \right) = 0 \text{ or } \pi;$$

the choice $\theta = 0$ is that consistent with deformation from a path that was originally along the real axis. In fact, what we have found is that the direction of steepest descent is along the real axis, a conclusion that we might have reached more or less intuitively.

Direct substitution into Eq. (12.108) with $g = t^{t+1}$, $F = e^{-t}$, $\theta = 0$, and $|w''| = -t$ yields

$$t! = \Gamma(t+1) \approx \sqrt{\frac{2\pi}{t}} t^{t+1} e^{-t} = \sqrt{2\pi} t^{t+1/2} e^{-t}. \tag{12.110}$$

This result is the leading term in Stirling's expansion of the gamma function. The method of steepest descents is probably the easiest way of obtaining this term. Further terms in the asymptotic expansion are developed in Section 13.4.

In this example the calculation was carried out assuming t to be real. This assumption is not necessary. We may show (Exercise 12.7.3) that Eq. (12.110) also holds when t is complex, provided only that its real part be required to be large and positive. ∎

Sometimes the application of the saddle point method to a real integral results in a contour that goes through a saddle point that is not on the real axis. Here is a relatively simple example. A more complicated case of practical importance appears in the chapter on Bessel functions (see Section 14.6).

Example 12.7.2   SADDLE POINT METHOD AVOIDS OSCILLATIONS

As a second example of the method of steepest descents, consider the integral

$$H(t) = \int_{-\infty}^{\infty} \frac{e^{-t(z^2-1/4)} \cos tz}{1+z^2} dz, \tag{12.111}$$

which we wish to evaluate for large positive t. When t is large, the integrand oscillates very rapidly, and ordinary quadrature methods become difficult. We proceed by bringing $H(t)$ to a form appropriate for applying the saddle point method, replacing $\cos tz$ by $\cos tz + i \sin tz = e^{itz}$ (a replacement that does not change the value of the integral because we added an odd term to the previously even integrand). We then have

$$H(t) = \int_C g(z) e^{-t(z^2-iz-1/4)} dz, \tag{12.112}$$

with $g(z) = 1/(1 + z^2)$. This form corresponds to $w(z) = -t(z^2 - iz - \frac{1}{4})$, so we have

$$w'(z) = -t(2z - i), \quad \text{which has a zero at } z_0 = i/2. \tag{12.113}$$

Then, at z_0, which is a saddle point,

$$w_0 = 0, \quad w''(z_0) = -2t, \quad g(z_0) = \frac{4}{3}. \tag{12.114}$$

We also need the phase θ of the steepest-descent direction. Noting that $\arg(w''(z_0)) = \pi$ and applying Eq. (12.106), we find $\theta = 0$ (or π).

We are now ready to apply Eq. (12.108). The result is

$$H(t) \approx \frac{\sqrt{2\pi}(4/3)(e^0)}{|-2t|} = \frac{4}{3}\sqrt{\frac{\pi}{t}}. \tag{12.115}$$

As a check, we compare this approximate formula for $H(t)$ with the result of a tedious numerical integration: For $t = 100$, $H_{\text{exact}} = 0.23284$, and $H_{\text{saddle}} = 0.23633$. ∎

Exercises

We present here a rather small number of exercises on the method of steepest descents. Several additional exercises appear elsewhere in this book, in particular in Section 14.6, where the technique is applied to the contour integral representations of Bessel functions.

12.7.1   Prove Jensen's theorem (that $|F(z)|^2$ can have no extremum in the interior of a region in which F is analytic) by showing that the mean value of $|F|^2$ on a circle about any point z_0 is equal to $|F(z_0)|^2$. Explain why you can then conclude that there cannot be an extremum of $|F|$ at z_0.

12.7.2   Find the steepest path and leading asymptotic expansion for the Fresnel integrals
$$\int_0^s \cos x^2 dx, \quad \int_0^s \sin x^2 dx.$$

Hint. Use $\int_0^1 e^{itz^2} dz$.

12.7.3   Show that the formula
$$\Gamma(1+s) \approx \sqrt{2\pi s} \, s^s e^{-s}$$

holds for complex values of s (with $\Re e(s)$ large and positive).

Hint. This involves assigning a phase to s and then demanding that $\Im m[sf(z)]$ be constant in the vicinity of the saddle point.

12.8   DISPERSION RELATIONS

The concept of dispersion relations entered physics with the work of Kronig and Kramers in optics. The name **dispersion** comes from optical dispersion, a result of the dependence of the index of refraction on wavelength, or angular frequency. As we shall soon see, the index of refraction n may have a real part determined by the phase velocity and a (negative) imaginary part determined by the absorption. Kronig and Kramers showed in 1926–1927 that the real part of $(n^2 - 1)$ could be expressed as an integral of the imaginary part. Generalizing this, we shall apply the label **dispersion relations** to any pair of equations giving the real part of a function as an integral of its imaginary part and the imaginary part as an integral of its real part (we develop this in more detail below). The existence of such integral relations might be suspected as an integral analog of the Cauchy-Riemann differential equations, Eq. (11.9).

The applications in modern physics are widespread. For instance, the real part of the function might describe the forward scattering of a gamma ray in a nuclear Coulomb field (a dispersive process). Then the imaginary part would describe the electron-positron pair production in that same Coulomb field (the absorptive process). As will be seen later, the dispersion relations may be taken as a consequence of causality and therefore are independent of the details of the particular interaction.

We consider a complex function $f(z)$ that is analytic in the upper half-plane and on the real axis. We also require that $f(z)$ approach zero for large $|z|$ in the upper half-plane sufficiently rapidly that its integral over the semicircular part of the contour in Fig. 12.6 will be negligible. The point of these conditions is that we may express $f(z)$ by the Cauchy integral formula, Eq. (11.30), using this contour, obtaining

$$f(z_0) = \frac{1}{2\pi i} \int_{-\infty}^{\infty} \frac{f(x)}{x - z_0} dx. \tag{12.116}$$

The integral over the contour shown in Fig. 12.6 has become an integral along the x-axis.

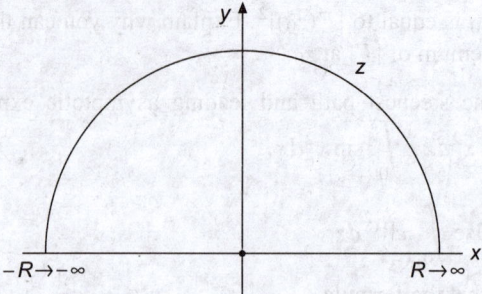

FIGURE 12.6   Contour for dispersion integral.

Equation (12.116) assumes that z_0 is in the upper half-plane, interior to the closed contour. If z_0 were in the lower half-plane, the integral would yield zero by the Cauchy integral theorem, Section 11.3. Now, if we move z_0 onto the real axis (then calling it x_0) and pass it via a small clockwise semicircle s in the upper half-plane, the contour integral (which would contain no singularities) would have nonzero contributions corresponding to a Cauchy principal value integral **minus** half the usual contribution from the pole at x_0, or

$$0 = \fint \frac{f(x)}{x - x_0} dx + \int_s \frac{f(z)}{z - x_0} dz$$

$$= \fint \frac{f(x)}{x - x_0} dx - \pi i f(x_0),$$

equivalent to the final formula

$$f(x_0) = \frac{1}{\pi i} \fint_{-\infty}^{\infty} \frac{f(x)}{x - x_0} dx. \tag{12.117}$$

Note that the cut integral sign denotes the Cauchy principal value. Splitting Eq. (12.117) into real and imaginary parts[6] yields

$$f(x_0) = u(x_0) + i v(x_0)$$

$$= \frac{1}{\pi} \fint_{-\infty}^{\infty} \frac{v(x)}{x - x_0} dx - \frac{i}{\pi} \fint_{-\infty}^{\infty} \frac{u(x)}{x - x_0} dx.$$

Finally, equating real part to real part and imaginary part to imaginary part, we obtain

$$u(x_0) = \frac{1}{\pi} \fint_{-\infty}^{\infty} \frac{v(x)}{x - x_0} dx,$$

$$\tag{12.118}$$

$$v(x_0) = -\frac{1}{\pi} \fint_{-\infty}^{\infty} \frac{u(x)}{x - x_0} dx.$$

---

[6]The second argument, $y = 0$, is dropped: $u(x_0, 0) \to u(x_0)$.

These are the **dispersion relations**. The real part of our complex function is expressed as an integral over the imaginary part. The imaginary part is expressed as an integral over the real part. Alternatively, the real part can be called an integral transform of the imaginary part (and vice versa); the particular transform involved is known as a **Hilbert transform**, and we note that (apart from a minus sign) the Hilbert transform is its own inverse. Note that these relations are meaningful only when $f(x)$ is a complex function of the real variable x. Compare Exercise 12.8.1.

From a physical point of view $u(x)$ and/or $v(x)$ may represent some physical measurements. Then $f(z) = u(z) + iv(z)$ is an analytic continuation over the upper half-plane, with the value on the real axis serving as a boundary condition.

Symmetry Relations

On occasion $f(x)$ will satisfy a symmetry relation and the integral from $-\infty$ to $+\infty$ may be replaced by an integral over positive values only. This is of considerable physical importance because the variable x might represent a frequency and only zero and positive frequencies are available for physical measurements. Suppose[7]

$$f(-x) = f^*(x). \tag{12.119}$$

Then

$$u(-x) + iv(-x) = u(x) - iv(x). \tag{12.120}$$

The real part of $f(x)$ is even and the imaginary part is odd.[8] In quantum mechanical scattering problems these relations, Eq. (12.120), are called **crossing conditions**. To exploit these crossing conditions, we rewrite the first of Eqs. (12.118) as

$$u(x_0) = \frac{1}{\pi} \int_{-\infty}^{0} \frac{v(x)}{x - x_0} dx + \frac{1}{\pi} \int_{0}^{\infty} \frac{v(x)}{x - x_0} dx. \tag{12.121}$$

Letting $x \to -x$ in the first integral on the right-hand side of Eq. (12.121) and substituting $v(-x) = -v(x)$ from Eq. (12.120), we obtain

$$u(x_0) = \frac{1}{\pi} \int_{0}^{\infty} v(x) \left(\frac{1}{x + x_0} + \frac{1}{x - x_0} \right) dx$$

$$= \frac{2}{\pi} \int_{0}^{\infty} \frac{x v(x)}{x^2 - x_0^2} dx. \tag{12.122}$$

---

[7]This is not just a curiosity. It ensures that the Fourier transform of $f(x)$ will be real. Or conversely, Eq. (12.119) is a consequence when $f(x)$ is obtained as the Fourier transform of a real function.

[8]$u(x, 0) = u(-x, 0)$, $v(x, 0) = -v(-x, 0)$. Compare these symmetry conditions with those that follow from the Schwarz reflection principle, Section 11.10.

Similarly,

$$^\bullet v(x_0) = -\frac{2}{\pi}\fint_0^\infty \frac{x_0 u(x)}{x^2 - x_0^2}\,dx. \tag{12.123}$$

The original Kronig-Kramers optical dispersion relations were in this form. The asymptotic behavior ($x_0 \to \infty$) of Eqs. (12.122) and (12.123) lead to quantum mechanical **sum rules**. See Exercise 12.8.4.

Optical Dispersion

The function $\exp[i(kx - \omega t)]$ can describe an electromagnetic wave moving along the x-axis in the positive direction with velocity $v = \omega/k$; ω is the angular frequency, k the wave number or propagation vector, and $n = ck/\omega$, the index of refraction. From Maxwell's equations with electric permittivity ε and magnetic permeability unity, and using Ohm's law with conductivity σ, the propagation vector k for a dielectric becomes[9]

$$k^2 = \varepsilon\frac{\omega^2}{c^2}\left(1 + i\frac{4\pi\sigma}{\omega\varepsilon}\right). \tag{12.124}$$

The presence of the conductivity (which means absorption) causes k^2 to have an imaginary part. The propagation vector k (and therefore the index of refraction n) have become complex.

For poor conductivity ($4\pi\sigma/\omega\varepsilon \ll 1$) a binomial expansion yields

$$k = \sqrt{\varepsilon}\frac{\omega}{c} + i\frac{2\pi\sigma}{c\sqrt{\varepsilon}}$$

and

$$e^{i(kx-\omega t)} = e^{i\omega(x\sqrt{\varepsilon}/c - t)}e^{-2\pi\sigma x/c\sqrt{\varepsilon}},$$

an attenuated wave.

Returning to the general expression for k^2, Eq. (12.124), we find that the index of refraction becomes

$$n^2 = \frac{c^2 k^2}{\omega^2} = \varepsilon + i\frac{4\pi\sigma}{\omega}. \tag{12.125}$$

We take n^2 to be a function of the **complex** variable ω (with ε and σ depending on ω). However, n^2 does not vanish as $\omega \to \infty$ but instead approaches unity. It therefore does not satisfy the condition needed for a dispersion relation, but this difficulty can be circumvented by working with $f(\omega) = n^2(\omega) - 1$. The Kronig-Kramers relations then take

---

[9]See J. D. Jackson, *Classical Electrodynamics*, 3rd ed. New York: Wiley (1999), Sections 7.7 and 7.10. Equation (12.124) is in Gaussian units.

the form

$$\Re e[n^2(\omega_0) - 1] = \frac{2}{\pi} \fint_0^\infty \frac{\omega \Im m[n^2(\omega) - 1]}{\omega^2 - \omega_0^2} d\omega,$$

(12.126)

$$\Im m[n^2(\omega_0) - 1] = -\frac{2}{\pi} \fint_0^\infty \frac{\omega_0 \Re e[n^2(\omega) - 1]}{\omega^2 - \omega_0^2} d\omega.$$

Knowledge of the absorption coefficient at all frequencies specifies the real part of the index of refraction, and vice versa.

The Parseval Relation

When the functions $u(x)$ and $v(x)$ are Hilbert transforms of each other, given by Eqs. (12.118), and each is square integrable,[10] the two functions satisfy the scaling condition

$$\int_{-\infty}^\infty |u(x)|^2 dx = \int_{-\infty}^\infty |v(x)|^2 dx.$$

(12.127)

This is the Parseval relation.

To derive Eq. (12.127), we start with

$$\int_{-\infty}^\infty |u(x)|^2 dx = \int_{-\infty}^\infty dx \left[\frac{1}{\pi} \fint_{-\infty}^\infty \frac{v(s)ds}{s - x} \right] \left[\frac{1}{\pi} \fint_{-\infty}^\infty \frac{v(t)dt}{t - x} \right],$$

using the formula for $u(x)$ from Eq. (12.118) twice. Integrating first with respect to x, we have

$$\int_{-\infty}^\infty |u(x)|^2 dx = \int_{-\infty}^\infty v(s)ds \int_{-\infty}^\infty v(t)dt \frac{1}{\pi^2} \fint_{-\infty}^\infty \frac{dx}{(s - x)(t - x)},$$

(12.128)

where both principal-value limits at the singularities of the integrand must now be taken for the x integration. As shown in Exercise 12.8.8, that integration yields a delta function[11]:

$$\frac{1}{\pi^2} \fint_{-\infty}^\infty \frac{dx}{(s - x)(t - x)} = \delta(s - t).$$

Thus,

$$\int_{-\infty}^\infty |u(x)|^2 dx = \int_{-\infty}^\infty v(t)dt \int_{-\infty}^\infty v(s)\delta(s - t)ds.$$

(12.129)

---

[10]This means that $\int_{-\infty}^\infty |u(x)|^2 dx$ and $\int_{-\infty}^\infty |v(x)|^2 dx$ are finite.

[11]Note that when $s = t$, the integrand has the same sign (for small ε) at $x = s - \varepsilon$ and at $x = s + \varepsilon$, so the limit defining the principal value then does not exist. The singularity in the integration is that which is needed to represent a delta function.

Then the s integration is carried out by inspection, using the defining property of the delta function:

$$\int_{-\infty}^{\infty} v(s)\delta(s-t)ds = v(t). \qquad (12.130)$$

Substituting Eq. (12.130) into Eq. (12.129), we have Eq. (12.127), the Parseval relation. Again, in terms of optics, the presence of refraction over some frequency range ($n \neq 1$) implies the existence of absorption, and vice versa.

Exercises

12.8.1   Assume that the function $f(z)$ satisfies the conditions for the dispersion relations. In addition, assume that $f(z) = f^*(z^*)$, i.e., that it meets the conditions of the Schwarz reflection principle, Eq. (11.127). Show that $f(z)$ is identically zero.

12.8.2   For $f(z)$ such that we may replace the closed contour of the Cauchy integral formula by an integral over the real axis we have

$$f(x_0) = \frac{1}{2\pi i}\left\{\int_{-\infty}^{x_0-\delta} \frac{f(x)}{x-x_0}dx + \int_{x_0+\delta}^{\infty} \frac{f(x)}{x-x_0}dx\right\} + \frac{1}{2\pi i}\int_{C} \frac{f(x)}{x-x_0}dx.$$

Here we take C to be a small semicircle about x_0 in the lower half-plane. Show that the formula for $f(x_0)$ reduces to

$$f(x_0) = \frac{1}{\pi i}\fint_{-\infty}^{\infty} \frac{f(x)}{x-x_0}dx,$$

which is Eq. (12.117).

12.8.3   (a)   The function $f(z) = e^{iz}$ does not vanish at the endpoints of the range of $\arg z$, a and π. Show, with the help of Jordan's lemma, Eq. (11.102), that Eq. (12.116) still holds.

(b)   For $f(z) = e^{iz}$ verify by direct integration the dispersion relations, Eq. (12.117) or Eqs. (12.118).

12.8.4   With $f(x) = u(x) + iv(x)$ and $f(x) = f^*(-x)$, show that as $x_0 \to \infty$,

(a) $u(x_0) \sim -\dfrac{2}{\pi x_0^2}\displaystyle\int_0^{\infty} xv(x)dx,$

(b) $v(x_0) \sim \dfrac{2}{\pi x_0}\displaystyle\int_0^{\infty} u(x)dx.$

In quantum mechanics relations of this form are often called **sum rules**.

12.8.5 (a) Given the integral equation (valid for all real x_0)

$$\frac{1}{1+x_0^2} = \frac{1}{\pi} \int\limits_{-\infty}^{\infty} \frac{u(x)}{x - x_0} dx,$$

use Hilbert transforms to determine $u(x_0)$.

(b) Verify that the $u(x_0)$ found as your answer to part (a) actually satisfies the integral equation.

(c) From $f(z)\,|_{y=0} = u(x) + iv(x)$, replace x by z and determine $f(z)$. Verify that the conditions for the Hilbert transforms are satisfied.

(d) Are the crossing conditions satisfied?

ANS. (a) $u(x_0) = \dfrac{x_0}{1 + x_0^2}$,   (c) $f(z) = (z + i)^{-1}$.

12.8.6 (a) If the real part of the complex index of refraction (squared) is constant (no optical dispersion), show that the imaginary part is zero (no absorption).

(b) Conversely, if there is absorption, show that there must be dispersion. In other words, if the imaginary part of $n^2 - 1$ is not zero, show that the real part of $n^2 - 1$ is not constant.

12.8.7 Given $u(x) = x/(x^2 + 1)$ and $v(x) = -1/(x^2 + 1)$, show by direct evaluation of each integral that

$$\int\limits_{-\infty}^{\infty} |u(x)|^2 dx = \int\limits_{-\infty}^{\infty} |v(x)|^2 dx.$$

ANS. $\displaystyle\int_{-\infty}^{\infty} |u(x)|^2 dx = \int_{-\infty}^{\infty} |v(x)|^2 dx = \frac{\pi}{2}$.

12.8.8 Take $u(x) = \delta(x)$, a delta function, and **assume** that the Hilbert transform equations hold.

(a) Show that

$$\delta(w) = \frac{1}{\pi^2} \int\limits_{-\infty}^{\infty} \frac{dy}{y(y - w)}.$$

(b) With changes of variables $w = s - t$ and $x = s - y$, transform the δ representation of part (a) into

$$\delta(s - t) = \frac{1}{\pi^2} \int\limits_{-\infty}^{\infty} \frac{dx}{(x - s)(x - t)}.$$

Note. The δ function is discussed in Section 1.11.

Additional Readings

Abramowitz, M., and I. A. Stegun, eds., *Handbook of Mathematical Functions with Formulas, Graphs, and Mathematical Tables* (AMS-55). Washington, DC: National Bureau of Standards (1972), reprinted, Dover (1974).

Lewin, L., *Polylogarithms and Associated Functions*. New York: North-Holland (1981). This is a definitive resource for the dilogarithm and its generalizations up through its publication date. It is clear and no more difficult than necessary.

McBride, E. B., *Obtaining Generating Functions*. New York: Springer-Verlag (1971). An introduction to methods of obtaining generating functions, both for sets of functions arising from ODEs and for those that do not.

Nussenzveig, H. M., *Causality and Dispersion Relations*, Mathematics in Science and Engineering Series, Vol. 95. New York: Academic Press (1972). This is an advanced text covering causality and dispersion relations in the first chapter and then moving on to develop implications in a variety of areas of theoretical physics.

Talman, J. D., *Special Functions*. New York: W. A. Benjamin (1968). Develops the theory of a number of special functions using their underlying group-theoretical properties, including presentation of their generating functions.

Wyld, H. W., *Mathematical Methods for Physics*. Reading, MA: Benjamin/Cummings (1976), Perseus Books (1999). This is a relatively advanced text that contains an extensive discussion of dispersion relations.

CHAPTER 13

GAMMA FUNCTION

The gamma function is probably the special function that occurs most frequently in the discussion of problems in physics. For integer values, as the factorial function, it appears in every Taylor expansion. As we shall later see, it also occurs frequently with half-integer arguments, and is needed for general nonintegral values in the expansion of many functions, e.g., Bessel functions of noninteger order.

It has been shown that the gamma function is one of a general class of functions that do not satisfy any differential equation with rational coefficients. Specifically, the gamma function is one of very few functions of mathematical physics that do not satisfy either the hypergeometric differential equation (Section 18.5) or the confluent hypergeometric equation (Section 18.6). Since most physical theories involve quantities governed by differential equations, the gamma function (by itself) does not usually describe a physical quantity of interest, but rather tends to appear as a factor in expansions of physically relevant quantities.

13.1 DEFINITIONS, PROPERTIES

At least three different convenient definitions of the gamma function are in common use. Our first task is to state these definitions, to develop some simple, direct consequences, and to show the equivalence of the three forms.

Infinite Limit (Euler)

The first definition, named after Euler, is

$$\Gamma(z) \equiv \lim_{n \to \infty} \frac{1 \cdot 2 \cdot 3 \cdots n}{z(z+1)(z+2) \cdots (z+n)} n^z, \quad z \neq 0, -1, -2, -3, \dots. \tag{13.1}$$

This definition of $\Gamma(z)$ is useful in developing the Weierstrass infinite-product form of $\Gamma(z)$, Eq. (13.16), and in obtaining the derivative of $\ln \Gamma(z)$ (Section 13.2). Here and elsewhere in this chapter z may be either real or complex. Replacing z with $z+1$, we have

$$\Gamma(z+1) = \lim_{n \to \infty} \frac{1 \cdot 2 \cdot 3 \cdots n}{(z+1)(z+2)(z+3) \cdots (z+n+1)} n^{z+1}$$

$$= \lim_{n \to \infty} \frac{nz}{z+n+1} \cdot \frac{1 \cdot 2 \cdot 3 \cdots n}{z(z+1)(z+2) \cdots (z+n)} n^{z}$$

$$= z\Gamma(z). \tag{13.2}$$

This is the basic functional relation for the gamma function. It should be noted that it is a **difference** equation.

Also, from the definition,

$$\Gamma(1) = \lim_{n \to \infty} \frac{1 \cdot 2 \cdot 3 \cdots n}{1 \cdot 2 \cdot 3 \cdots n(n+1)} n = 1. \tag{13.3}$$

Now, repeated application of Eq. (13.2) gives

$$\Gamma(2) = 1,$$

$$\Gamma(3) = 2\,\Gamma(2) = 2,$$

$$\Gamma(4) = 3\,\Gamma(3) = 2 \cdot 3, \quad \text{etc.,}$$

so

$$\Gamma(n) = 1 \cdot 2 \cdot 3 \cdots (n-1) = (n-1)!. \tag{13.4}$$

Definite Integral (Euler)

A second definition, also frequently called the Euler integral, and already presented in Table 1.2, is

$$\Gamma(z) \equiv \int_0^\infty e^{-t} t^{z-1} dt, \quad \Re e(z) > 0. \tag{13.5}$$

The restriction on z is necessary to avoid divergence of the integral. When the gamma function does appear in physical problems, it is often in this form or some variation, such as

$$\Gamma(z) = 2 \int_0^\infty e^{-t^2} t^{2z-1} dt, \quad \Re e(z) > 0, \tag{13.6}$$

or

$$\Gamma(z) = \int_0^1 \left[\ln\left(\frac{1}{t}\right) \right]^{z-1} dt, \quad \Re e(z) > 0. \tag{13.7}$$

When $z = \frac{1}{2}$, Eq. (13.6) is just the Gauss error integral, and, cf. Eq. (1.148), we have the interesting result

$$\Gamma\left(\frac{1}{2}\right) = \sqrt{\pi}. \tag{13.8}$$

Generalizations of Eq. (13.6), the Gaussian integrals, are considered in Exercise 13.1.10.

To show the equivalence of these two definitions, Eqs. (13.1) and (13.5), consider the function of two variables

$$F(z, n) = \int_0^n \left(1 - \frac{t}{n}\right)^n t^{z-1} dt, \quad \Re e(z) > 0, \tag{13.9}$$

with n a positive integer. This form was chosen because the exponential has the definition

$$\lim_{n \to \infty} \left(1 - \frac{t}{n}\right)^n \equiv e^{-t}. \tag{13.10}$$

Inserting Eq. (13.10) into Eq. (13.9), we see that the infinite-n limit of $F(z, n)$ corresponds to $\Gamma(z)$ as given by Eq. (13.5):

$$\lim_{n \to \infty} F(z, n) = F(z, \infty) = \int_0^\infty e^{-t} t^{z-1} dt \equiv \Gamma(z). \tag{13.11}$$

Our remaining task is to identify this limit also with Eq. (13.1).

Returning to $F(z, n)$, we evaluate it by carrying out successive integrations by parts. For convenience we make the substitution $u = t/n$. Then

$$F(z, n) = n^z \int_0^1 (1 - u)^n u^{z-1} du. \tag{13.12}$$

The first integration by parts yields

$$\frac{F(z, n)}{n^z} = (1 - u)^n \frac{u^z}{z} \Big|_0^1 + \frac{n}{z} \int_0^1 (1 - u)^{n-1} u^z du; \tag{13.13}$$

note that (because $z \neq 0$) the integrated part vanishes at both endpoints. Repeating this n times, with the integrated part vanishing at both endpoints each time, we finally get

$$F(z, n) = n^z \frac{n(n - 1) \cdots 1}{z(z + 1) \cdots (z + n - 1)} \int_0^1 u^{z+n-1} du$$

$$= \frac{1 \cdot 2 \cdot 3 \cdots n}{z(z + 1)(z + 2) \cdots (z + n)} n^z. \tag{13.14}$$

This is identical with the expression on the right side of Eq. (13.1). Hence

$$\lim_{n \to \infty} F(z, n) = F(z, \infty) \equiv \Gamma(z),$$

where $\Gamma(z)$ is in the form given by Eq. (13.1), thereby completing the proof.

Infinite Product (Weierstrass)

The third definition (Weierstrass' form) is the infinite product

$$\frac{1}{\Gamma(z)} \equiv z e^{\gamma z} \prod_{n=1}^{\infty} \left(1 + \frac{z}{n}\right) e^{-z/n}, \tag{13.15}$$

where γ is the Euler-Mascheroni constant

$$\gamma = 0.5772156619 \cdots, \tag{13.16}$$

which was introduced as a limit in Eq. (1.13). Existence of the limit was the topic of Exercise 1.2.13.

This infinite-product form is useful for proving various properties of $\Gamma(z)$. It can be derived from the original definition, Eq. (13.1), by rewriting it as

$$\Gamma(z) = \lim_{n \to \infty} \frac{1 \cdot 2 \cdot 3 \cdots n}{z(z+1) \cdots (z+n)} n^z = \lim_{n \to \infty} \frac{1}{z} \prod_{m=1}^{n} \left(1 + \frac{z}{m}\right)^{-1} n^z. \tag{13.17}$$

Taking the reciprocal of Eq. (13.17) and using

$$n^{-z} = e^{(-\ln n)z}, \tag{13.18}$$

we obtain

$$\frac{1}{\Gamma(z)} = z \lim_{n \to \infty} e^{(-\ln n)z} \prod_{m=1}^{n} \left(1 + \frac{z}{m}\right). \tag{13.19}$$

Multiplying and dividing the right-hand side of Eq. (13.19) by

$$\exp\left[\left(1 + \frac{1}{2} + \frac{1}{3} + \cdots + \frac{1}{n}\right) z\right] = \prod_{m=1}^{n} e^{z/m}, \tag{13.20}$$

we get

$$\frac{1}{\Gamma(z)} = z \left\{ \lim_{n \to \infty} \exp\left[\left(1 + \frac{1}{2} + \frac{1}{3} + \cdots + \frac{1}{n} - \ln n\right) z\right]\right\}$$

$$\times \left[\lim_{n \to \infty} \prod_{m=1}^{n} \left(1 + \frac{z}{m}\right) e^{-z/m}\right]. \tag{13.21}$$

Comparing with Eq. (1.13), we see that the parenthesized quantity in the exponent approaches as a limit the Euler-Mascheroni constant, thereby confirming Eq. (13.15).

Functional Relations

In Eq. (13.2) we already obtained the most important functional relation for the gamma function,

$$\Gamma(z+1) = z\,\Gamma(z). \tag{13.22}$$

Viewed as a complex-valued function, this formula permits the extension to negative z of values obtained via numerical evaluation of the integral representation, Eq. (13.5). While the Euler limit formula already tells us that $\Gamma(z)$ is an analytic function for all z except 0, $-1, \ldots$, stepwise extrapolation from the integral is a more efficient numerical approach.

The gamma function satisfies several other functional relations, of which one of the most interesting is the **reflection formula**,

$$\Gamma(z)\Gamma(1-z) = \frac{\pi}{\sin z\pi}. \tag{13.23}$$

This relation connects (for nonintegral z) values of $\Gamma(z)$ that are related by reflection about the line $z = 1/2$.

One way to prove the reflection formula starts from the product of Euler integrals,

$$\Gamma(z+1)\Gamma(1-z) = \int_0^\infty s^z e^{-s}\,ds \int_0^\infty t^{-z} e^{-t}\,dt$$

$$= \int_0^\infty \frac{v^z\,dv}{(v+1)^2} \int_0^\infty u\,e^{-u}\,du. \tag{13.24}$$

In obtaining the second line of Eq. (13.24) we transformed from the variables s, t to $u = s+t$, $v = s/t$, as suggested by combining the exponentials and the powers in the integrands. We also needed to insert the Jacobian of this transformation,

$$J^{-1} = - \begin{vmatrix} 1 & 1 \\ \dfrac{1}{t} & -\dfrac{s}{t^2} \end{vmatrix} = \frac{s+t}{t^2} = \frac{(v+1)^2}{u}\,;$$

the final substitution becomes obvious if we note that $v + 1 = u/t$.

Returning to Eq. (13.24), the u integration is elementary, being equal to 1!, while the v integration can be evaluated by contour-integration methods; it was the topic of Exercise 11.8.20, and has the value

$$\int_0^\infty \frac{v^z\,dv}{(v+1)^2} = \frac{\pi z}{\sin \pi z}. \tag{13.25}$$

Using these results, and then replacing $\Gamma(z+1)$ in Eq. (13.24) by $z\Gamma(z)$ and canceling z from the two sides of the resulting equation, we complete the demonstration of Eq. (13.23).

A special case of Eq. (13.23) results if we set $z = 1/2$. Then (taking the positive square root), we get

$$\Gamma\left(\tfrac{1}{2}\right) = \sqrt{\pi}, \tag{13.26}$$

in agreement with Eq. (13.8).

Another functional relation is **Legendre's duplication formula,**

$$\Gamma(1+z)\,\Gamma\left(z+\frac{1}{2}\right) = 2^{-2z}\sqrt{\pi}\ \Gamma(2z+1), \tag{13.27}$$

which we prove for general z in Section 13.3. However, it is instructive to prove it now for integer values of z. Assuming z to be a nonnegative integer n, we start the proof by writing $\Gamma(n+1) = n!$, $\Gamma(2n+1) = (2n)!$, and

$$\Gamma\left(n+\frac{1}{2}\right) = \Gamma\left(\frac{1}{2}\right) \cdot \left[\frac{1}{2} \cdot \frac{3}{2} \cdots \frac{2n-1}{2}\right] = \sqrt{\pi}\,\frac{1 \cdot 3 \cdots (2n-1)}{2^n} = \sqrt{\pi}\,\frac{(2n-1)!!}{2^n},$$
$$\tag{13.28}$$

where we have used Eq. (13.26) and the double factorial notation first introduced in Eqs. (1.75) and (1.76). The double factorial notation is used frequently enough in physics applications that a familiarity with it is essential, and will from here on be used without comment. Making the further observation that $n! = 2^{-n}(2n)!!$, Eq. (13.27) follows directly.

Incidentally, we call attention to the fact that gamma functions with half-integer arguments appear frequently in physics problems, and Eq. (13.28) shows how to write them in closed form.

Analytic Properties

The Weierstrass definition shows immediately that $\Gamma(z)$ has simple poles at $z = 0, -1, -2, -3, \ldots$ and that $[\Gamma(z)]^{-1}$ has no poles in the finite complex plane, which means that $\Gamma(z)$ has no zeros. This behavior may also be seen in Eq. (13.23), if we note that $\pi/(\sin \pi z)$ is never equal to zero. A plot of $\Gamma(z)$ for real z is shown in Fig. 13.1. We note sign changes for each unit interval of negative z, that $\Gamma(1) = \Gamma(2) = 1$, and that the gamma function has a minimum between $z = 1$ and $z = 2$, at $z_0 = 0.46143\ldots$, with $\Gamma(z_0) = 0.88560\ldots$. The residues R_n at the poles $z = -n$ (n an integer ≥ 0) are

$$R_n = \lim_{\varepsilon \to 0}\left(\varepsilon\,\Gamma(-n+\varepsilon)\right) = \lim_{\varepsilon \to 0}\frac{\varepsilon\,\Gamma(-n+1+\varepsilon)}{-n+\varepsilon} = \lim_{\varepsilon \to 0}\frac{\varepsilon\,\Gamma(-n+2+\varepsilon)}{(-n+\varepsilon)(-n+1+\varepsilon)}$$

$$= \lim_{\varepsilon \to 0}\frac{\varepsilon\,\Gamma(1+\varepsilon)}{(-n+\varepsilon)\cdots(\varepsilon)} = \frac{(-1)^n}{n!}, \tag{13.29}$$

showing that the residues alternate in sign, with that at $z = -n$ having magnitude $1/n!$.

Schlaefli Integral

A contour integral representation of the gamma function that we will find useful in developing asymptotic series for the Bessel functions is the **Schlaefli integral**

$$\int_C e^{-t}t^\nu\,dt = (e^{2\pi i\nu} - 1)\,\Gamma(\nu+1), \tag{13.30}$$

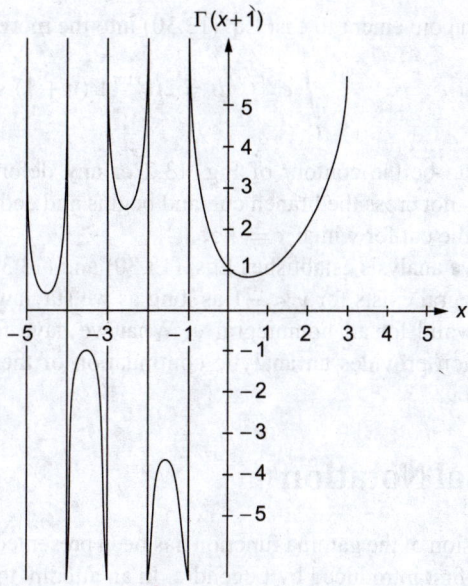

FIGURE 13.1   Gamma function $\Gamma(x+1)$ for real x.

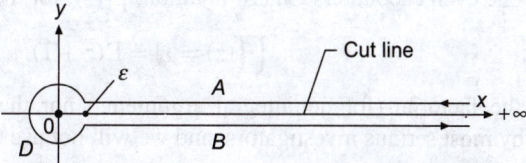

FIGURE 13.2   Gamma function contour.

where C is the contour shown in Fig. 13.2. This contour integral representation is only useful when ν is not an integer. For integer ν, the integrand is an entire function; both sides of Eq. (13.30) vanish and it yields no information. However, for noninteger ν, $t = 0$ is a branch point of the integrand and the right-hand side of Eq. (13.30) then evaluates to a nonzero result. Note that, unlike the contour representations we considered in earlier chapters, the present contour is open; we cannot close it at $z = +\infty$ because of the branch cut, nor can we close it with a large circle, as e^{-t} becomes infinite in the limit of large negative t.

To verify Eq. (13.30), we proceed (for $\nu + 1 > 0$) by evaluating the contributions from the various parts of the integration path. The integral from ∞ to $+\varepsilon$ on the real axis yields $-\Gamma(\nu + 1)$, choosing $\arg(z) = 0$. The integral $+\varepsilon$ to ∞ (in the fourth quadrant) then yields $e^{2\pi i \nu}\Gamma(\nu + 1)$, the argument of z having increased to 2π. Since the circle around the origin contributes nothing when $\nu > -1$, Eq. (13.30) follows. Now that this equation is established, we can deform the contour as desired (providing that we avoid the branch point and cut), since there are no other singularities we must avoid.

It is often convenient to cast Eq. (13.30) into the more symmetrical form

$$\int_C e^{-t} t^\nu \, dt = 2i e^{i\nu\pi} \Gamma(\nu + 1) \sin(\nu\pi),$$ (13.31)

where C can be the contour of Fig. 13.2 or any deformation thereof that encircles the origin, does not cross the branch cut, and begins and ends at any points respectively above and below the cut for which $x = +\infty$.

The above analysis establishes Eqs. (13.30) and (13.31) for $\nu > -1$. However, we note that the integral exists for $\nu < -1$ as long as we stay away from the origin, and therefore it remains valid for all nonintegral ν. What we have found is that this contour integral representation provides an analytic continuation of the Euler integral, Eq. (13.5), to all nonintegral ν.

Factorial Notation

Our discussion of the gamma function has been presented in terms of the classical notation, which was first introduced by Legendre. In an attempt to make a closer correspondence to the factorial notation (traditionally used for integers), and to simplify the Euler integral representation of the gamma function, Eq. (13.5), some authors have chosen to use the notation $z!$ as a synonym for $\Gamma(z + 1)$ even when z has an arbitrary complex value. Occasionally one even encounters Gauss' notation, $\prod(z)$, for the factorial function:

$$\prod(z) = z! = \Gamma(z + 1).$$

Neither the factorial (for nonintegral arguments) nor the Gauss notation are currently favored by most serious investigators, and we will not use them in this book.

Example 13.1.1   MAXWELL-BOLTZMANN DISTRIBUTION

In classical statistical mechanics, a state of energy E is occupied, according to the equation of Maxwell-Boltzmann statistics, with a probability proportional to $e^{-E/kT}$, where k is Boltzmann's constant and T is the absolute temperature; it is usual to define $\beta = 1/kT$ and to write the probability of occupancy of a state of energy E as $p(E) = Ce^{-\beta E}$. If the number of states in a small energy interval dE at energy E is given, using a density distribution function $n(E)$, as $n(E)\,dE$, then the total probability of states at energy E assumes the form $Cn(E)e^{-\beta E}\,dE$. Under those conditions, the total probability of occupancy in **any** state (namely, unity) must be

$$1 = C \int n(E) e^{-\beta E} \, dE,$$ (13.32)

which enables us to set the **normalization constant** C, and the average energy $\langle E \rangle$ of such a classical system will be

$$\langle E \rangle = C \int E n(E) e^{-\beta E} \, dE.$$ (13.33)

For a structureless ideal gas, it can be shown that $n(E)$ is proportional to $E^{1/2}$, with E, the kinetic energy of a gas molecule, in the range $(0, \infty)$. Then we may find C from

$$1 = C \int_0^\infty E^{1/2} e^{-\beta E}\, dE = C\, \frac{\Gamma(\frac{3}{2})}{\beta^{3/2}} = C\, \frac{\sqrt{\pi}}{2\beta^{3/2}}, \quad \text{or} \quad C = \frac{2\beta^{3/2}}{\sqrt{\pi}},$$

and

$$\langle E \rangle = C \int_0^\infty E^{3/2} e^{-\beta E}\, dE = C\, \frac{\Gamma(\frac{5}{2})}{\beta^{5/2}} = \left(\frac{2\beta^{3/2}}{\sqrt{\pi}} \right) \frac{\sqrt{\pi}}{\beta^{5/2}} \left(\frac{1}{2} \cdot \frac{3}{2} \right) = \frac{3}{2} kT,$$

the known value of the average kinetic energy per molecule for a structureless classical gas at temperature T.

In probability theory, the distribution used here is known as a **gamma distribution**; it is further discussed in Chapter 23. ∎

Exercises

13.1.1 Derive the recurrence relations

$$\Gamma(z + 1) = z\Gamma(z)$$

from the Euler integral, Eq. (13.5),

$$\Gamma(z) = \int_0^\infty e^{-t} t^{z-1} dt.$$

13.1.2 In a power-series solution for the Legendre functions of the second kind we encounter the expression

$$\frac{(n+1)(n+2)(n+3)\cdots(n+2s-1)(n+2s)}{2 \cdot 4 \cdot 6 \cdot 8 \cdots (2s-2)(2s) \cdot (2n+3)(2n+5)(2n+7)\cdots(2n+2s+1)},$$

in which s is a positive integer.

(a) Rewrite this expression in terms of factorials.

(b) Rewrite this expression using Pochhammer symbols; see Eq. (1.72).

13.1.3 Show that $\Gamma(z)$ may be written

$$\Gamma(z) = 2 \int_0^\infty e^{-t^2} t^{2z-1} dt, \quad \Re e(z) > 0,$$

$$\Gamma(z) = \int_0^1 \left[\ln\left(\frac{1}{t} \right) \right]^{z-1} dt, \quad \Re e(z) > 0.$$

13.1.4 In a Maxwellian distribution the fraction of particles of mass m with speed between v and $v + dv$ is

$$\frac{dN}{N} = 4\pi \left(\frac{m}{2\pi kT}\right)^{3/2} \exp\left(-\frac{mv^2}{2kT}\right) v^2 \, dv,$$

where N is the total number of particles, k is Boltzmann's constant, and T is the absolute temperature. The average or expectation value of v^n is defined as $\langle v^n \rangle = N^{-1} \int v^n \, dN$. Show that

$$\langle v^n \rangle = \left(\frac{2kT}{m}\right)^{n/2} \frac{\Gamma(\frac{n+3}{2})}{\Gamma(\frac{3}{2})}.$$

This is an extension of Example 13.1.1, in which the distribution was in kinetic energy $E = mv^2/2$, with $dE = mv \, dv$.

13.1.5 By transforming the integral into a gamma function, show that

$$-\int_0^1 x^k \ln x \, dx = \frac{1}{(k+1)^2}, \quad k > -1.$$

13.1.6 Show that

$$\int_0^\infty e^{-x^4} dx = \Gamma\left(\frac{5}{4}\right).$$

13.1.7 Show that

$$\lim_{x \to 0} \frac{\Gamma(ax)}{\Gamma(x)} = \frac{1}{a}.$$

13.1.8 Locate the poles of $\Gamma(z)$. Show that they are simple poles and determine the residues.

13.1.9 Show that the equation $\Gamma(x) = k$, $k \neq 0$, has an infinite number of real roots.

13.1.10 Show that, for integer s,

(a) $$\int_0^\infty x^{2s+1} \exp(-ax^2) dx = \frac{s!}{2a^{s+1}}.$$

(b) $$\int_0^\infty x^{2s} \exp(-ax^2) dx = \frac{\Gamma(s+\frac{1}{2})}{2a^{s+1/2}} = \frac{(2s-1)!!}{2^{s+1}a^s}\sqrt{\frac{\pi}{a}}.$$

These Gaussian integrals are of major importance in statistical mechanics.

13.1.11 Express the coefficient of the nth term of the expansion of $(1+x)^{1/2}$ in powers of x

(a) in terms of factorials of integers,

(b) in terms of the double factorial (!!) functions.

$$\text{ANS.} \quad a_n = (-1)^{n+1} \frac{(2n-3)!}{2^{2n-2}n!\,(n-2)!} = (-1)^{n+1} \frac{(2n-3)!!}{(2n)!!}, \, n = 2, 3, \ldots.$$

13.1.12 Express the coefficient of the nth term of the expansion of $(1+x)^{-1/2}$ in powers of x

(a) in terms of the factorials of integers,

(b) in terms of the double factorial (!!) functions.

$$\text{ANS.} \quad a_n = (-1)^n \frac{(2n)!}{2^{2n}(n!)^2} = (-1)^n \frac{(2n-1)!!}{(2n)!!}, \quad n = 1, 2, 3\ldots.$$

13.1.13 The Legendre polynomial P_n may be written as

$$P_n(\cos\theta) = 2\frac{(2n-1)!!}{(2n)!!}\left\{\cos n\theta + \frac{1}{1}\cdot\frac{n}{2n-1}\cos(n-2)\theta\right.$$

$$+ \frac{1\cdot 3}{1\cdot 2}\frac{n(n-1)}{(2n-1)(2n-3)}\cos(n-4)\theta$$

$$\left. + \frac{1\cdot 3\cdot 5}{1\cdot 2\cdot 3}\frac{n(n-1)(n-2)}{(2n-1)(2n-3)(2n-5)}\cos(n-6)\theta + \cdots\right\}.$$

Let $n = 2s + 1$. Then the above can be written

$$P_n(\cos\theta) = P_{2s+1}(\cos\theta) = \sum_{m=0}^{s} a_m \cos(2m+1)\theta.$$

Find a_m in terms of factorials and double factorials.

13.1.14 (a) Show that $\Gamma\left(\frac{1}{2}-n\right)\Gamma\left(\frac{1}{2}+n\right) = (-1)^n\pi$, where n is an integer.

(b) Express $\Gamma\left(\frac{1}{2}+n\right)$ and $\Gamma\left(\frac{1}{2}-n\right)$ separately in terms of $\pi^{1/2}$ and a double factorial function.

$$\text{ANS.} \quad \Gamma(\tfrac{1}{2}+n) = \frac{(2n-1)!!}{2^n}\pi^{1/2}.$$

13.1.15 Show that if $\Gamma(x+iy) = u+iv$, then $\Gamma(x-iy) = u-iv$.

This is a special case of the Schwarz reflection principle, Section 11.10.

13.1.16 Prove that $|\Gamma(\alpha+i\beta)| = |\Gamma(\alpha)|\prod_{n=0}^{\infty}\left[1+\frac{\beta^2}{(\alpha+n)^2}\right]^{-1/2}$.

This equation has been useful in calculations of beta decay theory.

13.1.17 Show that for n, a positive integer,

$$|\Gamma(n+ib+1)| = \left(\frac{\pi b}{\sinh \pi b}\right)^{1/2}\prod_{s=1}^{n}(s^2+b^2)^{1/2}.$$

13.1.18 Show that for all real values of x and y, $|\Gamma(x)| \geq |\Gamma(x+iy)|$.

13.1.19   Show that $|(\Gamma(\frac{1}{2}+iy)|^2 = \dfrac{\pi}{\cosh \pi y}$.

13.1.20   The probability density associated with the normal distribution of statistics is given by

$$f(x) = \frac{1}{\sigma (2\pi)^{1/2}} \exp\left[-\frac{(x-\mu)^2}{2\sigma^2}\right],$$

with $(-\infty, \infty)$ for the range of x. Show that

(a) $\langle x \rangle$, the mean value of x, is equal to μ,

(b)   the standard deviation $(\langle x^2 \rangle - \langle x \rangle^2)^{1/2}$ is given by σ.

13.1.21   For the gamma distribution

$$f(x) = \begin{cases} \dfrac{1}{\beta^\alpha \Gamma(\alpha)}\, x^{\alpha-1} e^{-x/\beta}, & x > 0, \\[2mm] 0, & x \le 0, \end{cases}$$

show that

(a) $\langle x \rangle$, the mean value of x, is equal to $\alpha\beta$,

(b) σ^2, its variance, defined as $\langle x^2 \rangle - \langle x \rangle^2$, has the value $\alpha\beta^2$.

13.1.22   The wave function of a particle scattered by a Coulomb potential is $\psi(r, \theta)$. Given that at the origin the wave function becomes

$$\psi(0) = e^{-\pi\gamma/2}\,\Gamma(1+i\gamma),$$

where $\gamma > 0$ is a dimensionless parameter, show that

$$|\psi(0)|^2 = \frac{2\pi\gamma}{e^{2\pi\gamma} - 1}.$$

13.1.23   Derive the contour integral representation of Eq. (13.31),

$$2i\Gamma(\nu + 1) \sin \nu\pi = \int_C e^{-t}(-t)^\nu\, dt.$$

13.2   DIGAMMA AND POLYGAMMA FUNCTIONS

Digamma Function

As may be noted from the three definitions in Section 13.1, it is inconvenient to deal with the derivatives of the gamma function directly. It is more productive to take the natural logarithm of the gamma function as given by Eq. (13.1), thereby converting the product to a sum, and then to differentiate. The most useful results are obtained if we start with $\Gamma(z+1)$:

$$\Gamma(z+1) = z\Gamma(z) = \lim_{n\to\infty} \frac{n!}{(z+1)(z+2)\cdots(z+n)} n^z, \qquad (13.34)$$

$$\ln\Gamma(z+1) = \lim_{n\to\infty}\left[\ln(n!) + z\ln n - \ln(z+1)\right.$$

$$\left. - \ln(z+2) - \cdots - \ln(z+n)\right], \qquad (13.35)$$

in which the logarithm of the limit is equal to tne limit of the logarithm. Differentiating with respect to z, we obtain

$$\frac{d}{dz}\ln\Gamma(z+1) \equiv \psi(z+1) = \lim_{n\to\infty}\left(\ln n - \frac{1}{z+1} - \frac{1}{z+2} - \cdots - \frac{1}{z+n}\right), \quad (13.36)$$

which defines $\psi(z+1)$, the **digamma function**. Note that this definition also corresponds to

$$\psi(z+1) = \frac{[\Gamma(z+1)]'}{\Gamma(z+1)}. \qquad (13.37)$$

To bring Eq. (13.36) to a better form, we add and subtract the harmonic number

$$H_n = \sum_{m=1}^{n} \frac{1}{m},$$

thereby obtaining

$$\psi(z+1) = \lim_{n\to\infty}\left[(\ln n - H_n) - \sum_{m=1}^{n}\left(\frac{1}{z+m} - \frac{1}{m}\right)\right]$$

$$= -\gamma + \sum_{m=1}^{\infty} \frac{z}{m(m+z)}. \qquad (13.38)$$

We have now arranged the contributions in a way that causes each group of terms to approach a finite limit as $n \to \infty$: in that limit $\ln n - H_n$ became (minus) the Euler-Mascheroni constant, defined in Eq. (1.13), and the summation is convergent.

Setting $z = 0$, we find[1]

$$\psi(1) = -\gamma = -0.577\ 215\ 664\ 901\cdots. \qquad (13.39)$$

For integer $n > 0$, Eq. (13.38) reduces to a form that is good for revealing its structure but less desirable for actual computation:

$$\psi(n+1) = -\gamma + H_n = -\gamma + \sum_{m=1}^{n}\frac{1}{m}. \qquad (13.40)$$

---

[1] γ has been computed to 1271 places by D. E. Knuth, *Math. Comput.* **16**: 275 (1962), and to 3566 decimal places by D. W. Sweeney, *ibid.* **17**: 170 (1963). It may be of interest that the fraction 228/395 gives γ accurate to six places.

Polygamma Function

The digamma function may be differentiated repeatedly, giving rise to the polygamma function:

$$\psi^{(m)}(z+1) \equiv \frac{d^{m+1}}{dz^{m+1}} \ln \Gamma(z+1)$$

$$= (-1)^{m+1} m! \sum_{n=1}^{\infty} \frac{1}{(z+n)^{m+1}}, \quad m = 1, 2, 3, \ldots. \tag{13.41}$$

Plots of $\Gamma(x)$, $\psi(x)$, and $\psi'(x)$ are presented in Fig. 13.3.

If we set $z = 0$ in Eq. (13.41), the series in that equation is that defining the Riemann zeta function,[2]

$$\zeta(m) \equiv \sum_{n=1}^{\infty} \frac{1}{n^m}, \tag{13.42}$$

and we have

$$\psi^{(m)}(1) = (-1)^{m+1} m! \zeta(m+1), \quad m = 1, 2, 3, \ldots. \tag{13.43}$$

The values of polygamma functions of the positive integral argument, $\psi^{(m)}(n+1)$, may be calculated recursively; see Exercise 13.2.8.

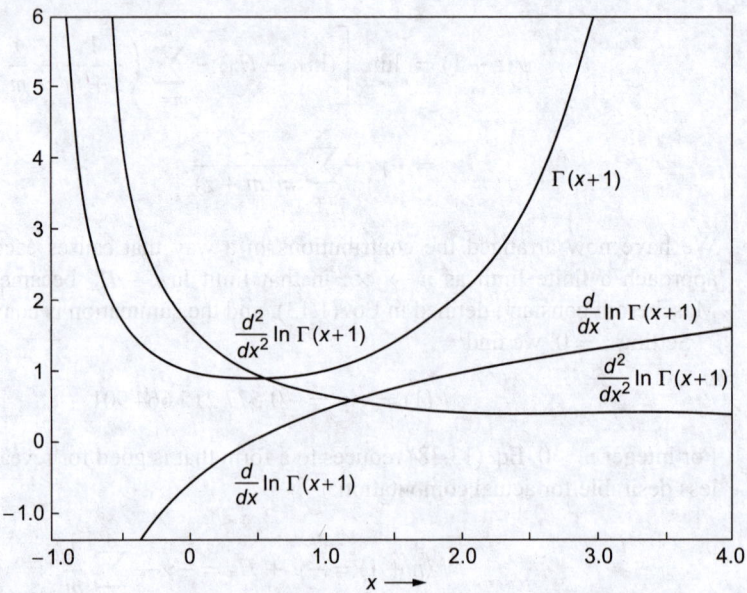

FIGURE 13.3   Gamma function and its first two logarithmic derivatives.

---

[2]For $z \neq 0$ this series has been used to define a generalization of $\zeta(m)$ known as the **Hurwitz zeta function**.

Maclaurin Expansion

It is now possible to write a Maclaurin expansion for $\ln \Gamma(z+1)$:

$$\ln \Gamma(z+1) = \sum_{n=1}^{\infty} \frac{z^n}{n!} \psi^{(n-1)}(1) = -\gamma z + \sum_{n=2}^{\infty} (-1)^n \frac{z^n}{n} \zeta(n). \qquad (13.44)$$

This expansion is convergent for $|z| < 1$; for $z = x$, the range is $-1 < x \leq 1$. Alternate forms of this series appear in Exercise 13.2.2. Equation (13.44) is a possible means of computing $\Gamma(z+1)$ for real or complex z, but Stirling's series (Section 13.4) is usually better, and in addition, an excellent table of values of the gamma function for complex arguments based on the use of Stirling's series and the functional relation, Eq. (13.22), is now available.[3]

Series Summation

The digamma and polygamma functions may also be used in summing series. If the general term of the series has the form of a rational fraction (with the highest power of the index in the numerator at least two less than the highest power of the index in the denominator), it may be transformed by the method of partial fractions; see Eq. (1.83). This transformation permits the infinite series to be expressed as a finite sum of digamma and polygamma functions. The usefulness of this method depends on the availability of tables of digamma and polygamma functions. Such tables and examples of series summation are given in AMS-55, chapter 6 (see Additional Readings for the reference).

Example 13.2.1   CATALAN'S CONSTANT

Catalan's constant, $\beta(2)$, Eq. (12.65), is given by

$$K = \beta(2) = \sum_{k=0}^{\infty} \frac{(-1)^k}{(2k+1)^2}.$$

Grouping the positive and negative terms separately and starting with the unit index, to match the form of $\psi^{(1)}$, Eq. (13.41), we obtain

$$K = 1 + \sum_{n=1}^{\infty} \frac{1}{(4n+1)^2} - \frac{1}{9} - \sum_{n=1}^{\infty} \frac{1}{(4n+3)^2}.$$

Now, identifying the summations in terms of $\psi^{(1)}$, we get

$$K = \frac{8}{9} + \frac{1}{16} \psi^{(1)}\left(1 + \frac{1}{4}\right) - \frac{1}{16} \psi^{(1)}\left(1 + \frac{3}{4}\right).$$

---

[3] *Table of the Gamma Function for Complex Arguments*, Applied Mathematics Series No. 34. Washington, DC: National Bureau of Standards (1954).

Using the values of $\psi^{(1)}$ from Table 6.1 of AMS-55 (see Additional Readings for the reference), we obtain

$$K = 0.91596559\ldots.$$

Compare this calculation of Catalan's constant with those carried out in earlier chapters (Exercises 1.1.12 and 12.4.4). ∎

Exercises

13.2.1   For "small" values of x,

$$\ln \Gamma(x+1) = -\gamma x + \sum_{n=2}^{\infty} (-1)^n \frac{\zeta(n)}{n} x^n,$$

where γ is the Euler-Mascheroni constant and $\zeta(n)$ the Riemann zeta function. For what values of x does this series converge?

ANS. $-1 < x \le 1$.

Note that if $x = 1$, we obtain

$$\gamma = \sum_{n=2}^{\infty} (-1)^n \frac{\zeta(n)}{n},$$

a series for the Euler-Mascheroni constant. The convergence of this series is exceedingly slow. For actual computation of γ, other, indirect, approaches are far superior (see Exercise 12.3.2).

13.2.2   Show that the series expansion of $\ln \Gamma(x+1)$ (Exercise 13.2.1) may be written as

(a) $\ln \Gamma(x+1) = \dfrac{1}{2} \ln \left(\dfrac{\pi x}{\sin \pi x} \right) - \gamma x - \displaystyle\sum_{n=1}^{\infty} \dfrac{\zeta(2n+1)}{2n+1} x^{2n+1},$

(b) $\ln \Gamma(x+1) = \dfrac{1}{2} \ln \left(\dfrac{\pi x}{\sin \pi x} \right) - \dfrac{1}{2} \ln \left(\dfrac{1+x}{1-x} \right) + (1-\gamma)x$

$$- \sum_{n=1}^{\infty} \left[\zeta(2n+1) - 1 \right] \frac{x^{2n+1}}{2n+1}.$$

Determine the range of convergence of each of these expressions.

13.2.3   Verify that for n, a positive integer, the following two forms of the digamma function are equal to each other:

$$\psi(n+1) = \sum_{j=1}^{n} \frac{1}{j} - \gamma \quad \text{and} \quad \psi(n+1) = \sum_{j=1}^{\infty} \frac{n}{j(n+j)} - \gamma.$$

13.2.4   Show that $\psi(z+1)$ has the series expansion

$$\psi(z+1) = -\gamma + \sum_{n=2}^{\infty} (-1)^n \zeta(n)\, z^{n-1}.$$

13.2.5   For a power-series expansion of $\ln \Gamma(z+1)$, AMS-55 (see Additional Readings for the reference) lists

$$\ln \Gamma(z+1) = -\ln(1+z) + z(1-\gamma) + \sum_{n=2}^{\infty} (-1)^n \left[\zeta(n) - 1 \right] \frac{z^n}{n}.$$

(a)   Show that this agrees with Eq. (13.44) for $|z| < 1$.

(b)   What is the range of convergence of this new expression?

13.2.6   Show that

$$\frac{1}{2} \ln \left(\frac{\pi z}{\sin \pi z} \right) = \sum_{n=1}^{\infty} \frac{\zeta(2n)}{2n} z^{2n}, \quad |z| < 1.$$

Hint. Use Eqs. (13.23) and (13.35).

13.2.7   Write out a Weierstrass infinite-product definition of $\ln \Gamma(z+1)$. Without differentiating, show that this leads directly to the Maclaurin expansion of $\ln \Gamma(z+1)$, Eq. (13.44).

13.2.8   Derive the difference relation for the polygamma function,

$$\psi^{(m)}(z+2) = \psi^{(m)}(z+1) + (-1)^m \frac{m!}{(z+1)^{m+1}}, \quad m = 0, 1, 2, \ldots.$$

13.2.9   The Pochhammer symbol $(a)_n$ is defined (for integral n) as

$$(a)_n = a(a+1) \cdots (a+n-1), \quad (a)_0 = 1.$$

(a)   Express $(a)_n$ in terms of factorials.

(b)   Find $(d/da)(a)_n$ in terms of $(a)_n$ and digamma functions.

$$ANS. \quad \frac{d}{da}(a)_n = (a)_n [\psi(a+n) - \psi(a)].$$

(c)   Show that

$$(a)_{n+k} = (a+n)_k \cdot (a)_n.$$

13.2.10 Verify the following special values of the ψ form of the digamma and polygamma functions:

$$\psi(1) = -\gamma, \quad \psi^{(1)}(1) = \zeta(2), \quad \psi^{(2)}(1) = -2\zeta(3).$$

13.2.11 Verify:

(a) $\displaystyle\int_0^\infty e^{-r} \ln r \, dr = -\gamma.$

(b) $\displaystyle\int_0^\infty r e^{-r} \ln r \, dr = 1 - \gamma.$

(c) $\displaystyle\int_0^\infty r^n e^{-r} \ln r \, dr = (n-1)! + n \int_0^\infty r^{n-1} e^{-r} \ln r \, dr, \quad n = 1, 2, 3, \dots.$

Hint. These may be verified by integration by parts, or by differentiating the Euler integral formula for $\Gamma(n+1)$ with respect to n.

13.2.12 Dirac relativistic wave functions for hydrogen involve factors such as $\Gamma[2(1 - \alpha^2 Z^2)^{1/2} + 1]$ where α, the fine structure constant, is $1/137$ and Z is the atomic number. Expand $\Gamma[2(1 - \alpha^2 Z^2)^{1/2} + 1]$ in a series of powers of $\alpha^2 Z^2$.

13.2.13 The quantum mechanical description of a particle in a Coulomb field requires a knowledge of the argument of $\Gamma(z)$ when z is complex. Determine the argument of $\Gamma(1 + ib)$ for small, real b.

13.2.14 Using digamma and polygamma functions, sum the series

(a) $\displaystyle\sum_{n=1}^\infty \frac{1}{n(n+1)},$ (b) $\displaystyle\sum_{n=2}^\infty \frac{1}{n^2 - 1}.$

Note. You can use Exercise 13.2.8 to calculate the needed digamma functions.

13.2.15 Show that

$$\sum_{n=1}^\infty \frac{1}{(n+a)(n+b)} = \frac{1}{(b-a)} \Big[\psi(1+b) - \psi(1+a) \Big],$$

where $a \neq b$, and neither a nor b is a negative integer. It is of some interest to compare this summation with the corresponding integral,

$$\int_1^\infty \frac{dx}{(x+a)(x+b)} = \frac{1}{b-a} \Big[\ln(1+b) - \ln(1+a) \Big].$$

The relation between $\psi(x)$ and $\ln x$ is made explicit in the analysis leading to Stirling's formula.

13.3   THE BETA FUNCTION

Products of gamma functions can be identified as describing an important class of definite integrals involving powers of sine and cosine functions, and these integrals, in turn, can be further manipulated to evaluate a large number of algebraic definite integrals. These properties make it useful to define the **beta function**, defined as

$$B(p, q) = \frac{\Gamma(p)\,\Gamma(q)}{\Gamma(p+q)}.$$ (13.45)

For whatever it is worth, note that the B in Eq. (13.45) is an upper-case beta.

To understand the virtue of this definition, let us write the product $\Gamma(p)\Gamma(q)$ using the integral representation given as Eq. (13.6), valid for $\Re e(p)$, $\Re e(q) > 0$:

$$\Gamma(p)\,\Gamma(q) = 4 \int_0^\infty s^{2p-1} e^{-s^2}\, ds \int_0^\infty t^{2q-1} e^{-t^2}\, dt.$$ (13.46)

The reason for using this integral representation is that the quadratic terms in the exponent, s^2 and t^2, combine in a convenient way if we change the integration variables from s, t to polar coordinates r, θ, with $s = r\cos\theta$, $t = r\sin\theta$, $r^2 = s^2 + t^2$, and $ds\, dt = r\, dr\, d\theta$. Equation (13.46) becomes

$$\Gamma(p)\,\Gamma(q) = 4 \int_0^\infty r^{2p+2q-1} e^{-r^2}\, dr \int_0^{\pi/2} \cos^{2p-1}\theta\, \sin^{2q-1}\theta\, d\theta$$

$$= 2\,\Gamma(p+q) \int_0^{\pi/2} \cos^{2p-1}\theta\, \sin^{2q-1}\theta\, d\theta,$$

where we have used Eq. (13.6) to recognize the r integration as $\Gamma(p+q)$. This gives us our first integral evaluation based on the beta function:

$$B(p, q) = 2 \int_0^{\pi/2} \cos^{2p-1}\theta\, \sin^{2q-1}\theta\, d\theta.$$ (13.47)

Because Eq. (13.47) is often used when p and q are integers, we rewrite for the case $p = m + 1$, $q = n + 1$,

$$\frac{m!\,n!}{(m+n+1)!} = 2 \int_0^{\pi/2} \cos^{2m+1}\theta\, \sin^{2n+1}\theta\, d\theta.$$ (13.48)

Because gamma functions of a half-integral argument are available in closed form, Eq. (13.47) also provides a route to these trigonometric integrals for even powers of the sine and/or cosine. Note also that from its definition it is obvious that $B(p, q) = B(q, p)$, showing that the integral in Eq. (13.47) does not change in value if the powers of the sine and cosine are interchanged.

Alternate Forms, Definite Integrals

The substitution $t = \cos^2 \theta$ converts Eq. (13.47) to

$$B(p+1, q+1) = \int_0^1 t^p (1-t)^q \, dt. \tag{13.49}$$

Replacing t by x^2, we obtain

$$B(p=1, q+1) = 2 \int_0^1 x^{2p+1} (1-x^2)^q \, dx. \tag{13.50}$$

The substitution $t = u/(1+u)$ in Eq. (13.49) yields still another useful form,

$$B(p+1, q+1) = \int_0^\infty \frac{u^p}{(1+u)^{p+q+2}} \, du. \tag{13.51}$$

The beta function as a definite integral is useful in establishing integral representations of the Bessel function (Exercise 14.1.17) and the hypergeometric function (Exercise 18.5.12).

Derivation of Legendre Duplication Formula

The Legendre duplication formula involves products of gamma functions, which suggests that the beta function may provide a useful route to its proof. We start by using Eq. (13.49) for $B\left(z + \frac{1}{2}, z + \frac{1}{2}\right)$:

$$B\left(z + \frac{1}{2}, z + \frac{1}{2}\right) = \int_0^1 t^{z-1/2} (1-t)^{z-1/2} \, dt. \tag{13.52}$$

Making the substitution $t = (1+s)/2$, we have

$$B\left(z + \frac{1}{2}, z + \frac{1}{2}\right) = 2^{-2z} \int_{-1}^1 (1-s^2)^{z-1/2} \, ds$$

$$= 2^{-2z+1} \int_0^1 (1-s^2)^{z-1/2} \, ds = 2^{-2z} B\left(\frac{1}{2}, z + \frac{1}{2}\right), \tag{13.53}$$

where we used the fact that the s integrand was even to change the integration range to $(0, 1)$, and then used Eq. (13.50) to evaluate the resulting integral. Now, inserting the definition, Eq. (13.45), for both instances of B in Eq. (13.53), we reach

$$\frac{\Gamma(z + \frac{1}{2})\Gamma(z + \frac{1}{2})}{\Gamma(2z + 1)} = 2^{-2z} \frac{\Gamma(\frac{1}{2})\Gamma(z + \frac{1}{2})}{\Gamma(z + 1)},$$

which is easily rearranged into

$$\Gamma(z+1)\Gamma\left(z+\frac{1}{2}\right) = \frac{\sqrt{\pi}}{2^{2z}}\,\Gamma(2z+1), \qquad (13.54)$$

the Legendre duplication formula, originally introduced as Eq. (13.27), but proved at that time only for integer values of z.

Although the integrals used in this derivation are defined only for $\Re e(z) > -1$, the result, Eq. (13.54), holds, by analytic continuation, for all z where the gamma functions are analytic.

Exercises

13.3.1 Verify the following beta function identities:

(a) $B(a,b) = B(a+1,b) + B(a,b+1),$

(b) $B(a,b) = \dfrac{a+b}{b} B(a,b+1),$

(c) $B(a,b) = \dfrac{b-1}{a} B(a+1,b-1),$

(d) $B(a,b)B(a+b,c) = B(b,c)B(a,b+c).$

13.3.2 (a) Show that

$$\int_{-1}^{1}(1-x^2)^{1/2}x^{2n}\,dx = \begin{cases} \pi/2, & n=0 \\ \pi\,\dfrac{(2n-1)!!}{(2n+2)!!}, & n=1,2,3,\dots. \end{cases}$$

(b) Show that

$$\int_{-1}^{1}(1-x^2)^{-1/2}x^{2n}\,dx = \begin{cases} \pi, & n=0, \\ \pi\,\dfrac{(2n-1)!!}{(2n)!!}, & n=1,2,3,\dots. \end{cases}$$

13.3.3 Show that

$$\int_{-1}^{1}(1-x^2)^n\,dx = \frac{2\,(2n)!!}{(2n+1)!!}, \qquad n=0,1,2,\dots.$$

13.3.4 Evaluate $\displaystyle\int_{-1}^{1}(1+x)^a(1-x)^b\,dx$ in terms of the beta function.

ANS. $2^{a+b+1}B(a+1,b+1).$

13.3.5   Show, by means of the beta function, that

$$\int_{t}^{z} \frac{dx}{(z-x)^{1-\alpha}(x-t)^{\alpha}} = \frac{\pi}{\sin \pi \alpha}, \quad 0 < \alpha < 1.$$

13.3.6   Show that the Dirichlet integral

$$\iint x^p y^q \, dx \, dy = \frac{p!\,q!}{(p+q+2)!} = \frac{B(p+1,q+1)}{p+q+2},$$

where the range of integration is the triangle bounded by the positive x- and y-axes and the line $x + y = 1$.

13.3.7   Show that

$$\int_{0}^{\infty}\int_{0}^{\infty} e^{-(x^2+y^2+2xy\cos\theta)} \, dx \, dy = \frac{\theta}{2\sin\theta}.$$

What are the limits on θ?

Hint. Consider oblique xy-coordinates.

ANS. $-\pi < \theta < \pi$.

13.3.8   Evaluate (using the beta function)

(a) $\displaystyle\int_{0}^{\pi/2} \cos^{1/2}\theta \, d\theta = \frac{(2\pi)^{3/2}}{16[\Gamma(5/4)]^2}$,

(b) $\displaystyle\int_{0}^{\pi/2} \cos^n \theta \, d\theta = \int_{0}^{\pi/2} \sin^n \theta \, d\theta = \frac{\sqrt{\pi}\,[(n-1)/2]!}{2(n/2)!}$

$$= \begin{cases} \dfrac{(n-1)!!}{n!!} & \text{for } n \text{ odd,} \\[2mm] \dfrac{\pi}{2} \cdot \dfrac{(n-1)!!}{n!!} & \text{for } n \text{ even.} \end{cases}$$

13.3.9   Evaluate $\displaystyle\int_{0}^{1} (1 - x^4)^{-1/2} dx$ as a beta function.

ANS. $\dfrac{[\Gamma(5/4)]^2 \cdot 4}{(2\pi)^{1/2}} = 1.311028777$.

13.3.10   Using beta functions, show that the integral representation

$$J_\nu(z) = \frac{2}{\pi^{1/2}\,\Gamma(\nu + \frac{1}{2})} \left(\frac{z}{2}\right)^\nu \int_{0}^{\pi/2} \sin^{2\nu}\theta \cos(z\cos\theta) \, d\theta, \quad \Re(\nu) > -\tfrac{1}{2},$$

reduces to the Bessel series

$$J_\nu(z) = \sum_{s=0}^{\infty} (-1)^s \frac{1}{s!\,\Gamma(s+\nu+1)} \left(\frac{z}{2}\right)^{2s+\nu},$$

thereby confirming its validity.

13.3.11 Given the associated Legendre function, defined in Chapter 15,

$$P_m^m(x) = (2m-1)!!\,(1-x^2)^{m/2},$$

show that

(a) $$\int_{-1}^{1} [P_m^m(x)]^2 \, dx = \frac{2}{2m+1}\,(2m)!, \quad m = 0, 1, 2, \ldots,$$

(b) $$\int_{-1}^{1} [P_m^m(x)]^2 \frac{dx}{1-x^2} = 2 \cdot (2m-1)!, \quad m = 1, 2, 3, \ldots.$$

13.3.12 Show that, for integers p and q,

(a) $$\int_{0}^{1} x^{2p+1}(1-x^2)^{-1/2}\, dx = \frac{(2p)!!}{(2p+1)!!},$$

(b) $$\int_{0}^{1} x^{2p}(1-x^2)^q \, dx = \frac{(2p-1)!!\,(2q)!!}{(2p+2q+1)!!}.$$

13.3.13 A particle of mass m moving in a symmetric potential that is well described by $V(x) = A|x|^n$ has a total energy $\frac{1}{2}m(dx/dt)^2 + V(x) = E$. Solving for dx/dt and integrating we find that the period of motion is

$$\tau = 2\sqrt{2m} \int_{0}^{x_{\max}} \frac{dx}{(E - Ax^n)^{1/2}},$$

where $x_{\max}$ is a classical turning point given by $A x_{\max}^n = E$. Show that

$$\tau = \frac{2}{n}\sqrt{\frac{2\pi m}{E}} \left(\frac{E}{A}\right)^{1/n} \frac{\Gamma(1/n)}{\Gamma(1/n + \frac{1}{2})}.$$

13.3.14 Referring to Exercise 13.3.13,

(a) Determine the limit as $n \to \infty$ of

$$\frac{2}{n}\sqrt{\frac{2\pi m}{E}} \left(\frac{E}{A}\right)^{1/n} \frac{\Gamma(1/n)}{\Gamma(1/n + \frac{1}{2})}.$$

(b)   Find $\lim_{n\to\infty} \tau$ from the behavior of the integrand $(E - Ax^n)^{-1/2}$.

(c)   Investigate the behavior of the physical system (potential well) as $n \to \infty$. Obtain the period from inspection of this limiting physical system.

13.3.15   Show that

$$\int_0^\infty \frac{\sinh^\alpha x}{\cosh^\beta x} dx = \frac{1}{2} B\left(\frac{\alpha + 1}{2}, \frac{\beta - \alpha}{2}\right), \quad -1 < \alpha < \beta.$$

Hint. Let $\sinh^2 x = u$.

13.3.16   The beta distribution of probability theory has a probability density

$$f(x) = \frac{\Gamma(\alpha + \beta)}{\Gamma(\alpha)\,\Gamma(\beta)} x^{\alpha-1}(1 - x)^{\beta-1},$$

with x restricted to the interval $(0, 1)$. Show that

(a) $\langle x \rangle$, the mean value, is $\dfrac{\alpha}{\alpha + \beta}$.

(b) σ^2, its variance, is $\langle x^2 \rangle - \langle x \rangle^2 = \dfrac{\alpha\beta}{(\alpha + \beta)^2(\alpha + \beta + 1)}$.

13.3.17   From

$$\lim_{n\to\infty} \frac{\int_0^{\pi/2} \sin^{2n}\theta\, d\theta}{\int_0^{\pi/2} \sin^{2n+1}\theta\, d\theta} = 1,$$

derive the Wallis formula for π:

$$\frac{\pi}{2} = \frac{2 \cdot 2}{1 \cdot 3} \cdot \frac{4 \cdot 4}{3 \cdot 5} \cdot \frac{6 \cdot 6}{5 \cdot 7} \cdots.$$

13.4   STIRLING'S SERIES

In statistical mechanics we encounter the need to evaluate $\ln(n!)$ for very large values of n, and we occasionally need $\ln \Gamma(z)$ for nonintegral z when $|z|$ is large enough that it is inconvenient or impractical to use the Maclaurin series, Eq. (13.44), possibly followed by repeated use of the functional relation $\Gamma(z + 1) = z\Gamma(z)$. These needs can be met by the asymptotic expansion for $\ln \Gamma(z)$ known as **Stirling's series** or **Stirling's formula**. While it is in principle possible to develop such an asymptotic formula by the method of steepest descents (and in fact we have already obtained the leading term of the expansion in this way; see Example 12.7.1), a relatively simple way of obtaining the full asymptotic expansion is by use of the Euler-Maclaurin integration formula in Section 12.3.

Derivation from Euler-Maclaurin Integration Formula

The Euler-Maclaurin formula for evaluating a definite integral on the range $(0, \infty)$, obtained by specializing Eq. (12.57) and ignoring the remainder, is

$$\int_0^\infty f(x)\,dx = \tfrac{1}{2} f(0) + f(1) + f(2) + f(3) + \cdots$$

$$+ \frac{B_2}{2!} f'(0) + \frac{B_4}{4!} f^{(3)}(0) + \frac{B_6}{6!} f^{(5)}(x) + \cdots, \qquad (13.55)$$

where B_n are Bernoulli numbers:

$$B_2 = \frac{1}{6}, \quad B_4 = -\frac{1}{30}, \quad B_6 = \frac{1}{42}, \quad B_8 = -\frac{1}{30}, \quad \cdots .$$

We proceed by applying Eq. (13.55) to the definite integral

$$\int_0^\infty \frac{dx}{(z+x)^2} = \frac{1}{z}$$

(for z not on the negative real axis). We note, by comparing with Eq. (13.41), that

$$f(1) + f(2) + \cdots = \sum_{n=1}^\infty \frac{1}{(z+n)^2} = \psi^{(1)}(z+1);$$

this makes a connection to the gamma function and is the reason for our current strategy. We also note that

$$f^{(2n-1)}(0) = \left(\frac{d}{dx}\right)^{2n-1} \frac{1}{(z+x)^2}\bigg|_{x=0} = -\frac{(2n)!}{z^{2n+1}},$$

so the expansion yields

$$\frac{1}{z} = \int_0^\infty \frac{dx}{(z+x)^2} = \frac{1}{2z^2} + \psi^{(1)}(z+1) - \frac{B_2}{z^3} - \frac{B_4}{z^5} - \cdots.$$

Solving for $\psi^{(1)}(z+1)$, we have

$$\psi^{(1)}(z+1) = \frac{d}{dz} \psi(z+1) = \frac{1}{z} - \frac{1}{2z^2} + \frac{B_2}{z^3} + \frac{B_4}{z^5} + \cdots$$

$$= \frac{1}{z} - \frac{1}{2z^2} + \sum_{n=1}^\infty \frac{B_{2n}}{z^{2n+1}}. \qquad (13.56)$$

Since the Bernoulli numbers diverge strongly, this series does not converge. It is a semi-convergent, or asymptotic, series, useful if one retains a small number of terms (compare with Section 12.6).

Integrating once, we get the digamma function

$$\psi(z+1) = C_1 + \ln z + \frac{1}{2z} - \frac{B_2}{2z^2} - \frac{B_4}{4z^4} - \cdots$$

$$= C_1 + \ln z + \frac{1}{2z} - \sum_{n=1}^{\infty} \frac{B_{2n}}{2nz^{2n}}, \tag{13.57}$$

where C_1 has a value still to be determined. In the next subsection we will show that $C_1 = 0$. Equation (13.57), then, gives us another expression for the digamma function, often more useful than Eq. (13.38) or Eq. (13.44).

Stirling's Formula

The indefinite integral of the digamma function, obtained by integrating Eq. (13.57), is

$$\ln \Gamma(z+1) = C_2 + \left(z + \frac{1}{2}\right) \ln z + (C_1 - 1)z + \frac{B_2}{2z} + \cdots + \frac{B_{2n}}{2n(2n-1)z^{2n-1}} + \cdots, \tag{13.58}$$

in which C_2 is another constant of integration. We are now ready to determine C_1 and C_2, which we can do by requiring that the asymptotic expansion be consistent with the Legendre duplication formula, Eq. (13.54). Substituting Eq. (13.58) into the logarithm of the duplication formula, we find that satisfaction of that formula dictates that $C_1 = 0$ and that C_2 must have the value

$$C_2 = \tfrac{1}{2} \ln 2\pi. \tag{13.59}$$

Thus, inserting also values of the B_{2n}, our final result is

$$\ln \Gamma(z+1) = \frac{1}{2} \ln 2\pi + \left(z + \frac{1}{2}\right) \ln z - z + \frac{1}{12z} - \frac{1}{360z^3} + \frac{1}{1260z^5} - \cdots. \tag{13.60}$$

This is Stirling's series, an asymptotic expansion. The absolute value of the error is less than the absolute value of the first term neglected.

The leading term in the asymptotic behavior of the gamma function was one of the examples used to illustrate the method of steepest descents. In Example 12.7.1, we found that

$$\Gamma(z+1) \sim \sqrt{2\pi} \, z^{z+1/2} e^{-z},$$

corresponding to

$$\ln \Gamma(z+1) \sim \frac{1}{2} \ln 2\pi + \left(z + \frac{1}{2}\right) \ln z - z,$$

yielding all the terms of Eq. (13.60) that do not vanish in the limit of large $|z|$.

To help convey a feeling of the remarkable precision of Stirling's series for $\Gamma(s+1)$, the ratio of the first term of Stirling's approximation to $\Gamma(s+1)$ is plotted in Fig. 13.4. In Table 13.1 we give the ratio of the first term in the expansion to $\Gamma(s+1)$ and a similar ratio when two terms are kept in the expansion to $\Gamma(s+1)$. The derivation of these forms is Exercise 13.4.1.

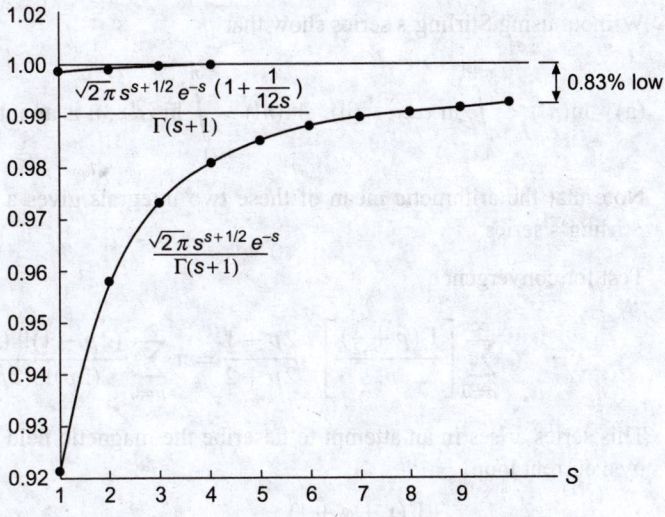

FIGURE 13.4   Accuracy of Stirling's formula.

Table 13.1   Ratios of One- and Two-Term Stirling Series to Exact Values of $\Gamma(s + 1)$

s	$\dfrac{1}{\Gamma(s+1)}\sqrt{2\pi}s^{s+1/2}e^{-s}$	$\dfrac{1}{\Gamma(s+1)}\sqrt{2\pi}s^{s+1/2}e^{-s}\left(1+\dfrac{1}{12s}\right)$
1	0.92213	0.99898
2	0.95950	0.99949
3	0.97270	0.99972
4	0.97942	0.99983
5	0.98349	0.99988
6	0.98621	0.99992
7	0.98817	0.99994
8	0.98964	0.99995
9	0.99078	0.99996
10	0.99170	0.99998

Exercises

13.4.1   Rewrite Stirling's series to give $\Gamma(z + 1)$ instead of $\ln \Gamma(z + 1)$.

$$\textit{ANS.} \quad \Gamma(z+1) = \sqrt{2\pi}\, z^{z+1/2}e^{-z}\left(1 + \frac{1}{12z} + \frac{1}{288z^2} - \frac{139}{51{,}840z^3} + \cdots\right).$$

13.4.2   Use Stirling's formula to estimate 52!, the number of possible rearrangements of cards in a standard deck of playing cards.

13.4.3   Show that the constants C_1 and C_2 in Stirling's formula have the respective values zero and $\frac{1}{2}\ln 2\pi$ by using the logarithm of the Legendre duplication formula (see Fig. 3.4).

13.4.4   Without using Stirling's series show that

(a) $\ln(n!) < \int_{1}^{n+1} \ln x \, dx,$ (b) $\ln(n!) > \int_{1}^{n} \ln x \, dx; n$ is an integer ≥ 2.

Note that the arithmetic mean of these two integrals gives a good approximation for Stirling's series.

13.4.5   Test for convergence

$$\sum_{p=0}^{\infty} \left[\frac{\Gamma(p + \frac{1}{2})}{p!} \right]^2 \frac{2p+1}{2p+2} = \pi \sum_{p=0}^{\infty} \frac{(2p-1)!! \, (2p+1)!!}{(2p)!! \, (2p+2)!!}.$$

This series arises in an attempt to describe the magnetic field created by and enclosed by a current loop.

13.4.6   Show that $\lim_{x \to \infty} x^{b-a} \dfrac{\Gamma(x+a+1)}{\Gamma(x+b+1)} = 1.$

13.4.7   Show that $\lim_{n \to \infty} \dfrac{(2n-1)!!}{(2n)!!} n^{1/2} = \pi^{-1/2}.$

13.4.8   A set of N distinguishable particles is assigned to states ψ_i, $i = 1, 2, \ldots, M$. If the numbers of particles in the various states are $n_1, n_2, \ldots, n_M$ (with $M \ll N$), the number of ways this can be done is

$$W = \frac{N!}{n_1! n_2! \cdots n_M!}.$$

The entropy associated with this assignment is $S = k \ln W$, where k is Boltzmann's constant. In the limit $N \to \infty$, with $n_i = p_i N$ (so p_i is the fraction of the particles in state i), find S as a function of N and the p_i.

(a)   In the limit of large N, find the entropy associated with an arbitrary set of n_i. Is the entropy an extensive function of the system size (i.e., is it proportional to N)?

(b)   Find the set of p_i that maximize S.

Hint. Remember that $\sum_i p_i = 1$ and that this is a constrained maximization (see Section 22.3).

Note. These formulas correspond to **classical**, or **Boltzmann**, statistics.

13.5   RIEMANN ZETA FUNCTION

We are now in a position to broaden our earlier survey of $\zeta(z)$, the Riemann zeta function. In so doing, we note an interesting degree of parallelism between some of the properties of $\zeta(z)$ and corresponding properties of the gamma function.

We open this section by repeating the definition of $\zeta(z)$, which is valid when the series converges:

$$\zeta(z) \equiv \sum_{n=1}^{\infty} n^{-z}. \tag{13.61}$$

The values of $\zeta(n)$ for integral n from 2 to 10 were listed in Table 1.1 on page 17.

We now want to consider the possibility of analytically continuing $\zeta(z)$ beyond the range of convergence of Eq. (13.61). As a first step toward doing so, we prove the integral representation that was given in Table 1.1:

$$\zeta(z) = \frac{1}{\Gamma(z)} \int_0^{\infty} \frac{t^{z-1}\, dt}{e^t - 1}. \tag{13.62}$$

Equation (13.62) has a range of validity that is limited by the behavior of its integrand at small t; since the denominator then approaches t, the overall small-t dependence is t^{z-2}. Writing $z = x + iy$ and $t^{z-2} = t^{x-2}e^{iy \ln t}$, we see that, like Eq. (13.61), Eq. (13.62) will only converge when $\Re e\, z > 1$.

We start from the right-hand side of Eq. (13.62), denoted I, by multiplying the numerator and denominator of its integrand by e^{-t} and expanding the denominator in powers of e^{-t}, reaching

$$I = \frac{1}{\Gamma(z)} \int_0^{\infty} \frac{t^{z-1}e^{-t}\, dt}{1 - e^{-t}} = \frac{1}{\Gamma(z)} \int_0^{\infty} \sum_{m=1}^{\infty} t^{z-1} e^{-mt}\, dt.$$

We next change the variable of integration for the individual terms so that all terms contain an identical factor e^{-t}:

$$I = \frac{1}{\Gamma(z)} \int_0^{\infty} \sum_{m=1}^{\infty} \left(\frac{t}{m}\right)^{z-1} e^{-t} \left(\frac{dt}{m}\right) = \frac{1}{\Gamma(z)} \left(\sum_{m=1}^{\infty} \frac{1}{m^z}\right) \int_0^{\infty} t^{z-1} e^{-t}\, dt$$

$$= \zeta(z) \frac{1}{\Gamma(z)} \int_0^{\infty} t^{z-1} e^{-t}\, dt = \zeta(z). \tag{13.63}$$

In the second line of Eq. (13.63) we recognize the summation as a zeta function and the integral as the Euler integral representation of $\Gamma(z)$, Eq. (13.5). It then cancels against the initial factor $1/\Gamma(z)$, leaving the desired final result, Eq. (13.62). In passing, we note that the only difference between the integral of Eq. (13.62) and the Euler integral for the gamma function is that we now have a denominator $e^t - 1$ instead of simply e^t.

The next step toward the analytic continuation we seek is to introduce a contour integral with the same integrand as Eq. (13.62), using the same open contour that was found useful for the gamma function, shown in Fig. 13.2. Just as for the gamma function, we do not wish to restrict z to integral values, so the integrand will in general have a branch point at $t = 0$, and again we have placed the branch cut on the positive real axis. Restricting consideration for now to z with $\Re e\, z > 1$, we evaluate the contour integral, denoted I, as the sum of its contributions from the sections of the contour, respectively, labeled A, B, and D in Fig. 13.2. For $\Re e\, z > 1$, the small circle D makes no contribution to the integral, while

$$I_A = \frac{1}{\Gamma(z)} \int_\infty^\varepsilon \frac{t^{z-1}\, dt}{e^t - 1} = -\zeta(z),$$

$$I_B = \frac{1}{\Gamma(z)} \int_\varepsilon^\infty \frac{t^{z-1} e^{2\pi i(z-1)}\, dt}{e^t - 1} = e^{2\pi i(z-1)} \zeta(z) = e^{2\pi i z} \zeta(z).$$

Combining the above, we get

$$I = \frac{1}{\Gamma(z)} \int_C \frac{t^{z-1}\, dt}{e^t - 1} = \left(e^{2\pi i z} - 1 \right) \zeta(z). \tag{13.64}$$

Note that Eq. (13.64) is useful as a relation involving $\zeta(z)$ only if z is not an integer.

We now wish to deform the contour of Eq. (13.64) in a way that will remove the restriction $\Re e\, z > 1$, which we originally needed to obtain that equation. The deformation corresponds to an analytic continuation of $\zeta(z)$ to a larger range of z, and will be effective because the deformation can avoid the divergence in the neighborhood of $t = 0$. When we consider possible deformations, we need to make the observation that, unlike the gamma function, the integrand of Eq. (13.64) has simple poles at the points $t = 2n\pi i$, $n = \pm 1, \pm 2, \dots$, so that if we deform the contour in a way that encloses any of these poles, we must allow for the change thereby produced in the value of the contour integral.

If we initially deform the contour by expanding the circle D to some finite radius less than $2\pi i$, we do not change the value of the integral I but extend its range of validity to negative z. If, for $z < 0$, we further expand D until it becomes an open circle of infinite radius (but not through any of the poles), the value of the contour integral is reduced to zero, with the change caused by the inclusion of the contribution from the poles that are then encircled. We therefore have the interesting result that the original contour integral had a value that was the negative of $2\pi i$ times the sum of the residues that were newly enclosed. Thus,

$$I = \left(e^{2\pi i z} - 1 \right) \zeta(z) = -\frac{2\pi i}{\Gamma(z)} \sum_{n=1}^\infty (\text{residues of } t^{z-1}/(e^t - 1) \text{ at } t = \pm 2n\pi i).$$

At the pole $t = +2\pi n i$, the residue is $\left(2n\pi e^{\pi i/2} \right)^{z-1}$, while at $t = -2\pi n i$ it is $\left(2n\pi e^{3\pi i/2} \right)^{z-1}$. Note that we must evaluate the residues taking cognizance of the branch cut. Inserting these values and rearranging a bit,

$$\left(e^{2\pi i z} - 1 \right) \zeta(z) = - \left(\sum_{n=1}^\infty \frac{1}{n^{-z+1}} \right) \frac{(2\pi)^z i}{\Gamma(z)} \left(e^{\pi i(z-1)/2} + e^{3\pi i(z-1)/2} \right)$$

$$= \zeta(1-z) \frac{(2\pi)^z}{\Gamma(z)} \left(e^{3\pi i z/2} - e^{\pi i z/2} \right). \tag{13.65}$$

Note that because $z < 0$, the summation over n converges and can be identified as $\zeta(1-z)$. Equation (13.65) can be simplified, but we already see its essential feature, namely that it provides a functional relation connecting $\zeta(z)$ and $\zeta(1-z)$, parallel to but more complicated than the reflection formula for the gamma function, Eq. (13.23). The derivation of Eq. (13.65) was carried out for $z < 0$, but now that we have obtained it, we can, appealing to analytic continuation, assert its validity for all z such that its constituent factors are nonsingular. This formula, in the simplified form we shall shortly obtain, was first found by Riemann.

The simplification of Eq. (13.65) can be accomplished by recognizing, with the aid of the gamma-function reflection formula, Eq. (13.23), that

$$\frac{e^{3\pi i z/2} - e^{\pi i z/2}}{e^{2\pi i z} - 1} = \frac{\sin(\pi z/2)}{\sin \pi z} = \frac{\Gamma(z)\,\Gamma(1-z)}{\Gamma(z/2)\,\Gamma(1-z/2)},$$

so

$$\zeta(z) = \zeta(1-z)\,\frac{\pi^z\, 2^z\, \Gamma(1-z)}{\Gamma(z/2)\,\Gamma(1-z/2)} = \zeta(1-z)\,\frac{\pi^{z-1/2}\,\Gamma((1-z)/2)}{\Gamma(z/2)}, \qquad (13.66)$$

where the final member of Eq. (13.66) was obtained by using the duplication formula, Eq. (13.27), with the value of z in the duplication formula set to the present $-z/2$. Equation (13.66) can now be rearranged to the more symmetrical form

$$\Gamma\left(\frac{z}{2}\right) \pi^{-z/2} \zeta(z) = \Gamma\left(\frac{1-z}{2}\right) \pi^{-(1-z)/2} \zeta(1-z). \qquad (13.67)$$

Equation (13.67), the **zeta-function reflection formula**, enables generation of $\zeta(z)$ in the half-plane $\Re e\ z < 0$ from values in the region $\Re e\ z > 1$, where the series definition converges.

It is possible to show that $\zeta(z)$ has no zeros in the region where the series definition converges, and, from Eq. (13.67), this implies that $\zeta(z)$ is also nonzero for all z in the half-plane $\Re e\ z < 0$ except at points where $\Gamma(z/2)$ is singular, namely $z = -2, -4, \ldots, -2n, \ldots$. $\Gamma(z/2)$ is also singular at $z = 0$ but, as we shall see shortly, the singularity at $\zeta(1)$ compensates the singularity at $\Gamma(0)$, with the result that $\zeta(0)$ is nonzero.

The zeros of $\zeta(z)$ at the negative even integers are called its **trivial zeros**, as they arise from the singularities of the gamma function. Any other zeros of $\zeta(z)$ (and there are an infinite number of them) must lie in the region $0 \le \Re e\ z \le 1$, which has been called the **critical strip** of the Riemann zeta function.

To obtain values of $\zeta(z)$ in the critical strip, we proceed by analytically continuing toward $\Re e\ z = 0$ the formula from Eq. (12.62) that defines the Dirichlet series $\eta(z)$ (clearly valid for $\Re e\ z > 1$),

$$\zeta(z) = \frac{\eta(z)}{1 - 2^{1-z}} = \frac{1}{1 - 2^{1-z}} \sum_{n=1}^{\infty} \frac{(-1)^{n-1}}{n^z}. \qquad (13.68)$$

This alternating series converges for all $\Re e\ z > 0$, thereby providing a formula for $\zeta(z)$ throughout the critical strip, but it is best used where the convergence is relatively rapid, namely for $\Re e\ z \ge \frac{1}{2}$. Values of $\zeta(z)$ for $\Re e\ z < \frac{1}{2}$ may be more conveniently obtained from those for $\Re e\ z \ge \frac{1}{2}$ using the reflection formula, Eq. (13.67).

Equation (13.68) may be used to verify that the singularity of $\zeta(z)$ at $z = 1$ is a simple pole and to find its residue. We proceed as follows:

$$\text{(Residue at } z = 1) = \lim_{z \to 1}(z - 1)\zeta(z) = \lim_{z \to 1}\left(\frac{z - 1}{1 - 2^{1-z}}\right)\sum_{n=1}^{\infty}\frac{(-1)^{n-1}}{n}$$

$$= \left(\frac{1}{\ln 2}\right)(\ln 2) = 1, \tag{13.69}$$

where we used l'Hôpital's rule, recognized that $d\,2^{1-z}/dz = -2^{1-z}\ln 2$, and identified the summation as that of Eq. (1.53). Returning now to Eq. (13.67), noting that

$$\lim_{z \to 0}\frac{\zeta(1 - z)}{\Gamma(z/2)} = \frac{-\text{residue of }\zeta(s)\text{ at }s = 1}{2\,(\text{residue of }\Gamma(s)\text{ at }s = 0)} = -\frac{1}{2},$$

we obtain the nonzero result

$$\zeta(0) = \Gamma(1/2)\pi^{-1/2}\left(-\frac{1}{2}\right) = -\frac{1}{2}. \tag{13.70}$$

In addition to the practical utility we have already noted for the Riemann zeta function, it plays a major role in current developments in analytic number theory. A starting point for such investigations is the celebrated Euler prime number product formula, which can be developed by forming

$$\zeta(s)(1 - 2^{-s}) = 1 + \frac{1}{2^s} + \frac{1}{3^s} + \cdots - \left(\frac{1}{2^s} + \frac{1}{4^s} + \frac{1}{6^s} + \cdots\right), \tag{13.71}$$

eliminating all the n^{-s}, where n is a multiple of 2. Then we write

$$\zeta(s)(1 - 2^{-s})(1 - 3^{-s}) = 1 + \frac{1}{3^s} + \frac{1}{5^s} + \frac{1}{7^s} + \frac{1}{9^s} + \cdots$$

$$- \left(\frac{1}{3^s} + \frac{1}{9^s} + \frac{1}{15^s} + \cdots\right),$$

eliminating all the remaining terms in which n is a multiple of 3. Continuing, we have $\zeta(s)(1 - 2^{-s})(1 - 3^{-s})(1 - 5^{-s})\cdots(1 - P^{-s})$, where P is a prime number, and all terms n^{-s}, in which n is a multiple of any integer up through P, are canceled out. In the limit $P \to \infty$, we reach

$$\zeta(s)(1 - 2^{-s})(1 - 3^{-s})\cdots(1 - P^{-s}) \longrightarrow \zeta(s)\prod_{P(\text{prime})=2}^{\infty}(1 - P^{-s}) = 1.$$

Therefore

$$\zeta(s) = \prod_{P(\text{prime})=2}^{\infty}(1 - P^{-s})^{-1}, \tag{13.72}$$

giving $\zeta(s)$ as an infinite product.[4] Incidentally, the cancellation procedure in the above derivation has a clear application in numerical computation. For example, Eq. (13.71) will give $\zeta(s)(1 - 2^{-s})$ to the same accuracy as Eq. (13.61) gives $\zeta(s)$, but with only half as many terms.

The asymptotic distribution of prime numbers can be related to the poles of ζ'/ζ, and in particular to the nontrivial zeros of the zeta function. Riemann conjectured that all the nontrivial zeros were on the **critical line** $\Re e\ z = \frac{1}{2}$, and there are potentially important results that can be proved if Riemann's conjecture is correct. Numerical work has verified that the first 300×10^9 nontrivial zeros of $\zeta(z)$ are simple and indeed fall on the critical line. See J. Van de Lune, H. J. J. Te Riele, and D. T. Winter, "On the zeros of the Riemann zeta function in the critical strip. IV," *Math. Comput.* **47**, 667 (1986).

Although many gifted mathematicians have attempted to establish what has come to be known as the **Riemann hypothesis**, it has for about 150 years remained unproven and is considered one of the premier unsolved problems in modern mathematics. Popular accounts of this fascinating problem can be found in M. du Santoy, *The Music of the Primes: Searching to Solve the Greatest Mystery in Mathematics*, New York: Harper-Collins (2003); J. Derbyshire, *Prime Obsession: Bernhard Riemann and the Greatest Unsolved Problem in Mathematics*, Washington, DC: Joseph Henry Press (2003); and K. Sabbagh, *The Riemann Hypothesis: The Greatest Unsolved Problem in Mathematics*, New York: Farrar, Straus and Giroux (2003).

Exercises

13.5.1   Show that the symmetrical functional relation

$$\Gamma\left(\frac{z}{2}\right)\pi^{-z/2}\zeta(z) = \Gamma\left(\frac{1-z}{2}\right)\pi^{-(1-z)/2}\zeta(1-z)$$

follows from the equation

$$\left(e^{2\pi i z} - 1\right)\zeta(z) = \zeta(1-z)\frac{(2\pi)^z}{\Gamma(z)}\left(e^{3\pi i z/2} - e^{\pi i z/2}\right).$$

13.5.2   Prove that

$$\int_0^\infty \frac{x^n e^x\, dx}{(e^x - 1)^2} = n!\,\zeta(n).$$

Assuming n to be real, show that each side of the equation diverges if $n = 1$. Hence the preceding equation carries the condition $n > 1$. Integrals such as this appear in the quantum theory of transport effects: thermal and electrical conductivity.

---

[4]For further discussion, the reader is referred to the works by Edwards, Ivíc, Patterson, and Titchmarsh in Additional Readings

13.5.3   The Bloch-Grüneisen approximation for the resistance in a monovalent metal at absolute temperature T is

$$\rho = C\frac{T^5}{\Theta^6} \int\limits_0^{\Theta/T} \frac{x^5 dx}{(e^x - 1)(1 - e^{-x})},$$

where Θ is the Debye temperature characteristic of the metal.

(a)   For $T \to \infty$, show that

$$\rho \approx \frac{C}{4} \cdot \frac{T}{\Theta^2}.$$

(b)   For $T \to 0$, show that

$$\rho \approx 5!\,\zeta(5)\,C\frac{T^5}{\Theta^6}.$$

13.5.4   Derive the following expansion of the Debye function for $n \geq 1$:

$$\int\limits_0^x \frac{t^n dt}{e^t - 1} = x^n\left[\frac{1}{n} - \frac{x}{2(n+1)} + \sum_{k=1}^\infty \frac{B_{2k}x^{2k}}{(2k+n)(2k)!}\right], \quad |x| < 2\pi.$$

The complete integral $(0, \infty)$ equals $n!\,\zeta(n+1)$ (Exercise 13.5.6).

13.5.5   The total energy radiated by a blackbody is given by

$$u = \frac{8\pi k^4 T^4}{c^3 h^3} \int\limits_0^\infty \frac{x^3}{e^x - 1}\,dx.$$

Show that the integral in this expression is equal to $3!\,\zeta(4)$. The final result is the Stefan-Boltzmann law.

13.5.6   As a generalization of the result in Exercise 13.5.5, show that

$$\int\limits_0^\infty \frac{x^s dx}{e^x - 1} = s!\,\zeta(s+1), \quad \Re(s) > 0.$$

13.5.7   Prove that

$$\int\limits_0^\infty \frac{x^s dx}{e^x + 1} = s!\,(1 - 2^{-s})\,\zeta(s+1), \quad \Re(s) > 0.$$

Exercises 13.5.6 and 13.5.7 give the Mellin integral transform of $1/(e^x \pm 1)$; this transform is defined in Eq. (20.9).

13.5.8   The neutrino energy density (Fermi distribution) in the early history of the universe is given by

$$\rho_\nu = \frac{4\pi}{h^3} \int\limits_0^\infty \frac{x^3}{\exp(x/kT)+1}\, dx.$$

Show that

$$\rho_\nu = \frac{7\pi^5}{30h^3}(kT)^4.$$

13.5.9   Prove that

$$\psi^{(n)}(z) = (-1)^{n+1} \int\limits_0^\infty \frac{t^n e^{-zt}}{1-e^{-t}}\, dt, \quad \Re e(z) > 0.$$

13.5.10   Show that $\zeta(s)$ is analytic in the entire finite complex plane except at $s = 1$, where it has a simple pole with a residue of $+1$.

Hint. The contour integral representation will be useful.

13.6   OTHER RELATED FUNCTIONS

Incomplete Gamma Functions

Generalizing the Euler-integral definition of the gamma function, Eq. (13.5), we define **incomplete gamma functions** by the variable-limit integrals

$$\gamma(a,x) = \int\limits_0^x e^{-t} t^{a-1}\, dt, \quad \Re(a) > 0,$$

$$\Gamma(a,x) = \int\limits_x^\infty e^{-t} t^{a-1}\, dt. \tag{13.73}$$

Clearly, these two functions are related, for

$$\gamma(a,x) + \Gamma(a,x) = \Gamma(a). \tag{13.74}$$

The choice of employing $\gamma(a,x)$ or $\Gamma(a,x)$ is purely a matter of convenience. If the parameter a is a positive integer, Eqs. (13.73) may be integrated completely to yield

$$\gamma(n,x) = (n-1)! \left(1 - e^{-x} \sum_{s=0}^{n-1} \frac{x^s}{s!}\right),$$

$$\Gamma(n,x) = (n-1)!\, e^{-x} \sum_{s=0}^{n-1} \frac{x^s}{s!}. \tag{13.75}$$

While the above expressions are valid only for positive integer n, the function $\Gamma(n, x)$ is well defined (providing $x > 0$) for $n = 0$ and corresponds to an exponential integral (see later subsection).

For nonintegral a, a power-series expansion of $\gamma(a, x)$ for small x and an asymptotic expansion of $\Gamma(a, x)$ are developed in Exercises 1.3.3 and 13.6.4:

$$\gamma(a, x) = x^a \sum_{n=0}^{\infty} (-1)^n \frac{x^n}{n!\,(a+n)}, \quad \text{small } x,$$

$$\Gamma(a, x) \sim x^{a-1} e^{-x} \sum_{n=0}^{\infty} \frac{\Gamma(a)}{\Gamma(a-n)} \cdot \frac{1}{x^n} \tag{13.76}$$

$$\sim x^{a-1} e^{-x} \sum_{n=0}^{\infty} (a-n)_n \frac{1}{x^n}, \quad \text{large } x,$$

where $(a - n)_n$ is a Pochhammer symbol. The final expression in Eq. (13.76) makes it clear how to obtain an asymptotic expansion for $\Gamma(0, x)$. Noting that $(-n)_n = (-1)^n n!$, we have

$$\Gamma(0, x) \sim \frac{e^{-x}}{x} \sum_{n=0}^{\infty} (-1)^n \frac{n!}{x^n}. \tag{13.77}$$

These incomplete gamma functions may also be expressed quite elegantly in terms of confluent hypergeometric functions (compare Section 18.6).

Incomplete Beta Function

Just as there are incomplete gamma functions, there is also an incomplete beta function, customarily defined for $0 \le x \le 1$, $p > 0$ (and, if $x = 1$, also $q > 0$) as

$$B_x(p, q) = \int_0^x t^{p-1} (1 - t)^{q-1} \, dt. \tag{13.78}$$

Clearly, $B_{x=1}(p, q)$ becomes the regular (complete) beta function, Eq. (13.49). A power-series expansion of $B_x(p, q)$ is the subject of Exercise 13.6.5. The relation to hypergeometric functions appears in Section 18.5.

The incomplete beta function makes an appearance in probability theory in calculating the probability of at most k successes in n independent trials.[5]

Exponential Integral

Although the incomplete gamma function $\Gamma(a, x)$ in its general form, Eq. (13.73), is only infrequently encountered in physical problems, a special case is quite common and very

---

[5] W. Feller, *An Introduction to Probability Theory and Its Applications*, 3rd ed. New York: Wiley (1968), Section VI.10.

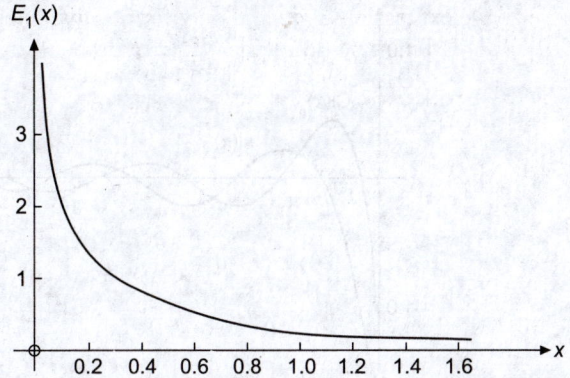

FIGURE 13.5   The exponential integral, $E_1(x) = -\text{Ei}(-x)$.

useful. We define the **exponential integral** by[6]

$$-\text{Ei}(-x) \equiv \int_x^\infty \frac{e^{-t}}{t}\, dt \equiv E_1(x). \tag{13.79}$$

For a graph of this function, see Fig. 13.5. To obtain a series expansion of $E_1(x)$ for small x, we will need to proceed with caution, because the integral in Eq. (13.78) diverges logarithmically as $x \to 0$. We start from

$$E_1(x) = \Gamma(0, x) = \lim_{a \to 0}\left[\Gamma(a) - \gamma(a, x)\right]. \tag{13.80}$$

Setting $a = 0$ in the convergent terms (those with $n \geq 1$) in the expansion of $\gamma(a, x)$ and moving them outside the scope of the limiting process, we rearrange Eq. (13.80) to

$$E_1(x) = \lim_{a \to 0}\left[\frac{a\Gamma(a) - x^a}{a}\right] - \sum_{n=1}^\infty \frac{(-1)^n x^n}{n \cdot n!}. \tag{13.81}$$

Using l'Hôpital's rule, Eq. (1.58), writing $a\Gamma(a) = \Gamma(a+1)$, and noting that $d\,x^a/da = x^a \ln x$, the limit in Eq. (13.81) reduces to

$$\left[\frac{d}{da}\Gamma(a+1) - \frac{d}{da}x^a\right]_{a=1} = \Gamma(1)\psi(1) - \ln x = -\gamma - \ln x, \tag{13.82}$$

where γ (without arguments) is the Euler-Mascheroni constant.[7] From Eqs. (13.81) and (13.82) we obtain the rapidly converging series

$$E_1(x) = -\gamma - \ln x - \sum_{n=1}^\infty \frac{(-1)^n x^n}{n \cdot n!}. \tag{13.83}$$

---

[6]The appearance of the two minus signs in $-\text{Ei}(-x)$ is a historical monstrosity. AMS-55, chapter 5, denotes this integral as $E_1(x)$. See Additional Readings for the reference.

[7]Having the notations $\gamma(a, x)$ and γ in the same discussion and with different meanings may seem unfortunate, but these are the traditional notations and should not lead to confusion if the reader is alert.

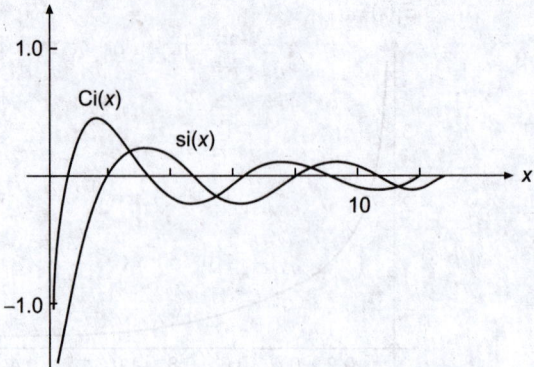

FIGURE 13.6   Sine and cosine integrals.

The asymptotic expansion for $E_1(x)$ is simply that given in Eq. (13.77) for $\Gamma(0, x)$. We repeat it here:

$$E_1(x) \sim e^{-x} \left[\frac{1}{x} - \frac{1!}{x^2} + \frac{2!}{x^3} - \frac{3!}{x^4} + \cdots \right]. \tag{13.84}$$

Further special forms related to the exponential integral are the sine integral, cosine integral (for both see Fig. 13.6), and the logarithmic integral, defined by[8]

$$\mathrm{si}(x) = - \int_x^\infty \frac{\sin t}{t} \, dt,$$

$$\mathrm{Ci}(x) = - \int_x^\infty \frac{\cos t}{t} \, dt, \tag{13.85}$$

$$\mathrm{li}(x) = \int_0^x \frac{dt}{\ln t} = \mathrm{Ei}(\ln x).$$

Viewed as functions of a complex variable, $\mathrm{Ci}(z)$ and $\mathrm{li}(z)$ are multivalued, with a branch cut conventionally chosen to be along the negative real axis from the branch point at $z = 0$. By transforming from real to imaginary argument, we can show that

$$\mathrm{si}(x) = \frac{1}{2i} \left[\mathrm{Ei}(ix) - \mathrm{Ei}(-ix) \right] = \frac{1}{2i} \left[E_1(ix) - E_1(-ix) \right], \tag{13.86}$$

whereas

$$\mathrm{Ci}(x) = \frac{1}{2} \left[\mathrm{Ei}(ix) + \mathrm{Ei}(-ix) \right] = -\frac{1}{2} \left[E_1(ix) + E_1(-ix) \right], \quad |\arg x| < \frac{\pi}{2}. \tag{13.87}$$

Adding these two relations, we obtain

$$\mathrm{Ei}(ix) = \mathrm{Ci}(x) + i\,\mathrm{si}(x), \tag{13.88}$$

---

[8] Another sine integral is denoted $\mathrm{Si}(x) = \mathrm{si}(x) + \pi/2$.

showing that the relation among these integrals is exactly analogous to that among e^{ix}, $\cos x$, and $\sin x$. In terms of E_1,

$$E_1(ix) = -\text{Ci}(x) + i \, \text{si}(x). \tag{13.89}$$

Asymptotic expansions of $\text{Ci}(x)$ and $\text{si}(x)$ were developed in Section 12.6, with explicit formulas in Eqs. (12.93) and (12.94). Power-series expansions about the origin for $\text{Ci}(x)$, $\text{si}(x)$, and $\text{li}(x)$ may be obtained from those for the exponential integral, $E_1(x)$, or by direct integration, Exercise 13.6.13. The exponential, sine, and cosine integrals are tabulated in AMS-55, chapter 5 (see Additional Readings for the reference), and can also be accessed by symbolic software such as Mathematica, Maple, Mathcad, and Reduce.

Error Function

The **error function** $\text{erf}(z)$ and the **complementary error function** $\text{erfc}(z)$ are defined by the integrals

$$\text{erf } z = \frac{2}{\sqrt{\pi}} \int_0^z e^{-t^2} \, dt, \quad \text{erfc } z = 1 - \text{erf } z = \frac{2}{\sqrt{\pi}} \int_z^\infty e^{-t^2} \, dt. \tag{13.90}$$

The factors $2/\sqrt{\pi}$ cause these functions to be scaled so that $\text{erf } \infty = 1$. For a plot of $\text{erf } x$, see Fig. 13.7.

The power-series expansion of $\text{erf } x$ follows directly from the expansion of the exponential in the integrand:

$$\text{erf } x = \frac{2}{\sqrt{\pi}} \sum_{n=0}^\infty \frac{(-1)^n x^{2n+1}}{(2n+1)\,n!}. \tag{13.91}$$

Its asymptotic expansion, the subject of Exercise 12.6.3, is

$$\text{erf } x \approx 1 - \frac{e^{-x^2}}{\sqrt{\pi}\,x} \left(1 - \frac{1}{2x^2} + \frac{1 \cdot 3}{2^2 x^4} - \frac{1 \cdot 3 \cdot 5}{2^3 x^6} + \cdots + (-1)^n \frac{(2n-1)!!}{2^n x^{2n}} \right). \tag{13.92}$$

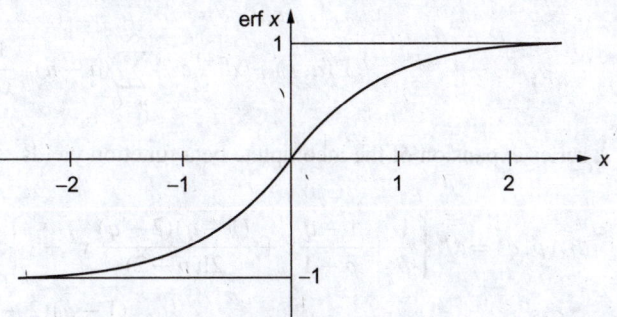

FIGURE 13.7   Error function, $\text{erf } x$.

From the general form of the integrands and Eq. (13.6) we expect that erf z and erfc z may be written as incomplete gamma functions with $a = \frac{1}{2}$. The relations are

$$\text{erf } z = \pi^{-1/2} \gamma(\tfrac{1}{2}, z^2), \quad \text{erfc } z = \pi^{-1/2} \Gamma(\tfrac{1}{2}, z^2). \tag{13.93}$$

Exercises

13.6.1   Show that $\gamma(a, x) = e^{-x} \sum_{n=0}^{\infty} \dfrac{(a-1)!}{(a+n)!} x^{a+n}$

    (a)   by repeatedly integrating by parts,

    (b)   by transforming it into Eq. (13.76).

13.6.2   Show that

    (a) $\dfrac{d^m}{dx^m}[x^{-a} \gamma(a, x)] = (-1)^m x^{-a-m} \gamma(a+m, x),$

    (b) $\dfrac{d^m}{dx^m}[e^x \gamma(a, x)] = e^x \dfrac{\Gamma(a)}{\Gamma(a-m)} \gamma(a-m, x).$

13.6.3   Show that $\gamma(a, x)$ and $\Gamma(a, x)$ satisfy the recurrence relations

    (a) $\gamma(a+1, x) = a\gamma(a, x) - x^a e^{-x},$

    (b) $\Gamma(a+1, x) = a\Gamma(a, x) + x^a e^{-x}.$

13.6.4   Show that the asymptotic expansion (for large x) of the incomplete gamma function $\Gamma(a, x)$ has the form

$$\Gamma(a, x) \sim x^{a-1} e^{-x} \sum_{n=0}^{\infty} \frac{\Gamma(a)}{\Gamma(a-n)} \cdot \frac{1}{x^n},$$

and that the above expression is equivalent to

$$\Gamma(a, x) \sim x^{a-1} e^{-x} \sum_{n=0}^{\infty} (a-n)_n \frac{1}{x^n}.$$

13.6.5   A series expansion of the incomplete beta function yields

$$B_x(p, q) = x^p \left\{ \frac{1}{p} + \frac{1-q}{p+1} x + \frac{(1-q)(2-q)}{2!(p+2)} x^2 + \cdots \right.$$

$$\left. + \frac{(1-q)(2-q)\cdots(n-q)}{n!(p+n)} x^n + \cdots \right\}.$$

Given that $0 \leq x \leq 1$, $p > 0$, and $q > 0$, test this series for convergence. What happens at $x = 1$?

13.6.6 Using the definitions of the various functions, show that

(a) $\text{si}(x) = \frac{1}{2i}[E_1(ix) - E_1(-ix)]$,

(b) $\text{Ci}(x) = -\frac{1}{2}[E_1(ix) + E_1(-ix)]$,

(c) $E_1(ix) = -\text{Ci}(x) + i\,\text{si}(x)$.

13.6.7 The potential produced by a $1s$ hydrogen electron is given by

$$V(r) = \frac{q}{4\pi\varepsilon_0 a_0}\left[\frac{1}{2r}\,\gamma(3, 2r) + \Gamma(2, 2r)\right].$$

(a) For $r \ll 1$, show that

$$V(r) = \frac{q}{4\pi\varepsilon_0 a_0}\left[1 - \frac{2}{3}r^2 + \cdots\right].$$

(b) For $r \gg 1$, show that

$$V(r) = \frac{q}{4\pi\varepsilon_0 a_0}\cdot\frac{1}{r}.$$

Here r is expressed in units of a_0, the Bohr radius.

Note. $V(r)$ is illustrated in Fig. 13.8.

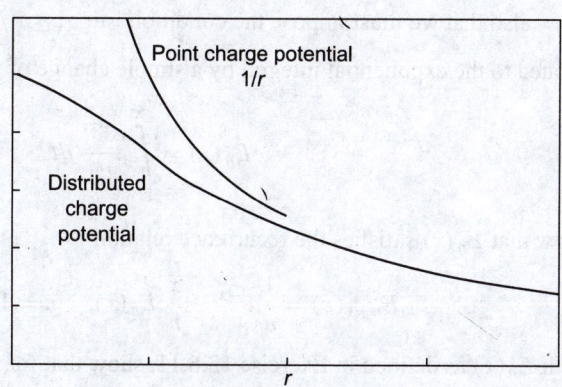

FIGURE 13.8 Distributed charge potential produced by a $1s$ hydrogen electron, Exercise 13.6.7.

13.6.8   The potential produced by a $2p$ hydrogen electron can be shown to be

$$V(\mathbf{r}) = \frac{1}{4\pi\varepsilon_0} \cdot \frac{q}{24a_0} \left[\frac{1}{r}\gamma(5, r) + \Gamma(4, r) \right]$$

$$- \frac{1}{4\pi\varepsilon_0} \cdot \frac{q}{120a_0} \left[\frac{1}{r^3}\gamma(7, r) + r^2\Gamma(2, r) \right] P_2(\cos\theta).$$

Here r is expressed in units of a_0, the Bohr radius. $P_2(\cos\theta)$ is a Legendre polynomial (Section 15.1).

(a)   For $r \ll 1$, show that

$$V(\mathbf{r}) = \frac{1}{4\pi\varepsilon_0} \cdot \frac{q}{a_0} \left[\frac{1}{4} - \frac{1}{120}r^2 P_2(\cos\theta) + \cdots \right].$$

(b)   For $r \gg 1$, show that

$$V(\mathbf{r}) = \frac{1}{4\pi\varepsilon_0} \cdot \frac{q}{a_0 r} \left[1 - \frac{6}{r^2}P_2(\cos\theta) + \cdots \right].$$

13.6.9   Prove that the exponential integral has the expansion

$$\int\limits_x^\infty \frac{e^{-t}}{t}\, dt = -\gamma - \ln x - \sum_{n=1}^\infty \frac{(-1)^n x^n}{n \cdot n!},$$

where γ is the Euler-Mascheroni constant.

13.6.10   Show that $E_1(z)$ may be written as

$$E_1(z) = e^{-z} \int\limits_0^\infty \frac{e^{-zt}}{1+t}\, dt.$$

Show also that we must impose the condition $|\arg z| \le \pi/2$.

13.6.11   Related to the exponential integral by a simple change of variable is the function

$$E_n(x) = \int\limits_1^\infty \frac{e^{-xt}}{t^n}\, dt.$$

Show that $E_n(x)$ satisfies the recurrence relation

$$E_{n+1}(x) = \frac{1}{n}\, e^{-x} - \frac{x}{n}\, E_n(x), \quad n = 1, 2, 3, \cdots.$$

13.6.12   With $E_n(x)$ as defined in Exercise 13.6.11, show that for $n > 1$,

$E_n(0) = 1/(n - 1)$.

13.6.13   Develop the following power-series expansions:

(a) $\text{si}(x) = -\dfrac{\pi}{2} + \sum\limits_{n=0}^{\infty} \dfrac{(-1)^n x^{2n+1}}{(2n+1)(2n+1)!}$,

(b) $\text{Ci}(x) = \gamma + \ln x + \sum\limits_{n=1}^{\infty} \dfrac{(-1)^n x^{2n}}{2n(2n)!}$.

13.6.14 An analysis of a center-fed linear antenna leads to the expression

$$\int_0^x \frac{1 - \cos t}{t}\, dt.$$

Show that this is equal to $\gamma + \ln x - \text{Ci}(x)$.

13.6.15 Using the relation

$$\Gamma(a) = \gamma(a, x) + \Gamma(a, x),$$

show that if $\gamma(a, x)$ satisfies the relations of Exercise 13.6.2, then $\Gamma(a, x)$ must satisfy the same relations.

13.6.16 For $x > 0$, show that

$$\int_x^{\infty} \frac{t^n\, dt}{e^t - 1} = \sum_{k=1}^{\infty} e^{-kx} \left[\frac{x^n}{k} + \frac{n x^{n-1}}{k^2} + \frac{n(n-1) x^{n-2}}{k^3} + \cdots + \frac{n!}{k^{n+1}} \right].$$

Additional Readings

Abramowitz, M., and I. A. Stegun, eds., *Handbook of Mathematical Functions with Formulas, Graphs, and Mathematical Tables* (AMS-55). Washington, DC: National Bureau of Standards (1972), reprinted, Dover (1974). Contains a wealth of information about gamma functions, incomplete gamma functions, exponential integrals, error functions, and related functions in chapters 4 to 6.

Artin, E., *The Gamma Function* (translated by M. Butler). New York: Holt, Rinehart and Winston (1964). Demonstrates that if a function $f(x)$ is smooth (log convex) and equal to $(n-1)!$ when $x = n =$ integer, it is the gamma function.

Davis, H. T., *Tables of the Higher Mathematical Functions*. Bloomington, IN: Principia Press (1933). Volume I contains extensive information on the gamma function and the polygamma functions.

Edwards, H. M., *Riemann's Zeta Function*. New York: Academic Press (1974) and Dover (2003).

Gradshteyn, I. S., and I. M. Ryzhik, *Table of Integrals, Series, and Products*. New York: Academic Press (1980).

Ivić, A., *The Riemann Zeta Function*. New York: Wiley (1985).

Luke, Y. L., *The Special Functions and Their Approximations*, Vol. 1. New York: Academic Press (1969).

Luke, Y. L., *Mathematical Functions and Their Approximations*. New York: Academic Press (1975). This is an updated supplement to *Handbook of Mathematical Functions with Formulas, Graphs, and Mathematical Tables* (AMS-55). Chapter 1 deals with the gamma function. Chapter 4 treats the incomplete gamma function and a host of related functions.

Patterson, S. J., *Introduction to the Theory of the Reimann Zeta Function*. Cambridge: Cambridge University Press (1988).

Titchmarsh, E. C., and D. R. Heath-Brown, *The Theory of the Riemann Zeta-Function*. Oxford: Clarendon Press (1986). A detailed, classic work.

CHAPTER 14

BESSEL FUNCTIONS

Bessel functions appear in a wide variety of physical problems. In Section 9.4 we saw that separation of the Helmholtz, or wave, equation in circular cylindrical coordinates led to Bessel's equation in the coordinate describing distance from the axis of the cylindrical system. In that same section, we also identified **spherical Bessel functions** (closely related to Bessel functions of half-integral order) in Helmholtz equations in spherical coordinates. In summarizing the forms of solutions to partial differential equations (PDEs) in these coordinate systems, we not only identified the original and spherical Bessel functions, but also those of imaginary argument (usually expressed as **modified Bessel functions** to avoid the explicit use of imaginary quantities). Since these PDEs can describe many types of problems ranging from stationary problems in quantum mechanics to those of spherical or cylindrical wave propagation, a good familiarity with Bessel functions is important to the practicing physicist.

Often problems in physics involve integrals that can be identified as Bessel functions, even when the original problem did not explicitly involve cylindrical or spherical geometry. Moreover, Bessel and closely related functions form a rich area of mathematical analysis with many representations, many interesting and useful properties, and many interrelations. Some of the major interrelations are developed in the present chapter. In addition to the material presented here, we call attention to further relations in terms of confluent hypergeometric functions; see Section 18.6.

14.1 BESSEL FUNCTIONS OF THE FIRST KIND, $J_\nu(x)$

Bessel functions **of the first kind**, normally labeled J_ν, are those obtained by the Frobenius method for solution of the Bessel ODE,

$$x^2 J_\nu'' + x J_\nu' + (x^2 - \nu^2) J_\nu = 0. \tag{14.1}$$

The term "first kind" reflects the fact that $J_\nu(x)$ includes the functions that, for non-negative integer ν, are regular at $x = 0$. All solutions to the Bessel ordinary differential equation (ODE) that are linearly independent of $J_\nu(x)$ are irregular at $x = 0$ for all ν; a specific choice for a second solution is denoted $Y_\nu(x)$ and is called a Bessel function **of the second kind**.[1]

Generating Function for Integral Order

We start our detailed study of Bessel functions by introducing a generating function yielding the J_n for integer n (of either sign). Because the J_n are not polynomials, the generating function cannot be found by the methods of Section 12.1, but we will be able to show that the functions defined by the generating function are indeed the solutions of the Bessel ODE obtained by the Frobenius method.

Our generating function formula, a Laurent series, is

$$g(x, t) = e^{(x/2)(t-1/t)} = \sum_{n=-\infty}^{\infty} J_n(x) t^n. \tag{14.2}$$

Although the Bessel ODE is homogeneous and its solutions are of arbitrary scale, Eq. (14.2) fixes a specific scale for $J_n(x)$. To relate Eq. (14.2) to the Frobenius solution, Eq. (7.48), we manipulate the exponential as follows:

$$g(x, t) = e^{xt/2} \cdot e^{-x/2t} = \sum_{r=0}^{\infty} \left(\frac{x}{2}\right)^r \frac{t^r}{r!} \sum_{s=0}^{\infty} (-1)^s \left(\frac{x}{2}\right)^s \frac{t^{-s}}{s!}$$

$$= \sum_{r=0}^{\infty} \sum_{s=0}^{\infty} (-1)^s \left(\frac{x}{2}\right)^{r+s} \frac{t^{r-s}}{r! s!}.$$

We now change the summation index r to $n = r - s$, yielding

$$g(x, t) = \sum_{n=-\infty}^{\infty} \left[\sum_s \frac{(-1)^s}{(n+s)! s!} \left(\frac{x}{2}\right)^{n+2s} \right] t^n, \tag{14.3}$$

where the s summation starts at $\max(0, -n)$. For $n \geq 0$, the coefficient of t^n is seen to be

$$J_n(x) = \sum_{s=0}^{\infty} \frac{(-1)^s}{s!(n+s)!} \left(\frac{x}{2}\right)^{n+2s}. \tag{14.4}$$

Comparing with Eq. (7.48), we confirm that for $n \geq 0$, J_n as given by Eq. (14.4) is the Frobenius solution, at the specific scale given here.

If now we replace n by $-n$, the summation in Eq. (14.3) becomes

$$J_{-n}(x) = \sum_{s=n}^{\infty} \frac{(-1)^s}{s!(s-n)!} \left(\frac{x}{2}\right)^{-n+2s};$$

---

[1] We use the notation of AMS-55, also used by Watson in his definitive treatise (for both sources, see Additional Readings). The Y_ν are sometimes also called **Neumann functions**; for that reason some workers write them as N_ν. They were denoted N_ν in previous editions of this book.

changing s to $s + n$, we reach

$$J_{-n}(x) = \sum_{s=0}^{\infty} \frac{(-1)^{s+n}}{s!(s+n)!} \left(\frac{x}{2}\right)^{n+2s} = (-1)^n J_n(x) \quad \text{(integral } n\text{)}, \tag{14.5}$$

confirming both that $J_{-n}(x)$ is a solution to the Bessel ODE and that it is linearly dependent on J_n.

If we now consider J_ν with ν nonintegral, we get no information from the generating function, but the Frobenius method then gives linearly independent solutions for both $+\nu$ and $-\nu$, which are both solutions of the Bessel ODE, Eq. (14.1), for the same value of ν^2. Looking at the details of the development of Eqs. (7.46) to (7.48), we see that the generalization of Eq. (14.4) to noninteger ν is

$$J_\nu(x) = \sum_{s=0}^{\infty} \frac{(-1)^s}{s!\Gamma(\nu+s+1)} \left(\frac{x}{2}\right)^{\nu+2s}, \quad (\nu \neq -1, -2, \dots), \tag{14.6}$$

and that $J_\nu(x)$ as given in Eq. (14.6) is a solution to the Bessel ODE.

For $\nu \geq 0$ the series of Eq. (14.6) is convergent for all x, and for small x is a practical way to evaluate $J_\nu(x)$. Graphs of J_0, J_1, and J_2 are shown in Fig. 14.1. The Bessel functions oscillate but are **not** periodic, except in the limit $x \to \infty$, with the amplitude of the oscillation decreasing asymptotically as $x^{-1/2}$. This behavior is discussed further in Section 14.6.

Recurrence Relations

The Bessel functions $J_n(x)$ satisfy recurrence relations connecting functions of contiguous n, as well as some connecting the derivative J_n' to various J_n. Such recurrence relations may all be obtained by operating on the series, Eq. (14.6), although this requires a bit of clairvoyance (or a lot of trial and error). However, if the recurrence relations are already known, their verification is straightforward; see Exercise 14.1.8. Our approach here will be to obtain them from the generating function $g(x, t)$, using a process similar to that illustrated in Example 12.1.2.

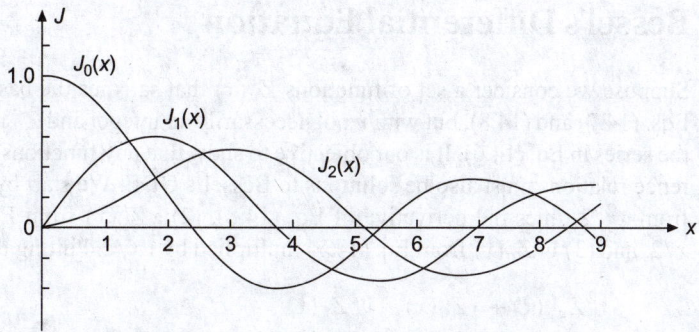

FIGURE 14.1   Bessel functions $J_0(x)$, $J_1(x)$, and $J_2(x)$.

We start by differentiating $g(x, t)$:

$$\frac{\partial}{\partial t} g(x, t) = \frac{x}{2}\left(1 + \frac{1}{t^2}\right) e^{(x/2)(t-1/t)} = \sum_{n=-\infty}^{\infty} n J_n(x) t^{n-1},$$

$$\frac{\partial}{\partial x} g(x, t) = \frac{1}{2}\left(t - \frac{1}{t}\right) e^{(x/2)(t-1/t)} = \sum_{n=-\infty}^{\infty} J_n'(x) t^n.$$

Inserting the right-hand side of Eq. (14.2) in place of the exponentials and equating the coefficients of equal powers of t (as illustrated in Example 12.1.2), we obtain the two basic Bessel-function recurrence formulas:

$$J_{n-1}(x) + J_{n+1}(x) = \frac{2n}{x} J_n(x), \tag{14.7}$$

$$J_{n-1}(x) - J_{n+1}(x) = 2J_n'(x). \tag{14.8}$$

Because Eq. (14.7) is a three-term recurrence relation, its use to generate J_n will require two starting values. For example, given J_0 and J_1, then J_2 (and any other integral order J_n including those for $n < 0$) may be computed.

An important special case of Eq. (14.8) is

$$J_0'(x) = -J_1(x). \tag{14.9}$$

Equations (14.7) and (14.8) can also be combined (Exercise 14.1.4) to form the useful additional formulas

$$\frac{d}{dx}\left[x^n J_n(x)\right] = x^n J_{n-1}(x), \tag{14.10}$$

$$\frac{d}{dx}\left[x^{-n} J_n(x)\right] = -x^{-n} J_{n+1}(x), \tag{14.11}$$

$$J_n(x) = \pm J_{n\pm1}' + \frac{n \pm 1}{x} J_{n\pm1}(x). \tag{14.12}$$

Bessel's Differential Equation

Suppose we consider a set of functions $Z_\nu(x)$ that satisfies the basic recurrence relations, Eqs. (14.7) and (14.8), but with ν not necessarily an integer and Z_ν not necessarily given by the series in Eq. (14.6). It is our objective to show that any functions that satisfy these recurrence relations must also be solutions to Bessel's ODE. We start by forming (1) $x^2 Z_\nu''(x)$ from $x^2/2$ times the derivative of Eq. (14.8), (2) $x Z_\nu'(x)$ from Eq. (14.8) multiplied by $x/2$, and (3) $\nu^2 Z_\nu(x)$ from Eq. (14.7) multiplied by $\nu x/2$. Putting these together we obtain

$$x^2 Z_\nu''(x) + x Z_\nu'(x) - \nu^2 Z_\nu(x)$$

$$= \frac{x^2}{2}\left[Z_{\nu-1}'(x) - Z_{\nu+1}'(x) - \frac{\nu-1}{x} Z_{\nu-1}(x) - \frac{\nu+1}{x} Z_{\nu+1}(x)\right]. \tag{14.13}$$

The terms within square brackets in Eq. (14.13) can now by use of Eq. (14.12) be simplified to $-2Z_\nu(x)$, so Eq. (14.13) can be rewritten

$$x^2 Z_\nu''(x) + x Z_\nu'(x) + (x^2 - \nu^2)Z_\nu(x) = 0, \tag{14.14}$$

which is Bessel's ODE. Reiterating, we have shown that any functions $Z_\nu(x)$ that satisfy the basic recurrence formulas, Eqs. (14.7) and (14.8), also satisfy Bessel's equation; that is, the Z_ν are Bessel functions. For later use, we note that if the argument of Z_ν is $k\rho$ rather than x, Eq. (14.14) becomes

$$\rho^2 \frac{d^2}{d\rho^2} Z_\nu(k\rho) + \rho \frac{d}{d\rho} Z_\nu(k\rho) + (k^2\rho^2 - \nu^2)Z_\nu(k\rho) = 0. \tag{14.15}$$

Integral Representation

It is of great value to have integral representations of Bessel functions. Starting from the generating-function formula, we can apply the residue theorem to evaluate the contour integral

$$\oint_C \frac{e^{(x/2)(t+1/t)}}{t^{n+1}} dt = \oint_C \sum_m J_m(x) t^{m-n-1} dt = 2\pi i J_n(x), \tag{14.16}$$

where the contour C encircles the singularity at $t = 0$. The integral on the left-hand side of Eq. (14.16) can now be brought to a convenient form by taking the contour to be the unit circle and changing the integration variable by making the substitution $t = e^{i\theta}$. Then $dt = ie^{i\theta}d\theta$, $e^{(x/2)(t-1/t)} = e^{ix\sin\theta}$, and we have

$$2\pi i J_n(x) = \int_0^{2\pi} \frac{e^{ix\sin\theta}}{e^{(n+1)i\theta}} i e^{i\theta} d\theta = \int_0^{2\pi} e^{i(x\sin\theta - n\theta)} i d\theta. \tag{14.17}$$

Assuming x to be real and taking the imaginary parts of both sides of Eq. (14.17), we find

$$J_n(x) = \frac{1}{2\pi} \int_0^{2\pi} \cos(x\sin\theta - n\theta)d\theta = \frac{1}{\pi} \int_0^{\pi} \cos(x\sin\theta - n\theta)\, d\theta, \tag{14.18}$$

where the last equality only holds because we are assuming n to be an integer. Though we will not need it now, the real part of this equation also gives an interesting formula:

$$\int_0^{2\pi} \sin(x\sin\theta - n\theta)d\theta = 0. \tag{14.19}$$

An oft-occurring special case of Eq. (14.18) is

$$J_0(x) = \frac{1}{2\pi} \int_0^{2\pi} e^{ix\cos\theta} d\theta = \frac{1}{\pi} \int_0^{\pi} \cos(x\sin\theta)\, d\theta. \tag{14.20}$$

Table 14.1   Zeros of the Bessel Functions and Their First Derivatives

Number of zeros	$J_0(x)$	$J_1(x)$	$J_2(x)$	$J_3(x)$	$J_4(x)$	$J_5(x)$
1	2.4048	3.8317	5.1356	6.3802	7.5883	8.7715
2	5.5201	7.0156	8.4172	9.7610	11.0647	12.3386
3	8.6537	10.1735	11.6198	13.0152	14.3725	15.7002
4	11.7915	13.3237	14.7960	16.2235	17.6160	18.9801
5	14.9309	16.4706	17.9598	19.4094	20.8269	22.2178
	$J_0'(x)$	$J_1'(x)$	$J_2'(x)$	$J_3'(x)$	$J_4'(x)$	$J_5'(x)$
1	3.8317	1.8412	3.0542	4.2012	5.3176	6.4156
2	7.0156	5.3314	6.7061	8.0152	9.2824	10.5199
3	10.1735	8.5363	9.9695	11.3459	12.6819	13.9872
4	13.3237	11.7060	13.1704	14.5858	15.9641	17.3128
5	16.4706	14.8636	16.3475	17.7887	19.1960	20.5755

Equation (14.18) is only one of many integral representations of J_n, and some of these can be derived (using an appropriately modified contour) for J_ν of a nonintegral order. This topic is explored in the subsection below entitled "Bessel Functions of Nonintegral Order".

Zeros of Bessel Functions

In many physical problems in which phenomena are described by Bessel functions, we are interested in the points where these functions (which have oscillatory character) are zero. For example, in a problem involving standing waves, these zeros identify the positions of the **nodes**. And in boundary value problems, we may need to choose the argument of our Bessel function to put a zero at an appropriate point.

There are no closed formulas for the zeros of Bessel functions; they must be found by numerical methods. Because the need for them arises frequently, tables of the zeros are available, both in compilations such as AMS-55 (see Additional Readings) and at a variety of sources online.[2] Table 14.1 lists the first few zeros of $J_n(x)$ for integer n from $n = 0$ through $n = 5$, giving also the positions of the zeros of J_n'.

Example 14.1.1   FRAUNHOFER DIFFRACTION, CIRCULAR APERTURE

In the theory of diffraction of radiation of wavelength λ, incident normal to a circular aperture of radius a, we encounter the integral

$$\Phi \sim \int_0^a r\, dr \int_0^{2\pi} e^{ibr\cos\theta}\, d\theta, \tag{14.21}$$

---

[2] Additional roots of the Bessel functions and those of their first derivatives may be found in C. L. Beattie, Table of first 700 zeros of Bessel functions, *Bell Syst. Tech. J.* **37**, 689 (1958), and Bell Monogr. **3055**. Roots may be also be accessed in Mathematica, Maple, and other symbolic software.

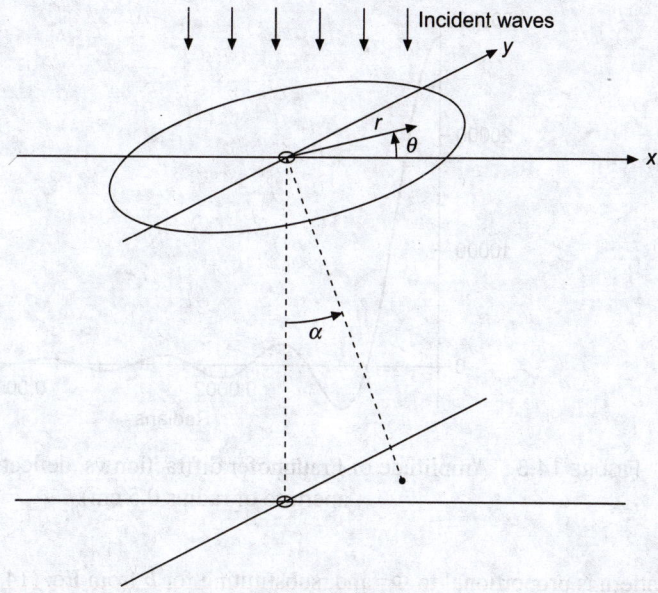

FIGURE 14.2   Geometry for Fraunhofer diffraction, circular aperture.

where Φ is the amplitude of the diffracted wave and (r, θ) identifies points in the aperture. The exponent $br \cos \theta$ is the phase of the radiation through (r, θ) that is diffracted to an angle α from the incident direction, with

$$b = \frac{2\pi}{\lambda} \sin \alpha. \tag{14.22}$$

The geometry is illustrated in Fig. 14.2. **Fraunhofer** diffraction, for which the above are the relevant formulas, applies in the limit that the outgoing radiation is detected at large distances from the aperture.

The behavior of the complex exponential will cause the amplitude to oscillate as α is increased, creating (for each wavelength) a diffraction pattern. To understand the patterns more fully, we need to evaluate the integral in Eq. (14.21). From Eq. (14.20) we may immediately reduce Eq. (14.21) to

$$\Phi \sim 2\pi \int_0^a J_0(br)r \, dr, \tag{14.23}$$

which can be integrated in r using Eq. (14.10):

$$\Phi \sim 2\pi \int_0^a \frac{1}{b^2} \frac{d}{dr}\big[(br)J_1(br)\big] dr = \frac{2\pi}{b^2}\big[br J_1(br)\big]_0^a = \frac{2\pi a}{b} J_1(ab), \tag{14.24}$$

where we have used the fact that $J_1(0) = 0$. The intensity of the light in the diffraction

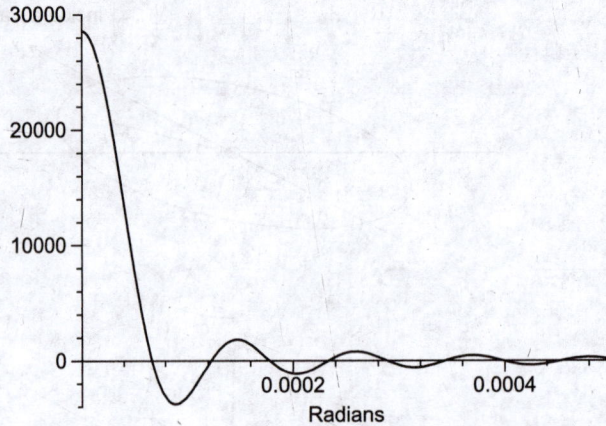

FIGURE 14.3   Amplitude of Fraunhofer diffraction vs. deflection angle (green light, aperture of radius 0.5 cm).

pattern is proportional to Φ^2 and, substituting for b from Eq. (14.22),

$$\Phi^2 \sim \left(\frac{J_1[(2\pi a/\lambda)\sin\alpha]}{\sin\alpha} \right)^2. \tag{14.25}$$

For visible light and apertures of reasonable size, $2\pi a/\lambda$ is quite small: for green light ($\lambda = 5.5 \times 10^{-5}$ cm) and an aperture with $a = 0.5$ cm, $2\pi a/\lambda = 57120$, and these parameter values lead to the pattern for Φ shown in Fig. 14.3. Note that the figure plots Φ (a plot of Φ^2 would make the oscillations too small to be observable on the same graph as the maximum at $\alpha = 0$). We see that Φ exhibits a central maximum at $\alpha = 0$ of amplitude $\sim 30,000$, with subsidiary extrema that by $\alpha = 0.001$ radian have decreased in magnitude to less than 1% of the central maximum. Remembering that the intensity is Φ^2, we see that the diffraction spreading of the incident light is exceedingly small. To make a quantitative analysis of the diffraction pattern, we need to identify the positions of its minima. They correspond to the zeros of J_1; for example, from Table 14.1 we find the first minimum to be where $(2\pi a/\lambda)\sin\alpha = 3.8317$, or $\alpha \approx 14$ seconds of arc. If this analysis had been known in the 17th century, the arguments against the wave theory of light would have collapsed.

In mid-20th century this same diffraction pattern appears in the scattering of nuclear particles by atomic nuclei, a striking demonstration of the wave properties of the nuclear particles. ∎

Further examples of the use of Bessel functions and their roots are provided by the following example and by the exercises of this section and Section 14.2.

Example 14.1.2   CYLINDRICAL RESONANT CAVITY

The propagation of electromagnetic waves in hollow metallic cylinders is important in many practical devices. If the cylinder has end surfaces, it is called a **cavity**. Resonant cavities play a crucial role in many particle accelerators.

The resonant frequencies of a cavity are those of the oscillatory solutions to Maxwell's equations that correspond to standing wave patterns. By combining Maxwell's equations, we derived in Example 3.6.2 the vector Laplace equation for the electric field $\mathbf{E}$ in a region free of electric charges and currents. Taking the z-axis along the axis of the cavity, our concern here is the equation for E_z, which from Eq. (3.71) we found to have the form

$$\nabla^2 E_z = -\frac{1}{c^2}\frac{\partial^2 E_z}{\partial t^2}, \tag{14.26}$$

which has standing-wave solutions $E_z(x, y, z, t) = E_z(x, y, z)f(t)$ where $f(t)$ has real solutions $\sin \omega t$ and $\cos \omega t$, corresponding to sinusoidal oscillations at angular frequency ω. We are implicitly assuming that our solution has a nonzero component E_z, and we will also set $B_z = 0$, so we intend to obtain solutions that are usually called the TM (for "transverse magnetic") modes of oscillation. Additional solutions, with $E_z = 0$ and B_z nonzero, correspond to TE (transverse electric) modes and are the subject of Exercise 14.1.25.

Thus, for the present problem, in which our cavity is that shown in Fig. 14.4, we seek solutions to the spatial PDE:

$$\nabla^2 E_z + k^2 E_z = 0, \quad k = \frac{\omega}{c}. \tag{14.27}$$

The aim of the present example is to find the values of ω for which Eq. (14.27) has solutions consistent with the boundary conditions at the cavity walls. Assuming the metallic walls to be perfect conductors, the boundary conditions are that the tangential components of the electric field vanish there. Taking the cavity to have planar end caps at $z = 0$ and $z = h$, and (in cylindrical coordinates ρ, φ) to be bounded by a curved surface at $\rho = a$, our boundary conditions are $E_x = E_y = 0$ on the end caps, and $E_\varphi = E_z = 0$ on the boundary at $\rho = a$.

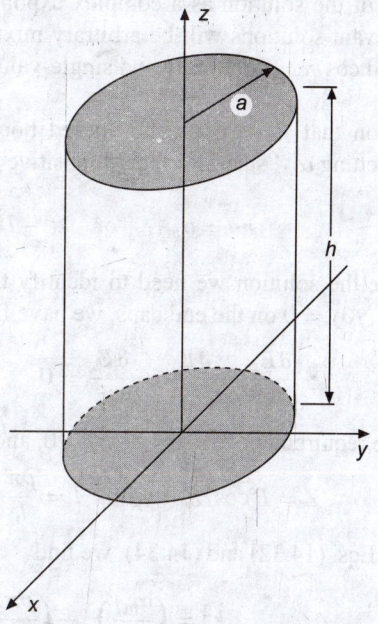

FIGURE 14.4   Resonant cavity.

Once a solution (with $B_z = 0$) has been found for E_z, then the remaining components of **B** and **E** have definite values. For further details, see J. D. Jackson, *Electrodynamics* in Additional Readings.

Equation (14.27) can be solved by the method of separation of variables, with solutions of the form given in Eq. (9.64):

$$E_z(\rho, \theta, z) = P_{lm}(\rho)\Phi_m(\varphi)Z_l(z), \tag{14.28}$$

with $\Phi_m(\theta) = e^{\pm im\varphi}$ or its equivalent in terms of sines and cosines, while $Z_l(z)$ and $P_{lm}(\rho)$ are solutions of the ODEs

$$\frac{d^2 Z_l}{dz^2} = -l^2 Z_l, \tag{14.29}$$

$$\frac{d}{d\rho}\left(\rho\frac{dP_{lm}}{d\rho}\right) + \left((k^2 - l^2)\rho^2 - m^2\right)P_{lm} = 0. \tag{14.30}$$

Equation (14.29) corresponds to Eq. (9.58), but with a different choice of the sign for the separation constant in anticipation of the fact that Z_l will turn out to be oscillatory. This change causes n^2 in Eq. (9.60) to become $k^2 - l^2$, and Eq. (14.30) is then seen to correspond exactly with Eq. (9.63).

Recognizing now Eq. (14.30) as Bessel's ODE and Eq. (14.29) as the ODE for a classical harmonic oscillator, we find, before imposing boundary conditions,

$$E_z = J_m(n\rho)e^{\pm im\varphi}\left[A\sin lz + B\cos lz\right], \tag{14.31}$$

and the general solution will be an arbitrary linear combination of the above for different values of n, m, and l. We have chosen the solution to Bessel's ODE to be of the first kind to maintain regularity at $\rho = 0$, since this ρ value is inside the cavity. We have written the φ dependence of the solution as a complex exponential for notational convenience. The physically relevant solutions will be arbitrary mixtures of the corresponding real quantities, $\sin m\varphi$ and $\cos m\varphi$. Continuity and single-valuedness in φ dictate that m have integer values.

The condition that $E_z = 0$ on the curved boundary translates into the requirement $J_m(na) = 0$. Letting α_{mj} stand for the jth positive zero of J_m, we find that

$$na = \alpha_{mj}, \quad \text{or} \quad k^2 - l^2 = \left(\frac{\alpha_{mj}}{a}\right)^2. \tag{14.32}$$

To complete the solution we need to identify the boundary condition on Z. Because $\partial E_x/\partial x = \partial E_y/\partial y = 0$ on the end caps, we have from the Maxwell equation for $\nabla \cdot \mathbf{E}$:

$$\frac{\partial E_x}{\partial x} + \frac{\partial E_y}{\partial y} + \frac{\partial E_z}{\partial z} = 0 \quad \longrightarrow \quad \frac{\partial E_z}{\partial z} = 0, \tag{14.33}$$

so we have the requirement $Z'(0) = Z'(h) = 0$, and we must choose

$$Z = B\cos lz, \quad \text{with} \quad l = \frac{p\pi}{h}, \quad p = 0, 1, 2, \ldots. \tag{14.34}$$

Combining Eqs. (14.32) and (14.34), we find

$$k^2 = \left(\frac{\alpha_{mj}}{a}\right)^2 + \left(\frac{p\pi}{h}\right)^2 = \frac{\omega^2}{c^2}, \tag{14.35}$$

thereby providing an equation for the resonant frequencies:

$$\omega_{mjp} = c\sqrt{\frac{\alpha_{mj}^2}{a^2} + \frac{p^2\pi^2}{h^2}}, \qquad \begin{cases} m = 0, 1, 2, \ldots, \\ j = 1, 2, 3, \ldots, \\ p = 0, 1, 2, \ldots. \end{cases} \qquad (14.36)$$

Recapitulating, the functions we have found, labeled by the indices m, j, and p, are the spatial parts of standing-wave solutions of TM character whose time dependence and overall amplitude are of the form $Ce^{\pm i\omega_{mjp}t}$. ∎

Bessel Functions of Nonintegral Order

While J_ν of noninteger ν are not produced from a generating-function approach, they are readily identified from the Taylor series expansion, and they are conventionally given a scale consistent with that of the J_n of integer n. They then satisfy the same recurrence relations as those derived from the generating function.

If ν is not an integer, there is actually an important simplification. The functions J_ν and $J_{-\nu}$ are then independent solutions of the same ODE, and a relation of the form of Eq. (14.5) does not exist. On the other hand, for $\nu = n$, an integer, we need another solution. The development of this second solution and an investigation of its properties form the subject of Section 14.3.

Schlaefli Integral

It is useful to modify the integral representation, Eq. (14.16), so that it can be applied for Bessel functions of nonintegral order. Our first step in doing so is to deform the circular contour by stretching it to infinity on the negative real axis and opening the contour there, as shown in Fig. 14.5. Our integral, written

$$F_\nu(x) = \frac{1}{2\pi i} \int\limits_C \frac{e^{(x/2)(t-1/t)}}{t^{\nu+1}} dt, \qquad (14.37)$$

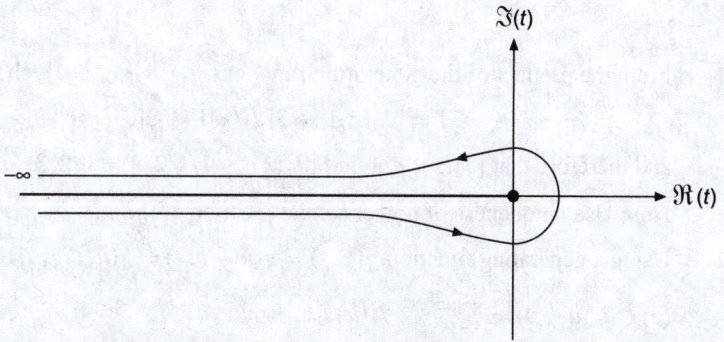

FIGURE 14.5   Contour, Schlaefli integral for J_ν.

now has a branch point at $t = 0$, and because we have opened the contour we can place the branch cut along the negative real axis. We might anticipate that this procedure will not affect our integral representation, as the integrand vanishes at $t = -\infty$ on both sides of the cut. However, that remains to be proved.

Our first step toward a proof that F_ν is actually J_ν is to verify that F_ν still satisfies Bessel's ODE. If we substitute F_ν and its x derivatives into the ODE, we can, after some manipulation, reach the expression

$$\frac{1}{2\pi i} \int\limits_C \frac{d}{dt} \left\{ \frac{e^{(x/2)(t-1/t)}}{t^\nu} \left[\nu + \frac{x}{2} \left(t + \frac{1}{t} \right) \right] \right\} dt, \tag{14.38}$$

and because the integration is within a region of analyticity of the integrand, the integral reduces to

$$\left\{ \frac{e^{(x/2)(t-1/t)}}{t^\nu} \left[\nu + \frac{x}{2} \left(t + \frac{1}{t} \right) \right] \right\}_{\text{end}} - \left\{ \frac{e^{(x/2)(t-1/t)}}{t^\nu} \left[\nu + \frac{x}{2} \left(t + \frac{1}{t} \right) \right] \right\}_{\text{start}}.$$

We therefore conclude that the ODE is satisfied if the above expression vanishes; in our present situation each of the quantities in braces is zero for large negative t and positive x, confirming that F_ν satisfies Bessel's ODE.

We still need to show that F_ν is the solution designated J_ν; to accomplish this we consider its value for small $x > 0$. Deforming the contour to a large open circle and making a change of variable to $u = e^{i\pi} xt/2$, we get (to lowest order in x)

$$F_\nu(x) \approx \frac{1}{2\pi i} \left(\frac{x}{2} \right)^\nu e^{i\nu\pi} \int\limits_{C'} \frac{e^{-u}}{u^{\nu+1}} du. \tag{14.39}$$

Because of the change of variable, the contour C' becomes that which we introduced when developing a Schlaefli integral representation of the gamma function, and, using Eq. (13.31), we reduce Eq. (14.39) to

$$F_\nu(x) \approx \left(\frac{x}{2} \right)^\nu \frac{\sin[(\nu+1)\pi]\Gamma(-\nu)}{\pi} = \frac{1}{\Gamma(\nu+1)} \left(\frac{x}{2} \right)^\nu, \tag{14.40}$$

where the last step used the reflection formula for the gamma function, Eq. (13.23). Since this is the leading term of the expansion for J_ν, our proof is complete.

Exercises

14.1.1   From the product of the generating functions $g(x, t)g(x, -t)$, show that

$$1 = [J_0(x)]^2 + 2[J_1(x)]^2 + 2[J_2(x)]^2 + \cdots$$

and therefore that $|J_0(x)| \le 1$ and $|J_n(x)| \le 1/\sqrt{2}, n = 1, 2, 3, \ldots$.

Hint. Use uniqueness of power series, (Section 1.2).

14.1.2   Using a generating function $g(x, t) = g(u + v, t) = g(u, t)g(v, t)$, show that

(a) $J_n(u + v) = \sum_{s=-\infty}^{\infty} J_s(u) J_{n-s}(v)$,

(b) $J_0(u + v) = J_0(u)J_0(v) + 2\sum_{s=1}^{\infty} J_s(u) J_{-s}(v)$.

These are addition theorems for the Bessel functions.

14.1.3   Using only the generating function

$$e^{(x/2)(t-1/t)} = \sum_{n=-\infty}^{\infty} J_n(x)t^n$$

and not the explicit series form of $J_n(x)$, show that $J_n(x)$ has odd or even parity according to whether n is odd or even, that is,

$$J_n(x) = (-1)^n J_n(-x).$$

14.1.4   Use the basic recurrence formulas, Eqs. (14.7) and (14.8), to prove the following formulas:

(a) $\frac{d}{dx}[x^n J_n(x)] = x^n J_{n-1}(x),$

(b) $\frac{d}{dx}[x^{-n} J_n(x)] = -x^{-n} J_{n+1}(x),$

(c) $J_n(x) = J'_{n+1} + \frac{n+1}{x} J_{n+1}(x).$

14.1.5   Derive the Jacobi-Anger expansion

$$e^{i\rho\cos\varphi} = \sum_{m=-\infty}^{\infty} i^m J_m(\rho)e^{im\varphi}.$$

This is an expansion of a plane wave in a series of cylindrical waves.

14.1.6   Show that

(a) $\cos x = J_0(x) + 2\sum_{n=1}^{\infty}(-1)^n J_{2n}(x),$

(b) $\sin x = 2\sum_{n=0}^{\infty}(-1)^n J_{2n+1}(x).$

14.1.7   To help remove the generating function from the realm of magic, show that it can be **derived** from the recurrence relation, Eq. (14.7).

Hint. (a) Assume a generating function of the form

$$g(x,t) = \sum_{m=-\infty}^{\infty} J_m(x)t^m.$$

(b) Multiply Eq. (14.7) by t^n and sum over n.

(c) Rewrite the preceding result as

$$\left(t + \frac{1}{t}\right)g(x,t) = \frac{2t}{x}\frac{\partial g(x,t)}{\partial t}.$$

(d) Integrate and adjust the "constant" of integration (a function of x) so that the coefficient of the zeroth power, t^0, is $J_0(x)$ as given by Eq. (14.6).

14.1.8   Show, by direct differentiation, that

$$J_\nu(x) = \sum_{s=0}^{\infty} \frac{(-1)^s}{s!\,\Gamma(s+\nu+1)} \left(\frac{x}{2}\right)^{\nu+2s}$$

satisfies the two recurrence relations

$$J_{\nu-1}(x) + J_{\nu+1}(x) = \frac{2\nu}{x} J_\nu(x),$$

$$J_{\nu-1}(x) - J_{\nu+1}(x) = 2J_\nu'(x),$$

and Bessel's differential equation

$$x^2 J_\nu''(x) + x J_\nu'(x) + (x^2 - \nu^2) J_\nu(x) = 0.$$

14.1.9   Prove that

$$\frac{\sin x}{x} = \int_0^{\pi/2} J_0(x\cos\theta)\cos\theta\,d\theta, \qquad \frac{1-\cos x}{x} = \int_0^{\pi/2} J_1(x\cos\theta)\,d\theta.$$

Hint. The definite integral

$$\int_0^{\pi/2} \cos^{2s+1}\theta\,d\theta = \frac{2\cdot4\cdot6\cdots(2s)}{1\cdot3\cdot5\cdots(2s+1)}$$

may be useful.

14.1.10   Derive

$$J_n(x) = (-1)^n x^n \left(\frac{1}{x}\frac{d}{dx}\right)^n J_0(x).$$

Hint. Try mathematical induction (Section 1.4).

14.1.11   Show that between any two consecutive zeros of $J_n(x)$ there is one and only one zero of $J_{n+1}(x)$.

Hint. Equations (14.10) and (14.11) may be useful.

14.1.12   An analysis of antenna radiation patterns for a system with a circular aperture involves the equation

$$g(u) = \int_0^1 f(r) J_0(ur) r\,dr.$$

If $f(r) = 1 - r^2$, show that

$$g(u) = \frac{2}{u^2} J_2(u).$$

14.1.13 The differential cross section in a nuclear scattering experiment is given by $d\sigma/d\Omega = |f(\theta)|^2$. An approximate treatment leads to

$$f(\theta) = \frac{-ik}{2\pi} \int_0^{2\pi} \int_0^R \exp[ik\rho \sin\theta \sin\varphi]\rho \, d\rho \, d\varphi.$$

Here θ is an angle through which the scattered particle is scattered. R is the nuclear radius. Show that

$$\frac{d\sigma}{d\Omega} = (\pi R^2)\frac{1}{\pi}\left[\frac{J_1(kR\sin\theta)}{\sin\theta}\right]^2.$$

14.1.14 A set of functions $C_n(x)$ satisfies the recurrence relations

$$C_{n-1}(x) - C_{n+1}(x) = \frac{2n}{x}C_n(x),$$

$$C_{n-1}(x) + C_{n+1}(x) = 2C_n'(x).$$

(a) What linear second-order ODE does the $C_n(x)$ satisfy?

(b) By a change of variable transform your ODE into Bessel's equation. This suggests that $C_n(x)$ may be expressed in terms of Bessel functions of transformed argument.

14.1.15 (a) Show by direct differentiation and substitution that

$$J_\nu(x) = \frac{1}{2\pi i}\int_C e^{(x/2)(t-1/t)}t^{-\nu-1}dt$$

(this is the Schlaefli integral representation of J_ν), and that the equivalent equation,

$$J_\nu(x) = \frac{1}{2\pi i}\left(\frac{x}{2}\right)^\nu \int_C e^{s-x^2/4s}s^{-\nu-1}ds,$$

both satisfy Bessel's equation. C is the contour shown in Fig. 14.5. The negative real axis is the cut line.

Hint. This exercise is aimed at providing details of the discussion that starts at Eq. (14.38).

(b) Show that the first integral (with n an integer) may be transformed into

$$J_n(x) = \frac{1}{2\pi}\int_0^{2\pi} e^{i(x\sin\theta - n\theta)}d\theta = \frac{i^{-n}}{2\pi}\int_0^{2\pi} e^{i(x\cos\theta + n\theta)}d\theta.$$

14.1.16 The contour C in Exercise 14.1.15 is deformed to the path $-\infty$ to -1, unit circle $e^{-i\pi}$ to $e^{i\pi}$, and finally -1 to $-\infty$. Show that

$$J_\nu(x) = \frac{1}{\pi}\int_0^\pi \cos(\nu\theta - x\sin\theta)d\theta - \frac{\sin\nu\pi}{\pi}\int_0^\infty e^{-\nu\theta - x\sinh\theta}d\theta.$$

This is Bessel's integral.

Hint. The negative values of the variable of integration u must be represented in a manner consistent with the presence of the branch cut, for example, by writing $u = te^{\pm ix}$.

14.1.17 (a) Show that

$$J_\nu(x) = \frac{2}{\pi^{1/2}\Gamma(\nu + \frac{1}{2})}\left(\frac{x}{2}\right)^\nu \int_0^{\pi/2} \cos(x\sin\theta)\cos^{2\nu}\theta\, d\theta,$$

where $\nu > -\frac{1}{2}$.

Hint. Here is a chance to use series expansion and term-by-term integration. The formulas of Section 13.3 will prove useful.

(b) Transform the integral in part (a) into

$$J_\nu(x) = \frac{1}{\pi^{1/2}\Gamma(\nu + \frac{1}{2})}\left(\frac{x}{2}\right)^\nu \int_0^\pi \cos(x\cos\theta)\sin^{2\nu}\theta\, d\theta$$

$$= \frac{1}{\pi^{1/2}\Gamma(\nu + \frac{1}{2})}\left(\frac{x}{2}\right)^\nu \int_0^\pi e^{\pm ix\cos\theta}\sin^{2\nu}\theta\, d\theta$$

$$= \frac{1}{\pi^{1/2}\Gamma(\nu + \frac{1}{2})}\left(\frac{x}{2}\right)^\nu \int_{-1}^1 e^{\pm ipx}(1 - p^2)^{\nu - 1/2}\, dp.$$

These are alternate integral representations of $J_\nu(x)$.

14.1.18 Given that C is the contour in Fig. 14.5,

(a) From

$$J_\nu(x) = \frac{1}{2\pi i}\left(\frac{x}{2}\right)^\nu \int_C t^{-\nu-1}e^{t-x^2/4t}\, dt$$

derive the recurrence relation

$$J_\nu'(x) = \frac{\nu}{x}J_\nu(x) - J_{\nu+1}(x).$$

(b) From

$$J_\nu(x) = \frac{1}{2\pi i}\int_C t^{-\nu-1}e^{(x/2)(t-1/t)}\, dt$$

derive the recurrence relation

$$J_\nu'(x) = \frac{1}{2}\left[J_{\nu-1}(x) - J_{\nu+1}(x)\right].$$

14.1.19   Show that the recurrence relation

$$J_n'(x) = \frac{1}{2}\big[J_{n-1}(x) - J_{n+1}(x) \big]$$

follows directly from differentiation of

$$J_n(x) = \frac{1}{\pi} \int_0^\pi \cos(n\theta - x\sin\theta)\, d\theta.$$

14.1.20   Evaluate

$$\int_0^\infty e^{-ax} J_0(bx)\, dx, \quad a, b > 0.$$

Actually the results hold for $a \geq 0$, $-\infty < b < \infty$. This is a Laplace transform of J_0.

Hint. Either an integral representation of J_0 or a series expansion will be helpful.

14.1.21   Using the symmetries of the trigonometric functions, confirm that for integer n,

$$\frac{1}{2\pi} \int_0^{2\pi} \cos(x\sin\theta - n\theta)\, d\theta = \frac{1}{\pi} \int_0^\pi \cos(x\sin\theta - n\theta)\, d\theta.$$

14.1.22   (a)   Plot the intensity, Φ^2 of Eq. (14.25), as a function of $(\sin\alpha/\lambda)$ along a diameter of the circular diffraction pattern. Locate the first two minima.

(b)   Estimate the fraction of the total light intensity that falls within the central maximum.

Hint. $[J_1(x)]^2/x$ may be written as a derivative and the area integral of the intensity integrated by inspection.

14.1.23   The fraction of light incident on a circular aperture (normal incidence) that is transmitted is given by

$$T = 2 \int_0^{2ka} J_2(x)\frac{dx}{x} - \frac{1}{2ka} \int_0^{2ka} J_2(x)\, dx.$$

Here a is the radius of the aperture and k is the wave number, $2\pi/\lambda$. Show that

(a) $T = 1 - \dfrac{1}{ka} \sum_{n=0}^\infty J_{2n+1}(2ka)$,   (b) $T = 1 - \dfrac{1}{2ka} \int_0^{2ka} J_0(x)\, dx$.

14.1.24   The amplitude $U(\rho, \varphi, t)$ of a vibrating circular membrane of radius a satisfies the wave equation

$$\nabla^2 U \equiv \frac{\partial^2 U}{\partial\rho^2} + \frac{1}{\rho}\frac{\partial U}{\partial\rho} + \frac{1}{\rho^2}\frac{\partial^2 U}{\partial\varphi^2} = \frac{1}{v^2}\frac{\partial^2 U}{\partial t^2}.$$

Here v is the phase velocity of the wave, determined by the properties of the membrane.

(a)   Show that a physically relevant solution is

$$U(\rho, \varphi, t) = J_m(k\rho)\left(c_1 e^{im\varphi} + c_2 e^{-im\varphi}\right)\left(b_1 e^{i\omega t} + b_2 e^{-i\omega t}\right).$$

(b)   From the Dirichlet boundary condition $J_m(ka) = 0$, find the allowable values of k.

14.1.25   Example 14.1.2 describes the TM modes of electromagnetic cavity oscillation. To obtain the transverse electric (TE) modes, we set $E_z = 0$ and work from the z component of the magnetic induction $\mathbf{B}$:

$$\nabla^2 B_z + \alpha^2 B_z = 0$$

with boundary conditions

$$B_z(0) = B_z(l) = 0 \quad \text{and} \quad \left.\frac{\partial B_z}{\partial \rho}\right|_{\rho = a} = 0.$$

Show that the TE resonant frequencies are given by

$$\omega_{mnp} = c\sqrt{\frac{\beta_{mn}^2}{a^2} + \frac{p^2 \pi^2}{l^2}}, \quad p = 1, 2, 3, \ldots,$$

and identify the quantities β_{mn}.

14.1.26   A conducting cylinder can accommodate traveling electromagnetic waves; when used for this purpose it is called a wave guide. The equations describing traveling waves are the same as those of Example 14.1.2, but there is no boundary condition on E_z at $z = 0$ or $z = h$ other than that its z dependence be oscillatory. For each TM mode (values of m and j of Example 14.1.2), there is a minimum frequency that can be transmitted through a wave guide of radius a. Explain why this is so, and give a formula for the cutoff frequencies.

14.1.27   Plot the three lowest TM and the three lowest TE angular resonant frequencies, ω_{mnp}, as a function of the ratio radius/length (a/l) for $0 \le a/l \le 1.5$.

Hint. Try plotting ω^2 (in units of c^2/a^2) vs. $(a/l)^2$. Why this choice?

14.1.28   Show that the integral

$$\int_0^a x^m J_n(x)\,dx, \quad m \ge n \ge 0,$$

(a)   is integrable for $m + n$ odd in terms of Bessel functions and powers of x, i.e., is expressible as linear combinations of $a^p J_q(a)$;

(b)   may be reduced for $m + n$ even to integrated terms plus $\int_0^a J_0(x)\,dx$.

14.1.29   Show that

$$\int_0^{\alpha_{0n}} \left(1 - \frac{y}{\alpha_{0n}}\right) J_0(y)\,y\,dy = \frac{1}{\alpha_{0n}} \int_0^{\alpha_{0n}} J_0(y)\,dy.$$

Here α_{0n} is the nth zero of $J_0(y)$. This relation is useful (see Exercise 14.2.9): The expression on the right is easier and quicker to evaluate, and is much more accurate. Taking the difference of two terms in the expression on the left leads to a large relative error.

14.2 ORTHOGONALITY

To identify the orthogonality properties of Bessel functions, it is convenient to start by writing Bessel's ODE in a form that we can recognize as a Sturm-Liouville eigenvalue problem, the general properties of which were discussed in detail starting from Eq. (8.15). If we divide Eq. (14.15) through by ρ^2 and rearrange slightly, we have

$$-\left(\frac{d^2}{d\rho^2} + \frac{1}{\rho}\frac{d}{d\rho} - \frac{v^2}{\rho^2}\right)Z_v(k\rho) = k^2 Z_v(k\rho), \tag{14.41}$$

showing that $Z_v(k\rho)$ is an eigenfunction of the operator

$$\mathcal{L} = -\left(\frac{d^2}{d\rho^2} + \frac{1}{\rho}\frac{d}{d\rho} - \frac{v^2}{\rho^2}\right) \tag{14.42}$$

with eigenvalue k^2. Since we are most often interested in problems whose solutions in cylindrical coordinates (ρ, φ, z) separate into products $P(\rho)\Phi(\varphi)Z(z)$ and which are for the region within a cylindrical boundary at some $\rho = a$, we usually have $\Phi(\varphi) = e^{im\varphi}$ with m an integer (thereby causing $v^2 \to m^2$), and find that $P(\rho) = J_m(k\rho)$. We choose P to be a Bessel function of the first kind because $\rho = 0$ is interior to our region and we want a solution that is nonsingular there.

From Sturm-Liouville theory, we find that the weight factor needed to make $\mathcal{L}$ of Eq. (14.42) self-adjoint (as an ODE) is $w(\rho) = \rho$, and the orthogonality integral for the two eigenfunctions $J_v(k\rho)$ and $J_v(k'\rho)$, a case of Eq. (8.20), is (whether or not v is an integer)

$$\frac{a\left[k' J_v(ka) J_v'(k'a) - k J_v'(ka) J_v(k'a)\right]}{k^2 - k'^2} = \int_0^a \rho J_v(k\rho) J_v(k'\rho)d\rho. \tag{14.43}$$

In writing Eq. (14.43) we have used the fact that the presence of a factor ρ in the boundary terms causes there to be no contribution from the lower limit $\rho = 0$.[3]

Equation (14.43) shows us that the $J_v(k)$ of different k will be orthogonal (with weight factor ρ) if we can cause the left-hand side of that equation to vanish. We may do so by choosing k and k' in such a way that $J_v(ka) = J_v(k'a) = 0$. In other words, we can require that k and k' be such that ka and $k'a$ are zeros of J_v, and our Bessel functions will then satisfy Dirichlet boundary conditions.

If now we let α_{vi} denote the ith zero of J_v, the above analysis corresponds to the following orthogonality formula for the interval $[0, a]$:

$$\int_0^a \rho J_v\left(\alpha_{vi}\frac{\rho}{a}\right) J_v\left(\alpha_{vj}\frac{\rho}{a}\right) d\rho = 0, \quad i \neq j. \tag{14.44}$$

---

[3]This will be true for all $v \geq -1$, as will become more evident when we discuss Bessel functions of the second kind.

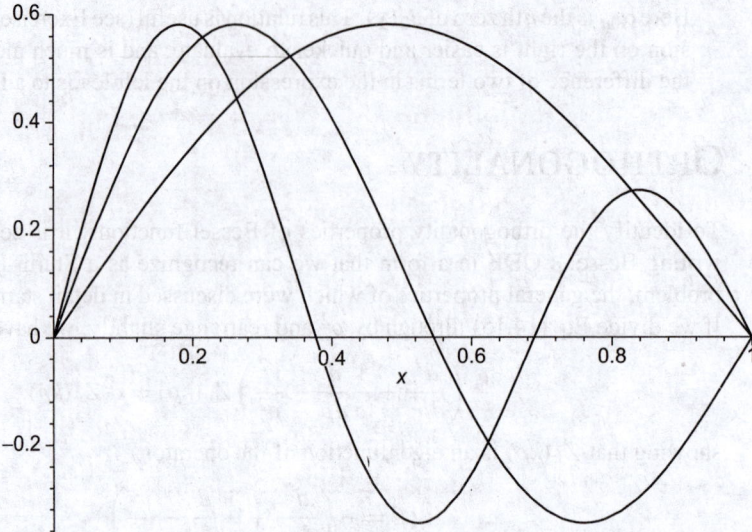

FIGURE 14.6   Bessel functions $J_1(\alpha_{1n}\rho)$, $n = 1, 2, 3$ on range $0 \leq \rho \leq 1$.

Note that all members of our orthogonal set of Bessel functions have the same value of the index ν, differing only in the scale of the argument of J_ν. Successive members of the orthogonal set will have increasing numbers of oscillations in the interval $(0, a)$. Note also that the weight factor, ρ, is just that which corresponds to **unweighted** orthogonality over the region within a circle of radius a. We show in Fig. 14.6 the first three Bessel functions of order $\nu = 1$ that are orthogonal within the unit circle.

An alternative to the foregoing analysis would be to ensure the vanishing of the boundary term of Eq. (14.43) at $\rho = a$ by choosing values of k corresponding to the Neumann boundary condition $J'_\nu(ka) = 0$. The functions obtained in this way would also form an orthogonal set.

Normalization

Our orthogonal sets of Bessel functions are not normalized, and to use them in expansions we need their normalization integrals. These integrals may be developed by returning to Eq. (14.43), which is valid for all k and k', whether or not the boundary terms vanish. We take the limits of both sides of that equation as $k' \to k$, evaluating the limit on the left-hand side using l'Hôpital's rule, which here corresponds to taking the derivatives of numerator and denominator with respect to k':

$$\int_0^a \rho\,[J_\nu(k\rho)]^2\,d\rho = \lim_{k' \to k} \frac{a\left[J_\nu(ka)\dfrac{d}{dk'}\left(k'J'_\nu(k'a)\right) - kJ'_\nu(ka)\dfrac{d}{dk'}\left(J_\nu(k'a)\right)\right]}{\dfrac{d}{dk'}(k^2 - k'^2)}.$$

We now simplify this equation for the case that $ka = \alpha_{vi}$, so we set $J_v(ka) = 0$ and reach

$$\int_0^a \rho \left[J_v \left(\alpha_{vi} \frac{\rho}{a} \right) \right]^2 d\rho = \frac{-a^2 k \left[J_v'(ka) \right]^2}{-2k} = \frac{a^2}{2} \left[J_v'(\alpha_{vi}) \right]^2. \tag{14.45}$$

Now, because α_{vi} is a zero of J_v, Eq. (14.12) permits us to recognize that $J_v'(\alpha_{vi}) = -J_{v+1}(\alpha_{vi})$. We then obtain from Eq. (14.45) the desired result,

$$\int_0^a \rho \left[J_v \left(\alpha_{vi} \frac{\rho}{a} \right) \right]^2 d\rho = \frac{a^2}{2} \left[J_{v+1}(\alpha_{vi}) \right]^2. \tag{14.46}$$

Bessel Series

If we assume that the set of Bessel functions $J_v(\alpha_{vj}\rho/a)$ for fixed v and for $j = 1, 2, 3, \ldots$ is complete, then any well-behaved but otherwise arbitrary function $f(\rho)$ may be expanded in a Bessel series

$$f(\rho) = \sum_{j=1}^{\infty} c_{vj} J_v \left(\alpha_{vj} \frac{\rho}{a} \right), \quad 0 \le \rho \le a, \quad v > -1. \tag{14.47}$$

The coefficients c_{vj} are determined by the usual rules for orthogonal expansions. With the aid of Eq. (14.46) we have

$$c_{vj} = \frac{2}{a^2 [J_{v+1}(\alpha_{vj})]^2} \int_0^a f(\rho) J_v \left(\alpha_{vj} \frac{\rho}{a} \right) \rho d\rho. \tag{14.48}$$

As pointed out earlier, it is also possible to obtain an orthogonal set of Bessel functions of given order v by imposing the Neumann boundary condition $J_v'(k\rho) = 0$ at $\rho = a$, corresponding to $k = \beta_{vj}/a$, where β_{vj} is the jth zero of J_v'. These functions can also be used for orthogonal expansions. This approach is explored in Exercises 14.2.2 and 14.2.5.

The following example illustrates the usefulness of Bessel series.

Example 14.2.1   ELECTROSTATIC POTENTIAL IN A HOLLOW CYLINDER

We consider a hollow cylinder, which in cylindrical coordinates (ρ, φ, z) is bounded by a curved surface at $\rho = a$ and end caps at $z = 0$ and $z = h$. The base $(z = 0)$ and curved surface are assumed to be grounded, and therefore at potential $\psi = 0$, while the end cap at $z = h$ has a known potential distribution $V(\rho, \varphi, h)$. Our problem is to determine the potential $V(\rho, \varphi, z)$ throughout the interior of the cylinder.

We proceed by finding separated-variable solutions to the Laplace equation in cylindrical coordinates, along the lines discussed in Section 9.4. Our first step is to identify product solutions, which, as in Eq. (9.64), must take the form[4]

$$\psi_{lm}(\rho, \varphi, z) = P_{lm}(\rho)\Phi_m(\varphi)Z_l(z),\tag{14.49}$$

with $\Phi_m = e^{\pm im\varphi}$, and

$$\frac{d^2}{dz^2}Z_l(z) = l^2 Z_l(z),\tag{14.50}$$

$$\rho^2\frac{d^2}{d\rho^2}P_{lm} + \rho\frac{d}{d\rho}P_{lm} + (l^2\rho^2 - m^2)P_{lm} = 0.\tag{14.51}$$

The equation for P_{lm} is Bessel's ODE, with solutions of relevance here $J_m(l\rho)$. To satisfy the boundary condition at $\rho = a$ we need to choose $l = \alpha_{mj}/a$, where j can be any positive integer and α_{mj} is the jth zero of J_m.

The equation for Z_l has solutions $e^{\pm lz}$; to satisfy the boundary condition at $z = 0$ we need to take the linear combination of these solutions that is equivalent to $\sinh lz$. Combining these observations, we see that possible solutions to the Laplace equation that satisfy all the boundary conditions other than that at $z = h$ can be written

$$\psi_{mj} = c_{mj}J_m\left(\alpha_{mj}\frac{\rho}{a}\right)e^{im\varphi}\sinh\left(\alpha_{mj}\frac{z}{a}\right).\tag{14.52}$$

Since Laplace's equation is homogeneous, any linear combination of the ψ_{mj} with arbitrary values of the c_{mj} will be a solution, and our remaining task is to find the linear combination of such solutions that satisfies the boundary condition at $z = h$. Therefore,

$$V(\rho, \varphi, z) = \sum_{m=-\infty}^{\infty}\sum_{j=1}^{\infty}\psi_{mj},\tag{14.53}$$

with the boundary condition at $z = h$ expressed as

$$\sum_{m=-\infty}^{\infty}\sum_{j=1}^{\infty}c_{mj}J_m\left(\alpha_{mj}\frac{\rho}{a}\right)e^{im\varphi}\sinh\left(\alpha_{mj}\frac{h}{a}\right) = V(\rho, \varphi, h).\tag{14.54}$$

Our solution is both a trigonometric series and a Bessel series, each with orthogonality properties that can be used to determine the coefficients. From Eq. (14.48) and the formula

$$\int_0^{2\pi}e^{-im\varphi}e^{im'\varphi} = 2\pi\delta_{mm'},\tag{14.55}$$

we find

$$c_{mj} = \left[\pi a^2\sinh\left(\alpha_{mj}\frac{h}{a}\right)J_{m+1}^2(\alpha_{mj})\right]^{-1}$$

$$\int_0^{2\pi}d\varphi\int_0^a V(\rho, \varphi, h)J_m\left(\alpha_{mj}\frac{\rho}{a}\right)e^{-im\varphi}\rho\,d\rho.\tag{14.56}$$

---

[4] Note that here Z_l is a function of z arising from the separation of variables; the notation is not intended to identify it as a Bessel function.

These are definite integrals, that is, numbers. Substituting back into Eq. (14.52), the series in Eq. (14.53) is specified and the potential $V(\rho, \varphi, z)$ is determined. ∎

Exercises

14.2.1   Show that

$$(k^2 - k'^2) \int_0^a J_\nu(kx) J_\nu(k'x) x\,dx = a[k' J_\nu(ka) J'_\nu(k'a) - k J'_\nu(ka) J_\nu(k'a)],$$

where $J'_\nu(ka) = \dfrac{d}{d(kx)} J_\nu(kx)\,|_{x=a}$, and that

$$\int_0^a [J_\nu(kx)]^2 x\,dx = \frac{a^2}{2} \left\{ [J'_\nu(ka)]^2 + \left(1 - \frac{\nu^2}{k^2 a^2}\right)[J_\nu(ka)]^2 \right\}, \quad \nu > -1.$$

These two integrals are usually called the **first and second Lommel integrals**.

14.2.2   (a)   If $\beta_{\nu m}$ is the mth zero of $(d/d\rho) J_\nu(\beta_{\nu m}\rho/a)$, show that the Bessel functions are orthogonal over the interval $[0, a]$ with an orthogonality integral

$$\int_0^a J_\nu\left(\beta_{\nu m} \frac{\rho}{a}\right) J_\nu\left(\beta_{\nu n} \frac{\rho}{a}\right) \rho\, d\rho = 0, \quad m \neq n, \quad \nu > -1.$$

(b)   Derive the corresponding normalization integral $(m = n)$.

$$ANS. \quad (b) \quad \frac{a^2}{2}\left(1 - \frac{\nu^2}{\beta_{\nu m}^2}\right)[J_\nu(\beta_{\nu m})]^2, \quad \nu > -1.$$

14.2.3   Verify that the orthogonality equation, Eq. (14.44), and the normalization equation, Eq. (14.46), hold for $\nu > -1$.

Hint. Using power-series expansions, examine the behavior of Eq. (14.43) as $\rho \to 0$.

14.2.4   From Eq. (11.49), develop a proof that $J_\nu(z)$, $\nu > -1$ has no complex roots (with a nonzero imaginary part).

Hint. (a) Use the series form of $J_\nu(z)$ to exclude pure imaginary roots.

(b) Assume $\alpha_{\nu m}$ to be complex and take $\alpha_{\nu n}$ to be $\alpha_{\nu m}^*$.

14.2.5   (a)   In the series expansion

$$f(\rho) = \sum_{m=1}^{\infty} c_{\nu m} J_\nu\left(\alpha_{\nu m} \frac{\rho}{a}\right), \quad 0 \leq \rho \leq a, \quad \nu > -1,$$

with $J_\nu(\alpha_{\nu m}) = 0$, show that the coefficients are given by

$$c_{\nu m} = \frac{2}{a^2 [J_{\nu+1}(\alpha_{\nu m})]^2} \int_0^a f(\rho) J_\nu\left(\alpha_{\nu m} \frac{\rho}{a}\right) \rho\, d\rho.$$

(b)   In the series expansion

$$f(\rho) = \sum_{m=1}^{\infty} d_{vm} J_v \left(\beta_{vm} \frac{\rho}{a} \right), \quad 0 \le \rho \le a, \quad v > -1,$$

with $(d/d\rho) J_v(\beta_{vm}\rho/a)\,|_{\rho=a} = 0$, show that the coefficients are given by

$$d_{vm} = \frac{2}{a^2(1 - v^2/\beta_{vm}^2)[J_v(\beta_{vm})]^2} \int_0^a f(\rho) J_v \left(\beta_{vm} \frac{\rho}{a} \right) \rho \, d\rho.$$

14.2.6   A right circular cylinder has an electrostatic potential of $\psi(\rho, \varphi)$ on both ends. The potential on the curved cylindrical surface is zero. Find the potential at all interior points.

Hint. Choose your coordinate system and adjust your z dependence to exploit the symmetry of your potential.

14.2.7   A function $f(x)$ is expressed as a Bessel series:

$$f(x) = \sum_{n=1}^{\infty} a_n J_m(\alpha_{mn}x),$$

with α_{mn} the nth root of J_m. Prove the Parseval relation,

$$\int_0^1 [f(x)]^2 x \, dx = \frac{1}{2} \sum_{n=1}^{\infty} a_n^2 [J_{m+1}(\alpha_{mn})]^2.$$

14.2.8   Prove that

$$\sum_{n=1}^{\infty} (\alpha_{mn})^{-2} = \frac{1}{4(m+1)}.$$

Hint. Expand x^m in a Bessel series and apply the Parseval relation.

14.2.9   A right circular cylinder of length l and radius a has on its end caps a potential

$$\psi \left(z = \pm \frac{l}{2} \right) = 100 \left(1 - \frac{\rho}{a} \right).$$

The potential on the curved surface (the side) is zero. Using the Bessel series from Exercise 14.2.6, calculate the electrostatic potential for $\rho/a = 0.0(0.2)1.0$ and $z/l = 0.0(0.1)0.5$. Take $a/l = 0.5$.

Hint. From Exercise 14.1.29 you have

$$\int_0^{\alpha_{0n}} \left(1 - \frac{y}{\alpha_{0n}}\right) J_0(y)\,y\,dy.$$

Show that this equals

$$\frac{1}{\alpha_{0n}} \int_0^{\alpha_{0n}} J_0(y)\,dy.$$

Numerical evaluation of this latter form rather than the former is both faster and more accurate.

Note. For $\rho/a = 0.0$ and $z/l = 0.5$ the convergence is slow, 20 terms giving only 98.4 rather than 100.

Check value.   For $\rho/a = 0.4$ and $z/l = 0.3$, $\psi = 24.558$.

14.3   NEUMANN FUNCTIONS, BESSEL FUNCTIONS OF THE SECOND KIND

From the theory of ODEs, it is known that Bessel's equation has two independent solutions. Indeed, for nonintegral order ν we have already found two solutions and labeled them $J_\nu(x)$ and $J_{-\nu}(x)$ using the infinite series, Eq. (14.6). The trouble is that when ν is integral, Eq. (14.5) holds and we have but one independent solution. A second solution may be developed by the methods of Section 7.6. This yields a perfectly good second solution of Bessel's equation. However, that solution is not the standard form, which is called a **Bessel function of the second kind** or alternatively, a **Neumann function**.

Definition and Series Form

The standard definition of the Neumann functions is the following linear combination of $J_\nu(x)$ and $J_{-\nu}(x)$:

$$Y_\nu(x) = \frac{\cos \nu\pi\, J_\nu(x) - J_{-\nu}(x)}{\sin \nu\pi}. \tag{14.57}$$

For nonintegral ν, $Y_\nu(x)$ clearly satisfies Bessel's equation, for it is a linear combination of known solutions, $J_\nu(x)$ and $J_{-\nu}(x)$. The behavior of $Y_\nu(x)$ for small x (and nonintegral ν) can be determined from the power-series expansion of $J_{-\nu}$, Eq. (14.6); we may write, calling upon Eq. (13.23),

$$
\begin{aligned}
Y_\nu(x) &= -\frac{1}{\sin\nu\pi}\left[\frac{1}{\Gamma(1-\nu)}\left(\frac{x}{2}\right)^{-\nu} - \cdots\right] \\
&= -\frac{\Gamma(\nu)\Gamma(1-\nu)}{\pi}\left[\frac{1}{\Gamma(1-\nu)}\left(\frac{x}{2}\right)^{-\nu} - \cdots\right] \\
&= -\frac{\Gamma(\nu)}{\pi}\left(\frac{x}{2}\right)^{-\nu} + \cdots.
\end{aligned}
\tag{14.58}
$$

However, for integral ν, Eq. (14.57) becomes indeterminate; in fact, $Y_n(x)$ for integral n is defined as

$$
Y_n(x) = \lim_{\nu\to n} Y_\nu(x).
\tag{14.59}
$$

To determine that the limit represented by Eq. (14.59) exists and is not identically zero (so that $Y_n(x)$ has a meaningful definition), we apply l'Hôpital's rule to Eq. (14.57), obtaining initially

$$
Y_n(x) = \frac{1}{\pi}\left[\frac{dJ_\nu}{d\nu} - (-1)^n \frac{dJ_{-\nu}}{d\nu}\right]_{\nu=n}.
\tag{14.60}
$$

Inserting the expansions of J_ν and $J_{-\nu}$ from Eq. (14.6), the differentiations of $(x/2)^{2s\pm\nu}$ combine to yield $(2/\pi)J_n(x)\ln(x/2)$, while the derivatives of $1/\Gamma(s\pm n+1)$ yield terms containing $\psi(s\pm n+1)/\Gamma(s\pm n+1)$, where ψ is the digamma function (Section 13.2). The final result, whose verification is the topic of Exercise 14.3.8, is

$$
Y_n(x) = \frac{2}{\pi}J_n(x)\ln\left(\frac{x}{2}\right) - \frac{1}{\pi}\sum_{k=0}^{n-1}\frac{(n-k-1)!}{k!}\left(\frac{x}{2}\right)^{2k-n}
$$
$$
-\frac{1}{\pi}\sum_{k=0}^{\infty}\frac{(-1)^k}{k!(n+k)!}\left[\psi(k+1)+\psi(n+k+1)\right]\left(\frac{x}{2}\right)^{2k+n},
\tag{14.61}
$$

An explicit form for $\psi(n)$ for integer n is given in Eq. (13.40).

Equation (14.61) shows that for $n > 0$, the most divergent term for small x is in agreement with the result for noninteger n given in Eq. (14.58). We also see that all solutions for integer n contain a logarithmic term with the regular function J_n multiplying the logarithm. In our earlier study of ODEs, we found that a second solution will usually have a contribution of this type when the indicial equation causes the exponents of the power-series expansion to be integers. We may also conclude from Eq. (14.61) that Y_n is linearly independent of J_n, confirming that we indeed have a second solution to Bessel's ODE.

It is of some interest to obtain the expansion of $Y_0(x)$ in a more explicit form. Returning to Eq. (14.61), we note that its first summation is vacant, and we have the relatively simple expansion

$$
\begin{aligned}
Y_0(x) &= \frac{2}{\pi}J_0(x)\ln\left(\frac{x}{2}\right) - \frac{2}{\pi}\sum_{k=0}^{\infty}\frac{(-1)^k}{k!k!}\left[-\gamma + H_k\right]\left(\frac{x}{2}\right)^{2k} \\
&= \frac{2}{\pi}J_0(x)\left[\gamma + \ln\left(\frac{x}{2}\right)\right] - \frac{2}{\pi}\sum_{k=1}^{\infty}\frac{(-1)^k}{k!k!}H_k\left(\frac{x}{2}\right)^{2k},
\end{aligned}
\tag{14.62}
$$

where H_k is the harmonic number $\sum_{m=1}^{k} m^{-1}$ and γ is the Euler-Mascheroni constant.

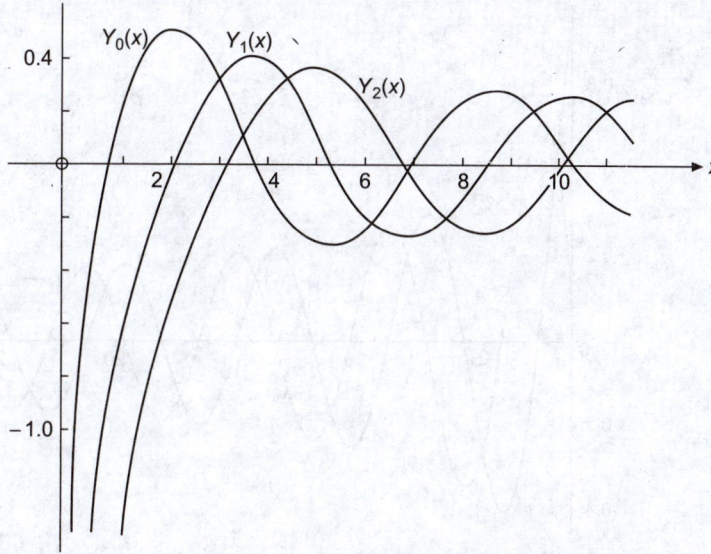

FIGURE 14.7 Neumann functions $Y_0(x)$, $Y_1(x)$, and $Y_2(x)$.

The Neumann functions $Y_n(x)$ are irregular at $x = 0$, but with increasing x become oscillatory, as may be seen from the graphs of Y_0, Y_1, and Y_2 in Fig. 14.7. The definition of Eq. (14.57) was specifically chosen to cause the oscillatory behavior to be at the same scale as that of J_n and displaced asymptotically in phase by $\pi/2$, similarly to the relative behavior of the sine and cosine. However, unlike the sine and cosine, J_n and Y_n only exhibit exact periodicity in the asymptotic limit. This point is covered in detail in Section 14.6. Figure 14.8 compares $J_0(x)$ and $Y_0(x)$ over a large range of x.

Integral Representations

As with all the other Bessel functions, $Y_\nu(x)$ has integral representations. For $Y_0(x)$ we have

$$Y_0(x) = -\frac{2}{\pi} \int_0^\infty \cos(x \cosh t) dt = -\frac{2}{\pi} \int_1^\infty \frac{\cos(xt)}{(t^2 - 1)^{1/2}} dt, \quad x > 0. \qquad (14.63)$$

See Exercise 14.3.7, which shows that the above integral is a solution to Bessel's ODE that is linearly independent of $J_0(x)$. Specific identification as Y_0 is the topic of Exercise 14.4.8.

Recurrence Relations

Substituting Eq. (14.57) for $Y_\nu(x)$ (nonintegral ν) into the recurrence relations for $J_n(x)$, Eqs. (14.7) and (14.8), we see immediately that $Y_\nu(x)$ satisfies these same recurrence relations. This actually constitutes a proof that Y_ν is a solution to the Bessel ODE. Note that the converse is not necessarily true. All solutions need not satisfy the same recurrence relations, as the relations depend on the scales assigned to the solutions of different ν. An example of this sort of trouble appears in Section 14.5.

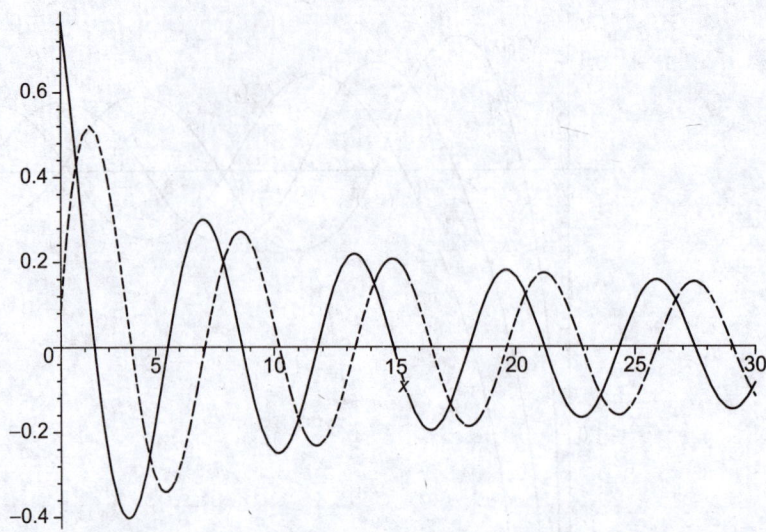

FIGURE 14.8   Oscillatory behavior of $J_0(x)$ (solid line) and $Y_0(x)$ (dashed line) for $1 \leq x \leq 30$.

Wronskian Formulas

An ODE $p(x)y'' + q(x)y' + r(x)y = 0$ in self-adjoint form (so $q = p'$) was found in Exercise 7.6.1 to have the following Wronskian formula connecting its solutions u and v:

$$u(x)v'(x) - u'(x)v(x) = \frac{A}{p(x)}. \tag{14.64}$$

To bring Bessel's equation to self-adjoint form, we need to write it as $xy'' + y' + (x - v^2/x)y = 0$, thereby showing that for our present purposes $p(x) = x$, and we therefore have for each noninteger v

$$J_v J'_{-v} - J'_v J_{-v} = \frac{A_v}{x}. \tag{14.65}$$

Since A_v is a constant but can be expected to depend on v, it may be identified for each v at any convenient point, such as $x = 0$. From the power-series expansion, Eq. (14.6), we obtain the following limiting behaviors for small x:

$$J_v \rightarrow \frac{1}{\Gamma(1+v)} \left(\frac{x}{2}\right)^v, \qquad J'_v \rightarrow \frac{v}{2\Gamma(1+v)} \left(\frac{x}{2}\right)^{v-1},$$

$$J_{-v} \rightarrow \frac{1}{\Gamma(1-v)} \left(\frac{x}{2}\right)^{-v}, \qquad J'_{-v} \rightarrow \frac{-v}{2\Gamma(1-v)} \left(\frac{x}{2}\right)^{-v-1}. \tag{14.66}$$

Substitution into Eq. (14.65) yields

$$J_v(x)J'_{-v}(x) - J'_v(x)J_{-v}(x) = \frac{-2v}{x\Gamma(1+v)\Gamma(1-v)} = -\frac{2\sin v\pi}{\pi x}, \tag{14.67}$$

using Eq. (13.23). Although Eq. (14.67) was obtained for $x \to 0$, comparison with Eq. (14.65) shows that it must be true for all x, and that $A_\nu = -(2/\pi) \sin \nu \pi$. Note that A_ν vanishes for integral ν, showing that the Wronskian of J_n and J_{-n} vanishes and that these Bessel functions are linearly dependent.

Using our recurrence relations, we may readily develop a large number of alternate forms, among which are

$$J_\nu J_{-\nu+1} + J_{-\nu} J_{\nu-1} = \frac{2 \sin \nu \pi}{\pi x}, \tag{14.68}$$

$$J_\nu J_{-\nu-1} + J_{-\nu} J_{\nu+1} = -\frac{2 \sin \nu \pi}{\pi x}, \tag{14.69}$$

$$J_\nu Y_\nu' - J_\nu' Y_\nu = \frac{2}{\pi x}, \tag{14.70}$$

$$J_\nu Y_{\nu+1} - J_{\nu+1} Y_\nu = -\frac{2}{\pi x}. \tag{14.71}$$

Many more will be found in the Additional Readings.

You will recall that in Chapter 7, Wronskians were of great value in two respects: (1) in establishing the linear independence or linear dependence of solutions of differential equations, and (2) in developing an integral form of a second solution. Here the specific forms of the Wronskians and Wronskian-derived combinations of Bessel functions are useful primarily in development of the general behavior of the various Bessel functions. Wronskians are also of great use in checking tables of Bessel functions.

Uses of Neumann Functions

The Neumann functions $Y_\nu(x)$ are of importance for a number of reasons:

1. They are second, independent solutions of Bessel's equation, thereby completing the general solution.
2. They are needed for physical problems in which they are not excluded by a requirement of regularity at $x = 0$. Specific examples include electromagnetic waves in coaxial cables and quantum mechanical scattering theory.
3. They lead directly to the two Hankel functions, whose definition and use, particularly in studies of wave propagation, are discussed in Section 14.4.

We close with one example in which Neumann functions play a vital role.

Example 14.3.1   COAXIAL WAVE GUIDES

We are interested in an electromagnetic wave confined between the concentric, conducting cylindrical surfaces $\rho = a$ and $\rho = b$. The equations governing the wave propagation are the same as those discussed in Example 14.1.2, but the boundary conditions are now different, and our interest is in solutions that are traveling waves (compare Exercise 14.1.26).

For wave propagation problems, it is convenient to write the solution in terms of complex exponentials, with the actual physical quantities involved ultimately identified as their real (or imaginary) parts. Thus, in place of Eq. (14.31) (the solution for standing waves in a cylindrical cavity), we now have for E_z solutions in which the ρ dependence must involve both J_m and Y_m (as the latter is not ruled out by a requirement for regularity at $\rho = 0$). Including the time dependence, we have for the TM (transverse magnetic) solutions the separated-variable forms

$$E_z = \left[c_{mn} J_m(\gamma_{mn}\rho) + d_{mn} Y_m(\gamma_{mn}\rho) \right] e^{\pm im\varphi} e^{i(lz-\omega t)}, \tag{14.72}$$

with l now permitted to have any real value (there is no boundary condition on z). The index n identifies different possible values of γ_{mn}. As in Eq. (14.30), the relation between γ_{mn}, l, and ω is

$$\frac{\omega^2}{c^2} = \gamma_{mn}^2 + l^2. \tag{14.73}$$

The most general TM traveling-wave solution will be an arbitrary linear combination of all functions of the form given by Eq. (14.72) with γ_{mn}, c_{mn}, and d_{mn} chosen so that E_z will vanish at $\rho = a$ and $\rho = b$. A main difference between this problem and that of Example 14.1.2 is that the condition on E_z is not given by the zeros of the Bessel functions J_m, but by zeros of linear combinations of J_m and Y_m. Specifically, we require that

$$c_{mn} J_m(\gamma_{mn}a) + d_{mn} Y_m(\gamma_{mn}a) = 0, \tag{14.74}$$

$$c_{mn} J_m(\gamma_{mn}b) + d_{mn} Y_m(\gamma_{mn}b) = 0. \tag{14.75}$$

These transcendental equations may be solved, for each relevant m, to yield an infinite set of solutions (indexed by n) for γ_{mn} and the ratio d_{mn}/c_{mn}. An example of this process is in Exercise 14.3.10.

Returning now to the equation for ω, we observe that the smallest value it can attain for the solution indexed by m and n is $c\gamma_{mn}$, showing that TM waves can only propagate if the angular frequency ω of the electromagnetic radiation is equal to or larger than this **cutoff**. In general, larger values of γ_{mn} correspond to higher degrees of transverse oscillation, and modes with greater transverse oscillation will therefore have higher cutoff frequencies.

As for the circular wave guide (the subject of Exercise 14.1.26, there will also be TE modes of propagation, also with mode-dependent cutoffs. However, the coaxial guide can also support traveling waves in TEM (transverse electric and magnetic) modes. These modes, not possible for a circular waveguide, do not exhibit a cutoff, are the confined equivalent of plane waves, and correspond to the flow of current (in opposite directions) on the coaxial conductors. ∎

Exercises

14.3.1   Prove that the Neumann functions Y_n (with n an integer) satisfy the recurrence relations

$$Y_{n-1}(x) + Y_{n+1}(x) = \frac{2n}{x} Y_n(x),$$

$$Y_{n-1}(x) - Y_{n+1}(x) = 2Y_n'(x).$$

Hint. These relations may be proved by differentiating the recurrence relations for J_ν or by using the limit form of Y_ν but **not** dividing everything by zero.

14.3.2   Show that for integer n

$$Y_{-n}(x) = (-1)^n Y_n(x).$$

14.3.3   Show that

$$Y_0'(x) = -Y_1(x).$$

14.3.4   If X and Z are any two solutions of Bessel's equation, show that

$$X_\nu(x) Z_\nu'(x) - X_\nu'(x) Z_\nu(x) = \frac{A_\nu}{x},$$

in which A_ν may depend on ν but is independent of x. This is a special case of Exercise 7.6.11.

14.3.5   Verify the Wronskian formulas

$$J_\nu(x) J_{-\nu+1}(x) + J_{-\nu}(x) J_{\nu-1}(x) = \frac{2 \sin \nu\pi}{\pi x},$$

$$J_\nu(x) Y_\nu'(x) - J_\nu'(x) Y_\nu(x) = \frac{2}{\pi x}.$$

14.3.6   As an alternative to letting x approach zero in the evaluation of the Wronskian constant, we may invoke the uniqueness of power-series expansions. The coefficient of x^{-1} in the series expansion of $u_\nu(x) v_\nu'(x) - u_\nu'(x) v_\nu(x)$ is then A_ν. Show by series expansion that the coefficients of x^0 and x^1 of $J_\nu(x) J_{-\nu}'(x) - J_\nu'(x) J_{-\nu}(x)$ are each zero.

14.3.7   (a) By differentiating and substituting into Bessel's ODE for $\nu = 0$, show that $\int_0^\infty \cos(x \cosh t) dt$ is a solution.
Hint. Rearrange the final integral to $\int_0^\infty \frac{d}{dt} \left[x \sin(x \cosh t) \sinh t \right] dt$.

(b) Show that $Y_0(x) = -\frac{2}{\pi} \int_0^\infty \cos(x \cosh t) dt$ is linearly independent of $J_0(x)$.

14.3.8   Verify the expansion formula for $Y_n(x)$ given in Eq. (14.61).

Hint. Start from Eq. (14.60) and perform the indicated differentiations on the power-series expansions of J_ν and $J_{-\nu}$. The digamma functions ψ arise from the differentiation of the gamma function. You will need the identity (not derived in this book) $\lim_{z \to -n} \psi(z)/\Gamma(z) = (-1)^{n-1} n!$, where n is a positive integer.

14.3.9   If Bessel's ODE (with solution J_ν) is differentiated with respect to ν, one obtains

$$x^2 \frac{d^2}{dx^2} \left(\frac{\partial J_\nu}{\partial \nu} \right) + x \frac{d}{dx} \left(\frac{\partial J_\nu}{\partial \nu} \right) + (x^2 - \nu^2) \frac{\partial J_\nu}{\partial \nu} = 2\nu J_\nu.$$

Use the above equation to show that $Y_n(x)$ is a solution to Bessel's ODE.

Hint. Equation (14.60) will be useful.

14.3.10   For the case $m = 0$, $a = 1$, and $b = 2$, the coaxial wave-guide TM boundary conditions become $f(\lambda) = 0$, with

$$f(x) = \frac{J_0(2x)}{Y_0(2x)} - \frac{J_0(x)}{Y_0(x)}.$$

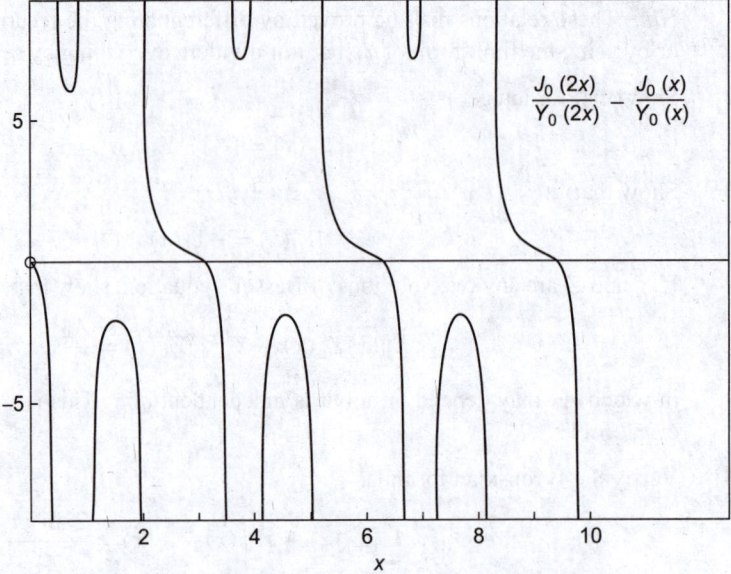

$$\frac{J_0\,(2x)}{Y_0\,(2x)} - \frac{J_0\,(x)}{Y_0\,(x)}$$

FIGURE 14.9   The function $f(x)$ of Exercise 14.3.10.

This function is plotted in Fig. 14.9.

(a)   Calculate $f(x)$ for $x = 0.0(0.1)10.0$ and plot $f(x)$ vs. x to find the approximate location of the roots.

(b)   Call a root-finding program to determine the first three roots to higher precision.

ANS.   (b) 3.1230, 6.2734, 9.4182.

Note. The higher roots can be expected to appear at intervals whose length approaches π. Why? AMS-55 (see Additional Readings) gives an approximate formula for the roots. The function $g(x) = J_0(x)Y_0(2x) - J_0(2x)Y_0(x)$ is much better behaved than the $f(x)$ previously discussed.

14.4   HANKEL FUNCTIONS

Hankel functions are solutions of Bessel's ODE with asymptotic properties that make them particularly useful in problems involving the propagation of spherical or cylindrical waves. Since the functions J_ν and Y_ν form the complete solution of this ODE, the Hankel functions cannot be anything completely new; they must be linear combinations of the solutions we have already found. We introduce them here via straightforward algebraic definitions; later in this section we identify integral representations that some authors have used as a starting point.

Definitions

Starting from the Bessel functions of the first and second kinds, namely $J_\nu(x)$ and $Y_\nu(x)$, we define the two Hankel functions $H_\nu^{(1)}(x)$ and $H_\nu^{(2)}(x)$ (sometimes, but nowadays infrequently referred to as **Bessel functions of the third kind**) as follows:

$$H_\nu^{(1)}(x) = J_\nu(x) + i Y_\nu(x), \tag{14.76}$$

$$H_\nu^{(2)}(x) = J_\nu(x) - i Y_\nu(x). \tag{14.77}$$

This is exactly analogous to taking

$$e^{\pm i\theta} = \cos\theta \pm i \sin\theta. \tag{14.78}$$

For real arguments, $H_\nu^{(1)}$ and $H_\nu^{(2)}$ are complex conjugates. The extent of the analogy will be seen even better when their asymptotic forms are considered. Indeed, it is their asymptotic behavior that makes the Hankel functions useful. This behavior is discussed in Section 14.6, and in that section we provide an illustrative example in which the asymptotic properties play a key role.

Series expansion of $H_\nu^{(1)}(x)$ and $H_\nu^{(2)}(x)$ may be obtained by combining Eqs. (14.6) and (14.62). Often only the first term is of interest; it is given by

$$H_0^{(1)}(x) \approx i\frac{2}{\pi}\ln x + 1 + i\frac{2}{\pi}(\gamma - \ln 2) + \cdots, \tag{14.79}$$

$$H_\nu^{(1)}(x) \approx -i\frac{\Gamma(\nu)}{\pi}\left(\frac{2}{x}\right)^\nu + \cdots, \quad \nu > 0, \tag{14.80}$$

$$H_0^{(2)}(x) \approx -i\frac{2}{\pi}\ln x + 1 - i\frac{2}{\pi}(\gamma - \ln 2) + \cdots, \tag{14.81}$$

$$H_\nu^{(2)}(x) \approx i\frac{\Gamma(\nu)}{\pi}\left(\frac{2}{x}\right)^\nu + \cdots, \quad \nu > 0. \tag{14.82}$$

In these equations γ is the Euler-Mascheroni constant, defined in Eq. (1.13).

Since the Hankel functions are linear combinations (with constant coefficients) of J_ν and Y_ν, they satisfy the same recurrence relations, Eqs. (14.7) and (14.8). For both $H_\nu^{(1)}(x)$ and $H_\nu^{(2)}(x)$,

$$H_{\nu-1}(x) + H_{\nu+1}(x) = \frac{2\nu}{x}H_\nu(x), \tag{14.83}$$

$$H_{\nu-1}(x) - H_{\nu+1}(x) = 2H_\nu'(x). \tag{14.84}$$

A variety of Wronskian formulas can be developed, including:

$$H_\nu^{(2)}H_{\nu+1}^{(1)} - H_\nu^{(1)}H_{\nu+1}^{(2)} = \frac{4}{i\pi x}, \tag{14.85}$$

$$J_{\nu-1}H_\nu^{(1)} - J_\nu H_{\nu-1}^{(1)} = \frac{2}{i\pi x}, \tag{14.86}$$

$$J_{\nu-1}H_\nu^{(2)} - J_\nu H_{\nu-1}^{(2)} = -\frac{2}{i\pi x}. \tag{14.87}$$

Contour Integral Representation of the Hankel Functions

The integral representation (Schlaefli integral) for $J_\nu(x)$ was introduced in Section 14.1, where we established that

$$J_\nu(x) = \frac{1}{2\pi i} \int_C e^{(x/2)(t-1/t)} \frac{dt}{t^{\nu+1}}, \tag{14.88}$$

with C the contour shown in Fig. 14.5. Recall that when ν is nonintegral, the integrand has a branch point at $t = 0$ and the contour had to avoid a cut line that was drawn along the negative real axis. In developing the Schlaefli integral for general ν, we began by showing that Bessel's ODE was satisfied for any open contour for which an expression of the form

$$\frac{e^{(x/2)(t-1/t)}}{t^\nu} \left[\nu + \frac{x}{2}\left(t + \frac{1}{t}\right) \right] \tag{14.89}$$

vanished at both endpoints of the contour.

We now make further use of those observations by noting that the expression in Eq. (14.89) not only vanishes at $t = -\infty$ on the real axis both below and above the cut, but that it also vanishes at $t = 0$ when that point is approached from positive t.

We therefore consider the contour shown in Fig. 14.10, calling attention to the fact that the upper half of the contour (from $t = 0+$ to $t = \infty e^{\pi i}$), labeled C_1, meets the conditions necessary to yield a solution to Bessel's ODE, and that the remaining (lower) half of the contour, labeled C_2, also yields a solution. What remains to be determined is the identification of these solutions: We will show that they are the Hankel functions. For $x > 0$, we assert that

$$H_\nu^{(1)}(x) = \frac{1}{\pi i} \int_{C_1} e^{(x/2)(t-1/t)} \frac{dt}{t^{\nu+1}}, \tag{14.90}$$

$$H_\nu^{(2)}(x) = \frac{1}{\pi i} \int_{C_2} e^{(x/2)(t-1/t)} \frac{dt}{t^{\nu+1}}. \tag{14.91}$$

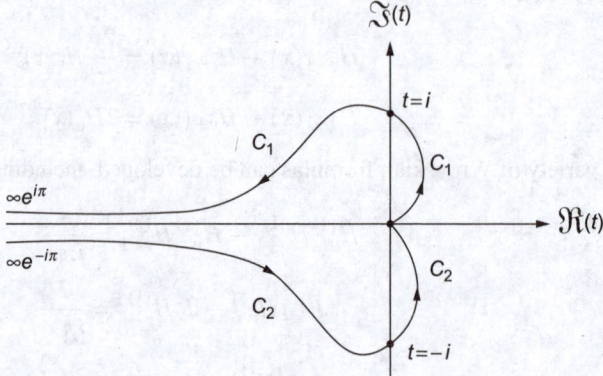

FIGURE 14.10   Hankel function contours.

These expressions are particularly convenient because they may be handled by the method of steepest descents (Section 12.7). $H_\nu^{(1)}(x)$ has a saddle point at $t = +i$, whereas $H_\nu^{(2)}(x)$ has a saddle point at $t = -i$.

There remains the problem of relating Eqs. (14.90) and (14.91) to our earlier definition of the Hankel functions, Eqs. (14.76) and (14.77). Since the contours of Eqs. (14.90) and (14.91) combine to produce a contour yielding J_ν, Eq. (14.88), we have, from the integral representations,

$$J_\nu(x) = \frac{1}{2}\left[H_\nu^{(1)}(x) + H_\nu^{(2)}(x) \right]. \tag{14.92}$$

If we can show (also from the integral representations) that

$$Y_\nu(x) = \frac{1}{2i}\left[H_\nu^{(1)}(x) - H_\nu^{(2)}(x) \right], \tag{14.93}$$

we will be able to recover the original definitions of the $H_\nu^{(i)}$.

We therefore rewrite Eq. (14.90) by replacing the integration variable t by $e^{i\pi}/s$, so the integrand of that equation becomes $-e^{(x/2)(s-1/s)}e^{-i\nu\pi}s^{\nu-1}$. After the substitution the contour (in s) is found to be the same as C_1, but traversed in the opposite direction (thereby compensating the initial minus sign in the transformed integrand). The result, with details left as Exercise 14.4.3, is that the contour integral representation of $H^{(1)}$ is consistent with the identification

$$H_\nu^{(1)}(x) = e^{-i\nu\pi} H_{-\nu}^{(1)}(x). \tag{14.94}$$

Similar processing of Eq. (14.91), with $t = e^{-i\pi}/s$, leads to

$$H_\nu^{(2)}(x) = e^{i\nu\pi} H_{-\nu}^{(2)}(x). \tag{14.95}$$

We now combine Eqs. (14.94) and (14.95) to reach

$$J_{-\nu}(x) = \frac{1}{2}\left[e^{i\nu\pi} H_\nu^{(1)}(x) + e^{-i\nu\pi} H_\nu^{(2)}(x) \right], \tag{14.96}$$

where again the $H_\nu^{(i)}$ refer to the contour integral representations. Substituting Eqs. (14.92) and (14.96) into the defining equation for Y_ν, Eq. (14.57), we confirm that Y_ν is described properly when the $H_\nu^{(i)}$ stand for their contour integral representations. This completes the proof that Eqs. (14.90) and (14.91) are consistent with the original definitions of the Hankel functions.

The reader may wonder why so much stress is placed on the development of integral representations. There are several reasons. The first is simply aesthetic appeal. Second, the integral representations facilitate manipulations, analysis, and the development of relations among the various special functions. We have already seen an example of this in the development of Eqs. (14.94) to (14.96). And, probably most important of all, integral representations are extremely useful in developing asymptotic expansions. Such expansions can often be obtained using the method of steepest descents (Section 12.7), or by methods involving expansion in negative powers of the expansion variable, as in Section 12.6.

In conclusion, the Hankel functions are introduced here for the following reasons:

- As analogs of $e^{\pm ix}$ they are useful for describing traveling waves. These applications are best studied when the asymptotic properties of the functions are in hand, and therefore are postponed to Section 14.6.

- They offer an alternate (contour integral) and rather elegant definition of Bessel functions.

- We will see in Section 14.5 that they offer a route to the definition of the quantities known as **modified Bessel functions**, and that in Section 14.6 they are useful for the development of the asymptotic properties of Bessel functions.

Exercises

14.4.1   Verify the Wronskian formulas

(a) $J_\nu(x)H_\nu^{(1)'}(x) - J_\nu'(x)H_\nu^{(1)}(x) = \frac{2i}{\pi x}$,

(b) $J_\nu(x)H_\nu^{(2)'}(x) - J_\nu'(x)H_\nu^{(2)}(x) = -\frac{2i}{\pi x}$,

(c) $Y_\nu(x)H_\nu^{(1)'}(x) - Y_\nu'(x)H_\nu^{(1)}(x) = -\frac{2}{\pi x}$,

(d) $Y_\nu(x)H_\nu^{(2)'}(x) - Y_\nu'(x)H_\nu^{(2)}(x) = -\frac{2}{\pi x}$,

(e) $H_\nu^{(1)}(x)H_\nu^{(2)'}(x) - H_\nu^{(1)'}(x)H_\nu^{(2)}(x) = -\frac{4i}{\pi x}$,

(f) $H_\nu^{(2)}(x)H_{\nu+1}^{(1)}(x) - H_\nu^{(1)}(x)H_{\nu+1}^{(2)}(x) = \frac{4}{i\pi x}$,

(g) $J_{\nu-1}(x)H_\nu^{(1)}(x) - J_\nu(x)H_{\nu-1}^{(1)}(x) = \frac{2}{i\pi x}$.

14.4.2   Show that the integral forms

(a) $\displaystyle \frac{1}{i\pi}\int_{0C_1}^{\infty e^{i\pi}} e^{(x/2)(t-1/t)}\frac{dt}{t^{\nu+1}} = H_\nu^{(1)}(x)$,

(b) $\displaystyle \frac{1}{i\pi}\int_{\infty e^{-i\pi}C_2}^{0} e^{(x/2)(t-1/t)}\frac{dt}{t^{\nu+1}} = H_\nu^{(2)}(x)$

satisfy Bessel's ODE. The contours C_1 and C_2 are shown in Fig. 14.10.

14.4.3   Show that the substitution $t = e^{i\pi}/s$ into Eq. (14.90) for $H_\nu^{(1)}(x)$ not only produces the integrand for the similar integral representation of $H_{-\nu}^{(1)}(x)$ but that the contour in s is identical to the original contour in t.

14.4.4   Using the integrals and contours given in Exercise 14.4.2, show that

$$\frac{1}{2i}[H_\nu^{(1)}(x) - H_\nu^{(2)}(x)] = Y_\nu(x).$$

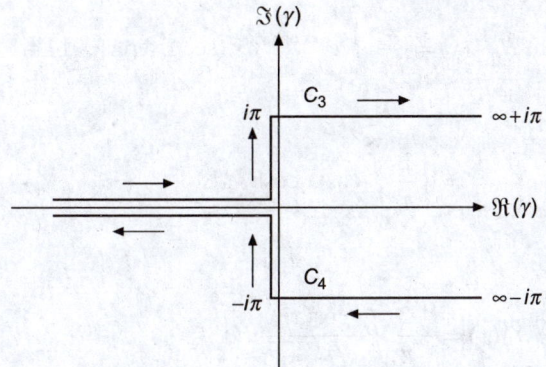

FIGURE 14.11   Hankel function contours for Exercise 14.4.5.

14.4.5   Show that the integrals in Exercise 14.4.2 may be transformed to yield

(a) $H_\nu^{(1)}(x) = \frac{1}{\pi i} \int_{C_3} e^{x \sinh \gamma - \nu \gamma} d\gamma$,

(b) $H_\nu^{(2)}(x) = \frac{1}{\pi i} \int_{C_4} e^{x \sinh \gamma - \nu \gamma} d\gamma$,

where C_3 and C_4 are the contours in Fig. 14.11.

14.4.6   (a)   Transform $H_0^{(1)}(x)$, Eq. (14.90), into

$$H_0^{(1)}(x) = \frac{1}{i\pi} \int_C e^{ix \cosh s} ds,$$

where the contour C runs from $-\infty - i\pi/2$ through the origin of the s-plane to $\infty + i\pi/2$.

(b)   Justify rewriting $H_0^{(1)}(x)$ as

$$H_0^{(1)}(x) = \frac{2}{i\pi} \int_0^{\infty + i\pi/2} e^{ix \cosh s} ds.$$

(c)   Verify that this integral representation actually satisfies Bessel's differential equation. (The $i\pi/2$ in the upper limit is not essential. It serves as a convergence factor. We can replace it by $ia\pi/2$ and take the limit $a \to 0$.)

14.4.7   From

$$H_0^{(1)}(x) = \frac{2}{i\pi} \int_0^{\infty} e^{ix \cosh s} ds$$

show that

(a) $J_0(x) = \frac{2}{\pi} \int_0^\infty \sin(x \cosh s) ds$,   (b) $J_0(x) = \frac{2}{\pi} \int_1^\infty \frac{\sin(xt)}{\sqrt{t^2 - 1}} dt$.

This last result is a Fourier sine transform.

14.4.8 From $H_0^{(1)}(x) = \dfrac{2}{i\pi} \displaystyle\int\limits_0^\infty e^{ix\cosh s}\,ds$ (see Exercises 14.4.5 and 14.4.6), show that

(a) $Y_0(x) = -\dfrac{2}{\pi} \displaystyle\int\limits_0^\infty \cos(x\cosh s)\,ds,$

(b) $Y_0(x) = -\dfrac{2}{\pi} \displaystyle\int\limits_1^\infty \dfrac{\cos(xt)}{\sqrt{t^2-1)}}\,dt.$

These are the integral representations in Eq. (14.63). This last result is a Fourier cosine transform.

14.5 MODIFIED BESSEL FUNCTIONS, $I_\nu(x)$ AND $K_\nu(x)$

The Laplace and Helmholtz equations, when separated in circular cylindrical coordinates, may lead to Bessel's ODE in the coordinate ρ that describes distance from the cylindrical axis. When that is the case, the behavior of the solutions as a function of ρ is inherently oscillatory; as we have already seen, the Bessel functions $J_\nu(k\rho)$, and also $Y_\nu(k\rho)$, have for any value of ν an infinite number of zeros, and this property may be useful in causing satisfaction of boundary conditions. However, as already shown in Section 9.4, the connection constants arising when the variables are separated may have a sign opposite to that required to yield Bessel's ODE, and the equation in the ρ coordinate then assumes the form

$$\rho^2 \frac{d^2}{d\rho^2} P_\nu(k\rho) + \rho \frac{d}{d\rho} P_\nu(k\rho) - (k^2\rho^2 + \nu^2) P_\nu(k\rho) = 0. \tag{14.97}$$

Equation (14.97), known as the **modified Bessel equation**, differs from the Bessel ODE only in the sign of the quantity $k^2\rho^2$, but this small change is sufficient to alter the nature of the solutions. As we shall shortly discuss in more detail, the solutions to Eq. (14.97), called **modified Bessel functions**, are **not** oscillatory and have behavior that is exponential (rather than trigonometric) in character.

Fortunately, the knowledge we have developed regarding the Bessel ODE can be put to good use for the modified Bessel equation, since the substitution $k \to ik$ converts the conventional Bessel ODE to its modified form, and shows that if $P_\nu(k\rho)$ is a solution to the Bessel ODE, then $P_\nu(ik\rho)$ must be a solution to the modified Bessel equation. One way of stating this fact is to note that the solutions of Eq. (14.97) are Bessel functions of imaginary argument.

Series Solution

Since any solution of Bessel's ODE can be converted into a solution of the modified ODE by insertion of i into its argument, let's start by looking at the series expansion

$$J_\nu(ix) = \sum_{s=0}^{\infty} \frac{(-1)^s}{s!\,\Gamma(s+\nu+1)} \left(\frac{ix}{2}\right)^{\nu+2s} = i^\nu \sum_{s=0}^{\infty} \frac{1}{s!\,\Gamma(s+\nu+1)} \left(\frac{x}{2}\right)^{\nu+2s}. \tag{14.98}$$

Since all the terms of the summation have the same sign, it is evident that $J_\nu(ix)$ cannot exhibit oscillatory behavior. It is convenient to choose the solutions of the modified Bessel equation in a way that causes them to be real, and we accordingly defined the **modified Bessel functions of the first kind**, denoted $I_\nu(x)$, as

$$I_\nu(x) = i^{-\nu} J_\nu(ix) = e^{-i\nu\pi/2} J_\nu(xe^{i\pi/2}) = \sum_{s=0}^{\infty} \frac{1}{s!\,\Gamma(s+\nu+1)} \left(\frac{x}{2}\right)^{\nu+2s}. \tag{14.99}$$

Like J_ν for $\nu \geq 0$, I_ν is finite at the origin, with a power-series expansion that is convergent for all x. At small x, its limiting behavior will be of the form

$$I_\nu(x) = \frac{x^\nu}{2^\nu \Gamma(\nu+1)} + \cdots . \tag{14.100}$$

From the relation between J_ν and $J_{-\nu}$, we may also conclude that I_ν and $I_{-\nu}$ are linearly independent unless ν is an integer n; taking cognizance of the factor i^{-n} in the definition of I_n, the linear dependence takes the form

$$I_n(x) = I_{-n}(x). \tag{14.101}$$

Graphs of I_0 and I_1 are shown in Fig. 14.12.

Recurrence Relations for I_ν

The recurrence relations satisfied by $I_\nu(x)$ may be developed from the series expansions, but it is perhaps easier to work from the existing recurrence relations for $J_\nu(x)$. Our starting point is Eq. (14.7), written for ix:

$$J_{\nu-1}(ix) + J_{\nu+1}(ix) = \frac{2n}{ix} J_n(ix). \tag{14.102}$$

We change J to I, related according to Eq. (14.99) by

$$J_\nu(ix) = i^\nu I_\nu(x), \tag{14.103}$$

thereby obtaining

$$i^{\nu-1} I_{\nu-1}(x) + i^{\nu+1} I_{\nu+1}(x) = \frac{2\nu}{ix} i^\nu I_\nu(x),$$

which simplifies to

$$I_{\nu-1}(x) - I_{\nu+1}(x) = \frac{2\nu}{x} I_\nu(x). \tag{14.104}$$

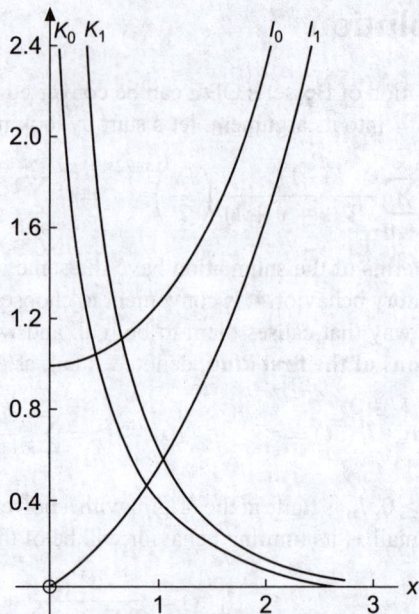

FIGURE 14.12   Modified Bessel functions.

In a similar fashion, Eq. (14.8) transforms into

$$I_{\nu-1}(x) + I_{\nu+1}(x) = 2I_\nu'(x). \tag{14.105}$$

The above analysis is also the topic of Exercise 14.1.14.

Second Solution K_ν

As already pointed out we have but one independent solution when ν is an integer, exactly as for the Bessel functions J_ν. The choice of a second, independent solution of Eq. (14.97) is essentially a matter of convenience. The second solution given here is selected on the basis of its asymptotic behavior, which we examine in the next section. The confusion of choice and notation for this solution is perhaps greater than anywhere else in this field.[5] There is also no universal nomenclature; the K_ν are sometimes referred to as Whittaker functions. Following AMS-55 (see Additional Readings for reference), we here define a second solution in terms of the Hankel function $H_\nu^{(1)}(x)$ as

$$K_\nu(x) \equiv \frac{\pi}{2} i^{\nu+1} H_\nu^{(1)}(ix) = \frac{\pi}{2} i^{\nu+1} \big[J_\nu(ix) + i Y_\nu(ix) \big]. \tag{14.106}$$

[5]Discussion and comparison of notations will be found in *Math. Tables Aids Comput.* **1**: 207–308 (1944) and in AMS-55 (see Additional Readings).

The factor $i^{\nu+1}$ makes $K_\nu(x)$ real when x is real.[6] Using Eqs. (14.57) and (14.99), we may transform Eq. (14.106) to[7]

$$K_\nu(x) = \frac{\pi}{2} \frac{I_{-\nu}(x) - I_\nu(x)}{\sin \nu\pi}, \tag{14.107}$$

somewhat analogous to Eq. (14.57) for $Y_\nu(x)$. The choice of Eq. (14.106) as a definition is somewhat unfortunate in that the function $K_\nu(x)$ does not satisfy the same recurrence relations as $I_\nu(x)$. The recurrence formulas for the K_ν are

$$K_{\nu-1}(x) - K_{\nu+1}(x) = -\frac{2\nu}{x} K_\nu(x), \tag{14.108}$$

$$K_{\nu-1}(x) + K_{\nu+1}(x) = -2K_\nu'(x). \tag{14.109}$$

To avoid this discrepancy in the recurrence relations, some authors[8] have included an additional factor of $\cos \nu\pi$ in the definition of K_ν. This would permit K_ν to satisfy the same recurrence relations as I_ν (see Exercise 14.5.8), but it has the disadvantage of making $K_\nu = 0$ for $\nu = \frac{1}{2}, \frac{3}{2}, \frac{5}{2}, \ldots$.

The series expansion of $K_\nu(x)$ follows directly from the series form of $H_\nu^{(1)}(ix)$, providing that we choose the branch of $\ln ix$ appropriately (see Exercise 14.5.9). Using Eqs. (14.79) and (14.80), the lowest-order terms are then found to be

$$K_0(x) = -\ln x - \gamma + \ln 2 + \cdots, \tag{14.110}$$

$$K_\nu(x) = 2^{\nu-1}\Gamma(\nu)x^{-\nu} + \cdots. \tag{14.111}$$

Because the modified Bessel function I_ν is related to the Bessel function J_ν, much as sinh is related to sine, the modified Bessel functions I_ν and K_ν are sometimes referred to as **hyperbolic Bessel functions**. K_0 and K_1 are shown in Fig. 14.12.

Integral Representations

$I_0(x)$ and $K_0(x)$ have the integral representations

$$I_0(x) = \frac{1}{\pi} \int_0^\pi \cosh(x \cos\theta)d\theta, \tag{14.112}$$

$$K_0(x) = \int_0^\infty \cos(x \sinh t)dt = \int_0^\infty \frac{\cos(xt)dt}{(t^2 + 1)^{1/2}}, \quad x > 0. \tag{14.113}$$

Equation (14.112) may be derived from Eq. (14.20) for $J_0(x)$ or may be taken as a special case of Exercise 14.5.14. The integral representation of K_0, Eq. (14.113), is derived in Section 14.6. A variety of other forms of integral representations (including $\nu \neq 0$) appear

---

[6]If ν is not an integer, $K_\nu(z)$ has a branch point at $z = 0$ due to the presence of a fractional power; if $\nu = n$, an integer, $K_n(z)$ has a branch point at $z = 0$ due to the term $\ln z$. We normally identify $K_n(z)$ as the branch that is real for real z.

[7]For integral index n we take the limit as $\nu \to n$.

[8]For example, Whittaker and Watson (see Additional Readings).

in the exercises. These integral representations are useful in developing asymptotic forms (Section 14.6) and in connection with Fourier transforms (Chapter 19).

Example 14.5.1 A GREEN'S FUNCTION

We wish to develop an expansion for the fundamental Green's function for the Laplace equation in cylindrical coordinates (ρ, φ, z). The defining equation is

$$\left[\frac{\partial^2}{\partial \rho_1^2} + \frac{1}{\rho_1} \frac{\partial}{\partial \rho_1} + \frac{1}{\rho_1^2} \frac{\partial^2}{\partial \varphi_1^2} + \frac{\partial^2}{\partial z_1^2} \right] G(\mathbf{r}_1, \mathbf{r}_2) = \delta(\rho_1 - \rho_2) \frac{1}{\rho_1^2} \delta(\varphi_1 - \varphi_2) \delta(z_1 - z_2).$$

(14.114)

We now write the Dirac delta function for the φ coordinate in the form corresponding to Eq. (5.27):

$$\delta(\varphi_1 - \varphi_2) = \frac{1}{2\pi} \sum_{m=-\infty}^{\infty} e^{im(\varphi_1 - \varphi_2)}.$$

For the z coordinate, we use the continuum limit of the above formula, or, equivalently, the large-n limit of Eq. (1.155),

$$\delta(z_1 - z_2) = \frac{1}{2\pi} \int_{-\infty}^{\infty} e^{ik(z_1 - z_2)} dk = \frac{1}{\pi} \int_{0}^{\infty} \cos k(z_1 - z_2) dk.$$

We use the last form of the above equation so that k will never be negative.

We now expand $G(\mathbf{r}_1, \mathbf{r}_2)$ as

$$G(\mathbf{r}_1, \mathbf{r}_2) = \frac{1}{2\pi^2} \sum_m \int_0^{\infty} dk\, g_m(k, \rho_1, \rho_2) e^{im(\varphi_1 - \varphi_2)} \cos k(z_1 - z_2).$$

(14.115)

For φ_1 and φ_2, this is simply an expansion in orthogonal functions; the dependence on z_1, z_2, and k is actually an integral transform that will be more completely justified in Chapter 20. For our present purposes, what is significant is that we can apply the orthogonality properties of the expansion to find that Eq. (14.114) will be satisfied if (for all relevant values of k and m)

$$\left[\frac{\partial^2}{\partial \rho_1^2} + \frac{1}{\rho_1} \frac{\partial}{\partial \rho_1} - \frac{m^2}{\rho_1^2} - k^2 \right] g_m(k, \rho_1, \rho_2) = \delta(\rho_1 - \rho_2).$$

(14.116)

We now have a one-dimensional (1-D) Green's function problem for which the homogeneous equation can be identified as the modified Bessel equation, with solutions $I_m(k\rho)$ and $K_m(k\rho)$. Keeping in mind that I_m is regular at the origin, that K_m is regular at infinity, and that the Green's function we seek must be regular at both these limits, we write our 1-D **axial Green's function** in the more explicit form

$$g_m(k\rho_1, k\rho_2) = -I_m(k\rho_<)K_m(k\rho_>),$$

(14.117)

where $\rho_<$ and $\rho_>$ are, respectively, the smaller and larger of ρ_1 and ρ_2. The coefficient in the above equation, -1, is evaluated according to Eq. (10.19), from

$$\left(p(k\rho)\left[K'_m(k\rho)I_m(k\rho) - I'_m(k\rho)K_m(k\rho)\right]\right)^{-1}.$$

The coefficient p is from the differential equation, and has here the value $k\rho$; the form involving modified Bessel functions is their Wronskian, and has the value $-1/k\rho$; that is the topic of Exercise 14.5.11.

Given our explicit formula for g_m, Eq. (14.115) assumes the final form

$$G(\mathbf{r}_1, \mathbf{r}_2) = \frac{1}{2\pi^2} \sum_m \int_0^\infty dk g_m(k\rho_1, k\rho_2)e^{im(\varphi_1-\varphi_2)} \cos k(z_1 - z_2). \tag{14.118}$$

This is the form quoted in Section 10.2. ∎

Summary

To put the modified Bessel functions $I_\nu(x)$ and $K_\nu(x)$ in proper perspective, note that we have introduced them here because:

- These functions are solutions of the frequently encountered modified Bessel equation, which arises in a variety of physically important problems,

- $K_\nu(x)$ will be found useful in determining the asymptotic behavior of all the Bessel and modified Bessel functions (Section 14.6), and

- $I_\nu(x)$ and $K_\nu(x)$ arise in our discussion of Green's functions (Example 14.5.1).

Exercises

14.5.1 Show that $e^{(x/2)(t+1/t)} = \sum_{n=-\infty}^{\infty} I_n(x)t^n$, thus generating modified Bessel functions, $I_n(x)$.

14.5.2 Verify the following identities

(a) $1 = I_0(x) + 2\sum_{n=1}^{\infty}(-1)^n I_{2n}(x)$,

(b) $e^x = I_0(x) + 2\sum_{n=1}^{\infty} I_n(x)$,

(c) $e^{-x} = I_0(x) + 2\sum_{n=1}^{\infty}(-1)^n I_n(x)$,

(d) $\cosh x = I_0(x) + 2\sum_{n=1}^{\infty} I_{2n}(x)$,

(e) $\sinh x = 2\sum_{n=1}^{\infty} I_{2n-1}(x)$.

14.5.3 (a) From the generating function of Exercise 14.5.1 show that

$$I_n(x) = \frac{1}{2\pi i} \oint e^{(x/2)(t+1/t)} \frac{dt}{t^{n+1}}.$$

(b) For $n = v$, not an integer, show that the preceding integral representation may be generalized to

$$I_v(x) = \frac{1}{2\pi i} \int_C e^{(x/2)(t+1/t)} \frac{dt}{t^{v+1}}.$$

The contour C is the same as that for $J_v(x)$ (Fig. 14.5).

14.5.4 For $v > -\frac{1}{2}$ show that $I_v(z)$ may be represented by

$$I_v(z) = \frac{1}{\pi^{1/2}\Gamma(v+\frac{1}{2})} \left(\frac{z}{2}\right)^v \int_0^\pi e^{\pm z\cos\theta} \sin^{2v}\theta \, d\theta$$

$$= \frac{1}{\pi^{1/2}\Gamma(v+\frac{1}{2})} \left(\frac{z}{2}\right)^v \int_{-1}^1 e^{\pm zp}(1-p^2)^{v-1/2} \, dp$$

$$= \frac{2}{\pi^{1/2}\Gamma(v+\frac{1}{2})} \left(\frac{z}{2}\right)^v \int_0^{\pi/2} \cosh(z\cos\theta) \sin^{2v}\theta \, d\theta.$$

14.5.5 The cylindrical cavity depicted in Fig. 14.4 has radius a and height h. For this exercise, the end caps $z = 0$ and h are at zero potential, while the cylindrical wall $\rho = a$ has a potential of functional form $V = V(\varphi, z)$.

(a) Show that the electrostatic potential $\Phi(\rho, \varphi, z)$ has the functional form

$$\Phi(\rho, \varphi, z) = \sum_{m=0}^\infty \sum_{n=1}^\infty I_m(k_n\rho)(a_{mn}\sin m\varphi + b_{mn}\cos m\varphi)\sin k_n z,$$

where $k_n = n\pi/h$.

(b) Show that the coefficients a_{mn} and b_{mn} are given by

$$\left. \begin{matrix} a_{mn} \\ b_{mn} \end{matrix} \right\} = \frac{2 - \delta_{m0}}{\pi l I_m(k_n a)} \int_0^{2\pi} \int_0^l V(\varphi, z) \left\{ \begin{matrix} \sin m\varphi \\ \cos m\varphi \end{matrix} \right\} \sin k_n z \, dz \, d\varphi.$$

Hint. Expand $V(\varphi, z)$ as a double series and use the orthogonality of the trigonometric functions.

14.5.6 Verify that $K_v(x)$ as defined in Eq. (14.106) is equivalent to

$$K_v(x) = \frac{\pi}{2} \frac{I_{-v}(x) - I_v(x)}{\sin v\pi}$$

and from this show that

$$K_v(x) = K_{-v}(x).$$

14.5.7 Show that $K_\nu(x)$ satisfies the following recurrence relations:

$$K_{\nu-1}(x) - K_{\nu+1}(x) = -\frac{2\nu}{x} K_\nu(x),$$

$$K_{\nu-1}(x) + K_{\nu+1}(x) = -2K_\nu'(x).$$

Note. These differ from the recurrence relations for I_ν.

14.5.8 If $\mathcal{K}_\nu = e^{\nu\pi i} K_\nu$, show that $\mathcal{K}_\nu$ satisfies the same recurrence relations as I_ν.

14.5.9 Show that when K_0 is evaluated from its series expansion about $x = 0$, the formula given as Eq. (14.110) only follows if a specific branch of its logarithmic term is chosen.

14.5.10 For $\nu > -\frac{1}{2}$ show that $K_\nu(z)$ may be represented by

$$K_\nu(z) = \frac{\pi^{1/2}}{\Gamma(\nu + \frac{1}{2})} \left(\frac{z}{2}\right)^\nu \int_0^\infty e^{-z\cosh t} \sinh^{2\nu} t \, dt, \quad -\frac{\pi}{2} < \arg z < \frac{\pi}{2}$$

$$= \frac{\pi^{1/2}}{\Gamma(\nu + \frac{1}{2})} \left(\frac{z}{2}\right)^\nu \int_1^\infty e^{-zp} (p^2 - 1)^{\nu - 1/2} dp.$$

14.5.11 Show that $I_\nu(x)$ and $K_\nu(x)$ satisfy the Wronskian relation

$$I_\nu(x)K_\nu'(x) - I_\nu'(x)K_\nu(x) = -\frac{1}{x}.$$

14.5.12 Verify that the coefficient in the axial Green's function of Eq. (14.117) is -1.

14.5.13 If $r = (x^2 + y^2)^{1/2}$, prove that

$$\frac{1}{r} = \frac{2}{\pi} \int_0^\infty \cos(xt) K_0(yt) dt.$$

This is a Fourier cosine transform of K_0.

14.5.14 Derive the integral representation

$$I_n(x) = \frac{1}{\pi} \int_0^\pi e^{x\cos\theta} \cos(n\theta) d\theta.$$

Hint. Start with the corresponding integral representation of $J_n(x)$. Equation (14.112) is a special case of this representation.

14.5.15 Show that

$$K_0(z) = \int_0^\infty e^{-z\cosh t} dt$$

satisfies the modified Bessel equation. How can you establish that this form is linearly independent of $I_0(z)$?

14.5.16   The cylindrical cavity of Exercise 14.5.5 has along the cylinder walls the potential walls:

$$V(z) = \begin{cases} 100\,\dfrac{z}{h}, & 0 \le \dfrac{z}{h} \le 1/2, \\[2mm] 100\Big(1 - \dfrac{z}{h}\Big), & 1/2 \le \dfrac{z}{h} \le 1. \end{cases}$$

With the radius-height ratio $a/h = 0.5$, calculate the potential for $z/h = 0.1(0.1)0.5$ and $\rho/a = 0.0(0.2)1.0$.

Check value. For $z/h = 0.3$ and $\rho/a = 0.8$, $V = 26.396$.

14.6   ASYMPTOTIC EXPANSIONS

Frequently in physical problems there is a need to know how a given Bessel or modified Bessel function behaves for large values of the argument, that is, its asymptotic behavior. This is one occasion when computers are not very helpful. One possible approach is to develop a power-series solution of the differential equation, but now using negative powers. This is Stokes' method, illustrated in Exercise 14.6.10. The limitation is that starting from some positive value of the argument (for convergence of the series), we do not know what mixture of solutions or multiple of a given solution we have. The problem is to relate the asymptotic series (useful for large values of the variable) to the power-series or related definition (useful for small values of the variable). This relationship can be established is various ways, one of which is to introduce a suitable **integral representation** whose asymptotic behavior can be studied by application of the method of steepest descents, Section 12.7.

We start this process with a study of the Hankel functions, for which a contour integral representation was introduced in Section 14.4.

Asymptotic Forms of Hankel Functions

In Section 14.4 it was shown that the Hankel functions, which satisfy Bessel's equation, may be defined by the contour integrals

$$H_\nu^{(1)}(t) = \frac{1}{\pi i} \int_{C_1} e^{(t/2)(z-1/z)} \frac{dz}{z^{\nu+1}}, \tag{14.119}$$

$$H_\nu^{(2)}(t) = \frac{1}{\pi i} \int_{C_2} e^{(t/2)(z-1/z)} \frac{dz}{z^{\nu+1}}, \tag{14.120}$$

where C_1 and C_2 are the contours shown in Fig. 14.10. We desire formulas based on these representations for the asymptotic behavior of the Hankel functions at large positive t.

The direct and exact evaluation of these integrals appears to be nearly impossible, but the situation does have features permitting us to use the method of steepest descents to make an asymptotic evaluation. Referring to the exposition of that method in Section 12.7, we have the approximate evaluation

$$\int_C g(z,t)e^{w(z,t)}dz \approx g(z_0,t)e^{w(z_0,t)}e^{i\theta}\sqrt{\frac{2\pi}{|w''(z_0,t)|}}, \tag{14.121}$$

where the contour C passes through a saddle point at $z = z_0$ and

$$\theta = -\frac{\arg(w''(z_0,t))}{2} + \left(\frac{\pi}{2} \text{ or } \frac{3\pi}{2}\right) \tag{14.122}$$

is a phase arising from the direction of passage through the saddle point.

We regard the common integrand of Eqs. (14.119) and (14.120) as possessing a slowly varying factor $g(z) = z^{-\nu-1}$ and an exponential e^w with $w = (t/2)(z - z^{-1})$, and seek saddle points by finding the zeros of

$$w' = \frac{t}{2}\left(1 + \frac{1}{z^2}\right). \tag{14.123}$$

Solving the above equation, we identify the two saddle points $z_0 = +i$ and $z_0 = -i$.

Limiting attention to $H_\nu^{(1)}(t)$, we see that we can deform the contour C_1 so that it passes through the saddle point at $z_0 = i$; there is neither the need nor the possibility to deform this contour to pass through $z_0 = -i$. Thus, at the saddle point, we have

$$w(+i) = it, \quad w''(+i) = -\frac{t}{z_0^3}\bigg|_{z_0=i} = -it. \tag{14.124}$$

The argument of $w''(z_0)$ is $-\pi/2$, so the possible values of the phase θ (the direction of descent from the saddle point) are $3\pi/4$ and $7\pi/4$. We must choose $\theta = 3\pi/4$ since we cannot get into position to cross the saddle point in the direction $\theta = 7\pi/4 = -\pi/4$ without first crossing a region where the integrand is larger in absolute value than its value at the saddle point.

We now have all the information needed to use Eq. (14.121) to estimate the integral. The result is

$$H_\nu^{(1)}(t) \approx \frac{1}{\pi i}e^{(i\pi/2)(-\nu-1)}e^{3i\pi/4}e^{it}\sqrt{\frac{2\pi}{t}}$$

$$\approx \sqrt{\frac{2}{\pi t}}e^{i(t-\nu\pi/2-\pi/4)}. \tag{14.125}$$

This is the leading term of the asymptotic expansion of the Hankel function $H_\nu^{(1)}(t)$ for large t. The other Hankel function can be treated similarly, but using the saddle point at $z = -i$, with result

$$H_\nu^{(2)}(t) \approx \sqrt{\frac{2}{\pi t}}e^{-i(t-\nu\pi/2-\pi/4)}. \tag{14.126}$$

Equations (14.125) and (14.126) permit us to obtain the leading terms in the asymptotic behavior of all the Bessel and modified Bessel functions. In particular, inserting the asymptotic form for $H^{(1)}(ix)$ into Eq. (14.106), which defines $K_\nu(x)$, we find

$$K_\nu(x) \sim \frac{\pi}{2} i^{\nu+1} \sqrt{\frac{2}{i\pi x}} e^{-x} e^{t - \nu\pi/2 - \pi/4},$$

$$\sim \sqrt{\frac{\pi}{2x}} e^{-x}, \tag{14.127}$$

Another solution to the modified Bessel equation can be obtained from $H^{(2)}(ix)$; its asymptotic behavior will be proportional to e^{+x}. Combining the present observations with Eqs. (14.100), (14.110), and (14.111), we can conclude that:

1. The modified Bessel function $K_\nu(x)$ will be irregular at $x = 0$ as given by Eqs. (14.110) or (14.111), and will decay exponentially at large x;
2. The modified Bessel function $I_\nu(x)$ will (for $\nu \geq 0$) be finite at the origin, as given by Eq. (14.100), and will increase exponentially at large x.

Rather than developing additional asymptotic forms from Eq. (14.127), we find it more interesting to obtain more complete asymptotic expansions by use of a particular integral representation of K_ν.

Expansion of an Integral Representation for K_ν

Here we start from the integral representation

$$K_\nu(z) = \frac{\pi^{1/2}}{\Gamma(\nu + \frac{1}{2})} \left(\frac{z}{2}\right)^\nu \int_1^\infty e^{-zx}(x^2 - 1)^{\nu-1/2}dx, \quad \nu > -\frac{1}{2}. \tag{14.128}$$

For the present let us take z to be real, although Eq. (14.128) may be established for $-\pi/2 < \arg z < \pi/2$ (i.e., for $\Re e(z) > 0$).

Before using Eq. (14.128) we need to verify that (1) the form claimed to be $K_\nu(z)$ satisfies the modified Bessel equation, (2) that it has the small-z behavior required for K_ν, and (3) that it has the required exponentially decaying asymptotic value. These three features suffice to establish the validity of Eq. (14.128).

The fact that Eq. (14.128) is a solution of the modified Bessel equation may be verified by direct substitution into Eq. (14.97). After some manipulation, we obtain

$$z^{\nu+1} \int_1^\infty \frac{d}{dx}\left[e^{-zx}(x^2 - 1)^{\nu+1/2}\right] dx = 0,$$

which transforms the combined integrand into the derivative of a function that vanishes at both endpoints.

We next consider how Eq. (14.128) behaves for small z. We proceed by substituting $x = 1 + t/z$:

$$\frac{\pi^{1/2}}{\Gamma(\nu + \frac{1}{2})} \left(\frac{z}{2}\right)^\nu \int_1^\infty e^{-zx}(x^2 - 1)^{\nu - 1/2} dx$$

$$= \frac{\pi^{1/2}}{\Gamma(\nu + \frac{1}{2})} \left(\frac{z}{2}\right)^\nu e^{-z} \int_0^\infty e^{-t} \left(\frac{t^2}{z^2} + \frac{2t}{z}\right)^{\nu - 1/2} \frac{dt}{z}$$

$$= \frac{\pi^{1/2}}{\Gamma(\nu + \frac{1}{2})} \frac{e^{-z}}{2^\nu z^\nu} \int_0^\infty e^{-t} t^{2\nu - 1} \left(1 + \frac{2z}{t}\right)^{\nu - 1/2} dt. \qquad (14.129)$$

This substitution has changed the limits of integration to a more convenient range and has isolated the negative exponential dependence e^{-z}. The integral in Eq. (14.129) may now (for $\nu > 0$) be evaluated for $z = 0$ to yield $\Gamma(2\nu)$. Then, using the duplication formula, Eq. (13.27), we have

$$\lim_{z \to 0} K_\nu(z) = \frac{\Gamma(\nu) 2^{\nu - 1}}{z^\nu}, \quad \nu > 0. \qquad (14.130)$$

Equation (14.130) agrees with Eq. (14.111), showing that Eq. (14.128) has the proper small-z behavior to represent K_ν. Note that for $\nu = 0$, Eq. (14.128) diverges logarithmically at $z = 0$ and the verification of its scale requires a different approach, which is the topic of Exercise 14.6.4.

Finally, to complete the identification of Eq. (14.128) with K_ν, we need to verify that it decays exponentially at large z. That feature will be a by-product of our main interest here, which is to develop an asymptotic series for $K_\nu(z)$. We do so by rewriting Eq. (14.129) as

$$K_\nu(z) = \sqrt{\frac{\pi}{2z}} \frac{e^{-z}}{\Gamma(\nu + \frac{1}{2})} \int_0^\infty e^{-t} t^{\nu - 1/2} \left(1 + \frac{t}{2z}\right)^{\nu - 1/2} dt. \qquad (14.131)$$

We next expand $(1 + t/2z)^{\nu - 1/2}$ by the binomial theorem and interchange the summation and integration (valid for the asymptotic series we plan to obtain), reaching

$$K_\nu(z) = \sqrt{\frac{\pi}{2z}} \frac{e^{-z}}{\Gamma(\nu + \frac{1}{2})} \sum_{r=0}^\infty \binom{\nu - \frac{1}{2}}{r} (2z)^{-r} \int_0^\infty e^{-t} t^{\nu + r - 1/2} dt$$

$$= \sqrt{\frac{\pi}{2z}} e^{-z} \sum_{r=0}^\infty \frac{\Gamma(\nu + r + \frac{1}{2})}{r! \Gamma(\nu - r + \frac{1}{2})} (2z)^{-r}. \qquad (14.132)$$

Equation (14.132) can now be rearranged to

$$K_\nu(z) \sim \sqrt{\frac{\pi}{2z}} e^{-z} \left[1 + \frac{(4\nu^2 - 1^2)}{1! 8z} + \frac{(4\nu^2 - 1^2)(4\nu^2 - 3^2)}{2!(8z)^2} + \cdots \right]. \qquad (14.133)$$

Equation (14.133) yields the anticipated exponential dependence, confirming that Eq. (14.128) actually represents K_ν.

Although the integral of Eq. (14.128), integrating along the real axis, was convergent only for $-\pi/2 < \arg z < \pi/2$, Eq. (14.133) may be extended to $-3\pi/2 < \arg z < 3\pi/2$. Considered as an infinite series, Eq. (14.133) is actually divergent. However, this series is asymptotic, in the sense that for large enough z, $K_\nu(z)$ may be approximated to any fixed degree of accuracy with a small number of terms. Compare Section 12.6 for a definition and discussion of asymptotic series. The asymptotic character arises because our binomial expansion was valid only for $t < 2z$ but we integrated t out to infinity. The exponential decrease of the integrand has prevented a disaster, but the series is only asymptotic and not convergent. By Table 7.1, $z = \infty$ is an essential singularity of the Bessel (and modified Bessel) equations. Fuchs' theorem does not guarantee a convergent series and we did not get one.

It is convenient to rewrite Eq. (14.133) as

$$K_\nu(z) = \sqrt{\frac{\pi}{2z}} e^{-z} \left[P_\nu(iz) + i Q_\nu(iz) \right], \qquad (14.134)$$

where

$$P_\nu(z) \sim 1 - \frac{(\mu - 1)(\mu - 9)}{2!(8z)^2} + \frac{(\mu - 1)(\mu - 9)(\mu - 25)(\mu - 49)}{4!(8z)^4} - \cdots, \qquad (14.135)$$

$$Q_\nu(z) \sim \frac{\mu - 1}{1!(8z)} - \frac{(\mu - 1)(\mu - 9)(\mu - 25)}{3!(8z)^3} + \cdots, \qquad (14.136)$$

and $\mu = 4\nu^2$. It should be noted that although $P_\nu(z)$ of Eq. (14.135) and $Q_\nu(z)$ of Eq. (14.136) have alternating signs, the series for $P_\nu(iz)$ and $Q_\nu(iz)$ in Eq. (14.134) have all positive signs. Finally, note that for z large, P_ν dominates.

Additional Asymptotic Forms

We started our detailed study of asymptotic behavior with K_ν because, with its properties in hand, we can deduce the asymptotic expansions of the other members of the family of Bessel-related functions.

1. Rearranging the definition of K_ν to

$$H_\nu^{(1)}(x) = \frac{2}{\pi} e^{-(i\pi/2)(\nu+1)} K_\nu(-ix), \qquad (14.137)$$

we have

$$H_\nu^{(1)}(z) = \sqrt{\frac{2}{\pi z}} \exp\left\{ i \left[z - \left(\nu + \frac{1}{2} \right) \frac{\pi}{2} \right] \right\} \left[P_\nu(z) + i Q_\nu(z) \right], \qquad (14.138)$$

which although originally derived for real values of $-ix$, can be analytically continued into the larger range $-\pi < \arg z < 2\pi$.

2. The second Hankel function is just (for real arguments) the complex conjugate of the first, and therefore

$$H_\nu^{(2)}(z) = \sqrt{\frac{2}{\pi z}} \exp\left\{ -i \left[z - \left(\nu + \frac{1}{2} \right) \frac{\pi}{2} \right] \right\} \left[P_\nu(z) - i Q_\nu(z) \right], \qquad (14.139)$$

valid for $-2\pi < \arg z < \pi$.

3. Since $J_\nu(z)$ is the real part of $H_\nu^{(1)}(z)$ for real z,

$$J_\nu(z) = \sqrt{\frac{2}{\pi z}} \left\{ P_\nu(z) \cos\left[z - \left(\nu + \frac{1}{2}\right)\frac{\pi}{2}\right] - Q_\nu(z) \sin\left[z - \left(\nu + \frac{1}{2}\right)\frac{\pi}{2}\right] \right\},$$

(14.140)

valid for $-\pi < \arg z < \pi$.

4. The Neumann function is the imaginary part of $H_\nu^{(1)}(z)$ for real z, or

$$Y_\nu(z) = \sqrt{\frac{2}{\pi z}} \left\{ P_\nu(z) \sin\left[z - \left(\nu + \frac{1}{2}\right)\frac{\pi}{2}\right] + Q_\nu(z) \cos\left[z - \left(\nu + \frac{1}{2}\right)\frac{\pi}{2}\right] \right\},$$

(14.141)

also valid for $-\pi < \arg z < \pi$.

5. Finally, the modified Bessel function $I_\nu(z)$ is given by

$$I_\nu(z) = i^{-\nu} J_\nu(iz),$$

(14.142)

so

$$I_\nu(z) = \frac{e^z}{\sqrt{2\pi z}}\left[P_\nu(iz) - i Q_\nu(iz) \right],$$

(14.143)

valid for $-\pi/2 < \arg z < \pi/2$.

Properties of the Asymptotic Forms

Having derived the asymptotic forms of the various Bessel functions, it is opportune to note their essential characteristics. Remembering that in the limit of large z, P_ν approaches unity while $Q_\nu \sim 1/z$, we see that at large z, all the Bessel functions have leading terms with a $1/z^{1/2}$ dependence, multiplied by either a real or complex exponential. The modified functions K_ν and I_ν, respectively, contain decreasing and increasing exponentials, while the ordinary Bessel functions J_ν and Y_ν have leading terms with sinusoidal oscillation (damped by the $z^{-1/2}$ factor). When multiplied by a time factor $e^{\pm i\omega t}$, the Hankel functions can describe incoming and outgoing traveling waves.

Looking at the oscillatory functions J_ν, Y_ν, $H_\nu^{(i)}$ in more detail, we see that exact sinusoidal behavior is only reached in the limit of large z, as for finite z the terms involving Q_ν will to some extent alter the periodicity. The reader may wish to compare the positions of the zeros of J_n in Table 14.1 with those predicted by its leading term, namely the zeros of

$$\cos\left[z - \left(n + \frac{1}{2}\right)\frac{\pi}{2}\right].$$

We see that J_n behaves asymptotically like a phase-shifted cosine function, with the phase shift a function of n. The asymptotic form of Y_n will be that of a sine function, with (for the same n) the same phase shift. This causes the zeros of J_n and Y_n for large z to alternate, as we saw for J_0 and Y_0 in Fig. 14.8.

The asymptotic behavior of the two solutions to a problem described by ordinary or modified Bessel functions may be sufficient to eliminate immediately one of these functions as a solution for a physical problem. This observation may enable us to use the behavior at $z = \infty$ as well as that at $z = 0$ to restrict the functional forms we need to consider.

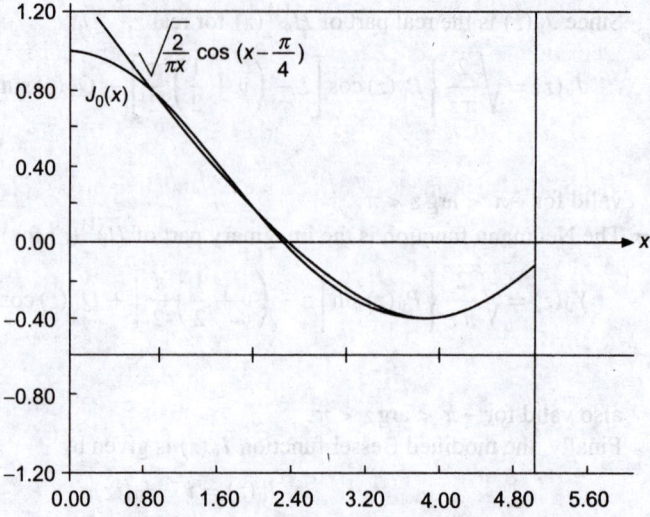

FIGURE 14.13   Asymptotic approximation of $J_0(x)$.

Finally, we note that the asymptotic series $P_\nu(z)$ and $Q_\nu(z)$, Eqs. (14.135) and (14.136), terminate for $\nu = \pm 1/2, \pm 3/2, \ldots$ and become polynomials (in negative powers of z). For these special values of ν the asymptotic approximations become exact solutions.

It is of some interest to consider the accuracy of the asymptotic forms, taking for example just the first term

$$J_n(x) \approx \sqrt{\frac{2}{\pi x}} \cos\left[x - \left(n + \frac{1}{2}\right)\left(\frac{\pi}{2}\right)\right]. \tag{14.144}$$

Clearly, the condition for Eq. (14.144) to be accurate is that the sine term of Eq. (14.140) be negligible; that is,

$$8x \gg 4n^2 - 1. \tag{14.145}$$

In Fig. 14.13 we plot $J_0(x)$ and the leading term of its asymptotic approximation. The agreement is nearly quantitative for $x > 5$. However, for n or $\nu > 1$ the asymptotic region may be far out.

Another use of the asymptotic formulas is to establish the constants in Wronskian formulas, where we know the Wronskian of any two Bessel functions of argument x has a $1/x$ functional dependence but with a premultiplying constant that depends on the Bessel functions involved.

Example 14.6.1   CYLINDRICAL TRAVELING WAVES

As an illustration of a problem in which we have chosen a specific Bessel function because of its asymptotic properties, consider a two-dimensional (2-D) wave problem similar to the vibrating circular membrane of Exercise 14.1.24. Now imagine that the waves are generated at $r = 0$ and move outward to infinity. We replace our standing waves by traveling ones. The differential equation remains the same, but the boundary conditions change. We now demand that for large r the wave behave like

$$U \sim e^{i(kr-\omega t)}, \tag{14.146}$$

to describe an outgoing wave with wavelength $2\pi/k$. We assume, for simplicity, that there is no azimuthal dependence, so we have circular symmetry, implying $m = 0$. The Bessel function of order zero with this asymptotic dependence is $H_0^{(1)}(kr)$, as can be seen from Eq. (14.138). This boundary condition at infinity then determines our wave solution as

$$U(r, t) = H_0^{(1)}(kr)e^{-i\omega t}. \tag{14.147}$$

This solution diverges as $r \to 0$, which is the behavior to be expected with a source at the origin. ∎

Exercises

14.6.1 Determine the asymptotic dependence of the modified Bessel functions $I_\nu(x)$, given

$$I_\nu(x) = \frac{1}{2\pi i} \int_C e^{(x/2)(t+1/t)} \frac{dt}{t^{\nu+1}}.$$

The contour starts and ends at $t = -\infty$, encircling the origin in a positive sense. There are two saddle points. Only the one at $z = +1$ contributes significantly to the asymptotic form.

14.6.2 Determine the asymptotic dependence of the modified Bessel function of the second kind, $K_\nu(x)$, by using

$$K_\nu(x) = \frac{1}{2} \int_0^\infty e^{(-x/2)(s+1/s)} \frac{ds}{s^{1-\nu}}.$$

14.6.3 Verify that the integral representations

$$I_n(z) = \frac{1}{\pi} \int_0^\pi e^{z \cos t} \cos(nt) dt,$$

$$K_\nu(z) = \int_0^\infty e^{-z \cosh t} \cosh(\nu t) dt, \quad \Re e(z) > 0,$$

satisfy the modified Bessel equation by direct substitution into that equation. How can you check the normalization?

14.6.4 (a) Show that when K_ν is defined by Eq. (14.128),

$$\frac{dK_0(z)}{dz} = -K_1(z).$$

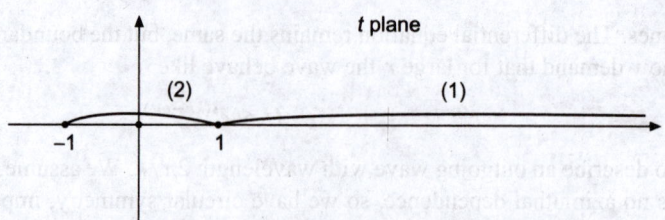

FIGURE 14.14   Modified Bessel function contours.

(b) Show that the indefinite integral of $-K_1(x)$ as defined by Eq. (14.128) has in the limit of small z the value $-\ln z + C$, and therefore, by comparison with Eq. (14.110), that K_0 as defined by Eq. (14.128) has the correct normalization.

14.6.5   Verify that Eq. (14.132) can be rearranged to the form given as Eq. (14.133).

14.6.6   (a) Show that

$$y(z) = z^\nu \int e^{-zt}(t^2 - 1)^{\nu-1/2}dt$$

satisfies the modified Bessel equation, provided the contour is chosen so that

$$e^{-zt}(t^2 - 1)^{\nu+1/2}$$

has the same value at the initial and final points of the contour.

(b) Verify that the contours shown in Fig. 14.14 are suitable for this problem.

14.6.7   Use the asymptotic expansions to verify the following Wronskian formulas:

(a) $J_\nu(x)J_{-\nu-1}(x) + J_{-\nu}(x)J_{\nu+1}(x) = -2\sin\nu\pi/\pi x$,

(b) $J_\nu(x)N_{\nu+1}(x) - J_{\nu+1}(x)N_\nu(x) = -2/\pi x$,

(c) $J_\nu(x)H_{\nu-1}^{(2)}(x) - J_{\nu-1}(x)H_\nu^{(2)}(x) = 2/i\pi x$,

(d) $I_\nu(x)K_\nu'(x) - I_\nu'(x)K_\nu(x) = -1/x$,

(e) $I_\nu(x)K_{\nu+1}(x) + I_{\nu+1}(x)K_\nu(x) = 1/x$.

14.6.8   Verify that the Green's function for the 2-D Helmholtz equation (operator $\nabla^2 + k^2$) with outgoing-wave boundary conditions is

$$G(\boldsymbol{\rho}_1, \boldsymbol{\rho}_2) = -\frac{i}{4}H_0^{(1)}(k|\boldsymbol{\rho}_1 - \boldsymbol{\rho}_2|).$$

Hint. $H_0^{(1)}(k\rho)$ is known to be an outgoing-wave solution to the homogeneous Helmholtz equation.

14.6.9   From the asymptotic form of $K_\nu(z)$, Eq. (14.134), derive the asymptotic form of $H_\nu^{(1)}(z)$, Eq. (14.138). Note particularly the phase, $(\nu + \frac{1}{2})\pi/2$.

14.6.10   Apply Stokes' method for obtaining an asymptotic expansion for the Hankel function $H_\nu^{(1)}$ as follows:

(a) Replace the Bessel function in Bessel's equation by $x^{-1/2}y(x)$ and show that $y(x)$ satisfies

$$y''(x) + \left(1 - \frac{\nu^2 - \frac{1}{4}}{x^2}\right)y(x) = 0.$$

(b) Develop a power-series solution with negative powers of x starting with the assumed form

$$y(x) = e^{ix}\sum_{n=0}^{\infty}a_n x^{-n}.$$

Obtain the recurrence relation giving a_{n+1} in terms of a_n. Check your result against the asymptotic series, Eq. (14.138).

(c) From Eq. (14.125), determine the initial coefficient, a_0.

14.6.11 Using the method of steepest descents, evaluate the second Hankel function given by

$$H_\nu^{(2)}(t) = \frac{1}{\pi i}\int_{C_2} e^{(t/2)(z-1/z)}\frac{dz}{z^{\nu+1}},$$

with contour C_2 as shown in Fig. 14.10.

$$ANS. \quad H_\nu^{(2)}(t) \approx \sqrt{\frac{2}{\pi t}}e^{-i(t-\pi/4-\nu\pi/2)}.$$

14.6.12 (a) In applying the method of steepest descents to the Hankel function $H_\nu^{(1)}(t)$, show that $w(z, t)$, which appears in Eq. (14.121), satisfies

$$\Re e[w(z, t)] < \Re e[w(z_0, t)] = 0$$

for z on the contour C_1 (Fig. 14.10) but away from the point $z = z_0 = i$.

(b) For general values of $z = re^{i\theta}$, show that

$$\Re e[w(z, t)] > 0 \quad \text{for} \quad 0 < r < 1, \quad \begin{cases} \dfrac{\pi}{2} < \theta \le \pi \\ -\pi \le \theta < \dfrac{\pi}{2} \end{cases}$$

and

$$\Re e[w(z, t)] < 0 \quad \text{for} \quad r > 1, \quad -\frac{\pi}{2} < \theta < \frac{\pi}{2}.$$

Your demonstration verifies that the distribution of the sign of w is as shown schematically in Fig. 14.15.

(c) Explain why the contour C_1 (Fig. 14.10) cannot be deformed to go through both saddle points, and why it may not go through the saddle point at $-i$ if it is to end at $z = -\infty$ with argument $+\pi$.

14.6.13 Calculate the first 15 partial sums of $P_0(x)$ and $Q_0(x)$, Eqs. (14.135) and (14.136). Let x vary from 4 to 10 in unit steps. Determine the number of terms to be retained for maximum accuracy and the accuracy achieved as a function of x. Specifically, how small may x be without raising the error above 3×10^{-6}?

$$ANS. \quad x_{min} = 6.$$

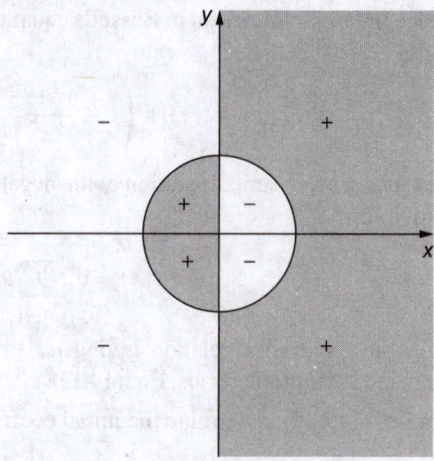

FIGURE 14.15   Sign of $w(z, t)$, occurring in Eq. (14.121), for integral representation of Hankel functions.

14.7   SPHERICAL BESSEL FUNCTIONS

In Section 9.4 we discussed the separation of the Helmholtz equation in spherical coordinates. We showed there that in the oft-occurring case that the boundary conditions of the problem have spherical symmetry, the radial equation has the form given in Eq. (9.80), namely,

$$r^2 \frac{d^2 R}{dr^2} + 2r \frac{dR}{dr} + \left[k^2 r^2 - l(l+1) \right] R = 0. \tag{14.148}$$

We remind the reader that the parameter k is that from the original Helmholtz equation, while $l(l+1)$ is the separation constant associated with solutions of the angular equations identified by the index l (which is required by the boundary conditions to be an integer).

In Section 9.4 we went on to discuss the fact that the substitution

$$R(kr) = \frac{Z(kr)}{(kr)^{1/2}} \tag{14.149}$$

permits us to rewrite Eq. (14.148) as

$$r^2 \frac{d^2 Z}{dr^2} + r \frac{dZ}{dr} + \left[k^2 r^2 - \left(l + \frac{1}{2} \right)^2 \right] Z = 0, \tag{14.150}$$

which we identified in Eq. (9.84) as Bessel's equation of order $l + \frac{1}{2}$.

We can now identify the general solution $Z(kr)$ as a linear combination of $J_{l+1/2}(kr)$ and $Y_{l+1/2}(kr)$, which in turn means that we can write $R(kr)$ in terms of these Bessel functions of half-integral order, illustrated (for $J_{l+1/2}$) by

$$R(kr) = \frac{C}{\sqrt{kr}} J_{l+1/2}(kr).$$

Since the $R(kr)$ describe radial functions in spherical coordinates, they are termed **spherical Bessel functions**. Note also that since Eq. (14.148) is homogeneous, we are free to define our spherical Bessel functions at any scale; the scale ordinarily used is that introduced in the next subsection.

Definitions

We define our spherical Bessel functions by the following equations. It is not ordinarily useful to introduce spherical Bessel functions with indices that are not integers, so we assume the index n to be integral (but not necessarily nonnegative).

$$j_n(x) = \sqrt{\frac{\pi}{2x}} \, J_{n+1/2}(x),$$

$$y_n(x) = \sqrt{\frac{\pi}{2x}} \, Y_{n+1/2}(x),$$

$$h_n^{(1)}(x) = \sqrt{\frac{\pi}{2x}} \, H_{n+1/2}^{(1)}(x) = j_n(x) + i y_n(x),$$

$$h_n^{(2)}(x) = \sqrt{\frac{\pi}{2x}} \, H_{n+1/2}^{(2)}(x) = j_n(x) - i y_n(x).$$

(14.151)

Referring to the definition of $Y_{n+1/2}$, we see that

$$Y_{n+1/2}(x) = \frac{\cos(n + \frac{1}{2})\pi \, J_{n+1/2}(x) - J_{-n-1/2}(x)}{\sin(n + \frac{1}{2})\pi} = (-1)^{n+1} J_{-n-\frac{1}{2}}(x),$$

which means that

$$y_n(x) = (-1)^{n+1} j_{-n-1}(x).$$

(14.152)

These spherical Bessel functions (Figs. 14.16 and 14.17) can be expressed in series form. Using Eq. (14.6), we have initially

$$j_n(x) = \sqrt{\frac{\pi}{2x}} \sum_{s=0}^{\infty} \frac{(-1)^s}{s! \Gamma(s + n + \frac{3}{2})} \left(\frac{x}{2}\right)^{2s+n+1/2}.$$

(14.153)

Writing

$$\Gamma(s + n + \tfrac{3}{2}) = \Gamma(n + \tfrac{3}{2})(n + \tfrac{3}{2})_s,$$

(14.154)

where $(..)_s$ is a Pochhammer symbol, defined in Eq. (1.72), we can bring Eq. (14.153) to the form

$$j_n(x) = \sqrt{\frac{\pi}{2x}} \left(\frac{x}{2}\right)^{n+1/2} \frac{1}{\Gamma(n + \frac{3}{2})} \sum_{s=0}^{\infty} \frac{(-1)^s}{s!(n + \frac{3}{2})_s} \left(\frac{x}{2}\right)^{2s}$$

$$= \frac{x^n}{(2n+1)!!} \sum_{s=0}^{\infty} \frac{(-1)^s}{s!(n + \frac{3}{2})_s} \left(\frac{x}{2}\right)^{2s}.$$

(14.155)

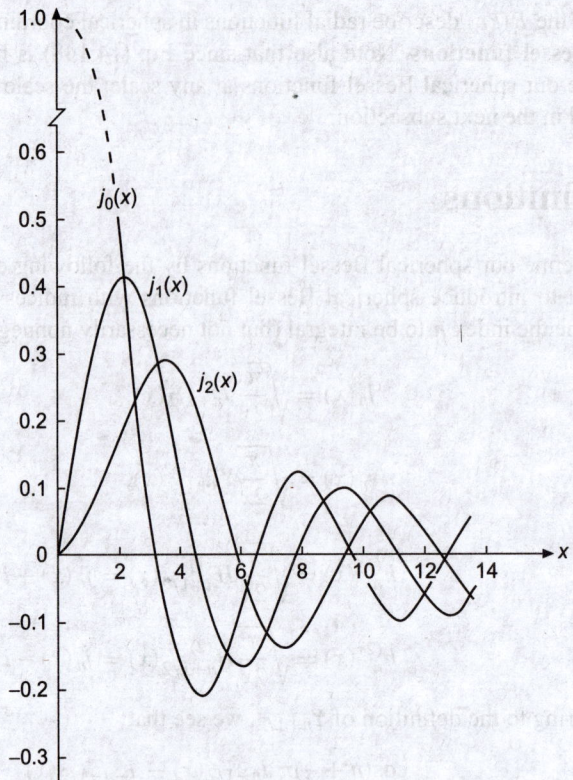

FIGURE 14.16   Spherical Bessel functions.

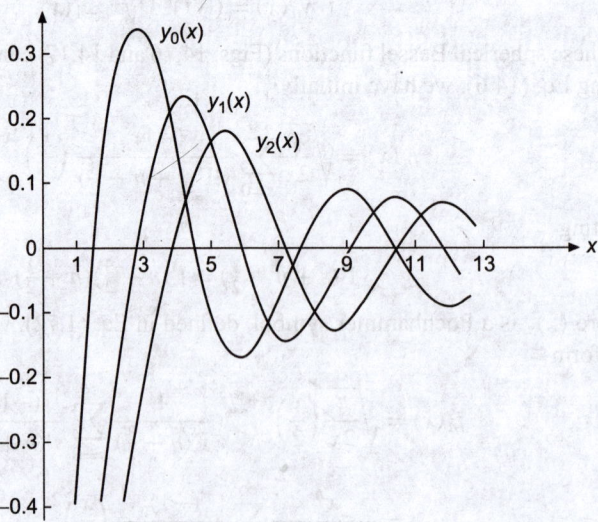

FIGURE 14.17   Spherical Neumann functions.

We reached the last line of Eq. (14.155) by writing $\Gamma(n + \frac{3}{2})$ using the double factorial notation (compare with Exercise 13.1.14).

If we now develop a series expansion for $y_n(x)$ by the same method that was used for $j_n(x)$, but starting from Eq. (14.152), we get

$$y_n(x) = -\frac{(2n-1)!!}{x^{n+1}} \sum_{s=0}^{\infty} \frac{(-1)^s}{s!(\frac{1}{2}-n)_s} \left(\frac{x}{2}\right)^{2s}. \tag{14.156}$$

The spherical Bessel functions are oscillatory, as can be seen from the graphs in Figs. 14.16 and 14.17. Note that $j_n(x)$ are regular at $x = 0$, with limiting behavior there proportional to x^n. The y_n are all irregular at $x = 0$, approaching that point as x^{-n-1}.

The infinite series in Eqs. (14.155) and (14.156) can be evaluated in closed form (but with increasing difficulty as n increases). For the special case $n = 0$, we can substitute into Eq. (14.155) $s! = 2^{-s}(2s)!!$ and $(3/2)_s = 2^{-s}(2s+1)!!$, reaching

$$j_0(x) = \sum_{s=0}^{\infty} \frac{(-1)^s 2^{2s}}{(2s)!!(2s+1)!!} \left(\frac{x}{2}\right)^{2s} = \sum_{s=0}^{\infty} \frac{(-1)^s}{(2s+1)!} x^{2s}$$

$$= \frac{\sin x}{x}. \tag{14.157}$$

A similar treatment of the expansion for y_0 yields

$$y_0(x) = -\frac{\cos x}{x}. \tag{14.158}$$

From the definition of the spherical Hankel functions, Eq. (14.151), we also have

$$h_0^{(1)}(x) = \frac{1}{x}(\sin x - i\cos x) = -\frac{i}{x} e^{ix}, \tag{14.159}$$

$$h_0^{(2)}(x) = \frac{1}{x}(\sin x + i\cos x) = \frac{i}{x} e^{-ix}. \tag{14.160}$$

Since we anticipate the availability of recurrence formulas for the spherical Bessel functions, and since y_0 is just $-j_{-1}$, we expect all the j_n and y_n to be linear combinations of sines and cosines. In fact, the recurrence formulas are good ways of getting these functions for small n. However, we identify here an alternate approach, which depends on the fact, noted in Section 14.6, that the asymptotic expansion for the Hankel functions actually terminates when the order is a half-integer, thereby yielding exact, closed expressions. We start from

$$h_n^{(1)}(x) = \sqrt{\frac{\pi}{2x}} H_{n+1/2}^{(1)}(x)$$

$$= (-i)^{n+1} \frac{e^{ix}}{x} \left[P_{n+1/2}(x) + i Q_{n+1/2}(x) \right], \tag{14.161}$$

where P_ν and Q_ν are given by Eqs. (14.135) and (14.136). Now, $P_{n+1/2}$ and $Q_{n+1/2}$ are **polynomials**, and we can bring Eq. (14.161) to the form

$$h_n^{(1)}(x) = (-i)^{n+1} \frac{e^{ix}}{x} \sum_{s=0}^{n} \frac{i^s}{s!(8x)^s} \frac{(2n+2s)!!}{(2n-2s)!!}$$

$$= (-i)^{n+1} \frac{e^{ix}}{x} \sum_{s=0}^{n} \frac{i^s}{s!(2x)^s} \frac{(n+s)!}{(n-s)!}. \tag{14.162}$$

For real x, $j_n(x)$ is the real part of this, $y_n(x)$ the imaginary part, and $h_n^{(2)}(x)$ the complex conjugate. Specifically,

$$h_1^{(1)}(x) = e^{ix}\left(-\frac{1}{x} - \frac{i}{x^2}\right), \tag{14.163}$$

$$h_2^{(1)}(x) = e^{ix}\left(\frac{i}{x} - \frac{3}{x^2} - \frac{3i}{x^3}\right), \tag{14.164}$$

$$j_1(x) = \frac{\sin x}{x^2} - \frac{\cos x}{x}, \tag{14.165}$$

$$j_2(x) = \left(\frac{3}{x^3} - \frac{1}{x}\right)\sin x - \frac{3}{x^2}\cos x, \tag{14.166}$$

$$y_1(x) = -\frac{\cos x}{x^2} - \frac{\sin x}{x}, \tag{14.167}$$

$$y_2(x) = -\left(\frac{3}{x^3} - \frac{1}{x}\right)\cos x - \frac{3}{x^2}\sin x. \tag{14.168}$$

Recurrence Relations

The recurrence relations to which we now turn provide a convenient way of developing the higher-order spherical Bessel functions. These recurrence relations may be derived from the power-series expansions, but it is easier to substitute into the known recurrence relations, Eqs. (14.8) and (14.9). This gives

$$f_{n-1}(x) + f_{n+1}(x) = \frac{2n+1}{x} f_n(x), \tag{14.169}$$

$$nf_{n-1}(x) - (n+1)f_{n+1}(x) = (2n+1)f_n'(x). \tag{14.170}$$

Rearranging these relations, or substituting into Eqs. (14.10) and (14.11), we obtain

$$\frac{d}{dx}[x^{n+1} f_n(x)] = x^{n+1} f_{n-1}(x), \tag{14.171}$$

$$\frac{d}{dx}[x^{-n} f_n(x)] = -x^{-n} f_{n+1}(x). \tag{14.172}$$

In these equations f_n may represent j_n, y_n, $h_n^{(1)}$, or $h_n^{(2)}$.

By mathematical induction (Section 1.4) we may establish the **Rayleigh formulas**:

$$j_n(x) = (-1)^n x^n \left(\frac{1}{x}\frac{d}{dx}\right)^n \left(\frac{\sin x}{x}\right), \tag{14.173}$$

$$y_n(x) = -(-1)^n x^n \left(\frac{1}{x}\frac{d}{dx}\right)^n \left(\frac{\cos x}{x}\right), \tag{14.174}$$

$$h_n^{(1)}(x) = -i(-1)^n x^n \left(\frac{1}{x}\frac{d}{dx}\right)^n \left(\frac{e^{ix}}{x}\right), \tag{14.175}$$

$$h_n^{(2)}(x) = i(-1)^n x^n \left(\frac{1}{x}\frac{d}{dx}\right)^n \left(\frac{e^{-ix}}{x}\right). \tag{14.176}$$

Limiting Values

For $x \ll 1$,[9] Eqs. (14.155) and (14.156) yield

$$j_n(x) \approx \frac{x^n}{(2n+1)!!}, \tag{14.177}$$

$$y_n(x) \approx -\frac{(2n-1)!!}{x^{n+1}}. \tag{14.178}$$

The limiting values of the spherical Hankel functions for small x go as $\pm i y_n(x)$.

The asymptotic values of j_n, y_n, $h_n^{(1)}$, and $h_n^{(2)}$ may be obtained from the asymptotic forms of the corresponding Bessel functions, as given in Section 14.6. We find

$$j_n(x) \sim \frac{1}{x} \sin\left(x - \frac{n\pi}{2}\right), \tag{14.179}$$

$$y_n(x) \sim -\frac{1}{x} \cos\left(x - \frac{n\pi}{2}\right), \tag{14.180}$$

$$h_n^{(1)}(x) \sim (-i)^{n+1}\frac{e^{ix}}{x} = -i\frac{e^{i(x-n\pi/2)}}{x}, \tag{14.181}$$

$$h_n^{(2)}(x) \sim i^{n+1}\frac{e^{-ix}}{x} = i\frac{e^{-i(x-n\pi/2)}}{x}. \tag{14.182}$$

The condition for these spherical Bessel forms is that $x \gg n(n+1)/2$. From these asymptotic values we see that $j_n(x)$ and $y_n(x)$ are appropriate for a description of **standing spherical waves**; $h_n^{(1)}(x)$ and $h_n^{(2)}(x)$ correspond to **traveling spherical waves**. If the time dependence for the traveling waves is taken to be $e^{-i\omega t}$, then $h_n^{(1)}(x)$ yields an outgoing traveling spherical wave, and $h_n^{(2)}(x)$ an incoming wave. Radiation theory in electromagnetism and scattering theory in quantum mechanics provide many applications.

---

[9]The condition that the second term in the series be negligible compared to the first is actually $x \ll 2[(2n+2)(2n+3)/(n+1)]^{1/2}$ for $j_n(x)$.

Orthogonality and Zeros

We may take the orthogonality integral for the ordinary Bessel functions, Eqs. (11.49) and (11.50),

$$\int_0^a J_\nu\left(\alpha_{\nu p}\frac{\rho}{a}\right) J_\nu\left(\alpha_{\nu q}\frac{\rho}{a}\right) \rho\, d\rho = \frac{a^2}{2}\left[J_{\nu+1}(\alpha_{\nu p})\right]^2 \delta_{pq},$$

and rewrite it in terms of j_n to obtain

$$\int_0^a j_n\left(\alpha_{np}\frac{r}{a}\right) j_n\left(\alpha_{nq}\frac{r}{a}\right) r^2\, dr = \frac{a^3}{2}\left[j_{n+1}(\alpha_{np})\right]^2 \delta_{pq}. \tag{14.183}$$

Here α_{np} is the p-th positive zero of j_n.

Note that in contrast to the formula for the orthogonality of the J_ν, Eq. (14.183) has the weight factor r^2, not r. This of course comes from the factors $x^{-1/2}$ in the definition of $j_n(x)$, but also has the effect that if the integration is construed as being over a **spherical volume** rather than a linear interval, it is the factor corresponding to uniform weight of all volume elements. (Remember that the weight ρ for the J_ν integral produces uniform weight if we construe the integration in that case as over the area within a circle.)

As for the ordinary Bessel functions, the functions that are orthogonal on $(0, a)$ all satisfy a Dirichlet boundary condition, with zeros at $r = a$. We therefore find it useful to know the values of the zeros of the j_n. The first few zeros for small n, and also the locations of the zeros of j_n', are listed in Table 14.2.

The following example illustrates a problem in which the zeros of the j_n play an essential role.

Table 14.2   Zeros of the Spherical Bessel Functions and Their First Derivatives

Number of zero	$j_0(x)$	$j_1(x)$	$j_2(x)$	$j_3(x)$	$j_4(x)$	$j_5(x)$
1	3.1416	4.4934	5.7635	6.9879	8.1826	9.3558
2	6.2832	7.7253	9.0950	10.4171	11.7049	12.9665
3	9.4248	10.9041	12.3229	13.6980	15.0397	16.3547
4	12.5664	14.0662	15.5146	16.9236	18.3013	19.6532
5	15.7080	17.2208	18.6890	20.1218	21.5254	22.9046
	$j_0'(x)$	$j_1'(x)$	$j_2'(x)$	$j_3'(x)$	$j_4'(x)$	$j_5'(x)$
1	4.4934	2.0816	3.3421	4.5141	5.6467	6.7565
2	7.7253	5.9404	7.2899	8.5838	9.8404	11.0702
3	10.9041	9.2058	10.6139	11.9727	13.2956	14.5906
4	14.0662	12.4044	13.8461	15.2445	16.6093	17.9472
5	17.2208	15.5792	17.0429	18.4681	19.8624	21.2311

Example 14.7.1   PARTICLE IN A SPHERE

An illustration of the use of the spherical Bessel functions is provided by the problem of a quantum mechanical particle of mass m in a sphere of radius a. Quantum theory requires that the wave function ψ, describing our particle, satisfy the Schrödinger equation

$$-\frac{\hbar^2}{2m}\nabla^2\psi = E\psi, \tag{14.184}$$

subject to the conditions that (1) $\psi(r)$ is finite for all $0 \leq r \leq a$, and (2) $\psi(a) = 0$. This corresponds to a square-well potential $V = 0$ for $r \leq a$, $V = \infty$ for $r > a$. Here $\hbar$ is Planck's constant divided by 2π. Equation (14.184) with its boundary conditions is an eigenvalue equation; its eigenvalues E are the possible values of the particle's energy.

Let us determine the **minimum** value of the energy for which our wave equation has an acceptable solution. Equation (14.184) is Helmholtz's equation, which after separation of variables leads to the radial equation previously presented as Eq. (14.148):

$$\frac{d^2R}{dr^2} + \frac{2}{r}\frac{dR}{dr} + \left[k^2 - \frac{l(l+1)}{r^2}\right]R = 0, \tag{14.185}$$

with

$$k^2 = 2mE/\hbar^2 \tag{14.186}$$

and l (determined from the angular equation) a nonnegative integer. Comparing with Eq. (14.150) and the definitions of the spherical Bessel functions, Eq. (14.151), we see that the general solution to Eq. (14.185) is

$$R = Aj_l(kr) + By_l(kr). \tag{14.187}$$

To satisfy the boundary conditions of the present problem, we must reject the solution y_l because it is singular at $r = 0$, and we must choose k such that $j_l(ka) = 0$. This boundary condition at $r = a$ can be satisfied if

$$k \equiv k_{li} = \frac{\alpha_{li}}{a}, \tag{14.188}$$

where α_{li} is the ith positive zero of j_l. From Eq. (14.186) we see that the smallest E will correspond to the smallest acceptable k, which in turn corresponds to the smallest α_{li}. Thus, scanning Table 14.2, we identify the smallest α_{li} as the first zero of j_0, a result which we would expect after we have learned that the value $l = 0$ is associated with an angular function with no kinetic energy.

We conclude this example by solving Eq. (14.186) for E with k assigned the value $\alpha_{01}/a = \pi/a$[10]:

$$E_{\min} = \frac{\pi^2\hbar^2}{2ma^2} = \frac{h^2}{8ma^2}. \tag{14.189}$$

---

[10]Most of the entries in Table 14.2 are only accessible numerically, but the zeros of j_0 are readily identified due to their simple form, $\alpha_{0m} = m\pi$.

This example illustrates several features common to bound-state problems in quantum mechanics. First, we see that for any finite sphere the particle will have a positive minimum or zero-point energy. Second, we note that the particle cannot have a continuous range of energy values; the energy is restricted to discrete values corresponding to the eigenvalues of the Schrödinger equation. Third, the possible energies in this spherically symmetric problem depend on l; as is evident from the table of zeros of j_l, the minimum energy for a given l increases with l. Finally, note that the orthogonality of the j_l under the conditions of this problem shows us that the eigenfunctions corresponding to the same l but different i are orthogonal (with the weight factor corresponding to spherical polar coordinates). ∎

We close this subsection with the observation that, in addition to orthogonality with respect to the scaling (to bring zeros to a specified r value), the spherical Bessel functions also possess orthogonality with respect to the indices:

$$\int_{-\infty}^{\infty} j_m(x) j_n(x)\, dx = 0, \quad m \neq n,\; m,\, n \geq 0. \tag{14.190}$$

The proof is left as Exercise 14.7.12. If $m = n$ (compare Exercise 14.7.13), we have

$$\int_{-\infty}^{\infty} [j_n(x)]^2\, dx = \frac{\pi}{2n+1}. \tag{14.191}$$

The spherical Bessel functions will enter again in connection with spherical waves, but further consideration is postponed until the corresponding angular functions, the Legendre functions, have been more thoroughly discussed.

Modifed Spherical Bessel Functions

Problems involving the radial equation

$$r^2 \frac{d^2 R}{dr^2} + 2r \frac{dR}{dr} - \left[k^2 r^2 + l(l+1) \right] R = 0, \tag{14.192}$$

which differs from Eq. (14.148) only in the sign of k^2, also arise frequently in physics. The solutions to this equation are spherical Bessel functions with imaginary arguments, leading us to define **modified spherical Bessel functions** (Fig. 14.18) as follows:

$$i_n(x) = \sqrt{\frac{\pi}{2x}} I_{n+1/2}(x), \tag{14.193}$$

$$k_n(x) = \sqrt{\frac{2}{\pi x}} K_{n+1/2}(x). \tag{14.194}$$

Note that the scale factor in the definition of k_n differs from that of the other spherical Bessel functions.

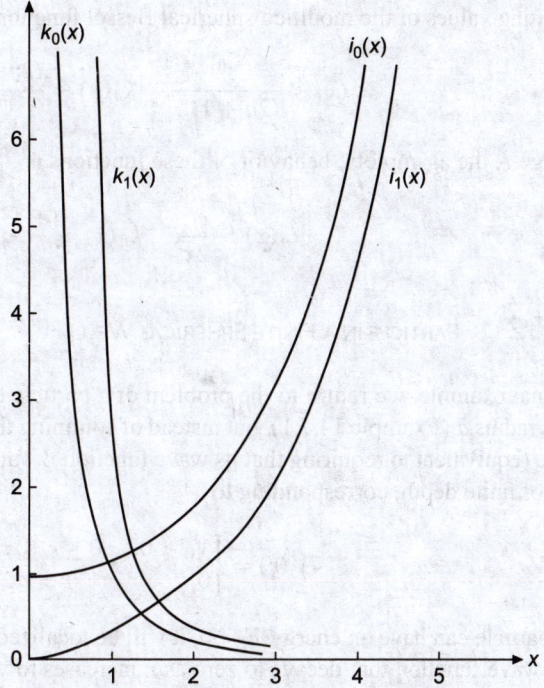

FIGURE 14.18   Modified spherical Bessel functions.

With the above definitions, these functions have the following recurrence relations:

$$i_{n-1}(x) - i_{n+1}(x) = \frac{2n+1}{x} i_n(x),$$

$$n i_{n-1}(x) + (n+1) i_{n+1}(x) = (2n+1) i_n'(x),$$

$$k_{n-1}(x) - k_{n+1}(x) = -\frac{2n+1}{x} k_n(x),$$ (14.195)

$$n k_{n-1}(x) + (n+1) k_{n+1}(x) = -(2n+1) k_n'(x).$$

The first few of these functions are

$$i_0(x) = \frac{\sinh x}{x}, \qquad\qquad k_0(x) = \frac{e^{-x}}{x},$$

$$i_1(x) = \frac{\cosh x}{x} - \frac{\sinh x}{x^2}, \qquad k_1(x) = e^{-x}\left(\frac{1}{x} + \frac{1}{x^2}\right),$$ (14.196)

$$i_2(x) = \sinh x\left(\frac{1}{x} + \frac{3}{x^3}\right) - \frac{3\cosh x}{x^2}, \quad k_2(x) = e^{-x}\left(\frac{1}{x} + \frac{3}{x^2} + \frac{3}{x^3}\right).$$

Limiting values of the modified spherical Bessel functions are, for small x,

$$i_n(x) \approx \frac{x^n}{(2n+1)!!}, \quad k_n(x) \approx \frac{(2n-1)!!}{x^{n+1}}. \qquad (14.197)$$

For large z, the asymptotic behavior of these functions is

$$i_n(x) \sim \frac{e^x}{2x}, \quad k_n(x) \sim \frac{e^{-x}}{x}. \qquad (14.198)$$

Example 14.7.2   PARTICLE IN A FINITE SPHERICAL WELL

As a final example, we return to the problem of a particle trapped in a spherical potential well of radius a (Example 14.7.1), but instead of confining the particle by a wall at potential $V = \infty$ (equivalent to requiring that its wave function ψ vanish at $r = a$), we now consider a well of finite depth, corresponding to

$$V(r) = \begin{cases} V_0 < 0, & 0 \le r \le a, \\ 0, & r > a. \end{cases}$$

If the particle can have an energy $E < 0$, it will be localized in and near the potential well, with a wave function that decays to zero as r increases to values greater than a. A simple case of this problem was one of our examples of an eigenvalue problem (Example 8.3.3), but in that case we did not proceed with enough generality to identify its solutions as Bessel functions.

This problem is governed by the Schrödinger equation, which now has the form

$$-\frac{\hbar^2}{2m} \nabla^2 \psi + V(r)\psi = E\psi.$$

This is an eigenvalue equation, to be solved for ψ and E over the full three-dimensional space, subject to the condition that ψ be continuous and differentiable for all r, and that it be normalizable (thus approaching zero asymptotically at large r). Here m is the mass of the particle and $\hbar$ is Planck's constant divided by 2π.

While this problem is more difficult than that of Example 14.7.1, it becomes manageable if we realize that it is equivalent to two separate problems for the respective regions $0 \le r \le a$ and $r > a$, within each of which the potential has a constant value, but constrained to (1) have the same eigenvalue E, and (2) connect smoothly (so the r derivative will exist) at $r = a$.

When our Schrödinger equation is processed by the method of separation of variables, we obtain as its radial component

$$\frac{d^2 R}{dr^2} + \frac{2}{r}\frac{dR}{dr} + \left(\frac{2m}{\hbar^2}\left[E - V(r) \right] - \frac{l(l+1)}{r^2} \right) R = 0,$$

which is either the spherical Bessel equation, Eq. (14.150), or the modified spherical Bessel equation, Eq. (14.192), depending on the sign of $E - V(r)$. We see that if $V_0 < E < 0$, then for $r \leq a$ we will have $E - V(r) > 0$, yielding a Bessel ODE with an acceptable solution involving j_l, while for $r > a$ we have $E - V(r) < 0$, leading to a modified Bessel ODE for which we can choose the k_l solution to obtain the necessary asymptotic behavior.

Summarizing the above, we have, for the two regions:

$$R_{\text{in}}(r) = A j_l(kr), \quad k^2 = \frac{2m}{\hbar^2}(E - V_0) \quad r \leq a,$$

$$R_{\text{out}}(r) = B k_l(k'r), \quad k'^2 = -\frac{2m}{\hbar^2} E \qquad r > a.$$

Smooth connection at $r = a$ then corresponds to the equations

$$R_{\text{in}}(a) = R_{\text{out}}(a) \quad \longrightarrow \quad A j_l(ka) = B k_l(k'r), \tag{14.199}$$

$$\left.\frac{dR_{\text{in}}}{dr}\right|_{r=a} = \left.\frac{dR_{\text{out}}}{dr}\right|_{r=a} \quad \longrightarrow \quad k A j_l'(ka) = k' B k_l'(k'a). \tag{14.200}$$

For $l = 0$ this problem reduces to that considered in Example 8.3.3, where we indicate a numerical procedure of solving it, but we are now in a position to obtain solutions for all l. . $\blacksquare$

Exercises

14.7.1   Show how one can obtain Eq. (14.162) starting from Eq. (14.161).

14.7.2   Show that if

$$y_n(x) = \sqrt{\frac{\pi}{2x}} Y_{n+1/2}(x),$$

it automatically equals

$$(-1)^{n+1} \sqrt{\frac{\pi}{2x}} J_{-n-1/2}(x).$$

14.7.3   Derive the trigonometric-polynomial forms of $j_n(z)$ and $y_n(z)$[11]:

$$j_n(z) = \frac{1}{z} \sin\left(z - \frac{n\pi}{2}\right) \sum_{s=0}^{[n/2]} \frac{(-1)^s (n + 2s)!}{(2s)!(2z)^{2s}(n - 2s)!}$$

$$+ \frac{1}{z} \cos\left(z - \frac{n\pi}{2}\right) \sum_{s=0}^{[(n-1)/2]} \frac{(-1)^s (n + 2s + 1)!}{(2s + 1)!(2z)^{2s}(n - 2s - 1)!},$$

---

[11] The upper summation limit $[n/2]$ means the largest **integer** that does not exceed $n/2$.

$$y_n(z) = \frac{(-1)^{n+1}}{z} \cos\left(z + \frac{n\pi}{2}\right) \sum_{s=0}^{[n/2]} \frac{(-1)^s (n+2s)!}{(2s)!(2z)^{2s}(n-2s)!}$$

$$+ \frac{(-1)^{n+1}}{z} \sin\left(z + \frac{n\pi}{2}\right) \sum_{s=0}^{[(n-1)/2]} \frac{(-1)^s (n+2s+1)!}{(2s+1)!(2z)^{2s+1}(n-2s-1)!} \, .$$

14.7.4   Use the integral representation of $J_\nu(x)$,

$$J_\nu(x) = \frac{1}{\pi^{1/2}\Gamma(\nu + \frac{1}{2})} \left(\frac{x}{2}\right)^\nu \int_{-1}^{1} e^{\pm ixp}(1 - p^2)^{\nu - 1/2} dp,$$

to show that the spherical Bessel functions $j_n(x)$ are expressible in terms of trigonometric functions; that is, for example,

$$j_0(x) = \frac{\sin x}{x}, \quad j_1(x) = \frac{\sin x}{x^2} - \frac{\cos x}{x}.$$

14.7.5   (a)   Derive the recurrence relations

$$f_{n-1}(x) + f_{n+1}(x) = \frac{2n+1}{x} f_n(x),$$

$$n f_{n-1}(x) - (n+1) f_{n+1}(x) = (2n+1) f_n'(x)$$

satisfied by the spherical Bessel functions $j_n(x)$, $y_n(x)$, $h_n^{(1)}(x)$, and $h_n^{(2)}(x)$.

   (b)   Show, from these two recurrence relations, that the spherical Bessel function $f_n(x)$ satisfies the differential equation

$$x^2 f_n''(x) + 2x f_n'(x) + \left[x^2 - n(n+1)\right] f_n(x) = 0.$$

14.7.6   Prove by mathematical induction (Section 1.4) that

$$j_n(x) = (-1)^n x^n \left(\frac{1}{x}\frac{d}{dx}\right)^n \left(\frac{\sin x}{x}\right)$$

for n, an arbitrary nonnegative integer.

14.7.7   From the discussion of orthogonality of the spherical Bessel functions, show that a Wronskian relation for $j_n(x)$ and $n_n(x)$ is

$$j_n(x) y_n'(x) - j_n'(x) y_n(x) = \frac{1}{x^2}.$$

14.7.8   Verify

$$h_n^{(1)}(x) h_n^{(2)'}(x) - h_n^{(1)'}(x) h_n^{(2)}(x) = -\frac{2i}{x^2}.$$

14.7.9   Verify Poisson's integral representation of the spherical Bessel function,

$$j_n(z) = \frac{z^n}{2^{n+1} n!} \int_0^{\pi} \cos(z\cos\theta) \sin^{2n+1}\theta \, d\theta.$$

14.7.10 A well-known integral representation for $K_\nu(x)$ has the form

$$K_\nu(x) = \frac{2^\nu \Gamma(\nu + \frac{1}{2})}{\sqrt{\pi} x^\nu} \int\limits_0^\infty \frac{\cos xt}{(t^2 + 1)^{\nu + 1/2}} dt.$$

Starting from this formula, show that

$$k_n(x) = \frac{2^{n+2}(n+1)!}{\pi x^{n+1}} \int\limits_0^\infty \frac{k^2 j_0(kx)}{(k^2 + 1)^{n+2}} dk.$$

14.7.11 Show that $\displaystyle\int\limits_0^\infty J_\mu(x) J_\nu(x) \frac{dx}{x} = \frac{2}{\pi} \frac{\sin[(\mu - \nu)\pi/2]}{\mu^2 - \nu^2}, \quad \mu + \nu > 0.$

14.7.12 Derive Eq. (14.190): $\displaystyle\int\limits_{-\infty}^\infty j_m(x) j_n(x) dx = 0, \quad \begin{cases} m \neq n, \\ m, n \geq 0. \end{cases}$

14.7.13 Derive Eq. (14.191): $\displaystyle\int\limits_{-\infty}^\infty \left[j_n(x) \right]^2 dx = \frac{\pi}{2n + 1}.$

14.7.14 The Fresnel integrals (Fig. 14.19 and Exercise 12.7.2) occurring in diffraction theory are given by

$$x(t) = \sqrt{\frac{\pi}{2}} C\left(\sqrt{\frac{\pi}{2}} t\right) = \int\limits_0^t \cos(v^2) dv,$$

$$y(t) = \sqrt{\frac{\pi}{2}} S\left(\sqrt{\frac{\pi}{2}} t\right) = \int\limits_0^t \sin(v^2) dv.$$

Show that these integrals may be expanded in series of spherical Bessel functions as follows:

$$x(s) = \frac{1}{2} \int\limits_0^s j_{-1}(u) u^{1/2} du = s^{1/2} \sum_{n=0}^\infty j_{2n}(s),$$

$$y(s) = \frac{1}{2} \int\limits_0^s j_0(u) u^{1/2} x du = s^{1/2} \sum_{n=0}^\infty j_{2n+1}(s).$$

Hint. To establish the equality of the integral and the sum, you may wish to work with their derivatives. The spherical Bessel analogs of Eqs. (14.8) and (14.12) may be helpful.

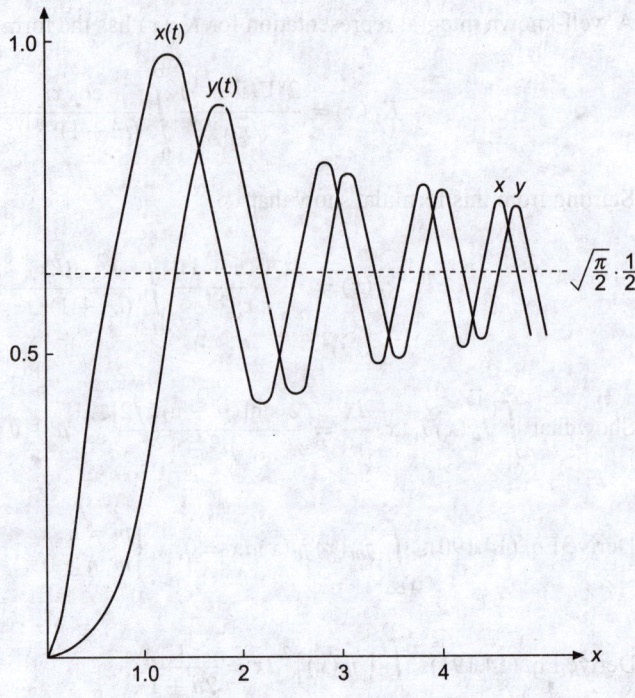

FIGURE 14.19   Fresnel integrals.

14.7.15 A hollow sphere of radius a (Helmholtz resonator) contains standing sound waves. Find the minimum frequency of oscillation in terms of the radius a and the velocity of sound v. The sound waves satisfy the wave equation

$$\nabla^2 \psi = \frac{1}{v^2} \frac{\partial^2 \psi}{\partial t^2}$$

and the boundary condition $\dfrac{\partial \psi}{\partial r} = 0, \quad r = a.$

The spatial part of this PDE is the same as the PDE discussed in Example 14.7.1, but here we have a Neumann boundary condition, in contrast to the Dirichlet boundary condition of that example.

$\qquad\qquad\qquad\qquad\qquad$ *ANS.* $\nu_{min} = 0.3313v/a, \quad \lambda_{max} = 3.018a.$

14.7.16 (a) Show that the parity of $i_n(x)$ (the behavior under $x \to -x$) is $(-1)^n$.

$\qquad$ (b) Show that $k_n(x)$ has no definite parity.

14.7.17 Show that the Wronskian of the spherical modified Bessel functions is given by

$$i_n(x)k_n'(x) - i_n'(x)k_n(x) = -\frac{1}{x^2}.$$

Additional Readings

Abramowitz, M., and I. A. Stegun, eds., *Handbook of Mathematical Functions with Formulas, Graphs, and Mathematical Tables* (AMS-55). Washington, DC: National Bureau of Standards (1972), reprinted, Dover (1974).

Jackson, J. D., *Classical Electrodynamics*, 3rd ed. New York: Wiley (1999).

Morse, P. M., and H. Feshbach, *Methods of Theoretical Physics*, 2 vols. New York: McGraw-Hill (1953). This work presents the mathematics of much of theoretical physics in detail but at a rather advanced level.

Watson, G. N., *A Treatise on the Theory of Bessel Functions*, 1st ed. Cambridge: Cambridge University Press (1922).

Watson, G. N., *A Treatise on the Theory of Bessel Functions*, 2nd ed. Cambridge: Cambridge University Press (1952). This is the definitive text on Bessel functions and their properties. Although difficult reading, it is invaluable as the ultimate reference.

Whittaker, E. T., and G. N. Watson, *A Course of Modern Analysis*, 4th ed. Cambridge: Cambridge University Press (1962), paperback.

CHAPTER 15

LEGENDRE FUNCTIONS

Legendre functions are important in physics because they arise when the Laplace or Helmholtz equations (or their generalizations) for central force problems are separated in spherical coordinates. They therefore appear in the descriptions of wave functions for atoms, in a variety of electrostatics problems, and in many other contexts. In addition, the Legendre polynomials provide a convenient set of functions that is orthogonal (with unit weight) on the interval $(-1, +1)$ that is the range of the sine and cosine functions. And from a pedagogical viewpoint, they provide a set of functions that are easy to work with and form an excellent illustration of the general properties of orthogonal polynomials. Several of these properties were discussed in a general way in Chapter 12. We collect here those results, expanding them with additional material that is of great utility and importance.

As indicated above, Legendre functions are encountered when an equation written in spherical polar coordinates (r, θ, φ), such as

$$-\nabla^2 \psi + V(r)\psi = \lambda \psi,$$

is solved by the method of separation of variables. Note that we are assuming that this equation is to be solved for a spherically symmetric region and that $V(r)$ is a function of the distance from the origin of the coordinate system (and therefore not a function of the three-component position vector $\mathbf{r}$). As in Eqs. (9.77) and (9.78), we write $\psi = R(r)\Theta(\theta)\Phi(\varphi)$ and decompose our original partial differential equation (PDE) into the three one-dimensional ordinary differential equations (ODEs):

$$\frac{d^2\Phi}{d\varphi^2} = -m^2\Phi, \tag{15.1}$$

$$\frac{1}{\sin\theta} \frac{d}{d\theta}\left(\sin\theta \frac{d\Theta}{d\theta}\right) - \frac{m^2\Theta}{\sin^2\theta} + l(l+1)\Theta = 0, \tag{15.2}$$

$$\frac{1}{r^2} \frac{d}{dr}\left(r^2 \frac{dR}{dr}\right) + \left[\lambda - V(r)\right]R - \frac{l(l+1)R}{r^2} = 0. \tag{15.3}$$

715

The quantities m^2 and $l(l+1)$ are constants that occur when the variables are separated; the ODE in φ is easy to solve and has natural boundary conditions (cf. Section 9.4), which dictate that m must be an integer and that the functions Φ can be written as $e^{\pm im\varphi}$ or as $\sin(m\varphi)$, $\cos(m\varphi)$.

The Θ equation can now be transformed by the substitution $x = \cos\theta$, cf. Eq. (9.79), reaching

$$(1-x^2)P''(x) - 2xP'(x) - \frac{m^2}{1-x^2}P(x) + l(l+1)P(x) = 0. \tag{15.4}$$

This is the **associated Legendre equation**; the special case with $m = 0$, which we will treat first, is the **Legendre** ODE.

15.1   LEGENDRE POLYNOMIALS

The Legendre equation,

$$(1-x^2)P''(x) - 2xP'(x) + \lambda P(x) = 0, \tag{15.5}$$

has regular singular points at $x = \pm 1$ and $x = \infty$ (see Table 7.1), and therefore has a series solution about $x = 0$ that has a unit radius of convergence, i.e., the series solution will (for all values of the parameter λ) converge for $|x| < 1$. In Section 8.3 we found that for most values of λ, the series solutions will diverge at $x = \pm 1$ (corresponding to $\theta = 0$ and $\theta = \pi$), making the solutions inappropriate for use in central force problems. However, if λ has the value $l(l+1)$, with l an integer, the series become truncated after x^l, leaving a polynomial of degree l.

Now that we have identified the desired solutions to the Legendre equations as polynomials of successive degrees, called **Legendre polynomials** and designated P_l, let us use the machinery of Chapter 12 to develop them from a generating-function approach. This course of action will set a scale for the P_l and provide a good starting point for deriving recurrence relations and related formulas.

We found in Example 12.1.3 that the generating function for the polynomial solutions of the Legendre ODE is given by Eq. (12.27):

$$g(x,t) = \frac{1}{\sqrt{1-2xt+t^2}} = \sum_{n=0}^{\infty} P_n(x)t^n. \tag{15.6}$$

To identify the scale that is given to P_n by Eq. (15.6), we simply set $x = 1$ in that equation, bringing its left-hand side to the form

$$g(1,t) = \frac{1}{\sqrt{1-2t+t^2}} = \frac{1}{1-t} = \sum_{n=0}^{\infty} t^n, \tag{15.7}$$

where the last step in Eq. (15.7) was to expand $1/(1-t)$ using the binomial theorem. Comparing with Eq. (15.6), we see that the scaling it predicts is $P_n(1) = 1$.

Next, consider what happens if we replace x by $-x$ and t by $-t$. The value of $g(x, t)$ in Eq. (15.6) is unaffected by this substitution, but the right-hand side takes a different form:

$$\sum_{n=0}^{\infty} P_n(x) t^n = g(x, t) = g(-x, -t) = \sum_{n=0}^{\infty} P_n(-x)(-t)^n, \tag{15.8}$$

showing that

$$P_n(-x) = (-1)^n P_n(x). \tag{15.9}$$

From this result it is obvious that $P_n(-1) = (-1)^n$, and that $P_n(x)$ will have the same parity as x^n.

Another useful special value is $P_n(0)$. Writing P_{2n} and P_{2n+1} to distinguish even and odd index values, we note first that because P_{2n+1} is odd under parity, i.e., $x \to -x$, we must have $P_{2n+1}(0) = 0$. To obtain $P_{2n}(0)$, we again resort to the binomial expansion:

$$g(0, t) = (1 + t^2)^{-1/2} = \sum_{n=0}^{\infty} \binom{-1/2}{n} t^{2n} = \sum_{n=0}^{\infty} P_{2n}(0) \, t^{2n}. \tag{15.10}$$

Then, using Eq. (1.74) to evaluate the binomial coefficient, we get

$$P_{2n}(0) = (-1)^n \frac{(2n-1)!!}{(2n)!!}. \tag{15.11}$$

It is also useful to characterize the leading terms of the Legendre polynomials. Applying the binomial theorem to the generating function,

$$(1 - 2xt + t^2)^{-1/2} = \sum_{n=0}^{\infty} \binom{-1/2}{n} (-2xt + t^2)^n, \tag{15.12}$$

from which we see that the maximum power of x that can multiply t^n will be x^n, and is obtained from the term $(-2xt)^n$ in the expansion of the final factor. Thus, the

$$\text{coefficient of } x^n \text{ in } P_n(x) \text{ is } \binom{-1/2}{n}(-2)^n = \frac{(2n-1)!!}{n!}. \tag{15.13}$$

These results are important, so we summarize:

$P_n(x)$ has sign and scaling such that $P_n(1) = 1$ and $P_n(-1) = (-1)^n$. $P_{2n}(x)$ is an even function of x; $P_{2n+1}(x)$ is odd. $P_{2n+1}(0) = 0$, and $P_{2n}(0)$ is given by Eq. (15.11). $P_n(x)$ is a polynomial of degree n in x, with the coefficient of x^n given by Eq. (15.13); $P_n(x)$ contains alternate powers of x: x^n, $x^{n-2}, \cdots, (x^0 \text{ or } x^1)$.

From the fact that P_n is of degree n with alternate powers, it is clear that $P_0(x) = $ constant and that $P_1(x) = (\text{constant}) x$. From the scaling requirements these must reduce to $P_0(x) = 1$ and $P_1(x) = x$.

Returning to Eq. (15.12), we can get explicit closed expressions for the Legendre polynomials. All we need to do is expand the quantity $(-2xt + t^2)^n$ and rearrange the summations to identify the x dependence associated with each power of t. The result, which is in general less useful than the recurrence formulas to be developed in the next subsection, is

$$P_n(x) = \sum_{k=0}^{[n/2]} (-1)^k \frac{(2n-2k)!}{2^n k! (n-k)! (n-2k)!} x^{n-2k}. \tag{15.14}$$

Here $[n/2]$ stands for the largest integer $\leq n/2$. This formula is consistent with the requirement that for n even, $P_n(x)$ has only even powers of x and even parity, while for n odd, it has only odd powers of x and odd parity. Proof of Eq. (15.14) is the topic of Exercise 15.1.2.

Recurrence Formulas

From the generating function equation we can generate recurrence formulas by differentiating $g(x,t)$ with respect to x or t. We start from

$$\frac{\partial g(x,t)}{\partial t} = \frac{x-t}{(1-2xt+t^2)^{3/2}} = \sum_{n=0}^{\infty} nP_n(x)t^{n-1}, \tag{15.15}$$

which we rearrange to

$$(1-2xt+t^2)\sum_{n=0}^{\infty} nP_n(x)t^{n-1} + (t-x)\sum_{n=0}^{\infty} P_n(x)t^n = 0, \tag{15.16}$$

and then expand, reaching

$$\sum_{n=0}^{\infty} nP_n(x)t^{n-1} - 2\sum_{n=0}^{\infty} nxP_n(x)t^n + \sum_{n=0}^{\infty} nP_n(x)t^{n+1}$$

$$+ \sum_{n=0}^{\infty} P_n(x)t^{n+1} - \sum_{n=0}^{\infty} xP_n(x)t^n = 0. \tag{15.17}$$

Collecting the coefficients of t^n from the various terms and setting the result to zero, Eq. (15.17) is seen to be equivalent to

$$(2n+1)xP_n(x) = (n+1)P_{n+1}(x) + nP_{n-1}(x), \quad n = 1, 2, 3, \ldots. \tag{15.18}$$

Equation (15.18) permits us to generate successive P_n from the starting values P_0 and P_1 that we have previously identified. For example,

$$2P_2(x) = 3xP_1(x) - P_0(x) \quad \longrightarrow \quad P_2(x) = \frac{1}{2}\left(3x^2 - 1\right). \tag{15.19}$$

Continuing this process, we can build the list of Legendre polynomials given in Table 15.1.

We can also obtain a recurrence formula involving P_n' by differentiating $g(x,t)$ with respect to x. This gives

$$\frac{\partial g(x,t)}{\partial x} = \frac{t}{(1-2xt+t^2)^{3/2}} = \sum_{n=0}^{\infty} P_n'(x)t^n,$$

Table 15.1   Legendre Polynomials

$$P_0(x) = 1$$
$$P_1(x) = x$$
$$P_2(x) = \tfrac{1}{2}(3x^2 - 1)$$
$$P_3(x) = \tfrac{1}{2}(5x^3 - 3x)$$
$$P_4(x) = \tfrac{1}{8}(35x^4 - 30x^2 + 3)$$
$$P_5(x) = \tfrac{1}{8}(63x^5 - 70x^3 + 15x)$$
$$P_6(x) = \tfrac{1}{16}(231x^6 - 315x^4 + 105x^2 - 5)$$
$$P_7(x) = \tfrac{1}{16}(429x^7 - 693x^5 + 315x^3 - 35x)$$
$$P_8(x) = \tfrac{1}{128}(6435x^8 - 12012x^6 + 6930x^4 - 1260x^2 + 35)$$

or

$$(1 - 2xt + t^2)\sum_{n=0}^{\infty} P_n'(x)t^n - t\sum_{n=0}^{\infty} P_n(x)t^n = 0. \tag{15.20}$$

As before, the coefficient of each power of t is set to zero and we obtain

$$P_{n+1}'(x) + P_{n-1}'(x) = 2x P_n'(x) + P_n(x). \tag{15.21}$$

A more useful relation may be found by differentiating Eq. (15.18) with respect to x and multiplying by 2. To this we add $(2n + 1)$ times Eq. (15.21), canceling the P_n' term. The result is

$$P_{n+1}'(x) - P_{n-1}'(x) = (2n + 1)P_n(x). \tag{15.22}$$

Starting from Eqs. (15.21) and (15.22), numerous additional relations can be developed,[1] including

$$P_{n+1}'(x) = (n + 1)P_n(x) + x P_n'(x), \tag{15.23}$$

$$P_{n-1}'(x) = -n P_n(x) + x P_n'(x), \tag{15.24}$$

$$(1 - x^2)P_n'(x) = n P_{n-1}(x) - nx P_n(x), \tag{15.25}$$

$$(1 - x^2)P_n'(x) = (n + 1)x P_n(x) - (n + 1)P_{n+1}(x). \tag{15.26}$$

Because we derived the generating function $g(x, t)$ from the Legendre ODE and then obtained the recurrence formulas using $g(x, t)$, that ODE will automatically be consistent with these recurrence relations. It is nevertheless of interest to verify this consistency, because then we can conclude that **any** set of functions satisfying the recurrence formulas will be a set of solutions to the Legendre ODE, and that observation will be relevant to

---

[1]Using the equation numbers in parentheses to indicate how they are to be combined, we may obtain some of these derivative formulas as follows:

$$2 \cdot \tfrac{d}{dx}(15.18) + (2n + 1) \cdot (15.21) \Rightarrow (15.22), \qquad \tfrac{1}{2}\{(15.21) + (15.22)\} \Rightarrow (15.23),$$

$$\tfrac{1}{2}\{(15.21) - (15.22)\} \Rightarrow (15.24), \qquad (15.23)_{n\to n-1} + x\,(15.24) \Rightarrow (15.25).$$

the Legendre functions of the second kind (solutions linearly independent of the polynomials P_l). A demonstration that functions satisfying the recurrence formulas also satisfy the Legendre ODE is the topic of Exercise 15.1.1.

Upper and Lower Bounds for $P_n(\cos\theta)$

Our generating function can be used to set an upper limit on $|P_n(\cos\theta)|$. We have

$$(1 - 2t\cos\theta + t^2)^{-1/2} = (1 - te^{i\theta})^{-1/2}(1 - te^{-i\theta})^{-1/2}$$

$$= \left(1 + \frac{1}{2}te^{i\theta} + \frac{3}{8}t^2e^{2i\theta} + \cdots\right)\left(1 + \frac{1}{2}te^{-i\theta} + \frac{3}{8}t^2e^{-2i\theta} + \cdots\right). \quad (15.27)$$

We may make two immediate observations from Eq. (15.27). First, when any term within the first set of parentheses is multiplied by any term from the second set of parentheses, the power of t in the product will be even if and only if m in the net exponential $e^{im\theta}$ is even. Second, for every term of the form $t^n e^{im\theta}$, there will be another term of the form $t^n e^{-im\theta}$, and the two terms will occur with the same coefficient, which must be positive (since all the terms in both summations are individually positive). These two observations mean that:

(1)   Taking the terms of the expansion two at a time, we can write the coefficient of t^n as a linear combination of forms

$$\frac{1}{2} a_{nm}(e^{im\theta} + e^{-im\theta}) = a_{nm}\cos m\theta$$

with all the a_{nm} **positive**, and

(2)   The parity of n and m must be the same (either they are both even, or both odd).

This, in turn, means that

$$P_n(\cos\theta) = \sum_{m=0 \text{ or } 1}^{n} a_{nm}\cos m\theta. \quad (15.28)$$

This expression is clearly a maximum when $\theta = 0$, where we already know, from the Summary following Eq. (15.11), that $P_n(1) = 1$. Thus,

> *The Legendre polynomial $P_n(x)$ has a global maximum on the interval $(-1, +1)$ at $x = 1$, with value $P_n(1) = 1$, and if n is even, also at $x = -1$. If n is odd, $x = -1$ will be a global minimum on this interval with $P_n(-1) = -1$.*

The maxima and minima of the Legendre polynomials can be seen from the graphs of P_2 through P_5, in which are plotted in Fig. 15.1.

Rodrigues Formula

In Section 12.1 we showed that orthogonal polynomials could be described by **Rodrigues formulas**, and that the repeated differentiations occurring therein were good

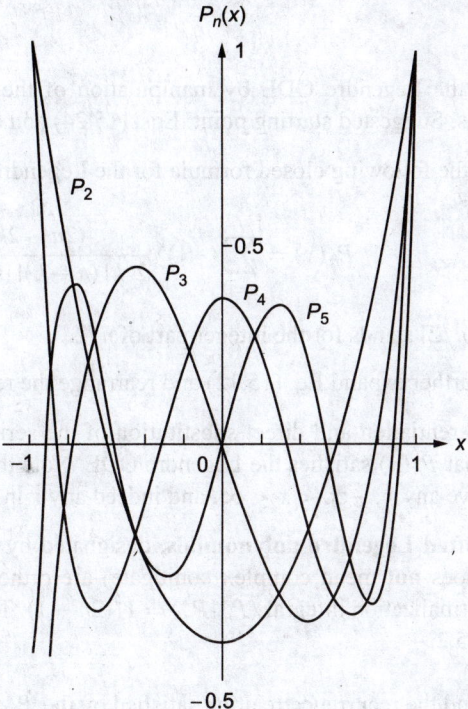

FIGURE 15.1   Legendre polynomials $P_2(x)$ through $P_5(x)$.

starting points for developing properties of these functions. Applying Eq. (12.9), we find that the Rodrigues formula for the Legendre polynomials must be proportional to

$$\left(\frac{d}{dx}\right)^n (1 - x^2)^n.$$ (15.29)

Equation (12.9) is not sufficient to set the scale of the orthogonal polynomials, and to bring Eq. (15.29) to the scaling already adopted via Eq. (15.6) we multiply Eq. (15.29) by $(-1)^n / 2^n n!$, so

$$P_n(x) = \frac{1}{2^n n!} \left(\frac{d}{dx}\right)^n (x^2 - 1)^n.$$ (15.30)

To establish that Eq. (15.30) has a scaling in agreement with our earlier analyses, it suffices to check the coefficient of a single power of x; we choose x^n. From the Rodrigues formula, this power of x can only arise from the term x^{2n} in the expansion of $(x^2 - 1)^n$, and the

coefficient of x^n in $P_n(x)$ (Rodrigues) is $\dfrac{1}{2^n n!} \dfrac{(2n)!}{n!} = \dfrac{(2n-1)!!}{n!}$,

in agreement with Eq. (15.13). This confirms the scale of Eq. (15.30).

Exercises

15.1.1   Derive the Legendre ODE by manipulation of the Legendre polynomial recurrence relations. Suggested starting point: Eqs. (15.24) and (15.25).

15.1.2   Derive the following closed formula for the Legendre polynomials $P_n(x)$.

$$P_n(x) = \sum_{k=0}^{[n/2]} (-1)^k \frac{(2n-2k)!}{2^n k! \, (n-k)! \, (n-2k)!} \, x^{n-2k},$$

where $[n/2]$ stands for the integer part of $n/2$.

Hint. Further expand Eq. (15.12) and rearrange the resulting double sum.

15.1.3   By differentiation and direct substitution of the series form given in Exercise 15.1.2, show that $P_n(x)$ satisfies the Legendre ODE. Note that there is no restriction on x. We may have any x, $-\infty < x < \infty$, and indeed any z in the entire finite complex plane.

15.1.4   The **shifted Legendre polynomials**, designated by the symbol $P_n^*(x)$ (where the asterisk does **not** mean complex conjugate) are orthogonal with unit weight on $[0, 1]$, with normalization integral $\langle P_n^* | P_n^* \rangle = 1/(2n+1)$. The P_n^* through $n = 6$ are shown in Table 15.2.

(a)   Find the recurrence relation satisfied by the P_n^*.
(b)   Show that all the coefficients of the P_n^* are integers.

Hint. Look at the closed formula in Exercise 15.1.2.

15.1.5   Given the series

$$\alpha_0 + \alpha_2 \cos^2 \theta + \alpha_4 \cos^4 \theta + \alpha_6 \cos^6 \theta = a_0 P_0 + a_2 P_2 + a_4 P_4 + a_6 P_6,$$

where the arguments of the P_n are $\cos\theta$, express the coefficients α_i as a column vector $\boldsymbol{\alpha}$ and the coefficients a_i as a column vector $\mathbf{a}$ and determine the matrices A and B such that

$$\mathsf{A}\boldsymbol{\alpha} = \mathbf{a} \quad \text{and} \quad \mathsf{B}\mathbf{a} = \boldsymbol{\alpha}.$$

Table 15.2   Shifted Legendre Polynomials

$P_0^*(x) = 1$
$P_1^*(x) = 2x - 1$
$P_2^*(x) = 6x^2 - 6x + 1$
$P_3^*(x) = 20x^3 - 30x^2 + 12x - 1$
$P_4^*(x) = 70x^4 - 140x^3 + 90x^2 - 20x + 1$
$P_5^*(x) = 252x^5 - 630x^4 + 560x^3 - 210x^2 + 30x - 1$
$P_6^*(x) = 924x^6 - 2772x^5 + 3150x^4 - 1680x^3 + 420x^2 - 42x + 1$

Check your computation by showing that **AB = 1** (unit matrix). Repeat for the odd case

$$\alpha_1 \cos\theta + \alpha_3 \cos^3\theta + \alpha_5 \cos^5\theta + \alpha_7 \cos^7\theta = a_1 P_1 + a_3 P_3 + a_5 P_5 + a_7 P_7.$$

Note. $P_n(\cos\theta)$ and $\cos^n\theta$ are tabulated in terms of each other in AMS-55 (see Additional Readings for the complete reference).

15.1.6 By differentiating the generating function $g(x, t)$ with respect to t, multiplying by $2t$, and then adding $g(x, t)$, show that

$$\frac{1 - t^2}{(1 - 2tx + t^2)^{3/2}} = \sum_{n=0}^{\infty} (2n + 1) P_n(x) t^n.$$

This result is useful in calculating the charge induced on a grounded metal sphere by a nearby point charge.

15.1.7 (a) Derive Eq. (15.26),

$$(1 - x^2) P_n'(x) = (n + 1) x P_n(x) - (n + 1) P_{n+1}(x).$$

(b) Write out the relation of Eq. (15.26) to preceding equations in symbolic form analogous to the symbolic forms for Eqs. (15.22) to (15.25).

15.1.8 Prove that

$$P_n'(1) = \frac{d}{dx} P_n(x)\,|_{x=1} = \frac{1}{2} n(n + 1).$$

15.1.9 Show that $P_n(\cos\theta) = (-1)^n P_n(-\cos\theta)$ by use of the recurrence relation relating P_n, P_{n+1}, and P_{n-1} and your knowledge of P_0 and P_1.

15.1.10 From Eq. (15.27) write out the coefficient of t^2 in terms of $\cos n\theta$, $n \leq 2$. This coefficient is $P_2(\cos\theta)$.

15.1.11 Derive the recurrence relation

$$(1 - x^2) P_n'(x) = n P_{n-1}(x) - nx P_n(x)$$

from the Legendre polynomial generating function.

15.1.12 Evaluate $\displaystyle\int_0^1 P_n(x)\, dx.$

> ANS. $n = 2s$,   1 for $s = 0$, 0 for $s > 0$;
>
> $n = 2s + 1$, $P_{2s}(0)/(2s + 2) = (-1)^s (2s - 1)!!/1(2s + 2)!!.$

Hint. Use a recurrence relation to replace $P_n(x)$ by derivatives and then integrate by inspection. Alternatively, you can integrate the generating function.

15.1.13 Show that **each** term in the summation

$$\sum_{r=[n/2]+1}^{n} \left(\frac{d}{dx}\right)^n \frac{(-1)^r n!}{r!\,(n - r)!} x^{2n-2r}$$

vanishes (r and n integral). Here $[n/2]$ is the largest integer $\leq n/2$.

15.1.14   Show that $\int_{-1}^{1} x^m P_n(x)\, dx = 0$ when $m < n$.

Hint. Use Rodrigues formula or expand x^m in Legendre polynomials.

15.1.15   Show that

$$\int_{-1}^{1} x^n P_n(x)\, dx = \frac{2\, n!}{(2n+1)!!}.$$

Note. You are expected to use the Rodrigues formula and integrate by parts, but also see if you can get the result from Eq. (15.14) by inspection.

15.1.16   Show that

$$\int_{-1}^{1} x^{2r} P_{2n}(x)\, dx = \frac{2^{2n+1}(2r)!\,(r+n)!}{(2r+2n+1)!\,(r-n)!}, \quad r \geq n.$$

15.1.17   As a generalization of Exercises 15.1.15 and 15.1.16, show that the Legendre expansions of x^s are

(a) $x^{2r} = \displaystyle\sum_{n=0}^{r} \frac{2^{2n}(4n+1)(2r)!\,(r+n)!}{(2r+2n+1)!\,(r-n)!}\, P_{2n}(x), \quad s = 2r,$

(b) $x^{2r+1} = \displaystyle\sum_{n=0}^{r} \frac{2^{2n+1}(4n+3)(2r+1)!\,(r+n+1)!}{(2r+2n+3)!\,(r-n)!}\, P_{2n+1}(x), \quad s = 2r+1.$

15.1.18   In numerical work (for e.g., the Gauss-Legendre quadrature), it is useful to establish that $P_n(x)$ has n real zeros in the interior of $[-1, 1]$. Show that this is so.

Hint. Rolle's theorem shows that the first derivative of $(x^2 - 1)^{2n}$ has one zero in the interior of $[-1, 1]$. Extend this argument to the second, third, and ultimately the nth derivative.

15.2   ORTHOGONALITY

Because the Legendre ODE is self-adjoint and the coefficient of $P''(x)$, namely $(1 - x^2)$, vanishes at $x = \pm 1$, its solutions of different n will automatically be orthogonal with unit weight on the interval $(-1, 1)$,

$$\int_{-1}^{1} P_n(x) P_m(x)\, dx = 0, \quad (n \neq m). \tag{15.31}$$

Because the P_n are real, no complex conjugation needs to be indicated in the orthogonality integral. Since P_n is often used with argument $\cos\theta$, we note that Eq. (15.31) is equivalent to

$$\int_0^\pi P_n(\cos\theta) P_m(\cos\theta) \sin\theta \, d\theta = 0, \quad (n \neq m). \tag{15.32}$$

The definition of the P_n does not guarantee that they are normalized, and in fact they are not. One way to establish the normalization starts by squaring the generating-function formula, yielding initially

$$(1 - 2xt + t^2)^{-1} = \left[\sum_{n=0}^\infty P_n(x) t^n \right]^2. \tag{15.33}$$

Integrating from $x = -1$ to $x = 1$ and dropping the cross terms because they vanish due to orthogonality, Eq. (15.31), we have

$$\int_{-1}^1 \frac{dx}{1 - 2tx + t^2} = \sum_{n=0}^\infty t^{2n} \int_{-1}^1 \left[P_n(x) \right]^2 dx. \tag{15.34}$$

Making now the substitution $y = 1 - 2tx + t^2$, with $dy = -2t \, dx$, we obtain

$$\int_{-1}^1 \frac{dx}{1 - 2tx + t^2} = \frac{1}{2t} \int_{(1-t)^2}^{(1+t)^2} \frac{dy}{y} = \frac{1}{t} \ln\left(\frac{1+t}{1-t} \right). \tag{15.35}$$

Expanding this result in a power series (Exercise 1.6.1),

$$\frac{1}{t} \ln\left(\frac{1+t}{1-t} \right) = 2 \sum_{n=0}^\infty \frac{t^{2n}}{2n+1}, \tag{15.36}$$

and equating the coefficients of powers of t in Eqs. (15.34) and (15.36), we must have

$$\int_{-1}^1 \left[P_n(x) \right]^2 dx = \frac{2}{2n+1}. \tag{15.37}$$

Combining Eqs. (15.31) and (15.37), we have the orthonormality condition

$$\int_{-1}^1 P_n(x) P_m(x) dx = \frac{2\delta_{nm}}{2n+1}. \tag{15.38}$$

This result can also be obtained using the Rodrigues formulas for P_n and P_m. See Exercise 15.2.1.

Legendre Series

The orthogonality of the Legendre polynomials makes it natural to use them as a basis for expansions. Given a function $f(x)$ defined on the range $(-1, 1)$, the coefficients in the expansion

$$f(x) = \sum_{n=0}^{\infty} a_n P_n(x) \tag{15.39}$$

are given by the formula

$$a_n = \frac{2n+1}{2} \int_{-1}^{1} f(x) P_n(x) dx. \tag{15.40}$$

The orthogonality property guarantees that this expansion is unique. Since we can (but perhaps will not wish to) convert our expansion into a power series by inserting the expansion of Eq. (15.14) and collecting the coefficients of each power of x, we can also obtain a power series, which we thereby know must be unique.

An important application of Legendre series is to solutions of the Laplace equation. We saw in Section 9.4 that when the Laplace equation is separated in spherical polar coordinates, its general solution (for spherical symmetry) takes the form

$$\psi(r, \theta, \varphi) = \sum_{l,m} (A_{lm} r^l + B_{lm} r^{-l-1}) P_l^m(\cos\theta)(A'_{lm} \sin m\varphi + B'_{lm} \cos m\varphi), \tag{15.41}$$

with l required to be an integer to avoid a solution that diverges in the polar directions. Here we consider solutions with no azimuthal dependence (i.e., with $m = 0$), so Eq. (15.41) reduces to

$$\psi(r, \theta) = \sum_{l=0}^{\infty} (a_l r^l + b_l r^{-l-1}) P_l(\cos\theta). \tag{15.42}$$

Often our problem is further restricted to a region either within or external to a boundary sphere, and if the problem is such that ψ must remain finite, the solution will have one of the two following forms:

$$\psi(r, \theta) = \sum_{l=0}^{\infty} a_l r^l P_l(\cos\theta) \quad (r \leq r_0), \tag{15.43}$$

$$\psi(r, \theta) = \sum_{l=0}^{\infty} a_l r^{-l-1} P_l(\cos\theta) \quad (r \geq r_0). \tag{15.44}$$

Note that this simplification is not always appropriate; see Example 15.2.2. Sometimes the coefficients (a_l) are determined from the boundary conditions of a problem rather than from the expansion of a known function. See the examples to follow.

Example 15.2.1   EARTH'S GRAVITATIONAL FIELD

An example of a Legendre series is provided by the description of the Earth's gravitational potential U at points exterior to the Earth's surface. Because gravitation is an inverse-square force, its potential in mass-free regions satisfies the Laplace equation, and therefore (if we neglect azimuthal effects, i.e., those dependent on longitude) it has the form given in Eq. (15.44).

To specialize to the current example, we define R to be the Earth's radius at the equator, and take as the expansion variable the dimensionless quantity R/r. In terms of the total mass of the Earth M and the gravitational constant G, we have

$$R = 6378.1 \pm 0.1 \, \text{km},$$

$$\frac{GM}{R} = 62.494 \pm 0.001 \, \text{km}^2/\text{s}^2,$$

and we write

$$U(r, \theta) = \frac{GM}{R} \left[\frac{R}{r} - \sum_{l=2}^{\infty} a_l \left(\frac{R}{r} \right)^{l+1} P_l(\cos\theta) \right]. \tag{15.45}$$

The leading term of this expansion describes the result that would be obtained if the Earth were spherically symmetric; the higher terms describe distortions. The P_1 term is absent because the origin from which r is measured is the Earth's center of mass.

Artificial satellite motions have shown that

$$a_2 = (1,082,635 \pm 11) \times 10^{-9},$$

$$a_3 = (-2,531 \pm 7) \times 10^{-9},$$

$$a_4 = (-1,600 \pm 12) \times 10^{-9}.$$

This is the famous pear-shaped deformation of the Earth. Other coefficients have been computed through a_{20}.

More recent satellite data permit a determination of the longitudinal dependence of the Earth's gravitational field. Such dependence may be described by a Laplace series (see Section 15.5). ∎

Example 15.2.2   SPHERE IN A UNIFORM FIELD

Another illustration of the use of a Legendre series is provided by the problem of a neutral conducting sphere (radius r_0) placed in a (previously) uniform electric field of magnitude E_0 (Fig. 15.2). The problem is to find the new, perturbed electrostatic potential ψ that satisfies Laplace's equation,

$$\nabla^2 \psi = 0.$$

We select spherical polar coordinates with origin at the center of the conducting sphere and the polar (z) axis oriented parallel to the original uniform field, a choice that will simplify

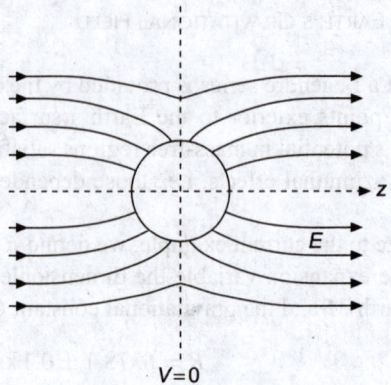

FIGURE 15.2   Conducting sphere in a uniform field.

the application of the boundary condition at the surface of the conductor. Separating variables, we note that because we require a solution to Laplace's equation, the potential for $r \geq r_0$ will be of the form of Eq. (15.42). Our solution will be independent of φ because of the axial symmetry of the problem.

Because the insertion of the conducting sphere will have an effect that is local, the asymptotic behavior of ψ must be of the form

$$\psi(r \to \infty) = -E_0 z = -E_0 r \cos \theta = -E_0 r P_1(\cos \theta), \qquad (15.46)$$

equivalent to

$$a_n = 0, \quad n > 1, \quad a_1 = -E_0. \qquad (15.47)$$

Note that if $a_n \neq 0$ for any $n > 1$, that term would dominate at large r and the boundary condition, Eq. (15.46), could not be satisfied. In addition, the neutrality of the conducting sphere requires that ψ not contain a contribution proportional to $1/r$, so we also must have $b_0 = 0$.

As a second boundary condition, the conducting sphere must be an equipotential, and without loss of generality we can set its potential to zero. Then, on the sphere $r = r_0$ we have

$$\psi(r_0, \theta) = a_0 + \left(\frac{b_1}{r_0^2} - E_0 r_0 \right) P_1(\cos \theta) + \sum_{n=2}^{\infty} b_n \frac{P_n(\cos \theta)}{r_0^{n+1}} = 0. \qquad (15.48)$$

In order that Eq. (15.48) may hold for all values of θ, we set

$$a_0 = 0, \quad b_1 = E_0 r_0^3 \quad b_n = 0, \quad n \geq 2. \qquad (15.49)$$

The electrostatic potential (outside the sphere) is then completely determined:

$$\psi(r, \theta) = -E_0 r P_1(\cos\theta) + \frac{E_0 r_0^3}{r^2} P_1(\cos\theta)$$

$$= -E_0 r P_1(\cos\theta)\left(1 - \frac{r_0^3}{r^3}\right) = -E_0 z\left(1 - \frac{r_0^3}{r^3}\right). \qquad (15.50)$$

In Section 9.5 we showed that Laplace's equation with Dirichlet boundary conditions on a closed boundary (parts of which may be at infinity) had a unique solution. Since we have now found a solution to our current problem, it must (apart from an additive constant) be the only solution.

It may further be shown that there is an induced surface charge density

$$\sigma = -\varepsilon_0 \frac{\partial\psi}{\partial r}\bigg|_{r=r_0} = 3\varepsilon_0 E_0 \cos\theta \qquad (15.51)$$

on the surface of the sphere and an induced electric dipole moment of magnitude

$$P = 4\pi r_0^3 \varepsilon_0 E_0. \qquad (15.52)$$

See Exercise 15.2.11. ∎

Example 15.2.3   ELECTROSTATIC POTENTIAL FOR A RING OF CHARGE

As a further example, consider the electrostatic potential produced by a thin conducting ring of radius a placed symmetrically in the equatorial plane of a spherical polar coordinate system and carrying a total electric charge q (Fig. 15.3). Again we rely on the fact that the potential ψ satisfies Laplace's equation. Separating the variables and recognizing that a solution for the region $r > a$ must go to zero as $r \to \infty$, we use the form given by

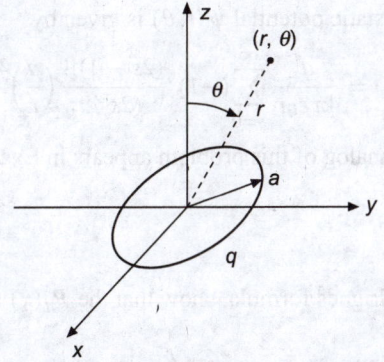

FIGURE 15.3   Charged, conducting ring.

Eq. (15.44), obtaining

$$\psi(r,\theta) = \sum_{n=0}^{\infty} c_n \frac{a^n}{r^{n+1}} P_n(\cos\theta), \quad r > a. \tag{15.53}$$

There is no φ (azimuthal) dependence because of the cylindrical symmetry of the system. Note also that by including an explicit factor a^n we cause all the coefficients c_n to have the same dimensionality; this choice simply modifies the definition of c_n and was, of course, not required.

Our problem is to determine the coefficients c_n in Eq. (15.53). This may be done by evaluating $\psi(r,\theta)$ at $\theta = 0$, $r = z$, and comparing with an independent calculation of the potential from Coulomb's law. In effect, we are using a boundary condition along the z-axis. From Coulomb's law (using the fact that all the charge is equidistant from any point on the z axis),

$$\psi(z,0) = \frac{q}{4\pi\varepsilon_0} \frac{1}{(z^2 + a^2)^{1/2}} = \frac{q}{4\pi\varepsilon_0 z} \sum_{s=0}^{\infty} \binom{-1/2}{s} \left(\frac{a^2}{z^2}\right)^s$$

$$= \frac{q}{4\pi\varepsilon_0 z} \sum_{s=0}^{\infty} (-1)^s \frac{(2s-1)!!}{(2s)!!} \left(\frac{a}{z}\right)^{2s}, \quad z > a, \tag{15.54}$$

where we have evaluated the binomial coefficient using Eq. (1.74).

Now, evaluating $\psi(z,0)$ from Eq. (15.53), remembering that $P_n(1) = 1$ for all n, we have

$$\psi(z,0) = \sum_{n=0}^{\infty} c_n \frac{a^n}{z^{n+1}}. \tag{15.55}$$

Since the power series expansion in z is unique, we may equate the coefficients of corresponding powers of z from Eqs. (15.54) and (15.55), reaching the conclusion that $c_n = 0$ for n odd, while for n even and equal to $2s$,

$$c_{2s} = \frac{q}{4\pi\varepsilon_0 z} (-1)^s \frac{(2s-1)!!}{(2s)!!}, \tag{15.56}$$

and our electrostatic potential $\psi(r,\theta)$ is given by

$$\psi(r,\theta) = \frac{q}{4\pi\varepsilon_0 r} \sum_{s=0}^{\infty} (-1)^s \frac{(2s-1)!!}{(2s)!!} \left(\frac{a}{r}\right)^{2s} P_{2s}(\cos\theta), \quad r > a. \tag{15.57}$$

The magnetic analog of this problem appears in Example 15.4.2.   ∎

Exercises

15.2.1   Using a Rodrigues formula, show that the $P_n(x)$ are orthogonal and that

$$\int_{-1}^{1} [P_n(x)]^2 dx = \frac{2}{2n+1}.$$

Hint. Integrate by parts.

15.2.2   You have constructed a set of orthogonal functions by the Gram-Schmidt process (Section 5.2), taking $u_n(x) = x^n$, $n = 0, 1, 2, \ldots$, in increasing order with $w(x) = 1$ and an interval $-1 \leq x \leq 1$. Prove that the nth such function constructed in this way is proportional to $P_n(x)$.

Hint. Use mathematical induction (Section 1.4).

15.2.3   Expand the Dirac delta function $\delta(x)$ in a series of Legendre polynomials using the interval $-1 \leq x \leq 1$.

15.2.4   Verify the Dirac delta function expansions

$$\delta(1 - x) = \sum_{n=0}^{\infty} \frac{2n + 1}{2} P_n(x),$$

$$\delta(1 + x) = \sum_{n=0}^{\infty} (-1)^n \frac{2n + 1}{2} P_n(x).$$

These expressions appear in a resolution of the Rayleigh plane wave expansion (Exercise 15.2.24) into incoming and outgoing spherical waves.

Note. Assume that the **entire** Dirac delta function is covered when integrating over $[-1, 1]$.

15.2.5   Neutrons (mass 1) are being scattered by a nucleus of mass A $(A > 1)$. In the center-of-mass system the scattering is isotropic. Then, in the laboratory system the average of the cosine of the angle of deflection of the neutron is

$$\langle \cos \psi \rangle = \frac{1}{2} \int_0^{\pi} \frac{A \cos \theta + 1}{(A^2 + 2A \cos \theta + 1)^{1/2}} \sin \theta \, d\theta.$$

Show, by expansion of the denominator, that $\langle \cos \psi \rangle = 2/(3A)$.

15.2.6   A particular function $f(x)$ defined over the interval $[-1, 1]$ is expanded in a Legendre series over this same interval. Show that the expansion is unique.

15.2.7   A function $f(x)$ is expanded in a Legendre series $f(x) = \sum_{n=0}^{\infty} a_n P_n(x)$. Show that

$$\int_{-1}^{1} [f(x)]^2 \, dx = \sum_{n=0}^{\infty} \frac{2a_n^2}{2n + 1}.$$

This is a statement that the Legendre polynomials form a complete set.

15.2.8   (a)   For

$$f(x) = \begin{cases} +1, & 0 < x < 1, \\ -1, & -1 < x < 0, \end{cases}$$

show that

$$\int_{-1}^{1} \left[f(x) \right]^2 dx = 2 \sum_{n=0}^{\infty} (4n+3) \left[\frac{(2n-1)!!}{(2n+2)!!} \right]^2.$$

(b) By testing the series, prove that it is convergent.

(c) The value of the integral in part (a) is 2. Check the rate at which the series converges by summing its first 10 terms.

15.2.9 Prove that

$$\int_{-1}^{1} x(1-x^2) P_n' P_m' \, dx = \frac{2n(n^2-1)}{4n^2-1} \delta_{m,n-1} + \frac{2n(n+2)(n+1)}{(2n+1)(2n+3)} \delta_{m,n+1}.$$

15.2.10 The coincidence counting rate, $W(\theta)$, in a gamma-gamma angular correlation experiment has the form

$$W(\theta) = \sum_{n=0}^{\infty} a_{2n} P_{2n}(\cos \theta).$$

Show that data in the range $\pi/2 \leq \theta \leq \pi$ can, in principle, define the function $W(\theta)$ (and permit a determination of the coefficients a_{2n}). This means that although data in the range $0 \leq \theta < \pi/2$ may be useful as a check, they are not essential.

15.2.11 A conducting sphere of radius r_0 is placed in an initially uniform electric field, $\mathbf{E}_0$. Show the following:

(a) The induced surface charge density is $\sigma = 3\varepsilon_0 E_0 \cos \theta$,

(b) The induced electric dipole moment is $P = 4\pi r_0^3 \varepsilon_0 E_0$.

Note. The induced electric dipole moment can be calculated either from the surface charge [part (a)] or by noting that the final electric field $\mathbf{E}$ is the result of superimposing a dipole field on the original uniform field.

15.2.12 Obtain as a Legendre expansion the electrostatic potential of the circular ring of Example 15.2.3, for points (r, θ) with $r < a$.

15.2.13 Calculate the **electric field** produced by the charged conducting ring of Example 15.2.3 for

(a) $r > a$,   (b) $r < a$.

15.2.14 As an extension of Example 15.2.3, find the potential $\psi(r, \theta)$ produced by a charged conducting disk, Fig. 15.4, for $r > a$, where a is the radius of the disk. The charge density σ (on each side of the disk) is

$$\sigma(\rho) = \frac{q}{4\pi a(a^2 - \rho^2)^{1/2}}, \quad \rho^2 = x^2 + y^2.$$

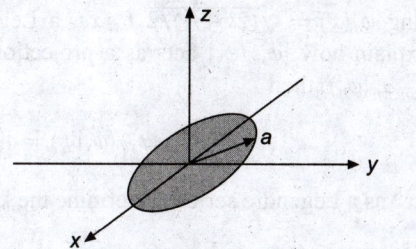

FIGURE 15.4   Charged conducting disk.

Hint. The definite integral you get can be evaluated as a beta function, Section 13.3. For more details see section 5.03 of Smythe in Additional Readings.

$$ANS. \quad \psi(r, \theta) = \frac{q}{4\pi\varepsilon_0 r} \sum_{l=0}^{\infty} (-1)^l \frac{1}{2l+1} \left(\frac{a}{r}\right)^{2l} P_{2l}(\cos\theta).$$

15.2.15 The hemisphere defined by $r = a$, $0 \le \theta < \pi/2$, has an electrostatic potential $+V_0$. The hemisphere $r = a$, $\pi/2 < \theta \le \pi$ has an electrostatic potential $-V_0$. Show that the potential at interior points is

$$V = V_0 \sum_{n=0}^{\infty} \frac{4n+3}{2n+2} \left(\frac{r}{a}\right)^{2n+1} P_{2n}(0) P_{2n+1}(\cos\theta)$$

$$= V_0 \sum_{n=0}^{\infty} (-1)^n \frac{(4n+3)(2n-1)!!}{(2n+2)!!} \left(\frac{r}{a}\right)^{2n+1} P_{2n+1}(\cos\theta).$$

Hint. You need Exercise 15.1.12.

15.2.16 A conducting sphere of radius a is divided into two electrically separate hemispheres by a thin insulating barrier at its equator. The top hemisphere is maintained at a potential V_0, and the bottom hemisphere at $-V_0$.

(a)   Show that the electrostatic potential **exterior** to the two hemispheres is

$$V(r, \theta) = V_0 \sum_{s=0}^{\infty} (-1)^s (4s+3) \frac{(2s-1)!!}{(2s+2)!!} \left(\frac{a}{r}\right)^{2s+2} P_{2s+1}(\cos\theta).$$

(b)   Calculate the electric charge density σ on the outside surface. Note that your series diverges at $\cos\theta = \pm 1$, as you expect from the infinite capacitance of this system (zero thickness for the insulating barrier).

$$ANS. \quad (b) \quad \sigma = \varepsilon_0 E_n = -\varepsilon_0 \frac{\partial V}{\partial r}\bigg|_{r=a}$$

$$= \varepsilon_0 V_0 \sum_{s=0}^{\infty} (-1)^s (4s+3) \frac{(2s-1)!!}{(2s)!!} P_{2s+1}(\cos\theta).$$

15.2.17 By writing $\varphi_s(x) = \sqrt{(2s+1)/2}\, P_s(x)$, a Legendre polynomial is renormalized to unity. Explain how $|\varphi_s\rangle\langle\varphi_s|$ acts as a projection operator. In particular, show that if $|f\rangle = \sum_n a'_n|\varphi_n\rangle$, then

$$|\varphi_s\rangle\langle\varphi_s|f\rangle = a'_s|\varphi_s\rangle.$$

15.2.18 Expand x^8 as a Legendre series. Determine the Legendre coefficients from Eq. (15.40),

$$a_m = \frac{2m+1}{2}\int_{-1}^{1} x^8 P_m(x)\, dx.$$

Check your values against AMS-55, Table 22.9. (For the complete reference, see Additional Readings.) This illustrates the expansion of a simple function $f(x)$.

Hint. Gaussian quadrature can be used to evaluate the integral.

15.2.19 Calculate and tabulate the electrostatic potential created by a ring of charge, Example 15.2.3, for $r/a = 1.5(0.5)5.0$ and $\theta = 0°(15°)90°$. Carry terms through $P_{22}(\cos\theta)$.

Note. The convergence of your series will be slow for $r/a = 1.5$. Truncating the series at P_{22} limits you to about four-significant-figure accuracy.

Check value. For $r/a = 2.5$ and $\theta = 60°$, $\psi = 0.40272(q/4\pi\varepsilon_0 r)$.

15.2.20 Calculate and tabulate the electrostatic potential created by a charged disk (Exercise 15.2.14), for $r/a = 1.5(0.5)5.0$ and $\theta = 0°(15°)90°$. Carry terms through $P_{22}(\cos\theta)$.

Check value. For $r/a = 2.0$ and $\theta = 15°$, $\psi = 0.46638(q/4\pi\varepsilon_0 r)$.

15.2.21 Calculate the first five (nonvanishing) coefficients in the Legendre series expansion of $f(x) = 1 - |x|$, evaluating the coefficients in the series by numerical integration. Actually these coefficients can be obtained in closed form. Compare your coefficients with those listed in Exercise 18.4.26.

ANS. $a_0 = 0.5000$, $a_2 = -0.6250$, $a_4 = 0.1875$, $a_6 = -0.1016$, $a_8 = 0.0664$.

15.2.22 Calculate and tabulate the exterior electrostatic potential created by the two charged hemispheres of Exercise 15.2.16, for $r/a = 1.5(0.5)5.0$ and $\theta = 0°(15°)90°$. Carry terms through $P_{23}(\cos\theta)$.

Check value. For $r/a = 2.0$ and $\theta = 45°$, $V = 0.27066V_0$.

15.2.23 (a) Given $f(x) = 2.0$, $|x| < 0.5$ and $f(x) = 0$, $0.5 < |x| < 1.0$, expand $f(x)$ in a Legendre series and calculate the coefficients a_n through a_{80} (analytically).
(b) Evaluate $\sum_{n=0}^{80} a_n P_n(x)$ for $x = 0.400(0.005)0.600$. Plot your results.

Note. This illustrates the Gibbs phenomenon of Section 19.3 and the danger of trying to calculate with a series expansion in the vicinity of a discontinuity.

15.2.24 A plane wave may be expanded in a series of spherical waves by the Rayleigh equation,

$$e^{ikr\cos\gamma} = \sum_{n=0}^{\infty} a_n j_n(kr) P_n(\cos\gamma).$$

Show that $a_n = i^n(2n+1)$.

Hint.

1. Use the orthogonality of the P_n to solve for $a_n j_n(kr)$.
2. Differentiate n times with respect to (kr) and set $r = 0$ to eliminate the r-dependence.
3. Evaluate the remaining integral by Exercise 15.1.15.

Note. This problem may also be treated by noting that both sides of the equation satisfy the Helmholtz equation. The equality can be established by showing that the solutions have the same behavior at the origin and also behave alike at large distances.

15.2.25 Verify the Rayleigh equation of Exercise 15.2.24 by starting with the following steps:

(a) Differentiate with respect to (kr) to establish

$$\sum_n a_n j_n'(kr) P_n(\cos\gamma) = i \sum_n a_n j_n(kr) \cos\gamma P_n(\cos\gamma).$$

(b) Use a recurrence relation to replace $\cos\gamma P_n(\cos\gamma)$ by a linear combination of P_{n-1} and P_{n+1}.
(c) Use a recurrence relation to replace j_n' by a linear combination of j_{n-1} and j_{n+1}.

15.2.26 From Exercise 15.2.24 show that

$$j_n(kr) = \frac{1}{2i^n} \int_{-1}^{1} e^{ikr\mu} P_n(\mu) d\mu.$$

This means that (apart from a constant factor) the spherical Bessel function $j_n(kr)$ is an integral transform of the Legendre polynomial $P_n(\mu)$.

15.2.27 Rewriting the formula of Exercise 15.2.26 as

$$j_n(z) = \tfrac{1}{2}(-i)^n \int_0^{\pi} e^{iz\cos\theta} P_n(\cos\theta) \sin\theta \, d\theta, \quad n = 0, 1, 2, \ldots,$$

verify it by transforming the right-hand side into

$$\frac{z^n}{2^{n+1} n!} \int_0^{\pi} \cos(z\cos\theta) \sin^{2n+1}\theta \, d\theta$$

and using Exercise 14.7.9.

15.3 PHYSICAL INTERPRETATION OF GENERATING FUNCTION

The generating function for the Legendre polynomials has an interesting and important interpretation. If we introduce spherical polar coordinates (r, θ, φ) and place a charge q at the point a on the positive z axis (see Fig. 15.5), the potential at a point (r, θ) (it is independent of φ) can be calculated, using the law of cosines, as

$$\psi(r, \theta) = \frac{q}{4\pi \varepsilon_0} \frac{1}{r_1} = \frac{q}{4\pi \varepsilon_0} (r^2 + a^2 - 2ar\cos\theta)^{-1/2}. \tag{15.58}$$

The expression in Eq. (15.58) is essentially that appearing in the generating function; to identify the correspondence we rewrite that equation as

$$\psi(r, \theta) = \frac{q}{4\pi \varepsilon_0 r} \left(1 - 2\frac{a}{r}\cos\theta + \frac{a^2}{r^2}\right)^{-1/2} = \frac{q}{4\pi \varepsilon_0 r} g\left(\cos\theta, \frac{a}{r}\right) \tag{15.59}$$

$$= \frac{q}{4\pi \varepsilon_0 r} \sum_{n=0}^{\infty} P_n(\cos\theta) \left(\frac{a}{r}\right)^n, \tag{15.60}$$

where we reached Eq. (15.60) by inserting the generating-function expansion.

The series in Eq. (15.60) only converges for $r > a$, with a rate of convergence that improves as r/a increases. If, on the other hand, we desire an expression for $\psi(r, \theta)$ when $r < a$, we can perform a different rearrangement of Eq. (15.58), to

$$\psi(r, \theta) = \frac{q}{4\pi \varepsilon_0 a} \left(1 - 2\frac{r}{a}\cos\theta + \frac{r^2}{a^2}\right)^{-1/2}, \tag{15.61}$$

which we again recognize as the generating-function expansion, but this time with the result

$$\psi(r, \theta) = \frac{q}{4\pi \varepsilon_0 a} \sum_{n=0}^{\infty} P_n(\cos\theta) \left(\frac{r}{a}\right)^n, \tag{15.62}$$

valid when $r < a$.

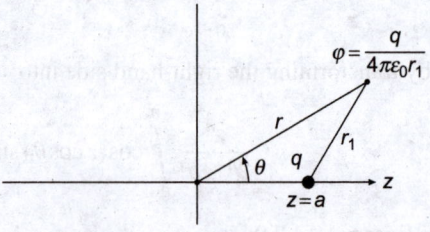

FIGURE 15.5 Electrostatic potential, charge q displaced from origin.

Expansion of $1/|\mathbf{r}_1 - \mathbf{r}_2|$

Equations (15.60) and (15.62) describe the interaction of a charge q at position $\mathbf{a} = a\hat{\mathbf{e}}_z$ with a unit charge at position $\mathbf{r}$. Dropping the factors needed for an electrostatics calculation, these equations yield formulas for $1/|\mathbf{r} - \mathbf{a}|$. The fact that $\mathbf{a}$ is aligned with the z-axis is actually of no importance for the computation of $1/|\mathbf{r} - \mathbf{a}|$; the relevant quantities are r, a, and the angle θ between $\mathbf{r}$ and $\mathbf{a}$. Thus, we may rewrite either Eq. (15.60) or (15.62) in a more neutral notation, to give the value of $1/|\mathbf{r}_1 - \mathbf{r}_2|$ in terms of the magnitudes r_1, r_2 and the angle between $\mathbf{r}_1$ and $\mathbf{r}_2$, which we now call χ. If we define $r_>$ and $r_<$ to be respectively the larger and the smaller of r_1 and r_2, Eqs. (15.60) and (15.62) can be combined into the single equation

$$\frac{1}{|\mathbf{r}_1 - \mathbf{r}_2|} = \frac{1}{r_>} \sum_{n=0}^{\infty} \left(\frac{r_<}{r_>}\right)^n P_n(\cos\chi), \tag{15.63}$$

which will converge everywhere except when $r_1 = r_2$.

Electric Multipoles

Returning to Eq. (15.60) and restricting consideration to $r > a$, we may note that its initial term (with $n = 0$) gives the potential we would get if the charge q were at the origin, and that further terms must describe corrections arising from the actual position of the charge. One way to obtain further understanding of the second and later terms in the expansion is to consider what would happen if we added a second charge, $-q$, at $z = -a$, as shown in Fig. 15.6. The potential due to the second charge will be given by an expression similar to that in Eq. (15.58), except that the signs of q and $\cos\theta$ must be reversed (the angle opposite r_2 in the figure is $\pi - \theta$). We now have

$$\psi = \frac{q}{4\pi\varepsilon_0} \left(\frac{1}{r_1} - \frac{1}{r_2}\right)$$

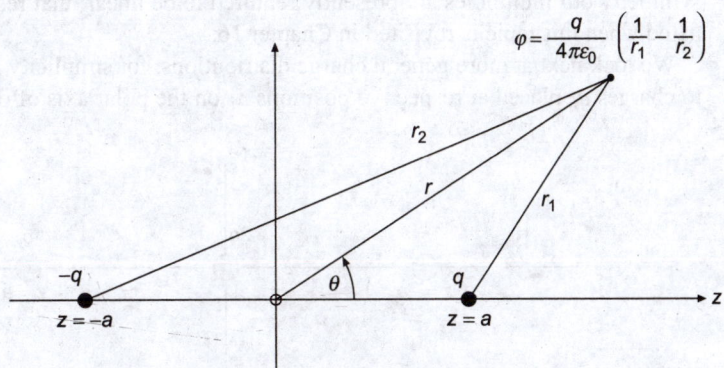

$$\varphi = \frac{q}{4\pi\varepsilon_0} \left(\frac{1}{r_1} - \frac{1}{r_2}\right)$$

FIGURE 15.6   Electric dipole.

$$= \frac{q}{4\pi\varepsilon_0 r}\left[\left(1 - 2\frac{a}{r}\cos\theta + \frac{a^2}{r^2}\right)^{-1/2} - \left(1 + 2\frac{a}{r}\cos\theta + \frac{a^2}{r^2}\right)^{-1/2}\right]$$

$$= \frac{q}{4\pi\varepsilon_0 r}\left[\sum_{n=0}^{\infty} P_n(\cos\theta)\left(\frac{a}{r}\right)^n - \sum_{n=0}^{\infty} P_n(\cos\theta)\left(-\frac{a}{r}\right)^n\right]. \tag{15.64}$$

If we combine the two summations in Eq. (15.64), alternate terms cancel, and we get

$$\psi = \frac{2q}{4\pi\varepsilon_0 r}\left[\frac{a}{r}P_1(\cos\theta) + \frac{a^3}{r^3}P_3(\cos\theta) + \cdots\right]. \tag{15.65}$$

This configuration of charges is called an **electric dipole**, and we note that its leading dependence on r goes as r^{-2}. The strength of the dipole (called the **dipole moment**) can be identified as $2qa$, equal to the magnitude of each charge multiplied by their separation $(2a)$. If we let $a \to 0$ while keeping the product $2qa$ constant at a value μ, all but the first term becomes negligible, and we have

$$\psi = \frac{\mu}{4\pi\varepsilon_0}\frac{P_1(\cos\theta)}{r^2}, \tag{15.66}$$

the potential of a **point dipole** of dipole moment μ, located at the origin of the coordinate system (at $r = 0$). Note that because we have limited the discussion to situations of cylindrical symmetry, our dipole is oriented in the polar direction; more general orientations can be considered after we have developed formulas for solutions of the associated Legendre equation (cases where the parameter m in Eq. (15.4) is nonzero).

We can extend the above analysis by combining a pair of dipoles of opposite orientation, for example, in the configuration shown in Fig. 15.7, thereby causing cancellation of their leading terms, leaving a potential whose leading contribution will be proportional to $r^{-3}P_2(\cos\theta)$. A charge configuration of this sort is called an **electric quadrupole**, and the P_2 term of the generating function expansion can be identified as the contribution of a **point quadrupole**, also located at $r = 0$. Further extensions, to 2^n-poles, with contributions proportional to $P_n(\cos\theta)/r^{n+1}$, permit us to identify each term of the generating expansion with the potential of a point multipole. We thus have a **multipole expansion**. Again we observe that because we have limited discussion to situations with cylindrical symmetry our multipoles are presently required to be linear; that restriction will be eliminated when this topic is revisited in Chapter 16.

We look next at more general charge distributions, for simplicity limiting consideration to charges q_i placed at respective positions a_i on the polar axis of our coordinate system.

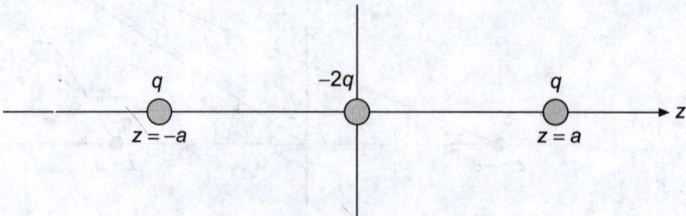

FIGURE 15.7   Linear electric quadrupole.

Adding together the generating-function expansions of the individual charges, our combined expansion takes the form

$$\psi = \frac{1}{4\pi\varepsilon_0 r}\left[\sum_i q_i + \sum_i \frac{q_i a_i}{r}P_1(\cos\theta) + \sum_i \frac{q_i a_i^2}{r^2}P_2(\cos\theta) + \cdots\right]$$

$$= \frac{1}{4\pi\varepsilon_0 r}\left[\mu_0 + \frac{\mu_1}{r}P_1(\cos\theta) + \frac{\mu_2}{r^2}P_2(\cos\theta) + \cdots\right], \tag{15.67}$$

where the μ_i are called the **multipole moments** of the charge distribution; μ_0 is the 2^0-pole, or **monopole** moment, with a value equal to the total net charge of the distribution; μ_1 is the 2^1-pole, or dipole moment, equal to $\sum_i q_i a_i$; μ_2 is the 2^2-pole, or quadrupole moment, given as $\sum_i q_i a_i^2$, etc. Our general (linear) multipole expansion will converge for values of r that are larger than all the a_i values of the individual charges. Put another way, the expansion will converge at points further from the coordinate origin than all parts of the charge distribution.

We next ask: What happens if we move the origin of our coordinate system? Or, equivalently, consider replacing r by $|\mathbf{r} - \mathbf{r_p}|$. For $r > r_p$, the binomial expansion of $1/|\mathbf{r} - \mathbf{r_p}|^n$ will have the generic form

$$\frac{1}{|\mathbf{r} - \mathbf{r_p}|^n} = \frac{1}{r^n} + C\frac{r_p}{r^{n+1}} + \cdots,$$

with the result that only the leading nonzero term of Eq. (15.67) will be unaffected by the change of expansion center. Translated into everyday language, this means that the lowest nonzero moment of the expansion will be independent of the choice of origin, but all higher moments will change when the expansion center is moved. Specifically, the total net charge (monopole moment) will always be independent of the choice of expansion center. The dipole moment will be independent of the expansion point only when the net charge is zero; the quadrupole moment will have such independence only if both the net charge and dipole moments vanish, etc.

We close this section with three observations.

- First, while we have illustrated our discussion with discrete arrays of point charges, we could have reached the same conclusions using continuous charge distributions, with the result that the summations over charges would become integrals over the **charge density**.

- Second, if we remove our restriction to linear arrays, our expansion would involve components of the multipole moments in different directions. In three-dimensional space, the dipole moment would have three components: a generalizes to (a_x, a_y, a_z), while the higher-order multipoles will have larger numbers of components ($a^2 \rightarrow a_x a_x, a_x a_y, \ldots$). The details of that analysis will be taken up when the necessary background is in place.

- Third, the multipole expansion is not restricted to electrical phenomena, but applies anywhere we have an inverse-square force. For example, planetary configurations are described in terms of mass multipoles. And gravitational radiation depends on the time behavior of mass quadrupoles.

Exercises

15.3.1 Develop the electrostatic potential for the array of charges shown in Fig. 15.7. This is a linear electric quadrupole.

15.3.2 Calculate the electrostatic potential of the array of charges shown in Fig. 15.8. Here is an example of two equal but oppositely directed quadrupoles. The quadrupole contributions cancel. The octopole terms do not cancel.

15.3.3 Show that the electrostatic potential produced by a charge q at $z = a$ for $r < a$ is

$$\varphi(\mathbf{r}) = \frac{q}{4\pi\varepsilon_0 a} \sum_{n=0}^{\infty} \left(\frac{r}{a}\right)^n P_n(\cos\theta).$$

15.3.4 Using $\mathbf{E} = -\nabla\varphi$, determine the components of the electric field corresponding to the (pure) electric dipole potential,

$$\varphi(\mathbf{r}) = \frac{2aq\,P_1(\cos\theta)}{4\pi\varepsilon_0 r^2}.$$

Here it is assumed that $r \gg a$.

$$ANS. \quad E_r = +\frac{4aq\cos\theta}{4\pi\varepsilon_0 r^3}, \quad E_\theta = +\frac{2aq\sin\theta}{4\pi\varepsilon_0 r^3}, \quad E_\varphi = 0.$$

15.3.5 Operating in **spherical polar coordinates**, show that

$$\frac{\partial}{\partial z}\left[\frac{P_l(\cos\theta)}{r^{l+1}}\right] = -(l+1)\frac{P_{l+1}(\cos\theta)}{r^{l+2}}.$$

This is the key step in the mathematical argument that the derivative of one multipole leads to the next higher multipole.

Hint. Compare with Exercise 3.10.28.

15.3.6 A point electric dipole of strength $p^{(1)}$ is placed at $z = a$; a second point electric dipole of equal but opposite strength is at the origin. Keeping the product $p^{(1)}a$ constant, let $a \to 0$. Show that this results in a point electric quadrupole.

Hint. Exercise 15.3.5 (when proved) will be helpful.

15.3.7 A point electric octopole may be constructed by placing a point electric quadrupole (pole strength $p^{(2)}$ in the z-direction) at $z = a$ and an equal but opposite point electric quadrupole at $z = 0$ and then letting $a \to 0$, subject to $p^{(2)}a = $ constant. Find the electrostatic potential corresponding to a point electric octopole. Show from the construction of the point electric octopole that the corresponding potential may be obtained by differentiating the point quadrupole potential.

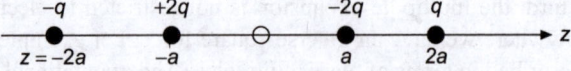

FIGURE 15.8   Linear electric octopole.

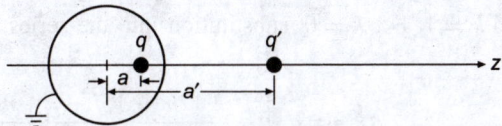

FIGURE 15.9   Image charges for Exercise 15.3.8.

15.3.8   A point charge q is in the interior of a hollow conducting sphere of radius r_0. The charge q is displaced a distance a from the center of the sphere. If the conducting sphere is grounded, show that the potential in the interior produced by q and the distributed induced charge is the same as that produced by q and its image charge q'. The image charge is at a distance $a' = r_0^2/a$ from the center, collinear with q and the origin (Fig. 15.9).

Hint. Calculate the electrostatic potential for $a < r_0 < a'$. Show that the potential vanishes for $r = r_0$ if we take $q' = -qr_0/a$.

15.4   ASSOCIATED LEGENDRE EQUATION

We need to extend our analysis to the associated Legendre equation because it is important to be able to remove the restriction to azimuthal symmetry that pervaded the discussion of the previous sections of this chapter. We therefore return to Eq. (15.4), which, before determining what its eigenvalue should be, assumed the form

$$(1 - x^2)P''(x) - 2xP'(x) + \left[\lambda - \frac{m^2}{1 - x^2}\right]P(x) = 0. \tag{15.68}$$

Trial and error (or great insight) suggests that the troublesome factor $1 - x^2$ in the denominator of this equation can be eliminated by making a substitution of the form $P = (1 - x^2)^p \mathcal{P}$, and further experimentation shows that a suitable choice for the exponent p is $m/2$. By straightforward differentiation, we find

$$P = (1 - x^2)^{m/2}\mathcal{P}, \tag{15.69}$$

$$P' = (1 - x^2)^{m/2}\mathcal{P}' - mx(1 - x^2)^{m/2-1}\mathcal{P}, \tag{15.70}$$

$$P'' = (1 - x^2)^{m/2}\mathcal{P}'' - 2mx(1 - x^2)^{m/2-1}\mathcal{P}'$$
$$+ \left[-m(1 - x^2)^{m/2-1} + (m^2 - 2m)x^2(1 - x^2)^{m/2-2}\right]\mathcal{P}. \tag{15.71}$$

Substitution of Eqs. (15.69)–(15.71) into Eq. (15.68), we obtain an equation that is potentially easier to solve, namely,

$$(1 - x^2)\mathcal{P}'' - 2x(m + 1)\mathcal{P}' + \left[\lambda - m(m + 1)\right]\mathcal{P} = 0. \tag{15.72}$$

We continue by seeking to solve Eq. (15.72) by the method of Frobenius, assuming a solution in the series form $\sum_j a_j x^{k+j}$. The indicial equation for this ODE has solutions

$k = 0$ and $k = 1$. For $k = 0$, substitution into the series solution leads to the recurrence formula

$$a_{j+2} = a_j \left[\frac{j^2 + (2m + 1)j - \lambda + m(m + 1)}{(j + 1)(j + 2)} \right]. \tag{15.73}$$

Just as for the original Legendre equation, we need solutions $\mathcal{P}(\cos\theta)$ that are nonsingular for the range $-1 \le \cos\theta \le +1$, but the recurrence formula leads to a power series that in general is divergent at ± 1.[2]

To avoid the divergence, we must cause the numerator of the fraction in Eq. (15.73) to become zero for some nonnegative even integer j, thereby causing $\mathcal{P}$ to be a polynomial. By direct substitution into Eq. (15.73), we can verify that a zero numerator is obtained for $j = l - m$ when λ is assigned the value $l(l + 1)$, a condition that can only be met if l is an integer at least as large as m and of the same parity. Further analysis for the other indicial equation solution, $k = 1$, extends our present result to values of l that are larger than m and of opposite parity.

Summarizing our results to this point, we have found that the regular solutions to the associated Legendre equation depend on integer indices l and m. Letting P_l^m, called an **associated Legendre function**, denote such a solution (note that the superscript m is **not** an exponent), we define

$$P_l^m(x) = (1 - x^2)^{m/2} \mathcal{P}_l^m(x), \tag{15.74}$$

where $\mathcal{P}_l^m$ is a polynomial of degree $l - m$ (consistent with our earlier observation that l must be at least as large as m), and with an explicit form and scale that we will now address.

A convenient explicit formula for $\mathcal{P}_l^m$ can be obtained by repeated differentiation of the regular Legendre equation. Admittedly, this strategy would have been difficult to devise without prior knowledge of the solution, but there are certain advantages to using the experience of those who have gone before. So, without apology, we apply Leibniz's formula for the mth derivative of a product (proved in Exercise 1.4.2),

$$\frac{d^m}{dx^m} \left[A(x) B(x) \right] = \sum_{s=0}^{m} \binom{m}{s} \frac{d^{m-s} A(x)}{dx^{m-s}} \frac{d^s B(x)}{dx^s}, \tag{15.75}$$

to the Legendre equation,

$$(1 - x^2) P_l'' - 2x P_l' + l(l + 1) P_l = 0,$$

reaching

$$(1 - x^2) u'' - 2x(m + 1)u' + \left[l(l + 1) - m(m + 1) \right] u = 0, \tag{15.76}$$

where

$$u \equiv \frac{d^m}{dx^m} P_l(x). \tag{15.77}$$

---

[2]The solution to the associated Legendre equation is $(1 - x^2)^{m/2} \mathcal{P}(x)$, suggesting the possibility that the $(1 - x^2)^{m/2}$ factor might compensate the divergence in $\mathcal{P}(x)$, yielding a convergent limit. It can be shown that such a compensation does not occur.

Comparing Eq. (15.76) with Eq. (15.72), we see that when $\lambda = l(l+1)$ they are identical, meaning that the polynomial solutions $\mathcal{P}$ of Eq. (15.72) for given l can be identified with the corresponding u. Specifically,

$$\mathcal{P}_l^m = (-1)^m \frac{d^m}{dx^m} P_l(x), \tag{15.78}$$

where the factor $(-1)^m$ is inserted to maintain agreement with AMS-55 (see Additional Readings), which has become the most widely accepted notational standard.[3]

We can now write a complete, explicit form for the associated Legendre functions:

$$P_l^m(x) = (-1)^m (1 - x^2)^{m/2} \frac{d^m}{dx^m} P_l(x). \tag{15.79}$$

Since the P_l^m with $m = 0$ are just the original Legendre functions, it is customary to omit the upper index when it is zero, so, for example, $P_l^0 \equiv P_l$.

Note that the condition on l and m can be stated in two ways:

(1)   For each m, there are an infinite number of acceptable solutions to the associated Legendre ODE with l values ranging from m to infinity, or

(2)   For each l, there are acceptable solutions with m values ranging from $l = 0$ to $l = m$.

Because m enters the associated Legendre equation only as m^2, we have up to this point tacitly considered only values $m \geq 0$. However, if we insert the Rodrigues formula for P_l into Eq. (15.73), we get the formula

$$P_l^m(x) = \frac{(-1)^m}{2^l \, l!} (1 - x^2)^{m/2} \frac{d^{l+m}}{dx^{l+m}} (x^2 - 1)^l, \tag{15.80}$$

which gives results for $-m$ that do not appear similar to those for $+m$. However, it can be shown that if we apply Eq. (15.75) for m values between zero and $-l$, we get

$$P_l^{-m}(x) = (-1)^m \frac{(l-m)!}{(l+m)!} P_l^m(x). \tag{15.81}$$

Equation (15.81) shows that P_l^m and P_l^{-m} are proportional; its proof is the topic of Exercise 15.4.3. The main reason for discussing both is that recurrence formulas we will develop for P_l^m with contiguous values of m will give results for $m < 0$ that can best be understood if we remember the relative scaling of P_l^m and P_l^{-m}.

Associated Legendre Polynomials

For further development of properties of the P_l^m, it is useful to develop a generating function for the polynomials $\mathcal{P}_l^m(x)$, which we can do by differentiating the Legendre generating function with respect to x. The result is

$$g_m(x, t) \equiv \frac{(-1)^m (2m - 1)!!}{(1 - 2xt + t^2)^{m+1/2}} = \sum_{s=0}^{\infty} \mathcal{P}_{s+m}^m(x) t^s. \tag{15.82}$$

---

[3]However, we note that the popular text, Jackson's *Electrodynamics* (see Additional Readings), does not include this phase factor. The factor is introduced to cause the definition of spherical harmonics (Section 15.5) to have the usual phase convention.

The factors t that result from differentiating the generating function have been used to change the powers of t that multiply the $\mathcal{P}$ on the right-hand side.

If we now differentiate Eq. (15.82) with respect to t, we obtain initially

$$(1 - 2tx + t^2)\frac{\partial g_m}{\partial t} = (2m + 1)(x - t)g_m(x, t),$$

which we can use together with Eq. (15.82) in a now-familiar way to obtain the recurrence formula,

$$(s + 1)\mathcal{P}_{s+m+1}^m(x) - (2m + 1 + 2s)x\mathcal{P}_{s+m}^m(x) + (s + 2m)\mathcal{P}_{s+m-1}^m = 0. \qquad (15.83)$$

Making the substitution $l = s + m$, we bring Eq. (15.83) to the more useful form,

$$(l - m + 1)\mathcal{P}_{l+1}^m - (2l + 1)x\mathcal{P}_l^m + (l + m)\mathcal{P}_{l-1}^m = 0. \qquad (15.84)$$

For $m = 0$ this relation agrees with Eq. (15.18).

From the form of $g_m(x, t)$, it is also clear that

$$(1 - 2xt + t^2)g_{m+1}(x, t) = -(2m + 1)g_m(x, t). \qquad (15.85)$$

From Eqs. (15.85) and (15.82) we may extract the recursion formula

$$\mathcal{P}_{s+m+1}^{m+1}(x) - 2x\mathcal{P}_{s+m}^{m+1}(x) + \mathcal{P}_{s+m-1}^{m+1}(x) = -(2m + 1)\mathcal{P}_{s+m}^m(x),$$

which relates the associated Legendre polynomials with upper index $m + 1$ to those with upper index m. Again we may simplify by making the substitution $l = s + m$:

$$\mathcal{P}_{l+1}^{m+1}(x) - 2x\mathcal{P}_l^{m+1}(x) + \mathcal{P}_{l-1}^{m+1}(x) = -(2m + 1)\mathcal{P}_l^m(x). \qquad (15.86)$$

Associated Legendre Functions

The recurrence relations for the associated Legendre polynomials or alternatively, differentiation of formulas for the original Legendre polynomials, enable the construction of recurrence formulas for the associated Legendre functions. The number of such formulas is extensive because these functions have two indices, and there exists a wide variety of formulas with different index combinations. Results of importance include the following:

$$P_l^{m+1}(x) + \frac{2mx}{(1 - x^2)^{1/2}}P_l^m(x) + (l + m)(l - m + 1)P_l^{m-1}(x) = 0, \qquad (15.87)$$

$$(2l + 1)xP_l^m(x) = (l + m)P_{l-1}^m(x) + (l - m + 1)P_{l+1}^m(x), \qquad (15.88)$$

$$(2l + 1)(1 - x^2)^{1/2}P_l^m(x) = P_{l-1}^{m+1}(x) - P_{l+1}^{m+1}(x) \qquad (15.89)$$

$$= (l - m + 1)(l - m + 2)P_{l+1}^{m-1}(x)$$

$$- (l + m)(l + m - 1)P_{l-1}^{m-1}(x), \qquad (15.90)$$

$$(1 - x^2)^{1/2}\left(P_l^m(x)\right)' = \frac{1}{2}(l + m)(l - m + 1)P_l^{m-1}(x) - \frac{1}{2}P_l^{m+1}(x), \qquad (15.91)$$

$$= (l + m)(l - m + 1)P_l^{m-1}(x) + \frac{mx}{(1 - x^2)^{1/2}}P_l^m(x). \qquad (15.92)$$

Table 15.3 Associated Legendre Functions

$$P_1^1(x) = -(1 - x^2)^{1/2} = -\sin\theta$$

$$P_2^1(x) = -3x(1 - x^2)^{1/2} = -3\cos\theta\sin\theta$$

$$P_2^2(x) = 3(1 - x^2) = 3\sin^2\theta$$

$$P_3^1(x) = -\tfrac{3}{2}(5x^2 - 1)(1 - x^2)^{1/2} = -\tfrac{3}{2}(5\cos^2\theta - 1)\sin\theta$$

$$P_3^2(x) = 15x(1 - x^2) = 15\cos\theta\sin^2\theta$$

$$P_3^3(x) = -15(1 - x^2)^{3/2} = -15\sin^3\theta$$

$$P_4^1(x) = -\tfrac{5}{2}(7x^3 - 3x)(1 - x^2)^{1/2} = -\tfrac{5}{2}(7\cos^3\theta - 3\cos\theta)\sin\theta$$

$$P_4^2(x) = \tfrac{15}{2}(7x^2 - 1)(1 - x^2) = \tfrac{15}{2}(7\cos^2\theta - 1)\sin^2\theta$$

$$P_4^3(x) = -105x(1 - x^2)^{3/2} = -105\cos\theta\sin^3\theta$$

$$P_4^4(x) = 105(1 - x^2)^2 = 105\sin^4\theta$$

It is obvious that, using Eq. (15.90), all the P_l^m with $m > 0$ can be generated from those with $m = 0$ (the Legendre polynomials), and that these, in turn, can be built recursively from $P_0(x) = 1$ and $P_1(x) = x$. In this fashion (or in other ways as suggested below), we can build a table of associated Legendre functions, the first members of which are listed in Table 15.3. The table shows the $P_l^m(x)$ both as functions of x and as functions of θ, where $x = \cos\theta$.

It is often easier to use recurrence formulas other than Eq. (15.90) to obtain the P_l^m, keeping in mind that when a formula contains P_{m-1}^m for $m > 0$, that quantity can be set to zero. It is also easy to obtain explicit formulas for certain values of l and m which can then be alternate starting points for recursion. See the example that follows.

Example 15.4.1 RECURRENCE STARTING FROM P_m^m

The associated Legendre function $P_m^m(x)$ is easily evaluated:

$$P_m^m(x) = \frac{(-1)^m}{2^m m!}(1 - x^2)^{m/2}\frac{d^{2m}}{dx^{2m}}(x^2 - 1)^m = \frac{(-1)^m}{2^m m!}(2m)!\,(1 - x^2)^{m/2}$$

$$= (-1)^m(2m - 1)!!\,(1 - x^2)^{m/2}. \tag{15.93}$$

We can now use Eq. (15.88) with $l = m$ to obtain P_{m+1}^m, dropping the term containing P_{m-1}^m because it is zero. We get

$$P_{m+1}^m(x) = (2m + 1)x P_m^m(x) = (-1)^m(2m + 1)!!\,x(1 - x^2)^{m/2}. \tag{15.94}$$

Further increases in l can now be obtained by straightforward application of Eq. (15.88).

Illustrating for a series of P_l^m with $m = 2$: $P_2^2(x) = (-1)^2(3!!)(1 - x^2) = 3(1 - x^2)$, in agreement with the table value. P_3^2 can be computed from Eq. (15.94) as $P_3^2(x) = (-1)^2(5!!)x(1 - x^2)$, which simplifies to the tabulated result. Finally, P_4^2 is obtained from the following case of Eq. (15.88):

$$7x P_3^2(x) = 5 P_2^2(x) + 2 P_4^2(x),$$

the solution of which for $P_4^2(x)$ is again in agreement with the tabulated value.   ∎

Parity and Special Values

We have already established that P_l has even parity if l is even and odd parity if l is odd. Since we can form P_l^m by differentiating P_l m times, with each differentiation changing the parity, and thereafter multiplying by $(1 - x^2)^{m/2}$, which has even parity, P_l^m must have a parity that depends on $l + m$, namely,

$$P_l^m(-x) = (-1)^{l+m} P_l^m(x). \tag{15.95}$$

We occasionally encounter a need for the value of $P_l^m(x)$ at $x = \pm 1$ or at $x = 0$. At $x = \pm 1$ the result is simple: The factor $(1 - x^2)^{m/2}$ causes $P_l^m(\pm 1)$ to vanish unless $m = 0$, in which case we recover the values $P_l(1) = 1$, $P_l(-1) = (-1)^l$. At $x = 0$, the value of P_l^m depends on whether $l + m$ is even or odd. The result, proof of which is left to Exercises 15.4.4 and 15.4.5, is

$$P_l^m(0) = \begin{cases} (-1)^{(l+m)/2} \dfrac{(l+m-1)!!}{(l-m)!!}, & l+m \text{ even}, \\ 0, & l+m \text{ odd}. \end{cases} \tag{15.96}$$

Orthogonality

For each m, the P_l^m of different l can be proved orthogonal by identifying them as eigenfunctions of a Sturm-Liouville system. However, it is instructive to demonstrate the orthogonality explicitly, and to do so by a method that also yields their normalization. We start by writing the orthogonality integral, with the P_l^m given by the Rodrigues formula in Eq. (15.80). For compactness and clarity, we introduce the abbreviated notation $R = x^2 - 1$, thereby getting

$$\int_{-1}^{1} P_p^m(x) P_q^m(x)\, dx = \frac{(-1)^m}{2^{p+q}\, p!\, q!} \int_{-1}^{1} R^m \left(\frac{d^{p+m} R^p}{dx^{p+m}} \right) \left(\frac{d^{q+m} R^q}{dx^{q+m}} \right) dx. \tag{15.97}$$

We consider first the case $p < q$, for which we plan to prove the integral in Eq. (15.97) vanishes. We proceed by carrying out repeated integrations by parts, in which we differentiate

$$u = R^m \left(\frac{d^{p+m} R^p}{dx^{p+m}} \right) \tag{15.98}$$

$p + m + 1$ times while integrating a like number of times the remainder of the integrand,

$$dv = \left(\frac{d^{q+m} R^q}{dx^{q+m}} \right) dx. \tag{15.99}$$

For each of these $p + m + 1 \leq q + m$ partial integrations the integrated (uv) terms will vanish because there will be at least one factor R that is not differentiated and will therefore vanish at $x = \pm 1$. After the repeated differentiation, we will have

$$\frac{d^{p+m+1}}{dx^{p+m+1}} u = \frac{d^{p+m+1}}{dx^{p+m+1}} \left[R^m \left(\frac{d^{p+m} R^p}{dx^{p+m}} \right) \right], \tag{15.100}$$

in which a quantity whose largest power of x is x^{2p+2m} contains also a $(2p + 2m + 1)$-fold differentiation. There is no way these components can yield a nonzero result. Since both the integrated terms and the transformed integral vanish, we get an overall vanishing result, confirming the orthogonality. Note that the orthogonality is with unit weight, independent of the value of m.

We now examine Eq. (15.97) for $p = q$, repeating the process we just carried out, but this time performing $p + m$ partial integrations. Again all the integrated terms vanish, but now there is a nonvanishing contribution from the repeated differentiation of u, see Eq. (15.98). Since the overall power of x is still x^{2p+2m} and the total number of differentiations is also $2p + 2m$, the only contributing terms are those in which the factor R^m is differentiated $2m$ times and the factor R^p is differentiated $2p$ times. Thus, applying Leibniz's formula, Eq. (15.75), to the $p + m$-fold differentiation of u, but keeping only the contributing term, we have

$$\frac{d^{p+m}}{dx^{p+m}} \left[R^m \left(\frac{d^{p+m} R^p}{dx^{p+m}} \right) \right] = \binom{p+m}{2m} \left(\frac{d^{2m} R^m}{dx^{2m}} \right) \left(\frac{d^{2p} R^p}{dx^{2p}} \right),$$
$$= \frac{(p+m)!}{(2m)! \, (p-m)!} (2m)! \, (2p)! = \frac{(p+m)!}{(p-m)!} (2p)!. \tag{15.101}$$

Inserting this result into the integration by parts, remembering that the transformed integration is accompanied by the sign factor $(-1)^{p+m}$, and recognizing that the repeated integration of dv, Eq. (15.99) with $q = p$, just yields R^p, we have, returning to Eq. (15.97),

$$\int_{-1}^{1} \left[P_p^m(x) \right]^2 dx = \frac{(-1)^{2m+p}}{2^{2p} \, p! \, p!} \frac{(p+m)!}{(p-m)!} (2p)! \int_{-1}^{1} R^p \, dx. \tag{15.102}$$

To complete the evaluation, we identify the integral of R^p as a beta function, with an evaluation given in Exercise 13.3.3 as

$$\int_{-1}^{1} R^p \, dx = (-1)^p \frac{2(2p)!!}{(2p+1)!!} = (-1)^p \frac{2^{2p+1} p! \, p!}{(2p+1)!}. \tag{15.103}$$

Inserting this result, and combining with the previously established orthogonality relation, we have

$$\int_{-1}^{1} P_p^m(x) P_q^m(x) \, dx = \frac{2}{2p+1} \frac{(p+m)!}{(p-m)!} \delta_{pq}. \tag{15.104}$$

Making the substitution $x = \cos\theta$, we obtain this formula in spherical polar coordinates:

$$\int_0^\pi P_p^m(\cos\theta) P_q^m(\cos\theta) \sin\theta \, d\theta = \frac{2}{2p+1} \frac{(p+m)!}{(p-m)!} \delta_{pq}. \tag{15.105}$$

Another way to look at the orthogonality of the associated Legendre functions is to rewrite Eq. (15.104) in terms of the associated Legendre polynomials $\mathcal{P}_l^m$. Invoking Eq. (15.74), Eq. (15.104) becomes

$$\int_{-1}^1 \mathcal{P}_p^m \mathcal{P}_q^m (1-x^2)^m dx = \frac{2}{2p+1} \frac{(p+m)!}{(p-m)!} \delta_{pq}, \tag{15.106}$$

showing that these **polynomials** are, for each m, orthogonal with the weight factor $(1 - x^2)^m$. From that viewpoint, we can observe that each value of m corresponds to a set of polynomials that are orthogonal with a different weight. However, since our main interest is in the functions that are in general **not** polynomials but are solutions of the associated Legendre equation, it is usually more relevant to us to note that these functions, which include the factor $(1 - x^2)^{m/2}$, are orthogonal **with unit weight**.

It is possible, but not particularly useful, to note that we can also have orthogonality of the P_l^m with respect to the upper index when the lower index is held constant:

$$\int_{-1}^1 P_l^m(x) P_l^n(x)(1-x^2)^{-1} dx = \frac{(l+m)!}{m(l-m)!} \delta_{mn}. \tag{15.107}$$

This equation is not very useful because in spherical polar coordinates the boundary condition on the azimuthal coordinate φ causes there already to be orthogonality with respect to m, and we are not usually concerned with orthogonality of the P_l^m with respect to m.

Example 15.4.2   CURRENT LOOP—MAGNETIC DIPOLE

An important problem in which we encounter associated Legendre functions is in the magnetic field of a circular current loop, a situation that may at first seem surprising since this problem has azimuthal symmetry.

Our starting point is the formula relating a current element $I d\mathbf{s}$ to the vector potential $\mathbf{A}$ that it produces (this is discussed in the chapter on Green's functions, and also in texts such as Jackson's *Classical Electrodynamics*; see Additional Readings). This formula is

$$d\mathbf{A}(\mathbf{r}) = \frac{\mu_0}{4\pi} \frac{I d\mathbf{s}}{|\mathbf{r} - \mathbf{r_s}|}, \tag{15.108}$$

where $\mathbf{r}$ is the point at which $\mathbf{A}$ is to be evaluated and $\mathbf{r}_s$ is the position of element ds of the current loop. We place our current loop, of radius a, in the equatorial plane of a spherical polar coordinate system, as shown in Fig. 15.10. Our task is to determine $\mathbf{A}$ as a function of position, and therefrom to obtain the components of the magnetic induction field $\mathbf{B}$.

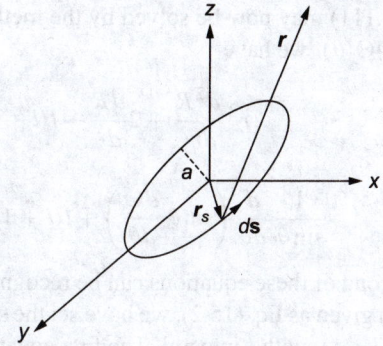

FIGURE 15.10   Circular current loop.

It is in principle possible to figure out the geometry and integrate Eq. (15.108) for the present problem, but a more practical approach will be to determine from general considerations the functional form of an expansion describing the solution, and then to determine the coefficients in the expansion by requiring correct results for points of high symmetry, where the calculation is not too difficult. This is an approach similar to that employed in Example 15.2.3, where we first identified the functional form of an expansion giving the potential generated by a circular ring of charge, after which we found the coefficients in the expansion from the easily computed potential on the axis of the ring.

From the form of Eq. (15.108) and the symmetry of the problem, we see immediately that for all $\mathbf{r}$, $\mathbf{A}$ must lie in a plane of constant z, and in fact it must be in the $\hat{\mathbf{e}}_\varphi$ direction, with A_φ independent of φ, i.e.,

$$\mathbf{A} = A_\varphi(r, \theta)\,\hat{\mathbf{e}}_\varphi. \tag{15.109}$$

If $\mathbf{A}$ had a component other than A_φ, it would have a nonzero divergence, as then $\mathbf{A}$ would have a nonzero inward or outward flux, resulting in a singularity on the axis of the loop.

Since everywhere except on the current loop itself there is no current, Maxwell's equation for the curl of $\mathbf{B}$ reduces to

$$\nabla \times \mathbf{B} = \nabla \times (\nabla \times \mathbf{A}) = 0,$$

and, since $\mathbf{A}$ has only a φ component, it further reduces to

$$\nabla \times \left[\nabla \times A_\varphi(r, \theta)\,\hat{\mathbf{e}}_\varphi\right] = 0. \tag{15.110}$$

The left-hand side of Eq. (15.110) was the subject of Example 3.10.4, and its evaluation was presented as Eq. (3.165). Setting that result to zero gives the equation that must be satisfied by $A_\varphi(r, \theta)$:

$$\frac{\partial^2 A_\varphi}{\partial r^2} + \frac{2}{r}\frac{\partial A_\varphi}{\partial r} + \frac{1}{r^2\sin\theta}\frac{\partial}{\partial\theta}\left(\sin\theta\frac{\partial A_\varphi}{\partial\theta}\right) - \frac{1}{r^2\sin^2\theta}A_\varphi = 0. \tag{15.111}$$

Equation (15.111) may now be solved by the method of separation of variables; setting $A_\varphi(r,\theta) = R(r)\Theta(\theta)$, we have

$$r^2 \frac{d^2R}{dr^2} + 2\frac{dR}{dr} - l(l+1)R = 0, \tag{15.112}$$

$$\frac{1}{\sin\theta}\frac{d}{d\theta}\left(\sin\theta\frac{d\Theta}{d\theta}\right) + l(l+1)\Theta - \frac{\Theta}{\sin^2\theta} = 0. \tag{15.113}$$

Because the second of these equations can be recognized as the associated Legendre equation, in the form given as Eq. (15.2), we have set the separation constant to the value it must have, namely $l(l+1)$, with l integral. The first equation is also familiar, with solutions for a given l being r^l and r^{-l-1}. The second equation has solutions $P_l^1(\cos\theta)$, i.e., its specific form dictates that the associated Legendre functions which solve it must have upper index $m = 1$. Since our main interest is in the pattern of $\mathbf{B}$ at r values larger than a, the radius of the current loop, we retain only the radial solution r^{-l-1}, and write

$$A_\varphi(r,\theta) = \sum_{l=1}^{\infty} c_l \left(\frac{a}{r}\right)^{l+1} P_l^1(\cos\theta). \tag{15.114}$$

When we obtain a more detailed solution, we will find that it converges only for $r > a$, so Eq. (15.114) and the value of $\mathbf{B}$ derived therefrom will only be valid outside a sphere containing the current loop. If we were also interested in solving this problem for $r < a$, we would need to construct a series solution using only the powers r^l.

From Eq. (15.114) we can compute the components of $\mathbf{B}$. Clearly, $B_\varphi = 0$. And, using Eq. (3.159), we have

$$B_r(r,\theta) = \nabla \times A_\varphi\,\hat{\mathbf{e}}_\varphi\Big|_r = \frac{\cot\theta}{r} A_\varphi + \frac{1}{r}\frac{\partial A_\varphi}{\partial\theta}, \tag{15.115}$$

$$B_\theta(r,\theta) = \nabla \times A_\varphi\,\hat{\mathbf{e}}_\varphi\Big|_\theta = -\frac{1}{r}\frac{\partial(rA_\varphi)}{\partial r}. \tag{15.116}$$

To evaluate the θ derivative in Eq. (15.115), we need

$$\frac{dP_l^1(\cos\theta)}{d\theta} = -\sin\theta\frac{dP_l^1(\cos\theta)}{d\cos\theta} = -l(l+1)P_l(\cos\theta) - \cot\theta P_l^1(\cos\theta), \tag{15.117}$$

a special case of Eq. (15.92) with $m = 1$ and $x = \cos\theta$. It is now straightforward to insert the expansion for A_φ into Eqs. (15.115) and (15.116); because of Eq. (15.117) the $\cot\theta$ term of Eq. (15.115) cancels, and we reach

$$B_r(r,\theta) = -\frac{1}{r}\sum_{l=1}^{\infty} l(l+1)\,c_l\left(\frac{a}{r}\right)^{l+1} P_l(\cos\theta), \tag{15.118}$$

$$B_\theta(r,\theta) = \frac{1}{r}\sum_{l=1}^{\infty} l\,c_l\left(\frac{a}{r}\right)^{l+1} P_l^1(\cos\theta). \tag{15.119}$$

To complete our analysis, we must determine the values of the c_l, which we do by using the Biot-Savart law to calculate B_r at points along the polar axis, where B_r is synonymous with B_z. Since $\theta = 0$ on the positive polar axis and $P_l(\cos\theta) = 1$, Eq. (15.118) reduces to

$$B_r(z,0) = -\frac{1}{z}\sum_{l=1}^{\infty} l(l+1)c_l\left(\frac{a}{z}\right)^{l+1} = -\frac{a^2}{z^3}\sum_{s=0}^{\infty}(s+1)(s+2)c_{s+1}\left(\frac{a}{z}\right)^s. \quad (15.120)$$

The symmetry of the problem permits one more simplification; the value of B_z must be the same at $-z$ as at z, from which we conclude that the coefficients $c_2, c_4, \ldots$ must all vanish, and we can rewrite Eq. (15.120) as

$$B_r(z,0) = -\frac{a^2}{z^3}\sum_{s=0}^{\infty} 2(s+1)(2s+1)c_{2s+1}\left(\frac{a}{z}\right)^{2s}. \quad (15.121)$$

The Biot-Savart law (in SI units) gives the contribution from the current element $I\,ds$ to **B** at a point whose displacement from the current element is $\mathbf{r_s}$ as

$$d\mathbf{B} = \frac{\mu_0}{4\pi} I\,\frac{d\mathbf{s}\times\hat{\mathbf{r}}_s}{r_s^2}. \quad (15.122)$$

We now compute **B** by integration of ds around the current loop. The geometry is shown in Fig. 15.11. Note that dB_z, which will be the same for all current elements $I\,ds$, has the value

$$dB_z = \frac{\mu_0 I}{4\pi r_s^2}\sin\chi\,ds,$$

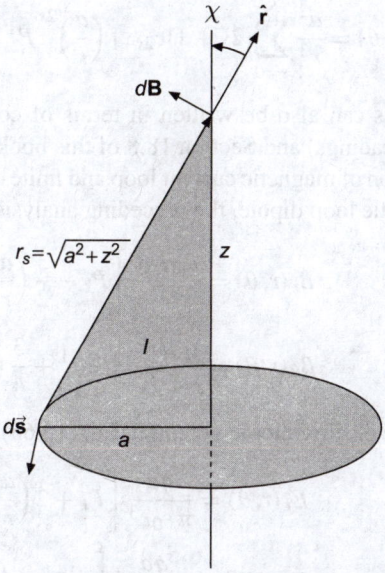

FIGURE 15.11   Biot-Savart law applied to a circular loop.

where χ is the labeled angle in Fig. 15.11 and r_s has the value indicated in the figure. The integration over s simply yields a factor $2\pi a$, and we see that $\sin\chi = a/(a^2 + z^2)^{1/2}$, so

$$
B_z = \frac{\mu_0 I a^2}{2}(a^2 + z^2)^{-3/2} = \frac{\mu_0 I a^2}{2z^3}\left(1 + \frac{a^2}{z^2}\right)^{-3/2}
$$

$$
= \frac{\mu_0 I a^2}{2z^3}\sum_{s=0}^{\infty}(-1)^s \frac{(2s+1)!!}{(2s)!!}\left(\frac{a}{z}\right)^{2s}. \tag{15.123}
$$

The binomial expansion in the second line of Eq. (15.123) is convergent for $z > a$.

We are now ready to reconcile Eqs. (15.121) and (15.123), finding that

$$
-2(s+1)(2s+1)c_{2s+1} = \frac{\mu_0 I}{2}(-1)^s \frac{(2s+1)!!}{(2s)!!},
$$

which reduces to

$$
c_{2s+1} = \frac{\mu_0 I}{2}(-1)^{s+1}\frac{(2s-1)!!}{(2s+2)!!}. \tag{15.124}
$$

We write final formulas for **A** and **B** in a form that recognizes that $c_{2s} = 0$, applicable for $r > a$:

$$
A_\varphi(r,\theta) = \frac{a^2}{r^2}\sum_{s=0}^{\infty}c_{2s+1}\left(\frac{a}{r}\right)^{2s} P_{2s+1}^1(\cos\theta), \tag{15.125}
$$

$$
B_r(r,\theta) = -\frac{a^2}{r^2}\sum_{s=0}^{\infty}(2s+1)(2s+2)c_{2s+1}\left(\frac{a}{r}\right)^{2s} P_{2s+1}(\cos\theta), \tag{15.126}
$$

$$
B_\theta(r,\theta) = \frac{a^2}{r^3}\sum_{s=0}^{\infty}(2s+1)c_{2s+1}\left(\frac{a}{r}\right)^{2s} P_{2s+1}^1(\cos\theta). \tag{15.127}
$$

These formulas can also be written in terms of complete elliptic integrals. See Smythe (Additional Readings) and Section 18.8 of this book.

A comparison of magnetic current loop and finite electric dipole fields may be of interest. For the magnetic loop dipole, the preceding analysis gives

$$
B_r(r,\theta) = \frac{\mu_0 I a^2}{2r^3}\left[P_1 - \frac{3}{2}\left(\frac{a}{r}\right)^2 P_3 + \cdots\right], \tag{15.128}
$$

$$
B_\theta(r,\theta) = \frac{\mu_0 I a^2}{4r^3}\left[-P_1^1 + \frac{3}{4}\left(\frac{a}{r}\right)^2 P_3^1 + \cdots\right]. \tag{15.129}
$$

From the finite electric dipole potential, Eq. (15.65), one can find

$$
E_r(r,\theta) = \frac{qa}{\pi\varepsilon_0 r^3}\left[P_1 + 2\left(\frac{a}{r}\right)^2 P_3 + \cdots\right], \tag{15.130}
$$

$$
E_\theta(r,\theta) = \frac{qa}{2\pi\varepsilon_0 r^3}\left[-P_1^1 - \left(\frac{a}{r}\right)^2 P_3^1 + \cdots\right]. \tag{15.131}
$$

The leading terms of both fields agree, and this is the basis for identifying both as dipole fields.

As with electric multipoles, it is sometimes convenient to discuss **point** magnetic multipoles. A point dipole can be formed by taking the limit $a \to 0$, $I \to \infty$, with Ia^2 held constant. The **magnetic moment m** is taken to be $I\pi a^2 \mathbf{n}$, where $\mathbf{n}$ is a unit vector perpendicular to the plane of the current loop and in the sense given by the right-hand rule. ∎

Exercises

15.4.1 Apply the Frobenius method to Eq. (15.72) to obtain Eq. (15.73) and verify that the numerator of that equation becomes zero if $\lambda = l(l+1)$ and $j = l - m$.

15.4.2 Starting from the entries for P_2^2 and P_2^1 in Table 15.3, apply a recurrence formula to obtain P_2^0 (which is P_2), P_2^{-1}, and P_2^{-2}. Compare your results with the value of P_2 from Table 15.1 and with values of P_2^{-1} and P_2^{-2} obtained by applying Eq. (15.81) to entries from Table 15.3.

15.4.3 Prove that

$$P_l^{-m}(x) = (-1)^m \frac{(l-m)!}{(l+m)!} P_l^m(x),$$

where $P_l^m(x)$ is defined by

$$P_l^m(x) = \frac{(-1)^m}{2^l l!} (1-x^2)^{m/2} \frac{d^{l+m}}{dx^{l+m}} (x^2-1)^l.$$

Hint. One approach is to apply Leibniz's formula to $(x+1)^l (x-1)^l$.

15.4.4 Show that

$$P_{2l}^1(0) = 0,$$

$$P_{2l+1}^1(0) = (-1)^{l+1} \frac{(2l+1)!!}{(2l)!!},$$

by each of these three methods:

(a) Use of recurrence relations,
(b) Expansion of the generating function,
(c) Rodrigues formula.

15.4.5 Evaluate $P_l^m(0)$ for $m > 0$.

$$\text{ANS.} \quad P_l^m(0) = \begin{cases} (-1)^{(l+m)/2} \dfrac{(l+m-1)!!}{(l-m)!!}, & l+m \text{ even}, \\[2mm] 0, & l+m \text{ odd}. \end{cases}$$

15.4.6 Starting from the potential of a finite dipole, Eq. (15.65), verify the formulas for the electric field components given as Eqs. (15.130) and (15.131).

15.4.7   Show that

$$P_l^l(\cos\theta) = (-1)^l (2l-1)!!\sin^l\theta, \quad l = 0, 1, 2, \ldots.$$

15.4.8   Derive the associated Legendre recurrence relation,

$$P_l^{m+1}(x) + \frac{2mx}{(1-x^2)^{1/2}} P_l^m(x) + \left[l(l+1) - m(m-1) \right] P_l^{m-1}(x) = 0.$$

15.4.9   Develop a recurrence relation that will yield $P_l^1(x)$ as

$$P_l^1(x) = f_1(x, l) P_l(x) + f_2(x, l) P_{l-1}(x).$$

Follow either of the procedures (a) or (b):

(a)   Derive a recurrence relation of the preceding form. Give $f_1(x, l)$ and $f_2(x, l)$ explicitly.

(b)   Find the appropriate recurrence relation in print.

(1)   Give the source.

(2)   Verify the recurrence relation.

$$ANS. \quad (a) \ P_l^1(x) = \frac{lx}{(1-x^2)^{1/2}} P_l - \frac{l}{(1-x^2)^{1/2}} P_{l-1}.$$

15.4.10   Show that $\sin\theta \dfrac{d}{d\cos\theta} P_n(\cos\theta) = P_n^1(\cos\theta)$.

15.4.11   Show that

(a) $$\int_0^\pi \left(\frac{dP_l^m}{d\theta} \frac{dP_{l'}^m}{d\theta} + \frac{m^2 P_l^m P_{l'}^m}{\sin^2\theta} \right) \sin\theta \, d\theta = \frac{2l(l+1)}{2l+1} \frac{(l+m)!}{(l-m)!} \delta_{ll'},$$

(b) $$\int_0^\pi \left(\frac{P_l^1}{\sin\theta} \frac{dP_{l'}^1}{d\theta} + \frac{P_{l'}^1}{\sin\theta} \frac{dP_l^1}{d\theta} \right) \sin\theta \, d\theta = 0.$$

These integrals occur in the theory of scattering of electromagnetic waves by spheres.

15.4.12   As a repeat of Exercise 15.2.9, show, using associated Legendre functions, that

$$\int_{-1}^1 x(1-x^2) P_n'(x) P_m'(x) \, dx = \frac{n+1}{2n+1} \frac{2}{2n-1} \frac{n!}{(n-2)!} \delta_{m,n-1}$$

$$+ \frac{n}{2n+1} \frac{2}{2n+3} \frac{(n+2)!}{n!} \delta_{m,n+1}.$$

15.4.13   Evaluate $\displaystyle\int_0^\pi \sin^2\theta \, P_n^1(\cos\theta) \, d\theta$.

15.4.14 The associated Legendre function $P_l^m(x)$ satisfies the self-adjoint ODE

$$(1 - x^2)\frac{d^2 P_l^m(x)}{dx^2} - 2x\frac{d P_l^m(x)}{dx} + \left[l(l+1) - \frac{m^2}{1-x^2}\right] P_l^m(x) = 0.$$

From the differential equations for $P_l^m(x)$ and $P_l^k(x)$ show that for $k \neq m$,

$$\int_{-1}^{1} P_l^m(x) P_l^k(x) \frac{dx}{1-x^2} = 0.$$

15.4.15 Determine the vector potential and the magnetic induction field of a magnetic quadrupole by differentiating the magnetic dipole potential.

$$ANS. \quad \mathbf{A}_{MQ} = -\frac{\mu_0}{2}(Ia^2)(dz)\frac{P_2^1(\cos\theta)}{r^3}\,\hat{\mathbf{e}}_\varphi + \text{higher-order terms},$$

$$\mathbf{B}_{MQ} = \mu_0(Ia^2)(dz)\left[\frac{3P_2(\cos\theta)}{r^4}\,\hat{\mathbf{e}}_r - \frac{P_2^1(\cos\theta)}{r^4}\,\hat{\mathbf{e}}_\theta\right] + \cdots.$$

This corresponds to placing a current loop of radius a at $z \to dz$ and an oppositely directed current loop at $z \to -dz$. The vector potential and magnetic induction field of a point dipole are given by the leading terms in these expansions if we take the limit $dz \to 0$, $a \to 0$, and $I \to \infty$ subject to $Ia^2\,dz = $ constant.

15.4.16 A single circular wire loop of radius a carries a constant current I.

(a) Find the magnetic induction $\mathbf{B}$ for $r < a$, $\theta = \pi/2$.

(b) Calculate the integral of the magnetic flux $(\mathbf{B} \cdot d\boldsymbol{\sigma})$ over the area of the current loop, that is,

$$\int_0^a r\,dr \int_0^{2\pi} d\varphi\, B_z\left(r, \theta = \frac{\pi}{2}\right).$$

$$ANS. \quad \infty.$$

The Earth is within such a ring current, in which I approximates millions of amperes arising from the drift of charged particles in the Van Allen belt.

15.4.17 The vector potential $\mathbf{A}$ of a magnetic dipole, dipole moment $\mathbf{m}$, is given by $\mathbf{A}(\mathbf{r}) = (\mu_0/4\pi)(\mathbf{m} \times \mathbf{r}/r^3)$. Show by direct computation that the magnetic induction $\mathbf{B} = \nabla \times \mathbf{A}$ is given by

$$\mathbf{B} = \frac{\mu_0}{4\pi}\frac{3\hat{\mathbf{r}}\,(\hat{\mathbf{r}} \cdot \mathbf{m}) - \mathbf{m}}{r^3}.$$

15.4.18 (a) Show that in the point dipole limit the magnetic induction field of the current loop becomes

$$B_r(r, \theta) = \frac{\mu_0}{2\pi} \frac{m}{r^3} P_1(\cos\theta),$$

$$B_\theta(r, \theta) = -\frac{\mu_0}{2\pi} \frac{m}{r^3} P_1^1(\cos\theta),$$

with $m = I\pi a^2$.

(b) Compare these results with the magnetic induction of the point magnetic dipole of Exercise 15.4.17. Take $\mathbf{m} = \hat{\mathbf{z}}m$.

15.4.19 A uniformly charged spherical shell is rotating with constant angular velocity.

(a) Calculate the magnetic induction $\mathbf{B}$ along the axis of rotation outside the sphere.

(b) Using the vector potential series of Example 15.4.2, find $\mathbf{A}$ and then $\mathbf{B}$ for all points outside the sphere.

15.4.20 In the liquid-drop model of the nucleus, a spherical nucleus is subjected to small deformations. Consider a sphere of radius r_0 that is deformed so that its new surface is given by

$$r = r_0 \left[1 + \alpha_2 P_2(\cos\theta) \right].$$

Find the area of the deformed sphere through terms of order α_2^2.

Hint.

$$dA = \left[r^2 + \left(\frac{dr}{d\theta} \right)^2 \right]^{1/2} r \sin\theta \, d\theta \, d\varphi.$$

$$ANS. \quad A = 4\pi r_0^2 \left[1 + \tfrac{4}{5}\alpha_2^2 + \mathcal{O}\left(\alpha_2^3\right) \right].$$

Note. The area element dA follows from noting that the line element ds for fixed φ is given by

$$ds = (r^2 \, d\theta^2 + dr^2)^{1/2} = \left[r^2 + \left(\frac{dr}{d\theta} \right)^2 \right]^{1/2} d\theta.$$

15.5 SPHERICAL HARMONICS

Our earlier discussion of separated-variable methods for solving the Laplace, Helmholtz, or Schrödinger equations in spherical polar coordinates showed that the possible angular solutions $\Theta(\theta)\Phi(\varphi)$ are always the same in spherically symmetric problems; in particular we found that the solutions for Φ depended on the single integer index m, and can be written in the form

$$\Phi_m(\varphi) = \frac{1}{\sqrt{2\pi}} \, e^{im\varphi}, \quad m = \ldots, -2, -1, 0, 1, 2, \ldots, \tag{15.132}$$

or, equivalently,

$$
\Phi_m(\varphi) = \begin{cases} \dfrac{1}{\sqrt{2\pi}}, & m = 0, \\[2ex] \dfrac{1}{\sqrt{\pi}} \cos m\varphi, & m > 0, \\[2ex] \dfrac{1}{\sqrt{\pi}} \sin |m|\varphi, & m < 0. \end{cases} \tag{15.133}
$$

The above equations contain the constant factors needed to make Φ_m normalized, and those of different m^2 are automatically orthogonal because they are eigenfunctions of a Sturm-Liouville problem. It is straightforward to verify that in either Eq. (15.132) or Eq. (15.133) our choices of the functions for $+m$ and $-m$ make Φ_m and Φ_{-m} orthogonal. Formally, our definitions are such that

$$
\int_0^{2\pi} \left[\Phi_m(\varphi) \right]^* \Phi_{m'}(\varphi) d\varphi = \delta_{mm'}. \tag{15.134}
$$

In Section 15.4 we found that the solutions $\Theta(\theta)$ could be identified as associated Legendre functions that can be labeled by the two integer indices l and m, with $-l \le m \le l$. From the orthonormality integral for these functions, Eq. (15.105), we can define the normalized solutions

$$
\Theta_{lm}(\cos\theta) = \sqrt{\frac{2l+1}{2} \frac{(l-m)!}{(l+m)!}} \; P_l^m(\cos\theta), \tag{15.135}
$$

satisfying the relation

$$
\int_0^{\pi} \left[\Theta_{lm}(\cos\theta) \right]^* \Theta_{l'm}(\cos\theta) \sin\theta \, d\theta = \delta_{ll'}. \tag{15.136}
$$

We have previously noted that an orthonormality condition of this type only applies if both functions Θ have the same value of the index m. The complex conjugate is not really necessary in Eq. (15.136) because the Θ are real, but we write it anyway to maintain consistent notation. Note also that when the argument of P_l^m is $x = \cos\theta$, then $(1 - x^2)^{1/2} = \sin\theta$, so the P_l^m are polynomials of overall degree l in $\cos\theta$ and $\sin\theta$.

The product $\Theta_{lm}\Phi_m$ is called a **spherical harmonic**, with that name usually implying that Φ_m is taken with the definition as a complex exponential; see Eq. (15.132). Therefore we define

$$
Y_l^m(\theta, \varphi) \equiv \sqrt{\frac{2l+1}{4\pi} \frac{(l-m)!}{(l+m)!}} \; P_l^m(\cos\theta) e^{im\varphi}. \tag{15.137}
$$

These functions, being normalized solutions of a Sturm-Liouville problem, are orthonormal over the spherical surface, with

$$
\int_0^{2\pi} d\varphi \int_0^{\pi} \sin\theta \, d\theta \left[Y_{l_1}^{m_1}(\theta, \varphi) \right]^* Y_{l_2}^{m_2}(\theta, \varphi) = \delta_{l_1 l_2} \delta_{m_1 m_2}. \tag{15.138}
$$

The definition we introduced for the associated Legendre functions leads to specific signs for the Y_l^m that are sometimes identified as the Condon-Shortley phase, after the authors of a classic text on atomic spectroscopy. This sign convention has been found to simplify various calculations, particularly in the quantum theory of angular momentum. One of the effects of this phase factor is to introduce an alternation of sign with m among the positive-m spherical harmonics. The word "harmonic" enters the name of Y_l^m because solutions of Laplace's equation are sometimes called harmonic functions.

The squares of the real parts of the first few spherical harmonics are sketched in Figure 15.12; their functional forms are given in Table 15.4.

Cartesian Representations

For some purposes it is useful to express the spherical harmonics using Cartesian coordinates, which can be done by writing $\exp(\pm i\varphi)$ as $\cos\varphi \pm i\sin\varphi$ and using the formulas for x, y, z in spherical polar coordinates (retaining, however, an overall dependence on r, necessary because the angular quantities must be independent of scale). For example,

$$\cos\theta = z/r, \quad \sin\theta\exp(\pm i\varphi) = \sin\theta\cos\varphi \pm i\sin\theta\sin\varphi = \frac{x}{r} \pm i\frac{y}{r}; \quad (15.139)$$

these quantities are all homogeneous (of degree zero) in the coordinates.

Continuing to higher values of l, we obtain fractions in which the numerators are homogeneous products of x, y, z of overall degree l, divided by a common factor r^l. Table 15.4 includes the Cartesian expression for each of its entries.

Overall Solutions

As we have already seen in Section 9.4, the separation of a Laplace, Helmholtz, or even a Schrödinger equation in spherical polar coordinates can be written in terms of equations of the generic form

$$R'' + \frac{2}{r}R' + \left[f(r) - l(l+1) \right]R = 0, \quad (15.140)$$

$$\left[\frac{1}{\sin\theta}\frac{d}{d\theta}\left(\sin\theta\frac{d}{d\theta} \right) + \frac{1}{\sin^2\theta}\frac{d^2}{d\varphi^2} + l(l+1) \right]Y_l^m(\theta,\varphi) = 0. \quad (15.141)$$

The function $f(r)$ in Eq. (15.140) is zero for the Laplace equation, k^2 for the Helmholtz equation, and $E - V(r)$ (V = potential energy, E = total energy, an eigenvalue) for the Schrödinger equation. We have combined the θ and φ equations into Eq. (15.141) and identified one of its solutions as Y_l^m. What is important to note right now is that the combined angular equation (and its boundary conditions and therefore its solutions) will be the same for all spherically symmetric problems, and that the angular solution affects the radial equation only through the separation constant $l(l+1)$. Thus, the radial equation will have solutions that depend on l but are independent of the index m.

In Section 9.4 we solved the radial equation for the Laplace and Helmholtz equations, with the results given in Table 9.2. For the Laplace equation $\nabla^2\psi = 0$, the general solution

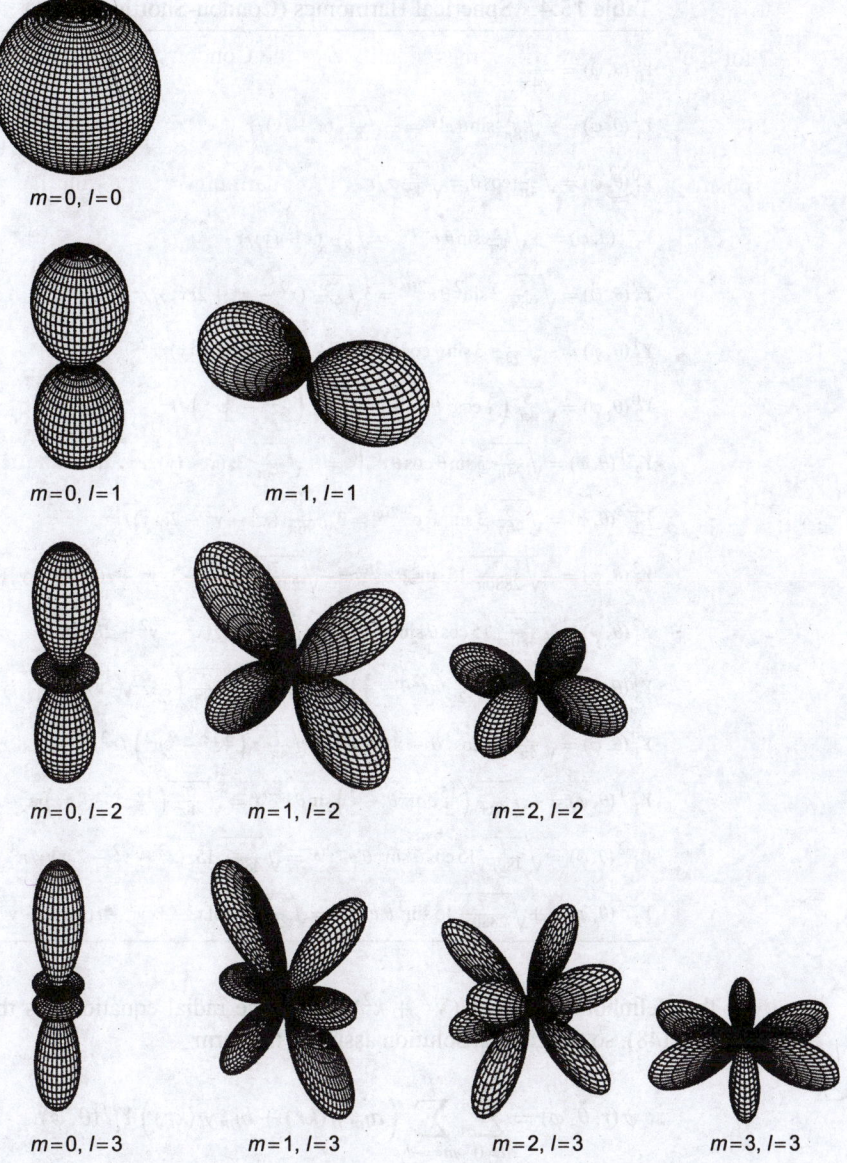

$m=0, l=0$

$m=0, l=1$ $m=1, l=1$

$m=0, l=2$ $m=1, l=2$ $m=2, l=2$

$m=0, l=3$ $m=1, l=3$ $m=2, l=3$ $m=3, l=3$

FIGURE 15.12 Shapes of $|\Re e Y_l^m(\theta, \varphi)|^2$ for $0 \leq l \leq 3$, $m = 0 \ldots l$.

in spherical polar coordinates is a sum, with arbitrary coefficients, of the solutions for the various possible values of l and m:

$$\psi(r, \theta, \varphi) = \sum_{l=0}^{\infty} \sum_{m=-l}^{l} \left(a_{lm} r^l + b_{lm} r^{-l-1} \right) Y_l^m(\theta, \varphi); \qquad (15.142)$$

Table 15.4   Spherical Harmonics (Condon-Shortley Phase)

$$Y_0^0(\theta, \varphi) = \frac{1}{\sqrt{4\pi}}$$

$$Y_1^1(\theta, \varphi) = -\sqrt{\frac{3}{8\pi}} \sin\theta\, e^{i\varphi} = -\sqrt{\frac{3}{8\pi}}\,(x+iy)/r$$

$$Y_1^0(\theta, \varphi) = \sqrt{\frac{3}{4\pi}} \cos\theta = \sqrt{\frac{3}{4\pi}}\,z/r$$

$$Y_1^{-1}(\theta, \varphi) = +\sqrt{\frac{3}{8\pi}} \sin\theta\, e^{-i\varphi} = \sqrt{\frac{3}{8\pi}}\,(x-iy)/r$$

$$Y_2^2(\theta, \varphi) = \sqrt{\frac{5}{96\pi}}\, 3\sin^2\theta\, e^{2i\varphi} = 3\sqrt{\frac{5}{96\pi}}\,(x^2-y^2+2ixy)/r^2$$

$$Y_2^1(\theta, \varphi) = -\sqrt{\frac{5}{24\pi}}\, 3\sin\theta\cos\theta\, e^{i\varphi} = -\sqrt{\frac{5}{24\pi}}\, 3z(x+iy)/r^2$$

$$Y_2^0(\theta, \varphi) = \sqrt{\frac{5}{4\pi}} \left(\tfrac{3}{2}\cos^2\theta - \tfrac{1}{2}\right) = \sqrt{\frac{5}{4\pi}} \left(\tfrac{3}{2}z^2 - \tfrac{1}{2}r^2\right)/r^2$$

$$Y_2^{-1}(\theta, \varphi) = \sqrt{\frac{5}{24\pi}}\, 3\sin\theta\cos\theta\, e^{-i\varphi} = +\sqrt{\frac{5}{24\pi}}\, 3z(x-iy)/r^2$$

$$Y_2^{-2}(\theta, \varphi) = \sqrt{\frac{5}{96\pi}}\, 3\sin^2\theta\, e^{-2i\varphi} = 3\sqrt{\frac{5}{96\pi}}\,(x^2-y^2-2ixy)/r^2$$

$$Y_3^3(\theta, \varphi) = -\sqrt{\frac{7}{2880\pi}}\, 15\sin^3\theta\, e^{3i\varphi} = -\sqrt{\frac{7}{2880\pi}}\, 15[x^3-3xy^2+i(3x^2y-y^3)]/r^3$$

$$Y_3^2(\theta, \varphi) = \sqrt{\frac{7}{480\pi}}\, 15\cos\theta\sin^2\theta\, e^{2i\varphi} = \sqrt{\frac{7}{480\pi}}\, 15z(x^2-y^2+2ixy)/r^3$$

$$Y_3^1(\theta, \varphi) = -\sqrt{\frac{7}{48\pi}} \left(\tfrac{15}{2}\cos^2\theta - \tfrac{3}{2}\right)\sin\theta\, e^{i\varphi} = -\sqrt{\frac{7}{48\pi}} \left(\tfrac{15}{2}z^2 - \tfrac{3}{2}r^2\right)(x+iy)/r^3$$

$$Y_3^0(\theta, \varphi) = \sqrt{\frac{7}{4\pi}} \left(\tfrac{5}{2}\cos^3\theta - \tfrac{3}{2}\cos\theta\right) = \sqrt{\frac{7}{4\pi}}\, z\left(\tfrac{5}{2}z^2 - \tfrac{3}{2}r^2\right)/r^3$$

$$Y_3^{-1}(\theta, \varphi) = +\sqrt{\frac{7}{48\pi}} \left(\tfrac{15}{2}\cos^2\theta - \tfrac{3}{2}\right)\sin\theta\, e^{-i\varphi} = \sqrt{\frac{7}{48\pi}} \left(\tfrac{15}{2}z^2 - \tfrac{3}{2}r^2\right)(x-iy)/r^3$$

$$Y_3^{-2}(\theta, \varphi) = \sqrt{\frac{7}{480\pi}}\, 15\cos\theta\sin^2\theta\, e^{-2i\varphi} = \sqrt{\frac{7}{480\pi}}\, 15z(x^2-y^2-2ixy)/r^3$$

$$Y_3^{-3}(\theta, \varphi) = +\sqrt{\frac{7}{2880\pi}}\, 15\sin^3\theta\, e^{-3i\varphi} = \sqrt{\frac{7}{2880\pi}}\, 15[x^3-3xy^2-i(3x^2y-y^3)]/r^3$$

for the Helmholtz equation $(\nabla^2 + k^2)\psi = 0$, the radial equation has the form given in Eq. (14.148), so the general solution assumes the form

$$\psi(r, \theta, \varphi) = \sum_{l=0}^{\infty} \sum_{m=-l}^{l} \left(a_{lm} j_l(kr) + b_{lm} y_l(kr) \right) Y_l^m(\theta, \varphi). \tag{15.143}$$

Laplace Expansion

Part of the importance of spherical harmonics lies in the completeness property, a consequence of the Sturm-Liouville form of Laplace's equation. Here this property means that any function $f(\theta, \varphi)$ (with sufficient continuity properties) evaluated over the surface of a sphere can be expanded in a uniformly convergent double series of spherical harmonics.[4]

---

[4] For a proof of this fundamental theorem, see E. W. Hobson (Additional Readings), chapter VII.

This expansion, known as a **Laplace series**, takes the form

$$f(\theta, \varphi) = \sum_{l=0}^{\infty} \sum_{m=-l}^{l} c_{lm} Y_l^m(\theta, \varphi), \tag{15.144}$$

with

$$c_{lm} = \left\langle Y_l^m \middle| f(\theta, \varphi) \right\rangle = \int_0^{2\pi} d\varphi \int_0^{\pi} \sin\theta \, d\theta \, Y_l^m(\theta, \varphi)^* f(\theta, \varphi). \tag{15.145}$$

A frequent use of the Laplace expansion is in specializing the general solution of the Laplace equation to satisfy boundary conditions on a spherical surface. This situation is illustrated in the following example.

Example 15.5.1   SPHERICAL HARMONIC EXPANSION

Consider the problem of determining the electrostatic potential within a charge-free spherical region of radius r_0, with the potential on the spherical bounding surface specified as an arbitrary function $V(r_0, \theta, \varphi)$ of the angular coordinates θ and φ. The potential $V(r, \theta, \varphi)$ is the solution of the Laplace equation satisfying the boundary condition at $r = r_0$ and regular for all $r \leq r_0$. This means it must be of the form of Eq. (15.142), with the coefficients b_{lm} set to zero to ensure a solution that is nonsingular at $r = 0$.

We proceed by obtaining the spherical harmonic expansion of $V(r_0, \theta, \varphi)$, namely Eq. (15.144), with coefficients

$$c_{lm} = \left\langle Y_l^m(\theta, \varphi) \middle| V(r_0, \theta, \varphi) \right\rangle.$$

Then, comparing Eq. (15.142), evaluated for $r = r_0$,

$$V(r_0, \theta, \varphi) = \sum_{l=0}^{\infty} \sum_{m=-l}^{l} a_{lm} r_0^l Y_l^m(\theta, \varphi),$$

with the expression from Eq. (15.144),

$$V(r_0, \theta, \varphi) = \sum_{l=0}^{\infty} \sum_{m=-l}^{l} c_{lm} Y_l^m(\theta, \varphi),$$

we see that $a_{lm} = c_{lm}/r_0^l$, so

$$V(r, \theta, \varphi) = \sum_{l=0}^{\infty} \sum_{m=-l}^{l} c_{lm} \left(\frac{r}{r_0}\right)^l Y_l^m(\theta, \varphi).$$

■

Example 15.5.2   LAPLACE SERIES—GRAVITY FIELDS

This example illustrates the notion that sometimes it is appropriate to replace the spherical harmonics by their real counterparts (in terms of sine and cosine functions). The gravity fields of the Earth, the Moon, and Mars have been described by a Laplace series of the form

$$U(r, \theta, \varphi) = \frac{GM}{R} \left[\frac{R}{r} - \sum_{l=2}^{\infty} \sum_{m=0}^{l} \left(\frac{R}{r} \right)^{l+1} \left[C_{lm} Y_{ml}^e(\theta, \varphi) + S_{lm} Y_{ml}^o(\theta, \varphi) \right] \right].$$

(15.146)

Here M is the mass of the body, R is its equatorial radius, and G is the gravitational constant. The real functions Y_{ml}^e and Y_{ml}^o are defined by Morse and Feshbach (see Additional Readings) as the unnormalized forms

$$Y_{ml}^e(\theta, \varphi) = P_l^m(\cos\theta)\cos m\varphi, \quad Y_{ml}^o(\theta, \varphi) = P_l^m(\cos\theta)\sin m\varphi.$$

Note that Morse and Feshbach place the m index before l. The normalization integrals for Y^e and Y^o are the topic of Exercise 15.5.6.

Satellite measurements have led to the numerical values for C_{20}, C_{22}, and S_{22} shown in Table 15.5.

Table 15.5   Gravity Field Coefficients, Eq. (15.145).

Coefficient[a]	Earth	Moon	Mars
C_{20}	1.083×10^{-3}	$(0.200 \pm 0.002) \times 10^{-3}$	$(1.96 \pm 0.01) \times 10^{-3}$
C_{22}	0.16×10^{-5}	$(2.4 \pm 0.5) \times 10^{-5}$	$(-5 \pm 1) \times 10^{-5}$
S_{22}	-0.09×10^{-5}	$(0.5 \pm 0.6) \times 10^{-5}$	$(3 \pm 1) \times 10^{-5}$

[a] C_{20} represents an equatorial bulge, whereas C_{22} and S_{22} represent an azimuthal dependence of the gravitational field.

∎

Symmetry of Solutions

The angular solutions of given l but different m are closely related in that they lead to the same solution for the radial equation. Except when $l = 0$, the individual solutions Y_l^m are not spherically symmetric, and we must recognize that a spherically symmetric problem can have solutions with less than the full spherical symmetry. A classical example of this phenomenon is provided by the Earth-Sun system, which has a spherically symmetric gravitational potential. However, the actual orbit of the Earth is planar. This apparent dilemma is resolved by noting that a solution exists for any orientation of the Earth's orbital plane; that actually occurring was determined by "initial conditions."

Returning now to the Laplace equation, we see that a radial solution for given l, i.e., r^l or r^{-l-1}, is associated with $2l + 1$ different angular solutions Y_l^m ($-l \le m \le l$), no one of which (for $l \ne 0$) has spherical symmetry. The most general solution for this l must be a linear combination of these $2l + 1$ mutually orthogonal functions. Put another way, the solution space of the angular solution of the Laplace equation for given l is a Hilbert space containing the $2l+1$ members $Y_l^{-l}(\theta, \varphi), \ldots, Y_l^{l}(\theta, \varphi)$. Now, if we write the Laplace equation in a coordinate system (θ', φ') oriented differently than the original coordinates, we must still have the same angular solution set, meaning that $Y_l^{m}(\theta', \varphi')$ must be a linear combination of the original Y_l^{m}. Thus, we may write

$$Y_l^{m}(\theta', \varphi') = \sum_{m'=-l}^{l} D_{m'm}^{l} Y_l^{m'}(\theta, \varphi), \qquad (15.147)$$

where the coefficients D depend on the coordinate rotation involved. Note that a coordinate rotation cannot change the r dependence of our solution to the Laplace equation, so Eq. (15.147) does not need to include a sum over all values of l. As a specific example, we see (Fig. 15.12) that for $l = 1$ we have three solutions that appear similar, but with different orientations. Alternatively, from Table 15.4 we see that the angular solutions Y_1^{m} have forms proportional to z/r, $(x+iy)/r$, and $(x-iy)/r$, meaning that they can be combined to form arbitrary combinations of x/r, y/r, and z/r. Since a rotation of the coordinate axes converts x, y, and z into linear combinations of each other, we can understand why the set of three functions Y_1^{m} ($m = 0, 1, -1$) is closed under coordinate rotations.

For $l = 2$, there are five possible m values, so the angular functions of this l value form a closed space containing five independent members. A fuller discussion of these spaces spanned by angular functions is part of what will be considered in Chapter 16.

Applying the preceding analysis to solutions of the Schrödinger equation, the eigenvalues of which are determined by solving its radial ODE for various values of the separation constant $l(l+1)$, we see that all solutions for the same l but different m will have the same eigenvalues E and radial functions, but will differ in the orientation of their angular parts. States of the same energy are called **degenerate**, and the independence of E with respect to m will cause a $(2l+1)$-fold degeneracy of the eigenstates of given l.

Example 15.5.3   SOLUTIONS FOR $l = 1$ AT ARBITRARY ORIENTATION

Let's do this problem in Cartesian coordinates. The angular solution Y_1^0 to Laplace's equation is shown in Table 15.4 to be proportional to z/r, which for our present purposes we write $(\mathbf{r} \cdot \hat{\mathbf{e}}_z)/r$, where $\hat{\mathbf{e}}_z$ is a unit vector in the z direction. We seek a similar solution, with $\hat{\mathbf{e}}_z$ replaced by an arbitrary unit vector $\hat{\mathbf{e}}_u = \cos\alpha\, \hat{\mathbf{e}}_x + \cos\beta\, \hat{\mathbf{e}}_y + \cos\gamma\, \hat{\mathbf{e}}_z$, where $\cos\alpha, \cos\beta$, and $\cos\gamma$ are the direction cosines of $\hat{\mathbf{e}}_u$. We get immediately

$$\frac{(\mathbf{r} \cdot \hat{\mathbf{e}}_u)}{r} = \frac{x}{r}\cos\alpha + \frac{y}{r}\cos\beta + \frac{z}{r}\cos\gamma.$$

Consulting the Cartesian-coordinate expressions for the spherical harmonics in Table 15.4, we see that the above expression can be written

$$\frac{(\mathbf{r} \cdot \hat{\mathbf{u}})}{r} = \sqrt{\frac{8\pi}{3}}\left(\frac{Y_1^{-1} - Y_1^{1}}{2}\right)\cos\alpha + \sqrt{\frac{8\pi}{3}}\left(\frac{-Y_1^{-1} - Y_1^{1}}{2i}\right)\cos\beta + \sqrt{\frac{4\pi}{3}}Y_1^{0}\cos\gamma.$$

This shows that all three Y_1^{m} are needed to reproduce Y_1^0 at an arbitrary orientation. Similar manipulations can be carried out for other l and m values.   ∎

Further Properties

The main properties of the spherical harmonics follow directly from those of the functions Θ_{lm} and Φ_m. We summarize briefly:

Special values. At $\theta = 0$, the polar direction in the spherical coordinates, the value of φ becomes immaterial, and all Y_l^m that have φ dependence must vanish. Using also the fact that $P_l(1) = 1$, we find in general

$$Y_l^m(0, \varphi) = \sqrt{\frac{2l+1}{4\pi}}\, \delta_{m0}. \tag{15.148}$$

A similar argument for $\theta = \pi$ leads to

$$Y_l^m(\pi, \varphi) = (-1)^l \sqrt{\frac{2l+1}{4\pi}}\, \delta_{m0}. \tag{15.149}$$

Recurrence formulas. Using the recurrence formulas developed for the associated Legendre functions, we get for the spherical harmonics with arguments (θ, φ):

$$\cos\theta\, Y_l^m = \left[\frac{(l-m+1)(l+m+1)}{(2l+1)(2l+3)}\right]^{1/2} Y_{l+1}^m$$

$$+ \left[\frac{(l-m)(l+m)}{(2l-1)(2l+1)}\right]^{1/2} Y_{l-1}^m, \tag{15.150}$$

$$e^{\pm i\varphi}\sin\theta\, Y_l^m = \mp \left[\frac{(l\pm m+1)(l\pm m+2)}{(2l+1)(2l+3)}\right]^{1/2} Y_{l+1}^{m\pm 1}$$

$$\pm \left[\frac{(l\mp m)(l\mp m-1)}{(2l-1)(2l+1)}\right]^{1/2} Y_{l-1}^{m\pm 1}. \tag{15.151}$$

Some integrals. These recurrence relations permit the ready evaluation of some integrals of practical importance. Our starting point is the orthonormalization condition, Eq. (15.138). For example, the matrix elements describing the dominant (electric dipole) mode of interaction of an electromagnetic field with a charged system in a spherical harmonic state are proportional to

$$\int \left[Y_{l'}^{m'}\right]^* \cos\theta\, Y_l^m\, d\Omega.$$

Using Eq. (15.150) and invoking the orthonormality of the Y_l^m, we find

$$\int \left[Y_{l'}^{m'}\right]^* \cos\theta\, Y_l^m\, d\Omega = \left[\frac{(l-m+1)(l+m+1)}{(2l+1)(2l+3)}\right]^{1/2} \delta_{m'm}\, \delta_{l',l+1}$$

$$+ \left[\frac{(l-m)(l+m)}{(2l-1)(2l+1)}\right]^{1/2} \delta_{m'm}\, \delta_{l',l-1}. \tag{15.152}$$

Equation (15.152) provides a basis for the well-known selection rule for dipole radiation.

Additional formulas involving products of three spherical harmonics and the detailed behavior of these quantities under coordinate rotations are more appropriately discussed in connection with a study of angular momentum and are therefore deferred to Chapter 16.

Exercises

15.5.1   Show that the parity of $Y_l^m(\theta, \varphi)$ is $(-1)^l$. Note the disappearance of any m dependence.

Hint. For the parity operation in spherical polar coordinates, see Exercise 3.10.25.

15.5.2   Prove that $Y_l^m(0, \varphi) = \left(\dfrac{2l+1}{4\pi}\right)^{1/2} \delta_{m0}$.

15.5.3   In the theory of Coulomb excitation of nuclei we encounter $Y_l^m(\pi/2, 0)$. Show that

$$Y_l^m\left(\frac{\pi}{2}, 0\right) = \left(\frac{2l+1}{4\pi}\right)^{1/2} \frac{[(l-m)!\,(l+m)!]^{1/2}}{(l-m)!!\,(l+m)!!}(-1)^{(l-m)/2}, \quad l+m \text{ even,}$$

$$= 0, \quad l+m \text{ odd.}$$

15.5.4   The orthogonal azimuthal functions yield a useful representation of the Dirac delta function. Show that

$$\delta(\varphi_1 - \varphi_2) = \frac{1}{2\pi} \sum_{m=-\infty}^{\infty} e^{im(\varphi_1 - \varphi_2)}.$$

Note. This formula assumes that φ_1 and φ_2 are restricted to $0 \leq \varphi < 2\pi$. Without this restriction there will be additional delta-function contributions at intervals of 2π in $\varphi_1 - \varphi_2$.

15.5.5   Derive the spherical harmonic closure relation

$$\sum_{l=0}^{\infty} \sum_{m=-l}^{+l} \left[Y_l^m(\theta_1, \varphi_1) \right]^* Y_l^m(\theta_2, \varphi_2) = \frac{1}{\sin\theta_1} \delta(\theta_1 - \theta_2)\,\delta(\varphi_1 - \varphi_2)$$

$$= \delta(\cos\theta_1 - \cos\theta_2)\,\delta(\varphi_1 - \varphi_2).$$

15.5.6   In some circumstances it is desirable to replace the imaginary exponential of our spherical harmonic by sine or cosine. Morse and Feshbach (see Additional Readings) define

$$Y_{ml}^e = P_l^m(\cos\theta)\cos m\varphi, \quad m \geq 0,$$

$$Y_{ml}^o = P_l^m(\cos\theta)\sin m\varphi, \quad m > 0,$$

and their normalization integrals are

$$\int_0^{2\pi} \int_0^{\pi} [Y_{mn}^{e\,\text{or}\,o}(\theta, \varphi)]^2 \sin\theta\, d\theta\, d\varphi = \frac{4\pi}{2(2n+1)} \frac{(n+m)!}{(n-m)!}, \quad n = 1, 2, \ldots$$

$$= 4\pi, \quad n = 0.$$

These spherical harmonics are often named according to the patterns of their positive and negative regions on the surface of a sphere: zonal harmonics for $m = 0$, sectoral harmonics for $m = n$, and tesseral harmonics for $0 < m < n$. For Y_{mn}^e, $n = 4$, $m = 0, 2, 4$, indicate on a diagram of a hemisphere (one diagram for each spherical harmonic) the regions in which the spherical harmonic is positive.

15.5.7   A function $f(r, \theta, \varphi)$ may be expressed as a Laplace series

$$f(r, \theta, \varphi) = \sum_{l,m} a_{lm} r^l Y_l^m(\theta, \varphi).$$

Letting $\langle \cdots \rangle_{\text{sphere}}$ denote the average over a sphere centered on the origin, show that

$$\left\langle f(r, \theta, \varphi) \right\rangle_{\text{sphere}} = f(0, 0, 0).$$

15.6   LEGENDRE FUNCTIONS OF THE SECOND KIND

The Legendre equation, a linear second-order ODE, has two independent solutions. Writing this equation in the form

$$y'' - \frac{2x}{1 - x^2} y' - \frac{l(l+1)}{1 - x^2} y = 0, \tag{15.153}$$

and restricting consideration to integer $l \geq 0$, our objective is to find a second solution that is linearly independent from the Legendre polynomials $P_l(x)$. Using the procedure of Section 7.6, and denoting the second solution $Q_l(x)$, we have

$$Q_l(x) = P_l(x) \int^x \frac{\exp\left[\int^x 2x/(1 - x^2)\, dx\right]}{[P_l(x)]^2} \, dx$$

$$= P_l(x) \int^x \frac{dx}{(1 - x^2)[P_l(x)]^2} \, dx. \tag{15.154}$$

Since any linear combination of P_l and the right-hand side of Eq. (15.154) is equally valid as a second solution of the Legendre ODE, we note that Eq. (15.154) defines both the scale and the specific functional form of Q_l.

Using Eq. (15.154), we can obtain explicit formulas for the Q_l. We find (remembering that $P_0 = 1$ and expanding the denominator in partial fractions):

$$Q_0(x) = \int^x \frac{1}{1 - x^2} \, dx = \frac{1}{2} \int \left[\frac{1}{1 + x} + \frac{1}{1 - x}\right] dx = \frac{1}{2} \ln\left(\frac{1 + x}{1 - x}\right). \tag{15.155}$$

Continuing to Q_1, the partial fraction expansion is a bit more involved, but leads to a simple result. Noting that $P_1(x) = x$, we have

$$Q_1(z) = x \int^x \frac{dx}{(1 - x^2)x^2}\, dx = \frac{x}{2} \ln\left(\frac{1+x}{1-x}\right) - 1. \tag{15.156}$$

With significantly more work, we can obtain Q_2:

$$Q_2(x) = \frac{1}{2}\, P_2(x) \ln\left(\frac{1+x}{1-x}\right) - \frac{3x}{2}. \tag{15.157}$$

This process can in principle be repeated for larger l, but it is easier and more instructive to verify that the forms of Q_0, Q_1, and Q_2 are consistent with the Legendre-function recurrence relations,[5] and then to obtain Q_l of larger l by recurrence. The recurrence formulas, originally written for P_l in Eq. (15.18), are

$$(l+1)Q_{l+1}(x) - (2l+1)x\, Q_l(x) + l Q_{l-1}(x) = 0, \tag{15.158}$$

$$(2l+1)Q_l(x) = Q'_{l+1}(x) - Q'_{n-1}(x). \tag{15.159}$$

Verification that Q_0, Q_1, and Q_2 satisfy these recurrence formulas is straightforward and is left as a exercise. Extension to higher l leads to the formula

$$Q_l(x) = \frac{1}{2}\, P_l(x) \ln\left(\frac{1+x}{1-x}\right) - \frac{2l-1}{1\cdot l}\, P_{l-1}(x) - \frac{2l-5}{3(l-1)}\, P_{l-3}(x) - \cdots. \tag{15.160}$$

Many applications using the functions $Q_l(x)$ involve values of x outside the range $-1 < x < 1$. If Eq. (15.160) is extended, say, beyond $+1$, then $1 - x$ will become negative and make a contribution $\pm i\pi$ to the logarithm, thereby making a contribution $\pm i\pi P_l$ to Q_l. Our solution will still remain a solution if this contribution is removed, and it is therefore convenient to define the second solution for x outside the range $(-1, +1)$ with

$$\ln\left(\frac{1+x}{1-x}\right) \quad \text{replaced by} \quad \ln\left(\frac{x+1}{x-1}\right).$$

From a complex-variable perspective, the logarithmic term in the solutions Q_l is related to the singularity in the ODE at $z = \pm 1$, reflecting the fact that to make the solutions single-valued it will be necessary to make a branch cut, traditionally taken on the real axis from -1 to $+1$. Then the Q_l with the $(1+x)/(1-x)$ logarithm are recovered on $-1 < x < 1$ if we average the results from the $(z+1)/(z-1)$ form on the two sides of the branch cut.

The behavior of the Q_l is illustrated by plots for $x < 1$ in Fig. 15.13 and for $x > 1$ in Fig. 15.14. Note that there is no singularity at $x = 0$ but all the Q_l exhibit a logarithmic singularity at $x = 1$.

---

[5]In Section 15.1 we showed that any set of functions that satisfies the recurrence relations reproduced here also satisfies the Legendre ODE.

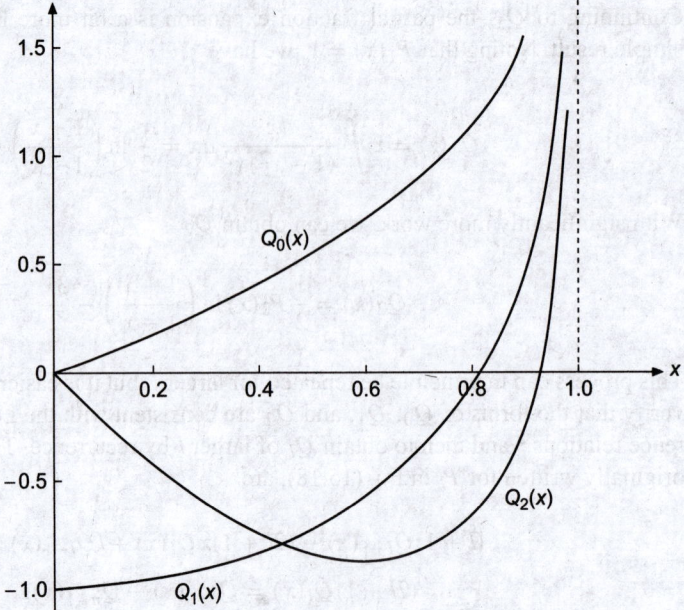

FIGURE 15.13   Legendre functions $Q_l(x)$, $0 \le x < 1$.

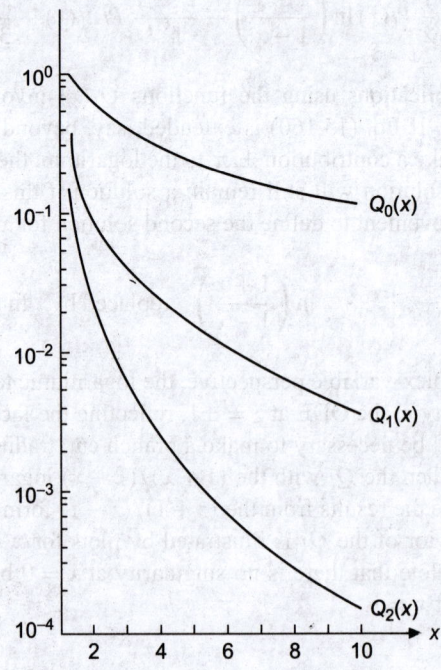

FIGURE 15.14   Legendre functions $Q_l(x)$, $x > 1$.

Properties

1. An examination of the formulas for $Q_l(x)$ reveals that if l is even, then $Q_l(x)$ is an odd function of x, while $Q_l(x)$ of odd l are even functions of x. More succinctly, $Q_l(-x) = (-1)^{l+1} Q_l(x)$.
2. The presence of the logarithmic term causes $Q_l(1) = \infty$ for all l.
3. Because $x = 0$ is a regular point of the Legendre ODE, $Q_l(0)$ must for all l be finite. The symmetry of Q_l causes $Q_l(0)$ to vanish for even l; it is shown in the next subsection that for odd l,

$$Q_{2s+1}(0) = (-1)^{s+1} \frac{(2s)!!}{(2s+1)!!}. \qquad (15.161)$$

4. From the result of Exercise 15.6.3, it can be shown that $Q_l(\infty) = 0$.

Alternate Formulations

Because the singular points of the Legendre ODE nearest to the origin are at the points ± 1, it should be possible to describe $Q_l(x)$ as a power series about the origin, with convergence for $|x| < 1$. Moreover, since the only other singular point of the Legendre equation is a regular singular point at infinity, it should also be possible to express one of its solutions as a power series in $1/x$, i.e., a series about the point at infinity, which must converge for $|x| > 1$.

To obtain a power series about $x = 0$, we return to the discussion of the Legendre ODE presented in Section 8.3, where we saw that an expansion of the form

$$y(x) = \sum_{j=0}^{\infty} a_j x^{s+j} \qquad (15.162)$$

led to an indicial equation with solutions $s = 0$ and $s = 1$, and with the a_j satisfying the recurrence formula, for eigenvalue $l(l+1)$,

$$a_{j+2} = a_j \frac{(s+j)(s+j+1) - l(l+1)}{(s+j+2)(s+j+1)}, \quad j = 0, 2, \dots. \qquad (15.163)$$

When l is even, we found that $P_l(x)$ was obtained as the solution $y(x)$ from the indicial-equation solution $s = 0$, and we did not make use (for even l) of the solution from $s = 1$ because that solution was not a polynomial and did not converge at $x = 1$. However, we are now seeking a second solution and are no longer restricting attention to those that converge at $x = \pm 1$. Thus, a second solution linearly independent of P_l must be that produced (again, for even l) as the series obtained when $s = 1$. This second solution will have odd parity, and therefore must be proportional to $Q_l(x)$.

Continuing, for even l, with $s = 1$, Eq. (15.163) becomes

$$a_{j+2} = a_j \frac{(l+j+2)(l-j-1)}{(j+2)(j+3)},$$

corresponding to

$$Q_l(x) = b_l \left[x - \frac{(l-1)(l+2)}{3!} x^3 + \frac{(l-3)(l-1)(l+2)(l+4)}{5!} x^5 - \cdots \right]. \quad (15.164)$$

Here b_l is the value of the coefficient of the expansion needed to give the formula for Q_l the proper scaling. For odd l, the corresponding formula, with $s = 0$, is an even function of x, and must therefore be proportional to Q_l:

$$Q_l(x) = b_l \left[1 - \frac{l(l+1)}{2!} x^2 + \frac{(l-2)l(l+1)(l+3)}{4!} x^4 \cdots \right]. \quad (15.165)$$

To find the values of the scale factors b_l, we turn now to the explicit forms for Q_0 and Q_1, Eqs. (15.155) and (15.156). Expanding the logarithm, we find (again keeping only the lowest-order terms)

$$Q_0(x) = x + \cdots, \quad Q_1(x) = -1 + \cdots.$$

From the recurrence formula, Eq. (15.158), keeping only the lowest-order contributions, we find

$$2Q_2 = 3x Q_1 - Q_0 \longrightarrow Q_2 = -2x + \cdots$$

$$3Q_3 = 5x Q_2 - 2Q_1 \longrightarrow Q_3 = 2/3 + \cdots$$

$$4Q_4 = 7x Q_3 - 3Q_2 \longrightarrow Q_4 = 8x/3 + \cdots$$

$$\cdots = \cdots$$

These results generalize to

$$b_l = \begin{cases} (-1)^p \dfrac{(2p)!!}{(2p-1)!!} & l \text{ even}, \quad l = 2p, \\[4mm] (-1)^{p+1} \dfrac{(2p)!!}{(2p+1)!!} & l \text{ odd}, \quad l = 2p+1. \end{cases} \quad (15.166)$$

One may now combine the values of the coefficients b_l with the expansions in Eqs. (15.164) and (15.165) to obtain entirely explicit series expansions of $Q_l(x)$ about $x = 0$. This is the topic of Exercise 15.6.2.

As mentioned earlier, the point $x = \infty$ is a regular singular point, and expansion about this point yields an expansion of $Q_l(x)$ in inverse powers of x. That expansion is considered in Exercise 15.6.3.

Exercises

15.6.1   Show that if l is even, $Q_l(-x) = -Q_l(x)$, and that if l is odd, $Q_l(-x) = Q_l(x)$.

15.6.2   Show that

(a)
$$Q_{2p}(x) = (-1)^p 2^{2p} \sum_{s=0}^{p} (-1)^s \frac{(p+s)!(p-s)!}{(2s+1)!(2p-2s)!} x^{2s+1}$$

$$+ 2^{2p} \sum_{s=p+1}^{\infty} \frac{(p+s)!(2s-2p)!}{(2s+1)!(s-p)!} x^{2s+1}, \quad |x| < 1,$$

(b)
$$Q_{2p+1}(x) = (-1)^{p+1} 2^{2p} \sum_{s=0}^{p} (-1)^s \frac{(p+s)!(p-s)!}{(2s)!(2p-2s+1)!} x^{2s}$$

$$+ 2^{2p+1} \sum_{s=p+1}^{\infty} \frac{(p+s)!(2s-2p-2)!}{(2s)!(s-p-1)!} x^{2s}, \quad |x| < 1.$$

15.6.3 (a) Starting with the assumed form

$$Q_l(x) = \sum_{j=0}^{\infty} b_{lj} x^{k-j},$$

show that

$$Q_l(x) = b_{l0} x^{-l-1} \sum_{s=0}^{\infty} \frac{(l+s)!(l+2s)!(2l+1)!}{s!(l!)^2 (2l+2s+1)!} x^{-2s}.$$

(b) The standard choice of b_{l0} is

$$b_{l0} = \frac{2^l (l!)^2}{(2l+1)!},$$

leading to the final result

$$Q_l(x) = x^{-l-1} \sum_{s=0}^{\infty} \frac{(l+2s)!}{(2s)!!(2l+2s+1)!!} x^{-2s}.$$

Show that this choice of b_{l0} brings this negative power-series form of $Q_n(x)$ into agreement with the closed-form solutions.

15.6.4 (a) Using the recurrence relations, prove (independent of the Wronskian relation) that

$$n\left[P_n(x) Q_{n-1}(x) - P_{n-1}(x) Q_n(x) \right] = P_1(x) Q_0(x) - P_0(x) Q_1(x).$$

(b) By direct substitution show that the right-hand side of this equation equals 1.

Additional Readings

Abramowitz, M., and I. A. Stegun, eds., *Handbook of Mathematical Functions with Formulas, Graphs, and Mathematical Tables* (AMS-55). Washington, DC: National Bureau of Standards (1972), reprinted, Dover (1974).

Hobson, E. W., *The Theory of Spherical and Ellipsoidal Harmonics*. New York: Chelsea (1955). This is a very complete reference, which is the classic text on Legendre polynomials and all related functions.

Jackson, J. D., *Classical Electrodynamics*, 3rd ed. New York: Wiley (1999).

Margenau, H., and G. M. Murphy, *The Mathematics of Physics and Chemistry*, 2nd ed. Princeton, NJ: Van Nostrand (1956).

Morse, P. M., and H. Feshbach, *Methods of Theoretical Physics*, 2 vols. New York: McGraw-Hill (1953). This work is detailed but at a rather advanced level.

Smythe, W. R., *Static and Dynamic Electricity*, 3rd ed. New York: McGraw-Hill (1968), reprinted, Taylor & Francis (1989), paperback. Advanced, detailed, and difficult. Includes use of elliptic integrals to obtain closed formulas.

Whittaker, E. T., and G. N. Watson, *A Course of Modern Analysis*, 4th ed. Cambridge, UK: Cambridge University Press (1962), paperback.

CHAPTER 16

ANGULAR MOMENTUM

The traditional quantum mechanical treatment of central force problems starts from solutions to the time-independent Schrödinger equation, which, for a single particle of mass m moving subject to a potential $V(r)$, is an eigenvalue problem of the general form

$$-\frac{\hbar^2}{2m}\nabla^2\psi(\mathbf{r}) + V(r)\psi(\mathbf{r}) = E\psi(\mathbf{r}). \tag{16.1}$$

Here $\hbar$ is Planck's constant divided by 2π, in SI units approximately 1.05×10^{-34} J-s (joule-seconds); the very small value of this constant causes quantum behavior to be perceptible under most circumstances only at small distances and for particles of small mass; the relevant ranges are typically at atomic scales of mass and length.

The basic interpretation of the Schrödinger equation is that if the energy E of the particle is measured, the result will be one of the eigenvalues of Eq. (16.1), and (subsequent to the measurement) the location of the particle will be described by a probability distribution

$$P(\mathbf{r})d^3r = |\psi(\mathbf{r})|^2 d^3r,$$

where $\psi(\mathbf{r})$ is an eigenfunction corresponding to E. As we have seen in Chapters 9 and 15, ψ will in general have angular as well as radial dependence, and its angular part can be written in terms of the spherical harmonics $Y_l^m(\theta, \varphi)$.

A more detailed interpretation of Eq. (16.1) is to identify it as an operator equation in which the momentum $\mathbf{p}$ is identified with the operator $-i\hbar\nabla$, while functions of position, such as the potential energy $V(r)$, are identified as multiplicative operators. Viewed in this way, the operator $-(\hbar^2/2m)\nabla^2$ is seen to represent $p^2/2m$ (i.e., the kinetic energy T), and Eq. (16.1) then becomes equivalent to

$$H\psi \equiv (T + V)\psi = E\psi, \tag{16.2}$$

where H, the Hamiltonian, is an operator whose eigenvalues are the possible values of the total energy.

The Hamiltonian H is a special operator in quantum mechanics because its eigenfunctions yield stationary probability distributions (they do not evolve into different distributions over time). However, H is just like any other quantum operator K representing a

773

dynamical quantity (with eigenvalues k that can be the result of measurement of K). If ψ is simultaneously an eigenfunction of H and of K, then we can have definite values of both E and k that will not evolve as a function of time, and the measuring of either will not disturb the definite value of the other. This state of affairs can only be achieved if H and K commute, because (see Section 6.4) $[H, K] = 0$ is a necessary and sufficient condition that H and K have a set of simultaneous eigenfunctions.

In earlier chapters, we examined commutators such as $[x, p_x] = i$ (here and except when noted, we use a unit system with $\hbar$ set to unity to avoid unnecessary notational complexity). The nonzero commutator of x and p_x tells us that we cannot simultaneously obtain unambiguous measurement of both these quantities (i.e., we do not have a complete set of states that are simultaneously eigenfunctions of x and p_x). This is the mathematical basis of the Heisenberg uncertainty principle in quantum mechanics.

The notion of simultaneous eigenfunctions and therefore commutation plays a key role in the study of angular momentum in quantum mechanics. Angular momentum is conserved in the classical central force problem, and one of the focal points of the present chapter is to understand the properties of angular momentum operators in quantum mechanics.

16.1 ANGULAR MOMENTUM OPERATORS

In classical physics, the kinetic energy of a particle of mass μ can be written in terms of its momentum $\mathbf{p}$ as $T_{\text{class}} = \mathbf{p}^2/2\mu$. Note that we are using μ for the particle mass to avoid confusion with the usual notation of the azimuthal wave functions φ_m. Most of the literature uses m for both quantities. Introducing spherical polar coordinates, T_{class} can be divided into radial and angular parts, with the angular kinetic energy of the form $\mathbf{L}^2_{\text{class}}/2\mu r^2$. Here $\mathbf{L}_{\text{class}}$ is the angular momentum, defined as $\mathbf{L}_{\text{class}} = \mathbf{r} \times \mathbf{p}$. Following the usual Schrödinger representation of quantum mechanics, the classical linear momentum $\mathbf{p}$ is replaced (in a unit system with $\hbar = 1$) by the **operator** $-i\nabla$. The quantum-mechanical kinetic energy operator is $T_{\text{QM}} = -\nabla^2/2\mu$, which in spherical polar coordinates can be written

$$T_{\text{QM}} = -\frac{1}{2\mu}\left[\frac{\partial^2}{\partial r^2} + \frac{2}{r}\frac{\partial}{\partial r}\right] - \frac{1}{2\mu r^2}\left[\frac{1}{\sin\theta}\frac{\partial}{\partial\theta}\left(\sin\theta\frac{\partial}{\partial\theta}\right) + \frac{1}{\sin^2\theta}\frac{\partial^2}{\partial\varphi^2}\right]. \quad (16.3)$$

Like the classical kinetic energy, T_{QM} can also be divided into radial and angular parts, with the angular part identified in terms of the angular momentum:

$$T_{\text{QM}} = T_{\text{radial,QM}} + \frac{1}{2\mu r^2}\mathbf{L}^2_{\text{QM}}, \quad (16.4)$$

$$T_{\text{radial,QM}} = -\frac{1}{2\mu}\left[\frac{\partial^2}{\partial r^2} + \frac{2}{r}\frac{\partial}{\partial r}\right], \quad (16.5)$$

$$\mathbf{L}^2_{\text{QM}} = -\frac{1}{\sin\theta}\frac{\partial}{\partial\theta}\left(\sin\theta\frac{\partial}{\partial\theta}\right) - \frac{1}{\sin^2\theta}\frac{\partial^2}{\partial\varphi^2}. \quad (16.6)$$

Since our focus here is on the quantum-mechanical operators, we drop the notation "QM" from now on.

The notation $\mathbf{L}^2$ in Eq. (16.6) is only really appropriate if it is consistent with the definition of the quantum-mechanical angular momentum operator, which must have the form

$$\mathbf{L} = \mathbf{r} \times \mathbf{p} = -i\mathbf{r} \times \nabla. \tag{16.7}$$

One way to confirm Eq. (16.6) is to start from the expression for $\mathbf{L}$ in spherical polar coordinates, which can be deduced by applying the operator $\mathbf{r} \times \mathbf{p}$ to an arbitrary function ψ:

$$\mathbf{L}\psi = -i\mathbf{r} \times \nabla \psi = -i r \hat{\mathbf{e}}_r \times \left[\hat{\mathbf{e}}_r \frac{\partial \psi}{\partial r} + \hat{\mathbf{e}}_\theta \frac{1}{r} \frac{\partial \psi}{\partial \theta} + \hat{\mathbf{e}}_\varphi \frac{1}{r \sin\theta} \frac{\partial \psi}{\partial \varphi} \right],$$

from which we extract the formula

$$\mathbf{L} = i \left(\hat{\mathbf{e}}_\theta \frac{1}{\sin\theta} \frac{\partial}{\partial \varphi} - \hat{\mathbf{e}}_\varphi \frac{\partial}{\partial \theta} \right). \tag{16.8}$$

We then rewrite $\mathbf{L}$ in Cartesian components L_x, L_y, L_z (but still expressed in polar coordinates) and evaluate

$$\mathbf{L}^2 = \mathbf{L} \cdot \mathbf{L} = L_x^2 + L_y^2 + L_z^2. \tag{16.9}$$

This process is the topic of Exercise 3.10.32, and leads, as expected, to Eq. (16.6).

In Section 15.5 we identified the solutions of the angular part of the Laplace and Schrödinger equations for central force problems as the spherical harmonics, denoted $Y_l^m(\theta, \varphi)$. Now that we have also written the angular part of these equations in terms of $\mathbf{L}^2$, we see that the Y_l^m can be identified as eigenfunctions of $\mathbf{L}^2$, i.e., that they are angular momentum eigenfunctions, satisfying an eigenvalue equation of the form

$$\mathbf{L}^2 Y_l^m(\theta, \varphi) = l(l+1) Y_l^m(\theta, \varphi). \tag{16.10}$$

Summarizing the discussion to this point, and drawing on previously established properties of the spherical harmonics:

The spherical harmonics Y_l^m are eigenfunctions of $\mathbf{L}^2$ with eigenvalue $l(l+1)$. The eigenfunctions for a given l are $(2l+1)$-fold degenerate and can be indexed by their m values, which range in unit steps from $-l$ to l.

We now strive for a deeper understanding of the role of angular momentum. The solutions to the time-independent Schrödinger equation are the eigenfunctions of its total energy operator, the Hamiltonian H. We have just observed that for central force problems the angular solutions are eigenfunctions of the angular momentum operator $\mathbf{L}^2$. In order for these two statements to be mutually consistent, it is necessary that H and $\mathbf{L}^2$ commute. For the systems under consideration here, this is clearly true, since we have assumed that H is of the form $T + V(r)$, so

$$H = T_{\text{radial}}(r) + \frac{1}{2\mu r^2} \mathbf{L}^2(\theta, \varphi) + V(r).$$

Since the only angle-dependent quantity in H is the operator $\mathbf{L}^2$, and since $\mathbf{L}^2$ obviously commutes with itself and is independent of r, we have

$$[H, \mathbf{L}^2] = 0.$$

The fact that H and $\mathbf{L}^2$ have simultaneous eigenfunctions in central force problems means that the stationary states of such systems can be characterized by definite values of both the energy and the angular momentum **quantum number** l. States of different l were ultimately identified with series of lines in the emission and absorption spectra of the hydrogen atom that had previously been labeled "sharp," "diffuse," "principal," and "fundamental." This identification caused physicists to use the initial letters of these names as synonyms for l values; hence it has become essential to know that the code letters for $l = 0, 1, 2,$ and 3 are respectively $s, p, d,$ and f. For $l > 3$, the code letters run alphabetically: $g, h \ldots$.

Turning now to the components of $\mathbf{L}$, we have (cf. Exercise 3.10.31)

$$[L_j, L_k] = i\varepsilon_{jkn}L_n \text{ and } [\mathbf{L}^2, L_j] = 0, \tag{16.11}$$

where j, k, n are different members of the set $(1,2,3)$ and ε_{jkn} is a Levi-Civita symbol. Although the L_j do not commute with each other, all commute with $\mathbf{L}^2$ and hence also with H, so $H, \mathbf{L}^2,$ and any one component of $\mathbf{L}$ mutually commute. We conclude that there exists a set of simultaneous eigenfunctions of $H, \mathbf{L}^2,$ and any one component of $\mathbf{L}$. For this purpose we usually pick L_z, motivated by the fact that, in spherical polar coordinates, it is, as found in Exercise 3.10.29,

$$L_z = -i\frac{\partial}{\partial\varphi}. \tag{16.12}$$

For reference, we copy here the far more complicated results for L_x and L_y, obtained from Exercise 3.10.30:

$$L_x = i\,\sin\varphi\frac{\partial}{\partial\theta} + i\,\cot\theta\cos\varphi\frac{\partial}{\partial\varphi},$$
$$L_y = -i\,\cos\varphi\frac{\partial}{\partial\theta} + i\,\cot\theta\sin\varphi\frac{\partial}{\partial\varphi}. \tag{16.13}$$

The spherical harmonics are, in fact, eigenfunctions of L_z. Since

$$L_z e^{im\varphi} = -i\frac{\partial}{\partial\varphi}e^{im\varphi} = me^{im\varphi}, \tag{16.14}$$

we see that Y_l^m is an eigenfunction of L_z with eigenvalue m. This is one of the reasons why the complex exponentials, rather than the trigonometric functions, were chosen in the definitions of the spherical harmonics. It is obvious that $\cos m\varphi$ is not an eigenfunction of L_z: $-i(\partial/\partial\varphi)\cos m\varphi = im\sin m\varphi$. Note, however, that $\exp(\pm im\varphi)$, $\cos m\varphi$, and $\sin m\varphi$ are all eigenfunctions of the operator $L_z^2 = -\partial^2/\partial\varphi^2$ with eigenvalue m^2.

Ladder Operators

The commutators of the angular momentum components permit the development of some useful algebraic relationships. While these relationships can be found from the specific forms of the operators (cf. Exercise 3.10.30), more general and valuable results are obtained by derivations based only on the commutators given in Eq. (16.11). We define the operators

$$L_+ = L_x + iL_y, \quad L_- = L_x - iL_y, \tag{16.15}$$

and consider the commutators

$$[L_z, L_+] = [L_z, L_x] + i[L_z, L_y] = iL_y + i(-iL_x) = L_+, \tag{16.16}$$

$$[L_z, L_-] = [L_z, L_x] - i[L_z, L_y] = iL_y - i(-iL_x) = -L_-. \tag{16.17}$$

We start by applying Eq. (16.16) to a function ψ_l^m, which is assumed to be a normalized simultaneous eigenfunction of $\mathbf{L}^2$, with eigenvalue λ_l, and of L_z, with eigenvalue m; the form of ψ_l^m (and even the space within which it resides) need not be specified to carry out the present discussion. Moreover, at this point we introduce no information about the possible values of λ_l and m. However, to visualize what we are doing, the reader can keep in mind that one possible interpretation of ψ_l^m is the spherical harmonic Y_l^m. We have

$$[L_z, L_+]\psi_l^m = L_z L_+ \psi_l^m - L_+ L_z \psi_l^m = L_+ \psi_l^m.$$

Since $L_z \psi_l^m = m\psi_l^m$, we can rewrite the central and right-hand members of the above equation as

$$L_z(L_+ \psi_l^m) - m(L_+ \psi_l^m) = (L_+ \psi_l^m),$$

which rearranges to

$$L_z(L_+ \psi_l^m) = (m + 1)(L_+ \psi_l^m). \tag{16.18}$$

This tells us that if $L_+ \psi_l^m$ is nonzero, it is an eigenfunction of L_z with eigenvalue $m + 1$; for that reason L_+ can be called a **raising operator**. By itself, this analysis tells us nothing about the value(s) of m, but only that L_+ increases m in unit steps. A similar development shows that L_- is a **lowering operator**, corresponding to the equation

$$L_z(L_- \psi_l^m) = (m - 1)(L_- \psi_l^m). \tag{16.19}$$

Raising and lowering operators are collectively referred to as **ladder operators**.

Next, we recall that $[\mathbf{L}^2, L_i] = 0$ for all components L_i. This means also that $[\mathbf{L}^2, L_+] = 0$, so

$$\mathbf{L}^2(L_+ \psi_l^m) = L_+ \mathbf{L}^2 \psi_l^m = \lambda_l(L_+ \psi_l^m),$$

showing that $(L_+ \psi_l^m)$ is still an eigenfunction of $\mathbf{L}^2$ with the same eigenvalue, λ_l, as ψ_l^m. Note that we did not need to know the value of λ_l to draw this conclusion. Summarizing, the operators $L_\pm$ convert ψ_l^m into quantities proportional to $\psi_l^{m\pm1}$, with the conversion failing only if $L_\pm \psi_l^m = 0$.

While Eqs. (16.18) and (16.19) tell us that $L_\pm$ are ladder operators, they do not tell us whether the quantities $L_\pm \psi_l^m$ are normalized. To address this problem, we write the normalization expression for $L_+ \psi_l^m$ in the form

$$\langle L_+ \psi_l^m | L_+ \psi_l^m \rangle = \langle \psi_l^m | L_- L_+ | \psi_l^m \rangle,$$

where we have used the fact that, because L_x and L_y are Hermitian, $(L_+)^\dagger = L_-$.

To obtain more information about L_-L_+, we rearrange $\mathbf{L}^2$ as follows:

$$\mathbf{L}^2 = \tfrac{1}{2}(L_+L_- + L_-L_+) + L_z^2 = L_-L_+ + \tfrac{1}{2}[L_+, L_-] + L_z^2, \tag{16.20}$$

a result that can be easily verified by expanding L_+, L_-, and the commutator. Then we introduce

$$[L_+, L_-] = [L_x + iL_y, L_x - iL_y] = -i[L_x, L_y] + i[L_y, L_x] = 2L_z, \tag{16.21}$$

and solve Eq. (16.20) for L_-L_+, obtaining

$$L_-L_+ = \mathbf{L}^2 - L_z^2 - L_z. \tag{16.22}$$

Using the fact that ψ_l^m is a normalized eigenfunction of both $\mathbf{L}^2$ and L_z, we can now perform the evaluation

$$\langle L_+\psi_l^m | L_+\psi_l^m \rangle = \langle \psi_l^m | L_-L_+ | \psi_l^m \rangle = \langle \psi_l^m | \mathbf{L}^2 - L_z^2 - L_z | \psi_l^m \rangle$$

$$= \lambda_l - m^2 - m. \tag{16.23}$$

A parallel analysis leads to the companion result

$$\langle L_-\psi_l^m | L_-\psi_l^m \rangle = \langle \psi_l^m | L_+L_- | \psi_l^m \rangle = \lambda_l - m^2 + m. \tag{16.24}$$

If we use the expressions in Eqs. (16.23) and (16.24) to account for the scale factors generated by the ladder operators, we can summarize their action as

$$L_+\psi_l^m = \sqrt{\lambda_l - m(m+1)}\,\psi_l^{m+1},$$
$$ \tag{16.25}$$
$$L_-\psi_l^m = \sqrt{\lambda_l - m(m-1)}\,\psi_l^{m-1},$$

where, the reader may recall, λ_l is the eigenvalue of $\mathbf{L}^2$ corresponding to quantum number l; the current analysis has not yet determined its value. The expressions in Eq. (16.25) have also incorporated the assumption that the signs of the ψ_l^m are related as shown. That is a matter of definition, and when the ψ_l^m are taken to be the spherical harmonics Y_l^m, the Condon-Shortley phase assignment was deliberately designed to make Eq. (16.25) consistent with the signs given the Y_l^m in Table 15.4.

Next, we return to Eq. (16.23) and note that since it describes a normalization integral, it is inherently nonnegative, and can be zero only if $L_+\psi_l^m$ is identically zero. The right-hand side of Eq. (16.23), however, will be become negative if m is permitted to get too large, so for any fixed l (and therefore a fixed λ_l), there must be some largest m, which we call $m_{\max}$, for which there exists a $\psi_l^{m_{\max}}$. But if we use Eq. (16.23) to evaluate $L_+\psi_l^{m_{\max}}$, we will, unless $\lambda_l - m_{\max}(m_{\max}+1) = 0$, generate a function with $m = m_{\max}+1$, thereby creating an inconsistency. Giving $m_{\max}$ the name l (permitted because within the current derivation we have not yet assigned a meaning to l), what we have found so far is that $\lambda_l = l(l+1)$ and that the maximum value of m is $m = l$. Remember that we still know nothing about possible values for l.

Turning now to Eq. (16.24), and inserting $l(l+1)$ for λ_l, we note that if m is permitted to become too negative we will again have an inconsistent situation, and that it is necessary that for some $m_{\min}$ the right-hand side of Eq. (16.24) must vanish. Thus, we require $l(l+1) - m_{\min}(m_{\min}-1) = 0$, an equation that is satisfied for $m_{\min} = l+1$ (which is clearly irrelevant), and for $m_{\min} = -l$ (the solution we want).

Finally, we observe that, starting from some ψ_l^m with $m = l$, we have the severe limitation that application of the lowering operator L_- will decrease the m value in unit steps, but must ultimately reach $m = -l$ to avoid the generation of an inconsistency. This state of affairs is possible if l is a nonnegative integer, in which case there are $2l + 1$ possible m values, ranging in unit steps from l to $-l$. However, it is also possible to assign l a half-integer value, as $m = l$ and $m = -l$ are then still connected by a series of unit steps. In this case, also, there will be $2l + 1$ different m values. This quantity, $2l + 1$, is sometimes called the **multiplicity** of the angular momentum states.

The fact that it is mathematically possible to have a series (**multiplet**) of states corresponding to either integral or half-integral l and satisfying the angular momentum commutation rules does not prove that such states are realizable in a particular algebraic system (such as that describing ordinary three-dimensional [3-D] space), or that such states are indeed relevant for physics. However, by solving Laplace's equation, we have already found that the angular momentum states of integral l can be described in ordinary space and that they can be identified as states of ordinary (so-called **orbital**) angular momentum. It is not possible to describe states of half-integral l as ordinary functions in 3-D space, so orbital angular momentum will only involve integral l.

Example 16.1.1   SPHERICAL HARMONICS LADDER

From Exercise 3.10.30, or alternatively by combining the formulas for L_x and L_y from Eq. (16.13), the orbital angular momentum ladder operator L_+ is found to be

$$L_+ = e^{i\varphi}\left(\frac{\partial}{\partial\theta} + i\cot\theta\,\frac{\partial}{\partial\varphi}\right).$$

Starting from $Y_1^0(\theta,\varphi) = \sqrt{3/4\pi}\cos\theta$, we can apply Eq. (16.25):

$$L_+ Y_1^0(\theta,\varphi) = \sqrt{\frac{3}{4\pi}}\,e^{i\varphi}\frac{\partial\cos\theta}{\partial\theta} = \sqrt{\frac{3}{4\pi}}\,e^{i\varphi}(-\sin\theta) = \sqrt{2}\,Y_1^1(\theta,\varphi), \tag{16.26}$$

which when solved for Y_1^1 gives (with proper scale and sign) the value tabulated in Table 15.4. The reader can verify that the application of L_+ to Y_1^1 gives zero. ∎

Spinors

It turns out that half-integral angular momentum states are needed to describe the intrinsic angular momentum of the electron and many other particles. Since these particles also have magnetic moments, an intuitive interpretation is that their charge distributions are spinning about some axis; hence the term **spin**. It is now understood that the spin phenomena cannot be explained consistently by describing these particles as ordinary charge distributions undergoing rotational motion, but are better treated by assigning these particles to states in an abstract space that, for the electron, has the l value $\frac{1}{2}$ (but in this context, we normally use s and write $s = \frac{1}{2}$), which means that the possible m values (often written m_s) are $m_s = +\frac{1}{2}$ and $m_s = -\frac{1}{2}$. It is not productive to try to think of this situation in terms of ordinary functions, but to accept an abstract formulation in which spin states are represented by symbols; popular choices are α or $|\uparrow\rangle$ for the state $m = +\frac{1}{2}$ and β or $|\downarrow\rangle$ for that with $m = -\frac{1}{2}$. These spin states can also be represented by two-component column vectors, with the angular momentum operators given in terms of the Pauli matrices as $\frac{1}{2}\sigma_i$.

The quantities forming a basis for the multiplets for half-integer angular momentum are called **spinors**. In addition to their manipulation using ladder operators, they have rotational properties that are discussed in more detail in Chapter 17.

Example 16.1.2   SPINOR LADDER

Calling the angular momentum operator **S**, we write S_x, S_y, S_z as the 2×2 matrices $\frac{1}{2}\sigma_i$, where σ_i are defined in Eq. (2.28):

$$S_x = \frac{1}{2}\begin{pmatrix} 0 & 1 \\ 1 & 0 \end{pmatrix}, \quad S_y = \frac{1}{2}\begin{pmatrix} 0 & -i \\ i & 0 \end{pmatrix}, \quad S_z = \frac{1}{2}\begin{pmatrix} 1 & 0 \\ 0 & -1 \end{pmatrix}. \tag{16.27}$$

By carrying out matrix operations we can verify that these matrices satisfy the angular momentum commutation rules. For example,

$$S_x S_y - S_y S_x = \frac{1}{4}\begin{pmatrix} 0 & 1 \\ 1 & 0 \end{pmatrix}\begin{pmatrix} 0 & -i \\ i & 0 \end{pmatrix} - \frac{1}{4}\begin{pmatrix} 0 & -i \\ i & 0 \end{pmatrix}\begin{pmatrix} 0 & 1 \\ 1 & 0 \end{pmatrix}$$

$$= \frac{i}{2}\begin{pmatrix} 1 & 0 \\ 0 & -1 \end{pmatrix} = i S_z.$$

We also find that

$$S_x^2 = S_y^2 = S_z^2 = (1/4)\mathbf{1},$$

and we therefore have

$$\mathbf{S}^2 = S_x^2 + S_y^2 + S_z^2 = \frac{1}{4}\Big[1 + 1 + 1\Big] = \frac{3}{4}\mathbf{1}.$$

Note that 3/4 is $S(S + 1)$ for $S = 1/2$.

The interpretation of these matrix relationships is that we have an abstract space spanned by the two functions

$$\psi_{1/2}^{1/2} \equiv \alpha \equiv |\uparrow\rangle = \begin{pmatrix} 1 \\ 0 \end{pmatrix}, \quad \psi_{1/2}^{-1/2} \equiv \beta \equiv |\downarrow\rangle = \begin{pmatrix} 0 \\ 1 \end{pmatrix},$$

and that the operators $\mathbf{S}^2$ and S_z operate on these functions as follows:

$$\mathbf{S}^2\alpha = \mathbf{S}^2\psi_{1/2}^{1/2} = \frac{3}{4}\begin{pmatrix} 1 & 0 \\ 0 & 1 \end{pmatrix}\begin{pmatrix} 1 \\ 0 \end{pmatrix} = \frac{3}{4}\begin{pmatrix} 1 \\ 0 \end{pmatrix} = \frac{3}{4}\psi_{1/2}^{1/2} = \frac{3}{4}\alpha,$$

$$S_z\alpha = S_z\psi_{1/2}^{1/2} = \frac{1}{2}\begin{pmatrix} 1 & 0 \\ 0 & -1 \end{pmatrix}\begin{pmatrix} 1 \\ 0 \end{pmatrix} = \frac{1}{2}\begin{pmatrix} 1 \\ 0 \end{pmatrix} = \frac{1}{2}\psi_{1/2}^{1/2} = \frac{1}{2}\alpha,$$

$$\mathbf{S}^2\beta = \mathbf{S}^2\psi_{1/2}^{-1/2} = \frac{3}{4}\begin{pmatrix} 1 & 0 \\ 0 & 1 \end{pmatrix}\begin{pmatrix} 0 \\ 1 \end{pmatrix} = \frac{3}{4}\begin{pmatrix} 0 \\ 1 \end{pmatrix} = \frac{3}{4}\psi_{1/2}^{-1/2} = \frac{3}{4}\beta,$$

$$S_z\beta = S_z\psi_{1/2}^{-1/2} = \frac{1}{2}\begin{pmatrix} 1 & 0 \\ 0 & -1 \end{pmatrix}\begin{pmatrix} 0 \\ 1 \end{pmatrix} = -\frac{1}{2}\begin{pmatrix} 0 \\ 1 \end{pmatrix} = -\frac{1}{2}\psi_{1/2}^{-1/2} = -\frac{1}{2}\beta.$$

The above formulas show that $\psi_{1/2}^{\pm 1/2}$ (also denoted α and β) are simultaneous eigenfunctions of $\mathbf{S}^2$ and S_z. To illustrate that they are not also eigenfunctions of S_x or S_y, we compute

$$S_x\alpha = S_x\psi_{1/2}^{1/2} = \frac{1}{2}\begin{pmatrix} 0 & 1 \\ 1 & 0 \end{pmatrix}\begin{pmatrix} 1 \\ 0 \end{pmatrix} = \frac{1}{2}\begin{pmatrix} 0 \\ 1 \end{pmatrix} = \frac{1}{2}\psi_{1/2}^{-1/2} = \frac{1}{2}\beta.$$

To make ladders, we now form

$$S_+ = S_x + iS_y = \begin{pmatrix} 0 & 1 \\ 0 & 0 \end{pmatrix}, \quad S_- = S_x - iS_y = \begin{pmatrix} 0 & 0 \\ 1 & 0 \end{pmatrix}.$$

Applying these operators to $\alpha = \psi_{1/2}^{1/2}$,

$$S_+\alpha = \begin{pmatrix} 0 & 1 \\ 0 & 0 \end{pmatrix}\begin{pmatrix} 1 \\ 0 \end{pmatrix} = 0, \quad S_-\alpha = \begin{pmatrix} 0 & 0 \\ 1 & 0 \end{pmatrix}\begin{pmatrix} 1 \\ 0 \end{pmatrix} = \begin{pmatrix} 0 \\ 1 \end{pmatrix} = \beta.$$

These results are in agreement with Eq. (16.25), for which, with the current parameters $\lambda = 3/4$, $m = 1/2$, its coefficients are

$$\sqrt{\lambda - m(m+1)} = 0, \quad \sqrt{\lambda - m(m-1)} = 1.$$

$\blacksquare$

Summary, Angular Momentum Formulas

The analysis of the preceding subsection applies to any system of operators satisfying the angular momentum commutation rules. Possible areas of application include orbital angular momentum (for which the eigenfunctions are the spherical harmonics), the intrinsic (spin) angular momentum we now know is associated with most fundamental particles, and even the overall angular momenta that result either from considering both the orbital and spin angular momenta of the same particle, or the total angular momentum of a collection of particles (as in a many-electron atom or even a nucleus).

It is useful to summarize the key results; we do so giving the operators the name J, to emphasize the fact that the results are not restricted to orbital angular momentum (for which the symbol L is nearly universally used), or to spin angular momentum (traditionally denoted S). Thus:

1. We assume that there exists a Hermitian operator $\mathbf{J}$ with components J_x, J_y, J_z such that $J_x^2 + J_y^2 + J_z^2 = \mathbf{J}^2$ and that these quantities satisfy the commutation relations

$$[J_k, J_l] = i\varepsilon_{kln} J_n, \quad [\mathbf{J}^2, J_k] = 0, \tag{16.28}$$

where k, l, n are x, y, z in any order and ε_{kln} is a Levi-Civita symbol. Other than the requirement of Eq. (16.28), $\mathbf{J}$ is arbitrary.

2. Because the operators $\mathbf{J}^2$ and J_z commute, there can exist functions (in some abstract space), generically denoted ψ_J^M, with ψ_J^M simultaneously a normalized eigenfunction of J_z with eigenvalue M and an eigenfunction of $\mathbf{J}^2$ with eigenvalue $J(J+1)$:

$$J_z \psi_J^M = M \psi_J^M, \quad \mathbf{J}^2 \psi_J^M = J(J+1)\psi_J^M, \quad \left\langle \psi_J^M | \psi_J^M \right\rangle = 1. \tag{16.29}$$

3. Operators satisfying the above conditions can be called angular momentum operators; those which were used as examples of angular momentum in ordinary space (**orbital angular momentum**) are clearly relevant for physics; similar operators in more abstract spaces are relevant only to the extent that they can be identified with physical phenomena.

We have already seen that these assumptions are sufficient to enable the introduction of ladder operators, and to reach the following conclusions:

1. The possible values of J are integral and half-integral; in ordinary 3-D space only functions of integral J can be realized.
2. For a given J, the possible values of M range in unit steps from $M = J$ to $M = -J$; this produces $2J + 1$ different M values.
3. Given any one ψ_J^M, we can generate others by use of the operators

$$J_+ = J_x + iJ_y, \quad J_- = J_x - iJ_y.$$

The result of applying these operators to ψ_J^M is, see Eq. (16.25),

$$J_+ \psi_J^M = \sqrt{(J-M)(J+M+1)}\,\psi_J^{M+1}, \tag{16.30}$$

$$J_- \psi_J^M = \sqrt{(J+M)(J-M+1)}\,\psi_J^{M-1}. \tag{16.31}$$

These formulas give zero results when J_+ is applied to ψ_J^J and when J_- is applied to ψ_J^{-J}.

Exercises

16.1.1   The quantum mechanical angular momentum operators $L_x \pm iL_y$ in 3-D physical space are given by

$$L_x + iL_y = e^{i\varphi}\left(\frac{\partial}{\partial\theta} + i\cot\theta\frac{\partial}{\partial\varphi}\right),$$

$$L_x - iL_y = -e^{-i\varphi}\left(\frac{\partial}{\partial\theta} - i\cot\theta\frac{\partial}{\partial\varphi}\right).$$

Show that

(a) $(L_x + iL_y)Y_L^M(\theta,\varphi) = \sqrt{(L-M)(L+M+1)}\,Y_L^{M+1}(\theta,\varphi),$

(b) $(L_x - iL_y)Y_L^M(\theta,\varphi) = \sqrt{(L+M)(L-M+1)}\,Y_L^{M-1}(\theta,\varphi).$

16.1.2   With $L_\pm$ given by

$$L_\pm = L_x \pm iL_y = \pm e^{\pm i\varphi}\left[\frac{\partial}{\partial\theta} \pm i\cot\theta\frac{\partial}{\partial\varphi}\right],$$

show that

(a) $Y_l^m = \sqrt{\dfrac{(l+m)!}{(2l)!(l-m)!}}\,(L_-)^{l-m}Y_l^l,$

(b) $Y_l^m = \sqrt{\dfrac{(l-m)!}{(2l)!(l+m)!}}\,(L_+)^{l+m}Y_l^{-l}.$

16.1.3   Using the known forms of L_+ and L_- (Exercise 16.1.2), show that

$$\int [Y_L^M]^* L_-(L_+Y_L^M)\,d\Omega = \int (L_+Y_L^M)^*(L_+Y_L^M)\,d\Omega.$$

Here $d\Omega$ is the element of solid angle $(\sin\theta\,d\theta\,d\varphi)$, and the integration is over the entire angular space.

16.1.4   (a)   Show that $\mathbf{J}^2 = \dfrac{1}{2}\Big[J_+J_- + J_-J_+ \Big] + J_z^2.$

(b)   Use the result from part (a) and the explicit formulas for L_+ and L_- from Exercise 16.1.2 to verify that all the spherical harmonics with $l=2$ are eigenfunctions of $\mathbf{L}^2$ with eigenvalue $l(l+1)=6$.

16.1.5   Derive the following relations without assuming anything about ψ_L^M other than that they are angular momentum eigenfunctions:

(a) $\psi_L^M(\theta,\varphi) = \sqrt{\dfrac{(L+M)!}{(2L)!(L-M)!}}\,(L_-)^{L-M}\psi_L^L(\theta,\varphi),$

(b) $\psi_L^M(\theta,\varphi) = \sqrt{\dfrac{(L-M)!}{(2L)!(L+M)!}}\,(L_+)^{L+M}\psi_L^{-L}(\theta,\varphi).$

16.1.6   Derive the operator equations

$$(L_+)^n Y_L^M(\theta, \varphi) = (-1)^n e^{in\varphi} \sin^{n+M} \theta \frac{d^n \sin^{-M} \theta Y_L^M(\theta, \varphi)}{(d\cos\theta)^n},$$

$$(L_-)^n Y_L^M(\theta, \varphi) = e^{-in\varphi} \sin^{n-M} \theta \frac{d^n \sin^M \theta Y_L^M(\theta, \varphi)}{(d\cos\theta)^n}.$$

Hint. Try mathematical induction (Section 1.4).

16.1.7   Show, using $(L_-)^n$, that

$$Y_L^{-M}(\theta, \varphi) = (-1)^M \left[Y_L^M(\theta, \varphi) \right]^*.$$

16.1.8   Verify by explicit calculation that

(a) $L_+ Y_1^0(\theta, \varphi) = -\sqrt{\dfrac{3}{4\pi}} \sin\theta e^{i\varphi} = \sqrt{2} Y_1^1(\theta, \varphi),$

(b) $L_- Y_1^0(\theta, \varphi) = +\sqrt{\dfrac{3}{4\pi}} \sin\theta e^{-i\varphi} = \sqrt{2} Y_1^{-1}(\theta, \varphi).$

The signs have the indicated values because the spherical harmonics were defined to be consistent with the results obtained using the ladder operators L_+ and L_- (Condon-Shortley phase).

16.2   ANGULAR MOMENTUM COUPLING

An important application of ladder operators is to systems in which a resultant angular momentum is the sum of two individual angular momenta. Because the angular momenta have directional properties, we anticipate a result that has some properties in common with vector addition, but because these are quantum mechanical quantities involving non-commuting operators, we need to study the problem in more detail.

If $\mathbf{j}_1$ and $\mathbf{j}_2$ are two individual angular momentum operators that act on different coordinate sets (as, e.g., the coordinates of two different particles), then they are unrelated and all components of each must commute with every component of the other. This will enable us to carry out a detailed analysis of operators of the combined system, for which the total angular momentum operator is $\mathbf{J} = \mathbf{j}_1 + \mathbf{j}_2$, with components $J_x = j_{1x} + j_{2x}$, $J_y = j_{1y} + j_{2y}$, $J_z = j_{1z} + j_{2z}$, with the overall operator $\mathbf{J}^2 = J_x^2 + J_y^2 + J_z^2$.

To discuss the problem, we will need the commutators

$$[j_{1k}, j_{1l}] = i\varepsilon_{kln} j_{1n}, \quad [j_{2k}, j_{2l}] = i\varepsilon_{kln} j_{2n}, \quad [j_{1k}, j_{2l}] = 0. \tag{16.32}$$

For the first two commutators, k, l, n are x, y, z in any order; the third commutator vanishes for all k, l including $k = l$. From the commutators in Eq. (16.32), it is easily established that the overall angular momentum components obey the commutation rules

$$[J_x, J_y] = iJ_z, \quad [J_y, J_z] = iJ_x, \quad [J_z, J_x] = iJ_y, \tag{16.33}$$

so these overall components satisfy the generic angular momentum commutation relations, meaning also that

$$[\mathbf{J}^2, J_i] = 0. \tag{16.34}$$

In addition,

$$[\mathbf{J}^2, \mathbf{j}_1^2] = [\mathbf{J}^2, \mathbf{j}_2^2] = 0. \tag{16.35}$$

However, it is **not** true that the components of $\mathbf{j}_1$ or $\mathbf{j}_2$, namely j_{1i} or j_{2i}, commute with $\mathbf{J}^2$, even though $\mathbf{J}^2$ and the sum $j_{1i} + j_{2i}$ do commute.

Example 16.2.1 COMMUTATION RULES FOR J COMPONENTS

To find the commutator $[\mathbf{J}^2, j_{1z}]$, write

$$\mathbf{J}^2 = (\mathbf{j}_1 + \mathbf{j}_2)^2 = \mathbf{j}_1^2 + \mathbf{j}_2^2 + 2\mathbf{j}_1 \cdot \mathbf{j}_2$$

$$= \mathbf{j}_1^2 + \mathbf{j}_2^2 + 2\left(j_{1x}j_{2x} + j_{1y}j_{2y} + j_{1z}j_{2z}\right),$$

so we have

$$[\mathbf{J}^2, j_{1z}] = [\mathbf{j}_1^2, j_{1z}] + [\mathbf{j}_2^2, j_{1z}] + 2\Big([j_{1x}j_{2x}, j_{1z}] + [j_{1y}j_{2y}, j_{1z}] + [j_{1z}j_{2z}, j_{1z}]\Big)$$

$$= 2\Big(j_{2x}[j_{1x}, j_{1z}] + j_{2y}[j_{1y}, j_{1z}]\Big) = 2i\left(j_{1x}j_{2y} - j_{1y}j_{2x}\right), \tag{16.36}$$

where we have dropped terms in which the commutators involve different particles and those, e.g., $[\mathbf{j}_1^2, j_{1z}]$, which vanish because the individual-particle operators are angular momenta.

Equation (16.36) clearly shows that $[\mathbf{J}^2, j_{1z}]$ is nonzero. However, its contributions are equal and opposite to those of $[\mathbf{J}^2, j_{2z}]$, explaining why $[\mathbf{J}^2, J_z]$ does vanish.

Consider next $[\mathbf{J}^2, \mathbf{j}_1^2]$. Again expanding $\mathbf{J}^2$, we get

$$[\mathbf{J}^2, \mathbf{j}_1^2] = [\mathbf{j}_1^2, \mathbf{j}_1^2] + [\mathbf{j}_2^2, \mathbf{j}_1^2] + 2\left([j_{1x}j_{2x}, \mathbf{j}_1^2] + [j_{1y}j_{2y}, \mathbf{j}_1^2] + [j_{1z}j_{2z}, \mathbf{j}_1^2]\right).$$

Every term of this equation vanishes, so $\mathbf{J}^2$ and $\mathbf{j}_1^2$ commute. ∎

We have noted that $\mathbf{j}_1^2$, $\mathbf{j}_2^2$, and J_z all commute with each other and with $\mathbf{J}^2$, j_{1z}, and j_{2z}, but that the last three of these operators do not all commute with each other. There are therefore different ways of selecting maximal sets of mutually commuting operators for which we can construct simultaneous eigenfunctions. One possibility is to select $\mathbf{j}_1^2$, $\mathbf{j}_2^2$, j_{1z}, j_{2z}, and J_z, which has the advantage that the simultaneous eigenfunctions are just products of the eigenstates for individual $\mathbf{j}_i$, but has the disadvantage that we will not have states of definite total angular momentum $\mathbf{J}^2$. This is a big disadvantage, because in reality different angular momenta in the same system actually interact to some extent. If we add to the Hamiltonian of our problem a small term (a **perturbation**) that causes the individual angular momenta not quite to be independent, our system will still strictly have conservation of $\mathbf{J}^2$ (i.e., H and $\mathbf{J}^2$ will still commute), but the perturbation added to the Hamiltonian will not commute with $\mathbf{j}_1$ and $\mathbf{j}_2$.

Alternatively, and for most purposes better, we could choose the mutually commuting operator set $\mathbf{J}^2$, $\mathbf{j}_1^2$, $\mathbf{j}_2^2$, and J_z, which would describe states of definite total angular momentum, but these states would be mixtures of the individual angular-momentum states and would not have definite values of j_{1z} or j_{2z}. It is the purpose of this section to relate these two descriptions by finding the equations that connect (i.e., **couple**) the individual angular momenta to form states of definite $\mathbf{J}^2$.

To simplify future discussion, we can refer to the product basis of the preceding paragraph as the m_1, m_2 basis, and call the alternative basis of definite J the J, M basis. The m_1, m_2 basis members also have definite values of M, but not J; most members of the J, M basis will not have definite values of either m_1 or m_2. If we stick with problems in which j_1 and j_2 are fixed, all members of both bases will have the same definite values of these quantum numbers.

Before getting into the details, let's make two observations. First, since we have raising and lowering operators that we can apply to the J, M basis, the functions in this basis must include all the M values for any J that is present at all. Second, since both bases have definite values of M, the transition from one basis to the other cannot mix functions of different M.

Vector Model

We begin with some qualitative observations. Since $J_z = j_{1z} + j_{2z}$ (with eigenvalues we call M) is part of both our commuting operator sets, we can conclude, from looking at the m_1, m_2 basis, that the maximum eigenvalue $M_{\max}$ of J_z will occur when $m_1 = j_1$ and $m_2 = j_2$, so $M_{\max} = j_1 + j_2$. Moving now to the J, M basis, which of course spans the same function space, we see that because $M_{\max}$ is the maximum M value, it must be a member of a multiplet with $J = M_{\max}$, and this must be the largest possible J. Thus, $J_{\max} = j_1 + j_2$.

To establish the minimum value possible for the quantum number J is a little trickier, and we will come back to that shortly. The result, which is simple, is that $J_{\min} = |j_1 - j_2|$. These maximum and minimum values of J correspond to the notion that the classical vector sum $\mathbf{j}_1 + \mathbf{j}_2$ has a maximum length equal to the sum of the lengths of these vectors and a minimum length equal to the absolute value of their difference; the quantum analog of this notion is not quantitatively exact because the magnitude of each $\mathbf{j}$ is actually $\sqrt{j(j+1)}$.

Further qualitative observations follow if we tabulate the various possible m_1, m_2 functions of various M values. The concept can be understood from a simple example. Suppose $j_1 = 2$, $j_2 = 1$. Then the members of the m_1, m_2 basis can be grouped as shown here. The kets in the table are labeled in more detail than usual to avoid potential confusion; those labeled m_1 have j value j_1, those labeled m_2 have $j = j_2$.

$$M = +3 \;\; |m_1 = +2\rangle |m_2 = +1\rangle$$
$$M = +2 \;\; |m_1 = +2\rangle |m_2 = 0\rangle \quad |m_1 = +1\rangle |m_2 = +1\rangle$$
$$M = +1 \;\; |m_1 = +2\rangle |m_2 = -1\rangle \quad |m_1 = +1\rangle |m_2 = 0\rangle \quad |m_1 = 0\rangle |m_2 = +1\rangle$$
$$M = 0 \;\; |m_1 = +1\rangle |m_2 = -1\rangle \quad |m_1 = 0\rangle |m_2 = 0\rangle \quad |m_1 = -1\rangle |m_2 = +1\rangle$$
$$M = -1 \;\; |m_1 = -2\rangle |m_2 = +1\rangle \quad |m_1 = -1\rangle |m_2 = 0\rangle \quad |m_1 = 0\rangle |m_2 = -1\rangle$$
$$M = -2 \;\; |m_1 = -2\rangle |m_2 = 0\rangle \quad |m_1 = -1\rangle |m_2 = -1\rangle$$
$$M = -3 \;\; |m_1 = -2\rangle |m_2 = -1\rangle$$

Because the basis transformations we are discussing only mix basis functions of the same M, a transition to the J, M basis will have the same number of functions of each M as are in the row of our table for that M. If there is only one function in the row, it must (without change) be a member of the J, M basis, and we may use it as a starting point for getting all the other members of the multiplet for the same J by application of the ladder operators. So in our current example, we can start from $|m_1 = +2\rangle|m_2 = +1\rangle$, and make one member of the multiplet for each M value in the table.

Once this has been done, we will have constructed as many J, M functions as there are entries in the first column of the table (but remember that in most cases they will not be the specific functions sitting in that column). But that observation does tell us that the numbers of functions that are still unused (but not their exact forms) will correspond with the numbers of functions in the remainder of the table. In particular, we see that there will in our example be one function left over with $M = 2$. Because it cannot have a $J = 3$ component, it must be a $|J = 2, M = 2\rangle$ eigenfunction and therefore must be orthogonal to the $|J = 3, M = 2\rangle$ function we have already found. That means that we can obtain it by Gram-Schmidt orthogonalization within the function space for $M = +2$.

From the $|J = 2, M = 2\rangle$ function, we can apply a ladder operator to find $|J = 2, M\rangle$ basis members with other M values, the number of which will correspond to the number of entries in the second column of our table. To continue to a third column, we would need to find a $M = +1$ function orthogonal to **both** the $|J = 3, M = +1\rangle$ and $|J = 2, M = +1\rangle$ functions. This process can be continued until the m_1, m_2 basis has been exhausted.

Taking now a further look at our table, we see that the number of columns with entries increases as we decrease M from its maximum value until M has reached $|j_1 - j_2|$; for smaller $|M|$ than that, the number of columns in use stays constant, because of limitations in the way the individual m values can be chosen to add up to M. That gives us a graphical indication that the smallest J value will be $|j_1 - j_2|$.

A more algebraic way of determining the smallest resultant J is based on a computation of the total number of J, M states generated if the possible J values run from an as yet undetermined value J_{min} to our previously determined maximum value J_{max}. Since the number of states for each J is $2J + 1$, the total number of J, M states we will have produced is

$$\sum_{J=J_{min}}^{J=J_{max}} (2J + 1) = (J_{max} - J_{min} + 1)(J_{max} + J_{min} + 1)$$

$$= (2j_1 + 1)(2j_2 + 1), \tag{16.37}$$

where the second line of this equation reflects the fact that the total number of states is readily counted in the m_1, m_2 basis. Inserting the value $J_{max} = j_1 + j_2$ and solving for J_{min}, we find

$$J_{min} = |j_1 - j_2|.$$

Another way of stating this result is to observe that the possible values of J satisfy a **triangle rule**, meaning that they occur in unit steps from a maximum of $j_1 + j_2$ to a minimum of $|j_1 - j_2|$.

Ladder Operator Construction

To develop a quantitative description of angular momentum coupling, we consider the case of general j_1 and j_2, and start from the lone member of the m_1, m_2 basis with $M = j_1 + j_2$. In line with our earlier discussion, this m_1, m_2 basis member must also be a function of the definite J value $J_{max} = j_1 + j_2$. Using a notation in which the lower entry in each ket is its J value and the upper entry gives the value of M, we indicate this by writing

$$\left| \begin{matrix} J_{max} \\ J_{max} \end{matrix} \right\rangle = \left| \begin{matrix} j_1 \\ j_1 \end{matrix} \right\rangle \left| \begin{matrix} j_2 \\ j_2 \end{matrix} \right\rangle. \tag{16.38}$$

We now generate additional states of the same J but with different M by applying the lowering operator J_- to Eq. (16.38); when we apply it to the right-hand side, we do so in the form $J_- = j_{1-} + j_{2-}$. The result, for the left side of Eq. (16.38), is

$$J_- \left| \begin{matrix} J_{max} \\ J_{max} \end{matrix} \right\rangle = \sqrt{2 J_{max}} \left| \begin{matrix} J_{max} - 1 \\ J_{max} \end{matrix} \right\rangle. \tag{16.39}$$

The coefficient $\sqrt{2 J_{max}}$ is that given by Eq. (16.31) for $J = M = J_{max}$. For the right side of Eq. (16.38), we get

$$(j_{1-} + j_{2-}) \left[\left| \begin{matrix} j_1 \\ j_1 \end{matrix} \right\rangle \left| \begin{matrix} j_2 \\ j_2 \end{matrix} \right\rangle \right] = \left[j_{1-} \left| \begin{matrix} j_1 \\ j_1 \end{matrix} \right\rangle \right] \left| \begin{matrix} j_2 \\ j_2 \end{matrix} \right\rangle + \left| \begin{matrix} j_1 \\ j_1 \end{matrix} \right\rangle \left[j_{2-} \left| \begin{matrix} j_2 \\ j_2 \end{matrix} \right\rangle \right]$$

$$= \sqrt{2 j_1} \left| \begin{matrix} j_1 - 1 \\ j_1 \end{matrix} \right\rangle \left| \begin{matrix} j_2 \\ j_2 \end{matrix} \right\rangle + \sqrt{2 j_2} \left| \begin{matrix} j_1 \\ j_1 \end{matrix} \right\rangle \left| \begin{matrix} j_2 - 1 \\ j_2 \end{matrix} \right\rangle, \tag{16.40}$$

where we have again obtained the coefficients from Eq. (16.31), but now evaluating them for the first term with $(J, M) = (j_1, j_1)$ and for the second term with $(J, M) = (j_2, j_2)$.

Combining these results, and solving for $\left| \begin{matrix} J_{max} - 1 \\ J_{max} \end{matrix} \right\rangle$,

$$\left| \begin{matrix} J_{max} - 1 \\ J_{max} \end{matrix} \right\rangle = \sqrt{\frac{j_1}{J_{max}}} \left| \begin{matrix} j_1 - 1 \\ j_1 \end{matrix} \right\rangle \left| \begin{matrix} j_2 \\ j_2 \end{matrix} \right\rangle + \sqrt{\frac{j_2}{J_{max}}} \left| \begin{matrix} j_1 \\ j_1 \end{matrix} \right\rangle \left| \begin{matrix} j_2 - 1 \\ j_2 \end{matrix} \right\rangle. \tag{16.41}$$

With escalating complexity, we could continue this process to smaller values of M.

As indicated in our earlier, more qualitative discussion, we can reach functions with $J = J_{max} - 1$ by starting from the unused member of the set of two functions

$$\left| \begin{matrix} j_1 - 1 \\ j_1 \end{matrix} \right\rangle \left| \begin{matrix} j_2 \\ j_2 \end{matrix} \right\rangle, \quad \left| \begin{matrix} j_1 \\ j_1 \end{matrix} \right\rangle \left| \begin{matrix} j_2 - 1 \\ j_2 \end{matrix} \right\rangle.$$

The quantity we seek,

$$\left| \begin{matrix} J_{max} - 1 \\ J_{max} - 1 \end{matrix} \right\rangle,$$

will be the function in the above-defined subspace that is orthogonal to

$$\left| \begin{matrix} J_{max} - 1 \\ J_{max} \end{matrix} \right\rangle$$

as given in Eq. (16.41), and therefore will be

$$\left| \begin{matrix} J_{max} - 1 \\ J_{max} - 1 \end{matrix} \right\rangle = -\sqrt{\frac{j_2}{J_{max}}} \left| \begin{matrix} j_1 - 1 \\ j_1 \end{matrix} \right\rangle \left| \begin{matrix} j_2 \\ j_2 \end{matrix} \right\rangle + \sqrt{\frac{j_1}{J_{max}}} \left| \begin{matrix} j_1 \\ j_1 \end{matrix} \right\rangle \left| \begin{matrix} j_2 - 1 \\ j_2 \end{matrix} \right\rangle. \tag{16.42}$$

At this point we note that the function produced by Eq. (16.42) could have been written with all its signs changed, as the orthogonalization process does not determine the sign of the orthogonal function. This only matters if we wish to correlate the signs of our J, M constructions with work by others. Irrespective of our choice of signs, we can apply J_- to reach the full set of M values, and then continue to states of smaller J until the m_1, m_2 space is exhausted.

The general result of the above-described processes is to obtain each J, M eigenstate as a linear combination of m_1, m_2 states of the same M, in a fashion summarized by the following equation (written in a less cumbersome notation now that the need for detail has disappeared):

$$|J, M\rangle = \sum_{m_1, m_2} C(j_1, j_2, J | m_1, m_2, M) |j_1, m_1; j_2, m_2\rangle. \tag{16.43}$$

Here $|j_1, m_1; j_2, m_2\rangle$ stands for $|j_1, m_1\rangle |j_2, m_2\rangle$ and we have given over to the coefficient $C(j_1, j_2, J | m_1, m_2, M)$ the responsibility to vanish when $m_1 + m_2 \neq M$. Thus, the apparent double summation in Eq. (16.43) is actually a single sum. The coefficients in Eq. (16.43) are called **Clebsch-Gordan coefficients**. To resolve the sign ambiguity resulting from the orthogonalization processes, they are defined to have signs specified by the Condon-Shortley phase convention.

It is important to realize that all the results of this section remain valid irrespective of whether j_1, j_2, or both are integral or half-integral. For example, if $j_1 = 1$ and $j_2 = \frac{1}{2}$ (corresponding to the coupling of the orbital and spin angular momenta of an electron), the possible J, M states will be a **quartet** for $J = 3/2$ (with M values $+3/2$, $+1/2$, $-1/2$, $-3/2$), and a **doublet** for $J = 1/2$ (with M values $+1/2$ and $-1/2$).

A second way to look at the Clebsch-Gordan coefficients is to identify them as the scalar products

$$C(j_1, j_2, J | m_1, m_2, M) = \langle J, M | j_1, m_1; j_2, m_2 \rangle. \tag{16.44}$$

Because of the method used for the construction of the $|J, M\rangle$, we can make one additional observation: The Clebsch-Gordan coefficients will all be real, even if the $|j_1, m_1\rangle$ and $|j_2, m_2\rangle$ used for their construction are not.

The Clebsch-Gordan expansion can be interpreted in yet another way. We can view the Clebsch-Gordan coefficients as the elements of a transformation matrix converting functions of the m_1, m_2 basis into those of the J, M basis; since both basis sets are orthonormal, the transformation must be unitary (and because it is real, orthogonal). This means that the inverse transformation, $(J, M) \rightarrow (m_1, m_2)$, must have a transformation matrix that is the transpose of that for the forward transformation $(m_1, m_2) \rightarrow (J, M)$. That means that we also have the equation

$$|j_1, m_1; j_2, m_2\rangle = \sum_{JM} C(j_1, j_2, J | m_1, m_2, M) | J, M\rangle. \tag{16.45}$$

This equation is correct and corresponds to our discussion. Note that instead of reversing the index order of the transformation matrix we have interchanged the index sets identifying the functions.

In passing, we make one further comment. While the Clebsch-Gordan coefficients can be identified as forming a transformation matrix, note that their row/column indexing differs from the pattern to which we are accustomed, since, instead of labels running from 1 to n (the dimension of the transformation), we are using in one dimension the compound index (m_1, m_2), and in the other dimension the compound quantity (J, M). This Clebsch-Gordan matrix will be somewhat sparse (containing many zero elements). The zeros occur because the coefficients vanish unless $M = m_1 + m_2$.

There is a significant literature on the practical computation of Clebsch-Gordan coefficients,[1] but to make the present discussion complete we simply give here a closed general formula:

$$C(j_1, j_2, J | m_1, m_2, M) = F_1 F_2 F_3, \tag{16.46}$$

where

$$F_1 = \sqrt{\frac{(j_1 + j_2 - J)!(J + j_1 - j_2)!(J + j_2 - j_1)!(2J + 1)}{(j_1 + j_2 + J + 1)!}}$$

$$F_2 = \sqrt{(J + M)!(J - M)!(j_1 + m_1)!(j_1 - m_1)!(j_2 + m_2)!(j_2 - m_2)!},$$

$$F_3 = \sum_s \frac{(-1)^s}{(j_1 - m_1 - s)!(j_2 + m_2 - s)!(J - j_2 + m_1 + s)!}$$

$$\times \frac{1}{(J - j_1 - m_2 + s)!(j_1 + j_2 - J - s)!s!}.$$

The F_3 summation is over all integer values of s for which the factorials all have non-negative arguments (which will be integral). The sum is therefore finite in extent and F_3 is a closed form. Equation (16.46) is only to be used for parameter values that satisfy the angular momentum and coupling conditions: j_1, j_2, J must satisfy the triangle condition, m_i is to be from the sequence $l_i, l_i - 1, \ldots, -l_i$ $(i = 1, 2)$, M to be from $J, J - 1, \ldots, -J$, and $M = m_1 + m_2$.

Finally, we call attention to the fact that Clebsch-Gordan coefficients have symmetries that are not obvious from the foregoing development. To expose the symmetries, it is convenient to convert them to the Wigner $3j$-symbols, defined as

$$\begin{pmatrix} j_1 & j_2 & j_3 \\ m_1 & m_2 & m_3 \end{pmatrix} = \frac{(-1)^{j_1 - j_2 - m_3}}{(2j_3 + 1)^{1/2}} C(j_1, j_2, j_3 | m_1, m_2, -m_3). \tag{16.47}$$

---

[1]See Biedenharn and Louck, Brink and Satchler, Edmonds, Rose, and Wigner in Additional Readings. Clebsch-Gordan coefficients are also tabulated in many places, and can easily be found online by a Web search.

Extensive discussion of $3j$-symbols and related quantities is beyond the scope of this book. This important, but advanced, topic is presented in most of the sources listed under Additional Readings.

The $3j$-symbols are invariant under even permutations of the indices (1,2,3), but under odd permutations $(1, 2, 3) \rightarrow (k, l, n)$ transform as follows:

$$\begin{pmatrix} j_1 & j_2 & j_3 \\ m_1 & m_2 & m_3 \end{pmatrix} = (-1)^{j_1+j_2+j_3} \begin{pmatrix} j_k & j_l & j_n \\ m_k & m_l & m_n \end{pmatrix}. \tag{16.48}$$

They also have the following symmetry under change of sign of their lower indices:

$$\begin{pmatrix} j_1 & j_2 & j_3 \\ m_1 & m_2 & m_3 \end{pmatrix} = (-1)^{j_1+j_2+j_3} \begin{pmatrix} j_1 & j_2 & j_3 \\ -m_1 & -m_2 & -m_3 \end{pmatrix}. \tag{16.49}$$

Even though some of the j_i may be half-integral, remember that j_3 must be equal to $j_1 + j_2$ or differ therefrom by an integer. This fact causes the powers of -1 in Eqs. (16.47) through (16.49) to be integral, so these factors are not multiple-valued and the sign assignments of the $3j$-symbols are unambiguous. These symmetry relations make a table of $3j$-symbols more compact than one of Clebsch-Gordan coefficients; such tables can be found in the literature,[2] and a short list is included here, as Table 16.1.

We close this section with two examples.

Table 16.1 Wigner $3j$-Symbols

$$\begin{pmatrix} \frac{1}{2} & \frac{1}{2} & 1 \\ \frac{1}{2} & -\frac{1}{2} & 0 \end{pmatrix} = \frac{1}{\sqrt{6}} \qquad \begin{pmatrix} \frac{1}{2} & \frac{1}{2} & 1 \\ \frac{1}{2} & \frac{1}{2} & -1 \end{pmatrix} = -\frac{1}{\sqrt{3}} \qquad \begin{pmatrix} \frac{1}{2} & \frac{1}{2} & 0 \\ \frac{1}{2} & -\frac{1}{2} & 0 \end{pmatrix} = \frac{1}{\sqrt{2}}$$

$$\begin{pmatrix} 1 & \frac{1}{2} & \frac{3}{2} \\ 1 & \frac{1}{2} & -\frac{3}{2} \end{pmatrix} = \frac{1}{2} \qquad \begin{pmatrix} 1 & \frac{1}{2} & \frac{3}{2} \\ 1 & -\frac{1}{2} & -\frac{1}{2} \end{pmatrix} = -\frac{1}{\sqrt{12}} \qquad \begin{pmatrix} 1 & \frac{1}{2} & \frac{3}{2} \\ 0 & \frac{1}{2} & -\frac{1}{2} \end{pmatrix} = -\frac{1}{\sqrt{6}}$$

$$\begin{pmatrix} 1 & 1 & 0 \\ 0 & 0 & 0 \end{pmatrix} = -\frac{1}{\sqrt{3}} \qquad \begin{pmatrix} 1 & 1 & 0 \\ 1 & -1 & 0 \end{pmatrix} = \frac{1}{\sqrt{3}} \qquad \begin{pmatrix} 1 & 1 & 1 \\ 0 & 0 & 0 \end{pmatrix} = 0$$

$$\begin{pmatrix} 1 & 1 & 1 \\ 1 & -1 & 0 \end{pmatrix} = \frac{1}{\sqrt{6}} \qquad \begin{pmatrix} 1 & 1 & 2 \\ 0 & 0 & 0 \end{pmatrix} = \sqrt{\frac{2}{15}} \qquad \begin{pmatrix} 1 & 1 & 2 \\ 1 & -1 & 0 \end{pmatrix} = \frac{1}{\sqrt{30}}$$

$$\begin{pmatrix} 1 & 1 & 2 \\ 1 & 0 & -1 \end{pmatrix} = -\frac{1}{\sqrt{10}} \qquad \begin{pmatrix} 1 & 1 & 2 \\ 1 & 1 & -2 \end{pmatrix} = \frac{1}{\sqrt{5}} \qquad \begin{pmatrix} 1 & 2 & 2 \\ 1 & -1 & 0 \end{pmatrix} = -\frac{1}{\sqrt{10}}$$

$$\begin{pmatrix} 1 & 2 & 2 \\ 1 & -2 & 1 \end{pmatrix} = \frac{1}{\sqrt{15}} \qquad \begin{pmatrix} 1 & 2 & 2 \\ 0 & 1 & -1 \end{pmatrix} = -\frac{1}{\sqrt{30}} \qquad \begin{pmatrix} 1 & 2 & 2 \\ 0 & 2 & -2 \end{pmatrix} = \sqrt{\frac{2}{15}}$$

$$\begin{pmatrix} 1 & 2 & 2 \\ 0 & 0 & 0 \end{pmatrix} = 0 \qquad \begin{pmatrix} 1 & 2 & 3 \\ 0 & 0 & 0 \end{pmatrix} = -\sqrt{\frac{3}{35}} \qquad \begin{pmatrix} 1 & 2 & 3 \\ 1 & -1 & 0 \end{pmatrix} = -\frac{1}{\sqrt{35}}$$

$$\begin{pmatrix} 1 & 2 & 3 \\ 1 & 0 & -1 \end{pmatrix} = \sqrt{\frac{2}{35}} \qquad \begin{pmatrix} 1 & 2 & 3 \\ 1 & -2 & 1 \end{pmatrix} = \frac{1}{\sqrt{105}} \qquad \begin{pmatrix} 1 & 2 & 3 \\ 1 & 1 & -2 \end{pmatrix} = -\sqrt{\frac{2}{21}}$$

$$\begin{pmatrix} 1 & 2 & 3 \\ 1 & 2 & -3 \end{pmatrix} = \frac{1}{\sqrt{7}} \qquad \begin{pmatrix} 1 & 2 & 3 \\ 0 & 1 & -1 \end{pmatrix} = \sqrt{\frac{8}{105}} \qquad \begin{pmatrix} 1 & 2 & 3 \\ 0 & 2 & -2 \end{pmatrix} = -\frac{1}{\sqrt{21}}$$

[2]See, for example, M. Rotenberg, R. Bivins, N. Metropolis, and J. K. Wooten, Jr., *The 3j- and 6j-Symbols*. Cambridge, MA: Massachusetts Institute of Technology Press (1959).

Example 16.2.2   Two Spinors

This example describes a problem that exists entirely in a abstract space, namely the coupling of two spin-$\frac{1}{2}$ particles (e.g., electrons) to form combined states of definite J. Letting α stand for a normalized single-particle state with $j = \frac{1}{2}$, $m = +\frac{1}{2}$, with β a normalized state with $j = \frac{1}{2}$, $m = -\frac{1}{2}$, we have the following four states in the m_1, m_2 basis:

$$
\begin{aligned}
M &= 1: & \alpha\alpha & \\
M &= 0: & \alpha\beta \quad & \beta\alpha \\
M &= -1: & \beta\beta &
\end{aligned}
$$

For all these two-particle states, the first symbol refers to particle 1, the second to particle 2. From Eq. (16.31) and Example 16.1.2, we have $j_-\alpha = \beta$, $j_-\beta = 0$, and we can use the following rearrangement of Eq. (16.31) to deal with the $|J, M\rangle$ states. Again we use a notation in which the lower entry in the ket is J; the upper entry is M:

$$
\left| \begin{matrix} M-1 \\ J \end{matrix} \right\rangle = \frac{1}{\sqrt{(J+M)(J-M+1)}} J_- \left| \begin{matrix} M \\ J \end{matrix} \right\rangle. \tag{16.50}
$$

The maximum M value in this system is $M = +1$, so the one state of this M value must have $J = 1$. showing that $\left| \begin{matrix} 1 \\ 1 \end{matrix} \right\rangle = \alpha\alpha$. Starting from it, we lower M:

$$
\left| \begin{matrix} 1 \\ 1 \end{matrix} \right\rangle = \alpha\alpha,
$$

$$
\left| \begin{matrix} 0 \\ 1 \end{matrix} \right\rangle = \frac{1}{\sqrt{2}} J_- \left| \begin{matrix} 1 \\ 1 \end{matrix} \right\rangle = \frac{1}{\sqrt{2}} \beta\alpha + \frac{1}{\sqrt{2}} \alpha\beta,
$$

$$
\left| \begin{matrix} -1 \\ 1 \end{matrix} \right\rangle = \frac{1}{\sqrt{2}} J_- \left| \begin{matrix} 0 \\ 1 \end{matrix} \right\rangle = \frac{1}{\sqrt{2}} \left[\frac{1}{\sqrt{2}} \beta\beta + \frac{1}{\sqrt{2}} \beta\beta \right] = \beta\beta.
$$

These are the well-known members of the $S = 1$ spin multiplet, which is known as a **triplet**. At $M = 0$, where there were two m_1, m_2 states, the state orthogonal to $\left| \begin{matrix} 0 \\ 1 \end{matrix} \right\rangle$ must be the $\left| \begin{matrix} 0 \\ 0 \end{matrix} \right\rangle$ state.

Even though we do not have an entirely explicit representation of the states α and β, we do know that they are normalized eigenstates of a Hermitian operator (J_z) with different eigenvalues, and therefore they must be orthogonal. Thus, we can apply the Gram-Schmidt process to the $M = 0$ subspace, using the relations

$$
\langle \alpha | \alpha \rangle = \langle \beta | \beta \rangle = 1, \quad \langle \alpha | \beta \rangle = 0.
$$

We easily find that the normalized function orthogonal to $(\alpha\beta + \beta\alpha)/\sqrt{2}$ is $(\alpha\beta - \beta\alpha)/\sqrt{2}$. It is the only member of the $S = 0$ multiplet, and is therefore known as a **singlet**. Note that we didn't have to know anything specific about spin operators to carry out this analysis.

Our tableau of states can now be written in the J, M basis:

$$J = 1 \qquad\qquad J = 0$$

$$M = 1 \qquad \alpha\alpha$$

$$M = 0 \qquad (\alpha\beta + \beta\alpha)/\sqrt{2} \qquad (\alpha\beta - \beta\alpha)/\sqrt{2}$$

$$M = -1 \qquad \beta\beta$$

From the J, M tableau, we can read out the Clebsch-Gordan coefficients:

$$C\left(\tfrac{1}{2}, \tfrac{1}{2}, 1 \middle| \tfrac{1}{2}, \tfrac{1}{2}, 1\right) = 1$$

$$C\left(\tfrac{1}{2}, \tfrac{1}{2}, 1 \middle| \tfrac{1}{2}, -\tfrac{1}{2}, 0\right) = C\left(\tfrac{1}{2}, \tfrac{1}{2}, 1 \middle| -\tfrac{1}{2}, \tfrac{1}{2}, 0\right) = \frac{1}{\sqrt{2}}$$

$$C\left(\tfrac{1}{2}, \tfrac{1}{2}, 0 \middle| \tfrac{1}{2}, -\tfrac{1}{2}, 0\right) = -C\left(\tfrac{1}{2}, \tfrac{1}{2}, 1 \middle| -\tfrac{1}{2}, \tfrac{1}{2}, 0\right) = \frac{1}{\sqrt{2}}$$

$$C\left(\tfrac{1}{2}, \tfrac{1}{2}, 1 \middle| -\tfrac{1}{2}, -\tfrac{1}{2}, -1\right) = 1$$

These coefficients can also be obtained from our table of $3j$-symbols. Using Eq. (16.47), we find the coefficients for $|J = 1, M = 0\rangle$ to be

$$C\left(\tfrac{1}{2}, \tfrac{1}{2}, 1 \middle| \tfrac{1}{2}, -\tfrac{1}{2}, 0\right) = \sqrt{3} \begin{pmatrix} \tfrac{1}{2} & \tfrac{1}{2} & 1 \\ \tfrac{1}{2} & -\tfrac{1}{2} & 0 \end{pmatrix},$$

$$C\left(\tfrac{1}{2}, \tfrac{1}{2}, 1 \middle| -\tfrac{1}{2}, \tfrac{1}{2}, 0\right) = \sqrt{3} \begin{pmatrix} \tfrac{1}{2} & \tfrac{1}{2} & 1 \\ -\tfrac{1}{2} & \tfrac{1}{2} & 0 \end{pmatrix}.$$

Both these $3j$-symbols correspond to the same entry in Table 16.1, and the symmetry rules give each the value $+1/\sqrt{6}$. Therefore, both these Clebsch-Gordan coefficients evaluate to $\sqrt{3}/\sqrt{6}$, or, as expected, $1/\sqrt{2}$.

For $|J = 0, M = 0\rangle$, we have, again calling on Eq. (16.47),

$$C\left(\tfrac{1}{2}, \tfrac{1}{2}, 0 \middle| \tfrac{1}{2}, -\tfrac{1}{2}, 0\right) = \begin{pmatrix} \tfrac{1}{2} & \tfrac{1}{2} & 0 \\ \tfrac{1}{2} & -\tfrac{1}{2} & 0 \end{pmatrix},$$

$$C\left(\tfrac{1}{2}, \tfrac{1}{2}, 0 \middle| -\tfrac{1}{2}, \tfrac{1}{2}, 0\right) = \begin{pmatrix} \tfrac{1}{2} & \tfrac{1}{2} & 0 \\ -\tfrac{1}{2} & \tfrac{1}{2} & 0 \end{pmatrix}.$$

Again these $3j$-symbols both correspond to the same tabulated entry (with value $1/\sqrt{2}$), but this time the symmetry rules cause them to have the respective values $+1/\sqrt{2}$ and $-1/\sqrt{2}$, in agreement with our explicit evaluation. ∎

Example 16.2.3   COUPLING OF p AND d ELECTRONS

As most physics students know, a p state is an angular momentum eigenstate with $l = 1$ (so m can be 1, 0, or -1). The three normalized functions constituting its multiplet are often denoted p_+, p_0, and p_-. A d state has $l = 2$; we denote the five normalized members of its multiplet d_{+2}, d_+, d_0, d_-, and d_{-2}. The m_1, m_2 basis has 15 members; grouped according to their M values, they consist of

$$
\begin{aligned}
M &= +3 & p_+d_{+2} & & \\
M &= +2 & p_+d_+ & \quad p_0d_{+2} & \\
M &= +1 & p_+d_0 & \quad p_0d_+ & \quad p_-d_{+2} \\
M &= \ \ 0 & p_+d_- & \quad p_0d_0 & \quad p_-d_+ \\
M &= -1 & p_+d_{-2} & \quad p_0d_- & \quad p_-d_0 \\
M &= -2 & p_0d_{-2} & \quad p_-d_- & \\
M &= -3 & p_-d_{-2} & &
\end{aligned}
$$

This is the same coupling of angular momenta $j = 1$ and $j = 2$ that was introduced at the beginning of the subsection entitled Vector Model, but we are now illustrating how to carry out the coupling computations using Clebsch-Gordan coefficients and $3j$-symbols. From this diagram, we expect one multiplet with $J = 3$, which in atomic spectroscopy is denoted F (multiparticle orbital angular momentum states are designated using upper-case letters); one with $J = 2$ (called D), and one with $J = 1$ (called P). Our plan is to construct these using the $3j$-symbols given in Table 16.1.

We start by writing, in the notation $|J, M\rangle$, the members of the F multiplet with $M \geq 1$ in terms of Clebsch-Gordan coefficients (those for $M < 1$ do not raise important new points):

$$|3, 3\rangle = C(1, 2, 3|1, 2, 3)\,p_+d_{+2},$$

$$|3, 2\rangle = C(1, 2, 3|1, 1, 2)\,p_+d_+ + C(1, 2, 3|0, 2, 2)\,p_0d_{+2},$$

$$|3, 1\rangle = C(1, 2, 3|1, 0, 1)\,p_+d_0 + C(1, 2, 3|0, 1, 1)\,p_0d_+ + C(1, 2, 3|-1, 2, 1)\,p_-d_{+2}.$$

The D and P multiplet members for $M \geq 1$ are

$$|2, 2\rangle = C(1, 2, 2|1, 1, 2)\,p_+d_+ + C(1, 2, 2|0, 2, 2)\,p_0d_{+2},$$

$$|2, 1\rangle = C(1, 2, 2|1, 0, 1)\,p_+d_0 + C(1, 2, 2|0, 1, 1)\,p_0d_+ + C(1, 2, 2|-1, 2, 1)\,p_-d_{+2},$$

$$|1, 1\rangle = C(1, 2, 1|1, 0, 1)\,p_+d_0 + C(1, 2, 1|0, 1, 1)\,p_0d_+ + C(1, 2, 1|-1, 2, 1)\,p_-d_{+2}.$$

We then express the Clebsch-Gordan coefficients in terms of $3j$-symbols. Doing just a representative few, using Eq. (16.47) and then the symmetry rules, Eqs. (16.48) and (16.49),

$$C(1, 2, 3|1, 2, 3) = +\sqrt{7}\begin{pmatrix} 1 & 2 & 3 \\ 1 & 2 & -3 \end{pmatrix} = 1,$$

$$C(1, 2, 2|1, 1, 2) = -\sqrt{5}\begin{pmatrix} 1 & 2 & 2 \\ 1 & 1 & -2 \end{pmatrix} = +\sqrt{5}\begin{pmatrix} 1 & 2 & 2 \\ 1 & -2 & 1 \end{pmatrix} = \sqrt{\tfrac{1}{3}},$$

$$C(1, 2, 1|-1, 2, 1) = \sqrt{3}\begin{pmatrix} 1 & 2 & 1 \\ -1 & 2 & -1 \end{pmatrix} = \sqrt{3}\begin{pmatrix} 1 & 1 & 2 \\ 1 & 1 & -2 \end{pmatrix} = \sqrt{\tfrac{3}{5}}.$$

Substituting these and other Clebsch-Gordan coefficients into the formulas for $|J, M\rangle$, we obtain the final results:

$$|3, 3\rangle = p_+d_{+2},$$

$$|3, 2\rangle = \sqrt{\frac{1}{3}}\, p_0 d_{+2} + \sqrt{\frac{2}{3}}\, p_+ d_+,$$

$$|3, 1\rangle = \sqrt{\frac{1}{15}}\, p_- d_{+2} + \sqrt{\frac{8}{15}}\, p_0 d_+ + \sqrt{\frac{2}{5}}\, p_+ d_0,$$

$$|2, 2\rangle = -\sqrt{\frac{2}{3}}\, p_0 d_{+2} + \sqrt{\frac{1}{3}}\, p_+ d_+.$$

$$|2, 1\rangle = -\sqrt{\frac{1}{3}}\, p_- d_{+2} - \sqrt{\frac{1}{6}}\, p_0 d_+ + \sqrt{\frac{1}{2}}\, p_+ d_0,$$

$$|1, 1\rangle = \sqrt{\frac{3}{5}}\, p_- d_{+2} - \sqrt{\frac{3}{10}}\, p_0 d_+ + \sqrt{\frac{1}{10}}\, p_+ d_0.$$

The reader may verify that states of the same M but different J have the required orthogonality. It is also easy to check that all these $|J, M\rangle$ states are normalized. ∎

Exercises

16.2.1 Derive recursion relations for Clebsch-Gordan coefficients. Use them to calculate $C(11J \mid m_1 m_2 M)$ for $J = 0, 1, 2$.

Hint. Use the known matrix elements of $J_+ = J_{1+} + J_{2+}$, J_{i+}, and $\mathbf{J}^2 = (\mathbf{J}_1 + \mathbf{J}_2)^2$, etc.

16.2.2 Defining $(Y_l\chi)_J^M$ by the formula

$$(Y_l\chi)_J^M = \sum C(l\tfrac{1}{2}J \mid m_l m_s M) Y_{lm_l} \chi_{m_s},$$

where $\chi_{\pm 1/2}$ are the spin up and down eigenfunctions of $\sigma_3 = \sigma_z$, show that $(Y_l\chi)_J^M$ is a J, M eigenfunction.

16.2.3 Find the (j, m) states of a p electron ($l = 1$), in which the orbital angular momentum of the electron is coupled to its spin angular momentum ($s = 1/2$) to form states whose conventional labelings are $^2p_{1/2}$ and $^2p_{3/2}$. The notation is of the general form $^{2s+1}(\text{symbol})_j$, where "symbol" is that indicating the l value (i.e., s, p, ...).

16.2.4 Repeat Exercise 16.2.3 for $l = 1$, $s = 3/2$. Apply the conventional labels to the j, m states.

16.2.5 A deuterium atom consists of a proton, a neutron, and an electron. Each of these particles has spin 1/2. The coupling of these three spins can produce J values of 3/2 and 1/2. We consider here only states with no orbital angular momentum.

(a) Show that these J, M states consist of one quartet ($J = 3/2$) and **two** linearly independent doublets ($J = 1/2$).

Hint. Make a vector-model diagram.

(b)   One way to analyze this problem is to couple the spins of the proton and neutron to form a nuclear triplet or singlet, and then to couple the resultant nuclear spin to the electron spin. Find the states that are obtained in this way (designate the single-particle states p_α, p_β, n_α, n_β, e_α, e_β).

(c)   Another way to analyze this problem is to couple the spins of the proton and electron to form an atomic triplet or singlet, and then to couple that resultant to the neutron spin. Find the states that result from this coupling scheme.

(d)   Show that the coupling schemes of parts (b) and (c) span the same Hilbert space.

Note. The actual interaction energies among these angular momenta cause the scheme of part (b) to be the better way of treating this problem (the triplet nuclear state is substantially the more stable), and the system actually looks like a spin-1 deuterium nucleus plus an electron.

16.3   SPHERICAL TENSORS

We have already seen that the set of spherical harmonics of given l transforms within itself under rotations. We now pursue this idea more formally. In Chapter 3 we saw that rotations could be characterized by the 3×3 unitary transformation matrices that transform a set of coordinates (their basis) into the new set corresponding to the rotation. These matrices could be viewed as second-rank tensors, but because they are restricted to rotational transformations, they are also known as **spherical tensors**.

We now wish to consider spherical tensors that transform more general sets of objects under rotation, and in particular those spherical tensors that have spherical harmonics as bases. Our new spherical tensors will then have dimensions other than 3×3; in fact, they must exist at all the sizes that correspond to sets of angular momentum eigenfunctions. Because we have already observed that a set of angular momentum eigenfunctions of a given J cannot be decomposed into subsets that transform only among themselves under rotation, we go one step further and call our spherical tensors **irreducible**.

Continuing for general angular momentum eigenfunctions $|L, M\rangle$, which we assume are representable in 3-D space as spherical harmonics or objects built from them by angular momentum coupling, we write the following defining equation for the spherical tensor describing the effect of a coordinate rotation R on $|L, M\rangle$:

$$R|L, M\rangle = \sum_{M'} D^L_{M'M}(R)|L, M'\rangle. \tag{16.51}$$

If the $|L, M\rangle$ are actually spherical harmonics (and not more complicated objects that resulted from angular momentum coupling), Eq. (16.51) can also be written as

$$Y^m_l(R\Omega) = \sum_{m'} D^l_{m'm}(R)Y^{m'}_l(\Omega). \tag{16.52}$$

Because we do not need to become embroiled in the details of the action of R on the coordinates, we have simply replaced (θ, φ) by the generic symbol Ω and have written $R\Omega$ to indicate the coordinates (θ', φ') that describe the point that was labeled (θ, φ) in the unrotated system. For any given l, $D^l_{m'm}(R)$ can be regarded as an element of a square matrix of dimension $2l + 1$ with rows and columns labeled by indices m' and m whose ranges are $(-l, \ldots, +l)$, not the more customary sequence starting from 1. The $D^l_{m'm}(\mathsf{R})$ are unitary, since they describe a transformation between two orthonormal sets. Because of their early exploitation by Eugene Wigner, they are sometimes called Wigner matrices. There is an extensive literature (see Additional Readings) on relationships satisfied by the $D^l_{m'm}(\mathsf{R})$ and on formulas for their evaluation. A related topic included in this book is the formula, Eq. (3.37), giving the transformation of the basis x, y, z by a rotation through Euler angles α, β, γ.

Addition Theorem

Equation (16.52) can be used to establish important rotational invariance properties. For example, consider a quantity A defined as

$$A = \sum_m Y_l^m(\Omega_1)^* Y_l^m(\Omega_2), \tag{16.53}$$

where Ω_1 and Ω_2 are two unrelated sets of angular coordinates. We apply a rotation R to the coordinate system, denoting the result $\mathsf{R}A$, and evaluating the right-hand side using Eq. (16.52):

$$\mathsf{R}A = \sum_m \left(\sum_\mu D^l_{\mu m}(\mathsf{R}) Y_l^\mu(\Omega_1) \right)^* \left(\sum_\nu D^l_{\nu m}(\mathsf{R}) Y_l^\nu(\Omega_2) \right). \tag{16.54}$$

We now reorder the summations in Eq. (16.54), and, in the second line of Eq. (16.55), use the fact that D is unitary to change D^* to the transpose of D^{-1}, thereby leading to the simplification in the third line. We have

$$\mathsf{R}A = \sum_{\mu\nu} \left(\sum_m D^l_{\mu m}(\mathsf{R})^* D^l_{\nu m}(\mathsf{R}) \right) Y_l^\mu(\Omega_1)^* Y_l^\nu(\Omega_2)$$

$$= \sum_{\mu\nu} \left(\sum_m \left[\mathsf{D}^l(\mathsf{R})^{-1} \right]_{m\mu} \left[\mathsf{D}^l(\mathsf{R}) \right]_{\nu m} \right) Y_l^\mu(\Omega_1)^* Y_l^\nu(\Omega_2)$$

$$= \sum_{\mu\nu} \delta_{\mu\nu} Y_l^\mu(\Omega_1)^* Y_l^\nu(\Omega_2) = \sum_\mu Y_l^\mu(\Omega_1)^* Y_l^\mu(\Omega_2) = A. \tag{16.55}$$

This shows that A is rotationally invariant, and is the starting point for an explanation of why a totally occupied atomic subshell (particles occupying all m values for a given l) leads to a spherically symmetric overall distribution.

The rotational invariance of A makes it easier for us to actually evaluate it, because we can choose to do so at a coordinate orientation for which the computation is relatively simple. Let's rotate the coordinates to place Ω_1 in the polar direction (so now $\theta_1 = 0$), and the θ value of Ω_2 in the rotated coordinates will be equal to the angle χ between the Ω_1 and Ω_2 directions, which is not affected by a coordinate rotation. In this new set of coordinates, $Y_l^m(\Omega_1)$ is $Y_l^m(0, \varphi)$ and is given, according to Eq. (15.148), as

$$Y_l^m(\Omega_1) = \sqrt{\frac{2l + 1}{4\pi}} \, \delta_{m0}.$$

The summation in Eq. (16.53) therefore reduces to its $m = 0$ term, and the only Ω_2 contribution we need is $Y_l^0(\chi, \varphi_2)$. But because $m = 0$, this Y does not actually depend on φ_2, and has the unambiguous value, from Eq. (15.137),

$$Y_l^0(\chi, \varphi_2) = \sqrt{\frac{2l+1}{4\pi}}\, P_l(\cos \chi).$$

These results enable us to obtain

$$A = \frac{2l+1}{4\pi} P_l(\cos \chi), \tag{16.56}$$

which, because of the rotational invariance, remains true whether or not the coordinate system was rotated. Inserting the original formula for A, and solving Eq. (16.56) for $P_l(\cos \chi)$, we obtain the **spherical harmonic addition theorem**,

$$P_l(\cos \chi) = \frac{4\pi}{2l+1} \sum_m Y_l^m(\Omega_1)^* Y_l^m(\Omega_2), \tag{16.57}$$

where χ is the angle between the directions Ω_1 and Ω_2.

Example 16.3.1   ANGLE BETWEEN TWO VECTORS

A useful special case of the addition theorem is for $l = 1$, for which $P_1(\cos \chi) = \cos \chi$. Then, writing $\Omega_i \equiv \theta_i, \varphi_i$, and evaluating all the spherical harmonics on the right-hand side of Eq. (16.57), we have

$$\cos \chi = \frac{1}{2} \left(\sin\theta_1 e^{-i\varphi_1} \right)^* \left(\sin\theta_2 e^{-i\varphi_2} \right) + \cos\theta_1 \cos\theta_2$$

$$+ \frac{1}{2} \left(-\sin\theta_1 e^{i\varphi_1} \right)^* \left(-\sin\theta_2 e^{i\varphi_2} \right)$$

$$= \cos\theta_1 \cos\theta_2 + \frac{1}{2} \sin\theta_1 \sin\theta_2 \left(e^{i(\varphi_1-\varphi_2)} + e^{i(\varphi_2-\varphi_1)} \right). \tag{16.58}$$

This reduces to the standard formula for the angle χ between directions (θ_1, φ_1) and (θ_2, φ_2):

$$\cos \chi = \cos\theta_1 \cos\theta_2 + \sin\theta_1 \sin\theta_2 \cos(\varphi_2 - \varphi_1). \tag{16.59}$$

∎

Spherical Wave Expansion

An important application of the addition theorem is the **spherical wave expansion**, which states

$$e^{i\mathbf{k}\cdot\mathbf{r}} = 4\pi \sum_{l=0}^{\infty} \sum_{m=-l}^{l} i^l j_l(kr) Y_l^m(\Omega_k)^* Y_l^m(\Omega_r) \tag{16.60}$$

$$= 4\pi \sum_{l=0}^{\infty} \sum_{m=-l}^{l} i^l j_l(kr) Y_l^m(\Omega_k) Y_l^m(\Omega_r)^*. \tag{16.61}$$

Here k and r are the magnitudes of $\mathbf{k}$ and $\mathbf{r}$, and Ω_k, Ω_r denote their respective angular coordinates. The two forms shown are equivalent because a change in the sign of m changes each harmonic to its complex conjugate (possibly with both harmonics undergoing a sign change). The quantity $j_l(kr)$ is a spherical Bessel function. This formula is particularly useful because it expresses the plane wave on its left-hand side as a series of spherical waves. This conversion is useful in scattering problems in which a plane wave, incident upon a scattering center, produces outgoing spherical waves with different spherical-harmonic (called **partial-wave**) components.

To establish Eq. (16.61), we write $\mathbf{k} \cdot \mathbf{r}$ as $kr \cos \chi$, where χ is the angle between $\mathbf{k}$ and $\mathbf{r}$, and then expand $\exp(ikr \cos \chi)$ as a series of Legendre polynomials:

$$e^{ikr \cos \chi} = \sum_{l=0}^{\infty} c_l P_l(\cos \chi), \tag{16.62}$$

with the coefficients c_l given by

$$c_l = \frac{2l+1}{2} \int_{-1}^{1} e^{ikrt} P_l(t) dt. \tag{16.63}$$

We now recognize the integral in Eq. (16.63) as proportional to an integral representation of j_l that was the topic of Exercise 15.2.26 and which we repeat here:

$$j_l(x) = \frac{i^{-l}}{2} \int_{-1}^{1} e^{ixt} P_l(t) dt. \tag{16.64}$$

This permits us to evaluate c_l, obtaining

$$c_l = (2l+1)i^l j_l(kr).$$

Inserting this expression for c_l into Eq. (16.62) and replacing $P_l(\cos \chi)$ in that equation by its equivalent as given by the addition theorem, Eq. (16.57), we have the desired verification of Eq. (16.61).

Laplace Spherical Harmonic Expansion

Another application of the addition theorem is to the Laplace expansion, where in Chapter 15 we found that the inverse distance between points $\mathbf{r}_1$ and $\mathbf{r}_2$ could be expanded in Legendre polynomials:

$$\frac{1}{|\mathbf{r}_1 - \mathbf{r}_2|} = \sum_{l=0}^{\infty} \frac{r_<^l}{r_>^{l+1}} P_l(\cos \chi). \tag{16.65}$$

Here $\mathbf{r}_1$ and $\mathbf{r}_2$ are measured from a common origin, with respective magnitudes r_1 and r_2; χ is the angle between $\mathbf{r}_1$ and $\mathbf{r}_2$. We define $r_>$ and $r_<$ as, respectively, the larger and the smaller of r_1 and r_2. If we now insert the addition theorem, we bring this expansion to the form

$$\frac{1}{|\mathbf{r}_1 - \mathbf{r}_2|} = \sum_{l=0}^{\infty} \frac{4\pi}{2l+1} \frac{r_<^l}{r_>^{l+1}} \sum_{m=-l}^{l} Y_l^m(\Omega_1)^* Y_l^m(\Omega_2), \tag{16.66}$$

where Ω_1 and Ω_2 are the angular coordinates of $\mathbf{r}_1$ and $\mathbf{r}_2$ in a coordinate system of arbitrary orientation.

Example 16.3.2   SPHERICAL GREEN'S FUNCTION

An explicit expansion of the Green's function for the 3-D Laplace equation may be obtained by considering its defining equation

$$\nabla_1^2 G(\mathbf{r}_1, \mathbf{r}_2) = \delta(r_1 - r_2) \frac{\delta(\Omega_1 - \Omega_2)}{r_1^2}, \tag{16.67}$$

where we have written ∇_1 to remind the reader that it acts only on $\mathbf{r}_1$. Also, note that on the right-hand side the factor $1/r_1^2$ is inserted to adjust the angular delta function to unit scale; it could equally well have been written $1/r_2^2$ because of the presence also of $\delta(r_1 - r_2)$.

We now insert into Eq. (16.67), the following general expansion for $G(\mathbf{r}_1, \mathbf{r}_2)$:

$$G(\mathbf{r}_1, \mathbf{r}_2) = \sum_{lm} \sum_{l'm'} g_{ll'mm'}(r_1, r_2) Y_{l'}^{m'}(\Omega_1) Y_l^m(\Omega_2)^*,$$

and the expansion of Exercise 16.3.9 for the angular delta function:

$$\delta(\Omega_1 - \Omega_2) = \sum_{lm} Y_l^m(\Omega_1) Y_l^m(\Omega_2)^*.$$

We also write the Laplacian in the form

$$\nabla_1^2 = \frac{\partial^2}{\partial r_1^2} + \frac{2}{r_1} \frac{\partial}{\partial r_1} - \frac{\mathbf{L}_1^2}{r_1^2},$$

where $\mathbf{L}_1$ operates only on functions of Ω_1.

We next take scalar products of the resulting expanded equation with all possible spherical harmonics of both Ω_1 and Ω_2, in addition taking note that $Y_l^m(\Omega_1)$ is an eigenfunction of $\mathbf{L}_1^2$ with eigenvalue $l(l+1)$. We find that many terms cancel, so the scalar products lead, for each l and m, to the following result:

$$\left[\frac{d^2}{dr_1^2} + \frac{2}{r_1} \frac{d}{dr_1} - l(l+1) \right] g_l(r_1, r_2) = \delta(r_1 - r_2). \tag{16.68}$$

We have collapsed the original four indices of $g_{ll'mm'}(r_1, r_2)$ into the single index l because all instances of Eq. (16.68) with $l \neq l'$ or $m \neq m'$ vanish, and g has the same value for all m.

Equation (16.68) is for each l an ODE which, with boundary conditions $g = 0$ at $r = 0$ and $r = \infty$, defines the **spherical Green's functions** we identified in Section 10.2. Since the homogeneous equation corresponding to Eq. (16.68) has solutions r^l and r^{-l-1}, its Green's function must have the form

$$g(r_1, r_2) = A_l \frac{r_<^l}{r_>^{l+1}}, \tag{16.69}$$

with $A_l = -1/(2l + 1)$, a result that can be obtained by application of Eq. (10.19).

Comparing Eq. (16.66) with the result for $G(\mathbf{r}_1, \mathbf{r}_2)$ obtained by using Eq. (16.69), we now have yet another way of verifying the result that is familiar from Coulomb's law:

$$G(\mathbf{r}_1, \mathbf{r}_2) = -\sum_{l=0}^{\infty} \frac{1}{2l+1} \frac{r_<^l}{r_>^{l+1}} \sum_{m=-l}^{l} Y_l^m(\Omega_1)^* Y_l^m(\Omega_2) \tag{16.70}$$

$$= -\frac{1}{4\pi} \frac{1}{|\mathbf{r}_1 - \mathbf{r}_2|}. \tag{16.71}$$

∎

General Multipoles

We are now ready to return to the multipole expansion. Given a set of charges q_i at respective points $\mathbf{r}_i$, all located within a sphere of radius a centered at the origin of a spherical polar coordinate system, we now consider the calculation of the electrostatic potential $\psi(\mathbf{r})$ at points outside the sphere, i.e., at points $\mathbf{r}$ such that $r > a$. Our starting point is the Laplace expansion of $1/|\mathbf{r}_1 - \mathbf{r}_2|$ in the form presented as Eq. (16.66). Since for all r_i we have $r_i < r$, we can write

$$\psi(\mathbf{r}) = \frac{1}{4\pi\epsilon_0} \sum_i q_i \sum_{l=0}^{\infty} \frac{4\pi}{2l+1} \frac{r_i^l}{r^{l+1}} \sum_{m=-l}^{l} Y_l^m(\theta_i, \varphi_i)^* Y_l^m(\theta, \varphi)$$

$$= \frac{1}{4\pi\varepsilon_0} \sum_{l=0}^{\infty} \sum_{m=-l}^{l} \frac{4\pi}{2l+1} \left[\sum_i q_i r_i^l Y_l^m(\theta_i, \varphi_i)^* \right] \frac{Y_l^m(\theta, \varphi)}{r^{l+1}}. \tag{16.72}$$

We see that this substitution has caused the entire effect of the charges q_i to be localized into the expressions

$$M_l^m = \frac{4\pi}{2l+1} \sum_i q_i r_i^l Y_l^m(\theta_i, \varphi_i)^*, \tag{16.73}$$

so that the potential due to the q_i, for points farther from $r = 0$ than all the charges, assumes the compact form,

$$\psi(\mathbf{r}) = \frac{1}{4\pi\varepsilon_0} \sum_{l=0}^{\infty} \sum_{m=-l}^{l} M_l^m \frac{Y_l^m(\theta, \varphi)}{r^{l+1}}. \tag{16.74}$$

Equation (16.74) is called the **multipole expansion**, and the M_l^m are known as the **multipole moments** of the charge distribution. At this point we note that different authors define the multipole moments with different scalings, making up the difference by the inclusion of an appropriate factor in their formulas corresponding to Eq. (16.74). One reason for the variety of notations is that M_l^m as defined in Eq. (16.73), which leads to the simplest formulas, does not yield the low-order moments at their "traditional" scalings. For example, the monopole moment, M_0^0, evaluates to $(4\pi)^{1/2}$ times the total charge, while M_1^0, the z-component of the dipole moment, comes out as $(4\pi/3)^{1/2} \sum_i q_i z_i$.

Of more fundamental interest is the relation between the multipole moments and the Cartesian forms that can represent them. We proceed by considering the M_l^m that result from a unit charge placed at (x, y, z). Using the Cartesian representations of the spherical harmonics given in Table 15.4, the first few M_l^m have the forms given here:

$$M_2^2 = \left(\frac{3\pi}{10}\right)^{1/2}(x^2 - y^2 + 2ixy)$$

$$M_1^1 = -\left(\frac{2\pi}{3}\right)^{1/2}(x + iy) \qquad M_2^1 = -\left(\frac{3\pi}{40}\right)^{1/2}z(x + iy)$$

$$M_0^0 = (4\pi)^{1/2} \qquad M_1^0 = \left(\frac{4\pi}{3}\right)^{1/2}z \qquad M_2^0 = \left(\frac{4\pi}{5}\right)^{1/2}\left[\frac{2z^2 - x^2 - y^2}{2}\right]$$

$$M_1^{-1} = \left(\frac{2\pi}{3}\right)^{1/2}(x - iy) \qquad M_2^{-1} = \left(\frac{3\pi}{40}\right)^{1/2}z(x - iy)$$

$$M_2^{-2} = \left(\frac{3\pi}{10}\right)^{1/2}(x^2 - y^2 - 2ixy)$$

The first point to note is that for any l value, the Cartesian representation of each M_l^m involves a homogeneous polynomial of combined degree l in x, y, and z. It is obviously necessary that the M_l^m of different m be linearly independent, and we see that for $l = 0$ and $l = 1$, the number of independent monomials is equal to $2l + 1$, the number of m values. Specifically, for $l = 0$ we have only the monomial 1, while for $l = 1$ we have x, y, and z. But for $l = 2$, there are six independent monomials $(x^2, y^2, z^2, xy, xz, yz)$, but only five values of m. The discrepancy is resolved by observing that one linear combination of these monomials, namely $r^2 = x^2 + y^2 + z^2$, remains invariant under all rotations of the coordinates, and it therefore has different symmetry properties than the five-dimensional space orthogonal to r^2. In fact, r^2 has the same symmetry as M_0^0, but has the wrong r dependence to contribute to a solution to the Laplace equation (and therefore to the potential of a charge distribution).

If we were to continue to $l = 3$, we would find that there are 10 linearly independent monomials of degree 3, but they divide into a group of seven functions (the space spanned by M_3^m) with an orthogonal complement (functions orthogonal to the first seven) of dimension 3. These three remaining functions have a rotational symmetry similar to M_1^m, but again with the wrong r dependence to contribute to the potential. This type of pattern continues to higher l, making logical the observation that a multipole moment of degree l (a "2^l-moment") has only $2l + 1$ components, despite the fact that in general the space of homogeneous polynomials of degree l has a larger dimension.

The multipole expansion is useful for continuous distributions of charge in addition to the discrete charge sets we have considered up to this point. The generalization of Eq. (16.73) is

$$M_l^m = \frac{4\pi}{2l + 1} \int \rho(\mathbf{r}')(r')^{l+2} Y_l^m(\theta', \varphi')^* \sin\theta' \, dr' \, d\theta' \, d\varphi', \qquad (16.75)$$

where $\rho(\mathbf{r})$ is the charge density. This expression will yield valid results when $\psi(\mathbf{r})$ is computed via Eq. (16.74) for r values greater than the largest r' for which $\rho(\mathbf{r})$ is nonzero.

Integrals of Three Spherical Harmonics

Our final spherical tensor application is to the integrals of three spherical harmonics (all of the same argument). These integrals arise in the evaluation of matrix elements of angle-dependent operators which themselves can be written in terms of spherical harmonics. While it is possible to evaluate some such integrals using the techniques illustrated in Eq. (15.152), a more general result is available. Note that this is not an angular momentum coupling problem of the type we considered in Section 16.2, because that section treated angular momenta with independent arguments that depended on different variables. Here we have a different and more specialized situation in which all three angular momentum functions have **the same argument**.

The formula we seek is most easily derived if we have access to values of some of the rotation coefficients $D^l_{m'm}$ (a.k.a. Wigner matrices) defined in Eq. (16.52). The coefficients we need can be easily deduced with the aid of the spherical harmonic addition theorem, so we start by establishing the following lemma (a **lemma** is a mathematical result needed to prove something else):

Lemma: Evaluation of $D^l_{m0}(\mathsf{R})$:

Writing first the spherical harmonic addition theorem, Eq. (16.57),

$$P_l(\cos\chi) = \frac{4\pi}{2l+1}\sum_m Y^m_l(\Omega_1)^* Y^m_l(\Omega_2),$$

where χ is the angle between the directions Ω_1 and Ω_2, we replace its left-hand side by the equivalent form

$$P_l(\cos\chi) = \sqrt{\frac{4\pi}{2l+1}}\, Y^0_l(\chi, 0),$$

thereby reaching

$$Y^0_l(\chi, 0) = \sqrt{\frac{4\pi}{2l+1}}\sum_m Y^m_l(\Omega_1)^* Y^m_l(\Omega_2). \tag{16.76}$$

We now compare this expression with Eq. (16.52), which we write here in a notation designed to make the comparison more obvious:

$$Y^0_l(\mathsf{R}\Omega_2) = \sum_m D^l_{m0}(\mathsf{R}) Y^m_l(\Omega_2). \tag{16.77}$$

If we select R to be a rotation that converts Ω_1 to the polar direction, then $\mathsf{R}\Omega_2$ will be $(\chi, 0)$; note that $Y^0_l(\mathsf{R}\Omega_2)$ is independent of φ so we can set its φ coordinate to zero. Thus, the comparison of Eqs. (16.76) and (16.77) yields

$$D^l_{m0}(\mathsf{R}) = \sqrt{\frac{4\pi}{2l+1}}\, Y^m_l(\Omega_1)^*. \tag{16.78}$$

We remind the reader that R is a rotation that converts Ω_1 to the polar direction.

Equation (16.78) has been derived under the assumption that the quantities being rotationally transformed are spherical harmonics (and not more complicated angular-momentum functions such as might be obtained via angular-momentum coupling). However, it is possible to show that the result generalizes, without change, to any angular momentum functions of integer l.   ∎

We now continue toward the goal of this subsection, namely the evaluation of integrals involving three spherical harmonics. The result we seek involves products of spherical harmonics with the same argument, but our method of obtaining that result proceeds by considering the rotational behavior of an angular momentum coupling formula (i.e., a product involving spherical harmonics of different arguments). So we now look at a special case of Eq. (16.45),

$$Y_{l_1}^0(\Omega_1)Y_{l_2}^0(\Omega_2) = \sum_L C(l_1, l_2, L|0, 0, 0)|L, 0\rangle, \tag{16.79}$$

where $|j_1, m_1; j_2, m_2\rangle$ of Eq. (16.45) is the product of spherical harmonics with $m_1 = m_2 = 0$ shown on the left-hand side of Eq. (16.79); the $|J, M\rangle$ state of Eq. (16.45) is now $|L, 0\rangle$. We next apply a rotation R to Eq. (16.79), using Eqs. (16.51) and (16.52) to get

$$\sum_{m_1 m_2} D_{m_1 0}^{l_1}(\mathsf{R}) D_{m_2 0}^{l_2}(\mathsf{R}) Y_{l_1}^{m_1}(\Omega_1) Y_{l_2}^{m_2}(\Omega_2) = \sum_{L,\sigma} C(l_1, l_2, L|0, 0, 0) D_{\sigma 0}^L(\mathsf{R})|L, \sigma\rangle. \tag{16.80}$$

Finally, we convert $|L, \sigma\rangle$ back to the m_1, m_2 basis, using Eq. (16.43):

$$\sum_{m_1 m_2} D_{m_1 0}^{l_1}(\mathsf{R}) D_{m_2 0}^{l_2}(\mathsf{R}) Y_{l_1}^{m_1}(\Omega_1) Y_{l_2}^{m_2}(\Omega_2) = \sum_{L,\sigma} C(l_1, l_2, L|0, 0, 0) D_{\sigma 0}^L(\mathsf{R})$$

$$\times \sum_{m_1 m_2} C(l_1, l_2, L|m_1, m_2, \sigma) Y_{l_1}^{m_1}(\Omega_1) Y_{l_2}^{m_2}(\Omega_2). \tag{16.81}$$

This relatively complicated equation must be satisfied for all values of Ω_1 and Ω_2, which will only be possible if its two sides are equal for each set of m_1, m_2 values. We therefore have the set of simpler equations,

$$D_{m_1 0}^{l_1}(\mathsf{R}) D_{m_2 0}^{l_2}(\mathsf{R}) = \sum_{L\sigma} C(l_1, l_2, L|0, 0, 0) C(l_1, l_2, L|m_1, m_2, \sigma) D_{\sigma 0}^L(\mathsf{R}), \tag{16.82}$$

satisfied separately for all values of the free parameters.

We are now ready to replace all the D^l in Eq. (16.82) by the result obtained in our lemma, Eq. (16.78). Since the rotation R is arbitrary, both in the lemma and in the present work, our use of Eq. (16.78) will produce some angular coordinates Ω that have nothing to do with the Ω_i we were previously using; the point that is important here is that because the same R occurs throughout Eq. (16.82), the application of Eq. (16.78) will everywhere produce the same Ω. Substitution of the lemma result yields

$$\frac{4\pi}{\sqrt{(2l_1+1)(2l_2+1)}}Y_{l_1}^{m_1}(\Omega)^*Y_{l_2}^{m_2}(\Omega)^* =$$

$$\sum_{L\sigma}C(l_1,l_2,L|0,0,0)C(l_1,l_2,L|m_1,m_2,\sigma)\sqrt{\frac{4\pi}{2L+1}}Y_L^{\sigma}(\Omega)^*.$$

Since the Y_l^m are the only potentially complex quantities appearing here, we may remove the complex conjugate signs by complex conjugating the entire equation. After other minor rearrangements and recognition of the fact that the only contributing σ value is $\sigma = m_1 + m_2$, we reach the final form

$$Y_{l_1}^{m_1}(\Omega)Y_{l_2}^{m_2}(\Omega) = \sum_L \sqrt{\frac{(2l_1+1)(2l_2+1)}{4\pi(2L+1)}}$$

$$\times C(l_1,l_2,L|0,0,0)C(l_1,l_2,L|m_1,m_2,m_1+m_2)Y_L^{m_1+m_2}(\Omega). \tag{16.83}$$

At last we can meet the objective of this subsection. Multiplying both sides of Eq. (16.83) by some $Y_{l_3}^{m_3}(\Omega)^*$ and integrating in Ω over the angular space, we get

$$\left\langle Y_{l_3}^{m_3}\left|Y_{l_1}^{m_1}\right|Y_{l_2}^{m_2}\right\rangle = \int_0^{2\pi}d\varphi\int_0^{\pi}\sin\theta d\theta Y_{l_3}^{m_3}(\theta,\varphi)^*Y_{l_1}^{m_1}(\theta,\varphi)Y_{l_2}^{m_2}(\theta,\varphi)$$

$$= \sqrt{\frac{(2l_1+1)(2l_2+1)}{4\pi(2L+1)}}C(l_1,l_2,l_3|0,0,0)C(l_1,l_2,l_3|m_1,m_2,m_3). \tag{16.84}$$

We do not have to include a Kronecker delta because the condition $m_3 = m_1 + m_2$ is taken care of by the fact that the Clebsch-Gordan coefficients vanish in the absence of this or any other condition needed for a nonzero result.

Some further insight can be obtained by considering the special case $m_1 = m_2 = m_3 = 0$ and writing the spherical harmonics in terms of Legendre polynomials. This brings us (after the substitution $t = \cos\theta$) to

$$\int_{-1}^1 P_{l_3}(t)P_{l_1}(t)P_{l_2}(t)dt = \frac{2}{2l_3+1}C(l_1,l_2,l_3|0,0,0)^2. \tag{16.85}$$

Since we know that the Legendre polynomial $P_l(t)$ of even l is an even function of t, while that of odd l is odd in t, we see from Eq. (16.85) that unless $l_1 + l_2 + l_3$ is even, the integral will vanish, telling us that $C(l_1,l_2,l_3|0,0,0)$ will only be nonzero if $l_1 + l_2 + l_3$ is even. In addition, if the product of any two of the $P_l(t)$ does not contain a power of t as large as the index of the third P_l, the integral will vanish due to the orthogonality of the Legendre functions. This observation translates into a **triangle condition**, namely that the integral will vanish unless $|l_1 - l_2| \le l_3 \le l_1 + l_2$. Since these are conditions on the Clebsch-Gordan coefficient $C(l_1,l_2,l_3|0,0,0)$, they apply also to the general integral formula, Eq. (16.84).

Summarizing, integrals of products of three spherical harmonics, evaluated in Eq. (16.84), *will only be nonzero if the three following conditions are satisfied:*

1. *The l values satisfy the triangle condition $|l_1 - l_2| \leq l_3 \leq l_1 + l_2$,*
2. *The m values satisfy the condition $m_3 = m_1 + m_2$,*
3. *The sum of the l values, $l_1 + l_2 + l_3$, is even.*

Exercises

16.3.1   For $l = 1$, Eq. (16.52) becomes

$$Y_1^m(\theta', \varphi') = \sum_{m'=-1}^{1} D_{m'm}^1(\alpha, \beta, \gamma) Y_1^{m'}(\theta, \varphi).$$

Rewrite these spherical harmonics in Cartesian form. Show that the resulting Cartesian coordinate equations are equivalent to the Euler rotation matrix $A(\alpha, \beta, \gamma)$, Eq. (3.37).

16.3.2   In proving the addition theorem, we assumed that $Y_l^k(\theta_1, \varphi_1)$ could be expanded in a series of $Y_l^m(\theta_2, \varphi_2)$, in which m varied from $-l$ to $+l$ but l was held fixed. What arguments can you develop to justify summing only over the upper index, m, and **not** over the lower index, l?

Hints. One possibility is to examine the homogeneity of the Y_l^m, that is, Y_l^m may be expressed entirely in terms of the form $\cos^{l-p} \theta \sin^p \theta$, or $x^{l-p-s} y^p z^s / r^l$. Another possibility is to examine the behavior of the Legendre equation under rotation of the coordinate system.

16.3.3   An atomic electron with angular momentum l and magnetic quantum number m has a wave function

$$\psi(r, \theta, \varphi) = f(r) Y_l^m(\theta, \varphi).$$

Show that the sum of the electron densities in a given complete shell is spherically symmetric; that is, $\sum_{m=-l}^{l} \psi^*(r, \theta, \varphi) \psi(r, \theta, \varphi)$ is independent of θ and φ.

16.3.4   The potential of an electron at point $\mathbf{r}_e$ in the field of Z protons at points $\mathbf{r}_p$ is

$$\Phi = -\frac{e^2}{4\pi \varepsilon_0} \sum_{p=1}^{Z} \frac{1}{|\mathbf{r}_e - \mathbf{r}_p|}.$$

Show that for r_e larger than all r_p, this may be written as

$$\Phi = -\frac{e^2}{4\pi \varepsilon_0 r_e} \sum_{p=1}^{Z} \sum_{L,M} \left(\frac{r_p}{r_e}\right)^L \frac{4\pi}{2L+1} Y_L^M(\theta_p, \varphi_p)^* Y_L^M(\theta_e, \varphi_e).$$

How should Φ be written for $r_e < r_p$?

16.3.5   Two protons are **uniformly** distributed within the same spherical volume. If the coordinates of one element of charge are $(r_1, \theta_1, \varphi_1)$ and the coordinates of the other are $(r_2, \theta_2, \varphi_2)$ and r_{12} is the distance between them, the element of repulsion energy will be given by

$$d\psi = \rho^2 \frac{d\tau_1 \, d\tau_2}{r_{12}} = \rho^2 \frac{r_1^2 \, dr_1 \sin\theta_1 d\theta_1 d\varphi_1 r_2^2 \, dr_2 \sin\theta_2 \, d\theta_2 \, d\varphi_2}{r_{12}},$$

where

$$\rho = \frac{\text{charge}}{\text{volume}} = \frac{3e}{4\pi R^3} \quad \text{and} \quad r_{12}^2 = r_1^2 + r_2^2 - 2r_1 r_2 \cos\gamma.$$

Here ρ is the charge density and γ is the angle between $\mathbf{r}_1$ and $\mathbf{r}_2$. Calculate the total electrostatic energy (of repulsion) of the two protons. This calculation is used in accounting for the mass difference in "mirror" nuclei, such as O^{15} and N^{15}.

$$ANS. \quad \frac{6}{5}\frac{e^2}{R}.$$

16.3.6   Each of the two $1s$ electrons in helium may be described by a hydrogenic wave function

$$\psi(\mathbf{r}) = \left(\frac{Z^3}{\pi a_0^3}\right)^{1/2} e^{-Zr/a_0}$$

in the absence of the other electron. Here Z, the atomic number, is 2. The symbol a_0 is the Bohr radius, $\hbar^2/me^2$. Find the mutual potential energy of the two electrons, given by

$$\int \psi^*(\mathbf{r}_1)\psi^*(\mathbf{r}_2)\frac{e^2}{|\mathbf{r}_1 - \mathbf{r}_2|}\psi(\mathbf{r}_1)\psi(\mathbf{r}_2)d^3r_1\,d^3r_2.$$

$$ANS. \quad \frac{5e^2 Z}{8a_0}.$$

16.3.7   The probability of finding a $1s$ hydrogen electron in a volume element $r^2 dr \sin\theta\,d\theta\,d\varphi$ is

$$\frac{1}{\pi a_0^3}e^{-2r/a_0}r^2\,dr\sin\theta\,d\theta\,d\varphi,$$

where r is the distance of the electron from the nucleus. Find the electrostatic potential of this charge distribution at points $\mathbf{r}_1$, where you may **not** assume that $\mathbf{r}_1$ is on the polar axis of your coordinate system. Calculate the potential from

$$V(\mathbf{r}_1) = -\frac{e}{4\pi\varepsilon_0}\int\frac{\rho(\mathbf{r}_2)}{r_{12}}d^3r_2,$$

where $r_{12} = |\mathbf{r}_1 - \mathbf{r}_2|$. Expand r_{12}. Apply the Legendre polynomial addition theorem and show that the angular dependence of $V(\mathbf{r}_1)$ drops out.

$$ANS. \quad V(\mathbf{r}_1) = -\frac{e}{4\pi\varepsilon_0}\left[\frac{1}{2r_1}\gamma\left(3,\frac{2r_1}{a_0}\right) + \frac{1}{a_0}\Gamma\left(2,\frac{2r_1}{a_0}\right)\right], \text{ where}$$

γ and Γ are incomplete gamma functions, Eq. (13.73).

16.3.8   A hydrogen electron in a $2p$ orbital has a charge distribution

$$\rho = -\frac{e}{64\pi a_0^5}r^2 e^{-r/a_0}\sin^2\theta,$$

where $a_0 = \hbar^2/me^2$ is the Bohr radius, and r is the distance between the electron and the nucleus. Find the electrostatic potential energy for this atomic state.

16.3.9 (a) As a Laplace series and as an example of Eq. (5.27), show that

$$\delta(\Omega_1 - \Omega_2) = \sum_{l=0}^{\infty} \sum_{m=-l}^{l} Y_l^m(\theta_2, \varphi_2)^* Y_l^m(\theta_1, \varphi_1).$$

(b) Show also that this **same** representation of the Dirac delta function may be written as

$$\delta(\Omega_1 - \Omega_2) = \sum_{l=0}^{\infty} \frac{2l+1}{4\pi} P_l(\cos \gamma),$$

and identify γ. Now, if you can justify equating the summations over l **term by term**, you have an alternate derivation of the spherical harmonic addition theorem.

16.3.10 Verify

(a) $\displaystyle \int Y_L^M(\theta, \varphi) Y_0^0(\theta, \varphi) Y_L^{M*}(\theta, \varphi) d\Omega = \frac{1}{\sqrt{4\pi}},$

(b) $\displaystyle \int Y_L^M Y_1^0 Y_{L+1}^{M*} d\Omega = \sqrt{\frac{3}{4\pi}} \sqrt{\frac{(L+M+1)(L-M+1)}{(2L+1)(2L+3)}},$

(c) $\displaystyle \int Y_L^M Y_1^1 Y_{L+1}^{M+1*} d\Omega = \sqrt{\frac{3}{8\pi}} \sqrt{\frac{(L+M+1)(L+M+2)}{(2L+1)(2L+3)}},$

(d) $\displaystyle \int Y_L^M Y_1^1 Y_{L-1}^{M+1*} d\Omega = -\sqrt{\frac{3}{8\pi}} \sqrt{\frac{(L-M)(L-M-1)}{(2L-1)(2L+1)}}.$

These integrals were used in an investigation of the angular correlation of internal conversion electrons.

16.3.11 Show that

(a) $\displaystyle \int_{-1}^{1} x P_L(x) P_N(x) dx = \begin{cases} \dfrac{2(L+1)}{(2L+1)(2L+3)}, & N = L+1, \\[4mm] \dfrac{2L}{(2L-1)(2L+1)}, & N = L-1, \end{cases}$

(b) $\displaystyle \int_{-1}^{1} x^2 P_L(x) P_N(x) dx = \begin{cases} \dfrac{2(L+1)(L+2)}{(2L+1)(2L+3)(2L+5)}, & N = L+2, \\[4mm] \dfrac{2(2L^2+2L-1)}{(2L-1)(2L+1)(2L+3)}, & N = L, \\[4mm] \dfrac{2L(L-1)}{(2L-3)(2L-1)(2L+1)}, & N = L-2. \end{cases}$

16.3.12   Since $x P_n(x)$ is a polynomial (of degree $n+1$), it may be represented by the Legendre series

$$x P_n(x) = \sum_{s=0}^{\infty} a_s P_s(x).$$

(a)   Show that $a_s = 0$ for $s < n-1$ and $s > n+1$.

(b)   Calculate a_{n-1}, a_n, and a_{n+1} and show that you have reproduced the recurrence relation, Eq. (15.18).

Note. This argument may be put in a general form to demonstrate the existence of a three-term recurrence relation for any of our complete sets of orthogonal polynomials:

$$x \varphi_n = a_{n+1} \varphi_{n+1} + a_n \varphi_n + a_{n-1} \varphi_{n-1}.$$

16.4   VECTOR SPHERICAL HARMONICS

Maxwell's equations lead naturally to applications involving a vector Helmholtz equation for the vector potential **A**, and various classical and quantum-mechanical problems in this area are usefully attacked by introducing **vector spherical harmonics**. Our first step in this direction will be to recognize that a set of unit vectors can be thought of as a spherical tensor of rank 1 and can be discussed in terms of the angular momentum formalism. We will later (in Chapter 17) pursue rotational symmetry in greater depth; for our present purposes it suffices to confirm the relationship between rotations in 3-D space and angular momentum operators.

A Spherical Tensor

We consider here vectors in 3-D space, of the form $\mathbf{u} = u_x \hat{\mathbf{e}}_x + u_y \hat{\mathbf{e}}_y + u_z \hat{\mathbf{e}}_z$, but, unlike our practice in Chapter 3, we will permit the u_j to be complex, and use the complex scalar product $\langle \mathbf{u} | \mathbf{u} \rangle^{1/2}$ as a measure of the magnitude of **u**. If we restrict the vectors **u** to be of unit length, they satisfy the conditions necessary to be identified as spherical tensors of rank 1.

We now introduce operators K_i defined by the following matrices:

$$K_1 = \begin{pmatrix} 0 & 0 & 0 \\ 0 & 0 & -i \\ 0 & i & 0 \end{pmatrix}, \quad K_2 = \begin{pmatrix} 0 & 0 & i \\ 0 & 0 & 0 \\ -i & 0 & 0 \end{pmatrix}, \quad K_3 = \begin{pmatrix} 0 & -i & 0 \\ i & 0 & 0 \\ 0 & 0 & 0 \end{pmatrix}. \tag{16.86}$$

The reader can easily verify that these matrices satisfy the angular momentum commutation rules, and in fact describe the result of applying the angular momentum operator $\mathbf{L} = \mathbf{r} \times \mathbf{p}$, where $\mathbf{p} = -i\nabla$, to the basis x, y, z. We next calculate

$$\mathbf{K}^2 = K_1^2 + K_2^2 + K_3^2 = 2 \begin{pmatrix} 1 & 0 & 0 \\ 0 & 1 & 0 \\ 0 & 0 & 1 \end{pmatrix},$$

showing that all members of the basis are eigenvectors of $\mathbf{K}^2$, with eigenvalue 2, which is $k(k+1)$ with $k = 1$. All members of our basis therefore have one unit of some abstract sort of angular momentum (often referred to as **spin**), and we can obtain a set of eigenvectors with values of an index m that can have values $+1$, 0, and -1. By diagonalizing the matrix K_3, we find its eigenvectors to be

$$\mathbf{k}_1 = \begin{pmatrix} -1\sqrt{2} \\ -i/\sqrt{2} \\ 0 \end{pmatrix}, \quad \mathbf{k}_0 = \begin{pmatrix} 0 \\ 0 \\ 1 \end{pmatrix}, \quad \mathbf{k}_{-1} = \begin{pmatrix} 1\sqrt{2} \\ -i/\sqrt{2} \\ 0 \end{pmatrix}. \tag{16.87}$$

While in principle the signs of these eigenvectors are arbitrary, they have been chosen here to agree with the Condon-Shortley phase convention.

Vector Coupling

The vector spherical harmonics are now defined as the quantities that result from the coupling of ordinary spherical harmonics and the vectors $\mathbf{e}_m$ to form states of definite J (the resultant of the orbital angular momentum of the spherical harmonic and the one unit possessed by the $\mathbf{e}_m$). It is customary to label the vector spherical harmonics to show both the L value from the ordinary (scalar) harmonic and the M value (the eigenvalue of J_z). Thus, the vector spherical harmonic will have three indices: J, L, and M. From the general formula for angular-momentum coupling, Eq. (16.43), we have

$$\mathbf{Y}_{JLM}(\theta, \varphi) = \sum_{mm'} C(L, 1, J | mm'M) Y_L^m(\theta, \varphi)\hat{\mathbf{e}}_{m'}. \tag{16.88}$$

Remember that M is M_J, not the m value of Y_L^m, and that $\hat{\mathbf{e}}_{m'}$ are the angular momentum eigenfunctions given in Eq. (16.87).

Because Eq. (16.88) couples an angular momentum L with one of magnitude $k = 1$, the L values in a vector spherical harmonic of given J are restricted to $J + 1$, J, and $J - 1$, a condition enforced by the values of the Clebsch-Gordan coefficients. Moreover, because the Clebsch-Gordan coefficients describe a unitary transformation, the obvious orthogonality of the states in the m, m' basis ($Y_l^m \hat{\mathbf{e}}_{m'}$) will cause the vector spherical harmonics also to be orthonormal:

$$\int \mathbf{Y}_{JLM}(\theta, \varphi) \cdot \mathbf{Y}_{J'L'M'}(\theta, \varphi) d\Omega = \delta_{JJ'}\delta_{LL'}\delta_{MM'}. \tag{16.89}$$

In addition, we can invert Eq. (16.89) using Eq. (16.45), reaching

$$Y_L^m(\theta, \varphi)\hat{\mathbf{e}}_{m'} = \sum_{JM} C(L, 1, J | mm'M)\mathbf{Y}_{JLM}. \tag{16.90}$$

The manipulation of expressions involving the vector spherical harmonics depends crucially on a few identities, of which perhaps the most important is the formula

$$\hat{\mathbf{r}}Y_L^M(\theta, \varphi) = -\left[\frac{L+1}{2L+1}\right]^{1/2} \mathbf{Y}_{L,L+1,M} + \left[\frac{L}{2L+1}\right]^{1/2} \mathbf{Y}_{L,L-1,M}. \tag{16.91}$$

To establish this formula, and at the same time to make its meaning more obvious, we start by noting that $\hat{\mathbf{r}}$ has a form that depends on the angular coordinates; specifically, it is

$$\hat{\mathbf{r}} = \frac{\mathbf{r}}{\sin\theta\cos\varphi\,\hat{\mathbf{e}}_x + \sin\theta\sin\varphi\,\hat{\mathbf{e}}_y + \cos\theta\,\hat{\mathbf{e}}_z}.$$

For our present purposes, it is more convenient to rearrange this to the form

$$\hat{\mathbf{r}} = \sin\theta\left(\frac{e^{i\varphi}\hat{\mathbf{e}}_{-1} - e^{-i\varphi}\hat{\mathbf{e}}_{+1}}{\sqrt{2}}\right) + \cos\theta\,\hat{\mathbf{e}}_0. \tag{16.92}$$

It is now clear that in order to prove Eq. (16.91) we must show that each $\hat{\mathbf{e}}_m$ has the same coefficient on both sides of the equation. Taking first the coefficient of $\hat{\mathbf{e}}_0$, the left-hand side of Eq. (16.91) yields, after use of Eq. (16.92),

$$\cos\theta\,Y_L^M(\theta,\varphi) = \left[\frac{(l-m+1)(l+m+1)}{(2l+1)(2l+3)}\right]^{1/2}Y_{l+1}^m$$
$$+ \left[\frac{(l-m)(l+m)}{(2l-1)(2l+1)}\right]^{1/2}Y_{l-1}^m, \tag{16.93}$$

a result previously exhibited as Eq. (15.150). The $\hat{\mathbf{e}}_0$ terms from the right-hand side of Eq. (16.91) consist of

$$-\left[\frac{L+1}{2L+1}\right]^{1/2}C(L+1,1,L|M,0,M)Y_{L+1}^M\hat{\mathbf{e}}_0$$

$$+\left[\frac{L}{2L+1}\right]^{1/2}C(L-1,1,L|M,0,M)Y_{L-1}^M\hat{\mathbf{e}}_0.$$

The Clebsch-Gordan coefficients appearing here have the values

$$C(L+1,1,L|M,0,M) = -\left[\frac{(L+M+1)(L-M+1)}{(L+1)(2L+3)}\right]^{1/2},$$

$$C(L-1,1,L|M,0,M) \doteq \left[\frac{L^2-M^2}{L(2L-1)}\right]^{1/2}.$$

These data permit confirmation of the $\mathbf{e}_0$ terms of Eq. (16.91). The terms in $\mathbf{e}_{+1}$ and $\mathbf{e}_{-1}$ can also be shown consistent; the formulas needed for that purpose are Eqs. (15.151) and (15.152).

Another useful formula, which can be obtained by using Eq. (16.91) to simplify the radial component when the gradient operator is applied to the form $f(r)Y_L^M(\theta,\varphi)$, is

$$\boldsymbol{\nabla}\left[f(r)Y_K^M(\theta,\varphi)\right] = -\left[\frac{L+1}{2L+1}\right]^{1/2}\left[\frac{\partial}{\partial r}-\frac{L}{r}\right]f(r)\mathbf{Y}_{L,L+1,M}(\theta,\varphi)$$

$$+\left[\frac{L}{2L+1}\right]^{1/2}\left[\frac{\partial}{\partial r}+\frac{L+1}{r}\right]f(r)\mathbf{Y}_{L,L-1,M}(\theta,\varphi). \tag{16.94}$$

Under coordinate inversion the vector spherical harmonics transform as

$$\mathbf{Y}_{L,L+1,M}(\theta',\varphi') = (-1)^{L+1}\mathbf{Y}_{L,L+1,M}(\theta,\varphi),$$

$$\mathbf{Y}_{L,L-1,M}(\theta',\varphi') = (-1)^{L+1}\mathbf{Y}_{L,L-1,M}(\theta,\varphi), \tag{16.95}$$

$$\mathbf{Y}_{LLM}(\theta',\varphi') = (-1)^{L}\mathbf{Y}_{LLM}(\theta,\varphi),$$

where

$$\theta' = \pi - \theta \quad \varphi' = \pi + \varphi.$$

Starting from Eqs. (16.91) and (16.94), a number of formulas can be derived for the divergence and curl of vector spherical harmonics. These formulas include the following:

$$\boldsymbol{\nabla} \cdot \left[f(r)\mathbf{Y}_{L,L+1,M}(\theta,\varphi) \right] = -\left[\frac{L+1}{2L+1}\right]^{1/2}\left[\frac{df(r)}{dr} + \frac{L+2}{r}f(r)\right]Y_L^M(\theta,\varphi),$$
$$\tag{16.96}$$

$$\boldsymbol{\nabla} \cdot \left[f(r)\mathbf{Y}_{L,L-1,M}(\theta,\varphi) \right] = \left[\frac{L}{2L+1}\right]^{1/2}\left[\frac{df(r)}{dr} - \frac{L-1}{r}f(r)\right]Y_L^M(\theta,\varphi), \tag{16.97}$$

$$\boldsymbol{\nabla} \cdot \left[f(r)\mathbf{Y}_{LLM}(\theta,\varphi) \right] = 0, \tag{16.98}$$

$$\boldsymbol{\nabla} \times \left[f(r)\mathbf{Y}_{L,L+1,M}(\theta,\varphi) \right] = i\left[\frac{L}{2L+1}\right]^{1/2}\left[\frac{df(r)}{dr} + \frac{L+2}{r}f(r)\right]\mathbf{Y}_{LLM}, \tag{16.99}$$

$$\boldsymbol{\nabla} \times \left[f(r)\mathbf{Y}_{LLM}(\theta,\varphi) \right] = i\left(\frac{L}{2L+1}\right)^{1/2}\left[\frac{df(r)}{dr} - \frac{L}{r}f(r)\right]\mathbf{Y}_{L,L+1,M}(\theta,\varphi),$$

$$+ i\left[\frac{L+1}{2L+1}\right]^{1/2}\left[\frac{df(r)}{dr} + \frac{L+1}{r}f(r)\right]\mathbf{Y}_{L,L-1,M}, \tag{16.100}$$

$$\boldsymbol{\nabla} \times \left[f(r)\mathbf{Y}_{L,L-1,M}(\theta,\varphi) \right] = i\left[\frac{L+1}{2L+1}\right]^{1/2}\left[\frac{df(r)}{dr} - \frac{L-1}{r}f(r)\right]\mathbf{Y}_{LLM}(\theta,\varphi). \tag{16.101}$$

For a complete derivation of Eqs. (16.96) to (16.101) we refer to the literature.[3] These relations play an important role in the partial wave expansion of classical and quantum electrodynamics.

The definitions of the vector spherical harmonics given here are dictated by convenience, primarily in quantum mechanical calculations, in which the angular momentum is a significant parameter. Further examples of the usefulness and power of the vector spherical harmonics will be found in Blatt and Weisskopf, in Morse and Feshbach, and in Jackson (all in Additional Readings).

In closing, we note that

---

[3] E. H. Hill, Theory of vector spherical harmonics, *Am. J. Phys.* **22**: 211 (1954). Note that Hill assigns phases in accordance with the Condon-Shortley phase convention. In Hill's notation, $\mathbf{X}_{LM} = \mathbf{Y}_{LLM}$, $\mathbf{V}_{LM} = \mathbf{Y}_{L,L+1,M}$, $\mathbf{W}_{LM} = \mathbf{Y}_{L,L-1,M}$.

- Vector spherical harmonics are developed from coupling L units of orbital angular momentum and one unit of spin angular momentum.

- An extension, coupling L units of orbital angular momentum and two units of spin angular momentum to form **tensor** spherical harmonics, is presented by Mathews.[4]

- The major application of tensor spherical harmonics is in the investigation of gravitational radiation.

Exercises

16.4.1   Construct the $l = 0, m = 0$ and $l = 1, m = 0$ vector spherical harmonics.

$$ANS. \quad \mathbf{Y}_{010} = -\hat{\mathbf{r}}(4\pi)^{-1/2}$$
$$\mathbf{Y}_{000} = 0$$
$$\mathbf{Y}_{120} = -\hat{\mathbf{r}}(2\pi)^{-1/2}\cos\theta - \hat{\boldsymbol{\theta}}(8\pi)^{-1/2}\sin\theta$$
$$\mathbf{Y}_{110} = \hat{\boldsymbol{\varphi}}i(3/8\pi)^{1/2}\sin\theta$$
$$\mathbf{Y}_{100} = \hat{\mathbf{r}}(4\pi)^{-1/2}\cos\theta - \hat{\boldsymbol{\theta}}(4\pi)^{-1/2}\sin\theta.$$

16.4.2   Verify that the parity of $\mathbf{Y}_{LL+1M}$ is $(-1)^{L+1}$, that of $\mathbf{Y}_{LLM}$ is $(-1)^L$, and that of $\mathbf{Y}_{LL-1M}$ is $(-1)^{L+1}$. What happened to the M-dependence of the parity?

Hint. $\hat{\mathbf{r}}$ and $\hat{\boldsymbol{\varphi}}$ have odd parity; $\hat{\boldsymbol{\theta}}$ has even parity (compare with Exercise 3.10.25).

16.4.3   Verify the orthonormality of the vector spherical harmonics $\mathbf{Y}_{JLM_J}$.

16.4.4   Jackson's *Classical Electrodynamics* (see Additional Readings) defines $\mathbf{Y}_{LLM}$ by the equation

$$\mathbf{Y}_{LLM}(\theta, \varphi) = \frac{1}{\sqrt{L(L+1)}} \mathbf{L} Y_L^M(\theta, \varphi),$$

in which the angular momentum operator $\mathbf{L}$ is given by

$$\mathbf{L} = -i(\mathbf{r} \times \nabla).$$

Show that this definition agrees with Eq. (16.88).

16.4.5   Show that

$$\sum_{M=-L}^{L} \mathbf{Y}_{LLM}^*(\theta, \varphi) \cdot \mathbf{Y}_{LLM}(\theta, \varphi) = \frac{2L+1}{4\pi}.$$

Hint. One way is to use Exercise 16.4.4 with $\mathbf{L}$ expanded in Cartesian coordinates and to apply raising and lowering operators.

[4]J. Mathews, Gravitational multipole radiation, *J. Soc. Ind. Appl. Math.* **10**: 768 (1963).

16.4.6   Show that

$$\int \mathbf{Y}_{LLM} \cdot (\hat{\mathbf{r}} \times \mathbf{Y}_{LLM}) d\Omega = 0.$$

The integrand represents an interference term in electromagnetic radiation that contributes to angular distributions but not to total intensity.

Additional Readings

Biedenharn, L. C., and J. D. Louck, *Angular Momentum in Quantum Physics: Theory and Application.* Encyclopedia of Mathematics and Its Applications, vol. 8. Reading, MA: Addison-Wesley (1981). An extremely detailed account, containing much material not easily found elsewhere.

Blatt, J. M., and V. Weisskopf, *Theoretical Nuclear Physics.* New York: Wiley (1952). Treats vector spherical harmonics.

Brink, D. M., and G. R. Satchler, *Angular Momentum.* New York: Oxford (1993). Contains a good presentation of graphical methods for the manipulation of $3j$, $6j$, and even $9j$ symbols. The $6j$ and $9j$ symbols are useful in dealing with the coupling of more than two angular momenta.

Condon, E. U., and G. H. Shortley, *Theory of Atomic Spectra.* Cambridge: Cambridge University Press (1935). This is the original and standard work on spin-orbit coupling in atomic states. It is extremely thorough and not for the beginner.

Edmonds, A. R., *Angular Momentum in Quantum Mechanics.* Princeton, NJ: Princeton University Press (1957). A good introductory text, with detailed discussion of the symmetries of $3j$, $6j$, and $9j$ symbols.

Jackson, J. D., *Classical Electrodynamics*, 3rd ed. New York: Wiley (1999). Applies vector spherical harmonics to multipole radiation and related problems.

Morse, P. M., and H. Feshbach, *Methods of Theoretical Physics*, 2 vols. New York: McGraw-Hill (1953). Includes material on vector spherical harmonics.

Rose, M. E., *Elementary Theory of Angular Momentum.* New York: Wiley (1957), reprinted, Dover (1995). As part of the development of the quantum theory of angular momentum, Rose includes a detailed and readable account of the rotation group.

Wigner, E. P., *Group Theory and Its Application to the Quantum Mechanics of Atomic Spectra* (translated by J. J. Griffin). New York: Academic Press (1959). This is the classic reference on group theory for the physicist. The rotation group is treated in considerable detail. There is a wealth of applications to atomic physics. The translation from the original German edition included a conversion from a left-handed to a right-handed coordinate system. This conversion introduced a few errors that can be resolved by comparison with the untranslated book.

CHAPTER 17

GROUP THEORY

*Disciplined judgment, about what is neat
and symmetrical and elegant, has time and
time again proved an excellent guide to
how nature works.*

MURRAY GELL-MANN

17.1 INTRODUCTION TO GROUP THEORY

Symmetry has long been important in the study of physical systems. Connections between the geometric symmetry of crystalline systems and their x-ray diffraction spectra were found to be crucial to the interpretation of the diffraction patterns and the extraction therefrom of information locating the atoms in the crystal. The geometric symmetries of molecules determine which vibrational modes will be active in absorbing or emitting radiation; the symmetries of periodic systems have implications as to their energy bands, their ability to conduct electricity, and even their superconductivity. The invariance of physical laws with respect to position or orientation (i.e., the symmetry of space) gives rise to **conservation laws** for linear and angular momentum. Sometimes the implications of symmetry invariance are far more complicated or sophisticated than might at first be supposed; the invariance of the forces predicted by electromagnetic theory when measurements are made in observation frames moving uniformly at different speeds (**inertial frames**) was an important clue leading Einstein to the discovery of special relativity. With the advent of quantum mechanics, considerations of angular momentum and spin introduced new symmetry concepts into physics. These ideas have since catalyzed the modern development of particle theory.

Central to all these symmetry notions is the fact that complete sets of symmetry operations form what in mathematics are known as groups. The elements of a group may be finite in number, in which case the group is then termed **finite** or **discrete**, as for example the symmetry operations shown for the object depicted in Fig. 17.2. But alternatively, the

815

symmetry operations may be infinite in number and described by continuously variable parameter(s); such groups are termed **continuous**. An example of a continuous group is the set of possible rotational displacements of a circular object about its axis (in which case the parameter is the rotation angle).

Definition of a Group

A group G is defined as a set of objects or operations (e.g., rotations or other transformations), called the elements of G, that may be combined, by a procedure to be called **multiplication** and denoted by *, to form a well-defined **product**, subject to the following four conditions:

1. If a and b are any two elements of G, then the product $a * b$ is also an element of G; more formally, $a * b$ associates an element of G with the ordered pair (a, b) of elements of G. In other words, G is **closed** under multiplication of its own elements.
2. This multiplication is associative: $(a * b) * c = a * (b * c)$.
3. There is a unique identity element[1] I in G, such that $I * a = a * I = a$ for every element a in G.
4. Each element a of G has an inverse, denoted a^{-1}, such that $a * a^{-1} = a^{-1} * a = I$.

The above simple rules have a number of direct consequences, including the following:

*   It can be shown that the inverse of any element a is unique: If a^{-1} and $\hat{a}^{-1}$ are both inverses of a, then $\hat{a}^{-1} = \hat{a}^{-1} * (a * o^{-1}) = (\hat{a}^{-1} * a) * a^{-1} = a^{-1}$.

*   The products $g * a$, where a is fixed and g ranges over all elements of the group, consist (in some order) of all the elements of the group. If g and g' produce the same element, then $g * a = g' * a$. Multiplying on the right by a^{-1}, we get $(g * a) * a^{-1} = (g' * a) * a^{-1}$, which reduces to $g = g'$.

Here are some useful conventions and further definitions:

*   The * for multiplication is tedious to write; when no ambiguity will result it is customary to drop it, and instead of $a * b$ we write ab.

*   When a and b are operations, and ab is to be applied to an object appearing to their right, b is deemed to act first, with a then applied to the result of operation with b.

*   If a discrete group possesses n elements (including I), its **order** is n; a continuous group of order n has elements that are defined by n parameters.

*   If $ab = ba$ for all a, b of G, the multiplication is **commutative**, and the group is called **abelian**.

*   If a group possesses an element a such that the sequence I, a, $a^2 (= aa)$, a^3, $\cdots$ includes all elements of the group, it is termed **cyclic**. If a group is cyclic, it must also be abelian. However, not all abelian groups are cyclic.

---

[1] Following E. Wigner, the identity element of a group is often labeled E, from the German **Einheit**, that is, unit; some other authors just write 1.

- Two groups $\{I, a, b, \cdots\}$ and $\{I', a', b', \cdots\}$ are **isomorphic** if their elements can be put into one-to-one correspondence such that for all a and b, $ab = c \iff a'b' = c'$. If the correspondence is many-to-one, the groups are **homomorphic**.

- If a subset G' of G is closed under the multiplication defined for G, it is also a group and called a **subgroup** of G. The identity I of G always forms a subgroup of G.

Examples of Groups

Example 17.1.1 D_3, SYMMETRY OF AN EQUILATERAL TRIANGLE

The symmetry operations of an equilateral triangle form a finite group with six elements; our triangle can be placed either side up, and with any vertex in the top position. The six operations that convert the initial orientation into symmetry equivalents are I (the identity operation that makes no orientation change), C_3, an operation which rotates the triangle counterclockwise by 1/3 of a revolution, C_3^2 (two successive C_3 operations), C_2, rotation by 1/2 a revolution (for this group the rotation is about an axis in the plane of the triangle), and C_2' and C_2'' (180° rotations about additional axes in the plane of the triangle). Figure 17.1 is a schematic diagram indicating these symmetry operations, and Fig. 17.2 shows their result, with the vertices of the triangle numbered to show the effect of each operation. The multiplication table for the group is shown in Table 17.1, where the product ab (which describes the result of first applying operation b, and then operation a) is

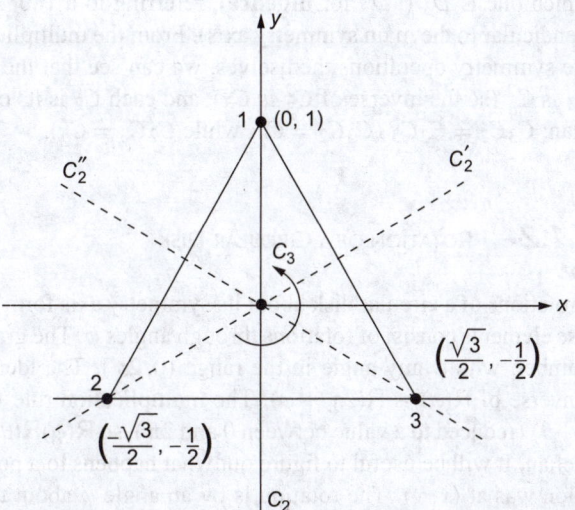

FIGURE 17.1   Diagram identifying symmetry operations of an equilateral triangle. I is the identity operation (the diagram as shown here). C_3 and C_3^2 are counterclockwise rotations, by, respectively, 120° and 240°; C_2, C_2', C_2'' are operations that turn the triangle over by rotation about the indicated axes.

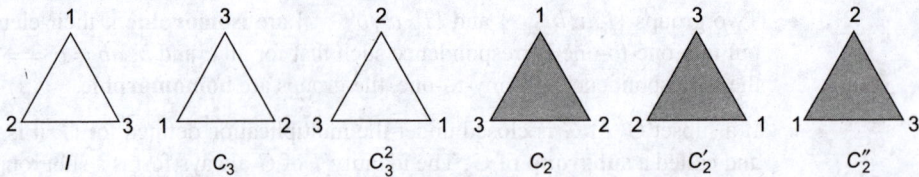

FIGURE 17.2   Result of applying the symmetry operations identified in Fig. 17.1 to an equilateral triangle. One side of the triangle is shaded to make it obvious when that side is up.

Table 17.1   Multiplication Table for Group D_3

	I	C_3	C_3^2	C_2	C_2'	C_2''
I	I	C_3	C_3^2	C_2	C_2'	C_2''
C_3	C_3	C_3^2	I	C_2''	C_2	C_2'
C_3^2	C_3^2	I	C_3	C_2'	C_2''	C_2
C_2	C_2	C_2'	C_2''	I	C_3	C_3^2
C_2'	C_2'	C_2''	C_2	C_3^2	I	C_3
C_2''	C_2''	C_2	C_2'	C_3	C_3^2	I

Operations are pictured in Fig. 17.2. The table entry for row a and column b is the product element ab. For example, $C_2 C_3 = C_2'$.

the group element listed in row a and column b of the table. This group has several names, of which one is D_3 ("D" for **dihedral**, referring to a 180° rotation axis lying in a plane perpendicular to the main symmetry axis). From the multiplication table or by examination of the symmetry operations themselves, we can see that the inverse of I is I, the inverse of C_3 is C_3^2 (so the inverse of C_3^2 is C_3), and each C_2 is its own inverse. This group is not abelian; $C_3 C_2 \neq C_2 C_3$ ($C_3 C_2 = C_2''$, while $C_2 C_3 = C_2'$).   ■

Example 17.1.2   ROTATION OF A CIRCULAR DISK

The rotations of a circular disk about its symmetry axis form a continuous group of order 1 whose elements consist of rotations through angles φ. The group elements $R(\varphi)$ are infinite in number, with φ any angle in the range $(0, 2\pi)$. The identity element is clearly $R(0)$; the inverse of $R(\varphi)$ is $R(2\pi - \varphi)$. The multiplication rule for this group is $R(\varphi)R(\theta) = R(\varphi + \theta)$ (reduced to a value between 0 and 2π), so $R(\varphi)R(\theta) = R(\theta)R(\varphi)$, and this group is abelian. It will be useful to figure out what happens to a point on the disk that before the rotation was at (x, y). The rotation is by an angle φ about the z axis, clockwise, looking down from positive z, a choice made to be consistent with the counterclockwise rotations of the coordinate axes used elsewhere in this book. The final location of this point, (x', y'), is given by the matrix equation

$$\begin{pmatrix} x' \\ y' \end{pmatrix} = \begin{pmatrix} \cos\varphi & \sin\varphi \\ -\sin\varphi & \cos\varphi \end{pmatrix} \begin{pmatrix} x \\ y \end{pmatrix}. \tag{17.1}$$

■

Example 17.1.3   AN ABSTRACT GROUP

Groups do not need to represent geometric operations. Consider a set of four quantities (elements) I, A, B, C, with our knowledge about them only that when any two are multiplied, the result is an element of the set. The multiplication table of this four-element set is shown in Table 17.2. These elements form a group, because each has an inverse (itself), there is an identity element (I), and the set is closed under multiplication.

Table 17.2 Multiplication Table for the Vierergruppe

	I	A	B	C
I	I	A	B	C
A	A	I	C	B
B	B	C	I	A
C	C	B	A	I

The table entry for row a and column b is the product element ab.

■

Example 17.1.4   ISOMORPHISM AND HOMOMORPHISM: C_4 GROUP

The symmetry operations of a square that cannot be turned over form a four-membered group sometimes called C_4 whose elements can be named I, C_4 (90° rotation), C_2 (180° rotation), C_4' (270° rotation). The four complex numbers $1, i, -1, -i$ also form a group when the group operation is ordinary multiplication. These groups are isomorphic, and can be put into correspondence in two different ways:

$$I \leftrightarrow 1, \quad C_4 \leftrightarrow i, \quad C_2 \leftrightarrow -1, \quad C_4' \leftrightarrow -i \quad \text{or} \quad I \leftrightarrow 1, \quad C_4 \leftrightarrow -i, \quad C_2 \leftrightarrow -1, \quad C_4' \leftrightarrow i.$$

This group is also cyclic, as $C_4^2 = C_2$, $C_4^3 = C_4'$, or equivalently $i^2 = -1$, $i^3 = -i$.

The group C_4 has a two-to-one correspondence with the ordinary multiplicative group containing only 1 and -1: I and $C_2 \leftrightarrow 1$, while C_4 and $C_4' \leftrightarrow -1$. This is a homomorphism. A more trivial homomorphism, possessed by all groups, is obtained when every element is assigned to correspond to the identity.

■

Exercises

17.1.1   The **Vierergruppe** (German: four-membered group) is a group different from the C_4 group introduced in Example 17.1.4. The Vierergruppe has the multiplication table shown in Table 17.2. Determine whether this group is cyclic and whether it is abelian.

17.1.2   (a)   Show that the permutations of n distinct objects satisfy the group postulates.

   (b)   Construct the multiplication table for the permutations of three objects, giving each permutation a name of some sort. (Suggestion: Use I for the permutation that leaves the order unchanged.)

   (c)   Show that this permutation group (named S_3) is isomorphic with D_3 and identify corresponding operations. Is your identification unique?

17.1.3   **Rearrangement theorem:** Given a group of distinct elements $(I, a, b, \ldots, n)$, show that the set of products $(aI, a^2, ab, ac, \ldots, an)$ reproduces all the group elements in a new order.

17.1.4   A group G has a subgroup H with elements h_i. Let x be a fixed element of the original group G and **not** a member of H. The transform

$$x h_i x^{-1}, \quad i = 1, 2, \ldots$$

generates a **conjugate subgroup** $x H x^{-1}$. Show that this conjugate subgroup satisfies each of the four group postulates and therefore is a group.

17.1.5   (a)   A particular group is abelian. A second group is created by replacing g_i by g_i^{-1} for each element in the original group. Show that the two groups are isomorphic.

   Note. This means showing that if $ab = c$, then $a^{-1}b^{-1} = c^{-1}$.

   (b)   Continuing part (a), show that the second group is also abelian.

17.1.6   Consider a cubic crystal consisting of identical atoms at $\mathbf{r} = (la, ma, na)$, with $l, m,$ and n taking on all integral values.

   (a)   Show that each Cartesian axis is a fourfold symmetry axis.

   (b)   The cubic **point group** will consist of all operations (rotations, reflections, inversion) that leave the simple cubic crystal invariant and that do not move the atom at $l = m = n = 0$. From a consideration of the permutation of the positive and negative coordinate axes, predict how many elements this cubic group will contain.

17.1.7   A plane is covered with regular hexagons, as shown in Fig. 17.3.

   (a)   Determine the rotational symmetry of an axis perpendicular to the plane through the common vertex of three hexagons (A). That is, if the axis has n-fold symmetry, show (with careful explanation) what n is.

   (b)   Repeat part (a) for an axis perpendicular to the plane through the geometric center of one hexagon (B).

   (c)   Find all the different kinds of axes within the plane of hexagons about which a $180°$ rotation is a symmetry element (this corresponds to turning the plane over by rotation about that axis).

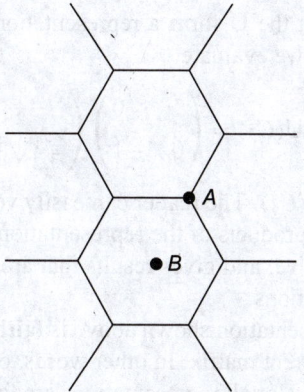

FIGURE 17.3 Plane covered by hexagons.

17.2 REPRESENTATION OF GROUPS

All discrete groups and the continuous groups we study here can be represented by square matrices. By this we mean that to each element of the group we can associate a matrix, and that if $U(a)$ is the matrix associated with a and $U(b)$ the matrix associated with b, then the matrix product $U(a)U(b)$ will be the matrix associated with ab. In other words, the matrices have the same multiplication table as the group. We call these matrices U because they can be chosen to be unitary. It is not necessary that U have a dimension equal to the order of the group.

Sometimes we need to identify representations with a label. For specific representations we can use their generally adopted names; when we need a generic label, we will use K or K'. Thus, we can refer to representation K, consisting of matrices $U^K(a)$.

Example 17.2.1   A UNITARY REPRESENTATION

Here is a unitary representation of the group D_3 illustrated in Fig. 17.2:

$$U(I) = \begin{pmatrix} 1 & 0 \\ 0 & 1 \end{pmatrix}, \qquad U(C_3) = \begin{pmatrix} -\frac{1}{2} & \frac{1}{2}\sqrt{3} \\ -\frac{1}{2}\sqrt{3} & -\frac{1}{2} \end{pmatrix},$$

$$U(C_3^2) = \begin{pmatrix} -\frac{1}{2} & -\frac{1}{2}\sqrt{3} \\ \frac{1}{2}\sqrt{3} & -\frac{1}{2} \end{pmatrix}, \qquad U(C_2) = \begin{pmatrix} 1 & 0 \\ 0 & -1 \end{pmatrix},$$

$$U(C_2') = \begin{pmatrix} -\frac{1}{2} & \frac{1}{2}\sqrt{3} \\ \frac{1}{2}\sqrt{3} & \frac{1}{2} \end{pmatrix}, \qquad U(C_2'') = \begin{pmatrix} -\frac{1}{2} & -\frac{1}{2}\sqrt{3} \\ -\frac{1}{2}\sqrt{3} & \frac{1}{2} \end{pmatrix}. \qquad (17.2)$$

Several features of this representation are apparent:

• The unit operation is represented by a unit matrix.

• The inverse of an operation is represented by the inverse of its matrix.

We can check that the U form a representation: From the multiplication table, we have $C_2\,C_3 = C_2'$. Now we evaluate

$$\mathsf{U}(C_2)\mathsf{U}(C_3) = \begin{pmatrix} 1 & 0 \\ 0 & -1 \end{pmatrix} \begin{pmatrix} -\frac{1}{2} & \frac{1}{2}\sqrt{3} \\ -\frac{1}{2}\sqrt{3} & -\frac{1}{2} \end{pmatrix} = \begin{pmatrix} -\frac{1}{2} & \frac{1}{2}\sqrt{3} \\ \frac{1}{2}\sqrt{3} & \frac{1}{2} \end{pmatrix},$$

which is indeed $\mathsf{U}(C_2')$. The reader can easily verify that other products of group elements correspond to the products of the representation matrices. Matrix multiplication is in general not commutative, and gives results that are consistent with the lack of commutativity of the group operations.

The 2×2 representation shown above is **faithful**, meaning that each group element corresponds to a different matrix. In other words, our 2×2 representation is isomorphic with the original group. Not all representations are faithful; consider the relatively trivial representation in which every group element is represented by the 1×1 matrix (1). Every group will possess this representation. A somewhat less trivial, but still unfaithful, representation of D_3 is one in which

$$\mathsf{U}(I) = \mathsf{U}(C_3) = \mathsf{U}(C_3^2) = 1, \quad \mathsf{U}(C_2) = \mathsf{U}(C_2') = \mathsf{U}(C_2'') = -1. \tag{17.3}$$

This representation distinguishes elements according to whether they involve turning the triangle over. Not all groups will possess this 1×1 representation; if we had not permitted the triangle to be turned over, this representation would have been excluded. These unfaithful representations are homomorphic with the original group. ∎

An important feature of a representation of a group G is that its essential features are invariant if we make the same unitary transformation on the matrices representing all the group elements. To see this, consider what happens when we replace each $\mathsf{U}(g)$ by $\mathsf{V}\mathsf{U}(g)\mathsf{V}^{-1}$. Then the product $\mathsf{U}(g)\mathsf{U}(g')$, which is some $\mathsf{U}(g'')$, becomes $(\mathsf{V}\mathsf{U}(g)\mathsf{V}^{-1})(\mathsf{V}\mathsf{U}(g')\mathsf{V}^{-1}) = \mathsf{V}\mathsf{U}(g)\mathsf{U}(g')\mathsf{V}^{-1} = \mathsf{V}\mathsf{U}(g'')\mathsf{V}^{-1}$, so the transformed matrices still form a representation of G. Representations that can be transformed into each other by application of a unitary transformation are termed **equivalent**.

The possibility of unitary transformation also enables us to consider whether a representation of G is **reducible**. An **irreducible** representation of G is defined as one that cannot be broken into a **direct sum** of representations of smaller dimension by application of the same unitary transformation to all members of the representation. What we mean by a direct sum of representations is that each matrix will be block diagonal (all with the same sequence of blocks). Since different blocks will not mix under matrix multiplication, corresponding blocks of the representation members will themselves define representations (see Fig. 17.4). If a representation named K is a direct sum of smaller representations K_1 and K_2, that fact can be indicated by the notation

$$K = K_1 \oplus K_2.$$

It is not always obvious whether a representation is reducible. We will shortly encounter theorems that provide (for discrete groups) ways of determining what irreducible representations are present in a representation that may be reducible. Moreover, if a group is **abelian**, then the fact that all its elements commute means that the matrices representing them can all be diagonalized simultaneously. From that fact we can conclude that all irreducible representations of abelian groups are 1×1.

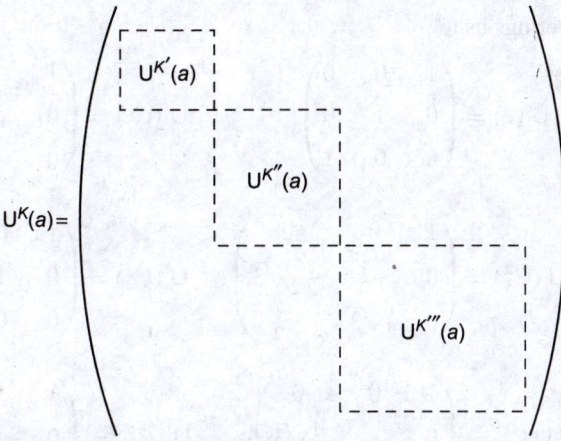

$$U^K(a) = \begin{pmatrix} U^{K'}(a) & & \\ & U^{K''}(a) & \\ & & U^{K'''}(a) \end{pmatrix}$$

FIGURE 17.4   A member of a reducible representation in direct-sum form. All members will have the same block structure, so individual blocks define representations of smaller dimension.

It is important to understand that **reducibility** implies the **existence** of a unitary transformation that brings all members of a representation to the same block-diagonal form; a reducible representation may not exhibit the block-diagonal form if it has not been subjected to a suitable unitary transformation. Here is an example illustrating that point.

Example 17.2.2   A REDUCIBLE REPRESENTATION

Here is a reducible representation for our equilateral triangle:

$$\mathsf{U}(I) = \begin{pmatrix} 1 & 0 & 0 \\ 0 & 1 & 0 \\ 0 & 0 & 1 \end{pmatrix}, \quad \mathsf{U}(C_3) = \begin{pmatrix} 0 & 1 & 0 \\ 0 & 0 & 1 \\ 1 & 0 & 0 \end{pmatrix}, \quad \mathsf{U}(C_3^2) = \begin{pmatrix} 0 & 0 & 1 \\ 1 & 0 & 0 \\ 0 & 1 & 0 \end{pmatrix},$$

$$\mathsf{U}(C_2) = \begin{pmatrix} 0 & 0 & 1 \\ 0 & 1 & 0 \\ 1 & 0 & 0 \end{pmatrix}, \quad \mathsf{U}(C_2') = \begin{pmatrix} 1 & 0 & 0 \\ 0 & 0 & 1 \\ 0 & 1 & 0 \end{pmatrix}, \quad \mathsf{U}(C_2'') = \begin{pmatrix} 0 & 1 & 0 \\ 1 & 0 & 0 \\ 0 & 0 & 1 \end{pmatrix}. \quad (17.4)$$

Note that some of these matrices are not in any direct-sum form. To show that the representation of Eq. (17.4) is reducible, we transform all the U to $\mathsf{U}' = \mathsf{VUV}^{-1}$, using

$$\mathsf{V} = \begin{pmatrix} 1/\sqrt{3} & 1/\sqrt{3} & 1/\sqrt{3} \\ 1/\sqrt{6} & -\sqrt{2/3} & 1/\sqrt{6} \\ 1/\sqrt{2} & 0 & -1/\sqrt{2} \end{pmatrix},$$

which brings us to

$$U'(I) = \begin{pmatrix} 1 & 0 & 0 \\ 0 & 1 & 0 \\ 0 & 0 & 1 \end{pmatrix}, \qquad U'(C_3) = \begin{pmatrix} 1 & 0 & 0 \\ 0 & -\frac{1}{2} & \frac{1}{2}\sqrt{3} \\ 0 & -\frac{1}{2}\sqrt{3} & -\frac{1}{2} \end{pmatrix},$$

$$U'(C_3^2) = \begin{pmatrix} 1 & 0 & 0 \\ 0 & -\frac{1}{2} & -\frac{1}{2}\sqrt{3} \\ 0 & \frac{1}{2}\sqrt{3} & -\frac{1}{2} \end{pmatrix}, \quad U'(C_2) = \begin{pmatrix} 1 & 0 & 0 \\ 0 & 1 & 0 \\ 0 & 0 & -1 \end{pmatrix},$$

$$U'(C_2') = \begin{pmatrix} 1 & 0 & 0 \\ 0 & -\frac{1}{2} & \frac{1}{2}\sqrt{3} \\ 0 & \frac{1}{2}\sqrt{3} & \frac{1}{2} \end{pmatrix}, \quad U'(C_2'') = \begin{pmatrix} 1 & 0 & 0 \\ 0 & -\frac{1}{2} & -\frac{1}{2}\sqrt{3} \\ 0 & -\frac{1}{2}\sqrt{3} & \frac{1}{2} \end{pmatrix}. \qquad (17.5)$$

All the matrices of this representation are block diagonal, and are direct sums that consist of an upper 1×1 block that is the trivial representation, all of whose elements are (1), and a lower 2×2 block that is exactly the 2×2 representation illustrated in Eq. (17.2). There exists no unitary transformation that will simultaneously reduce the 2×2 blocks of all members of the representation to direct sums of 1×1 blocks, so we have reduced the representation of Eq. (17.4) to its irreducible components.[2]   ∎

Example 17.2.3   REPRESENTATIONS OF A CONTINUOUS GROUP

Example 17.1.2 presented a continuous group of order 1 whose elements are rotations $R(\varphi)$ about the symmetry axis of a circular disk. These rotations were taken to be **defined** by the matrix equation presented as Eq. (17.1). The 2×2 matrix in that equation can also be viewed as a representation of $R(\varphi)$:

$$U(\varphi) = \begin{pmatrix} \cos\varphi & \sin\varphi \\ -\sin\varphi & \cos\varphi \end{pmatrix}.$$

Because this group is abelian (two successive rotations yield the same result if applied in either order), we know that this representation is reducible. If we apply the unitary transformation

$$U'(\varphi) = VU(\varphi)V^{-1}, \quad \text{with} \quad V = \begin{pmatrix} 1/\sqrt{2} & -i/\sqrt{2} \\ 1/\sqrt{2} & i/\sqrt{2} \end{pmatrix},$$

the result is

$$U'(\varphi) = \begin{pmatrix} \cos\varphi + i\sin\varphi & 0 \\ 0 & \cos\varphi - i\sin\varphi \end{pmatrix} = \begin{pmatrix} e^{i\varphi} & 0 \\ 0 & e^{-i\varphi} \end{pmatrix}. \qquad (17.6)$$

---

[2]We know this because some of these 2×2 matrices do not commute with each other and therefore cannot be diagonalized simultaneously.

Equation (17.6) applies to every element of our rotation group after transforming with V, and we see that every rotation now has a diagonal representation. In other words, $U(\varphi)$ has been transformed into a direct sum of two one-dimensional (1-D) representations, $U' = U_1 \oplus U_{(-1)}$, with $U_1(\varphi) = e^{i\varphi}$ and $U_{(-1)}(\varphi) = e^{-i\varphi}$. In fact, these are only two of an infinite number of irreducible representations, all of dimension 1:

$$U_n(\varphi) = e^{in\varphi},$$

where n can have any positive or negative integer value, including zero. The reason n is limited to integer values is to assure that $U(2\pi) = U(0)$. Note that only the n values ± 1 lead to faithful representations. ∎

Exercises

17.2.1   For any representation K of a group, and for any group element a, show that

$$\left[U^K(a)\right]^{-1} = U^K(a^{-1}).$$

17.2.2   Show that these four matrices form a representation of the Vierergruppe, whose multiplication table is in Table 17.2.

$$1 = \begin{pmatrix} 1 & 0 \\ 0 & 1 \end{pmatrix}, \quad A = \begin{pmatrix} -1 & 0 \\ 0 & -1 \end{pmatrix}, \quad B = \begin{pmatrix} 0 & 1 \\ 1 & 0 \end{pmatrix}, \quad C = \begin{pmatrix} 0 & -1 \\ -1 & 0 \end{pmatrix}.$$

17.2.3   Show that the matrices 1, A, B, and C of Exercise 17.2.2 are reducible. Reduce them.

Note. This means transforming B and C to diagonal form (by the same unitary transformation).

17.2.4   (a)   Once you have a matrix representation of any group, a 1-D representation can be obtained by taking the determinants of the matrices. Show that the multiplicative relations are preserved in this determinant representation.

(b)   Use determinants to obtain a 1-D representation of D_3 from the 2×2 representation in Eq. (17.2).

17.2.5   Show that the cyclic group of n objects, C_n, may be represented by r^m, $m = 0, 1, 2, \ldots, n - 1$. Here r is a generator given by

$$r = \exp(2\pi i s/n).$$

The parameter s takes on the values $s = 1, 2, 3, \ldots, n$, with each value of s yielding a different 1-D (irreducible) representation of C_n.

17.2.6   Develop the irreducible 2×2 matrix representation of the group of rotations (including those that turn it over) that transform a square into itself. Give the group multiplication table.

Note. This group has the name D_4 (see Fig. 17.5).

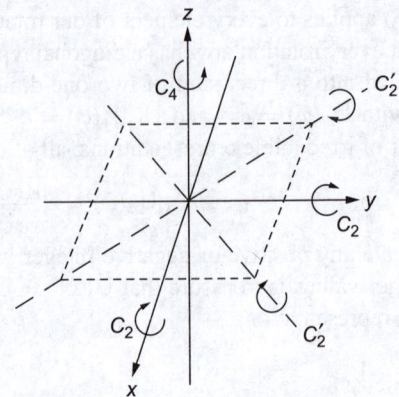

FIGURE 17.5 D_4 symmetry group.

17.3 SYMMETRY AND PHYSICS

Representations of groups provide a key connection between group theory and the symmetry properties of physical systems. Our discussion will be directed mainly at quantum systems, but much of it will also apply to systems that can be described using classical physics.

Consider a quantum system whose Hamiltonian H possesses certain geometric symmetries. If we write $H = T + V$, the symmetries will be those of the potential energy V, since the kinetic energy operator T is invariant with respect to rotations and displacements of the coordinate axes. A concrete example that illustrates the concept would be the determination of the wave function of an electron in the presence of nuclei in some fixed configuration possessing symmetry, such as the equilibrium locations of the nuclei in a symmetric molecule.

The symmetry of H corresponds to a requirement that H be invariant with respect to the application of any element of its symmetry group. Letting R denote such a symmetry element, the invariance of H means that if φ is a solution of the Schrödinger equation with energy E, then $R\varphi$ must also be a solution with the same energy eigenvalue:

$$H(R\varphi) = E(R\varphi).$$

By successively applying the elements of our symmetry group to φ, we can generate a set of eigenfunctions, all with the same eigenvalue. If φ happened to have the full symmetry of H, this set would contain only one member and the situation would be easy to understand. But if φ had less symmetry,[3] our eigenfunction set would have more than one member, with its maximum possible size being the number of elements in our symmetry group. When the eigenfunction set has more than one member, the eigenfunctions do not individually have the complete symmetry of the Hamiltonian, but they form a closed set that permits the partial symmetry to be expressed in all symmetry-equivalent ways. For example, the hydrogenic eigenfunctions known as p states form a three-membered set;

---

[3] This is possible; an example is a hydrogen-atom p state.

none has the full spherical symmetry of the hydrogen atom Hamiltonian, but linear combinations of the three p states can describe a p orbital at an arbitrary orientation (obvious because a vector in an arbitrary direction can be written as a linear combination of vectors in the coordinate directions).

So let's assume that, starting from some chosen φ, we have found a full set of symmetry-related eigenfunctions, have eliminated from them any linear dependence, and have formed an orthonormal eigenfunction set, denoted φ_i, $i = 1 \ldots N$.

Because of the way in which the φ_i were constructed, they will transform linearly among themselves if we apply to them any operation R from our symmetry group, so we may write

$$R\varphi_i = \sum_j U_{ji}(R)\varphi_j. \tag{17.7}$$

If we apply two symmetry operations (R followed by S), the transformation rule for the result will be

$$SR\varphi_i = \sum_{jk} U_{kj}(S)\, U_{ji}(R)\varphi_k. \tag{17.8}$$

Equations (17.7) and (17.8) show that the transformation for the group element SR is the matrix product of those for S and R, so the matrices $\mathsf{U}(S)$ and $\mathsf{U}(R)$ have properties that make them members of a representation of our symmetry group. What is new here is that we have identified U as a representation **associated with the basis** $\{\varphi_i\}$.

At this point we do not know whether the representation formed from our $\{\varphi_i\}$ basis is reducible; its reducibility depends on the quantum system under study and the particular choice made for the initial function φ. If our U are reducible, let's assume we now apply a transformation that will convert them into the direct-sum form. The transformation to obtain the direct-sum separation corresponds to a division of the basis into smaller sets of functions that transform only among themselves. Our overall conclusion from the above analysis is:

> If a Hamiltonian H is fully symmetric under the operations of a symmetry group, all its eigenfunctions can be classified into sets, with each set forming a **basis** for an irreducible representation of the symmetry group. The members of a symmetry-related set of eigenfunctions will be degenerate and are referred to as a **multiplet**. Ordinarily different multiplets will correspond to different eigenvalues; any degeneracy between eigenfunctions of different irreducible representations arises from sources other than the symmetry under study.

Because the eigenfunctions of a Hamiltonian possessing geometric symmetry can be identified with irreducible representations of its symmetry group, it is natural to use **approximate** eigenfunctions with similar symmetry restrictions.

Example 17.3.1   AN EVEN HAMILTONIAN

Consider a Hamiltonian $H(x)$, which is **even** in x, meaning that $H(-x) = H(x)$, but has no other symmetry. Letting σ stand for the reflection operator $x \to -x$ (σ is the usual notation for a reflection operation), our symmetry group, called C_s, consists only of the two operations I and σ, and its multiplication table is

$$I\,I = \sigma\,\sigma = I, \quad I\sigma = \sigma I = \sigma.$$

This group is abelian, and has two irreducible representations of dimension 1: one (A_1) that is completely symmetric, $U(I) = U(\sigma) = 1$, and one (A_2) with sign alternation, $U(I) = 1$, $U(\sigma) = -1$. The eigenfunctions of H will therefore be even or odd, and there is no inherent symmetry requirement that even and odd states be degenerate with each other.

If we start with a function $\varphi(x)$ that is even, we will have $I\varphi = \sigma\varphi = \varphi$, so our basis will consist only of φ, and $U(I) = U(\sigma) = 1$, indicating that the representation constructed using this basis will be the fully symmetric A_1.

On the other hand, if our starting function $\varphi(x)$ was odd, then $I\varphi = \varphi$ but $\sigma\varphi = -\varphi$; again our basis will consist only of $\varphi(x)$, but now the representation constructed from it will consist of $U(I) = 1$, $U(\sigma) = -1$, and will be the alternating-sign representation A_2.

But if we start with a function $\varphi(x)$ that is neither even nor odd, then $I\varphi(x) = \varphi(x)$, but $\sigma\varphi(x) = \varphi(-x)$. Our assumption that $\varphi(x)$ is neither even nor odd means that $\varphi(x)$ and $\varphi(-x)$ are linearly independent, so our basis will consist of two members (and therefore be of dimension 2). Since the symmetry group has only A_1 and A_2 as irreducible representations, the representation built from our two-membered basis will be reducible, and will reduce to $A_1 \oplus A_2$. The basis will separate into the two members $\varphi(x) + \varphi(-x)$ (a 1-D A_1 basis) and $\varphi(x) - \varphi(-x)$ (an A_2 basis).

Given a problem with an even Hamiltonian, one may use the above-identified symmetry analysis to seach for solutions that are restricted to have either even or odd symmetry. This strategy may greatly simplify the process of finding solutions. The notion can be extended to problems with different or greater degrees of symmetry. ∎

It is important to note that all geometric symmetry groups (other than the trivial group, which has only the element I) will possess representations other than A_1, which means that they will have bases of less symmetry than the original group. In Example 17.3.1, our Hamiltonian was even, but could have eigenfunctions that are either even (A_1) or odd (A_2). A Hamiltonian with D_3 symmetry (which we have already seen has irreducible representations of dimensions 1 and 2) can have A_1 eigenfunctions of the full three-dimensional (3-D) symmetry or A_2 eigenfunctions with alternating-sign symmetry. It can also have sets of two degenerate eigenfunctions corresponding to the representation in Eq. (17.2), where (as indicated by the 2×2 matrices) the symmetry operations can convert either of the basis members into linear combinations of both. The irreducibility means that there exists no single function built from this two-member basis that will remain the same (except for a possible sign or phase factor) under all the group operations. The existence of an irreducible basis with more than one member is a consequence of the fact that the symmetry group is not abelian.

Although the elements of a symmetry group may not all commute with each other, they all commute with a Hamiltonian (or other operator) having the full group symmetry. To show this, note that for any eigenfunction ψ and any group element R,

$$H\psi = E\psi \longrightarrow H(R\psi) = E(R\psi) = R(E\psi) = RH\psi \longrightarrow HR = RH.$$

The last step follows because the previous steps are valid for all members of a complete set of eigenfunctions ψ.

Sometimes, especially for continuous groups, we will know in advance how to construct bases for irreducible representations. For example, the spherical harmonics of a given l value form a basis for representation of the 3-D rotation group. From Chapter 16, we know that these spherical harmonics form a closed set under rotation, but only if the set includes all m values. This information, together with the orthonormality of the Y_l^m, tells us that Y_l^m, $m = -l, \ldots, l$ is an orthonormal basis of dimension $2l + 1$ for an irreducible representation of the 3-D rotation group, which is named $SO(3)$. In contrast to the situation for discrete groups, continuous groups (even of low order) may possess an infinite number of finite-dimensional irreducible representations.

An experienced investigator can often find bases for irreducible representations by inspection or educated insight. However, if simple methods for finding a basis prove insufficient, general methods can be used to construct basis functions if the matrices defining the relevant irreducible representation are available. Details of the process can be found in the works by Falicov, Hamermesh, and Tinkham (see Additional Readings).

Example 17.3.2   QUANTUM MECHANICS, TRIANGULAR SYMMETRY

Let's consider a Hamiltonian that has the D_3 symmetry of an equilateral triangle that can be turned over, and our problem is such that its solution can be approximated as a wave function that is distributed over orbitals centered at the three vertices $\mathbf{R}_i$ of the triangle, of the form $\psi(\mathbf{r}) = a_1\varphi(r_1) + a_2\varphi(r_2) + a_3\varphi(r_3)$, where r_i is the distance $|\mathbf{r} - \mathbf{R}_i|$, and φ is a spherically symmetric orbital. The function

$$\psi_0 = \varphi(r_1) + \varphi(r_2) + \varphi(r_3)$$

is a basis for the trivial (A_1) representation of the D_3 group. But because we have three orbitals, there will be two other linear combinations of them that are linearly independent of ψ_0, and one way to choose them is

$$\psi_1 = \frac{1}{\sqrt{2}}\big[\varphi(r_1) - \varphi(r_3)\big], \quad \psi_2 = \frac{1}{\sqrt{6}}\big[-\varphi(r_1) + 2\varphi(r_2) - \varphi(r_3)\big].$$

Neither of these functions (nor any linear combination of them) has enough symmetry to be either A_1 or A_2 basis functions, and they therefore must (together) form a basis for a 2×2 irreducible representation of the D_3 symmetry group that is called E. Knowing that this would be the case, we chose these functions in a way that makes them orthogonal and at a consistent normalization, and they are in fact a basis for the irreducible representation given in Eq. (17.2).

We can check this by applying group operations to ψ_1 and ψ_2, verifying that the result corresponds to the appropriate column of the matrix for the operation. We make one such check here: Applying C_3 to ψ_1, we get $C_3\psi_1 = [\varphi(r_3) - \varphi(r_2)]/\sqrt{2}$, while the first column of $\mathsf{U}(C_3)$ in Eq. (17.2) yields

$$C_3\psi_1 = -\frac{1}{2}\psi_1 - \frac{\sqrt{3}}{2}\psi_2 = -\frac{1}{2}\left(\frac{\varphi(r_1) - \varphi(r_3)}{\sqrt{2}}\right) - \frac{\sqrt{3}}{2}\left(\frac{-\varphi(r_1) + 2\varphi(r_2) - \varphi(r_3)}{\sqrt{6}}\right).$$

The reader can verify that these two expressions for $C_3\psi_1$ are equal, and can make further checks if desired.

One might think that because of the triangular symmetry there would be an irreducible representation of dimension 3. But mathematics is not that simple; all D_3 representations of dimension 3 are reducible! ∎

The symmetries required of solutions to Schrödinger equations have implications beyond their role in causing or explaining degeneracy. The dominant interaction between an electromagnetic field and a molecule can occur only if the molecule has an electric dipole moment, and the presence of a dipole moment depends on the symmetry of the electronic wave function. Another context in which symmetry is important is in the evaluation of the expectation values of quantum operators. These expectation values will vanish unless the integrals that define them have integrands with a fully symmetric part. In addition, it is worth mentioning that many quantum calculations are simplified by limiting them to contributions that do not vanish by reason of symmetry. All these issues can be framed in terms of the irreducible representations for which our wave functions are bases.

In the next sections, we develop some key results of group representation theory, first for discrete groups because the analysis is simpler, and then (in less detail) for continuous groups that have become important in particle theory and relativity.

Exercises

17.3.1   Consider a quantum mechanics problem with D_3 symmetry, with the threefold symmetry axis taken as the z direction, and with orbitals $\varphi(\mathbf{r} - \mathbf{R}_j)$ located at the vertices of an equilateral triangle. This is the same system geometry as in Example 17.3.2, but in the present problem φ will no longer be chosen to have spherical symmetry.

Given that $\varphi(\mathbf{r}) = (z/r)f(r)$ (so φ has the symmetry of a p orbital oriented along the symmetry axis), construct linear combinations of the φ that are bases for irreducible representations of D_3, for each basis indicating its representation.

17.4   DISCRETE GROUPS

Classes

It has been found useful to divide the elements of a finite group G into sets called **classes**. Starting from a group element a_1, one can apply similarity transformations of the form ga_1g^{-1}, where g can be any member of G. If we let a_1 be transformed in this way, using all the elements g of G, the result will be a set of elements that we can denote $a_1, \ldots, a_k$, where k may or may not be larger than 1. Certainly this set will include a_1 itself, as that result is obtained when $g = I$ and also when $g = a_1$ or $g = a_1^{-1}$. The set of elements obtained in this way is called a **class** of G, and can be identified by specifying one of its members. If we choose $a_1 = I$, we find that I is in a class all by itself; often classes will have larger numbers of members.

A class will have the same members no matter which of its elements is assigned the role of a_1. This is clear, since if $a_i = ga_1g^{-1}$ then also $a_1 = g^{-1}a_ig$, showing that we can get a_1 from any other element of the class, and therefrom all the elements reachable from a_1.

Example 17.4.1 CLASSES OF THE TRIANGULAR GROUP D_3

As observed already in general, one class of D_3 will consist solely of I. The class including C_3 contains also C_3^2 (the result of $C_2 C_3 C_2^{-1}$). Finally, C_2, C_2', and C_2'' constitute a third class. ∎

Classes are important because:

- For a given representation (whether or not reducible), all matrices of the same class will have the same value of their trace—obvious because trace$(gag^{-1}) = $ trace$(ag^{-1}g) = $ trace(a). In the group theory world, the trace is also known as the **character**, customarily identified with the symbol Γ.

- It can be shown that the number of inequivalent irreducible representations of a finite group is equal to its number of classes. (For proof and fuller discussion, see Additional Readings at the end of this chapter.)

It can be shown (again, see Additional Readings) that the set of characters for all elements and irreducible representations of a finite group defines an orthogonal finite-dimensional vector space. Writing $\Gamma^K(g)$ as the character of group element g in irreducible representation K, we have the key relations, for a group of order n:

$$n_g \sum_K \Gamma^K(g)\Gamma^K(g') = n\,\delta_{gg'}, \qquad \sum_g \Gamma^K(g)\Gamma^{K'}(g) = n\,\delta_{KK'}. \tag{17.9}$$

Here n_g is the number of elements in the class containing g. These relations enable any reducible representation to be decomposed into a direct sum of irreducible representations, and can also be of aid in finding the characters of irreducible representations if they were not already known.

Another theorem of great importance in the theory of finite groups, sometimes called the **dimensionality theorem**, is that the sum of the squares of the dimensions n_K of the inequivalent irreducible representations is equal to the order, n, of the group:

$$\sum_K n_K^2 = n. \tag{17.10}$$

This theorem, together with the theorem that the number of irreducible K equals the number of classes, imposes stringent limits on the number and size of the irreducible representations of a group. These two requirements are often enough to determine completely the inventory of irreducible representations.

Since the finite groups of interest in physics have been well studied, the most frequent use of these orthogonality relations is to extract from a basis that may be reducible (i.e., a basis for a possibly reducible representation) the irreducible bases that may be included therein. This task is usually carried out with a table of irreducible representations at hand.

Example 17.4.2 ORTHOGONALITY RELATIONS, GROUP D_3

The usual scheme for tabulating discrete group characters is called a **character table**; that for our triangle group D_3 is shown in Table 17.3. The rows of the table are labeled with

Table 17.3   Character Table for Group D_3

	I	$2C_3$	$3C_2$
A_1	1	1	1
A_2	1	1	−1
E	2	−1	0
Ψ	3	0	1

Each row corresponds to an irreducible representation, and each column corresponds to a class. The table entry is the character for each element of that irreducible representation and class. The row below the boxed table (labeled Ψ) is not part of the table but is used in connection with Example 17.4.4.

the usual names assigned the irreducible representations: The labels A and B (the latter not used for this group) are reserved for 1×1 representations. Representations of dimension 2 are normally assigned a label E, and those of dimension 3 (also not occurring here) are called T. Each column of the character table is labeled with a typical member of the class, preceded by a number indicating the number of group elements in the class. This number is omitted if the class contains only one element.

Because the representation of group element I is a unit matrix, the characters (traces) in column I directly indicate the dimensions of the representations. We see that A_1 is a 1×1 representation, so each A_1 matrix contains a single number equal to the character shown, meaning that A_1 is the trivial totally symmetric representation. We see that A_2 is also 1×1, but the three group elements for which the triangle was turned over are now represented by -1. Finally, representation E is seen to be 2×2, and is the representation we found long ago in Eq. (17.2).

Checking the first orthogonality relation for $g = g' = I$, for which $n_g = 1$, we have $1(1^2 + 1^2 + 2^2) = 6$, as expected. For $g = I$, $g' = C_3$, we have $1[1(1) + 1(1) + 2(-1)] = 0$, and for $g = g' = C_3$, we note that $n_g = 2$ and we have $2[1^2 + 1^2 + (-1)^2] = 6$. The reader can check other cases of this orthogonality relation.

Moving to the second orthogonality relation, we take $K = K' = E$, finding $1(2^2) + 2(-1)^2 + 3(0^2) = 6$; the 1, 2, and 3 multiplying individual terms allow for the fact that the sum is over all **elements**, not just over **classes**. Other cases follow similarly.   ∎

Example 17.4.3   COUNTING IRREDUCIBLE REPRESENTATIONS

We consider two cases, first the group C_4, which was the subject of Example 17.1.4. This group is cyclic, with elements I, a, a^2, a^3; those are all the elements, because $a^4 = I$. As already indicated, a faithful representation of this group consists of 1, i, -1, $-i$, with the group operation being ordinary multiplication. Another realization of C_4 is an object that is symmetric under $90°$ rotation about a single axis. This group is abelian, as $a^p a^q = a^q a^p$. Then $gag^{-1} = a$ for any group elements a and g, so each element is in a class by itself. So we have four classes, and hence four irreducible representations. We also have, from the dimension theorem,

$$\sum_{K=1}^{4} n_K^2 = 4.$$

The only way to satisfy this equation is to have four irreducible representations, each of dimension 1. This result should have been expected, since C_4 is abelian. Our irreducible representations can be built from the four following choices of $U(a)$: $1, i, -1, -i$, leading to the following character table.

	I	a	a^2	a^3
A_1	1	1	1	1
A_2	1	i	-1	$-i$
A_3	1	-1	1	-1
A_4	1	$-i$	-1	i

Our second case is D_3, which has six elements and the three classes identified in Example 17.4.1. This means that it has three irreducible representations with dimensions whose squares add to six. The only set of dimensions satisfying this requirements is 1, 1, and 2. ∎

Example 17.4.2 can be generalized to deal with reducible representations; any representation whose characters do not match any row of the character table must be reducible (unless just wrong!). If we were to transform a reducible representation to direct-sum form, it would then be obvious that its trace will be the sum of the traces of its blocks, and that property will hold even if we do not know how to make the block-diagonalizing transformation. In group-theory lingo we would say that the characters of a reducible representation will be the sum of the characters of the irreducible representations it contains. Note that if a given irreducible representation occurs more than once, its characters must be added a corresponding number of times.

Now suppose that we have a reducible representation Ψ of a group of order n. Even if we do not yet know its decomposition into irreducible components, we can write its characters for group elements g in the form

$$\Gamma^{\Psi}(g) = \sum_K c_K \Gamma^K(g), \tag{17.11}$$

where c_K is the number of times irreducible representation K is contained in Ψ. If we multiply both sides of this equation by $\Gamma^{K'}(g)$ and sum over g, the orthogonality kicks in, and

$$\sum_g \Gamma^{K'}(g)\Gamma^{\Psi}(g) = \sum_g \sum_K c_K \Gamma^{K'}(g)\Gamma^K(g) = nc_{K'}. \tag{17.12}$$

Evaluating the left-hand side of Eq. (17.12), we easily solve for $c_{K'}$. We can repeat this sequence of steps with different K' until all the irreducible representations in Ψ have been found.

Example 17.4.4   DECOMPOSING A REDUCIBLE REPRESENTATION

Suppose we start from the following set of three basis functions for the triangular group D_3[4]:

$$\psi_1 = x^2, \quad \psi_2 = y^2, \quad \psi_3 = \sqrt{2}xy, \tag{17.13}$$

where x, y, z are Cartesian coordinates with origin at the center of the triangle, and the axes are in the directions shown in Fig. 17.1. Since $C_3 x = -\frac{1}{2} x + \frac{1}{2}\sqrt{3}\, y$, $C_3 y = -\frac{1}{2}\sqrt{3}\, x - \frac{1}{2}\, y$, we can (somewhat tediously) determine that

$$C_3 x^2 = \frac{1}{4} x^2 + \frac{3}{4} y^2 - \sqrt{\frac{3}{8}}(\sqrt{2}xy),$$

$$C_3 y^2 = \frac{3}{4} x^2 + \frac{1}{4} y^2 + \sqrt{\frac{3}{8}}(\sqrt{2}xy),$$

$$C_3 (\sqrt{2}xy) = \sqrt{\frac{3}{8}} x^2 - \sqrt{\frac{3}{8}} y^2 - \frac{1}{2}(\sqrt{2}xy),$$

so in the ψ basis,

$$\mathsf{U}^\Psi(C_3) = \begin{pmatrix} \frac{1}{4} & \frac{3}{4} & \sqrt{\frac{3}{8}} \\ \frac{3}{4} & \frac{1}{4} & -\sqrt{\frac{3}{8}} \\ -\sqrt{\frac{3}{8}} & \sqrt{\frac{3}{8}} & -\frac{1}{2} \end{pmatrix}. \tag{17.14}$$

Similar analysis can be used to obtain the matrix of C_2, which is easier because the operation involved is just $x \longrightarrow -x$, with y remaining unchanged. We get

$$\mathsf{U}^\Psi(C_2) = \begin{pmatrix} 1 & 0 & 0 \\ 0 & 1 & 0 \\ 0 & 0 & -1 \end{pmatrix}. \tag{17.15}$$

The representation of I is, of course, just the 3×3 unit matrix. Since the only data we need right now are the traces of one representative of each class, we are ready to proceed, and we see that

$$\Gamma^\Psi(I) = 3, \quad \Gamma^\Psi(C_3) = 0, \quad \Gamma^\Psi(C_2) = 1.$$

We are labeling the characters with superscript Ψ as a reminder that the representation is that associated with the ψ_i. These characters have been appended below their respective columns in Table 17.3.

Now we use the fact that the Ψ representation must decompose into

$$\Psi = c_1 A_1 \oplus c_2 A_2 \oplus c_3 E, \tag{17.16}$$

---

[4] These basis functions have been chosen in a way that makes the reducible representation unitary. The factor $\sqrt{2}$ in ψ_3 is needed to make all the ψ_i at the same scale.

and we find the c_i by applying Eq. (17.12). Using the data in Table 17.3, and taking K' to be in turn A_1, A_2, and E,

$$A_1 \; : \; (1)(3) + 2(1)(0) + 3(1)(1) = 6 = 6c_1, \text{ so } c_1 = 1,$$

$$A_2 \; : \; (1)(3) + 2(1)(0) + 3(-1)1) = 0 = 6c_2, \text{ so } c_2 = 0,$$

$$E \; : \; (2)(3) + 2(-1)(0) + 3(0)(1) = 6 = 6c_3, \text{ so } c_3 = 1.$$

Thus, $\Psi = A_1 \oplus E$. We can check our work by summing the A_1 and E entries from the character table. As they must, they add to give the entries for Ψ. ∎

For some purposes it is insufficient just to know which irreducible representations are included in a reducible basis for a group G. We may also need to know how to transform the basis so that each basis member will be associated with a specific irreducible representation of G. Sometimes it is easy to see how to do this. For the above example, the basis function for A_1 must have the full group symmetry, while the E basis functions must be orthogonal to the A_1 basis. These considerations lead us to

$$A_1 \; : \; \varphi = \psi_1 + \psi_2 = x^2 + y^2, \tag{17.17}$$

$$E \; : \; \varphi_1 = \psi_1 - \psi_2 = x^2 - y^2, \quad \varphi_2 = \sqrt{2}\,\psi_3 = 2xy. \tag{17.18}$$

However, if finding the irreducible basis functions by inspection proves difficult, there are formulas that can be used to find them. See Additional Readings.

Other Discrete Groups

Most of the examples we have used have been for one group, D_3, in which we have considered symmetry operations that involve rotations about axes through the center of the system. Groups keeping a central point fixed are called **point groups**, and they arise, among other places, when studying phenomena that depend on the geometric symmetries of molecules. Some point groups have additional symmetries associated with inversion or reflection. It is possible for a point group to have a single n-fold axis for any positive integer n (meaning that a symmetry element is a rotation through an angle $2\pi/n$). However, the number of point groups having multiple symmetry axes with $n \geq 3$ is very limited; they correspond to the Platonic regular polyhedra, and therefore can only be tetrahedral, cubic/octahedral, and dodecahedral/icosahedral.

Other discrete groups arise when we consider permutational symmetry; the **symmetric group** is important in many-body physics and is the subject of a separate section of this chapter.

Exercises

17.4.1   The Vierergruppe has the multiplication table shown in Table 17.2.

  (a)   Divide its elements into classes.

  (b)   Using the class information, determine for the Vierergruppe its number of inequivalent irreducible representations and their dimensions.

  (c)   Construct a character table for the Vierergruppe.

17.4.2   The group D_3 may be discussed as a **permutation** group of three objects. Operation C_3, for instance, moves vertex 1 to the position formerly occupied by vertex 2; likewise vertex 2 moves to the original position of vertex 3 and vertex 3 moves to the original position of vertex 1. So this shuffling could be described as the permutation of $(1,2,3)$ to $(2,3,1)$. Using now letters a, b, c to avoid notational confusion, this permutation $(abc) \to (bca)$ corresponds to the matrix equation

$$C_3 \begin{pmatrix} a \\ b \\ c \end{pmatrix} = \begin{pmatrix} 0 & 1 & 0 \\ 0 & 0 & 1 \\ 1 & 0 & 0 \end{pmatrix} \begin{pmatrix} a \\ b \\ c \end{pmatrix} = \begin{pmatrix} b \\ c \\ a \end{pmatrix},$$

thereby identifying a 3×3 representation of the operation C_3.

(a)   Develop analogous 3×3 representations for the other elements of D_3.

(b)   Reduce your 3×3 representation to the direct sum of a 1×1 and a 2×2 representation. *Note:* This 3×3 representation must be reducible or Eq. (17.10) would be violated.

17.4.3   The group named D_4 has a fourfold axis of symmetry, and twofold axes in four directions perpendicular to the fourfold axis. See Fig. 17.5. D_4 has the following classes (the numbers preceding the class descriptors indicate the number of elements in the class): $I, 2C_4, C_2, 2C_2', 2C_2''$. The twofold axes marked with primes are in the plane of fourfold symmetry.

(a)   Find the number and dimensions of the irreducible representations.

(b)   Given that all the characters of the representations of dimension 1 are ± 1 and that $C_2 = C_4^2$, use the orthogonality conditions to construct a complete character table for D_4.

17.4.4   The eight functions $\pm x^3, \pm x^2 y, \pm xy^2, \pm y^3$ form a reducible basis for D_4, with C_4 a $90°$ counterclockwise rotation in the xy plane, $C_2 = C_4^2$, $C_2' = (x \to -x, y \to y)$, $C_2'' = (x \to y, y \to x)$, and the remaining members of D_4 are additional members of the classes containing the above operations. Find the characters of the reducible representation for which these functions form a basis, and find the direct sum of irreducible representations of which it consists.

17.4.5   The group C_{4v} has a fourfold symmetry axis in the z direction, reflection symmetries (σ_v) about the xz and yz planes, and additional reflection symmetries ($\sigma_d, d =$ dihedral) about planes that contain the z axis but are $45°$ from the x and y axes. See Fig. 17.6. The character table for C_{4v} follows.

	I	$2C_4$	C_2	$2\sigma_v$	$2\sigma_d$
A_1	1	1	1	1	1
A_2	1	1	1	-1	-1
B_1	1	-1	1	1	-1
B_2	1	-1	1	-1	1
E	2	0	-2	0	0

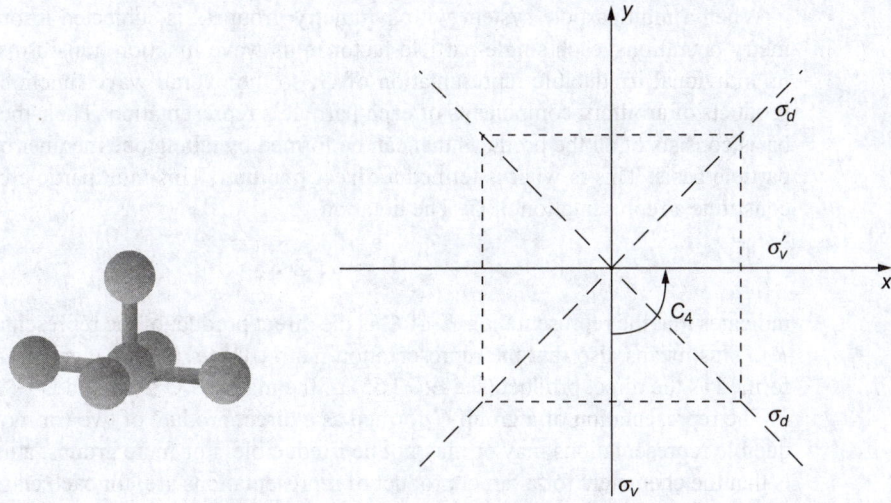

FIGURE 17.6 C_{4v} symmetry group. At left, a molecule with this symmetry.
At right, a diagram identifying the reflection planes, which are perpendicular to the
plane of the diagram.

(a)   Construct the matrix representing one member of each class of C_{4v} using as a
basis a p_z orbital at each of the points $(x, y) = (a, 0), (0, a), (-a, 0), (0, -a)$, and
therefrom extract the characters of the reducible representation for which these p_z
orbitals form a basis. A p_z orbital has functional form $(z/r) f(r)$.

(b)   Determine the irreducible representations contained in our reducible p_z representation.

(c)   Form those linear combinations of our p_z functions that are bases for each of the
irreducible representations found in part (a).

17.4.6   Using the notation and geometry of Exercise 17.4.5, repeat that exercise for the eight-
member basis consisting of a p_x and a p_y orbital at each of the points $(x, y) = (a, 0)$,
$(0, a), (-a, 0), (0, -a)$.

17.5   DIRECT PRODUCTS

Many multiparticle quantum-mechanical systems are described using wave functions that
are products of individual-particle states. This approach is that of an independent-particle
model, which at a higher degree of approximation can include interparticle interactions.
The single-particle states can then be chosen to reflect the symmetry of the system, meaning that each one-particle state will be a basis member of some irreducible representation
of the system's symmetry group. This idea is obvious, for example, in atomic structure,
where we encounter notations such as $1s^2 2s^2 2p^3$ (the ground-state electron configuration
of the N atom).

When a multiparticle system with symmetry group G is subjected to one of its symmetry operations, each single-particle factor in its wave function transforms according to its individual irreducible representation of G, so the overall wave function may contain products of arbitrary components of each particle's representation. Thus, the multiparticle basis consists of all the products that can be formed by taking one member of each single-particle basis. This is what is termed a **direct product**. This multiparticle basis will also constitute a representation of G. The notation

$$K = K_1 \otimes K_2$$

indicates that the representation K of G is the direct product of the representations K_1 and K_2. This means also that the representation matrix $\mathsf{U}^K(a)$ of any element a of G can be formed as the direct product (see Eq. 2.55) of the matrices $\mathsf{U}^{K_1}(a)$ and $\mathsf{U}^{K_2}(a)$.

The representation of a group G formed as a direct product of two (or more) of its irreducible representations may or may not be irreducible. For finite groups, a useful theorem is that the characters for a direct product of representations are, for each class, the product of the individual characters for that class. Once the characters for the direct product have been constructed, the methods of the previous section can be used to find the irreducible components of the product states.

Example 17.5.1   EVEN-ODD SYMMETRY

Sometimes the analysis of a direct product is simple. Consider a system of n independent particles subject to a potential whose only symmetry element (other than I) is inversion (denoted i) through the origin of the coordinate system, so $V(-\mathbf{r}) = V(\mathbf{r})$. In this case, G (conventionally named C_i) has the two elements I and i, with the following character table.

	I	i
A_g	1	1
A_u	1	-1

Individual particles with A_1 wave functions, which remain unchanged under inversion, are conventionally labeled g (from the German word **gerade**). Particles with A_2 wave functions, which change sign on inversion, are labeled u, for **ungerade**. In fact, the usual notation for the character table of the C_i group writes A_g and A_u in place of A_1 and A_2, thereby conveying more information about the symmetries of the corresponding basis functions.

Now suppose that this system is in a state with j of the particles in u states and $n - j$ of the particles in g states. Intuitively, we know that if j is an odd number, the overall wave function will change sign on inversion, but will not change sign if j is even. Formally, we examine the direct product representation K:

$$K = u(1) \otimes u(2) \otimes \cdots \otimes u(j) \otimes g(j+1) \otimes \cdots \otimes g(n).$$

Using the theorem that the characters of representation K can be obtained by multiplying those of its constituent factors, we find $\Gamma^K(I) = 1$, $\Gamma^K(i) = (-1)^j$. Irrespective of the value of j, K will be irreducible: It is A_g if j is even, and A_u if j is odd. ∎

Example 17.5.2   Two Quantum Particles in D_3 Symmetry

This case is not as simple. Suppose both particles are in states of E symmetry, a situation spectroscopists would identify with the notation e^2; they use lower-case symbols to identify individual-particle states, reserving capital letters for the overall symmetry designation. For definiteness, let's further suppose[5] that each particle has a wave function of the form found in Eq. (17.18), so particle i will have the two-member basis

$$\varphi_a(i) = \left(x_i^2 - y_i^2 \right), \quad \varphi_b(i) = 2x_i y_i,$$

and the product basis will therefore have the four members

$$\Phi_{aa} = \varphi_a(1)\varphi_a(2), \quad \Phi_{ab} = \varphi_a(1)\varphi_b(2),$$
$$\Phi_{ba} = \varphi_b(1)\varphi_a(2), \quad \Phi_{bb} = \varphi_b(1)\varphi_b(2). \tag{17.19}$$

The matters at issue are (1) to find the overall symmetries this system can exhibit, and (2) to identify the basis functions for each symmetry.

Consulting Table 17.3, we compute the products for $e \otimes e$:

$$\begin{array}{cccc}
 & I & 2C_3 & 3C_2 \\
e \otimes e: & 4 & 1 & 0.
\end{array}$$

Since this representation has dimension 4 while the largest irreducible representation has dimension 2, it must be reducible. Applying the technique of Example 17.4.4, we can find that it decomposes into $e \otimes e = A_1 \oplus A_2 \oplus E$, a result that is easily checked by adding entries in the D_3 character table.

A set of basis functions corresponding to the decomposition into irreducible representations are

$$\psi^{A1} = (x_1^2 - y_1^2)(x_2^2 - y_2^2) + 4x_1 y_1 x_2 y_2, \tag{17.20}$$

$$\psi^{A2} = 2\left[(x_1^2 - y_1^2)x_2 y_2 - x_1 y_1(x_2^2 - y_2^2) \right], \tag{17.21}$$

$$\psi_1^E = (x_1^2 - y_1^2)(x_2^2 - y_2^2) - 4x_1 x_1 y_1 x_2 y_2, $$
$$\psi_2^E = 2\left[(x_1^2 - y_1^2)x_2 y_2 + x_1 y_1(x_2^2 - y_2^2) \right]. \tag{17.22}$$

Finding these could be challenging; verifying them is less so. ∎

For continuous groups, it is usually simpler to decompose direct-product representations in other ways. For example, in Chapter 16 we used ladder operators to identify overall

---

[5] An actual problem will have a wave function that, in addition to the functional dependence shown here, will have a completely symmetric additional factor that is not relevant for the present group-theoretic discussion.

Table 17.4   Character Table, Group C_{4v}

	I	$2C_4$	C_2	$2\sigma_v$	$2\sigma_d$
A_1	1	1	1	1	1
A_2	1	1	1	-1	-1
B_1	1	-1	1	1	-1
B_2	1	-1	1	-1	1
E	2	0	-2	0	0

angular-momentum states (irreducible representations) formed from products of individual angular momenta. The resulting multiplets correspond to the irreducible representations, and the angular momentum functions that we found are their bases.

Exercises

17.5.1   The group C_{4v} has eight elements, corresponding to the rotational and reflection symmetries of a square that **cannot** be turned over. See Fig. 17.6. Symmetry rotations about the z axis are denoted C_4, C_2, C_4'. Reflections relative to the xz and yz planes are named σ_v and σ_v'; those at $45°$ relative to the xz and yz planes are called σ_d and σ_d' (d indicates "dihedral"). The character table for C_{4v} is in Table 17.4.

(a)   Find the direct sum of irreducible representations of C_{4v} corresponding to the direct product $E \otimes E$.

(b)   A basis for E (in the context of Fig. 17.5) consists of the two functions $\varphi_1 = x$, $\varphi_2 = y$. Apply a few of the group operations to this basis and verify the entries for E in the character table.

(c)   Assume now that we have two sets of variables, x_1, y_1 and x_2, y_2, and we form the direct-product basis x_1x_2, x_1y_2, y_1x_2, y_1y_2. Determine how the direct-product basis functions can be combined to form bases for each of the irreducible representations in the direct sum corresponding to $E \otimes E$.

17.6   SYMMETRIC GROUP

The **symmetric group** S_n is the group of permutations of n distinguishable objects, and is therefore of order $n!$. To see this, note that to make a permutation, we may choose the first object in n different ways, then the second in $n - 1$ ways, etc., until we reach the nth object, which can be chosen in only one way. The total number of possible permutations is therefore $n(n - 1) \ldots (1) = n!$. This group is important in the physics of identical-particle systems, whose wave functions must be either symmetric with respect to particle interchanges (particles with this symmetry are called **bosons**), or antisymmetric under pairwise particle interchanges (these particles are called **fermions**). This means that an n-boson wave function $\Psi_B(1, 2, \ldots, n)$ must satisfy

$$P\Psi_B(1, \ldots, n) = \Psi_B(1, \ldots, n), \qquad (17.23)$$

where P is any permutation of the particle numbers. From a group-theoretical viewpoint this means that Ψ_B is a sole basis function for the trivial A_1 representation of $\mathbf{S}_n$: 1×1, with all members of the representation equal to (1). Many-fermion wave functions $\Psi_F(1, \ldots, n)$ satisfy

$$P\Psi_F(1, \ldots, n) = \epsilon_P \Psi_F(1, \ldots, n), \tag{17.24}$$

where ϵ_P is the n-particle Levi-Civita symbol with an index string corresponding to P; in simple language this means $\epsilon_P = 1$ if P is an **even** permutation of the particle numbers (one requiring an even number of pairwise interchanges), and $\epsilon_P = -1$ if P is **odd**. This means that Ψ_F is the sole basis function for the 1×1 totally antisymmetric representation of $\mathbf{S}_n$ with members (ϵ_P), which we will call A_2.

Since the representations needed for either bosons or fermions are simple and of dimension 1×1, it might seem that sophisticated group-theoretic considerations would be unnecessary. But that is an oversimplification, because many-fermion systems (and some boson systems) consist of direct products of spatial and spin functions, and the spin functions may form a basis of $\mathbf{S}_n$ of dimension larger than one.

Example 17.6.1   TWO AND THREE IDENTICAL FERMIONS

In elementary quantum mechanics, the ground state of a two-fermion system such as the two electrons of the He atom can be treated using a simple wave function of the form

$$\Psi_F = \Big(f(1)g(2) + g(1)f(2)\Big)\Big(\alpha(1)\beta(2) - \beta(1)\alpha(2)\Big).$$

Here f and g are single-particle spatial functions, and α, β describe single-particle spin states. We continue, using a streamlined notation in which the particle numbers are suppressed, understanding that they always occur in ascending numerical order, so Ψ_F will henceforth be written $(fg + gf)(\alpha\beta - \beta\alpha)$. It is obvious that Ψ_F has the fermion (anti)symmetry; we note that it is an A_2 basis function, which is the product of a symmetric A_1 spatial function and an antisymmetric A_2 spin function. The physics of this problem demands that the overall ground-state wave function Ψ_F contain spin function $\alpha\beta - \beta\alpha$ because it is a two-particle spin eigenstate. The two-particle example shows that the A_2 overall representation was obtained as $A_1 \otimes A_2$.

For three particles, things are different. To treat the ground state of the Li atom, we cannot form a completely antisymmetric spin function using only the two single-particle spin functions α and β. The actual spin functions relevant for the ground state form a 2×2 representation of $\mathbf{S}_n$, which we will call E:

$$\theta_1 = \frac{1}{\sqrt{6}}(2\alpha\alpha\beta - \alpha\beta\alpha - \beta\alpha\alpha), \quad \theta_2 = \frac{1}{\sqrt{2}}(\beta\alpha\alpha - \alpha\beta\alpha). \tag{17.25}$$

Since permutations mix θ_1 and θ_2, the overall wave function for this three-particle system must be of the form

$$\Psi_F = \chi_1\theta_1 + \chi_2\theta_2,$$

where χ_1 and χ_2 are three-body spatial functions such that Ψ_F has the required A_2 symmetry. If the χ_i are built from spatial orbitals f, g, and h, one possible set of χ_i are

$$\chi_1 = \frac{1}{2}(ghf - hfg - hgf + fhg),$$

$$\chi_2 = \frac{1}{\sqrt{3}}\left(fgh + gfh - \frac{1}{2}ghf - \frac{1}{2}hfg - \frac{1}{2}hgf - \frac{1}{2}fhg\right),$$

(17.26)

a result that is difficult to find by trial and error. Since the spin functions, and therefore also the spatial functions, become more complicated as the system size increases, the value of a group-theoretic description clearly becomes more urgent. ∎

We consider now, from a formal viewpoint, only the many-fermion case. As illustrated in Example 17.6.1, we deal with space-spin functions in which the spin function has, for reasons we will not discuss here, been chosen to be built from an irreducible representation K of the symmetric group, whose member for permutation P is a unitary matrix designated $\mathsf{U}^K(P)$, and whose basis is a set of spin functions θ_i, $i = 1, \ldots, n_K$, where n_K is the dimension of the spin representation. This means that

$$P\,\theta_i = \sum_{j=1}^{n_K} U_{ji}^K(P)\theta_j.$$

(17.27)

We shall now show that an antisymmetric overall space-spin function can result if we form

$$\Psi_F = \sum_{i=1}^{n_K} \chi_i\,\theta_i,$$

(17.28)

where the χ_i are basis functions for a representation K', of the same dimension as K, meaning that

$$P\,\chi_i = \sum_{k=1}^{n_K} U_{ki}^{K'}(P)\chi_k.$$

(17.29)

The representation K' is assumed to have members that satisfy

$$\mathsf{U}^{K'}(P) = \epsilon_P\mathsf{U}^K(P)^*.$$

(17.30)

The representation K' must exist, since it is (apart from a complex conjugate) the direct product of representations K and A_2. Because A_2 only imparts sign changes to various U^K, the representation K' will be irreducible because representation K is. The representation K' is termed **dual** to representation K.

To verify that the assumed form of Ψ_F has the required A_2 symmetry, we take it, as given in Eq. (17.28), and apply to it an arbitrary permutation P:

$$P\Psi_F = \sum_{i=1}^{n_K} (P\chi_i)(P\theta_i) = \sum_i \left(\sum_k U_{ki}^{K'}(P)\chi_k \right) \left(\sum_j U_{ji}^K(P)\theta_j \right)$$

$$= \sum_{jk} \left(\sum_i U_{ki}^{K'}(P) U_{ji}^K(P) \right) \chi_k \theta_j$$

$$= \sum_{jk} \left(\sum_i \epsilon_P U_{ki}^K(P)^* U_{ji}^K(P) \right) \chi_k \theta_j. \tag{17.31}$$

The steps taken in the processing of Eq. (17.31) are substitutions of Eqs. (17.27) and (17.29) for $P\chi_i$ and $P\theta_i$, followed by a conversion from $\mathsf{U}^{K'}$ to U^K through the use of Eq. (17.30). We complete our analysis by recognizing that because U is unitary, $U_{ki}(P)^* = (\mathsf{U}^{-1})_{ik}(P)$, so

$$\sum_i \epsilon_P U_{ki}^K(P)^* U_{ji}^K(P) = \epsilon_P \delta_{jk},$$

leading to the final result

$$P\Psi_F = \sum_{jk} \epsilon_P \delta_{jk} \chi_k \theta_j = \epsilon_P \sum_k \chi_k \theta_k = \epsilon_P \Psi_F. \tag{17.32}$$

Equation (17.32) shows that the overall wave function Ψ_F has the required fermion antisymmetry.

Our only remaining problem is to construct spatial functions χ_k, which are bases for representation K'. We state without proof (see Additional Readings) that this can be accomplished using the formula

$$\chi_i^j = \sum_P U_{ij}^{K'}(P)^* P\chi_0, \tag{17.33}$$

where χ_0 is a single spatial function whose permutations will be used to construct the χ_i. The index j identifies an entire set of χ_i; if χ_0 has no permutational symmetry, we can create sets of χ_i in $n_{K'}$ in different ways, each corresponding to a different value of j.

Example 17.6.2   CONSTRUCTION OF MANY-BODY SPATIAL FUNCTIONS

We consider a three-electron problem in which the spin states are given by Eq. (17.25). We need the representation of $\mathbf{S}_3$ for which these θ_i are a basis. We are fortunate to already have this representation, as $\mathbf{S}_3$ is isomorphic (in 1–1 correspondence) with D_3, so we can use the set of 2×2 representation matrices given in Eq. (17.2), if we make the identification $C_2 \leftrightarrow P(12)$, $C_2' \leftrightarrow P(13)$, $C_2'' \leftrightarrow P(23)$, where $P(ij)$ denotes the permutation that interchanges the ith and jth items in the ordered list to which the permutation is applied. The permutation $P(123 \rightarrow 312)$ corresponds to C_3, and $P(123 \rightarrow 231)$ corresponds to C_3^2.

We now apply Eq. (17.33); an easy way to do this is to start by generating the matrix T that results from keeping all i and j. In the present case, that means forming the matrix sum

$$\mathsf{T} = \mathsf{U}(I)\chi_0 - \mathsf{U}(C_2)P(12)\chi_0 - \mathsf{U}(C_2')P(13)\chi_0 - \mathsf{U}(C_2'')P(23)\chi_0$$
$$+ \mathsf{U}(C_3)P(123 \to 312)\chi_0 + \mathsf{U}(C_3^2)P(123 \to 231)\chi_0.$$

The minus signs for the $\mathsf{U}(C_2)$ terms arise from the ϵ_P which is needed to convert U^K into $\mathsf{U}^{K'}$.

Taking χ_0 as the product $f(1)g(2)h(3)$, hereafter written fgh, and inserting numerical values for the U, we reach

$$\mathsf{T} = \begin{pmatrix} fgh - gfh - \frac{1}{2}(ghf & \frac{1}{2}\sqrt{3}(ghf - hfg \\ +hfg - hgf - fhg) & -hgf + fhg) \\ \frac{1}{2}\sqrt{3}(-ghf + hfg & fgh + gfh - \frac{1}{2}(ghf \\ -hgf + fhg) & +hfg + hgf + fhg) \end{pmatrix}. \tag{17.34}$$

Each column of Eq. (17.34) defines a set of χ_i, in a form that is not guaranteed to be normalized. From the second column, dividing through by $\sqrt{3}$ for normalization, we obtain the χ_i that were listed as a possible wave function in Example 17.6.1 at Eq. (17.26). The first column of Eq. (17.34) shows that there is a second possibility for an antisymmetric wave function built from the spatial product fgh, namely one that can be written

$$\Psi_F' = \chi_1'\theta_1 + \chi_2'\theta_2,$$

with the normalized spatial functions

$$\chi_1' = \frac{1}{\sqrt{3}}\left(fgh - gfh - \frac{1}{2}ghf - \frac{1}{2}hfg + \frac{1}{2}hgf + \frac{1}{2}fhg\right),$$

$$\chi_2' = \frac{1}{2}(-ghf + hfg - hgf + fhg).$$

∎

Exercises

17.6.1 (a) The objects $(abcd)$ are permuted to $(dacb)$. Write out a 4×4 matrix representation of this one permutation.

Hint: Compare with Exercise 17.4.2.

(b) Is the permutation $(abdc) \to (dacb)$ odd or even?

(c) Is this permutation a possible member of the D_4 group, which was the subject of Exercise 17.4.3? Why or why not?

17.6.2 (a) The permutation group of four objects, S_4, has $4! = 24$ elements. Treating the four elements of the cyclic group, C_4, as permutations, set up a 4×4 matrix representation of C_4. Note that C_4 is a subgroup of P_4.

(b) How do you know that this 4×4 matrix representation of C_4 **must** be reducible?

17.6.3   The permutation group of four objects, S_4, has five classes.

(a)   Determine the number of elements in each class of S_4 and identify one element of each class as a product of cycles.

(b)   Two of the irreducible representations of S_4 are of dimension 1 (and are usually denoted A_1 and A_2). Noting that permutations can be classified as even or odd, find the characters of A_1 and A_2.

Hint. Set up a character table and fill in the A_1 and A_2 lines.

(c)   One irreducible representation of S_4 (usually denoted E) is of dimension 2. Determine the dimensions of all the irreducible representations of S_4 other than A_1, A_2, and E.

(d)   Complete the character table of S_4.

Hint. Only the even permutations have nonzero characters in the E representation.

17.7   CONTINUOUS GROUPS

Several continuous groups whose importance in physics was recognized long ago correspond to rotational symmetry in two- or three-dimensional space. Here the group elements are the rotations, the angles of which can vary continuously and thereby assume an infinite number of values. For rotations, the group multiplication rule corresponds to the application of successive rotations, which we have seen can be described by matrix multiplication. Rotations clearly form a group since they contain an identity element (no rotation), successive rotations are equivalent to a single rotation, and every rotation has an inverse (its reverse).

Rotations in two-dimensional (2-D) space can be described by 2×2 orthogonal matrices with determinant $+1$; the group consisting of these rotations is named SO(2) (SO stands for "special orthogonal"). If we also include reflections, so that the determinant can be ± 1, the group is named O(2). Since a 2-D rotation is completely specified by a single angle, SO(2) is a one-parameter group. A matrix representation of SO(2) was introduced in Eq. (17.1); the group parameter is the rotation angle φ.

Rotations in 3-D space are described by 3×3 orthogonal matrices. The resulting groups are designated O(3) and SO(3); for SO(3), three angles (e.g., the Euler angles) are group parameters. Generalizing to $n \times n$ matrices, the groups are named O(n) and SO(n); the number of parameters needed to specify fully an $n \times n$ real orthogonal matrix is $n(n-1)/2$, and that is the number of independent parameters (generalizations of the Euler angles) needed in SO(n). If we further generalize to unitary matrices, we have the groups SU(n) and U(n). Proof that these sets of unitary matrices form groups is left as an exercise.

Let's introduce some nomenclature. The $n \times n$ matrices referred to above can be thought of as the defining, or **fundamental**, representations of the groups involved. The **order** of a continuous group is defined as the number of independent parameters needed to specify its fundamental representation, so the order of SO(n) is the previously stated $n(n-1)/2$; the order of the group SU(n) is $n^2 - 1$.

In addition to their use for the treatment of rotational symmetry, continuous groups are also relevant to the classification of elementary (and not so elementary) particles. It has been experimentally observed that regularities in the masses and charges of sets of particles can be explained if their wave functions are identified as basis members of an irreducible representation of an appropriate group. Note that now the group does not describe rotations in ordinary space, but refers to a more abstract space relevant to an understanding of the physics involved. The earliest example of this idea was **electron spin**; spin wave functions are objects in an abstract $SU(2)$ space, together with rules to unravel their observational properties. A further abstraction began with the notion that the proton and neutron might form a basis for an abstract $SU(2)$ representation, and has since blossomed with the introduction of $SU(3)$ and other continuous groups into particle physics. A brief survey of these ideas is presented in our specific discussion of $SU(3)$.

Lie Groups and Their Generators

It is extremely useful to manage groups such as $SO(n)$ or $SU(n)$ in ways that do not explicitly involve an infinite number of elements; a formalism for doing so was devised by the Norwegian mathematician Sophus Lie. Groups for which Lie's analysis is applicable, called Lie groups, have elements that depend continuously on parameters that vary over closed intervals (meaning that the parameter set includes the limit of any converging sequence of parameters). The groups $SO(n)$ and $SU(n)$ are Lie groups.

Lie's essential idea was to describe a group in terms of its **generators**, a minimal set of quantities that could be used in a specific way (multiplied by parameters) to produce any element of the group. Our starting point is, for each parameter φ controlling a group operation, to introduce a generator S with the property that when φ is infinitesimal (and therefore written $\delta\varphi$) the group element with parameter $\delta\varphi$ (which must be close to the identity element of the group) can be represented by

$$U(\delta\varphi) = \mathbf{1} + i\,\delta\varphi\,S. \tag{17.35}$$

The factor i in Eq. (17.35) could have been included in S but it is more convenient not to do so. Group operations corresponding to larger values of φ can now be generated from repeated operation (N times) by φ/N, where φ/N is small. We therefore identify $U(\varphi)$ as the limit

$$U(\varphi) = \lim_{N\to\infty} \left(1 + \frac{i\,\varphi\,S}{N}\right)^N;$$

This large-N limit defines the exponential, so we have the general result

$$U(\varphi) = \exp(i\varphi\,S). \tag{17.36}$$

Given any representation U of our continuous group, we can find the generator S corresponding to the parameter φ for that representation by differentiation of Eq. (17.36), evaluated at the identity element of our group. In particular,

$$-i\left[\frac{dU(\varphi)}{d\varphi}\right]_{\varphi=0} = S, \tag{17.37}$$

revealing that the entire behavior of a representation U can be deduced from its behavior in an infinitesimal parameter-space neighborhood of the identity operation. However, to obtain complete knowledge of the structure of a Lie group we need to study the behavior of its generators for a representation that is **faithful**; for that purpose it is desirable to use the fundamental representation.

Example 17.7.1   SO(2) GENERATOR

SO(2) involves rotational symmetry about a single axis, and its operations are counterclockwise rotations of the coordinate axes through angles φ. Working with the 2×2 fundamental representation of SO(2), an infinitesimal rotation $\delta\varphi$ causes (to first order) $(x', y') = (x + y\,\delta\varphi, y - x\,\delta\varphi)$, or

$$
\begin{pmatrix} x' \\ y' \end{pmatrix} = \begin{pmatrix} 1 & \delta\varphi \\ -\delta\varphi & 1 \end{pmatrix} \begin{pmatrix} x \\ y \end{pmatrix} = \left[\begin{pmatrix} 1 & 0 \\ 0 & 1 \end{pmatrix} + \delta\varphi \begin{pmatrix} 0 & 1 \\ -1 & 0 \end{pmatrix} \right] \begin{pmatrix} x \\ y \end{pmatrix} = \mathbf{1} + i\,\delta\varphi\mathsf{S},
$$

with

$$
i\mathsf{S} = \begin{pmatrix} 0 & 1 \\ -1 & 0 \end{pmatrix}, \quad \text{or} \quad \mathsf{S} = \begin{pmatrix} 0 & -i \\ i & 0 \end{pmatrix} = \boldsymbol{\sigma}_2, \tag{17.38}
$$

where $\boldsymbol{\sigma}_2$ is a Pauli matrix. A general rotation is then represented by Eq. (17.36) as

$$
\mathsf{U}(\varphi) = e^{i\varphi\mathsf{S}} = \mathbf{1}_2 \cos\varphi + i\boldsymbol{\sigma}_2 \sin\varphi = \begin{pmatrix} \cos\varphi & \sin\varphi \\ -\sin\varphi & \cos\varphi \end{pmatrix}, \tag{17.39}
$$

where we have evaluated the exponential of the matrix in Eq. (17.39) using the Euler identity, Eq. (2.80). This equation can be recognized as the transformation law for a 2-D coordinate rotation, Eq. (3.23), verifying that the generator formalism works as expected.

If we had started from the final expression for $\mathsf{U}(\varphi)$ given in Eq. (17.39), we could have generated S from it by applying the differentiation formula, Eq. (17.37). ∎

The generator form, Eq. (17.36), has some nice features:

1. For the groups SO(n) and SU(n), any U will be unitary (remember, "orthogonal" is a special case of "unitary"). This means that

$$
\mathsf{U}^{-1} = \exp(-i\varphi\mathsf{S}) = U^\dagger = \exp(-i\varphi\mathsf{S}^\dagger), \tag{17.40}
$$

so $\mathsf{S} = \mathsf{S}^\dagger$, showing that S is Hermitian. That is the proximate reason for inclusion of i in the defining equation for S.

2. Because for both SO(n) and SU(n), det(U) = 1, we also have, invoking the trace formula, Eq. (2.84),

$$
\det(\mathsf{U}) = \exp\big(\operatorname{trace}(\ln\mathsf{U})\big) = \exp\big(i\varphi\,\operatorname{trace}(\mathsf{S})\big) = 1. \tag{17.41}
$$

This condition is satisfied for general φ only if trace(S) = 0. So S is not only Hermitian, but traceless.

3. It can be shown (but is not proved here) that the number of independent generators of a Lie group is equal to the order of the group.

One of Lie's key observations was that by focusing on infinitesimal group elements, various properties of the generators could be deduced. We have already seen that if the form of U in terms of its parameters is known, the generators S can be obtained by differentiation of Eq. (17.36) in the limit corresponding to the identity group element.

Second, relations between the generators can be developed, as follows: Let us consider two operations $U_j(\epsilon_j)$ and $U_k(\epsilon_k)$ of a group G, that respectively correspond to the generators S_j and S_k. The values of ϵ_j and ϵ_k are assumed small, so the resulting U_j and U_k differ, but only slightly, from the identity element. Expanding the exponentials and keeping terms through second order in ϵ,

$$U_j = \exp(i\epsilon_j S_j) = 1 + i\epsilon_j S_j - \frac{1}{2}\epsilon_j^2 S_j^2 + \cdots,$$

$$U_k = \exp(i\epsilon_k S_k) = 1 + i\epsilon_k S_k - \frac{1}{2}\epsilon_k^2 S_k^2 + \cdots,$$

we evaluate the leading term (in ϵ) of the matrix product $U_k^{-1}U_j^{-1}U_kU_j$. The linear terms all cancel, as do several of the quadratic terms. The remaining quadratic terms can be grouped so as to reach the result

$$U_k^{-1}U_j^{-1}U_kU_j = 1 + \epsilon_j\epsilon_k[S_j, S_k] + \cdots$$
$$= 1 + i\epsilon_j\epsilon_k \sum_l f_{jkl}S_l + \cdots. \qquad (17.42)$$

The last line of Eq. (17.42) reflects the fact that the left-hand side of the equation must correspond to some group element, and that element must, to first order in the generators, be of the form shown. Note that the premultipliers $i\epsilon_j\epsilon_k$ are not a form restriction, as their presence simply changes the value of f_{jkl}.

Comparing the two lines of Eq. (17.42), we obtain the important **closure** relation among the generators of the group G:

$$[S_j, S_k] = i \sum_l f_{jkl}S_l. \qquad (17.43)$$

The coefficients f_{jkl} are called the **structure constants** of G. It can be shown that f_{jkl} is antisymmetric with respect to index permutations, so $f_{jkl} = f_{klj} = f_{ljk} = -f_{kjl} = -f_{lkj} = -f_{jlkj}$. The structure constants provide a representation-independent characterization of a Lie group, but as already mentioned, to determine them we will need to work with a faithful representation, such as the group's fundamental representation. We will shortly do so for the groups we study in detail.

As is obvious from the foregoing analysis, Lie group generators will not in general commute. In 3-D, rotations about different axes do not commute, and therefore their generators cannot commute either. An additional indicator for group classification is the maximum number of independent generators that all mutually commute. This number is called the **rank** of the group; it is significant because the generators can be subjected to unitary transformations without changing the ultimate group structure, and the mutually commuting generators can therefore be brought simultaneously to diagonal form. Once this is done, the basis members of the generator set can be labeled using the diagonal elements (the eigenvalues) of the commuting generators. The values of the labels (and the physical phenomena related thereto) depend on the representation in use.

For the orthogonal groups $SO(n)$ and unitary groups $SU(n)$ the commutation relations, Eq. (17.43), can be developed along the lines of angular momentum, leading to generalized ladder operators (and selection rules) in conjunction with the mutually commuting operators. For these central aspects of (the so-called classical) Lie groups we refer to the work by Greiner and Mueller (see Additional Readings).

Summarizing, the rank of a group indicates the number of indices needed to label the basis. In applications to quantum mechanics, these indices are often referred to as quantum numbers. For example, in $SO(3)$, which is of rank 1, the index is usually taken to be M_L, usually identified physically as the z component of an angular momentum; when $SU(2)$, also of rank 1, is used for the description of electron spin, the index is usually called M_S. The possible values of M_L or M_S depend on the representation, and we saw in Chapter 16 that the values range, in unit steps, between $+L$ and $-L$ (or $+S$ and $-S$), so that diagrams identifying these basis members can be plotted on a line. In contrast, we will see that $SU(3)$ is of rank 2, so its basis members are labeled with two quantum numbers. Diagrams identifying the label assignments will in that case need to be 2-D.

It is also possible to label entire representations. One way to label them is to use the eigenvalues of operators that commute with all the generators of the group; such operators are called **Casimir operators**; the number of independent Casimir operators is equal to the rank of the group. $SO(3)$ has therefore one Casimir operator; it is the operator usually known in angular-momentum applications as L^2 or J^2.

Groups $SO(2)$ and $SO(3)$

$SO(2)$ and $SO(3)$ are rotation groups; $SO(2)$ corresponds to rotational symmetry about one axis, which we will take to be the z axis when the symmetry is for a 3-D system. $SO(2)$ will therefore have only one generator, that already found in Eq. (17.38):

$$S_z = \sigma_2 = \begin{pmatrix} 0 & -i \\ i & 0 \end{pmatrix}. \tag{17.44}$$

To use S_z as one of the generators of $SO(3)$, we extend to a 3×3 basis, calling the generator S_3, obtaining

$$S_3 = \begin{pmatrix} 0 & -i & 0 \\ i & 0 & 0 \\ 0 & 0 & 0 \end{pmatrix}. \tag{17.45}$$

$SO(3)$ has two other generators, S_1 and S_2. To obtain S_1, the generator corresponding to

$$U_x(\psi) = \begin{pmatrix} 1 & 0 & 0 \\ 0 & \cos\psi & \sin\psi \\ 0 & -\sin\psi & \cos\psi \end{pmatrix}, \tag{17.46}$$

we apply Eq. (17.37):

$$S_1 = -i \left[\frac{dR_x(\phi)}{d\psi} \right]_{\psi=0} = -i \begin{pmatrix} 0 & 0 & 0 \\ 0 & -\sin\psi & \cos\psi \\ 0 & -\cos\psi & -\sin\psi \end{pmatrix}_{\psi=0} = \begin{pmatrix} 0 & 0 & 0 \\ 0 & 0 & -i \\ 0 & i & 0 \end{pmatrix}. \quad (17.47)$$

In a similar fashion, starting from

$$U_y(\theta) = \begin{pmatrix} \cos\theta & 0 & -\sin\theta \\ 0 & 1 & 0 \\ \sin\theta & 0 & \cos\theta \end{pmatrix}, \quad (17.48)$$

we find

$$S_2 = \begin{pmatrix} 0 & 0 & i \\ 0 & 0 & 0 \\ -i & 0 & 0 \end{pmatrix}. \quad (17.49)$$

Summarizing, the structure of $SO(2)$ is trivial, as it has only a single generator, and has order 1 and rank 1. However, the structure of $SO(3)$ is not entirely trivial. Because no two of S_1, S_2, and S_3 commute, $SO(3)$ will have order 3, but rank 1. By matrix multiplication, we may compute its structure constants. It is easily verified that

$$[S_j, S_k] = i\epsilon_{jkl}S_l, \quad (17.50)$$

where ϵ_{jkl} is a Levi-Civita symbol. Thus, the Levi-Civita symbols are the structure constants for $SO(3)$. Note also that the S_j obey the angular momentum commutation rules. In fact, these are the same matrices that were called K_i in Eq. (16.86) in Chapter 16, and they were identified there as matrices describing the components of angular momentum in a basis consisting of x, y, and z. This observation can be generalized to reach the conclusion that for any representation of $SO(3)$, the generators can be taken to be the angular momentum components L_j ($j = 1, 2, 3$) as expressed in any basis for that representation.

Example 17.7.2   GENERATORS DEPEND ON BASIS

To show that the generators indeed have a form that depends on the choice of basis, consider a basis for $SO(3)$ proportional to the spherical harmonics for $l = 1$ with standard phases,

$$\psi_1 = -\frac{1}{\sqrt{2}}(x + iy), \quad \psi_2 = z, \quad \psi_3 = \frac{1}{\sqrt{2}}(x - iy). \quad (17.51)$$

We now apply $L_x = -i[y\partial/\partial z - z\partial/\partial y]$ to the basis members, getting the result $L_x\psi_1 = z/\sqrt{2} = \psi_2/\sqrt{2}$, $L_x\psi_2 = -iy = (\psi_1 + \psi_3)/\sqrt{2}$, $L_x\psi_3 = z/\sqrt{2} = \psi_2/\sqrt{2}$, meaning that the matrix representation of L_x, and therefore of a generator we will call S_x, is

$$S_x = \frac{1}{\sqrt{2}} \begin{pmatrix} 0 & 1 & 0 \\ 1 & 0 & 1 \\ 0 & 1 & 0 \end{pmatrix}. \quad (17.52)$$

Applying L_y and L_z to the spherical harmonic basis, we obtain generators S_y and S_z:

$$S_y = \frac{1}{\sqrt{2}} \begin{pmatrix} 0 & -i & 0 \\ i & 0 & -i \\ 0 & i & 0 \end{pmatrix}, \quad S_z = \begin{pmatrix} 1 & 0 & 0 \\ 0 & 0 & 0 \\ 0 & 0 & -1 \end{pmatrix}. \tag{17.53}$$

These generators, though different from those given in Eqs. (17.45), (17.47), and (17.49), are equivalent to them in the sense that they define the same irreducible representation of SO_3. ∎

Group SU(2) and SU(2)–SO(3) Homomorphism

A complete set of generators for the fundamental representation of $SU(2)$ must span the space of traceless 2×2 Hermitian matrices; since there is only one off-diagonal element above the diagonal that can have an arbitrary complex value, it can, if nonzero, be assigned in two linearly independent ways (such as 1 and $-i$). The below-diagonal element is then completely determined by Hermiticity. There is only one independent way to assign the diagonal elements, as there are two and they must be real and sum to zero. Thus, a simple set of matrices satisfying the necessary conditions consists of the three Pauli matrices σ_j, $j = 1, 2, 3$. Noting also that there would be advantages to having the generators scaled so that they would satisfy the angular momentum commutation relations, we choose the definition

$$S_j = \frac{1}{2} \sigma_j, \quad j = 1, 2, 3. \tag{17.54}$$

Then, based on our many previous encounters or by performing the matrix multiplications, we can confirm

$$[S_j, S_k] = i \epsilon_{jkl} S_l. \tag{17.55}$$

In addition, for rotation parameters denoted as α_j in connection with generators S_j, we have, calling the corresponding $SU(2)$ members U_j,

$$U_j(\alpha_j) = \exp(i \alpha_j \sigma_j / 2), \quad j = 1, 2, 3. \tag{17.56}$$

Invoking the Euler identity, Eq. (2.80), we can rewrite Eq. (17.56) as

$$U_j(\alpha_j) = 1_2 \cos\left(\frac{\alpha_j}{2}\right) + i \sigma_j \sin\left(\frac{\alpha_j}{2}\right). \tag{17.57}$$

The group $SU(2)$ was first recognized as relevant for physics when it was observed that spin states of the electron form a basis for its fundamental representation. We already know, from Chapter 16, that orbital angular momentum multiplets come in sets with odd numbers of members ($2L + 1$, with L integral). But we also observed that abstract quantities that obey the angular momentum commutation rules with half-integer L values come in multiplets with even numbers of members. The multiplet with two members is the fundamental basis for the group $SU(2)$. These basis functions are conventionally written $|\uparrow\rangle$ and $|\downarrow\rangle$, (or just α and β), and in matrix notation are

$$|\uparrow\rangle = \begin{pmatrix} 1 \\ 0 \end{pmatrix}, \quad |\downarrow\rangle = \begin{pmatrix} 0 \\ 1 \end{pmatrix}. \tag{17.58}$$

Since the structure constants for $SU(2)$ show that its generators satisfy the angular momentum commutation rules, we may conclude that all angular momentum multiplets define representations of $SU(2)$; in Chapter 16 we found that the multiplets of odd dimension ($2L + 1$ with L integral) can be chosen to be the spherical harmonics of angular momentum L and are therefore also a basis for a representation of $SO(3)$. Angular momentum multiplets of even dimension do not have a 3-D spatial representation and cannot correspond to a representation of $SO(3)$. They are the more abstract quantities we call spinors, have half-integer angular-momentum quantum numbers, and are bases only for representations of $SU(2)$.

Further understanding of the situation can be obtained by applying $U_x(\varphi)$, a synonym for $U_1(\varphi)$, to the spin function $|\uparrow\rangle$. Taking $\varphi = \pi$, this corresponds to a 180° rotation about the x axis, which we might expect would convert $|\uparrow\rangle$ into $|\downarrow\rangle$. Applying Eq. (17.57), which for the current case assumes the form $U_x = i\sigma_1$, we have

$$U_x |\uparrow\rangle = i \begin{pmatrix} 0 & 1 \\ 1 & 0 \end{pmatrix} \begin{pmatrix} 1 \\ 0 \end{pmatrix} = i \begin{pmatrix} 0 \\ 1 \end{pmatrix} = i |\downarrow\rangle. \tag{17.59}$$

So far, so good. But let's now try a similar rotation with $\varphi = 2\pi$. We then have $U_x = -1_2$, meaning that a complete 360° rotation does not restore $|\uparrow\rangle$, but gives instead $-|\uparrow\rangle$, namely the expected state, but with a change of sign. To recover $|\uparrow\rangle$ with its original (+) sign would require a rotation $\varphi = 4\pi$, i.e., two revolutions. Each rotation between $\varphi = 2\pi$ and $\varphi = 4\pi$ is, with opposite sign, equivalent to one in the $(0, 2\pi)$ range.

We now see the essential difference between $SU(2)$ and $SO(3)$: The angular range of the rotation parameters in $SU(2)$ is twice that in $SO(3)$, so each $SO(3)$ element is generated twice in each dimension (with different signs) in $SU(2)$. Thus the correspondence between the two groups is not one-to-one (an isomorphism), but is two-to-one, a homomorphism. The existence of this homomorphism is not important for irreducible representations of odd dimension (corresponding to integer L or, in more general contexts, J), since then $U(2\pi) = U(0)$ and the range $(2\pi, 4\pi)$ simply duplicates $(0, 2\pi)$. But the homomorphism remains important for even-dimension representations of $SU(2)$, which correspond to half-integer J and are not representations of $SO(3)$. However, the fact that all representations of $SO(3)$ are also representations of $SU(2)$ means that we can form within $SU(2)$ direct products that include representations of both even and odd dimension. This observation validates our analysis of states with both orbital and spin angular momentum.

In summary, we observe that half-integer angular momentum basis functions, which in earlier discussion we have already labeled as **spinors**, not only are objects that cannot be represented as functions in ordinary 3-D space, but are also objects whose rotational properties are unusual in that their angular periodicity is 4π, not the value 2π that would ordinarily be expected. They are thus somewhat abstract quantities whose relevance to physics rests on their ability to explain the "spin" properties of electrons and other fermions.

Group $SU(3)$

Starting in the 1930s, physicists began to give considerable attention to the symmetries of **baryons**, particles that, as the prefix "bary" implies, are heavy in comparison to electrons, and that interact subject to a force called the **strong interaction**. The earliest conjecture, by Heisenberg, was to the effect that the approximate charge independence of the nuclear forces involving protons and neutrons suggested that they could be viewed as different quantum states of the same particle (called the **nucleon**), with the nucleon having a symmetry appropriate to the existence of a doublet of states. The nucleon was postulated to have the same symmetry as electron spin, namely that of the continuous group SU(2). Although the nucleon symmetry has nothing to do with spin, it is referred to as **isospin**, with the isospin symmetry described by the matrices τ_i, $i = 1, 2, 3$ (equal to the corresponding Pauli spin matrices σ_i), and the isospin states can be classified by the eigenvalue of τ_3 (designated I_3), with $I_3 = +1/2$ corresponding to the proton, $I_3 = -1/2$ corresponding to the neutron.

By the early 1960s, a large number of additional baryons with strong interactions had been identified, of which eight (proton, neutron, and six others) were rather similar in mass. The masses of the baryons discussed in this section are listed in Table 17.5.

In 1961, Gell-Mann, and independently Ne'eman, suggested that these eight baryons might be symmetry-related, and proposed that they be identified with an irreducible representation of the group SU(3), with the relatively small mass differences attributed to forces weaker than the strong interaction and with different symmetry. The states describing these eight particles would be a basis for the generators of an SU_3 representation of dimension 8. Subsequently, it was proposed that all eight of these particles were actually formed from combinations of three smaller, and presumably more fundamental, particles called **quarks**, and the three types of quarks initially postulated, given the names **up** (u), **down** (d), and **strange** (s), were ultimately identified as forming a basis for the generators of SU(3). This original insight then led to the identification of a set of mesons involved with strong interaction as species consisting of one quark and one antiquark, thereby also corresponding to basis members of representations of SU(3).

The situation described in the preceding paragraph can be more fully understood by proceeding to a somewhat detailed discussion of the group SU(3). This group is defined by its generators, of which there are eight. The maximum number that commute with each other is two, so the group is of order $3^2 - 1 = 8$ and rank 2. The simplest useful way to specify the

Table 17.5 Baryon Octet

		Mass	Y	I_3
Ξ :	Ξ^-	1321.32	-1	$-\frac{1}{2}$
	Ξ^0	1314.9	-1	$+\frac{1}{2}$
Σ :	Σ^-	1197.43	0	-1
	Σ^0	1192.55	0	0
	Σ^+	1189.37	0	$+1$
Λ :	Λ	1115.63	0	0
N :	n	939.566	1	$-\frac{1}{2}$
	p	938.272	1	$+\frac{1}{2}$

Masses are given as rest-mass energies, in MeV (1 MeV = 10^6 eV).

generators is to write them as 3×3 matrices in the $SU(3)$ fundamental representation. Like other continuous groups, $SU(3)$ has an infinite number of other irreducible representations of various sizes, but the key properties of the generators (specifically, their commutation rules) will be the same as those of the fundamental representation. We accordingly write the eight $SU(3)$ generators in terms of zero-trace Hermitian matrices λ_1 through λ_8, with

$$S_i = \frac{1}{2}\lambda_i, \tag{17.60}$$

where the λ_i, known as the **Gell-Mann matrices**, are

$$\lambda_1 = \begin{pmatrix} 0 & 1 & 0 \\ 1 & 0 & 0 \\ 0 & 0 & 0 \end{pmatrix}, \quad \lambda_2 = \begin{pmatrix} 0 & -i & 0 \\ i & 0 & 0 \\ 0 & 0 & 0 \end{pmatrix},$$

$$\lambda_3 = \begin{pmatrix} 1 & 0 & 0 \\ 0 & -1 & 0 \\ 0 & 0 & 0 \end{pmatrix}, \quad \lambda_4 = \begin{pmatrix} 0 & 0 & 1 \\ 0 & 0 & 0 \\ 1 & 0 & 0 \end{pmatrix},$$

$$\lambda_5 = \begin{pmatrix} 0 & 0 & -i \\ 0 & 0 & 0 \\ i & 0 & 0 \end{pmatrix}, \quad \lambda_6 = \begin{pmatrix} 0 & 0 & 0 \\ 0 & 0 & 1 \\ 0 & 1 & 0 \end{pmatrix},$$

$$\lambda_7 = \begin{pmatrix} 0 & 0 & 0 \\ 0 & 0 & -i \\ 0 & i & 0 \end{pmatrix}, \quad \lambda_8 = \frac{1}{\sqrt{3}} \begin{pmatrix} 1 & 0 & 0 \\ 0 & 1 & 0 \\ 0 & 0 & -2 \end{pmatrix}. \tag{17.61}$$

In our use of $SU(3)$, we will associate the rows and columns of this representation (in order) to the quarks u, d, and s. Note that λ_1, λ_2, and λ_3 are block diagonal with the upper block being the $SU(2)$ isospin matrices, signaling the presence of an $SU(2)$ subgroup with generators $\lambda_1/2$, $\lambda_2/2$, and $\lambda_3/2$. If we combine λ_3 and λ_8 so as to choose the generators in different ways, we can replace λ_3 with one of the following:

$$\lambda_3' = \sqrt{3}\,\lambda_8 - \lambda_3 = \begin{pmatrix} 0 & 0 & 0 \\ 0 & 1 & 0 \\ 0 & 0 & -1 \end{pmatrix}, \tag{17.62}$$

$$\lambda_3'' = \sqrt{3}\,\lambda_8 + \lambda_3 = \begin{pmatrix} 1 & 0 & 0 \\ 0 & 0 & 0 \\ 0 & 0 & -1 \end{pmatrix}, \tag{17.63}$$

indicating the existence of another $SU(2)$ subgroup with generators $S_1' = \lambda_6/2$, $S_2' = \lambda_7/2$, $S_3' = \lambda_3'/2$, and a third $SU(2)$ subgroup, with generators $S_1'' = \lambda_4/2$, $S_2'' = \lambda_5/2$, $S_3'' = \lambda_3''/2$. These observations support the notion that isospin multiplets can exist within an $SU(3)$ basis.

Because $SU(3)$ is of rank 2, the members of its representations can be labeled according to the eigenvalues of two commuting generators, in contrast to the single label, S_z or I_z, that we employed to label $SU(2)$ members. It is customary to use for this purpose the two generators (λ_3 and λ_8) already in diagonal form. Continuing with the notation introduced for the nucleon, the eigenvalue of the $SU(3)$ generator S_3 is identified as I_3, while S_8 is used to construct the identifier Y (known as **hypercharge**), defined as the eigenvalue of $2S_8/\sqrt{3}$. An oft-used alternative to Y is the **strangeness** $S \equiv Y - 1$.

Example 17.7.3   QUANTUM NUMBERS OF QUARKS

From

$$S_3 = \frac{1}{2}\begin{pmatrix} 1 & 0 & 0 \\ 0 & -1 & 0 \\ 0 & 0 & 0 \end{pmatrix},$$

we can read out the quark I_3 values $+\frac{1}{2}$ for u, $-\frac{1}{2}$ for d, and 0 for s. From

$$2S_8/\sqrt{3} = \lambda_8/\sqrt{3} = \frac{1}{3}\begin{pmatrix} 1 & 0 & 0 \\ 0 & 1 & 0 \\ 0 & 0 & -2 \end{pmatrix},$$

we find the Y values $\frac{1}{3}$ for u and d, and $-\frac{2}{3}$ for s.   ∎

From the definitions of the S_i in Eq. (17.60), one can readily carry out the matrix operations needed to establish their commutation rules. Note that even though the commutation rules will be obtained by examining the specific representation introduced in Eq. (17.60), they apply to all representations of the SU(3) generators.

We will use the commutation rules in a ladder-operator approach to the analysis of the symmetry properties of the three-quark multiplets. It is helpful to systematize the work by temporarily renaming S_1, S_2 as I_1, I_2; S_6, S_7 as U_1, U_2; and S_4, S_5 as V_1, V_2. Then we introduce

$$I_+ = I_1 + iI_2, \qquad I_- = I_1 - iI_2,$$

$$U_+ = U_1 + iU_2, \quad U_- = U_1 - iU_2, \qquad (17.64)$$

$$V_+ = V_1 + iV_2, \quad V_- = V_1 - iV_2,$$

and write some relevant commutators as

$$[S_3, I_\pm] = \pm I_\pm, \quad [S_3, U_\pm] = \mp\frac{1}{2}U_\pm, \qquad [S_3, V_\pm] = \pm\frac{1}{2}V_\pm,$$

$$\qquad (17.65)$$

$$[S_8, I_\pm] = 0, \qquad [S_8, U_\pm] = \pm\frac{1}{2}\sqrt{3}\,U_\pm, \quad [S_8, V_\pm] = \pm\frac{1}{2}\sqrt{3}\,V_\pm.$$

Using the logic of ladder operators (described in detail for applications to angular momentum operators in Section 16.1), the above commutators can be used to show that, starting from a basis function $\psi(I_3, Y)$, we can apply $I_\pm$, $U_\pm$, or $V_\pm$ to obtain basis functions with other label sets. For example,

$$[S_8, U_+]\psi(I_3, Y) = S_8 U_+ \psi(I_3, Y) - U_+ S_8 \psi(I_3, Y) = \frac{1}{2}\sqrt{3}\,U_+\psi(I_3, Y).$$

Replacing $S_8\psi(I_3, Y)$ by $\frac{1}{2}\sqrt{3}\,Y\psi(I_3, Y)$, this equation can be rearranged to

$$S_8\Big(U_+\psi(I_3, Y)\Big) = \frac{1}{2}\sqrt{3}\,(Y + 1)\Big(U_+\psi(I_3, Y)\Big),$$

which shows that if it does not vanish, $U_+\psi(I_3, Y)$ is an eigenvector of S_8 with an eigenvalue corresponding to an increase of one unit in Y. Similarly, from the relation $[S_3, U_+]\psi(I_3, Y) = -\frac{1}{2}U_+\psi(I_3, Y)$, we find that $U_+\psi(I_3, Y)$, if nonvanishing, is an eigenvector of S_3 with an eigenvalue less by 1/2 than that of $\psi(I_3, Y)$. These observations correspond to the equation $U_+\psi(I_3, Y) = C\psi(I_3 - \frac{1}{2}, Y + 1)$. This and other ladder identities are summarized in the following equations:

$$I_\pm\psi(I_3, Y) = C_I\,\psi(I_3 \pm 1, Y),$$

$$U_\pm\psi(I_3, Y) = C_U\,\psi(I_3 \mp \frac{1}{2}, Y \pm 1), \qquad (17.66)$$

$$V_\pm\psi(I_3, Y) = C_V\,\psi(I_3 \pm \frac{1}{2}, Y \pm 1).$$

The constants C will depend on the representation under study and on the values of I_3 and Y; if the result of an operation according to any of these equations leads to an (I_3, Y) set that is not part of the representation's basis, the C associated with that equation will vanish and the ladder construction will terminate.

It is important to stress that the operators in Eq. (17.66) only move **within** the representation under study, so if we start with a basis member of an irreducible representation, all the functions we will be able to reach will also be members of the same representation.

Example 17.7.4   QUARK LADDERS

As a preliminary to our study of baryon and meson symmetries, let's see how the ladder operators work, with the quarks, symbolically $\psi(I_3, Y)$, represented by

$$u = \psi\left(\frac{1}{2}, \frac{1}{3}\right) = \begin{pmatrix} 1 \\ 0 \\ 0 \end{pmatrix}, \quad d = \psi\left(-\frac{1}{2}, \frac{1}{3}\right) = \begin{pmatrix} 0 \\ 1 \\ 0 \end{pmatrix}, \quad s = \psi\left(0, -\frac{2}{3}\right) = \begin{pmatrix} 0 \\ 0 \\ 1 \end{pmatrix}.$$

As explained in Example 17.7.3, the values of I_3 and Y are obtained from the diagonal elements (the eigenvalues) of S_3 and S_8. The 3×3 matrices representing the ladder operators in this example are

$$I_+ = \begin{pmatrix} 0 & 1 & 0 \\ 0 & 0 & 0 \\ 0 & 0 & 0 \end{pmatrix}, \quad U_+ = \begin{pmatrix} 0 & 0 & 1 \\ 0 & 0 & 0 \\ 0 & 0 & 0 \end{pmatrix}, \quad V_+ = \begin{pmatrix} 0 & 0 & 0 \\ 0 & 0 & 1 \\ 0 & 0 & 0 \end{pmatrix},$$

$$\qquad\qquad\qquad\qquad\qquad\qquad\qquad\qquad\qquad\qquad\qquad\qquad (17.67)$$

$$I_- = \begin{pmatrix} 0 & 0 & 0 \\ 1 & 0 & 0 \\ 0 & 0 & 0 \end{pmatrix}, \quad U_- = \begin{pmatrix} 0 & 0 & 0 \\ 0 & 0 & 0 \\ 1 & 0 & 0 \end{pmatrix}, \quad V_- = \begin{pmatrix} 0 & 0 & 0 \\ 0 & 0 & 0 \\ 0 & 1 & 0 \end{pmatrix}.$$

By straightforward matrix multiplication, we find $I_-u = d$, $I_+d = u$, $U_-d = s$, $U_+s = d$, $V_-u = s$, $V_+s = u$; all other operations yield vanishing results. These relationships can be represented in the 2-D graph shown as Fig. 17.7 with Y in the vertical direction and I_3 horizontal. The arrows in the graph are labeled to indicate the results of application of the ladder operators. $\blacksquare$

Continuing now to the baryons, we consider representations appropriate to three quarks, which we can form as the direct product of three single-quark representations. Using the notation **3** as shorthand for the fundamental representation (which is of dimension 3), the

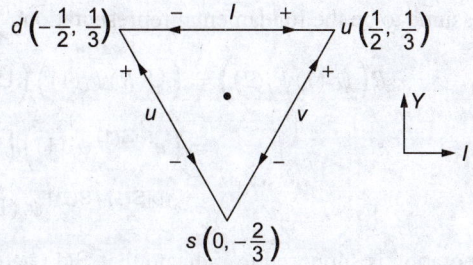

FIGURE 17.7   Conversions between u, d, and s quarks by application of ladder operators $I_\pm$, $U_\pm$, and $V_\pm$. The coordinates of each particle are its (I, Y).

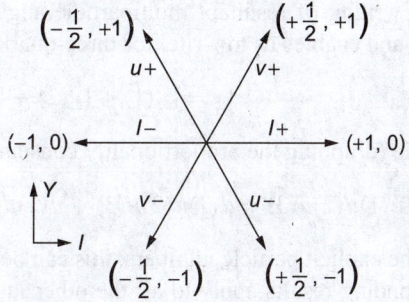

FIGURE 17.8   Root diagram of $SU(3)$. Each operator is labeled by the changes it causes: $(\Delta I, \Delta Y)$.

direct product we need is $\mathbf{3} \otimes \mathbf{3} \otimes \mathbf{3}$. This direct product is a reducible representation, which decomposes into the direct sum

$$\mathbf{3} \otimes \mathbf{3} \otimes \mathbf{3} = \mathbf{10} \oplus \mathbf{8} \oplus \mathbf{8} \oplus \mathbf{1}, \tag{17.68}$$

where $\mathbf{10}$, $\mathbf{8}$, and $\mathbf{1}$ refer to irreducible representations of the indicated dimensions.

A standard way to decompose product representations such as we have here uses diagrams known as Young tableaux. Because development of the rules for construction and use of Young tableaux would take us beyond the scope of this text, we pursue here an alternate route that uses the ladder operators of Eq. (17.66). Use of the ladder operators also has the advantage that it yields explicit expressions for the I_3, Y eigenfunctions. Since the direction in which ladder operators connect states in an I_3, Y diagram is general, we can draw a picture that summarizes their properties. Such a picture is called a **root diagram**; that for $SU(3)$ is shown in Fig. 17.8.

Example 17.7.5   GENERATORS FOR DIRECT PRODUCTS

If we apply an operation R depending on a parameter φ to a product of basis functions for different particles, each function will transform according to its representation, which we presently assume to be the fundamental representation:

$$R\Big(\psi_i(1)\psi_j(2)\Big) = \Big(U(R)\psi_i(1)\Big)\Big(U(R)\psi_j(2)\Big)$$

$$= \Big(e^{i\varphi S(1)}\psi_i(1)\Big)\Big(e^{i\varphi S(2)}\psi_j(2)\Big)$$

$$= e^{i\varphi[S(1)+S(2)]}\psi_i(1)\psi_j(2),$$

where the notation is supposed to indicate that $S(1)$ acts only on particle 1 and $S(2)$ acts only on particle 2 (this can be arranged by an appropriate definition of the direct-product matrices and the operators to which they correspond). The important point here is that because generators appear in an exponent, a **product** of single-particle operations can be obtained using a **sum** of single-particle generators. This observation is a generalization of our earlier writing of resultant multiparticle angular momenta as sums of individual contributions, and enables us to write, for three-quark products, expressions such as

$$I_\pm = I_\pm(1) + I_\pm(2) + I_\pm(3);$$

so, for example (dropping the proportionality constant C_I),

$$I_- u(1)u(2)u(3) = d(1)u(2)u(3) + u(1)d(2)u(3) + u(1)u(2)d(3).$$

Suppressing the explicit particle numbers, this can be shortened to $I_- uuu = duu + udu + uud$. Corresponding results apply to all the other ladder operators and to all three-quark products, and to the application of the diagonal generators, such as

$$S_3\, u(1)u(2)u(3) = \Big(S_3(1)u(1)\Big)u(2)u(3) + u(1)\Big(S_3(2)u(2)\Big)u(3)$$

$$+ u(1)u(2)\Big(S_3(3)u(3)\Big) = \frac{3}{2}u(1)u(2)u(3),$$

or $S_3\, uuu = \frac{3}{2}uuu$, equivalent to assigning $I_3 = \frac{3}{2}$ to uuu. Similar analysis can yield results such as $I_3 = \frac{1}{2}$ for uud, or $(2S_8/\sqrt{3})dss = -dss$, showing that dss has $Y = -1$. ∎

We are now ready to return to the verification of Eq. (17.68).

Example 17.7.6 DECOMPOSITION OF BARYON MULTIPLETS

There are 27 three-quark products, which, using the analysis of Example 17.7.5, have the (I_3, Y) values shown here.

$(+\frac{3}{2}, 1)$	uuu	$(0, 0)$	$uds, dus, usd, dsu, sud, sdu$
$(+\frac{1}{2}, 1)$	uud, udu, duu	$(-1, 0)$	dds, dsd, sdd
$(-\frac{1}{2}, 1)$	udd, dud, ddu	$(+\frac{1}{2}, -1)$	uss, sus, ssu
$(-\frac{3}{2}, 1)$	ddd	$(-\frac{1}{2}, -1)$	dss, sds, ssd
$(+1, 0)$	uus, usu, suu	$(0, -2)$	sss

We can find the irreducible representations in our direct product in a relatively mechanical way. We start by placing the 27 quark products at their coordinate positions in an I_3, Y diagram. We note that the point $(\frac{3}{2}, 1)$ is occupied by only one product, uuu, so it must, by itself, be a member of some irreducible representation of SU_3. Starting there, we may take steps in any of the directions indicated in the root diagram, providing there is a function at each point to which we move. Since all we are doing is identifying possible states, we need not make any sophisticated computations as we proceed. Since uuu is completely symmetric under permutations, the basis function at each point will be a symmetric sum of the products at each point reached. When we have reached all the points, we will have identified a total of 10 basis functions, all members of the same irreducible representation, the one we called **10**. This set of 10 basis functions is called a **decuplet**. The graph for these basis functions, called a **weight diagram**, is shown in Fig. 17.9.

At the points where there was more than one quark product, there will be products left over after accounting for **10**; if we want to be quantitative, they will be linear combinations that are orthogonal to the symmetric forms used in **10**. Continuing with either of the two leftover functions at $(\frac{1}{2}, 1)$, we may construct another set of basis functions from the leftovers; these sets will contain eight members, with the weight diagram shown in Fig. 17.10. (There are only seven points still occupied in the diagram, but the one at (0,0) yields two different functions when approached from different directions; the function obtained when (0,0) is reached horizontally can, via a subgroup analysis, be related to the members of its representation at $(\pm 1, 0)$. These points are elaborated in Exercise 17.7.4.) After accounting for these two **octets**, corresponding to representations **8**, there will be one completely antisymmetric function left at (0,0); it is a basis for **1**.   ■

Both the representations **8** and **10** are relevant for particle physics. The rationalization of the similar-mass baryon octet was based on assignment of those particles to members of **8**, with the small mass differences associated with the breaking of the strong-interaction symmetry by a weaker force which retained some of the $SU(2)$ subgroup symmetries, and by the (weaker still) electromagnetic forces that also broke the $SU(2)$ symmetries. The identification of the octet members with the basis functions of **8** is included in Fig. 17.10, and the energetics of the overall situation is indicated schematically in Fig. 17.11.

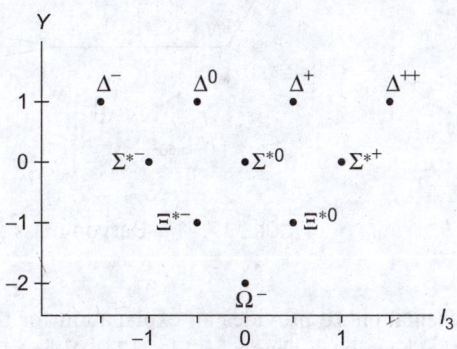

FIGURE 17.9   Weight diagram, baryon decuplet. The symbols at the various points are the names of particles assigned to the basis.

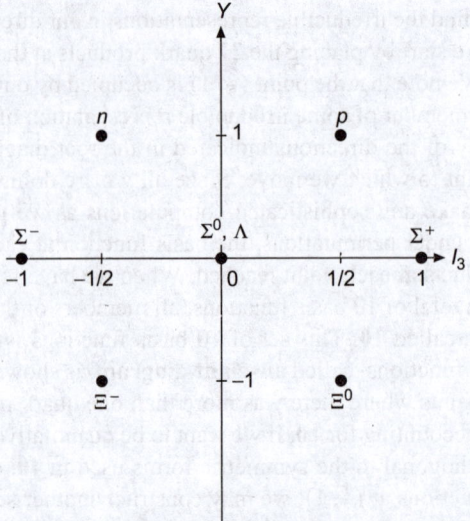

FIGURE 17.10   Weight diagram, baryon octet.

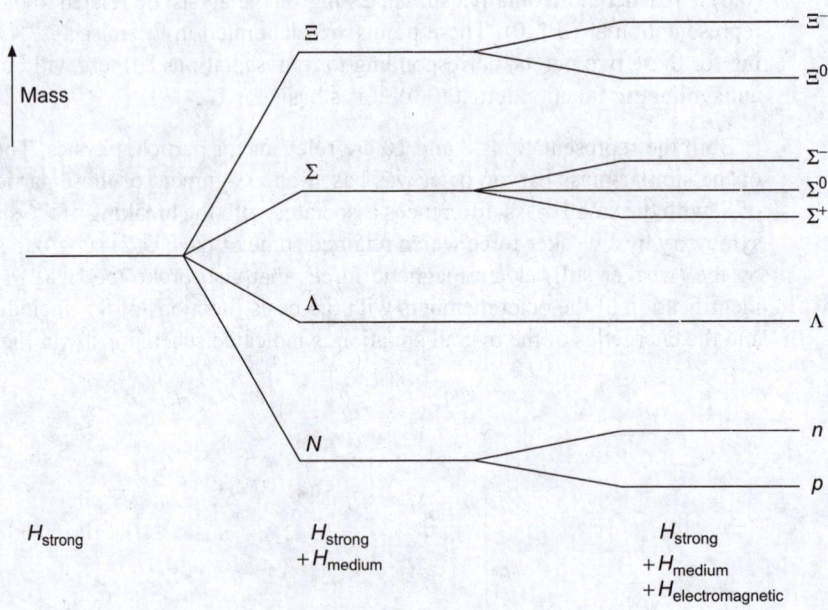

FIGURE 17.11   Baryon mass splitting.

The representation **10** provides an explanation for the set of 10 excited-state baryons whose weight diagram is shown in Fig. 17.9. When Gell-Mann fitted the then existent data to the decuplet representation, the Ω^- particle had not yet been discovered, and its prediction and subsequent detection provided a strong indication of the relevance of SU(3) to physics. Yet another instance of the importance of SU(3) is provided by the existence of a meson octet (displaced by one unit in Y relative to the primary baryon octet).

Finally, we caution the reader that the foregoing discussion is by no means complete. It does not take full account of fermion antisymmetry requirements, the consideration of which led to the SU(3)-color gauge theory of the strong interaction called quantum chromodynamics (QCD). QCD also, at a minimum, involves the group SU(3). We have also left much unsaid about subgroup decompositions of the overall symmetry group, qualitatively alluded to in the discussion supporting Fig. 17.9.

To keep group theory and its very real value in proper perspective, we should emphasize that group theory identifies and formalizes symmetries. It classifies (and sometimes predicts) particles. But apart from saying, e.g., that one part of the Hamiltonian has SU(2) symmetry and another part has SU(3) symmetry, group theory says nothing about the particle interaction. Likewise, a spherically symmetric Hamiltonian has (in ordinary space) SO(3) symmetry, but this fact tells us nothing about the radial dependence of either the potential or the wave function.

Exercises

17.7.1   Determine three SU(2) subgroups of SU(3).

17.7.2   Prove that the matrices U(n) (unitary matrices of order n) form a group, and that SU(n) (those with determinant unity) form a subgroup of U(n).

17.7.3   Using Eq. (17.56) for the matrix elements of SU(2) corresponding to rotations about the coordinate axes, find the matrix corresponding to a rotation defined by Euler angles (α, β, γ). The Euler angles are defined in Section 3.4.

17.7.4   For a product of three quarks, the member of SU(3) representation **10** with $(I_3, Y) = (+\frac{3}{2}, 1)$ is uuu.

   (a)   Apply operators in the root diagram for SU(3), Fig. 17.8, to obtain all the remaining members of the decuplet comprising the representation **10**.

   (b)   The two representations **8** can be chosen to have for $I_3 = \frac{1}{2}$, $Y = 1$ the respective members $\psi_1\left(\frac{1}{2}, 1\right) = (ud - du)u$ and $\psi_2\left(\frac{1}{2}, 1\right) = 2uud - udu - duu$. Briefly explain why this choice is possible.

   (c)   Using the operators in the root diagram and the above $\psi_1\left(\frac{1}{2}, 1\right)$, find expressions for $\psi_1\left(-\frac{1}{2}, 1\right)$, $\psi_1(-1, 0)$, $\psi_1(1, 0)$, $\psi_1\left(-\frac{1}{2}, -1\right)$, and $\psi_1\left(\frac{1}{2}, -1\right)$.

   (d)   Taking each of the six ψ_1 functions you now have, apply an operator that will convert it into $\psi_1(0, 0)$. Show that you obtain exactly two linearly independent $\psi_1(0, 0)$, thereby justifying the claim that the ψ_1 are an octet at the points shown in Fig. 17.10.

   (e)   Show that the octet built starting from $\psi_2(\frac{1}{2}, 1)$ is linearly independent from that built from ψ_1.

   (f)   Find the wave function $\psi(0, 0)$ that is linearly independent of all the $\psi(0, 0)$ functions found in parts (a)–(e). It is the sole member of the representation **1**.

17.8   LORENTZ GROUP

It has long been accepted that the laws of physics should be **covariant**, meaning that they should have forms that are (1) independent of the origin of the coordinates used to describe them (leading from an isolated system to the law of conservation of linear momentum); (2) independent of the orientation of our coordinates (leading to a conservation law for angular momentum); and (3) independent of the zero from which time is measured. Most of our experience suggests that velocities should add like ordinary vectors; for example, a person walking toward the front of a moving train would, as viewed by a stationary observer, have a net velocity equal to the sum of that of the train and the walker's velocity relative to the train. This rule for velocity addition is identified as **Galilean**, and is correct in the limit of small velocities. However, it is now known that transformations between coordinate systems with a constant nonzero relative velocity must lead to a non-intuitive velocity addition law that causes the velocity of light to be the same as measured by observers in all coordinate systems (reference frames). As Einstein showed in 1905, the necessary velocity addition law could be obtained if coordinate-system changes were described by **Lorentz transformations**. Einstein's theory, now known as **special relativity** (its extension to curved space-time to describe gravitation is called **general relativity**), also helped to complete an understanding of the way in which electric and magnetic phenomena become interconverted when charges at rest in one coordinate system are viewed as moving in another.

The transformations that are consistent with the symmetry of space-time form a group known as the **inhomogeneous Lorentz group** or the **Poincaré group**. The Poincaré group consists of space and time displacements and all Lorentz transformations; here we shall only discuss the Lorentz transformations, which by themselves form the **Lorentz group**, sometimes for clarity referred to as the **homogeneous Lorentz group**.

Homogeneous Lorentz Group

Lorentz transformations can be likened to rotations that affect both the spatial and the time coordinates. An ordinary spatial rotation about the origin, in which $(x_1, x_2) \rightarrow (x'_1, x'_2)$, has the property that the length of the associated vector is unchanged by the rotation, so that $x_1^2 + x_2^2 = x_1'^2 + x_2'^2$. But we now consider transformations involving a spatial coordinate (let's choose z) and a time coordinate t, but with $z^2 - c^2t^2 = z'^2 - c^2t'^2$, so that the velocity of light, c, computed for travel from the origin $(0, 0)$ to (z, t) will be the same as that for travel from the origin to (z', t'). We are therefore abandoning the notion that the time variable is universal, assuming instead that it changes together with changes in the spatial variable(s) in a way that keeps the velocity of light constant. We also see that it is natural to rescale the t coordinate to $x_0 = ct$, so that the invariant of the transformation becomes $z^2 - x_0^2$.

Let's now examine a situation in which the coordinate system is moving in the $+z$ direction at an infinitesimal velocity $c\,\delta\rho$ (so that a Galilean transformation applies to z):

$$z' = z - c(\delta\rho)t = z - (\delta\rho)x_0.$$

But we assume that t also changes, to

$$t' = t - a(\delta\rho)z, \quad \text{or} \quad x'_0 = x_0 - ac(\delta\rho)z,$$

with a chosen to keep $z^2 - x_0^2$ constant to first order in $\delta\rho$. The value of a that satisfies this requirement is $a = +1/c$, so our infinitesimal Lorentz transformation is

$$\begin{pmatrix} x_0' \\ z' \end{pmatrix} = \begin{pmatrix} 1 & -\delta\rho \\ -\delta\rho & 1 \end{pmatrix} \begin{pmatrix} x_0 \\ z \end{pmatrix} = \left[\mathbf{1}_2 - \delta\rho \begin{pmatrix} 0 & 1 \\ 1 & 0 \end{pmatrix} \right] \begin{pmatrix} x_0 \\ z \end{pmatrix}.$$

To identify this equation in terms of a generator, we note that

$$-\delta\rho \begin{pmatrix} 0 & 1 \\ 1 & 0 \end{pmatrix} = i(\delta\rho)\,\mathsf{S}, \quad \text{or} \quad \mathsf{S} = i \begin{pmatrix} 0 & 1 \\ 1 & 0 \end{pmatrix} = i\sigma_1, \tag{17.69}$$

where σ_1 is a Pauli matrix. Extending now to a finite velocity just as we did for ordinary rotations in the passage from Eq. (17.35) to Eq. (17.36), we have an expression that is similar to Eq. (17.39), except that we now have σ_1 instead of σ_2, while in place of φ we now have $i\rho$. The result is

$$U(\rho) = \exp(i\rho[i\sigma_1]) = \cos(i\rho) + i\sigma_1 \sin(i\rho) = \cosh(\rho) - \sigma_1 \sinh(\rho)$$

$$= \begin{pmatrix} \cosh\rho & -\sinh\rho \\ -\sinh\rho & \cosh\rho \end{pmatrix}. \tag{17.70}$$

While $\delta\rho$ was an infinitesimal velocity (in units of c), it does not follow that ρ, the result of repeated $\delta\rho$ transformations, is proportional to the resultant velocity in the final transformed coordinates. However, from the equation $z' = z\cosh\rho - x_0\sinh\rho$, we identify the resultant velocity as $v = c\sinh\rho/\cosh\rho = c\tanh\rho$.

Summarizing, and introducing the symbols usually used in relativistic mechanics, we identify

$$\beta \equiv \frac{v}{c}, \quad \tanh\rho = \beta, \quad \cosh\rho = \frac{1}{\sqrt{1-\beta^2}} \equiv \gamma, \quad \sinh\rho = \beta\gamma. \tag{17.71}$$

The range of ρ (sometimes called the **rapidity**) is unlimited, but $\tanh\rho < 1$, thereby showing that c is an upper limit to v (which cannot be reached for finite ρ).

A Lorentz transformation that does not also involve a spatial rotation is known as a **boost** or a **pure Lorentz transformation**. Successive boosts can be analyzed using the group property of the Lorentz transformations: A boost of rapidity ρ followed by another, of rapidity ρ', both in the z direction, must have transformation matrix

$$U(\rho')U(\rho) = \begin{pmatrix} \cosh\rho' & -\sinh\rho' \\ -\sinh\rho' & \cosh\rho' \end{pmatrix} \begin{pmatrix} \cosh\rho & -\sinh\rho \\ -\sinh\rho & \cosh\rho \end{pmatrix}$$

$$= \begin{pmatrix} \cosh\rho'\cosh\rho + \sinh\rho'\sinh\rho & -\cosh\rho'\sinh\rho - \sinh\rho'\cosh\rho \\ \sinh\rho'\cosh\rho - \cosh\rho'\sinh\rho & \sinh\rho'\sinh\rho + \cosh\rho'\cosh\rho \end{pmatrix}$$

$$= \begin{pmatrix} \cosh(\rho+\rho') & -\sinh(\rho+\rho') \\ -\sinh(\rho+\rho') & \cosh(\rho+\rho') \end{pmatrix} = U(\rho+\rho'),$$

showing that the rapidity (not the velocity) is the additive parameter for successive boosts in the same direction. The result we have just obtained is obvious if we write it in the generator notation; it is

$$U(\rho')U(\rho) = \exp(-\rho'\boldsymbol{\sigma}_1)\exp(-\rho\boldsymbol{\sigma}_1) = \exp(-(\rho'+\rho)\boldsymbol{\sigma}_1) = U(\rho'+\rho). \qquad (17.72)$$

Because of the group property, successive boosts in different spatial directions must yield a resultant Lorentz transformation, but the result is not equivalent to any single boost, and corresponds to a boost plus a spatial rotation. This rotation is the origin of the Thomas precession that arises in the treatment of spin-orbit coupling terms in atomic and nuclear physics. A good discussion of the Thomas precession frequency is in the work by Goldstein (Additional Readings).

Example 17.8.1   ADDITION OF COLLINEAR VELOCITIES

Let's now apply Eq. (17.72) to two successive boosts in the z direction, identifying each by its individual velocity (v' for the first boost, v'' for the second), or equivalently $\beta' = v'/c$, $\beta'' = v''/c$. The corresponding rapidities will be denoted ρ' and ρ'', so

$$\tanh\rho' = \beta' = \frac{v'}{c}, \quad \tanh\rho'' = \beta'' = \frac{v''}{c}.$$

The resultant of the two successive boosts will have rapidity $\rho = \rho'+\rho''$, and will therefore be associated with a resultant velocity v satisfying $\tanh(\rho' + \rho'') = v/c = \beta$. From the summation formula for the hyperbolic tangent, we have

$$\frac{v}{c} = \beta = \tanh(\rho'+\rho'') = \frac{\tanh\rho' + \tanh\rho''}{1 + \tanh\rho'\tanh\rho''} = \frac{\dfrac{v'}{c} + \dfrac{v''}{c}}{1 + \dfrac{v'v''}{c^2}} = \frac{\beta'+\beta''}{1+\beta'\beta''}. \qquad (17.73)$$

Equation (17.73) shows that when v' and v'' are both small compared to c, the velocity addition is approximately Galilean, becoming exactly Galilean in the small-velocity limit. But as the individual velocities increase, their resultant decreases relative to their arithmetic sum, and never exceeds c. This behavior is to be expected, since (for real arguments) the hyperbolic tangent cannot exceed unity.   ∎

Minkowski Space

If we make the definition $x_4 = ict$, the formulas we have just obtained, and many others as well, can be written in a systematic form that does not have minus signs explicitly present for the time coordinate. Then Lorentz transformations act like rotations in a space with basis (x_1, x_2, x_3, x_4), and the conserved quantity is $x_1^2 + x_2^2 + x_3^2 + x_4^2$. This approach is appealing and is widely used.

An alternative way to proceed, which has the disadvantage of being a bit more cumbersome, but with the advantage of providing a framework suitable for the extension to general relativity, is to use real coordinates (as was done in the preceding subsection), but to handle the difference in behavior of the spatial and time coordinates by introducing a suitably defined metric tensor. One possibility (for basis $x_0 = ct$, x_1, x_2, x_3), where x_i

($i = 1, 2, 3$) are Cartesian spatial coordinates, is to use the **Minkowski** metric tensor, first introduced in Example 4.5.2,

$$(g^{\mu\nu}) = (g_{\mu\nu}) = \begin{pmatrix} 1 & 0 & 0 & 0 \\ 0 & -1 & 0 & 0 \\ 0 & 0 & -1 & 0 \\ 0 & 0 & 0 & -1 \end{pmatrix}, \qquad (17.74)$$

where it is understood that Greek indices run over the four-index set 0 to 3, and that displacements are rendered as scalar products of the form $x^{\mu} g_{\mu\nu} x'^{\nu}$ or $x_{\mu} g^{\mu\nu} x'_{\nu}$, where the repeated indices are understood to be summed (the Einstein summation convention). Note that because all the analysis in this section is in Cartesian coordinates, the distinction between contravariant and covariant indices is limited to the insertion of minus signs in some elements of products that involve the metric tensor.

As was pointed out in Example 4.6.2, this metric tensor sometimes appears with the signs of all its diagonal elements reversed. Either choice of signs is valid and yields proper results for problems of physics if used consistently, but trouble can arise if material from inconsistent sources is combined. The cited example also indicates how Maxwell's equations can be written in a manifestly covariant form.

Note that the transformation matrices S and U must be mixed tensors, since they convert a vector (whether covariant or contravariant) into another vector of the same variance status. Since for a pure boost these matrices are symmetric, either index can be deemed to be covariant (the other then being contravariant).

Exercises

17.8.1 Show that in $3 + 1$ dimensions (this means three spatial dimension plus time), a boost in the xy plane at an angle θ from the x direction has, in coordinates (x_0, x_1, x_2, x_3), the generator

$$S = i \begin{pmatrix} 0 & \cos\theta & \sin\theta & 0 \\ \cos\theta & 0 & 0 & 0 \\ \sin\theta & 0 & 0 & 0 \\ 0 & 0 & 0 & 0 \end{pmatrix}.$$

17.8.2 (a) Show that the generator in Exercise 17.8.1 produces a Lorentz transformation matrix for rapidity ρ given by

$$U(\rho; \theta) = \begin{pmatrix} \cosh\rho & -\cos\theta\sinh\rho & -\sin\theta\sinh\rho & 0 \\ -\cos\theta\sinh\rho & \sin^2\theta + \cos^2\theta\cosh\rho & \cos\theta\sin\theta(\cosh\rho - 1) & 0 \\ -\sin\theta\sinh\rho & \cos\theta\sin\theta(\cosh\rho - 1) & \cos^2\theta + \sin^2\theta\cosh\rho & 0 \\ 0 & 0 & 0 & 1 \end{pmatrix}.$$

Note. This transformation matrix is symmetric. All single boosts (in any spatial direction) have symmetric transformation matrices.

(b) Verify that the transformation matrix of part (a) is consistent with (1) rotating the spatial coordinates to align the boost direction with a coordinate axis, (2) performing a boost in the direction of that axis using Eq. (17.70), and (3) rotating back to the original coordinate system.

17.8.3   Obtain the Lorentz transformation matrix for a boost of finite amount ρ' in the x direction followed by a finite boost ρ'' in the y direction. Show that there are no values of ρ and θ that can bring this transformation to the form given in Exercise 17.8.2.

17.9   LORENTZ COVARIANCE OF MAXWELL'S EQUATIONS

We start our discussion of Lorentz covariance by recalling how the magnetic and electric fields **B** and **E** depend on the vector and scalar potentials **A** and φ:

$$\mathbf{B} = \nabla \times \mathbf{A},$$

$$\mathbf{E} = -\frac{\partial \mathbf{A}}{\partial t} - \nabla \varphi. \tag{17.75}$$

Restricting consideration to situations where ε and μ have their free-space values ε_0 and μ_0 (with $\varepsilon_0 \mu_0 = 1/c^2$), it can be shown that **A** and φ form a four-vector whose components $\mathcal{A}^\mu$ (in contravariant form) are

$$\mathcal{A}^i = c\varepsilon_0 A_i, \quad i = 1, 2, 3,$$

$$\mathcal{A}^0 = \varepsilon_0 \varphi. \tag{17.76}$$

We now form the tensor $F^{\mu\lambda}$ with elements

$$F^{\mu\lambda} = \frac{\partial \mathcal{A}^\lambda}{\partial x_\mu} - \frac{\partial \mathcal{A}^\mu}{\partial x_\lambda}, \tag{17.77}$$

which we evaluate (consistently with our choice of Minkowski metric) using

$$\frac{\partial}{\partial x_0} = \frac{\partial}{c\partial t}, \quad \frac{\partial}{\partial x_1} = -\frac{\partial}{\partial x}, \quad \frac{\partial}{\partial x_2} = -\frac{\partial}{\partial y}, \quad \frac{\partial}{\partial x_3} = -\frac{\partial}{\partial z}. \tag{17.78}$$

The resulting form for $F^{\mu\lambda}$, known as the **electromagnetic field tensor**, is

$$F^{\mu\lambda} = \varepsilon_0 \begin{pmatrix} 0 & -E_x & -E_y & -E_z \\ E_x & 0 & -cB_z & cB_y \\ E_y & cB_z & 0 & -cB_x \\ E_z & -cB_y & cB_x & 0 \end{pmatrix}. \tag{17.79}$$

The quantity $F^{\mu\lambda}$ is, as its name implies, a second-order tensor that must have the transformation properties associated with the Lorentz group. We know this to be the case because we constructed $F^{\mu\lambda}$ as a linear combination of terms, each of which was the derivative of a four-vector; differentiation of a vector (in a Cartesian system) generates a second-order tensor.

An interesting aside to the above analysis is provided by the discussion of Maxwell's equations in the language of differential forms. In Example 4.6.2 we showed that the differential form

$$F = -E_x \, dt \wedge dx - E_y \, dt \wedge dy - E_z \, dt \wedge dz + B_x \, dy \wedge dz + B_y \, dz \wedge dx + B_z \, dx \wedge dy$$

was a starting point from which Maxwell's equations could be derived; we now observe that the individual terms of this differential form correspond to the elements of the tensor under discussion here.

Lorentz Transformation of E and B

Returning to the main matter of present concern, we now apply a Lorentz transformation to $F^{\mu\lambda}$. For simplicity we take a pure boost in the z direction, which will have matrix elements similar to those of Eq. (17.70); using the notations introduced in Eq. (17.71), our transformation matrix can be written

$$
\mathsf{U} = \begin{pmatrix} \gamma & 0 & 0 & -\beta\gamma \\ 0 & 1 & 0 & 0 \\ 0 & 0 & 1 & 0 \\ -\beta\gamma & 0 & 0 & \gamma \end{pmatrix}.
\tag{17.80}
$$

Noting that we must apply our Lorentz transformation to both indices of $F^{\mu\lambda}$, and keeping in mind that U is symmetric and, as pointed out in Section 17.8, a mixed tensor, we can write

$$
\mathsf{F}' = \mathsf{U}\mathsf{F}\mathsf{U},
\tag{17.81}
$$

where F and F' are both contravariant matrices. If we now compare the individual elements of F' with those of F, we obtain formulas for the components of $\mathbf{E}'$ and $\mathbf{B}'$ in terms of the components of $\mathbf{E}$ and $\mathbf{B}$. For the transformation at issue here, the results are (where v is the velocity of the transformed coordinate system, in the z direction, relative to the original coordinates):

$$
\begin{aligned}
E'_x &= \gamma\left(E_x - \beta c B_y\right) = \gamma\left(E_x - v B_y\right), \\
E'_y &= \gamma\left(E_y + \beta c B_x\right) = \gamma\left(E_y + v B_x\right), \\
E'_z &= E_z,
\end{aligned}
\tag{17.82}
$$

$$
\begin{aligned}
B'_x &= \gamma\left(B_x + \frac{\beta}{c}E_y\right) = \gamma\left(B_x + \frac{v}{c^2}E_y\right), \\
B'_y &= \gamma\left(B_y - \frac{\beta}{c}E_x\right) = \gamma\left(B_y - \frac{v}{c^2}E_x\right), \\
B'_z &= B_z.
\end{aligned}
\tag{17.83}
$$

We can generalize the above to a boost $\mathbf{v}$ in an arbitrary direction:

$$
\begin{aligned}
\mathbf{E}' &= \gamma\left(\mathbf{E} + \mathbf{v}\times\mathbf{B}\right) + (1-\gamma)\mathbf{E}_v, \\
\mathbf{B}' &= \gamma\left(\mathbf{B} - \frac{\mathbf{v}\times\mathbf{E}}{c^2}\right) + (1-\gamma)\mathbf{B}_v,
\end{aligned}
\tag{17.84}
$$

where $\mathbf{E}_v = (\mathbf{E} \cdot \hat{\mathbf{v}})\hat{\mathbf{v}}$ and $\mathbf{B}_v = (\mathbf{B} \cdot \hat{\mathbf{v}})\hat{\mathbf{v}}$ are the projections of $\mathbf{E}$ and $\mathbf{B}$ in the direction of $\mathbf{v}$. In the limit $v \ll c$, these equations reduce to

$$\mathbf{E}' = \mathbf{E} + \mathbf{v} \times \mathbf{B},$$

$$\mathbf{B}' = \mathbf{B} - \frac{\mathbf{v} \times \mathbf{E}}{c^2}. \tag{17.85}$$

Note that the coordinate transformation changes the velocity with which charges move and therefore changes the magnetic force. It is now clear that the Lorentz transformation explains how the total force (electric plus magnetic) can be independent of the **reference frame** (i.e., the relative velocities of the coordinate systems). In fact, the need to make the total electromagnetic force independent of the reference frame was first noted by Lorentz and Poincaré. This was where Lorentz transformations were first recognized as relevant for physics, and that may have provided Einstein with a clue as he developed his formulation of special relativity.

Example 17.9.1   TRANSFORMATION TO BRING CHARGE TO REST

Consider a charge q moving at a velocity $\mathbf{v}$, with $v \ll c$. By giving the coordinate system a boost $\mathbf{v}$, we transform to a frame in which the charge is at rest and experiences only an electric force $q\mathbf{E}'$. But since the total force is independent of the reference frame, it is also given, according to Eq. (17.86), as

$$\mathbf{F} = q(\mathbf{E} + \mathbf{v} \times \mathbf{B}), \tag{17.86}$$

which is just the classical Lorentz force.   ∎

The ability to write Maxwell's equations in a tensor form that gives the experimentally observed results under Lorentz transformation is an important achievement because it guarantees that the formulation is consistent with special relativity. This is one of the reasons that modern theories of quantum electrodynamics and elementary particles are often written in this **manifestly covariant** form. Conversely, the insistence on such a tensor form has been a useful guide in the construction of these theories.

We close with the following general observations:

> The Lorentz group is the symmetry group of electrodynamics, of the electroweak gauge theory, and of the strong interactions described by quantum chromodynamics. It appears necessary that mechanics in general have the symmetry of the Lorentz group, and that requirement corresponds to the general applicability of special relativity. With respect to electrodynamics, the Lorentz symmetry explains the fact that the velocity of light is the same in all inertial frames, and it explains how electric and magnetic forces are interrelated and yield physical results that are frame-independent. While a detailed study of relativistic mechanics is beyond the scope of this book, the extension to special relativity of Newton's equations of motion is straightforward and leads to a variety of results, some of which challenge human intuition.

Exercises

17.9.1   Apply the Lorentz transformation of Eq. (17.80) to $F^{\mu\lambda}$ as given in Eq. (17.79). Verify that the result is a matrix F' whose elements confirm the results given in Eqs. (17.82) and (17.83).

17.9.2   Confirm that the generalization of Eqs. (17.82) and (17.83) to a boost corresponding to an arbitrary velocity $\mathbf{v}$ is properly given by Eq. (17.84).

17.10   SPACE GROUPS

Perfect crystals exhibit translational symmetry, meaning that they can be considered as a space-filling array of parallelepipeds stacked end-to-end and side-to-side, with each containing an identical set of identically placed atoms. A single parallelepiped is referred to as the **unit cell** of the crystal; a unit cell can be specified by giving the vectors that define its edges. Calling these vectors $\mathbf{h}_1$, $\mathbf{h}_2$, $\mathbf{h}_3$, equivalent points in any two unit cells are separated from each other by vectors

$$\mathbf{b} = n_1\mathbf{h}_1 + n_2\mathbf{h}_2 + n_3\mathbf{h}_3,$$

where n_1, n_2, n_3 can be any integers (positive, negative, or zero). The set of these equivalent points is called the **Bravais lattice** of the crystal.

A Bravais lattice will have a symmetry that depends on the angles and relative lengths of the lattice vectors; in three dimensions there are 14 different symmetries possible for Bravais lattices. There are 32 3-D point groups that are symmetry-compatible with at least one Bravais lattice; these are called **crystallographic point groups** to distinguish them from the infinite number of point groups that can exist in the absence of any compatibility requirement.

Example 17.10.1   TILING A FLOOR

To understand the notion of crystallographic point group, consider what would happen (in two dimensions) if we try to tile a floor with identical tiles in the shape of a regular polygon. We will have success with squares and triangles, and even with hexagons. These work because an integer number of tiles can be placed so that they have vertices at the same point. A triangle has an internal angle of $60°$, so six of them can meet at a point; similarly, four squares can meet at a point, as can three hexagons (internal angle $120°$). But we cannot tile with regular pentagons (internal angle $108°$) or any regular polygon with more than six sides.   ∎

Combining Bravais lattices and compatible point groups, there is a total of 230 different groups in 3-D that exhibit translational symmetry and some sort of point-group symmetry. These 230 groups are called **space groups**. Their study and use in crystallography (e.g., to determine the detailed structure of a crystal from its x-ray scattering) is the topic of several of the larger books in the Additional Readings.

Systems with periodicity in only one or two dimensions also exist in nature; some linear polymers are 1-D periodic systems; surface systems and single-layer arrays such as **graphene** (a macroscopic hexagonal array of carbon atoms) exhibit periodicity in two dimensions. There is even a kind of translational symmetry that involves elements that form helical structures. The recognition of this type of symmetry in crystallographic studies of DNA was the key contribution leading to the discovery that DNA existed as a double helix.

Additional Readings

Buerger, M. J., *Elementary Crystallography*. New York: Wiley (1956). A comprehensive discussion of crystal symmetries. Buerger develops all 32 point groups and all 230 space groups. Related books by this author include *Contemporary Crystallography*. New York: McGraw-Hill (1970); *Crystal Structure Analysis*. New York: Krieger (1979) (reprint, 1960); and *Introduction to Crystal Geometry*. New York: Krieger (1977) (reprint, 1971).

Burns, G., and A. M. Glazer, *Space Groups for Solid-State Scientists*. New York: Academic Press (1978). A well-organized, readable treatment of groups and their application to the solid state.

de-Shalit, A., and I. Talmi, *Nuclear Shell Model*. New York: Academic Press (1963). We adopt the Condon-Shortley phase conventions of this text.

Falicov, L. M., *Group Theory and Its Physical Applications*. Notes compiled by A. Luehrmann. Chicago: University of Chicago Press (1966). Group theory, with an emphasis on applications to crystal symmetries and solid-state physics.

Gell-Mann, M., and Y. Ne'eman, *The Eightfold Way*. New York: Benjamin (1965). A collection of reprints of significant papers on SU(3) and the particles of high-energy physics. Several introductory sections by Gell-Mann and Ne'eman are especially helpful.

Goldstein, H., *Classical Mechanics*, 2nd ed. Reading, MA: Addison-Wesley (1980). Chapter 7 contains a short but readable introduction to relativity from a viewpoint consonant with that presented here.

Greiner, W., and B. Müller, *Quantum Mechanics Symmetries*. Berlin: Springer (1989). We refer to this textbook for more details and numerous exercises that are worked out in detail.

Hamermesh, M., *Group Theory and Its Application to Physical Problems*. Reading, MA: Addison-Wesley (1962). A detailed, rigorous account of both finite and continuous groups. The 32 point groups are developed. The continuous groups are treated, with Lie algebra included. A wealth of applications to atomic and nuclear physics.

Hassani, S., *Foundations of Mathematical Physics*. Boston: Allyn and Bacon (1991).

Heitler, W., *The Quantum Theory of Radiation*, 2nd ed. Oxford: Oxford University Press (1947), reprinting, Dover (1983).

Higman, B., *Applied Group-Theoretic and Matrix Methods*. Oxford: Clarendon Press (1955). A rather complete and unusually intelligible development of matrix analysis and group theory.

Jackson, J. D., *Classical Electrodynamics*, 3rd ed. New York: Wiley (1998).

Messiah, A., *Quantum Mechanics*, vol. II. Amsterdam: North-Holland (1961).

Panofsky, W. K. H., and M. Phillips, *Classical Electricity and Magnetism*, 2nd ed. Reading, MA: Addison-Wesley (1962). The Lorentz covariance of Maxwell's equations is developed for both vacuum and material media. Panofsky and Phillips use contravariant and covariant tensors.

Park, D., Resource letter SP-1 on symmetry in physics. *Am. J. Phys.* **36**: 577–584 (1968). Includes a large selection of basic references on group theory and its applications to physics: atoms, molecules, nuclei, solids, and elementary particles.

Ram, B., Physics of the SU(3) symmetry model. *Am. J. Phys.* **35**: 16 (1967). An excellent discussion of the applications of SU(3) to the strongly interacting particles (baryons). For a sequel to this see R. D. Young, Physics of the quark model. *Am. J. Phys.* **41**: 472 (1973).

Tinkham, M., *Group Theory and Quantum Mechanics*. New York: McGraw-Hill (1964), reprinting, Dover (2003). Clear and readable.

Wigner, E. P., *Group Theory and Its Application to the Quantum Mechanics of Atomic Spectra* (translated by J. J. Griffin). New York: Academic Press (1959). This is the classic reference on group theory for the physicist. The rotation group is treated in considerable detail. There is a wealth of applications to atomic physics.

CHAPTER 18

MORE SPECIAL FUNCTIONS

In this chapter we shall study four sets of orthogonal polynomials: Hermite, Laguerre, and Chebyshev[1] of the first and second kinds. Although these four sets are of less importance in mathematical physics than are the Bessel and Legendre functions of Chapters 14 and 15, they are used and therefore deserve attention. For example, Hermite polynomials occur in solutions of the simple harmonic oscillator of quantum mechanics and Laguerre polynomials in wave functions of the hydrogen atom. Because the general mathematical techniques duplicate those used for Bessel and Legendre functions, the development of these functions is only outlined. Detailed proofs are for the most part left to the reader.

The sets of polynomials treated in this chapter can be related to the more general quantities known as **hypergeometric** and **confluent hypergeometric** functions (solutions of the hypergeometric ODE). For practical reasons we defer most discussion of these relationships until we have had an opportunity to define the hypergeometric functions and the associated nomenclature. The benefit accruing from the connection to hypergeometric functions is that the hypergeometic recurrence formulas and other general properties translate into useful relationships for the polynomial sets that we are presently studying.

We conclude the chapter with a short section on elliptic integrals. Although the importance of this subject has declined as the power of computers has increased, there are some physical problems for which they are useful and it is not yet time to eliminate them from this text.

18.1 HERMITE FUNCTIONS

We start by identifying **Hermite functions** as solutions of the **Hermite** ODE,

$$H_n''(x) - 2x H_n'(x) + 2n H_n(x) = 0. \tag{18.1}$$

---

[1] This is the spelling choice of AMS-55 (for the complete reference, see Abramowitz in Additional Readings). However, various names, such as Tschebyscheff, are encountered in the literature.

Here n is a parameter. When $n \geq 0$ is integral, this ODE will have a solution $H_n(x)$ which is a polynomial of degree n; these solutions are known as **Hermite polynomials**.

In the presence of appropriate boundary conditions, the Hermite ODE is a Sturm-Liouville system; polynomial solutions to such ODEs was the topic of Section 12.1. We showed there, in Example 12.1.1, that the Hermite polynomials could be generated from their **Rodrigues formula**, Eq. (12.17), and that, in turn, a Rodrigues formula can be obtained from the underlying ODE. We also showed in that same section how we can go from the Rodrigues formula to a generating function for a given polynomial set, presenting in Table 12.1 a list of generating functions that could be found in this way. That list included the following generating function for the Hermite polynomials:

$$g(x, t) = e^{-t^2 + 2tx} = \sum_{n=0}^{\infty} H_n(x) \frac{t^n}{n!}. \tag{18.2}$$

Here we elect not to depend on the analysis of Section 12.1 but rather to take the viewpoint that Eq. (18.2) can be regarded as a **definition** of the Hermite polynomials, thereby making the present analysis completely self-contained. Accordingly, we proceed by verifying that these polynomials satisfy the Hermite ODE, have the expected Rodrigues formula, and exhibit the other properties that can be developed starting from the generating function.

Recurrence Relations

Note the absence of a superscript, which distinguishes Hermite polynomials from the unrelated Hankel functions. From the generating function we find that the Hermite polynomials satisfy the recurrence relations

$$H_{n+1}(x) = 2x H_n(x) - 2n H_{n-1}(x) \tag{18.3}$$

and

$$H_n'(x) = 2n H_{n-1}(x). \tag{18.4}$$

The Hermite polynomials were used in Example 12.1.2 as a detailed illustration of the method for obtaining recurrence formulas from generating functions; we summarize the process here. By differentiating the generating function formula with respect to t we obtain

$$\frac{\partial g}{\partial t} = (-2t + 2x)e^{-t^2 + 2tx} = \sum_{n=0}^{\infty} H_{n+1}(x) \frac{t^n}{n!}, \quad \text{or}$$

$$-2 \sum_{n=0}^{\infty} H_n(x) \frac{t^{n+1}}{n!} + 2x \sum_{n=0}^{\infty} H_n(x) \frac{t^n}{n!} = \sum_{n=0}^{\infty} H_{n+1}(x) \frac{t^n}{n!}.$$

Because this equation must be satisfied separately for each power of t, we arrive at Eq. (18.3). Similarly, differentiation with respect to x leads to

$$\frac{\partial g}{\partial x} = 2t e^{-t^2 + 2tx} = \sum_{n=0}^{\infty} H_n'(x) \frac{t^n}{n!} = 2 \sum_{n=0}^{\infty} H_n(x) \frac{t^{n+1}}{n!},$$

from which we can obtain Eq. (18.4).

The Maclaurin expansion of the generating function

$$e^{-t^2+2tx} = \sum_{n=0}^{\infty} \frac{(2tx-t^2)^n}{n!} = 1 + (2tx - t^2) + \cdots \tag{18.5}$$

gives $H_0(x) = 1$ and $H_1(x) = 2x$, and then the recursion formula, Eq. (18.3), permits the construction of any $H_n(x)$ desired. For convenient reference the first several Hermite polynomials are listed in Table 18.1 and presented graphically in Fig. 18.1.

Special Values

Special values of the Hermite polynomials follow from the generating function for $x = 0$:

$$e^{-t^2} = \sum_{n=0}^{\infty} \frac{(-t^2)^n}{n!} = \sum_{n=0}^{\infty} H_n(0) \frac{t^n}{n!},$$

Table 18.1   Hermite Polynomials

$H_0(x) = 1$

$H_1(x) = 2x$

$H_2(x) = 4x^2 - 2$

$H_3(x) = 8x^3 - 12x$

$H_4(x) = 16x^4 - 48x^2 + 12$

$H_5(x) = 32x^5 - 160x^3 + 120x$

$H_6(x) = 64x^6 - 480x^4 + 720x^2 - 120$

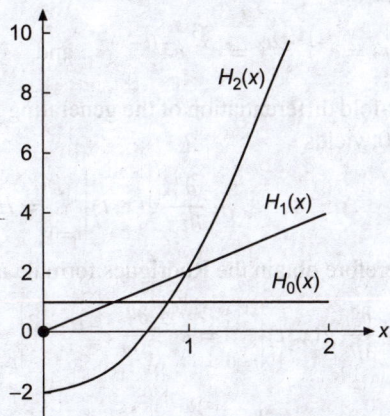

FIGURE 18.1   Hermite polynomials.

that is,

$$H_{2n}(0) = (-1)^n \frac{(2n)!}{n!}, \quad H_{2n+1}(0) = 0, \quad n = 0, 1, \cdots. \tag{18.6}$$

We also obtain from the generating function the important parity relation

$$H_n(x) = (-1)^n H_n(-x) \tag{18.7}$$

by noting that Eq. (18.3) yields

$$g(-x, -t) = \sum_{n=0}^{\infty} H_n(-x) \frac{(-t)^n}{n!} = g(x, t) = \sum_{n=0}^{\infty} H_n(x) \frac{t^n}{n!}.$$

Hermite ODE

If we substitute the recursion formula Eq. (18.4) into Eq. (18.3), we can eliminate the index $n - 1$, obtaining

$$H_{n+1}(x) = 2x H_n(x) - H_n'(x).$$

If we differentiate this recurrence relation and substitute Eq. (18.4) for the index $n + 1$, we find

$$H_{n+1}'(x) = 2(n + 1) H_n(x) = 2H_n(x) + 2x H_n'(x) - H_n''(x),$$

which can be rearranged to the second-order Hermite ODE, Eq. (18.1). This completes the process of establishing the identification of the Hermite polynomials obtained from the generating function as solutions of the Hermite ODE.

Rodrigues Formula

A simple way to generate the Rodrigues formula for the Hermite polynomials starts from the observations that

$$g(x, t) = e^{-t^2 + 2tx} = e^{x^2} e^{-(t-x)^2} \quad \text{and} \quad \frac{\partial}{\partial t} e^{-(t-x)^2} = -\frac{\partial}{\partial x} e^{-(t-x)^2}.$$

We note that n-fold differentiation of the generating function formula, Eq. (18.2), followed by setting $t = 0$, yields

$$\left. \frac{\partial^n}{\partial t^n} g(x, t) \right|_{t=0} = H_n(x),$$

and we can therefore obtain the Rodrigues formula as

$$H_n(x) = \left. \frac{\partial^n}{\partial t^n} g(x, t) \right|_{t=0} = e^{x^2} \left. \frac{\partial^n}{\partial t^n} e^{-(t-x)^2} \right|_{t=0} = (-1)^n e^{x^2} \left. \frac{\partial^n}{\partial x^n} e^{-(t-x)^2} \right|_{t=0}$$

$$= (-1)^n e^{x^2} \frac{\partial^n}{\partial x^n} e^{-x^2}. \tag{18.8}$$

Series Expansion

Starting from the Maclaurin expansion, Eq. (18.5), we can derive our Hermite polynomial $H_n(x)$ in series form: Using the binomial expansion of $(2x - t)^\nu$, we initially get

$$e^{-t^2+2tx} = \sum_{\nu=0}^{\infty} \frac{t^\nu}{\nu!}(2x - t)^\nu = \sum_{\nu=0}^{\infty} \frac{t^\nu}{\nu!} \sum_{s=0}^{\nu} \binom{\nu}{s}(2x)^{\nu-s}(-t)^s$$

$$= \sum_{\nu=0}^{\infty} \sum_{s=0}^{\nu} \frac{t^{\nu+s}}{(\nu+s)!} \frac{(-1)^s(\nu+s)!\,(2x)^{\nu-s}}{(\nu-s)!\,s!}.$$

Changing the first summation index from ν to $n = \nu + s$, and noting that this change causes the s summation to range from zero to $[n/2]$, the largest integer less than or equal to $n/2$, our expansion takes the form

$$e^{-t^2+2tx} = \sum_{n=0}^{\infty} \frac{t^n}{n!} \sum_{s=0}^{[n/2]} \frac{(-1)^s n!}{(n-2s)!\,s!}(2x)^{n-2s},$$

from which we can read out the formula for H_n:

$$H_n(x) = \sum_{s=0}^{[n/2]} \frac{(-1)^s n!}{(n-2s)!\,s!}(2x)^{n-2s}. \tag{18.9}$$

Finally, we note that $H_n(x)$ can be written as a Schlaefli integral. Comparing with Eq. (12.18),

$$H_n(x) = \frac{n!}{2\pi i} \oint t^{-n-1} e^{-t^2+2tx}\,dt. \tag{18.10}$$

Orthogonality and Normalization

The orthogonality of the Hermite polynomials is demonstrated by identifying them as arising in a Sturm-Liouville system. The Hermite ODE, however, is clearly **not** self-adjoint, but can be made so by multiplying it by $\exp(-x^2)$ (see Exercise 8.2.2). With $\exp(-x^2)$ as a weighting factor, we obtain the orthogonality integral

$$\int_{-\infty}^{\infty} H_m(x)H_n(x)\,e^{-x^2}\,dx = 0, \quad m \neq n. \tag{18.11}$$

The interval $(-\infty, \infty)$ is chosen to obtain the Hermitian operator boundary conditions (see Section 8.2).

It is sometimes convenient to absorb the weighting function into the Hermite polynomials. We may define

$$\varphi_n(x) = e^{-x^2/2} H_n(x), \tag{18.12}$$

with $\varphi_n(x)$ no longer a polynomial. Substitution into Eq. (18.1) yields the differential equation for $\varphi_n(x)$,

$$\varphi_n''(x) + (2n + 1 - x^2)\varphi_n(x) = 0. \tag{18.13}$$

Equation (18.13) is self-adjoint, and the solutions $\varphi_n(x)$ are orthogonal on the interval $-\infty < x < \infty$ with a unit weighting function.

We still need to normalize these functions. One approach is to combine two instances of the generating function formula (using variables s and t), after which we multiply by e^{-x^2} and integrate over x from $-\infty$ to ∞. These steps yield

$$\int_{-\infty}^{\infty} e^{-x^2} e^{-s^2+2sx} e^{-t^2+2tx} dx = \sum_{m,n=0}^{\infty} \frac{s^m t^n}{m! n!} \int_{-\infty}^{\infty} e^{-x^2} H_m(x) H_n(x) dx. \tag{18.14}$$

We next note that the exponentials on the left-hand side of Eq. (18.14) can be combined into $e^{2st} e^{-(x-s-t)^2}$, after which the integral can be evaluated:

$$\int_{-\infty}^{\infty} e^{-x^2} e^{-s^2+2sx} e^{-t^2+2tx} dx = e^{2st} \int_{-\infty}^{\infty} e^{-(x-s-t)^2} dx = \pi^{1/2} e^{2st}.$$

Inserting this result into Eq. (18.14) after expanding it in a power series, we get

$$\pi^{1/2} e^{2st} = \pi^{1/2} \sum_{n=0}^{\infty} \frac{2^n s^n t^n}{n!} = \sum_{m,n=0}^{\infty} \frac{s^m t^n}{m! n!} \int_{-\infty}^{\infty} e^{-x^2} H_m(x) H_n(x) dx.$$

By equating coefficients of equal powers of s and t, we both confirm the orthogonality and obtain the normalization integral

$$\int_{-\infty}^{\infty} e^{-x^2} \left[H_n(x) \right]^2 dx = 2^n \pi^{1/2} n!. \tag{18.15}$$

Exercises

18.1.1   Assume that the Hermite polynomials are known to be solutions of the Hermite ODE, Eq. (18.1). Assume further that the recurrence relation, Eq. (18.3), and the values of $H_n(0)$ are also known. Given the existence of a generating function

$$g(x, t) = \sum_{n=0}^{\infty} H_n(x) \frac{t^n}{n!},$$

(a)   Differentiate $g(x, t)$ with respect to x and using the recurrence relation develop a first-order PDE for $g(x, t)$.

(b)   Integrate with respect to x, holding t fixed.
(c)   Evaluate $g(0, t)$ using the known values of $H_n(0)$.
(d)   Finally, show that $g(x, t) = \exp(-t^2 + 2tx)$.

18.1.2   In developing the properties of the Hermite polynomials, start at a number of different points, such as:

1.   Hermite's ODE, Eq. (18.1),
2.   Rodrigues's formula, Eq. (18.8),
3.   Integral representation, Eq. (18.10),
4.   Generating function, Eq. (18.2),
5.   Gram-Schmidt construction of a complete set of orthogonal polynomials over $(-\infty, \infty)$ with a weighting factor of $\exp(-x^2)$ (Section 5.2).

Outline how you can go from any one of these starting points to all the other points.

18.1.3   Prove that $|H_n(x)| \le |H_n(ix)|$.

18.1.4   Rewrite the series form of $H_n(x)$, Eq. (18.9), as an **ascending** power series.

$$ANS. \quad H_{2n}(x) = (-1)^n \sum_{s=0}^{n} (-1)^{2s} (2x)^{2s} \frac{(2n)!}{(2s)!(n-s)!},$$

$$H_{2n+1}(x) = (-1)^n \sum_{s=0}^{n} (-1)^s (2x)^{2s+1} \frac{(2n+1)!}{(2s+1)!(n-s)!}.$$

18.1.5   (a)   Expand x^{2r} in a series of even-order Hermite polynomials.
(b)   Expand x^{2r+1} in a series of odd-order Hermite polynomials.

$$ANS. \quad (a) \ x^{2r} = \frac{(2r)!}{2^{2r}} \sum_{n=0}^{r} \frac{H_{2n}(x)}{(2n)!(r-n)!}$$

$$(b) \ x^{2r+1} = \frac{(2r+1)!}{2^{2r+1}} \sum_{n=0}^{r} \frac{H_{2n+1}(x)}{(2n+1)!(r-n)!}, \quad r = 0, 1, 2, \dots.$$

Hint. Use a Rodrigues representation and integrate by parts.

18.1.6   Show that

(a) $\displaystyle \int_{-\infty}^{\infty} H_n(x) \exp\left[-\frac{x^2}{2}\right] dx = \begin{cases} 2\pi n! / (n/2)!, & n \text{ even} \\ \\ 0, & n \text{ odd.} \end{cases}$

(b) $\displaystyle \int_{-\infty}^{\infty} x H_n(x) \exp\left[-\frac{x^2}{2}\right] dx = \begin{cases} 0, & n \text{ even} \\ \\ 2\pi \dfrac{(n+1)!}{((n+1)/2)!}, & n \text{ odd.} \end{cases}$

18.1.7   (a) Using the Cauchy integral formula, develop an integral representation of $H_n(x)$ based on Eq. (18.2) with the contour enclosing the point $z = -x$.

$$\text{ANS.} \quad H_n(x) = \frac{n!}{2\pi i} e^{x^2} \oint \frac{e^{-z^2}}{(z+x)^{n+1}} \, dz.$$

(b) Show by direct substitution that this result satisfies the Hermite equation.

18.2   APPLICATIONS OF HERMITE FUNCTIONS

One of the most important applications of Hermite functions in physics arises from the fact that the functions $\varphi_n(x)$ of Eq. (18.12) are the eigenstates of the quantum-mechanical simple harmonic oscillator, which describes motion subject to a quadratic (also known as a **harmonic** or a **Hooke's-law**) potential. This fact causes Hermite polynomials not only to appear in elementary quantum-mechanics problems, but also in analyses of the vibrational states of molecules, where the lowest-order description of the interatomic potential is harmonic. In view of the importance of these topics, we now proceed to examine them in some detail.

Simple Harmonic Oscillator

The quantum mechanical simple harmonic oscillator is governed by a Schrödinger equation of the form

$$-\frac{\hbar^2}{2m} \frac{d^2 \psi(z)}{dz^2} + \frac{k}{2} z^2 \psi(z) = E \psi(z), \tag{18.16}$$

where m is the mass of the oscillator, k is the force constant for its Hooke's law force directed toward $z = 0$, $\hbar$ is Planck's constant divided by 2π, and E is an eigenvalue giving the energy of the oscillator. Equation (18.16) is to be solved subject to the boundary condition that $\psi(z)$ vanish at $z = \pm\infty$. It is convenient to make a change of variable that eliminates the various constants from the equation, and we therefore make the substitutions

$$z = \frac{\hbar^{1/2} x}{(km)^{1/4}}, \quad \frac{k}{2} z^2 = \frac{\hbar}{2} \sqrt{\frac{k}{m}} x^2, \quad \frac{\hbar^2}{2m} \frac{d^2}{dz^2} = \frac{\hbar}{2} \sqrt{\frac{k}{m}} \frac{d^2}{dx^2},$$

which converts Eq. (18.16) into

$$-\frac{1}{2} \frac{d^2 \varphi(x)}{dx^2} + \frac{x^2}{2} \varphi(x) = \lambda \varphi(x), \tag{18.17}$$

with boundary conditions at $x = \pm\infty$. The eigenvalue λ in this equation is related to E by

$$E = \hbar\lambda \sqrt{\frac{k}{m}}. \tag{18.18}$$

The solutions of Eq. (18.17) that satisfy the boundary conditions can now be identified as given by Eq. (18.13), and we can identify λ_n, the eigenvalue of Eq. (18.17) corresponding to $\varphi_n(x)$, as having the value $n + \frac{1}{2}$. Turning to Eq. (18.12), and expressing x in terms of the original variable z, the eigenstates of Eq. (18.16) can be characterized (including a normalization constant N_n) as

$$\psi_n(z) = N_n e^{-(\alpha z)^2/2} H_n(\alpha z), \quad E_n = (n + \tfrac{1}{2})\hbar\sqrt{\frac{k}{m}}, \quad \alpha = \frac{\hbar^{1/2}}{(km)^{1/4}}, \quad (18.19)$$

with n restricted to the integer values $0, 1, 2, \cdots$. The normalization constant can be deduced from Eq. (18.15). Noting that the normalization integral is to be over the variable z, we find it to be

$$N_n = \left(\frac{\alpha}{2^n \pi^{1/2} n!}\right)^{1/2}. \quad (18.20)$$

It is of interest to examine a few of the eigenstates of this oscillator problem. For reference, a classical oscillator of mass m and force constant k will have the angular oscillation frequency

$$\omega_{\text{class}} = \sqrt{\frac{k}{m}},$$

and can have an arbitrary energy of oscillation, while our quantum oscillator is restricted to oscillation energies $(n + \tfrac{1}{2})\hbar\omega_{\text{class}}$, with n a nonnegative integer. We note that the quantum oscillator must have at least the total energy $\tfrac{1}{2}\hbar\omega_{\text{class}}$; this is usually referred to as its **zero-point energy** and is a consequence of the fact that its spatial distribution must be described by a wave function of finite extent.

The three lowest-energy eigenfunctions of the quantum oscillator are shown in Fig. 18.2. We note that these wave functions predict a position distribution that extends to $\pm\infty$, albeit with exponentially decaying amplitude for larger $|z|$. The corresponding classical oscillator will have excursions in z that are strictly bounded by $kz_{\text{max}}^2/2 = E$, where E can be assigned any value greater than or equal to zero. We have marked in Fig. 18.2 the excursion range of a classical oscillator with an energy equal to the eigenvalue of the quantum oscillator; note that the exponential decay of the quantum wave function begins at the ends of the classical range.

Operator Approach

While the analysis of the preceding subsection is straightforward and provides a complete set of eigenstates for the simple quantum oscillator, additional insight can be obtained by an alternative approach that uses the commutation and other algebraic properties of the quantum-mechanical operators. Our starting point for this development is the recognition that the differential operator $-d^2/dx^2$ of Eq. (18.17) arose as a representation of the dynamical quantity p^2, where (in units with $\hbar = 1$) $p \longleftrightarrow -i\, d/dx$. Then our Schrödinger equation of Eq. (18.17) can be written

$$\mathcal{H}\varphi = \frac{p^2 + x^2}{2}\,\varphi = \lambda\varphi, \quad (18.21)$$

where $\mathcal{H}$ is the Hamiltonian operator, with eigenvalues λ.

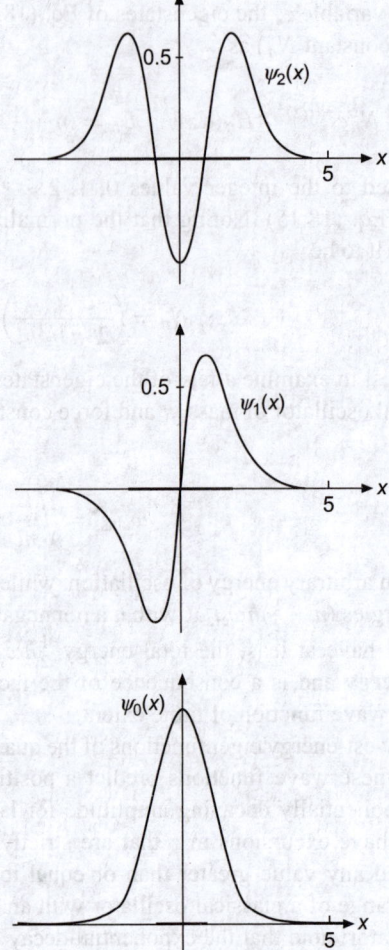

FIGURE 18.2   Quantum mechanical oscillator wave functions. The heavy bar on the x-axis indicates the allowed range of the classical oscillator with the same total energy.

The key to an approach starting from Eq. (18.21) is that x and p satisfy the basic commutation relation

$$[x, p] = xp - px = i, \qquad (18.22)$$

a result discussed in detail in the analysis leading to Eq. (5.43). In fact, if we proceed under the assumption that Eq. (18.22) is all that we know about x and p, there is the additional advantage that any results we obtain will be more general than those from our original oscillator problem in ordinary space. This observation underlies much recent work in which physical theory has evolved in more abstract directions.

With a knowledge of the way in which angular momentum theory was developed in terms of raising and lowering operators, one can easily motivate a somewhat similar procedure here, by defining the two operators

$$a = \frac{1}{\sqrt{2}}(x + ip), \quad a^\dagger = \frac{1}{\sqrt{2}}(x - ip). \tag{18.23}$$

Since we typically use a to denote a constant, we remind the reader that in the present development it is an operator (involving x and d/dx). With suitable Sturm-Liouville boundary conditions, x and p are both Hermitian. But the presence of the imaginary unit i causes a not to be Hermitian, and (as indicated by the notation) changing the sign of the term ip converts a into its adjoint, $a^\dagger$.

Our first use of Eq. (18.23) is to form $a^\dagger a$ and $aa^\dagger$:

$$a^\dagger a = \frac{1}{2}(x - ip)(x + ip) = \frac{1}{2}(x^2 + p^2) + \frac{i}{2}(xp - px) = \mathcal{H} + \frac{i}{2}[x, p] = \mathcal{H} - \frac{1}{2},$$

$$aa^\dagger = \frac{1}{2}(x + ip)(x - ip) = \frac{1}{2}(x^2 + p^2) - \frac{i}{2}(xp - px) = \mathcal{H} - \frac{i}{2}[x, p] = \mathcal{H} + \frac{1}{2}.$$

From these equations we obtain the useful formulas

$$\mathcal{H} = a^\dagger a + \tfrac{1}{2}, \tag{18.24}$$

$$[a, a^\dagger] = aa^\dagger - a^\dagger a = 1, \tag{18.25}$$

and therefrom

$$[\mathcal{H}, a] = [a^\dagger a + \tfrac{1}{2}, a] = [a^\dagger a, a] = a^\dagger aa - aa^\dagger a = (a^\dagger a - aa^\dagger)a = -a. \tag{18.26}$$

Applying $[\mathcal{H}, a]$ to an eigenfunction φ_n with eigenvalue λ_n (assumed not yet known), we write

$$[\mathcal{H}, a]\varphi_n = H(a\varphi_n) - aH\varphi_n = H(a\varphi_n) - \lambda_n(a\varphi_n) = -(a\varphi_n),$$

which we easily rearrange to the form

$$\mathcal{H}(a\varphi_n) = (\lambda_n - 1)(a\varphi_n). \tag{18.27}$$

Equation (18.27) shows that we can interpret a as a **lowering** operator that converts an eigenfunction with eigenvalue λ_n into another eigenfunction that has eigenvalue $\lambda_n - 1$. A similar analysis, left to the reader, shows that from the commutator $[\mathcal{H}, a^\dagger]$ we find $a^\dagger$ to be a **raising** operator, according to

$$\mathcal{H}(a^\dagger \varphi_n) = (\lambda_n + 1)(a^\dagger \varphi_n). \tag{18.28}$$

These formulas show that, given any eigenfunction φ_n, we can construct a **ladder** of eigenstates whose eigenvalues differ by unit steps. The only limitation that would terminate the construction of an infinite ladder would be the possibility that for some φ_n, either $a\varphi_n$ or $a^\dagger \varphi_n$ might be zero.

To investigate the circumstances under which $a\varphi_n$ might vanish, let's form the scalar product $\langle a\varphi_n | a\varphi_n \rangle$. We find

$$\langle a\varphi_n | a\varphi_n \rangle = \langle \varphi_n | a^\dagger a | \varphi_n \rangle = \langle \varphi_n | \mathcal{H} - \tfrac{1}{2} | \varphi_n \rangle = \langle \varphi_n | \lambda_n - \tfrac{1}{2} | \varphi_n \rangle. \tag{18.29}$$

Equation (18.29) shows that only if $\lambda_n = \frac{1}{2}$ will we have $a\varphi_n = 0$. That equation also shows that if $\lambda_n < \frac{1}{2}$ we have the mathematical inconsistency that the norm of $a\varphi_n$ is predicted to be negative. These observations together imply that the only possible values of λ_n are positive half-integers, as otherwise by repeated application of the lowering operator a we can move to a λ value prohibited by Eq. (18.29). We leave to the reader the verification that the application of the raising operator $a^\dagger$ to any valid φ_n produces a new eigenfunction $a^\dagger\varphi_n$ with a positive norm.

Our overall conclusion is that any system with a Hamiltonian of the form given by Eq. (18.21), whether or not represented by an ODE in ordinary space, will have eigenstates whose eigenvalues form a ladder of unit spacing, with the smallest eigenvalue equal to $\frac{1}{2}$. This makes it natural to label the states φ_n by integers $n \geq 0$, and therefore to write

$$\mathcal{H}\varphi_n = \lambda_n \varphi_n, \quad \lambda_n = n + \tfrac{1}{2}, \quad n = 0, 1, 2 \cdots, \tag{18.30}$$

in agreement with what we found from our original approach; compare Eq. (18.19).

Before leaving this exercise in operator algebra, it may be worth noting that the notion of raising and lowering operators also arises in contexts where the states thereby reached can be interpreted as those containing different numbers of particles (or **quasiparticles**, a physics jargon that refers to objects, such as photons, whose population is easily changed by interaction with their surroundings). In such contexts, a raising operator is then often referred to as a **creation operator**, with a lowering operator then called an **annihilation** (or sometimes a **destruction**) operator. Obviously these terms have to be interpreted with an understanding of the underlying physics.

Returning to the description of p as a differential operator, the equation $a\varphi_0 = 0$ can be identified as a differential equation satisfied by the ground (lowest-energy) state of our oscillator. More specifically,

$$\sqrt{2}\, a\varphi_0 = (x + ip)\varphi_0 = \left[x + i\left(-i\frac{d}{dx} \right) \right]\varphi_0 = \left[x + \frac{d}{dx} \right]\varphi_0 = 0, \tag{18.31}$$

which has the advantage of being a **first-order** ODE. This ODE is separable, and can be integrated:

$$\frac{d\varphi_0}{\varphi_0} = -x\, dx, \quad \ln\varphi_0 = -\frac{x^2}{2} + \ln c_0, \quad \varphi_0 = c_0\, e^{-x^2/2},$$

in agreement with our previous analysis.

Eigenstates for arbitrary n can now be generated by repeated application of $a^\dagger$ to φ_0. Doing so is left as an exercise.

Molecular Vibrations

In the dynamics and spectroscopy of molecules in the Born-Oppenheimer approximation, the motion of a molecule is separated into electronic, vibrational, and rotational motion. In treating the vibrational motion, the departure of nuclei from their equilibrium positions is to lowest order described by a quadratic potential, and the resulting oscillations are identified as **harmonic**. These harmonic motions can be treated as coupled simple harmonic oscillators, and we can decouple the individual nuclear motions by making a transformation to **normal** coordinates, as was illustrated in Example 6.5.2. In this harmonic oscillation limit, the vibrational wave functions have the form given in the preceding subsection, and the computation of properties associated with these wave functions then involve integrals in which products of Hermite functions appear.

The simplest integrals occurring in vibrational problems are of the form

$$\int_{-\infty}^{\infty} x^r e^{-x^2} H_n(x) H_m(x) dx.$$

Examples for $r = 1$ and $r = 2$ (with $n = m$) are included in the exercises at the end of this section. A large number of other examples can be found in the work by Wilson, Decius, and Cross.[2] Some of the vibrational properties of molecules require the evaluation of integrals containing as many as four Hermite functions. In the remainder of this subsection we illustrate some of the possibilities and the associated mathematical procedures.

Example 18.2.1   THREEFOLD HERMITE FORMULA

Consider the following integral involving three Hermite polynomials

$$I_3 \equiv \int_{-\infty}^{\infty} e^{-x^2} H_{m_1}(x) H_{m_2}(x) H_{m_3}(x) dx, \tag{18.32}$$

where $N_i \geq 0$ are integers. The formula (due to E. C. Titchmarsh, *J. Lond. Math. Soc.* **23**: 15 (1948); see Gradshteyn and Ryzhik, p. 804, in Additional Readings) generalizes the I_2 case needed for the orthogonality and normalization of Hermite polynomials. To start, we note that the integrand of I_3 will be even if the index sum $m_1 + m_2 + m_3$ is even, and odd if that index sum is odd, so I_3 will vanish unless $m_1 + m_2 + m_3$ is even. In addition, we see that if the product $H_{m_1} H_{m_2}$ is expanded and written as a sum of Hermite polynomials, the resulting polynomial of largest index will be $H_{m_1+m_2}$, so I_3 will vanish due to orthogonality unless $m_1 + m_2$ is at least as large as m_3. This condition must continue to hold if the roles of the m_i are permuted; a convenient way of summarizing these observations is to state that the m_i must satisfy a **triangle** condition. Both the even index sum and the triangle condition parallel similar conditions on integrals of Legendre polynomials which we encountered in Section 16.3 and discussed in detail at Eq. (16.85).

[2]E. B. Wilson, Jr., J. C. Decius, and P. C. Cross, *Molecular Vibrations*, New York: McGraw-Hill (1955), reprinted, Dover (1980).

To derive I_3, we start with the product of three generating functions of Hermite polynomials, multiply by e^{-x^2}, and integrate over x:

$$Z_3 \equiv \int_{-\infty}^{\infty} e^{-x^2} \prod_{j=1}^{3} e^{2xt_j - t_j^2} dx = \int_{-\infty}^{\infty} e^{-(t_1+t_2+t_3-x)^2 + 2(t_1 t_2 + t_1 t_3 + t_2 t_3)} dx$$

$$= \sqrt{\pi} \, e^{2(t_1 t_2 + t_1 t_3 + t_2 t_3)} = \sqrt{\pi} \sum_{N=0}^{\infty} \frac{2^N}{N!} \sum_{\substack{n_1,n_2,n_3 \geq 0 \\ n_1+n_2+n_3=N}} \frac{N!}{n_1! \, n_2! \, n_3!} t_1^{n_2+n_3} t_2^{n_1+n_3} t_3^{n_1+n_2}.$$

$$(18.33)$$

In reaching Eq. (18.33), we recognized the x integration as an error integral, Eq. (1.148), and then expanded the resulting exponential, first as a power series in $w = 2(t_1 t_2 + t_1 t_3 + t_2 t_3)$, and then expanding the powers of w by the generalization of the binomial theorem given as Eq. (1.80). Note that the index for the power of $t_i t_j$ in the polynomial expansion was designated n_k, where i, j, k are (in some order) $1, 2, 3$.

We next expand the generating functions in terms of Hermite polynomials and set the result equal to a slightly simplified version of the expression just obtained for Z_3:

$$Z_3 = \sum_{m_1,m_2,m_3=0}^{\infty} \frac{t_1^{m_1} t_2^{m_2} t_3^{m_3}}{m_1! \, m_2! \, m_3!} \int_{-\infty}^{\infty} e^{-x^2} H_{m_1}(x) H_{m_2}(x) H_{m_3}(x) dx$$

$$= \sqrt{\pi} \sum_{n_1,n_2,n_3=0}^{\infty} \frac{2^N t_1^{n_2+n_3} t_2^{n_1+n_3} t_3^{n_1+n_2}}{n_1! \, n_2! \, n_3!}, \qquad (18.34)$$

with $N = n_1 + n_2 + n_3$. In Eq. (18.34) we now equate the coefficients of equal powers of the t_j, finding that $m_1 = n_2 + n_3$, $m_2 = n_1 + n_3$, $m_3 = n_1 + n_2$, that

$$N = \frac{m_1 + m_2 + m_3}{2},$$

and that $n_1 = N - m_1$, $n_2 = N - m_2$, $n_3 = N - m_3$. From the coefficients of $t_1^{m_1} t_2^{m_2} t_3^{m_3}$, we obtain the final result

$$I_3 = \frac{\sqrt{\pi} \, 2^N m_1! \, m_2! \, m_3!}{(N-m_1)! \, (N-m_2)! \, (N-m_3)!}. \qquad (18.35)$$

Equation (18.35) explicitly reflects the necessity of the triangle condition. If it is not satisfied but the sum of the m_i is even, at least one of the factorials in the denominator of Eq. (18.35) will have a negative integer argument, thereby causing I_3 to be zero. The requirement that the sum of the m_i be even is not explicit in the form of Eq. (18.35), but the formula for I_3 is restricted to that case because the right-hand side of Eq. (18.34) only contains terms in which the sum of the powers of the t_i is even. ∎

Hermite Product Formula

The integrals I_m with $m > 3$ can be obtained in closed form, but as finite sums. The starting point for that analysis is a formula for the product of two Hermite polynomials due to

E. Feldheim, *J. Lond. Math. Soc.* **13**: 22 (1938). To derive Feldheim's formula, we can start from a product of two generating functions, written as

$$e^{2x(t_1+t_2)-t_1^2-t_2^2} = \sum_{m_1,m_2=0}^{\infty} H_{m_1}(x)H_{m_2}(x)\frac{t_1^{m_1}}{m_1!}\frac{t_2^{m_2}}{m_2!}$$

$$= e^{2x(t_1+t_2)-(t_1+t_2)^2}\,e^{2t_1t_2} = \sum_{n=0}^{\infty}H_n(x)\frac{(t_1+t_2)^n}{n!}\sum_{\nu=0}^{\infty}\frac{(2t_1t_2)^\nu}{\nu!}.$$

Applying the binomial expansion to $(t_1+t_2)^n$ and then comparing like powers of t_1 and t_2 in the two lines of the above equation, we find

$$H_{m_1}(x)H_{m_2}(x) = \sum_{\nu=0}^{\min(m_1,m_2)} H_{m_1+m_2-2\nu}(x)\frac{m_1!\,m_2!\,2^\nu}{\nu!\,(m_1+m_2-2\nu)!}\binom{m_1+m_2-2\nu}{m_1-\nu}$$

$$= \sum_{\nu=0}^{\min(m_1,m_2)} H_{m_1+m_2-2\nu}(x)\,2^\nu\nu!\binom{m_1}{\nu}\binom{m_2}{\nu}. \tag{18.36}$$

For $\nu = 0$ the coefficient of $H_{N_1+N_2}$ is obviously unity. Special cases, such as

$$H_1^2 = H_2 + 2,\ \ H_1H_2 = H_3 + 4H_1,\ \ H_2^2 = H_4 + 8H_2 + 8,\ \ H_1H_3 = H_4 + 6H_2$$

can be derived from Table 13.1 and agree with the general twofold product formula.

The product formula has been generalized to products of $m > 2$ Hermite polynomials, thereby providing a new way of evaluating the integrals I_m. For details we refer the reader to work by Liang, Weber, Hayashi, and Lin.[3]

Example 18.2.2   FOURFOLD HERMITE FORMULA

An important application of the Hermite product formula is a newly reported evaluation of the integral I_4 containing a product of four Hermite polynomials. The analysis is that of one of the present authors and his colleagues.[3]

The integral we are about to study is of the form

$$I_4 = \int_{-\infty}^{\infty} e^{-x^2}H_{m_1}(x)H_{m_2}(x)H_{m_3}(x)H_{m_4}(x)dx. \tag{18.37}$$

It is convenient to order the indices of the Hermite polynomials so that $m_1 \geq m_2 \geq m_3 \geq m_4$. Our approach will be to apply the product formula to $H_{m_1}H_{m_2}$ and to $H_{m_3}H_{m_4}$, thereby

---

[3]K. K. Liang, H. J. Weber, M. Hayashi, and S. H. Lin, Computational aspects of Franck-Condon overlap intervals. In Pandalai, S. G., ed., *Recent Research Developments in Physical Chemistry*, Vol. 8, Transworld Research Network (2005).

initially obtaining

$$I_4 = \sum_{\mu=0}^{\min(m_1,m_2)} 2^\mu \mu! \binom{m_1}{\mu}\binom{m_2}{\mu} \sum_{\nu=0}^{\min(m_3,m_4)} 2^\nu \nu! \binom{m_3}{\nu}\binom{m_4}{\nu}$$

$$\times \int_{-\infty}^{\infty} e^{-x^2} H_{m_1+m_2-2\mu}(x) H_{m_3+m_4-2\nu}(x)\,dx. \tag{18.38}$$

Invoking the orthogonality of the H_m with the weighting factor shown, the integral in Eq. (18.38) can be evaluated, yielding

$$\int_{-\infty}^{\infty} e^{-x^2} H_{m_1+m_2-2\mu}(x) H_{m_3+m_4-2\nu}(x)\,dx$$

$$= \sqrt{\pi}\, 2^{m_3+m_4-2\nu}(m_3 + m_4 - 2\nu)!\, \delta_{m_1+m_2-2\mu,\, m_3+m_4-2\nu}. \tag{18.39}$$

The Kronecker delta in Eq. (18.39) limits the value of μ to the single value, if any, that satisfies

$$\mu = \frac{m_1 + m_2 - m_3 - m_4}{2} + \nu, \tag{18.40}$$

so the double summation collapses to a single sum over ν. Moreover, when the powers of 2 in Eqs. (18.38) and (18.39) are combined, their resultant is 2^M, where

$$M = \frac{m_1 + m_2 + m_3 + m_4}{2}. \tag{18.41}$$

We now rewrite Eq. (18.38), removing the μ summation and assigning μ the value from Eq. (18.40), writing the binomial coefficients in terms of their constituent factorials, and introducing M wherever it will result in simplification. We reach

$$I_4 = \sum_\nu \frac{\sqrt{\pi}\, 2^M\, (m_3 + m_4 - 2\nu)!\, m_1!\, m_2!\, m_3!\, m_4!}{(M - m_3 - m_4 + \nu)!\, (M - m_1 - \nu)!\, (M - m_2 - \nu)!\, (m_3 - \nu)!\, (m_4 - \nu)!\, \nu!}. \tag{18.42}$$

This formula for I_4 will only be valid when the sum of the m_i is even, equivalent to the requirement that M (and therefore also μ) be integral. If the sum of the m_i is odd, then I_4 will have an odd integrand and will vanish by symmetry. The summation in Eq. (18.42) will be over the nonnegative integral values of ν for which none of the factorials in the denominator of that summation has a negative argument. Note that there will be no value of ν that satisfies this condition if $m_1 > m_2 + m_3 + m_4$, because $M - m_1$ will then be negative, and then $I_4 = 0$. Thus we have a generalization of the triangle condition that applied to the threefold Hermite formula: If the largest of the m_i is greater than the sum of the others, the H_m of smaller m cannot combine to yield a Hermite polynomial of sufficiently large index to avoid an orthogonality zero.

Further examination of the factorials in the denominator of Eq. (18.42) reveals that the lower limit of the summation will (if $m_1 \leq m_2 + m_3 + m_4$) always be $\nu = 0$; note that

$M - m_3 - m_4$ will always be nonnegative. The upper limit of the summation will be the smaller of m_4 and $M - m_1$. ∎

The Hermite polynomial product formula can also be applied to products of Hermite polynomials with a different exponential weighting function than in the examples we have presented. To evaluate such integrals we use the generalized product formula in conjunction with the integral (see Gradshteyn and Ryzhik, p. 803, in the Additional Readings),

$$\int_{-\infty}^{\infty} e^{-a^2 x^2} H_m(x) H_n(x) dx = \frac{2^{m+n}}{a^{m+n+1}} (1 - a^2)^{(m+n)/2} \Gamma\left(\frac{m+n+1}{2}\right)$$

$$\times \sum_{\nu=0}^{\min(m,n)} \frac{(-m)_\nu (-n)_\nu}{\nu! \left(\frac{1-m-n}{2}\right)_\nu} \left(\frac{a^2}{2(a^2-1)}\right)^\nu, \qquad (18.43)$$

instead of the standard orthogonality integral for the product of two Hermite polynomials. The quantity $(-m)_\nu$ is a Pochhammer symbol, and causes the ν summation in Eq. (18.43) to be a finite sum. The summation can also be identified as a hypergeometric function; see Exercise 18.5.11. The process we have sketched yields a result that is similar to I_m but somewhat more complicated. We omit details.

The oscillator potential has also been employed extensively in calculations of nuclear structure (nuclear shell model), as well as in quark models of hadrons and the nuclear force.

Exercises

18.2.1   Prove that $\left(2x - \dfrac{d}{dx}\right)^n 1 = H_n(x)$.

Hint. Check out the cases $n = 0$ and $n = 1$ and then use mathematical induction (Section 1.4).

18.2.2   Show that $\displaystyle\int_{-\infty}^{\infty} x^m e^{-x^2} H_n(x) dx = 0$ for m an integer, $0 \le m \le n - 1$.

18.2.3   The transition probability between two oscillator states m and n depends on

$$\int_{-\infty}^{\infty} x e^{-x^2} H_n(x) H_m(x) dx.$$

Show that this integral equals $\pi^{1/2} 2^{n-1} n! \, \delta_{m,n-1} + \pi^{1/2} 2^n (n+1)! \, \delta_{m,n+1}$. This result shows that such transitions can occur only between states of adjacent energy levels, $m = n \pm 1$.

Hint. Multiply the generating function, Eq. (18.2), by itself using two different sets of variables (x, s) and (x, t). Alternatively, the factor x may be eliminated by the recurrence relation, Eq. (18.3).

18.2.4   Show that $\int_{-\infty}^{\infty} x^2 e^{-x^2} H_n(x) H_n(x) dx = \pi^{1/2} 2^n n! \left(n + \frac{1}{2}\right)$.

This integral occurs in the calculation of the mean-square displacement of our quantum oscillator.

Hint. Use the recurrence relation, Eq. (18.3), and the orthogonality integral.

18.2.5   Evaluate

$$\int_{-\infty}^{\infty} x^2 e^{-x^2} H_n(x) H_m(x) dx$$

in terms of n and m and appropriate Kronecker delta functions.

ANS. $2^{n-1} \pi^{1/2} (2n+1) n! \, \delta_{nm} + 2^n \pi^{1/2} (n+2)! \, \delta_{n+2,m} + 2^{n-2} \pi^{1/2} n! \, \delta_{n-2,m}$.

18.2.6   Show that $\int_{-\infty}^{\infty} x^r e^{-x^2} H_n(x) H_{n+p}(x) dx = \begin{cases} 0, & p > r \\ 2^n \pi^{1/2} (n+r)!, & p = r, \end{cases}$

with n, p, and r nonnegative integers.

Hint. Use the recurrence relation, Eq. (18.3), p times.

18.2.7   With $\psi_n(x) = e^{-x^2/2} \dfrac{H_n(x)}{(2^n n! \, \pi^{1/2})^{1/2}}$, verify that

$$a\psi_n(x) = \frac{x - ip}{\sqrt{2}} = \frac{1}{\sqrt{2}} \left(x + \frac{d}{dx}\right) \psi_n(x) = n^{1/2} \psi_{n-1}(x),$$

$$a^\dagger \psi_n(x) = \frac{x + ip}{\sqrt{2}} = \frac{1}{\sqrt{2}} \left(x - \frac{d}{dx}\right) \psi_n(x) = (n+1)^{1/2} \psi_{n+1}(x).$$

Note. The usual quantum mechanical operator approach establishes these raising and lowering properties before the form of $\psi_n(x)$ is known.

18.2.8   (a)   Verify the operator identity

$$x + ip = x - \frac{d}{dx} = -\exp\left[\frac{x^2}{2}\right] \frac{d}{dx} \exp\left[-\frac{x^2}{2}\right].$$

(b)   The normalized simple harmonic oscillator wave function is

$$\psi_n(x) = (\pi^{1/2} 2^n n!)^{-1/2} \exp\left[-\frac{x^2}{2}\right] H_n(x).$$

Show that this may be written as

$$\psi_n(x) = (\pi^{1/2} 2^n n!)^{-1/2} \left(x - \frac{d}{dx}\right)^n \exp\left[-\frac{x^2}{2}\right].$$

Note. This corresponds to an *n*-fold application of the raising operator of Exercise 18.2.7.

18.3   LAGUERRE FUNCTIONS

Rodrigues Formula and Generating Function

Let's start from the Laguerre ODE,

$$xy''(x) + (1 - x)y'(x) + ny(x) = 0. \tag{18.44}$$

This ODE is not self-adjoint, but the weighting factor needed to make it self-adjoint can be computed from the usual formula,

$$w(x) = \frac{1}{x} \exp\left[\int \frac{1 - x}{x} \, dx\right] = \frac{1}{x} \exp(\ln x - x) = e^{-x}. \tag{18.45}$$

Given $w(x)$, we may now use the method developed in Section 12.1 to obtain a Rodrigues formula and generating function for the Laguerre polynomials. Letting $L_n(x)$ denote the *n*th Laguerre polynomial, the Rodrigues formula is (apart from a scale factor) given by Eq. (12.9):

$$L_n(x) = \frac{1}{w(x)} \left(\frac{d}{dx}\right)^n (w(x)p(x)^n),$$

where $p(x)$ is the coefficient of y'' in the ODE. Inserting the expressions for $w(x)$ and $p(x)$, and inserting a factor $1/n!$ to bring the Laguerre polynomials to their conventional scaling, the Rodrigues formula takes the more complete and explicit form,

$$L_n(x) = \frac{e^x}{n!} \left(\frac{d}{dx}\right)^n (x^n e^{-x}). \tag{18.46}$$

A generating function can now be written as a sum of contour integrals of the Schlaefli type, as in Eq. (12.25):

$$g(x, t) = \sum_{t=0}^{\infty} L_n(x)t^n = \frac{1}{w(x)} \sum_{n=0}^{\infty} \frac{c_n t^n n!}{2\pi i} \oint_C \frac{w(z)[p(z)]^n}{(z - x)^{n+1}} \, dz,$$

where the contour surrounds the point x and no other singularities. Specializing to our current problem, and noting that the coefficient c_n has the value $1/n!$, this formula becomes

$$g(x, t) = \frac{e^x}{2\pi i} \sum_{n=0}^{\infty} \oint_C \frac{e^{-z}(tz)^n}{(z - x)^{n+1}} \, dz = \frac{e^x}{2\pi i} \oint_C \frac{e^{-z} \, dz}{(z - x)} \sum_{n=0}^{\infty} \left(\frac{tz}{z - x}\right)^n. \tag{18.47}$$

We now recognize the *n* summation as a geometric series, so our generating function becomes

$$g(x, t) = \frac{e^x}{2\pi i} \oint_C \frac{e^{-z} \, dz}{z - x - tz}. \tag{18.48}$$

Our integrand has a simple pole at $z = x/(1-t)$, with residue $e^{-x/(1-t)}/(1-t)$, and $g(x,t)$ reduces to

$$g(x,t) = \frac{e^x\, e^{-x/(1-t)}}{1-t} = \frac{e^{-xt/(1-t)}}{1-t} = \sum_{n=0}^{\infty} L_n(x)t^n, \tag{18.49}$$

the form given in Table 12.1.

Not all workers define Laguerre polynomials at the scale chosen here and represented by the specific formulas in Eq. (18.46) and (18.49). However, our choice is probably the most common, and is consistent with that in AMS-55 (see Abramowitz in Additional Readings).

Properties of Laguerre Polynomials

By differentiating the generating function in Eq. (18.45) with respect to x and t, we obtain recurrence relations for the Laguerre polynomials as follows. Using the product rule for differentiation we verify the identities

$$(1-t)^2 \frac{\partial g}{\partial t} = (1 - x - t)g(x,t), \quad (t-1)\frac{\partial g}{\partial x} = tg(x,t). \tag{18.50}$$

Writing the left-hand and right-hand sides of the first identity in terms of Laguerre polynomials using the expansion given in Eq. (18.49), we obtain

$$\sum_n \left[(n+1)L_{n+1}(x) - 2nL_n(x) + (n-1)L_{n-1}(x) \right] t^n$$

$$= \sum_n \left[(1-x)L_n(x) - L_{n-1}(x) \right] t^n.$$

Equating coefficients of z^n yields

$$(n+1)L_{n+1}(x) = (2n+1-x)L_n(x) - nL_{n-1}(x). \tag{18.51}$$

To get the second recursion relation we use both identities of Eqs. (18.50) to verify a third identity,

$$x\frac{\partial g}{\partial x} = t\frac{\partial g}{\partial t} - t\frac{\partial (tg)}{\partial t},$$

which, when written similarly in terms of Laguerre polynomials, is seen to be equivalent to

$$xL_n'(x) = nL_n(x) - nL_{n-1}(x). \tag{18.52}$$

To use these recurrence formulas we need starting values. From the Rodrigues formula, we easily find $L_0(x) = 1$ and $L_1(x) = 1 - x$. Applying Eq. (18.51) we continue to $L_n(x)$ with $n > 1$, obtaining the results given in Table 18.2. The first three Laguerre polynomials are plotted in Fig. 18.3.

Table 18.2 Laguerre Polynomials

$L_0(x) = 1$

$L_1(x) = -x + 1$

$2! L_2(x) = x^2 - 4x + 2$

$3! L_3(x) = -x^3 + 9x^2 - 18x + 6$

$4! L_4(x) = x^4 - 16x^3 + 72x^2 - 96x + 24$

$5! L_5(x) = -x^5 + 25x^4 - 200x^3 + 600x^2 - 600x + 120$

$6! L_6(x) = x^6 - 36x^5 + 450x^4 - 2400x^3 + 5400x^2 - 4320x + 720$

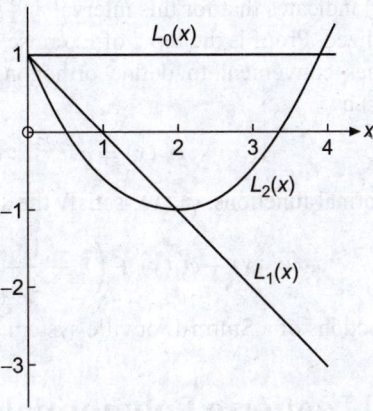

FIGURE 18.3 Laguerre polynomials.

From the recurrence relations or the Rodrigues formula, we find the the power series expansion of $L_n(x)$:

$$L_n(x) = \frac{(-1)^n}{n!} \left[x^n - \frac{n^2}{1!} x^{n-1} + \frac{n^2(n-1)^2}{2!} x^{n-2} - \cdots + (-1)^n n! \right]$$

$$= \sum_{m=0}^{n} \frac{(-1)^m n! \, x^m}{(n-m)! \, m! \, m!} = \sum_{s=0}^{n} \frac{(-1)^{n-s} n! \, x^{n-s}}{(n-s)! \, (n-s)! \, s!}. \tag{18.53}$$

Also, from Eq. (18.49) we find

$$g(0, t) = \frac{1}{1-t} = \sum_{n=0}^{\infty} t^n = \sum_{n=0}^{\infty} L_n(0) t^n,$$

which shows that at $x = 0$ the Laguerre polynomials have the special value

$$L_n(0) = 1. \tag{18.54}$$

The form of the generating function, that of Laguerre's ODE, and Table 18.2 all show that the Laguerre polynomials have neither odd nor even symmetry under the parity transformation $x \rightarrow -x$.

As we already observed at the beginning of this section, the Laguerre ODE is not self-adjoint but can be made so by appending the weighting factor e^{-x}. Noting also that with this weighting factor, the Laguerre polynomials satisfy Sturm-Liouville boundary conditions at $x = 0$ and $x = \infty$, we see that the $L_n(x)$ must satisfy an orthogonality condition of the form

$$\int_0^\infty e^{-x} L_m(x) L_n(x) dx = \delta_{mn}. \tag{18.55}$$

Equation (18.55) indicates that for this interval and weighting factor the Laguerre polynomials are normalized. Proof is the topic of Exercise 18.3.3.

It is sometimes convenient to define orthogonalized Laguerre functions (with unit weighting factor) by

$$\varphi_n(x) = e^{-x/2} L_n(x). \tag{18.56}$$

Our new orthonormal functions, $\varphi_n(x)$, satisfy the self-adjoint ODE

$$x\varphi_n''(x) + \varphi_n'(x) + \left(n + \frac{1}{2} - \frac{x}{4}\right) \varphi_n(x) = 0, \tag{18.57}$$

and are eigenfunctions of a Sturm-Liouville system on the range $(0 \leq x < \infty)$.

Associated Laguerre Polynomials

In many applications, particularly in quantum mechanics, we need the associated Laguerre polynomials defined by[4]

$$L_n^k(x) = (-1)^k \frac{d^k}{dx^k} L_{n+k}(x). \tag{18.58}$$

By differentiating the power series for $L_n(x)$ given in Eq. (18.53) (compare Table 18.2), we can get the explicit forms shown in Table 18.3. In general,

$$L_n^k(x) = \sum_{m=0}^n (-1)^m \frac{(n+k)!}{(n-m)!\,(k+m)!\,m!} x^m, \quad k \geq 0. \tag{18.59}$$

One of the present authors[5] has recently found a new generating function for the associated Laguerre polynomials with the remarkably simple form

$$g_l(x, t) = e^{-tx}(1+t)^l = \sum_{n=0}^\infty L_n^{l-n}(x) t^n. \tag{18.60}$$

---

[4] Some authors use $\mathfrak{L}_{n+k}^k(x) = (d^k/dx^k)[L_{n+k}(x)]$. Hence our $L_n^k(x) = (-1)^k \mathfrak{L}_{n+k}^k(x)$.

[5] H. J. Weber, Connections between real polynomial solutions of hypergeometric-type differential equations with Rodrigues formula, *Cent. Eur. J. Math.* **5**: 415–427 (2007).

Table 18.3 Associated Laguerre Polynomials

$L_0^k = 1$

$1! L_1^k = -x + (k+1)$

$2! L_2^k = x^2 - 2(k+2)x + (k+1)_2$

$3! L_3^k = -x^3 + 3(k+3)x^2 - 3(k+2)_2x + (k+1)_3$

$4! L_4^k = x^4 - 4(k+4)x^3 + 6(k+3)_2 - 4(k+2)_3 + (k+1)_4$

$5! L_5^k = -x^5 + 5(k+5)x^4 - 10(k+4)_2x^3 + 10(k+3)_3x^2 - 5(k+2)_4x + (k+1)_5$

$6! L_6^k = x^6 - 6(k+6)x^5 + 15(k+5)_2x^4 - 20(k+4)_3x^3 + 15(k+3)_4x^2$
$\qquad - 6(k+2)_5x + (k+1)_6$

$7! L_7^k = -x^7 + 7(k+7)x^6 - 21(k+6)_2x^5 + 35(k+5)_3x^4 - 35(k+4)_4x^3$
$\qquad + 21(k+3)_5x^2 - 7(k+2)_6x + (k+1)_7$

The notations $(k+n)_m$ are Pochhammer symbols, defined in Eq. (1.72).

Rather than deriving this formula, we verify it by showing that it produces the defining relation for the L_n^k, Eq. (18.58), and is consistent with the previously presented formulas for the ordinary Laguerre polynomials (i.e., the L_n^k with $k = 0$).

If we multiply both members of Eq. (18.60) by $1 - t$, the coefficients of t^n yield the recurrence formula

$$L_n^{l-n} + L_{n-1}^{l-n+1} = L_n^{l-n+1}, \quad \text{or} \quad L_n^k - L_n^{k+1} = -L_{n-1}^{k+1}. \tag{18.61}$$

On the other hand, differentiation of Eq. (18.60) with respect to x and writing

$$\frac{\partial g_l(x,t)}{\partial x} = \sum_n \frac{dL_n^{l-n}(x)}{dx} t^n = -te^{-tx}(1+t)^l = e^{-tx}(1+t)^l - e^{-tx}(1+t)^{l+1},$$

the coefficients of t^n yield a formula for $dL_n^{l-n}(x)/dx$, namely (with $k = l - n$)

$$\frac{dL_n^k(x)}{dx} = L_n^k(x) - L_n^{k+1}(x), \tag{18.62}$$

and substituting the result from Eq. (18.61), we reach

$$\frac{dL_n^k(x)}{dx} = -L_{n-1}^{k+1}, \tag{18.63}$$

thereby confirming that our generating function yields Eq. (18.58).

The verification that our generating function is correct is now completed by using it to find $L_n^0(x)$, which is the coefficient of t^n in $e^{-tx}(1+t)^n$. Using the binomial expansion of $(1+t)^n$ and the Maclaurin series for the exponential, we get

$$L_n^0(x) = \sum_{m=0}^{n} \binom{n}{n-m} \frac{(-x)^m}{m!} = \sum_{m=0}^{n} \frac{(-1)^m n!}{(n-m)! \, m! \, m!} x^m,$$

in agreement with Eq. (18.53).

We can also confirm the series expansion given as Eq. (18.59) for L_n^k. It is the coefficient of t^n in $e^{-tx}(1+t)^{k+n}$, obtained in a manner similar to the procedure we just carried out for L_n^0.

The generating function provides convenient routes to other properties of the associated Laguerre polynomials. Special values for $x = 0$ can be obtained from

$$\sum_n L_n^{l-n}(0)t^n = (1+t)^l = \sum_{n=0}^l \binom{l}{n} t^n.$$

We therefore have

$$L_n^k(0) = \binom{n+k}{n}. \tag{18.64}$$

A formula for recurrence in the index n of $L_n^k(x)$ can be obtained by differentiating the generating function formula with respect to t. Doing so, from the coefficient of t^n and setting $l = k + n$,

$$(n+1)L_{n+1}^{k-1}(x) = (k+n)L_n^{k-1}(x) - xL_n^k(x). \tag{18.65}$$

Using Eq. (18.61) to raise the upper index in the two terms for which it is $k - 1$, we find after collecting similar terms,

$$(n+1)L_{n+1}^k(x) - (2n+k+1-x)L_n^k(x) + (n+k)L_{n-1}^k(x) = 0, \tag{18.66}$$

a lower-index recurrence formula.

Finally, returning to Eq. (18.65), differentiating it once with respect to x, and identifying $\left[L_{n+1}^{k-1}\right]' = -L_n^k$, we get

$$(n+k)\left[L_n^{k-1}\right]' = x\left[L_n^k\right]' + L_n^k - (n+1)L_n^k = x\left[L_n^k\right]' - nL_n^k. \tag{18.67}$$

A second differentiation brings us to

$$x\left[L_n^k\right]'' + (1-n)\left[L_n^k\right]' = (n+k)\left[L_n^{k-1}\right]'' = (n+k)\left[L_n^{k-1}\right]' - (n-k)\left[L_n^k\right]', \tag{18.68}$$

where the final member of Eq. (18.68) was the result of substituting the derivative of Eq. (18.62) with $k \to k - 1$. Using Eq. (18.67) to replace $(n+k)\left[L_n^{k-1}\right]'$ by a form in which the upper index is k, we reach an ODE for L_n^k:

$$x\frac{d^2L_n^k(x)}{dx^2} + (k+1-x)\frac{dL_n^k(x)}{dx} + nL_n^k(x) = 0. \tag{18.69}$$

This ODE is known as the **associated Laguerre equation**. When associated Laguerre polynomials appear in a physical problem it is usually because that physical problem involves Eq. (18.69). The most important application is their use to describe the bound states of the hydrogen atom, which are derived in upcoming Example 18.3.1.

The associated Laguerre equation, Eq. (18.69), is not self-adjoint, but the weighting function needed to bring it to self-adjoint form (for upper index k) can be found in the usual way:

$$w_k(x) = \frac{1}{x} \exp\left[\int \frac{k+1-x}{x} \, dx\right] = x^k e^{-x}. \qquad (18.70)$$

When we also note that Sturm-Liouville boundary conditions are satisfied at $x = 0$ and $x = \infty$, we see that the associated Laguerre polynomials are orthogonal according to the equation

$$\int_0^\infty e^{-x} x^k L_n^k(x) L_m^k(x) \, dx = \frac{(n+k)!}{n!} \delta_{mn}. \qquad (18.71)$$

The value of the integral in Eq. (18.71) for $m = n$ can be established using the generating function, Eq. (18.58). Doing so is left as an exercise.

Equation (18.71) shows the same orthogonality interval $(0, \infty)$ as that for the Laguerre polynomials, but with a different weighting function for each k. We see that for each k the associated Laguerre polynomials define a new set of orthogonal polynomials.

A Rodrigues representation of the associated Laguerre polynomials is useful and can be found in various ways. A fairly direct approach is simply to use Eq. (12.9) with $p(x) = x$, the coefficient of the second-derivative term in Eq. (18.69) and the value of $w_k(x)$ given in Eq. (18.70). The result is

$$L_n^k(x) = \frac{e^x x^{-k}}{n!} \frac{d^n}{dx^n} (e^{-x} x^{n+k}). \qquad (18.72)$$

Note that this and all our earlier formulas involving the $L_n^k(x)$ reduce properly to corresponding expressions involving $L_n(x)$ when $k = 0$.

By letting $\psi_n^k(x) = e^{-x/2} x^{k/2} L_n^k(x)$, we find that $\psi_n^k(x)$ satisfies the self-adjoint ODE,

$$x \frac{d^2 \psi_n^k(x)}{dx^2} + \frac{d\psi_n^k(x)}{dx} + \left(-\frac{x}{4} + \frac{2n+k+1}{2} - \frac{k^2}{4x}\right) \psi_n^k(x) = 0. \qquad (18.73)$$

The $\psi_n^k(x)$ are sometimes called **Laguerre functions**. Equation (18.57) is the special case $k = 0$ of Eq. (18.73).

A further useful form is given by defining[6]

$$\Phi_n^k(x) = e^{-x/2} x^{(k+1)/2} L_n^k(x). \qquad (18.74)$$

Substitution into the associated Laguerre equation yields

$$\frac{d^2 \Phi_n^k(x)}{dx^2} + \left(-\frac{1}{4} + \frac{2n+k+1}{2x} - \frac{k^2-1}{4x^2}\right) \Phi_n^k(x) = 0. \qquad (18.75)$$

The $\Phi_n^k(x)$ are orthogonal with weighting function x^{-1}.

The associated Laguerre ODE, Eq. (18.69), has solutions even if n is not an integer, but they are then not polynomials and diverge proportionally to $x k e^x$ as $x \to \infty$. This fact is useful in the following example.

---

[6]This corresponds to modifying the function ψ in Eq. (18.73) to eliminate the first derivative.

Example 18.3.1   THE HYDROGEN ATOM

The most important application of the Laguerre polynomials is in the solution of the Schrödinger equation for the hydrogen-like atom (H, He$^+$, Li^{2+}, etc.). For a system consisting of a nucleus of charge Ze fixed at the origin and one electron whose distribution is described by a wave function ψ, this equation is

$$-\frac{\hbar^2}{2m}\nabla^2\psi - \frac{Ze^2}{4\pi\epsilon_0 r}\psi = E\psi, \tag{18.76}$$

in which $Z = 1$ for hydrogen, $Z = 2$ for He$^+$, and so on. Separating variables in spherical polar coordinates and recognizing that the angular part of the solution to this equation must be a spherical harmonic, we set $\psi(\mathbf{r}) = R(r)Y_L^M(\theta, \varphi)$ with $R(r)$ satisfying the ODE

$$-\frac{\hbar^2}{2m}\frac{1}{r^2}\frac{d}{dr}\left(r^2\frac{dR}{dr}\right) - \frac{Ze^2}{4\pi\epsilon_0 r}R + \frac{\hbar^2}{2m}\frac{L(L+1)}{r^2}R = E. \tag{18.77}$$

For bound states, $R \to 0$ as $r \to \infty$, and it can be shown that these conditions can only be met if $E < 0$. In addition, R must be finite at $r = 0$. We do not consider unbound (continuum) states with positive energy. Only when the latter are included do hydrogenic wave functions form a complete set.

By use of the abbreviations (resulting from rescaling r to the dimensionless radial variable ρ)

$$\alpha = \left[-\frac{8mE}{\hbar^2}\right]^{1/2}, \quad \rho = \alpha r, \quad \lambda = \frac{mZe^2}{2\pi\epsilon_0\alpha\hbar^2}, \quad \chi(\rho) = R(r), \tag{18.78}$$

Eq. (13.85) becomes

$$\frac{1}{\rho^2}\frac{d}{d\rho}\left(\rho^2\frac{d\chi(\rho)}{d\rho}\right) + \left(\frac{\lambda}{\rho} - \frac{1}{4} - \frac{L(L+1)}{\rho^2}\right)\chi(\rho) = 0. \tag{18.79}$$

For our present purposes, it is useful to rewrite the first term of Eq. (18.79) using the identity

$$\frac{1}{\rho^2}\frac{d}{d\rho}\left(\rho^2\frac{d\chi}{d\rho}\right) = \frac{1}{\rho}\frac{d^2}{d\rho^2}(\rho\chi)$$

and then multiply the resulting equation by ρ, reaching

$$\frac{d}{d\rho^2}(\rho\chi) + \left(\frac{\lambda}{\rho} - \frac{1}{4} - \frac{L(L+1)}{\rho^2}\right)(\rho\chi) = 0. \tag{18.80}$$

A comparison with Eq. (18.75) for $\Phi_n^k(x)$ shows that Eq. (18.80) is satisfied by

$$\rho\chi(\rho) = e^{-\rho/2}\rho^{L+1}L_{\lambda-L-1}^{2L+1}(\rho), \tag{18.81}$$

where k and n of Eq. (18.75) have been, respectively, replaced by $2L + 1$ and $\lambda - L - 1$.

The parameter λ must be restricted to values such that $\lambda - L - 1$ is both integral and nonnegative. If this requirement is violated, $L_{\lambda-L-1}^{2L+1}$ will diverge too rapidly to permit $\rho\chi(\rho)$ to go to zero at large r, which is required for a bound-state electron distribution.

Since we already know that L, a spherical harmonic index, must be integral and nonnegative, we see that the possible values of λ are integers n at least as large as $L + 1$.[7]

This restriction on λ, imposed by our boundary condition, has the effect of quantizing the energy. Inserting $\lambda = n$, the definitions in Eqs. (18.78) lead to

$$E_n = -\frac{Z^2 m}{2n^2 \hbar^2} \left(\frac{e^2}{4\pi \epsilon_0}\right)^2.$$

(18.82)

Since our Schrödinger equation implicitly set the potential energy to zero when the electron is at an infinite separation from the nucleus, the negative sign reflects the fact that we are dealing here with bound states in which the electron cannot escape to infinity. The other quantities introduced in Eq. (18.78) can also be expressed in terms of n:

$$\alpha = \frac{me^2}{2\pi \epsilon_0 \hbar^2} \frac{Z}{n} = \frac{2Z}{na_0}, \quad \rho = \frac{2Z}{na_0} r, \quad \text{with } a_0 = \frac{4\pi \epsilon_0 \hbar^2}{me^2}.$$

(18.83)

The quantity a_0, of dimension length, is known as the **Bohr radius**, and its appearance as a scale factor causes the potential energy (for $n = 1$, the smallest possible value) to have an average value corresponding to this electron-nuclear separation.

Summarizing, the final normalized hydrogen wave function is

$$\psi_{nLM}(r, \theta, \varphi) = \left[\left(\frac{2Z}{na_0}\right)^3 \frac{(n - L - 1)!}{2n(n + L)!}\right]^{1/2} e^{-\alpha r/2} (\alpha r)^L L_{n-L-1}^{2L+1}(\alpha r) Y_L^M(\theta, \varphi).$$

(18.84)

Note that the energy corresponding to ψ_{nLM} depends only on n, which is called the **principal quantum number** of this system. Note also that if n is assigned a specific integral value, the condition on λ requires that $L \le n - 1$, thereby explaining the well-known pattern of possible hydrogenic energy states: If $n = 1$, L can only be zero; for $n = 2$, we can have $L = 0$ or $L = 1$, etc. ∎

Exercises

18.3.1   Show with the aid of the Leibniz formula that the series expansion of $L_n(x)$, Eq. (18.53), follows from the Rodrigues representation, Eq. (18.72).

18.3.2   (a)   Using the explicit series form, Eq. (18.53), show that

$$L'_n(0) = -n, \quad L''_n(0) = \tfrac{1}{2}n(n - 1).$$

(b)   Repeat without using the explicit series form of $L_n(x)$.

18.3.3   Derive the normalization relation, Eq. (18.71) for the associated Laguerre polynomials, thereby also confirming Eq. (18.55) for the L_n.

---

[7]This is the conventional notation for λ. It is not the same n as the index n in $\Phi_n^k(x)$.

18.3.4   Expand x^r in a series of associated Laguerre polynomials $L_n^k(x)$, with k fixed and n ranging from 0 to r (or to ∞ if r is not an integer).

Hint. The Rodrigues form of $L_n^k(x)$ will be useful.

$$ANS. \quad x^r = (r+k)!\, r! \sum_{n=0}^{r} \frac{(-1)^n L_n^k(x)}{(n+k)!(r-n)!}, \quad 0 \le x < \infty.$$

18.3.5   Expand e^{-ax} in a series of associated Laguerre polynomials $L_n^k(x)$, with k fixed and n ranging from 0 to ∞.

(a)   Evaluate directly the coefficients in your assumed expansion.
(b)   Develop the desired expansion from the generating function.

$$ANS. \quad e^{-ax} = \frac{1}{(1+a)^{1+k}} \sum_{n=0}^{\infty} \left(\frac{a}{1+a}\right)^n L_n^k(x), \quad 0 \le x < \infty.$$

18.3.6   Show that $\displaystyle \int_0^\infty e^{-x} x^{k+1} L_n^k(x) L_n^k(x)\, dx = \frac{(n+k)!}{n!}\, (2n+k+1).$

Hint. Note that $x L_n^k = (2n+k+1) L_n^k - (n+k) L_{n-1}^k - (n+1) L_{n+1}^k$.

18.3.7   Assume that a particular problem in quantum mechanics has led to the ODE

$$\frac{d^2 y}{dx^2} - \left[\frac{k^2-1}{4x^2} - \frac{2n+k+1}{2x} + \frac{1}{4}\right] y = 0$$

for nonnegative integers n, k. Write $y(x)$ as $y(x) = A(x)B(x)C(x)$, with the requirement that

(a) $A(x)$ be a **negative** exponential giving the required asymptotic behavior of $y(x)$, and
(b) $B(x)$ be a **positive** power of x giving the behavior of $y(x)$ for $0 \le x \ll 1$.

Determine $A(x)$ and $B(x)$. Find the relation between $C(x)$ and the associated Laguerre polynomial.

$$ANS. \quad A(x) = e^{-x/2}, \quad B(x) = x^{(k+1)/2}, \quad C(x) = L_n^k(x).$$

18.3.8   From Eq. (18.84) the normalized radial part of the hydrogenic wave function is

$$R_{nL}(r) = \left[\alpha^3 \frac{(n-L-1)!}{2n(n+L)!}\right]^{1/2} e^{-\alpha r} (\alpha r)^L L_{n-L-1}^{2L+1}(\alpha r),$$

in which $\alpha = 2Z/na_0 = 2Zme^2/4\pi\epsilon_0\hbar^2$. Evaluate

$$(a) \quad \langle r \rangle = \int_0^\infty r R_{nL}(\alpha r) R_{nL}(\alpha r) r^2\, dr,$$

(b) $\langle r^{-1}\rangle = \int\limits_{0}^{\infty} r^{-1} R_{nL}(\alpha r) R_{nL}(\alpha r) r^2\, dr.$

The quantity $\langle r\rangle$ is the average displacement of the electron from the nucleus, whereas $\langle r^{-1}\rangle$ is the average of the reciprocal displacement.

$$ANS. \quad \langle r\rangle = \frac{a_0}{2}\left[3n^2 - L(L+1)\right], \qquad \langle r^{-1}\rangle = \frac{1}{n^2 a_0}.$$

18.3.9   Derive a recurrence formula for the hydrogen wave function expectation values:

$$\frac{s+2}{n^2}\langle r^{s+1}\rangle - (2s+3)a_0\langle r^s\rangle + \frac{s+1}{4}\left[(2L+1)^2 - (s+1)^2\right]a_0^2\langle r^{s-1}\rangle = 0,$$

with $s \geq -2L - 1$.

Hint. Transform Eq. (18.80) into a form analogous to Eq. (18.73). Multiply by $\rho^{s+2}u' - c\rho^{s+1}u$, with $u = \rho\Phi$. Adjust c to cancel terms that do not yield expectation values.

18.3.10   Show that $\int\limits_{-\infty}^{\infty} x^n e^{-x^2} H_n(xy)dx = \sqrt{\pi}\, n!\, P_n(y)$, where P_n is a Legendre polynomial.

18.4   CHEBYSHEV POLYNOMIALS

The generating function for the Legendre polynomials can be generalized to the following form:

$$\frac{1}{(1 - 2xt + t^2)^\alpha} = \sum_{n=0}^{\infty} C_n^{(\alpha)}(x)t^n. \tag{18.85}$$

The coefficients $C_n^{(\alpha)}(x)$ are known as the **ultraspherical polynomials** (also called **Gegenbauer polynomials**). For $\alpha = 1/2$, we recover the Legendre polynomials; the special cases $\alpha = 0$ and $\alpha = 1$ yield two types of Chebyshev polynomials that are the subject of this section. The primary importance of the Chebyshev polynomials is in numerical analysis.

Type II Polynomials

With $\alpha = 1$ and $C_n^{(1)}(x)$ written as $U_n(x)$, Eq. (18.85) gives

$$\frac{1}{1 - 2xt + t^2} = \sum_{n=0}^{\infty} U_n(x)t^n, \quad |x| < 1, \quad |t| < 1. \tag{18.86}$$

These functions are called type II Chebyshev polynomials. Although these polynomials have few applications in mathematical physics, one unusual application is in the development of four-dimensional spherical harmonics used in angular momentum theory.

Type I Polynomials

With $\alpha = 0$ there is a difficulty. Indeed, our generating function reduces to the constant 1. We may avoid this problem by first differentiating Eq. (18.85) with respect to t. This yields

$$\frac{-\alpha(-2x + 2t)}{(1 - 2xt + t^2)^{\alpha+1}} = \sum_{n=1}^{\infty} n C_n^{(\alpha)}(x) t^{n-1},$$

or

$$\frac{x - t}{(1 - 2xt + t^2)^{\alpha+1}} = \sum_{n=1}^{\infty} \frac{n}{2} \left[\frac{C_n^{(\alpha)}(x)}{\alpha} \right] t^{n-1}. \tag{18.87}$$

We define $C_n^{(0)}(x)$ as

$$C_n^{(0)}(x) = \lim_{\alpha \to 0} \frac{C_n^{(\alpha)}(x)}{\alpha}. \tag{18.88}$$

The purpose of differentiating with respect to t was to get α in the denominator and to create an indeterminate form. Now multiplying Eq. (18.87) by $2t$ and adding 1 in the form $(1 - 2xt + t^2)/(1 - 2xt + t^2)$, we obtain

$$\frac{1 - t^2}{1 - 2xt + t^2} = 1 + 2 \sum_{n=1}^{\infty} \frac{n}{2} C_n^{(0)}(x) t^n. \tag{18.89}$$

We define $T_n(x)$ as

$$T_n(x) = \begin{cases} 1, & n = 0, \\ \dfrac{n}{2} C_n^{(0)}(x), & n > 0. \end{cases} \tag{18.90}$$

Note the special treatment for $n = 0$. We will encounter a similar treatment of the $n = 0$ term when we study Fourier series in Chapter 19. Also, note that $C_n^{(0)}$ is the limit indicated in Eq. (18.88) and not a literal substitution of $\alpha = 0$ into the generating function series. With these new labels,

$$\frac{1 - t^2}{1 - 2xt + t^2} = T_0(x) + 2 \sum_{n=1}^{\infty} T_n(x) t^n, \quad |x| \le 1, \quad |t| < 1. \tag{18.91}$$

We call $T_n(x)$ the type I Chebyshev polynomials. Note that the notation and spelling of the name for these functions differ from reference to reference. Here we follow the usage of AMS-55 (Additional Readings).

Recurrence Relations

Differentiating the generating function, Eq. (18.91), with respect to t and multiplying by the denominator, $1 - 2xt + t^2$, we obtain

$$-t - (t - x)\left[T_0(x) + 2\sum_{n=1}^{\infty} T_n(x)t^n \right] = (1 - 2xt + t^2)\sum_{n=1}^{\infty} nT_n(x)t^{n-1}$$

$$= \sum_{n=1}^{\infty}\left[nT_nt^{n-1} - 2xnT_nt^n + nT_nt^{n+1}\right],$$

from which after several simplification steps we reach the recurrence relation

$$T_{n+1}(x) - 2xT_n(x) + T_{n-1}(x) = 0, \quad n > 0. \tag{18.92}$$

A similar treatment of Eq. (18.86) yields the corresponding recursion relation for U_n:

$$U_{n+1}(x) - 2xU_n(x) + U_{n-1}(x) = 0, \quad n > 0. \tag{18.93}$$

Using the generating functions directly for $n = 0$ and 1, and then applying these recurrence relations for the higher-order polynomials, we get Table 18.4. Plots of the T_n and U_n are presented in Figs. 18.4 and 18.5.

Differentiation of the generating functions for $T_n(x)$ and $U_n(x)$ with respect to the variable x leads to a variety of recurrence relations involving derivatives. For example, from Eq. (18.89) we thus obtain

$$(1 - 2xt + t^2)2\sum_{n=1}^{\infty} T_n'(x)t^n = 2t\left[T_0(x) + 2\sum_{n=1}^{\infty} T_n(x)t^n \right],$$

from which we extract the recursion formula

$$2T_n(x) = T_{n+1}'(x) - 2xT_n'(x) + T_{n-1}'(x). \tag{18.94}$$

Other useful recurrence formulas we can find in this way are

$$(1 - x^2)T_n'(x) = -nxT_n(x) + nT_{n-1}(x) \tag{18.95}$$

Table 18.4   Chebyshev Polynomials: Type I (Left), Type II (Right)

$T_0 = 1$	$U_0 = 1$
$T_1 = x$	$U_1 = 2x$
$T_2 = 2x^2 - 1$	$U_2 = 4x^2 - 1$
$T_3 = 4x^3 - 3x$	$U_3 = 8x^3 - 4x$
$T_4 = 8x^4 - 8x^2 + 1$	$U_4 = 16x^4 - 12x^2 + 1$
$T_5 = 16x^5 - 20x^3 + 5x$	$U_5 = 32x^5 - 32x^3 + 6x$
$T_6 = 32x^6 - 48x^4 + 18x^2 - 1$	$U_6 = 64x^6 - 80x^4 + 24x^2 - 1$

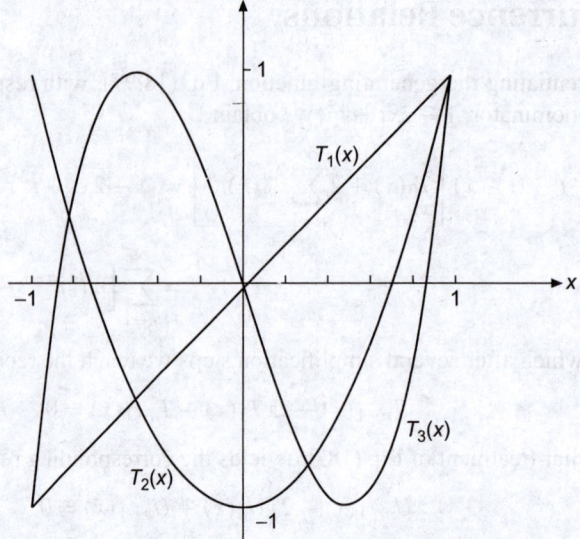

FIGURE 18.4   The Chebyshev polynomials T_1, T_2, and T_3.

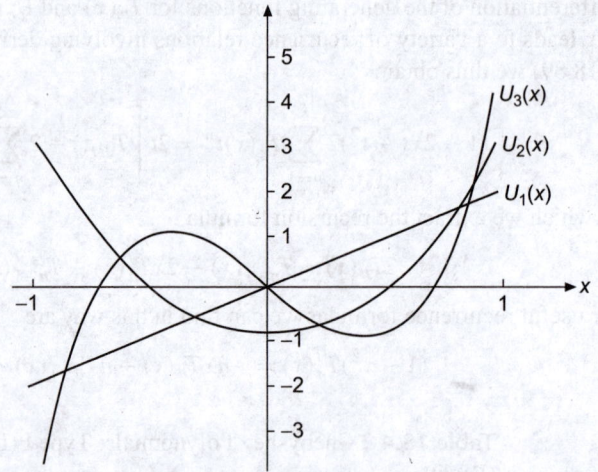

FIGURE 18.5   The Chebyshev polynomials U_1, U_2, and U_3.

and

$$(1 - x^2)U_n'(x) = -nxU_n(x) + (n + 1)U_{n-1}(x). \tag{18.96}$$

Manipulating a variety of these formulas as in Section 15.1 for Legendre polynomials one can eliminate the index $n - 1$ in favor of T_n'' and establish that $T_n(x)$, the Chebyshev polynomial type I, satisfies the ODE

$$(1 - x^2)T_n''(x) - xT_n'(x) + n^2 T_n(x) = 0. \tag{18.97}$$

The Chebyshev polynomial of type II, $U_n(x)$, satisfies

$$(1 - x^2)U_n''(x) - 3xU_n'(x) + n(n + 2)U_n(x) = 0. \tag{18.98}$$

We could have defined the Chebyshev polynomials starting from these ODEs, but we chose instead a development based on generating functions.

Processes similar to those used for the Chebyshev polynomials can be applied to the general ultraspherical polynomials; the result is the **ultraspherical ODE**

$$(1 - x^2)\frac{d^2}{dx^2} C_n^{(\alpha)}(x) - (2\alpha + 1)x\frac{d}{dx} C_n^{(\alpha)}(x) + n(n + 2\alpha)C_n^{(\alpha)}(x) = 0. \tag{18.99}$$

Special Values

Again, from the generating functions, we can obtain the special values of various polynomials:

$$T_n(1) = 1, \quad T_n(-1) = (-1)^n,$$

$$T_{2n}(0) = (-1)^n, \quad T_{2n+1}(0) = 0;$$

$$U_n(1) = n + 1, \quad U_n(-1) = (-1)^n(n + 1), \tag{18.100}$$

$$U_{2n}(0) = (-1)^n, \quad U_{2n+1}(0) = 0.$$

Verification of Eq. (18.100) is left to the exercises.

The polynomials T_n and U_n satisfy parity relations that follow from their generating functions with the substitutions $t \to -t, x \to -x$, which leave them invariant; these are

$$T_n(x) = (-1)^n T_n(-x), \quad U_n(x) = (-1)^n U_n(-x). \tag{18.101}$$

Rodrigues representations of $T_n(x)$ and $U_n(x)$ are

$$T_n(x) = \frac{(-1)^n \pi^{1/2}(1 - x^2)^{1/2}}{2^n \Gamma(n + \frac{1}{2})} \frac{d^n}{dx^n}\left[(1 - x^2)^{n-1/2}\right] \tag{18.102}$$

and

$$U_n(x) = \frac{(-1)^n (n + 1)\pi^{1/2}}{2^{n+1}\Gamma(n + \frac{3}{2})(1 - x^2)^{1/2}} \frac{d^n}{dx^n}\left[(1 - x^2)^{n+1/2}\right]. \tag{18.103}$$

Trigonometric Form

At this point in the development of the properties of the Chebyshev polynomials it is beneficial to change variables, replacing x by $\cos\theta$. With $x = \cos\theta$ and $d/dx = (-1/\sin\theta)(d/d\theta)$, we verify that

$$(1-x^2)\frac{d^2 T_n}{dx^2} = \frac{d^2 T_n}{d\theta^2} - \cot\theta\frac{dT_n}{d\theta}, \quad x T_n' = -\cot\theta\frac{dT_n}{d\theta}.$$

Adding these terms, Eq. (18.97) becomes

$$\frac{d^2 T_n}{d\theta^2} + n^2 T_n = 0, \tag{18.104}$$

the simple harmonic oscillator equation with solutions $\cos n\theta$ and $\sin n\theta$. The special values (boundary conditions at $x = 0$ and 1) identify

$$T_n = \cos n\theta = \cos(n\arccos x). \tag{18.105}$$

For $n \neq 0$ a second linearly independent solution of Eq. (18.104) is labeled

$$V_n = \sin n\theta = \sin(n\arccos x). \tag{18.106}$$

The corresponding solutions of the type II Chebyshev equation, Eq. (18.98), become

$$U_n = \frac{\sin(n+1)\theta}{\sin\theta}, \tag{18.107}$$

$$W_n = \frac{\cos(n+1)\theta}{\sin\theta}. \tag{18.108}$$

The two sets of solutions, type I and type II, are related by

$$V_n(x) = (1-x^2)^{1/2} U_{n-1}(x), \tag{18.109}$$

$$W_n(x) = (1-x^2)^{-1/2} T_{n+1}(x). \tag{18.110}$$

As already seen from the generating functions, $T_n(x)$ and $U_n(x)$ are polynomials. Clearly, $V_n(x)$ and $W_n(x)$ are **not** polynomials. From

$$T_n(x) + i V_n(x) = \cos n\theta + i\sin n\theta$$

$$= (\cos\theta + i\sin\theta)^n = \left[x + i(1-x^2)^{1/2}\right]^n, \quad |x| \leq 1 \tag{18.111}$$

we can apply the binomial theorem to obtain expansions

$$T_n(x) = x^n - \binom{n}{2}x^{n-2}(1-x^2) + \binom{n}{4}x^{n-4}(1-x^2)^2 - \cdots \tag{18.112}$$

and, for $n > 0$

$$V_n(x) = \sqrt{1-x^2}\left[\binom{n}{1}x^{n-1} - \binom{n}{3}x^{n-3}(1-x^2) + \cdots\right]. \tag{18.113}$$

From the generating functions, or from the ODEs, power-series representations are

$$T_n(x) = \frac{n}{2} \sum_{m=0}^{[n/2]} (-1)^m \frac{(n-m-1)!}{m!\,(n-2m)!} (2x)^{n-2m} \tag{18.114}$$

for $n \geq 1$, with $[n/2]$ the integer part of $n/2$ and

$$U_n(x) = \sum_{m=0}^{[n/2]} (-1)^m \frac{(n-m)!}{m!\,(n-2m)!} (2x)^{n-2m}. \tag{18.115}$$

Application to Numerical Analysis

An important feature of the Chebyshev polynomials $T_n(x)$ with $n > 0$ is that as x is varied, they oscillate between the extreme values $T_n = +1$ and $T_n = -1$. This behavior is readily seen from Eq. (18.105) and is illustrated for T_{12} in Fig. 18.6. If a function is expanded in the T_n and the expansion is extended sufficiently that the contributions of successive T_n are decreasing rapidly, a good approximation to the truncation error will be proportional to the first T_n not included in the expansion. In this approximation, there will be negligible error at the n values of x where T_n is zero, and there will be maximum errors (all of the same magnitude but alternating in sign) at the extrema of T_n that fall between the zeros. In that sense, the errors satisfy a minimax principle, meaning that the maximum of the error has been minimized by distributing it evenly into the regions between the points of negligible error.

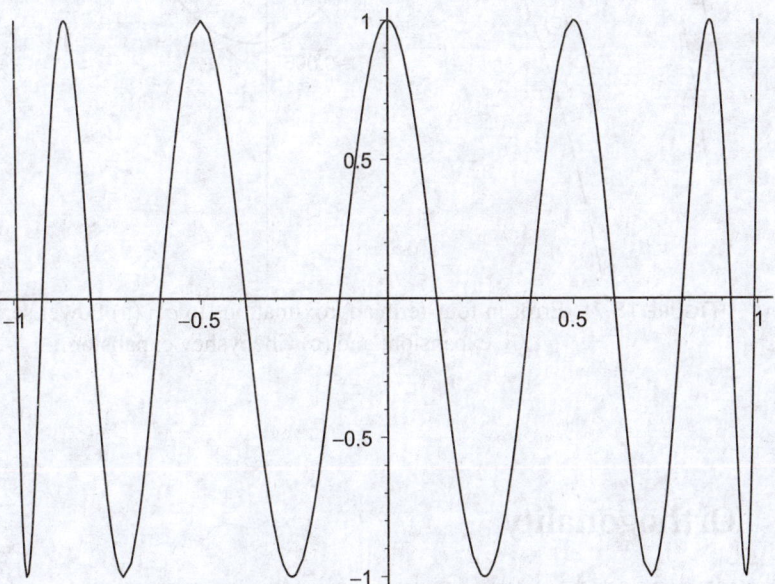

FIGURE 18.6   The Chebyshev polynomial T_{12}.

Example 18.4.1   MINIMIZING THE MAXIMUM ERROR

Figure 18.7 shows the errors in four-term expansions of e^x on the range $[-1, 1]$ carried out in various ways: (a) Maclaurin series, (b) Legendre expansion, and (c) Chebyshev expansion. The power series is optimum at the point $x = 0$ and the error increases with increasing values of $|x|$. The orthogonal expansions produce a fit over the region $[-1, 1]$, with the maximum errors occurring at $x = \pm 1$ and three intermediate values of x. However, the Legendre expansion has larger errors at ± 1 than it has at the interior points, while the Chebyshev expansion yields smaller errors at ± 1 (with a concomitant increase in the error at the other maxima) with the result that all the error maxima are comparable. This choice approximately minimizes the maximum error.

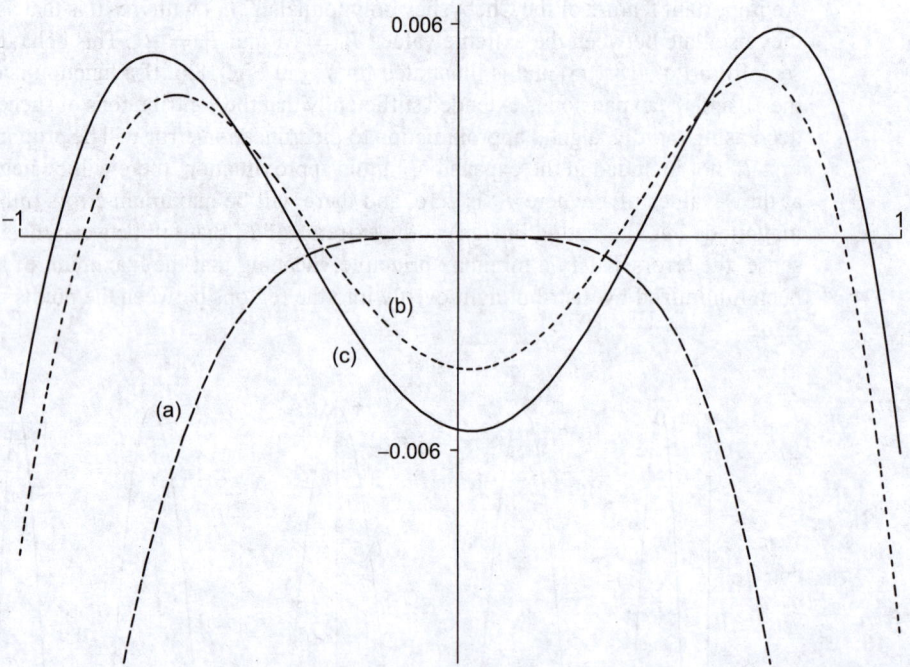

FIGURE 18.7   Error in four-term approximations to e^x: (a) Power series; (b) Legendre expansion; and (c) Chebyshev expansion.

Orthogonality

If Eq. (18.97) is put into self-adjoint form (Section 8.2), we obtain $w(x) = (1 - x^2)^{-1/2}$ as a weighting factor. For Eq. (18.98) the corresponding weighting factor is $(1 - x^2)^{+1/2}$.

The resulting orthogonality integrals,

$$\int_{-1}^{1} T_m(x)T_n(x)(1-x^2)^{-1/2}\, dx = \begin{cases} 0, & m \neq n, \\ \dfrac{\pi}{2}, & m = n \neq 0, \\ \pi, & m = n = 0, \end{cases} \tag{18.116}$$

$$\int_{-1}^{1} V_m(x)V_n(x)(1-x^2)^{-1/2}\, dx = \begin{cases} 0, & m \neq n, \\ \dfrac{\pi}{2}, & m = n \neq 0, \\ 0, & m = n = 0, \end{cases} \tag{18.117}$$

$$\int_{-1}^{1} U_m(x)U_n(x)(1-x^2)^{1/2}\, dx = \frac{\pi}{2}\,\delta_{mn}, \tag{18.118}$$

and

$$\int_{-1}^{1} W_m(x)W_n(x)(1-x^2)^{1/2}\, dx = \frac{\pi}{2}\,\delta_{mn}, \tag{18.119}$$

are a direct consequence of the Sturm-Liouville theory. The normalization values may best be obtained by making the substitution $x = \cos\theta$.

Exercises

18.4.1   By evaluating the generating function for special values of x, verify the special values
$$T_n(1) = 1, \quad T_n(-1) = (-1)^n, \quad T_{2n}(0) = (-1)^n, \quad T_{2n+1}(0) = 0.$$

18.4.2   By evaluating the generating function for special values of x, verify the special values
$$U_n(1) = n+1, \quad U_n(-1) = (-1)^n(n+1), \quad U_{2n}(0) = (-1)^n, \quad U_{2n+1}(0) = 0.$$

18.4.3   Another Chebyshev generating function is
$$\frac{1-xt}{1-2xt+t^2} = \sum_{n=0}^{\infty} X_n(x)t^n, \quad |t| < 1.$$

How is $X_n(x)$ related to $T_n(x)$ and $U_n(x)$?

18.4.4   Given
$$(1-x^2)U_n''(x) - 3xU_n'(x) + n(n+2)U_n(x) = 0,$$

show that $V_n(x)$, Eq. (18.106), satisfies
$$(1-x^2)V_n''(x) - xV_n'(x) + n^2 V_n(x) = 0,$$

which is Chebyshev's equation.

18.4.5   Show that the Wronskian of $T_n(x)$ and $V_n(x)$ is given by

$$T_n(x)V_n'(x) - T_n'(x)V_n(x) = -\frac{n}{(1-x^2)^{1/2}}.$$

This verifies that T_n and V_n ($n \neq 0$) are independent solutions of Eq. (18.97). Conversely, for $n = 0$, we do not have linear independence. What happens at $n = 0$? Where is the "second" solution?

18.4.6   Show that $W_n(x) = (1-x^2)^{-1/2}T_{n+1}(x)$ is a solution of

$$(1-x^2)W_n''(x) - 3x W_n'(x) + n(n+2)W_n(x) = 0.$$

18.4.7   Evaluate the Wronskian of $U_n(x)$ and $W_n(x) = (1-x^2)^{-1/2}T_{n+1}(x)$.

18.4.8 $V_n(x) = (1-x^2)^{1/2}U_{n-1}(x)$ is not defined for $n = 0$. Show that a second and independent solution of the Chebyshev differential equation for $T_n(x)$ ($n = 0$) is $V_0(x) = \arccos x$ (or $\arcsin x$).

18.4.9   Show that $V_n(x)$ satisfies the same three-term recurrence relation as $T_n(x)$, Eq. (18.92).

18.4.10   Verify the series solutions for $T_n(x)$ and $U_n(x)$, Eqs. (18.114) and (18.115).

18.4.11   Transform the series form of $T_n(x)$, Eq. (18.114), into an **ascending** power series.

$$ANS.\ \ T_{2n}(x) = (-1)^n n \sum_{m=0}^{n}(-1)^m \frac{(n+m-1)!}{(n-m)!(2m)!}(2x)^{2m}, \quad n \geq 1,$$

$$T_{2n+1}(x) = \frac{2n+1}{2}\sum_{m=0}^{n}\frac{(-1)^{m+n}(n+m)!}{(n-m)!(2m+1)!}(2x)^{2m+1}.$$

18.4.12   Rewrite the series form of $U_n(x)$, Eq. (18.115), as an ascending power series.

$$ANS.\ \ \ U_{2n}(x) = (-1)^n \sum_{m=0}^{n}(-1)^m \frac{(n+m)!}{(n-m)!(2m)!}(2x)^{2m},$$

$$U_{2n+1}(x) = (-1)^n \sum_{m=0}^{n}(-1)^m \frac{(n+m+1)!}{(n-m)!(2m+1)!}(2x)^{2m+1}.$$

18.4.13   (a)   From the differential equation for T_n (in self-adjoint form) show that

$$\int_{-1}^{1}\frac{dT_m(x)}{dx}\frac{dT_n(x)}{dx}(1-x^2)^{1/2}dx = 0, \quad m \neq n.$$

(b)   Confirm the preceding result by showing that

$$\frac{dT_n(x)}{dx} = nU_{n-1}(x).$$

18.4.14   The substitution $x = 2x' - 1$ converts $T_n(x)$ into the **shifted** Chebyshev polynomials $T_n^*(x')$. Verify that this produces the shifted polynomials shown in Table 18.5 and that

Table 18.5   Shifted Type I Chebyshev Polynomials

$T_0^* = 1$

$T_1^* = 2x - 1$

$T_2^* = 8x^2 - 8x + 1$

$T_3^* = 32x^3 - 48x^2 + 18x - 1$

$T_4^* = 128x^4 - 256x^3 + 160x^2 - 32x + 1$

$T_5^* = 512x^5 - 1280x^4 + 120x^3 - 400x^2 + 50x - 1$

$T_6^* = 2048x^6 - 6144x^5 + 6912x^4 - 3584x^3 + 840x^2 - 72x + 1$

they satisfy the orthonormality condition

$$\int_0^1 T_n^*(x') T_m(x') [x(1-x)]^{-1/2} \, dx = \frac{\delta_{mn} \pi}{2 - \delta_{n0}}.$$

18.4.15   The expansion of a power of x in a Chebyshev series leads to the integral

$$I_{mn} = \int_{-1}^{1} x^m T_n(x) \frac{dx}{\sqrt{1-x^2}}.$$

(a)   Show that this integral vanishes for $m < n$.

(b)   Show that this integral vanishes for $m + n$ odd.

18.4.16   Evaluate the integral

$$I_{mn} = \int_{-1}^{1} x^m T_n(x) \frac{dx}{\sqrt{1-x^2}}$$

for $m \geq n$ and $m + n$ even by each of two methods:

(a)   Replacing $T_n(x)$ by its Rodrigues representation.

(b)   Using $x = \cos\theta$ to transform the integral to a form with θ as the variable.

$$\text{ANS.} \quad I_{mn} = \pi \frac{m!}{(m-n)!} \frac{(m-n-1)!!}{(m+n)!!}, \quad m \geq n, \ m+n \text{ even.}$$

18.4.17   Establish the following bounds, $-1 \leq x \leq 1$:

(a) $|U_n(x)| \leq n+1$,   (b) $\left| \dfrac{d}{dx} T_n(x) \right| \leq n^2$.

18.4.18   (a)   Show that for $-1 \leq x \leq 1$, $\quad |V_n(x)| \leq 1$.

(b)   Show that $W_n(x)$ is unbounded in $-1 \leq x \leq 1$.

18.4.19 Verify the orthogonality-normalization integrals for

(a) $T_m(x), T_n(x)$,   (b) $V_m(x), V_n(x)$,

(c) $U_m(x), U_n(x)$,   (d) $W_m(x), W_n(x)$.

Hint. All these can be converted to trigonometric integrals.

18.4.20 Show whether

(a) $T_m(x)$ and $V_n(x)$ are or are not orthogonal over the interval $[-1, 1]$ with respect to the weighting factor $(1 - x^2)^{-1/2}$.

(b) $U_m(x)$ and $W_n(x)$ are or are not orthogonal over the interval $[-1, 1]$ with respect to the weighting factor $(1 - x^2)^{1/2}$.

18.4.21 Derive

(a) $T_{n+1}(x) + T_{n-1}(x) = 2xT_n(x)$,

(b) $T_{m+n}(x) + T_{m-n}(x) = 2T_m(x)T_n(x)$, from the "corresponding" cosine identities.

18.4.22 A number of equations relate the two types of Chebyshev polynomials. As examples show that

$$T_n(x) = U_n(x) - xU_{n-1}(x)$$

and

$$(1 - x^2)U_n(x) = xT_{n+1}(x) - T_{n+2}(x).$$

18.4.23 Show that

$$\frac{dV_n(x)}{dx} = -n\frac{T_n(x)}{\sqrt{1 - x^2}}$$

(a) using the trigonometric forms of V_n and T_n,

(b) using the Rodrigues representation.

18.4.24 Starting with $x = \cos\theta$ and $T_n(\cos\theta) = \cos n\theta$, expand

$$x^k = \left(\frac{e^{i\theta} + e^{-i\theta}}{2}\right)^k$$

and show that

$$x^k = \frac{1}{2^{k-1}}\left[T_k(x) + \binom{k}{1}T_{k-2}(x) + \binom{k}{2}T_{k-4} + \cdots\right],$$

the series in brackets terminating after the term containing T_1 or T_0.

18.4.25   Develop the following Chebyshev expansions (for $[-1, 1]$):

(a) $\quad (1-x^2)^{1/2} = \dfrac{2}{\pi}\left[1 - 2\sum_{s=1}^{\infty}(4s^2-1)^{-1}T_{2s}(x)\right]$,

(b) $\quad \left.\begin{array}{cc} +1, & 0 < x \le 1 \\ -1, & -1 \le x < 0 \end{array}\right\} = \dfrac{4}{\pi}\sum_{s=0}^{\infty}(-1)^s(2s+1)^{-1}T_{2s+1}(x)$.

18.4.26   (a)   For the interval $[-1, 1]$ show that

$$|x| = \frac{1}{2} + \sum_{s=1}^{\infty}(-1)^{s+1}\frac{(2s-3)!!}{(2s+2)!!}(4s+1)P_{2s}(x)$$

$$= \frac{2}{\pi} + \frac{4}{\pi}\sum_{s=1}^{\infty}(-1)^{s+1}\frac{1}{4s^2-1}T_{2s}(x).$$

(b)   Show that the ratio of the coefficient of $T_{2s}(x)$ to that of $P_{2s}(x)$ approaches $(\pi s)^{-1}$ as $s \to \infty$. This illustrates the relatively rapid convergence of the Chebyshev series.

Hint. With the Legendre recurrence relations, rewrite $xP_n(x)$ as a linear combination of derivatives. The trigonometric substitution $x = \cos\theta$, $T_n(x) = \cos n\theta$ is most helpful for the Chebyshev part.

18.4.27   Show that

$$\frac{\pi^2}{8} = 1 + 2\sum_{s=1}^{\infty}(4s^2-1)^{-2}.$$

Hint. Apply Parseval's identity (or the completeness relation) to the results of Exercise 18.4.26.

18.4.28   Show that

(a) $\quad \cos^{-1}x = \dfrac{\pi}{2} - \dfrac{4}{\pi}\sum_{n=0}^{\infty}\dfrac{1}{(2n+1)^2}T_{2n+1}(x)$.

(b) $\quad \sin^{-1}x = \dfrac{4}{\pi}\sum_{n=0}^{\infty}\dfrac{1}{(2n+1)^2}T_{2n+1}(x)$.

18.5   HYPERGEOMETRIC FUNCTIONS

In Chapter 7 the hypergeometric equation[8]

$$x(1-x)y''(x) + [c - (a+b+1)x]y'(x) - ab\,y(x) = 0 \qquad (18.120)$$

---

[8] This is sometimes called Gauss' ODE. The solutions are then referred to as Gauss functions.

was introduced as a canonical form of a linear second-order ODE with regular singularities at $x = 0, 1$, and ∞. One solution, designated $_2F_1$, is

$$y(x) = {}_2F_1(a, b; c; x)$$

$$= 1 + \frac{a\,b}{c}\frac{x}{1!} + \frac{a(a+1)b(b+1)}{c(c+1)}\frac{x^2}{2!} + \cdots, \quad c \neq 0, -1, -2, -3, \ldots,$$

which is known as the **hypergeometric function** or **hypergeometric series**. For real a, b, and c (the only case considered here), the range of convergence for $c > a + b$ is $-1 \leq x \leq 1$, while for $a + b - 1 < c \leq a + b$ the convergence range is $-1 \leq x < 1$. For $c \leq a + b - 1$ the hypergeometric series diverges.

The terms of the hypergeometric series are conveniently written in terms of the Pochhammer symbol, introduced at Eq. (1.72); we repeat the definition here:

$$(a)_n = a(a+1)(a+2)\cdots(a+n-1), \quad (a)_0 = 1.$$

Using this notation, the hypergeometric function becomes

$$_2F_1(a, b; c; x) = \sum_{n=0}^{\infty} \frac{(a)_n (b)_n}{(c)_n} \frac{x^n}{n!}. \tag{18.121}$$

In this form the significance of the subscripts 2 and 1 becomes clear. The leading subscript 2 indicates that two Pochhammer symbols appear in the numerator and the trailing subscript 1 indicates one Pochhammer symbol in the denominator. The subscripts 2 and 1 are only useful if one intends to discuss analogs of the "standard" hypergeometric function that involve different numbers of Pochhammer symbols. We retain the subscripts because we will shortly identify **confluent hypergeometric functions** with forms similar to Eq. (18.121) but with only one Pochhammer symbol in the numerator, therefore of the form $_1F_1(a; c; z)$. Note also that the numerator and denominator parameters are set off by semicolons (actually making the subscripts unnecessary). We retain them to conform to the most widely used notations for these functions.

Looking further at Eq. (18.121), we note that the series will reduce to zero (for all x) if c is either zero or a negative integer (unless the denominator is fortuitously cancelled by a particular choice of a or b). On the other hand, if a or b equals 0 or a negative integer, the series terminates and the hypergeometric function becomes a polynomial. Many more or less elementary functions can be represented by the hypergeometric function.[9] For example,

$$\ln(1 + x) = x \, {}_2F_1(1, 1; 2; -x). \tag{18.122}$$

The hypergeometric equation as a second-order linear ODE has a second independent solution. The usual form is

$$y(x) = x^{1-c} \, {}_2F_1(a+1-c, b+1-c; 2-c; x), \quad c \neq 2, 3, 4, \ldots. \tag{18.123}$$

If c is an integer either the two solutions coincide or (barring a rescue by integral a or integral b) one of the solutions will blow up (see Exercise 18.5.1). In such a case the second solution is expected to include a logarithmic term.

---

[9]With three parameters, a, b, and c, we can represent almost anything.

Alternate forms of the hypergeometric ODE include

$$(1-z^2)\frac{d^2}{dz^2}\left[\left(\frac{1-z}{2}\right)y\right] - \left[(a+b+1)z - (a+b+1-2c)\right]\frac{d}{dz}\left[\left(\frac{1-z}{2}\right)y\right]$$

$$- ab\left[\left(\frac{1-z}{2}\right)y\right] = 0, \tag{18.124}$$

$$(1-z^2)\frac{d^2}{dz^2}y(z^2) - \left[(2a+2b+1)z + \frac{1-2c}{z}\right]\frac{d}{dz}y(z^2) - 4ab\,y(z^2) = 0. \tag{18.125}$$

Contiguous Function Relations

The parameters a, b, and c enter in the same way as the parameter n of Bessel, Legendre, and other special functions. As we found with these functions, we expect recurrence relations involving unit changes in the parameters a, b, and c. Hypergeometric functions that differ by ± 1 in a parameter are referred to as **contiguous functions**. Generalizing this term to include simultaneous unit changes in more than one parameter, we find 26 functions contiguous to $_2F_1(a, b; c; x)$. Taking them two at a time, we can develop the formidable total of 325 equations among the contiguous functions. Two typical examples are

$$(a-b)\left\{c(a+b-1) + 1 - a^2 - b^2 + [(a-b)^2 - 1](1-x)\right\}\,_2F_1(a, b; c; x)$$

$$= (c-a)(a-b+1)b\,_2F_1(a-1, b+1; c; x)$$

$$+ (c-b)(a-b-1)a\,_2F_1(a+1, b-1; c; x), \tag{18.126}$$

$$[2a - c + (b-a)x]\,_2F_1(a, b; c; x) = a(1-x)\,_2F_1(a+1, b; c; x)$$

$$- (c-a)\,_2F_1(a-1, b; c; x). \tag{18.127}$$

Many more contiguous relations can be found in AMS-55 or in Olver *et al.* (Additional Readings).

Hypergeometric Representations

A number of the special functions introduced in this book can be expressed in terms of hypergeometric functions. The identification can usually be made by noting that these functions are solutions of ODEs that are special cases of the hypergeometric ODE. It is also necessary to determine the factors needed to express the functions at the agreed-upon scale. We cite several examples.

1. The ultraspherical functions $C_n^{(\alpha)}(x)$ satisfy the ODE given as Eq. (18.99), and since that equation is a special case of the hypergeometric equation, Eq. (18.120), we see that ultraspherical functions (and Legendre and Chebyshev functions) may be expressed as

hypergeometric functions. For the ultraspherical function we obtain

$$C_n^{(\alpha)}(x) = \frac{(n+2\alpha)!}{2^\alpha n!\,\Gamma(\alpha+1)}\, {}_2F_1\left(-n, n+2\alpha+1; 1+\alpha; \frac{1-x}{2}\right), \qquad (18.128)$$

with the factor preceding the ${}_2F_1$ function determined by requiring $C_n^{(\alpha)}$ to have the proper scale.

2. For Legendre and associated Legendre functions we find

$$P_n(x) = {}_2F_1\left(-n, n+1; 1; \frac{1-x}{2}\right), \qquad (18.129)$$

$$P_n^m(x) = \frac{(n+m)!}{(n-m)!}\frac{(1-x^2)^{m/2}}{2^m m!}\, {}_2F_1\left(m-n, m+n+1; m+1; \frac{1-x}{2}\right). \qquad (18.130)$$

Alternate forms for the Legendre functions are

$$P_{2n}(x) = (-1)^n \frac{(2n)!}{2^{2n} n!\, n!}\, {}_2F_1\left(-n, n+\frac{1}{2}; \frac{1}{2}; x^2\right)$$

$$= (-1)^n \frac{(2n-1)!!}{(2n)!!}\, {}_2F_1\left(-n, n+\frac{1}{2}; \frac{1}{2}; x^2\right), \qquad (18.131)$$

$$P_{2n+1}(x) = (-1)^n \frac{(2n+1)!}{2^{2n} n!\, n!}\, x\, {}_2F_1\left(-n, n+\frac{3}{2}; \frac{3}{2}; x^2\right)$$

$$= (-1)^n \frac{(2n+1)!!}{(2n)!!}\, x\, {}_2F_1\left(-n, n+\frac{3}{2}; \frac{3}{2}; x^2\right). \qquad (18.132)$$

3. The Chebyshev functions have representations

$$T_n(x) = {}_2F_1\left(-n, n; \frac{1}{2}; \frac{1-x}{2}\right), \qquad (18.133)$$

$$U_n(x) = (n+1)\, {}_2F_1\left(-n, n+2; \frac{3}{2}; \frac{1-x}{2}\right), \qquad (18.134)$$

$$V_n(x) = n\sqrt{1-x^2}\, {}_2F_1\left(-n+1, n+1; \frac{3}{2}; \frac{1-x}{2}\right). \qquad (18.135)$$

The leading factors are determined by direct comparison of complete power series, comparison of coefficients of particular powers of the variable, or evaluation at $x = 0$ or 1.

The hypergeometric series may be used to define functions with nonintegral indices. The physical applications are minimal.

Exercises

18.5.1   (a)   For c, an integer, and a and b nonintegral, show that

$$_2F_1(a, b; c; x) \quad \text{and} \quad x^{1-c} \, _2F_1(a + 1 - c, b + 1 - c; 2 - c; x)$$

yield only one solution to the hypergeometric equation.

(b)   What happens if a is an integer, say, $a = -1$, and $c = -2$?

18.5.2   Find the Legendre, Chebyshev I, and Chebyshev II recurrence relations corresponding to the hypergeometric contiguous function relation given as Eq. (18.126).

18.5.3   Transform the following polynomials into hypergeometric functions of argument x^2:

(a) $T_{2n}(x)$;

(b) $x^{-1}T_{2n+1}(x)$;

(c) $U_{2n}(x)$;

(d) $x^{-1}U_{2n+1}(x)$.

> *ANS.*   (a) $T_{2n}(x) = (-1)^n \, _2F_1(-n, n; \frac{1}{2}; x^2)$.
>
> (b) $x^{-1}T_{2n+1}(x) = (-1)^n (2n + 1) \, _2F_1\left(-n, n + 1; \frac{3}{2}; x^2\right)$.
>
> (c) $U_{2n}(x) = (-1)^n \, _2F_1\left(-n, n + 1; \frac{1}{2}; x^2\right)$.
>
> (d) $x^{-1}U_{2n+1}(x) = (-1)^n (2n + 2) \, _2F_1\left(-n, n + 2; \frac{3}{2}; x^2\right)$.

18.5.4   Derive or verify the leading factor in the hypergeometric representations of the Chebyshev functions.

18.5.5   Verify that the Legendre function of the second kind, $Q_\nu(z)$, is given by

$$Q_\nu(z) = \frac{\pi^{1/2}\nu!}{\Gamma(\nu + \frac{3}{2})(2z)^{\nu+1}} \, _2F_1\left(\frac{\nu}{2} + \frac{1}{2}, \frac{\nu}{2} + 1; \frac{\nu}{2} + \frac{3}{2}; z^{-2}\right),$$

where $|z| > 1$, $|\arg z| < \pi$, and $\nu \neq -1, -2, -3, \cdots$.

18.5.6   The incomplete beta function was defined in Eq. (13.78) as

$$B_x(p, q) = \int_0^x t^{p-1}(1 - t)^{q-1}\, dt.$$

Show that

$$B_x(p, q) = p^{-1}x^p \, _2F_1(p, 1 - q; p + 1; x).$$

18.5.7   Verify the integral representation

$$_2F_1(a, b; c; z) = \frac{\Gamma(c)}{\Gamma(b)\Gamma(c - b)} \int_0^1 t^{b-1}(1 - t)^{c-b-1}(1 - tz)^{-a}\, dt.$$

What restrictions must be placed on the parameters b and c?

Note. Although the power series used to establish this integral representation is only valid for $|z| < 1$, the representation is valid for general z, as can be established by analytic continuation. For nonintegral a the real axis in the z-plane from 1 to ∞ is a cut line.

Hint. The integral is suspiciously like a beta function and can be expanded into a series of beta functions.

ANS. $c > b > 0.$

18.5.8   Prove that

$$_2F_1(a, b; c; 1) = \frac{\Gamma(c)\Gamma(c - a - b)}{\Gamma(c - a)\Gamma(c - b)}, \quad c \neq 0, -1, -2, \ldots, \quad c > a + b.$$

Hint. Here is a chance to use the integral representation in Exercise 18.5.7.

18.5.9   Prove that

$$_2F_1(a, b; c; x) = (1 - x)^{-a} \, _2F_1\left(a, c - b; c; \frac{-x}{1 - x}\right).$$

Hint. Try an integral representation.

Note. This relation is useful in developing a Rodrigues representation of $T_n(x)$ (see Exercise 18.5.10).

18.5.10   Derive the Rodrigues representation of $T_n(x)$,

$$T_n(x) = \frac{(-1)^n \pi^{1/2} (1 - x^2)^{1/2}}{2^n (n - \frac{1}{2})!} \frac{d^n}{dx^n}\left[(1 - x^2)^{n - 1/2}\right].$$

Hint. One possibility is to use the hypergeometric function relation

$$_2F_1(a, b; c; z) = (1 - z)^{-a} \, _2F_1\left(a, c - b; c; \frac{-z}{1 - z}\right),$$

with $z = (1 - x)/2$. An alternate approach is to develop a first-order differential equation for $y = (1 - x^2)^{n - 1/2}$. Repeated differentiation of this equation leads to the Chebyshev equation.

18.5.11   Show that the summation in Eq. (18.43),

$$\sum_{v=0}^{\min(m,n)} \frac{(-m)_v (-n)_v}{v! \left(\dfrac{1 - m - n}{2}\right)_v} \left(\frac{a^2}{2(a^2 - 1)}\right)^v,$$

can be written as a hypergeometric function.

18.5.12   Verify that

$$_2F_1(-n, b; c; 1) = \frac{(c - b)_n}{(c)_n}.$$

Hint. Here is a chance to use the contiguous function relation Eq. (18.127) and mathematical induction (Section 1.4). Alternatively, use the integral representation and the beta function.

18.6 CONFLUENT HYPERGEOMETRIC FUNCTIONS

The confluent hypergeometric equation,[10]

$$xy''(x) + (c - x)y'(x) - ay(x) = 0, \tag{18.136}$$

has a regular singularity at $x = 0$ and an irregular one at $x = \infty$. It is obtained from the hypergeometric equation of Section 18.5 in the limit that one of the singularities at finite x is merged with that at infinity, causing that singularity to become irregular. One solution of the confluent hypergeometric equation is

$$y(x) = {}_1F_1(a; c; x) = M(a, c, x)$$

$$= 1 + \frac{a}{c}\frac{x}{1!} + \frac{a(a+1)}{c(c+1)}\frac{x^2}{2!} + \cdots, \quad c \neq 0, -1, -2, \cdots. \tag{18.137}$$

The notation $M(a, c, x)$ (with commas, not semicolons) has become standard for this solution. It is convergent for all finite x (or complex z). In terms of the Pochhammer symbols, we have

$$M(a, c, x) = \sum_{n=0}^{\infty} \frac{(a)_n}{(c)_n} \frac{x^n}{n!}. \tag{18.138}$$

Clearly, $M(a, c, x)$ becomes a polynomial if the parameter a is 0 or a negative integer. Numerous more or less elementary functions may be represented by the confluent hypergeometric function. Examples are the error function and the incomplete gamma function:

$$\text{erf}(x) = \frac{2}{\pi^{1/2}} \int_0^x e^{-t^2} dt = \frac{2}{\pi^{1/2}} x M\left(\frac{1}{2}, \frac{3}{2}, -x^2\right), \tag{18.139}$$

$$\gamma(a, x) = \int_0^x e^{-t} t^{a-1} dt = a^{-1} x^a M(a, a+1, -x), \quad \Re(a) > 0. \tag{18.140}$$

A second solution of Eq. (18.136) is given by

$$y(x) = x^{1-c} M(a + 1 - c, 2 - c, x), \quad c \neq 2, 3, 4, \cdots. \tag{18.141}$$

Clearly, this coincides with the first solution for $c = 1$.

The standard form of the second solution of Eq. (18.136) is a linear combination of Eqs. (18.137) and (18.141):

$$U(a, c, x) = \frac{\pi}{\sin \pi c} \left[\frac{M(a, c, x)}{\Gamma(a - c + 1)\Gamma(c)} - \frac{x^{1-c} M(a + 1 - c, 2 - c, x)}{\Gamma(a)\Gamma(-c)} \right]. \tag{18.142}$$

Note the resemblance to our definition of the Neumann function, Eq. (14.57). As with the Neumann function, this definition of $U(a, c, x)$ becomes indeterminate for certain parameter values, namely when c is an integer.

---

[10]This is often called **Kummer's equation**. The solutions, then, are **Kummer functions**.

An alternate form of the confluent hypergeometric equation is obtained by changing the independent variable from x to x^2:

$$\frac{d^2}{dx^2}y(x^2) + \left[\frac{2c-1}{x} - 2x\right]\frac{d}{dx}y(x^2) - 4ay(x^2) = 0. \tag{18.143}$$

As with the hypergeometric functions, contiguous functions exist in which the parameters a and c are changed by ± 1. Including the cases of simultaneous changes in the two parameters, we have eight possibilities. Taking the original function and pairs of the contiguous functions, we can develop a total of 28 equations. The recurrence relations for Bessel, Hermite, and Laguerre functions are special cases of these equations.

Integral Representations

It is frequently convenient to have the confluent hypergeometric functions in integral form. We find (Exercise 18.6.10)

$$M(a, c, x) = \frac{\Gamma(c)}{\Gamma(a)\Gamma(c-a)} \int_0^1 e^{xt} t^{a-1}(1-t)^{c-a-1}dt, \quad c > a > 0, \tag{18.144}$$

$$U(a, c, x) = \frac{1}{\Gamma(a)} \int_0^\infty e^{-xt} t^{a-1}(1+t)^{c-a-1}dt, \quad \Re e(x) > 0, a > 0. \tag{18.145}$$

Three important techniques for deriving or verifying integral representations are as follows:

1. Transformation of generating function expansions and Rodrigues representations: The Bessel and Legendre functions provide examples of this approach.
2. Direct integration to yield a series: This direct technique is useful for a Bessel function representation (Exercise 14.1.17) and a hypergeometric integral (Exercise 18.5.7).
3. (a) Verification that the integral representation satisfies the ODE. (b) Exclusion of the other solution. (c) Verification of normalization. This is the method used in Section 14.6 to establish an integral representation of the modified Bessel function $K_\nu(z)$. It will work here to establish Eqs. (18.144) and (18.145).

Confluent Hypergeometric Representations

Special functions that can be represented in terms of confluent hypergeometric functions include the following:

1. **Bessel functions**:

$$J_\nu(x) = \frac{e^{-ix}}{\Gamma(\nu+1)}\left(\frac{x}{2}\right)^\nu M\left(\nu + \frac{1}{2}, 2\nu+1, 2ix\right), \tag{18.146}$$

whereas for the modified Bessel functions of the first kind,

$$I_\nu(x) = \frac{e^{-x}}{\Gamma(\nu+1)} \left(\frac{x}{2}\right)^\nu M\left(\nu + \frac{1}{2}, 2\nu + 1, 2x\right). \tag{18.147}$$

2. **Hermite functions**:

$$H_{2n}(x) = (-1)^n \frac{(2n)!}{n!} M\left(-n, \frac{1}{2}, x^2\right). \tag{18.148}$$

$$H_{2n+1}(x) = (-1)^n \frac{2(2n+1)!}{n!} x M\left(-n, \frac{3}{2}, x^2\right), \tag{18.149}$$

using Eq. (13.150).

3. **Laguerre functions**:

$$L_n(x) = M(-n, 1, x). \tag{18.150}$$

The constant is fixed as unity by noting Eq. (18.54) for $x = 0$. For the associated Laguerre functions,

$$L_n^m(x) = (-1)^m \frac{d^m}{dx^m} L_{n+m}(x) = \frac{(n+m)!}{n!\,m!} M(-n, m+1, x). \tag{18.151}$$

Alternate verification is obtained by comparing Eq. (18.151) with the power-series solution, Eq. (18.59). Note that in the hypergeometric form, as distinct from a Rodrigues representation, the indices n and m need not be integers, but if they are not integers, $L_n^m(x)$ will not be a polynomial.

Further Observations

There are certain advantages in expressing our special functions in terms of hypergeometric and confluent hypergeometric functions. If the general behavior of the latter functions is known, the behavior of the special functions we have investigated follows as a series of special cases. This may be useful in determining asymptotic behavior or evaluating normalization integrals. The asymptotic behavior of $M(a, c, x)$ and $U(a, c, x)$ may be conveniently obtained from integral representations of these functions, Eqs. (18.144) and (18.145). The further advantage is that the relations between the special functions are clarified. For instance, an examination of Eqs. (18.148), (18.149), and (18.151) suggests that the Laguerre and Hermite functions are related.

The confluent hypergeometric equation, Eq. (18.136), is clearly not self-adjoint. For this and other reasons it is convenient to define

$$M_{k\mu}(x) = e^{-x/2} x^{\mu+1/2} M(\mu - k + \tfrac{1}{2}, 2\mu + 1, x). \tag{18.152}$$

This new function, $M_{k\mu}(x)$, is called a Whittaker function; it satisfies the self-adjoint equation

$$M_{k\mu}''(x) + \left(-\frac{1}{4} + \frac{k}{x} + \frac{\frac{1}{4} - \mu^2}{x^2}\right) M_{k\mu}(x) = 0. \tag{18.153}$$

The corresponding second solution is

$$W_{k\mu}(x) = e^{-x/2}x^{\mu+1/2}U(\mu - k + \tfrac{1}{2}, 2\mu + 1, x). \tag{18.154}$$

Exercises

18.6.1   Verify the confluent hypergeometric representation of the error function

$$\text{erf}(x) = \frac{2x}{\pi^{1/2}} M\left(\frac{1}{2}, \frac{3}{2}, -x^2\right).$$

18.6.2   Show that the Fresnel integrals $C(x)$ and $s(x)$ of Exercise 12.6.1 may be expressed in terms of the confluent hypergeometric function as

$$C(x) + is(x) = x M\left(\frac{1}{2}, \frac{3}{2}, \frac{i\pi x^2}{2}\right).$$

18.6.3   By direct differentiation and substitution verify that

$$y = ax^{-a} \int_0^x e^{-t} t^{a-1}\, dt = ax^{-a}\gamma(a, x)$$

satisfies

$$xy'' + (a + 1 + x)y' + ay = 0.$$

18.6.4   Show that the modified Bessel function of the second kind, $K_\nu(x)$, is given by

$$K_\nu(x) = \pi^{1/2}e^{-x}(2x)^\nu U(\nu + \tfrac{1}{2}, 2\nu + 1, 2x).$$

18.6.5   Show that the cosine and sine integrals of Section 13.6 may be expressed in terms of confluent hypergeometric functions as

$$\text{Ci}(x) + i\,\text{si}(x) = -e^{ix}U(1, 1, -ix).$$

This relation is useful in numerical computation of $\text{Ci}(x)$ and $\text{si}(x)$ for large values of x.

18.6.6   Verify the confluent hypergeometric form of the Hermite polynomial $H_{2n+1}(x)$, Eq. (18.149), by showing that

(a) $H_{2n+1}(x)/x$ satisfies the confluent hypergeometric equation with $a = -n, c = 3/2$ and argument x^2,

(b) $\lim\limits_{x \to 0} \dfrac{H_{2n+1}(x)}{x} = (-1)^n \dfrac{2(2n + 1)!}{n!}.$

18.6.7   Show that the contiguous confluent hypergeometric function equation

$$(c - a)M(a - 1, c, x) + (2a - c + x)M(a, c, x) - aM(a + 1, c, x) = 0$$

leads to the associated Laguerre function recurrence relation, Eq. (18.66).

18.6.8   Verify the Kummer transformations:

(a) $M(a, c, x) = e^x M(c - a, c, -x),$

(b) $U(a, c, x) = x^{1-c} U(a - c + 1, 2 - c, x).$

18.6.9   Prove that

(a) $\dfrac{d^n}{dx^n} M(a, c, x) = \dfrac{(a)_n}{(b)_n} M(a + n, b + n, x),$

(b) $\dfrac{d^n}{dx^n} U(a, c, x) = (-1)^n (a)_n U(a + n, c + n, x).$

18.6.10   Verify the following integral representations:

(a) $M(a, c, x) = \dfrac{\Gamma(c)}{\Gamma(a)\Gamma(c - a)} \displaystyle\int_0^1 e^{xt} t^{a-1} (1 - t)^{c-a-1} dt, \ c > a > 0,$

(b) $U(a, c, x) = \dfrac{1}{\Gamma(a)} \displaystyle\int_0^\infty e^{-xt} t^{a-1} (1 + t)^{c-a-1} dt, \quad \Re(x) > 0, a > 0.$

Under what conditions can you accept $\Re(x) = 0$ in part (b)?

18.6.11   From the integral representation of $M(a, c, x)$, Exercise 18.6.10(a), show that

$$M(a, c, x) = e^x M(c - a, c, -x).$$

Hint. Replace the variable of integration t by $1 - s$ to release a factor e^x from the integral.

18.6.12   From the integral representation of $U(a, c, x)$ in Exercise 18.6.10(b), show that the exponential integral is given by

$$E_1(x) = e^{-x} U(1, 1, x).$$

Hint. Replace the variable of integration t in $E_1(x)$ by $x(1 + s)$.

18.6.13   From the integral representations of $M(a, c, x)$ and $U(a, c, x)$ in Exercise 18.6.10, develop asymptotic expansions of

(a) $M(a, c, x)$,   (b) $U(a, c, x)$.

Hint. You can use the technique that was employed with $K_\nu(z)$ in Section 14.6.

ANS.

(a) $\dfrac{\Gamma(c)}{\Gamma(a)} \dfrac{e^x}{x^{c-a}} \left\{ 1 + \dfrac{(1 - a)(c - a)}{1! \, x} + \dfrac{(1 - a)(2 - a)(c - a)(c - a + 1)}{2! \, x^2} + \cdots \right\},$

(b) $\dfrac{1}{x^a} \left\{ 1 + \dfrac{a(1 + a - c)}{1! \, (-x)} + \dfrac{a(a + 1)(1 + a - c)(2 + a - c)}{2! \, (-x)^2} + \cdots \right\}.$

18.6.14 Show that the Wronskian of the two confluent hypergeometric functions $M(a, c, x)$ and $U(a, c, x)$ is given by

$$MU' - M'U = -\frac{(c-1)!}{(a-1)!}\frac{e^x}{x^c}.$$

What happens if a is 0 or a negative integer?

18.6.15 The Coulomb wave equation (radial part of the Schrödinger equation with Coulomb potential) is

$$\frac{d^2y}{dr^2} + \left[1 - \frac{2\eta}{r} - \frac{L(L+1)}{r^2}\right]y = 0.$$

Show that a regular solution $y = F_L(\eta, r)$ is given by

$$F_L(\eta, r) = C_L(\eta)r^{L+1}e^{-ir}M(L + 1 - i\eta, 2L + 2, 2ir).$$

18.6.16 (a) Show that the radial part of the hydrogen-atom wave function, Eq. (18.81), may be written as

$$e^{-\alpha r/2}(\alpha r)^L L_{n-L-1}^{2L+1}(\alpha r) =$$

$$\frac{(n+L)!}{(n-L-1)!(2L+1)!}e^{-\alpha r/2}(\alpha r)^L M(L + 1 - n, 2L + 2, \alpha r).$$

(b) It was assumed previously that the total (kinetic + potential) energy E of the electron was negative. Rewrite the (unnormalized) radial wave function for an unbound hydrogenic electron, $E > 0$.

ANS. $e^{i\alpha r/2}(\alpha r)^L M(L + 1 - in, 2L + 2, -i\alpha r)$, outgoing wave. This representation provides a powerful alternative technique for the calculation of photoionization and recombination coefficients.

18.6.17 Evaluate

(a) $\displaystyle\int_0^\infty [M_{k\mu}(x)]^2 dx$,   (b) $\displaystyle\int_0^\infty [M_{k\mu}(x)]^2 \frac{dx}{x}$,   (c) $\displaystyle\int_0^\infty [M_{k\mu}(x)]^2 \frac{dx}{x^{1-a}}$,

where $2\mu = 0, 1, 2, \ldots,$ $k - \mu - \frac{1}{2} = 0, 1, 2, \ldots,$ $a > -2\mu - 1$.

ANS. (a) $2k(2\mu)!$, (b) $(2\mu)!$, (c) $(2k)^a(2\mu)!$.

18.7   DILOGARITHM

The **dilogarithm**, defined as

$$\text{Li}_2(z) = -\int_0^z \frac{\ln(1-t)}{t} dt \tag{18.155}$$

and its analytic continuation beyond the range of convergence of the above integral, arises in the evaluation of matrix elements in few-body problems of atomic physics and in various perturbation-theoretic contributions to quantum electrodynamics. Because of a historic lack of familiarity with this special function among physicists, many places of its occurrence have only been recognized in recent years.

Expansion and Analytic Properties

Expanding the logarithm in Eq. (18.155), using the series in Eq. (1.97), we directly obtain the series expansion

$$\text{Li}_2(z) = \sum_{n=1}^{\infty} \frac{z^n}{n^2}. \tag{18.156}$$

Note that we have inserted the logarithm without an additional multiple of $2\pi i$, thereby obtaining the branch of Li_2 that is nonsingular at $z = 0$.

Further applications of the operator that converts $-\ln(1 - z)$ into $\text{Li}_2(z)$ produce **polylogarithms**, which also occur in physics, albeit less frequently:

$$\text{Li}_p(z) = \int_0^z \text{Li}_{p-1}(t) \frac{dt}{t} = \sum_{n=1}^{\infty} \frac{z^n}{n^p} \quad p = 3, \, 4, \dots. \tag{18.157}$$

However, in this text we limit consideration to the first member of this sequence, Li_2.

The series expansion of Li_2, Eq. (18.156), has circle of convergence $|z| = 1$, with convergence for all z on this circle. The singularity limiting the radius of convergence is not apparent from the form of the expansion, but, looking at Eq. (18.155), we identify it as a branch point located at $z = 1$. It is customary to draw a branch cut from $z = 1$ to $z = \infty$ along, and just below the positive real axis, and to define the principal value of Li_2 as that which corresponds to Eq. (18.156) and its analytic continuation.

From the form of Eq. (18.156), it is apparent that for real z in the interval $-1 \leq z \leq +1$, $\text{Li}_2(z)$ will also be real. For $z > 1$, we see from Eq. (18.155) that for part of the range of integration, the factor $\ln(1 - t)$ will necessarily be complex, with the result that $\text{Li}_2(z)$ will no longer be real, even for real z. However, there is no similar problem for negative real z, as the principal value of $\ln(1 - t)$ remains real for all negative real values of t.

Analyzing further the behavior of the integral in Eq. (18.155), we note that if we reach a point z by carrying out the integral, along a path (in t) that goes first from $t = 0$ to just above the branch point at $t = 1$, and then in a straight line to z, we will for the last segment of the path alter the argument of $1 - t$ by some amount θ in the clockwise direction, thereby adding an amount $-i\theta$ to the numerator of the integrand. See Fig. 18.8.

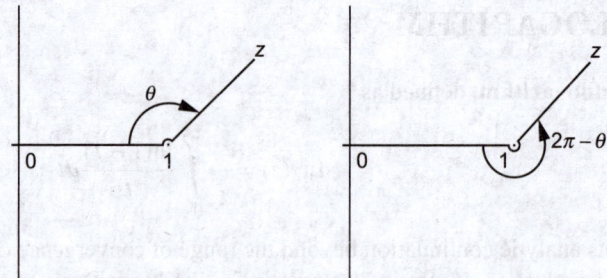

FIGURE 18.8   Contours for integral representation of dilogarithm.

This addition to the numerator means that the evaluation of $\mathrm{Li}_2(z)$ will have the form

$$\mathrm{Li}_2(z) = -\int_0^1 \frac{\ln(1-t)}{t}\, dt - \int_1^z \frac{\ln(|1-t|)}{t}\, dt + i\theta \int_1^z \frac{dt}{t}$$

$$= \mathrm{Li}_2(1) - \int_1^z \frac{\ln(|1-t|)}{t}\, dt + i\theta \ln z \quad \text{(path above } z=1\text{)}. \qquad (18.158)$$

If we repeat the above analysis to reach the same point z by a path (in t) that passes around $z = 1$ below the real axis, the argument of $1 - t$ will be changed by an amount $2\pi - \theta$ in the counterclockwise direction, and

$$\mathrm{Li}_2(z) = \mathrm{Li}_2(1) - \int_1^z \frac{\ln(|1-t|)}{t}\, dt - i(2\pi - \theta) \ln z \quad \text{(path below } z=1\text{)}. \qquad (18.159)$$

Comparing Eqs. (18.158) and (18.159), we see that the values of $\mathrm{Li}_2(z)$, for the same z, but on these two different branches the values, will differ by an amount $2\pi i \ln z$. If z is complex, the difference will affect both the real and imaginary parts of $\mathrm{Li}_2(z)$, in ways more complicated than either changing the phase or adding a multiple of π to the imaginary part. When working with the dilogarithm, it is therefore essential to make a careful determination of the branch on which it is to be evaluated. In fact, whenever possible formulas involving the dilogarithm and (because of the context) known to be real-valued should be manipulated (using formulas such as those in the next subsection) to cause each dilogarithm in the formula to be for a value of z that is real and with $z < 1$.

Properties and Special Values

From Eq. (18.156), we see that $\mathrm{Li}_2(0) = 0$. Setting $z = 1$, we note that we get the series for $\zeta(2)$, so $\mathrm{Li}_2(1) = \zeta(2) = \pi^2/6$. We also have $\mathrm{Li}_2(-1) = -\eta(2)$, where $\eta(2)$ is the Dirichlet series in Eq. (12.62), so $\mathrm{Li}_2(-1) = -\pi^2/12$.

The dilogarithm has a derivative that follows directly from Eq. (18.155),

$$\frac{d\,\text{Li}_2(z)}{dz} = -\frac{\ln(1-z)}{z}, \tag{18.160}$$

and possesses several functional relations enabling an easy analytic continuation beyond the convergence range of Eq. (18.156). Some of these are the following:

$$\text{Li}_2(z) + \text{Li}_2(1-z) = \frac{\pi^2}{6} - \ln z \ln(1-z) \tag{18.161}$$

$$\text{Li}_2(z) + \text{Li}_2(z^{-1}) = -\frac{\pi^2}{6} - \frac{1}{2}\ln^2(-z) \tag{18.162}$$

$$\text{Li}_2(z) + \text{Li}_2\left(\frac{z}{z-1}\right) = -\frac{1}{2}\ln^2(1-z). \tag{18.163}$$

These relationships are most easily established by showing that the derivatives of both sides of the equations are equal and that the values of the two sides correspond for some convenient value of z. These functional relations enable the determination of $\text{Li}_2(z)$ for all real z from values on the real line in the range $|z| \leq \frac{1}{2}$, for which the series in Eq. (18.155) converges rapidly.

From the functional relations it is possible to identify a few more specific values of z for which the principal value of $\text{Li}_2(z)$ can be expressed in terms of elementary functions. For example, $\text{Li}_2(1/2) = -\frac{1}{2}\ln^2(2) + \pi^2/12$. But for most z, closed expressions are not available.

Example 18.7.1   CHECK USEFULNESS OF FORMULA

The integral

$$I = \frac{1}{8\pi^2} \iint d^3r_1 d^3r_2 \, \frac{e^{-\alpha r_1 - \beta r_2 - \gamma r_{12}}}{r_1^2 r_2^2 r_{12}}$$

arises in computations of the electronic structure of the He atom. Here $\mathbf{r}_i$ are the positions of two electrons relative to the nucleus (which is at the origin of our coordinate system), the integration is over the full three-dimensional spaces of $\mathbf{r}_1$ and $\mathbf{r}_2$, $r_i = |\mathbf{r}_i|$, and $r_{12} = |\mathbf{r}_1 - \mathbf{r}_2|$.

This integral is found to have the value

$$I = \frac{1}{\gamma}\left[\frac{\pi^2}{6} + \text{Li}_2\left(\frac{\gamma - \beta}{\alpha + \gamma}\right) + \text{Li}_2\left(\frac{\gamma - \alpha}{\beta + \gamma}\right) + \frac{1}{2}\ln^2\left(\frac{\alpha + \gamma}{\beta + \gamma}\right)\right].$$

We now ask: Are its individual terms real?

We note from the definition of I that it will be convergent only if $\alpha + \beta$, $\alpha + \gamma$, and $\beta + \gamma$ are all positive. If that is not the case, in the portion of the space in which some particle is far from the other two, the overall exponential will increase without limit. Looking now at the formula for the integral, we see immediately that the $\ln^2$ term will be real, as its argument is the quotient of two positive numbers. The first Li_2 term can be written

$$\text{Li}_2\left(\frac{\gamma - \beta}{\alpha + \gamma}\right) = \text{Li}_2\left(1 - \frac{\alpha + \beta}{\alpha + \gamma}\right),$$

showing that the argument of Li_2 is real and less than $+1$, meaning that this Li_2 will evaluate to a real result. Similar observations apply to the second instance of Li_2. We conclude that our formula is in a proper form for unambiguous computation using principal values of its multivalued functions. ■

Exercises

18.7.1 Prove that the expansion of $\text{Li}_2(z)$, Eq. (18.156), converges everywhere on the circle $|z| = 1$.

18.7.2 Use the functional relations, Eqs. (18.161) to (18.163), to find the principal value of $\text{Li}_2(1/2)$.

18.7.3 Find all the multiple values of $\text{Li}_2(1/2)$.

18.7.4 Explain why Eq. (18.161) gives the expected result for $z = 0$ when on the principal branch of the dilogarithm.

18.7.5 Show that

$$\text{Li}_2\left(\frac{1 + z^{-1}}{2}\right) = -\text{Li}_2\left(\frac{1 + z}{1 - z}\right) - \frac{1}{2}\ln^2\left(\frac{1 - z^{-1}}{2}\right).$$

18.7.6 The following integral arises in the computation of the electronic energy of the Li atom using a correlated wave function (one that explicitly includes the electron-electron distances as well as the distances of electrons from the nucleus):

$$I = \iiint d^3r_1 d^3r_2 d^3r_3 \, \frac{e^{-\alpha_1 r_1 - \alpha_2 r_2 - \alpha_3 r_3}}{r_1 r_2 r_3 r_{12} r_{13} r_{23}},$$

where $r_i = |\mathbf{r}_i|$, $r_{ij} = |\mathbf{r}_i - \mathbf{r}_j|$, and the integrations are over the entire three-dimensional space of each $\mathbf{r}_i$. For convergence of I, we require all $\alpha_j > 0$, but there are no restrictions on their relative magnitudes.

In terms of the auxiliary quantities

$$\zeta_1 = \frac{\alpha_1}{\alpha_2 + \alpha_3}, \quad \zeta_2 = \frac{\alpha_2}{\alpha_1 + \alpha_3}, \quad \zeta_3 = \frac{\alpha_3}{\alpha_1 + \alpha_2},$$

this integral has the value

$$I = \frac{32\pi^3}{\alpha_1 \alpha_2 \alpha_3}\left(-\frac{\pi^2}{2} + \sum_{j=1}^{3}\left[\text{Li}_2(\zeta_j) - \text{Li}_2(-\zeta_j) + \ln \zeta_j \ln\left(\frac{1 - \zeta_j}{1 + \zeta_j}\right)\right]\right)$$

Rearrange I to a form (first found by Remiddi[11]), in which all terms in the final expression are guaranteed to evaluate to real quantities and can be evaluated as principal values.

18.8 ELLIPTIC INTEGRALS

Elliptic integrals occasionally arise in physical problems and therefore it is worthwhile to summarize their definitions and properties. Before the advent of computers, it was also important for physicists and engineers to be familiar with methods for hand computation of elliptic integrals, but that need has diminished with time and expansion methods for these functions will not be emphasized here. We do, however, illustrate problems in which elliptic integrals arise; the following example is a case in point.

Example 18.8.1   PERIOD OF A SIMPLE PENDULUM

For small-amplitude oscillations, a pendulum (Fig. 18.9) has simple harmonic motion with a period $T = 2\pi(l/g)^{1/2}$. But for a maximum amplitude θ_M large enough that $\sin\theta_M$ cannot be approximated by θ_M, a direct application of Newton's second law of motion and solution of the resulting ODE becomes difficult. In that situation a good way to proceed is to write the equation for conservation of energy. Setting the zero of potential energy at the point from which the pendulum is suspended, the potential energy of a pendulum of mass m and length l at angle θ is $-mgl\cos\theta$, and its total energy (the potential energy at angle θ_M) is $-mgl\cos\theta_M$. The pendulum has kinetic energy $ml^2(d\theta/dt)^2/2$, so energy conservation requires

$$\frac{1}{2}ml^2\left(\frac{d\theta}{dt}\right)^2 - mgl\cos\theta = -mgl\cos\theta_M. \tag{18.164}$$

Solving for $d\theta/dt$ we obtain

$$\frac{d\theta}{dt} = \pm\left(\frac{2g}{l}\right)^{1/2}(\cos\theta - \cos\theta_M)^{1/2}, \tag{18.165}$$

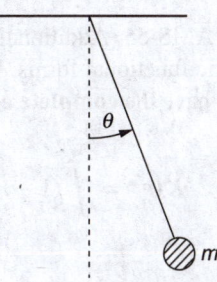

FIGURE 18.9   Simple pendulum.

[11]E. Remiddi, Analytic value of the atomic three-electron correlation integral with Slater wave functions. *Phys. Rev. A* **44**: 5492 (1991).

with the mass m canceling out. At $t = 0$ we choose as initial conditions $\theta = 0$ and $d\theta/dt > 0$. An integration from $\theta = 0$ to $\theta = \theta_M$ yields

$$\int_0^{\theta_M} (\cos\theta - \cos\theta_M)^{-1/2} d\theta = \left(\frac{2g}{l}\right)^{1/2} \int_0^t dt = \left(\frac{2g}{l}\right)^{1/2} t. \tag{18.166}$$

This is $\frac{1}{4}$ of a cycle, and therefore the time t is $\frac{1}{4}$ of the period T. We note that $\theta \leq \theta_M$, and with a bit of clairvoyance we try the half-angle substitution

$$\sin\left(\frac{\theta}{2}\right) = \sin\left(\frac{\theta_M}{2}\right) \sin\varphi. \tag{18.167}$$

With this, Eq. (18.166) becomes

$$T = 4\left(\frac{l}{g}\right)^{1/2} \int_0^{\pi/2} \left(1 - \sin^2\left(\frac{\theta_M}{2}\right) \sin^2\varphi\right)^{-1/2} d\varphi. \tag{18.168}$$

The integral in Eq. (18.168) does not reduce to an elementary function; in fact, it is an **elliptic integral** of a standard type. Further examples of elliptic integrals in physical problems can be found in the exercises. ∎

Definitions

The **elliptic integral of the first kind** is defined as

$$F(\varphi\backslash\alpha) = \int_0^\varphi (1 - \sin^2\alpha \sin^2\theta)^{-1/2} d\theta, \tag{18.169}$$

or

$$F(x|m) = \int_0^x \left[(1 - t^2)(1 - mt^2)\right]^{-1/2} dt, \quad 0 \leq m < 1. \tag{18.170}$$

This is the notation of AMS-55 (Additional Readings). Note the use of the separators $\backslash$ and $|$ to identify the specific functional forms. When the upper limit in these integrals is set to $\varphi = \pi/2$ or $x = 1$, we have the **complete elliptic integral of the first kind**,

$$K(m) = \int_0^{\pi/2} (1 - m\sin^2\theta)^{-1/2} d\theta$$

$$= \int_0^1 \left[(1 - t^2)(1 - mt^2)\right]^{-1/2} dt, \tag{18.171}$$

with $m = \sin^2\alpha, 0 \leq m < 1$.

The **elliptic integral of the second kind** is defined by

$$E(\varphi \backslash \alpha) = \int_0^\varphi (1 - \sin^2 \alpha \sin^2 \theta)^{1/2} d\theta \tag{18.172}$$

or

$$E(x|m) = \int_0^x \left(\frac{1 - mt^2}{1 - t^2} \right)^{1/2} dt, \quad 0 \le m \le 1. \tag{18.173}$$

Again, for the case $\varphi = \pi/2$, $x = 1$, we have the **complete elliptic integral of the second kind**:

$$E(m) = \int_0^{\pi/2} (1 - m \sin^2 \theta)^{1/2} d\theta$$

$$\tag{18.174}$$

$$= \int_0^1 \left(\frac{1 - mt^2}{1 - t^2} \right)^{1/2} dt, \quad 0 \le m \le 1.$$

Series Expansions

For our range $0 \le m < 1$, the denominator of $K(m)$ may be expanded by the binomial series in Eq. (1.74):

$$(1 - m \sin^2 \theta)^{-1/2} = \sum_{n=0}^\infty \frac{(2n - 1)!!}{(2n)!!} m^n \sin^{2n} \theta,$$

after which the resulting series is then integrated term by term. The integrals of the individual terms are beta functions (see Exercise 13.3.8), and we get

$$K(m) = \frac{\pi}{2} \left\{ 1 + \sum_{n=1}^\infty \left[\frac{(2n - 1)!!}{(2n)!!} \right]^2 m^n \right\}. \tag{18.175}$$

Similarly (see Exercise 18.8.2),

$$E(m) = \frac{\pi}{2} \left\{ 1 - \sum_{n=1}^\infty \left[\frac{(2n - 1)!!}{(2n)!!} \right]^2 \frac{m^n}{2n - 1} \right\}. \tag{18.176}$$

These series can be identified as hypergeometric functions. Comparing with the general definitions in Section 18.5, we have

$$K(m) = \frac{\pi}{2} {}_2F_1(\tfrac{1}{2}, \tfrac{1}{2}; 1; m),$$

$$\tag{18.177}$$

$$E(m) = \frac{\pi}{2} {}_2F_1(-\tfrac{1}{2}, \tfrac{1}{2}; 1; m).$$

The complete elliptic integrals are plotted in Fig. 18.10.

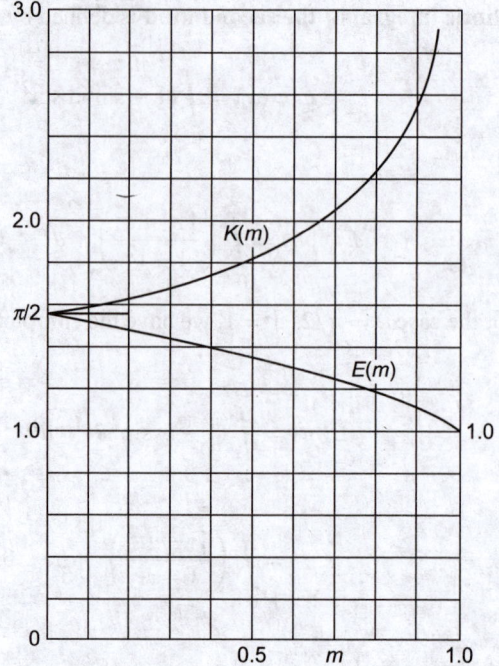

FIGURE 18.10   Complete elliptic integrals, $K(m)$ and $E(m)$.

Limiting Values

From the series Eqs. (18.175) and (18.176), or from the defining integrals,

$$\lim_{m \to 0} K(m) = \frac{\pi}{2}, \quad \lim_{m \to 0} E(m) = \frac{\pi}{2}. \tag{18.178}$$

For $m \to 1$ the series expansions are of little use. However, the integrals yield

$$\lim_{m \to 1} K(m) = \infty, \quad \lim_{m \to 1} E(m) = 1. \tag{18.179}$$

The divergence in $K(m)$ is logarithmic.

Elliptic integrals have been used extensively in the past for evaluating integrals. For instance, general integrals of the form

$$I = \int_0^x R\left(t, \sqrt{a_4 t^4 + a_3 t^3 + a_2 t^2 + a_1 t^1 + a_0}\right) dt,$$

where R is a rational function of its arguments, may be expressed in terms of elliptic integrals. Jahnke and Emde (Additional Readings) give pages of such transformations. With computers available for direct numerical evaluation, interest in these elliptic integral techniques has declined. A more extensive account of elliptic functions, integrals, and the related Jacobi theta functions can be found in Whittaker and Watson's treatise. Many formulas and tables of elliptic integrals are in AMS-55 and even more formulas are in Olver *et al.* (all of these sources are in the Additional Readings).

Exercises

18.8.1 The ellipse $x^2/a^2 + y^2/b^2 = 1$ may be represented parametrically by $x = a \sin \theta$, $y = b \cos \theta$. Show that the length of arc within the first quadrant is

$$a \int_0^{\pi/2} (1 - m \sin^2 \theta)^{1/2} d\theta = a E(m).$$

Here $0 \le m = (a^2 - b^2)/a^2 \le 1$.

18.8.2 Derive the series expansion

$$E(m) = \frac{\pi}{2} \left\{ 1 - \left(\frac{1}{2} \right)^2 \frac{m}{1} - \left(\frac{1 \cdot 3}{2 \cdot 4} \right)^2 \frac{m^2}{3} - \cdots \right\}.$$

18.8.3 Show that

$$\lim_{m \to 0} \frac{(K - E)}{m} = \frac{\pi}{4}.$$

18.8.4 A circular loop of wire in the xy-plane, as shown in Fig. 18.11, carries a current I. Given that the vector potential is

$$A_\varphi(\rho, \varphi, z) = \frac{a \mu_0 I}{2\pi} \int_0^\pi \frac{\cos \alpha \, d\alpha}{(a^2 + \rho^2 + z^2 - 2a\rho \cos \alpha)^{1/2}},$$

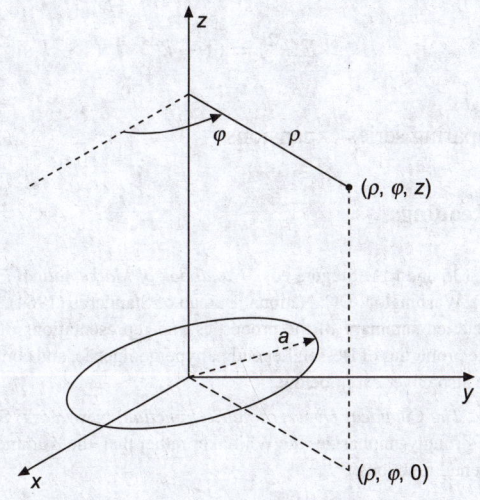

FIGURE 18.11 Circular wire loop.

show that

$$A_\varphi(\rho, \varphi, z) = \frac{\mu_0 I}{\pi k} \left(\frac{a}{\rho}\right)^{1/2} \left[\left(1 - \frac{k^2}{2}\right) K(k^2) - E(k^2)\right],$$

where

$$k^2 = \frac{4a\rho}{(a + \rho)^2 + z^2}.$$

Note. For extension of this exercise to **B**, see Smythe.[12]

18.8.5   An analysis of the magnetic vector potential of a circular current loop leads to the expression

$$f(k^2) = k^{-2}\left[(2 - k^2)K(k^2) - 2E(k^2)\right],$$

where $K(k^2)$ and $E(k^2)$ are the complete elliptic integrals of the first and second kinds. Show that for $k^2 \ll 1$ ($r \gg$ radius of loop)

$$f(k^2) \approx \frac{\pi k^2}{16}.$$

18.8.6   Show that

(a) $\dfrac{dE(k^2)}{dk} = \dfrac{1}{k}(E - K),$

(b) $\dfrac{dK(k^2)}{dk} = \dfrac{E}{k(1 - k^2)} - \dfrac{K}{k}.$

Hint. For part (b) show that

$$E(k^2) = (1 - k^2) \int_0^{\pi/2} (1 - k \sin^2 \theta)^{-3/2} d\theta$$

by comparing series expansions.

Additional Readings

Abramowitz, M., and I. A. Stegun, eds., *Handbook of Mathematical Functions*, Applied Mathematics Series-55 (AMS-55). Washington, DC: National Bureau of Standards (1964), paperback edition, Dover (1974). Chapter 22 is a detailed summary of the properties and representations of orthogonal polynomials. Other chapters summarize properties of Bessel, Legendre, hypergeometric, and confluent hypergeometric functions and much more. See also Olver *et al.*, below.

Buchholz, H., *The Confluent Hypergeometric Function*. New York: Springer Verlag (1953), translated (1969). Buchholz strongly emphasizes the Whittaker rather than the Kummer forms. Applications to a variety of other transcendental functions.

---

[12] W. R. Smythe, *Static and Dynamic Electricity*, 3rd ed. New York: McGraw-Hill (1969), p. 270.

Erdelyi, A., W. Magnus, F. Oberhettinger, and F. G. Tricomi, *Higher Transcendental Functions*, 3 vols. New York: McGraw-Hill (1953), reprinted, Krieger (1981). A detailed, almost exhaustive listing of the properties of the special functions of mathematical physics.

Fox, L., and I. B. Parker, *Chebyshev Polynomials in Numerical Analysis*. Oxford: Oxford University Press (1968). A detailed, thorough, but very readable account of Chebyshev polynomials and their applications in numerical analysis.

Gradshteyn, I. S., and I. M. Ryzhik, *Table of Integrals, Series and Products* (A. Jeffrey and D. Zwillinger, eds.), 7th ed. New York: Academic Press (2007).

Jahnke, E., and F. Emde, *Tables of Functions with Formulae and Curves*. Leipzig: Teubner (1933), Dover (1945).

Jahnke, E., F. Emde, and F. Lösch, *Tables of Higher Functions*, 6th ed. New York: McGraw-Hill (1960). An enlarged update of the work by Jahnke and Emde.

Lebedev, N. N., *Special Functions and Their Applications* (translated by R. A. Silverman). Englewood Cliffs, NJ: Prentice-Hall (1965), paperback, Dover (1972).

Luke, Y. L., *The Special Functions and Their Approximations*, 2 vols. New York: Academic Press (1969). Volume 1 is a thorough theoretical treatment of gamma functions, hypergeometric functions, confluent hypergeometric functions, and related functions. Volume 2 develops approximations and other techniques for numerical work.

Luke, Y. L., *Mathematical Functions and Their Approximations*. New York: Academic Press (1975). This is an updated supplement to *Handbook of Mathematical Functions with Formulas, Graphs and Mathematical Tables* (AMS-55).

Magnus, W., F. Oberhettinger, and R. P. Soni, *Formulas and Theorems for the Special Functions of Mathematical Physics*. New York: Springer (1966). An excellent summary of just what the title says.

Olver, F. W. J., D. W. Lozier, R. F. Boisvert, and C. W. Clark, eds., *NIST Handbook of Mathematical Functions*. Cambridge: Cambridge University Press (2010). Update of AMS-55 (Abramowitz and Stegun, above), but links to computer programs are provided instead of tables of data.

Rainville, E. D., *Special Functions*. New York: Macmillan (1960), reprinted, Chelsea (1971). This book is a coherent, comprehensive account of almost all the special functions of mathematical physics that the reader is likely to encounter.

Sansone, G., *Orthogonal Functions* (translated by A. H. Diamond). New York: Interscience (1959), reprinted, Dover (1991).

Slater, L. J., *Confluent Hypergeometric Functions*. Cambridge: Cambridge University Press (1960). This is a clear and detailed development of the properties of the confluent hypergeometric functions and of relations of the confluent hypergeometric equation to other ODEs of mathematical physics.

Sneddon, I. N., *Special Functions of Mathematical Physics and Chemistry*, 3rd ed. New York: Longman (1980).

Whittaker, E. T., and G. N. Watson, *A Course of Modern Analysis*. Cambridge: Cambridge University Press, reprinted (1997). The classic text on special functions and real and complex analysis.

CHAPTER 19

FOURIER SERIES

Periodic phenomena involving waves, rotating machines (harmonic motion), or other repetitive driving forces are described by periodic functions. Fourier series are a basic tool for solving ordinary differential equations (ODEs) and partial differential equations (PDEs) with periodic boundary conditions. Fourier integrals for nonperiodic phenomena are developed in Chapter 20. The common name for the field is **Fourier analysis**.

19.1 GENERAL PROPERTIES

A Fourier series is defined as an expansion of a function or representation of a function in a series of sines and cosines, such as

$$f(x) = \frac{a_0}{2} + \sum_{n=1}^{\infty} a_n \cos nx + \sum_{n=1}^{\infty} b_n \sin nx. \tag{19.1}$$

The coefficients a_0, a_n, and b_n are related to $f(x)$ by definite integrals:

$$a_n = \frac{1}{\pi} \int_0^{2\pi} f(s) \cos ns \, ds, \quad n = 0, 1, 2, \ldots, \tag{19.2}$$

$$b_n = \frac{1}{\pi} \int_0^{2\pi} f(s) \sin ns \, ds, \quad n = 1, 2, \ldots, \tag{19.3}$$

which are subject to the requirement that the integrals exist. Note that a_0 is singled out for special treatment by the inclusion of the factor $\frac{1}{2}$. This is done so that Eq. (19.2) will apply to all a_n, $n = 0$ as well as $n > 0$.

The conditions imposed on $f(x)$ to make Eq. (19.1) valid are that $f(x)$ have only a finite number of finite discontinuities and only a finite number of extreme values (maxima and minima) in the interval $[0, 2\pi]$.[1] Functions satisfying these conditions may be

---

[1] These conditions are **sufficient** but not **necessary**.

935

called **piecewise regular**. The conditions themselves are known as the **Dirichlet conditions**. Although there are some functions that do not obey these conditions, they can be considered pathological for purposes of Fourier expansions. In the vast majority of physical problems involving a Fourier series, the Dirichlet conditions will be satisfied.

Expressing $\cos nx$ and $\sin nx$ in exponential form, we may rewrite Eq. (19.1) as

$$f(x) = \sum_{n=-\infty}^{\infty} c_n e^{inx}, \tag{19.4}$$

in which

$$c_n = \frac{1}{2}(a_n - ib_n), \quad c_{-n} = \frac{1}{2}(a_n + ib_n), \quad n > 0, \tag{19.5}$$

and

$$c_0 = \frac{1}{2} a_0. \tag{19.6}$$

Sturm-Liouville Theory

The ODE

$$-y''(x) = \lambda y(x)$$

on the interval $[0, 2\pi]$ with boundary conditions $y(0) = y(2\pi)$, $y'(0) = y'(2\pi)$ is a Sturm-Liouville problem, and these boundary conditions make it Hermitian. Therefore its eigenfunctions, either $\cos nx$ ($n = 0, 1, \ldots$) and $\sin nx$ ($n = 1, 2, \ldots$), or $\exp(inx)$ ($n = \ldots, -1, 0, 1, \ldots$), form a complete set, with eigenfunctions of different eigenvalues orthogonal. Since the eigenfunctions have respective values n^2, those of different $|n|$ will automatically be orthogonal, while those of the same $|n|$ can be orthogonalized if necessary. Defining the scalar product for this problem as

$$\langle f|g \rangle = \int_{-0}^{2\pi} f^*(x) g(x)\, dx,$$

it is easy to check that $\langle e^{inx} | e^{-inx} \rangle = 0$ for $n \neq 0$, and if we write $\cos nx$ and $\sin nx$ as complex exponentials, it is also easy to see that $\langle \sin nx | \cos nx \rangle = 0$. To make the eigenfunctions normalized, a simple approach is to note that the average value of $\sin^2 nx$ or $\cos^2 nx$ over an integer number of oscillations is $1/2$ (again for $n \neq 0$), so

$$\int_0^{2\pi} \sin^2 nx\, dx = \int_0^{2\pi} \cos^2 nx\, dx = \pi \quad (n \neq 0),$$

and $\langle e^{inx} | e^{inx} \rangle = 2\pi$.

The relationships identified above indicate that the eigenfunctions $\varphi_n = e^{inx}/\sqrt{2\pi}$, ($n = \ldots, -1, 0, 1, \ldots$) form an orthonormal set, as do

$$\varphi_0 = \frac{1}{\sqrt{2\pi}}, \quad \varphi_n = \frac{\cos nx}{\sqrt{\pi}}, \quad \varphi_{-n} = \frac{\sin nx}{\sqrt{\pi}}, \quad (n = 1, 2, \ldots),$$

so expansions in these functions have the forms given in Eqs. (19.1) to (19.3) or Eqs. (19.4) to (19.6). Since we know that the eigenfunctions of a Sturm-Liouville operator form a complete set, we know that our Fourier-series expansions of L^2 functions will at least converge in the mean.

Discontinuous Functions

There are significant differences between the behavior of Fourier- and power-series expansions. A power series is essentially an expansion about a point, using only information from that point about the function to be expanded (including, of course, the values of its derivatives). We already know that such expansions only converge within a radius of convergence defined by the position of the nearest singularity. However, a Fourier series (or any expansion in orthogonal functions) uses information from the entire expansion interval, and therefore can describe functions that have "nonpathological" singularities within that interval. However, we also know that the representation of a function by an orthogonal expansion is only guaranteed to converge **in the mean**. This feature comes into play for the expansion of functions with discontinuities, where there is no unique value to which the expansion must converge. However, for Fourier series, it can be shown that if a function $f(x)$ satisfying the Dirichlet conditions is discontinuous at a point x_0, its Fourier series evaluated at that point will be the arithmetic average of the limits of the left and right approaches:

$$f_{\text{Fourier series}}(x_0) = \lim_{\varepsilon \to 0} \left[\frac{f(x_0 + \varepsilon) + f(x_0 - \varepsilon)}{2} \right]. \tag{19.7}$$

For proof of Eq. (19.7), see Jeffreys and Jeffreys or Carslaw (Additional Readings). It can also be shown that if the function to be expanded is continuous but has a finite discontinuity in its first derivative, its Fourier series will then exhibit uniform convergence (see Churchill, Additional Readings). These features make Fourier expansions useful for functions with a variety of types of discontinuities.

Example 19.1.1   SAWTOOTH WAVE

An idea of the convergence of a Fourier series and the error in using only a finite number of terms in the series may be obtained by considering the expansion of

$$f(x) = \begin{cases} x, & 0 \le x < \pi, \\ x - 2\pi, & \pi < x \le 2\pi. \end{cases} \tag{19.8}$$

This is a sawtooth wave form, as shown in Fig. 19.1. Using Eqs. (19.2) and (19.3), we find the expansion to be

$$f(x) = 2 \left[\sin x - \frac{\sin 2x}{2} + \frac{\sin 3x}{3} - \cdots + (-1)^{n+1} \frac{\sin nx}{n} + \cdots \right]. \tag{19.9}$$

Figure 19.2 shows $f(x)$ for $0 \le x < 2\pi$ for the sum of 4, 6, and 10 terms of the series. Three features deserve comment.

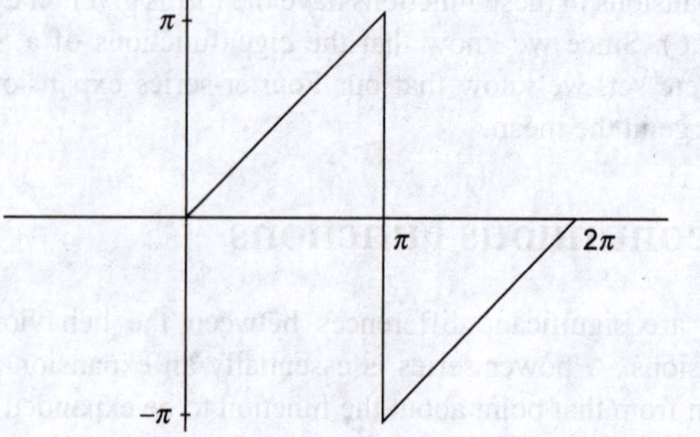

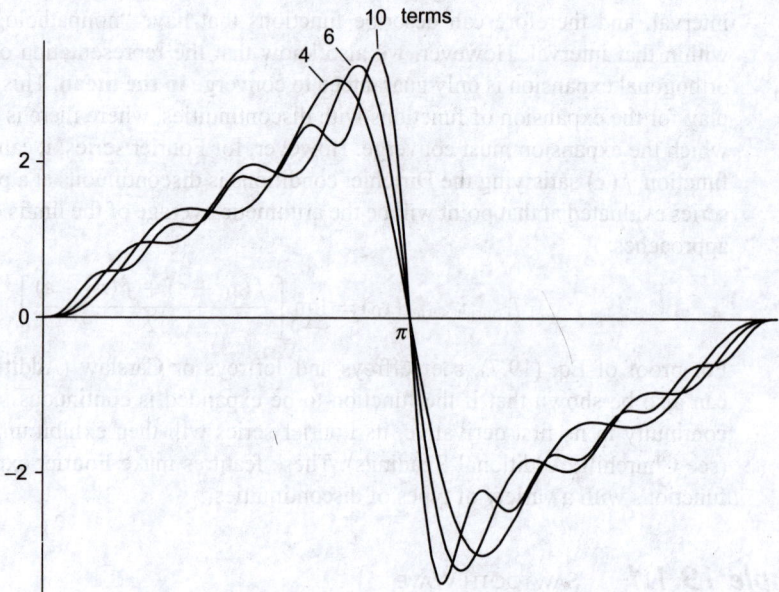

FIGURE 19.1   Sawtooth wave form.

FIGURE 19.2   Expansion of sawtooth wave form, range $[0, 2\pi]$.

1. There is a steady increase in the accuracy of the representation as the number of terms included is increased.
2. At $x = \pi$, where $f(x)$ changes discontinuously from $+\pi$ to $-\pi$, all the curves pass through the average of these two values, namely $f(\pi) = 0$.
3. In the vicinity of the discontinuity at $x = \pi$, there is an overshoot that persists and shows no sign of diminishing.

As a matter of incidental interest, setting $x = \pi/2$ in Eq. (19.9) leads to

$$f\left(\frac{\pi}{2}\right) = \frac{\pi}{2} = 2\left[1 - 0 - \frac{1}{3} - 0 + \frac{1}{5} - 0 - \frac{1}{7} + \cdots\right],$$

thereby yielding an alternate derivation of Leibniz's formula for $\pi/4$, which was obtained by another method in Exercise 1.3.2.   ∎

Periodic Functions

Fourier series are used extensively to represent periodic functions, especially wave forms for signal processing. The form of the series is inherently periodic; the expansions in Eqs. (19.1) and (19.4) are periodic with period 2π, with $\sin nx$, $\cos nx$, and $\exp(inx)$, each completing n cycles of oscillation in that interval. Thus, while the coefficients in a Fourier expansion are determined from an interval of length 2π, the expansion itself (if the function involved is actually periodic) applies for an indefinite range of x. The periodicity also means that the interval used for determining the coefficients need not be $[0, 2\pi]$ but may be any other interval of that length. Often one encounters situations in which the formulas in Eqs. (19.2) and (19.3) are changed so that their integrations run between $-\pi$ and π. In fact, it would have been natural to have restated Example 19.1.1 as dealing with $f(x) = x$, for $-\pi < x < \pi$. This of course does not remove the discontinuity or change the form of the Fourier series. The discontinuity has simply been moved to the ends of the interval in x.

In actual situations, the natural interval for a Fourier expansion will be the wavelength of our wave form, so it may make sense to redefine our Fourier series so that Eq. (19.1) becomes

$$f(x) = \frac{a_0}{2} + \sum_{n=1}^{\infty} a_n \cos \frac{n\pi x}{L} + \sum_{n=1}^{\infty} b_n \sin \frac{n\pi x}{L}, \tag{19.10}$$

with

$$a_n = \frac{1}{L} \int_{-L}^{L} f(s) \cos \frac{n\pi s}{L} \, ds, \quad n = 0, 1, 2, \ldots, \tag{19.11}$$

$$b_n = \frac{1}{L} \int_{-L}^{L} f(s) \sin \frac{n\pi s}{L} \, ds, \quad n = 1, 2, \ldots. \tag{19.12}$$

In many problems the x dependence of a Fourier expansion describes the spatial dependence of a wave distribution that is moving (say, toward $+x$) with **phase velocity** v. This means that in place of x we need to write $x - vt$, and this substitution carries the implicit assumption that the wave form retains the same shape as it moves forward.[2] The individual terms of the Fourier expansion can now be given an interesting interpretation. Taking as an example the term

$$\cos\left[\frac{n\pi}{L}(x - vt)\right],$$

---

[2] For waves in physical media, this assumption is by no means always true, as it depends on the time-dependent response properties of the medium.

we note that it describes a contribution of wavelength $2L/n$ (when x increases this much at constant t, the argument of the cosine function increases by 2π). We also note that the period of the oscillation (the change in t at constant x for one cycle of the cosine function) is $T = 2L/nv$, corresponding to the oscillation frequency $v = nv/2L$. If we call the frequency for $n = 1$ the **fundamental frequency** and denote it $v_0 = v/2L$, we identify the terms for each $n > 1$ in the Fourier series as describing overtones, or **harmonics** of the fundamental frequency, with individual frequencies nv_0.

A typical problem for which Fourier analysis is suitable is one in which a particle undergoing oscillatory motion is subject to a periodic driving force. If the problem is described by a linear ODE, we may make a Fourier expansion of the driving force and solve for each harmonic individually. This makes the Fourier expansion a practical tool as well as a nice analytical device. We stress, however, that its utility depends crucially on the linearity of our problem; in nonlinear problems an overall solution is not a superposition of component solutions.

As suggested earlier, we have proceeded on the assumption that v, the phase velocity, is the same for all terms of the Fourier series. We now see that this assumption corresponds to the notion that the medium supporting the wave motion can respond equally well to forces at all frequencies. If, for example, the medium consists of particles too massive to respond quickly at high frequency, those components of the wave form will become attenuated and damped out of a propagating wave. Conversely, if the system contains components that resonate at certain frequencies, the response at those frequencies will be enhanced. Fourier expansions give physicists (and engineers) a powerful tool for analyzing wave forms and for designing media (e.g., circuits) that yield desired behaviors.

One question that is sometimes raised is: "Were the harmonics there all along, or were they created by our Fourier analysis?" One answer compares the functional resolution into harmonics with the resolution of a vector into rectangular components. The components may have been present, in the sense that they may be isolated and observed, but the resolution is certainly not unique. Hence many authors prefer to say that the harmonics were created by our choice of expansion. Other expansions in other sets of orthogonal functions would produce a different decomposition. For further discussion, we refer to a series of notes and letters in the *American Journal of Physics*.[3]

What if a function is not periodic? We can still obtain its Fourier expansion, but (a) the results will of course depend on how the expansion interval is chosen (both as to position and length), and (b) because no information outside the expansion interval was used in obtaining the expansion, we can have no realistic expectation that the expansion will produce there a reasonable approximation to our function.

Symmetry

Suppose we have a function $f(x)$ that is either an even or an odd function of x. If it is even, then its Fourier expansion cannot contain any odd terms (since all terms are linearly independent, no odd term can be removed by retaining others). Our expansion, developed

---

[3]B. L. Robinson, Concerning frequencies resulting from distortion. *Am. J. Phys.* **21**: 391 (1953); F. W. Van Name, Jr., Concerning frequencies resulting from distortion. *Am J. Phys.* **22**: 94 (1954).

for the interval $[-\pi, \pi]$, then must take the form

$$f(x) = \frac{a_0}{2} + \sum_{n=1}^{\infty} a_n \cos nx, \quad f(x) \text{ even.} \tag{19.13}$$

On the other hand, if $f(x)$ is odd, we must have

$$f(x) = \sum_{n=1}^{\infty} b_n \sin nx, \quad f(x) \text{ odd.} \tag{19.14}$$

In both cases, when determining the coefficients we only need consider the interval $[0, \pi]$, referring to Eqs. (19.2) and (19.3), as the adjoining interval of length π will make a contribution identical to that considered. The series in Eqs. (19.13) and (19.14) are sometimes called **Fourier cosine** and **Fourier sine** series.

If we have a function defined on the interval $[0, \pi]$, we can represent it either as a Fourier sine series or as a Fourier cosine series (or, if it has no interfering singularities, as a power series), with similar results on the interval of definition. However, the results outside that interval may differ markedly because these expansions carry different assumptions as to symmetry and periodicity.

Example 19.1.2 DIFFERENT EXPANSIONS OF $f(x) = x$

We consider three possible ways to expand $f(x) = x$ based on its values on the range $[0, \pi]$:

- Its power-series expansion will (obviously) have the power-series expansion $f(x) = x$.

- Comparing with Example 19.1.1, its Fourier sine series will have the form given in Eq. (19.9).

- Its Fourier cosine series will have coefficients determined from

$$a_n = \frac{2}{\pi} \int_0^\pi x \cos nx \, dx = \begin{cases} \pi, & n = 0, \\ -\dfrac{4}{n^2 \pi}, & n = 1, 3, 5, \ldots, \\ 0, & n = 2, 4, 6, \ldots, \end{cases}$$

corresponding to the expansion

$$f(x) = \frac{\pi}{2} - \sum_{n=0}^{\infty} \frac{4}{\pi} \frac{\cos(2n+1)x}{(2n+1)^2}.$$

All three of these expansions represent $f(x)$ well in the range of definition, $[0, \pi]$, but their behavior becomes strikingly different outside that range. We compare the three expansions for a range larger than $[0, \pi]$ in Fig. 19.3. ∎

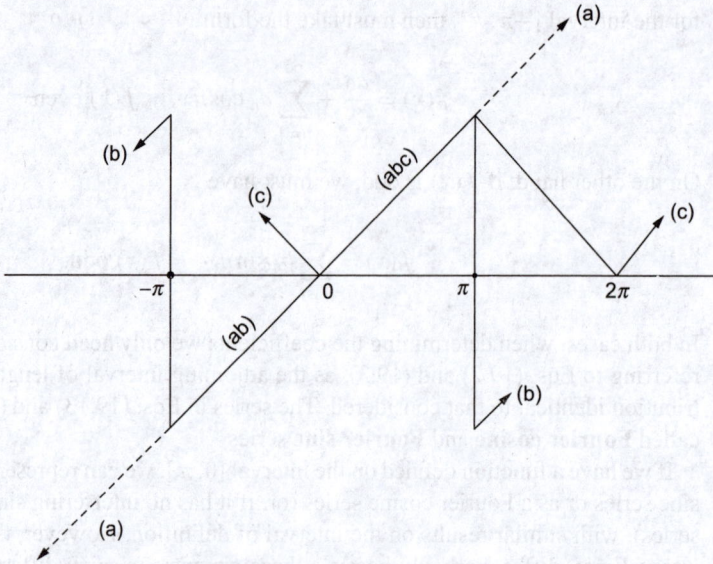

FIGURE 19.3   Expansions of $f(x) = x$ on $[0, \pi]$: (a) power series, (b) Fourier sine series, (c) Fourier cosine series.

Operations on Fourier Series

Term-by-term integration of the series

$$f(x) = \frac{a_0}{2} + \sum_{n=1}^{\infty} a_n \cos nx + \sum_{n=1}^{\infty} b_n \sin nx \qquad (19.15)$$

yields

$$\int_{x_0}^{x} f(x)\, dx = \frac{a_0 x}{2}\bigg|_{x_0}^{x} + \sum_{n=1}^{\infty} \frac{a_n}{n} \sin nx \bigg|_{x_0}^{x} - \sum_{n=1}^{\infty} \frac{b_n}{n} \cos nx \bigg|_{x_0}^{x}. \qquad (19.16)$$

Clearly, the effect of integration is to place an additional power of n in the denominator of each coefficient. This results in more rapid convergence than before. Consequently, a convergent Fourier series may always be integrated term by term, the resulting series converging uniformly to the integral of the original function. Indeed, term-by-term integration may be valid even if the original series, Eq. (19.15), is not itself convergent. The function $f(x)$ need only be integrable. A discussion will be found in Jeffreys and Jeffreys (Additional Readings).

Strictly speaking, Eq. (19.16) may not be a Fourier series; that is, if $a_0 \neq 0$, there will be a term $\frac{1}{2} a_0 x$. However,

$$\int_{x_0}^{x} f(x)\, dx - \frac{1}{2} a_0 x \qquad (19.17)$$

will still be a Fourier series.

The situation regarding differentiation is quite different from that of integration. Here the word is caution. Consider the series for

$$f(x) = x, \quad -\pi < x < \pi. \tag{19.18}$$

We readily found (in Example 19.1.1) that the Fourier series is

$$x = 2 \sum_{n=1}^{\infty} (-1)^{n+1} \frac{\sin nx}{n}, \quad -\pi < x < \pi. \tag{19.19}$$

Differentiating term by term, we obtain

$$1 = 2 \sum_{n=1}^{\infty} (-1)^{n+1} \cos nx, \tag{19.20}$$

which is not convergent. **Warning**: Check your derivative for convergence.

For the triangular wave shown in Fig. 19.4 (and treated in Exercise 19.2.9), the Fourier expansion is

$$f(x) = \frac{\pi}{2} - \frac{4}{\pi} \sum_{n=1,\text{odd}}^{\infty} \frac{\cos nx}{n^2}, \tag{19.21}$$

which converges more rapidly than the expansion of Eq. (19.19); in fact, it exhibits uniform convergence. Differentiating term by term we get

$$f'(x) = \frac{4}{\pi} \sum_{n=1,\text{odd}}^{\infty} \frac{\sin nx}{n}, \tag{19.22}$$

which is the Fourier expansion of a square wave,

$$f'(x) = \begin{cases} 1, & 0 < x < \pi, \\ -1, & -\pi < x < 0. \end{cases} \tag{19.23}$$

Inspection of Fig. 19.3 verifies that this is indeed the derivative of our triangular wave.

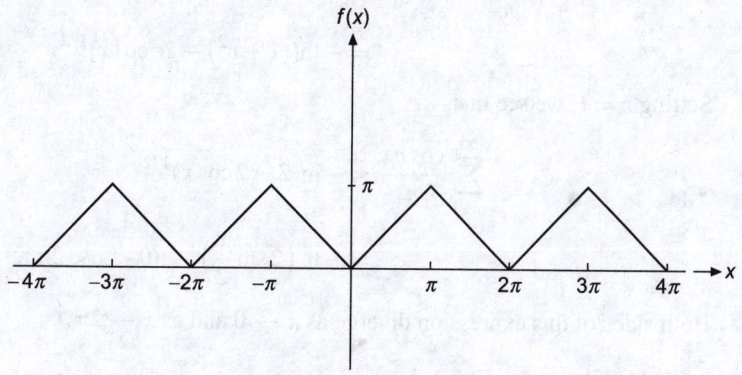

FIGURE 19.4   Triangular wave.

- As the inverse of integration, the operation of differentiation has placed an additional factor n in the numerator of each term. This reduces the rate of convergence and may, as in the first case mentioned, render the differentiated series divergent.

- In general, term-by-term differentiation is permissible if the series to be differentiated is uniformly convergent.

Summing Fourier Series

Often the most efficient way to identify the function represented by a Fourier series is simply to identify the expansion in a table. But if it is our desire to sum the series ourselves, a useful approach is to replace the trigonometric functions by their complex exponential forms, and then identifying the Fourier series as one or more power series in $e^{\pm ix}$.

Example 19.1.3   Summation of a Fourier Series

Consider the series $\sum_{n=1}^{\infty} (1/n) \cos nx, x \in (0, 2\pi)$. Since this series is only conditionally convergent (and diverges at $x = 0$), we take

$$\sum_{n=1}^{\infty} \frac{\cos nx}{n} = \lim_{r \to 1} \sum_{n=1}^{\infty} \frac{r^n \cos nx}{n},$$

absolutely convergent for $|r| < 1$. Our procedure is to try forming power series by transforming the trigonometric functions into exponential form:

$$\sum_{n=1}^{\infty} \frac{r^n \cos nx}{n} = \frac{1}{2} \sum_{n=1}^{\infty} \frac{r^n e^{inx}}{n} + \frac{1}{2} \sum_{n=1}^{\infty} \frac{r^n e^{-inx}}{n}.$$

Now, these power series may be identified as Maclaurin expansions of $-\ln(1-z)$, with $z = re^{ix}$ or re^{-ix}. From Eq. (1.97),

$$\sum_{n=1}^{\infty} \frac{r^n \cos nx}{n} = -\frac{1}{2}[\ln(1 - re^{ix}) + \ln(1 - re^{-ix})]$$

$$= -\ln[(1 + r^2) - 2r \cos x]^{1/2}.$$

Setting $r = 1$, we see that

$$\sum_{n=1}^{\infty} \frac{\cos nx}{n} = -\ln(2 - 2\cos x)^{1/2}$$

$$= -\ln\left(2 \sin \frac{x}{2}\right), \quad (0 < x < 2\pi). \tag{19.24}$$

Both sides of this expression diverge as $x \to 0$ and as $x \to 2\pi$.[4]   ∎

---

[4]Note that the range of validity of Eq. (19.24) may be shifted to $[-\pi, \pi]$ (excluding $x = 0$) if we replace x by $|x|$ on the right-hand side.

Exercises

19.1.1   A function $f(x)$ (quadratically integrable) is to be represented by a **finite** Fourier series. A convenient measure of the accuracy of the series is given by the integrated square of the deviation,

$$\Delta_p = \int_0^{2\pi} \left[f(x) - \frac{a_0}{2} - \sum_{n=1}^{p} (a_n \cos nx + b_n \sin nx) \right]^2 dx.$$

Show that the requirement that Δ_p be minimized, that is,

$$\frac{\partial \Delta_p}{\partial a_n} = 0, \quad \frac{\partial \Delta_p}{\partial b_n} = 0,$$

for all n, leads to choosing a_n and b_n as given in Eqs. (19.2) and (19.3).

Note. Your coefficients a_n and b_n are independent of p. This independence is a consequence of orthogonality and would not hold if we expanded $f(x)$ in a power series.

19.1.2   In the analysis of a complex waveform (ocean tides, earthquakes, musical tones, etc.), it might be more convenient to have the Fourier series written as

$$f(x) = \frac{a_0}{2} + \sum_{n=1}^{\infty} \alpha_n \cos(nx - \theta_n).$$

Show that this is equivalent to Eq. (19.1) with

$$a_n = \alpha_n \cos \theta_n, \qquad \alpha_n^2 = a_n^2 + b_n^2,$$
$$b_n = \alpha_n \sin \theta_n, \qquad \tan \theta_n = b_n / a_n.$$

Note. The coefficients α_n^2 as a function of n define what is called the **power spectrum**. The importance of α_n^2 lies in their invariance under a shift in the phase θ_n.

19.1.3   A function $f(x)$ is expanded in an exponential Fourier series

$$f(x) = \sum_{n=-\infty}^{\infty} c_n e^{inx}.$$

If $f(x)$ is real, $f(x) = f^*(x)$, what restriction is imposed on the coefficients c_n?

19.1.4   Assuming that $\int_{-\pi}^{\pi} [f(x)]^2 dx$ is finite, show that

$$\lim_{m \to \infty} a_m = 0, \quad \lim_{m \to \infty} b_m = 0.$$

Hint. Integrate $[f(x) - s_n(x)]^2$, where $s_n(x)$ is the nth partial sum, and use Bessel's inequality (Section 5.1). For our finite interval the assumption that $f(x)$ is square integrable ($\int_{-\pi}^{\pi} |f(x)|^2 \, dx$ is finite) implies that $\int_{-\pi}^{\pi} |f(x)| \, dx$ is also finite. The converse does not hold.

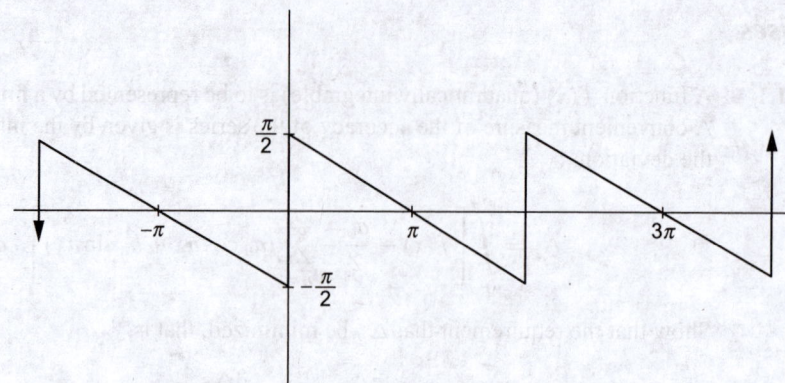

FIGURE 19.5   Reverse sawtooth wave.

19.1.5   Apply the summation technique of this section to show that

$$\sum_{n=1}^{\infty} \frac{\sin nx}{n} = \begin{cases} \frac{1}{2}(\pi - x), & 0 < x \le \pi, \\ -\frac{1}{2}(\pi + x), & -\pi \le x < 0. \end{cases}$$

This is the reverse sawtooth wave shown in Fig. 19.5.

19.1.6   Sum the series $\sum_{n=1}^{\infty}(-1)^{n+1}\frac{\sin nx}{n}$ and show that it equals $x/2$.

19.1.7   Sum the trigonometric series $\sum_{n=0}^{\infty}\frac{\sin(2n+1)x}{2n+1}$ and show that it equals

$$\begin{cases} \pi/4, & 0 < x < \pi, \\ -\pi/4, & -\pi < x < 0. \end{cases}$$

19.1.8   Let $f(z) = \ln(1 + z) = \sum_{n=1}^{\infty}\frac{(-1)^{n+1}z^n}{n}$. This series converges to $\ln(1 + z)$ for $|z| \le 1$, except at the point $z = -1$.

(a)   From the real parts show that

$$\ln\left(2\cos\frac{\theta}{2}\right) = \sum_{n=1}^{\infty}(-1)^{n+1}\frac{\cos n\theta}{n}, \quad -\pi < \theta < \pi.$$

(b)   Using a change of variable, transform part (a) into

$$-\ln\left(2\sin\frac{\theta}{2}\right) = \sum_{n=1}^{\infty}\frac{\cos n\theta}{n}, \quad 0 < \theta < 2\pi.$$

19.1.9   (a)   Expand $f(x) = x$ in the interval $(0, 2L)$. Sketch the series you have found (right-hand side of ANS.) over $(-2L, 2L)$.

$$ANS. \quad x = L - \frac{2L}{\pi}\sum_{n=1}^{\infty}\frac{1}{n}\sin\left(\frac{n\pi x}{L}\right).$$

(b) Expand $f(x) = x$ as a sine series in the **half** interval $(0, L)$. Sketch the series you have found (right-hand side of Ans.) over $(-2L, 2L)$.

$$ANS. \quad x = \frac{4L}{\pi} \sum_{n=0}^{\infty} \frac{1}{2n+1} \sin\left(\frac{(2n+1)\pi x}{L}\right).$$

19.1.10   In some problems it is convenient to approximate $\sin \pi x$ over the interval $[0, 1]$ by a parabola $ax(1-x)$, where a is a constant. To get a feeling for the accuracy of this approximation, expand $4x(1-x)$ in a Fourier sine series $(-1 \le x \le 1)$:

$$f(x) = \begin{Bmatrix} 4x(1-x), & 0 \le x \le 1 \\ 4x(1+x), & -1 \le x \le 0 \end{Bmatrix} = \sum_{n=1}^{\infty} b_n \sin n\pi x.$$

$$ANS. \quad b_n = \frac{32}{\pi^3} \frac{1}{n^3}, \quad n \text{ odd},$$
$$b_n = 0, \quad n \text{ even}.$$

This approximation is shown in Fig. 19.6.

19.1.11   Verify that $\delta(\varphi_1 - \varphi_2) = \frac{1}{2\pi} \sum_{m=-\infty}^{\infty} e^{im(\varphi_1-\varphi_2)}$ is a Dirac delta function by showing that it satisfies the definition,

$$\int_{-\pi}^{\pi} f(\varphi_1) \frac{1}{2\pi} \sum_{m=-\infty}^{\infty} e^{im(\varphi_1-\varphi_2)} d\varphi_1 = f(\varphi_2).$$

Hint. Represent $f(\varphi_1)$ by an exponential Fourier series.

19.1.12   Show that integration of the Fourier expansion of $f(x) = x$, $-\pi < x < \pi$, leads to

$$\frac{\pi^2}{12} = \sum_{n=1}^{\infty} \frac{(-1)^{n+1}}{n^2} = 1 - \frac{1}{4} + \frac{1}{9} - \frac{1}{16} + \cdots.$$

Note. The series for $f(x) = x$ was the subject of Example 19.1.1. Confirm that the change in the defined range from $[0, 2\pi]$ to $[-\pi, \pi]$ has no effect on the expansion.

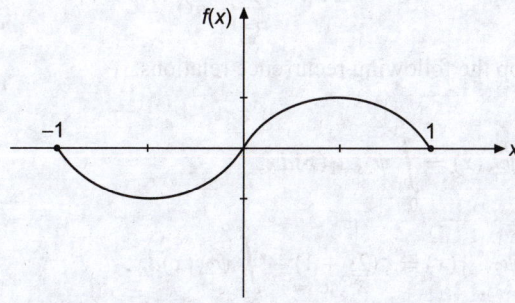

FIGURE 19.6   Parabolic approximation to sine wave.

19.1.13   (a)   Assuming that the Fourier expansion of $f(x)$ is uniformly convergent, show that

$$\frac{1}{\pi} \int_{-\pi}^{\pi} \left[f(x) \right]^2 dx = \frac{a_0^2}{2} + \sum_{n=1}^{\infty} (a_n^2 + b_n^2).$$

This is Parseval's identity. Note that it is a completeness relation for the Fourier expansion.

(b)   Given $x^2 = \dfrac{\pi^2}{3} + 4 \sum_{n=1}^{\infty} \dfrac{(-1)^n \cos nx}{n^2}, \quad -\pi \leq x \leq \pi,$

apply Parseval's identity to obtain $\zeta(4)$ in closed form.

(c)   The condition of uniform convergence is not necessary. Show this by applying the Parseval identity to the square wave

$$f(x) = \begin{cases} -1, & -\pi < x < 0 \\ 1, & 0 < x < \pi \end{cases}$$

$$= \frac{4}{\pi} \sum_{n=1}^{\infty} \frac{\sin(2n-1)x}{2n-1}.$$

19.1.14   Given

$$\varphi_1(x) \equiv \sum_{n=1}^{\infty} \frac{\sin nx}{n} = \begin{cases} -\dfrac{1}{2}(\pi + x), & -\pi \leq x < 0, \\ \dfrac{1}{2}(\pi - x), & 0 < x \leq \pi, \end{cases}$$

show by integrating that

$$\varphi_2(x) \equiv \sum_{n=1}^{\infty} \frac{\cos nx}{n^2} = \begin{cases} \dfrac{1}{4}(\pi + x)^2 - \dfrac{\pi^2}{12}, & -\pi \leq x \leq 0, \\ \dfrac{1}{4}(\pi - x)^2 - \dfrac{\pi^2}{12}, & 0 \leq x \leq \pi. \end{cases}$$

19.1.15   Given

$$\psi_{2s}(x) = \sum_{n=1}^{\infty} \frac{\sin nx}{n^{2s}}, \quad \psi_{2s+1}(x) = \sum_{n=1}^{\infty} \frac{\cos nx}{n^{2s+1}},$$

develop the following recurrence relations:

(a) $\psi_{2s}(x) = \displaystyle\int_0^x \psi_{2s-1}(x) dx,$

(b) $\psi_{2s+1}(x) = \zeta(2s+1) - \displaystyle\int_0^x \psi_{2s}(x) dx.$

Note. The functions $\psi_s(x)$ and $\varphi_s(x)$ of this and the preceding exercise are known as **Clausen functions**. In theory they may be used to improve the rate of convergence of a Fourier series. As is often the case, there is the question of how much analytical work we do and how much arithmetic work we demand that a computer do. As computers become steadily more powerful, the balance progressively shifts so that we are doing less and demanding that computers do more.

19.1.16   Show that $f(x) = \sum_{n=1}^{\infty} \frac{\cos nx}{n+1}$ may be written as

$$f(x) = \psi_1(x) - \varphi_2(x) + \sum_{n=1}^{\infty} \frac{\cos nx}{n^2(n+1)},$$

where $\psi_1(x)$ and $\varphi_2(x)$ are the Clausen functions defined in Exercises 19.1.14 and 19.1.15.

19.2 APPLICATIONS OF FOURIER SERIES

We present in this section two typical problems and a short table of useful Fourier series, followed by a substantial number of exercises that illustrate some of the techniques that arise in applications.

Example 19.2.1   SQUARE WAVE

One application of Fourier series, the analysis of a "square" wave (Fig. 19.7) in terms of its Fourier components, occurs in electronic circuits designed to handle sharply rising pulses. Suppose that our wave is defined by

$$f(x) = 0, \quad -\pi < x < 0,$$
$$f(x) = h, \quad 0 < x < \pi. \tag{19.25}$$

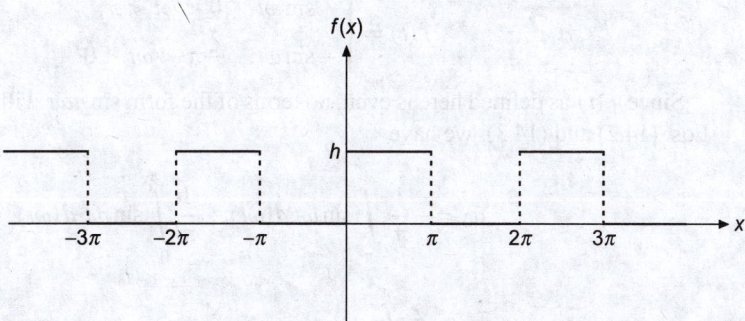

FIGURE 19.7   Square wave.

From Eqs. (19.2) and (19.3), we find

$$a_0 = \frac{1}{\pi} \int_0^\pi h \, dt = h,$$

$$a_n = \frac{1}{\pi} \int_0^\pi h \cos nt \, dt = 0, \quad n = 1, 2, 3, \ldots,$$

$$b_n = \frac{1}{\pi} \int_0^\pi h \sin nt \, dt = \frac{h}{n\pi}(1 - \cos n\pi)$$

$$= \begin{cases} \dfrac{2h}{n\pi}, & n \text{ odd}, \\ 0, & n \text{ even}. \end{cases}$$

The resulting series is

$$f(x) = \frac{h}{2} + \frac{2h}{\pi}\left(\frac{\sin x}{1} + \frac{\sin 3x}{3} + \frac{\sin 5x}{5} + \cdots \right). \tag{19.26}$$

Except for the first term, which represents an average of $f(x)$ over the interval $[-\pi, \pi]$, all the cosine terms have vanished. Since $f(x) - h/2$ is odd, we have a Fourier sine series. Although only the odd terms in the sine series occur, they fall only as n^{-1}. This **conditional convergence** is like that of the alternating harmonic series. Physically this means that our square wave contains a lot of **high-frequency components**. If the electronic apparatus will not pass these components, our square-wave input will emerge more or less rounded off, perhaps as an amorphous blob.   ∎

Example 19.2.2   FULL-WAVE RECTIFIER

As a second example, let us ask how well the output of a full-wave rectifier approaches pure direct current. Our rectifier may be thought of as passing the positive peaks of an incoming sine wave and inverting the negative peaks, as shown in Fig. 19.8. This yields

$$f(t) = \begin{cases} \sin \omega t, & 0 < \omega t < \pi, \\ -\sin \omega t, & -\pi < \omega t < 0. \end{cases} \tag{19.27}$$

Since $f(t)$ as defined here is even, no terms of the form $\sin n\omega t$ will appear. Again, from Eqs. (14.2) and (14.3), we have

$$a_0 = -\frac{1}{\pi} \int_{-\pi}^0 \sin \omega t \, d(\omega t) + \frac{1}{\pi} \int_0^\pi \sin \omega t \, d(\omega t)$$

$$= \frac{2}{\pi} \int_0^\pi \sin \omega t \, d(\omega t) = \frac{4}{\pi},$$

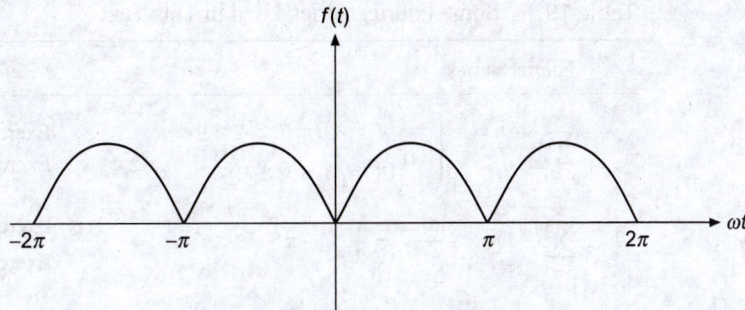

FIGURE 19.8   Full wave rectifier.

$$a_n = \frac{2}{\pi} \int_0^\pi \sin \omega t \cos n\omega t \; d(\omega t)$$

$$= \begin{cases} -\dfrac{2}{\pi} \dfrac{2}{n^2 - 1}, & n \text{ even,} \\[2mm] 0, & n \text{ odd.} \end{cases}$$

Note that $[0, \pi]$ is not an orthogonality interval for both sines and cosines together and we do not get zero when n is even. The resulting series is

$$f(t) = \frac{2}{\pi} - \frac{4}{\pi} \sum_{n=2,4,6,\ldots}^{\infty} \frac{\cos n\omega t}{n^2 - 1}. \tag{19.28}$$

The original frequency, ω, has been eliminated; in fact, all its odd harmonics are also absent. The lowest-frequency oscillation is 2ω. The high-frequency components fall off as n^{-2}, showing that the full-wave rectifier does a fairly good job of approximating direct current. Whether this good approximation is adequate depends on the particular application. If the remaining alternating current components are objectionable, they may be further suppressed by appropriate filter circuits.   ∎

These examples bring out two features characteristic of Fourier expansions:[5]

- If $f(x)$ has discontinuities, as in the square wave in Example 19.2.1, we can expect the nth coefficient to be decreasing as $\mathcal{O}(1/n)$. Convergence is conditional only.

- If $f(x)$ is continuous (although possibly with discontinuous derivatives as in the full-wave rectifier of Example 19.2.2), we can expect the nth coefficient to be decreasing as $1/n^2$, that is, absolute convergence.

We close this section by providing, in Table 19.1, a list of Fourier series that have been introduced either as examples or in the exercises of this chapter. More extensive lists can be found in the Additional Readings, particularly in the work by Oberhettinger, but also in the texts by Carslaw, Churchill, and Zygmund.

[5] G. Raisbeek, Order of magnitude of Fourier coefficients. *Am. Math. Mon.* **62**: 149 (1955).

Table 19.1   Some Fourier Series Used in This Text

	Fourier Series	Reference
1.	$\displaystyle\sum_{n=1}^{\infty}\frac{\sin nx}{n}=\begin{cases}-\frac{1}{2}(\pi+x), & -\pi\le x<0\\ \frac{1}{2}(\pi-x), & 0\le x<\pi\end{cases}$	Exercise 19.1.5 Exercise 19.2.8
2.	$\displaystyle\sum_{n=1}^{\infty}(-1)^{n+1}\frac{\sin nx}{n}=\frac{x}{2},\quad -\pi<x<\pi$	Exercise 19.1.6 Exercise 19.2.7
3.	$\displaystyle\sum_{n=0}^{\infty}\frac{\sin(2n+1)x}{2n+1}=\begin{cases}-\pi/4, & -\pi<x<0\\ +\pi/4, & 0<x<\pi\end{cases}$	Exercise 19.1.7 Eq. (19.26)
4.	$\displaystyle\sum_{n=1}^{\infty}\frac{\cos nx}{n}=-\ln\left[2\sin\left(\frac{\lvert x\rvert}{2}\right)\right],\quad -\pi<x<\pi$	Exercise 19.1.8(b) Eq. (19.24)
5.	$\displaystyle\sum_{n=1}^{\infty}(-1)^{n}\frac{\cos nx}{n}=-\ln\left[2\cos\left(\frac{x}{2}\right)\right],\quad -\pi<x<\pi$	Exercise 19.1.8(a)
6.	$\displaystyle\sum_{n=0}^{\infty}\frac{\cos(2n+1)x}{2n+1}=\frac{1}{2}\ln\left[\cot\frac{\lvert x\rvert}{2}\right],\quad -\pi<x<\pi$	Exercise 19.2.5

Exercises

19.2.1   Transform the Fourier expansion of a square wave, Eq. (19.26), into a power series. Show that the coefficients of x^1 form a **divergent** series. Repeat for the coefficients of x^3.

Note. A power series cannot handle a discontinuity. These infinite coefficients are the result of attempting to beat this basic limitation on power series.

19.2.2   Derive the Fourier series expansion of the Dirac delta function $\delta(x)$ in the interval $-\pi<x<\pi$.

(a)   What significance can be attached to the constant term?

(b)   In what region is this representation valid?

(c)   With the identity

$$\sum_{n=1}^{N}\cos nx=\frac{\sin(Nx/2)}{\sin(x/2)}\cos\left[\left(N+\frac{1}{2}\right)\frac{x}{2}\right],$$

show that your Fourier representation of $\delta(x)$ is consistent with Eq. (5.27).

19.2.3   Expand $\delta(x-t)$ in a Fourier series. Compare your result with the bilinear form of Eq. (5.27).

$$ANS. \quad \delta(x-t) = \frac{1}{2\pi} + \frac{1}{\pi}\sum_{n=1}^{\infty}(\cos nx \cos nt + \sin nx \sin nt)$$

$$= \frac{1}{2\pi} + \frac{1}{\pi}\sum_{n=1}^{\infty}\cos n(x-t).$$

19.2.4 Show that integrating the Fourier expansion of the Dirac delta function (Exercise 19.2.2) leads to the Fourier representation of the square wave, Eq. (19.26), with $h = 1$.

Note. Integrating the constant term $(1/2\pi)$ leads to a term $x/2\pi$. What are you going to do with this?

19.2.5 Starting from the Fourier series given as lines 4 and 5 of Table 19.1, show that:

$$\sum_{n=0}^{\infty} \frac{\cos(2n+1)x}{2n+1} = \frac{1}{2}\ln\left[\cot\frac{|x|}{2}\right].$$

19.2.6 Develop the Fourier series representation of

$$f(t) = \begin{cases} 0, & -\pi \leq \omega t \leq 0, \\ \sin \omega t, & 0 \leq \omega t \leq \pi. \end{cases}$$

This is the output of a simple half-wave rectifier. It is also an approximation of the solar thermal effect that produces "tides" in the atmosphere.

$$ANS. \quad f(t) = \frac{1}{\pi} + \frac{1}{2}\sin \omega t - \frac{2}{\pi}\sum_{n=2,4,6,\ldots}^{\infty}\frac{\cos n\omega t}{n^2-1}.$$

19.2.7 A sawtooth wave is given by

$$f(x) = x, \quad -\pi < x < \pi.$$

Show that

$$f(x) = 2\sum_{n=1}^{\infty}\frac{(-1)^{n+1}}{n}\sin nx.$$

19.2.8 A different sawtooth wave is described by

$$f(x) = \begin{cases} -\frac{1}{2}(\pi+x), & -\pi \leq x < 0 \\ +\frac{1}{2}(\pi-x), & 0 < x \leq \pi. \end{cases}$$

Show that $f(x) = \sum_{n=1}^{\infty}(\sin nx/n)$.

19.2.9 A triangular wave (Fig. 19.4) is represented by

$$f(x) = \begin{cases} x, & 0 < x < \pi \\ -x, & -\pi < x < 0. \end{cases}$$

Represent $f(x)$ by a Fourier series.

$$ANS. \quad f(x) = \frac{\pi}{2} - \frac{4}{\pi} \sum_{n=1,3,5,\dots} \frac{\cos nx}{n^2}.$$

19.2.10   Expand

$$f(x) = \begin{cases} 1, & x^2 < x_0^2 \\ 0, & x^2 > x_0^2 \end{cases}$$

in the interval $[-\pi, \pi]$.

Note. This variable-width square wave is of some importance in electronic music.

19.2.11   A metal cylindrical tube of radius a is split lengthwise into two nontouching halves. The top half is maintained at a potential $+V$, the bottom half at a potential $-V$. See Fig. 19.9. Separate the variables in Laplace's equation and solve for the electrostatic potential for $r \le a$. Observe the resemblance between your solution for $r = a$ and the Fourier series for a square wave.

19.2.12   A metal cylinder is placed in a (previously) uniform electric field, E_0, with the axis of the cylinder perpendicular to that of the original field.

(a)   Find the perturbed electrostatic potential.

(b)   Find the induced surface charge on the cylinder as a function of angular position.

19.2.13   (a)   Find the Fourier series representation of

$$f(x) = \begin{cases} 0, & -\pi < x \le 0 \\ x, & 0 \le x < \pi. \end{cases}$$

(b)   From the Fourier expansion show that

$$\frac{\pi^2}{8} = 1 + \frac{1}{3^2} + \frac{1}{5^2} + \cdots.$$

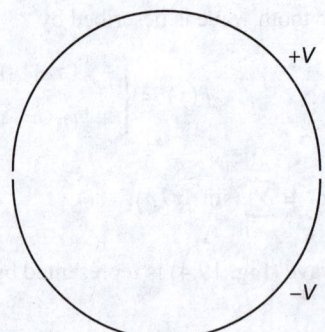

FIGURE 19.9   Cross section of split tube.

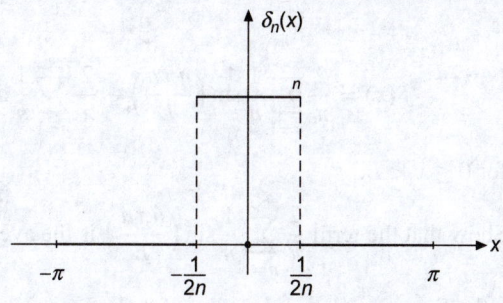

FIGURE 19.10   Rectangular pulse.

19.2.14   Integrate the Fourier expansion of the unit step function

$$f(x) = \begin{cases} 0, & -\pi < x < 0 \\ 1, & 0 < x < \pi. \end{cases}$$

Show that your integrated series agrees with Exercise 19.2.13.

19.2.15   In the interval $(-\pi, \pi)$, $\delta_n(x) = \begin{cases} n, & |x| < 1/2n, \\ 0, & |x| > 1/2n. \end{cases}$

This wave form is the pulse shown in Fig. 19.10.

(a)   Expand $\delta_n(x)$ as a Fourier cosine series.

(b)   Show that your Fourier series agrees with a Fourier expansion of $\delta(x)$ in the limit
as $n \to \infty$.

19.2.16   Confirm the delta function nature of your Fourier series of Exercise 19.2.15 by showing
that for any $f(x)$ that is finite in the interval $[-\pi, \pi]$ and continuous at $x = 0$,

$$\int_{-\pi}^{\pi} f(x) \, [\text{Fourier expansion of } \delta_\infty(x)] \, dx = f(0).$$

19.2.17   (a)   Show that the Dirac delta function $\delta(x - a)$, expanded in a Fourier sine series in
the half-interval $(0, L)$ $(0 < a < L)$ is given by

$$\delta(x - a) = \frac{2}{L} \sum_{n=1}^{\infty} \sin\left(\frac{n\pi a}{L}\right) \sin\left(\frac{n\pi x}{L}\right).$$

Note that this series actually describes $-\delta(x + a) + \delta(x - a)$ in the interval
$(-L, L)$.

(b)   By integrating both sides of the preceding equation from 0 to x, show that the
cosine expansion of the square wave

$$f(x) = \begin{cases} 0, & 0 \leq x < a \\ 1, & a < x < L, \end{cases}$$

is

$$f(x) = \frac{2}{\pi} \sum_{n=1}^{\infty} \frac{1}{n} \sin\left(\frac{n\pi a}{L}\right) - \frac{2}{\pi} \sum_{n=1}^{\infty} \frac{1}{n} \sin\left(\frac{n\pi a}{L}\right) \cos\left(\frac{n\pi x}{L}\right),$$

for $0 \le x < L$.

(c)   Show that the term $\dfrac{2}{\pi} \sum_{n=1}^{\infty} \dfrac{1}{n} \sin\left(\dfrac{n\pi a}{L}\right)$ is the average of $f(x)$ on $(0, L)$.

19.2.18   Verify the Fourier cosine expansion of the square wave, Exercise 19.2.17(b), by direct calculation of the Fourier coefficients.

19.2.19   (a)   A string is clamped at both ends $x = 0$ and $x = L$. Assuming small-amplitude vibrations, we find that the amplitude $y(x, t)$ satisfies the wave equation

$$\frac{\partial^2 y}{\partial x^2} = \frac{1}{v^2} \frac{\partial^2 y}{\partial t^2}.$$

Here v is the wave velocity. The string is set in vibration by a sharp blow at $x = a$. Hence we have

$$y(x, 0) = 0, \qquad \frac{\partial y(x, t)}{\partial t} = L v_0 \delta(x - a) \text{ at } t = 0.$$

The constant L is included to compensate for the dimensions (inverse length) of $\delta(x - a)$. With $\delta(x - a)$ given by Exercise 19.2.17(a), solve the wave equation subject to these initial conditions.

$$ANS. \quad y(x, t) = \frac{2 v_0 L}{\pi v} \sum_{n=1}^{\infty} \frac{1}{n} \sin \frac{n\pi a}{L} \sin \frac{n\pi x}{L} \sin \frac{n\pi v t}{L}.$$

(b)   Show that the transverse velocity of the string $\partial y(x, t)/\partial t$ is given by

$$\frac{\partial y(x, t)}{\partial t} = 2 v_0 \sum_{n=1}^{\infty} \sin \frac{n\pi a}{L} \sin \frac{n\pi x}{L} \cos \frac{n\pi v t}{L}.$$

19.2.20   A string, clamped at $x = 0$ and at $x = L$, is vibrating freely. Its motion is described by the wave equation

$$\frac{\partial^2 u(x, t)}{\partial t^2} = v^2 \frac{\partial^2 u(x, t)}{\partial x^2}.$$

Assume a Fourier expansion of the form

$$u(x, t) = \sum_{n=1}^{\infty} b_n(t) \sin \frac{n\pi x}{L}$$

and determine the coefficients $b_n(t)$. The initial conditions are

$$u(x, 0) = f(x) \quad \text{and} \quad \frac{\partial}{\partial t} u(x, 0) = g(x).$$

Note. This is only half the conventional Fourier orthogonality integral interval. However, as long as only the sines are included here, the Sturm-Liouville boundary conditions are still satisfied and the functions are orthogonal.

$$ANS. \quad b_n(t) = A_n \cos \frac{n\pi vt}{L} + B_n \sin \frac{n\pi vt}{L},$$

$$A_n = \frac{2}{L} \int_0^L f(x) \sin \frac{n\pi x}{L} \, dx, \quad B_n = \frac{2}{n\pi v} \int_0^L g(x) \sin \frac{n\pi x}{L} \, dx.$$

19.2.21   (a)   Let us continue the vibrating string problem in Exercise 19.2.20. We assume now that the presence of a resisting medium will damp the vibrations according to the equation

$$\frac{\partial^2 u(x,t)}{\partial t^2} = v^2 \frac{\partial^2 u(x,t)}{\partial x^2} - k \frac{\partial u(x,t)}{\partial t}.$$

Introduce a Fourier expansion

$$u(x,t) = \sum_{n=1}^{\infty} b_n(t) \sin \frac{n\pi x}{L}$$

and again determine the coefficients $b_n(t)$. Take the initial and boundary conditions to be the same as in Exercise 19.2.20. Assume the damping to be small.

(b)   Repeat, but assume the damping to be large.

ANS.

(a) $b_n(t) = e^{-kt/2}[A_n \cos \omega_n t + B_n \sin \omega_n t], \quad \omega_n^2 = \left(\frac{n\pi v}{L}\right) - \left(\frac{k}{2}\right)^2 > 0,$

$$A_n = \frac{2}{L} \int_0^L f(x) \sin \frac{n\pi x}{L} \, dx, \quad B_n = \frac{2}{\omega_n L} \int_0^L g(x) \sin \frac{n\pi x}{L} dx + \frac{k}{2\omega_n} A_n.$$

(b) $b_n(t) = e^{-kt/2}[A_n \cosh \sigma_n t + B_n \sinh \sigma_n t], \quad \sigma_n^2 = \left(\frac{k}{2}\right)^2 - \left(\frac{n\pi v}{L}\right)^2 > 0,$

$$A_n = \frac{2}{L} \int_0^L f(x) \sin \frac{n\pi x}{L} \, dx, \quad B_n = \frac{2}{\sigma_n L} \int_0^L g(x) \sin \frac{n\pi x}{L} \, dx + \frac{k}{2\sigma_n} A_n.$$

19.3   GIBBS PHENOMENON

The Gibbs phenomenon is an overshoot, a peculiarity of the Fourier series and other eigenfunction series at a simple discontinuity. An example is seen in Fig. 19.2.

Partial Summation of Fourier Series

To better understand the Gibbs phenomenon we examine methods for the partial summation of Fourier series. This procedure is unlikely to lead to convenient solutions of practical problems for which Fourier series are ideal, but it may provide insight that is needed for our present study.

We start from the Fourier series of a function $f(x)$ in exponential form, truncating it to retain terms only for $n \leq |r|$ and labeling the truncated expansion $f_r(x)$:

$$f_r(x) = \sum_{n=-r}^{r} c_n e^{inx}, \quad c_n = \frac{1}{2\pi} \int_{-\pi}^{\pi} f(t) e^{-int} \, dt.$$

Combining these equations in a way useful for the present discussion, we have

$$f_r(x) = \frac{1}{2\pi} \int_{-\pi}^{\pi} f(t) \sum_{n=-r}^{r} e^{i(x-t)} dt. \tag{19.29}$$

The summation in Eq. (19.29) is a geometric series. Using a result easily obtained from Eq. (1.96),

$$\sum_{n=-r}^{r} y^n = \frac{y^{-r} - y^{r+1}}{1 - y} = \frac{y^{r+\frac{1}{2}} - y^{-(r+\frac{1}{2})}}{y^{1/2} - y^{-1/2}},$$

we set $y = e^{i(x-t)}$, after which we can identify the resulting expression as a quotient of sine functions:[6]

$$\sum_{n=-r}^{r} e^{in(x-t)} = \frac{e^{i(r+\frac{1}{2})(x-t)} - e^{-i(r+\frac{1}{2})(x-t)}}{e^{i(x-t)/2} - e^{-i(x-t)/2}} = \frac{\sin[(r+\frac{1}{2})(x-t)]}{\sin\frac{1}{2}(x-t)}. \tag{19.30}$$

Inserting Eq. (19.30) into Eq. (19.29), we reach

$$f_r(x) = \frac{1}{2\pi} \int_{-\pi}^{\pi} f(t) \frac{\sin[(r+\frac{1}{2})(x-t)]}{\sin\frac{1}{2}(x-t)} dt. \tag{19.31}$$

This is convergent at all points, including $t = x$. Equation (19.31) shows that the quantity

$$\frac{1}{2\pi} \frac{\sin[(r+\frac{1}{2})(x-t)]}{\sin\frac{1}{2}(x-t)}$$

is in the large-r limit a Dirac delta distribution.

Square Wave

For convenience of numerical calculation we consider the behavior of the Fourier series that represents the periodic square wave

$$f(x) = \begin{cases} \dfrac{h}{2}, & 0 < x < \pi, \\[2mm] -\dfrac{h}{2}, & -\pi < x < 0. \end{cases} \tag{19.32}$$

---

[6]This series also occurs in the analysis of a diffraction grating consisting of r slits.

This is essentially the square wave used in Example 19.2.1, and we immediately see that its Fourier expansion is

$$f(x) = \frac{2h}{\pi} \left(\frac{\sin x}{1} + \frac{\sin 3x}{3} + \frac{\sin 5x}{5} + \cdots \right).$$ (19.33)

Applying Eq. (19.31) to our square wave, we have

$$f_r(x) = \frac{h}{4\pi} \int_0^\pi \frac{\sin[(r + \frac{1}{2})(x - t)]}{\sin \frac{1}{2}(x - t)} dt - \frac{h}{4\pi} \int_{-\pi}^0 \frac{\sin[(r + \frac{1}{2})(x - t)]}{\sin \frac{1}{2}(x - t)} dt.$$

Making the substitution $x - t = s$ in the first integral and $x - t = -s$ in the second, we obtain

$$f_r(x) = \frac{h}{4\pi} \int_{-\pi+x}^x \frac{\sin(r + \frac{1}{2})s}{\sin \frac{1}{2}s} ds - \frac{h}{4\pi} \int_{-\pi-x}^{-x} \frac{\sin(r + \frac{1}{2})s}{\sin \frac{1}{2}s} ds.$$ (19.34)

It is important to note that both the integrals in Eq. (19.34) have the same integrand, and therefore have the same indefinite integral, which we denote $\Phi(t)$. We may therefore write

$$f(r) = \frac{h}{4\pi} \Big[\Phi(x) - \Phi(-\pi + x) \Big] - \frac{h}{4\pi} \Big[\Phi(-x) - \Phi(-\pi - x) \Big]$$

$$= \frac{h}{4\pi} \Big[\Phi(x) - \Phi(-x) \Big] - \frac{h}{4\pi} \Big[\Phi(-\pi + x) - \Phi(-\pi - x) \Big],$$ (19.35)

where the second line of Eq. (19.35) is an obvious rearrangement of the first. However, this second line is useful because it shows that we can also write $f_r(x)$ as

$$f_r(x) = \frac{h}{4\pi} \int_{-x}^x \frac{\sin(r + \frac{1}{2})s}{\sin \frac{1}{2}s} ds - \frac{h}{4\pi} \int_{-\pi-x}^{-\pi+x} \frac{\sin(r + \frac{1}{2})s}{\sin \frac{1}{2}s} ds.$$ (19.36)

We are now ready to consider the partial sums in the vicinity of the discontinuity, $x = 0$. For small x, the denominator of the second integrand approaches -1, and the second integral therefore becomes negligible in the limit $x \to 0$. On the other hand, the first integrand becomes large near $s = 0$, and the value of the first integral depends on the magnitudes of r and x. If we now introduce the new variables $p = r + \frac{1}{2}$ and $\xi = ps$, we have (noting that the integrand is an even function of s)

$$f_r(x) \approx \frac{h}{2\pi} \int_0^{px} \frac{\sin \xi}{\sin(\xi/2p)} \frac{d\xi}{p}.$$ (19.37)

Calculation of Overshoot

We are now prepared to make a computation of the Fourier series overshoot. From Eq. (19.37), we see that for any finite r, $f_r(0)$ will be zero, giving at $x = 0$ the average of the two square-wave values ($+h/2$ and $-h/2$). However (keeping r fixed), Eq. (19.37) also tells us that $f_r(x)$ will increase as px becomes nonzero, reaching a maximum when

$px = \pi$. This maximum, which we will shortly show constitutes an overshoot, will therefore occur at $x = \pi/p$, which is approximately $x = \pi/r$. We thus see that the location of the overshoot maximum will differ from $x = 0$ in a manner approximately inversely proportional to the number of terms taken in the Fourier expansion.

To estimate the maximum value of $f_r(x)$, we substitute $px = \pi$ into Eq. (19.37), which we then simplify by making the good approximation $\sin(\xi/2p) \approx \xi/2p$:

$$f_r(x_{max}) = \frac{h}{2\pi} \int_0^{\pi} \frac{\sin\xi \, d\xi}{p \sin(\xi/2p)} \approx \frac{h}{\pi} \int_0^{\pi} \frac{\sin\xi}{\xi} \, d\xi. \tag{19.38}$$

If the upper limit of the final integral of Eq. (19.38) were replaced by infinity, we would have

$$\int_0^{\infty} \frac{\sin\xi}{\xi} \, d\xi = \frac{\pi}{2}, \tag{19.39}$$

a result found in Example 11.8.5. Note that this replacement would cause $f_r(x)$ to have the value $h/2$, which is the exact value of $f(x)$ for $x > 0$.

The integral we would have to add to that of Eq. (19.38) to obtain the infinite range is

$$\int_{\pi}^{\infty} \frac{\sin\xi}{\xi} \, d\xi = -\text{si}(\pi) ; \tag{19.40}$$

we have identified this integral as the sine integral function $\text{si}(x)$ introduced in Table 1.2 and plotted in Fig. 13.6. Thus,

$$\int_0^{\pi} \frac{\sin\xi}{\xi} \, d\xi = \frac{\pi}{2} + \text{si}(\pi). \tag{19.41}$$

The graph of $\text{si}(x)$ shows that $\text{si}(\pi) > 0$, indicating an overshoot. A direct demonstration that our integral is larger than $\pi/2$ can also be deduced by writing

$$\left(\int_0^{\infty} - \int_{\pi}^{3\pi} - \int_{3\pi}^{5\pi} - \cdots \right) \frac{\sin\xi}{\xi} \, d\xi = \int_0^{\pi} \frac{\sin\xi}{\xi} \, d\xi. \tag{19.42}$$

The first integral on the left-hand side has value $\pi/2$, while each of those to be subtracted is negative (and therefore makes a further positive contribution).

A Gaussian quadrature or a power-series expansion and term-by-term integration yields

$$\frac{2}{\pi} \int_0^{\pi} \frac{\sin\xi}{\xi} \, d\xi = 1.1789797\ldots, \tag{19.43}$$

which means that the Fourier series tends to overshoot the positive corner of the square wave by some 18% and to undershoot the negative corner by the same amount. This behavior is illustrated in Fig. 19.11. The inclusion of more terms (increasing r) does nothing to

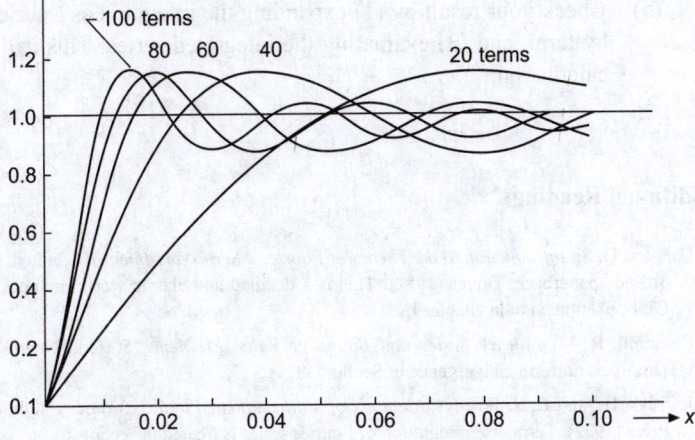

FIGURE 19.11   Square wave: Gibbs phenomenon.

remove this overshoot but merely moves it closer to the point of discontinuity. The overshoot is the Gibbs phenomenon, and because of it the Fourier series representation may be highly unreliable for precise numerical work, especially in the vicinity of a discontinuity.

The Gibbs phenomenon is not limited to the Fourier series. It occurs with other eigenfunction expansions. For more details, see W. J. Thompson, Fourier series and the Gibbs phenomenon, *Am. J. Phys.* **60**: 425 (1992).

Exercises

19.3.1   With the partial-sum summation techniques of this section, show that at a discontinuity in $f(x)$ the Fourier series for $f(x)$ takes on the arithmetic mean of the right- and left-hand limits:

$$f(x_0) = \tfrac{1}{2}[f(x_0 + 0) + f(x_0 - 0)].$$

In evaluating $\lim_{r \to \infty} s_r(x_0)$, you may find it convenient to identify part of the integrand as a Dirac delta function.

19.3.2   Determine the partial sum, s_n, of the series in Eq. (19.33) by using

(a) $\dfrac{\sin mx}{m} = \int_0^x \cos my \, dy,$ (b) $\displaystyle\sum_{p=1}^{n} \cos(2p - 1)y = \dfrac{\sin 2ny}{2 \sin y}.$

Do you agree with the result given in Eq. (19.40)?

19.3.3   (a)   Calculate the value of the Gibbs phenomenon integral

$$I = \frac{2}{\pi} \int_0^{\pi} \frac{\sin t}{t} \, dt$$

by numerical quadrature accurate to 12 significant figures.

(b) Check your result by (1) expanding the integrand as a series, (2) integrating term by term, and (3) evaluating the integrated series. This calls for double-precision calculation.

$$ANS. \quad I = 1.178979744472.$$

Additional Readings

Carslaw, H. S., *Introduction to the Theory of Fourier's Series and Integrals*, 2nd ed. London: Macmillan (1921); 3rd ed., paperback, Dover (1952). This is a detailed and classic work; includes considerable discussion of Gibbs phenomenon in chapter IX.

Churchill, R. V., *Fourier Series and Boundary Value Problems*, 5th ed., New York: McGraw-Hill (1993). Discusses uniform convergence in Section 38.

Jeffreys, H., and B. S. Jeffreys, *Methods of Mathematical Physics*, 3rd ed. Cambridge: Cambridge University Press (1972). Termwise integration of Fourier series is treated in section 14.06.

Kufner, A., and J. Kadlec, *Fourier Series*. London: Iliffe (1971). This book is a clear account of Fourier series in the context of Hilbert space.

Lanczos, C., *Applied Analysis*. Englewood Cliffs, NJ: Prentice-Hall (1956), reprinted, Dover (1988). The book gives a well-written presentation of the Lanczos convergence technique (which suppresses the Gibbs phenomenon oscillations). This and several other topics are presented from the point of view of a mathematician who wants useful numerical results and not just abstract existence theorems.

Oberhettinger, F., *Fourier Expansions; A Collection of Formulas*. New York: Academic Press (1973).

Zygmund, A., *Trigonometric Series*. Cambridge: Cambridge University Press (1988). The volume contains an extremely complete exposition, including relatively recent results in the realm of pure mathematics.

CHAPTER 20

INTEGRAL TRANSFORMS

20.1 INTRODUCTION

Frequently in mathematical physics we encounter pairs of functions related by an expression of the form

$$g(x) = \int_a^b f(t) K(x, t) dt, \tag{20.1}$$

where it is understood that a, b, and $K(x, t)$ (called the **kernel**) will be the same for all function pairs f and g. We can write the relationship expressed in Eq. (20.1) in the more symbolic form

$$g(x) = \mathcal{L} f(t), \tag{20.2}$$

thereby emphasizing the fact that Eq. (20.1) can be interpreted as an operator equation. The function $g(x)$ is called the integral transform of $f(t)$ by the operator $\mathcal{L}$, with the specific transform determined by the choice of a, b, and $K(x, t)$. The operator defined by Eq. (20.1) will be linear:

$$\int_a^b [f_1(t) + f_2(t)] K(x, t) dt = \int_a^b f_1(t) K(x, t) dt + \int_a^b f_2(t) K(x, t) dt, \tag{20.3}$$

$$\int_a^b c f(t) K(\alpha, t) dt = c \int_a^b f(t) K(\alpha, t) dt. \tag{20.4}$$

In order for transforms to be useful, we will shortly see that we need to be able to "undo" their effect. From a practical viewpoint, this means that not only must there exist an operator $\mathcal{L}^{-1}$, but also that we have a reasonably convenient and powerful method of evaluating

$$\mathcal{L}^{-1}g(x) = f(t) \qquad (20.5)$$

for an acceptably broad range of $g(x)$. The procedure for inverting a transform takes a wide variety of forms that depend on the specific properties of $K(x, t)$, so we cannot write a formula that is as general as that for $\mathcal{L}$ in Eq. (20.1).

Not all superficially reasonable choices for the kernel $K(x, t)$ will lead to operators $\mathcal{L}$ that have inverses, and even for strategically chosen kernels it may be the case that $\mathcal{L}$ and $\mathcal{L}^{-1}$ will only exist for substantially restricted classes of functions. Thus, the entire development of the present chapter is restricted (for any given integral transform) to functions for which the indicated operations can be carried out.

Before embarking on a study of integral transforms, we may well ask, "Why are integral transforms useful?" Their most common applications are in situations illustrated schematically in Fig. 20.1, where we have a problem that can be solved only with difficulty, if at all, in its original formulation (usually in ordinary space, sometimes called **direct** or **physical space**). However, it may happen that the transform of the problem can be solved relatively easily. Our strategy, then, will be to formulate and solve our problem in the transform space, after which we transform the solution back to direct space. This strategy often works because the most popular integral transforms are changed in simple ways by differentiation and integration operators, with the result that differential and integral equations assume relatively simple forms. This feature will be discussed and illustrated at length later in this chapter.

Another frequent use of integral transforms is to use one, together with its inverse, to form an **integral representation** of a function that we originally had in an explicit form. This move (which appears to be in the direction of generating greater complexity) has value that arises from the relatively simple behavior of the transforms of differentiation and integration operators. Procedures involving integral representations are also presented in later sections of this chapter.

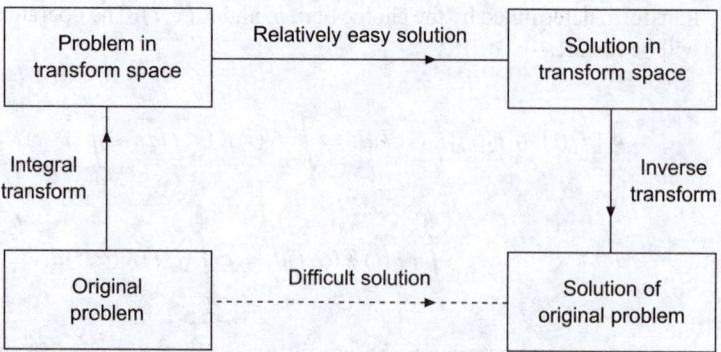

FIGURE 20.1   Schematic: use of integral transforms.

Some Important Transforms

The integral transform that has seen the widest use is the **Fourier transform**, defined as

$$g(\omega) = \frac{1}{\sqrt{2\pi}} \int\limits_{-\infty}^{\infty} f(t) e^{i\omega t} \, dt. \tag{20.6}$$

The notation for this transform is not entirely universal; some writers omit the prefactor $1/\sqrt{2\pi}$; we keep it because it causes the transform and its inverse to have formulas that are more symmetrical. In applications involving periodic systems, one occasionally encounters a definition with kernel $\exp(2\pi i\omega t/a_0)$, where a_0 is a lattice constant. These differences in notation do not change the mathematics, but cause formulas to differ by powers of 2π or a_0. Caution is therefore advised when combining material from different sources.

We have defined the Fourier transform in a notation that assigns the symbol ω to the transform variable. We did so because, in studying signal processing (an important use of Fourier transforms), the function $f(t)$ usually represents the time behavior of a signal (typically a wave distribution of some kind). Its Fourier transform, $g(\omega)$, can then be identified as the corresponding frequency distribution. However, it is worth pointing out that Fourier transforms turn up in contexts far removed from signal-processing problems; they can be used to advantage in evaluating integrals, in alternative formulations of quantum mechanics, and in a wide range of other mathematical procedures.

A second transform that has historically been of great importance is the **Laplace transform**,

$$F(s) = \int\limits_{0}^{\infty} e^{-ts} f(t) \, dt. \tag{20.7}$$

One of its useful features is the fact that under transformation, differential equations become algebraic equations (as we shall see in detail in Section 20.8). Since algebraic equations are usually easier to solve than differential equations, this feature lends itself to the strategy illustrated in Fig. 20.1. A disadvantage of the Laplace transform is that the formula for its inverse is relatively difficult to use. Historically, this difficulty was dealt with by developing tables of Laplace transforms (which can be used to identify inverses). As digital computers have become more powerful, the use of Laplace transforms has declined, but they remain sufficiently useful that we treat them in some detail in the present chapter.

Among other transforms that have seen significant use, we mention here two:

1. The **Hankel transform**,

$$g(\alpha) = \int\limits_{0}^{\infty} f(t) \, t \, J_n(\alpha t) \, dt. \tag{20.8}$$

This transform represents the continuum limit of the Bessel series we studied in Eqs. (14.47) and (14.48).

2. The **Mellin transform**,

$$g(\alpha) = \int_0^\infty f(t)\, t^{\alpha-1}\, dt. \tag{20.9}$$

We have actually used the Mellin transform without calling it by name; for example, $g(\alpha) = \Gamma(\alpha)$ is the Mellin transform of $f(t) = e^{-t}$. Many Mellin transforms are given in a text by Titchmarsh (see Additional Readings).

20.2   FOURIER TRANSFORM

We proceed now to a more detailed discussion of the Fourier transform,

$$g(\omega) = \frac{1}{\sqrt{2\pi}} \int_{-\infty}^\infty f(t) e^{i\omega t}\, dt. \tag{20.10}$$

If we rewrite the exponential in Eq. (20.10) in terms of the sine and cosine, and then restrict consideration to functions that are assumed to be either even or odd functions of x, we obtain variants of the original form that are also useful integral transforms:

$$g_c(\omega) = \sqrt{\frac{2}{\pi}} \int_0^\infty f(t) \cos \omega t\, dt, \tag{20.11}$$

$$g_s(\omega) = \sqrt{\frac{2}{\pi}} \int_0^\infty f(t) \sin \omega t\, dt. \tag{20.12}$$

These formulas define the **Fourier cosine** and **Fourier sine** transforms. Their kernels, which are real, are natural for use in studies of wave motion and for extracting information from waves, particularly when phase information is involved. The output of a stellar interferometer, for instance, involves a Fourier transform of the brightness across a stellar disk. The electron distribution in an atom may be obtained from a Fourier transform of the amplitude of scattered x-rays.

Example 20.2.1   SOME FOURIER TRANSFORMS

1. $f(t) = e^{-\alpha|t|}$, with $\alpha > 0$. To deal with the absolute value, we break the transform integral into two regions:

$$g(\omega) = \sqrt{\frac{1}{2\pi}} \int_{-\infty}^0 e^{\alpha t + i\omega t}\, dt + \sqrt{\frac{1}{2\pi}} \int_0^\infty e^{-\alpha t + i\omega t}\, dt$$

$$= \sqrt{\frac{1}{2\pi}} \left[\frac{1}{\alpha + i\omega} + \frac{1}{\alpha - i\omega} \right] = \sqrt{\frac{1}{2\pi}} \frac{2\alpha}{\alpha^2 + \omega^2}. \tag{20.13}$$

We note two features of this result: (1) It is real; from the form of the transform, we can see that if $f(t)$ is even, its transform will be real. (2) The more localized is $f(t)$, the less localized will be $g(\omega)$. The transform will have an appreciable value until $\omega \gg \alpha$; larger α corresponds to greater localization of $f(t)$.

2. $f(t) = \delta(t)$. We easily find

$$g(\omega) = \sqrt{\frac{1}{2\pi}} \int_{-\infty}^{\infty} \delta(t) e^{i\omega t}\, dt = \sqrt{\frac{1}{2\pi}}. \tag{20.14}$$

This is the ultimately localized $f(t)$, and we see that $g(\omega)$ is completely delocalized; it has the same value for all ω.

3. $f(t) = 2\alpha\sqrt{1/2\pi} / (\alpha^2 + t^2)$, with $\alpha > 0$. One way to evaluate this transform is by contour integration. It is convenient to start by writing initially

$$g(\omega) = \frac{1}{2\pi} \int_{-\infty}^{\infty} \frac{2\alpha\, e^{i\omega t}}{(t - i\alpha)(t + i\alpha)}\, dt.$$

The integrand has two poles: one at $t = i\alpha$ with residue $e^{-\alpha\omega}/i$ and one at $t = -i\alpha$ with residue $e^{+\alpha\omega}/(-i)$. If $\omega > 0$, our integrand will become negligible on a large semicircle in the upper half-plane, so an integral over the contour shown in Fig. 20.2(a) will be that needed for $g(\omega)$. This contour encloses only the pole at $t = i\alpha$, so we get

$$g(\omega) = \frac{1}{2\pi} (2\pi i) \frac{e^{-\alpha\omega}}{i} \quad (\omega > 0). \tag{20.15}$$

However, if $\omega < 0$, we must close the contour in the lower half-plane, as in Fig. 20.2(b), circling the pole at $t = -i\alpha$ in a clockwise sense (thereby generating a minus sign). This procedure yields

$$g(\omega) = \frac{1}{2\pi} (-2\pi i) \frac{e^{+\alpha\omega}}{-i} \quad (\omega < 0). \tag{20.16}$$

If $\omega = 0$, we cannot perform a contour integration on either of the paths shown in Fig. 20.2, but we then do not need this sophisticated an approach, as we have the

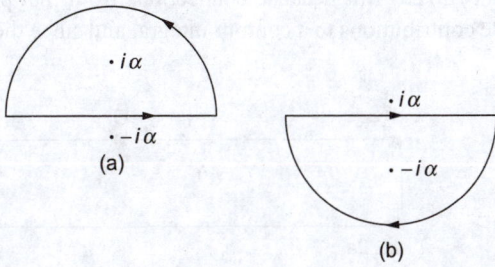

$\cdot\, i\alpha$

$\cdot -i\alpha$

(a)

$\cdot\, i\alpha$

$\cdot -i\alpha$

(b)

FIGURE 20.2   Contours for third transform in Example 20.2.1.

elementary integral

$$g(0) = \frac{1}{2\pi} \int\limits_{-\infty}^{\infty} \frac{2\alpha}{t^2 + \alpha^2} \, dt = 1. \tag{20.17}$$

Combining Eqs. (20.15)–(20.17) and simplifying, we have

$$g(\omega) = e^{-\alpha|\omega|}.$$

Here we Fourier transformed the transform from our first example, recovering the original untransformed function. This provides an interesting clue as to the form to be expected for the inverse Fourier transform. It is only a clue, because our example involved a transform that was real (i.e., not complex). ∎

An important Fourier transform follows.

Example 20.2.2   FOURIER TRANSFORM OF GAUSSIAN

The Fourier transform of a Gaussian function e^{-at^2}, with $a > 0$,

$$g(\omega) = \frac{1}{\sqrt{2\pi}} \int\limits_{-\infty}^{\infty} e^{-at^2} e^{i\omega t} \, dt,$$

can be evaluated analytically by completing the square in the exponent,

$$-at^2 + i\omega t = -a \left(t - \frac{i\omega}{2a} \right)^2 - \frac{\omega^2}{4a},$$

which we can check by evaluating the square. Substituting this identity and changing the integration variable from t to $s = t - i\omega/2a$, we obtain (in the limit of large T)

$$g(\omega) = \frac{1}{\sqrt{2\pi}} e^{-\omega^2/4a} \int\limits_{-T-i\omega/2a}^{T-i\omega/2a} e^{-as^2} \, ds. \tag{20.18}$$

The s integration, shown in Fig. 20.3, is on a path parallel to, but below the real axis by an amount $i\omega/2a$. But because connections from that path to the real axis at $\pm T$ make negligible contributions to a contour integral and since the contours in Fig. 20.3 enclose no

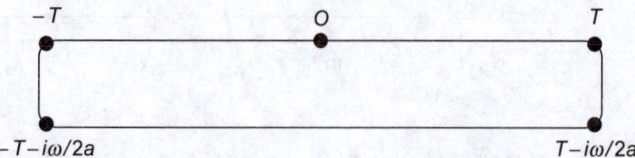

FIGURE 20.3   Contour for transform of Gaussian in Example 20.2.2.

singularities, the integral in Eq. (20.18) is equivalent to one along the real axis. Changing the integration limits to $\pm\infty$ and rescaling to the new variable $\xi = s/\sqrt{a}$, we reach

$$\int_{-\infty}^{\infty} e^{-as^2} dt = \frac{1}{\sqrt{a}} \int_{-\infty}^{\infty} e^{-\xi^2} d\xi = \sqrt{\frac{\pi}{a}},$$

where we have used Eq. (1.148) to evaluate the error-function integral. Substituting these results we find

$$g(\omega) = \frac{1}{\sqrt{2a}} \exp\left(-\frac{\omega^2}{4a}\right), \tag{20.19}$$

again a Gaussian, but in ω-space. An increase in a makes the original Gaussian e^{-at^2} narrower, while making wider its Fourier transform, the behavior of which is dominated by the exponential $e^{-\omega^2/4a}$. ∎

Fourier Integral

When we first encountered the delta function, its representation which is the large-n limit of

$$\delta_n(t) = \frac{1}{2\pi} \int_{-n}^{n} e^{i\omega t} d\omega, \tag{20.20}$$

was identified as particularly useful in Fourier analysis. We now use that representation to obtain an important result known as the **Fourier integral**. We write the fairly obvious equation,

$$f(x) = \lim_{n\to\infty} \int_{-\infty}^{\infty} f(t)\,\delta_n(t-x)dt$$

$$= \lim_{n\to\infty} \frac{1}{2\pi} \int_{-\infty}^{\infty} f(t) \left[\int_{-n}^{n} e^{i\omega(t-x)} d\omega\right] dt. \tag{20.21}$$

We now interchange the order of integration and take the limit $n \to \infty$, reaching

$$f(x) = \frac{1}{2\pi} \int_{-\infty}^{\infty} d\omega \int_{-\infty}^{\infty} dt f(t) e^{i\omega(t-x)}.$$

Finally, we rearrange this equation to the form

$$f(x) = \frac{1}{2\pi} \int_{-\infty}^{\infty} e^{-i\omega x} d\omega \int_{-\infty}^{\infty} f(t) e^{i\omega t} dt. \tag{20.22}$$

Equation (20.22), the **Fourier integral**, is an integral representation of $f(x)$, and will be more obviously recognized as such if the inner integration (over t) is performed, leaving unevaluated that over ω. In fact, if we identify the inner integration as (apart from a factor $\sqrt{1/2\pi}$) the Fourier transform of $f(t)$, and label it $g(\omega)$ as in Eq. (20.10), then Eq. (20.22) can be rewritten

$$f(t) = \sqrt{\frac{1}{2\pi}} \int_{-\infty}^{\infty} g(\omega)e^{-i\omega t} d\omega, \tag{20.23}$$

showing that whenever we have the Fourier transform of a function $f(t)$ we can use it to make a **Fourier integral representation** of that function.

The Fourier integral formula, written as in Eq. (20.23), illustrates the value of Fourier analysis in signal processing. If $f(t)$ is an arbitrary signal, Eq. (20.23) describes the signal as composed of a superposition of waves $e^{-i\omega t}$ at angular frequencies[1] ω, with respective amplitudes $g(\omega)$. Thus, the Fourier integral is the underlying justification that one can express a signal either by its time dependence $f(t)$ or by its (angular) frequency distribution $g(\omega)$.

Before leaving the Fourier integral, we should remark that our derivation of it did not provide a rigorous justification for the reversal of the order of integration and the passage to the infinite-n limit. The interested reader can find a more rigorous treatment in, for example, the work *Fourier Transforms* by I. N. Sneddon (Additional Readings).

Example 20.2.3   FOURIER INTEGRAL REPRESENTATION

From the first transform of Example 20.2.1, we found that $f(t) = e^{-\alpha|t|}$ has Fourier transform $g(\omega) = \sqrt{1/2\pi}\, 2\alpha/(\alpha^2 + \omega^2)$. If we substitute these data into Eq. (20.23), we obtain

$$e^{-\alpha|t|} = f(t) = \frac{1}{2\pi} \int_{-\infty}^{\infty} \frac{2\alpha e^{-i\omega t}}{\alpha^2 + \omega^2} d\omega = \frac{\alpha}{\pi} \int_{-\infty}^{\infty} \frac{e^{-i\omega t}}{\alpha^2 + \omega^2} d\omega. \tag{20.24}$$

Equation (20.24) provides an integral representation for $\exp(-\alpha|t|)$ that contains no absolute value signs and may constitute a useful starting point for various analytical manipulations. We will shortly encounter some more substantive examples with immediate applications for physics.   ■

Inverse Fourier Transform

As the reader may have noticed, Eq. (20.23) is a formula for the **inverse Fourier transform**. Note that the regular ("direct") and inverse Fourier transforms are given by very similar (but not quite identical) formulas. The only difference is in the sign of the complex exponential. This change of sign causes two successive applications of the Fourier transform not to be identical with applying the transform and then its inverse, and the difference shows up when $g(\omega)$ is not real.[2]

---

[1] The wave $e^{-i\omega t}$ has period $2\pi/\omega$, thus frequency $\nu = \omega/2\pi$. Its angular frequency (radians per unit time rather than cycles) is $2\pi\nu = \omega$.

[2] Even functions have real Fourier transforms; the transforms of odd functions are imaginary. A function that is neither even nor odd will have a Fourier transform that is complex.

The analysis of the preceding subsection can also be applied to the Fourier cosine and sine transforms. For convenience, we summarize the formulas for all three varieties of the Fourier transform and their respective inverses.

$$g(\omega) = \frac{1}{\sqrt{2\pi}} \int_{-\infty}^{\infty} f(t)e^{i\omega t}\,dt, \qquad (20.25)$$

$$f(t) = \frac{1}{\sqrt{2\pi}} \int_{-\infty}^{\infty} g(\omega)e^{-i\omega t}\,d\omega, \qquad (20.26)$$

$$g_c(\omega) = \sqrt{\frac{2}{\pi}} \int_{0}^{\infty} f(t)\cos\omega t\,dt, \qquad (20.27)$$

$$f_c(t) = \sqrt{\frac{2}{\pi}} \int_{0}^{\infty} g(\omega)\cos\omega t\,d\omega, \qquad (20.28)$$

$$g_s(\omega) = \sqrt{\frac{2}{\pi}} \int_{0}^{\infty} f(t)\sin\omega t\,dt, \qquad (20.29)$$

$$f_s(t) = \sqrt{\frac{2}{\pi}} \int_{0}^{\infty} g(\omega)\sin\omega t\,d\omega. \qquad (20.30)$$

Note that the Fourier sine and cosine transforms only use data for $0 \leq t < \infty$. Therefore, even though it is possible to evaluate the corresponding inverse transforms for negative t, the results may be irrelevant to the actual situation at those t values. But if our function $f(t)$ is even, then the cosine transform will reproduce it faithfully for negative t; odd functions will be properly described for negative t by the sine transform.

Example 20.2.4   FINITE WAVE TRAIN

An important application of the Fourier transform is the resolution of a finite pulse into sinusoidal waves. Imagine that an infinite wave train $\sin\omega_0 t$ is clipped by Kerr cell or saturable dye cell shutters so that we have

$$f(t) = \begin{cases} \sin\omega_0 t, & |t| < \dfrac{N\pi}{\omega_0}, \\[2mm] 0, & |t| > \dfrac{N\pi}{\omega_0}. \end{cases} \qquad (20.31)$$

This corresponds to N cycles of our original wave train (Fig. 20.4). Since $f(t)$ is odd, we use the Fourier sine transform, Eq. (20.28), to obtain

$$g_s(\omega) = \sqrt{\frac{2}{\pi}} \int_0^{N\pi/\omega_0} \sin \omega_0 t \sin \omega t \, dt. \tag{20.32}$$

Integrating, we find our amplitude function:

$$g_s(\omega) = \sqrt{\frac{2}{\pi}} \left[\frac{\sin[(\omega_0 - \omega)(N\pi/\omega_0)]}{2(\omega_0 - \omega)} - \frac{\sin[(\omega_0 + \omega)(N\pi/\omega_0)]}{2(\omega_0 + \omega)} \right]. \tag{20.33}$$

It is of considerable interest to see how $g_s(\omega)$ depends on frequency. For large ω_0' and $\omega \approx \omega_0$, only the first term will be of any importance because of the denominators. It is plotted in Fig. 20.5. This is the amplitude curve for the single-slit diffraction pattern. It has zeros at

$$\frac{\omega_0 - \omega}{\omega_0} = \frac{\Delta\omega}{\omega_0} = \pm\frac{1}{N}, \pm\frac{2}{N}, \quad \text{and so on.} \tag{20.34}$$

For large N, $g_s(\omega)$ may also be interpreted as proportional to a Dirac delta distribution.

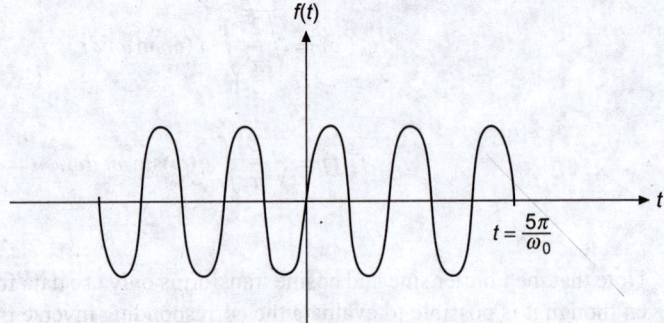

FIGURE 20.4   Finite wave train.

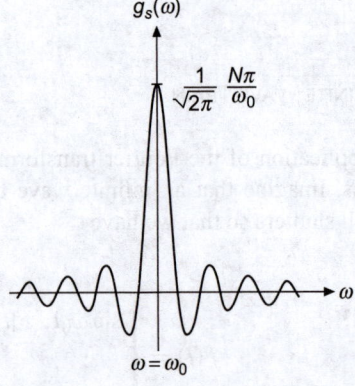

FIGURE 20.5   Fourier transform of finite wave train.

Since a large fraction of the frequency distribution falls within its central maximum, the half-width of that maximum,

$$\Delta\omega = \frac{\omega_0}{N},\qquad(20.35)$$

is a good measure of the spread in angular frequency of our wave pulse. Clearly, if N is large (a long pulse), the frequency spread will be small. On the other hand, if our pulse is clipped short, N small, the frequency distribution will be wider.

The inverse relationship between frequency spread and pulse length is a fundamental property of finite wave distributions; the precision with which a signal can be identified as a specific frequency depends on the pulse length. This same principle finds expression as the **Heisenberg uncertainty principle** of quantum mechanics, in which position uncertainty (the quantum variable corresponding to pulse length) is inversely related to momentum uncertainty (quantum analog of frequency). It is worth noting that the uncertainty principle in quantum mechanics is a consequence of the wave nature of matter and does not depend on additional *ad hoc* postulates.   ∎

Transforms in 3-D Space

Applying the Fourier transform operator in each dimension of a three-dimensional (3-D) space, we obtain the extremely useful formulas

$$g(\mathbf{k}) = \frac{1}{(2\pi)^{3/2}} \int f(\mathbf{r})e^{i\mathbf{k}\cdot\mathbf{r}}\, d^3r,\qquad(20.36)$$

$$f(\mathbf{r}) = \frac{1}{(2\pi)^{3/2}} \int g(\mathbf{k})e^{-i\mathbf{k}\cdot\mathbf{r}}\, d^3k.\qquad(20.37)$$

These integrals are over all space. Verification, if desired, follows immediately by substituting the left-hand side of one equation into the integrand of the other equation and choosing the integration order that permits the complex exponentials to be identified as delta functions in each of the three dimensions. Equation (20.37) may be interpreted as an expansion of a function $f(\mathbf{r})$ in a continuum of plane waves; $g(\mathbf{k})$ then becomes the amplitude of the wave $\exp(-i\mathbf{k}\cdot\mathbf{r})$.

Example 20.2.5   SOME 3-D TRANSFORMS

1. Let's find the Fourier transform of the Yukawa potential, $e^{-\alpha r}/r$. Using the notation $[\cdots]^T$ to denote the Fourier transform of the included object, we seek

$$\left[\frac{e^{-\alpha r}}{r}\right]^T(\mathbf{k}) = \frac{1}{(2\pi)^{3/2}} \int \frac{e^{-\alpha r}}{r}\, e^{i\mathbf{k}\cdot\mathbf{r}}\, d^3r.\qquad(20.38)$$

Perhaps the simplest way to proceed is to introduce the spherical wave expansion for $\exp(i\mathbf{k}\cdot\mathbf{r})$, Eq. (16.61). Equation (20.38), written in spherical polar coordinates, then assumes the form

$$\left[\frac{e^{-\alpha r}}{r}\right]^{T}(\mathbf{k}) = \frac{4\pi}{(2\pi)^{3/2}} \int_{0}^{\infty} r\,dr \int d\Omega_{r} \sum_{lm} i^{l} e^{-\alpha r} j_{l}(kr) Y_{l}^{m}(\Omega_{k})^{*} Y_{l}^{m}(\Omega_{r}). \quad (20.39)$$

All terms of the angular integration vanish except that with $l = m = 0$. For that term, each Y_{0}^{0} has the constant value $1/\sqrt{4\pi}$, and Eq. (20.39) reduces to

$$\left[\frac{e^{-\alpha r}}{r}\right]^{T}(\mathbf{k}) = \frac{4\pi}{(2\pi)^{3/2}} \int_{0}^{\infty} r\,e^{-\alpha r} j_{0}(kr)\,dr. \quad (20.40)$$

Inserting $j_{0}(kr) = \sin kr/kr$, the r integration becomes elementary, and we reach

$$\left[\frac{e^{-\alpha r}}{r}\right]^{T}(\mathbf{k}) = \frac{1}{(2\pi)^{3/2}} \frac{4\pi}{k^{2}+\alpha^{2}}. \quad (20.41)$$

We wrote Eq. (20.41) as we did to make obvious that if the transform were scaled without the factor $1/(2\pi)^{3/2}$, we would have the well-known result $4\pi/(k^{2}+\alpha^{2})$.

2. Even more important than the Fourier transform of the Yukawa potential is that of the Coulomb potential, $1/r$. An attempt to evaluate this transform directly leads to convergence problems, but it is easy to evaluate it as the limiting case of the Yukawa potential with $\alpha = 0$. Thus, we have the extremely important result,

$$\left[\frac{1}{r}\right]^{T}(\mathbf{k}) = \frac{1}{(2\pi)^{3/2}} \frac{4\pi}{k^{2}}. \quad (20.42)$$

3. From the relation between the Fourier transform and its inverse, Eq. (20.42) can effectively be inverted to yield

$$\left[\frac{1}{r^{2}}\right]^{T}(\mathbf{k}) = \left(\frac{\pi}{2}\right)^{1/2} \frac{1}{k}. \quad (20.43)$$

4. Another useful Fourier transform is that of the hydrogenic $1s$ orbital, which (in unnormalized form) is $\exp(-Zr)$. A simple way to evaluate this transform is to differentiate the transform for the Yukawa potential with respect to its parameter, α in Eq. (20.41). Noting that differentiation with respect to this parameter commutes with the transform operator (which involves integration with respect to other variables), we have

$$-\frac{\partial}{\partial Z}\left[\frac{e^{-Zr}}{r}\right]^{T}(\mathbf{k}) = \left[e^{-Zr}\right]^{T}(\mathbf{k}) = \frac{1}{(2\pi)^{3/2}} \frac{8\pi Z}{(k^{2}+Z^{2})^{2}}. \quad (20.44)$$

5. Consider next an arbitrary function whose angular dependence is a spherical harmonic (i.e., an angular momentum eigenfunction). Using spherical polar coordinates, we look at

$$\left[f(r) Y_l^m(\Omega_r) \right]^T(\mathbf{k}) = \frac{1}{(2\pi)^{3/2}} \int\limits_0^\infty f(r) r^2 \, dr \int d\Omega_r Y_l^m(\Omega_r) e^{i\mathbf{k}\cdot\mathbf{r}}$$

$$= \frac{4\pi}{(2\pi)^{3/2}} \int\limits_0^\infty f(r) r^2 \, dr \int d\Omega_r Y_l^m(\Omega_r)$$

$$\times \sum_{l'm'} i^{l'} j_{l'}(kr) Y_{l'}^{m'}(\Omega_k) Y_{l'}^{m'}(\Omega_r)^*,$$

where we have inserted the spherical wave expansion, Eq. (16.61), for $\exp(i\mathbf{k}\cdot\mathbf{r})$. Because the Y_l^m are orthonormal, the summation reduces to a single term, and we have

$$\left[f(r) Y_l^m(\Omega_r) \right]^T(\mathbf{k}) = \frac{4\pi i^l}{(2\pi)^{3/2}} Y_l^m(\Omega_k) \int\limits_0^\infty f(r) j_l(kr) r^2 dr. \tag{20.45}$$

Equation (20.45) shows that a function with spherical harmonic angular dependence has a transform containing the same spherical harmonic and that the radial dependence of the transform is essentially a Hankel transform. Compare with Eq. (20.8).

6. As a final example, consider the Fourier transform of a 3-D Gaussian. Again using spherical polar coordinates and the spherical wave expansion (a procedure generally applicable for transforms of spherically symmetric functions), we get

$$\left[e^{-ar^2} \right]^T(\mathbf{k}) = \frac{4\pi}{(2\pi)^{3/2}} \int\limits_0^\infty r^2 e^{-ar^2} j_0(kr) dr. \tag{20.46}$$

Using methods similar to those of Example 20.2.2, we find

$$\left[e^{-ar^2} \right]^T(\mathbf{k}) = \frac{1}{(2a)^{3/2}} e^{-k^2/4a}. \tag{20.47}$$

This result could also be obtained using Cartesian coordinates and using the result of Example 20.2.2 in each of the three dimensions. ∎

Exercises

20.2.1 (a) Show that $g(-\omega) = g^*(\omega)$ is a necessary and sufficient condition for $f(x)$ to be real.

(b) Show that $g(-\omega) = -g^*(\omega)$ is a necessary and sufficient condition for $f(x)$ to be pure imaginary.

Note. The condition of part (a) is used in the development of the dispersion relations of Section 12.8.

20.2.2   The function

$$f(x) = \begin{cases} 1, & |x| < 1 \\ 0, & |x| > 1 \end{cases}$$

is a symmetrical finite step function.

(a)   Find $g_c(\omega)$, Fourier cosine transform of $f(x)$.

(b)   Taking the inverse cosine transform, show that

$$f(x) = \frac{2}{\pi} \int_0^\infty \frac{\sin \omega \cos \omega x}{\omega} \, d\omega.$$

(c)   From part (b) show that

$$\int_0^\infty \frac{\sin \omega \cos \omega x}{\omega} \, d\omega = \begin{cases} 0, & |x| > 1, \\ \dfrac{\pi}{4}, & |x| = 1, \\ \dfrac{\pi}{2}, & |x| < 1. \end{cases}$$

20.2.3   (a)   Show that the Fourier sine and cosine transforms of e^{-at} are

$$g_s(\omega) = \sqrt{\frac{2}{\pi}} \frac{\omega}{\omega^2 + a^2}, \quad g_c(\omega) = \sqrt{\frac{2}{\pi}} \frac{a}{\omega^2 + a^2}.$$

Hint. Each of the transforms can be related to the other by integration by parts.

(b)   Show that

$$\int_0^\infty \frac{\omega \sin \omega x}{\omega^2 + a^2} \, d\omega = \frac{\pi}{2} e^{-ax}, \quad x > 0,$$

$$\int_0^\infty \frac{\cos \omega x}{\omega^2 + a^2} \, d\omega = \frac{\pi}{2a} e^{-ax}, \quad x > 0.$$

These results can also be obtained by contour integration (Exercise 11.8.12).

20.2.4   Find the Fourier transform of the triangular pulse (Fig. 20.6),

$$f(x) = \begin{cases} h(1 - a|x|), & |x| < 1/a, \\ 0, & |x| > 1/a. \end{cases}$$

Note. This function provides another delta sequence with $h = a$ and $a \to \infty$.

20.2.5   Consider the sequence

$$\delta_n(x) = \begin{cases} n, & |x| < 1/2n, \\ 0, & |x| > 1/2n. \end{cases}$$

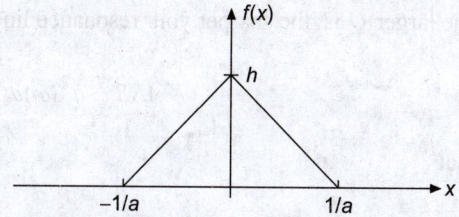

FIGURE 20.6   Triangular pulse.

This is Eq. (1.152). Express $\delta_n(x)$ as a Fourier integral (via the Fourier integral theorem, inverse transform, etc.). Finally, show that we may write

$$\delta(x) = \lim_{n \to \infty} \delta_n(x) = \frac{1}{2\pi} \int_{-\infty}^{\infty} e^{-ikx}\, dk.$$

20.2.6   Using the sequence

$$\delta_n(x) = \frac{n}{\sqrt{\pi}} \exp(-n^2 x^2),$$

show that

$$\delta(x) = \frac{1}{2\pi} \int_{-\infty}^{\infty} e^{-ikx}\, dk.$$

Hint. Remember that $\delta(x)$ is defined in terms of its behavior as part of an integrand.

20.2.7   The formula

$$\delta(t - x) = \frac{1}{2\pi} \int_{-\infty}^{\infty} e^{i\omega(t-x)}\, d\omega = \frac{1}{2\pi} \int_{-\infty}^{\infty} e^{i\omega t} e^{-i\omega x}\, d\omega$$

can be identified as the continuum limit of an eigenfunction expansion. Derive sine and cosine representations of $\delta(t - x)$ that are comparable to the exponential representation just given.

$$ANS. \quad \frac{2}{\pi} \int_{0}^{\infty} \sin \omega t\, \sin \omega x\, d\omega, \quad \frac{2}{\pi} \int_{0}^{\infty} \cos \omega t\, \cos \omega x\, d\omega.$$

20.2.8   In a resonant cavity, an electromagnetic oscillation of frequency ω_0 dies out as

$$A(t) = \begin{cases} A_0\, e^{-\omega_0 t/2Q}\, e^{-i\omega_0 t}, & t > 0, \\ 0, & t < 0. \end{cases}$$

The parameter Q is a measure of the ratio of stored energy to energy loss per cycle. Calculate the frequency distribution of the oscillation, $a^*(\omega)a(\omega)$, where $a(\omega)$ is the Fourier transform of $A(t)$.

Note. The larger Q is, the sharper your resonance line will be.

$$ANS. \quad a^*(\omega)a(\omega) = \frac{A_0^2}{2\pi} \frac{1}{(\omega - \omega_0)^2 + (\omega_0/2Q)^2}.$$

20.2.9   Prove that

$$\frac{\hbar}{2\pi i} \int_{-\infty}^{\infty} \frac{e^{-i\omega t} d\omega}{E_0 - i\Gamma/2 - \hbar\omega} = \begin{cases} \exp\left(-\frac{\Gamma t}{2\hbar}\right) \exp\left(-i\frac{E_0 t}{\hbar}\right), & t > 0, \\ 0, & t < 0. \end{cases}$$

This Fourier integral appears in a variety of problems in quantum mechanics: barrier penetration, scattering, time-dependent perturbation theory, and so on.

Hint. Try contour integration.

20.2.10   Verify that the following are Fourier integral transforms of one another:

(a) $$\begin{cases} \sqrt{\frac{2}{\pi}} \cdot \frac{1}{\sqrt{a^2 - x^2}}, & |x| < a, \\ 0, & |x| > a, \end{cases} \quad \text{and } J_0(ay),$$

(b) $$\begin{cases} 0, & |x| < a, \\ -\sqrt{\frac{2}{\pi}} \frac{1}{\sqrt{x^2 + a^2}}, & |x| > a, \end{cases} \quad \text{and } Y_0(a|y|),$$

(c) $$\sqrt{\frac{\pi}{2}} \frac{1}{\sqrt{x^2 + a^2}} \quad \text{and} \quad K_0(a|y|).$$

(d)   Can you suggest why $I_0(ay)$ is not included in this list?

Hint. J_0, Y_0, and K_0 may be transformed most easily by using an exponential representation, reversing the order of integration, and employing the Dirac delta function exponential representation, Eq. (20.20). These cases can be treated equally well as Fourier cosine transforms.

20.2.11   Show that the following are Fourier transforms of each other:

$$i^n J_n(t) \quad \text{and} \quad \begin{cases} \sqrt{\frac{2}{\pi}} T_n(x)(1 - x^2)^{-1/2}, & |x| < 1, \\ 0, & |x| > 1. \end{cases}$$

$T_n(x)$ is the nth-order Chebyshev polynomial.

Hint. With $T_n(\cos\theta) = \cos n\theta$, the transform of $T_n(x)(1 - x^2)^{-1/2}$ leads to an integral representation of $J_n(t)$.

20.2.12   Show that the Fourier exponential transform of

$$f(\mu) = \begin{cases} P_n(\mu), & |\mu| \leq 1 \\ 0, & |\mu| > 1 \end{cases}$$

is $(2i^n/2\pi) j_n(kr)$. Here $P_n(\mu)$ is a Legendre polynomial and $j_n(kr)$ is a spherical Bessel function.

20.2.13   (a)   Show that $f(x) = x^{-1/2}$ is a **self-reciprocal** under both Fourier cosine and sine transforms; that is,

$$\sqrt{\frac{2}{\pi}} \int_0^\infty x^{-1/2} \cos xt \, dx = t^{-1/2},$$

$$\sqrt{\frac{2}{\pi}} \int_0^\infty x^{-1/2} \sin xt \, ds = t^{-1/2}.$$

(b)   Use the preceding results to evaluate the Fresnel integrals

$$\int_0^\infty \cos(y^2) dy \quad \text{and} \quad \int_0^\infty \sin(y^2) dy.$$

20.2.14   Show that $\left[\dfrac{1}{r^2}\right]^T (\mathbf{k}) = \left(\dfrac{\pi}{2}\right)^{1/2} \dfrac{1}{k}.$

20.2.15   The Fourier transform formulas for a function of two variables are

$$F(u, v) = \frac{1}{2\pi} \iint f(x, y) e^{i(ux+vy)} \, dx \, dy,$$

$$f(x, y) = \frac{1}{2\pi} \iint F(u, v) e^{-i(ux+vy)} \, du \, dv,$$

where the integrations are over the entire xy or uv plane. For $f(x, y) = f([x^2 + y^2]^{1/2}) = f(r)$, show that the zero-order Hankel transforms

$$F(\rho) = \int_0^\infty r f(r) J_0(\rho r) dr,$$

$$f(r) = \int_0^\infty \rho F(\rho) J_0(\rho r) d\rho,$$

are a special case of the Fourier transforms.

Note. This technique may be generalized to derive the Hankel transforms of order $\nu = 0$, $\frac{1}{2}, 1, \frac{3}{2}, \ldots$. See the two texts by Sneddon (Additional Readings). It might also be noted that the Hankel transforms of half-integral orders $\nu = \pm\frac{1}{2}$ reduce to Fourier sine and cosine transforms.

20.2.16   Show that the 3-D Fourier exponential transform of a radially symmetric function may be rewritten as a Fourier sine transform:

$$\frac{1}{(2\pi)^{3/2}} \int_{-\infty}^{\infty} f(r) e^{i\mathbf{k}\cdot\mathbf{r}} d^3 x = \frac{1}{k}\sqrt{\frac{2}{\pi}} \int_{0}^{\infty} r f(r) \sin kr\, dr.$$

20.3 PROPERTIES OF FOURIER TRANSFORMS

Fourier transforms have a number of useful properties, many of which follow directly from the transform definition. Using the 3-D transform as an illustration, and letting $g(\mathbf{k})$ be the Fourier transform of $f(\mathbf{r})$:

$$\left[f(\mathbf{r} - \mathbf{R}) \right]^T (\mathbf{k}) = e^{i\mathbf{k}\cdot\mathbf{R}} g(\mathbf{k}), \qquad \text{(translation)}, \tag{20.48}$$

$$\left[f(\alpha\mathbf{r}) \right]^T (\mathbf{k}) = \frac{1}{\alpha^3} g(\alpha^{-1}\mathbf{k}), \qquad \text{(change of scale)}, \tag{20.49}$$

$$\left[f(-\mathbf{r}) \right]^T (\mathbf{k}) = g(-\mathbf{k}), \qquad \text{(sign change)}, \tag{20.50}$$

$$\left[f^*(-\mathbf{r}) \right]^T (\mathbf{k}) = g^*(\mathbf{k}), \qquad \text{(complex conjugation)}, \tag{20.51}$$

$$\left[\nabla f(\mathbf{r}) \right]^T (\mathbf{k}) = -i\mathbf{k}\, g(\mathbf{k}), \qquad \text{(gradient)}, \tag{20.52}$$

$$\left[\nabla^2 f(\mathbf{r}) \right]^T (\mathbf{k}) = -k^2\, g(\mathbf{k}), \qquad \text{(Laplacian)}. \tag{20.53}$$

The first four of the above formulas can be obtained by carrying out appropriate operations on the defining equation of the transform; details are left to the exercises. Equations (20.52) and (20.53) are easily established from the inverse transform formula. For example, from Eq. (20.37),

$$\nabla f(\mathbf{r}) = \frac{1}{(2\pi)^{3/2}} \int g(\mathbf{k}) \left[\nabla_r e^{-i\mathbf{k}\cdot\mathbf{r}} \right] d\mathbf{k}$$

$$= \frac{1}{(2\pi)^{3/2}} \int g(\mathbf{k}) \left[(-i\mathbf{k}) e^{-i\mathbf{k}\cdot\mathbf{r}} \right] d\mathbf{k}$$

$$= \frac{1}{(2\pi)^{3/2}} \int \left[-i\mathbf{k}\, g(\mathbf{k}) \right] e^{-i\mathbf{k}\cdot\mathbf{r}} d\mathbf{k}, \tag{20.54}$$

showing that $-i\mathbf{k}\, g(\mathbf{k})$ is indeed the Fourier transform of $\nabla f(\mathbf{r})$. It should be noted that this demonstration requires the existence of the integrals involved.

The translation formula is of considerable practical value, as it enables a function that is most conveniently described relative to an origin at $\mathbf{R}$ to have a transform whose natural representation is about the origin in the $\mathbf{k}$ space, albeit with a complex phase factor, $\exp(i\mathbf{k}\cdot\mathbf{R})$. This feature will become important, for example, in problems involving atoms centered at different spatial points, because the transforms of atomic orbitals on such atoms can all be written as centered at a single point in the transform space. Thus, the translation formula can convert a spatially complex problem into a single-center problem (though now with oscillatory character due to the phase factors).

The formulas for the gradient and Laplacian, as well as their one-dimensional (1-D) variants,

$$\left[f'(t) \right]^T (\omega) = -i\omega\, g(\omega), \qquad \text{(first derivative)}, \qquad (20.55)$$

$$\left[\frac{d^n}{dt^n} f(t) \right]^T (\omega) = (-i\omega)^n\, g(\omega), \qquad \text{(nth derivative)}, \qquad (20.56)$$

make the application of these differential operators have simple forms in the transform space. As we see from Eq. (20.55), the operation of differentiation corresponds in the transform space to multiplication by $-i\omega$.

Example 20.3.1   WAVE EQUATION

Fourier transform techniques may be used to advantage in handling partial differential equations (PDEs). To illustrate the technique, let us derive a familiar expression from elementary physics. An infinitely long string is vibrating freely. The amplitude y of the (small) vibrations satisfies the wave equation

$$\frac{\partial^2 y}{\partial x^2} = \frac{1}{v^2} \frac{\partial^2 y}{\partial t^2}, \qquad (20.57)$$

where v is the phase velocity of the wave propagation. We take as initial conditions

$$y(x, 0) = f(x), \qquad \left. \frac{\partial y(x, t)}{\partial t} \right|_{t=0} = 0, \qquad (20.58)$$

where f is assumed localized, meaning that $\lim_{x=\pm\infty} f(x) = 0$.

Our method for solving the PDE of Eq. (20.57) will be to take the Fourier transforms (in x) of its two members, using α as the transform variable. This is equivalent to multiplying Eq. (20.57) by $e^{i\alpha x}$ and integrating over x. Before simplifying, we have

$$\int_{-\infty}^{\infty} \frac{\partial^2 y(x, t)}{\partial x^2} e^{i\alpha x} dx = \frac{1}{v^2} \int_{-\infty}^{\infty} \frac{\partial^2 y(x, t)}{\partial t^2} e^{i\alpha x} dx. \qquad (20.59)$$

If we recognize

$$Y(\alpha, t) = \frac{1}{\sqrt{2\pi}} \int_{-\infty}^{\infty} y(x, t) e^{i\alpha x} dx \qquad (20.60)$$

as the transform (from our initial variable x to our transform variable α) of the solution $y(x, t)$ of our PDE, we can rewrite Eq. (20.59) as

$$(-i\alpha)^2 Y(\alpha, t) = \frac{1}{v^2} \frac{\partial^2 Y(\alpha, t)}{\partial t^2}. \qquad (20.61)$$

Here we have used Eq. (20.56) for the transform of $\partial^2 y/\partial x^2$ and moved the operator $\partial^2/\partial t^2$, which is irrelevant to the transform operator, outside the integral, leaving behind just $Y(\alpha, t)$.

Our original problem has now been converted into Eq. (20.61), but this new equation has the important simplifying feature that the only derivative appearing in it is that with respect to t; we have therefore succeeded in replacing our original PDE (in x and t) with an ordinary differential equation (ODE) (in t only). The dependence of our problem on α (the variable to which x was converted) is only algebraic.

This transformation, from a PDE to an ODE, is a significant achievement. We are now ready to solve Eq. (20.61), subject to the initial conditions, which we need to express in terms of Y. Taking transforms of the quantities in Eq. (20.58), we have

$$\begin{cases} Y(\alpha, 0) = \dfrac{1}{\sqrt{2\pi}} \displaystyle\int_{-\infty}^{\infty} f(x) e^{i\alpha x} dx = F(\alpha), \\[4mm] \dfrac{\partial Y(\alpha, t)}{\partial t}\bigg|_{t=0} = 0. \end{cases} \tag{20.62}$$

It is important to recognize that $F(\alpha)$ is (in principle) known; it is the Fourier transform of the known initial amplitude $f(x)$.

Solving Eq. (20.61) subject to the initial conditions on Y given in Eq. (20.62), we obtain

$$Y(\alpha, t) = F(\alpha) \frac{e^{i\alpha vt} + e^{-i\alpha vt}}{2}. \tag{20.63}$$

We could have written the t dependence as $\cos(\alpha vt)$, but the exponential form is better suited to what we will do next.

Since we really want our solution in terms of x rather than α, our final step will be to apply inverse Fourier transforms to both sides of Eq. (20.63):

$$\frac{1}{\sqrt{2\pi}} \int_{-\infty}^{\infty} Y(\alpha, t) e^{-i\alpha x} d\alpha = \frac{1}{\sqrt{2\pi}} \int_{-\infty}^{\infty} F(\alpha) \frac{e^{i\alpha vt - i\alpha x} + e^{-i\alpha vt - i\alpha x}}{2} d\alpha. \tag{20.64}$$

The left-hand side of Eq. (20.64) is clearly $y(x, t)$; each term on the right-hand side is an inverse transform of F (and is therefore f), but the first exponential, if written $e^{-i\alpha(x - vt)}$, can be seen to lead to an inverse transform of argument $x - vt$, while the second exponential leads to an inverse transform of argument $x + vt$. Thus, our final simplification of Eq. (20.64) takes the form

$$y(x, t) = \frac{1}{2}\Big[f(x - vt) + f(x + vt) \Big]. \tag{20.65}$$

Our solution thus consists of a superposition in which half the amplitude of the original wave form is moving toward $+x$ (at velocity v) while the other half of the original wave form is moving (also at velocity v) in the $-x$ direction.   ∎

Example 20.3.2   HEAT FLOW PDE

To illustrate another transformation of a PDE into an ODE, let us Fourier transform the 1-D heat-flow PDE,

$$\frac{\partial \psi}{\partial t} = a^2 \frac{\partial^2 \psi}{\partial x^2},$$

where the solution $\psi(x, t)$ is the temperature at position x and time t.

We transform the x dependence, with the transform variable denoted y, writing the transform of $\psi(x, t)$ as $\Psi(y, t)$, and identifying the transform of $\partial^2 \psi(x, t)/\partial x^2$ as $-y^2 \Psi(y, t)$. Our heat flow equation then takes the form

$$\frac{\partial \Psi(y, t)}{\partial t} = -a^2 y^2 \Psi(y, t),$$

with general solution

$$\ln \Psi(y, t) = -a^2 y^2 t + \ln C(y), \quad \text{or} \quad \Psi = C(y)e^{-a^2 y^2 t}.$$

The physical significance of $C(y)$ is that it is the initial spatial distribution of Ψ or, in other words, the Fourier transform of the initial temperature profile $\psi(x, 0)$. Thus, if we assume the initial temperature distribution is known, then so also is $C(y)$, and our PDE solution, the inverse transform of Ψ, assumes the form

$$\psi(x, t) = \frac{1}{2\pi} \int\limits_{-\infty}^{\infty} C(y)e^{-a^2 y^2 t} e^{-iyx} dy. \tag{20.66}$$

Further progress depends on the specific form of $C(y)$. If we assume the initial temperature to be a delta-function spike at $x = 0$, corresponding to an instantaneous pulse of thermal energy at $x = t = 0$, we then have as its Fourier transform $C(y) =$ constant, see Eq. (20.14). We can now evaluate the integral in Eq. (20.66) to obtain an explicit form for $\psi(x, t)$. With C constant, the functional form of Eq. (20.66) is (apart from the sign of i) just that encountered in Example 20.2.2 for the Fourier transform of a Gaussian, and we can evaluate the integral to obtain

$$\psi(x, t) = \frac{C}{a\sqrt{2t}} \exp\left(-\frac{x^2}{4a^2 t}\right).$$

This form for ψ was obtained in Section 9.7, but it arose there as a clever guess that was ultimately justified because it led to a solution of the diffusion PDE.   ∎

Example 20.3.3   COULOMB GREEN'S FUNCTION

The Green's function associated with the Poisson equation satisfies the PDE

$$\nabla_r^2 G(\mathbf{r}, \mathbf{r}') = \delta(\mathbf{r} - \mathbf{r}'). \tag{20.67}$$

We take the Fourier transform of both sides of this equation with respect to $\mathbf{r}$, designating $g(\mathbf{k}, \mathbf{r}')$ as the transform of G. Note that $\mathbf{r}'$ is unaffected by the transformation.

Using Eq. (20.53), the left-hand side of Eq. (20.67) becomes $-k^2 g(\mathbf{k}, \mathbf{r}')$, while the right-hand side, in which the delta function has been translated an amount $\mathbf{r}'$, has according to Eq. (20.48) the transform $e^{i\mathbf{k}\cdot\mathbf{r}'}\delta^T(\mathbf{k})$. Thus, Eq. (20.67) transforms into

$$-k^2 g(\mathbf{k}, \mathbf{r}') = \frac{1}{(2\pi)^{3/2}} e^{i\mathbf{k}\cdot\mathbf{r}'},$$

where the transform of the delta function has been evaluated as the 3-D equivalent of Eq. (20.14). We may now solve for g:

$$g(\mathbf{k}, \mathbf{r}') = -\frac{1}{(2\pi)^{3/2}} \frac{e^{i\mathbf{k}\cdot\mathbf{r}'}}{k^2},$$

and recover G by taking the inverse transform,

$$G(\mathbf{r}, \mathbf{r}') = -\frac{1}{(2\pi)^3} \int \frac{e^{i\mathbf{k}\cdot\mathbf{r}'}}{k^2} e^{-i\mathbf{k}\cdot\mathbf{r}} d^3k = -\frac{1}{(2\pi)^3} \int \frac{d^3k}{k^2} e^{-i\mathbf{k}\cdot(\mathbf{r}-\mathbf{r}')}.$$

We see that the evaluation is proportional to that of the inverse transform of $1/k^2$, but for argument $\mathbf{r} - \mathbf{r}'$. Using Eq. (20.43) (which applies also for the inverse transform because it is real), we reach

$$G(\mathbf{r}, \mathbf{r}') = -\frac{1}{(2\pi)^{3/2}} \left(\frac{\pi}{2}\right)^{1/2} \frac{1}{|\mathbf{r} - \mathbf{r}'|} = -\frac{1}{4\pi} \frac{1}{|\mathbf{r} - \mathbf{r}'|},$$

a result we have previously obtained by other methods (cf. Section 10.2). Note that we did not assume G to be a function of $\mathbf{r} - \mathbf{r}'$; we **found** it to have that form. ∎

Successes and Limitations

Some of the above examples illustrate an important role played by the Fourier transform:

- *Use of the Fourier transform can convert a PDE into an ODE, thereby reducing the "degree of transcendence" of the problem.*

All the examples also illustrate the procedure sketched schematically in Fig. 20.1:

- *Fourier transformation can often convert a difficult problem into one which we are able to solve. A useful form for our solution can then be obtained by transforming it back to physical space.*

Despite these successes, it is worth noting that not all problems posed as differential equations are amenable to Fourier-transform solution methods. Some of the limitations arise from the implicit requirement that the necessary transforms and their inverses exist. We can also expect Fourier methods to work only when the solution is unique, as the process of taking a transform and then solving an algebraic equation produces a single result, and not a set of two or more linearly independent solutions.

Usually the boundary conditions are the proximate reason that a differential equation solution is unique, and the requirement that an (exponential) Fourier transform exist imposes Dirichlet boundary conditions at infinity. For 1-D systems on the semi-infinite range $0 \le x < \infty$, use of the Fourier sine transform imposes a Dirichlet condition at the finite boundary $x = 0$, while use of the cosine transform corresponds to a Neumann boundary condition there.

Additional opportunities for solving differential equations by transform methods are provided by use of the Laplace transform, for which it is more natural to introduce boundary data. See the later sections of this chapter.

Exercises

20.3.1   Write the 1-D equivalents of the equations for translation, scale change, sign change, and complex conjugation that were given for 3-D transforms in Eqs. (20.48) to (20.51).

20.3.2   (a)   Show that by replacement of $\mathbf{r}$ by $\mathbf{r} - \mathbf{R}$ in the formula for the Fourier transform of $f(\mathbf{r})$, one can derive the translation formula, Eq. (20.48).

        (b)   Using methods similar to those for part (a), establish the formulas for scale change, sign change, and complex conjugation, Eqs. (20.49) to (20.51).

20.3.3   Derive Eq. (20.53), the formula for the Fourier transform of $\nabla^2 f(\mathbf{r})$.

20.3.4   Verify Eqs. (20.55) and (20.56), the formulas for the derivatives of 1-D Fourier transforms.

20.3.5   Derive the inverse of Eq. (20.56), namely that

$$\left[t^n f(t) \right]^T (\omega) = i^{-n} \frac{d^n}{d\omega^n} \, g(\omega).$$

20.3.6   The 1-D neutron diffusion equation with a (plane) source is

$$-D \frac{d^2 \varphi(x)}{dx^2} + K^2 D \varphi(x) = Q \, \delta(x),$$

where $\varphi(x)$ is the neutron flux, $Q \, \delta(x)$ is the (plane) source at $x = 0$, and D and K^2 are constants. Apply a Fourier transform. Solve the equation in transform space. Transform your solution back into x-space.

ANS. $\varphi(x) = \dfrac{Q}{2KD} \, e^{-|Kx|}.$

20.4   FOURIER CONVOLUTION THEOREM

An important relationship satisfied by Fourier transforms is that known as the **convolution theorem**. As we shall soon see, this theorem is useful in the solution of differential equations, in establishing the normalization of momentum wave functions, in the evaluation of integrals arising in many branches of physics, and in a variety of signal-processing applications.

We define the **convolution** of two functions $f(x)$ and $g(x)$, understood here to be over the interval $(-\infty, \infty)$, as the following operation designated $f * g$:

$$(f * g)(x) \equiv \frac{1}{\sqrt{2\pi}} \int\limits_{-\infty}^{\infty} g(y)f(x-y)dy. \tag{20.68}$$

The corresponding definition in three dimensions is

$$(f * g)(\mathbf{r}) \equiv \frac{1}{(2\pi)^{3/2}} \int g(\mathbf{r}')f(\mathbf{r}-\mathbf{r}')d^3r', \tag{20.69}$$

where the integral is over the full 3-D space.

This operation is sometimes referred to as **Faltung**, the German term for "folding." To better understand the origin of this name, look at Fig. 20.7, where we have plotted $f(y) = e^{-y}$ and $f(x-y) = e^{-(x-y)}$. Clearly, $f(y)$ and $f(x-y)$ are related by reflection relative to the vertical line $y = x/2$; that is, we could generate $f(x-y)$ by folding over $f(y)$ on the line $y = x/2$.

Our interest here is not primarily in the nomenclature, but rather to understand what happens if we take the Fourier transform of a convolution. Letting $F(t)$ and $G(t)$, respectively, be the Fourier transforms of f and g, we find

$$(f * g)^T(t) = \frac{1}{\sqrt{2\pi}} \int\limits_{-\infty}^{\infty} dx \left[\frac{1}{\sqrt{2\pi}} \int\limits_{-\infty}^{\infty} dy\, g(y)f(x-y) \right] e^{itx}$$

$$= \left[\frac{1}{\sqrt{2\pi}} \int\limits_{-\infty}^{\infty} dy\, g(y)e^{ity} \right] \left[\frac{1}{\sqrt{2\pi}} \int\limits_{-\infty}^{\infty} dx\, f(x-y)e^{it(x-y)} \right]$$

$$= \left[\frac{1}{\sqrt{2\pi}} \int\limits_{-\infty}^{\infty} dy\, g(y)e^{ity} \right] \left[\frac{1}{\sqrt{2\pi}} \int\limits_{-\infty}^{\infty} dz\, f(z)e^{itz} \right]$$

$$= G(t)F(t). \tag{20.70}$$

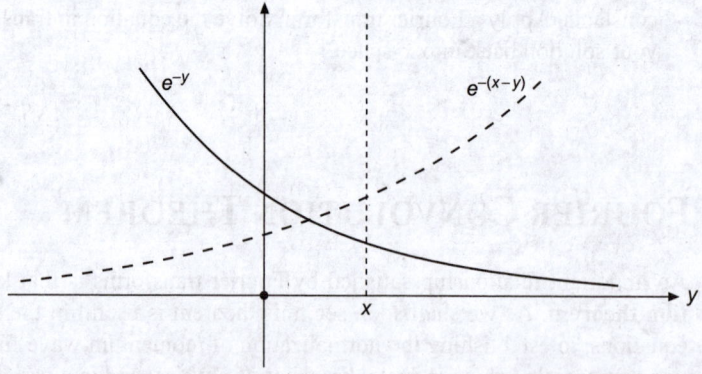

e^{-y} $e^{-(x-y)}$

FIGURE 20.7   Factors in a Faltung.

In the second line of the above equation set we simply divided e^{itx} into the two factors e^{ity} and $e^{it(x-y)}$; the third line was reached by changing the integration variable of the second integral from x to $z = x - y$. After this change, y only appears in the first set of square brackets and z only appears in the second bracket set. We are then able to continue to the fourth line where we identify the integrals as Fourier transforms.

We often encounter integrals that have the form of a convolution $f * g$. The convolution theorem then enables the construction of the Fourier transform of the integral, and the integral itself will then be given by taking the inverse transform of $(f * g)^T$. This process corresponds to

$$\int_{-\infty}^{\infty} g(y)f(x-y)dy = \sqrt{2\pi}(f * g)(x) = \sqrt{2\pi}\frac{1}{\sqrt{2\pi}}\int_{-\infty}^{\infty} (f * g)^T(t)e^{-ixt}\,dt$$

$$= \int_{-\infty}^{\infty} G(t)F(t)e^{-ixt}dt. \tag{20.71}$$

Once again we see an appealing feature inherent to Fourier analysis. While the two functions in our original integral, $g(y)$ and $f(x-y)$, had different arguments, their transforms, $G(t)$ and $F(t)$, have the same argument. We still have an integral to evaluate after using the convolution theorem, but (as just observed) the integrand consists of a product of quantities both of which are evaluated at the **same** point. The cost of the transformation is the presence of a complex exponential, which imparts oscillatory character to the integral. We have thus traded geometric complexity for oscillational complexity. Often this will be an advantageous trade-off.

For the record, here is the 3-D equivalent of Eq. (20.71):

$$\int g(\mathbf{r}')f(\mathbf{r}-\mathbf{r}')d^3r' = \int F(\mathbf{k})G(\mathbf{k})e^{-i\mathbf{k}\cdot\mathbf{r}}d^3k. \tag{20.72}$$

Parseval Relation

If we specialize Eq. (20.71) to $x = 0$, we get the relatively simple result

$$\int_{-\infty}^{\infty} f(-y)g(y)dy = \int_{-\infty}^{\infty} F(t)G(t)dt. \tag{20.73}$$

This equation becomes more easily interpreted if we change $f(y)$ to $f^*(-y)$. Then we must replace $f(-y)$ in Eq. (20.73) by $f^*(y)$, while $F(t)$ becomes $[f^*(-y)]^T$, which, invoking Eq. (20.51), can be written $F^*(t)$. With these changes, we have

$$\int_{-\infty}^{\infty} f^*(y)g(y)dy = \int_{-\infty}^{\infty} F^*(t)G(t)dt. \tag{20.74}$$

This equation is known as the **Parseval relation**; some authors prefer to call it **Rayleigh's theorem**.

The integrals in Eq. (20.74) are of the form of scalar products, and will exist if f and g (and therefore also F and G) are quadratically integrable (i.e., members of an $\mathcal{L}^2$ space). Letting $\mathcal{F}$ denote the Fourier transform operator, we can rewrite Eq. (20.74) in the compact form

$$\langle f|g\rangle = \langle \mathcal{F}f|\mathcal{F}g\rangle. \tag{20.75}$$

If we now move the $\mathcal{F}$ out of the left half-bracket, writing instead its adjoint in the right half-bracket, we reach

$$\langle f|g\rangle = \langle f|\mathcal{F}^\dagger\mathcal{F}g\rangle. \tag{20.76}$$

Since this equation must hold for all f and g in our Hilbert space, it is necessary that $\mathcal{F}^\dagger\mathcal{F}$ reduce to the identity operator, meaning that

$$\mathcal{F}^\dagger = \mathcal{F}^{-1}. \tag{20.77}$$

Our conclusion is that the Fourier transform operator is **unitary**.

If, next, we consider the special case $g = f$, Eq. (20.75) takes the form

$$\langle f|f\rangle = \langle F|F\rangle, \tag{20.78}$$

showing that f and its transform, F, have the same norm, a result that is hardly surprising since we already know that transforming f twice brings us back to at worst f multiplied by a complex phase factor.

An interesting consequence of the unitarity property is illustrated by the formulas governing Fraunhofer diffraction optics. The amplitude of the diffraction pattern appears as the Fourier transform of the function describing the aperture (compare Exercise 20.4.3). With intensity proportional to the square of the amplitude, the Parseval relation implies that the energy passing through the aperture (the integral of $|f|^2$) is equal to that in the diffraction pattern, whose total energy is the integral of $|F|^2$. In this problem the Parseval relation corresponds to energy conservation.

We close this topic with two observations. First, note how the clarity and simplicity of our discussion of the Parseval relation was greatly enhanced by introducing appropriate notation. Much of our insight and intuition regarding mathematical concepts flows directly from the use of good notations for their description. Secondly, we call attention to the fact that Parseval's relation can be developed independently of the inverse Fourier transform and then used rigorously to derive the inverse transform. Details can be found in the text by Morse and Feshbach (Additional Readings).

Here are some examples illustrating use of the convolution theorem.

Example 20.4.1   POTENTIAL OF CHARGE DISTRIBUTION

We require the potential at all points $\mathbf{r}$ produced by a charge distribution $\rho(\mathbf{r}')$. From Coulomb's law, or equivalently from the Green's function for Poisson's equation, we have

$$\psi(\mathbf{r}) = \frac{1}{4\pi} \int \frac{\rho(\mathbf{r}')}{|\mathbf{r}-\mathbf{r}'|} d^3r. \tag{20.79}$$

The integral for ψ is of the convolution form, and its presence in this problem suggests that convolutions will arise in a wide variety of problems in which there is a distributed source of almost any kind and an effect therefrom that depends on relative position.

Taking $f(\mathbf{r}) = 1/r$, so that $f(\mathbf{r} - \mathbf{r}') = 1/|\mathbf{r} - \mathbf{r}'|$, and $g(\mathbf{r}) = \rho(\mathbf{r})$, application of the convolution formula Eq. (20.72) yields

$$\psi(\mathbf{r}) = \frac{1}{4\pi} \int f^T(\mathbf{k}) g^T(\mathbf{k}) e^{-i\mathbf{k}\cdot\mathbf{r}} d^3k.$$

Since

$$f^T(\mathbf{k}) = \frac{1}{(2\pi)^{3/2}} \frac{4\pi}{k^2} \quad \text{and} \quad g^T(\mathbf{k}) = \rho^T(\mathbf{k}),$$

we have

$$\psi(\mathbf{r}) = \frac{1}{(2\pi)^{3/2}} \int \frac{\rho^T(\mathbf{k})}{k^2} e^{-i\mathbf{k}\cdot\mathbf{r}} d^3k. \tag{20.80}$$

Depending on the functional form of ρ, Eq. (20.80) may or may not be easier to evaluate than the original equation for ψ, Eq. (20.79). ∎

Example 20.4.2   TWO-CENTER OVERLAP INTEGRAL

In quantum mechanics problems involving molecules, one often encounters the so-called **overlap integral**, which is the scalar product of two atomic orbitals, one, φ_a, centered at a point $\mathbf{A}$, and another, φ_b, centered at a different point $\mathbf{B}$. This overlap integral, denoted S_{ab}, can be written

$$S_{ab} = \int \varphi_a^*(\mathbf{r} - \mathbf{A}) \varphi_b(\mathbf{r} - \mathbf{B}) d^3r. \tag{20.81}$$

The integral is over the full 3-D space. One way to evaluate S_{ab} starts by changing to coordinates in which the origin is at $\mathbf{A}$; this amounts to the substitution $\mathbf{r}' = \mathbf{r} - \mathbf{A}$, in terms of which $\mathbf{r} - \mathbf{B} = \mathbf{r}' - (\mathbf{B} - \mathbf{A})$, so

$$S_{ab} = \int \varphi_a^*(\mathbf{r}') \varphi_b(\mathbf{r}' - \mathbf{R}) d^3r',$$

where $\mathbf{R} = \mathbf{B} - \mathbf{A}$. We note the physically expected feature that the value of S_{ab} does not depend on $\mathbf{A}$ and $\mathbf{B}$ separately but only on the vector $\mathbf{R}$ describing their relative position.

This integral for S_{ab} is almost in the standard form for a convolution (it differs therefrom by having $\mathbf{r}' - \mathbf{R}$ instead of $\mathbf{R} - \mathbf{r}'$). This discrepancy can be handled by invoking Eq. (20.50); the net effect is to change the sign of the transform variable $\mathbf{k}$ when we evaluate φ_b^T.

Again using Eq. (20.72), we write

$$S_{ab} = \int \left[\varphi_a^*\right]^T(\mathbf{k}) \varphi_b^T(-\mathbf{k}) e^{-i\mathbf{k}\cdot\mathbf{R}} d^3k.$$

We continue with the specific case that φ_a and φ_b are Slater-type orbitals (STOs), both with the same screening parameter ζ. These STOs, and their Fourier transforms (which can be obtained by differentiating Eq. (20.41) with respect to its parameter α), are

$$\varphi = \varphi^* = e^{-\zeta r}, \qquad \varphi^T = \frac{1}{(2\pi)^{3/2}} \frac{8\pi\zeta}{(k^2 + \zeta^2)^2}.$$

Inserting the formula for φ^T into the integral for S_{ab}, we get

$$S_{ab} = \frac{(8\pi\zeta)^2}{(2\pi)^3} \int \frac{e^{-i\mathbf{k}\cdot\mathbf{R}}}{(k^2 + \zeta^2)^4} \, d^3k.$$

At this point we already see an advantage of the convolution-based procedure. This integral (whether or not we can easily evaluate it) has assumed a single-center character, with the interorbital spacing relegated to the complex exponential factor.

To complete the evaluation, we now insert the spherical wave expansion for $\exp(-i\mathbf{k}\cdot\mathbf{R})$, Eq. (16.61), and we note the further simplification that the only term surviving the integration over the angular coordinates of $\mathbf{k}$ is the $l = 0$ term of the expansion. Keeping in mind that $Y_0^0 = 1/\sqrt{4\pi}$, that term is seen to be just $j_0(kR)$, so our formula for S_{ab} becomes

$$S_{ab} = \frac{(8\pi\zeta)^2}{(2\pi)^3} \int_0^\infty \frac{j_0(kR)}{(k^2 + \zeta^2)^4} \, 4\pi k^2 \, dk.$$

We now have a known 1-D integral, which in fact we encountered in Exercise 14.7.10:

$$k_n(x) = \frac{2^{n+2}\,(n+1)!}{\pi\,x^{n+1}} \int_0^\infty \frac{k^2\, j_0(kx)}{(k^2 + 1)^{n+2}} \, dk.$$

Changing x in this formula to ζR and replacing k by k/ζ, we reach

$$S_{ab} = \frac{\pi R^3}{3} k_2(\zeta R) = \frac{\pi e^{-\zeta R}}{3\zeta^3}\left(\zeta^2 R^2 + 3\zeta R + 3\right). \tag{20.82}$$

Note that when we insert the explicit form for k_2, we obtain a relatively simple final result.

There are other ways to obtain this formula (one of which is to use prolate ellipsoidal coordinates with $\mathbf{A}$ and $\mathbf{B}$ as foci), but the method we have chosen here provides a good illustration of the issues and formulas that arise when the convolution method is applicable.   ∎

Multiple Convolutions

Some important problems take the form of multiple convolutions, which we illustrate in one dimension by the convolution of a function h first with a function g followed by the convolution of that result with f, i.e., $f * (g * h)$. Thus,

$$\left[f * (g * h) \right](x) = \frac{1}{\sqrt{2\pi}} \int\limits_{-\infty}^{\infty} dy f(y) (g * h)(x - y)$$

$$= \frac{1}{2\pi} \int\limits_{-\infty}^{\infty} dy \int\limits_{-\infty}^{\infty} dt f(y) g(t) h(x - y - t),$$

which after making the substitution $t = z - y$ (and therefore $x - y - t = x - z$) becomes

$$\left[f * (g * h) \right](x) = \frac{1}{2\pi} \int\limits_{-\infty}^{\infty} dy \int\limits_{-\infty}^{\infty} dz \, f(y) g(z - y) h(x - z). \tag{20.83}$$

Letting F, G, and H be the Fourier transforms of f, g, and h, this case of the convolution theorem is

$$\left[f * g * h \right]^T (\omega) = F(\omega) G(\omega) H(\omega). \tag{20.84}$$

We have now omitted the parentheses surrounding $g * h$ since we would have gotten the same result if we convoluted f, g, and h in any order. Then, taking the inverse transform, we have

$$\int\limits_{-\infty}^{\infty} dy \int\limits_{-\infty}^{\infty} dz \, f(y) g(z - y) h(x - z) = (2\pi)^{1/2} \int\limits_{-\infty}^{\infty} F(\omega) G(\omega) H(\omega) e^{-i\omega x} d\omega. \tag{20.85}$$

In three dimensions, the corresponding formulas are

$$\left[f * (g * h) \right](\mathbf{r}) = \frac{1}{(2\pi)^3} \int d^3 r' \int d^3 r'' f(\mathbf{r}') g(\mathbf{r}'' - \mathbf{r}') h(\mathbf{r} - \mathbf{r}''), \tag{20.86}$$

$$\left[f * (g * h) \right]^T (\mathbf{k}) = F(\mathbf{k}) G(\mathbf{k}) H(\mathbf{k}), \tag{20.87}$$

$$\int d^3 r' \int d^3 r'' f(\mathbf{r}') g(\mathbf{r}'' - \mathbf{r}') h(\mathbf{r} - \mathbf{r}'') = (2\pi)^{3/2} \int F(\mathbf{k}) G(\mathbf{k}) H(\mathbf{k}) e^{-i\mathbf{k} \cdot \mathbf{r}} d^3 k. \tag{20.88}$$

Example 20.4.3   INTERACTION OF TWO CHARGE DISTRIBUTIONS

The electrostatic interaction of two charge distributions $\rho_1(\mathbf{r})$ and $\rho_2(\mathbf{r})$ is given by the integral

$$V = \int d^3 r' \int d^3 r'' \frac{\rho_1(\mathbf{r}') \rho_2(\mathbf{r}'')}{|\mathbf{r}'' - \mathbf{r}'|}, \tag{20.89}$$

which is a double convolution, as in Eq. (20.88), but with the free argument $\mathbf{r}$ set to zero and with a sign discrepancy in the argument of h (which is ρ_2 of the present example).

Taking the above into account and applying Eq. (20.88), we have

$$V = (2\pi)^{3/2} \int d^3k \, \rho_1^T(\mathbf{k}) \left[\frac{1}{r}\right]^T (\mathbf{k}) \rho_2^T(-\mathbf{k})$$

$$= 4\pi \int \frac{d^3k}{k^2} \rho_1^T(\mathbf{k}) \, \rho_2^T(-\mathbf{k}), \tag{20.90}$$

where we have inserted the value of $(1/r)^T$ from Eq. (20.42). This expression has the obvious advantage that it is a 3-D integral in place of the original six-fold integration in Eq. (20.89). The price we have to pay for this simplification is the cost of taking the Fourier transforms of ρ_1 and ρ_2. ∎

Transform of a Product

The similarity between the formulas for the direct and inverse Fourier transforms suggest that we may be able to identify the Fourier transform of a product as a convolution. Accordingly, we rewrite Eq. (20.71) with x replaced by $-x$ and also change the variable of integration in that equation from y to $-y$. We then have (multiplying the equation by $1/\sqrt{2\pi}$)

$$\frac{1}{\sqrt{2\pi}} \int\limits_{-\infty}^{\infty} g(-y) f(y-x) dy = \frac{1}{\sqrt{2\pi}} \int\limits_{-\infty}^{\infty} G(t) F(t) e^{ixt} \, dt = \left[G(t) \, F(t)\right]^T (x). \tag{20.91}$$

If we now make the further identifications

$$\left[G(t)\right]^T(y) = g(-y) \quad \text{and} \quad \left[F(t)\right]^T(x-y) = f(y-x),$$

we have

$$(F^T * G^T)(x) = \left[G(t) \, F(t)\right]^T(x). \tag{20.92}$$

Rewriting Eq. (20.92) with the functions renamed f and g and their respective transforms denoted F and G, we have our desired final result:

$$\left[f g\right]^T = F * G. \tag{20.93}$$

Equation (20.93) will be useful only if f and g individually have Fourier transforms. It is possible that this condition is not satisfied despite the fact that fg possesses a transform. We therefore proceed to consider the case that f not have a transform, but instead possesses a Maclaurin expansion, and therefore can be represented by a series in positive integer powers of x. Then, starting from the relation

$$\left[x^n g(x)\right]^T(t) = i^{-n} \frac{d^n}{dt^n} G(t),$$

the topic of Exercise 20.3.5, we can write

$$\left[f g\right]^T(t) = f\left(-i\frac{d}{dt}\right) G(t), \tag{20.94}$$

where the expression $-i(d/dt)$ is the **argument** of f (and not a multiplicative factor). Unless f is quite simple, this expression may be of limited practical value.

Momentum Space

Hamilton's equations of classical mechanics formalize a symmetry between position variables q and the corresponding (**conjugate**) momentum variables p. This same correspondence carries over into quantum mechanics, where (in one dimension, in units with $\hbar = 1$), the fundamental relationship is the commutator $[x, p] = i$. The time-independent Schrödinger equation (for a particle of mass m) is

$$H\psi \equiv \left[\frac{1}{2m} p^2 + V(x) \right] \psi = E \psi,$$

and it is usually made more explicit by taking $p = -i(d/dx)$, in which case the wave function ψ is a function of x: $\psi = \psi(x)$. In principle we could have chosen p as the fundamental variable, in which case the proper value of the commutator is recovered if we take $x = +i(d/dp)$, and ψ (which we will now give the name φ) will be a function of p: $\varphi = \varphi(p)$. These two representations of the Schrödinger equation in one dimension correspond, respectively, to the two ODEs:

$$-\frac{1}{2m} \frac{d^2}{dx^2} \psi(x) + V(x)\psi(x) = E\psi(x), \tag{20.95}$$

$$\frac{p^2}{2m} \varphi(p) + V\left(i\frac{d}{dp} \right) \varphi(p) = E\varphi(p). \tag{20.96}$$

Note that in the second of these two equations, the argument of V is a differential operator, and unless the form of V is relatively simple, the momentum-space ODE will be quite complicated and correspondingly difficult to solve.

In the **coordinate representation** $(x, -id/dx)$, a wave function $\exp(ikx)$ is an eigenfunction of momentum with eigenvalue k:

$$p\,e^{ikx} = -i\,\frac{d}{dx}\,e^{ikx} = -i(ik)e^{ikx} = k\,e^{ikx},$$

and this fact suggests that momentum wave functions will be Fourier transforms of their coordinate counterparts. We therefore seek to verify the consistency of Eqs. (20.95) and (20.96) by Fourier transforming the first of these two equations, letting $g(t)$ represent the transform of ψ and using Eq. (20.56) to take the transform of the second derivative.[3] In the case that V has a Maclaurin expansion, we then use Eq. (20.94), obtaining

$$\frac{t^2}{2m}g(t) + V\left(-i\frac{d}{dt} \right) g(t) = Eg(t).$$

This equation can be brought into agreement with Eq. (20.96) if we take its complex conjugate (assuming V to be real), so we can make the identification $\varphi(p) \longleftrightarrow g^*(t)$.

---

[3] Here t is the transform variable; in the present context it has nothing to do with time.

On the other hand, if V has a transform we can use the convolution formula, Eq. (20.93), thereby converting Eq. (20.95) into an integral equation:

$$\frac{p^2}{2m}\,\varphi(p) + \frac{1}{\sqrt{2\pi}} \int\limits_{-\infty}^{\infty} V^T(p - p')\,\varphi(p')\,dp' = E\,\varphi(p). \qquad (20.97)$$

Example 20.4.4   MOMENTUM-SPACE SCHRÖDINGER EQUATION

The time-independent Schrödinger equation for the hydrogen atom has (in **hartree atomic units** $\hbar = m = e = 1$) the coordinate representation

$$-\frac{1}{2}\nabla^2 \psi(\mathbf{r}) - \frac{1}{r}\psi(\mathbf{r}) = E\,\psi(\mathbf{r}).$$

Taking the Fourier transform of this equation, we get for the **momentum-space** wave function $\varphi(\mathbf{k})$

$$\frac{k^2}{2}\,\varphi(\mathbf{k}) - \frac{1}{(2\pi)^3} \int \frac{4\pi}{|\mathbf{k} - \mathbf{k}'|^2}\,\varphi(\mathbf{k}')d^3k' = E\,\varphi(\mathbf{k}). \qquad (20.98)$$

In reaching Eq. (20.98), we have used the 3-D version of Eq. (20.97), inserting for the transform of V the result from Eq. (20.42).

In principle one can solve Eq. (20.98) for $\varphi(\mathbf{k})$ and the corresponding eigenvalues E, and the results should be equivalent to the original equation. That is a more difficult task than we will undertake now, but it is straightforward to verify that the Fourier transform of the known solution for the hydrogen ground state is a solution to Eq. (20.98).

From Eq. (20.44), the hydrogen $1s$ wave function e^{-r} is seen to have Fourier transform

$$\varphi(\mathbf{k}) = \frac{C}{(k^2 + 1)^2},$$

where C is independent of k and has a value that is irrelevant here. Inserting this result into Eq. (20.98), we find

$$\frac{1}{2}\frac{Ck^2}{(k^2 + 1)^2} - \frac{C}{2\pi^2} \int \frac{d^3k'}{|\mathbf{k} - \mathbf{k}'|^2(k'^2 + 1)^2} = E\,\frac{C}{(k^2 + 1)^2}. \qquad (20.99)$$

Writing $|\mathbf{k} - \mathbf{k}'|^2 = k^2 + 2kk'\cos\theta + k'^2$, the integral, though a bit tedious, is found to be elementary. Inserting its value, Eq. (20.99) becomes (canceling the common factor C),

$$\frac{1}{2}\frac{k^2}{(k^2 + 1)^2} - \frac{1}{2}\frac{1}{k^2 + 1} = E\,\frac{1}{(k^2 + 1)^2}.$$

This equation is satisfied if $E = -1/2$, the correct energy (in hartree atomic units) for the hydrogen $1s$ state.   ∎

Exercises

20.4.1 Work out the convolution equation corresponding to Eq. (20.71) for

(a) Fourier sine transforms

$$\frac{1}{2}\int_0^\infty g(y)\Big[f(y+x)+f(y-x)\Big]dy = \int_0^\infty F_s(s)G_s(s)\cos sx\,ds,$$

where f and g are odd functions.

(b) Fourier cosine transforms

$$\frac{1}{2}\int_0^\infty g(y)\Big[f(y+x)+f(x-y)\Big]dy = \int_0^\infty F_c(s)G_c(s)\cos sx\,ds,$$

where f and g are even functions.

20.4.2 Show that for both Fourier sine and Fourier cosine transforms Parseval's relation has the form

$$\int_0^\infty F(t)G(t)dt = \int_0^\infty f(y)g(y)dy.$$

20.4.3 (a) A rectangular pulse is described by

$$f(x) = \begin{cases} 1, & |x| < a, \\ 0, & |x| > a. \end{cases}$$

Show that the Fourier exponential transform is

$$F(t) = \sqrt{\frac{2}{\pi}}\frac{\sin at}{t}.$$

This is the single-slit diffraction problem of physical optics. The slit is described by $f(x)$. The diffraction pattern **amplitude** is given by the Fourier transform $F(t)$.

(b) Use the Parseval relation to evaluate

$$\int_{-\infty}^\infty \frac{\sin^2 t}{t^2}dt.$$

This integral may also be evaluated by using the calculus of residues (Exercise 11.8.9).

ANS. (b) π.

20.4.4   Solve Poisson's equation, $\nabla^2 \psi(\mathbf{r}) = -\rho(\mathbf{r})/\varepsilon_0$, by the following sequence of operations:

(a)   Take the Fourier transform of both sides of this equation. Solve for the Fourier transform of $\psi(\mathbf{r})$.

(b)   Carry out the Fourier inverse transform.

20.4.5   (a)   Given $f(x) = 1 - |x/2|$ for $-2 \le x \le 2$, with $f(x) = 0$ elsewhere, show that the Fourier transform of $f(x)$ is

$$F(t) = \sqrt{\frac{2}{\pi}} \left(\frac{\sin t}{t} \right)^2 .$$

(b)   Using the Parseval relation, evaluate

$$\int_{-\infty}^{\infty} \left(\frac{\sin t}{t} \right)^4 dt .$$

$$ANS. \quad (b) \ \frac{2\pi}{3}.$$

20.4.6   With $F(t)$ and $G(t)$ the Fourier transforms of $f(x)$ and $g(x)$, respectively, show that

$$\int_{-\infty}^{\infty} \left| f(x) - g(x) \right|^2 dx = \int_{-\infty}^{\infty} \left| F(t) - G(t) \right|^2 dt .$$

If $g(x)$ is an approximation to $f(x)$, the preceding relation indicates that the mean square deviation in t-space is equal to the mean square deviation in x-space.

20.4.7   Use the Parseval relation to evaluate

$$(a) \ \int_{-\infty}^{\infty} \frac{d\omega}{(\omega^2 + a^2)^2}, \qquad (b) \ \int_{-\infty}^{\infty} \frac{\omega^2 \, d\omega}{(\omega^2 + a^2)^2}.$$

Hint. Compare Exercise 20.2.3.

$$ANS. \quad (a) \ \frac{\pi}{2a^3}, \quad (b) \ \frac{\pi}{2a}.$$

20.4.8   The nuclear form factor $F(\mathbf{k})$ and the charge distribution $\rho(\mathbf{r})$ are 3-D Fourier transforms of each other:

$$F(\mathbf{k}) = \frac{1}{(2\pi)^{3/2}} \int \rho(\mathbf{r}) e^{i\mathbf{k}\cdot\mathbf{r}} d^3 r .$$

If the measured form factor is

$$F(\mathbf{k}) = (2\pi)^{-3/2} \left(1 + \frac{k^2}{a^2} \right)^{-1}$$

find the corresponding charge distribution.

$$ANS. \quad \rho(\mathbf{r}) = \frac{a^2}{4\pi} \frac{e^{-ar}}{r}.$$

20.4.9 Using convolution methods, find an integral whose value is the electrostatic interaction energy between a charge distribution $\rho(\mathbf{r} - \mathbf{A})$ and a unit point charge at $\mathbf{C}$.

20.4.10 With $\psi(\mathbf{r})$ a wave function in ordinary space and $\varphi(\mathbf{p})$ the corresponding momentum function, show that

(a) $\quad \dfrac{1}{(2\pi\hbar)^{3/2}} \displaystyle\int \mathbf{r}\psi(\mathbf{r})e^{-i\mathbf{r}\cdot\mathbf{p}/\hbar}\, d^3r = i\hbar\nabla_p\,\varphi(\mathbf{p}),$

(b) $\quad \dfrac{1}{(2\pi\hbar)^{3/2}} \displaystyle\int \mathbf{r}^2\psi(\mathbf{r})e^{-\mathbf{r}\cdot\mathbf{p}/\hbar}\, d^3r = (i\hbar\nabla_p)^2\varphi(\mathbf{p}).$

Note. ∇_p is the gradient in momentum space:

$$\hat{\mathbf{e}}_x\frac{\partial}{\partial p_x} + \hat{\mathbf{e}}_y\frac{\partial}{\partial p_y} + \hat{\mathbf{e}}_z\frac{\partial}{\partial p_z}.$$

These results may be extended to any positive integer power of $\mathbf{r}$ and therefore to any (analytic) function that may be expanded as a Maclaurin series in $\mathbf{r}$.

20.4.11 The ordinary space wave function $\psi(\mathbf{r}, t)$ satisfies the time-dependent Schrödinger equation,

$$i\hbar\frac{\partial\psi(\mathbf{r}, t)}{\partial t} = -\frac{\hbar^2}{2m}\nabla^2\psi + V(\mathbf{r})\psi.$$

Show that the corresponding time-dependent momentum wave function satisfies the analogous equation

$$i\hbar\frac{\partial\varphi(\mathbf{p}, t)}{\partial t} = \frac{p^2}{2m}\varphi + V(i\hbar\,\nabla_p)\varphi.$$

Note. Assume that $V(\mathbf{r})$ may be expressed by a Maclaurin series and use Exercise 20.4.10. $V(i\hbar\nabla_p)$ is the same function of the variable $i\hbar\,\nabla_p$ that $V(\mathbf{r})$ is of the variable $\mathbf{r}$.

20.5 SIGNAL-PROCESSING APPLICATIONS

A time-dependent electrical pulse $f(t)$ may be regarded as a superposition of waves of many frequencies. For angular frequency ω, we have a contribution

$$F(\omega)e^{i\omega t}.$$

Then the complete pulse may be written as

$$f(t) = \frac{1}{2\pi}\int\limits_{-\infty}^{\infty} F(\omega)e^{i\omega t}\, d\omega. \tag{20.100}$$

Because the angular frequency ω is related to the linear frequency ν by

$$\nu = \frac{\omega}{2\pi},$$

most physicists associate the entire $1/2\pi$ factor with this integral, so this formula differs by a factor $(2\pi)^{-1/2}$ from the definition we have adopted for the Fourier transform.

But if ω is a frequency, what about the negative frequencies? The negative ω may be looked on as a mathematical device to avoid dealing with two functions ($\cos \omega t$ and $\sin \omega t$) separately.

Because Eq. (20.100) has the form of a Fourier transform, we may solve for $F(\omega)$ by taking the inverse transform. Keeping in mind the scale at which we wrote Eq. (20.100), we get

$$F(\omega) = \int\limits_{-\infty}^{\infty} f(t)e^{-i\omega t}\,dt. \tag{20.101}$$

Equation (20.101) represents a **resolution of the pulse** $f(t)$ into its angular frequency components. Equation (20.100) is a **synthesis of the pulse** from its components.

Now consider some device, such as a servomechanism or a stereo amplifier, with an input $f(t)$ and an output $g(t)$. For an input of a single frequency f_ω with input $f_\omega(t) = F(\omega)e^{i\omega t}$, the device will alter the amplitude and may also change the phase. For the situations we discuss here, we assume a linear response, which means that we are assuming that g_ω (the output corresponding to f_ω) will be a signal at the same frequency as f_ω, will scale linearly with f_ω, and be independent of the simultaneous presence of signals at other frequencies. However, the responses of interesting devices will depend on the frequency. Hence, our assumption is that g_ω and f_ω are related by an equation of the form

$$g_\omega(t) = \varphi(\omega) f_\omega(t). \tag{20.102}$$

This amplitude- and phase-modifying function, $\varphi(\omega)$, is called a **transfer** function. When making schematic diagrams of electronic circuits, it is customary to designate a device characterized by a transfer function by a suitably labeled box with input and output conductors, as shown in (Fig. 20.8).

Because we have assumed the operation corresponding to the transfer function to be linear, the total output from a pulse containing many frequencies may be obtained by integrating over the entire input, as modified by the transfer function,

$$g(t) = \frac{1}{2\pi} \int\limits_{-\infty}^{\infty} \varphi(\omega) F(\omega) e^{i\omega t}\,d\omega. \tag{20.103}$$

The transfer function is characteristic of the device to which it applies. Once it is known (either by calculation or measurement), the output $g(t)$ can be calculated for any input $f(t)$.

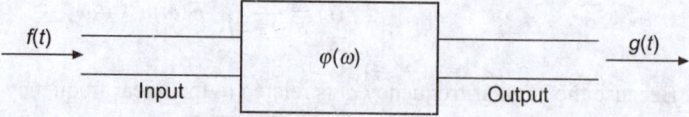

FIGURE 20.8   Schematic for device described by transfer function.

Equation (20.103) can be brought to a convenient form if we recognize that it is simply the formula for the Fourier transform of the product $\varphi(\omega)F(\omega)$. We already know that $F(\omega)$ has transform $f(t)$. Letting $\Phi(t)$ be (at the scaling of this section) the transform of $\varphi(\omega)$, we may then use Eq. (20.93) to rewrite Eq. (20.103) as the convolution of the transforms f and Φ:

$$g(t) = \int\limits_{-\infty}^{\infty} f(t')\Phi(t - t')dt'. \tag{20.104}$$

Interpreting Eq. (20.104), we have an input (a "cause"), namely $f(t')$, modified by $\Phi(t - t')$, producing an output (an "effect"), namely $g(t)$. Adopting the concept of **causality** (that the cause precedes the effect), we must obtain contributions to $g(t)$ only from times t' such that $t' < t$. We do this by requiring

$$\Phi(t - t') = 0, \quad t' > t. \tag{20.105}$$

Then Eq. (20.104) becomes

$$g(t) = \int\limits_{-\infty}^{t} f(t')\Phi(t - t')dt'. \tag{20.106}$$

Since Eq. (20.106) must yield real output $g(t)$ for arbitrary real input $f(t)$, we see that in addition to the requirement in Eq. (20.105), we also know that $\Phi(t)$ must be real.

The adoption of Eq. (20.106) and the reality of Φ have profound consequences here and equivalently in dispersion theory (Section 12.8).

Example 20.5.1   TRANSFER FUNCTION: HIGH-PASS FILTER

A **high-pass filter** permits almost complete transmission of high-frequency electrical signals but strongly attenuates those at lower frequencies. A very simple high-pass filter is shown in Fig. 20.9. Its transfer function describes the steady-state behavior of the filter in the absence of loading (meaning that the output terminals are not connected to anything), so we can assume that, for a signal at frequency ω, the input, output, and current are the real parts of the respective quantities $V_{in}e^{i\omega t}$, $V_{out}e^{i\omega t}$, $Ie^{i\omega t}$. Possible phase differences in these quantities are allowed for by permitting V_{in}, V_{out}, and I to be complex.

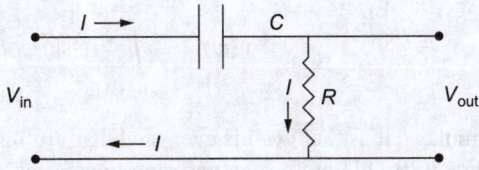

FIGURE 20.9   Simple high-pass filter.

Following the usual procedure for electrical circuit analysis, we solve Kirchhoff's equation (the condition that the net change in potential around any loop of the circuit vanishes):

$$V_{\text{in}}e^{i\omega t} = \int^{t} \frac{I}{C} e^{i\omega t}\, dt + R I e^{i\omega t}. \tag{20.107}$$

Differentiating with respect to t (to eliminate the integral), we have

$$V_{\text{in}} \frac{d}{dt} e^{i\omega t} = \frac{I}{C} e^{i\omega t} + R I \frac{d}{dt} e^{i\omega t},$$

which, evaluating the derivatives, reduces to

$$i\omega V_{\text{in}} = \frac{I}{C} + i\omega R I, \quad \text{with solution} \quad I = \frac{i\omega C V_{\text{in}}}{1 + i\omega R C}. \tag{20.108}$$

Since $V_{\text{out}} = I R$, we easily find the transfer function

$$\varphi(\omega) = \frac{V_{\text{out}}}{V_{\text{in}}} = \frac{i\omega R C}{1 + i\omega R C}. \tag{20.109}$$

To confirm the behavior of the filter, note that in the limit of large ω, $\varphi(\omega) \to 1$, while at small ω, $\varphi(\omega) \to i\omega R C$, which vanishes in the limit of small ω. The transition between these two limiting behaviors is a function of the product RC. ∎

Limitations on Transfer Functions

Let us write the transfer function $\varphi(\omega)$ as the inverse Fourier transform of $\Phi(t)$ (still using the scaling of this section), keeping in mind that $\Phi(t)$ vanishes for $t < 0$,

$$\varphi(\omega) = \int_{0}^{\infty} \Phi(t) e^{-i\omega t}\, dt. \tag{20.110}$$

Now, separating φ into its real and imaginary parts: $\varphi(\omega) = u(\omega) + i v(\omega)$, and making the same separation for the right-hand side of Eq. (20.110), we have

$$u(\omega) = \int_{0}^{\infty} \Phi(t) \cos \omega t\, dt,$$

$$v(\omega) = - \int_{0}^{\infty} \Phi(t) \sin \omega t\, dt. \tag{20.111}$$

These formulas tell us that $u(\omega)$ is even, and that $v(\omega)$ is odd.

Since Eqs. (20.111) are cosine and sine transforms, they can be inverted to give two alternative formulas for $\Phi(t)$ in the range of applicability of these transforms, namely for

$t > 0$. Continuing to use the transform scaling of this section,

$$\Phi(t) = \frac{2}{\pi} \int_0^\infty u(\omega)\cos \omega t \, d\omega,$$

$$(t > 0) \qquad (20.112)$$

$$= -\frac{2}{\pi} \int_0^\infty v(\omega)\sin \omega t \, d\omega.$$

The present significance of these results is that

$$\int_0^\infty u(\omega)\cos \omega t \, d\omega = - \int_0^\infty v(\omega)\sin \omega t \, d\omega, \quad (t > 0). \qquad (20.113)$$

The imposition of causality has led to a mutual interdependence of the real and imaginary parts of the transfer function. The present result is similar to those involving causality that were discussed in Section 12.8.

We close this subsection by verifying that the conditions on u and v are consistent with the properties required of Φ. Writing

$$\Phi(t) = \frac{1}{2\pi} \int_{-\infty}^\infty \varphi(\omega)e^{i\omega t} \, dt,$$

then inserting $e^{i\omega t} = \cos \omega t + i \sin \omega t$ and $\varphi = u + iv$, we have

$$\Phi(t) = \frac{1}{2\pi} \int_{-\infty}^\infty \left[u(\omega)\cos \omega t - v(\omega)\sin \omega t \right] d\omega$$

$$+ \frac{i}{2\pi} \int_{-\infty}^\infty \left[u(\omega)\sin \omega t + v(\omega)\cos \omega t \right] d\omega. \qquad (20.114)$$

The imaginary part of Eq. (20.114) vanishes because its integrand is an odd function of ω. If $t > 0$, we know from Eq. (20.113) that the two terms of the real part of Eq. (20.114) are equal, and we get the expected nonzero result. But if $t < 0$, the sign of the second term of the real part is changed and they then add to zero.

Exercises

20.5.1   Find the transfer function $\varphi(\omega)$ for the circuit shown in the left panel of Fig. 20.10. Is this a high-pass, a low-pass, or a more complicated filter?

20.5.2   Find the transfer function $\varphi(\omega)$ for the circuit shown in the right panel of Fig. 20.11.

Hint. The potential difference across an inductor is given by $L \, dI/dt$.

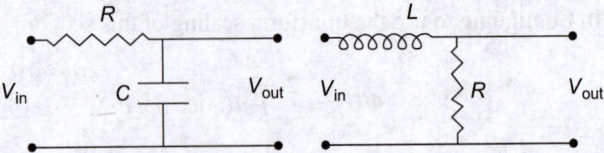

FIGURE 20.10   Circuits for Exercise 20.5.1 (left) and Exercise 20.5.2 (right).

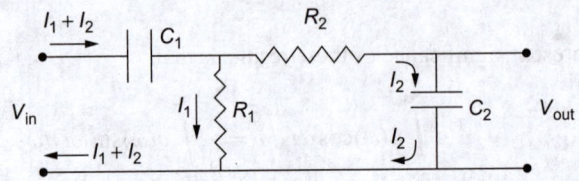

FIGURE 20.11   Circuit for Exercise 20.5.3.

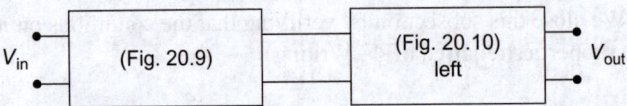

FIGURE 20.12   Representation of the circuit in Fig. 20.11 in terms of successive transfer functions.

20.5.3   Find the transfer function $\varphi(\omega)$ for the circuit shown in Fig. 20.11. This is a **band-pass filter**.

Hint. Assume the currents in the various parts of the circuit to have the values shown in the figure.

20.5.4   The circuit elements for Exercise 20.5.3 correspond to the successive transfer functions shown in Fig. 20.12. Explain why the transfer function for this exercise is only the product of the individual transfer functions in the limit $R_2 \gg R_1$.

20.6   DISCRETE FOURIER TRANSFORM

For many physicists the Fourier transform is automatically the continuous Fourier transform whose analytical properties we have been discussing in previous sections of this chapter. The use of digital computers, however, presents an opportunity to work with numerically determined Fourier transforms, which consist of values given at a discrete set of points. Integrations are therefore converted into finite summations. Transforms defined on discrete point sets have properties worth pursuing, and analysis in that area is the topic of this section.

Orthogonality on Discrete Point Sets

Throughout the earlier chapters of this book we have introduced and made use of the properties of orthogonal functions, where orthogonality has been defined as the vanishing of an integral whose integrand contains a product of the functions under study. The alternative, to be discussed here, is to define orthogonality over a discrete point set as the vanishing of a sum of products computed at the individual points. It turns out that sines, cosines, and imaginary exponentials have the remarkable property that they are also orthogonal over a series of discrete, equally spaced points on an orthogonality interval.

To analyze this situation, we take a set of N equally spaced points x_k, on the interval $(0, 2\pi)$:

$$x_k = \frac{2\pi k}{N}, \quad k = 0, 1, 2, \ldots, N-1, \tag{20.115}$$

and we consider functions $\varphi_p(x)$, defined only on the points x_k and for integer p, as

$$\varphi_p(x) = e^{ipx}. \tag{20.116}$$

In line with our introductory discussion, we define the scalar products of these functions as

$$\langle \varphi_p \,|\, \varphi_q \rangle = \sum_{k=0}^{N-1} \varphi_p^*(x_k)\, \varphi_q(x_k). \tag{20.117}$$

Inserting Eq. (20.115) for the x_k, the scalar product takes the form

$$\langle \varphi_p \,|\, \varphi_q \rangle = \sum_{k=0}^{N-1} e^{2\pi i k(q-p)/N} = \sum_{k=0}^{N-1} r^k, \tag{20.118}$$

where $r = e^{2\pi i(q-p)/N}$. This is a finite geometric series; if $r = 1$ its sum has the value N; otherwise the sum evaluates to $(1 - r^N)/(1 - r)$. But $r^N = e^{2\pi i(q-p)}$, and because p and q were restricted to integer values, we have $r^N = 1$, so the sum vanishes. To complete our understanding of the situation, we need to determine the conditions under which $r = 1$. We clearly have $r = 1$ when $q = p$. Note that we also have $r = 1$ when $q - p$ is any integer multiple of N. Thus, a formal statement relative to this scalar product is

$$\langle \varphi_p \,|\, \varphi_q \rangle = N \sum_{n=-\infty}^{\infty} \delta_{q-p,nN}. \tag{20.119}$$

Note that at most only one of the infinite sum of Kronecker deltas will be nonzero, and all will be zero unless $q - p$ is a multiple of N (one of which is $q - p = 0$).

Equation (20.119) is more complicated than necessary. Because the functions φ_p are defined by their values at N points, only N of them are linearly independent. In fact,

$$\varphi_{p+N}(x_k) = e^{2\pi i(p+N)k/N} = e^{2\pi i p k/N} = \varphi_p(x_k).$$

We can therefore restrict p and q in Eq. (20.119) to the range $(0, N - 1)$, and our orthogonality relation then becomes

$$\langle \varphi_p | \varphi_q \rangle = N \delta_{pq}, \quad 0 \le p, q \le N - 1. \tag{20.120}$$

Obviously, if function values on a discrete point set are to be used to represent a continuous function, the amount of detail that is retained in the analysis will depend on the size of the point set. We will come back to this issue in a later part of the present section.

Discrete Fourier Transform

By analogy with the definitions introduced for the conventional Fourier transform, we define the discrete transform g_p $(p = 0, \ldots, N - 1)$ of a function f defined only on the points x_k by the formula

$$g_p = N^{-1/2} \sum_{k=0}^{N-1} e^{2\pi i k p / N} f_k. \tag{20.121}$$

We are now writing f_k as a shorthand for $f(x_k)$, and that substitution has pretty much decoupled the problem from the original interval of definition $0 \le x \le 2\pi$. In essence, we are now discussing transformations between two N-member sets of function values.

The transformation inverse to Eq. (20.121) is

$$f_j = N^{-1/2} \sum_{p=0}^{N-1} e^{-2\pi i j p / N} g_p; \tag{20.122}$$

Eq. (20.122) can be verified by substituting into it the formula for g_p, yielding

$$f_j = N^{-1} \sum_{p=0}^{N-1} \sum_{k=0}^{N-1} e^{2\pi i (k-j) p / N} f_k = \sum_{k=0}^{N-1} \delta_{kj} f_k = f_j,$$

as required.

These discrete transforms have properties similar to those of their continuous cousins. For example, the transform of f_{k-j}, where j is an integer, corresponding to translation by j steps in the f array, is

$$[f_{k-j}]_p^T = N^{-1/2} \sum_{k=0}^{N-1} e^{2\pi i k p / N} f_{k-j} = e^{2\pi i j p / N} N^{-1/2} \sum_{k=0}^{N-1} e^{2\pi i (k-j) p / N} f_{k-j}.$$

Because of the periodicity of the f_k, we note that

$$N^{-1/2} \sum_{k=0}^{N-1} e^{2\pi i (k-j) p / N} f_{k-j} = N^{-1/2} \sum_{k'=-j}^{N-j-1} e^{2\pi i k' p / N} f_{k'} = N^{-1/2} \sum_{k'=0}^{N-1} e^{2\pi i k' p / N} f_{k'},$$

which is the formula for the p coefficient in the transform of f. We therefore have the translation formula

$$[f_{k-j}]_p^T = e^{2\pi ijp/N} g_p. \tag{20.123}$$

We examine next the convolution theorem, where the discrete convolution of two point sets f and g is defined as

$$[f * g]_k = N^{-1/2} \sum_{j=0}^{N-1} f_j g_{k-j}. \tag{20.124}$$

Taking the transform of this convolution, we have

$$N^{-1} \sum_{k=0}^{N-1} e^{2\pi ikp/N} \sum_{j=0}^{N-1} f_j g_{k-j}$$

$$= \left[N^{-1/2} \sum_{j=0}^{N-1} e^{2\pi ijp/N} f_j \right] \left[N^{-1/2} \sum_{k=0}^{N-1} e^{2\pi i(k-j)p/N} g_{k-j} \right].$$

As in the continuous case, we have split the complex exponential into two factors. We now redefine the index of the second summation from k to $l = k - j$, thereby making the two square brackets completely independent. Each can then be recognized as a transform (for the second, we need to use the fact that the g_k are periodic). The final result is

$$[f * g]_p^T = F_p G_p, \tag{20.125}$$

where F and G are the respective discrete transforms of f and g. This result is completely analogous with the convolution theorem for the continuous transform.

We close this discussion with the observation that the discrete transform and its inverse are linear transformations on coefficient arrays (vectors) of finite dimension N. Therefore, each transform operator can be represented as an $N \times N$ matrix whose rows and columns correspond to the points k or p. The fact that the transform and its inverse are complex conjugates means that the transformation matrices are unitary. Moreover, from the forms of the transform and its inverse, we see that all the elements of these matrices are proportional to complex exponentials.

Limitations

As mentioned earlier, the ability of discrete transforms to reproduce phenomena that are actually based on continuous functions will depend on the size of the point set in use. A large amount of detail on errors and limitations in the use of the discrete Fourier transform is provided by Hamming (see Additional Readings). We illustrate the potential problems in the following example.

Example 20.6.1   DISCRETE FOURIER TRANSFORM: ALIASING

Let's consider the simple case $f(x) = \cos 3x$ on the interval $0 \leq x \leq 2\pi$, which we (ill-advisedly) attempt to treat by the discrete Fourier transform method with $N = 4$. Our four points are at $x = 0$, $\pi/2$, π, and $3\pi/2$, and the four corresponding values of f_k are $(1, 0, -1, 0)$. The problem is that these same four values would be produced from $g(x) = \cos x$, so neither our discrete transform nor any information derived therefrom can properly reflect any difference in behavior between $f(x)$ and $g(x)$. If all that we are given are the four values $(1, 0, -1, 0)$, the most straightforward thing to do is take the discrete transform, yielding $(0, 1, 0, 1)$, which (from the formula for the inverse transform) corresponds to

$$\frac{1}{2}(0, 1, 0, 1) \longrightarrow \frac{e^{i\pi x/2} + e^{3i\pi x/2}}{2}.$$

If evaluated only at the chosen points, this expression is correct, but if used as an approximation over the continuous range $(0, 2\pi)$ it cannot distinguish between $\cos x$, $\cos 3x$, or any linear combination of the two with unit overall weight.

Situations in which the behavior at one wavelength or frequency is mistaken for that at another is called **aliasing**. The best way to avoid aliasing errors is to use point sets of sufficient size to accommodate the expected extent of oscillatory character in our problem.   ∎

Fast Fourier Transform

The fast Fourier transform (FFT) is a particular way of factoring and rearranging the terms in the sums of the discrete Fourier transform. Brought to the attention of the scientific community by Cooley and Tukey,[4] its importance lies in the drastic reduction in the number of numerical operations required. The reduction is possible because the transformation matrix contains large numbers of duplicate entries, and the FFT procedure organizes the computation in a way permitting identical sets of coefficients to be computed only once. Because of the tremendous increase in speed achieved (and reduction in cost), the fast Fourier transform has been hailed as one of the few really significant advances in numerical analysis in the past few decades.

For N data points, a direct calculation of a discrete Fourier transform would require about N^2 multiplications. For N a power of 2, the fast Fourier transform technique of Cooley and Tukey cuts the number of multiplications required to $(N/2) \log_2 N$. If $N = 1024$ (2^{10}), the fast Fourier transform achieves a computational reduction by a factor of over 200. This is why the fast Fourier transform is called fast and why it has revolutionized

---

[4]J. W. Cooley and J. W. Tukey, *Math. Comput.* **19**: 297 (1965).

the digital processing of waveforms. Details on its internal operation will be found in the paper by Cooley and Tukey and in other sources.[5]

Exercises

20.6.1   Derive the trigonometric forms of discrete orthogonality corresponding to Eq. (20.120):

$$\sum_{k=0}^{N-1} \cos(2\pi pk/N)\sin(2\pi qk/N) = 0$$

$$\sum_{k=0}^{N-1} \cos(2\pi pk/N)\cos(2\pi qk/N) = \begin{cases} 0, & p \neq q \\ N/2, & p = q \neq 0, N/2 \\ N, & p = q = 0, N/2 \end{cases}$$

$$\sum_{k=0}^{N-1} \sin(2\pi pk/N)\sin(2\pi qk/N) = \begin{cases} 0, & p \neq q \\ N/2, & p = q \neq 0, N/2 \\ 0, & p = q = 0, N/2. \end{cases}$$

Note. If N is odd, p and q will never have the value $N/2$.

Hint. Consider the use of trigonometric identities such as

$$\sin A \cos B = \frac{1}{2}\Big[\sin(A+B) + \sin(A-B)\Big].$$

20.6.2   Show in detail how to go from

$$F_p = \frac{1}{N^{1/2}} \sum_{k=0}^{N-1} f_k e^{2\pi ipk} \quad \text{to} \quad f_k = \frac{1}{N^{1/2}} \sum_{p=0}^{N-1} F_p e^{-2\pi ipk}.$$

20.6.3   The N-membered point sets f_k and F_p are discrete Fourier transforms of each other. Derive the following symmetry relations:

(a)   If f_k is real, F_p is Hermitian symmetric; that is, $F_p = F_{N-p}^*$.

(b)   If f_k is pure imaginary, then $F_p = -F_{N-p}^*$.

Note. The symmetry of part (a) is an illustration of aliasing. If F_p describes an amplitude at a frequency proportional to p, we necessarily predict an equal amplitude at the frequency proportional to $N - p$.

---

[5] See, for example, G. D. Bergland, A guided tour of the fast Fourier transform, *IEEE Spectrum* **6**: 41 (1969). A good discussion can also be found in W. H. Press, B. P. Flannery, S. A. Teukolsky, and W. T. Vetterling, *Numerical Recipes*, 2nd ed., Cambridge: Cambridge University Press (1996), section 12.3.

20.7   LAPLACE TRANSFORMS

Definition

The Laplace transform $f(s)$ of a function $F(t)$ is defined by[6]

$$f(s) = \mathcal{L}\{F(t)\} = \int_0^\infty e^{-st} F(t) dt. \tag{20.126}$$

A few comments on the existence of the integral are in order. The infinite integral of $F(t)$,

$$\int_0^\infty F(t) dt,$$

need not exist. For instance, $F(t)$ may diverge exponentially for large t. However, if there are some constants s_0, M, and $t_0 \geq 0$ such that for all $t > t_0$

$$|e^{-s_0 t} F(t)| \leq M, \tag{20.127}$$

the Laplace transform will exist for $s > s_0$; $F(t)$ is then said to be of **exponential order**. As a counterexample, $F(t) = e^{t^2}$ does not satisfy the condition given by Eq. (20.127) and is **not** of exponential order. Thus, $\mathcal{L}\left\{e^{t^2}\right\}$ does **not** exist.

The Laplace transform may also fail to exist because of a sufficiently strong singularity in the function $F(t)$ as $t \to 0$. For example,

$$\int_0^\infty e^{-st} t^n \, dt$$

diverges at the origin for $n \leq -1$. The Laplace transform $\mathcal{L}\{t^n\}$ does not exist for $n \leq -1$.

Since, for two functions $F(t)$ and $G(t)$ for which the integrals exist,

$$\mathcal{L}\left\{ aF(t) + bG(t) \right\} = a\mathcal{L}\{F(t)\} + b\mathcal{L}\{G(t)\}, \tag{20.128}$$

the operation denoted by $\mathcal{L}$ is **linear**.

Elementary Functions

To introduce the Laplace transform, let us apply the operation to some of the elementary functions. In all cases we assume that $F(t) = 0$ for $t < 0$. If

$$F(t) = 1, \quad t > 0,$$

---

[6]This is sometimes called a **one-sided Laplace transform**; the integral from $-\infty$ to $+\infty$ is referred to as a **two-sided Laplace transform**. Some authors introduce an additional factor of s. This extra s appears to have little advantage and continually gets in the way; for further comments, see section 14.13 in the text by Jeffreys and Jeffreys (Additional Readings). Generally, we take s to be real and positive. It is possible to let s become complex, provided $\Re e(s) > 0$.

then

$$\mathcal{L}\{1\} = \int_0^\infty e^{-st}\, dt = \frac{1}{s}, \quad \text{for} \quad s > 0. \tag{20.129}$$

Next, let

$$F(t) = e^{kt}, \quad t > 0.$$

The Laplace transform becomes

$$\mathcal{L}\{e^{kt}\} = \int_0^\infty e^{-st} e^{kt}\, dt = \frac{1}{s-k}, \quad \text{for} \quad s > k. \tag{20.130}$$

Using this relation, we obtain the Laplace transform of certain other functions. Since

$$\cosh kt = \tfrac{1}{2}(e^{kt} + e^{-kt}), \quad \sinh kt = \tfrac{1}{2}(e^{kt} - e^{-kt}), \tag{20.131}$$

we have

$$\mathcal{L}\{\cosh kt\} = \frac{1}{2}\left(\frac{1}{s-k} + \frac{1}{s+k}\right) = \frac{s}{s^2 - k^2}, \tag{20.132}$$

$$\mathcal{L}\{\sinh kt\} = \frac{1}{2}\left(\frac{1}{s-k} - \frac{1}{s+k}\right) = \frac{k}{s^2 - k^2}, \tag{20.133}$$

both valid for $s > k$.

From the relations

$$\cos kt = \cosh ikt, \quad \sin kt = -i \sinh ikt,$$

it is evident that we can obtain transforms of the sine and cosine if k is replaced by ik in Eqs. (20.132) and (20.133):

$$\mathcal{L}\{\cos kt\} = \frac{s}{s^2 + k^2}, \tag{20.134}$$

$$\mathcal{L}\{\sin kt\} = \frac{k}{s^2 + k^2}, \tag{20.135}$$

both valid for $s > 0$. Another derivation of this last transform is given in Example 20.8.1. It is a curious fact that $\lim_{s \to 0} \mathcal{L}\{\sin kt\} = 1/k$ despite the fact that $\int_0^\infty \sin kt\, dt$ does not exist.

Finally, for $F(t) = t^n$, we have

$$\mathcal{L}\{t^n\} = \int_0^\infty e^{-st} t^n\, dt,$$

which is just a gamma function. Hence

$$\mathcal{L}\{t^n\} = \frac{\Gamma(n+1)}{s^{n+1}}, \quad s > 0,\ n > -1. \tag{20.136}$$

Note that in all these transforms we have the variable s in the denominator, so that it occurs as a negative power. From the definition of the transform, Eq. (20.126) and the existence condition, Eq. (20.127), it is clear that if $f(s)$ is a Laplace transform, then $\lim_{s \to \infty} f(s) = 0$. The significance of this point is that if $f(s)$ behaves asymptotically for large s as a positive power of s, then no inverse transform can exist.

Heaviside Step Function

In Exercise 1.11.9 we encountered the Heaviside step function $u(t)$. Because of its utility in describing discontinuous signal pulses, its Laplace transform occurs frequently. We therefore remind the reader of the definition

$$u(t - k) = \begin{cases} 0, & t < k, \\ 1, & t > k. \end{cases} \tag{20.137}$$

Taking the transform, we have

$$\mathcal{L}\{u(t - k)\} = \int_{k}^{\infty} e^{-st} \, dt = \frac{1}{s} e^{-ks}. \tag{20.138}$$

Example 20.7.1   TRANSFORM OF SQUARE PULSE

Let's compute the transform of a square pulse $F(t)$ of height A that is on from $t = 0$ to $t = t_0$; see Fig. 20.13. Using the Heaviside step function, the pulse can be represented as

$$F(t) = A\Big[u(t) - u(t - t_0)\Big].$$

Its transform is therefore

$$\mathcal{L}\{F(t)\} = \frac{1}{s}(1 - e^{-t_0 s}).$$

∎

Dirac Delta Function

For use with differential equations one further transform is helpful, namely that of the Dirac delta function. From the properties of the delta function, we have

$$\mathcal{L}\{\delta(t - t_0)\} = \int_{0}^{\infty} e^{-st} \delta(t - t_0) dt = e^{-st_0}, \quad \text{for} \quad t_0 > 0. \tag{20.139}$$

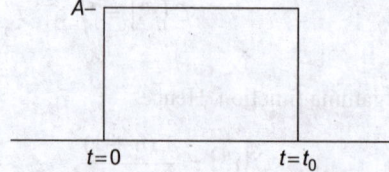

FIGURE 20.13   Square pulse.

For $t_0 = 0$ we must be a bit more careful, as the sequences we have used for defining the delta function involve contributions symmetrically distributed about t_0, and the integration defining the Laplace transform is restricted to $t \geq 0$. Consistent results when using Laplace transforms, however, are obtained if we consider delta sequences that are entirely within the range $t \geq t_0$, which is equivalent to

$$\mathcal{L}\{\delta(t)\} = 1. \tag{20.140}$$

This delta function is frequently called the **impulse** function because it is so useful in describing impulsive forces, that is, forces lasting only a short time.

Inverse Transform

As we have already seen in our discussion of the Fourier transform, the taking of an integral transform will ordinarily have little value unless we can carry out the inverse transform. That is, with

$$\mathcal{L}\{F(t)\} = f(s),$$

then it is desirable to be able to compute

$$\mathcal{L}^{-1}\{f(s)\} = F(t). \tag{20.141}$$

However, this inverse transform is not entirely unique. Two functions $F_1(t)$ and $F_2(t)$ can have the same transform, $f(s)$, if their difference, $N(t) = F_1(t) - F_2(t)$, is a **null function**, meaning that for all $t_0 > 0$ it satisfies

$$\int_0^{t_0} N(t)dt = 0.$$

This result is known as **Lerch's theorem**, and is not quite equivalent to $F_1 = F_2$, because it permits F_1 and F_2 to differ at isolated points. However, in most problems studied by physicists or engineers this ambiguity is not important and we will not consider it further.

The inverse transform can be determined in various ways.

1. A table of transforms can be built up and used to identify inverse transformations, exactly as a table of logarithms can be used to look up antilogarithms. The preceding transforms constitute the beginnings of such a table. More complete sets of Laplace transforms are in several of the Additional Readings, and a relatively short table of transforms appears in the present text as Table 20.1. Many functional forms not in Table 20.1 can be reduced to tabular entries using a partial fraction expansion or other properties of the Laplace transform presented later in this chapter. Of particular value in this regard are the translation and derivative formulas. There is some justification for suspecting that these tables are probably of more value in solving textbook exercises than in solving real-world problems.
2. A general technique for $\mathcal{L}^{-1}$ will be developed in Section 20.10 by using the calculus of residues.
3. Transforms and their inverses can be represented numerically. See the work by Krylov and Skoblya in Additional Readings.

Table 20.1   Laplace Transforms[a]

	$f(s)$	$F(t)$	Limitation	Equation
1.	1	$\delta(t)$	Singularity at $+0$	(20.140)
2.	$\dfrac{1}{s}$	1	$s > 0$	(20.129)
3.	$\dfrac{\Gamma(n+1)}{s^{n+1}}$	t^n	$s > 0,\ n > -1$	(20.136)
4.	$\dfrac{1}{s-k}$	e^{kt}	$s > k$	(20.130)
5.	$\dfrac{1}{(s-k)^2}$	te^{kt}	$s > k$	(20.176)
6.	$\dfrac{s}{s^2-k^2}$	$\cosh kt$	$s > k$	(20.132)
7.	$\dfrac{k}{s^2-k^2}$	$\sinh kt$	$s > k$	(20.133)
8.	$\dfrac{s}{s^2+k^2}$	$\cos kt$	$s > 0$	(20.134)
9.	$\dfrac{k}{s^2+k^2}$	$\sin kt$	$s > 0$	(20.135)
10.	$\dfrac{s-a}{(s-a)^2+k^2}$	$e^{at}\cos kt$	$s > a$	(20.159)
11.	$\dfrac{k}{(s-a)^2+k^2}$	$e^{at}\sin kt$	$s > a$	(20.158)
12.	$\dfrac{s^2-k^2}{(s^2+k^2)^2}$	$t\cos kt$	$s > 0$	(20.177)
13.	$\dfrac{2ks}{(s^2+k^2)^2}$	$t\sin kt$	$s > 0$	(20.178)
14.	$(s^2+a^2)^{-1/2}$	$J_0(at)$	$s > 0$	(20.182)
15.	$(s^2-a^2)^{-1/2}$	$I_0(at)$	$s > a$	Exercise 20.8.13
16.	$\dfrac{1}{a}\cot^{-1}\left(\dfrac{s}{a}\right)$	$j_0(at)$	$s > 0$	Exercise 20.8.14
17.	$\left.\begin{array}{c}\dfrac{1}{2a}\ln\dfrac{s+a}{s-a}\\[2ex]\dfrac{1}{a}\coth^{-1}\left(\dfrac{s}{a}\right)\end{array}\right\}$	$i_0(at)$	$s > a$	Exercise 20.8.14
18.	$\dfrac{(s-a)^n}{s^{n+1}}$	$L_n(at)$	$s > 0$	Exercise 20.8.16
19.	$\dfrac{1}{s}\ln(s+1)$	$E_1(x)$	$s > 0$	Exercise 20.8.17
20.	$\dfrac{\ln s}{s}$	$-\ln t - \gamma$	$s > 0$	Exercise 20.10.9

[a] γ is the Euler-Mascheroni constant.

Example 20.7.2   PARTIAL FRACTION EXPANSION

The function $f(s) = k^2/s(s^2 + k^2)$ does not appear as a transform listed in Table 20.1, but we may obtain it from the tabulated transforms by observing that it has the partial fraction expansion

$$f(s) = \frac{k^2}{s(s^2 + k^2)} = \frac{1}{s} - \frac{s}{s^2 + k^2}.$$

The partial fraction technique was discussed in Section 1.5, and the present example was the subject of Example 1.5.3.

Each of the two partial fractions corresponds to an entry in Table 20.1, and we can therefore take the inverse transform of $f(s)$ term by term:

$$\mathcal{L}^{-1}\{f(s)\} = 1 - \cos kt.$$

Remember that the range of the inverse transform is restricted to $t \geq 0$. ∎

Example 20.7.3   A STEP FUNCTION

This example shows how Laplace transforms can be used to evaluate a definite integral. Consider

$$F(t) = \int_0^\infty \frac{\sin tx}{x} dx. \tag{20.142}$$

Suppose we take the Laplace transform of this definite (and improper) integral, naming it $f(s)$:

$$f(s) = \mathcal{L}\left\{ \int_0^\infty \frac{\sin tx}{x} dx \right\} = \int_0^\infty e^{-st} \int_0^\infty \frac{\sin tx}{x} dx\, dt.$$

Now, interchanging the order of integration (which is justified),[7] we get

$$f(s) = \int_0^\infty \frac{1}{x} \left[\int_0^\infty e^{-st} \sin tx\, dt \right] dx = \int_0^\infty \frac{dx}{s^2 + x^2}, \tag{20.143}$$

since the factor in square brackets is just the Laplace transform of $\sin tx$. The integral on the right-hand side is elementary, with evaluation

$$f(s) = \int_0^\infty \frac{dx}{s^2 + x^2} = \frac{1}{s} \tan^{-1}\left(\frac{x}{s}\right)\Big|_0^\infty = \frac{\pi}{2s}. \tag{20.144}$$

Using entry #2 in Table 20.1, we carry out the inverse transformation to obtain

$$F(t) = \frac{\pi}{2}, \quad t > 0, \tag{20.145}$$

---

[7] See Chapter 1 in Jeffreys and Jeffreys (Additional Readings) for a discussion of uniform convergence of integrals.

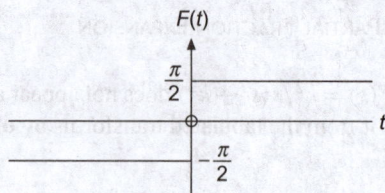

FIGURE 20.14 $F(t) = \int_0^\infty \frac{\sin tx}{x} dx$, a step function.

in agreement with an evaluation by the calculus of residues, Eq. (11.107). It has been assumed that $t > 0$ in $F(t)$. For $F(-t)$ we need note only that $\sin(-tx) = -\sin tx$, giving $F(-t) = -F(t)$. Finally, if $t = 0$, $F(0)$ is clearly zero. Therefore,

$$\int\limits_0^\infty \frac{\sin tx}{x} dx = \frac{\pi}{2} [2u(t) - 1] = \begin{cases} \dfrac{\pi}{2}, & t > 0 \\ 0, & t = 0 \\ -\dfrac{\pi}{2}, & t < 0. \end{cases} \tag{20.146}$$

Here $u(t)$ is the Heaviside unit step function, Eq. (20.137). Thus, $\int\limits_0^\infty (\sin tx/x) dx$, taken as a function of t, describes a step function (Fig. 20.14), with a step of height π at $t = 0$. ■

The technique in the preceding example was to (1) introduce a second integration, namely the Laplace transform, (2) reverse the order of integration and integrate once, and (3) take the inverse Laplace transform. This is a technique that will apply to many problems.

Exercises

20.7.1   Prove that

$$\lim_{s \to \infty} sf(s) = \lim_{t \to +0} F(t).$$

Hint. Assume that $F(t)$ can be expressed as $F(t) = \sum_{n=0}^\infty a_n t^n$.

20.7.2   Show that

$$\frac{1}{\pi} \lim_{s \to 0} \mathcal{L}\{\cos xt\} = \delta(x).$$

20.7.3   Verify that

$$\mathcal{L}\left\{ \frac{\cos at - \cos bt}{b^2 - a^2} \right\} = \frac{s}{(s^2 + a^2)(s^2 + b^2)}, \quad a^2 \neq b^2.$$

20.7.4 Using partial fraction expansions, show that

(a) $\mathcal{L}^{-1}\left\{\dfrac{1}{(s+a)(s+b)}\right\} = \dfrac{e^{-at} - e^{-bt}}{b-a}, \quad a \neq b.$

(b) $\mathcal{L}^{-1}\left\{\dfrac{s}{(s+a)(s+b)}\right\} = \dfrac{ae^{-at} - be^{-bt}}{a-b}, \quad a \neq b.$

20.7.5 Using partial fraction expansions, show that for $a^2 \neq b^2$,

(a) $\mathcal{L}^{-1}\left\{\dfrac{1}{(s^2+a^2)(s^2+b^2)}\right\} = -\dfrac{1}{a^2-b^2}\left\{\dfrac{\sin at}{a} - \dfrac{\sin bt}{b}\right\}.$

(b) $\mathcal{L}^{-1}\left\{\dfrac{s^2}{(s^2+a^2)(s^2+b^2)}\right\} = \dfrac{1}{a^2-b^2}\{a\sin at - b\sin bt\}.$

20.7.6 Show that

(a) $\displaystyle\int_0^\infty \frac{\cos s}{s^\nu}\,ds = \frac{\pi}{2(\nu-1)!\cos(\nu\pi/2)}, \quad 0 < \nu < 1.$

(b) $\displaystyle\int_0^\infty \frac{\sin s}{s^\nu}\,ds = \frac{\pi}{2(\nu-1)!\sin(\nu\pi/2)}, \quad 0 < \nu < 2.$

Why is ν restricted to (0, 1) for (a), to (0, 2) for (b)? These integrals may be interpreted as Fourier transforms of $s^{-\nu}$ and as Mellin transforms of $\sin s$ and $\cos s$.

Hint. Replace $s^{-\nu}$ by a Laplace transform integral: $\mathcal{L}\{t^{\nu-1}\}/\Gamma(\nu)$. Then integrate with respect to s. The resulting integral can be treated as a beta function (Section 13.3).

20.7.7 A function $F(t)$ can be expanded in a Maclaurin series,

$$F(t) = \sum_{n=0}^\infty a_n t^n.$$

Then

$$\mathcal{L}\{F(t)\} = \int_0^\infty e^{-st}\sum_{n=0}^\infty a_n t^n\,dt = \sum_{n=0}^\infty a_n \int_0^\infty e^{-st}t^n\,dt.$$

Show that $f(s)$, the Laplace transform of $F(t)$, contains no powers of s greater than s^{-1}. Check your result by calculating $\mathcal{L}\{\delta(t)\}$, and comment on this fiasco.

20.7.8 Show that the Laplace transform of the confluent hypergeometric function $M(a, c; x)$ is

$$\mathcal{L}\{M(a, c; x)\} = \frac{1}{s}\,{}_2F_1\left(a, 1; c; \frac{1}{s}\right).$$

20.8   PROPERTIES OF LAPLACE TRANSFORMS

Transforms of Derivatives

Perhaps the main application of Laplace transforms is in converting differential equations into simpler forms that may be solved more easily. It will be seen, for instance, that coupled differential equations with constant coefficients transform to simultaneous linear algebraic equations. For the study of differential equations we need formulas for the Laplace transforms of the derivatives of a function.

Let us transform the first derivative of $F(t)$:

$$\mathcal{L}\{F'(t)\} = \int_0^\infty e^{-st} \frac{dF(t)}{dt}\, dt.$$

Integrating by parts, we obtain

$$\mathcal{L}\{F'(t)\} = e^{-st} F(t)\Big|_0^\infty + s \int_0^\infty e^{-st} F(t)\, dt$$

$$= s\mathcal{L}\{F(t)\} - F(0). \tag{20.147}$$

Strictly speaking, $F(0) = F(+0)$,[8] and dF/dt is required to be at least piecewise continuous for $0 \le t < \infty$. Naturally, both $F(t)$ and its derivative must be such that the integrals do not diverge. An extension to higher derivatives gives

$$\mathcal{L}\left\{F^{(2)}(t)\right\} = s^2 \mathcal{L}\{F(t)\} - sF(+0) - F'(+0), \tag{20.148}$$

$$\mathcal{L}\{F^{(n)}(t)\} = s^n \mathcal{L}\{F(t)\} - s^{n-1} F(+0) - \cdots - F^{(n-1)}(+0). \tag{20.149}$$

The Laplace transform, like the Fourier transform, replaces differentiation with multiplication. In the following examples ODEs become algebraic equations. Here is the power and the utility of the Laplace transform. But see Example 20.8.7 for what may happen if the coefficients are not constant.

Note how the initial conditions, $F(+0)$, $F'(+0)$, and so on, are incorporated into the transform. This situation is different than for the Fourier transform, and arises from the finite lower limit ($t = 0$) of the integral defining the transform. This property makes the Laplace transform more powerful for obtaining solutions to differential equations subject to initial conditions.

---

[8]This notation means that zero is approached from the positive side.

Example 20.8.1   USE OF DERIVATIVE FORMULA

Here is an example showing how the derivative formula has uses even in contexts not involving the solution to a differential equation. Starting from the identity

$$-k^2 \sin kt = \frac{d^2}{dt^2} \sin kt, \qquad (20.150)$$

we apply on both sides of the equation the Laplace transform operation, reaching

$$-k^2 \mathcal{L}\{\sin kt\} = \mathcal{L}\left\{\frac{d^2}{dt^2} \sin kt\right\}$$

$$= s^2 \mathcal{L}\{\sin kt\} - s \sin(0) - \frac{d}{dt} \sin kt \Big|_{t=0}.$$

Since $\sin(0) = 0$ and $d/dt \sin kt \,|_{t=0} = k$, the above equation has solution

$$\mathcal{L}\{\sin kt\} = \frac{k}{s^2 + k^2}.$$

This result confirms Eq. (20.135).   ∎

Examples involving the solutions of differential equations follow.

Example 20.8.2   SIMPLE HARMONIC OSCILLATOR

As a physical example, consider a mass m oscillating under the influence of an ideal spring, spring constant k. As usual, friction is neglected. Then Newton's second law becomes

$$m\frac{d^2 X(t)}{dt^2} + kX(t) = 0. \qquad (20.151)$$

We take as initial conditions

$$X(0) = X_0, \quad X'(0) = 0.$$

Applying the Laplace transform, we obtain

$$m\mathcal{L}\left\{\frac{d^2 X}{dt^2}\right\} + k\mathcal{L}\{X(t)\} = 0. \qquad (20.152)$$

Letting $x(s)$ denote the presently unknown transform $\mathcal{L}\{X(t)\}$ and using Eq. (20.148), we convert Eq. (20.152) to the form

$$ms^2 x(s) - msX_0 + kx(s) = 0,$$

which has solution

$$x(s) = X_0 \frac{s}{s^2 + \omega_0^2}, \quad \text{with } \omega_0^2 \equiv \frac{k}{m}.$$

From Table 20.1 this is seen to be the transform of $\cos \omega_0 t$, which gives the expected result:

$$X(t) = X_0 \cos \omega_0 t. \qquad (20.153)$$

∎

Example 20.8.3   EARTH'S NUTATION

A somewhat more involved example is the nutation of the Earth's poles (force-free precession). We treat the Earth as a rigid (oblate) spheroid, with z-axis through its direction of symmetry. We assume the spheroid to have moments of inertia I_z and $I_x = I_y$ and to be rotating about its x, y, and z axes at the respective angular velocities $X(t) = \omega_x(t)$, $Y(t) \equiv \omega_y(t)$, $\omega_z =$ constant. The Euler equations of motion for X and Y reduce to

$$\frac{dX}{dt} = -aY, \quad \frac{dY}{dt} = +aX, \tag{20.154}$$

where $a \equiv [(I_z - I_x)/I_z]\omega_z$. For the Earth, the initial values of X and Y are not both zero, so the axis of rotation is not aligned with the symmetry axis (see Fig. 20.15), and because of this lack of alignment, the axis of rotation precesses about the axis of symmetry. For the Earth, the deviation between the rotation and symmetry axes is small, only about 15 meters (measured at the Earth's surface at the poles).

Our first step in solving these coupled ODEs is to take their Laplace transforms, obtaining

$$sx(s) - X(0) = -ay(s), \quad sy(s) - Y(0) = ax(s).$$

Combining to eliminate $y(s)$, we have

$$s^2 x(s) - sX(0) + aY(0) = -a^2 x(s),$$

or

$$x(s) = X(0)\frac{s}{s^2 + a^2} - Y(0)\frac{a}{s^2 + a^2}. \tag{20.155}$$

Recognizing these functions of s as transforms listed in Table 20.1,

$$X(t) = X(0)\cos at - Y(0)\sin at.$$

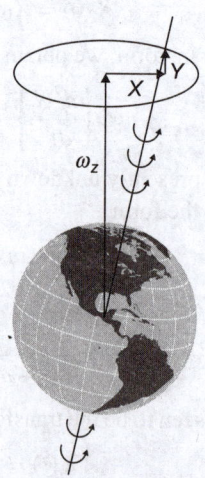

FIGURE 20.15   Earth's rotation axis and its components.

Similarly,

$$Y(t) = X(0)\sin at + Y(0)\cos at.$$

This is seen to be a rotation of the vector (X, Y) counterclockwise (for $a > 0$) about the z-axis with angle $\theta = at$ and angular velocity a.

A direct interpretation may be found by choosing the x and y axes so that $Y(0) = 0$. Then

$$X(t) = X(0)\cos at, \quad Y(t) = X(0)\sin at,$$

which are the parametric equations for rotation of (X, Y) in a circular orbit of radius $X(0)$, with angular velocity a in the counterclockwise sense.

For the Earth, a as defined here corresponds to a period $(2\pi/a)$ of some 300 days. Actually, because of departures from the idealized rigid body assumed in setting up Euler's equations, the period is about 427 days.[9]

These same equations arise in electromagnetic theory. If in Eq. (20.154) we set

$$X(t) = L_x, \quad Y(t) = L_y,$$

where L_x and L_y are the x- and y-components of the angular momentum $\mathbf{L}$ of a charged particle moving in a uniform magnetic field $B_z \mathbf{e}_z$, and then assign a the value $a = -g_L B_z$, where g_L is the **gyromagnetic ratio** of the particle, then Eq. (20.148) determines its Larmor precession in the magnetic field. ∎

Example 20.8.4   IMPULSIVE FORCE

For an impulsive force acting on a particle of mass m, Newton's second law takes the form

$$m\frac{d^2 X}{dt^2} = P\delta(t),$$

where P is a constant. Transforming, we obtain

$$ms^2 x(s) - ms X(0) - m X'(0) = P.$$

For a particle starting from rest, $X'(0) = 0$. We shall also take $X(0) = 0$. Then

$$x(s) = \frac{P}{ms^2},$$

and, taking the inverse transform,

$$X(t) = \frac{P}{m} t,$$

$$\frac{dX(t)}{dt} = \frac{P}{m}, \quad \text{a constant.}$$

The effect of the impulse $P\delta(t)$ is to transfer (instantaneously) P units of linear momentum to the particle.

---

[9]D. Menzel, ed., *Fundamental Formulas of Physics*, Englewood Cliffs, NJ: Prentice-Hall (1955), reprinted, Dover (1960), p. 695.

A similar analysis applies to the ballistic galvanometer. The torque on the galvanometer is given initially by $k\iota$, in which ι is a pulse of current and k is a proportionality constant. Since ι is of short duration, we set

$$k\iota = kq\,\delta(t),$$

where q is the total charge carried by the current ι. Then, with I the moment of inertia,

$$I\frac{d^2\theta}{dt^2} = kq\,\delta(t),$$

and transforming, as before, we find that the effect of the current pulse is a transfer of kq units of **angular** momentum to the galvanometer.   ■

Change of Scale

If we replace t by at in the defining formula for the Laplace transform, we readily obtain

$$\mathcal{L}\{F(at)\} = \int_0^\infty e^{-st}\,F(at)dt = \frac{1}{a}\int_0^\infty e^{-(s/a)(at)}\,F(at)\,d(at)$$

$$= \frac{1}{a}\,f\left(\frac{s}{a}\right). \tag{20.156}$$

Substitution

If we replace the parameter s by $s - a$ in the definition of the Laplace transform, Eq. (20.126), we have

$$f(s - a) = \int_0^\infty e^{-(s-a)t}\,F(t)dt = \int_0^\infty e^{-st}e^{at}\,F(t)dt$$

$$= \mathcal{L}\left\{e^{at}\,F(t)\right\}. \tag{20.157}$$

Hence the replacement of s with $s - a$ corresponds to multiplying $F(t)$ by e^{at}, and conversely. This result can used to check some entries in our table of transforms. From Eq. (20.157) we find immediately that

$$\mathcal{L}\left\{e^{at}\sin kt\right\} = \frac{k}{(s-a)^2 + k^2}, \quad (s > a), \tag{20.158}$$

and

$$\mathcal{L}\left\{e^{at}\cos kt\right\} = \frac{s-a}{(s-a)^2 + k^2}, \quad s > a. \tag{20.159}$$

These are entries 10 and 11 of Table 20.1.

Example 20.8.5   DAMPED OSCILLATOR

Equations (20.158) and (20.159) are useful when we consider an oscillating mass with damping proportional to the velocity. Equation (20.151), with such damping added, becomes

$$mX''(t) + bX'(t) + kX(t) = 0, \tag{20.160}$$

in which b is a proportionality constant. Let us assume that the particle starts from rest at $X(0) = X_0$, so $X'(0) = 0$. The transformed equation is

$$m[s^2 x(s) - sX_0] + b[sx(s) - X_0] + kx(s) = 0,$$

with solution

$$x(s) = X_0 \frac{ms + b}{ms^2 + bs + k}.$$

This transform does not appear in our table, but may be handled by completing the square of the denominator:

$$s^2 + \frac{b}{m}s + \frac{k}{m} = \left(s + \frac{b}{2m}\right)^2 + \left(\frac{k}{m} - \frac{b^2}{4m^2}\right).$$

Considering further only the case that the damping is small enough that $b^2 < 4km$, then the last term is positive and will be denoted by ω_1^2. We then rearrange $x(s)$ to the form

$$x(s) = X_0 \frac{s + b/m}{(s + b/2m)^2 + \omega_1^2}$$

$$= X_0 \frac{s + b/2m}{(s + b/2m)^2 + \omega_1^2} + X_0 \frac{\omega_1(b/2m\omega_1)}{(s + b/2m)^2 + \omega_1^2}.$$

These are the same transforms we encountered in Eqs. (20.158) and (20.159), so we may take the inverse transform of our formula for $x(s)$, reaching

$$X(t) = X_0 e^{-(b/2m)t}\left(\cos\omega_1 t + \frac{b}{2m\omega_1}\sin\omega_1 t\right)$$

$$= X_0 \frac{\omega_0}{\omega_1} e^{-(b/2m)t} \cos(\omega_1 t - \varphi). \tag{20.161}$$

Here we have made the substitutions

$$\tan\varphi = \frac{b}{2m\omega_1}, \quad \omega_0^2 = \frac{k}{m}.$$

Of course, as $b \to 0$, this solution goes over to the undamped solution, given in Example 20.8.2. ∎

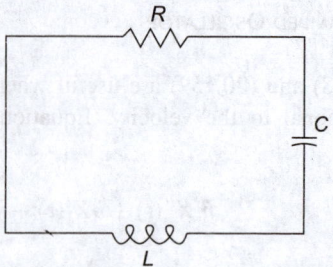

FIGURE 20.16   *RLC* circuit.

RLC Analog

It is worth noting the similarity between the damped simple harmonic oscillation of a mass (Example 20.8.5) and an *RLC* circuit (resistance, inductance, and capacitance). See Fig. 20.16. At any instant, the sum of the potential differences around the loop must be zero (Kirchhoff's law, conservation of energy). This gives

$$L\frac{dI}{dt} + RI + \frac{1}{C}\int_0^t I\,dt = 0. \tag{20.162}$$

Differentiating Eq. (20.162) with respect to time (to eliminate the integral), we have

$$L\frac{d^2I}{dt^2} + R\frac{dI}{dt} + \frac{1}{C}I = 0. \tag{20.163}$$

If we replace $I(t)$ with $X(t)$, L with m, R with b, and C^{-1} with k, then Eq. (20.163) is identical with the mechanical problem. It is but one example of the unification of diverse branches of physics by mathematics. A more complete discussion will be found in a book by Olson.[10]

Translation

This time let $f(s)$ be multiplied by e^{-bs}, with $b > 0$:

$$e^{-bs}f(s) = e^{-bs}\int_0^\infty e^{-st}F(t)dt$$

$$= \int_0^\infty e^{-s(t+b)}F(t)dt. \tag{20.164}$$

---

[10]H. F. Olson, *Dynamical Analogies*, New York: Van Nostrand (1943).

Now let $t + b = \tau$. Equation (20.164) becomes

$$e^{-bs} f(s) = \int\limits_{b}^{\infty} e^{-s\tau} F(\tau - b) d\tau. \tag{20.165}$$

Since $F(t)$ is assumed to be equal to zero for $t < 0$, so that $F(\tau - b) = 0$ for $0 \le \tau < b$, we can change the lower limit in Eq. (20.165) to zero without changing the value of the integral. Then renaming τ as our standard Laplace transform variable t, we have

$$e^{-bs} f(s) = \mathcal{L}\{F(t - b)\}. \tag{20.166}$$

If instead of relying on the assumption that $F(t) = 0$ for negative t we insert a Heaviside unit step function $u(\tau - b)$ to restrict the contributions from F to positive arguments, Eq. (20.165) takes the form

$$e^{-bs} f(s) = \int\limits_{0}^{\infty} e^{-s\tau} F(\tau - b) u(\tau - b) d\tau.$$

For this reason the translation formula, Eq. (20.166), is often called the **Heaviside shifting theorem**.

Example 20.8.6   ELECTROMAGNETIC WAVES

The electromagnetic wave equation with $E = E_y$ or E_z, a transverse wave propagating along the x-axis, is

$$\frac{\partial^2 E(x,t)}{\partial x^2} - \frac{1}{v^2} \frac{\partial^2 E(x,t)}{\partial t^2} = 0. \tag{20.167}$$

We want to solve this PDE for the situation that a source at $x = 0$ generates a time-dependent signal $E(0, t)$ starting at time $t = 0$ and propagating only toward positive x, with initial conditions that for $x > 0$,

$$E(x, 0) = 0, \qquad \frac{\partial E(x,t)}{\partial t}\bigg|_{t=0} = 0.$$

Transforming Eq. (20.167) with respect to t, we get

$$\frac{\partial^2}{\partial x^2} \mathcal{L}\{E(x,t)\} - \frac{s^2}{v^2} \mathcal{L}\{E(x,t)\} + \frac{s}{v^2} E(x, 0) + \frac{1}{v^2} \frac{\partial E(x,t)}{\partial t}\bigg|_{t=0} = 0,$$

which due to the initial conditions simplifies to

$$\frac{\partial^2}{\partial x^2} \mathcal{L}\{E(x,t)\} = \frac{s^2}{v^2} \mathcal{L}\{E(x,t)\}. \tag{20.168}$$

The general solution of Eq. (20.168) (which is an **ODE** in x) is

$$\mathcal{L}\{E(x,t)\} = f_1(s)e^{-(s/v)x} + f_2(s)e^{+(s/v)x}. \tag{20.169}$$

To understand more fully this result consider first the case $f_2(s) = 0$. Then Eq. (20.169) becomes

$$\mathcal{L}\{E(x,t)\} = e^{-(x/v)s} f_1(s), \tag{20.170}$$

which we recognize as of the same form as Eq. (20.166), meaning that

$$E(x,t) = F\left(t - \frac{x}{v}\right),$$

where F is the function whose Laplace transform is f_1, namely $E(0,t)$.[11] Since F is assumed to vanish when its argument is negative, this formula can be written in the more explicit form

$$E(x,t) = \begin{cases} F\left(t - \dfrac{x}{v}\right) = E\left(0, t - \dfrac{x}{v}\right), & t \geq \dfrac{x}{v}, \\ 0, & t < \dfrac{x}{v}. \end{cases} \tag{20.171}$$

This solution represents a wave (or pulse) moving in the positive x-direction with velocity v. Note that for $x > vt$ the region remains undisturbed; the pulse has not had time to get there. If we had decided to take the solution of Eq. (20.169) with $f_1(s) = 0$, we would have obtained

$$E(x,t) = \begin{cases} F\left(t + \dfrac{x}{v}\right) = E\left(0, t + \dfrac{x}{v}\right), & t \geq -\dfrac{x}{v}, \\ 0, & t < -\dfrac{x}{v}, \end{cases} \tag{20.172}$$

which we must reject because (for propagation toward positive x) it violates causality.

Our solution to this problem, Eq. (20.171), can be verified by differentiation and substitution into the original PDE, Eq. (20.167). ■

Derivative of a Transform

When $F(t)$, which is at least piecewise continuous, and s are chosen so that $e^{-st}F(t)$ converges exponentially for large s, the integral

$$\int_0^\infty e^{-st} F(t)\,dt$$

---

[11] Consider Eq. (20.170) with x set to zero.

is uniformly convergent and may be differentiated (under the integral sign) with respect to s. Then

$$f'(s) = \int_0^\infty (-t)e^{-st}F(t)dt = \mathcal{L}\{-tF(t)\}. \tag{20.173}$$

Continuing this process, we obtain

$$f^{(n)}(s) = \mathcal{L}\{(-t)^n F(t)\}. \tag{20.174}$$

All the integrals so obtained will be uniformly convergent because of the decreasing exponential behavior of $e^{-st}F(t)$.

This technique may be applied to generate more transforms. For example,

$$\mathcal{L}\{e^{kt}\} = \int_0^\infty e^{-st}e^{kt}\,dt = \frac{1}{s-k}, \quad s > k. \tag{20.175}$$

Differentiating with respect to s (or with respect to k), we obtain

$$\mathcal{L}\{te^{kt}\} = \frac{1}{(s-k)^2}, \quad s > k. \tag{20.176}$$

If we replace k by ik and separate Eq. (20.176) into its real and imaginary parts, we get

$$\mathcal{L}\{t\cos kt\} = \frac{s^2 - k^2}{(s^2 + k^2)^2}, \tag{20.177}$$

$$\mathcal{L}\{t\sin kt\} = \frac{2ks}{(s^2 + k^2)^2}. \tag{20.178}$$

These expressions are valid for $s > 0$.

Example 20.8.7   BESSEL'S EQUATION

An interesting application of a differentiated Laplace transform appears in the solution of Bessel's equation with $n = 0$. From Chapter 14 we have

$$x^2 y''(x) + x y'(x) + x^2 y(x) = 0.$$

This ODE cannot be solved by the method illustrated in Example 20.8.2 because the derivatives are multiplied by functions of the independent variable x. However, an alternate approach depending on Eq. (20.174) is available. Dividing by x and substituting $t = x$ and $F(t) = y(x)$ to agree with the present notation, we see that the Bessel equation becomes

$$t F''(t) + F'(t) + t F(t) = 0. \tag{20.179}$$

We need a regular solution, and it appears possible for $F(0)$ to be nonzero, so we scale the solution by setting $F(0) = 1$. Then, setting $t = 0$ in Eq. (20.179), we find that $F'(+0) = 0$. In addition, we assume that our unknown $F(t)$ has a transform. Transforming Eq. (20.179), using Eqs. (20.147) and (20.148) for the derivatives and Eq. (20.173) to append factors of t, we have

$$-\frac{d}{ds}\left[s^2 f(s) - s\right] + sf(s) - 1 - \frac{d}{ds} f(s) = 0. \tag{20.180}$$

Rearranging and simplifying, we obtain

$$(s^2 + 1) f'(s) + sf(s) = 0,$$

or

$$\frac{df}{f} = -\frac{s\,ds}{s^2 + 1},$$

a first-order ODE. By integration,

$$\ln f(s) = -\frac{1}{2} \ln(s^2 + 1) + \ln C,$$

which may be rewritten as

$$f(s) = \frac{C}{\sqrt{s^2 + 1}}. \tag{20.181}$$

To confirm that our transform yields the power-series expansion of J_0, we expand $f(s)$ as given in Eq. (20.181) in a series of negative powers of s, convergent for $s > 1$:

$$f(s) = \frac{C}{s} \left(1 + \frac{1}{s^2}\right)^{-1/2}$$

$$= \frac{C}{s} \left[1 - \frac{1}{2s^2} + \frac{1 \cdot 3}{2^2 \cdot 2!s^4} - \cdots + \frac{(-1)^n (2n)!}{(2^n n!)^2 s^{2n}} + \cdots\right].$$

Inverting, term by term, we obtain

$$F(t) = C \sum_{n=0}^{\infty} \frac{(-1)^n t^{2n}}{(2^n n!)^2}.$$

When C is set equal to 1, as required by the initial condition $F(0) = 1$, we recover $J_0(t)$, our familiar Bessel function of order zero. Hence,

$$\mathcal{L}\{J_0(t)\} = \frac{1}{\sqrt{s^2 + 1}}. \tag{20.182}$$

This simple, closed form is the Laplace transform of $J_0(t)$. After making a scale change to form $J_0(at)$ using Eq. (20.156), we confirm entry 14 of Table 20.1.

Note that in our derivation of Eq. (20.182) we assumed $s > 1$. The proof for $s > 0$ is the topic of Exercise 20.8.10. ∎

It is worth noting that this application was successful and relatively easy because we took $n = 0$ in Bessel's equation. This made it possible to divide out a factor of x (or t). If this had not been done, the terms of the form $t^2 F(t)$ would have introduced a second derivative of $f(s)$. The resulting equation would have been no easier to solve than the original one. This observation illustrates the point that when we go beyond linear ODEs with constant coefficients, the Laplace transform may still be applied, but there is no guarantee that it will be helpful.

The application to Bessel's equation, $n \neq 0$, will be found in the Additional Readings. Alternatively, given the result

$$\mathcal{L}\{J_n(at)\} = \frac{a^{-n}(\sqrt{s^2 + a^2} - s)^n}{\sqrt{s^2 + a^2}}, \tag{20.183}$$

we can confirm its validity by expressing $J_n(t)$ as an infinite series and transforming term by term.

Integration of Transforms

Again, with $F(t)$ at least piecewise continuous and x large enough so that $e^{-xt} F(t)$ decreases exponentially (as $x \to \infty$), the integral

$$f(x) = \int_0^\infty e^{-xt} F(t) dt$$

is uniformly convergent with respect to x. This justifies reversing the order of integration in the following equation:

$$\int_s^\infty f(x) dx = \int_s^\infty dx \int_0^\infty dt \, e^{-xt} F(t) = \int_0^\infty e^{-st} \frac{F(t)}{t} \, dt,$$

$$= \mathcal{L}\left\{\frac{F(t)}{t}\right\}, \tag{20.184}$$

where the last member of the first line is obtained by integrating with respect to x. The lower limit s must be chosen large enough so that $f(s)$ is within the region of uniform convergence. Equation (20.184) is valid when $F(t)/t$ is finite at $t = 0$ or diverges less strongly than t^{-1} (so that $\mathcal{L}\{F(t)/t\}$ will exist).

For convenience we summarize the definition and properties of the Laplace transform in Table 20.2. Included in the table are formulas for convolution and inversion that will be discussed in Sections 20.9 and Sections 20.10.

Table 20.2 Laplace Transform Operations

	Operation	Equation
1. Laplace transform	$f(s) = \mathcal{L}\{F(t)\} = \int_{0}^{\infty} e^{-st} F(t)dt$	(15.99)
2. Transform of derivative	$sf(s) - F(+0) = \mathcal{L}\{F'(t)\}$	(15.123)
	$s^2 f(s) - sF(+0) - F'(+0) = \mathcal{L}\{F''(t)\}$	(15.124)
3. Transform of integral	$\dfrac{1}{s} f(s) = \mathcal{L}\left\{\displaystyle\int_{0}^{t} F(x)dx\right\}$	Exercise 20.9.1
4. Change of scale	$\dfrac{1}{a} f\left(\dfrac{s}{a}\right) = \mathcal{L}\{F(at)\}$	(20.156)
5. Substitution	$f(s - a) = \mathcal{L}\{e^{at} F(t)\}$	(15.152)
6. Translation	$e^{-bs} f(s) = \mathcal{L}\{F(t - b)\}$	(15.164)
7. Derivative of transform	$f^{(n)}(s) = \mathcal{L}\{(-t)^n F(t)\}$	(15.173)
8. Integral of transform	$\displaystyle\int_{s}^{\infty} f(x)dx = \mathcal{L}\left\{\dfrac{F(t)}{t}\right\}$	(15.189)
9. Convolution	$f_1(s) f_2(s) = \mathcal{L}\left\{\displaystyle\int_{0}^{t} F_1(t - z) F_2(z)dz\right\}$	(15.193)
10. Inverse transform, Bromwich integral[a]	$\dfrac{1}{2\pi i} \displaystyle\int_{\beta - i\infty}^{\beta + i\infty} e^{st} f(s)ds = F(t)$	(15.212)

[a] β must be large enough that $e^{-\beta t} F(t)$ vanishes as $t \to +\infty$.

Exercises

20.8.1 Use the expression for the transform of a second derivative to obtain the transform of $\cos kt$.

20.8.2 A mass m is attached to one end of an unstretched spring, spring constant k (Fig. 20.17). Starting at time $t = 0$, the free end of the spring experiences a constant acceleration a, away from the mass. Using Laplace transforms,

(a) find the position x of m as a function of time.

(b) determine the limiting form of $x(t)$ for small t.

$$ANS. \quad (a) \quad x = \frac{1}{2} at^2 - \frac{a}{\omega^2}(1 - \cos\omega t), \quad \omega^2 = \frac{k}{m},$$

$$(b) \quad x = \frac{a\omega^2}{4!} t^4, \quad \omega t \ll 1.$$

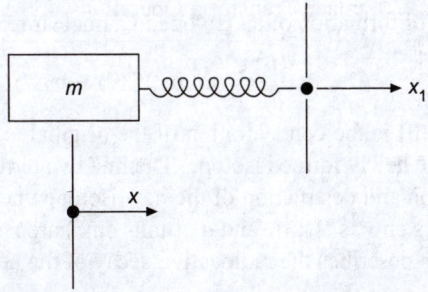

FIGURE 20.17   Spring, Exercise 20.8.2.

20.8.3   Radioactive nuclei decay according to the law

$$\frac{dN}{dt} = -\lambda N,$$

with N the concentration of a given nuclide and λ its particular decay constant. This equation may be interpreted as stating that the rate of decay is proportional to the number of these radioactive nuclei present. They all decay independently.

Consider now a radioactive series of n different nuclides, with Nuclide 1 decaying into Nuclide 2, Nuclide 2 into Nuclide 3, etc., until reaching Nuclide n, which is stable. The concentrations of the various nuclides satisfy the system of ODEs

$$\frac{dN_1}{dt} = -\lambda_1 N_1, \quad \frac{dN_2}{dt} = \lambda_1 N_1 - \lambda_2 N_2, \quad \cdots, \quad \frac{dN_n}{dt} = \lambda_{n-1} N_{n-1}.$$

(a)   For the case $n = 3$ find $N_1(t)$, $N_2(t)$, and $N_3(t)$, with $N_1(0) = N_0$ and $N_2(0) = N_3(0) = 0$.

(b)   Find an approximate expression for N_2 and N_3, valid for small t when $\lambda_1 \approx \lambda_2$.

(c)   Find approximate expressions for N_2 and N_3, valid for large t, when (1) $\lambda_1 \gg \lambda_2$, (2) $\lambda_1 \ll \lambda_2$.

ANS.   (a) $N_1(t) = N_0 e^{-\lambda_1 t}$, $\quad N_2(t) = N_0 \dfrac{\lambda_1}{\lambda_2 - \lambda_1} (e^{-\lambda_1 t} - e^{-\lambda_2 t})$,

$$N_3(t) = N_0 \left(1 - \frac{\lambda_2}{\lambda_2 - \lambda_1} e^{-\lambda_1 t} + \frac{\lambda_1}{\lambda_2 - \lambda_1} e^{-\lambda_2 t} \right).$$

(b) $N_2 \approx N_0 \lambda_1 t$, $\quad N_3 \approx \dfrac{N_0}{2} \lambda_1 \lambda_2 t^2$.

(c)   (1) $N_2 \approx N_0 e^{\lambda_2 t}$

$N_3 \approx N_0 (1 - e^{-\lambda_2 t})$, $\quad \lambda_1 t \gg 1$.

(2) $N_2 \approx N_0 (\lambda_1/\lambda_2) e^{-\lambda_1 t}$,

$N_3 \approx N_0 (1 - e^{-\lambda_1 t})$, $\quad \lambda_2 t \gg 1$.

20.8.4   The rate of formation of an isotope in a nuclear reactor is given by

$$\frac{dN_2}{dt} = \varphi \left[\sigma_1 N_1(0) - \sigma_2 N_2(t) \right] - \lambda_2 N_2(t).$$

Here $N_1(0)$ is the concentration of the original isotope (assumed constant), and N_2 is that of the newly formed isotope. The first two terms on the right-hand side describe the production and destruction of the new isotope via neutron absorption; φ is the neutron flux (units $cm^{-2}s^{-1}$); σ_1 and σ_2 (units cm^2) are neutron absorption cross sections. The final term describes the radioactive decay of the new isotope, with decay constant λ_2.

(a)   Find the concentration N_2 of the new isotope as a function of time.

(b)   For original isotope ^{153}Eu, $\sigma_1 = 400$ barns $= 400 \times 10^{-24}$ cm^2, $\sigma_2 = 1000$ barns $= 1000 \times 10^{-24}$ cm^2, and $\lambda_2 = 1.4 \times 10^{-9}$ s^{-1}. If $N_1(0) = 10^{20}$ and $\varphi = 10^9$ cm^{-2}s^{-1}, find N_2, the concentration of ^{154}Eu, after 1 year of continuous irradiation. Is the assumption that N_1 is constant justified?

20.8.5   In a nuclear reactor ^{135}Xe is formed as both a direct fission product of ^{235}U and by decay of ^{135}I (another fission product), half-life 6.7 hours. The half-life of ^{135}Xe is 9.2 hours. Because ^{135}Xe strongly absorbs thermal neutrons, thereby "poisoning" the nuclear reactor, its concentration is a matter of great interest. The relevant equations are

$$\frac{dN_I}{dt} = \varphi \gamma_I (\sigma_f N_U) - \lambda_I N_I,$$

$$\frac{dN_{Xe}}{dt} = \varphi \left[\gamma_{Xe}(\sigma_f N_U) - \sigma_{Xe} N_{Xe} \right] + \lambda_I N_I - \lambda_{Xe} N_{Xe}.$$

Here N_I, N_{Xe}, N_U are the concentrations of ^{135}I, ^{135}Xe, ^{235}U, with N_U assumed to be constant. The neutron flux φ in the reactor causes fission of ^{235}U with cross section σ_f and removes ^{135}Xe by neutron absorption with cross section $\sigma_{Xe} = 3.5 \times 10^6$ barns $= 3.5 \times 10^{-18}$ cm^2. Neutron absorption by ^{135}I is negligible. The yield of ^{135}I and ^{135}Xe per fission are, respectively, $\gamma_I = 0.060$ and $\gamma_{Xe} = 0.003$.

(a)   Find $N_{Xe}(t)$ in terms of neutron flux φ and the product $\sigma_f N_U$.

(b)   Find $N_{Xe}(t \to \infty)$.

(c)   After N_{Xe} has reached equilibrium, the reactor is shut down: $\varphi = 0$. Find $N_{Xe}(t)$ following shutdown. Note the short-term increase in N_{Xe}, which may for a few hours interfere with starting the reactor up again.

Hint. The half-life $t_{1/2}$ of a radioactive isotope is the time required for decay of half of the nuclides in a sample. For a decay rate $dN/dt = -\lambda N$, the half-life has the value $t_{1/2} = \ln 2/\lambda$, so λ can be computed as $\lambda = \ln 2/t_{1/2} = 0.693/t_{1/2}$.

20.8.6   Solve Eq. (20.160), which describes a damped simple harmonic oscillator, for $X(0) = X_0$, $X'(0) = 0$, and

(a) $b^2 = 4mk$ (critically damped),

(b) $b^2 > 4mk$ (overdamped).

$$ANS. \quad (a)\ X(t) = X_0 e^{-(b/2m)t} \left(1 + \frac{b}{2m} t \right).$$

20.8.7   Again solve Eq. (20.160), which describes a damped simple harmonic oscillator, but this time for $X(0) = 0$, $X'(0) = v_0$, and

(a) $b^2 < 4mk$ (underdamped),

(b) $b^2 = 4mk$ (critically damped),

(c) $b^2 > 4mk$ (overdamped).

$$ANS. \quad (a)\ X(t) = \frac{v_0}{\omega_1} e^{-(b/2m)t} \sin \omega_1 t,$$
$$(b)\ X(t) = v_0 t e^{-(b/2m)t}.$$

20.8.8   The motion of a body falling in a resisting medium may be described by

$$m\frac{d^2 X(t)}{dt^2} = mg - b\frac{dX(t)}{dt}$$

when the retarding force is proportional to the velocity. Find $X(t)$ and $dX(t)/dt$ for the initial conditions

$$X(0) = \left.\frac{dX}{dt}\right|_{t=0} = 0.$$

20.8.9   **Ringing circuit**. In certain electronic devices, resistance, inductance, and capacitance are placed in a circuit as shown in Fig. 20.18. A constant voltage is maintained across the capacitance, keeping it charged. At time $t = 0$ the circuit is disconnected from the voltage source. Find the voltages across each of the elements R, L, and C as a function of time. Assume R to be small.

Hint. By Kirchhoff's laws

$$I_{RL} + I_C = 0 \quad \text{and} \quad E_R + E_L = E_C,$$

where

$$E_R = I_{RL}R, \quad E_L = L\frac{dI_{RL}}{dt}, \quad E_C = \frac{q_0}{C} + \frac{1}{C}\int_0^t I_C\, dt,$$

$q_0 =$ initial charge of capacitor.

20.8.10   With $J_0(t)$ expressed as a contour integral, apply the Laplace transform operation, reverse the order of integration, and thus show that

$$\mathcal{L}\{J_0(t)\} = (s^2 + 1)^{-1/2}, \quad \text{for } s > 0.$$

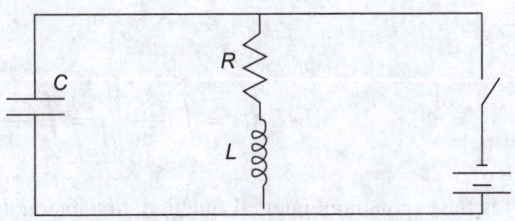

FIGURE 20.18   Ringing circuit.

20.8.11   Develop the Laplace transform of $J_n(t)$ from $\mathcal{L}\{J_0(t)\}$ by using the Bessel function recurrence relations.

Hint. Here is a chance to use mathematical induction (Section 1.4).

20.8.12   A calculation of the magnetic field of a circular current loop in circular cylindrical coordinates leads to the integral

$$\int_0^\infty e^{-kz} k J_1(ka)\, dk, \quad \Re\, z \geq 0.$$

Show that this integral is equal to $a/(z^2 + a^2)^{3/2}$.

20.8.13   Show that

$$\mathcal{L}\{I_0(at)\} = (s^2 - a^2)^{-1/2}, \quad s > a.$$

20.8.14   Verify the following Laplace transforms:

(a) $\mathcal{L}\{j_0(at)\} = \mathcal{L}\left\{\dfrac{\sin at}{at}\right\} = \dfrac{1}{a}\cot^{-1}\left(\dfrac{s}{a}\right),$

(b) $\mathcal{L}\{y_0(at)\}$ does not exist.

(c) $\mathcal{L}\{i_0(at)\} = \mathcal{L}\left\{\dfrac{\sinh at}{at}\right\} = \dfrac{1}{2a}\ln\dfrac{s+a}{s-a} = \dfrac{1}{a}\coth^{-1}\left(\dfrac{s}{a}\right),$

(d) $\mathcal{L}\{k_0(at)\}$ does not exist.

20.8.15   Develop a Laplace transform solution of Laguerre's equation,

$$tF''(t) + (1-t)F'(t) + nF(t) = 0.$$

Note that you need a derivative of a transform and a transform of derivatives. Go as far as you can with a general value of n; then (and only then) set $n = 0$.

20.8.16   Show that the Laplace transform of the Laguerre polynomial $L_n(at)$ is given by

$$\mathcal{L}\{L_n(at)\} = \dfrac{(s-a)^n}{s^{n+1}}, \quad s > 0.$$

20.8.17   Show that

$$\mathcal{L}\{E_1(t)\} = \dfrac{1}{s}\ln(s+1), \quad s > 0,$$

where

$$E_1(t) = \int_t^\infty \dfrac{e^{-\tau}}{\tau}\, d\tau = \int_1^\infty \dfrac{e^{-xt}}{x}\, dx.$$

$E_1(t)$ is the exponential integral function, first encountered in this book in Table 1.2.

20.8.18 (a) From Eq. (20.184) show that

$$\int_0^\infty f(x)dx = \int_0^\infty \frac{F(t)}{t}\,dt,$$

provided the integrals exist.

(b) From the preceding result show that

$$\int_0^\infty \frac{\sin t}{t}\,dt = \frac{\pi}{2},$$

in agreement with Eqs. (20.146) and (11.107).

20.8.19 (a) Show that

$$\mathcal{L}\left\{\frac{\sin kt}{t}\right\} = \cot^{-1}\left(\frac{s}{k}\right).$$

(b) Using this result (with $k = 1$), prove that

$$\mathcal{L}\{\text{si}(t)\} = -\frac{1}{s}\tan^{-1}s,$$

where

$$\text{si}(t) = -\int_t^\infty \frac{\sin x}{x}\,dx, \quad \text{the sine integral.}$$

20.8.20 If $F(t)$ is periodic (Fig. 20.19) with a period a so that $F(t+a) = F(t)$ for all $t \geq 0$, show that

$$\mathcal{L}\{F(t)\} = \frac{1}{1 - e^{-as}}\int_0^a e^{-st}F(t)dt.$$

Note that the integration is now over only the **first period** of $F(t)$.

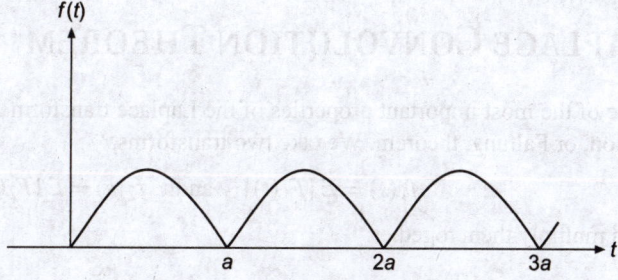

FIGURE 20.19 Periodic function.

20.8.21   Find the Laplace transform of the square wave (period a) defined by

$$F(t) = \begin{cases} 1, & 0 < t < a/2, \\ 0, & a/2 < t < a. \end{cases}$$

$$ANS. \quad f(s) = \frac{1}{s} \frac{1 - e^{-as/2}}{1 - e^{-as}}.$$

20.8.22   Show that

(a) $\mathcal{L}\{\cosh at \cos at\} = \dfrac{s^3}{s^4 + 4a^4},$

(b) $\mathcal{L}\{\cosh at \sin at\} = \dfrac{as^2 + 2a^3}{s^4 + 4a^4},$

(c) $\mathcal{L}\{\sinh at \cos at\} = \dfrac{as^2 - 2a^3}{s^4 + 4a^4},$

(d) $\mathcal{L}\{\sinh at \sin at\} = \dfrac{2a^2 s}{s^4 + 4a^4}.$

20.8.23   Show that

(a) $\mathcal{L}^{-1}\left\{(s^2 + a^2)^{-2}\right\} = \dfrac{1}{2a^3} \sin at - \dfrac{t}{2a^2} \cos at,$

(b) $\mathcal{L}^{-1}\left\{s(s^2 + a^2)^{-2}\right\} = \dfrac{t}{2a} \sin at,$

(c) $\mathcal{L}^{-1}\left\{s^2(s^2 + a^2)^{-2}\right\} = \dfrac{1}{2a} \sin at + \dfrac{t}{2} \cos at,$

(d) $\mathcal{L}^{-1}\left\{s^3(s^2 + a^2)^{-2}\right\} = \cos at - \dfrac{at}{2} \sin at.$

20.8.24   Show that

$$\mathcal{L}\{(t^2 - k^2)^{-1/2} u(t - k)\} = K_0(ks).$$

Hint. Try transforming an integral representation of $K_0(ks)$ into the Laplace transform integral.

20.9   LAPLACE CONVOLUTION THEOREM

One of the most important properties of the Laplace transform is that given by the convolution, or Faltung, theorem. We take two transforms,

$$f_1(s) = \mathcal{L}\{F_1(t)\} \quad \text{and} \quad f_2(s) = \mathcal{L}\{F_2(t)\},$$

and multiply them together:

$$f_1(s) f_2(s) = \int_0^\infty e^{-sx} F_1(x)dx \int_0^\infty e^{-sy} F_2(y)dy. \qquad (20.185)$$

If we introduce the new variable $t = x + y$ and integrate over t and y instead of x and y, the limits of integration become $(0 \leq t \leq \infty)$, $(0 \leq y \leq t)$. Noting that the Jacobian of the transformation from (x, y) to (t, y) is unity, we have

$$f_1(s) f_2(s) = \int_0^\infty e^{-st} dt \int_0^t F_1(t - y) F_2(y) dy$$

$$= \mathcal{L} \left\{ \int_0^t F_1(t - y) F_2(y) dy \right\}$$

$$= \mathcal{L} \{ F_1 * F_2 \}, \tag{20.186}$$

where, similarly to the Fourier transform, we use the notation

$$\int_0^t F_1(t - z) F_2(z) dz \equiv F_1 * F_2, \tag{20.187}$$

and call this operation the **convolution** of F_1 and F_2. It can be shown that convolution is symmetric:

$$F_1 * F_2 = F_2 * F_1. \tag{20.188}$$

Carrying out the inverse transform, we also find

$$\mathcal{L}^{-1} \{ f_1(s) f_2(s) \} = \int_0^t F_1(t - z) F_2(z) dz = F_1 * F_2. \tag{20.189}$$

Convolution formulas are useful for finding new transforms or, in some cases, as an alternative to a partial fraction expansion. They also find use in the solution of integral equations, as is illustrated in Chapter 21.

Example 20.9.1   Driven Oscillator with Damping

As one illustration of the use of the convolution theorem, let us return to the mass m on a spring, with damping and a driving force $F(t)$. The equation of motion, Eq. (20.160), now becomes

$$m X''(t) + b X'(t) + k X(t) = F(t). \tag{20.190}$$

Initial conditions $X(0) = 0$, $X'(0) = 0$ are used to simplify this illustration, and the transformed equation is

$$m s^2 x(s) + b s x(s) + k x(s) = f(s),$$

with solution

$$x(s) = \frac{f(s)}{m} \frac{1}{(s + b/2m)^2 + \omega_1^2}, \tag{20.191}$$

where, as in Example 20.8.5,

$$\omega_0^2 \equiv \frac{k}{m}, \quad \omega_1^2 \equiv \omega_0^2 - \frac{b^2}{4m^2}. \tag{20.192}$$

We identify the right-hand side of Eq. (20.191) as the product of two known transforms:

$$\frac{f(s)}{m} = \frac{1}{m} \mathcal{L}\{F(t)\}, \quad \frac{1}{(s+b/2m)^2 + \omega_1^2} = \frac{1}{\omega_1} \mathcal{L}\{e^{-(b/2m)t} \sin \omega_1 t\},$$

where the second of these is a case of Eq. (20.158).

Now applying the convolution theorem, Eq. (20.189), we obtain the solution to our original problem as an integral:

$$X(t) = \mathcal{L}^{-1}\{x(s)\} = \frac{1}{m\omega_1} \int_0^t F(t-z)e^{-(b/2m)z} \sin \omega_1 z \, dz. \tag{20.193}$$

We go on to consider two specific choices for the driving force $F(t)$. We first take the impulsive force $F(t) = P\delta(t)$. Then

$$X(t) = \frac{P}{m\omega_1} e^{-(b/2m)t} \sin \omega_1 t. \tag{20.194}$$

Here P represents the momentum transferred by the impulse, and the constant P/m takes the place of an initial velocity $X'(0)$.

As a second case, let $F(t) = F_0 \sin \omega t$. We could again use Eq. (20.193), but a partial fraction expansion is perhaps more convenient. With

$$f(s) = \frac{F_0\omega}{s^2 + \omega^2}$$

Eq. (20.191) can be written in the partial fraction form,

$$x(s) = \frac{F_0\omega}{m} \frac{1}{s^2 + \omega^2} \frac{1}{(s+b/2m)^2 + \omega_1^2}$$

$$= \frac{F_0\omega}{m} \left[\frac{a's + b'}{s^2 + \omega^2} + \frac{c's + d'}{(s+b/2m)^2 + \omega_1^2} \right], \tag{20.195}$$

with coefficients a', b', c', and d' (independent of s) to be determined. Direct calculation shows for a' and b'

$$-\frac{1}{a'} = \frac{b}{m}\omega^2 + \frac{m}{b}(\omega_0^2 - \omega^2)^2,$$

$$-\frac{1}{b'} = -\frac{m}{b}(\omega_0^2 - \omega^2)\left[\frac{b}{m}\omega^2 + \frac{m}{b}(\omega_0^2 - \omega^2)^2\right].$$

The terms of $x(s)$ containing a' and b' lead upon inversion of the Laplace transform to the steady-state component of the solution:

$$X(t) = \frac{F_0}{[b^2\omega^2 + m^2(\omega_0^2 - \omega^2)^2]^{1/2}} \sin(\omega t - \varphi), \tag{20.196}$$

where

$$\tan \varphi = \frac{b\omega}{m(\omega_0^2 - \omega^2)}.$$

Differentiating the denominator, we find that the amplitude has a maximum when $\omega = \omega_2$, with

$$\omega_2^2 = \omega_0^2 - \frac{b^2}{2m^2} = \omega_1^2 - \frac{b^2}{4m^2}. \tag{20.197}$$

This is the resonance condition.[12] At resonance the amplitude becomes $F_0/b\omega_1$, showing that the mass m goes into infinite oscillation at resonance if damping is neglected ($b = 0$).

This calculation differs from those used for the determination of transfer functions (compare Example 20.5.1) in that a steady-state solution at a fixed frequency is not assumed. Use of the Laplace transform (rather than the Fourier transform) permits solution for transient as well as steady-state components of the solution. The transients, which we will not work out in detail, arise from the terms of Eq. (20.195) involving c' and d'. These terms contain the quantity $(s + b/2m)^2$ in the denominator, and its presence will generate terms of the inverse transform that contain the exponential factor $e^{-bt/2m}$. In other words, these terms describe exponentially decaying transients.

It is worth noting that we have had three different characteristic frequencies:

Resonance for forced oscillations with damping: $\omega_2^2 = \omega_0^2 - \dfrac{b^2}{2m^2}$,

Free oscillation frequency, with damping: $\omega_1^2 = \omega_0^2 - \dfrac{b^2}{4m^2}$,

Free oscillation frequency, no damping: $\omega_0^2 = \dfrac{k}{m}$.

These frequencies coincide only if the damping is zero.   ∎

Recall that Eq. (20.190) is our ODE for the response of a dynamical system to an arbitrary driving force. The final response clearly depends on both the driving force and the characteristics of our system. This dual dependence is separated in the transform space. In Eq. (20.191) the transform of the response (output) appears as the product of two factors, one describing the driving force (input) and the other describing the dynamical system. This is a factorization similar to that we found when discussing the use of Fourier transforms in signal-processing applications in Section 20.5.

Exercises

20.9.1   From the convolution theorem show that

$$\frac{1}{s} f(s) = \mathcal{L}\left\{ \int_0^t F(x)dx \right\},$$

where $f(s) = \mathcal{L}\{F(t)\}$.

---

[12]The amplitude (squared) has the typical resonance denominator (the Lorentz line shape), found in Exercise 20.2.8.

20.9.2   If $F(t) = t^a$ and $G(t) = t^b$, $a > -1$, $b > -1$,

(a)   Show that the convolution $F * G$ is given by

$$F * G = t^{a+b+1} \int_0^1 y^a (1-y)^b \, dy.$$

(b)   By using the convolution theorem, show that

$$\int_0^1 y^a (1-y)^b \, dy = \frac{a! \, b!}{(a+b+1)!} = B(a+1, b+1),$$

where B is the beta function.

20.9.3   Using the convolution integral, calculate

$$\mathcal{L}^{-1} \left\{ \frac{s}{(s^2 + a^2)(s^2 + b^2)} \right\}, \quad a^2 \neq b^2.$$

20.9.4   An undamped oscillator is driven by a force $F_0 \sin \omega t$. Find the displacement $X(t)$ as a function of time, subject to initial conditions $X(0) = X'(0) = 0$. Note that the solution is a linear combination of two simple harmonic motions, one with the frequency of the driving force and one with the frequency ω_0 of the free oscillator.

$$ANS. \quad X(t) = \frac{F_0/m}{\omega^2 - \omega_0^2} \left(\frac{\omega}{\omega_0} \sin \omega_0 t - \sin \omega t \right).$$

20.10   INVERSE LAPLACE TRANSFORM

Bromwich Integral

We now develop an expression for the inverse Laplace transform $\mathcal{L}^{-1}$ appearing in the equation

$$F(t) = \mathcal{L}^{-1} \{ f(s) \}. \tag{20.198}$$

One approach lies in the Fourier transform, for which we know the inverse relation. There is a difficulty, however. Our Fourier transformable function had to satisfy the Dirichlet conditions. In particular, we required that in order for $g(\omega)$ to be a valid Fourier transform,

$$\lim_{\omega \to \infty} g(\omega) = 0, \tag{20.199}$$

so that the infinite integral would be well defined.[13] Now we wish to treat functions $F(t)$ that may diverge exponentially. To surmount this difficulty, we extract an exponential factor, $e^{\beta t}$, from our (possibly) divergent $F(t)$ and write

$$F(t) = e^{\beta t} G(t). \tag{20.200}$$

---

[13] We made an exception to deal with the delta function, but even in that case $g(\omega)$ was bounded for all ω.

If $F(t)$ diverges as $e^{\alpha t}$, we require β to be greater than α so that $G(t)$ will be **convergent**. Now, with $G(t) = 0$ for $t < 0$ and otherwise suitably restricted so that it may be represented by a Fourier integral, as in Eq. (20.22), we have

$$G(t) = \frac{1}{2\pi} \int_{-\infty}^{\infty} e^{iut} \, du \int_{0}^{\infty} G(v)e^{-iuv} \, dv. \tag{20.201}$$

Inserting Eq. (20.201) into Eq. (20.200), we have

$$F(t) = \frac{e^{\beta t}}{2\pi} \int_{-\infty}^{\infty} e^{iut} \, du \int_{0}^{\infty} F(v)e^{-\beta v}e^{-iuv} \, dv. \tag{20.202}$$

We now make a change of variable to $s = \beta + iu$, causing the integral over v in Eq. (20.202) to assume the form of a Laplace transform:

$$\int_{0}^{\infty} F(v)e^{-sv} \, dv = f(s).$$

The variable s is now complex, but must be restricted to $\Re e(s) \geq \beta$ in order to guarantee convergence. Note that the Laplace transform has extended a function specified on the positive real axis onto the complex plane, $\Re e \, s \geq \beta$.[14]

We now need to rewrite Eq. (20.202) using the variable s in place of u. The range $-\infty < u < \infty$ corresponds to a contour in the complex plane of s, which is a vertical line from $\beta - i\infty$ to $\beta + i\infty$; we also need to substitute $du = ds/i$. Making these changes, Eq. (20.202) becomes

$$F(t) = \frac{1}{2\pi i} \int_{\beta-i\infty}^{\beta+i\infty} e^{st} f(s) \, ds. \tag{20.203}$$

Here is our **inverse transform**. The path has become an infinite vertical line in the complex plane. Note that the constant β was chosen so that $f(s)$ would be nonsingular for $s \geq \beta$. It can be shown that the nonsingularity of $f(s)$ extends to complex s provided that $\Re e \, s \geq \beta$, so the integrand of Eq. (20.203) can have singularities only to the left of the integration path. See Fig. 20.20.

The inverse transformation given by Eq. (20.203) is known as the **Bromwich integral**, although sometimes it is referred to as the **Fourier-Mellin theorem** or **Fourier-Mellin integral**. This integral may now be evaluated by the regular methods of contour integration (Chapter 11). If $t > 0$ and $f(s)$ is analytic except for isolated singularities (and no branch points), and is also small at large $|s|$, the contour may be closed by an infinite semicircle in the left half-plane that does not contribute to the integral. Then by the residue theorem (Section 11.8),

$$F(t) = \sum (\text{residues included for } \Re e \, s < \beta). \tag{20.204}$$

---

[14]For a derivation of the inverse Laplace transform using only real variables, see C. L. Bohn and R. W. Flynn, Real variable inversion of Laplace transforms: An application in plasma physics, *Am. J. Phys.* **46**: 1250 (1978).

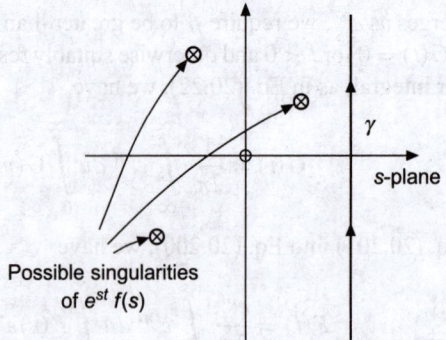

FIGURE 20.20   Possible singularities of $e^{st} f(s)$.

It is worth mentioning that in many cases of interest $f(s)$ may become large in the left half-plane or have branch points, and evaluation of the Bromwich integral may then present significant challenges.

Possibly this means of evaluation with $\Re e\ s$ ranging through negative values seems paradoxical in view of our previous requirement that $\Re e\ s \geq \beta$. The paradox disappears when we recall that the requirement $\Re e\ s \geq \beta$ was imposed to guarantee convergence of the Laplace transform integral that defined $f(s)$. Once $f(s)$ is obtained, we may then proceed to exploit its properties as an analytic function in the complex plane wherever we choose.

Perhaps a pair of examples may clarify the evaluation of Eq. (20.203).

Example 20.10.1   INVERSION VIA CALCULUS OF RESIDUES

If $f(s) = a/(s^2 - a^2)$, then the integrand for the Bromwich integral will be

$$e^{st} f(s) = \frac{ae^{st}}{s^2 - a^2} = \frac{ae^{st}}{(s+a)(s-a)}. \tag{20.205}$$

From the form of Eq. (20.205), we see that this integrand has poles at $s = \pm a$, and the value of β for the integral must be larger than $|a|$. Since these are simple poles, it is easy to verify that the residue at $s = a$ must be $e^{at}/2$, while the residue at $s = -a$ will be $-e^{-at}/2$. The form of the integrand also permits us to close the contour in the left half-plane. We find, in accord with Eq. (20.204),

$$\text{Residues} = \left(\frac{1}{2}\right)(e^{at} - e^{-at}) = \sinh at = F(t). \tag{20.206}$$

Equation (20.206) is in agreement with entry #7 of our table of Laplace transforms, Table 20.1. ∎

Example 20.10.2 MULTIREGION INVERSION

If $f(s) = (1 - e^{-as})/s$, the Bromwich integral then has integrand

$$e^{st} f(s) = e^{st} \left(\frac{1 - e^{-as}}{s} \right),$$

(20.207)

and the possibilities for closing the contour depend on the relative magnitudes of t and a.

Considering first $t > a$, we may close the contour for the Bromwich integral in the left half-plane without changing its value. Our integrand is an entire function (analytic everywhere in the finite s-plane; note that the s in the denominator cancels when the numerator is expanded in a Maclaurin series). Since no singularities are enclosed, we conclude that for $t > a$, $F(t) = 0$.

For t in the range $0 < t < a$, a different situation is encountered. Expanding the integrand into the two terms

$$\frac{e^{st}}{s} - \frac{e^{s(t-a)}}{s},$$

we see that the first becomes small in the left half-plane (but large in the right half-plane), while the second terms behaves in an opposite fashion (large in the left half-plane, small in the right). The obvious solution is to use different contours for the two terms, each of which is individually singular, with a pole at $s = 0$. We therefore close the contour for the first term in the left half-plane, but close that for the second term in the right half-plane. Since the vertical portion of the contour is at $\Re e \, s = \beta > 0$, we see that the integral of the first term encloses the singularity, while the integral of the second term does not. Therefore the first integral will have a value equal to the residue of the integrand at the singularity (this residue is 1), while the second integral will vanish. These contours are illustrated in Fig. 20.21.

Finally, for $t < 0$, the entire integrand becomes small in the right half-plane, the contour (for the entire integrand) surrounds no singularities, and the integral is zero. Summarizing these three cases,

$$F(t) = u(t) - u(t - a) = \begin{cases} 0, & t < 0, \\ 1, & 0 < t < a, \\ 0, & t > a, \end{cases}$$

(20.208)

a step function of unit height and length a (Fig. 20.22). ∎

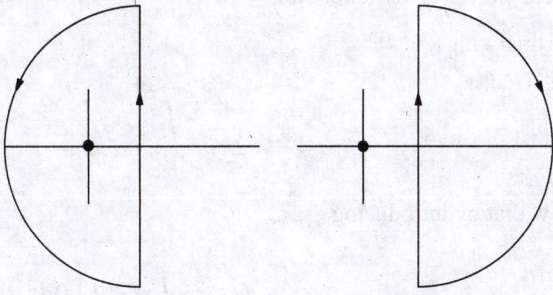

FIGURE 20.21 Contours for Example 20.10.2.

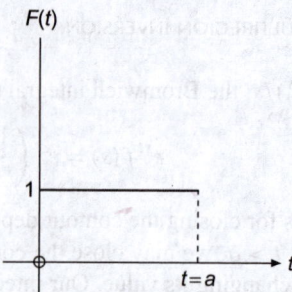

FIGURE 20.22   Finite-length step function $u(t) - u(t - a)$.

Two general comments may be in order. First, these two examples hardly begin to show the usefulness and power of the Bromwich integral. It is always available for inverting a complicated transform when the tables prove inadequate.

Second, this derivation is not presented as a rigorous one. Rather, it is given more as a plausibility argument, although it can be made rigorous. The determination of the inverse transform is somewhat similar to the solution of a differential equation. It makes little difference how you get the inverse transform. Guess at it if you want. It can always be checked by verifying that

$$\mathcal{L}\{F(t)\} = f(s).$$

Two alternate derivations of the Bromwich integral are the subjects of Exercises 20.10.1 and (20.10.2).

Exercises

20.10.1   Derive the Bromwich integral from Cauchy's integral formula.

Hint. Apply the inverse transform $\mathcal{L}^{-1}$ to

$$f(s) = \frac{1}{2\pi i} \lim_{\alpha \to \infty} \int_{\beta - i\alpha}^{\beta + i\alpha} \frac{f(z)}{s - z} \, dz,$$

where $f(z)$ is analytic for $\Re e \, z \geq \beta$.

20.10.2   Starting with

$$\frac{1}{2\pi i} \int_{\beta - i\infty}^{\beta + i\infty} e^{st} f(s) \, ds,$$

show that by introducing

$$f(s) = \int_{0}^{\infty} e^{-sz} F(z) \, dz$$

we can convert our integral into the Fourier representation of a Dirac delta function. From this derive the inverse Laplace transform.

20.10.3 Derive the Laplace transformation convolution theorem by use of the Bromwich integral.

20.10.4 Find

$$\mathcal{L}^{-1}\left\{\frac{s}{s^2 - k^2}\right\}$$

(a) by a partial fraction expansion.

(b) Repeat, using the Bromwich integral.

20.10.5 Find

$$\mathcal{L}^{-1}\left\{\frac{k^2}{s(s^2 + k^2)}\right\}$$

(a) by using a partial fraction expansion.

(b) Repeat using the convolution theorem.

(c) Repeat using the Bromwich integral.

ANS. $F(t) = 1 - \cos kt$.

20.10.6 Use the Bromwich integral to find the function whose transform is $f(s) = s^{-1/2}$. Note that $f(s)$ has a branch point at $s = 0$. The negative x-axis may be taken as a cut line. See Fig. 20.23.

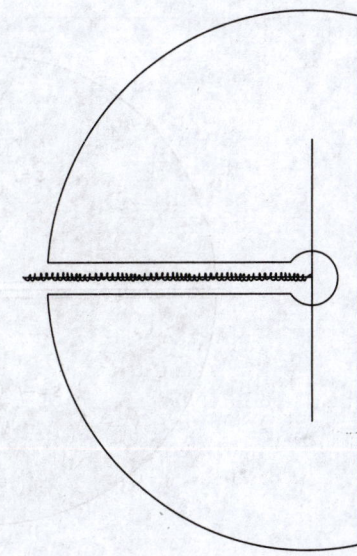

FIGURE 20.23 Contour for Exercise 20.10.6.

Hint. A portion of the path needed to close the contour will yield nonzero contributions to the contour integral. These will need to be taken into account to get the proper value for the Bromwich integral.

ANS. $F(t) = (\pi t)^{-1/2}$.

20.10.7   Show that

$$\mathcal{L}^{-1}\left\{(s^2+1)^{-1/2}\right\} = J_0(t)$$

by evaluation of the Bromwich integral.

Hint. Convert your Bromwich integral into an integral representation of $J_0(t)$. Figure 20.24 shows a possible contour.

20.10.8   Evaluate the inverse Laplace transform

$$\mathcal{L}^{-1}\left\{(s^2-a^2)^{-1/2}\right\}$$

by each of the following methods:

(a)   Expansion in a series and term-by-term inversion.

(b)   Direct evaluation of the Bromwich integral.

(c)   Change of variable in the Bromwich integral: $s = (a/2)(z + z^{-1})$.

20.10.9   Show that

$$\mathcal{L}^{-1}\left\{\frac{\ln s}{s}\right\} = -\ln t - \gamma,$$

where $\gamma = 0.5772\ldots$ is the Euler-Mascheroni constant.

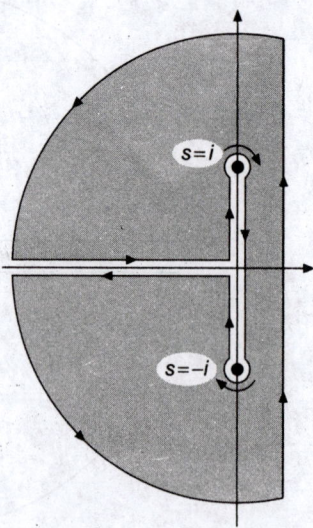

FIGURE 20.24   A possible contour for the inversion of $J_0(t)$.

20.10.10 Evaluate the Bromwich integral for

$$f(s) = \frac{s}{(s^2 + a^2)^2}.$$

20.10.11 Heaviside expansion theorem. If the transform $f(s)$ may be written as a ratio

$$f(s) = \frac{g(s)}{h(s)},$$

where $g(s)$ and $h(s)$ are analytic functions, with $h(s)$ having simple, isolated zeros at $s = s_i$, show that

$$F(t) = \mathcal{L}^{-1}\left\{\frac{g(s)}{h(s)}\right\} = \sum_i \frac{g(s_i)}{h'(s_i)}\, e^{s_i t}.$$

Hint. See Exercise 11.6.3.

20.10.12 Using the Bromwich integral, invert $f(s) = s^{-2}e^{-ks}$. Express $F(t) = \mathcal{L}^{-1}\{f(s)\}$ in terms of the (shifted) unit step function $u(t-k)$.

$$\textit{ANS.} \quad F(t) = (t-k)u(t-k).$$

20.10.13 You have a Laplace transform:

$$f(s) = \frac{1}{(s+a)(s+b)}, \quad a \neq b.$$

Invert this transform by each of three methods:

(a) Partial fractions and use of tables,

(b) Convolution theorem,

(c) Bromwich integral.

$$\textit{ANS.} \quad F(t) = \frac{e^{-bt} - e^{-at}}{a-b}, \ a \neq b.$$

Additional Readings

Abramowitz, M., and I. A. Stegun, eds., *Handbook of Mathematical Functions with Formulas, Graphs, and Mathematical Tables* (AMS-55). Washington, DC: National Bureau of Standards (1972), reprinted, Dover (1974). Chapter 29 contains tables of Laplace transforms.

Champeney, D. C., *Fourier Transforms and Their Physical Applications*. New York: Academic Press (1973). Fourier transforms are developed in a careful, easy-to-follow manner. Approximately 60% of the book is devoted to applications of interest in physics and engineering.

Erdelyi, A., W. Magnus, F. Oberhettinger, and F. G. Tricomi, *Tables of Integral Transforms*, 2 vols. New York: McGraw-Hill (1954). This text contains extensive tables of Fourier sine, cosine, and exponential transforms, Laplace and inverse Laplace transforms, Mellin and inverse Mellin transforms, Hankel transforms, and other more specialized integral transforms.

Hamming, R. W., *Numerical Methods for Scientists and Engineers*, 2nd ed. New York: McGraw-Hill (1973), reprinted, Dover (1987). Chapter 33 provides an excellent description of the fast Fourier transform.

Hanna, J. R., *Fourier Series and Integrals of Boundary Value Problems*. Somerset, NJ: Wiley (1990). This book is a broad treatment of the Fourier solution of boundary value problems. The concepts of convergence and completeness are given careful attention.

Jeffreys, H., and B. S. Jeffreys, *Methods of Mathematical Physics*, 3rd ed. Cambridge: Cambridge University Press (1972).

Krylov, V. I., and N. S. Skoblya, *Handbook of Numerical Inversion of Laplace Transform* (translated by D. Louvish). Jerusalem: Israel Program for Scientific Translations (1969).

Lepage, W. R., *Complex Variables and the Laplace Transform for Engineers*. New York: McGraw-Hill (1961); Dover (1980). A complex variable analysis that is carefully developed and then applied to Fourier and Laplace transforms. It is written to be read by students, but intended for the serious student.

McCollum, P. A., and B. F. Brown, *Laplace Transform Tables and Theorems*. New York: Holt, Rinehart and Winston (1965).

Miles, J. W., *Integral Transforms in Applied Mathematics*. Cambridge: Cambridge University Press (1971). This is a brief but interesting and useful treatment for the advanced undergraduate. It emphasizes applications rather than abstract mathematical theory.

Morse, P. M., and H. Feshbach, *Methods of Theoretical Physics*. New York: McGraw-Hill (1953). Parseval's relations are derived independently of the inverse Fourier transform in Section 4.8 of this comprehensive, but difficult text.

Papoulis, A., *The Fourier Integral and Its Applications*. New York: McGraw-Hill (1962). This is a rigorous development of Fourier and Laplace transforms and includes extensive applications in science and engineering.

Roberts, G. E., and H. Kaufman, *Table of Laplace Transforms*. Philadelphia: Saunders (1966).

Sneddon, I. N., *Fourier Transforms*. New York: McGraw-Hill (1951), reprinted, Dover (1995). A detailed comprehensive treatment, this book is loaded with applications to a wide variety of fields of modern and classical physics.

Sneddon, I. N., *The Use of Integral Transforms*. New York: McGraw-Hill (1974). Written for students in science and engineering in terms they can understand, this book covers all the integral transforms mentioned in this chapter as well as in several others. Many applications are included.

Titchmarsh, E. C., *Introduction to the Theory of Fourier Integrals*, 2nd ed. New York: Oxford University Press (1937).

Van der Pol, B., and H. Bremmer, *Operational Calculus Based on the Two-sided Laplace Integral*, 3rd ed. Cambridge, UK: Cambridge University Press (1987). Here is a development based on the integral range $-\infty$ to $+\infty$, rather than the useful 0 to ∞. Chapter V contains a detailed study of the Dirac delta function (impulse function).

Wolf, K. B., *Integral Transforms in Science and Engineering*. New York: Plenum Press (1979). This book is a very comprehensive treatment of integral transforms and their applications.

CHAPTER 21

INTEGRAL EQUATIONS

21.1 INTRODUCTION

With the exception of the integral transforms of Chapter 20, we have for the most part been considering relations between an unknown function $\varphi(x)$ and one or more of its derivatives. We now proceed to investigate equations containing the unknown function within an integral. As with differential equations, we shall confine our attention to linear relations, which are called **linear integral equations**. These integral equations are classified in two ways:

- If the **limits of integration are fixed**, we call the equation a **Fredholm** equation; if **one limit is variable**, it is a **Volterra** equation.

- If the **unknown function** appears **only under the integral** sign, we label it **first kind**. If it appears both **inside and outside** the integral, it is labeled **second kind**.

Here are some examples of these definitions. In each of the following equations, $\varphi(t)$ is an unknown function whose value we seek. $K(x, t)$, which we call the **kernel**, and $f(x)$ are assumed to be known. When $f(x) = 0$, the equation is said to be **homogeneous**. This is a **Fredholm equation of the first kind**,

$$f(x) = \int_a^b K(x, t)\varphi(t)\, dt. \tag{21.1}$$

Next we have a **Fredholm equation of the second kind**, which is an eigenvalue equation with λ the eigenvalue,

$$\varphi(x) = f(x) + \lambda \int_a^b K(x, t)\varphi(t)\, dt. \tag{21.2}$$

1047

Here we have a **Volterra equation of the first kind,**

$$f(x) = \int_a^x K(x,t)\varphi(t)\,dt; \tag{21.3}$$

and a **Volterra equation of the second kind,**

$$\varphi(x) = f(x) + \int_a^x K(x,t)\varphi(t)\,dt. \tag{21.4}$$

Why do we bother about integral equations? After all, the differential equations have done a rather good job of describing our physical world so far. However, there are several reasons for introducing integral equations.

First, we have placed considerable emphasis on the solution of differential equations **subject to particular boundary conditions.** For instance, the boundary condition at $r = 0$ determines whether the Neumann function $Y_n(r)$ is present when Bessel's equation is solved. The boundary condition for $r \to \infty$ determines whether $I_n(r)$ is present in our solution of the modified Bessel equation. To the contrary, an integral equation relates the unknown function not only to its values at neighboring points (derivatives) but also to its values throughout a region, including the boundary. In a very real sense the boundary conditions are built into the integral equation rather than imposed at the final stage of the solution. It will be seen later in this section that if we construct an integral equation that is equivalent to a differential equation with its boundary conditions, the form of that integral equation depends on the boundary conditions.

A second feature of integral equations is that their compact and completely self-contained form may turn out to be a more convenient or powerful formulation of a problem than a differential equation and its boundary conditions. Mathematical problems such as existence, uniqueness, and completeness may often be handled more easily and elegantly in integral form. And finally, whether or not we like it, there are problems, such as some diffusion and transport phenomena, that cannot be represented by differential equations. If we wish to solve such problems, we are forced to handle integral equations.

Example 21.1.1   MOMENTUM REPRESENTATION IN QUANTUM MECHANICS

The Schrödinger equation (in ordinary space representation) for a particle of mass m subject to a potential $V(\mathbf{r})$ is

$$-\frac{\hbar^2}{2m}\nabla^2\psi(\mathbf{r}) + V(\mathbf{r})\psi(\mathbf{r}) = E\psi(\mathbf{r}), \tag{21.5}$$

and we previously found, extending the 1-D result from Eq. (20.97), that in momentum space the equivalent equation (for the Coulomb potential in hartree atomic units) is

$$\frac{\mathbf{k}^2}{2m}\varphi(\mathbf{k}) + \frac{1}{(2\pi)^{3/2}}\int\frac{4\pi}{|\mathbf{k}-\mathbf{k}'|^2}\varphi(\mathbf{k}')d^3k' = E\varphi(\mathbf{k}). \tag{21.6}$$

This is an integral-equation eigenvalue problem. Note that the kernel of Eq. (21.6) is a function of $\mathbf{k} - \mathbf{k}'$; this functional dependence, which arises from the convolution theorem, is typical of an ordinary potential in which the direct-space wave function is multiplied by a function that depends only on position. ∎

Transformation of a Differential Equation into an Integral Equation

Often we find that we have a choice. The physical problem may be represented by a differential or an integral equation. Let us assume that we have the differential equation and wish to transform it into an integral equation. Starting with a **linear** second-order ordinary differential equation (ODE),

$$y'' + A(x)y' + B(x)y = g(x), \tag{21.7}$$

with initial conditions

$$y(a) = y_0, \qquad y'(a) = y_0',$$

we integrate to obtain

$$y'(x) = -\int_a^x A(t)y'(t)\,dt - \int_a^x B(t)y(t)\,dt + \int_a^x g(t)\,dt + y_0'.$$

Integrating the first integral on the right by parts yields

$$y'(x) = -A(x)y(x) - \int_a^x \left[B(t) - A'(t) \right] y(t)\,dt + \int_a^x g(t)\,dt + A(a)y_0 + y_0'.$$

Integrating a second time, we obtain

$$y(x) = -\int_a^x A(t)y(t)\,dt - \int_a^x du \int_a^u \left[B(t) - A'(t) \right] y(t)\,dt$$

$$+ \int_a^x du \int_a^u g(t)\,dt + \left[A(a)y_0 + y_0' \right](x - a) + y_0. \tag{21.8}$$

To transform this equation into a neater form, we use the relation

$$\int_a^x du \int_a^u f(t)\,dt = \int_a^x f(t)\,dt \int_t^x du = \int_a^x (x - t)f(t)\,dt. \tag{21.9}$$

Applying this result to Eq. (21.8), we obtain

$$y(x) = -\int_a^x \left(A(t) + (x-t)\Big[B(t) - A'(t) \Big] \right) y(t) \, dt$$

$$+ \int_a^x (x-t)g(t)\, dt + \Big[A(a)y_0 + y_0' \Big](x-a) + y_0. \tag{21.10}$$

If we now introduce the abbreviations

$$K(x,t) = (t-x)\Big[B(t) - A'(t) \Big] - A(t),$$

$$f(x) = \int_a^x (x-t)g(t)\, dt + \Big[A(a)y_0 + y_0' \Big](x-a) + y_0,$$

Eq. (21.10) becomes

$$y(x) = f(x) + \int_a^x K(x,t)y(t)\, dt, \tag{21.11}$$

which is a Volterra equation of the second kind. Note that $f(x)$ in Eq. (21.11) has a form that includes the initial conditions from the original differential equation.

Another method for obtaining an integral equation equivalent to a differential equation plus its boundary conditions was presented in Section 10.1, where we found that the Green's function for a differential equation appeared as the kernel of the equivalent integral equation.

Example 21.1.2   Linear Oscillator Equation

Let's find an integral equation equivalent to the linear oscillator equation

$$y'' + \omega^2 y = 0 \tag{21.12}$$

with boundary conditions

$$y(0) = 0, \qquad y'(0) = 1.$$

This corresponds to Eq. (21.7) with

$$A(x) = 0, \qquad B(x) = \omega^2, \qquad g(x) = 0.$$

Substituting into Eq. (21.10), we find that the integral equation becomes

$$y(x) = x + \omega^2 \int_0^x (t-x)y(t)\, dt. \tag{21.13}$$

This integral equation, Eq. (21.13), is equivalent to the original differential equation plus the initial conditions. A check shows that each form is indeed satisfied by $y(x) = (1/\omega)\sin \omega x$.

Let us reconsider the linear oscillator equation, Eq. (21.12), but now with the boundary conditions

$$y(0) = 0, \qquad y(b) = 0.$$

Since $y'(0)$ is not given, we must modify the procedure. The first integration gives

$$y' = -\omega^2 \int\limits_0^x y\, dx + y'(0).$$

Integrating a second time and again using Eq. (21.9), we have

$$y = -\omega^2 \int\limits_0^x (x - t)y(t)\, dt + xy'(0). \tag{21.14}$$

To eliminate the unknown $y'(0)$, we now impose the condition $y(b) = 0$. This gives

$$\omega^2 \int\limits_0^b (b - t)y(t)\, dt = by'(0).$$

Substituting this back into Eq. (21.14), we obtain

$$y(x) = -\omega^2 \int\limits_0^x (x - t)y(t)\, dt + \omega^2 \frac{x}{b} \int\limits_0^b (b - t)y(t)\, dt.$$

Now let us break the interval $[0, b]$ into two intervals, $[0, x]$ and $[x, b]$. Since

$$\frac{x}{b}(b - t) - (x - t) = \frac{t}{b}(b - x),$$

we find

$$y(x) = \omega^2 \int\limits_0^x \frac{t}{b}(b - x)y(t)\, dt + \omega^2 \int\limits_x^b \frac{x}{b}(b - t)y(t)\, dt. \tag{21.15}$$

Finally, if we define the kernel

$$K(x, t) = \begin{cases} \dfrac{t}{b}(b - x), & t < x, \\[2mm] \dfrac{x}{b}(b - t), & t > x, \end{cases} \tag{21.16}$$

we have

$$y(x) = \omega^2 \int\limits_0^b K(x,t)y(t)\,dt, \tag{21.17}$$

a homogeneous Fredholm equation of the second kind.

Our new kernel, $K(x,t)$, illustrated in Fig. 21.1, has some interesting properties.

1. It is symmetric, $K(x,t) = K(t,x)$.
2. It is continuous, in the sense that

$$\left.\frac{t}{b}(b-x)\right|_{t=x} = \left.\frac{x}{b}(b-t)\right|_{t=x}.$$

3. Its derivative with respect to t is **discontinuous**. As t increases through the point $t = x$, there is a discontinuity of -1 in $\partial K(x,t)/\partial t$.

Comparing with the discussion in Section 10.1, we identify $K(x,t)$ as the Green's function for this ODE **with the specified boundary conditions**. Note in particular Eq. (10.30), which corresponds exactly to what was found here. ∎

The above example shows how the initial or boundary conditions play a decisive role in the conversion of a linear second-order ODE into an integral equation. Summarizing,

> *If we have* **initial** *conditions (only one end of our interval), the differential equation transforms into a Volterra integral equation. But if we have a* **boundary value problem** *(boundary conditions at both ends of our interval), the differential equation leads to a Fredholm-type integral equation with a kernel that will be the Green's function appropriate to the given boundary conditions.*

In closing, we call attention to the fact that the reverse transformation (integral equation to differential equation) is not always possible. There exist integral equations for which no corresponding differential equation is known.

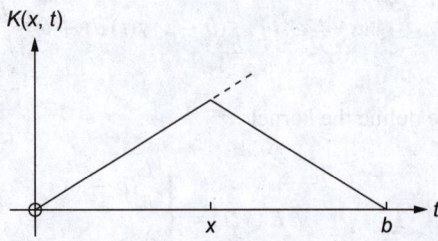

FIGURE 21.1   Kernel, Eq. (21.16), for linear oscillator boundary-value problem.

Exercises

21.1.1 Starting with the ODE, integrate twice and derive the Volterra integral equation corresponding to

(a) $y''(x) - y(x) = 0; \quad y(0) = 0, \quad y'(0) = 1.$

$$ANS. \quad y = \int_0^x (x - t)y(t)\, dt + x.$$

(b) $y''(x) - y(x) = 0; \quad y(0) = 1, \quad y'(0) = -1.$

$$ANS. \quad y = \int_0^x (x - t)y(t)\, dt - x + 1.$$

Check your results with Eq. (21.11).

21.1.2 Starting with the given answers of Exercise 21.1.1, differentiate and recover the original ODEs **and the boundary conditions**.

21.1.3 Given $\varphi(x) = x - \int_0^x (t - x)\varphi(t)\, dt,$

solve this integral equation by converting it to an ODE (plus boundary conditions) and solving the ODE (by inspection).

21.1.4 Show that the homogeneous Volterra equation of the second kind

$$\psi(x) = \lambda \int_0^x K(x, t)\psi(t)\, dt$$

has no solution (apart from the trivial solution $\psi = 0$).

Hint. Develop a Maclaurin expansion of $\psi(x)$. Assume that $\psi(x)$ and $K(x, t)$ are differentiable with respect to x as needed.

21.2 SOME SPECIAL METHODS

It is well known that general methods are available both for differentiating functions and (compare Chapters 7 and 9) for solving linear differential equations, while there is no general direct method for evaluating integrals. Integrations are carried out using a variety of tools of limited applicability, and the process is ultimately one of pattern recognition and the application of experience. Similar observations apply to the solution of integral equations. We consider here some special methods that work when the integral equation under study has suitable characteristics.

Integral-Transform Methods

When the kernel of an integral equation (and its integration limits) match the specification of an integral transform for which we have an inversion formula, we can use that identification to solve the integral equation. Formulas based on four integral transforms are listed here for reference, in each case with $f(x)$ a known function and $\varphi(x)$ to be determined.

If our integral equation is $f(x) = \frac{1}{\sqrt{2\pi}} \int_{-\infty}^{\infty} e^{ixt} \varphi(t)\,dt$, then its solution is

$$\varphi(x) = \frac{1}{\sqrt{2\pi}} \int_{-\infty}^{\infty} e^{-ixt} f(t)\,dt \quad \text{(Fourier transform).} \tag{21.18}$$

If our integral equation is $f(x) = \int_0^{\infty} e^{-xt} \varphi(t)\,dt$, then its solution is

$$\varphi(x) = \frac{1}{2\pi i} \int_{\gamma - i\infty}^{\gamma + i\infty} e^{xt} f(t)\,dt \quad \text{(Laplace transform).} \tag{21.19}$$

If our integral equation is $f(x) = \int_0^{\infty} t^{x-1} \varphi(t)\,dt$, then its solution is

$$\varphi(x) = \frac{1}{2\pi i} \int_{\gamma - i\infty}^{\gamma + i\infty} x^{-t} f(t)\,dt \quad \text{(Mellin transform).} \tag{21.20}$$

If our integral equation is $f(x) = \int_0^{\infty} t\varphi(t) J_\nu(xt)\,dt$, then its solution is

$$\varphi(x) = \int_0^{\infty} t f(t) J_\nu(xt)\,dt \quad \text{(Hankel transform).} \tag{21.21}$$

Note that these formulas can also be applied "in reverse," i.e., with $\varphi(x)$ known and $f(x)$ to be determined. This observation, however, is of somewhat limited utility since nothing significantly new appears for the inverse Fourier and Hankel transforms, while the integration limits for the inverse Laplace and Mellin transforms make them unlikely to appear in an integral equation.

Actually the usefulness of the integral transform technique extends a bit beyond these four rather specialized forms. We illustrate with two examples.

Example 21.2.1   FOURIER TRANSFORM SOLUTION

Let's consider a Fredholm equation of the first kind with a kernel of the general type $k(x - t)$, where k is a function (not a constant),

$$f(x) = \int_{-\infty}^{\infty} k(x - t)\varphi(t)\,dt, \tag{21.22}$$

in which $\varphi(t)$ is our unknown function. **Assuming that the needed transforms exist**, we apply the Fourier convolution theorem, Eq. (20.71), to obtain

$$f(x) = \int_{-\infty}^{\infty} K(\omega)\Phi(\omega)e^{-i\omega x}d\omega. \tag{21.23}$$

The functions $K(\omega)$ and $\Phi(\omega)$ are, respectively, the Fourier transforms of $k(x)$ and $\varphi(x)$. Taking the Fourier transform of both sides of Eq. (21.23), the formula for which is Eq. (21.18), we find

$$K(\omega)\Phi(\omega) = \frac{1}{2\pi}\int_{-\infty}^{\infty} f(x)e^{i\omega x}dx = \frac{F(\omega)}{\sqrt{2\pi}}, \tag{21.24}$$

where $F(\omega)$ is the Fourier transform of $f(x)$. Since $\Phi(\omega)$ is the only unknown in Eq. (21.24), we may solve for it, obtaining

$$\Phi(\omega) = \frac{1}{\sqrt{2\pi}}\frac{F(\omega)}{K(\omega)}, \tag{21.25}$$

and, using the inverse Fourier transform, we have the solution to Eq. (21.22):

$$\varphi(x) = \frac{1}{2\pi}\int_{-\infty}^{\infty} \frac{F(\omega)}{K(\omega)}e^{-i\omega x}d\omega. \tag{21.26}$$

A rigorous justification of this result is presented by Morse and Feshbach (see Additional Readings). An extension of this transformation solution appears as Exercise 21.2.1. ∎

Example 21.2.2   GENERALIZED ABEL EQUATION

The generalized Abel equation is a Volterra equation of the first kind:

$$f(x) = \int_{0}^{x} \frac{\varphi(t)}{(x-t)^{\alpha}}\, dt, \quad 0 < \alpha < 1, \quad \text{with} \begin{cases} f(x) & \text{known,} \\ \varphi(t) & \text{unknown.} \end{cases} \tag{21.27}$$

Taking the Laplace transform of both sides of this equation, we obtain

$$\mathcal{L}\{f(x)\} = \mathcal{L}\left\{\int_{0}^{x} \frac{\varphi(t)}{(x-t)^{\alpha}}\, dt\right\} = \mathcal{L}\{x^{-\alpha}\}\mathcal{L}\{\varphi(x)\},$$

the last step following by the Laplace convolution theorem, Eq. (20.186). Then, evaluating $\mathcal{L}\{x^{-\alpha}\}$ from entry 3 of Table 20.1,

$$\mathcal{L}\{\varphi(x)\} = \frac{s^{1-\alpha}\mathcal{L}\{f(x)\}}{\Gamma(1-\alpha)}. \tag{21.28}$$

In principle, our integral equation is solved, since all that remains is to take the inverse transform of Eq. (21.28). A clever way of obtaining the inverse transform proceeds as follows, with its initial step being to divide Eq. (21.28) by s.[1] We get

$$\frac{1}{s}\mathcal{L}\{\varphi(x)\} = \frac{s^{-\alpha}\mathcal{L}\{f(x)\}}{\Gamma(1-\alpha)} = \frac{\mathcal{L}\{x^{\alpha-1}\}\mathcal{L}\{f(x)\}}{\Gamma(\alpha)\Gamma(1-\alpha)}.$$

Combining the gamma functions according to Eq. (13.23) and applying the Laplace convolution theorem again, we discover that

$$\frac{1}{s}\mathcal{L}\{\varphi(x)\} = \frac{\sin\pi\alpha}{\pi}\mathcal{L}\left\{\int_0^x \frac{f(t)}{(x-t)^{1-\alpha}}\,dt\right\}.$$

Inverting with the aid of Entry 3 of Table 20.2, we get

$$\int_0^x \varphi(t)\,dt = \frac{\sin\pi\alpha}{\pi}\int_0^x \frac{f(t)}{(x-t)^{1-\alpha}}\,dt,$$

and finally, by differentiating, we have the solution to our generalized Abel equation:

$$\varphi(x) = \frac{\sin\pi\alpha}{\pi}\frac{d}{dx}\int_0^x \frac{f(t)}{(x-t)^{1-\alpha}}\,dt. \tag{21.29}$$

∎

Generating-Function Method

Occasionally, the reader may encounter integral equations that involve generating functions. Suppose we have the admittedly special case,

$$f(x) = \int_{-1}^1 \frac{\varphi(t)}{(1-2xt+x^2)^{1/2}}\,dt, \quad -1 \le x \le 1, \tag{21.30}$$

where $f(x)$ is known and $\varphi(t)$ is to be determined.

We note two important features:

1. $(1-2xt+x^2)^{-1/2}$ generates the Legendre polynomials.
2. $[-1, 1]$ is the orthogonality interval for the Legendre polynomials.

---

[1] This division converts $s^{1-\alpha}$, which cannot be inverted when $0 < \alpha < 1$, into $s^{-\alpha}$, which is the transform of $x^{\alpha-1}/\Gamma(\alpha)$.

These features make it possible to expand the denominator in Legendre polynomials, suggesting that it may be useful also to represent $\varphi(t)$ as an expansion in these same functions. Thus, we introduce the expansions

$$\frac{1}{(1 - 2xt + x^2)^{1/2}} = \sum_{n=0}^{\infty} P_n(t) x^n, \qquad \varphi(t) = \sum_{m=0}^{\infty} a_m P_m(t).$$

Substituting these expansions into our integral equation, Eq. (21.30),

$$f(x) = \sum_{n=0}^{\infty} \sum_{m=0}^{\infty} a_m x^n \int_{-1}^{1} P_n(t) P_m(t)\, dt = \sum_{n=0}^{\infty} \sum_{m=0}^{\infty} a_m x^n \frac{2\delta_{nm}}{2n+1}$$

$$= \sum_{n=0}^{\infty} \frac{2a_n}{2n+1} x^n. \tag{21.31}$$

If we now insert into Eq. (21.31) the Maclaurin series expansion for $f(x)$,

$$f(x) = \sum_{n=0}^{\infty} \frac{f^{(n)}(0)}{n!},$$

we may equate powers of x, reaching, for each n,

$$\frac{f^{(n)}(0)}{n!} = \frac{2a_n}{2n+1},$$

so the solution to our integral equation is

$$\varphi(t) = \sum_{n=0}^{\infty} \frac{2n+1}{2} \frac{f^{(n)}(0)}{n!} P_n(t). \tag{21.32}$$

Similar results may be obtained with other generating functions (see the list in Table 12.1).

This technique of expanding in a series of special functions is always available. It is worth a try whenever the expansion is possible (and convenient) and the interval is appropriate.

Separable Kernel

We consider here the special case that the kernel of our integral equation is separable, in the sense that

$$K(x, t) = \sum_{j=1}^{n} M_j(x) N_j(t), \tag{21.33}$$

where n, the upper limit of the sum, is **finite**. Such kernels are sometimes called **degenerate**. Our class of separable kernels includes all polynomials and many of the elementary transcendental functions. For example, $K(x, t) = \cos(t - x)$ is separable:

$$\cos(t - x) = \cos t \cos x + \sin t \sin x.$$

Integral equations with separable kernels have the desirable property that they can be related to eigenvalue equations and permit the application of methods of linear algebra.

Let's consider a Fredholm equation of the second kind, Eq. (21.2), with a separable kernel of the form given in Eq. (21.33). Inserting this formula for $K(x, t)$ and bringing the summation outside the integral, we have

$$\varphi(x) = f(x) + \lambda \sum_{j=1}^{n} M_j(x) \int_a^b N_j(t)\varphi(t)\, dt. \tag{21.34}$$

We now see that the integral with respect to t will for each j be a constant (with values that are currently not known):

$$\int_a^b N_j(t)\varphi(t)\, dt = c_j. \tag{21.35}$$

Hence Eq. (16.71) becomes

$$\varphi(x) = f(x) + \lambda \sum_{j=1}^{n} c_j M_j(x). \tag{21.36}$$

Once the constants c_i have been determined, Eq. (21.36) will give us $\varphi(x)$, the solution to our integral equation. Equation (21.36) further tells us that the form of $\varphi(x)$ will consist of $f(x)$ plus a linear combination of the x-dependent factors in the separable kernel.

We may find the c_i by multiplying Eq. (21.36) by $N_i(x)$ and integrating to eliminate the x-dependence. Use of Eq. (21.35) yields

$$c_i = b_i + \lambda \sum_{j=1}^{n} a_{ij}c_j, \tag{21.37}$$

where

$$b_i = \int_a^b N_i(x)f(x)dx, \qquad a_{ij} = \int_a^b N_i(x)M_j(x)dx. \tag{21.38}$$

It is perhaps helpful to write Eq. (21.37) in matrix form , with $\mathsf{A} = (a_{ij})$:

$$\mathbf{b} = \mathbf{c} - \lambda \mathsf{A}\mathbf{c} = (1 - \lambda\mathsf{A})\mathbf{c}, \tag{21.39}$$

or

$$\mathbf{c} = (1 - \lambda\mathsf{A})^{-1}\mathbf{b}. \tag{21.40}$$

Equation (21.39) is equivalent to a set of simultaneous linear algebraic equations

$$(1 - \lambda a_{11})c_1 - \lambda a_{12}c_2 - \lambda a_{13}c_3 - \cdots = b_1,$$
$$-\lambda a_{21}c_1 + (1 - \lambda a_{22})c_2 - \lambda a_{23}c_3 - \cdots = b_2, \tag{21.41}$$
$$-\lambda a_{31}c_1 - \lambda a_{32}c_2 + (1 - \lambda a_{33})c_3 - \cdots = b_3, \quad \text{and so on.}$$

If our integral equation is homogeneous, so $f(x) = 0$, then $\mathbf{b} = 0$. To get a solution in that case, we set the determinant of the coefficients of c_i equal to zero:

$$|1 - \lambda A| = 0, \tag{21.42}$$

exactly as for any matrix eigenvalue problem. The roots of Eq. (21.42) yield our eigenvalues. Substituting into $(1 - \lambda A)\mathbf{c} = 0$, we find the c_i and then Eq. (21.36) gives our solution.

Example 21.2.3   HOMOGENEOUS FREDHOLM EQUATION

To illustrate this technique for determining eigenvalues and eigenfunctions of the homogeneous Fredholm equation of the second kind, we consider

$$\varphi(x) = \lambda \int_{-1}^{1} (t + x)\varphi(t)\, dt. \tag{21.43}$$

Writing the kernel of this equation as $M_1(x)N_1(t) + M_2(x)N_2(t)$, we have

$$M_1(x) = 1, \qquad M_2(x) = x,$$
$$N_1(t) = t, \qquad N_2(t) = 1.$$

Using the notation of Eqs. (21.33) to (21.42), we find from Eq. (21.38):

$$a_{11} = a_{22} = 0, \quad a_{12} = \frac{2}{3}, \quad a_{21} = 2; \quad b_1 = b_2 = 0.$$

Equation (21.42), our secular equation, becomes[2]

$$\begin{vmatrix} 1 & -\dfrac{2\lambda}{3} \\ -2\lambda & 1 \end{vmatrix} = 0. \tag{21.44}$$

Expanding, we obtain

$$1 - \frac{4\lambda^2}{3} = 0, \qquad \lambda = \pm\frac{\sqrt{3}}{2}. \tag{21.45}$$

Substituting the eigenvalues $\lambda = \pm\sqrt{3}/2$ into Eq. (21.39), we have

$$c_1 \mp \frac{c_2}{\sqrt{3}} = 0. \tag{21.46}$$

Finally, with the choice $c_1 = 1$, Eq. (21.36) gives the two solutions

$$\varphi_1(x) = \frac{\sqrt{3}}{2}(1 + \sqrt{3}x), \quad \lambda = \frac{\sqrt{3}}{2}, \tag{21.47}$$

---

[2] This equation would look more like our usual secular equations if each row of the determinant were divided by λ. Then we would have the secular equation in a familiar form, but with $1/\lambda$ identified as the eigenvalue.

$$\varphi_2(x) = -\frac{\sqrt{3}}{2}(1 - \sqrt{3}x), \quad \lambda = -\frac{\sqrt{3}}{2}. \tag{21.48}$$

Since our equation is homogeneous, the normalization of $\varphi(x)$ is arbitrary. ∎

If the kernel of an integral equation is not separable in the sense of Eq. (21.33), there is still the possibility that it may be approximated by a kernel that is separable. Then we can get the exact solution of an approximate equation, which we can treat as an approximation to the solution of the original equation.

Exercises

21.2.1   The kernel of a Fredholm equation of the second kind,

$$\varphi(x) = f(x) + \lambda \int_{-\infty}^{\infty} K(x,t)\varphi(t)\, dt,$$

is of the form $k(x - t)$.[3] Assuming that the required transforms exist, show that

$$\varphi(x) = \frac{1}{\sqrt{2\pi}} \int_{-\infty}^{\infty} \frac{F(t)e^{-ixt}\, dt}{1 - \sqrt{2\pi}\lambda K(t)}.$$

$F(t)$ and $K(t)$ are the Fourier transforms of $f(x)$ and $k(x)$, respectively.

21.2.2   (a) The kernel of a Volterra equation of the first kind,

$$f(x) = \int_{0}^{x} K(x,t)\varphi(t)\, dt,$$

has the form $k(x - t)$. Assuming that the required transforms exist, show that

$$\varphi(x) = \frac{1}{2\pi i} \int_{\gamma-i\infty}^{\gamma+i\infty} \frac{F(s)}{K(s)} e^{xs}\, ds,$$

where $F(s)$ and $K(s)$ are, respectively, the Laplace transforms of $f(x)$ and $k(x)$.

(b) In terms of the notation of part (a), show that the Volterra equation of the second kind,

$$\varphi(x) = f(x) + \lambda \int_{0}^{x} K(x,t)\varphi(t)\, dt,$$

---

[3]This kernel and a range $0 \leq x < \infty$ are the characteristics of integral equations of the Wiener-Hopf type. Details will be found in Chapter 8 of Morse and Feshbach (1953); see the Additional Readings.

has solution

$$\varphi(x) = \frac{1}{2\pi i} \int\limits_{\gamma-i\infty}^{\gamma+i\infty} \frac{F(s)}{1 - \lambda K(s)} e^{xs} ds.$$

21.2.3   Using the Laplace transform solution (Exercise 21.2.2), solve

(a) $\varphi(x) = x + \int\limits_0^x (t - x)\varphi(t)\, dt.$

ANS. $\varphi(x) = \sin x.$

(b) $\varphi(x) = x - \int\limits_0^x (t - x)\varphi(t)\, dt.$

ANS. $\varphi(x) = \sinh x.$

Check your results by substituting back into the original integral equations.

21.2.4   Reformulate the equations of Example 21.2.1 for integrals on the range $(0, \infty)$ using Fourier cosine transforms.

21.2.5   Given the Fredholm integral equation,

$$e^{-x^2} = \int\limits_{-\infty}^{\infty} e^{-(x-t)^2} \varphi(t)\, dt,$$

apply the Fourier convolution technique of Example 21.2.1 to solve for $\varphi(t)$.

21.2.6   Solve Abel's equation,

$$f(x) = \int\limits_0^x \frac{\varphi(t)}{(x - t)^\alpha}\, dt, \quad 0 < \alpha < 1,$$

by the following method:

(a)   Multiply both sides by $(z - x)^{\alpha-1}$ and integrate with respect to x over the range $0 \le x \le z$.

(b)   Reverse the order of integration and evaluate the integral on the right-hand side (with respect to x) by recognizing it as a beta function.

Note.

$$\int\limits_t^z \frac{dx}{(z - x)^{1-\alpha}(x - t)^\alpha} = B(1 - \alpha, \alpha) = \Gamma(\alpha)\Gamma(1 - \alpha) = \frac{\pi}{\sin \pi \alpha}.$$

21.2.7 Given the generalized Abel equation with $f(x) = 1$,

$$1 = \int_0^x \frac{\varphi(t)}{(x-t)^\alpha}\, dt, \quad 0 < \alpha < 1,$$

solve for $\varphi(t)$ and verify that $\varphi(t)$ is a solution of the given equation.

ANS. $\varphi(t) = \dfrac{\sin \pi\alpha}{\pi} t^{\alpha-1}.$

21.2.8 A Fredholm equation of the first kind has a kernel $e^{-(x-t)^2}$:

$$f(x) = \int_{-\infty}^\infty e^{-(x-t)^2} \varphi(t)\, dt.$$

Show that the solution is

$$\varphi(x) = \frac{1}{\sqrt{\pi}} \sum_{n=0}^\infty \frac{f^{(n)}(0)}{2^n n!} H_n(x),$$

in which $H_n(x)$ is an nth-order Hermite polynomial.

21.2.9 Solve the integral equation

$$f(x) = \int_{-1}^1 \frac{\varphi(t)}{(1 - 2xt + x^2)^{1/2}}\, dt, \quad -1 \leq x \leq 1,$$

for the unknown function $\varphi(t)$, if

(a) $f(x) = x^{2s}$,

(b) $f(x) = x^{2s+1}$.

ANS.   (a) $\varphi(t) = \dfrac{4s+1}{2} P_{2s}(t),$ (b) $\varphi(t) = \dfrac{4s+3}{2} P_{2s+1}(t).$

21.2.10 Find the eigenvalues and eigenfunctions of

$$\varphi(x) = \lambda \int_{-1}^1 (t - x)\varphi(t)\, dt.$$

21.2.11 Find the eigenvalues and eigenfunctions of

$$\varphi(x) = \lambda \int_0^{2\pi} \cos(x - t)\varphi(t)\, dt.$$

ANS. $\lambda_1 = \lambda_2 = \dfrac{1}{\pi},$ $\varphi(x) = A\cos x + B\sin x.$

21.2.12 Find the eigenvalues and eigenfunctions of

$$y(x) = \lambda \int_{-1}^{1} (x-t)^2 y(t)\, dt.$$

Hint. This problem may be treated by the separable-kernel method or by a Legendre expansion.

21.2.13 Use the separable-kernel technique to show that

$$\psi(x) = \lambda \int_{0}^{\pi} \cos x \, \sin t\, \psi(t)\, dt$$

has **no** solution (apart from $\psi = 0$). Explain this result in terms of separability and symmetry.

21.2.14 Given $\varphi(x) = \lambda \int_{0}^{1} (1+xt)\varphi(t)\, dt,$

solve for the eigenvalues and the eigenfunctions by the separable-kernel technique.

21.2.15 Knowing the form of the solutions of an integral equation can be a great advantage. For

$$\varphi(x) = \lambda \int_{0}^{1} (1+xt)\varphi(t)\, dt,$$

assume $\varphi(x)$ to have the form $1 + bx$. Substitute into the integral equation. Integrate and solve for b and λ.

21.2.16 The equation

$$f(x) = \int_{a}^{b} K(x,t)\varphi(t)\, dt$$

has a degenerate kernel $K(x,t) = \sum_{i=1}^{n} M_i(x)N_i(t)$.

(a) Show that this integral equation has no solution unless $f(x)$ can be written as

$$f(x) = \sum_{i=1}^{n} f_i M_i(x),$$

where the f_i are constants.

(b) Show that to any solution $\varphi(x)$ we may add $\psi(x)$, provided that $\psi(x)$ is orthogonal to all $N_i(x)$:

$$\int_{a}^{b} N_i(x)\psi(x)dx = 0 \quad \text{for all } i.$$

21.2.17   A Kirchhoff diffraction theory analysis of a laser leads to the integral equation

$$v(\mathbf{r}_2) = \gamma \iint K(\mathbf{r}_1, \mathbf{r}_2) v(\mathbf{r}_1) dA.$$

The unknown, $v(\mathbf{r}_1)$, gives the geometric distribution of the radiation field over one mirror surface; the range of integration is over the surface of that mirror. For square confocal spherical mirrors, the integral equation becomes

$$v(x_2, y_2) = \frac{-i\gamma e^{ikb}}{\lambda b} \int_{-a}^{a} \int_{-a}^{a} e^{-(ik/b)(x_1x_2 + y_1y_2)} v(x_1, y_1) dx_1 dy_1,$$

in which b is the centerline distance between the laser mirrors. This can be put in a somewhat simpler form by the substitutions

$$\frac{kx_i^2}{b} = \xi_i^2, \quad \frac{ky_i^2}{b} = \eta_i^2, \quad \text{and} \quad \frac{ka^2}{b} = \frac{2\pi a^2}{\lambda b} = \alpha^2.$$

(a)   Show that the variables separate and we get two integral equations.

(b)   Show that the new limits, $\pm\alpha$, may be approximated by $\pm\infty$ for a mirror dimension $a \gg \lambda$.

(c)   Solve the resulting integral equations.

21.3   NEUMANN SERIES

Many and probably most integral equations cannot be solved by the specialized techniques of the preceding section. Here we develop a rather general technique for solving integral equations. The method, due largely to Neumann, Liouville, and Volterra, develops the unknown function $\varphi(x)$ as a power series in λ, where λ is a given constant. The method is applicable whenever the series converges.

We solve a linear integral equation of the second kind by successive approximations; let's take as an example the Fredholm equation

$$\varphi(x) = f(x) + \lambda \int_a^b K(x, t) \varphi(t) \, dt, \tag{21.49}$$

in which $f(x) \neq 0$. If the upper limit of the integral is a variable (Volterra equation), the following development will still hold, but with minor modifications. Let us make the following initial approximation to our unknown function:

$$\varphi(x) \approx \varphi_0(x) = f(x). \tag{21.50}$$

This choice is not mandatory. If you can make a better guess, go ahead and guess. The choice here is equivalent to saying that the term of the equation containing the integral is small relative to $f(x)$. To improve this first crude approximation, we feed $\varphi_0(x)$ back into the integral in Eq. (21.49), getting

$$\varphi_1(x) = f(x) + \lambda \int_a^b K(x,t)f(t)\,dt. \tag{21.51}$$

Substituting the new $\varphi_1(x)$ back into Eq. (21.49), we obtain a second approximation to $\varphi(x)$:

$$\varphi_2(x) = f(x) + \lambda \int_a^b K(x,t_1)f(t_1)\,dt_1$$

$$+ \lambda^2 \int_a^b \int_a^b K(x,t_1)K(t_1,t_2)f(t_2)\,dt_2\,dt_1.$$

This process can be repeated indefinitely, defining after n steps the nth order approximation

$$\varphi_n(x) = \sum_{i=0}^n \lambda^i u_i(x), \tag{21.52}$$

where

$$u_0(x) = f(x)$$

$$u_1(x) = \int_a^b K(x,t_1)f(t_1)\,dt_1$$

$$\tag{21.53}$$

$$u_2(x) = \int_a^b \int_a^b K(x,t_1)K(t_1,t_2)f(t_2)\,dt_2\,dt_1$$

$$u_n(x) = \int_a^b \int_a^b \cdots \int_a^b K(x,t_1)K(t_1,t_2)\cdots K(t_{n-1},t_n)f(t_n)\,dt_n\cdots dt_1.$$

We expect that our solution $\varphi(x)$ will be

$$\varphi(x) = \lim_{n\to\infty} \varphi_n(x) = \lim_{n\to\infty} \sum_{i=0}^n \lambda^i u_i(x), \tag{21.54}$$

provided that our infinite series converges.

We may conveniently check the convergence by the Cauchy ratio test, Section 1.1, noting that

$$|\lambda^n u_n(x)| \le |\lambda^n| \cdot |f|_{\max} \cdot |K|_{\max}^n \cdot |b-a|^n,$$

using $|f|_{\max}$ to represent the **maximum** value of $|f(x)|$ in the interval $[a, b]$ and $|K|_{\max}$ to represent the maximum value of $|K(x, t)|$ in its domain in the xt-plane. A sufficient condition for convergence is

$$|\lambda| \cdot |K|_{\max} \cdot |b - a| < 1. \tag{21.55}$$

Note that $\lambda|u_n(\max)|$ is being used as a **comparison** series. If it converges, our actual series must converge. If this condition is not satisfied, we may or may not have convergence, and a more sensitive test would be required to determine the convergence. Of course, even if the Neumann series diverges, there still may be a solution to our integral equation obtainable by another method.

To gain more understanding of our iterative manipulation, we may find it helpful to rewrite the Neumann series solution, Eq. (21.54), in operator form. We start by rewriting Eq. (21.49) as

$$\varphi = \lambda K \varphi + f,$$

where K represents the **integral operator** $\int_a^b K(x, t)[\,]\,dt$. Solving symbolically for φ, we obtain

$$\varphi = (1 - \lambda K)^{-1} f.$$

Binomial expansion leads to Eq. (21.54). The **convergence** of the Neumann series is a demonstration that the inverse operator $(1 - \lambda K)^{-1}$ exists.

Example 21.3.1   NEUMANN SERIES SOLUTION

To illustrate the Neumann method, we consider the integral equation

$$\varphi(x) = x + \frac{1}{2} \int_{-1}^{1} (t - x)\varphi(t)\,dt. \tag{21.56}$$

To start the Neumann series, we take

$$\varphi_0(x) = x.$$

Then

$$\varphi_1(x) = x + \frac{1}{2} \int_{-1}^{1} (t - x)t\,dt = x + \frac{1}{2} \left(\frac{1}{3}t^3 - \frac{1}{2}t^2 x \right)\bigg|_{-1}^{1} = x + \frac{1}{3}.$$

Substituting $\varphi_1(x)$ back into Eq. (21.56), we get

$$\varphi_2(x) = x + \frac{1}{2} \int_{-1}^{1} (t - x)t\,dt + \frac{1}{2} \int_{-1}^{1} (t - x)\frac{1}{3}dt = x + \frac{1}{3} - \frac{x}{3}.$$

Continuing this process of substituting back into Eq. (21.56), we obtain

$$\varphi_3(x) = x + \frac{1}{3} - \frac{x}{3} - \frac{1}{3^2},$$

and by mathematical induction (Section 1.4),

$$\varphi_{2n}(x) = x + \sum_{s=1}^{n} (-1)^{s-1} 3^{-s} - x \sum_{s=1}^{n} (-1)^{s-1} 3^{-s}. \tag{21.57}$$

Letting $n \to \infty$, we get

$$\varphi(x) = \frac{3}{4}x + \frac{1}{4}. \tag{21.58}$$

This solution can (and should) be checked by substituting back into the original equation, Eq. (21.56).

It is interesting to note that our series converged easily even though Eq. (21.55) is **not** satisfied in this particular case. Actually Eq. (21.55) is a rather crude upper bound on λ. It can be shown that a necessary and sufficient condition for the convergence of our series solution is that $|\lambda| < |\lambda_e|$, where λ_e is the eigenvalue of smallest magnitude of the corresponding homogeneous equation (that with $f(x) = 0$). For this particular example, $\lambda_e = \sqrt{3}/2$. Clearly, $\lambda = \frac{1}{2} < \lambda_e$. ∎

The technique illustrated by the Neumann series occurs in a number of contexts in quantum mechanics. For example, one approach to the calculation of time-dependent perturbations in quantum mechanics starts with the integral equation for the evolution operator

$$U(t, t_0) = 1 - \frac{i}{\hbar} \int_{t_0}^{t} dt_1 V(t_1) U(t_1, t_0). \tag{21.59}$$

Iteration leads to

$$U(t, t_0) = 1 - \frac{i}{\hbar} \int_{t_0}^{t} dt_1 V(t_1) + \left(\frac{i}{\hbar}\right)^2 \int_{t_0}^{t} dt_1 \int_{t_0}^{t_1} dt_2 V(t_1) V(t_2) + \cdots. \tag{21.60}$$

The evolution operator is obtained as a series of multiple integrals of the perturbing potential $V(t)$, closely analogous to the Neumann series, Eq. (21.52).

A second and similar relationship between the Neumann series and quantum mechanics appears when the Schrödinger wave equation for scattering is reformulated as an integral equation. See Example 10.2.2. The first term in a Neumann series solution is the incident (unperturbed) wave. The second term is the first-order Born approximation, Eq. (10.51).

The Neumann method may also be applied to Volterra integral equations of the second kind, corresponding to replacing the fixed upper limit b in Eq. (21.49) by a variable, x. In the Volterra case the Neumann series converges for all λ as long as the kernel is square integrable.

Exercises

21.3.1   Using the Neumann series, solve

(a) $\varphi(x) = 1 - 2 \int_0^x t\varphi(t)\,dt,$

ANS.   (a) $\varphi(x) = e^{-x^2}$.

(b) $\varphi(x) = x + \int_0^x (t - x)\varphi(t)\,dt,$

(c) $\varphi(x) = x - \int_0^x (t - x)\varphi(t)\,dt.$

21.3.2   Solve

$$\psi(x) = x + \int_0^1 (1 + xt)\psi(t)\,dt$$

by each of the following methods:

(a)   The Neumann series technique,

(b)   The separable-kernel technique,

(c)   Educated guessing.

21.3.3   Solve

$$\varphi(x) = 1 + \lambda^2 \int_0^x (x - t)\varphi(t)\,dt$$

by each of the following methods:

(a)   Reduction to an ODE (find the boundary conditions),

(b)   The Neumann series,

(c)   The use of Laplace transforms.

ANS. $\varphi(x) = \cosh \lambda x$.

21.3.4   (a)   In Eq. (21.59), take $V = V_0$, independent of t. Without using Eq. (21.60), show that Eq. (21.59) leads directly to

$$U(t - t_0) = \exp\left[-\frac{i}{\hbar}(t - t_0)V_0\right].$$

(b)   Repeat for Eq. (21.60) without using Eq. (21.59).

21.4   HILBERT-SCHMIDT THEORY

Symmetrization of Kernels

The Hilbert-Schmidt theory deals with linear integral equations of the Fredholm type with symmetric kernels:

$$K(x, t) = K(t, x). \tag{21.61}$$

The symmetry is of great importance, both because we will find it leads to results parallel to those found for the Sturm-Liouville theory of differential equations, and also because many problems of physical relevance can be written as Fredholm integral equations with symmetric kernels.

Before plunging into the theory, we note that some important nonsymmetric kernels can be symmetrized. If we have the equation

$$\varphi(x) = f(x) + \lambda \int_a^b K(x, t)\rho(t)\varphi(t)\, dt, \tag{21.62}$$

the total kernel is actually $K(x, t)\rho(t)$, clearly not symmetric if $K(x, t)$ alone is symmetric. However, if we multiply Eq. (21.62) by $\sqrt{\rho(x)}$ and substitute

$$\sqrt{\rho(x)}\varphi(x) = \psi(x),$$

we obtain

$$\psi(x) = \sqrt{\rho(x)} f(x) + \lambda \int_a^b \left[K(x, t)\sqrt{\rho(x)\rho(t)} \right] \psi(t)\, dt, \tag{21.63}$$

with a symmetric total kernel $K(x, t)\sqrt{\rho(x)\rho(t)}$.

Orthogonal Eigenfunctions

We now focus on the homogeneous Fredholm equation of the second kind:

$$\varphi(x) = \lambda \int_a^b K(x, t)\varphi(t)\, dt. \tag{21.64}$$

We assume that the kernel $K(x, t)$ is symmetric and real. Perhaps one of the first questions we might ask about the equation is: "Does it make sense?" or more precisely, "Does an eigenvalue λ satisfying this equation exist?" This question can be answered in the affirmative. Courant and Hilbert (in their work cited in the Additional Readings, chapter III, section 4) show that if $K(x, t)$ is continuous, there is at least one such eigenvalue and possibly an infinite number of them.

It is useful to recognize that Eq. (21.64) represents a linear-operator eigenvalue problem: The integral on its right-hand side converts φ into (in general) some other function, which we can indicate symbolically by the equation

$$\psi(x) = \int_a^b K(x, t)\varphi(t)\, dt \equiv \mathcal{K}\varphi(x), \tag{21.65}$$

so our eigenvalue problem is

$$\mathcal{K}\varphi(x) = \frac{1}{\lambda}\varphi(x). \tag{21.66}$$

We do not have to worry about the possibility that $\lambda = 0$, since we can read directly from Eq. (21.64) that in that case the solution to our integral equation will be uniquely $\varphi(x) = 0$.

The integral operator $\mathcal{K}$ is **linear**, since it is obviously true that

$$\mathcal{K}\Big(a\varphi_1(x) + b\varphi_2(x)\Big) = a\mathcal{K}\varphi_1(x) + b\mathcal{K}\varphi_2(x).$$

In addition, if we define the scalar product as an integral on the range (a, b):

$$\langle \psi | \varphi \rangle \equiv \int_a^b \psi^*(x)\varphi(x)dx, \tag{21.67}$$

we then see that our requirement that the kernel $K(x, t)$ be real and symmetric will make $\mathcal{K}$ a self-adjoint operator:

$$\langle \psi | \mathcal{K}\varphi \rangle = \int_a^b \psi^*(x)\left[\int_a^b K(x, t)\varphi(t)\, dt \right] dx = \int_a^b dt \left[\int_a^b dx\, K(t, x)\psi(x) \right]^* \varphi(t)$$

$$= \langle \mathcal{K}\psi | \varphi \rangle. \tag{21.68}$$

The linearity and self-adjointness indicate that we can expect to confirm that $\mathcal{K}$ has the key properties of self-adjoint operators, namely that its eigenvalues are real and (except in the case of degeneracy) its eigenvectors are orthogonal.

While the above constitutes a complete demonstration of the orthogonality of our solutions to the homogeneous Fredholm equation, let's confirm these properties more explicitly.

We can start from the two equations,

$$\frac{1}{\lambda_i}\varphi_i(x) = \int_a^b K(x,t)\varphi_i(t)\,dt, \tag{21.69}$$

$$\frac{1}{\lambda_j}\varphi_j(x) = \int_a^b K(x,t)\varphi_j(t)\,dt. \tag{21.70}$$

If we multiply Eq. (21.69) by $\varphi_j^*(x)$ and Eq. (21.70) by $\varphi_i^*(x)$ and then integrate with respect to x, the two equations become[4]

$$\frac{1}{\lambda_i}\int_a^b \varphi_j^*(x)\varphi_i(x)dx = \int_a^b\int_a^b K(x,t)\varphi_j^*(t)\varphi_i(x)dtdx, \tag{21.71}$$

$$\frac{1}{\lambda_j}\int_a^b \varphi_i^*(x)\varphi_j(x)dx = \int_a^b\int_a^b K(x,t)\varphi_i^*(t)\varphi_j(x)dtdx. \tag{21.72}$$

Since we have demanded that $K(x,t)$ be real and symmetric, we may take the complex conjugate of Eq. (21.72) and then interchange the roles of x and t in the integral, reaching

$$\frac{1}{\lambda_j^*}\int_a^b \varphi_i(x)\varphi_j^*(x)dx = \int_a^b\int_a^b K(x,t)\varphi_i(x)\varphi_j^*(t)dtdx. \tag{21.73}$$

Subtracting Eq. (21.73) from Eq. (21.71), we obtain

$$\left(\frac{1}{\lambda_i} - \frac{1}{\lambda_j^*}\right)\int_a^b \varphi_j^*(x)\varphi_i(x)dx = 0. \tag{21.74}$$

Just as in our earlier derivation from Sturm-Liouville theory, we conclude that if $i = j$ the integral in Eq. (21.74) is necessarily nonzero; so $1/\lambda_i = 1/\lambda_i^*$, meaning that λ_i must be real. But if $\lambda_i \neq \lambda_j$,

$$\int_a^b \varphi_i^*(x)\varphi_j(x)dx = 0, \quad \lambda_i \neq \lambda_j, \tag{21.75}$$

proving orthogonality. The derivation can also be completed if $K(x,t)$ is Hermitian, meaning that $K(t,x) = K^*(x,t)$. See Exercise 21.4.1. Since we are mostly concerned with real

---

[4]We assume that the necessary integrals exist. For an example of a simple pathological case, see Exercise 21.4.4.

K, it is appropriate to assume also that φ is real, and for the remainder of this chapter we will often omit the complex conjugate asterisks that occur, for example, in Eq. (21.75).

If the eigenvalue λ_i is **degenerate**,[5] the eigenfunctions for that particular eigenvalue may be orthogonalized by the Gram-Schmidt method (Section 5.2). Our orthogonal eigenfunctions may, of course, be normalized, and we assume that this has been done. The result is

$$\int_a^b \varphi_i^*(x)\varphi_j(x)\,dx = \delta_{ij}. \tag{21.76}$$

It can be shown that the eigenfunctions of our integral equations form a complete set,[6] in the sense that if a function $g(x)$ can be generated by the integral

$$g(x) = \int K(x,t)h(t)\,dt,$$

with $h(t)$ a piecewise continuous function, then $g(x)$ can be represented by a series of eigenfunctions,

$$g(x) = \sum_{n=1}^{\infty} a_n \varphi_n(x). \tag{21.77}$$

The series in Eq. (21.77) can be shown to converge uniformly and absolutely.

Let us extend this to the kernel $K(x,t)$ by asserting that

$$K(x,t) = \sum_{n=1}^{\infty} a_n \varphi_n(t), \tag{21.78}$$

and $a_n = a_n(x)$. Substituting into the original integral equation, Eq. (21.64), and using the orthogonality integral, we obtain

$$\varphi_i(x) = \lambda_i a_i(x). \tag{21.79}$$

Therefore, for our homogeneous Fredholm equation of the second kind, the kernel may be expressed in terms of the eigenfunctions and eigenvalues as

$$K(x,t) = \sum_{n=1}^{\infty} \frac{\varphi_n(x)\varphi_n(t)}{\lambda_n}. \tag{21.80}$$

Equation (21.80) is not actually a new result. In the Green's function chapter, Section 10.1, we identified $K(x,t)$, there called $G(x,t)$, as the Green's function appearing in Eq. (10.30), with the expansion given in Eq. (10.14). However, it is possible that the

---

[5] As for differential operators, if more than one distinct eigenfunction of Eq. (21.64) corresponds to the same eigenvalue, that eigenvalue is said to be degenerate.

[6] For a proof of this statement, see Courant and Hilbert (1953), chapter III, section 5, in the Additional Readings.

expansion given by Eq. (21.80) may not exist. As an illustration of the sort of pathological behavior that may occur, you are invited to apply this analysis to

$$\varphi(x) = \lambda \int_0^\infty e^{-xt} \varphi(t)\, dt.$$

Compare Exercise 21.4.4.

It should be emphasized that this Hilbert-Schmidt theory is concerned with the establishment of properties of the eigenvalues (real) and eigenfunctions (orthogonality, completeness), properties that may be of great interest and value. The Hilbert-Schmidt theory does **not solve** the homogeneous integral equation for us any more than the Sturm-Liouville theory for differential equations solved the ODEs. The solutions of the integral equation come by the application of techniques such as were introduced in Sections 21.2 and 21.3, or perhaps even by numerical methods.

Inhomogeneous Integral Equation

We now continue with the Hilbert-Schmidt theory by seeking solutions of the inhomogeneous equation

$$\varphi(x) = f(x) + \lambda \int_a^b K(x,t)\varphi(t)\, dt. \tag{21.81}$$

We assume that the solutions of the corresponding homogeneous integral equation are already known:

$$\varphi_n(x) = \lambda_n \int_a^b K(x,t)\varphi_n(t)\, dt, \tag{21.82}$$

the solution $\varphi_n(x)$ corresponding to the eigenvalue λ_n. Note that at this point we are assuming nothing about λ; it is a constant that has no specific relationship to the eigenvalues λ_n of the homogeneous integral equation.

We expand both $\varphi(x)$ and $f(x)$ in terms of this set of eigenfunctions:

$$\varphi(x) = \sum_{n=1}^\infty a_n \varphi_n(x) \quad (a_n \text{ unknown}), \tag{21.83}$$

$$f(x) = \sum_{n=1}^\infty b_n \varphi_n(x) \quad (b_n \text{ known}). \tag{21.84}$$

Substituting into Eq. (21.81), we obtain

$$\sum_{n=1}^\infty a_n \varphi_n(x) = \sum_{n=1}^\infty b_n \varphi_n(x) + \lambda \int_a^b K(x,t) \sum_{n=1}^\infty a_n \varphi_n(t)\, dt. \tag{21.85}$$

By interchanging the order of integration and summation, we may evaluate the integral by Eq. (21.82), and we get

$$\sum_{n=1}^{\infty} a_n \varphi_n(x) = \sum_{n=1}^{\infty} b_n \varphi_n(x) + \lambda \sum_{n=1}^{\infty} \frac{a_n \varphi_n(x)}{\lambda_n}. \tag{21.86}$$

If we multiply by $\varphi_i(x)$ and integrate from $x = a$ to $x = b$, the orthogonality of our eigenfunctions leads to

$$a_i = b_i + \lambda \frac{a_i}{\lambda_i}. \tag{21.87}$$

This can be rewritten as

$$a_i = b_i + \frac{\lambda}{\lambda_i - \lambda} b_i. \tag{21.88}$$

We now multiply Eq. (21.88) by $\varphi_i(x)$ and sum over i, giving

$$\varphi(x) = f(x) + \lambda \sum_{i=1}^{\infty} \frac{\varphi_i(x)}{\lambda_i - \lambda} b_i$$

$$= f(x) + \lambda \sum_{i=1}^{\infty} \frac{\varphi_i(x)}{\lambda_i - \lambda} \int_a^b f(t) \varphi_i(t) \, dt. \tag{21.89}$$

Here it is assumed that the eigenfunctions $\varphi_i(x)$ are normalized to unity. **Note that if $f(x) = 0$, there is no solution unless** λ is equal to one of the λ_i, thereby confirming that the homogeneous integral equation has only the solutions $\varphi_i(x)$.

In the event that λ for the inhomogeneous equation, Eq. (21.81), is equal to one of the eigenvalues λ_p of the homogeneous equation, our solution, Eq. (21.89), blows up. It can be shown that the inhomogeneous equation then has no solution unless the coefficient b_p vanishes, meaning that there is no solution unless the inhomogeneous term $f(x)$ is orthogonal to the eigenfunction φ_p. If the eigenvalue λ_p is degenerate, there will be no solution unless $f(x)$ is orthogonal to all the degenerate eigenfunctions.

For the case that $b_p = 0$, we can return to Eq. (21.87), which then reduces for a_p to

$$a_p = b_p + a_p = a_p, \tag{21.90}$$

which gives no information about a_p. Note that if $b_p \neq 0$ this equation cannot be satisfied, a signal that a solution cannot be obtained.

Under the assumption that $b_p = 0$ we now can rewrite Eq. (21.86), identifying its first two summations, respectively, as $\varphi(x)$ and $f(x)$, separating the final summation into the single term $a_p \varphi_p(x)$ plus a sum over all n other than p, thereby reaching

$$\varphi(x) = f(x) + a_p \varphi_p + \lambda_p \sum_{i=1}^{\infty}{}' \frac{\varphi_i(x)}{\lambda_i - \lambda_p} \int_a^b f(t) \varphi_i(t) \, dt. \tag{21.91}$$

In this solution the a_p remains as an undetermined constant,[7] and the prime indicates that $i = p$ is to be omitted from the sum.

It is of interest to relate Eq. (21.89) to what might be expected if we tried to develop a similar equation by Green's-function methods. To do this, we start by rewriting Eq. (21.81) as an operator equation of the form

$$\mathcal{K}\varphi(x) - \frac{1}{\lambda}\varphi(x) = -\frac{f(x)}{\lambda}, \tag{21.92}$$

where $\mathcal{K}$ is the operator that we introduced in Eq. (21.65). Next, we note that, from Eq. (21.82), the φ_n are eigenfunctions of $\mathcal{K}$ with eigenvalues $1/\lambda_n$:

$$\mathcal{K}\varphi_n(x) = \frac{\varphi_n(x)}{\lambda_n}. \tag{21.93}$$

Then, applying Eq. (10.39), the Green's function of the entire left-hand side of Eq. (21.92) will be (assuming φ is real):

$$
\begin{aligned}
G(x, t) &= \sum_n \frac{\varphi_n(x)\varphi_n(t)}{\lambda_n^{-1} - \lambda^{-1}} = \lambda \sum_n \frac{\lambda_n}{\lambda - \lambda_n} \varphi_n(x)\varphi_n(t) \\
&= -\lambda \sum_n \varphi_n(x)\varphi_n(t) + \lambda^2 \sum_n \frac{\varphi_n(x)\varphi_n(t)}{\lambda - \lambda_n} \\
&= -\lambda \delta(t - x) - \lambda^2 \sum_n \frac{\varphi_n(x)\varphi_n(t)}{\lambda_n - \lambda}.
\end{aligned}
\tag{21.94}
$$

To reach the last line of Eq. (21.94) we used the eigenfunction expansion of the delta function, Eq. (5.27). Applying this Green's function to the right-hand side of Eq. (21.92), we get

$$
\begin{aligned}
\varphi(x) &= -\frac{1}{\lambda} \int_a^b G(x, t) f(t)\, dt \\
&= -\frac{1}{\lambda} \int_a^b \left[-\lambda \delta(t - x) - \lambda^2 \sum_n \frac{\varphi_n(x)\varphi_n(t)}{\lambda_n - \lambda} \right] f(t)\, dt \\
&= f(x) + \lambda \sum_n \frac{\varphi_n(x)}{\lambda_n - \lambda} \int_a^b \varphi_n(t) f(t)\, dt,
\end{aligned}
\tag{21.95}
$$

which agrees with Eq. (21.89).

---

[7]This is like the inhomogeneous linear ODE. We may add to its solution any constant times a solution of the corresponding homogeneous ODE.

Example 21.4.1   INHOMOGENEOUS FREDHOLM EQUATION

Let's seek solutions to the inhomogeneous Fredholm equation

$$\varphi(x) = x^3 + \lambda \int_{-1}^{1} (t+x)\varphi(t)\,dt, \tag{21.96}$$

for the two λ values $\lambda = 1$ and $\lambda = \sqrt{3}/2$. The corresponding homogeneous equation, treated in Example 21.2.3, has solutions only for the two eigenvalues $\pm\sqrt{3}/2$. In normalized form, they are:

$$\lambda_1 = \frac{\sqrt{3}}{2}, \quad \varphi_1 = \frac{\sqrt{3}}{2}\left(x + \frac{1}{\sqrt{3}}\right); \quad \lambda_2 = -\frac{\sqrt{3}}{2}, \quad \varphi_2 = \frac{\sqrt{3}}{2}\left(x - \frac{1}{\sqrt{3}}\right).$$

Taking first $\lambda = 1$, which is not an eigenvalue of the homogeneous equation, we have

$$\varphi(x) = x^3 + \sum_{i=1}^{2} \frac{\varphi_i(x)}{\lambda_i - 1}\int_{-1}^{1} t^3\varphi_i(t)\,dt$$

$$= x^3 + \frac{\frac{\sqrt{3}}{2}\left(x + \frac{1}{\sqrt{3}}\right)}{\frac{\sqrt{3}}{2} - 1}\frac{\sqrt{3}}{2}\int_{-1}^{1} t^3\left(t + \frac{1}{\sqrt{3}}\right)dt$$

$$+ \frac{\frac{\sqrt{3}}{2}\left(x - \frac{1}{\sqrt{3}}\right)}{-\frac{\sqrt{3}}{2} - 1}\frac{\sqrt{3}}{2}\int_{-1}^{1} t^3\left(t - \frac{1}{\sqrt{3}}\right)dt$$

$$= x^3 - \frac{6}{5}(2x + 1). \tag{21.97}$$

Continuing now to $\lambda = \sqrt{3}/2$, we note that it is the eigenvalue λ_1 of the homogeneous integral equation. That means the integral equation will have no solution unless $\langle\varphi_1|f\rangle = 0$. For the present problem,

$$\langle\varphi_1|f\rangle = \frac{\sqrt{3}}{2}\int_{-1}^{1}\left(x + \frac{1}{\sqrt{3}}\right)x^3\,dx \neq 0,$$

so our integral equation will have no solution for $\lambda = \sqrt{3}/2$. If in spite of this observation we attempted to generate a solution using Eq. (21.91), the function $\varphi(x)$ we obtained would not satisfy the integral equation, irrespective of the value we might choose to assign to a_p. The immediate reason we cannot obtain a solution is that the integral

$$\int_{-1}^{1}(t+x)f(t)\,dt = \int_{-1}^{1}(t+x)t^3\,dt = \frac{2}{5}$$

evaluates to a quantity that cannot be represented as a linear combination of the eigenfunctions φ_i other than φ_p (in the present case, this means that 2/5 is not proportional to φ_2). There is therefore no way to add an additional component to $f(x)$ to obtain a cancellation of the 2/5. ∎

Exercises

21.4.1   In the Fredholm equation

$$\varphi(x) = \lambda \int_a^b K(x,t)\varphi(t)\,dt,$$

assume that the kernel $K(x,t)$ is self-adjoint or Hermitian:

$$K(x,t) = K^*(t,x).$$

Extend the analysis of the present section to show that

(a)   the eigenfunctions are orthogonal, in the sense that

$$\int_a^b \varphi_m^*(x)\varphi_n(x)\,dx = 0, \quad m \neq n(\lambda_m \neq \lambda_n).$$

(b)   the eigenvalues are real.

21.4.2   (a)   Show that the eigenfunctions of Exercise 21.2.12 are orthogonal.

(b)   Show that the eigenfunctions of Exercise 21.2.14 are orthogonal.

21.4.3   Use the Hilbert-Schmidt method to solve the inhomogeneous integral equation

$$\varphi(x) = x + \tfrac{1}{2}\int_{-1}^1 (t+x)\varphi(t)\,dt.$$

The corresponding homogeneous integral equation was treated in Example 21.2.3.

Note. The application of the Hilbert-Schmidt technique here is somewhat like using a shotgun to kill a mosquito, especially when the equation can be solved quickly by expanding in Legendre polynomials.

21.4.4   The Fredholm integral equation

$$\varphi(x) = \lambda \int_0^\infty e^{-xt}\varphi(t)\,dt$$

has an infinite number of solutions, of which one is

$$\varphi(x) = x^{-1/2}, \quad \lambda = \pi^{-1/2}.$$

Verify that this is a solution and that it is **not** normalizable.

Note. A basic reason for this anomalous behavior is that the range of integration is infinite, making this a "singular" integral equation. Note also that a series expansion of the kernel e^{-xt} would permit a solution by the separable-kernel method (Section 21.2), except that the series is infinite. This observation is consistent with the fact that this integral equation has an infinite number of eigenvalues and eigenfunctions.

21.4.5   Given

$$y(x) = x + \lambda \int_0^1 xt \; y(t) \, dt:$$

(a)   Determine $y(x)$ as a Neumann series.

(b)   Find the range of λ for which your Neumann series solution is convergent. Compare with the value obtained from

$$|\lambda| \cdot |K|_{\max} < 1.$$

(c)   Find the eigenvalue and the eigenfunction of the corresponding homogeneous integral equation.

(d)   By the separable-kernel method show that the solution is

$$y(x) = \frac{3x}{3 - \lambda}.$$

(e)   Find $y(x)$ by the Hilbert-Schmidt method.

21.4.6   In Exercise 21.2.11 it was found that the integral equation

$$\varphi(x) = \lambda \int_0^{2\pi} \cos(x - t)\varphi(t) \, dt$$

had (unnormalized) eigenfunctions $\cos x$ and $\sin x$, both with eigenvalue $\lambda_i = 1/\pi$. Show that the kernel of this integral equation has an expansion of the form

$$K(x, t) = \sum_{n=1}^{2} \frac{\varphi_n(x)\varphi_n(t)}{\lambda_n}.$$

21.4.7   The integral equation $\varphi(x) = \lambda \int_0^1 (1 + xt)\varphi(t) \, dt$

has eigenvalues $\lambda_1 = 0.7889$ and $\lambda_2 = 15.211$. The corresponding eigenfunctions are $\varphi_1 = 1 + 0.5352x$ and $\varphi_2 = 1 - 1.8685x$.

(a)   Show that these eigenfunctions are orthogonal over the interval $[0, 1]$.

(b)   Normalize the eigenfunctions to unity.

(c)   Show that

$$K(x,t) = \frac{\varphi_1(x)\varphi_1(t)}{\lambda_1} + \frac{\varphi_2(x)\varphi_2(t)}{\lambda_2}.$$

ANS.   (b) $\varphi_1(x) = 0.7831 + 0.4191x,$

$\varphi_2(x) = 1.8403 - 3.4386x.$

21.4.8   An alternate form of the solution to the inhomogeneous integral equation, Eq. (21.81), is

$$\varphi(x) = \sum_{i=1}^{\infty} \frac{b_i \lambda_i}{\lambda_i - \lambda} \varphi_i(x).$$

(a)   Derive this form without using Eq. (21.89).

(b)   Show that this form and Eq. (21.89) are equivalent.

Additional Readings

Bocher, M., *An Introduction to the Study of Integral Equations*, Cambridge Tracts in Mathematics and Mathematical Physics, No. 10. New York: Hafner (1960). This is a helpful introduction to integral equations.

Byron, F. W., Jr., and R. W. Fuller, *Mathematics of Classical and Quantum Physics*. Reading, MA: Addison-Wesley (1969), reprinted, Dover (1992). The treatment of integral equations is rather advanced.

Cochran, J. A., *The Analysis of Linear Integral Equations*. New York: McGraw-Hill (1972). This is a comprehensive treatment of linear integral equations intended for applied mathematicians and mathematical physicists. It assumes a moderate to high level of mathematical competence on the part of the reader.

Courant, R., and D. Hilbert, *Methods of Mathematical Physics*, Vol. 1 (English edition). New York: Interscience (1953). This is one of the classic works of mathematical physics. Originally published in German in 1924, the revised English edition is an excellent reference for a rigorous treatment of integral equations, Green's functions, and a wide variety of other topics on mathematical physics.

Golberg, M. A., ed., *Solution Methods of Integral Equations*. New York: Plenum Press (1979). This is a set of papers from a conference on integral equations. The initial chapter is excellent for up-to-date orientation and a wealth of references.

Kanval, R. P., *Linear Integral Equations*. New York: Academic Press (1971), reprinted, Birkhäuser (1996). This book is a detailed but readable treatment of a variety of techniques for solving linear integral equations.

Morse, P. M., and H. Feshbach, *Methods of Theoretical Physics*. New York: McGraw-Hill (1953). Detailed, rigorous, and difficult.

Muskhelishvili, N. I., *Singular Integral Equations*, 2nd ed. New York: Dover (1992).

Stakgold, I., *Green's Functions and Boundary Value Problems*. New York: Wiley (1979).

CHAPTER 22

CALCULUS OF VARIATIONS

The calculus of variations deals with problems where we search for a function or curve, rather than a value of some variable, that makes a given quantity stationary, usually an energy or action integral. Because a function is varied, these problems are called **variational**. Variational principles, such as those of D'Alembert, Lagrange, and Hamilton, have been developed in classical mechanics; Fermat's principle (that of the shortest optical path) finds use in electrodynamics. Lagrangian variational techniques also occur in quantum mechanics and field theory. Before plunging into this rather different branch of mathematical physics, let us summarize some of its uses in both physics and mathematics.

1. **In existing physical theories**:
   a. Unification of diverse areas of physics using energy as a key concept
   b. Convenience in analysis: Lagrange equations, Section 22.2
   c. Elegant treatment of constraints, Section 22.4

2. **Starting point for new, complex areas of physics and engineering**. In general relativity, the geodesic is taken as the minimum path of a light pulse or the free-fall path of a particle in curved Riemannian space. Variational principles appear in quantum field theory. Variational principles have been applied extensively in control theory.

3. **Mathematical unification**. Variational analysis provides a proof of the completeness of the Sturm-Liouville eigenfunctions, and can be used to establish bounds for the eigenvalues. Similar results follow for the eigenvalues and eigenfunctions in the Hilbert-Schmidt theory of integral equations.

22.1 EULER EQUATION

The calculus of variations typically involves problems in which a quantity to be minimized (or maximized) appears as a **functional**, meaning that it is a quantity whose argument(s) are themselves function(s), not just variable(s). As a simple, yet fairly general case, let J

be a functional of y, defined as

$$J[y] = \int_{x_1}^{x_2} f\left(y(x), \frac{dy(x)}{dx}, x\right) dx. \tag{22.1}$$

Here f is a fixed function of the three variables y, dy/dx, and x, while J will have a value dependent on the choice of y. The square-bracket notation is frequently used to remind the reader that J is a functional. Because J is given as an integral, its value depends on the behavior of $y(x)$ throughout the entire range of x (here $x_1 \leq x \leq x_2$). A typical problem in the calculus of variations is to find (usually subject to some constraints) a continuous and differentiable function $y(x)$ that makes J stationary relative to small changes in y anywhere (or everywhere) in its range of definition. These stationary values of J will in many problems be minima or maxima, but they can also be saddle points. The conditions of physical problems will normally require that variations in y be restricted to those that preserve its continuity and differentiability

It is convenient to introduce a notation that makes our discussions less cumbersome; we usually rewrite Eq. (22.1) in a notation with dy/dx denoted y_x and with the arguments x and $[y]$ suppressed, and we indicate the variation in J produced by a (small) variation in y as

$$\delta J = \delta \int_{x_1}^{x_2} f(y, y_x, x) \, dx. \tag{22.2}$$

Note that we wrote δ rather than d or ∂; this distinction reminds us that the variation is that of a function (here y) rather than that of a variable.

In visualizing the situation described by Eq. (22.2), it is helpful to think of $y(x)$ as a **path** or curve connecting the values $y(x_1)$ and $y(x_2)$; in fact, a common problem in the calculus of variations will be to determine $y(x)$ subject to the constraint that $y(x_1)$ and $y(x_2)$ have specified values (and often subject to further constraints that may also be integrals). To illustrate the class of problems represented by Eq. (22.2), here are two simple examples:

- Determination of the minimum-energy configuration of a rope or chain of given length attached to fixed points at both ends, in the presence of a uniform gravitational field.

- Determination of the track between two points at different heights that will minimize the travel time of an object that, starting from rest, slides without friction along the track subject only to a uniform gravitational field (this is known as the **brachistochrone problem**).

The problems here under consideration are much more difficult than typical minimizations in differential calculus, where the minimum in a function can be found by comparing its values, say $y(x)$, at neighboring points (by looking at dy/dx). What we can do, instead, is to start by assuming the existence of an optimum path, i.e., a function $y(x)$ for which J is stationary, and then compare J for our (unknown) optimum path with that obtained from neighboring paths, of which there are an infinite number. See Fig. 22.1. Even this strategy may sometimes fail, as there exist functionals J for which there is no optimum path.

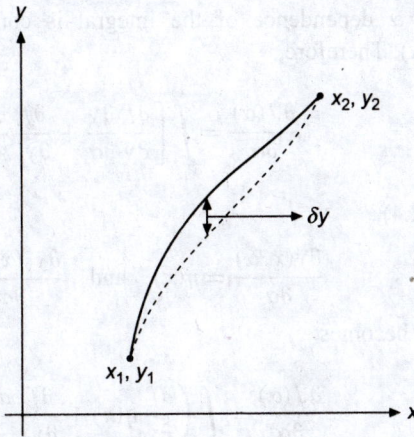

FIGURE 22.1 Neighboring paths.

Restricting attention to functions $y(x)$ for which the endpoints $y(x_1)$ and $y(x_2)$ are fixed, we consider a deformation of $y(x)$, called the **variation** of y and denoted δy. We describe δy by introducing a new function, $\eta(x)$, and a scale factor α that controls the magnitude of the variation. The function $\eta(x)$ is arbitrary except for being continuous and differentiable, and, to keep the endpoints fixed, with

$$\eta(x_1) = \eta(x_2) = 0. \tag{22.3}$$

With these definitions, our path, now a function of α, is

$$y(x, \alpha) = y(x, 0) + \alpha \eta(x), \tag{22.4}$$

and we choose $y(x, 0)$ as the (unknown) path that will minimize J. Relative to $y(x, 0)$, the variation δy is then

$$\delta y = \alpha \eta(x). \tag{22.5}$$

Using Eq. (22.4), our formula for J can now be written

$$J(\alpha) = \int_{x_1}^{x_2} f\left(y(x, \alpha), y_x(x, \alpha), x\right) dx, \tag{22.6}$$

and we see that we have reached a simpler formulation in which J is now a **function** of α rather than a **functional** of y. This means that we now know how to optimize it.[1]

We proceed now to obtain a stationary value of J by imposing the condition

$$\left[\frac{\partial J(\alpha)}{\partial \alpha}\right]_{\alpha=0} = 0, \tag{22.7}$$

analogous to the vanishing of the derivative dy/dx in differential calculus.

---

[1] The arbitrary nature of the dependence of $J(\alpha)$ on $\eta(x)$ will come into play later.

Now, the α dependence of the integral is contained in $y(x, \alpha)$ and $y_x(x, \alpha) = (\partial/\partial x)y(x, \alpha)$. Therefore,[2]

$$\frac{\partial J(\alpha)}{\partial \alpha} = \int_{x_1}^{x_2} \left[\frac{\partial f}{\partial y} \frac{\partial y}{\partial \alpha} + \frac{\partial f}{\partial y_x} \frac{\partial y_x}{\partial \alpha} \right] dx = 0. \tag{22.8}$$

From Eq. (22.4),

$$\frac{\partial y(x, \alpha)}{\partial \alpha} = \eta(x) \quad \text{and} \quad \frac{\partial y_x(x, \alpha)}{\partial \alpha} = \frac{d\eta(x)}{dx}, \tag{22.9}$$

so Eq. (22.8) becomes

$$\frac{\partial J(\alpha)}{\partial \alpha} = \int_{x_1}^{x_2} \left(\frac{\partial f}{\partial y} \eta(x) + \frac{\partial f}{\partial y_x} \frac{d\eta(x)}{dx} \right) dx = 0. \tag{22.10}$$

Integrating the second term by parts to get $\eta(x)$ as a common factor, we convert it to

$$\int_{x_1}^{x_2} \frac{d\eta(x)}{dx} \frac{\partial f}{\partial y_x} dx = \eta(x) \frac{\partial f}{\partial y_x} \Big|_{x_1}^{x_2} - \int_{x_1}^{x_2} \eta(x) \frac{d}{dx} \frac{\partial f}{\partial y_x} dx. \tag{22.11}$$

The integrated part vanishes by Eq. (22.3), and Eq. (22.10) becomes

$$\frac{\partial J(\alpha)}{\partial \alpha} = \int_{x_1}^{x_2} \left[\frac{\partial f}{\partial y} - \frac{d}{dx} \frac{\partial f}{\partial y_x} \right] \eta(x)\, dx = 0. \tag{22.12}$$

Equation (22.12), which must be satisfied for arbitrary $\eta(x)$, is to be understood as a condition on $y(x)$. Occasionally we will see Eq. (22.12) multiplied by $\delta\alpha$, which gives, upon using $\eta(x)\delta\alpha = \delta y$,

$$\delta J = \int_{x_1}^{x_2} \left(\frac{\partial f}{\partial y} - \frac{d}{dx} \frac{\partial f}{\partial y_x} \right) \delta y\, dx = 0. \tag{22.13}$$

Equation (22.13) is to be solved for arbitrary δy with $\delta y(x_1) = \delta y(x_2) = 0$.

We now take up the solution of Eq. (22.12). That equation can be satisfied for arbitrary $\eta(x)$ only if the bracketed expression forming the remainder of its integrand vanishes "almost everywhere," meaning everywhere except possibly at isolated points.[3] The condition for our stationary value is thus formally a partial differential equation (PDE),

$$\frac{\partial f}{\partial y} - \frac{d}{dx} \frac{\partial f}{\partial y_x} = 0, \tag{22.14}$$

known as the **Euler equation**. Since the form of f is known, it will actually reduce (because there is really only one independent variable, x) to an ordinary differential equation (ODE) for y with boundary conditions at x_1 and x_2. In that connection, it is important

---

[2] Note that y and y_x are being treated as **independent** variables because they occur as different arguments of f.

[3] Compare the discussion of convergence in the mean, at Eq. (5.22).

to note that the derivative d/dx occurs in the Euler equation, and that it has a meaning distinct from the partial derivative $\partial/\partial x$. In particular, if $f = f(y(x), y_x, x)$, then df/dx, which stands for the change in f (from all sources) due to a change in x, has the evaluation

$$\frac{df}{dx} = \frac{\partial f}{\partial x} + \frac{\partial f}{\partial y}\frac{dy}{dx} + \frac{\partial f}{\partial y_x}\frac{d^2 y}{dx^2},$$

where the last term has the form given because $dy_x/dx = d^2 y/dx^2$. Note that the first term on the right gives the **explicit** x-dependence of f; the second and third terms give its **implicit** x-dependence via y and y_x.

The Euler equation, Eq. (22.14), is a necessary, but by no means sufficient condition that there be a function $y(x)$ that is continuous and differentiable on the range (x_1, x_2) and yields a stationary value of J.[4] A nice example of a lack of sufficiency is provided by the problem of determining stationary paths between points on the surface of a sphere (this example was provided by Courant and Robbins; see Additional Readings). The minimum-distance path from point A to point B on a spherical surface is the arc of a great circle, shown as Path 1 in Fig. 22.2. But Path 2 also satisfies the Euler equation. Path 2 is a maximum, but only if we demand that it be a great circle and then only if we make less than one circuit (as Path 2 plus n complete revolutions is also a solution). If the path is not required to be a great circle, any deviation from Path 2 will increase the length. This is hardly the property of a local maximum, and that illustrates why it is important to check solutions of the Euler equation to see if they satisfy the physical conditions of the given problem.

Sometimes a problem admits a discontinuous solution that has physical relevance and will not be found by straightforward application of the Euler equation. An example is provided by the soap film of Example 22.1.3, where such a solution describes what happens if the film becomes unstable and breaks.

Following are examples of the use of the Euler equation.

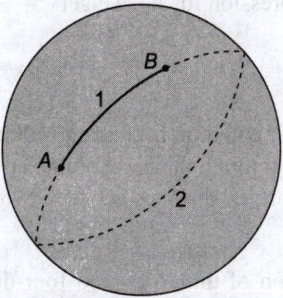

FIGURE 22.2   Stationary paths over a sphere.

---

[4]For a discussion of sufficiency conditions and the development of the calculus of variations as a part of mathematics, see the works by Ewing and Sagan in Additional Readings.

Example 22.1.1   STRAIGHT LINE

Perhaps the simplest application of the Euler equation is in the determination of the shortest distance between two points in the Euclidean xy-plane. Since the element of distance is

$$ds = [(dx)^2 + (dy)^2]^{1/2} = [1 + y_x^2]^{1/2}\, dx,$$

the distance J may be written as

$$J = \int_{x_1,y_1}^{x_2,y_2} ds = \int_{x_1}^{x_2} [1 + y_x^2]^{1/2}\, dx. \tag{22.15}$$

Comparison with Eq. (22.2) shows that

$$f(y, y_x, x) = (1 + y_x^2)^{1/2}.$$

Substituting into Eq. (22.14) and noting that $\partial f/\partial y$ vanishes, we obtain

$$-\frac{d}{dx}\left[\frac{1}{(1 + y_x^2)^{1/2}}\right] = 0,$$

or

$$\frac{1}{(1 + y_x^2)^{1/2}} = C, \quad \text{a constant.}$$

This equation is satisfied if

$$y_x = a, \quad \text{a second constant.}$$

Integrating this expression for y_x, we get

$$y = ax + b, \tag{22.16}$$

which is the familiar equation for a straight line. The constants a and b are now chosen so that the line passes through the two points (x_1, y_1) and (x_2, y_2). Hence the Euler equation predicts that the shortest[5] distance between two fixed points in Euclidean space is a straight line.   ■

The generalization of this to curved four-dimensional space-time leads to the important concept of the geodesic in general relativity. A further discussion of geodesics is in Section 22.2.

---

[5]Technically, we have only found a $y(x)$ of stationary J. By inspection of the solution, we easily determine the distance to be a minimum.

Example 22.1.2   OPTICAL PATH NEAR A BLACK HOLE

We now wish to determine the optical path in an atmosphere where the velocity of light increases in proportion to the height y according to $v(y) = y/b$, with $b > 0$ some parameter describing the light speed. So $v = 0$ at $y = 0$, which simulates the conditions at the surface of a black hole, called its **event horizon**, where the gravitational force is so strong that the velocity of light goes to zero, thus trapping light.

Our variational principle (Fermat's principle) is that light will take the path of shortest travel time from (x_1, y_1) to (x_2, y_2), namely

$$\Delta t = \int dt = \int_{x_1,y_1}^{x_2,y_2} \frac{ds}{v} = \int_{x_1,y_1}^{x_2,y_2} \frac{b}{y} ds = b \int_{x_1,y_1}^{x_2,y_2} \frac{\sqrt{dx^2 + dy^2}}{y} = \text{minimum}. \qquad (22.17)$$

The path is along a line defined by the relation between y and x. While we have in previous equations taken x to be the independent variable, there is no inherent requirement to do so, and our work on the present problem will be simplified if we choose y as the independent variable, and we write Eq. (22.17) in the form

$$\Delta t = \int_{y_1}^{y_2} \frac{\sqrt{x_y^2 + 1}}{y} dy, \qquad (22.18)$$

where x_y stands for dx/dy. Then our Euler equation will be

$$\frac{\partial f}{\partial x} - \frac{d}{dy} \frac{\partial f}{\partial x_y} = 0, \quad \text{with} \quad f(x, x_y, y) = \frac{\sqrt{x_y^2 + 1}}{y}.$$

Noting that $\partial f/\partial x = 0$ and differentiating $\partial f/\partial x_y$, we have

$$-\frac{d}{dy} \frac{x_y}{y\sqrt{x_y^2 + 1}} = 0.$$

This equation can be integrated, giving

$$\frac{x_y}{y\sqrt{x_y^2 + 1}} = C_1 = \text{constant}, \quad \text{or} \quad x_y = \frac{C_1 y}{\sqrt{1 - C_1^2 y^2}}.$$

Writing $x_y = dx/dy$ and separating dx and dy in this first-order ODE, we find the integral

$$\int^x dx = \int^y \frac{C_1 y\, dy}{\sqrt{1 - C_1^2 y^2}},$$

which yields

$$x + C_2 = -\frac{\sqrt{1 - C_1^2 y^2}}{C_1}, \quad \text{or} \quad (x + C_2)^2 + y^2 = \frac{1}{C_1^2}.$$

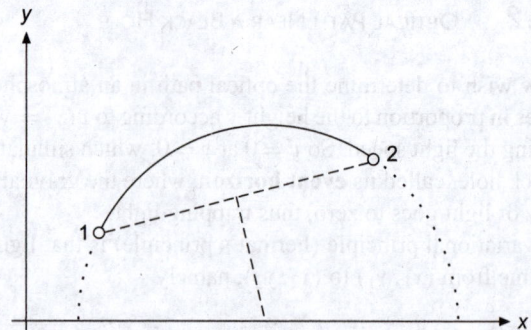

FIGURE 22.3   Circular optical path in medium.

Irrespective of the values of C_1 and C_2, this light path is the arc of a circle whose center is on the line $y = 0$, namely the event horizon. The actual path of light passing from (x_1, y_1) to (x_2, y_2) will be on the circle through those points centered on $y = 0$; the construction of the path can be performed geometrically as shown in Fig. 22.3. Note that light will not escape completely from the black hole with this model for $v(y)$ unless $x_1 = x_2$ (a path perpendicular to the event horizon).

This example may be adapted to a mirage (Fata Morgana) in a desert with hot air near the ground and cooler air aloft (the index of refraction changes with height in cool vs. hot air). For the mirage problem, the relevant velocity law is $v(y) = v_0 - y/b$. In that case, the circular light path is no longer convex with center on the x-axis, but becomes concave. ∎

Alternate Forms of Euler Equations

Another form of the Euler equation, which is often useful (Exercise 22.1.1), is

$$\frac{\partial f}{\partial x} - \frac{d}{dx}\left(f - y_x \frac{\partial f}{\partial y_x}\right) = 0. \tag{22.19}$$

In problems in which $f = f(y, y_x)$, i.e., in which x does not appear explicitly, Eq. (22.19) reduces to

$$\frac{d}{dx}\left(f - y_x \frac{\partial f}{\partial y_x}\right) = 0, \tag{22.20}$$

or

$$f - y_x \frac{\partial f}{\partial y_x} = \text{constant}. \tag{22.21}$$

Example 22.1.3   SOAP FILM

As our next illustrative example, consider two parallel coaxial wire circles to be connected by a surface of minimum area that is generated by revolving a curve $y(x)$ about the x-axis.

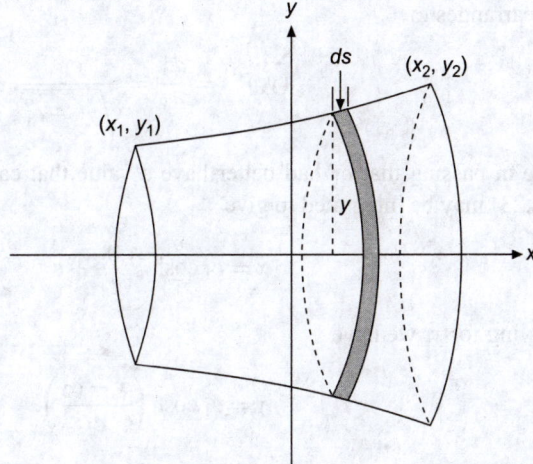

FIGURE 22.4   Surface of rotation, soap-film problem.

See Fig. 22.4. The curve is required to pass through fixed endpoints (x_1, y_1) and (x_2, y_2). The variational problem is to choose the curve $y(x)$ so that the area of the resulting surface will be a minimum. A physical situation corresponding to this problem is that of a soap film suspended between the wire circles.

For the element of area shown in Fig. 22.4,

$$dA = 2\pi y \, ds = 2\pi y (1 + y_x^2)^{1/2} \, dx.$$

The variational equation is then

$$J = \int_{x_1}^{x_2} 2\pi y (1 + y_x^2)^{1/2} \, dx.$$

Neglecting the 2π, we identify

$$f(y, y_x, x) = y(1 + y_x^2)^{1/2}.$$

Since $\partial f / \partial x = 0$, we may apply Eq. (22.20) and get

$$y(1 + y_x^2)^{1/2} - \frac{y \, y_x^2}{(1 + y_x^2)^{1/2}} = c_1,$$

which simplifies to

$$\frac{y}{(1 + y_x^2)^{1/2}} = c_1. \qquad (22.22)$$

Squaring, we get

$$\frac{y^2}{1 + y_x^2} = c_1^2,$$

which rearranges to

$$(y_x)^{-1} = \frac{dx}{dy} = \frac{c_1}{\sqrt{y^2 - c_1^2}}. \tag{22.23}$$

We note in passing that c_1 had better have a value that causes dy/dx to be real. Equation (22.23) may be integrated to give

$$x = c_1 \cosh^{-1} \frac{y}{c_1} + c_2,$$

and, solving for y, we have

$$y = c_1 \cosh\left(\frac{x - c_2}{c_1}\right). \tag{22.24}$$

Finally, c_1 and c_2 are determined by requiring the solution to pass through the points (x_1, y_1) and (x_2, y_2). Our "minimum"-area surface is a special case of a catenary of revolution, or a **catenoid**.   ∎

Soap Film: Minimum Area

This calculus of variations contains many pitfalls for the unwary. Remember, the Euler equation is a **necessary** condition, and assumes a **differentiable solution**. The sufficiency conditions are quite involved. Again, see the Additional Readings for details. Respect for some of these hazards may be developed by further considering the soap-film problem in Example 22.1.3, with $(x_1, y_1) = (-x_0, 1)$, $(x_2, y_2) = (+x_0, 1)$. We are therefore considering a soap film stretched between two rings of unit radius at $x = \pm x_0$. The problem is to predict the curve $y(x)$ assumed by the soap film.

By referring to Eq. (22.24), we find that $c_2 = 0$ because our problem is symmetric about $x = 0$. Then

$$y = c_1 \cosh\left(\frac{x}{c_1}\right), \tag{22.25}$$

and our endpoint conditions become

$$c_1 \cosh\left(\frac{x_0}{c_1}\right) = 1. \tag{22.26}$$

If we take $x_0 = \frac{1}{2}$ we obtain the following transcendental equation for c_1:

$$1 = c_1 \cosh\left(\frac{1}{2c_1}\right). \tag{22.27}$$

We find that this equation has two solutions: $c_1 = 0.2350$, leading to a "deep" curve, and $c_1 = 0.8483$, leading to a "shallow" curve. Which curve is assumed by the soap film?

Before answering this question, consider the physical situation with the rings moved apart so that $x_0 = 1$. Then Eq. (22.26) becomes

$$1 = c_1 \cosh\left(\frac{1}{c_1}\right), \tag{22.28}$$

which has **no real solutions**. The physical significance is that as the unit-radius rings were moved out from the origin, a point was reached at which the soap film could no longer maintain the same horizontal force over each vertical section. Stable equilibrium was no longer possible. The soap film broke (irreversible process) and formed a circular film over each ring (with a total area of $2\pi = 6.2832\ldots$). This is known as the Goldschmidt discontinuous solution to the soap-film problem.

The next question is: How large may x_0 be and still give a real solution for Eq. (22.26)? Solving Eq. (22.26) for x_0,

$$x_0 = c_1 \cosh^{-1}(1/c_1), \tag{22.29}$$

we find that x_0 will be real only for $c_1 \leq 1$ and that its maximum value is attained when $dx_0/dc_1 = 0$. A plot of x_0 vs. c_1 is shown in Fig. 22.5; it helps to explain the behavior we observed at $x_0 = \frac{1}{2}$. We see from the plot (and more precisely from Exercise 22.1.6) that the Euler equation has no solutions for $x_0 > x_{max}$, where $x_{max} \approx 0.6627$, and that this x_0 value occurs when $c_1 \approx 0.5524$. For values of x_0 smaller than x_{max}, there are solutions for two different values of c_1, corresponding to the "deep" and "shallow" curves found earlier for $x_0 = \frac{1}{2}$.

Returning to the question as to which solution of Eq. (22.26) describes the soap film, let us calculate the area corresponding to each solution. Using Eq. (22.22) to reach the last

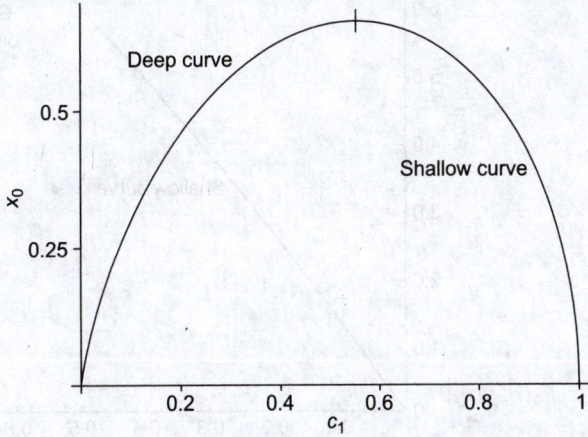

Deep curve

Shallow curve

x_0

0.5

0.25

0.2   0.4   0.6   0.8   1

c_1

FIGURE 22.5   Solutions of Eq. (22.26) for unit-radius rings at $x = \pm x_0$.

member of the first line below, we have

$$A = 4\pi \int_0^{x_0} y(1 + y_x^2)^{1/2}\, dx = \frac{4\pi}{c_1} \int_0^{x_0} y^2\, dx$$

$$= 4\pi c_1 \int_0^{x_0} \left(\cosh \frac{x}{c_1}\right)^2 dx = \pi c_1^2 \left[\sinh\left(\frac{2x_0}{c_1}\right) + \frac{2x_0}{c_1}\right]. \tag{22.30}$$

For $x_0 = \frac{1}{2}$, Eq. (22.30) leads to

$$c_1 = 0.2350 \quad \rightarrow \quad A = 6.8456,$$

$$c_1 = 0.8483 \quad \rightarrow \quad A = 5.9917,$$

showing that the former can at most be only a local minimum. A more detailed investigation (compare Bliss, Additional Readings, chapter IV) shows that this surface is not even a local minimum. For $x_0 = \frac{1}{2}$, the soap film will be described by the shallow curve

$$y = 0.8483 \cosh\left(\frac{x}{0.8483}\right).$$

This shallow catenoid (catenary of revolution) will be an absolute minimum for $0 \le x_0 < 0.528$. However, for $0.528 < x < 0.6627$, its area is greater than that of the Goldschmidt discontinuous solution (6.2832) and it is only a relative minimum. See Fig. 22.6.

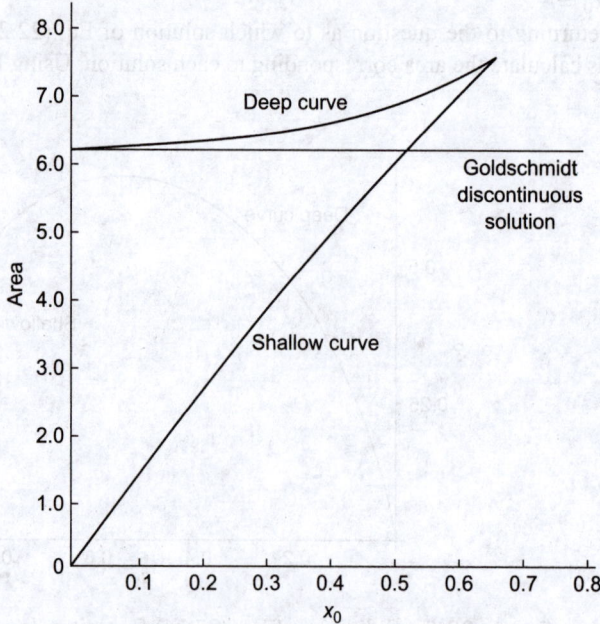

FIGURE 22.6   Catenoid area and that of the discontinuous solution of the soap-film problem (unit-radius rings at $x = \pm x_0$).

For an excellent discussion of both the mathematical problems and experiments with soap films, we refer to Courant and Robbins in Additional Readings. The larger message of this subsection is the extent to which one must use caution in accepting solutions of the Euler equations.

Exercises

22.1.1 For $dy/dx \equiv y_x \neq 0$, show the equivalence of the two forms of Euler's equation:

$$\frac{\partial f}{\partial x} - \frac{d}{dx}\frac{\partial f}{\partial y_x} = 0$$

and

$$\frac{\partial f}{\partial y} - \frac{d}{dx}\left(f - y_x\frac{\partial f}{\partial y_x}\right) = 0.$$

22.1.2 Derive Euler's equation by expanding the integrand of

$$J(\alpha) = \int_{x_1}^{x_2} f\left(y(x,\alpha), y_x(x,\alpha), x\right) dx$$

in powers of α.

Note. The stationary condition is $\partial J(\alpha)/\partial\alpha = 0$, evaluated at $\alpha = 0$. The terms quadratic in α may be useful in establishing the nature of the stationary solution (maximum, minimum, or saddle point).

22.1.3 Find the Euler equation corresponding to Eq. (22.14) if $f = f(y_{xx}, y_x, y, x)$, assuming that y and y_x have fixed values at the endpoints of their interval of definition.

$$\text{ANS.} \quad \frac{d^2}{dx^2}\left(\frac{\partial f}{\partial y_{xx}}\right) - \frac{d}{dx}\left(\frac{\partial f}{\partial y_x}\right) + \frac{\partial f}{\partial y} = 0.$$

22.1.4 The integrand $f(y, y_x, x)$ of Eq. (22.2) has the form

$$f(y, y_x, x) = f_1(x, y) + f_2(x, y)y_x.$$

(a) Show that the Euler equation leads to

$$\frac{\partial f_1}{\partial y} - \frac{\partial f_2}{\partial x} = 0.$$

(b) What does this imply for the dependence of the integral J on the choice of path?

22.1.5 Show that the condition that $J = \int f(x, y)\,dx$ has a stationary value

(a) leads to $f(x, y)$ independent of y and

(b) yields no information about any x-dependence.

We get no (continuous, differentiable) solution. To be a meaningful variational problem, dependence on y or higher derivatives is essential.

Note. The situation will change when constraints are introduced (compare to Exercise 22.4.6).

22.1.6 A soap film stretched between two rings of unit radius centered at $\pm x_0$ will have its closest approach to the x-axis at $x = 0$, with the distance from the axis given by c_1, with x_0 and c_1 related by Eq. (22.26) or Eq. (22.29).

(a) Show that dc_1/dx_0 becomes infinite when $x_0 \sinh(x_0/c_1) = 1$, indicating that the soap film becomes unstable if x_0 is increased beyond the value satisfying this condition.

(b) Show that the condition of part (a) is equivalent to

$$\frac{x_0}{c_1} = \coth\left(\frac{x_0}{c_1}\right).$$

(c) Solve the transcendental equation of part (b) to obtain the critical value of x_0/c_1 and show that the separate values of x_0 and c_1 are then approximately $x_0 \approx 0.6627$ and $c_1 \approx 0.5524$.

22.1.7 A soap film is stretched across the space between two rings of unit radius centered at $\pm x_0$ on the x-axis and perpendicular to the x-axis. Using the solution developed in Example 22.1.3, set up the transcendental equations for the condition that x_0 is such that the area of the curved surface of rotation equals the area of the two rings (Goldschmidt discontinuous solution). Solve for x_0.

22.1.8 In Example 22.1.1, expand $J[y(x, \alpha)] - J[y(x, 0)]$ in powers of α. The term linear in α leads to the Euler equation and to the straight-line solution, Eq. (22.16). Investigate the α^2 term and show that the stationary value of J, the straight-line distance, is a **minimum**.

22.1.9 (a) Show that the integral

$$J = \int_{x_1}^{x_2} f(y, y_x, x)\, dx, \quad \text{with} \quad f = y(x),$$

has **no** extreme values.

(b) If $f(y, y_x, x) = y^2(x)$, find a discontinuous solution similar to the Goldschmidt solution for the soap-film problem.

22.1.10 Fermat's principle of optics states that a light ray in a medium for which n is the (position-dependent) index of refraction will follow the path $y(x)$ for which

$$\int_{x_1, y_1}^{x_2, y_2} n(y, x)\, ds$$

is a minimum. For $y_2 = y_1 = 1$, $-x_1 = x_2 = 1$, find the ray path if

(a) $n = e^y$,   (b) $n = a(y - y_0)$, $y > y_0$.

22.1.11 A particle moves, starting at rest, from point A on the surface of the Earth to point B (also on the surface) by sliding frictionlessly through a tunnel. Find the differential equation satisfied by the path if the transit time is to be a minimum. Assume the Earth to be a nonrotating sphere of uniform density.

Hint. The potential energy of a particle of mass m a distance $r < R$ from the center of the Earth, with R the Earth's radius, is $\frac{1}{2}mg(R^2 - r^2)/R$, where g is the gravitational acceleration at the Earth's surface. It is convenient to describe the path of the particle (in the plane through A, B, and the center of the Earth) by plane polar coordinates (r, θ), with A at $(R, -\varphi)$ and B at (R, φ).

ANS.   Letting r_0 be the minimum value of r (reached at $\theta = 0$),

$$\text{Eq. (22.21) yields } r_\theta^2 = \frac{r^2 R^2 (r^2 - r_0^2)}{r_0^2 (R^2 - r^2)} \text{ (the constant in}$$

that equation has the value such that $r_\theta = 0$ at $\theta = 0$).

The solution for the path is a hypocycloid, generated by a circle of radius $\frac{1}{2}(R - r_0)$ rolling inside the circle of radius R. You might like to show that the transit time is

$$t = \pi \frac{(R^2 - r_0^2)^{1/2}}{(Rg)^{1/2}}.$$

For details see P. W. Cooper, *Am. J. Phys.* **34**: 68 (1966); G. Veneziano, *et al.,* **34**: 701 (1966).

22.1.12   A ray of light follows a straight-line path in a first homogeneous medium, is refracted at an interface, and then follows a new straight-line path in the second medium. See Fig. 22.7. Use Fermat's principle of optics to derive Snell's law of refraction:

$$n_1 \sin\theta_1 = n_2 \sin\theta_2.$$

Hint. Keep the points (x_1, y_1) and (x_2, y_2) fixed and vary x_0 to satisfy Fermat's principle.

Note. This is **not** an Euler equation problem, because the light path is not differentiable at x_0.

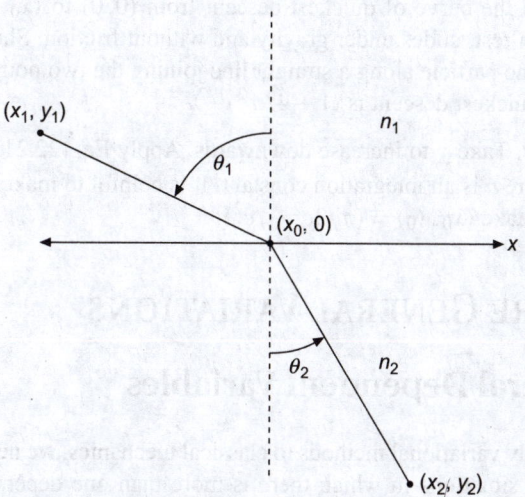

FIGURE 22.7   Snell's law.

22.1.13   A second soap-film configuration for the unit-radius rings at $x = \pm x_0$ consists of a circular disk, radius a, in the $x = 0$ plane and two catenoids of revolution, one joining the disk and each ring. One catenoid may be described by

$$y = c_1 \cosh\left(\frac{x}{c_1} + c_3\right).$$

(a)   Impose boundary conditions at $x = 0$ and $x = x_0$.

(b)   Although not necessary, it is convenient to require that the catenoids form an angle of $120°$ where they join the central disk. Express this third boundary condition in mathematical terms.

(c)   Show that the total area of catenoids plus central disk is then

$$A = c_1^2\left[\sinh\left(\frac{2x_0}{c_1} + 2c_3\right) + \frac{2x_0}{c_1}\right].$$

Note. Although this soap-film configuration is physically realizable and stable, the area is larger than that of the simple catenoid for all ring separations for which both films exist.

$$ANS. \quad (a) \begin{cases} 1 = c_1 \cosh\left(\dfrac{x_0}{c_1} + c_3\right) \\ a = c_1 \cosh c_3 \end{cases} \quad (b)\ \frac{dy}{dx} = \tan 30° = \sinh c_3.$$

22.1.14   For the soap film described in Exercise 22.1.13, find (numerically) the maximum value of x_0.

Note. This calls for a calculator with hyperbolic functions or a table of hyperbolic cotangents.

$$ANS. \quad x_{0\,\text{max}} = 0.4078.$$

22.1.15   Find the curve of quickest descent from $(0, 0)$ to (x_0, y_0) for a particle that, starting from rest, slides under gravity and without friction. Show that the ratio of times taken by the particle along a straight line joining the two points compared to along the curve of quickest descent is $(1 + 4/\pi^2)^{1/2}$.

Hint. Take y to increase downwards. Apply Eq. (22.21) to obtain $y_x^2 = (1 - c^2 y)/c^2 y$, where c is an integration constant. It is helpful to make the substitution $c^2 y = \sin^2 \varphi/2$ and take $(x_0, y_0) = (\pi/2c^2, 1/c^2)$.

22.2   MORE GENERAL VARIATIONS

Several Dependent Variables

To apply variational methods to classical mechanics, we need to generalize the Euler equation to situations in which there is more than one dependent variable in roles like y in

Eq. (22.2). The generalization corresponds to functionals J of the form

$$J = \int_{x_1}^{x_2} f\Big(u_1(x), u_2(x), \ldots, u_n(x), u_{1x}(x), u_{2x}(x), \ldots, u_{nx}(x), x\Big) dx. \qquad (22.31)$$

We are now calling the dependent variables u_i to be consistent with notations we will shortly introduce, and as before we use the subscript x to denote differentiation with respect to x, so that $u_{ix} = du_i/dx$ and (later) $\eta_{ix} = d\eta_i/dx$. As in Section 22.1, we determine stationary values of J by comparing neighboring paths for each u_i. Let

$$u_i(x, \alpha) = u_i(x, 0) + \alpha \eta_i(x), \qquad i = 1, 2, \ldots, n, \qquad (22.32)$$

with the η_i independent of one other but subject to the continuity and endpoint restrictions discussed in Section 22.1. By differentiating J from Eq. (22.31) with respect to α and setting $\alpha = 0$ (the condition that J be stationary), we obtain

$$\int_{x_1}^{x_2} \sum_i \left(\frac{\partial f}{\partial u_i} \eta_i + \frac{\partial f}{\partial u_{ix}} \eta_{ix} \right) dx = 0. \qquad (22.33)$$

Again, each of the terms $(\partial f/\partial u_{ix})\eta_{ix}$ is integrated by parts. The integrated part vanishes and Eq. (22.33) becomes

$$\int_{x_1}^{x_2} \sum_i \left(\frac{\partial f}{\partial u_i} - \frac{d}{dx} \frac{\partial f}{\partial u_{ix}} \right) \eta_i \, dx = 0. \qquad (22.34)$$

Since the η_i are arbitrary and **independent** of one another,[6] each of the terms in the sum must vanish **independently**. We have

$$\frac{\partial f}{\partial u_i} - \frac{d}{dx} \frac{\partial f}{\partial u_{ix}} = 0, \quad i = 1, 2, \ldots, n, \qquad (22.35)$$

a whole set of Euler equations, each of which must be satisfied for a stationary value of J.

Hamilton's Principle

The most important application of Eq. (22.31) occurs when the integrand f is taken to be a Lagrangian L. The Langrangian (for nonrelativistic systems; see Exercise 22.2.5 for a relativistic particle) is defined as the **difference** of kinetic and potential energies of a system:

$$L \equiv T - V. \qquad (22.36)$$

Using time as an independent variable instead of x and $x_i(t)$ as the dependent variables, our conversion of Eq. (22.31) involves the replacements

$$x \to t, \qquad y_i \to x_i(t), \qquad y_{ix} \to \dot{x}_i(t);$$

---

[6]For example, we could set $\eta_2 = \eta_3 = \eta_4 \cdots = 0$, eliminating all but one term of the sum, and then treat η_1 exactly as in Section 22.1.

$x_i(t)$ is the position and $\dot{x}_i = dx_i/dt$ is the velocity of particle i as a function of time. The equation $\delta J = 0$ is then a mathematical statement of Hamilton's principle of classical mechanics,

$$\delta \int_{t_1}^{t_2} L(x_1, x_2, \ldots, x_n, \dot{x}_1, \dot{x}_2, \ldots, \dot{x}_n; t)\, dt = 0. \tag{22.37}$$

In words, Hamilton's principle asserts that the motion of the system from time t_1 to t_2 is such that the time integral of the Lagrangian L, or action, has a stationary value. The resulting Euler equations are usually called the **Lagrangian equations of motion**,

$$\frac{d}{dt} \frac{\partial L}{\partial \dot{x}_i} - \frac{\partial L}{\partial x_i} = 0 \qquad (\text{each } i). \tag{22.38}$$

These Lagrangian equations can be derived from Newton's equations of motion, and Newton's equations can be derived from Lagrange's. The two sets of equations are equally "fundamental."

The Lagrangian formulation has advantages over the conventional Newtonian laws. Whereas Newton's equations are vector equations, we see that Lagrange's equations involve only scalar quantities. The coordinates $x_1, x_2, \ldots$ need not be a standard set of coordinates or lengths. They can be selected to match the conditions of the physical problem. The Lagrange equations are invariant with respect to the choice of coordinate system. Newton's equations (in component form) are not manifestly invariant. For example, Exercise 3.10.27 shows what happens when $\mathbf{F} = m\mathbf{a}$ is resolved in spherical polar coordinates.

Exploiting the concept of energy, we may easily extend the Lagrangian formulation from mechanics to diverse fields, such as electrical networks and acoustical systems. Extensions to electromagnetism appear in the exercises. The result is a unification of otherwise separate areas of physics. In the development of new areas, the quantization of Lagrangian particle mechanics provided a model for the quantization of electromagnetic fields and led to the gauge theory of quantum electrodynamics.

One of the most valuable advantages of Hamilton's principle (the Lagrange equation formulation) is the ease in seeing a relation between a symmetry and a conservation law. As an example, let $x_i = \varphi$, an azimuthal angle. If our Lagrangian is independent of φ (that is, φ is said to be an **ignorable coordinate**), there are two consequences: (1) the conservation or invariance of the component of angular momentum associated with (**conjugate to**) φ, and (2) from Eq. (22.38), $\partial L/\partial \dot{\varphi} = \text{constant}$. Similarly, invariance under translation leads to conservation of linear momentum.

Example 22.2.1   MOVING PARTICLE, CARTESIAN COORDINATES

A particle of mass m moves in one dimension with its position described by a Cartesian coordinate x, subject to a potential $V(x)$. Its kinetic energy is given by $T = m\dot{x}^2/2$, so its Lagrangian L has the form

$$L = T - V = \frac{1}{2}m\dot{x}^2 - V(x).$$

We will need

$$\frac{\partial L}{\partial \dot{x}} = m\dot{x}, \qquad \frac{\partial L}{\partial x} = -\frac{dV(x)}{dx} = F(x). \tag{22.39}$$

We have identified the force F as the negative gradient of the potential. Inserting the results from Eq. (22.39) into the Lagrangian equation of motion, Eq. (22.38), we get

$$\frac{d}{dt}(m\dot{x}) - F(x) = 0,$$

which is Newton's second law of motion. ■

Example 22.2.2   MOVING PARTICLE, CIRCULAR CYLINDRICAL COORDINATES

Now let us consider a particle of mass m moving in the xy-plane, that is, $z = 0$. We use cylindrical coordinates ρ, φ. The kinetic energy is

$$T = \frac{1}{2}m(\dot{x}^2 + \dot{y}^2) = \frac{1}{2}m(\dot{\rho}^2 + \rho^2\dot{\varphi}^2), \tag{22.40}$$

and we take $V = 0$ for simplicity.

We could have converted $\dot{x}^2 + \dot{y}^2$ into circular cylindrical coordinates by taking $x(\rho, \varphi) = \rho \cos \varphi$, $y(\rho, \varphi) = \rho \sin \varphi$, and then differentiating with respect to time and squaring. What we actually did was to recognize that the cylindrical coordinates are an orthogonal system with scale factors $h_\rho = 1$, $h_\varphi = \rho$, so the velocity v has in the cylindrical system components $v_\rho = \dot{\rho}$ and $v_\varphi = \rho\dot{\varphi}$.

We now apply the Lagrangian equations of motion first to the ρ coordinate and then to φ:

$$\frac{d}{dt}(m\dot{\rho}) - m\rho\dot{\varphi}^2 = 0, \qquad \frac{d}{dt}(m\rho^2\dot{\varphi}) = 0.$$

The second equation is a statement of conservation of angular momentum. The first may be interpreted as radial acceleration[7] equated to centrifugal force. In this sense the centrifugal force is a real force. It is of some interest that this interpretation of centrifugal force as a real force is supported by the general theory of relativity. ■

Hamilton's Equations

Hamilton was the first to show that Euler's equation for the Lagrangian enabled the equations of motion to be reduced to the set of coupled first-order PDEs called **Hamilton's equations**. A starting point for this analysis is the definition of the **canonical momentum** p_i conjugate to the coordinate q_i, defined as

$$p_i = \frac{\partial L}{\partial \dot{q}_i}. \tag{22.41}$$

---

[7]Here is a second method of attacking Exercise 3.10.13.

This definition is consistent with the elementary definition of momentum in Cartesian coordinates, where (in one dimension) $T = m\dot{q}^2/2$, $p = m\dot{q}$. From Eq. (22.41) and the Lagrangian equations of motion, Eq. (22.38), we have by direct substitution

$$\dot{p}_i = \frac{\partial L}{\partial q_i}, \tag{22.42}$$

and this permits us to write the variation of L in the form

$$dL = \sum_i \left(\frac{\partial L}{\partial q_i} dq_i + \frac{\partial L}{\partial \dot{q}_i} d\dot{q}_i \right) + \frac{\partial L}{\partial t} dt = \sum_i (\dot{p}_i \, dq_i + p_i \, d\dot{q}_i) + \frac{\partial L}{\partial t} dt. \tag{22.43}$$

We now define the **Hamiltonian** as

$$H = \sum_i p_i \dot{q}_i - L, \tag{22.44}$$

and compute

$$dH = \sum_i (p_i d\dot{q}_i + \dot{q}_i dp_i) - \left(\sum_i (\dot{p}_i dq_i + p_i d\dot{q}_i) + \frac{\partial L}{\partial t} dt \right) = \sum_i (\dot{q}_i dp_i - \dot{p}_i dq_i) - \frac{\partial L}{\partial t} dt. \tag{22.45}$$

But from the chain rule for differentiation, we also have

$$dH = \sum_i \left(\frac{\partial H}{\partial p_i} dp_i + \frac{\partial H}{\partial q_i} dq_i \right) + \frac{\partial H}{\partial t} dt. \tag{22.46}$$

Equating the coefficients of dp_i, dq_i, and dt in Eqs. (22.45) and (22.46), we obtain Hamilton's equations:

$$\frac{\partial H}{\partial p_i} = \dot{q}_i, \qquad \frac{\partial H}{\partial q_i} = -\dot{p}_i, \qquad \frac{\partial H}{\partial t} = -\frac{\partial L}{\partial t}. \tag{22.47}$$

In conservative systems, $\partial H/\partial t = 0$, and H has a constant value equal to the total energy of the system.

Several Independent Variables

Sometimes the integrand f in an equation analogous to Eq. (22.2) will contain an unknown function, u, that is a function of several independent variables, $u = u(x, y, z)$. In the three-dimensional case, for example, that equation becomes

$$J = \iiint f\left(u, u_x, u_y, u_z, x, y, z\right) dx \, dy \, dz, \tag{22.48}$$

where $u_x = \partial u/\partial x$, $u_y = \partial u/\partial y$, $u_z = \partial u/\partial z$, and u is assumed to have specified values on the boundary of the region of integration.

Generalizing the analysis of Section 22.1, we represent the variation of u as

$$u(x, y, z, \alpha) = u(x, y, z, 0) + \alpha \eta(x, y, z),$$

where η is arbitrary except that it must vanish on the boundary. Our integral J is now, as in Section 22.1, a function of α, and our variational problem is to make J stationary with respect to α.

Differentiating the integral Eq. (22.48) with respect to the parameter α and then setting $\alpha = 0$, we obtain

$$\frac{\partial J}{\partial \alpha}\bigg|_{\alpha=0} = \iiint \left(\frac{\partial f}{\partial u} \eta + \frac{\partial f}{\partial u_x} \eta_x + \frac{\partial f}{\partial u_y} \eta_y + \frac{\partial f}{\partial u_z} \eta_z \right) dx \, dy \, dz = 0.$$

We continue to use a notation similar to that used previously: η_x is shorthand for $\partial \eta / \partial x$, etc.

Again, we integrate each of the terms $(\partial f / \partial u_i) \eta_i$ by parts. The integrated part vanishes at the boundary (because the deviation η is required to go to zero there) and we get

$$\iiint \left(\frac{\partial f}{\partial u} - \frac{\partial}{\partial x} \frac{\partial f}{\partial u_x} - \frac{\partial}{\partial y} \frac{\partial f}{\partial u_y} - \frac{\partial}{\partial z} \frac{\partial f}{\partial u_z} \right) \eta(x, y, z) \, dx \, dy \, dz = 0. \tag{22.49}$$

We must now digress to clarify the notation in Eq. (22.49). The derivative $\partial/\partial x$ enters that equation as a result of the integration by parts, and it therefore must act on all the x dependence of $\partial f / \partial u_x$, not just on the explicit appearance of x in f. The reader may recall that this derivative was written d/dx when it arose in Section 22.1, but that notation is not entirely appropriate here as the functions involved also depend on y and z.

We conclude our analysis with the now-familiar observation that since the variation $\eta(x, y, z)$ is arbitrary, the term in large parentheses is set equal to zero. This yields the Euler equation for (three) independent variables,

$$\frac{\partial f}{\partial u} - \frac{\partial}{\partial x} \frac{\partial f}{\partial u_x} - \frac{\partial}{\partial y} \frac{\partial f}{\partial u_y} - \frac{\partial}{\partial z} \frac{\partial f}{\partial u_z} = 0. \tag{22.50}$$

Remember that the derivative $\partial/\partial x$ operates on both the explicit and implicit x dependence of $\partial f / \partial u_x$; similar remarks apply to $\partial/\partial y$ and $\partial/\partial z$.

Example 22.2.3 LAPLACE'S EQUATION

A variational problem with several independent variables is provided by electrostatics. An electrostatic field has

$$\text{energy density} = \frac{1}{2} \varepsilon \mathbf{E}^2,$$

where $\mathbf{E}$ is the electric field. In terms of the static potential φ,

$$\text{energy density} = \frac{1}{2} \varepsilon (\nabla \varphi)^2.$$

Now let us impose the requirement that the electrostatic energy (associated with the field) in a given charge-free volume be a minimum subject to specific conditions on φ at the boundary. The assumption that the volume is charge-free makes φ continuous and differentiable throughout the volume, and we therefore have a situation to which an Euler equation applies. We have the volume integral

$$J = \iiint (\nabla \varphi)^2 \, dx \, dy \, dz = \iiint (\varphi_x^2 + \varphi_y^2 + \varphi_z^2) \, dx \, dy \, dz,$$

where φ_x stands for $\partial\varphi/\partial x$. Thus,

$$f(\varphi, \varphi_x, \varphi_y, \varphi_z, x, y, z) = \varphi_x^2 + \varphi_y^2 + \varphi_z^2,$$

so Euler's equation, Eq. (22.50), yields (with u in that equation replaced by φ)

$$-2(\varphi_{xx} + \varphi_{yy} + \varphi_{zz}) = 0,$$

which in the usual vector notation is equivalent to

$$\nabla^2\varphi(x, y, z) = 0.$$

This is Laplace's equation of electrostatics.

Closer investigation shows that this stationary value is indeed a minimum. Thus the demand that the field energy be minimized leads to Laplace's PDE. ∎

Several Dependent and Independent Variables

In some cases our integrand f contains more than one dependent variable and more than one independent variable. Consider

$$f = f\left(p(x, y, z), p_x, p_y, p_z, q(x, y, z), q_x, q_y, q_z, r(x, y, z), r_x, r_y, r_z, x, y, z \right).$$
$$\tag{22.51}$$

We proceed as before with

$$p(x, y, z, \alpha) = p(x, y, z, 0) + \alpha\xi(x, y, z),$$

$$q(x, y, z, \alpha) = q(x, y, z, 0) + \alpha\eta(x, y, z),$$

$$r(x, y, z, \alpha) = r(x, y, z, 0) + \alpha\zeta(x, y, z), \quad \text{and so on.}$$

Keeping in mind that ξ, η, and ζ are independent of one another, as were the η_i in Eq. (22.32), the same differentiation and then integration by parts will lead to

$$\frac{\partial f}{\partial p} - \frac{\partial}{\partial x}\frac{\partial f}{\partial p_x} - \frac{\partial}{\partial y}\frac{\partial f}{\partial p_y} - \frac{\partial}{\partial z}\frac{\partial f}{\partial p_z} = 0, \tag{22.52}$$

with similar equations for functions q and r. Replacing $p, q, r, \ldots$ with y_i and $x, y, z, \ldots$ with x_i, we can put Eq. (22.52) in a more compact form:

$$\frac{\partial f}{\partial y_i} - \sum_j \frac{\partial}{\partial x_j}\left(\frac{\partial f}{\partial y_{ij}}\right) = 0, \quad i = 1, 2, \ldots, \tag{22.53}$$

in which

$$y_{ij} \equiv \frac{\partial y_i}{\partial x_j}.$$

An application of Eq. (22.53) appears in Exercise 22.2.10.

Geodesics

Particularly in general relativity, it is of interest to identify the shortest path between two points in a "curved space," i.e., a space characterized by a metric tensor more general than that of Euclidean or even Minkoswki space. A path that is a "local minimum" (calculated using the relevant metric), meaning that it is shorter than other paths that can be reached from it by small deformations, is referred to as a **geodesic**. This definition causes both the two great-circle paths of Fig. 22.2 to be identified as geodesics, because even the longer path is of minimum length relative to small deformations. In practice, it is usually easy to identify which of several geodesics in fact corresponds to the shortest path.

The calculus of variations is the natural tool for identifying geodesics, and in fact it was used in Example 22.1.1 to verify that a straight line is the geodesic connecting given points in Euclidean space. To extend the analysis to more general metric spaces, we start by relating the distance between two neighboring points, ds, with the changes in their coordinates, $dq^i, i = 1, 2, \ldots$. Note that we distinguish between covariant and contravariant quantities, using superscripts for the latter (coordinate displacements are contravariant; compare with Section 4.3). The distance ds is a scalar, given by

$$ds^2 = g_{ij}\, dq^i\, dq^j. \tag{22.54}$$

Here g_{ij} is the metric tensor, which is symmetric but in many cases of interest not diagonal. Note that we are using the Einstein summation convention, so i and j in Eq. (22.54) are summed, causing ds^2 to be a scalar. This formula is an obvious generalization of that for Euclidean space,

$$ds^2 = dx^2 + dy^2 + dz^2,$$

but differs therefrom in that the coordinates q_i are not assumed to be mutually orthogonal, so ds^2 contains cross terms $dq^i dq^j$ with $i \neq j$.

A path in our curved space can be described parametrically by giving the q_i as functions of an independent variable that we will call u, and the distance between two points A and B can then be represented as

$$J = \int\limits_A^B \frac{ds}{du}\, du = \int\limits_A^B \frac{\sqrt{g_{ij}\, dq^i\, dq^j}}{du}\, du = \int\limits_A^B \sqrt{g_{ij} \frac{dq^i}{du} \frac{dq^j}{du}}\, du$$

$$= \int\limits_A^B \sqrt{g_{ij}\, \dot{q}^i\, \dot{q}^j}\, du, \tag{22.55}$$

where we are borrowing the dot notation, $\dot{q}^i \equiv dq^i/du$.

One could now proceed to find the $q^i(u)$ that minimize J, but this is a relatively difficult problem. Instead we rely on the Lagrangian formulation of relativistic mechanics, where, for a particle not subject to a potential (other than a gravitational force whose effect is described by the metric), the Lagrangian reduces to

$$L = \frac{m}{2} g_{ij}\, \dot{q}^i\, \dot{q}^j. \tag{22.56}$$

Here the dot notation refers to derivatives with respect to the proper time τ (or to any other variable related thereto by an **affine transformation** (meaning the new variable, e.g., u, is related to τ by a transformation of the form $u = a\tau + b$). This means that we can replace the minimization of J by that of the **action**:

$$\delta \int_A^B g_{ij} \dot{q}^i \dot{q}^j \, du = 0, \tag{22.57}$$

in effect simplifying our problem by eliminating the radical that was present in Eq. (22.55).

The minimization in Eq. (22.57) is a relatively simple standard problem in the calculus of variations; for solving it we note that each g_{ij} is in general a function of all the q^k (but not the derivatives $\dot{q}^k$). There will be an Euler equation for each k; before simplification they take the form

$$\frac{\partial g_{ij} \dot{q}^i \dot{q}^j}{\partial q^k} - \frac{d}{du} \frac{\partial g_{ij} \dot{q}^i \dot{q}^j}{\partial \dot{q}^k} = 0. \tag{22.58}$$

Starting to evaluate Eq. (22.58), we get

$$\frac{\partial g_{ij}}{\partial q^k} \dot{q}^i \dot{q}^j - \frac{d}{du} g_{ij} \frac{\partial}{\partial \dot{q}^k} \left(\dot{q}^i \dot{q}^j \right) = \frac{\partial g_{ij}}{\partial q^k} \dot{q}^i \dot{q}^j - \frac{d}{du} \left(g_{kj} \dot{q}^j + g_{ik} \dot{q}^i \right) = 0. \tag{22.59}$$

Some simplification is achieved by using the relations

$$\frac{d\dot{q}^j}{du} = \ddot{q}^j \quad \text{and} \quad \frac{dg_{kj}}{du} = \frac{\partial g_{kj}}{\partial q^i} \dot{q}^i$$

(remember that the Einstein summation convention is still in use). Equation (22.59) reduces to

$$\frac{1}{2} \dot{q}^i \dot{q}^j \left[\frac{\partial g_{ij}}{\partial q^k} - \frac{\partial g_{kj}}{\partial q^i} - \frac{\partial g_{ik}}{\partial q^j} \right] - g_{ik} \ddot{q}^i = 0. \tag{22.60}$$

As a final simplification, we multiply Eq. (22.60) by g^{kl} and use the identity $g^{kl} g_{ik} = \delta_i^l$, reaching (in a more expanded notation) the **geodesic equation**

$$\frac{d^2 q^l}{du^2} + \frac{dq^i}{du} \frac{dq^j}{du} \frac{1}{2} g^{kl} \left[\frac{\partial g_{kj}}{\partial q^i} + \frac{\partial g_{ik}}{\partial q^j} - \frac{\partial g_{ij}}{\partial q^k} \right] = 0. \tag{22.61}$$

Comparing with the formula for the Christoffel symbol, Eq. (4.63), we can rewrite Eq. (22.61) as

$$\frac{d^2 q^l}{du^2} + \frac{dq^i}{du} \frac{dq^j}{du} \Gamma^l_{ij} = 0. \tag{22.62}$$

Note that although Eq. (22.62) gives the differential equation describing geodesics in curved space, it is a long way from that equation to its explicit solution for significant problems in general relativity. The exploration of such solutions is a topic of current research and beyond the scope of the present text.

Relation to Physics

The calculus of variations as developed so far provides an elegant description of a wide variety of physical phenomena. The physics includes classical mechanics, as in Examples 22.2.1 and 22.2.2; relativistic mechanics, Exercise 22.2.5; electrostatics, Example 22.2.3; and electromagnetic theory in Exercise 22.2.10. The convenience should not be minimized, but at the same time we should be aware that in these cases the calculus of variations has only provided an alternate description of what was already known. The situation does change with incomplete theories.

> *If the basic physics is not yet known, a postulated variational principle can be a useful starting point.*

Exercises

22.2.1   (a)   Develop the equations of motion corresponding to $L = \frac{1}{2}m(\dot{x}^2 + \dot{y}^2)$.

(b)   In what sense do your solutions minimize the integral $\int_{t_1}^{t_2} L\, dt$?
Compare the result for your solution with $x = $ constant, $y = $ constant.

22.2.2   From the Lagrangian equations of motion, Eq. (22.38), show that a system in stable equilibrium has a minimum potential energy.

22.2.3   Write out the Lagrangian equations of motion of a particle in spherical coordinates for potential V equal to a constant. Identify the terms corresponding to (a) centrifugal force and (b) Coriolis force.

22.2.4   The spherical pendulum consists of a mass on a wire of length l, free to move in polar angle θ and azimuth angle φ (Fig. 22.8).

(a)   Set up the Lagrangian for this physical system.

(b)   Develop the Lagrangian equations of motion.

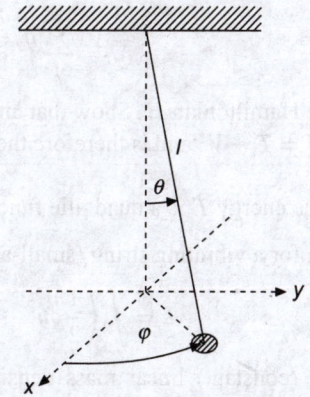

FIGURE 22.8   Spherical pendulum.

22.2.5   Show that the Lagrangian

$$L = m_0 c^2 \left(1 - \sqrt{1 - \frac{v^2}{c^2}} \right) - V(\mathbf{r})$$

leads to a relativistic form of Newton's second law of motion,

$$\frac{d}{dt} \left(\frac{m_0 v_i}{\sqrt{1 - v^2/c^2}} \right) = F_i,$$

in which the force components are $F_i = -\partial V / \partial x_i$.

22.2.6   The Lagrangian for a particle with charge q in an electromagnetic field described by scalar potential φ and vector potential $\mathbf{A}$ is

$$L = \frac{1}{2} m v^2 - q\varphi + q\mathbf{A} \cdot \mathbf{v}.$$

Find the equation of motion of the charged particle.

Hint. $(d/dt)A_j = \partial A_j / \partial t + \sum_i (\partial A_j / \partial x_i) \dot{x}_i$. The dependence of the force fields $\mathbf{E}$ and $\mathbf{B}$ on the potentials φ and $\mathbf{A}$ is developed in Section 3.9; see in particular Eq. (3.108).

ANS. $m\ddot{x}_i = q[\mathbf{E} + \mathbf{v} \times \mathbf{B}]_i$.

22.2.7   Consider a system in which the Lagrangian is given by

$$L(q_i, \dot{q}_i) = T(q_i, \dot{q}_i) - V(q_i),$$

where q_i and $\dot{q}_i$ represent sets of variables. The potential energy V is independent of velocity and neither T nor V has any explicit time dependence.

(a)   Show that

$$\frac{d}{dt} \left(\sum_j \dot{q}_j \frac{\partial L}{\partial \dot{q}_j} - L \right) = 0.$$

(b)   The constant quantity

$$\sum_j \dot{q}_j \frac{\partial L}{\partial \dot{q}_j} - L$$

defines the Hamiltonian H. Show that under the preceding assumed conditions, H satisfies $H = T + V$, and is therefore the total energy.

Note. The kinetic energy T is a quadratic function of the $\dot{q}_i$.

22.2.8   The Lagrangian for a vibrating string (small-amplitude vibrations) is

$$L = \int \left(\frac{1}{2} \rho u_t^2 - \frac{1}{2} \tau u_x^2 \right) dx,$$

where ρ is the (constant) linear mass density and τ is the (constant) tension. The x-integration is over the length of the string. Show that application of Hamilton's principle to the Lagrangian density (the integrand), now with two independent variables, leads to the classical wave equation,

$$\frac{\partial^2 u}{\partial x^2} = \frac{\rho}{\tau} \frac{\partial^2 u}{\partial t^2}.$$

22.2.9 Show that the stationary value of the total energy of the electrostatic field of Example 22.2.3 is a **minimum**.

Hint. Investigate the α^2 terms of J.

22.2.10 The Lagrangian (per unit volume) of an electromagnetic field with a charge density ρ and current density $\mathbf{J}$ is given by

$$L = \frac{1}{2}\left(\varepsilon_0 \mathbf{E}^2 - \frac{1}{\mu_0}\mathbf{B}^2\right) - \rho\varphi + \mathbf{J}\cdot\mathbf{A}.$$

Show that Lagrange's equations lead to two of Maxwell's equations. (The remaining two are a consequence of the definition of $\mathbf{E}$ and $\mathbf{B}$ in terms of $\mathbf{A}$ and φ.)

Hint. Take φ and the components of $\mathbf{A}$ as **dependent** variables; and x, y, z, and t as **independent** variables. $\mathbf{E}$ and $\mathbf{B}$ are given in terms of $\mathbf{A}$ and φ by Eq. (3.108).

22.3 Constrained Minima/Maxima

In preparation for dealing with problems in the calculus of variations in which an integral is to be minimized subject to constraints (which may either be algebraic equations or fixed values of other integrals), we look now at situations in which we seek a constrained extremum of an ordinary function.

A typical constrained problem of the type now under consideration is the minimization of a function of several variables, here illustrated as $f(x, y, z)$, subject to the constraint that $g(x, y, z)$ be kept constant. Since the equation $g(x, y, z) = C$ defines a surface, our constrained problem is that of minimizing $f(x, y, z)$ on a surface of constant g. The presence of the constraint means that only two of the three variables x, y, z are actually independent, and in principle one could solve the constraint equation to obtain z as a function of x and y: $z = z(x, y)$, after which one could obtain the desired minimum by setting to zero the derivatives

$$\frac{\partial}{\partial x} f\left(x, y, z(x, y)\right) \quad \text{and} \quad \frac{\partial}{\partial y} f\left(x, y, z(x, y)\right).$$

However, it may be cumbersome, or in some cases nearly impossible to solve the constraint equation, and in any case this approach does not treat the variables x, y, z on an explicitly equivalent basis. For these reasons it is useful to employ an alternate procedure, known as the method of **Lagrangian multipliers**.

Lagrangian Multipliers

Continuing with our three-dimensional illustration in which we seek to minimize $f(x, y, z)$ subject to the constraint $g(x, y, z) = C$, our starting point is that the constraint equation implies

$$dg = \left(\frac{\partial g}{\partial x}\right)_{yz} dx + \left(\frac{\partial g}{\partial y}\right)_{xz} dy + \left(\frac{\partial g}{\partial z}\right)_{xy} dz = 0,$$

where (as indicated here explicitly) the partial derivatives of g are taken viewing x, y, and z as independent. Proceeding as for the derivation of Eq. (1.144), we have

$$\left(\frac{\partial z}{\partial x}\right)_y = -\frac{\left(\frac{\partial g}{\partial x}\right)_{yz}}{\left(\frac{\partial g}{\partial z}\right)_{xy}} \quad \text{and} \quad \left(\frac{\partial z}{\partial y}\right)_x = -\frac{\left(\frac{\partial g}{\partial y}\right)_{xz}}{\left(\frac{\partial g}{\partial z}\right)_{xy}}. \tag{22.63}$$

Now setting $(\partial f/\partial x)_y$ to zero, we have (imposing the constraint $dg = 0$)

$$\left(\frac{\partial f}{\partial x}\right)_y = \left(\frac{\partial f}{\partial x}\right)_{yz} + \left(\frac{\partial f}{\partial z}\right)_{xy} \left(\frac{\partial z}{\partial x}\right)_y = \left(\frac{\partial f}{\partial x}\right)_{yz} - \frac{\left(\frac{\partial f}{\partial z}\right)_{xy}}{\left(\frac{\partial g}{\partial z}\right)_{xy}} \left(\frac{\partial g}{\partial x}\right)_{yz}$$

$$= \left(\frac{\partial f}{\partial x}\right)_{yz} - \lambda \left(\frac{\partial g}{\partial x}\right)_{yz} = 0, \tag{22.64}$$

where

$$\lambda = \frac{\left(\frac{\partial f}{\partial z}\right)_{xy}}{\left(\frac{\partial g}{\partial z}\right)_{xy}}. \tag{22.65}$$

The quantity λ is called a **Lagrangian multiplier**.

Now taking Eq. (22.64), its equivalent with y replacing x, and a rearranged form of Eq. (22.65), we have the symmetrical set of formulas

$$\left(\frac{\partial f}{\partial x}\right)_{yz} - \lambda \left(\frac{\partial g}{\partial x}\right)_{yz} = 0,$$

$$\left(\frac{\partial f}{\partial y}\right)_{xz} - \lambda \left(\frac{\partial g}{\partial y}\right)_{xz} = 0, \tag{22.66}$$

$$\left(\frac{\partial f}{\partial z}\right)_{xy} - \lambda \left(\frac{\partial g}{\partial z}\right)_{xy} = 0.$$

The generalization of Eqs. (22.66) to n variables and k constraints is

$$\frac{\partial f}{\partial x_i} - \sum_{j=1}^{k} \lambda_j \frac{\partial g_j}{\partial x_i} = 0, \quad i = 1, 2, \ldots, n. \tag{22.67}$$

The n equations, Eqs. (22.67), contain $n + k$ unknowns (the n x_i and the k λ_j), and they are to be solved subject also to the k constraint equations. In some problems it is never necessary to evaluate explicitly the Lagrangian multipliers, and for this reason the method is sometimes referred to as that of **(Lagrange's) undetermined multiplier(s)**.

Note that the formulation provided above does not only identify minima; the same equations will locate maxima and saddle points. It is necessary to determine the nature of the stationary points from the specific problem at hand.

While the derivation of Eq. (22.66) was asymmetric in that λ was obtained considering z to be a dependent variable, we could have carried out the analysis with x or y in place of z. This gives us an alternate route to the final formulas in the special case that $(\partial g/\partial z)$ vanishes, in which case Eq. (22.65) becomes undefined. The method only fails if all the derivatives of a constraint function vanish at the stationary point.

Example 22.3.1   MINIMIZING SURFACE-TO-VOLUME RATIO

Consider a right circular cylinder of radius r and height h. We wish to find the ratio h/r that will minimize the surface area for a fixed enclosed volume. The relevant formulas are: surface area $S = 2\pi(rh + r^2)$, volume $V = \pi r^2 h$.

Applying Eqs. (22.67) for the case of one constraint and two independent variables, we have

$$\frac{\partial S}{\partial r} - \lambda \frac{\partial V}{\partial r} = 2\pi(h + 2r) - \lambda(2\pi rh) = 0,$$

$$\frac{\partial S}{\partial h} - \lambda \frac{\partial V}{\partial h} = 2\pi r - \lambda \pi r^2 = 0.$$

Eliminating λ from these equations, we find $h/r = 2$. Because we have not also used the constraint equation, we get only the ratio of the two variables h and r (which is the information that is relevant for the present problem). However, if we specify the volume V (i.e., use the constraint equation), we then get individual values of h and r.

We close with two more observations: (1) Our solution obviously provides a *minimum* S/V ratio, but in principle this has to be determined by closer study of the problem. In the present case, there is no maximum, as S/V increases without limit as h/r approaches zero. (2) We note that minimizing S for fixed V is the same thing as maximizing V for fixed S, and leads to equivalent Lagrangian multiplier equations.   ∎

Exercises

22.3.0   The following problems are to be solved by using Lagrangian multipliers.

22.3.1   The ground-state energy of a quantum particle of mass m in a pillbox (right-circular cylinder) is given by

$$E = \frac{\hbar^2}{2m}\left(\frac{(2.4048)^2}{R^2} + \frac{\pi^2}{H^2} \right),$$

in which R is the radius and H is the height of the pillbox. Find the ratio of R to H that will minimize the energy for a fixed volume.

22.3.2   The U.S. Post Office limits first-class mail to Canada to a total of 36 inches, length plus girth. Using Lagrange multipliers, find the dimensions of the rectangular parallelepiped of maximum volume subject to this constraint.

22.3.3   A thermal nuclear reactor is subject to the constraint

$$\varphi(a,b,c) = \left(\frac{\pi}{a}\right)^2 + \left(\frac{\pi}{b}\right)^2 + \left(\frac{\pi}{c}\right)^2 = B^2, \quad \text{a constant,}$$

where the reactor is a rectangular parallelepiped of sides a, b, and c. Find the ratios of a, b, and c that maximize the reactor volume.

ANS. $a = b = c$, cube.

22.3.4   For a lens of focal length f, the object distance p and the image distance q are related by $1/p + 1/q = 1/f$. Find the minimum object-image distance $(p + q)$ for fixed f. Assume real object and image (p and q both positive).

22.3.5   You have an ellipse $(x/a)^2 + (y/b)^2 = 1$. Find the inscribed rectangle of maximum area. Show that the ratio of the area of the maximum-area rectangle to the area of the ellipse is $2/\pi = 0.6366$.

22.3.6   A rectangular parallelepiped is inscribed in an ellipsoid of semiaxes a, b, and c. Maximize the volume of the inscribed rectangular parallelepiped. Show that the ratio of the maximum volume to the volume of the ellipsoid is $2/\pi\sqrt{3} \approx 0.367$.

22.3.7   Find the maximum value of the directional derivative of $\varphi(x, y, z)$,

$$\frac{d\varphi}{ds} = \frac{\partial\varphi}{\partial x}\cos\alpha + \frac{\partial\varphi}{\partial y}\cos\beta + \frac{\partial\varphi}{\partial z}\cos\gamma,$$

subject to the constraint,

$$\cos^2\alpha + \cos^2\beta + \cos^2\gamma = 1.$$

22.4 VARIATION WITH CONSTRAINTS

As in earlier sections, we seek the path that will make the integral

$$J = \int f\left(y_i, \frac{\partial y_i}{\partial x_j}, x_j\right) dx_j \tag{22.68}$$

stationary. This is the general case in which x_j represents a set of independent variables and y_i a set of dependent variables. Now, however, we introduce one or more constraints. This means that the y_i are no longer independent of each other. Then, if we vary the y_i by writing $y_i(\alpha) = y_i(0) + \alpha \eta_i$, not all the η_i may then be varied arbitrarily, and the Euler equations would not apply.

Our approach will be to use Lagrange's method of undetermined multipliers. We consider first the possibility that the kth constraint takes the form of an equation:

$$\varphi_k\left(y_i, \frac{\partial y_i}{\partial x_j}, x_j\right) = 0. \tag{22.69}$$

This will ordinarily not be meaningful unless there is more than one dependent or independent variable, so that Eq. (22.69) restricts, but does not fully determine y_i. Remember that y_i and x_j are here used to denote **sets** of variables. To introduce an undetermined multiplier and remain in harmony with our study of the calculus of variations, we note that the constraint, Eq. (22.69), can be stated in the form

$$\int \lambda_k(x_j) \varphi_k\left(y_i, \frac{\partial y_i}{\partial x_j}, x_j\right) dx_j = 0, \tag{22.70}$$

with $\lambda_k(x_j)$ an arbitrary function of the x_j. Equation (22.70) is clearly satisfied if

$$\delta \int \lambda_k(x_j) \varphi_k\left(y_i, \frac{\partial y_i}{\partial x_j}, x_j\right) dx_j = 0. \tag{22.71}$$

Alternatively, we may have a constraint in the form of an integral (now dependent on both the y_i and their derivatives throughout the interval on which the problem is defined):

$$\int \varphi_k\left(y_i, \frac{\partial y_i}{\partial x_j}, x_j\right) dx_j = \text{constant}. \tag{22.72}$$

The effect of this constraint can be brought to a form consistent with Eq. (22.71) by writing

$$\delta \int \lambda_k \varphi_k\left(y_i, \frac{\partial y_i}{\partial x_j}, x_j\right) dx_j = 0. \tag{22.73}$$

Note that in this equation λ_k does not depend on the x_j but is simply a constant, as it is only the integral of φ_k that is required to be stationary.

At this point, our constraints have been written as integrals that are dependent on the undetermined multipliers λ_k, where λ_k means either $\lambda_k(x_j)$ or just λ_k, depending on whether the constraint was from Eq. (22.71) or (22.73). We therefore have our problem in a form suitable for applying the method of Lagrangian multipliers as developed in

Section 22.3, and may use a formula analogous to Eq. (22.67). In our present notation, we obtain

$$\delta \int \left[f\left(y_i, \frac{\partial y_i}{\partial x_j}, x_j \right) + \sum_k \lambda_k \varphi_k \left(y_i, \frac{\partial y_i}{\partial x_j}, x_j \right) \right] dx_j = 0. \tag{22.74}$$

Remember that the Lagrangian multiplier λ_k may depend on the x_j when $\varphi(y_i, x_j)$ is given in the form of Eq. (22.69).

We now continue by treating the entire integrand as a new function whose integral is to be made stationary:

$$g\left(y_i, \frac{\partial y_i}{\partial x_j}, x_j \right) = f + \sum_k \lambda_k \varphi_k. \tag{22.75}$$

If we have N dependent variables y_i $(i = 1, 2, \ldots, N)$ and m constraints $(k = 1, 2, \ldots, m)$, then $N - m$ of the η_i may be taken as arbitrary. In place of arbitrary variation of the m remaining η_i, we may instead set the m multipliers λ_k to the (presently unknown) values that permit the Euler equations to be satisfied. The overall result is that we may require satisfaction of an Euler equation for each of the dependent variables y_i, but the m quantities λ_k that appear in the solution of the Euler equations must be assigned values consistent with the constraints that have been imposed. In other words, it will be necessary to solve simultaneously the Euler equations and the equations of constraint to find the function g (and hence f) yielding a stationary value.

Lagrangian Formulation with Constraints

In the absence of constraints, Lagrange's equations of motion Eq. (17.52) were found to be[8]

$$\frac{d}{dt} \frac{\partial L}{\partial \dot{q}_i} - \frac{\partial L}{\partial q_i} = 0,$$

with t (time) the one independent variable and $q_i(t)$ (the particle positions) a set of dependent variables. Usually the generalized coordinates q_i are chosen to eliminate the forces of constraint, but this is not necessary and not always desirable. In the presence of **holonomic** constraints (those that can be expressed via mathematical expressions, e.g., $\varphi_k = 0$), Hamilton's principle is

$$\delta \int \left[L(q_i, \dot{q}_i, t) + \sum_k \lambda_k(t)\, \varphi_k(q_i, t) \right] dt = 0, \tag{22.76}$$

and the constrained Lagrangian equations of motion are

$$\frac{d}{dt} \frac{\partial L}{\partial \dot{q}_i} - \frac{\partial L}{\partial q_i} = \sum_k a_{ik} \lambda_k. \tag{22.77}$$

---

[8] The symbol q is customary in classical mechanics. It serves to emphasize that the variable is not necessarily a Cartesian variable (and not necessarily a length).

Usually the constraint is of the form $\varphi_k = \varphi_k(q_i, t)$, independent of the generalized velocities $\dot{q}_i$. In this case the coefficient a_{ik} is given by

$$a_{ik} = \frac{\partial \varphi_k}{\partial q_i}. \tag{22.78}$$

Then $a_{ik}\lambda_k$ (no summation) represents the force of the kth constraint in the $\hat{q}_i$-direction, appearing in Eq. (22.77) in exactly the same way as $-\partial V/\partial q_i$.

Example 22.4.1   SIMPLE PENDULUM

To illustrate, consider the simple pendulum, a mass m, constrained by a wire of length l to swing in an arc (Fig. 22.9) under a gravitational force characterized by a constant acceleration g. In the absence of the one constraint,

$$\varphi_1 = r - l = 0, \tag{22.79}$$

there are two generalized coordinates r and θ (assuming the motion to be restricted to a vertical plane). The Lagrangian is

$$L = T - V = \frac{1}{2}m(\dot{r}^2 + r^2\dot{\theta}^2) + mgr\cos\theta, \tag{22.80}$$

taking the potential V to be zero when the pendulum is horizontal, at $\theta = \pi/2$. Noting that

$$a_{r1} = \frac{\partial \varphi_1}{\partial r} = 1, \quad a_{\theta 1} = \frac{\partial \varphi_1}{\partial \theta} = 0,$$

the equations of motion obtained from Eq. (22.77) are

$$\frac{d}{dt}\frac{\partial L}{\partial \dot{r}} - \frac{\partial L}{\partial r} = \lambda_1, \quad \frac{d}{dt}\frac{\partial L}{\partial \dot{\theta}} - \frac{\partial L}{\partial \theta} = 0, \tag{22.81}$$

or

$$\frac{d}{dt}(m\dot{r}) - mr\dot{\theta}^2 - mg\cos\theta = \lambda_1,$$

$$\frac{d}{dt}(mr^2\dot{\theta}) + mgr\sin\theta = 0.$$

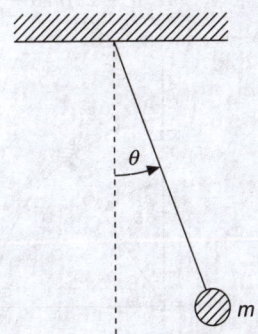

FIGURE 22.9   Simple pendulum.

Substituting from the equation of constraint ($r = l$, $\dot{r} = 0$), these equations become

$$ml\dot{\theta}^2 + mg\cos\theta = -\lambda_1, \qquad ml^2\ddot{\theta} + mgl\sin\theta = 0. \tag{22.82}$$

The second equation may be solved for $\theta(t)$ to yield simple harmonic motion if the amplitude is small ($\sin\theta \approx \theta$), whereas the first equation expresses the tension in the wire in terms of θ and $\dot{\theta}$. Note that since the equation of constraint, Eq. (22.79), is in the form of Eq. (22.69), the Lagrange multiplier λ_1 will be a function of t. Since the second equation suffices to determine $\theta(t)$ (assuming a choice of initial conditions), the left-hand side of the first equation can be evaluated if an explicit form for λ_1 is desired.   ∎

Example 22.4.2   SLIDING OFF A LOG

Another example from mechanics is the problem of a particle sliding on a cylindrical surface, as shown in Fig. 22.10. The object is to find the critical angle θ_c at which the particle flies off from the surface. This critical angle is the angle at which the radial force of constraint goes to zero, and it will depend on the initial velocity with which the particle departs from a position atop the cylinder. To make the problem well-defined, we seek the maximum value that can be attained by θ_c, corresponding to its limit at low initial velocity.

To illustrate the present constrained-minimization method, we take

$$L = T - V = \tfrac{1}{2}m(\dot{r}^2 + r^2\dot{\theta}^2) - mgr\cos\theta \tag{22.83}$$

and the one equation of constraint,

$$\varphi_1 = r - l = 0. \tag{22.84}$$

Proceeding as in Example 22.4.1, with

$$a_{r1} = \frac{\partial\varphi_1}{\partial r} = 1, \qquad a_{\theta 1} = \frac{\partial\varphi_1}{\partial\theta} = 0,$$

we reach

$$m\ddot{r} - mr\dot{\theta}^2 + mg\cos\theta = \lambda_1(\theta),$$

$$mr^2\ddot{\theta} + 2mr\dot{r}\dot{\theta} - mgr\sin\theta = 0.$$

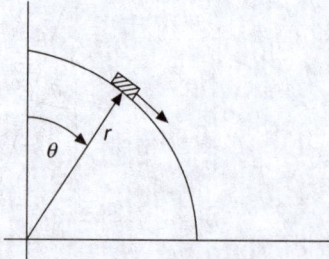

FIGURE 22.10   A particle sliding on a cylindrical surface.

We have chosen to identify the constraining force λ_1 as a function of the angle θ, a valid choice since θ is a single-valued function of the independent variable t.

Inserting the constrained values $r = l$, $\ddot{r} = \dot{r} = 0$, these equations reduce to

$$-ml\dot{\theta}^2 + mg\cos\theta = \lambda_1(\theta), \tag{22.85}$$

$$ml^2\ddot{\theta} - mgl\sin\theta = 0. \tag{22.86}$$

Differentiating Eq. (22.85) with respect to time and remembering that

$$\frac{df(\theta)}{dt} = \frac{df(\theta)}{d\theta}\dot{\theta},$$

we obtain

$$-2ml\ddot{\theta} - mg\sin\theta = \frac{d\lambda_1(\theta)}{d\theta}. \tag{22.87}$$

Combining Eqs. (22.86) and (22.87) to eliminate the $\ddot{\theta}$ term, we have

$$\frac{d\lambda_1}{d\theta} = -3mg\sin\theta,$$

which integrates to

$$\lambda_1(\theta) = 3mg\cos\theta + C. \tag{22.88}$$

To fix the constant C, we evaluate Eq. (22.88) for $\theta = 0$:

$$-ml\dot{\theta}^2\Big|_{\theta=0} + mg = 3mg + C,$$

which shows that $C \le -2mg$, with $C = -2mg$ when the initial velocity $\dot{\theta}(0)$ is zero. Using this value of C (which leads to the largest critical angle), we have

$$\lambda_1(\theta) = mg(3\cos\theta - 2). \tag{22.89}$$

The particle will stay on the surface as long as the force of constraint is nonnegative, that is, as long as the surface has to push outward on the particle, corresponding to $\lambda_1(\theta) > 0$. From Eq. (22.89) we find that the critical angle, at which $\lambda_1(\theta_c) = 0$, satisfies

$$\cos\theta_c = \frac{2}{3}, \quad \text{or} \quad \theta_c = 48°11'$$

from the vertical. At or before this angle (neglecting all friction) our particle takes off.

It must be admitted that this result can be obtained more easily by considering a varying centripetal force furnished by the radial component of the gravitational force. The example was chosen to illustrate the use of Lagrange's undetermined multiplier without confusing the reader with a complicated physical system. ∎

Example 22.4.3   SCHRÖDINGER WAVE EQUATION

As a final illustration of a constrained minimum, let us find the Euler equations for the quantum mechanical problem of a particle of mass m subject to a potential V,

$$\delta J = \int \psi^*(\mathbf{r}) H \psi(\mathbf{r}) d^3r, \tag{22.90}$$

with the constraint that ψ is the normalized wave function of a bound state:

$$\int \psi^*(\mathbf{r}) \psi(\mathbf{r}) d^3r = 1. \tag{22.91}$$

Equation (22.90) is a statement that the energy of the system is stationary, with H its Hamiltonian operator

$$H = -\frac{\hbar^2}{2m} \nabla^2 + V(\mathbf{r}). \tag{22.92}$$

In Eq. (22.90) ψ and ψ^* are dependent variables; since they are in principle complex we can treat each as a separate variable; this point was discussed in Chapter 5, footnote 3.

The integrand in Eq. (17.121) involves **second** derivatives, but it is convenient to convert them to first derivatives using Green's theorem, Eq. (3.86):

$$\int \psi^*(\mathbf{r}) \nabla^2 \psi(\mathbf{r}) d^3r = \int_S \psi^* \nabla \psi \cdot d\boldsymbol{\sigma} - \int \nabla \psi^* \cdot \nabla \psi d^3r.$$

We now observe that the surface terms vanish due to the requirement that ψ be continuous, and our variational principle becomes

$$\delta \int \left[\frac{\hbar^2}{2m} \nabla \psi^* \cdot \nabla \psi + V \psi^* \psi \right] d^3r = 0. \tag{22.93}$$

The function g for our constrained variation is therefore

$$g = \frac{\hbar^2}{2m} \nabla \psi^* \cdot \nabla \psi + V \psi^* \psi - \lambda \psi^* \psi$$

$$= \frac{\hbar^2}{2m} (\psi_x^* \psi_x + \psi_y^* \psi_y + \psi_z^* \psi_z) + V \psi^* \psi - \lambda \psi^* \psi, \tag{22.94}$$

again using the subscript x to denote $\partial/\partial x$. For $y_i = \psi^*$, our Euler equation becomes

$$\frac{\partial g}{\partial \psi^*} - \frac{\partial}{\partial x} \frac{\partial g}{\partial \psi_x^*} - \frac{\partial}{\partial y} \frac{\partial g}{\partial \psi_y^*} - \frac{\partial}{\partial z} \frac{\partial g}{\partial \psi_z^*} = 0.$$

This yields

$$V\psi - \lambda \psi - \frac{\hbar^2}{2m} (\psi_{xx} + \psi_{yy} + \psi_{zz}) = 0,$$

or

$$-\frac{\hbar^2}{2m} \nabla^2 \psi + V \psi = \lambda \psi. \tag{22.95}$$

The Euler equation for $y_i = \psi$ gives the complex conjugate of Eq. (22.95), and therefore provides no further information. Reference to Eq. (22.92) enables us to identify λ physically as the energy of the quantum mechanical system. With this interpretation, Eq. (22.95) is the celebrated Schrödinger wave equation. ∎

Rayleigh-Ritz Technique

A number of physically important problems can be related to variational principles of the general form

$$\delta J = \delta \int_a^b \left(p(x)y_x^2 + q(x)y^2 \right) dx = 0, \tag{22.96}$$

where $y(a)$ and $y(b)$ have fixed values, and the variation is subject to the constraint

$$\int_a^b y^2 w(x) dx = \text{constant.} \tag{22.97}$$

Treating Eqs. (22.96) and (22.97) as a constrained minimization, its Euler equation takes the form

$$\frac{d}{dx}\left(p(x)\frac{dy}{dx} \right) - q(x)y + \lambda wy = 0, \tag{22.98}$$

where λ is a Lagrange multiplier. This situation usually arises in contexts such that $w(x)$ is a nonnegative weight function and $y(a)$ and $y(b)$ satisfy Sturm-Liouville boundary conditions, meaning that

$$p(x)y_x y \Big|_a^b = 0. \tag{22.99}$$

From the above we conclude that although originally introduced as a Lagrange multiplier, λ must also be an eigenvalue of the Sturm-Liouville system described by Eqs. (22.98) and (22.99). This identification was already noted in Example 22.4.3.

Often problems of the type now under discussion are presented as unconstrained minimizations of the form

$$\delta J = \delta \left(\frac{\int_a^b \left(p(x)y_x^2 + q(x)y^2 \right) dx}{\int_a^b y^2 w(x) dx} \right) = 0. \tag{22.100}$$

Equation (22.100) is equivalent to the earlier formulation because $py_x^2 + qy^2$ is homogeneous in y and the denominator normalizes y without otherwise changing its functional form. The J satisfying Eq. (22.100) evaluates to the eigenvalue λ.

In the frequently occurring case that $p(x)$ is actually independent of x, we can manipulate the y_x^2 term in the integrand of J, causing Eqs. (22.96), (22.97), and (22.100) to assume the useful forms,

$$\delta J = \delta \int_a^b \left(- p\, y_{xx} + q(x) y^2 \right) dx = 0, \qquad \text{(constrained minimum)}, \qquad (22.101)$$

$$p \frac{d^2 y}{dx^2} - q(x) y + \lambda w y = 0, \qquad (22.102)$$

$$\delta J = \delta \left(\frac{\int_a^b \left(- p\, y\, y_{xx} + q(x) y^2 \right) dx}{\int_a^b y^2 w(x)\, dx} \right) = 0, \qquad \text{(unconstrained, } J = \lambda). \qquad (22.103)$$

The Rayleigh-Ritz technique uses the direct evaluation of any one of the above forms for $\delta J = 0$ as a means of obtaining solutions to the eigenvalue problem shown as Eq. (22.98) or (22.102). Application of the technique can be as simple as guessing a form for y and evaluating J, but more accurate results are obtained by taking a form for $y(x)$ that contains adjustable parameters, and then varying the parameters to minimize J within the parameter space. The quality of the results obtained obviously depends on whether the actual minimum form for y has been well approximated.

Ground State Eigenfunction

Suppose that we seek to compute the ground-state eigenfunction y_0 and eigenvalue λ_0 of some complicated atomic or nuclear system.[9] A classic example, for which no exact analytical solution has been found, is the helium atom problem. The eigenfunction y_0 is **unknown**, but we shall assume that we can make a pretty good guess at an approximation to it, which we will call y. Although we do not know either y_0 or any other eigenfunctions y_i $(i = 1, 2 \ldots)$, or the corresponding eigenvalues λ_i, we do know, because the eigenfunctions can be chosen to form a complete orthogonal set, that we can write the expansion

$$y = c_0 y_0 + \sum_{i=1}^{\infty} c_i y_i. \qquad (22.104)$$

We shall assume that we picked y sensibly enough that it is not orthogonal to the ground state, so $c_0 \neq 0$. Invoking the orthogonality property, E_y, the expectation value of the

---

[9]This means that λ_0 is the smallest eigenvalue.

energy for wave function y, is

$$E_y = \frac{\langle y|H|y \rangle}{\langle y|y \rangle} = \frac{\displaystyle\sum_{i=0}^{\infty} |c_i|^2 \lambda_i}{\displaystyle\sum_{i=0}^{\infty} |c_i|^2}, \tag{22.105}$$

where H, the operator defining the Schrödinger equation, typically has the form

$$H = -\frac{\hbar^2}{2m} \frac{d^2}{dx^2} + V(x).$$

The Schrödinger equation and its approximate solution E_y are then seen to correspond to Eqs. (22.102) and (22.103). The final member of Eq. (22.105) results from the substitution of Eq. (22.104). This substitution is similar to that carried out in Eq. (6.30), but note that in that equation the function (there called ψ) was assumed normalized. As we already observed in Section 6.4, the expression for E_y is a weighted average of the eigenvalues (with all the weights $|c_i|^2 \geq 0$), so E_y must be at least as large as y_0, and in fact must be larger if y contains any admixture of eigenfunctions whose λ_i are larger than λ_0.

It is useful to scale y so $c_0 = 1$ and rearrange Eq. (22.105) to

$$E_y = \lambda_0 + \frac{\displaystyle\sum_{i=1}^{\infty} c_i^2 \lambda_i}{1 + \displaystyle\sum_{i=1}^{\infty} c_i^2}, \tag{22.106}$$

a form that makes clear that the error in E_y will be quadratic in the c_i, even though the difference between y and y_0 is linear in the c_i.

Our analysis therefore contains two important results.

(1) *Whereas the error in the eigenfunction y was $\mathcal{O}(c_i)$, the error in λ is only $\mathcal{O}(c_i^2)$. Even a poor approximation of the eigenfunctions may yield an accurate calculation of the eigenvalue.*

(2) *If λ_0 is the lowest eigenvalue (ground state), then $E_y > \lambda_0$, so our approximation is always on the high side, but converges to λ_0 as our approximate eigenfunction y improves ($c_i \to 0$).*

In practical problems in quantum mechanics, y often depends on parameters that may be varied to minimize E_y and thereby improve the estimate of the ground-state energy λ_0. This is the "variational method" discussed in quantum mechanics texts. It was illustrated in Example 8.4.1.

Example 22.4.4   QUANTUM OSCILLATOR

The ground state of a quantum-mechanical particle of mass m constrained to the region $0 \leq x < \infty$ and subject also to a potential $V = kx^2/2$ is described (in a unit system with

$\hbar = 1$) by the lowest-eigenvalue eigenstate of the Schrödinger equation,

$$-\frac{1}{2m}\frac{d^2\psi}{dx^2} + \frac{kx^2}{2}\psi = E\psi, \tag{22.107}$$

subject to the boundary conditions $\psi(0) = \psi(\infty) = 0$. A guessed wave function consistent with the boundary conditions is $y(x) = xe^{-\alpha x}$. Let's find the value of α making the approximate eigenvalue a minimum.

Our Schrödinger equation is of the type represented by Eq. (22.102), so we can use Eq. (22.103) and find the unconstrained value of J as given there with $p = 1/2m$, $q = kx^2/2$, $w = 1$, and integration range $(0, \infty)$. Noting that $y_{xx} = \alpha(\alpha x - 2)e^{-\alpha x}$, we have

$$J = \frac{\displaystyle\int_0^\infty \left(-\frac{\alpha x}{2m}(\alpha x - 2) + \frac{kx^4}{2}\right)e^{-2\alpha x}\,dx}{\displaystyle\int_0^\infty x^2 e^{-2\alpha x}\,dx} = \frac{\dfrac{1}{8m\alpha} + \dfrac{3k}{8\alpha^5}}{\dfrac{1}{4\alpha^3}} = \frac{\alpha^2}{2m} + \frac{3k}{2\alpha^2}. \tag{22.108}$$

Differentiating Eq. (22.108) with respect to α^2 and setting the result to zero, we get

$$\frac{1}{2m} - \frac{3k}{2\alpha^4} = 0, \quad \text{or} \quad \alpha = (3mk)^{1/4}.$$

Inserting this α value into the expression for J, Eq. (22.108), we find

$$J = \frac{(3mk)^{1/2}}{2m} + \frac{3k}{2(3mk)^{1/2}} = \sqrt{\frac{3k}{m}} \approx 1.732\sqrt{\frac{k}{m}}. \tag{22.109}$$

This value of J is an upper bound to the ground-state energy, the exact value of which is $1.5\sqrt{k/m}$.

Taking a somewhat more complicated (and flexible) wave function, of the form $y = (x + cx^2)e^{-\alpha x}$, and optimizing both α and c, the approximate energy improves to $1.542\sqrt{k/m}$. The approximate wave functions of this example are compared with the exact wave function in Fig. 22.11. Note that the second approximation yields an eigenvalue that is in error

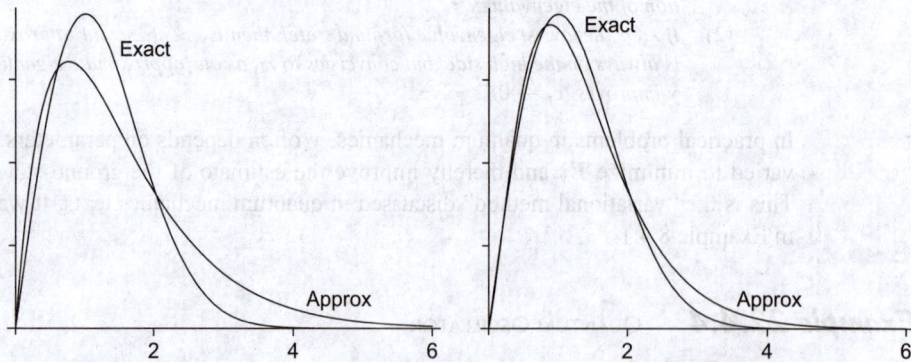

FIGURE 22.11   Exact and approximate ground-state wave functions for quantum oscillator, Example 22.4.4, plotted for $k/m = 1$. Left: Single-term approximation $y = xe^{-\alpha x}$. Right: Two-term approximation $y = (x + cx^2)e^{-\alpha x}$.

by less than 3%, even though the approximate wave function exhibits considerably larger relative errors.   ∎

Example 22.4.5   VARIATION OF LINEAR PARAMETERS

A frequent use of the Rayleigh-Ritz technique is the approximation of an eigenfunction of a Schrödinger equation,

$$H\psi(x) = E\psi(x),$$

as a truncated expansion in a fixed orthonormal set of functions. The advantage of this procedure is that the parameters in the wave function all occur linearly, and the optimization reduces to a matrix eigenvalue problem.

Given an approximate function (often called a **trial function**) of the form

$$y(x) = \sum_{i=1}^{N} c_i \varphi_i(x), \tag{22.110}$$

we seek to minimize

$$J = \langle y|H|y \rangle \quad \text{subject to} \quad \langle y|y \rangle = 1. \tag{22.111}$$

Again we emphasize that the φ_i have no specific relation to the eigenfunction we seek; they are simply members of an orthonormal set that has two desirable features: (1) they are such that a few of them can provide a reasonable representation of the eigenfunction, and (2) they are tractable in the sense that it is convenient to evaluate the matrix elements we are about to define.

Defining a matrix H of elements $H_{ij} = \langle \varphi_i|H|\varphi_j \rangle$ and a column vector $\mathbf{c}$ with components c_i, we can restate Eq. (22.111) as the minimization of

$$J = \mathbf{c}^\dagger H \mathbf{c} \quad \text{subject to} \quad \mathbf{c}^\dagger \mathbf{c} = 1. \tag{22.112}$$

This formulation, in turn, can be reduced using Lagrangian multipliers to the unconstrained matrix eigenvalue problem

$$H\mathbf{c} = \lambda \mathbf{c}, \tag{22.113}$$

which we can solve (using matrix methods) for λ (the approximate value of J). This application of the Rayleigh-Ritz technique is therefore seen to be equivalent to the approximation of an operator equation by a finite matrix equation.   ∎

Exercises

22.4.1   A particle of mass m is on a frictionless horizontal surface. In terms of plane polar coordinates (r, θ), it is constrained to move so that $\theta = \omega t$ (accomplished by pushing it with a rotating radial arm against which it can slide frictionlessly). With the initial conditions

$$t = 0, \quad r = r_0, \quad \dot{r} = 0:$$

(a)   Find the radial position as a function of time.

$$ANS. \quad r(t) = r_0 \cosh \omega t.$$

(b)   Find the force exerted on the particle by the constraint.

$$ANS. \quad F^{(c)} = 2m\dot{r}\omega = 2mr_0\omega^2 \sinh \omega t.$$

22.4.2   A point mass m is moving on a flat, horizontal, frictionless plane. The mass is constrained by a string to move radially inward at a constant rate. Using plane polar coordinates (r, θ), $r = r_0 - kt$:

(a)   Set up the Lagrangian.

(b)   Obtain the constrained Lagrange equations.

(c)   Solve the θ-dependent Lagrange equation to obtain $\omega(t)$, the angular velocity. What is the physical significance of the constant of integration that you get from your "free" integration?

(d)   Using the $\omega(t)$ from part (b), solve the r-dependent (constrained) Lagrange equation to obtain $\lambda(t)$. In other words, explain what is happening to the **force** of constraint as $r \to 0$.

22.4.3   A flexible cable is suspended from two fixed points. The length of the cable is fixed. Find the curve that will minimize the total gravitational potential energy of the cable.

$$ANS. \quad \text{Hyperbolic cosine.}$$

22.4.4   A fixed volume of water is rotating in a cylinder with constant angular velocity ω. Find the curve of the water surface that will minimize the total potential energy of the water in the combined gravitational-centrifugal force field.

$$ANS. \quad \text{Parabola.}$$

22.4.5   (a)   Show that for a fixed-length perimeter the plane figure with maximum area is a circle.

(b)   Show that for a fixed planar area the boundary with minimum perimeter is a circle.

Hint. The radius of curvature R is given by

$$R = \frac{(r^2 + r_\theta^2)^{3/2}}{r r_{\theta\theta} - 2r_\theta^2 - r^2}.$$

Note. The problems of this section, variation subject to constraints, are often called *isoperimetric*. The term arose from problems of maximizing area subject to a fixed perimeter, as in part (a) of this problem.

22.4.6   Show that requiring J, given by

$$J = \int_a^b \int_a^b K(x, t)\varphi(x)\varphi(t)dx\, dt,$$

to have a stationary value subject to the normalizing condition

$$\int_a^b \varphi^2(x)dx = 1$$

leads to a Hilbert-Schmidt integral equation of the form given in Eq. (20.64).

Note. The kernel $K(x,t)$ is symmetric.

22.4.7   An unknown function satisfies the differential equation

$$y'' + \left(\frac{\pi}{2}\right)^2 y = 0$$

and the boundary conditions $y(0) = 1$, $y(1) = 0$.

(a)   Calculate the approximation $\lambda = F[y_{trial}]$ for $y_{trial} = 1 - x^2$.

(b)   Compare with the exact eigenvalue.

ANS.   (a) $\lambda = 2.5$.   (b) $\lambda/\lambda_{exact} = 1.013$.

22.4.8   In Exercise 22.4.7 use a trial function $y = 1 - x^n$.

(a)   Find the value of n that will minimize $F[y_{trial}]$.

(b)   Show that the optimum value of n drives the ratio λ/λ_{exact} down to 1.003.

ANS.   (a) $n = 1.7247$.

22.4.9   A quantum mechanical particle in a sphere (Example 14.7.1) satisfies

$$\nabla^2 \psi + k^2 \psi = 0,$$

with $k^2 = 2mE/\hbar^2$. The boundary condition is that $\psi = 0$ at $r = a$, where a is the radius of the sphere. For the ground state [where $\psi = \psi(r)$], try an approximate wave function,

$$\psi_a(r) = 1 - \left(\frac{r}{a}\right)^2,$$

and calculate an approximate eigenvalue k_a^2.

Hint. To determine $p(r)$ and $w(r)$, put your equation in self-adjoint form (in spherical polar coordinates).

ANS. $k_a^2 = \dfrac{10.5}{a^2}$, $k_{exact}^2 = \dfrac{\pi^2}{a^2}$.

22.4.10   The wave equation for a quantum mechanical oscillator may be written as

$$\frac{d^2\psi(x)}{dx^2} + (\lambda - x^2)\psi(x) = 0,$$

with $\lambda = 1$ for the ground state; see Eq. (18.17). Take

$$\psi_{\text{trial}} = \begin{cases} 1 - \dfrac{x^2}{a^2}, & x^2 \leq a^2 \\ 0, & x^2 > a^2 \end{cases}$$

for the ground-state wave function (with a^2 an adjustable parameter) and calculate the corresponding ground-state energy. How much error do you have?

Note. Your parabola is really not a very good approximation to a Gaussian exponential. What improvements can you suggest?

22.4.11   The Schrödinger equation for a central potential may be written as

$$\mathcal{L}u(r) + \frac{\hbar^2 l(l+1)}{2Mr^2}\, u(r) = Eu(r).$$

The $l(l+1)$ term, the angular momentum barrier, comes from splitting off the angular dependence. Compare Eq. (9.80) (divide that equation through by $-r^2$). Use the Rayleigh-Ritz technique to show that $E > E_0$, where E_0 is the energy eigenvalue of $\mathcal{L}u_0 = E_0 u_0$ corresponding to $l = 0$. This means that the ground state will have $l = 0$, zero angular momentum.

Hint. You can expand $u(r)$ as $u_0(r) + \sum_{i=1}^{\infty} c_i u_i$, where $\mathcal{L}u_i = E_i u_i,\ E_i > E_0$.

Additional Readings

Bliss, G. A., *Calculus of Variations*. The Mathematical Association of America. LaSalle, IL: Open Court Publishing Co. (1925). As one of the older texts, this is still a valuable reference for details of problems such as minimum-area problems.

Courant, R., and H. Robbins, *What Is Mathematics?* 2nd ed. New York: Oxford University Press (1996). Chapter VII contains a fine discussion of the calculus of variations, including soap-film solutions to minimum-area problems.

Ewing, G. M., *Calculus of Variations with Applications*. New York: Norton (1969). Includes a discussion of sufficiency conditions for solutions of variational problems.

Lanczos, C., *The Variational Principles of Mechanics*, 4th ed. Toronto: University of Toronto Press (1970), reprinted, Dover (1986). This book is a very complete treatment of variational principles and their applications to the development of classical mechanics.

Sagan, H., *Boundary and Eigenvalue Problems in Mathematical Physics*. New York: Wiley (1961), reprinted, Dover (1989). This delightful text could also be listed as a reference for Sturm-Liouville theory, Legendre and Bessel functions, and Fourier series. Chapter 1 is an introduction to the calculus of variations, with applications to mechanics. Chapter 7 picks up the calculus of variations again and applies it to eigenvalue problems.

Sagan, H., *Introduction to the Calculus of Variations*. New York: McGraw-Hill (1969), reprinted, Dover (1983). This is an excellent introduction to the modern theory of the calculus of variations, which is more sophisticated and complete than his 1961 text. Sagan covers sufficiency conditions and relates the calculus of variations to problems of space technology.

Weinstock, R., *Calculus of Variations*. New York: McGraw-Hill (1952), New York: Dover (1974). A detailed, systematic development of the calculus of variations and applications to Sturm-Liouville theory and physical problems in elasticity, electrostatics, and quantum mechanics.

Yourgrau, W., and S. Mandelstam, *Variational Principles in Dynamics and Quantum Theory*, 3rd ed. Philadelphia: Saunders (1968), New York: Dover (1979). This is a comprehensive, authoritative treatment of variational principles. The discussions of the historical development and the many metaphysical pitfalls are of particular interest.

CHAPTER 23

PROBABILITY AND STATISTICS

Probabilities arise in many problems dealing with random events or large numbers of particles defining random variables. An event is called **random** if it is practically impossible to predict from the initial state. This includes cases where we have merely incomplete information about initial states and/or the dynamics. For example, in statistical mechanics we deal with systems containing large numbers of particles, but our knowledge is ordinarily limited to a few average or macroscopic quantities such as the total energy, the volume, the pressure, or the temperature. Because the values of these macroscopic variables are consistent with very large numbers of different microscopic configurations of our system, we are prevented from predicting the behavior of individual atoms or molecules. Often the average properties of many similar events are predictable, as in quantum theory. This is why probability theory can be and has been developed.

Random variables are also involved when data depend on chance, such as weather reports and stock prices. The theory of probability describes mathematical models of chance processes in terms of probability distributions of random variables that describe how some "random events" are more likely than others. In this sense, probability is a measure of our ignorance, giving quantitative meaning to qualitative statements, such as "It will probably rain tomorrow" and "I'm unlikely to draw the queen of hearts." Probabilities are of fundamental importance in quantum mechanics and statistical mechanics and are applied in meteorology, economics, games, and many other areas of daily life.

Because experiments in the sciences are always subject to measurement errors, theories of errors and their propagation involve probabilities. **Statistics** is the area of mathematics that connects observations on data samples to inferences about the probable content of the entire population from which the sample(s) came. It is an extensive and sophisticated branch of mathematics, and in the present text only a few of the most basic concepts can be presented. The material found here may be adequate to provide a conceptual basis for statistical mechanics, but can at best be an elementary introduction to the ideas needed to gain maximum information from data-intensive experimental studies such as those arising from the study of cosmic rays or the data from high-energy particle accelerators. A more complete picture of the role of statistics in physics and engineering can be obtained from a number of the texts in the Additional Readings.

23.1   PROBABILITY: DEFINITIONS, SIMPLE PROPERTIES

All possible **mutually exclusive**[1] outcomes of an experiment that is subject to chance represent the events (or points) of a **sample space** S. Suppose we toss a coin, and record that it lands either "heads" or "tails." These are mutually exclusive events, so our sample space for a single coin toss can be deemed to be spanned by a discrete random variable x, with possible values x_i, which (based on our experiment, called a **trial**), will have one of the two values x_1 (for heads) or x_2 (for tails). Now suppose, with the same sample space, we carry out larger numbers of trials. Some will have the result x_1 (heads), others x_2 (tails). It is of interest to define the **probability** of an outcome in our sample space by the ratio

$$P(x_i) \equiv \frac{\text{number of times event } x_i \text{ occurs}}{\text{total number of trials}}, \tag{23.1}$$

where it is assumed that the number of trials is large enough that $P(x_i)$ approaches a constant limiting value. In the event that we are able to enumerate all the possible events that produce outcomes in our sample space and can also assume that each event is equally likely, we may then define the theoretical probability of an outcome x_i as

$$P(x_i) \equiv \frac{\text{number of outcomes } x_i}{\text{total number of all events}}. \tag{23.2}$$

An example of the use of this theoretical probability can be illustrated using coin tosses. For example, suppose that we toss a coin twice and take our random variable x to be the number of heads obtained in a two-toss trial. Our sample S now contains three possible values of x, which we designate x_0, x_1, x_2, where we are now letting x_i stand for the occurrence of i heads in the two tosses. Obviously, the only possible values of x are 0, 1, and 2. But we also know that the four possible results of two successive tosses are (heads, then heads), (heads, then tails), (tails, then heads), (tails, then tails); these possibilities are mutually exclusive and it is reasonable to assume that they are equally likely. Then, using Eq. (23.2), we conclude that the probabilities of x_2 (two heads) and x_0 (no heads) will each be 1/4, while the probability of x_1 (one heads) will be 1/2.

The experimental definition, Eq. (23.1), is the more appropriate when the total number of events is not well defined (or is difficult to obtain) or we cannot identify equally likely outcomes. A large, thoroughly mixed pile of black and white sand grains of the same size and in equal proportions is a relevant example, because it is impractical to count them all. But we can count the grains in a small sample volume that we pick. This way we can check that white and black grains turn up with roughly equal probability 1/2, provided that we put back each sample and mix the pile again. It is found that the larger the sample volume,

---

[1] This means that given that one particular event did occur, the others could not have occurred.

the smaller the spread in probability about $1/2$ will be. Moreover, the more trials we run, the closer the average of all the individual trial probabilities will be to $1/2$. We could even pick single grains and check if the probability $1/4$ of picking two black grains in a row equals that of two white grains, etc. There are lots of statistics questions we can pursue. Thus, piles of colored sand provide for instructive experiments.

The following axioms are self-evident.

- Probabilities satisfy $0 \leq P \leq 1$. Probability 1 means certainty; probability 0 means impossibility.

- The entire sample has probability 1. For example, drawing an arbitrary card from a deck of cards has probability 1.

- The probabilities for mutually exclusive events add. The probability for getting exactly one head in two coin tosses is $1/4 + 1/4 = 1/2$ because it is $1/4$ for head first and then tail, plus $1/4$ for tail first and then head.

Example 23.1.1   PROBABILITY FOR A OR B

Before proceeding with this example, we must clarify the definition of "or." In probability theory, "A or B" means A, B, or **both** A and B. The specification "A or B but not both" is referred to as the **exclusive or** of A and B (sometimes abbreviated **xor**).

What is the probability for drawing a club or a jack from a shuffled deck of cards?[2] To answer this question we need to identify equally probable mutually exclusive events. We note that because there are 52 cards in a deck, the drawing of each being equally likely (with 13 cards for each suit and 4 jacks), there are 13 clubs including the club jack, and 3 other jacks; that is, there are 16 mutually exclusive draws that meet our specification out of the total of 52, giving the probability $(13 + 3)/52 = 16/52 = 4/13$.   ■

Sets, Unions, and Intersections

If we represent a sample space by a set S of points, then events meeting certain specifications can be identified as subsets $A, B, \ldots$ of S, denoted as $A \subset S$, etc. Two sets A, B are equal if A is contained in B, denoted $A \subset B$, and B is contained in A, denoted $B \subset A$. The **union** $A \cup B$ consists of all points (events) that are in A or B or both (see Fig. 23.1). The **intersection** $A \cap B$ consists of all points that are in both A and B. If A and B have no common points, their intersection is the **empty set** (which has no elements), and we write $A \cap B = \emptyset$. The set of points in A that are not in the intersection of A and B is denoted by $A - A \cap B$, thereby **defining a subtraction of sets**. If we take the club suit in Example 23.1.1 as set A and the four jacks as set B, then their union comprises all clubs and jacks, and their intersection is the club jack only.

Each subset A has its probability $P(A) \geq 0$. In terms of these set-theory concepts and notations, the probability laws we just discussed become

$$0 \leq P(A) \leq 1.$$

---

[2]Note that these events are not mutually exclusive.

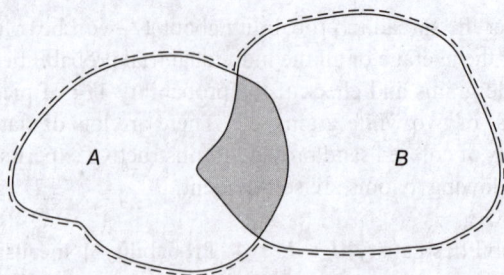

FIGURE 23.1   The shaded area gives the intersection $A \cap B$, corresponding to the A **and** B event sets; the dashed line encloses $A \cup B$, corresponding to the event set A **or** B.

The entire sample space has $P(S) = 1$. The probability of the union $A \cup B$ of mutually exclusive events is the sum

$$P(A \cup B) = P(A) + P(B), \quad \text{where} \quad A \cap B = \emptyset. \tag{23.3}$$

The **addition rule** for probabilities of arbitrary sets is given by the following theorem:

$$\textbf{Addition rule:} \quad P(A \cup B) = P(A) + P(B) - P(A \cap B). \tag{23.4}$$

To prove Eq. (23.4), we write the union as two mutually exclusive sets: $A \cup B = A \cup (B - B \cap A)$, where we have subtracted the intersection of A and B from B before joining them. The respective probabilities of these mutually exclusive sets are $P(A)$ and $P(B) - P(B \cap A)$, which we add. We could also have written $A \cup B = (A - A \cap B) \cup B$, from which our theorem follows similarly by adding these probabilities: $P(A \cup B) = [P(A) - P(A \cap B)] + P(B)$. Note that $A \cap B = B \cap A$. The relationships among these sets can be checked by referring to Fig. 23.1.

Sometimes the rules and definitions of probabilities that we have discussed so far are not sufficient, and we need to introduce the notion of conditional probability. Let A and B denote sets of events in our sample space. The **conditional probability** $P(B|A)$ is defined to be the probability that an event which is a member of A is also a member of B. To understand the need for this somewhat formal definition, consider the following example.

Example 23.1.2   CONDITIONAL PROBABILITY

Consider a box of 10 identical red and 20 identical blue pens, from which we remove pens successively in a random order without putting them back. Suppose we draw a red pen first, event R, followed by the draw of a blue pen, event B. One way to compute $P(R, B)$ is to note that our sample space consists of 30×29 mutually exclusive and equally probable points (each a two-event ordered sequence), of which 10×20 meet our specifications, leading to the computation $P(R, B) = (10 \times 20)/(30 \times 29) = 20/87$. Note that in this example, $P(R, B)$ refers to **ordered** events.

Another way of making the same computation is to start by noting that the initial drawing of a red pen will occur with probability $P(R) = 10/30$. But now the probability of drawing a blue pen in the next round, event B, however, will depend on the fact that we drew a red pen in the first round, and is given by the **conditional probability** $P(B|R)$. Since there are now 29 pens of which 20 are blue, we easily compute $P(B|R) = 20/29$, and the probability of the sequence "red, then blue" is

$$P(R, B) = \frac{10}{30}\frac{20}{29} = \frac{20}{87},\tag{23.5}$$

equal to the result we obtained previously.   ∎

The generalization of the result in Eq. (23.5) is the very useful formula

$$P(A, B) = P(A)P(B|A),\tag{23.6}$$

which has the obvious interpretation that the probability that A and B both occur can be written as the probability of A, multiplied by the conditional probability $P(B|A)$ that B occurs, given the occurrence of A.

Two observations relative of Eq. (23.6) are in order. First, it can be rearranged to reach an explicit formula for $P(B|A)$:

$$P(B|A) = \frac{P(A, B)}{P(A)}.\tag{23.7}$$

Second, if the conditional probability $P(B|A) = P(B)$ is independent of A, then the events A and B are called **independent**, and the combined probability is simply the **product of both probabilities**, or

$$P(A, B) = P(A)P(B), \quad (A \text{ and } B \text{ independent}).\tag{23.8}$$

If A and B are defined in a way that neither depends on the other (a condition not satisfied in Example 23.1.2), we can rewrite Eq. (23.7) as

$$P(B|A) = \frac{P(A \cap B)}{P(A)}.\tag{23.9}$$

Example 23.1.3   SCHOLASTIC APTITUDE TESTS

Colleges and universities rely on the verbal and mathematics SAT scores, among others, as predictors of a student's success in passing courses and graduating. A research university is known to admit mostly students with a combined verbal and mathematics score of 1400 points or more. The graduation rate is 95%; that is, 5% drop out or transfer elsewhere. Of those who graduate, 97% have an SAT score of at least 1400 points, while 80% of those who drop out have an SAT score below 1400. Suppose a student has an SAT score below 1400. What is his/her probability of graduating?

Let A represent all students with an SAT test score below 1400, and let B represent those with scores ≥ 1400. These are mutually exclusive events with $P(A) + P(B) = 1$. Let C represent those students who graduate, and let $\tilde{C}$ represent those who do not. Our problem here is to determine the conditional probabilities $P(C|A)$ and $P(C|B)$. To apply Eq. (23.9) we need the four probabilities $P(A)$, $P(B)$, $P(A \cap C)$, and $P(B \cap C)$.

Among the 95% of students who graduate, 3% are in set A and 97% are in set B, so

$$P(A \cap C) = (0.95)(0.03) = 0.0285, \quad P(B \cap C) = (0.95)(0.97) = 0.9215.$$

Among the 5% of students who do not graduate, 80% are in set A and 20% are in set B, so

$$P(A \cap \tilde{C}) = (0.05)(0.80) = 0.0400, \quad P(B \cap \tilde{C}) = (0.05)(0.20) = 0.0100.$$

Since $P(A) = P(A \cap C) + P(A \cap \tilde{C})$, and likewise for $P(B)$, we have

$$P(A) = 0.0285 + 0.0400 = 0.0685, \quad P(B) = 0.9215 + 0.0100 = 0.9315.$$

Now, applying Eq. (23.9), we obtain the final results

$$P(C|A) = \frac{P(A \cap C)}{P(A)} = \frac{0.0285}{0.0685} \approx 41.6\%,$$

$$P(C|B) = \frac{P(B \cap C)}{P(B)} = \frac{0.9215}{0.9315} \approx 98.9\%;$$

that is, a little less than 42% is the probability for a student with a score below 1400 to graduate at this particular university. ■

As a corollary to the equation for conditional probability, Eq. (23.9), we now compare $P(A|B) = P(A \cap B)/P(B)$ and $P(B|A) = P(A \cap B)/P(A)$, obtaining a result known as **Bayes' theorem:**

$$P(A|B) = \frac{P(A)}{P(B)} P(B|A). \tag{23.10}$$

Bayes' theorem is a special case of the following more general theorem:

If the random events A_i with probabilities $P(A_i) > 0$ are mutually exclusive and their union represents the entire sample S, then an arbitrary random event $B \subset S$ has the probability

$$P(B) = \sum_{i=1}^{n} P(A_i) P(B|A_i). \tag{23.11}$$

The decomposition law given by Eq. (23.11) resembles the expansion of a vector into a basis of unit vectors defining its components. This relation follows from the obvious decomposition $B = \cup_i (B \cap A_i)$ (this notation indicates the union of all the quantities $B \cap A_i$, see Fig. 23.2), which implies $P(B) = \sum_i P(B \cap A_i)$ because the components $B \cap A_i$ are mutually exclusive. For each i, we know from Eq. (23.9) that $P(B \cap A_i) = P(A_i) P(B|A_i)$, which proves the theorem.

Counting Permutations and Combinations

Counting the events in samples can help us find probabilities; this procedure is found to be of great importance in statistical mechanics.

If we have n different molecules, let us ask in how many ways we can arrange them in a row, that is, permute them. This number is defined as the number of their **permutations**. Thus, by definition, the **order matters in permutations**. There are n choices of picking the first molecule, $n - 1$ for the second, etc. Altogether there are $n!$ permutations of n **different** molecules or objects.

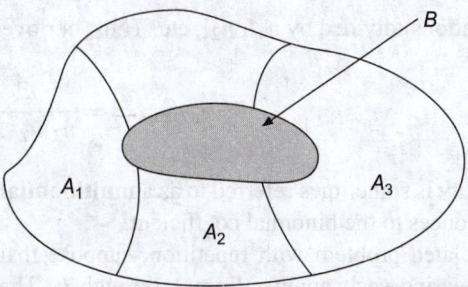

FIGURE 23.2   The shaded area B is composed of mutually exclusive subsets of B
belonging also to A_1, A_2, A_3, where the A_i are mutually exclusive.

Generalizing this, suppose there are n people but only $k < n$ chairs to seat them. In how
many ways can we seat k people in the chairs? Counting as before, we get

$$n(n-1)\cdots(n-k+1) = \frac{n!}{(n-k)!} \tag{23.12}$$

for the number of permutations of k objects which can be formed by selection from a set
originally containing n objects.

We now consider the counting of **combinations** of objects, where the term **combination**
is defined to refer to sets in which the object order is irrelevant. For example, three letters
a, b, c can be combined, two letters at a time, in three ways: ab, ac, bc. If letters can be
repeated, then we also have the pairs aa, bb, cc and have a total of six combinations.
These examples illustrate the fact that a **combination** of different particles differs from a
permutation in that the particles' order **does not matter**. Combinations may occur with
repetition or without; the essential point is that no two combinations contain the same
particles.

The number of different combinations of n numbered (and thereby distinguishable) particles, k at a time and without repetitions, is given by the binomial coefficient

$$\frac{n(n-1)\cdots(n-k+1)}{k!} = \binom{n}{k}. \tag{23.13}$$

To prove Eq. (23.13), we start from the number $n!/(n-k)!$ of permutations in which k
particles were chosen from n, and divide out the number $k!$ of permutations of the group
of k particles because their order does not matter in a combination.

A generalization of the above is a situation in which we have a total of n distinguishable
(numbered) objects, and we place n_1 of these into Box 1, n_2 into Box 2, etc. We wish to
know how many different ways this can be done (this is a **combination** problem because
the objects in each box do not form ordered sets). A simple way to solve this problem is to
identify each permutation of the n objects with an assignment into boxes; the first n_1 of the
permuted objects is placed in Box 1, the next n_2 in Box 2, etc. However, permutations
that differ only in the ordering of objects destined for the same box do not constitute
different distributions, so the total number of distributions will be $n!$ (the overall number

of permutations) divided by $n_1!$, $n_2!$, etc. Thus, our overall formula is

$$B(n_1, n_2, \ldots) = \frac{n!}{n_1! n_2! \ldots}. \tag{23.14}$$

This quantity is sometimes referred to as a **multinomial coefficient**; if there were only two boxes it reduces to the binomial coefficient.

For a related problem with repetition, suppose that we have an unlimited supply of particles bearing each number from 1 through k. Then the number of distinct ways in which n particles can be chosen can be shown to be

$$\binom{n + k - 1}{n} = \binom{n + k - 1}{k - 1}. \tag{23.15}$$

The following example provides a proof of Eq. (23.15).

Example 23.1.4   COMBINATIONS WITH REPETITION

The physical relevance of the situation giving rise to Eq. (23.15) is that it is mathematically equivalent to the number of ways that n identical, indistinguishable particles can be placed in k boxes. To see that these problems are equivalent, note that the number on each particle of Eq. (23.15) can be used to identify the box in which that particle will be placed.

A simple way to count the possible assignments is to consider the distinguishable ways that n indistinguishable particles and $k - 1$ indistinguishable partitions can be placed in a line containing $n + k - 1$ items. The particles (if any) that occur in the line earlier than the first partition are assigned to Box 1; those between the first and second partitions are assigned to Box 2, etc., with the particles (if any) occurring later than the $(k - 1)$th (the last) partition are assigned to Box k. Each different placement of the partitions yields a unique assignment of particles to boxes, and the number of different partition placements is the number of combinations given by the binomial coefficient in Eq. (23.15). ∎

In statistical mechanics, we frequently need to know the number of ways in which it is possible to put n particles in k boxes subject to various additional specifications. If we are working in classical theory, our more complete specification includes the notion that the particles are **distinguishable**, and we refer to the probability computation as that given by **Maxwell-Boltzmann statistics**. In the quantum domain, it is assumed that identical particles are inherently indistinguishable; in fact, we cannot even identify them by their trajectories, as the notion of path is blurred by the Heisenberg uncertainty principle. This indistinguishability leads to the requirement that many-particle states must have symmetry under the interchange of identical particles, and in nature we find two cases: Either the wave function is symmetric under interchange of the coordinates of a pair of identical particles (such particles are said to exhibit **Bose-Einstein statistics**), or the coordinate interchange causes a reversal in the sign of the wave function (the case called **Fermi-Dirac statistics**). The symmetry (or antisymmetry) under particle interchange influences the way in which particles can be assigned to states (boxes): In Bose-Einstein statistics any number of **indistinguishable** particles may be placed in the same box; in Fermi-Dirac statistics no box may contain more than one **indistinguishable** particle.

Application of the various kinds of statistics in general problems is outside the scope of this text; however, the basic case in which we simply count the number of assignments that are possible is easily approached. If we have n particles and k available states:

- In Maxwell-Boltzmann (classical) statistics, the number of possible assignments of particles to states is k^n (each particle can independently be assigned to any state).

- In Bose-Einstein statistics, the number of possible assignments is given by Eq. (23.15).

- In Fermi-Dirac statistics, the number of possible assignments is $\binom{k}{n}$. This formula gives the number of ways that n of the k states can be selected for occupancy. Note that the number of assignments is zero if $n > k$, indicating that we cannot make any assignment (with a maximum of one particle per state) unless there are at least as many states as there are particles.

Exercises

23.1.1 A card is drawn from a shuffled deck. (a) What is the probability that it is black, (b) a red nine, (c) or a queen of spades?

23.1.2 Find the probability of drawing two kings from a shuffled deck of cards (a) if the first card is put back before the second is drawn, and (b) if the first card is not put back after being drawn.

23.1.3 When two fair dice are thrown, what is the probability of (a) observing a number less than 4, or (b) a number greater than or equal to 4 but less than 6?

23.1.4 Rolling three fair dice, what is the probability of obtaining six points?

23.1.5 Determine the probability $P(A \cap B \cap C)$ in terms of $P(A)$, $P(B)$, $P(C)$, $P(A \cup B)$, $P(A \cup C)$, $P(B \cup C)$, and $P(A \cup B \cup C)$.

23.1.6 Determine directly or by mathematical induction (Section 1.4) the probability of a distribution of N (Maxwell-Boltzmann) particles in k boxes with N_1 in Box 1, N_2 in Box 2, ..., N_k in the kth box for any numbers $N_j \geq 1$ with $N_1 + N_2 + \cdots + N_k = N$, $k < N$. Repeat this for Fermi-Dirac and Bose-Einstein particles.

23.1.7 Show that $P(A \cup B \cup C) = P(A) + P(B) + P(C) - P(A \cap B) - P(A \cap C) - P(B \cap C) + P(A \cap B \cap C)$.

23.1.8 Determine the probability that a positive integer $n \leq 100$ is divisible by a prime number $p \leq 100$. Verify your result for $p = 3, 5, 7$.

23.1.9 Put two particles obeying Maxwell-Boltzmann (Fermi-Dirac, or Bose-Einstein) statistics in three boxes. How many ways of doing so are there in each case?

23.2   RANDOM VARIABLES

In this section we define properties that characterize the probability distributions of random variables, by which we mean variables that will assume various numerical values with individual probabilities. Thus, the name of a color (e.g., "black" or "white") cannot be the value assigned a random variable, but we can define a random variable to have one numerical value for "black" and another for "white"; the usefulness of our definition may depend on the problem we are attempting to solve.

Having defined a random variable and given its distribution, we are interested in particular in its **mean** or **average** value, and in measures of the width or spread of its values. The width is of particular importance when the random variable represents repeated measurements of the same quantity but subject to experimental error. In addition, we introduce properties that characterize the extent to which the value of one random variable depends on (i.e., is **correlated** with) those of another.

Random variables can be **discrete**, as for example those introduced in the previous section to describe the outcomes of coin tosses, or they may be **continuous**, either inherently so (as, for example, the wave function in a quantum mechanical system) or because they consist of so many closely spaced discrete points that it is impractical to work with them individually.

Example 23.2.1   DISCRETE RANDOM VARIABLE

The possible outcomes of the tossing of a die define a random variable X with values $x_1, x_2, \ldots, x_6$, each with probability $1/6$; we can denote this by writing $P(x_i) = 1/6$, $i = 1 \ldots 6$.

If we toss two dice and record the sum of the points shown in each trial, then this sum is also a discrete random variable, which takes on the value 2 when both dice show 1 with probability $(1/6)^2$; the value 3 in either of the two cases in which one die has 1 and the other 2, hence with probability $(1/6)^2 + (1/6)^2 = 1/18$. Continuing, the value 4 is reached in three equally probable ways: $2 + 2$, $3 + 1$, and $1 + 3$ with total probability $3(1/6)^2 = 1/12$; the values 5 and 6 are reached with the respective probabilities $4(1/6)^2 = 1/9$ and $5(1/6)^2 = 5/36$; and the value 7 occurs with the maximum probability, $6(1/6)^2 = 1/6$. The value 8 is reached in five ways $(6 + 2, 5 + 3, 4 + 4, 3 + 5, 2 + 6)$, with probability $5(1/6)^2 = 5/36$, and further increases in x lead to smaller probabilities, finally at $x = 12$ reaching probability $(1/6)^2 = 1/36$. This probability distribution is symmetric about $x = 7$, and can be represented graphically as in Fig. 23.3 or algebraically as

$$P(x) = \frac{x-1}{36} = \frac{6 - (7 - x)}{36}, \quad x = 2, 3, \ldots, 7,$$

$$P(x) = \frac{13 - x}{36} = \frac{6 + (7 - x)}{36}, \quad x = 7, 8, \ldots, 12.$$

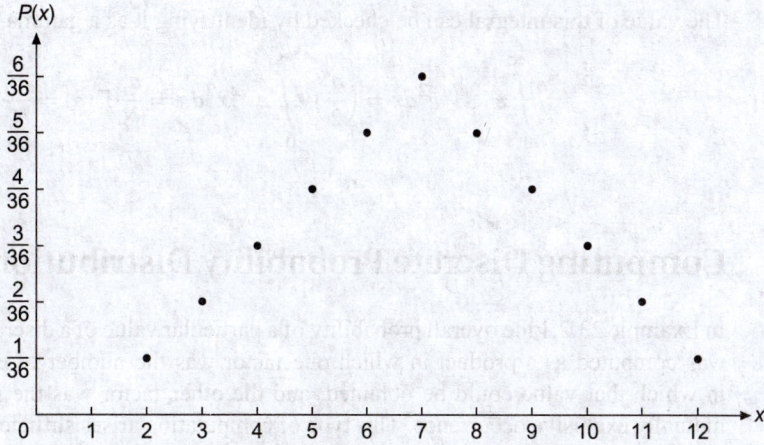

FIGURE 23.3   Probability distribution $P(x)$ of the sum of points when two dice are tossed.

In summary, then,

- If a discrete random variable X can assume the values x_i, each value occurs by chance with a probability $P(X = x_i) = p_i \geq 0$ that is a discrete-valued function of the random variable X, and the probabilities satisfy $\sum_i p_i = 1$.

- We define the probability density $f(x)$ of a **continuous random variable** X as

$$P(x \leq X \leq x + dx) = f(x)dx; \tag{23.16}$$

that is, $f(x)dx$ is the probability that X lies in the interval $x \leq X \leq x + dx$. For $f(x)$ to be a probability density, it has to satisfy $f(x) \geq 0$ and $\int f(x)dx = 1$.

- The generalization to probability distributions depending on several random variables is straightforward. Quantum physics abounds in examples.

Example 23.2.2   CONTINUOUS RANDOM VARIABLE: HYDROGEN ATOM

Quantum mechanics gives the probability $|\psi|^2 \, d^3r$ of finding a $1s$ electron in a hydrogen atom in volume[3] d^3r, where $\psi = Ne^{-r/a}$ is the $1s$ wave function, a is the Bohr radius, and $N = (\pi a^3)^{-1/2}$ is a normalization constant such that

$$\int |\psi|^2 \, d^3r = 4\pi N^2 \int\limits_0^\infty e^{-2r/a} r^2 dr = \pi a^3 N^2 = 1.$$

---

[3]Note that $|\psi|^2 4\pi r^2 dr$ gives the probability for the electron to be found between r and $r + dr$, at any angle.

The value of this integral can be checked by identifying it as a gamma function:

$$\int_0^\infty e^{-2r/a} r^2 \, dr = \left(\frac{a}{2}\right)^3 \int_0^\infty e^{-x} x^2 \, dx = \frac{a^3}{8} \Gamma(3) = \frac{a^3}{4}.$$

∎

Computing Discrete Probability Distributions

In Example 23.2.1 the overall probability of a particular value of a discrete random variable was computed as a product in which one factor was the number of equally likely ways in which that value could be obtained, and the other factor was the probability of each mutually exclusive occurrence. This type of computation arises sufficiently frequently that we should learn how to deal with it in general. Therefore, consider a situation in which N independent events take place (examples of such events include tosses of an individual die, selection of a card from a deck, energy state occupied by a molecule, orientation of the magnetic moment of a particle), and that each such event has one of a set of m mutually exclusive outcomes (e.g., number showing on the die, identity of the card, energy state, or magnetic moment orientation).

We assume that the outcomes $x_1, x_2, \ldots, x_m$ of an individual event will have the respective probabilities $p_1, p_2, \ldots, p_m$, with $p_1 + p_2 + \cdots + p_m = 1$ (so that we have included all the possible outcomes). Then, we compute the probability that any n_1 of the events have outcome x_1, any n_2 events have outcome x_2, etc.:

$$P(n_1, n_2, \ldots, n_m) = B(n_1, n_2, \ldots, n_m)(p_1)^{n_1}(p_2)^{n_2} \ldots (p_m)^{n_m}, \tag{23.17}$$

where $n_1 + n_2 + \cdots + n_m = N$, and $B(n_1, n_2, \ldots, n_m)$ is the number of ways that, for each i, n_i of the events have outcome x_i.

Now $B(n_1, n_2, \ldots, n_m)$ is just the multinomial coefficient encountered earlier; in the present context the numbered objects correspond to events numbered from 1 to N and each box corresponds to an individual-event outcome. Thus, our final formula for the probability of a distribution defined by n_1, n_2, etc., is

$$P(n_1, n_2, \ldots, n_m) = \frac{N!}{n_1! n_2! \ldots n_m!}(p_1)^{n_1}(p_2)^{n_2} \ldots (p_m)^{n_m}. \tag{23.18}$$

Mean and Variance

When we make n measurements of a quantity x, obtaining the values x_j, we define the **average value**

$$\bar{x} = \frac{1}{n} \sum_{j=1}^n x_j \tag{23.19}$$

of the trials, also called the **mean** or **expectation value**, where this formula assumes that every observed value x_i is equally likely and occurs with probability $1/n$. This connection is the key link of experimental data with probability theory. This observation and practical experience suggest defining the **mean value for a discrete random variable** X as

$$\langle X \rangle \equiv \sum_i x_i \, p_i, \tag{23.20}$$

while defining the mean value for a **continuous random variable** x characterized by probability density $f(x)$ as

$$\langle X \rangle = \int x f(x) dx. \tag{23.21}$$

Other notations for the mean in the literature are $\bar{X}$ and $E(X)$.

The use of the arithmetic mean $\bar{x}$ of n measurements as the average value is suggested by simplicity and plain experience, again assuming equal probability for each x_i. But why do we not consider the geometric mean

$$x_g = (x_1 x_2 \ldots x_n)^{1/n}$$

or the harmonic mean x_h determined by the relation

$$\frac{1}{x_h} = \frac{1}{n}\left(\frac{1}{x_1} + \frac{1}{x_1} + \cdots + \frac{1}{x_n}\right)$$

or the value $\tilde{x}$ that minimizes the sum of absolute deviations $|x_i - \tilde{x}|$? Here the x_i are taken to increase monotonically. When we plot $O(x) = \sum_{i=1}^{2n+1} |x_i - x|$, as in Fig. 23.4(a), for an odd number of points, we realize that it has a minimum at its central value $i = n$, while for an even number of points $E(x) = \sum_{i=1}^{2n} |x_i - x|$ is flat in its central region, as shown in Fig. 23.4(b). These properties make these functions unacceptable for determining average values. Instead, when we minimize (with respect to x) the sum of quadratic deviations,

$$\sum_{i=1}^{n} (x - x_i)^2 = \text{minimum}, \tag{23.22}$$

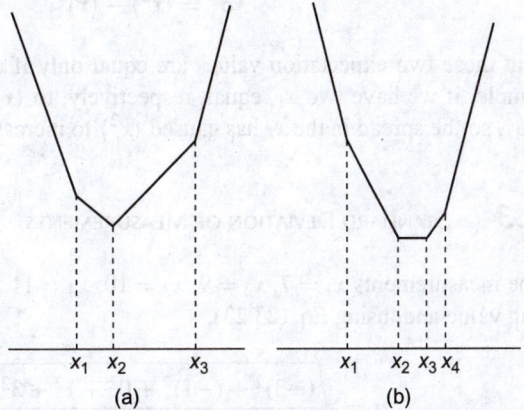

(a)

(b)

FIGURE 23.4   (a) $\sum_{i=1}^{3} |x_i - x|$ for an odd number of points. (b) $\sum_{i=1}^{4} |x_i - x|$ for an even number of points.

setting the derivative equal to zero yields $2\sum_i(x - x_i) = 0$, or

$$x = \frac{1}{n}\sum_i x_i \equiv \bar{x},$$

that is, the arithmetic mean. The arithmetic mean has another important property: If we denote by $v_i = x_i - \bar{x}$ the deviations, then $\sum_i v_i = 0$, that is, the sum of positive deviations equals the sum of negative deviations. This principle of minimizing the quadratic sum of deviations, called the **method of least squares**, is due to C. F. Gauss, among others.

The ability of a mean value to represent a set of data points depends on the spread of the individual measurements from this mean. Again, we reject the average sum of deviations $\sum_{i=1}^{n}|x_i - \bar{x}|/n$ as a measure of the spread because it selects the central measurement as the best value for no good reason. A more appropriate definition of the spread is based on the average of the squares of the deviations from the mean. This quantity, known as the **standard deviation**, is defined as

$$\sigma = \sqrt{\frac{1}{n}\sum_{i=1}^{n}(x_i - \bar{x})^2},\tag{23.23}$$

where the square root is motivated by dimensional analysis.

If we square Eq. (23.23) and expand $(x_i - \bar{x})^2$, written as $(x_i - \langle x \rangle)^2$, we get

$$n\sigma^2 = \sum_{i=1}^{n}x_i^2 - 2\langle x \rangle\sum_{i=1}^{n}x_i + n\langle x \rangle^2$$

$$= n\left(\langle x^2 \rangle - \langle x \rangle^2\right).$$

Dividing through by n, we obtain the very useful formula,

$$\sigma^2 = \langle x^2 \rangle - \langle x \rangle^2.\tag{23.24}$$

Note that these two expectation values are equal only if all the x_i have the same value; for example, if we have two x_i, equal, respectively, to $\langle x \rangle + \delta$ and $\langle x \rangle - \delta$, then $\langle x^2 \rangle = \langle x \rangle^2 + \delta^2$, so the spread in the x_i has caused $\langle x_i^2 \rangle$ to increase.

Example 23.2.3   STANDARD DEVIATION OF MEASUREMENTS

From the measurements $x_1 = 7$, $x_2 = 9$, $x_3 = 10$, $x_4 = 11$, $x_5 = 13$, we extract $\bar{x} = 10$ for the mean value and, using Eq. (23.23),

$$\sigma = \sqrt{\frac{(-3)^2 + (-1)^2 + 0^2 + 1^2 + 3^2}{5}} = 2.2361$$

for the standard deviation, or spread. ∎

There is yet another interpretation of the standard deviation, in terms of the sum of squares of measurement differences:

$$\sum_{i<k}(x_i - x_k)^2 = \frac{1}{2}\sum_{i=1}^{n}\sum_{k=1}^{n}\left(x_i^2 + x_k^2 - 2x_ix_k\right)$$

$$= \frac{1}{2}\left[2n^2\langle x^2\rangle - 2n^2\langle x\rangle^2\right] = n^2\sigma^2. \tag{23.25}$$

The last step in the above equation made use of Eq. (23.24).

Now we are ready to generalize the spread in a set of n measurements with equal probability $1/n$ to the **variance** of an arbitrary probability distribution. For a discrete random variable X with probabilities p_i at $X = x_i$, we define the **variance**

$$\sigma^2 = \sum_j \left(x_j - \langle X\rangle\right)^2 p_j; \tag{23.26}$$

for a continuous probability distribution the definition becomes

$$\sigma^2 = \int_{-\infty}^{\infty} (x - \langle X\rangle)^2 f(x)dx. \tag{23.27}$$

We now develop some relationships satisfied by random variables:

1. The variance σ^2 of a random variable X has the property

$$\sigma^2 = \langle X^2\rangle - \langle X\rangle^2. \tag{23.28}$$

This formula, previously derived as Eq. (23.24) only for a discrete random variable with all x_i equally probable, is true in general. The proof is left as Exercise 23.2.3.

2. If random variables X and Y are related by the linear equation $Y = aX + b$, then Y has mean value $\langle Y\rangle = a\langle X\rangle + b$ and variance $\sigma^2(Y) = a^2\sigma^2(X)$.

    We prove this theorem only for a continuous distribution, leaving the case of a discrete random variable as an exercise for the reader. Directly from the definitions, we have

$$\langle Y\rangle = \int_{-\infty}^{\infty} (ax + b)f(x)dx = a\langle X\rangle + b.$$

where the integral multiplying b simplifies because $\int f(x)dx = 1$. For the variance we similarly obtain

$$\sigma^2(Y) = \int_{-\infty}^{\infty}(ax + b - a\langle X\rangle - b)^2 f(x)dx = \int_{-\infty}^{\infty}a^2(x - \langle X\rangle)^2 f(x)dx$$

$$= a^2\sigma^2(X).$$

3.   Probabilities of random variables satisfy the **Chebyshev inequality**,

$$P(|x - \langle X \rangle| \geq k\sigma) \leq \frac{1}{k^2},\qquad (23.29)$$

which demonstrates why the standard deviation serves as a measure of the spread of an arbitrary probability distribution from its mean value $\langle X \rangle$. We first derive the simpler inequality

$$P(Y \geq K) \leq \frac{\langle Y \rangle}{K}$$

for a continuous random variable Y with values y restricted to $y \geq 0$. (The proof for a discrete random variable follows along similar lines.) This inequality follows from

$$\langle Y \rangle = \int_0^\infty yf(y)dy = \int_0^K yf(y)dy + \int_K^\infty yf(y)dy$$

$$\geq \int_K^\infty yf(y)dy \geq K \int_K^\infty f(y)dy = KP(Y \geq K).$$

Next we apply the same method to the positive variance integral,

$$\sigma^2 = \int (x - \langle X \rangle)^2 f(x)dx \geq \int_{|x-\langle X \rangle| \geq k\sigma} (x - \langle X \rangle)^2 f(x)dx$$

$$\geq k^2\sigma^2 \int_{|x-\langle X \rangle| \geq k\sigma} f(x)dx = k^2\sigma^2 P(|x - \langle X \rangle| \geq k\sigma),$$

where we have first decreased the right-hand side by omitting the part of the positive integral with $|x - \langle X \rangle| \leq k\sigma$ and then decreased it further by replacing $(x - \langle X \rangle)^2$ in the remaining integral by its minimum value, $k^2\sigma^2$. We now divide the first and last members of this sequence of inequalities by the positive quantity $k^2\sigma^2$, thereby proving the Chebyshev inequality. For $k = 3$ we have the conventional three-standard-deviation estimate,

$$P(|x - \langle X \rangle| \geq 3\sigma) \leq \frac{1}{3^2} = \frac{1}{9}.\qquad (23.30)$$

Moments of Probability Distributions

It is straightforward to generalize the mean value to higher moments of probability distributions relative to the mean value $\langle X \rangle$:

$$\left\langle (X - \langle X \rangle)^k \right\rangle = \sum_j \left(x_j - \langle X \rangle \right)^k p_j, \qquad \text{discrete distribution,}$$

(23.31)

$$\left\langle (X - \langle X \rangle)^k \right\rangle = \int_{-\infty}^{\infty} (x - \langle X \rangle)^k f(x) dx, \quad \text{continuous distribution.}$$

The **moment-generating function**

$$\langle e^{tX} \rangle = \int e^{tx} f(x) dx = 1 + t\langle X \rangle + \frac{t^2}{2!} \langle X^2 \rangle + \cdots$$

(23.32)

is a weighted sum of the moments of the continuous random variable X, which is obtained by substituting the Taylor expansion of the exponential functions. Therefore,

$$\langle X \rangle = \frac{d\langle e^{tX} \rangle}{dt} \bigg|_{t=0}, \quad \langle X^2 \rangle = \frac{d^2 \langle e^{tX} \rangle}{dt^2} \bigg|_{t=0}, \dots, \quad \langle X^n \rangle = \frac{d^n \langle e^{tX} \rangle}{dt^n} \bigg|_{t=0}.$$

(23.33)

Note that the moments here are not relative to the expectation value, but are relative to $x = 0$; they are called **central moments**.

Example 23.2.4   MOMENT-GENERATING FUNCTION

Suppose we have four cards, numbered from 1 through 4, from which we draw two at random and add their numbers. Letting this sum of the drawn numbers be values of a random variable X, we find that X has the following values and respective probabilities $P(x)$:

$$P(3) = 1/6, \quad P(4) = 1/6, \quad P(5) = 1/3, \quad P(6) = 1/6, \quad P(7) = 1/6.$$

Verifying these probabilities is the topic of Exercise 23.2.1.

The moment-generating function for this system has the form

$$M = \frac{1}{6} \left(e^{3t} + e^{4t} + 2e^{5t} + e^{6t} + e^{7t} \right),$$

and its first two derivatives are

$$M' = \frac{1}{6} \left(3e^{3t} + 4e^{4t} + 10e^{5t} + 6e^{6t} + 7e^{7t} \right),$$

$$M'' = \frac{1}{6} \left(9e^{3t} + 16e^{4t} + 50e^{5t} + 36e^{6t} + 49e^{7t} \right).$$

Setting $t = 0$, we get

$$\langle X \rangle = M'(0) = 5, \quad \langle X^2 \rangle = M''(0) = \frac{80}{3}.$$

Thus, the mean of X is found to be 5, and its variance is given by

$$\sigma^2 = \langle X^2 \rangle - \langle X \rangle^2 = \frac{80}{3} - 25 = \frac{5}{3}.$$

In this example we see that the moment-generating function does (in a systematic way) the same thing as direct formation of the moments; in a later example, Example 23.3.2, we see a situation in which the use of the moment-generating function provides an opportunity to compute moments with rather little computational work. ∎

Mean values, central moments, and variance can be defined analogously for probability distributions that depend on several random variables. We illustrate for the case of two random variables X and Y, for which the mean values and the variance of each variable take the forms

$$\langle X \rangle = \int\limits_{-\infty}^{\infty} \int\limits_{-\infty}^{\infty} x f(x, y) dx \, dy,$$

$$\langle Y \rangle = \int\limits_{-\infty}^{\infty} \int\limits_{-\infty}^{\infty} y f(x, y) dx \, dy, \tag{23.34}$$

$$\sigma^2(X) = \int\limits_{-\infty}^{\infty} \int\limits_{-\infty}^{\infty} (x - \langle X \rangle)^2 \, f(x, y) dx \, dy,$$

$$\sigma^2(Y) = \int\limits_{-\infty}^{\infty} \int\limits_{-\infty}^{\infty} (y - \langle Y \rangle)^2 \, f(x, y) dx \, dy. \tag{23.35}$$

Covariance and Correlation

Two random variables are said to be **independent if the probability density** $f(x, y)$ **factorizes** into a product $f(x)g(y)$ of probability distributions of one random variable each.

The covariance, defined as

$$\text{cov}(X, Y) = \langle (X - \langle X \rangle) (Y - \langle Y \rangle) \rangle, \tag{23.36}$$

is a measure of how much the random variables X and Y are correlated (or related): It is zero for independent random variables because

$$\text{cov}(X, Y) = \int (x - \langle X \rangle)(y - \langle Y \rangle) f(x, y) dx\, dy$$

$$= \int (x - \langle X \rangle) f(x) dx \int (y - \langle Y \rangle) g(y) dy$$

$$= (\langle X \rangle - \langle X \rangle)(\langle Y \rangle - \langle Y \rangle) = 0.$$

The normalized covariance $\text{cov}(X, Y)/\sigma(X)\sigma(Y)$, which has values between -1 and $+1$, is often called **correlation**.

In order to demonstrate that the correlation is bounded by

$$-1 \leq \frac{\text{cov}(X, Y)}{\sigma(X)\sigma(Y)} \leq 1,$$

we analyze the positive mean value

$$Q = \langle [a(X - \langle X \rangle) + c(Y - \langle Y \rangle)]^2 \rangle$$

$$= a^2 \langle [X - \langle X \rangle]^2 \rangle + 2ac \langle [X - \langle X \rangle][Y - \langle Y \rangle] \rangle + c^2 \langle [Y - \langle Y \rangle]^2 \rangle$$

$$= a^2 \sigma(X)^2 + 2ac\, \text{cov}(X, Y) + c^2 \sigma(Y)^2 \geq 0. \tag{23.37}$$

For this quadratic form to be nonnegative for all values of the constants a and c, its discriminant must satisfy $\text{cov}(X, Y)^2 - c(X)^2 \sigma(Y)^2 \leq 0$, which proves the desired inequality.

The usefulness of the correlation as a quantitative measure is emphasized by the following theorem:

The probability $P(Y = aX + b)$ will be unity if, and only if, the correlation $\text{cov}(X, Y)/\sigma(X)\sigma(Y)$ is equal to ± 1.

This theorem states that a $\pm 100\%$ correlation between X and Y implies not only some functional relation between both random variables but that the relation between them is linear.

Our first step in proving this theorem is to show that $P(Y = aX + b) = 1$ (meaning that $Y = aX + b$) implies that $\text{cov}(X, Y)/\sigma(X)\sigma(Y) = \pm 1$. For the mean $\langle Y \rangle$, we simply compute

$$\langle Y \rangle = \langle aX + b \rangle = a\langle X \rangle + b.$$

For the variance,

$$\sigma(Y)^2 = \langle Y^2 \rangle - \langle Y \rangle^2 = \langle (aX + b)^2 \rangle - (a\langle X \rangle + b)^2$$

$$= a^2 \langle X^2 \rangle + 2ab\langle X \rangle + b^2 - \left(a^2 \langle X \rangle^2 + 2ab\langle X \rangle + b^2 \right)$$

$$= a^2 \left(\langle X^2 \rangle - \langle X \rangle^2 \right) = a^2 \sigma(X)^2,$$

which is equivalent to $\sigma(Y) = \pm a\sigma(X)$. We also need $\text{cov}(X, Y)$, which is

$$\text{cov}(X, Y) = \langle (X - \langle X \rangle)\left((aX + b) - (a\langle X \rangle + b)\right) \rangle$$

$$= a\left(\langle X^2 \rangle - \langle X \rangle^2\right) = a\sigma^2(X) = \pm\sigma(X)\sigma(Y),$$

where the last equality was obtained by identifying $a\sigma(X)$ as $\pm\sigma(Y)$. This result completes the first step in our proof of the theorem.

To complete the proof, we must establish the converse of the relation we have just proved, namely that $\text{cov}(X, Y)/\sigma(X)\sigma(Y) = \pm 1$ implies $P(Y = aX + b) = 1$ for some set of values (a, b). We proceed by forming the quadratic expectation value

$$\left\langle \left[(\sigma(Y)X \mp \sigma(X)Y) - \langle \sigma(Y)X \mp \sigma(X)Y \rangle \right]^2 \right\rangle,$$

where the symbol $\mp$ indicates that we choose a sign opposite to that of the correlation $\text{cov}(X, Y)/\sigma(X)\sigma(Y)$. Our plan is to show that this expectation value is zero. Since the expectation value is that of an inherently nonnegative quantity, we may then conclude that $\sigma(Y)X \mp \sigma(X)Y$ is (almost) everywhere equal to its expectation value, the value of which is some constant C. We therefore have

$$\sigma(Y)X \mp \sigma(X)Y = C, \quad \text{equivalent to} \quad Y = \pm\frac{\sigma(Y)X - C)}{\sigma(X)},$$

the linear relation we seek.

It remains to confirm that the quadratic expectation value vanishes. Rearranging it first to the form

$$\left\langle \left[\sigma(Y)(X - \langle X \rangle) \mp \sigma(X)(Y - \langle Y \rangle) \right]^2 \right\rangle$$

and then expanding the square, we reach

$$\left\langle \sigma(Y)^2(X - \langle X \rangle)^2 + \sigma(X)^2(Y - \langle Y \rangle)^2 \mp 2\sigma(X)\sigma(Y)(X - \langle X \rangle)(Y - \langle Y \rangle) \right\rangle.$$

Making now the substitutions $(X - \langle X \rangle)^2 = \sigma(X)^2$, $(Y - \langle Y \rangle)^2 = \sigma(Y)^2$, and $\langle (X - \langle X \rangle)(Y - \langle Y \rangle) \rangle = \pm\sigma(X)\sigma(Y)$, our quadratic expectation value reduces to zero.

Marginal Probability Distributions

It is sometimes useful to integrate out (i.e., average over) one of the random variables in a multivariable distribution. When we do so, we are left with the probability distribution of the other random variables. For a two-variable distribution, we can eliminate either of the two variables:

$$F(x) = \int f(x, y)dy, \quad \text{or} \quad G(y) = \int f(x, y)dx, \tag{23.38}$$

and analogously for discrete probability distributions. When one or more random variables are integrated out, the remaining probability distribution is called **marginal**, the name motivated by the geometric aspects of projection. It is straightforward to show that these marginal distributions satisfy all the requirements of properly normalized probability distributions.

Here is a comprehensive example that illustrates the computation of probability distributions and their mean values, variances, covariance, and correlation.

Example 23.2.5   REPEATED DRAWS OF CARDS

This example deals with independent repeated draws from a deck of playing cards. To make sure that these events stay independent, we draw the first card at random from a bridge deck containing 52 cards and then put it back at a random place and reshuffle the deck. Now we repeat the process for a second card. Let's define the random variables:

- X = number of so-called honors, that is, tens, jacks, queens, kings, or aces;
- Y = number of twos or threes.

In a single draw the probability of Event a (drawing an honor) is $p_a = 20/52 = 5/13$, while the probability of Event b (drawing a two or three) is $p_b = 2(4/52) = 2/13$. The probability of Event c (drawing anything else) is $p_c = (13 - 5 - 2)/13 = 6/13$. Since that exhausts all the mutually exclusive possibilities, we have $a + b + c = 1$.

In two drawings, it is possible to draw zero, one, or two honors (i.e., $x = 0$, 1, or 2). Likewise, we may draw zero, one, or two cards of value 2 or 3 (i.e., $y = 0$, 1, or 2). But because we are only drawing two cards, we have the additional condition $0 \leq x + y \leq 2$.

The probability function $P(X = x, Y = y)$, which we will write in the simpler form $P(x, y)$, is given by a formula of the type presented in Eq. (23.18), with N (the number of events) equal to 2 and with the three individual-event probabilities p_a, p_b, and p_c. The number of events a is x, the number of events b is y, and therefore the number of events c is $2 - x - y$, and, by Eq. (23.18),

$$P(x, y) = \frac{2!}{x!\, y!\, (2 - x - y)!} (p_a)^x (p_b)^y (p_c)^{2-x-y}$$

$$= \frac{2!}{x!\, y!\, (2 - x - y)!} \left(\frac{5}{13}\right)^x \left(\frac{2}{13}\right)^y \left(\frac{6}{13}\right)^{2-x-y}, \tag{23.39}$$

with $0 \leq x + y \leq 2$. More explicitly, $P(x, y)$ has the following values:

$$P(0, 0) = \left(\frac{6}{13}\right)^2, \quad P(1, 0) = 2 \cdot \frac{5}{13} \cdot \frac{6}{13} = \frac{60}{13^2},$$

$$P(2, 0) = \left(\frac{5}{13}\right)^2, \quad P(0, 1) = 2 \cdot \frac{2}{13} \cdot \frac{6}{13} = \frac{24}{13^2},$$

$$P(0, 2) = \left(\frac{2}{13}\right)^2, \quad P(1, 1) = 2 \cdot \frac{5}{13} \cdot \frac{2}{13} = \frac{20}{13^2}.$$

The probability distribution is properly normalized. Its expectation values are given by

$$\langle X \rangle = \sum_{0 \leq x+y \leq 2} x P(x, y) = P(1, 0) + P(1, 1) + 2P(2, 0)$$

$$= \frac{60}{13^2} + \frac{20}{13^2} + 2\left(\frac{5}{13}\right)^2 = \frac{130}{13^2} = \frac{10}{13} = 2p_a,$$

and

$$\langle Y \rangle = \sum_{0 \leq x+y \leq 2} y P(x, y) = P(0, 1) + P(1, 1) + 2P(0, 2)$$

$$= \frac{24}{13^2} + \frac{20}{13^2} + 2\left(\frac{2}{13}\right)^2 = \frac{52}{13^2} = \frac{4}{13} = 2p_b.$$

The values $2p_a$ and $2p_b$ are expected because we are drawing a card two times. The variances are

$$\sigma^2(X) = \sum_{0 \leq x+y \leq 2} \left(x - \frac{10}{13}\right)^2 P(x, y)$$

$$= \left(-\frac{10}{13}\right)^2 [P(0, 0) + P(0, 1) + P(0, 2)] + \left(\frac{3}{13}\right)^2 [P(1, 0) + P(1, 1)] + \left(\frac{16}{13}\right)^2 P(2, 0)$$

$$= \frac{10^2 \cdot 64 + 3^2 \cdot 80 + 16^2 \cdot 5^2}{13^4} = \frac{4^2 \cdot 5 \cdot 169}{13^4} = \frac{80}{13^2},$$

$$\sigma^2(Y) = \sum_{0 \leq x+y \leq 2} \left(y - \frac{4}{13}\right)^2 P(x, y)$$

$$= \left(-\frac{4}{13}\right)^2 [P(0, 0) + P(1, 0) + P(2, 0)] + \left(\frac{9}{13}\right)^2 [P(0, 1) + P(1, 1)] + \left(\frac{22}{13}\right)^2 P(0, 2)$$

$$= \frac{4^2 \cdot 11^2 + 9^2 \cdot 44 + 22^2 \cdot 2^2}{13^4} = \frac{11 \cdot 4 \cdot 169}{13^4} = \frac{44}{13^2}.$$

The covariance is given by

$$\text{cov}(X, Y) = \sum_{0 \leq x+y \leq 2} \left(x - \frac{10}{13}\right)\left(y - \frac{4}{13}\right) P(x, y) = \frac{10 \cdot 4}{13^2} \cdot \frac{6^2}{13^2} - \frac{10 \cdot 9}{13^2} \cdot \frac{24}{13^2}$$

$$- \frac{10 \cdot 22}{13^2} \cdot \frac{4}{13^2} - \frac{3 \cdot 4}{13^2} \cdot \frac{60}{13^2} + \frac{3 \cdot 9}{13^2} \cdot \frac{20}{13^2} - \frac{16 \cdot 4}{13^2} \cdot \frac{5^2}{13^2} = -\frac{20}{13^2}.$$

Therefore, the correlation of the random variables X, Y is given by

$$\frac{\text{cov}(X, Y)}{\sigma(X)\sigma(Y)} = -\frac{20}{8\sqrt{5 \cdot 11}} = -\frac{1}{2}\sqrt{\frac{5}{11}} = -0.3371,$$

which means that there is a small (negative) correlation between these random variables, because if an honor is drawn, that drawing is not available to yield a 2 or a 3, and vice versa.

Finally, let us determine the marginal distribution,

$$P(X = x) = \sum_{y=0}^{2} P(x, y),$$

or explicitly,

$$P(X = 0) = P(0, 0) + P(0, 1) + P(0, 2) = \left(\frac{6}{13}\right)^2 + \frac{24}{13^2} + \left(\frac{2}{13}\right)^2 = \left(\frac{8}{13}\right)^2,$$

$$P(X = 1) = P(1, 0) + P(1, 1) = \frac{60}{13^2} + \frac{20}{13^2} = \frac{80}{13^2},$$

$$P(X = 2) = P(2, 0) = \left(\frac{5}{13}\right)^2,$$

which is properly normalized because

$$P(x = 0) + P(X = 1) + P(X = 2) = \frac{64 + 80 + 25}{13^2} = \frac{169}{13^2} = 1.$$

The mean value and variance of X can be computed from the marginal probabilities:

$$\langle X \rangle = \sum_{x=0}^{2} x P(X = x) = P(X = 1) + 2P(X = 2) = \frac{80 + 2 \cdot 25}{13^2} = \frac{130}{13^2} = \frac{10}{13},$$

$$\sigma_F = \sum_{x=0}^{2} \left(x - \frac{10}{13}\right)^2 P(X = x) = \left(-\frac{10}{13}\right)^2 \left(\frac{8}{13}\right)^2 + \left(\frac{3}{13}\right)^2 \frac{80}{13^2} + \left(\frac{16}{13}\right)^2 \left(\frac{5}{13}\right)^2$$

$$= \frac{80 \cdot 169}{13^4} = \frac{80}{13^2}.$$

These data agree with our earlier computations of the same quantities. ∎

Conditional Probability Distributions

If we are interested in the distribution of a random variable X for a definite value $y = y_0$ of another random variable, then we deal with a **conditional probability distribution** $P(X = x | Y = y_0)$. The corresponding continuous probability density is $f(x, y_0)$.

Exercises

23.2.1   Verify the probabilities for the outcomes of the two-card draws in Example 23.2.4, and by direct computation of the mean and variance check the results given in that example.

23.2.2   Show that adding a constant c to a random variable X changes the expectation value $\langle X \rangle$ by that same constant but not the variance. Show also that multiplying a random variable by a constant multiplies both the mean and variance by that constant. Show that the random variable $X - \langle X \rangle$ has mean value zero.

23.2.3   Using the definition given in Eq. (23.27) for the variance σ^2 of a continuous random variable, show that

$$\sigma^2 = \langle X^2 \rangle - \langle X \rangle^2.$$

23.2.4   A velocity $v_j = x_j/t_j$ is measured by recording the distances x_j at the corresponding times t_j. Show that $\bar{x}/\bar{t}$ is a good approximation for the average velocity v, provided that all the errors are small: $|x_j - \bar{x}| \ll |\bar{x}|$ and $|t_j - \bar{t}| \ll |\bar{t}|$.

23.2.5   Redefine the random variable Y in Example 23.2.5 as the number of fours through nines. Then determine the correlation of the X and Y random variables for the drawing of two cards (with replacement, as in the example).

23.2.6   The probability that a particle of an ideal gas travels a distance x between collisions is proportional to $e^{-x/f}\, dx$, where f is the constant mean free path. Verify that f is the average distance between collisions, and determine the probability of a free path of length $l \geq 3f$.

23.2.7   Determine the probability density for a particle in simple harmonic motion in the interval $-A \leq x \leq A$.

Hint. The probability that the particle is between x and $x + dx$ is proportional to the time it takes to travel across the interval.

23.3   BINOMIAL DISTRIBUTION

In this and the next two sections, we explore specific random variable distributions that are of importance both in physics and in the mathematical theories of probability and statistics. The topic of the present section is the **binomial distribution**, which typically occurs in the study of repeated independent trials of random events.

Example 23.3.1   REPEATED TOSSES OF DICE

What is the probability of three sixes in four tosses, all trials being independent? Getting one six in a single toss of a fair die has probability $a = 1/6$, and getting anything else has probability $b = 5/6$ with $a + b = 1$. Let the random variable $S = s$ be the number of sixes. In four tosses, $0 \leq s \leq 4$. The probability distribution $P(S = s)$ is given by the product of the two possibilities, a^s and b^{4-s}, times the number of ways that s sixes can be obtained from four tosses. This number is given by Eq. (23.18), and our probability is

$$P(S = s) = \frac{4!}{s!(4-s)!} a^s b^{4-s} = \binom{4}{s} a^s b^{4-s}. \tag{23.40}$$

We can now check that our probability is properly normalized by verifying that the sum of $P(S = s)$ for all s adds to unity. From properties of the binomial coefficients, we find

$$\sum_{s=0}^{4} \binom{4}{s} a^s b^{4-s} = (a+b)^4 = \left(\frac{1}{6} + \frac{5}{6}\right)^4 = 1. \tag{23.41}$$

Writing out the cases of Eq. (23.40) explicitly, we have

$$f(0) = b^4, \quad f(1) = 4ab^3, \quad f(2) = 6a^2b^2, \quad f(3) = 4a^3b, \quad f(4) = a^4,$$

so we can answer our original question: The probability of three sixes in four tosses is

$$4a^3 b = 4 \left(\frac{1}{6}\right)^3 \frac{5}{6} = \frac{5}{4 \cdot 3^4},$$

which is fairly small.   ∎

This case dealt with repeated independent trials, each with two possible outcomes of constant probability p for a hit and $q = 1 - p$ for a miss, and it is typical of many applications, including practical issues such as the random instances of defective products. The generalization to $S = s$ successes in n trials is given by the **binomial probability distribution**:

$$P(S = s) = \frac{n!}{s!(n-s)!} p^s q^{n-s} = \binom{n}{s} p^s q^{n-s}. \tag{23.42}$$

Figure 23.5 shows histograms for cases with 20 trials and various hit probabilities p.

Example 23.3.2   USE OF MOMENT-GENERATING FUNCTION

If we view our probability distribution as the result of adding together n random variables S_i, each having the value $s_i = 1$ with probability p and the value $s_i = 0$ with probability q, we can use the moment-generating function of Eq. (23.32) to obtain more information about the binomial distribution. We write

$$\langle e^{tS} \rangle = \langle e^{t(S_1 + S_2 + \cdots + S_n)} \rangle = \langle e^{tS_1} \rangle \langle e^{tS_2} \rangle \cdots \langle e^{tS_n} \rangle = \left[\langle e^{tS_1} \rangle \right]^n, \tag{23.43}$$

where we have used the fact that the trials are independent to write $\langle e^{tS} \rangle$ as a product of single-trial expectation values, all of which are identical.

We continue by evaluating $\langle e^{tS_1} \rangle$, which is an average for the two values $s_1 = 1$, with probability p, and $s_1 = 0$, with probability q. We get

$$\langle e^{tS_1} \rangle = pe^t + qe^0 = pe^t + q, \tag{23.44}$$

so Eq. (23.43) reduces to

$$\langle e^{tS} \rangle = (pe^t + q)^n. \tag{23.45}$$

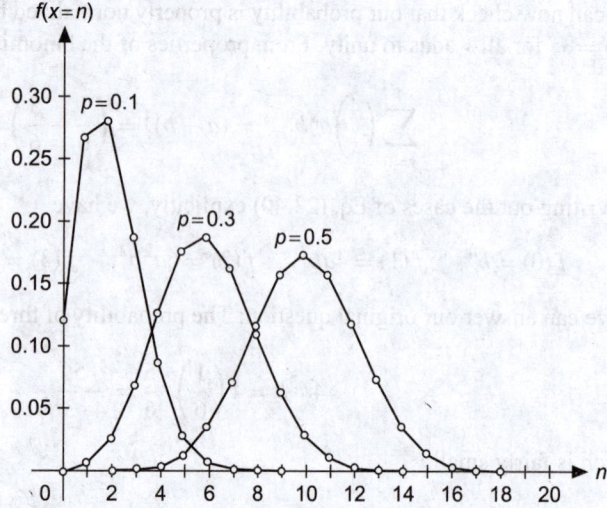

FIGURE 23.5   Binomial probability distributions for $n = 20$ and $p = 0.1, 0.3, 0.5$.

Note that the fact the trials were independent enabled us to obtain the moment-distribution function without enumerating all the many-trial possibilities.

Now that we have $\langle e^{tS} \rangle$ we can differentiate it, as in Eq. (23.33), to obtain moments of our distribution. Using

$$\frac{\partial \langle e^{tS} \rangle}{\partial t} = npe^t(pe^t + q)^{n-1},$$

$$\langle S \rangle = \sum_i s_i f(s_i) = \left. \frac{\partial \langle e^{tS} \rangle}{\partial t} \right|_{t=0} = np,$$

$$\frac{\partial^2 \langle e^{tS} \rangle}{\partial t^2} = npe^t(pe^t + q)^{n-1} + n(n-1)p^2 e^{2t}(pe^t + q)^{n-2},$$

$$\langle S^2 \rangle = \sum_i s_i^2 f(s_i) = \left. \frac{\partial^2 \langle e^{tS} \rangle}{\partial t^2} \right|_{t=0} = np + n(n-1)p^2,$$

we obtain, applying Eq. (23.28),

$$\sigma^2(S) = \langle S^2 \rangle - \langle S \rangle^2 = np + n(n-1)p^2 - n^2 p^2$$

$$= np(1 - p) = npq.$$

For a given n, we see that the variance is largest when $p = q = 1/2$. This behavior is apparent in Fig. 23.5, where we see that the distribution broadens as p is increased from 0.1 to 0.3 to 0.5. ∎

Exercises

23.3.1 Show that the variable $X = x$, defined as the number of heads in n coin tosses, is a random variable and determine its probability distribution. Describe the sample space. What are its mean value, the variance, and the standard deviation? Plot the probability function $P(x) = [n!/x!(n-x)!]2^{-n}$ for $n = 10, 20$, and 30 using graphics software.

23.3.2 Plot the binomial probability function for the probabilities $p = 1/6$, $q = 5/6$, and $n = 6$ throws of a die.

23.3.3 A hardware company knows that the probability of mass-producing nails includes a small probability $p = 0.03$ of defective nails (usually without a sharp tip). What is the probability of finding more than two defective nails in its commercial box of 100 nails?

23.3.4 Four cards are drawn from a shuffled bridge deck. What is the probability that they are all red? That they are all hearts? That they are honors? Compare the probabilities when each card is put back at a random place before drawing the next card, with the probabilities when the cards are not replaced in the deck.

23.3.5 Show that for the binomial distribution of Eq. (23.42), the most probable value of x is np.

23.4 POISSON DISTRIBUTION

The Poisson distribution is often used to describe situations in which an event occurs repeatedly at a constant rate of probability. Typical applications involve the decay of radioactive samples, but only in the approximation that the decay rate is slow enough that depletion in the population of the decaying species can be neglected. Other applications of interest include so-called **Poisson noise**, where fluctuations in a low rate of arrival of particles at a detector cause statistically predictable fluctuations in the detector signal.

The Poisson distribution can be developed by considering the probabilities that varying numbers of events are detected over an interval during which events occur at a constant rate of probability. The essential features of the development are that it assumes that (1) the event rate is small enough that there will be observationally accessible intervals in which at most one event occurs (i.e., one can consider intervals containing either zero or one event), and (2) the total number of events is small enough that it is useful to model their occurrence by a discrete probability distribution.

Let's proceed by defining the probability $P_n(t)$ that exactly n events occur in a time t, and that the probability of one event occurring in a short time interval dt will be μdt, where μ is a constant such that $\mu dt \ll 1$. This time interval dt is therefore short enough that we can neglect the possibility that more than one event occurs within it. Based on this hypothesis, we can set up a recursion relation for $P_n(t)$ by considering the two following mutually exclusive possibilities for the occurrence of n events in a time $d + dt$: (1) that n events occur during a time t and no events occur in a subsequent time interval dt, and (2) that $n - 1$ events occur during the time t and one event occurs during the subsequent interval dt. We therefore write

$$P_n(t + dt) = P_n(t)P_0(dt) + P_{n-1}(t)P_1(dt).$$

Then, inserting $P_1(dt) = \mu dt$ and $P_0(dt) = 1 - P_1(dt)$ and dividing through by dt, we get, after minor rearrangement,

$$\frac{dP_n(t)}{dt} = \frac{P_n(t+dt) - P_n(t)}{dt} = \mu P_{n-1}(t) - \mu P_n(t). \tag{23.46}$$

As a first step in solving this recursion relation, we note that for $n = 0$ it simplifies (because the possibility involving P_{n-1} does not exist) to

$$\frac{dP_0(t)}{dt} = -\mu P_0(t). \tag{23.47}$$

This equation, with initial condition $P_0(0) = 1$ (meaning that it is certain that no events are observed in an interval of zero length), has solution $P_0(t) = e^{-\mu t}$. Our solution informs us that the probability that no events have occurred before time t decays exponentially with t, at a rate dependent on the magnitude of μ. From this starting point and the further initial conditions $P_n(0) = 0$ for $n \geq 1$ (again, no detection of events occurs during an interval of zero length), the recursion relation can be solved to yield

$$P_n(t) = \frac{(\mu t)^n}{n!} e^{-\mu t}. \tag{23.48}$$

Equation (23.48) can be checked by substituting it into the recursion formula, Eq. (23.46), and by verifying that it satisfies the initial conditions $P_n(0) = \delta_{n0}$.

Equation (23.48) is taken as the definition of the Poisson distribution, regarded as a function of the quantity μt. Replacing μt by μ, we write the Poisson-distribution probabilities given for a discrete random variable X in the standard form,

$$p(n) = \frac{\mu^n}{n!} e^{-\mu}, \quad X = n = 0, 1, 2, \ldots. \tag{23.49}$$

We can check that the probabilities in Eq. (23.49) are properly normalized by noting that $\sum_n \mu^n / n!$ evaluates to e^μ. An example of a Poisson distribution is given in Fig. 23.6.

The mean value and variance of a Poisson distribution are easily calculated:

$$\langle X \rangle = \sum_{n=1}^{\infty} n \frac{\mu^n}{n!} e^{-\mu} = e^{-\mu} \sum_{n=1}^{\infty} \frac{\mu^n}{(n-1)!} = \mu, \tag{23.50}$$

$$\langle X^2 \rangle = \sum_{n=1}^{\infty} n^2 \frac{\mu^n}{n!} e^{-\mu} = e^{-\mu} \sum_{n=1}^{\infty} \left[\frac{\mu^n}{(n-2)!} + \frac{\mu^n}{(n-1)!} \right] = \mu^2 + \mu, \tag{23.51}$$

$$\sigma^2 = \langle X^2 \rangle - \langle X \rangle^2 = \mu(\mu+1) - \mu^2 = \mu. \tag{23.52}$$

The moments can also be calculated from the moment-generating function

$$\left\langle e^{tX} \right\rangle = \sum_{n=0}^{\infty} \frac{\mu^n}{n!} e^{-\mu} e^{tn} = e^{-\mu} \sum_{n=0}^{\infty} \frac{(\mu e^t)^n}{n!} = e^{\mu(e^t - 1)}.$$

Recall that the procedure for obtaining moments is to differentiate with respect to t and read out the derivatives evaluated at $t = 0$.

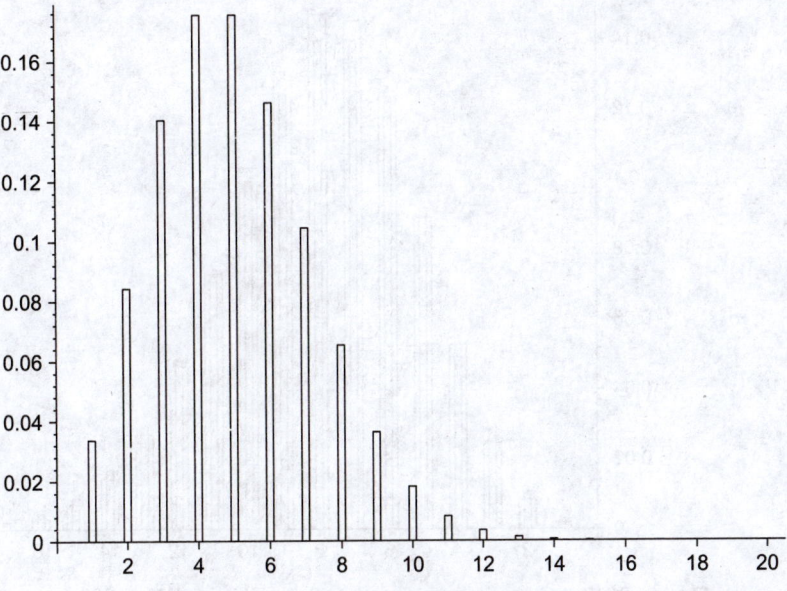

FIGURE 23.6   Poisson distribution, $\mu = 5$.

Relation to Binomial Distribution

A Poisson distribution becomes a good approximation of the binomial distribution for a large number n of trials and small probability $p \sim \mu/n$, with μ held constant.

Theorem: *In the limit $n \to \infty$ and $p \to 0$ so that the mean value $np \to \mu$ stays finite, the binomial distribution becomes a Poisson distribution.*

To prove this theorem, we need to find the large-n limit of the binomial distribution formula, Eq. (23.42). To do so, we apply Stirling's formula, in the form $n! \sim \sqrt{2\pi n}(n/e)^n$ for large n. See Eq. (12.110). For the quotient of the two n-dependent factorials occurring in Eq. (23.42), we have (keeping s finite while letting $n \to \infty$):

$$\frac{n!}{(n-s)!} \sim \left(\frac{n}{e}\right)^n \left(\frac{e}{n-s}\right)^{n-s} \sim \left(\frac{n}{e}\right)^s \left(\frac{n}{n-s}\right)^{n-s} \sim \left(\frac{n}{e}\right)^s \left(1 + \frac{s}{n-s}\right)^{n-s}.$$

The factor in the final expression raised to the power $n - s$ is, in the limit of large n, an expression of value e^s (in fact, it is, with $n - s$ changed to n, one of the often-used definitions of the exponential). The final result is

$$\frac{n!}{(n-s)!} \sim n^s. \tag{23.53}$$

We use a similar defining expression for the exponential to evaluate the factor q^{n-s} in Eq. (23.42). Writing $q^{n-s} = (1-p)^{n-s}$ and replacing p by its limiting value $p = \mu/n$,

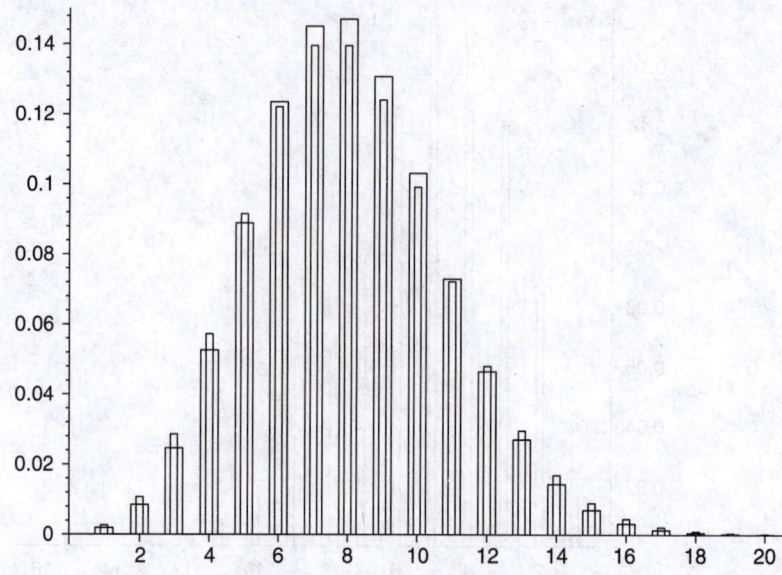

FIGURE 23.7   Comparison of binomial distribution ($N = 80$, $p = 0.1$), wide bars, and
Poisson distribution ($\mu = 8$), narrow bars.

we have

$$q^{n-s} = (1 - p)^{n-s} \sim \left(1 - \frac{\mu}{n}\right)^n \left(1 - \frac{\mu}{n}\right)^{-s} \sim e^{-\mu}\,(1) \sim e^{-\mu}. \qquad (23.54)$$

Inserting the large-n limiting values from Eqs. (23.53) and (23.54) into the formula for the
binomial distribution, we reach

$$P(S = s) = \frac{n!}{s!(n-s)!}\, p^s q^{n-s} \sim \frac{n^s}{s!}\, p^s e^{-\mu} \sim \frac{\mu^s}{s!} e^{-\mu}, \qquad (23.55)$$

where in the last step we have combined n^s and p^s into μ^s.

Equation (23.55) establishes our theorem, and thereby completes the connection between the Poisson and binomial distributions. This result, which becomes valid in the limit
of a large number of trials, each of small probability, is sometimes referred to as an example of the **laws of large numbers**. A comparison of the binomial and Poisson distributions
is presented as Fig. 23.7.

Exercises

23.4.1   Radioactive decays for long-lived isotopes are governed by the Poisson distribution. In
a Rutherford-Geiger experiment, the numbers of emitted α particles are counted in each
of $n = 2608$ time intervals of 7.5 seconds each. In Table 23.1 n_i is the number of time
intervals in which i particles were emitted. Determine the average number λ of particles
emitted per time interval, and compare the n_i of Table 23.1 with np_i computed from
the Poisson distribution with mean value λ.

Table 23.1   Data for Exercise 23.4.1

$i \rightarrow$	0	1	2	3	4	5	6	7	8	9	10
$n_i \rightarrow$	57	203	383	525	532	408	273	139	45	27	16

23.4.2 Derive the standard deviation of a Poisson distribution of mean value μ.

23.4.3 The number of α-particles emitted by the decay of a radium sample is counted per minute for 40 hours. The total number is 5000. How many 1-minute intervals are expected with (a) 2, and (b) 5 α-particles?

23.4.4 For a radioactive sample, 10 decays are counted on average in 100 seconds. Use the Poisson distribution to estimate the probability of counting 3 decays in 10 seconds.

23.4.5 ^{238}U has a half-life of 4.51×10^9 years. Its decay series ends with the stable lead isotope ^{206}Pb. The ratio of the number of ^{206}Pb to ^{238}U atoms in a rock sample is measured as 0.0058. Estimate the age of the rock assuming that all the lead in the rock is from the initial decay of the ^{238}U, which determines the rate of the entire decay process, because the subsequent steps take place far more rapidly.

Hint. This is not a Poisson distribution problem, but is an application of the decay law $N(t) = Ne^{-\lambda t}$, where λ, the decay constant, is related to the half-life T by $T = \ln 2/\lambda$.

ANS. 3.8×10^7 years.

23.4.6 The probability of hitting a target in one shot is known to be 20%. If five shots are fired independently, what is the probability of striking the target at least once?

23.5   GAUSS' NORMAL DISTRIBUTION

The bell-shaped Gauss distribution is defined by the probability density

$$f(x) = \frac{1}{\sigma\sqrt{2\pi}} \exp\left(-\frac{[x-\mu]^2}{2\sigma^2}\right), \quad -\infty < x < \infty, \tag{23.56}$$

with mean value μ and variance σ^2. In part because it represents continuous limits of both the binomial and Poisson distributions, it is by far the most important continuous probability distribution and is displayed in Fig. 23.8.

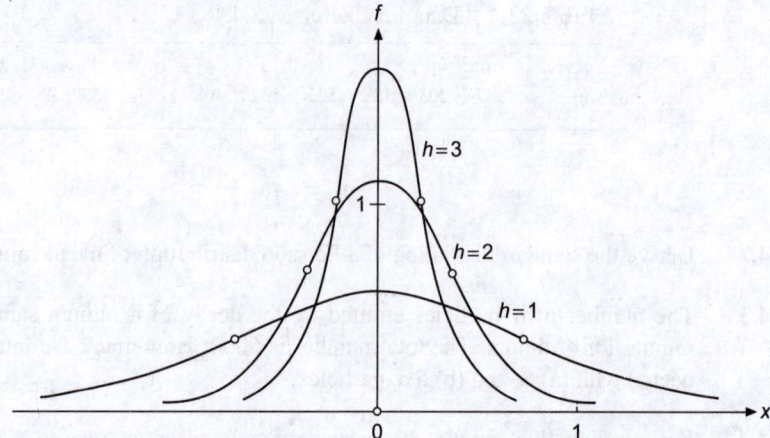

FIGURE 23.8   Gauss normal distribution for mean value zero and various standard deviations (marked by circles). Curves are labeled by $h = 1/\sigma\sqrt{2}$.

It is properly normalized because, substituting $y = (x - \mu)/\sigma\sqrt{2}$, we obtain

$$\frac{1}{\sigma\sqrt{2\pi}} \int_{-\infty}^{\infty} e^{-(x-\mu)^2/2\sigma^2} dx = \frac{1}{\sqrt{\pi}} \int_{-\infty}^{\infty} e^{-y^2} dy = \frac{2}{\sqrt{\pi}} \int_{0}^{\infty} e^{-y^2} dy = 1.$$

To check the mean value, we can make the substitution $y = x - \mu$, and find that

$$\langle X \rangle - \mu = \int_{-\infty}^{\infty} \frac{x - \mu}{\sigma\sqrt{2\pi}} e^{-(x-\mu)^2/2\sigma^2} dx = \int_{-\infty}^{\infty} \frac{y}{\sigma\sqrt{2\pi}} e^{-y^2/2\sigma^2} dy = 0, \qquad (23.57)$$

showing that $\langle X \rangle = \mu$. The zero result in Eq. (23.57) occurs because the integrand is odd in y, so the integral over $y > 0$ cancels that over $y < 0$. A check that the variance of this normal distribution is indeed σ^2 is the topic of Exercise 23.5.1.

We can compute conditional probabilities for the normal distribution. In particular, making for convenience the substitution $y = (x - \langle X \rangle)/\sigma$,

$$P(|X - \langle X \rangle| > k\sigma) = P\left(\frac{|X - \langle X \rangle|}{\sigma} > k\right) = P(|Y| > k)$$

$$= \sqrt{\frac{2}{\pi}} \int_{k}^{\infty} e^{-y^2/2} dy = \sqrt{\frac{4}{\pi}} \int_{k/\sqrt{2}}^{\infty} e^{-z^2} dz = \text{erfc}(k/\sqrt{2}),$$

we can evaluate the integral for $k = 1, 2, 3$, and thus extract the following numerical relations for a normally distributed random variable:

$$P(|X - \langle X \rangle| \geq \sigma) \approx 0.3173, \quad P(|X - \langle X \rangle| \geq 2\sigma) \approx 0.0455,$$

$$P(|X - \langle X \rangle| \geq 3\sigma) \approx 0.0027. \qquad (23.58)$$

It is interesting to compare the last of these quantities with Chebyshev's inequality, which gives 1/9 for the probability that an event falls further than 3σ from the mean. The 1/9 applies to an **arbitrary** probability distribution, and is in strong contrast to the much smaller 0.0027 given by the 3σ-rule for the **normal** distribution.

Limits of Poisson and Binomial Distributions

In a special limit, the discrete Poisson probability distribution is closely related to the continuous Gauss distribution. This limit theorem is another example of the **laws of large numbers**, which are often dominated by the bell-shaped normal distribution.

> **Theorem:** *For large n and mean value μ, the Poisson distribution approaches a Gauss distribution.*

To prove this theorem, in the limit $n \to \infty$, we approximate for large n the factorial in the Poisson probability $p(n)$ by Stirling's asymptotic formula, $n! \sim \sqrt{2n\pi}\,(n/e)^n$, and choose the deviation $v = n - \mu$ from the mean value as the new variable. We let the mean value μ approach ∞ and treat v/μ as small, but assume v^2/μ to be finite. Substituting $n = \mu + v$, we obtain

$$\ln p(n) = \ln\left(\frac{\mu^n e^{-\mu}}{n!}\right) = n \ln \mu - \mu - \ln\sqrt{2n\pi} - n \ln n + n$$

$$= (\mu + v)\ln\left(\frac{\mu}{\mu + v}\right) + v - \ln\sqrt{2(\mu + v)\pi}$$

$$= (\mu + v)\ln\left(1 - \frac{v}{\mu + v}\right) + v - \ln\sqrt{2\pi(\mu + v)}.$$

We next expand the first logarithmic term in powers of $v/(\mu + v)$, reaching

$$\ln p(n) = -\sum_{t=1}^{\infty} \frac{v^t}{t(\mu + v)^{t-1}} + v - \ln\sqrt{2\pi(\mu + v)}. \tag{23.59}$$

The first two terms of the t summation yield nonvanishing contributions in the large-μ limit; further terms vanish because the power of v in the numerator is less than twice that of μ in the denominator. Replacing $\mu + v$ by μ, Eq. (23.59) reduces to

$$\ln p(n) \sim -\frac{v^2}{2\mu} - \ln\sqrt{2\pi\mu}, \quad \text{equivalent to} \quad p(n) \sim \frac{1}{\sqrt{2\pi\mu}}e^{-v^2/2\mu}. \tag{23.60}$$

This is a Gauss distribution of the continuous variable v with mean value 0 and standard deviation $\sigma = \sqrt{\mu}$.

In another special limit, the discrete binomial probability distribution is also closely related to the continuous Gauss distribution. This limit theorem is yet another example of the **laws of large numbers**.

Theorem: *In the limit $n \to \infty$, with p a finite trial probability such that the mean value $np \to \infty$, the binomial distribution becomes a Gauss normal distribution. Recall from Section 23.4 that, when $np \to \mu < \infty$, the binomial distribution becomes a Poisson distribution.*

Instead of the large number s of successes in n trials, we use the deviation $v = s - pn$ from the (large) mean value pn as our new continuous random variable, under the condition that as $n \to \infty$, $|v| \ll pn$ (so $v/n \to 0$) but v^2/n is finite. Thus, we replace s by $pn + v$ and $n - s$ by $qn - v$ in the factorials of the formula for the binomial distribution, Eq. (23.42). Writing now $W(v)$ as our probability distribution in the large-pn limit, we apply Stirling's formula as we have done several times before, obtaining initially

$$W(v) = \frac{p^s q^{n-s} n^{n+1/2} e^{-n+s+(n-s)}}{\sqrt{2\pi}(pn+v)^{s+1/2}(qn-v)^{n-s+1/2}}. \tag{23.61}$$

Next we factor out the dominant powers of n and cancel powers of p and q to find

$$W(v) = \frac{1}{\sqrt{2\pi pqn}} \left(1 + \frac{v}{pn}\right)^{-(pn+v+1/2)} \left(1 - \frac{v}{qn}\right)^{-(qn-v+1/2)}. \tag{23.62}$$

Taking the logarithm of $W(v)$ and expanding in powers of v, we retain only the terms through v^2, yielding

$$\ln W(v) = -\ln\sqrt{2\pi pqn}$$
$$- \left[\frac{v}{n}\left(\frac{1}{2p} - \frac{1}{2q}\right) - \frac{v^2}{n^2}\left(\frac{1}{4p^2} + \frac{1}{4q^2}\right) + \frac{v^2}{n}\left(\frac{1}{2p} + \frac{1}{2q}\right) + \cdots\right]. \tag{23.63}$$

Setting v/n to zero, noting that

$$\left(\frac{1}{2p} + \frac{1}{2q}\right) = \frac{p+q}{2pq} = \frac{1}{2pq},$$

and dropping all terms v^t with $t > 2$, we obtain our large-n limit

$$W(v) = \frac{1}{\sqrt{2\pi pqn}} e^{-v^2/2pqn}, \tag{23.64}$$

which is a Gauss distribution in the deviations $s - pn$, with mean value 0 and standard deviation $\sigma = \sqrt{npq}$. The large values assumed for both pn and qn (and the discarded terms) restrict the validity of the theorem to the central part of the Gaussian bell shape, and exclude the tails.

Exercises

23.5.1 Show that the variance of the normal distribution given by Eq. (23.56) is σ^2, the symbol in that equation.

23.5.2 Show that Eq. (23.62) can be obtained by manipulation of the formula Eq. (23.61) for $W(v)$.

23.5.3 With $W(v)$ the expression in Eq. (23.62), show that the expansion of $\ln W(v)$ in powers of v leads to Eq. (23.63).

23.5.4 What is the probability for a normally distributed random variable to differ by more than 4σ from its mean value? Compare your result with the corresponding one from Chebyshev's inequality. Explain the difference in your own words.

23.5.5 An instructor grades a final exam of a large undergraduate class, obtaining the mean value of points M and the variance σ^2. Assuming a normal distribution for the number M of points, he defines a grade F when $M < m - 3\sigma/2$, D when $m - 3\sigma/2 < M < m - \sigma/2$, C when $m - \sigma/2 < M < m + \sigma/2$, B when $m + \sigma/2 < M < m + 3\sigma/2$, and A when $M > m + 3\sigma/2$. What is the percentage of As, Fs; Bs, Ds; and Cs? Redesign the cutoffs so that there are equal percentages of As and Fs (5%), 25% Bs and Ds, and 40% Cs.

23.6 TRANSFORMATIONS OF RANDOM VARIABLES

We have already encountered some elementary transformations involving random variables: In Section 23.2 we observed that a random variable $Y = aX + b$ will have mean value $\langle Y \rangle = a\langle X \rangle + b$ and variance $\sigma^2(Y) = a^2\sigma^2(X)$. Here we consider more general transformations, with particular focus on continuous probability distributions.

First, consider a simple change of random variable from X to Y, where $y = y(x)$. If the probability distribution of X is $f(x)dx$, then the contribution at x to some quantity $M(y)$ is

$$P\{M[y(x)]\}dx = M[y(x)]f(x)dx. \tag{23.65}$$

But we may wish to express the probability in terms of the distribution of Y, writing

$$P[M(y)]dy = M(y)g(y)dy, \tag{23.66}$$

for y evaluated at the point corresponding to x, i.e., $y = y(x)$. To make these equations consistent, it is necessary that

$$g(y)dy = f(x)dx, \quad \text{or} \quad g(y) = f[x(y)]\frac{dx}{dy}. \tag{23.67}$$

For example, if $y = x^2$, then $dx/dy = 1/(2x) = y^{-1/2}/2$ and $g(y) = f(\sqrt{y})y^{-1/2}/2$.

Let's now address the transformation of two random variables X, Y into $U(X, Y)$, $V(X, Y)$. Again we treat the continuous case. If

$$u = u(x, y), \quad v = v(x, y), \quad x = x(u, v), \quad y = y(u, v) \tag{23.68}$$

describe the transformation and its inverse; integrals of the probability density will transform by formulas that include the Jacobian of the transformation (see Section 4.4). The transformed probability density becomes

$$g(u, v) = f(x(u, v), y(u, v))|J|, \tag{23.69}$$

where the Jacobian is

$$J = \frac{\partial(x, y)}{\partial(u, v)} = \begin{vmatrix} \dfrac{\partial x}{\partial u} & \dfrac{\partial x}{\partial v} \\[2mm] \dfrac{\partial y}{\partial u} & \dfrac{\partial y}{\partial v} \end{vmatrix}. \tag{23.70}$$

This is a generalization of Eq. (23.67).

Addition of Random Variables

Let's apply this analysis to a situation in which Z is the sum of two random variables X and Y, or $Z = X + Y$. We transform to new variables X and Z, so the transformation is $x = x, z = x + y$; or $x = x, y = z - x$. The Jacobian for this transformation is

$$J = \begin{vmatrix} \dfrac{\partial x}{\partial x} & \dfrac{\partial x}{\partial z} \\[2mm] \dfrac{\partial(z - x)}{\partial x} & \dfrac{\partial(z - x)}{\partial z} \end{vmatrix} = \begin{vmatrix} 1 & 0 \\ -1 & 1 \end{vmatrix} = 1.$$

If our original probability distribution was $f(x, y)$, it therefore transforms into $g(x, z) = f(x, z - x)$. We are usually interested in the marginal distribution in Z, obtained by integrating over x, and

$$P(Z = z) \equiv g(z) = \int_{-\infty}^{\infty} f(x, z - x) dx. \tag{23.71}$$

In the oft-occurring case that X and Y are independent random variables, so $f(x, y) = f_1(x) f_2(y)$, Eq. (23.71) assumes the form

$$g(z) = \int_{-\infty}^{\infty} f_1(x) f_2(z - x) dx, \tag{23.72}$$

which we recognize as a Fourier convolution, see Eq. (20.68):

$$g(z) = \int_{-\infty}^{\infty} f_1(x) f_2(z - x) dx = \sqrt{2\pi}(f_1 * f_2)(z). \tag{23.73}$$

Equation (23.72) gives us a general formula whereby we can obtain the distribution of $Z = X + Y$ from the distributions of independent variables X and Y, while Eq. (23.73) shows that it may be useful to consider the use of Fourier transforms for evaluating the integral. In fact, the moment-generating function, Eq. (23.32), is (if t is replaced by it) proportional to the Fourier transform of the probability density, and

$$\langle e^{itX} \rangle = \int e^{itx} f(x) dx = \sqrt{2\pi} f^T(t) \tag{23.74}$$

is known as the **characteristic function** in probability theory.

Applying the Fourier convolution theorem, Eq. (20.70), we therefore write

$$[P(Z = z)]^T (t) \equiv g^T (t) = \sqrt{2\pi} f_1^T (t) f_2^T (t), \tag{23.75}$$

showing that we can obtain $g(z)$ as the inverse Fourier transform

$$g(z) = \int e^{-izt} f_1^T (t) f_2^T (t) dt. \tag{23.76}$$

Connection with statistics texts will be improved by restating Eqs. (23.75) and (23.76) using the characteristic function notation. Equation (23.75) is equivalent to

$$\langle e^{itZ} \rangle = \langle e^{it(X+Y)} \rangle = \langle e^{itX} \rangle \langle e^{itY} \rangle. \tag{23.77}$$

Equation (23.76) states that $g(z)$ is the distribution that corresponds to $\langle e^{itZ} \rangle$; since Fourier transforms have inverses it can be assured that such a distribution exists.

Example 23.6.1 ADDITION THEOREM, NORMAL DISTRIBUTION

A good example of the analysis for a random variable $Z = X + Y$ is provided when X and Y are taken to be Gauss normal distributions with zero mean value and the same variance. This situation corresponds to a relationship known as the **addition theorem** for normal distributions.

> **Theorem:** *If the* **independent** *random variables* X, Y *have identical normal distributions, that is, the same mean value and variance, then* $Z = X + Y$ *has normal distribution with twice the mean value and twice the variance of* X *and* Y.

To prove this theorem, we assume without loss of generality that the normal distributions each have variance $\sigma = 1$, so, from Eq. (23.56), each has the form

$$f(x) = \frac{1}{\sqrt{2\pi}} e^{-(x-\mu)^2/2}.$$

From Eq. (20.18) and the translation formula, Eq. (20.67), we find the Fourier transform of $f(x)$ to be

$$f^T (t) = \frac{1}{\sqrt{2\pi}} e^{it\mu} e^{-t^2/2}.$$

Now, applying Eq. (23.75), we have

$$g^T (t) = \frac{1}{\sqrt{2\pi}} e^{2it\mu} e^{-t^2}.$$

Taking the inverse transform, noting that the complex exponential shifts the origin by an amount 2μ, we get

$$g(z) = \frac{1}{2\sqrt{\pi}} e^{-(z-2\mu)^2/4},$$

which shows that the mean and variance of Z are twice those of X and Y, so the theorem is satisfied. ∎

Multiplication or Division of Random Variables

Consider now the product $Z = XY$, taking X, Z as the new variables. This corresponds to the transformation $x = \tilde{x}$, $y = z/x$, with Jacobian

$$
J = \begin{vmatrix} \dfrac{\partial x}{\partial x} & \dfrac{\partial x}{\partial z} \\ \dfrac{\partial (z/x)}{\partial x} & \dfrac{\partial (z/x)}{\partial z} \end{vmatrix} = \begin{vmatrix} 1 & 0 \\ -z/x^2 & 1/x \end{vmatrix} = \frac{1}{x},
$$

so the marginal distribution of Z is given by

$$
g(z) = \int_{-\infty}^{\infty} f\left(x, \frac{z}{x}\right) \frac{dx}{|x|}. \tag{23.78}
$$

If the random variables X, Y are independent with densities f_1, f_2, then

$$
g(z) = \int_{-\infty}^{\infty} f_1(x) f_2\left(\frac{z}{x}\right) \frac{dx}{|x|}. \tag{23.79}
$$

Finally, let $Z = X/Y$, taking Y, Z as the new variables, corresponding to $x = yz$, $y = y$, with Jacobian

$$
J = \begin{vmatrix} \dfrac{\partial (yz)}{\partial y} & \dfrac{\partial (yz)}{\partial z} \\ \dfrac{\partial y}{\partial y} & \dfrac{\partial y}{\partial z} \end{vmatrix} = \begin{vmatrix} z & y \\ 1 & 0 \end{vmatrix} = -y,
$$

and the probability distribution of Z is given by

$$
g(z) = \int_{-\infty}^{\infty} f(yz, y)|y|dy. \tag{23.80}
$$

If the random variables X, Y are independent with densities f_1, f_2, then

$$
g(z) = \int_{-\infty}^{\infty} f_1(yz) f_2(y)|y|dy. \tag{23.81}
$$

Gamma Distribution

Up to this point the only specific continuous probability distribution we have introduced is the Gauss normal distribution. However, if we make a change in the random variable of that distribution from X to $Y = X^2$, there will result a different distribution of significant utility, known as a **gamma distribution**. Let's start the present discussion with the now quite familiar normal distribution of mean value zero and variance σ^2. It has probability distribution

$$f(x) = \frac{1}{\sigma\sqrt{2\pi}}e^{x^2/2\sigma^2}.$$

As indicated just after Eq. (23.67), a transformation to write the distribution in terms of $y = x^2$ leads us to

$$g(y) = \frac{e^{-y/2\sigma^2}}{\sigma\sqrt{2\pi}}\frac{y^{-1/2}}{2}.$$

However, this equation does not take into account the fact that y must be restricted to nonnegative values, and that the same value of y will be encountered for two different values of x, namely $x = +\sqrt{y}$ and $x = -\sqrt{y}$. These considerations make a more proper and complete formula for $g(y)$ the following:

$$g(y) = \begin{cases} 0, & y \leq 0, \\ \dfrac{y^{-1/2}e^{-y/2\sigma^2}}{(2\sigma^2)^{1/2}\sqrt{\pi}}, & y > 0. \end{cases} \tag{23.82}$$

This expression for $g(y)$ is normalized (it must be, due to the way in which it was obtained). However, it is instructive to check, which is best done by changing to a new variable $z = y/2\sigma^2$, in terms of which we have

$$\int_0^\infty g(z)dz = \frac{1}{\sqrt{\pi}}\int_0^\infty z^{-1/2}e^{-z}\,dz = \frac{\Gamma(\frac{1}{2})}{\sqrt{\pi}} = 1,$$

where we have identified the integral as $\Gamma\left(\frac{1}{2}\right)$ and also noted that $\Gamma\left(\frac{1}{2}\right) = \sqrt{\pi}$.

Because the functional form of $g(y)$ is essentially that of the integrand of the integral representation of the gamma function, the distribution given by $g(y)$ is called a **gamma distribution**, and in particular, a gamma distribution with parameters $p = 1/2$ (the argument of the gamma function) and σ^2 (the variance of the underlying normal distribution). We generalize to gamma distributions of general p and σ:

$$g(p, \sigma; y) \equiv \begin{cases} 0, & y \leq 0, \\ \dfrac{y^{p-1}e^{-y/2\sigma^2}}{(2\sigma^2)^p\Gamma(p)}, & y > 0. \end{cases} \tag{23.83}$$

The gamma distribution often appears in contexts where the random variables involved need to be added together. It is therefore useful to take note of the Fourier transform of $g(p, \sigma; y)$:

$$[g(p, \sigma)]^T(t) = \frac{1}{\sqrt{2\pi}}\frac{1}{(1 - 2i\sigma^2 t)^p}. \tag{23.84}$$

Using the characteristic-function notation as introduced at Eq. (23.74), and defining X to be a (p, σ) gamma-distributed random variable, Eq. (23.84) takes the alternative form

$$\langle e^{itX} \rangle = \frac{1}{(1 - 2i\sigma^2 t)^p}. \tag{23.85}$$

Example 23.6.2   ADDITION OF GAMMA-DISTRIBUTION RANDOM VARIABLES

Let's compute the distribution of a random variable $Y = X_1 + X_2$, where X_1 has gamma distribution $g(p_1, \sigma; x_1)$ and X_2 has gamma distribution $g(p_2, \sigma; x_2)$. Note that both X_1 and X_2 have the same variance.

Using Eq. (23.77) for the characteristic function of $X_1 + X_2$ and Eq. (23.85) to evaluate $\langle e^{itX_j} \rangle$, we get

$$\langle e^{itY} \rangle = \frac{1}{(1 - 2i\sigma^2 t)^{p_1 + p_2}}.$$

Recognizing this result as the characteristic function for a gamma distribution of parameter $p = p_1 + p_2$, we see that

$$g(y) = g(p_1 + p_2, \sigma; y).$$

Generalizing this result to an arbitrary number of X_j:

> The probability distribution for a sum of gamma-distributed random variables X_j of parameters p_j but all of the same σ is a gamma distribution for that σ and with $p = \sum_j p_j$.

A corollary to the above is obtained if we consider the probability distribution of a sum of the form

$$Z = \sum_{j=1}^{n} X_j^2, \tag{23.86}$$

where the X_j are Gauss normal distributions, all with the same variance σ^2. Because the quantities being summed are **squares** of random variables, it is useful first to make the substitutions $Y_j = X_j^2$, changing each distribution of X_j to that of a Y_j gamma distribution with $p = 1/2$, and finally combining the n gamma distributions to form the distribution of Z; the result will be a gamma distribution with $p = n/2$ and the common value of σ. Summarizing,

> The probability distribution for the sum of the squares of n Gauss normal random variables with a common variance σ^2, as in Eq. (23.86), will be a gamma distribution with parameters $p = n/2$ and the common value of σ.

∎

Exercises

23.6.1   Let $X_1, X_2, \ldots, X_n$ be independent normal random variables with the same mean $\bar{x}$ and variance σ^2. Show that

$$\frac{\sum_i X_i / n - \bar{x}}{\sigma \sqrt{n}}$$

is normal with mean zero and variance 1.

23.6.2   If the random variable X is normal with mean value 29 and standard deviation 3, what can you say about the distributions of $2X - 1$ and $3X + 2$?

23.6.3 For a normal distribution of mean value m and variance σ^2, find the distance r such that half the area under the bell shape is between $m - r$ and $m + r$.

23.6.4 If $\langle X \rangle$, $\langle Y \rangle$ are the average values of two independent random variables X, Y, what is the expectation value of the product XY?

23.6.5 If X and Y are two independent random variables with different probability densities and the function $f(x, y)$ has derivatives of any order, express $\langle f(X, Y) \rangle$ in terms of $\langle X \rangle$ and $\langle Y \rangle$. Develop similarly the covariance and correlation.

23.6.6 Let $f(x, y)$ be the joint probability density of two random variables X, Y. Find the variance $\sigma^2(aX + bY)$, where a, b are constants. What happens when X, Y are independent?

23.6.7 Obtain an addition theorem for the distribution of a random variable $Y = X_1 + X_2$ where X_1 and X_2 are Gauss normal distributions with different mean values μ_j and variances σ_j^2.

ANS. Y is normal with mean $\mu_1 + \mu_2$ and variance $\sigma_1^2 + \sigma_2^2$.

23.6.8 Show that the Fourier transform of the gamma-distribution probability density, Eq. (23.83), has the functional form given in Eq. (23.84).

23.7 STATISTICS

In statistics, probability theory is applied to the evaluation of data from random experiments or to samples to test some hypothesis because the data have random fluctuations due to lack of complete control over the experimental conditions. Typically one attempts to estimate the mean value and variance of the distributions from which the samples derive, and to generalize properties valid for a sample to the rest of the events at a prescribed confidence level. Any assumption about an unknown probability distribution is called a **statistical hypothesis**. The concepts of tests and confidence intervals are among the most important developments of statistics.

Error Propagation

When we measure a quantity x repeatedly, obtaining the values x_j, or select a sample for testing, we can compute

$$\bar{x} = \frac{1}{n} \sum_{j=1}^{n} x_j, \quad \sigma^2 = \frac{1}{n} \sum_{j=1}^{n} (x_j - \bar{x})^2,$$

where $\bar{x}$ is the mean value and σ^2 is the variance, a measure of the spread of the points about the mean value. We can write $x_j = \bar{x} + e_j$, where e_j is the deviation from the mean value, and we know that $\sum_j e_j = 0$.

Now suppose we want to estimate the value of a known function $f(x)$ based on these measurements x_j; that is, we want to assign a value of f given the set $f_j = f(x_j)$.

Substituting $x_j = \bar{x} + e_j$ and forming the mean value

$$\bar{f} = \frac{1}{n} \sum_j f(x_j) = \frac{1}{n} \sum_j f(\bar{x} + e_j)$$

$$= f(\bar{x}) + \frac{1}{n} f'(\bar{x}) \sum_j e_j + \frac{1}{2n} f''(\bar{x}) \sum_j e_j^2 + \cdots$$

$$= f(\bar{x}) + \frac{1}{2} \sigma^2 f''(\bar{x}) + \cdots, \tag{23.87}$$

we obtain the average value $\bar{f}$ as $f(\bar{x})$ in lowest order, as expected. But in second order there is a correction given by the variance with a scale factor $f''(\bar{x})/2$.

It is also of interest to determine the spread predicted for the values of $f(x_j)$. To lowest order, this is given by the average of the sum of squares of the deviations. Approximating f_j as $\bar{f} + f'(\bar{x})e_j$, we get

$$\sigma^2(f) \equiv \frac{1}{n} \sum_j (f_j - \bar{f})^2 \approx [f'(\bar{x})]^2 \frac{1}{n} \sum_j e_j^2 = [f'(\bar{x})]^2 \sigma^2. \tag{23.88}$$

In summary, we may formulate somewhat symbolically

$$f(\bar{x} \pm \sigma) = f(\bar{x}) \pm f'(\bar{x})\sigma$$

as the simplest form of error propagation for a function of one measured variable.

For a function $f(x_j, y_k) \equiv f_{jk}$ of two quantities $x_j = \bar{x} + u_j$, $y_k = \bar{y} + v_k$, where the x_j and y_k are measured independently of each other and we have r values of j and s values of k, we obtain similarly

$$\bar{f} = \frac{1}{rs} \sum_{j=1}^{r} \sum_{k=1}^{s} f_{jk} = f(\bar{x}, \bar{y}) + \frac{1}{r} f_x \sum_j u_j + \frac{1}{s} f_y \sum_k v_k + \cdots$$

$$\approx f(\bar{x}, \bar{y}). \tag{23.89}$$

The error in $\bar{f}$ is seen to be second-order in the u_j and v_k. In writing Eq. (23.89) we have used the relations $\sum_j u_j = \sum_k v_k = 0$ and have introduced the definitions

$$f_x = \frac{\partial f}{\partial x} \Big|_{\bar{x}, \bar{y}}, \quad f_y = \frac{\partial f}{\partial y} \Big|_{\bar{x}, \bar{y}}. \tag{23.90}$$

The variance of f is (to first order)

$$\sigma^2(f) = \frac{1}{rs} \sum_{j=1}^{r} \sum_{k=1}^{s} (f_{jk} - \bar{f})^2 = \frac{1}{rs} \sum_{j,k} (u_j f_x + v_k f_y)^2 = \frac{f_x^2}{r} \sum_j u_j^2 + \frac{f_y^2}{s} \sum_k v_k^2,$$

where we have dropped the zero cross term $\sum_{j,k} u_j v_k = \sum_j u_j \sum_k v_k$. Noting that $\sum_j u_j^2 = r\sigma_x^2$ and $\sum_k v_k^2 = s\sigma_y^2$, we reach the final result

$$\sigma^2(f) = \frac{1}{rs} \sum_{j,k} (f_{jk} - \bar{f})^2 = f_x^2 \sigma_x^2 + f_y^2 \sigma_y^2. \tag{23.91}$$

Symbolically, the error propagation for a function of two measured variables may be summarized as

$$f(\bar{x} \pm \sigma_x, \bar{y} \pm \sigma_y) = f(\bar{x}, \bar{y}) \pm \sqrt{f_x^2 \sigma_x^2 + f_y^2 \sigma_y^2}.$$

Example 23.7.1   REPEATED MEASUREMENTS

As an application and generalization of the result given in Eq. (23.91), let's consider what happens when we regard the mean of n measurements x_j as a function

$$\bar{x} = f(x_1, x_2, \ldots + x_n) = (x_1 + x_2 + \cdots + x_n)/n$$

of the variables $x_1, \ldots, x_n$, each with variance σ^2. Then we have $f_{x_j} = 1/n$ for each j, and, according to Eq. (23.91),

$$\sigma^2(\bar{x}) = \sum_{j=1}^n f_{x_j}^2 \sigma^2 = \sum_{j=1}^n \frac{\sigma^2}{n^2} = \frac{\sigma^2}{n}. \tag{23.92}$$

This result indicates that the standard deviation of the mean value, $\sigma(\bar{x})$, will decrease with the number of repeated measurements, approaching zero as $\sigma/\sqrt{n}$. It is important to recognize the distinction between the variance of the mean value, denoted $\sigma^2(\bar{x})$, and the corresponding quantity for the individual measurements (denoted σ^2).

If we refer now to our earlier result that the sum of n identically distributed, Gauss normal random variables is also a normal random variable with a variance equal to n times that of each variable (see Example 23.6.1), and note also that division of the sum by n (to form the mean) causes division of the variance by n^2, as discussed following Eq. (23.28), we find a result identical to that developed in the present example, but with the additional feature that the mean is also normally distributed.   ∎

The arithmetic mean $\bar{x}$ will, because of the distribution in the x_j, differ from the true (but unknown) value μ, with μ and $\bar{x}$ differing by some amount α, or $\bar{x} = \mu + \alpha$. However, as the number n of measurements increases, we expect that the error α will tend to zero, and that, according to Example 23.7.1, we can estimate α to fall in the range $(-\sigma/\sqrt{n} < \alpha < \sigma/\sqrt{n})$. We can refine this estimate by considering the spread of the x_j measured with respect to the true value μ, meaning that we compute the variance using the average of v_j^2, where $v_j = x_j - \mu$, instead of that of e_j^2, where, as before, $e_j = x_j - \bar{x}$. Calling this version of the variance s^2, we write

$$s^2 = \frac{1}{n} \sum_{j=1}^n v_j^2 = \frac{1}{n} \sum_{j=1}^n (e_j + \alpha)^2 = \frac{1}{n} \sum_{j=1}^n e_j^2 + \alpha^2, \tag{23.93}$$

where the term linear in e_j vanishes because $\sum_j e_j = 0$. Inserting now an estimate of α, in the form $\alpha^2 \approx s^2/n$ (this approximation good to first order), Eq. (23.93) rearranges to

$$s^2 \left(1 - \frac{1}{n}\right) = \frac{1}{n} \sum_{j=1}^{n} e_j^2, \tag{23.94}$$

equivalent to

$$s = \sqrt{\frac{\sum_j (x_j - \bar{x})^2}{n-1}}. \tag{23.95}$$

The quantity s is referred to as the **sample standard deviation**. Equation (23.95) is not well defined when $n = 1$, but that is not an issue because a single data point is insufficient to determine a spread. The presence of $n - 1$, in contrast to the factor n in Eq. (23.23), allows for the probable error in $\bar{x}$, and is known as **Bessel's correction** to the standard deviation formula.

Fitting Curves to Data

Suppose we have a sample of measurements y_j taken at times t_j, where the time is known precisely but the y_j are subject to experimental error. An example would be snapshots of the position of a particle in uniform motion at the times t_j. Our statistical hypothesis, motivated by Newton's first law and the initial condition that $y = 0$ when $t = 0$, is that $y(t)$ satisfies an equation of the form $y = at$, where the constant a is to be determined from the measurements.

To fit our equation to the data, we first minimize the sum of the squares of deviations $S = \sum_j (at_j - y_j)^2$ to determine the slope parameter a, also called **regression coefficient**, using the method of least squares. Differentiating S with respect to a we obtain

$$2 \sum_j (at_j - y_j)t_j = 0,$$

which we can solve for a:

$$a = \frac{\sum_j t_j y_j}{\sum_j t_j^2}. \tag{23.96}$$

Note that the numerator is built like a sample covariance, the scalar product of the variables t, y of the sample. As shown in Fig. 23.9, the measured values y_j do not as a rule lie on the line. They have the **sample standard deviation**, computed from Eq. (23.95),

$$s = \sqrt{\frac{\sum_j (y_j - at_j)^2}{n-1}}.$$

Alternatively, suppose that the y_j values are known precisely while the t_j are measurements subject to experimental error. As suggested by Fig. 23.10, in this case we need to

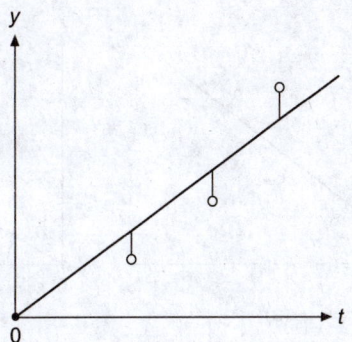

FIGURE 23.9   Straight line fit to data points (t_j, y_j) with t_j known, y_j measured.

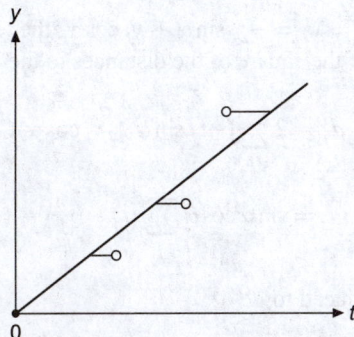

FIGURE 23.10   Straight line fit to data points (t_j, y_j) with y_j known, t_j measured.

interchange the roles of t and y and to fit the line $t = by$ to the data points. We minimize $S = \sum_j (by_j - t_j)^2$, setting $dS/db = 0$, and find similarly the slope parameter

$$b = \frac{\sum_j t_j y_j}{\sum_j y_j^2}.$$

(23.97)

In case both t_j and y_j have errors (we take t and y to have the same measurement precision), we have to minimize the sum of squares of the deviations of both variables. It is convenient to fit to a parameterization $t \sin\alpha - y \cos\alpha = 0$, so $y/t = \sin\alpha/\cos\alpha = \tan\alpha$, meaning that α is the angle the fitting line makes with the t-axis (see Fig. 23.11). Our task will therefore be to determine α. We also see from Fig. 23.11 that the fitting line has to be drawn so that the sum of the squares of the distances d_j of the points (t_j, y_j) from the line becomes a minimum. To find d_j, we rotate our coordinate system the angle α, which moves (t_j, y_j) to (t'_j, y'_j) according to

$$\begin{pmatrix} t'_j \\ y'_j \end{pmatrix} = \begin{pmatrix} \cos\alpha & \sin\alpha \\ -\sin\alpha & \cos\alpha \end{pmatrix} \begin{pmatrix} t_j \\ y_j \end{pmatrix},$$

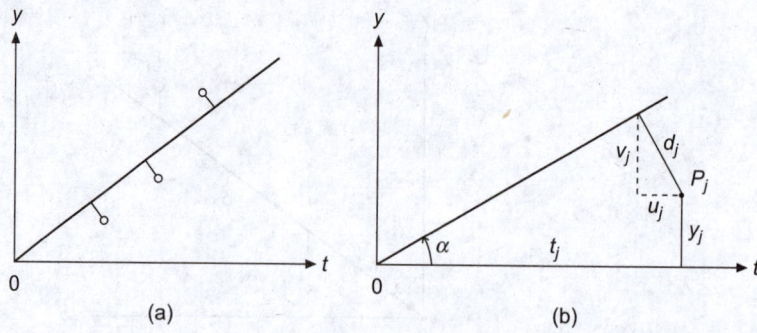

FIGURE 23.11   (a) Straight line fit to data points (t_j, y_j). (b) Geometry of deviations u_j, v_j, d_j.

which yields $d_j = y_j' = -t_j \sin\alpha + y_j \cos\alpha$, the (signed) distance to the line at angle α. The minimum of the square of the distances to the line is found from

$$\frac{d}{d\alpha} \sum_j d_j^2 = 2 \sum_j (-t_j \sin\alpha + y_j \cos\alpha)(-t_j \cos\alpha - y_j \sin\alpha)$$

$$= \sin\alpha \cos\alpha \sum_j \left(t_j^2 - y_j^2\right) - \left(\cos^2\alpha - \sin^2\alpha\right) \sum_j t_j y_j = 0,$$

which can be reduced to

$$\tan 2\alpha = \frac{2 \sum_j t_j y_j}{\sum_j \left(t_j^2 - y_j^2\right)}. \tag{23.98}$$

This least-squares fitting is appropriate when the measurement errors are unknown, as it gives equal weight to the deviation of each point from the fitting line.

Finally, if we have information that permits the assignment of different probable errors to different points, we have the alternative of making a "weighted" least-squares fit called a **chi square** fit, which we discuss in the next subsection.

The χ^2 Distribution

Given a set of u_j corresponding to values t_j of an independent variable (which is not necessarily a time), we seek to fit these data to a function $u(t, a_1, a_2, \ldots)$, where the a_i are parameters that are adjusted to optimize the fit. The optimization is carried out by minimizing a **weighted sum** of the squares of the deviations, where the weights are controlled by the assumed standard deviations σ_j of the respective measurements u_j. The quantity to be minimized is traditionally labeled χ^2 and called **chi-square**, and its precise definition is

$$\chi^2 = \sum_{j=1}^{n} \left(\frac{u_j - u(t_j, a, \ldots)}{\sigma_j}\right)^2, \tag{23.99}$$

where n is the number of data points. This quadratic merit function gives more weight to points with small measurement uncertainties σ_j.

The key assumptions adopted to analyze the probability distribution corresponding to the **chi-square** fit are (1) that each data point is an independent Gauss normal random variable X_j with zero mean and unit variance, with the unit variance assured by the presence of the σ_j in each term, and (2) that the distribution χ^2 is related to the X_j by

$$\chi^2 = \sum_{j=1}^{n} X_j^2.$$ (23.100)

Making a chi-square fit requires no knowledge of statistics; we simply apply standard analytical or numerical methods to minimize χ^2 for our set of data points. On the other hand, a knowledge of the chi-square probability distribution will be needed to determine whether we are getting the expected quality from our chi-square fit. In particular, if we wish to determine the probability of the occurrence of our data set based on the chi-square distribution (and possibly assess the adequacy of our assumptions regarding the individual-point variances σ_j^2), we must undertake further analysis.

Our earlier discussion of transformations of random variables included the analysis of sums of normally distributed X_j^2 of the form given in Eq. (23.100), with the result developed in Example 23.6.2. Specializing to the case at hand, we note that χ^2 will have a gamma probability distribution with parameters $p = n/2$ and $\sigma = 1$, so

$$g(\chi^2 = y) = \frac{y^{(n/2)-1}e^{-y/2}}{2^{n/2}\Gamma(n/2)}.$$ (23.101)

Plots of $g(y)$ for several values of n are given in Fig. 23.12.

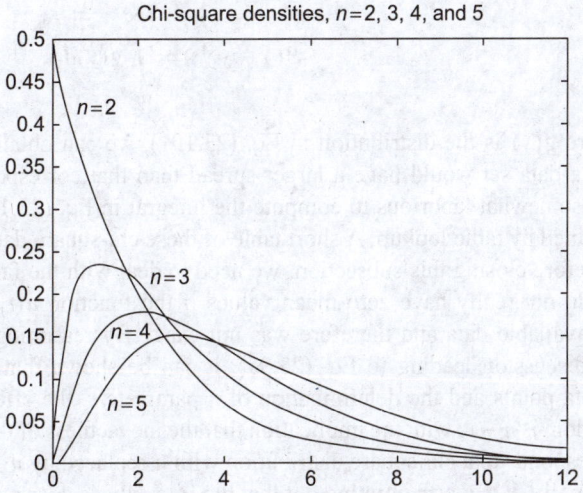

FIGURE 23.12 χ^2 probability density $g_n(y)$.

Table 23.2 χ^2 Distribution

n	$v = 0.8$	$v = 0.7$	$v = 0.5$	$v = 0.4$	$v = 0.3$	$v = 0.2$	$v = 0.1$
1	0.064	0.148	0.455	0.708	1.074	1.642	2.706
2	0.446	0.713	1.386	1.833	2.408	3.219	4.605
3	1.005	1.424	2.366	2.946	3.665	4.642	6.251
4	1.649	2.195	3.357	4.045	4.878	5.989	7.779
5	2.343	3.000	4.351	5.132	6.064	7.289	9.236
6	3.070	3.828	5.348	6.211	7.231	8.558	10.645

Note: A data set with n degrees of freedom will have probability v that its value of χ^2 exceeds the tabulated value.

It is also useful to note the moment-generating function for this distribution:

$$\langle e^{t\chi^2} \rangle = \frac{1}{(1 - 2t)^{n/2}}, \tag{23.102}$$

a result that follows directly from Eq. (23.85). Differentiating Eq. (23.102), we find

$$\langle \chi^2 \rangle = \frac{d(1 - 2t)^{-n/2}}{dt}\bigg|_{t=0} = n, \quad \langle (\chi^2)^2 \rangle = \frac{d^2(1 - 2t)^{-n/2}}{dt^2}\bigg|_{t=0} = n(n+2), \tag{23.103}$$

and therefore

$$\sigma^2(\chi^2) = \langle (\chi^2)^2 \rangle - \langle \chi^2 \rangle^2 = n(n+2) - n^2 = 2n. \tag{23.104}$$

These results suggest that typical data with realistically assigned individual-measurement variances would yield a value of χ^2 comparable to the number of data points. However, by calculating

$$P(\chi^2 > y_0) = \int_{y_0}^{\infty} g(y)dy, \tag{23.105}$$

where $g(y)$ is the distribution in Eq. (23.101), we can obtain for any y_0 the probability that a data set would have a larger spread than that corresponding to $\chi^2 = y_0$. Because it is somewhat laborious to compute the integral in Eq. (23.105), its values are generally obtained by table lookup. A short table of these chi-square data are given in Table 23.2.

Before closing this subsection, we need to deal with the fact that our random variables X_j do not really have zero mean values if the function $u(t_j, \ldots)$ was chosen based on the available data and therefore was not exact. By reasoning similar to that involved in the discussion leading to Eq. (23.95), it can be shown that if a chi-square fit involves n data points and the determination of r parameters, the effective number of degrees of freedom is $n - r$, with the implication that the inexactness of the fit in r degrees of freedom corresponds to a chi-square distribution with n replaced by $n - r$.

Finally, it is worth pointing out that the χ^2 analysis does not really test the assumptions that the data points are independent normal random variables. If these assumptions are not approximately valid, it is unlikely that good chi-square fits can be achieved.

Example 23.7.2 CHI-SQUARE FIT

Let us apply the χ^2 function to a straight-line fit of the type shown in Fig. 23.9, with the three measured points and their individual standard deviations, written as $(t_j, u_j \pm \sigma_j)$, having the values

$$(1, 0.8 \pm 0.1), \quad (2, 1.5 \pm 0.05), \quad (3, 2.7 \pm 0.2).$$

Before proceeding to the chi-square fit, we first fit a line assuming the points to be equally weighted, corresponding to using Eq. (23.96) for the slope a. We find

$$a = \frac{1(0.8) + 2(1.5) + 3(2.7)}{1^2 + 2^2 + 3^2} = \frac{11.9}{14} = 0.850.$$

The sample variance of the points from the line is

$$\sigma^2 = \frac{1}{2} \left([0.8 - 1(0.850)]^2 + [1.5 - 2(0.850)]^2 + (2.7 - 3(0.850)]^2 \right) = 0.0325,$$

and the variance of a is

$$\sigma^2(a) = \sum_j \left(\frac{\partial a}{\partial u_j} \right)^2 \sigma^2 = \sum_j \left(\frac{t_j}{\sum_k t_k^2} \right)^2 \sigma^2 = \frac{\sigma^2}{\sum_k t_k^2} = \frac{0.0325}{14} = 0.00232.$$

Thus, the unweighted fit yields $a = 0.850 \pm \sqrt{0.00232} = 0.850 \pm 0.048$.

Turning now to the chi-square fit, we next minimize

$$\chi^2 = \sum_j \left(\frac{u_j - at_j}{\sigma_j} \right)^2$$

with respect to a. This process yields

$$\frac{\partial \chi^2}{\partial a} = -2 \sum_j \frac{t_j(u_j - at_j)}{\sigma_j^2} = 0,$$

or

$$a = \sum_j \frac{t_j u_j}{\sigma_j^2} \bigg/ \sum_j \frac{t_j^2}{\sigma_j^2}.$$

In our case

$$a = \frac{\dfrac{1(0.8)}{0.1^2} + \dfrac{2(1.5)}{0.05^2} + \dfrac{3(2.7)}{0.2^2}}{\dfrac{1^2}{0.1^2} + \dfrac{2^2}{0.05^2} + \dfrac{3^2}{0.2^2}} = \frac{1482.5}{1925} = 0.770.$$

The value we obtained for a is dominated by the middle point, the smallest σ_j; if that point were the only one used, we would have gotten $a = 1.5/2 = 0.75$. The variance of a, $\sigma^2(a)$, is now

$$\sigma^2(a) = \sum_j \left(\frac{\partial a}{\partial u_j} \right)^2 \sigma_j^2 = \sum_j \left(\frac{t_j/\sigma_j^2}{\sum_k t_k^2/\sigma_k^2} \right)^2 \sigma_j^2 = \frac{1}{\sum_k t_k^2/\sigma_k^2} = \frac{1}{1925} = 0.000519.$$

The chi-square estimate of a is therefore $a = 0.770 \pm \sqrt{0.000519} = 0.770 \pm 0.023$.

Our fit has for χ^2 the value

$$\chi^2 = \frac{[0.8 - 1(0.770)]^2}{0.1^2} + \frac{[1.5 - 2(0.770)]^2}{0.05^2} + \frac{[2.7 - 3(0.770)]^2}{0.2^2} = 4.533.$$

Our problem involves three points and one parameter, and therefore its chi-square distribution has two degrees of freedom and, according to Eqs. (23.103) and (23.104), has a mean value of 2 and a variance of 4. Our value of χ^2, 4.533, is significantly larger than the mean value of the distribution and therefore describes a data set with more spread than would normally be expected for the stated values of σ_j. We can obtain a more quantitative measure of the probability that χ^2 would be at least as large as our value by comparing with the entries in Table 23.2. Using the row of the table for $n = 2$, we see that the probability of getting a spread larger than that of our present data is quite small, only slightly above 0.1.   ∎

Student t Distribution

The Student t distribution (sometimes just called the t **distribution**) is designed for use with small data sets for which the variance is unknown. This distribution was first described by W. S. Gosset, who published his work under the pen name "Student" because his employer, the Guinness brewery, would not permit him to publish it under his own name.

Gosset considered the probability distribution of a random variable T, of the form

$$T = \frac{Y\sqrt{n}}{\sqrt{S/n}}. \tag{23.106}$$

For the applications under consideration here,

$$Y = \frac{1}{n}\sum_{j=1}^{n} X_j - \mu = \bar{X} - \mu, \tag{23.107}$$

$$S = \sum_{j=1}^{n} X_j^2. \tag{23.108}$$

Here the X_j are a set of n independent Gauss normal random variables, each of the same unknown variance σ^2. The quantity μ is the (unknown) value of the mean of X. An important feature of Gosset's choice for T is that (as we shall shortly show) its probability distribution $f_n(t)$ is independent of the variance of the X_j.

The procedure for obtaining the probability distribution of T depends on the fact that Y and S are independent random variables. That is so, but proof is beyond the scope of the present abbreviated discussion. We start by noting that S is a gamma distribution, with probability distribution $g(n, \sigma; s)$, as given in Eq. (23.85). Next, we proceed to the distribution of $U = \sqrt{S/n}$, which we denote $h(u)$. Making a change of variable from s to nu^2, and observing that $ds = (ds/du)du$, we find

$$h(u) = g(n, \sigma; nu^2)(2nu). \tag{23.109}$$

This is the probability distribution of the denominator of T. To get the distribution of the numerator, we note that Y is a normal distribution with variance σ^2/n (see Eq. (23.92)), and mean zero. It, therefore (see Eq. (23.56)), has the distribution we denote $r(y)$, of the form

$$r(y) = \sqrt{\frac{n}{2\pi\sigma^2}} e^{-ny^2/2\sigma^2}. \tag{23.110}$$

The numerator, $Z = Y\sqrt{n}$, will therefore have a distribution $k(z)$, where $z = y\sqrt{n}$, so

$$k(z) = r(z/\sqrt{n})(dy/dz) = \frac{1}{\sqrt{2\pi\sigma^2}} e^{z^2/2\sigma^2}; \tag{23.111}$$

the presence of the factor $\sqrt{n}$ causes the numerator to have variance σ^2. Finally, we use the formula for the ratio of two independent distributions, Eq. (23.81), to obtain

$$f(t) = \int_0^\infty k(ut)h(u)u\,du. \tag{23.112}$$

The integration only extends from zero to infinity because the gamma distribution in $h(u)$ is only nonzero for positive u. Inserting expressions for the quantities in Eq. (23.112),

$$f_n(t) = \frac{1}{\sqrt{2\pi\sigma^2}} \int_0^\infty e^{-u^2 t^2/2\sigma^2} g(n, \sigma; nu^2)(2nu^2)\,du$$

$$= \frac{1}{\sqrt{2\pi\sigma^2}} \frac{1}{2^{n/2}\sigma^n \Gamma(n/2)} \int_0^\infty e^{-u^2 t^2/2\sigma^2} (nu^2)^{(n/2)-1} e^{-nu^2/2\sigma^2} (2nu^2)\,du$$

$$= \frac{2}{\sigma^{n+1}\sqrt{\pi n}} \left(\frac{n}{2}\right)^{(n+1)/2} \frac{1}{\Gamma(n/2)} \int_0^\infty e^{-u^2(t^2+n)/2\sigma^2} u^n\,du. \tag{23.113}$$

To complete the evaluation, we change variables in the integral to $z = u^2(t^2 + n)/2\sigma^2$, thereby making the integral identifiable as a gamma function, so

$$\int_0^\infty e^{-u^2(t^2+n)/2\sigma^2} u^n\,du = \frac{1}{2}\left(\frac{2\sigma^2}{t^2+n}\right)^{(n+1)/2} \int_0^\infty z^{(n-1)/2} e^{-z}\,dz$$

$$= \frac{1}{2}\left(\frac{2\sigma^2}{t^2+n}\right)^{(n+1)/2} \Gamma\left(\frac{n+1}{2}\right). \tag{23.114}$$

Inserting this result into Eq. (23.113) and simplifying, we note that the instances of σ entirely cancel, and we are left with

$$f_n(t) = \frac{\Gamma\left(\dfrac{n+1}{2}\right)}{\sqrt{\pi n}\,\Gamma\left(\dfrac{n}{2}\right)} \left(1 + \frac{t^2}{n}\right)^{-(n+1)/2} \tag{23.115}$$

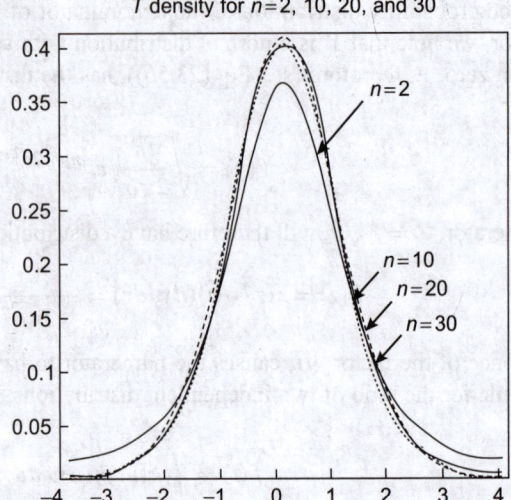

FIGURE 23.13   Student t probability density $f_n(t)$ for $n = 2, 10, 20,$ and 30.

Equation (23.115) is the probability density for the t distribution with n degrees of free-dom. This equation shows that we have achieved the desired result, namely that the dis-tribution T is independent of the variance of the input random variables X_j. Since it is our intention to use the t distribution for the reduction of experimental data of unknown variance, we have achieved our current objective. Figure 23.13 shows densities $f_n(t)$ for several n; an important feature of these curves is that they depend very weakly on n.

Confidence Intervals

A **confidence interval** for a random variable X is the range within which x will fall, not with certainty but with a high probability, the confidence level, which we can choose. If X has a probability distribution $f(x)$, the confidence interval for probability p will be the range of x, usually symmetrically centered about some value x_0, that contains the fraction p of its probability distribution. If this range is bounded by $x_0 - dx$ and $x_0 + dx$, it is customary to write that $x = x_0 \pm dx$ with $(100p)\%$ confidence. If, for example, a computed value of x is 0.50 and 90% of its probability distribution falls between $x = 0.40$ and $x = 0.60$, we say that x has the value $x = 0.50 \pm 0.10$ with 90% confidence.

Confidence intervals are usually found by what is called the **pivotal method**, which involves relating the variable for which we desire a confidence interval to a known proba-bility distribution. The identification and selection of pivotal quantities is in general outside the scope of this text, but for a Gauss normal random variable with zero mean, a suitable pivot is its t distribution. Referring to Eq. (23.106), this means we can estimate a confi-dence interval for Y (the deviations of the observed mean $\bar{X}$ from its true value) from the equation

$$Y = \bar{X} - \mu = \frac{T\sqrt{S/n}}{\sqrt{n}}, \qquad (23.116)$$

where T is the random variable corresponding to the t distribution and S is the single value obtained by inserting the observed values of the X_i into Eq. (23.108). We use Eq. (23.116) by inserting into it the range of T that corresponds to a total probability p, calculating therefrom the corresponding range of Y. Note that we do not insert a probability distribution for S; we use the value of S arising from our data.

The distribution of T is an even function of t with a maximum at $t = 0$, as is obvious from Eq. (23.115) and Fig. 23.13, and our confidence interval for T will naturally be centered about zero. Therefore, a confidence interval of probability p will correspond to a symmetric range of t, $(-C_p < t < +C_p)$, such that

$$P(-C_p < t < +C_p) = p.$$

Because $f(t)$ is even, we also have

$$P(-\infty < t < +C_p) = \tfrac{1}{2} + (-C_p < t < C_p)/2,$$

which is equivalent to

$$P(-\infty < t < +C_p) = \frac{1+p}{2} \equiv \hat{p}. \tag{23.117}$$

Because of the frequent need to use values of C corresponding to various values of $\hat{p}$ and degrees of freedom n, these C values have been tabulated and appear in many statistics texts. A short table is included here (Table 23.3).

Given a confidence interval for T, we may insert it into Eq. (23.116), which when solved for μ becomes

$$\mu = \bar{X} - T\frac{\sqrt{S/n}}{\sqrt{n}} = \bar{x} - \frac{T\sigma}{\sqrt{n}}. \tag{23.118}$$

From the limiting values for T, we get the corresponding range for μ, which is valid with the probability of the T range. Note that except for the range of T, all the quantities on the right-hand side of Eq. (23.118) are to be computed from our sample data. In particular, we need the mean value $\bar{X}$ for our sample and the standard deviation of our data points, $\sigma = \sqrt{S/n}$. Note further that, as with the chi-square distribution, when measured data are used to generate the sample mean and sample standard deviation, the appropriate t distribution to use for n data points is that with $n - 1$ degrees of freedom, and in using

Table 23.3   Student t Distribution

$\hat{p}$	$n = 1$	$n = 2$	$n = 3$	$n = 4$	$n = 5$
0.8	1.38	1.06	0.98	0.94	0.92
0.9	3.08	1.89	1.64	1.53	1.48
0.95	6.31	2.92	2.35	2.13	2.02
0.975	12.7	4.30	3.18	2.78	2.57
0.99	31.8	6.96	4.54	3.75	3.36
0.999	318.3	22.3	10.2	7.17	5.89

Note: Entries are the values C in $\int_{-\infty}^{C} f_n(t)dt = \hat{p}$, where $f_n(t)$ is given in Eq. (23.115), with n the number of degrees of freedom.

Eq. (23.118) it is customary to take σ as the sample standard deviation, as defined in Eq. (23.95). These points are explained more fully in several of the Additional Readings.

Example 23.7.3   CONFIDENCE INTERVAL

Suppose we have the following random data from a population that can be assumed to have a Gauss normal distribution:

$$7.12 \quad 4.95 \quad 6.18 \quad 5.69 \quad 2.90 \quad 8.47,$$

and we wish to determine 90% and 95% confidence intervals for the population mean.

Since we have neither the population mean nor variance, but have assumed the population distribution to be normal, we can use the t distribution as just outlined. As a preliminary to doing so, we need to calculate the sample mean and standard deviation. Since we have six data points, the number of degrees of freedom will be $n = 5$. We have

$$\bar{X} = (7.12 + 4.95 + 6.18 + 5.60 + 2.90 + 8.47)/6 = 5.885,$$

$$\sigma = \left[\frac{1}{5} \left((7.12 - 5.885)^2 + \cdots + (8.47 - 5.885)^2 \right) \right]^{1/2} = 1.9035.$$

Considering first the 90% confidence interval that corresponds to the range $(-C_{90} < t < C_{90})$ with $\hat{p} = (1 + p)/2 = 0.95$, we read from Table 23.3 the value $C_{90} = 2.02$. Thus,

$$\mu = 5.885 \pm \frac{(2.02)(1.9035)}{\sqrt{5}} = 5.885 \pm 1.720 \quad (90\% \text{ confidence}).$$

For 95% confidence, we need C_{95}, again for $n = 5$. This time, $\hat{p} = 0.975$, so $C_{95} = 2.57$, and

$$\mu = 5.885 \pm \frac{(2.57)(1.9035)}{\sqrt{5}} = 5.885 \pm 2.188 \quad (95\% \text{ confidence}).$$

A few final observations are in order. First, we see that by demanding an increase in the confidence level, the interval probably containing the true mean becomes wider. Note that at high confidence levels the probable width can become much larger than the sample standard deviation. Finally, note that even the confidence intervals are sample-dependent. Other data from the same population could generate intervals of different widths. Perhaps oversimplifying, these analyses show that there is no way of converting probability data into significant statements that have complete certainty. ∎

Exercises

23.7.1   Let ΔA be the error of a measurement of A, etc. Use error propagation to show that

$$\left(\frac{\sigma(C)}{C} \right)^2 = \left(\frac{\sigma(A)}{A} \right)^2 + \left(\frac{\sigma(B)}{B} \right)^2$$

holds for the product $C = AB$ and the ratio $C = A/B$.

23.7.2   Find the mean value and standard deviation of the sample of measurements $x_1 = 6.0$, $x_2 = 6.5$, $x_3 = 5.9$, $x_4 = 6.1$, $x_5 = 6.2$. If the point $x_6 = 6.1$ is added to the sample, how does the change affect the mean value and standard deviation?

23.7.3   Carry out a χ^2 analysis of the fit corresponding to Fig. 23.10 using the same points as in Example 23.7.2, but with the errors now associated with the t_i rather than the y_i.

23.7.4   Using the data from Exercise 23.7.2 (including the point x_6), find the 90% and 95% confidence intervals for the mean of the x_i.

Additional Readings

Bevington, P. R., and D. K. Robinson, *Data Reduction and Error Analysis for the Physical Sciences*, 3rd ed. New York: McGraw-Hill (2003).

Chung, K. L., *A Course in Probability Theory Revised*, 3rd ed. New York: Academic Press (2000).

DeGroot, M. H., *Probability and Statistics*, 2nd ed. Reading, MA: Addison-Wesley (1986).

Devore, J. L., *Probability and Statistics for Engineering and the Sciences*, 5th ed. New York: Duxbury Press (1999).

Freund, J. E., and R. E. Walpole, *Mathematical Statistics*, 4th ed. Englewood Cliffs, NJ: Prentice Hall (1987). This well-regarded text is at a level comparable to the exposition in this chapter. Clear and with many statistical tables.

Kreyszig, E., *Introductory Mathematical Statistics: Principles and Methods*. New York: Wiley (1970).

Montgomery, D. C., and G. C. Runger, *Applied Statistics and Probability for Engineers*, 2nd ed. New York: Wiley (1998).

Papoulis, A., *Probability, Random Variables, and Stochastic Processes*, 3rd ed. New York: McGraw-Hill (1991).

Ramachandran, K. M., and C. P. Tsokos, *Mathematical Statistics with Applications*. New York: Academic Press (2009). Relatively detailed but readable and self-contained.

Ross, S. M., *First Course in Probability*, 5th ed., vol. A. New York: Prentice Hall (1997).

Ross, S. M., *Introduction to Probability and Statistics for Engineers and Scientists*, 2nd ed. New York: Academic Press (1999).

Ross, S. M., *Introduction to Probability Models*, 7th ed. New York: Academic Press (2000).

Suhir, E., *Applied Probability for Engineers and Scientists*. New York: McGraw-Hill (1997).

INDEX

Page numbers followed by '*f*' and '*t*' indicate figures and tables, respectively.

Numbers

0-forms, 233
1-D axial Green's function, 684
1-forms, 233
2-D integration, 74*f*
   region, 70, 71*f*
2-forms, 233
3-forms, 233

A

Abel equation, generalized, 1055–1056
Abel's test, 23
abelian group, 816, 822
absolute convergence, 13, 23, 29
abstract group, 819, 819*t*
addition
   of gamma-distribution random variables, 1164
   of tensors, 208
   of random variables, 1160–1161
addition by scalar, 255
addition rule, for probabilities, 1128
addition theorem
   application
      Laplace expansion, 799–801
      spherical wave expansion, 798–799
   for spherical harmonics, 797–798
   for normal distributions, 1161
adjoint matrix, 105
adjoint operator, 277, 297
   and scalar product, 278
   basis expansion of, 281–282
   finding, 278
affine transformation, 1104
algebraic formula, 51
aliasing, 1006
alternating series
   absolute convergence, 13
   Leibniz criterion, 11–12
angular momentum, 126, 126*f*, 299
   angular momentum operators, 774–776
      angular momentum formulas, 781–782
      exercises, 782–784
      ladder operators, 776–779
      spinor, 779–781

coupling, 784–786
   Clebsch-Gordan coefficients, 789–791
   exercises, 795–796
   ladder operators construction, 788–795
   of *p* and *d* electrons, 793–795
   spinors, 792–793
   vector model, 786–788
angular momentum formulas, 781–782
angular momentum operators, 774–776
   angular momentum formulas, 781–782
   exercises, 782–784
   ladder operators, 776–779
   spinor, 779–781
annihilation operator, 882
anti-Hermitian, 277
anti-Hermitian matrices, 108, 319
antiderivation, 239
antisymmetric stretching mode, 323
antisymmetric tensor, 208, 216
arbitrary probability distribution, 1157
arbitrary-vector technique, 167
Argand diagram, 56, 56*f*, 57, 470, 492
arithmetic mean, 1137
associated Laguerre equation, 894
associated Laguerre polynomials
   generating function, 892–895
associated Legendre equation, 425, 716, 741–743
   exercises, 753–756
   magnetic field of current loop, 748–753
   orthogonality, 746–748
   parity and special values, 746
associated Legendre functions, 425, 744–745,
      745*t*
associated Legendre polynomials, 743–744
associative, 96, 97
asymptotic expansions, 581
   asymptotic forms, 692–693
      of Hankel functions, 688–690
      properties of, 693–695
   exercises, 695–698
   of an integral representation, 690–692
   Stokes' method, 688

asymptotic series, 577
   Bessel functions, 691
   cosine and sine integrals, 580–582
   definition of, 582–583
   exercises, 583–584
   exponential integral, 578–580
   integral representation expansion, 690–692
   overview, 577
asymptotic values, Bessel functions, 690, 703
atomic interaction integral, 72
average value, 1136
axial Green's function, 464
axial vectors, 136, 215

B

Baker-Hausdorff formula, 114
band-pass filter, 1002*f*
baryons, 852, 853*t*
   multiplets, decomposition of, 858–861, 859*f*,
      860*f*
basis expansion, adjoint, 281–282
basis functions, 252, 253
Bayes' theorem, 1130
Bernoulli equation, 330, 378
Bernoulli numbers, 556, 562*t*
   contour of integration for, 563*f*
   exercises, 566–567
   generating-function, 560
   overview, 560–565
   polynomials, 565–566
   Riemann zeta function, 564
Bernoulli polynomials, 565–566
   Euler-Maclaurin integration formula, 567
Bessel functions, 67
   asymptotic expansions
      asymptotic forms, 692–695
      exercises, 695–698
      Hankel functions, asymptotic forms of,
         688–690
      of an integral representation, 690–692
   asymptotic values, 690
   of first kind
      Bessel's differential equation, 646–647
      confluent hypergeometric representation, 919
      cylindrical resonant cavity, 650–653
      exercises, 654–661
      Fraunhofer diffraction, circular aperture,
         648–650
      Frobenius method, 643
      generating function for integral order,
         644–645
      integral representation, 647–648
      modified, 681
      orthogonality, 661
      recurrence relations, 645–646

      second kind, 644
      Wronskian, 670–671
   Hankel functions
      contour integral representation of, 676–678
      definitions, 674–675
      exercises, 678–680
   Helmholtz equation, 680, 698, 705
   hyperbolic, 683
   Laplace equation, 651
   modified, 428, 643, 678, 682*f*
      asymptotic expansion, 688
      contours, 696*f*
      exercises, 688
      Fourier transforms, 684
      Green's function, 684–685
      Hankel function, 682
      hyperbolic Bessel functions, 683
      integral representation, 683–684, 690–692
      Laplace equations, 680
      recurrence relations, 681–682
      series expansion, 681
      Whittaker functions, 682
   Neumann functions, Bessel functions of second
      kind
      coaxial wave guides, 672
      definition and series form, 667–669
      exercises, 674
      integral representations, 669
      recurrence relations, 669–670
      uses of, 671
      Wronskian formulas, 670–671
   orthogonality
      Bessel series, 663
      electrostatic potential in a hollow cylinder,
         663–664
      exercises, 665–667
      Neumann boundary condition, 662
      normalization, 662
      Sturm-Liouville theory, 661
   PDEs, 643
   recurrence relations, 645–646
   of second kind, 667
   Schlaefli integral, 653–654
   spherical, 643
      asymptotic values, 703
      definitions, 702
      exercises, 709–712
      Helmholtz equation, 698
      limiting values, 703
      modified, 709
      orthogonality and zeros, 703
      particle in a sphere, 704–706
      recurrence relations, 702
      waves, 703

of third kind, 675
  in wave guides, 671–672
  zeros, 648–653
Bessel series, 663
Bessel's correction, 1168
Bessel's differential equation, 646–647
Bessel's equation, 344–345, 366–367, 1025–1027
  limitations of series approach, 351–353
Bessel's inequality, 262
beta function, 617
  definite integrals, alternate forms, 618
  derivation of Legendre duplication formula,
    618–619
  exercises, 619–622
binomial coefficients, 34
binomial distribution, 1148–1151
  limits of, 1157–1158
  and Poisson distribution, 1153–1154, 1154f
binomial expansion, application of, 41–42
binomial probability distribution, 1149, 1150f
binomial theorem, 33–36, 493–494, 581, 716
  exercise, 36–40
Biot-Savart law, 750, 751, 751f
black hole, optical path near event horizon of,
    1087–1088, 1088f
Bohr radius, 897, 1135
Born approximation, quantum mechanical
    scattering, 465–466
Bose-Einstein statistics, 1132, 1133
bosons, 840
boundary conditions, 381, 405
  Cauchy, 412
  Dirichlet, 412, 985
  Green's function, 452–454
  hollow cylinder, 664
  homogeneous, 448
  Neumann, 412
  ring of charge, 730
  specific, 438–439
  sphere in uniform electric field, 728
  sphere with, 428–430
  waveguide, coaxial cable, 671
boundary curve, 406
boundary value problem, 1052
brachistochrone problem, 1082
branch cut (cut line), 500, 508f
  exploiting, 534–537
  using, 534–535
branch points, 499–503, 499f, 500f, 502f, 503f,
    503t, 536–537
  avoidance of, 532–534
  of order 2, 500
Bravais lattice, 869
Bromwich integral, 1038–1040, 1040f
brute-force approach, 32

C

calculus of residues
  Cauchy principal value, 512–515, 512f, 515f
  computing residues, 510–511
  counting poles and zeros, 518–519
  exercises, 520–522
  pole expansion of meromorphic functions,
    515–518
  product expansion of entire functions, 519–520
  residue theorem, 509–510, 509f
calculus of variations
  Euler equation, 1081–1085
    alternate forms of, 1088
    exercises, 1093–1096
    optical path near event horizon of a black
      hole, 1087–1088, 1088f
    soap film, 1088–1090, 1089f
    soap film–minimum area, 1090–1093, 1092f
    straight line, 1086
  Lagrangian multipliers, 1107–1109
  Rayleigh-Ritz variational technique, 1117–1118
    ground state eigenfunction, 1118–1119
  several dependent variables, 1096–1097, 1102
    exercises, 1105–1107
    Hamilton's principle, 1097–1098
    Laplace's equation, 1101–1102
    moving particle–Cartesian coordinates,
      1098–1099
    moving particle–circular cylindrical
      coordinates, 1099
  several independent variables, 1100–1102
  variation with constraints, 1111–1112
    exercises, 1121–1124
    Lagrangian equations, 1112–1113
    Schrödinger wave equation, 1116–1117
    simple pendulum, 1113–1114, 1113f
    sliding off a log, 1114–1115, 1114f
canonical momentum, 1099
Cartesian coordinate system, 47
Cartesian coordinates, 415–420
  spherical harmonics using, 758
Casimir operators, 849
Catalan's constant, 13, 572, 613
catenoid, catenary of revolution, 1090
Cauchy (Maclaurin) integral test, 5–8
Cauchy boundary conditions, 412
Cauchy criterion, 2
Cauchy inequality, 490
Cauchy principal value, 512–515, 512f, 515f,
Cauchy ratio test, 1065
Cauchy root test, 4
Cauchy's integral formula, 486–487, 554, 591
  applications of, 490
  derivatives, 488
  exercises, 491–492

Cauchy's integral formula (*continued*)
Morera's theorem, 489–490
Cauchy's integral theorem
contour integrals, 477–478, 478*f*
exercises, 485, 486*f*
Goursat proof, 481–482, 481*f*
Laurent expansion, 492–497
multiply connected regions, 483–484, 483*f*
statement of, 478–481, 480*f*
Cauchy-Riemann conditions, 471–477
analytic functions, 472–474
derivatives of, 474–475
exercises, 476–477
overview, 471–472
point at infinity, 475
Cauchy-Riemann differential equations, 591
causality, 591
cavities, cylindrical, 650–653
central field potential, Laplacian of, 154
central force, 192
central force problems, 426
central moments, 1141
chain rule, 63
chaotic behaviour, 377
character, 831, 832*t*
characteristic curves, 405
characteristic equation, 303
characteristic function in probability theory, 1160
characteristic polynomial, 303
characteristics of PDEs, 404–406
charge density, 739
Chebyshev differential equation, 388
Chebyshev inequality, 1140
Chebyshev polynomials
exercises, 907–911
generating functions, 899
hypergeometric representations, 914
numerical analysis, 905–906
orthogonality, 906–907
recurrence relations, 901–903
shifted, 908
trigonometric form, 904–905
type I, 900
type II, 899
ultraspherical polynomials, 899
chi square fit, 1170, 1173–1174
chi-square (χ^2) distribution, 1170–1174
Christoffel symbols, 222
evaluating, 223–224
circle of convergence, 493
circular contour
z^n on, 479
circular cylindrical coordinates, 187–190, 188*f*, 421, 431
cylindrical eigenvalue problem, 422–424

circular disk, rotations of, 818
circular functions, 58–59
circular membrane, Bessel functions, 659
circular optical path, 1088*f*
circular wave guide, 672
circular wire loop, 931*f*
classes, 830–835
Clausen functions, 949
Clebsch-Gordan coefficients, 789–791
Clifford algebra, 112
closed loop, 499–501, 499*f*, 500*f*
closure relation, 264
coaxial wave guides, 671–672
coefficient vector, 261
colatitude, 72
collinear velocities, addition of, 864
column vector, 95, 123, 125
extraction of, 108
combinations, counting of, 1130–1133
commutation rules, 785–786
commutative, 96, 816
commutative operation, 47
commutator, 97, 276
comparison tests, 3–4
completeness, 255, 262
of Hilbert-Schmidt of integral equations, 1073
complex conjugation, 54, 470
complex exponentials, integrals with, 527–531, 529*f*
complex numbers
and functions, 53
Cartesian components, 53
circular and hyperbolic functions, 58–59
complex domain, 55–56
exercises, 60–61
imaginary numbers, 54
logarithm, 60
polar representation, 56–58
powers and roots, 59
multiplication of, 54
of unit magnitude, 57
complex plane, 56
complex variable theory, 53
complex variables, *see also* Cauchy-Riemann conditions; mapping; singularities
algebra using, permanence of algebraic form, 55
Cauchy's integral formula, 591
causality, 591
dispersion relations

exercises, 596–597
optical dispersion, 594–595
overview, 591–593
Parseval relation, 595–596
symmetry relations, 593
functions of, 470
computing residues, 510–511
conditional convergence, 13
conditional probability, 1128
conditional probability distributions, 1147
Condon-Shortley phase, 758, 760*t*
confidence interval, 1176–1178
confluent hypergeometric functions, 912
asymptotic expansions, 919
Bessel and modified Bessel functions, 918–919
exercises, 920–922
Hermite functions, 919
Laguerre functions, 919
Whittaker function, 919
Wronskian, 922
conformal mapping, 549
conjugate subgroup, 820
conjugation, complex, 56, 105
connected, simply, 164
conservation laws, 815
conservative force, 171, 244
constant B field, vector potentials of, 172
constant coefficients, with ODEs, 342–343
constrained minima/maxima, 1107–1109
exercises, 1110
contiguous function relations, 913
continuous deformation, 484
continuous groups, 816, 845–846
exercises, 861
homomorphism SU(2)–SO(3), 851–852
Lie groups and their generators, 846–849
of representation, 824–825
SO(2) and SO(3), 849–851
SU(3), 852
continuous random variable, 1135–1137
contour integral, 477–478, 478*f*
contour integral representation, 676–678
contour integration, 967, 967*f*
singularity on, 530–531
methods, 572, 603
contraction, 209–210
contravariant basis vectors, 220–221
contravariant metric tensor, 219
contravariant tensors, 206–207
contravariant vectors, 206, 219
convergence
infinite products, 575
infinite series, partial sum approximation, 579
of Neumann series, 1066
convergence in the mean, 262

convergence of infinite series
absolute, 13, 23
of power series, 29
rate, 16
tests, *see also* Cauchy (Maclaurin) integral test
comparison, 3–4
Gauss', 9
improvement of, 16–17
Kummer's, 8–10
uniform and nonuniform, 21–22
convergence, rate of, 16
convolution (Faltungs) theorem
driven oscillator with damping, 1035–1037
Parseval relation, 987–990
coordinate transformations
exercises, 138–139
of orthogonal, 135
of reflections, 136–137, 137*f*
of rotations, 133–135
of successive operations, 137–138
coordinates, *see also* Cartesian coordinates;
circular cylindrical coordinates; orthogonal
coordinates; spherical polar coordinates
curvilinear, 182
correlation, 1142–1144
cosines
asymptotic expansion, 581, 582
confluent hypergeometric representation, 920
infinite products, 575
integral of in denominator, 523–524
integrals cos in asymptotic series, 580–582
Coulomb's law, 447, 730
counting poles and zeros, 518–519
coupling, angular momentum, *see* angular
momentum
covariance, 1142–1144
covariance of Maxwell's equations, Lorentz, *see*
Lorentz covariance of Maxwell's equations
covariant, 862
covariant basis vectors, 218, 220–221
covariant derivatives, 222–223
covariant metric tensor, 219
covariant tensors, 206–207
covariant vector, 206
Cramer's rule, 84
creation operator, 882
criterion, Leibniz, 11–12
cross derivatives, 62
cross product, 126–128, 126*f*, 127*f*, *see also* triple
vector product
crossing conditions, 593
crystallographic point groups, 869
curl, $\nabla \times$, 149–153
circular cylindrical coordinates, 193
in curvilinear coordinates, 186–187, 186*f*

curvilinear coordinates, 182
  differential operators in, 185–187, 185f, 186f
  exercises, 196–203
  integrals in, 184–185
cut line (branch cut), 500, 508f
  exploiting, 534
  using, 534–535
cylindrical symmetry, 443
cylindrical traveling waves, 694–695

D

d'Alembert ratio test, 4–5, 55, 578
d'Alembert's solution, of wave equation, 436
damped oscillator, 1021
de Moivre's Theorem, 59
decuplet, 859, 859f
defective matrices, 324
definite integral (Euler), 600–601
definite integrals, 580
  evaluation of, 522
    exercises, 538–544
degeneracy, 307–308
degenerate, 1057, 1072
delta function, Dirac, 263–265, 1010–1011
  δ-sequence function, 76f
  Dirichlet kernel, 77
  exercise, 80–81
  Fourier series, 77
  Kronecker delta, 79–80
  properties of, 78–79
  sequence, 76
  spherical polar coordinates, 79
denominator, integral of cos in, 523–524
dependent variable, 329
derivative operators, tensor, *see* tensor derivative
    operators
derivatives, *see also* exterior derivatives
  chain rule, 63
  cross derivatives, 62
  exercises, 64
  mixed derivatives, 401
  partial derivatives, 62, 401
  stationary points, 63–64
determinants, 295
  and linear dependence, 89–90
  derivatives of, 102
  exercises, 93–94
  homogeneous linear equations, 83–84
  inhomogeneous linear equations, 84
  product theorem, 103–104
  properties of, 87
deuteron, 391–393
diagonal matrices, 99
  eigenvalues, 313
  eigenvector, 312

diagonalization
  matrices, 311–314
  simultaneous, 314–315
differentiable manifolds, 233
differential equations
  first-order differential equations, 331–342
    exact differential equations, 333
    exercises, 339–342
    homogeneous equations, 334–335
    isobaric equations, 335
    linear first-order ODEs, 336–339
    nonseparable ODEs, 333–334
    parachutist, 331–332
    RL circuit, 338–339
    separable equations, 331
  Fuchs' theorem, 355
  linear independence of solutions, 358–360
    second solution, 362–363
    series form of the second solution, 364–366
  nonlinear, 377–380
  number of solutions, 361
  partial differential equations, 329
  particular solution, 337
  second solution
    exercises, 370–374
    finding, 362–363
    for linear oscillator equation, 363
    logarithmic term, 668
    Neumann functions, 368–369
    of Bessel's equation, 366–367
  series solutions, Frobenius method, 346–350,
      350f
    exercises, 355–358
    expansion about, 350
    Fuchs' theorem, 355
    limitations of series approach, Bessel's
        equation, 351–353
    regular and irregular singularities, 353–354
    symmetry of solutions, 350–351
  singular points, 343–345, 345t
differential forms, 232
  0-forms, 233
  1-forms, 233
  2-forms, 233
  3-forms, 233
  complementary, 235–236
  exercises, 238, 243, 248
  exterior algebra, 233–235
  exterior derivatives, 238–243
  Hodge operator, 235
    in Minkowski space, 236–237
  integration of, 243–248
  Maxwell's equations, 241–243
  miscellaneous, 237–238
  simplifying, 234

Stokes' theorem on, 245
three-dimensional (3-D), 407
differential operators, 275
differential vector operators, 143
gradient, 143
properties, 153–157
exercises, 157–159
differentiate parameter, 67
differentiation
of forms, 238–243
power series, 30
diffraction, 648–650
diffusion partial differential equations, 437–444
digamma and polygamma functions, 610
digamma functions, 610–611
exercises, 614–616
Maclaurin expansion, computation, 613
polygamma function, 612
series summation, 613
dihedral, 818
dilogarithm
exercises, 926
expansion and analytic properties, 923–924
properties and special values, 924–926
dimensionality theorem, 831
dipole moment, 738
Dirac braket notation, 265
Dirac delta distribution, 972
Dirac delta function, *see* delta function, Dirac
Dirac gamma matrices, 112
Dirac half-braket notation, 265
Dirac matrices, 111
Dirac notation, 265–266
Dirac's relativistic theory, 38
direct product, 108–112, 837–839
exercises, 837f, 840, 840t
generators for, 857–858
of tensors, 210–211
direct space, 964
Dirichlet boundary conditions, 385, 412, 704
Dirichlet conditions, 936, 985
Dirichlet kernel, 77
Dirichlet series
exercises, 573–574
overview, 571–572
discontinuous functions, 937–939
expansions in, 262–263
discrete Fourier transform, 1002–1007
aliasing, 1006
exercises, 1007
fast Fourier transform, 1006–1007
limitations, 1005
orthogonality over discrete points, 1002–1004
discrete groups, 815
classes, 830–835

exercises, 835–837, 836t, 837f
other, 835
discrete probability distributions, computing, 1136
discrete random variables, 1134–1135
discrete spectrum, 420
dispersion integral contour for, 592f
dispersion relations
causality, 591
crossing conditions, 593
exercises, 596–597
Hilbert transforms, 593, 595
optical dispersion, 594–595
overview, 591–593
Parseval relation, 595–596
sum rules, 596
symmetry relations, 593–594
divergence, ∇, 146–149, 149f
curvilinear coordinates, 185–186, 185f
divergent series, 4
division, of random variables, 1162
Doppler shift, 37
dot products, 49–50
gradient of, 143, 157
double factorial notation, 35
double series, rearrangement of, 18–19
driven oscillator with damping, 1035–1037
dual tensors, 216–217

E

Earth's gravitational field, 727
Earth's nutation, 1018–1019, 1018f
eigenfunction, 299
eigenfunction completeness of Hilbert-Schmidt
of integral equations, 1073
orthogonal, 1069–1073
eigenfunction expansion of Green's function,
460–461
eigenvalue problem, 422–424
eigenvalues
equations, 299–300
basic expansions, 300
equivalence of operator and matrix form, 300
of Hermitian matrices, 310
of Hilbert-Schmidt theory, 1073
eigenvectors, 300
normalizing, 304
of Hermitian matrices, 310–311
Einstein convention, 207
electric dipole, 738, 737f
electric multipoles, 737–739
electric quadrupole, 738
electromagnetic field tensor, 866
electromagnetic wave equation, 156
electromagnetic waves, 1023–1024
electromagnetism, potentials in, 174

electron spin, 846
electrostatic potential
    for ring of charge, 729–730
    in hollow cylinder, 663–664
elementary functions, 1008–1010
elliptic integrals
    definitions of, 928–929
    exercises, 931–932
    of first kind, 928
    limiting values, 930
    period of simple pendulum, 927–928
    of second kind, 928
    series expansion, 929–930
elliptic partial differential equations (PDEs), 410
empty set, 1127
energy, relativistic, 35–36
entire function, 519–520
equality of matrices, 96
equation of continuity, 148
equations, *see also* Maxwell's equations
    motion and field, 213
equilateral triangle, symmetry of, 817, 817f, 818f
error function, 637
error propagation, 1165–1168
essential (irregular) singular point, 344
essential singularities, 344, 498
Euclidean space, 237
Euler angles, 140, 140f
Euler equation, 1081–1085
    alternate forms of, 1088
    exercises, 1093–1096
    soap film, 1088–1090, 1089f
    soap film–minimum area, 1090–1093, 1092f
    straight line, 1086
Euler identity, 113
Euler transformation, 43, 44
Euler-Maclaurin integration formula, 566
    Bernoulli polynomials, 567
    example, 569–570
    exercises, 570–571
    overview, 567–569
Euler-Mascheroni constant, 7, 33, 367, 675
event horizon, 1087
evolution operator, 1067
exact ODEs, 333–334
expansion, 736, *see also* Taylor's expansion
    Laplace expansion, 760–762, 799–801
    pole, of meromorphic functions, 498, 515–518
    product, of entire function, 519–520
    spherical harmonic, 761
    spherical wave, 798–799
expectation value, 283, 285, 297, 1136
    in transformation basis, 295
exponential function, of Maclaurin theorem,
        27–28

exponential integral, 578–580, 634–637
exterior algebra, 233
exterior derivatives, 238–243
exterior products, 233
extrema, 62–64

F

factorial function, asymptotic form of, 588
factorial notation, 606
faithful group, 822
Faraday's law, 168
fast Fourier transform (FFT), 1006–1007
Feldheim's formula, 885
Fermi-Dirac statistics, 1132, 1133
fermions, 840
FFT, *see* fast Fourier transform
field equations, 213
finite wave train, 971–973, 972f
first-order Born approximation, 1067
first-order differential equations, 331–342
    exact differential equations, 333
    exercises, 339–342
    homogeneous equations, 334–335
    isobaric equations, 335
    linear first-order ODEs, 336–339
    nonseparable ODEs, 333–334
    parachutist, 331–332
    RL circuit, 338–339
    separable equations, 331
first-order partial differential equations, 403
    characteristics of, 404–406
    exercises, 408–409
    general, 406–407
fixed and movable singularities, special solutions,
        378–379
flux, 148
Fourier convolution theorem, 1055
    exercises, 994–997
    multiple convolutions, 990–992
Fourier cosine series, 941
Fourier cosine, sine transforms, 966
Fourier expansions, characteristic of, 951
Fourier integral representation, 969–970
Fourier series, 77
    applications of, 949–957
        exercises, 952–957
        full-wave rectifier, 950–951, 951f, 952t
        square wave, high frequencies, 949–950,
            949f
    definition of, 935
    general properties, 935–949
        discontinuous functions, 937–939
        exercises, 945–949
        periodic functions, 939–940
        sawtooth wave, 937–939, 938f

Sturm-Liouville theory, 936–937
summation of a Fourier series, 944
symmetry, 940–941, 942f
Gibbs phenomenon
calculation of overshoot, 959–961
exercises, 961–962
square wave, 958–959
summation of series, 957–958
operations on, 942–944
Fourier sine series, 941
Fourier transform, 965–968
aliasing, 1006
convolution theorem, 985–987
of derivatives
heat flow PDE, 983
wave equation, 981–982
discrete, see discrete Fourier transforms
exercises, 975–980, 985
fast, 1006–1007
of Gaussian, 969, 968f
inverse, 970–973
limitations on transfer functions, 1000–1001
momentum space representation, 993–994
of product, 992
properties of, 980–984
solution, 1054–1055
successes and limitations of, 984–985
in 3-D space, 973–975
unitary operator, 988
Fourier transforms–inversion theorem, finite wave
train, 971–973, 972f
Fourier-Mellin integral, 1039
Fraunhofer diffraction, Bessel function, 648–650
Fredholm equation, 1047, 1052, 1054, 1058, 1064
homogeneous, 1059–1060, 1069
inhomogeneous, 1076–1077
Fresnel integrals, 712f
Frobenius method, 643, 645
series solutions, 346–350, 350f
Fuchs' theorem, 355, 692
full-wave rectifier, 950–951, 951f, 952t
functions, 143
Chebyshev polynomials
exercises, 907–911
generating functions, 899
numerical analysis, 905–906
orthogonality, 906–907
recurrence relations, 901–903
trigonometric form, 904–905
type I, 900
type II, 899
ultraspherical polynomials, 899
confluent hypergeometric functions
Bessel and modified Bessel functions,
918–919

exercises, 920–922
Hermite functions, 919
Laguerre functions, 919
Whittaker function, 919
dilogarithm
exercises, 926
expansion and analytic properties, 923–924
properties and special values, 924–926
Dirac delta, 263–265
discontinuous, 262–263
entire, 498
exponential, of Maclaurin theorem, 27–28
Hermite functions
applications of the product formulas,
885–887
direct expansion of products of Hermite
polynomials, 884–887
exercises, 876–878, 887–888
Hermite product formula, 884–887
molecular vibration, 882–883
orthogonality and normalization, 875–876
quantum mechanical simple harmonic
oscillator, 878–879
recurrence relations, 872–873
Rodrigues formula, 874
threefold Hermite formula, 883–884
values of, 873–874
hypergeometric functions, 911
confluent, 912
contiguous function relations, 913
exercises, 915–916
hypergeometric representations, 913–914
Pochhammer symbol, 912
Laguerre functions
associated Laguerre polynomials, 892–895
differential equation–Laguerre polynomials,
890–892
exercises, 897–899
hydrogen atom, 896–897
Rodrigues formula and generating function,
889–890
of complex variables, 470
of operators, 282
orthonormal, 269–271
series expansions, 41–44
excercise, 44–45
series of
Abel's test, 23
exercises, 24–25, 32–33
uniform and nonuniform convergence, 21–22
Weierstrass M test, 22–23
square-wave, 263

G

Galilean, 862
gamma distribution, 607, 1162–1164

gamma function, *see also* factorial function
  analytic properties, 604
  asymptotic form of, 588–589
  beta function
    definite integrals, alternate forms, 618
    derivation of Legendre duplication formula,
      618–619
    exercises, 619–622
  definitions, simple properties, 599
    definite integral (Euler), 600–601
    factorial notation, 606
    infinite limit (Euler), 599–600
    infinite product (Weierstrass), 602
  incomplete beta function, 634
  incomplete gamma functions and related
      functions, 633–634
    error function, 637
    exercises, 638–641
    exponential integral, 634–637
    Riemann zeta function, 626–631
    Stirling's series, 622
      derivation from Euler-Maclaurin integration
        formula, 623–624
gamma function contour, 605f
gamma functional relation, 506
gauge condition, 174
gauge transformations, 174
Gauss elimination, 91–93
Gauss technique, 91
Gauss' fundamental theorem of algebra, 490
Gauss' law, 175–176, 175f
Gauss' normal distribution, 1155–1159
Gauss' test, 9
  Legendre series, 9–10
Gauss' theorem, 164–165, 165f, 176, 248
  Green's theorem, 165–166
Gegenbauer polynomials, *see* ultraspherical
    polynomials
Gell-Mann matrices, 854
general coordinates, tensor in
  covariant derivatives, 222–223
  exercises, 226
  metric tensor in, 218–219
general relativity, 862
generalized Abel equation, 1055–1056
generating function, 555, 1056
  associated Laguerre polynomials, 892–895
  Bernoulli numbers, 560
  Bessel functions, modified, 919
  Chebyshev polynomials, 899
  electric multipoles, 737–739
  exercises, 740–741
  expansion, 736–737
  Hermite polynomials, 555–556, 872
  for integral order, 644–645

  Laguerre polynomials, 889–890
  Legendre polynomials, 557–558
  physical interpretation of, 735
  Taylor expansion of, 565
generators of continuous groups, 846–849
geodesics, 1103–1104
geometric properties, 47
geometric series, 2–3
Gibbs phenomenon
  calculation of overshoot, 959–961
  exercises, 961–962
  square wave, 958–959
  summation of series, 957–958
Goldschmidt discontinuous solution, 1091, 1092f
Goursat proof of Cauchy's integral, 481–482,
    481f
gradient, ∇
  as differential vector operator, 143–146
  in curvilinear coordinates, 185
  of dot product, 157
Gram-Schmidt orthogonalization
  example, 270–272
  exercises, 273–275
  orthonormalizing physical vectors, 273
  overview, 269–270
  physical vectors, 272
  vectors by, 269–275
Gram-Schmidt process, 308
Gram-Schmidt transformation, 293
graphene, 869
Grassmann algebra, *see* exterior algebra
gravitational potential, 172
Green's function, 447–467, 684–685, 983–984,
    1050, 1052, 1072, 1075
  advantage of, 452
  axial, 464
  boundary conditions, 452–454
    accomodating, 464
    at infinity, 454
    initial value problem, 453–454
  differential vs. integral formulation, 456
  eigenfunction expansion of, 460–461
  exercises, 456–459, 466–467
  features of, 448, 459–460
  form of, 450–452, 461–466
  fundamental, 462, 463t
  general properties of, 449–450
  Helmholtz equation, 463
  Laplace's equation, 462, 464
  one-dimensional, 448–459
  relation to integral equation, 454–456
  self-adjoint problems, 460
  spherical, 463, 800–801
  two and three dimension problems, 459–467
Green's theorem, 165–166, 246–247

Gregory series, 39
ground state, 391
ground state eigenfunction, 1118–1119
group theory, *see also* generators of continuous
    groups; homogeneous Lorentz group
  definition of, 816–817, 817, 818*f*, 818*t*
  discrete
    classes, 830–835
    other, 835
  exercises, 820, 821*f*
  faithfulness, 822
  homomorphic, 817
  homomorphism and isomorphism, 819
  isomorphic, 817
  Lorentz covariance of Maxwell's equations,
    866–868
  vierergruppe, 820

H

Hamilton's equations, 1099–1100
Hamilton's principle, 1097, 1098
Hankel functions, 682
  asymptotic forms, 692, 693
  contour integral representation of, 676–678
  definition, 674–675
  integral representation of, 698*f*
  series expansion, 675
  spherical, 701
  Wronskian formulas, 675
Hankel transforms, 965, 1054
harmonic functions, 473
harmonic numbers, 3
harmonic oscillator, 878–879, 1017
harmonic series, 3
harmonics, 799, *see also* spherical harmonics;
    vector spherical harmonics
Hartree atomic units, 396
heat flow partial differential equations, 437–444,
  983
Heaviside shifting theorem, 1023
Heaviside step function, 1010
Heisenberg uncertainty principle, 973
Helmholtz equation, 415, 422, 439, 705
  Bessel functions, 680, 698
  Green's function, 463
  spherical coordinates, 698
Helmholtz's theorem, 177–180
Hermite equation, 390–391
Hermite functions
  applications of the product formulas, 885–887
  confluent hypergeometric functions, 919
  direct expansion of products of Hermite
    polynomials, 884–887
  exercises, 876–878, 887–888
  Hermite polynomials, 872

Hermite product formula, 884–887
  molecular vibration, 882–883
  orthogonality and normalization, 875–876
  quantum mechanical simple harmonic
    oscillator, 878–879
  recurrence relations, 872–873
  Rodrigues formula, 874
  threefold Hermite formula, 883–884
  values of, 873–874
Hermite polynomial, *see also* Legendre
    polynomials
Hermite polynomials, 280, 391, 554, 873*f*
  direct expansion of products of, 884–887
  example, 554–556
  generating function, 555–556, 872
  orthogonality integral, 875
  recurrence relations, 872–873
  Rodrigues representation, 874
Hermitian matrices, 108, 301
  anti-, 319
  diagonalization, 311–313
    example, 313
    exercises, 317–318
    expectation values, 316
    finding diagonalizing transformation,
      313–314
    positive definite and singular operators, 317
    simultaneous, 314–315
    spectral decomposition, 315–316
  of eigenvalues, 310
  unitary transformation, 313
Hermitian operator, 277, 284
  expectation value, 316
  self-adjoint ODEs, 384
Hilbert space, 255–256, 278, 279, 289
Hilbert transforms, 593, 595
Hilbert-Schmidt theory
  homogeneous Fredholm equation, 1069
  inhomogeneous Fredholm equation, 1076–1077
  inhomogeneous integral equation, 1073–1077
  orthogonal eigenfunctions, 1069–1073
  symmetrization of kernels, 1069
Hodge operator, 235
homogeneous boundary condition, 448
homogeneous equations, 334–335
homogeneous Fredholm equation, 1059–1060,
  1069
homogeneous linear equations, 83–84
  ODEs, 330
homogeneous Lorentz group, 862–864
homogeneous ODEs, 335, 338, 351
  second-order, 344
homomorphic group, 817
homomorphism, 819
  SU(2) and SU(2)–SO(3), 851–852

Hooke's law spring, 342–343
Hubble's law, 52
hydrogen atom, 896–897
   Schrödinger's wave equation, 896
hyperbolic functions, 58–59
hyperbolic partial differential equations (PDEs),
      410
hypercharge, 854
hypergeometric equation
   alternate forms, 918
   singularities, 345, 912, 917
hypergeometric functions, 911
   confluent, 912
   contiguous function relations, 913
   exercises, 915–916
   hypergeometric representations, 913–914
   Pochhammer symbol, 912
hypergeometric series, *see* hypergeometric
      function

I

identity operator, 277
imaginary axis, 56
imaginary numbers, 54
imaginary part, 56
improper rotations, of coordinate system, 215
impulse function, 1011
impulsive force, 1020
incomplete beta function, 634
incomplete gamma functions, 633–634
   of first kind confluent hypergeometric
         representation, 917
indefinite integral of $f(z)$, 489
independence, linear, 671
independent variables, 329, 407–408, 411
indeterminate forms, 31
indicial equation, 348
indistinguishable particles, 1133
inertial frames, 815
infinite limit (Euler), 599–600
infinite product (Weierstrass), 602
infinite products
   convergence, 575
   evaluate, 575
   exercises, 576–577
   overview, 574–575
   sine and cosines, 575
infinite series, 1, *see also* Taylor's expansion;
      power series
   algebra of
      alternating series, 11–13
      convergence, 13
      convergence: absolute, 13
      convergence: Cauchy integral, 5–8
      convergence: Cauchy root, 4

convergence: comparison, 3–4
convergence: conditional, Leibniz criterion,
      15–16
convergence: d'Alembert ratio, 4–5
convergence: Gauss', 9
convergence: Kummer's, 8–10
convergence: Maclaurin integral, 5–8
convergence: test of, 3–11
convergence: uniform, 21–22, 29
divergence of squares, 15–16
double series, 18–19
exercises, 20–21
rearrangement of double, 18–19
exercises, 10–11, 13–14
fundamental concepts
   geometric series, 2–3
   harmonic, 3
of functions
   Abel's test, 23
   exercises, 24–25
   uniform and nonuniform convergence, 21–22
   Weierstrass M test, 22–23
power series, 29–30
infinity, boundary conditions at, 454
inhomogeneous Fredholm equation, 1076–1077
inhomogeneous integral equation, 1073–1077
inhomogeneous linear equations, 84
inhomogeneous linear ODEs, 375–377
   exercises, 377
inhomogeneous Lorentz group, 862
inner product and matrix multiplication, 97–98
integer powers, 59
integers, sum of, 40–41, 41
integral equations
   boundary condition, 1048
   exercises, 1060–1064
   feature of, 1048
   Fredholm equation, 1047, 1052, 1054,
         1058–1060, 1069
   generating-function, 1056–1057
   Green's function, 454–456
   Hilbert-Schmidt theory
      exercises, 1077–1079
      homogeneous Fredholm equation,
            1059–1060
      orthogonal eigenfunctions, 1069–1073
      symmetrization of kernels, 1069
integral-transforms
   Fourier transform solution, 1054–1055
   generalized Abel equation, 1055–1056
introduction, 1047–1048
   definition, 1047
   exercises, 1053
   linear oscillator equation, 1050–1052

momentum representation in quantum
      mechanics, 1048–1049
   transformation of differential equation into
      integral equation, 1049–1050
linear, 1047
Neumann series
   exercises, 1068
   overview, 1064–1066
   solution, 1066–1067
separable kernel, 1057–1059
Volterra equation, 1047, 1048, 1050, 1055
integral form, Neumann functions, 671
integral operator, 275, 1066
linear, 1070
integral representations, 647–648, 964
   of dilogarithm, 924f
   expansion of, 690–692
   of Hankel functions, 698f
   modified Bessel functions, 684
integral test, Cauchy, see Cauchy (Maclaurin)
      integral test
integral theorems
   exercises, 169–170
   Gauss' theorem, 164–165, 165f
   Green's theorem, 165–166
   Stokes' theorem, 167–168, 167f, 168f
integral transforms, 1054
   convolution (Faltungs) theorem, driven
      oscillator with damping, 1035–1037
   convolution theorem, 985–987
      Parseval relation, 987–990
   Fourier transform of derivatives
      heat flow PDE, 983
      wave equation, 981–982
   Fourier transform of Gaussian, 968–969, 968f
   Fourier transform solution, 1054–1055
   generalized Abel equation, 1055–1056
   inverse Laplace transform
      Bromwich integral, 1038–1040, 1040f
      exercises, 1042–1045
      inversion via calculus of residues, 1040
      multiregion inversion, 1041–1042, 1041f,
         1042f
   Laplace transform of derivatives, 1016–1020
      Earth's nutation, 1018–1019, 1018f
      impulsive force, 1019–1020
      simple harmonic oscillator, 1017
      use of derivative formula, 1017
   Laplace transforms, 1008–1034
      definition, 1008
      Dirac delta function, 1010–1011
      elementary functions, 1008–1010
      exercises, 1014–1015
      Heaviside step function, 1010
      inverse transform, 1012t, 1011–1014, 1014f

partial fraction expansion, 1013
   properties of, 1016–1034
   step function, 1013–1014, 1014f
Laplace, Mellin, and Hankel transforms,
      965–966
   use of, 964f
integrals, 67, 764, 927, see also Cauchy
      (Maclaurin) integral test; definite integrals;
      elliptic integrals
   containing logarithm, 532–534, 533f
   contour, 581, 592, 581f
   cosine, 580–582
   definite, 580
   evaluation of, 65
      1-D integral, 66
      differentiate parameter, 67
      exercises, 74–75
      integration by parts, 65
      integration variables, 72–74
      multiple integrals, 70–72
      recursion, 69
      trigonometric integral, 69
   exponential, 578–580
   of meromorphic function, 526–527, 527f
   of three spherical harmonics, 803–805
   oscillatory, 529–530
   range, 525–527, 525f
   sine, 580–582
   trigonometric, 522–524
   with complex exponentials, 527–531, 529f
integrating factors, 334
integration
   by parts, 65, 568, 578
   by parts of volume integrals, 163
   contour of, 530–531
   of power series, 30, 583
   order, reversing, 70–71
   technique, 531–532
   variables, 72–74
intersections, 1127–1130, 1128f
invariants
   example, 295
   exercises, 296
   overview, 294–295
inverse Fourier transform, 1055
inverse Laplace transform
   Bromwich integral, 1038–1040, 1040f
   exercises, 1042–1045
   inversion via calculus of residues, 1040
   multiregion inversion, 1041–1042, 1041f,
      1042f
inverse matrix, 99–102
inverse transform, 211, 1011–1014, 1012t
inversion
   multiregion, 1041–1042, 1041f, 1042f

inversion (*continued*)
  of power series, 32
  via calculus of residues, 1040
inversion operation, 136
irreducible representations, 822
irreducible spherical tensors, 796
irregular (essential) singular point, 344
irregular sign changes, series with, 12–13
irregular singularities, 353–354
irregular solution, 369
irrotational, 152, 154–155
isobaric ODEs, 335
isomorphic group, 817
isomorphism, 819
isospin, SU(2), 852–861
isotropic tensors, 209

J

Jacobi method, 314
Jacobi-Anger expansion, 655
Jacobian, 73
  2-D and 3-D, 229–230
  definiton, 227
  direct approaches to, 231
  exercises, 231–232
  inverse of, 230–231
Jacobian determinant, 229
Jacobian matrix, 229
Jensen's theorem, 585
Jordan's lemma, 528

K

Kepler's laws of planetary motion, 189–190
kernel, 963
  of integral equation, 455
kernel equation, 1047, 1052f
  separable, 1057–1059
kernel function, 447
Kirchoff diffraction theory, 166
Kirchoff's law, 338
Korteweg-deVries equation, 413
Kronecker delta, 79–80, 209, 258, 805
Kronig-Kramers optical dispersion relations, 591, 594
Kummer's test, 8–10

L

L'Hôpital's rule, 31, 517, 516, 576, 662
ladder operators, 776–779
  construction, 788–795
Lagrangian equations, 1112–1113
  of motion, 1098
Lagrangian mechanics, 63
Lagrangian multipliers, 1107–1109
Laguerre functions

associated Laguerre polynomials, 892–895
differential equation–Laguerre polynomials, 890–892
exercises, 897–899
hydrogen atom, 896–897
Rodrigues formula and generating function, 889–890
Laguerre polynomials
  associated
    confluent hypergeometric representation, 919
    generating function, 892–895
    integral representation, 895
    orthogonality, 895
    recurrence relations, 893
    Rodrigues' representation, 895
    Schrödinger's wave equation, 896
  confluent hypergeometric representation, 919
  differential equation, 890–892
  generating function, 889–890
  recurrence relations, 890, 893
  Rodrigues' formula, 889–890
  self-adjoint form, 894
Laplace convolution theorem, 1034–1038
  exercises, 1037–1038
Laplace equation, 154, 433–434, 726, 1101–1102
  Bessel functions, 651
  for parallelepiped, 417–419
  Green's function, 462, 464
Laplace expansion, 760–761
Laplace series
  expansion theorem, 762
  gravity fields, 762
Laplace spherical harmonic expansion, 799–801
Laplace transforms, 965, 1008–1034, 1054
  convolution theorem, 1056
  of derivatives, 1016–1020
    Earth's nutation, 1018–1019, 1018f
    impulsive force, 1019–1020
    simple harmonic oscillator, 1017
    use of derivative formula, 1017
  definition, 1008
  Dirac delta function, 1010–1011
  elementary functions, 1008–1010
  exercises, 1014–1015
  Heaviside step function, 1010
  inverse transform, 1011–1014, 1012t, 1014f
  one-sided, 1008
  operations, 1028t
  other properties
    Bessel's equation, 1025–1027
    change of scale, 1020
    damped oscillator, 1021
    derivative of a transform, 1024–1025
    electromagnetic waves, 1023–1024
    exercises, 1028–1034

integration of transforms, 1027
RLC analog, 1022, 1022*f*
substitution, 1020
translation, 1022–1023
partial fraction expansion, 1013
properties of, 1016–1034
step function, 1013–1014, 1014*f*
two-sided, 1008
Laplacian, 154
development by minors, 88
in circular cylindrical coordinates, 192
of vector, 155–156
Laurent expansion
exercises, 496–497
Laurent series, 494–496
Taylor expansion, 492–494, 493*f*
Laurent series, 33, 494–496, 644
least squares, method of, 1138
Legendre duplication formula, derivation of,
618–619
Legendre equation, 425, 716
Legendre functions, 425, 715, 768*f*
associated, 744–745, 745*t*
hypergeometric representation, 914
recurrence formulas for, 745–746, 764
associated Legendre equation, 741–743
exercises, 753–756
magnetic field of current loop, 748–753
orthogonality, 748
parity and special values, 746
generating function
electric multipoles, 737–739
exercises, 740–741
expansion, 736–737
physical interpretation of, 735
Legendre polynomials, 716
associated, 743–744
exercises, 722–724
recurrence formulas, 718–720
Rodrigues formulas, 720–721
upper and lower bounds for $P_n(\cos\theta)$, 720
of second kind, 766
alternate formulations, 769–770
exercises, 770–771
properties, 769
orthogonality, 724
Earth's gravitational field, 727
electrostatic potential for ring of charge,
729–730
exercises, 730–735
Legendre series, 726–730
sphere in uniform field, 727–729, 728*f*
spherical harmonics, 756
Cartesian representations, 758
exercises, 765–766

Laplace expansion, 760–762
properties of, 764–765
solutions, 758–760
symmetry of solutions, 762–763
Legendre ordinary differential equations (ODEs),
716
Legendre polynomials, 270–271, 425, 557–558
719*t*
associated, 743–744
exercises, 722–724
generating function, 557–558, 716, 735
orthogonality of, 726
recurrence formulas, 718–720
Rodrigues formulas, 720–721
Schlaefli integral, 557
upper and lower bounds for $P_n(\cos\theta)$, 720
Legendre series, 9–10, 726–730
Legendre's differential equation, 276, 388
Legendre's duplication formula, 604
Legendre's equation, 389–390
Leibniz criterion, 11–12
Leibniz's formula, 553, 742
Lerch's theorem, 1011
level lines, 586
Levi-Civita symbol, 85, 87, 216, 841, 850
line integrals, 159–160, 160*f*
linear electric quadrupole, 738*f*
linear equation, 88–89
linear equation system, 102–103
linear first-order ODEs, 336–339
linear Hermitian operator, 311
linear independence of solutions, 358–360
linear integral equations, 1047
linear integral operator, 1070
linear operation, 329
linear operators, 275, 329, 401
linear oscillator, 347–350
linear oscillator equation, 347, 363, 1050–1052
linear parameters, variation of, 1121
linear vector space, 252
linearly dependent equations, 90–91
Liouville's theorem, 490
Lippmann-Schwinger equation, 466
logarithm, 60
Lommel integrals, 665
Lorentz covariance of Maxwell's equations,
866–868
exercises, 868–869
Lorentz gauge, 174
Lorentz group, *see* homogeneous Lorentz group
exercises, 865–866
Lorentz transformation, 862
of E and B, 867–868
lowering operator, 777

M

Maclaurin expansion, 64
  computation, 613
Maclaurin integral test, 5–8
  Riemann Zeta function, 7
Maclaurin series, 27, 44, 253
Maclaurin theorem, 27
  exponential function, 27–28
  logarithm, 28–29
magnetic dipole, 748–753
magnetic field of current loop, 748–753
magnetic moment, 753
magnetic vector potential, 173–174, 193
manifestly covariant form, 868
mapping, 57
  complex variables, 547–549, 548f
    exercises, 549–550
  conformal, 549
matching conditions, 391
mathematical induction, 40–41
  excercise, 41
matrices, 95
  addition and subtraction, 96
  adjoint matrix, 105
  defective, 324
  definitions, 95–96
  diagonalization, 311–314
  Dirac notation in, 266
  direct product, 108–112
  equality, 96
  functions of, 113–114
  Hermitian matrices, 108, 315
  multiplication, 97, 279
    inner product, 97–98
    by scalar, 96
  normal
    exercises, 324–326
    normal modes of vibration, 322–324
    overview, 319–320
  null matrix, 96
  numerical inversion of, 100
  orthogonal matrices, 107
  product theorem, 103–104
  rank of, 104
  symmetric, 105
  trace matrix, 105
  transpose matrix, 104
  unitary matrices, 107, 314
matrix algebra, 95
matrix eigenvalue equation, 300
matrix eigenvalue problems, 301
  example, 301–303
    2-D ellipsoidal basin, 303–305
    block-diagonal matrix, 305–307
  exercises, 308–310

matrix elements, 279
  of operator, 280–281
matrix invariant, 295
matrix products, operations on, 106
Maxwell's equations, 155, 241–243, 594
  Gauss' law, 176
  Lorentz covariance of, 866–868
Maxwell-Boltzmann distribution, 606–607
Maxwell-Boltzmann statistics, 1132, 1133
mean value, 1136–1140
mean value theorem, 26, 62
measurement errors, 1125, 1170
Mellin transforms, 966, 1054
meromorphic, 498, 515
meromorphic functions
  integral of, 526–527, 527f
  pole expansion of, 515–518
metric spaces, 218
metric tensor, 218–219
  Christoffel symbols as derivatives of, 223
metric, curvilinear coordinates, 184
Milne's model, 37
Minkowski space, 236–237, 864
miscellaneous vector identities, 156–157
Mittag-Leffler theorem, 515–516
mixed derivatives, 401
mixed tensor, 209, 210
modified Bessel functions, 678, 680, 682f
  asymptotic expansion, 688
  contours, 696f
  exercises, 688
  Fourier transforms, 684
  Green's function, 684–685
  Hankel function, 682
  hyperbolic Bessel functions, 683
  integral representation, 684, 690–692
  Laplace equations, 680
  recurrence relations, 681–682
  series expansion, 681
  Whittaker functions, 682
modified spherical Bessel functions, 428
modulus, 56, 470
molecular vibration, 882–883
moment-generating function, 1141–1142,
  1149–1150
momentum, *see* angular momentum
momentum representation
  in quantum mechanics, 1048–1049
  Schrödinger wave equation, 994
monopole moment of charge distribution, 739
monotonic decreasing function, 5
movable singularities, 378–379
moving particle, Cartesian coordinates,
  1098–1099
multinomial coefficient, 1132

multiple integrals, 70–72

multiplet, 827, 851

multiplication

   by scalar, 255

   of matrices, inner product, 97–98

   operator, 275

   of random variables, 1162

multiply connected regions, 483–484, 483*f*

multipole expansion, 738, 739, 801–803

multipole moments of charge distribution, 739, 801

multivalued function, 500

mutually commuting operator, 785

mutually exclusive events, 1126

N

Navier-Stokes equations, 190, 377

NDEs, *see* nonlinear differential equations

negative definite operators, 317

neighboring paths, 1082, 1083*f*

Neumann boundary conditions, 385, 412, 428, 662

Neumann functions, 367–369, 693, 917

   Bessel functions of second kind

      coaxial wave guides, 672

      definition and series form, 667–669

      exercises, 674

      integral representations, 669

      recurrence relations, 669–670

      uses of, 671

      Wronskian formulas, 670–671

   integral form, 671

   recurrence relations, 669–670

   spherical, 700*f*

   Wronskian formulas, 670–671

Neumann series, 1064–1066

   exercises, 1068

Newton's equations of motion, 213

Newton's law, 331, 342

Newton's second law of motion, 322, 1106

nodes of standing wave, 435

nonlinear differential equations (NDEs), 377–380

   Bernoulli and Riccati equations, 378

   exercises, 379–380

   fixed and movable singularities, special solutions, 378–379

nonlinear dispersive equation, 413

nonlinear methods and chaos

   nonlinear differential equations (NDEs)

      Bernoulli and Riccati equations, 378

      exercises, 379–380

      fixed and movable singularities, special solutions, 378–379

   nonlinear ODEs, 377–380

nonnormal matrices, 322–324

nonuniform convergence, 21–22

nonunitary transformations, 293

normal distributions, addition theorem for, 1161

normal eigensystem, 320–321

normal matrices

   defective, 324

   example, 320–321

   exercises, 324–328

   normal modes of vibration, 322–324

   overview, 319–320

normalization, 662

normalization constant, 606

nucleon, 853

null matrix, 96

numerical evaluation, 91–93

O

ODEs, *see* ordinary differential equations

Oersted's law, 168

Olbers' paradox, 11

one-dimensional problems, Green's function, 448–459

one-sided Laplace transform, 1008

operators

   adjoint, 277

   basis expansions of, 279–280

   commutation of, 276–277

   example, 277, 278, 280–282

   exercises, 282–283

   expression, 285–286

   functions of, 282

   identity, inverse, adjoint, 277–278

   matrix elements, 280–281

   overview, 275–276

   self-adjoint, 277, 284–285

      example, 284–286

      overview, 283–284

   transformations of, 291

      exercises, 294

      nonunitary transformations, 293

   unitary

      successive transformations, 290

      unitary transformations, 287–288

operators, differential vector, *see* differential vector operators

optical dispersion, 594–595

optical path near event horizon of black hole, 1087–1088, 1088*f*

orbital angular momentum, 782

order 2 branch points, 500

ordinary differential equations (ODEs), 329, 330, 381, 644, 715, 982, 1084

   exact, 333–334

   Hermite, 554

   homogeneous linear, 330

   homogenous, 335

ordinary differential equations (*continued*)
 inhomogeneous linear, 375–377
  exercises, 377
 isobaric, 335
 Legendre, 557, 716
 linear first-order, 336–339
 linear second-order, 1049
  initial/boundary conditions in, 1052
 nonlinear, 413
 nonseparable exact, 333–334
 Rodrigues formulas, 551, 552
 second order, 452
 second-order linear, 343–346
 second-order Sturm-Liouville, 551
 separable, 331–332
 singularities of, 345*t*
 with constant coefficients, 342–343
ordinary points of the ODE, 344
orthogonal, 124
 transformations, 135
orthogonal coordinates, $\mathbb{R}^3$, 182–184, 182*f*, 183*f*
orthogonal eigenfunctions, 1069–1073
orthogonal functions, expansions in, 258–259
orthogonal matrices, 107, 135
orthogonal polynomials, 272*f*
 exercises, 558–560
 generating function, 555, 556
 Hermite, 555–556
 Rodrigues formula, 551–554
 Schlaefli integral, 554
orthogonal unitary, 277
orthogonality, 51, 703, 724, 906–907
 associated Legendre equation, 746–748
 Bessel series, 663
 Earth's gravitational field, 727
 electrostatic potential for ring of charge, 729–730
 electrostatic potential in a hollow cylinder, 663–664
 exercises, 665–667, 730–735
 integral, Hermite polynomials, 875
 Legendre series, 726–730
 Neumann boundary condition, 662
 normalization, 662
 over discrete points, 1002–1004
 sphere in uniform field, 727–729, 728*f*
 Sturm-Liouville differential equations, 1073
 Sturm-Liouville theory, 661
orthogonalization
 Gram-Schmidt
  overview, 269–270
  example, 270–272
  exercises, 273–275
  orthonormalizing physical vectors, 272–273
orthogonalized Laguerre functions, 892

orthonormal set, 258
orthonormalization, physical vectors, 272–273
oscillator
 damping, 1035–1037
 driven, 1035–1037
 harmonic, 878–879
oscillatory integral, 529–530
oscillatory series, 2
outward flow, 148
overlap integral, 989–990
overlap matrix, 317
overshoot, calculation of, 959–961

P

parabolic partial differential equations (PDEs), 410
parallelepiped, Laplace equation for, 417–419
parity
 and special values, 746
 Bessel functions, 655
Parseval relation, 595–596, 987–990
partial derivatives, 62, 401
partial differential equations (PDEs), 329, 643, 981–982
 boundary conditions, 405, 411–413
 characteristics of, 404–406
 classes of, 409–411
 elliptic, 410
 examples of, 402–403
 exercises, 408–409
 first-order, 403–408
 heat flow, or diffusion, 983
  alternate solutions, 439–441
  exercises, 444
  special boundary condition again, 441–442
  specific boundary condition, 437
  spherically symmetric heat flow, 442–444
 homogeneous, 402
 hyperbolic, 410
 nonlinear, 413–414
 parabolic, 410
 second-order, 409–411
 separation of variables, 414, 430–432
  Cartesian coordinates, 415–420
  circular cylindrical coordinates, 421–424, 431
  exercises, 432–433
  spherical polar coordinates, 424–430
 types of, 402
partial fraction expansion, 42, 43, 767, 1013
partial sum approximation, 579
partial-wave components, 799
particle, in a sphere, 704–706
passive rotations, of coordinate system, 215
Pauli matrices, 112

PDEs, *see* partial differential equations
periodic functions, 939–940
permutation group, 845
permutations, counting of, 1130–1133
physical space, 964
piecewise regular, 936
pivotal method, 1176
plane triangle, 131, 131*f*
Pochhammer symbol, 35, 699, 912, 917
Poincaré group, 862
Poincaré's lemma, 239, 240
point groups, 820, 835
point quadrupole, 738
Poisson distribution, 1151, 1153*f*
  exercises, 1154–1155
  limits of, 1157–1158
  relation to binomial distribution, 1153–1154,
    1154*f*
Poisson noise, 1151
Poisson's equation, 176–177, 433–434
polar coordinates, 442, *see also* spherical polar
    coordinates
  evaluation, 72
polar vectors, 136
polarization matrix, 212
pole expansion of meromorphic functions, 498,
    515–518
poles, 497–498
polygamma function, 612
polylogarithms, 923
polynomials, 701, 748
  Bernoulli, 565–566
  Hermite, 280, 554
    example, 554–555, 556
  Legendre, 270–272, 557–558
  orthogonal, 272*f*
    exercises, 558–560
    generating function, 555
    Hermite, 555–556
    Rodrigues formulas, 551–554
    Schlaefli integral, 554
positive definite operators, 317
potential theory
  exercises, 180–182
  Gauss' law, 175–176, 175*f*
  Helmholtz's theorem, 177–180
  Poisson's equation, 176–177
  scalar potential, 171–172
  vector potential, 172–175
potential, of charge distribution, 988–989
power series, convergence, uniform and absolute,
    29
  differentiation and integration, 30
  inversion of, 32
  uniqueness theorem, L'Hôpital's rule, 31

power spectrum, 945
power-series expansion, 670
principal axes, 300, 305
principal quantum number, 897
principal value, 501
probability
  binomial distribution
    exercises, 1151
    limits of, 1157–1158
    moment-generating function, 1149–1150
    repeated tosses of dice, 1148–1149
  definitions, simple properties, 1126
    conditional probability, 1128–1129
    counting permutations and combinations,
      1130–1133
    exercises, 1133
    probability for A or B, 1127
    scholastic aptitude tests, 1129–1130
  Gauss' normal distribution, 1155–1159
  Poisson distribution, 1151, 1153*f*
    exercises, 1154–1155
    limits of, 1157–1158
    relation to binomial distribution, 1153–1154,
      1154*f*
  random variables
    addition of, 1160–1161
    computing discrete probability distributions,
      1136
    continuous random variable: hydrogen atom,
      1135–1136
    discrete, 1134–1135, 1137
    exercises, 1147–1148
    mean and variance, 1136–1140
    multiplication or division of, 1162
    repeated draws of cards, 1145–1147
    standard deviation of measurements,
      1138–1140
    transformations of, 1159–1160
  statistics
    chi-square (χ^2) distribution, 1170–1174
    confidence interval, 1176–1178
    error propagation, 1165–1168
    exercises, 1178–1179
    fitting curves to data, 1168–1170
    student t distribution, 1174–1176
  theory of, 1125
probability density, student t, 1176*f*
probability distributions
  arbitrary, 1157
  conditional, 1147
  marginal, 1144–1147
  moments of, 1141–1142
product expansion of entire functions, 519–520
products, *see* cross product; direct product
  expansion of entire functions, 519–520

products (*continued*)
  infinite
    convergence of, 575
    exercises, 576–577
    overview, 574–575
    sine, cosine functions, 575
pseudoscalar, 137
pseudotensors, 215–216
  and dual tensors, 216–217
  exercises, 217–218
  Levi-Civita symbol, 216
pseudovectors, 136, 137f, 215

Q

QCD, *see* quantum chromodynamics
quantum chromodynamics (QCD), 861
quantum mechanical oscillator wave functions,
  880f
quantum mechanical scattering, Born
  approximation, 465–466
quantum mechanical simple harmonic oscillator,
  878–879
quantum mechanics
  momentum representation in, 1048–1049
  of triangular symmetry, 829–830
  Schrödinger equation of, 330, 1048
  sum rules, 594, 596
  time-dependent perturbations, 1067
quantum number, 776
quantum oscillator, 1120f, 1119–1121
quantum particle, 419–420
quantum theory, 704
quarks, 853
  ladders, 856–857, 857f
  quantum numbers of, 855–856
quotient rule, 211–213

R

radius of convergence, 494
radius vector, 48
raising operator, 777
random variables, 1125
  addition of, 1160–1161
    gamma-distribution, 1164
  computing discrete probability distributions,
    1136
  continuous random variable: hydrogen atom,
    1135–1136
  discrete, 1134–1135, 1137
  exercises, 1147–1148
  mean and variance, 1136–1140
  multiplication or division of, 1162
  repeated draws of cards, 1145–1147
  standard deviation of measurements,
    1138–1140

transformations of, 1159–1160
  exercises, 1164–1165
rank, 848
  tensor of, 205, 207–208
rapidity, 863
ratio test, Cauchy, d'Alembert, 4–5
Rayleigh formulas, 702
Rayleigh's theorem, *see* Parseval relation
Rayleigh-Ritz variational technique, 1117–1118,
  1121
  ground state eigenfunction, 1118–1119
real axis, 56
real part, 56
rearrangement of double series, 18–19
rearrangement theorem, 820
reciprocal lattice, 129
recurrence formulas, 556, 718–720, 764
recurrence relations, 348
  Bessel functions, 645–646
    spherical, 702
  Chebyshev polynomials, 901–903
  confluent hypergeometric functions, 918
  Hankel functions, 675
  Hermite polynomials, 872–873
  Laguerre polynomials, associated, 893
  modified Bessel functions, 681–682
  Neumann functions, 669–670
  spherical Bessel functions, 702
recursion, 69
reducible representation, 823–824
reference frame, 868
reflection formula, 603
reflections
  in spherical coordinates, 196
  of coordinate transformations, 136–137, 137f
regression coefficient, 1168
regular singularities, 353–354
regular solution, 369
relativistic energy, 35–36
representation
  counting irreducible, 832–833, 833t
  decomposing a reducible, 834–835
  exercises, 825, 826f
  of continuous groups, 824–825
  of group, 821
  reducible, 823–824
  unitary, 821–823, 823f
residue theorem, 509–510, 509f
resolution of identity, 266, 297
resonant cavity, 650–653
Riccati equations, 378
Riemann Zeta function, 7, 16–17, 571, 626–631
  exercises, 631–633
Riemann's theorem, 15
Riemannian spaces, *see* metric spaces

RL circuit, 338–339
RLC analog, 1022, 1022*f*
Rodrigues formula, 551–554, 720–721
   for Hermite ODE, 554
     Laguerre polynomials, 889–890
      associated, 895
Rodrigues representation, Hermite polynomials, 874
root diagram, 857
root test, Cauchy, 4
rotations
   groups SO(2) and SO(3), 849–851
   in $\mathbb{R}^3$, 139–142, 140*f*
     exercises, 142–143
   in spherical coordinates, 194–196, 195*f*
   of circular disk, 818
   of coordinate system, 215
   of coordinate transformations, 133–135
Rouché's theorem, 518–519
row vectors, 95, 123, 125
   extraction of, 108

S

saddle points, 63, 433
   argument, 586
   asymptotic forms
     factorial function, 588
     of gamma function, 588–589
   for avoiding oscillations, 589
   method, 587–588
   overview, 585–587
sample space, 1126
sample standard deviation, 1168
sawtooth wave, 937–939, 938*f*,
scalar, 205
scalar field, 143
scalar potential, 171–172
scalar product, 51, 254–255, 271, 285, 295, 297
   and adjoint operator, 278
   in spin space, 259
   triple, 128–130, 129*f*,
scalar quantities, 46
scattering cross section, 465
Schlaefli integral, 554, 604, 653*f*, 676
   Legendre polynomials, 557
scholastic aptitude tests, 1129–1130
Schrödinger equation, 708, 1048, 1116–1117
   hydrogen atom, 896
   momentum space representation, 994
   of quantum mechanics, 330
Schwarz inequality, 51, 257
Schwarz reflection principle, 547
   exercises, 549–550
second-order linear ODEs, 343–346
second-order partial differential equations (PDEs)
   boundary conditions, 411–413
   classes of, 409–411
   exercises, 414
   nonlinear, 413–414
second-order Sturm-Liouville ordinary differential
     equations (ODEs), 551
second-rank tensor, 207–208
secular determinant, 302
secular equation, 302, 306
self-adjoint matrices, 108
self-adjoint ODEs
   boundary conditions, 381
   deuteron, 391–393
   eigenvalues, 389
   exercises, 393–395
   Hermitian operators, 384
   Legendre's equation, 389–390
self-adjoint operators, 277, 284–286, 1070
   example, 284–286
   exercises, 286–287
   overview, 283–284
self-adjoint poblems, Green's function, 460
self-adjoint theory, 384
semi-convergent series, 579
separable kernel, 1057–1059
   homogeneous Fredholm equation, 1059–1060
separable ODEs, 331–332
separation of variables, 403, 414, 430–432
   Cartesian coordinates, 415–420
   circular cylindrical coordinates, 421–424, 431
   exercises, 432–433
   spherical polar coordinates, 424–430
series approach
   Bessel's equation, limitations of, 351–353
   Chebyshev, 25
   hypergeometric, 912
   Legendre, 9–10
   shifted polynomials, Chebyshev, 908
   ultraspherical, 25
series expansion, 681
series solutions, Frobenius method, 346–350, 350*f*
   exercises, 355–358
   expansion about, 350
   Fuchs' theorem, 355
   limitations of series approach, Bessel's
     equation, 351–353
   regular and irregular singularities, 353–354
   symmetry of solutions, 350–351
sets, 1127–1130
several dependent and independent variables,
     relation to physics, 1105
sign changes, series with alternating, 12–13
signal-processing applications, 997–1001
   exercises, 1001–1002
similarity transformations, 208, 293

simple pendulum, 927–928, 1113–1114, 1113f
simple pole, 498
simultaneous diagonalization, 314–315
sine
   infinite products, 575
   integrals in asymptotic series, 580–582
single-electron wave function, 396
single-slit diffraction pattern, 972
singular points, 343–345, 345t
   essential (irregular), 344
   irregular (essential), 344
   isolated, 497
singularities
   analytic continuation, 503–507, 504f, 505f
   exercises, 507–508
   fixed, 378–379
   movable, 378–379
   on contour of integration, 530–531
   poles, 497–498
Slater-type orbitals (STOs), 990
Snell's law, 1095, 1095f
SO(2) rotation groups, 849–851
SO(3) rotation groups, 849–851
soap film, 1088–1090, 1089f
soap film–minimum area, 1090–1093, 1092f
solar products, 256–257
solenoidal, 149, 154–155
soliton, 413
source term, 447
space groups, 869
special relativity, 862
special unitary groups, SU(3), Gell-Mann
      matrices, 852–861
special values, 764
   parity and, 746
spectral decomposition, 315–316
sphere in uniform field, 727–729, 728f
sphere with boundary conditions, 428–430
spherical Bessel functions, 427, 428
   asymptotic values, 703
   definitions, 702
   exercises, 709–712
   Helmholtz equation, 698
   limiting values, 703
   modified, 709
   orthogonality and zeros, 703
   particle in a sphere, 704–706
   recurrence relations, 702
spherical coordinates, Helmholtz equation, 698
spherical Green's functions, 463, 800–801
spherical harmonics, 445, 473, 756
   addition theorem for, 797–798
   Cartesian representations, 758
   Condon-Shortley phase, 758, 760t
   exercises, 765–766

integrals of three, 803–805
ladder, 779
Laplace expansion, 760–761, 799–801
Laplace series–gravity fields, 762
properties of, 764–765
symmetry of solutions, 762–763
vector, 809–813
spherical pendulum, 1105, 1105f
spherical polar coordinates, 79, 183, 190–194,
      194f, 424–430
spherical tensors, 796
   addition theorem, 797–798
      Laplace expansion, 799–801
      spherical wave expansion, 798–799
   exercises, 806–809
   integrals of three spherical harmonics, 803–805
spherical volume, 704
spherical waves
   Bessel functions, 703
   expansion, 798–799
spin operator, adjoint of, 282
spin space, 259–260
   of electron, 253
spinor ladder, 780–781
spinors, 213, 779–780, 832
square integrable, 595
square integration contour, z^n on, 479–481, 480f,
square pulse, transform of, 1010, 1010f
square wave, 949–950, 949f, 958–959
   expansion of, 264f
squares of random variables, 1164
squares of series, divergent, 15–16
standard deviation, 1138
   of measurements, 1138–1140
   sample, 1168
standing waves, 382–384, 435
star operator, *see* Hodge operator
stationary, 63
stationary paths, 1085, 1085f
stationary points, 433
statistical hypothesis, 1165
statistics, 1125
   chi-square (χ^2) distribution, 1170–1174
   confidence interval, 1176–1178
   error propagation, 1165–1168
   exercises, 1178–1179
   fitting curves to data, 1168–1170
   student t distribution, 1174–1176
steepest descent
   method of, 585
      asymptotic form of gamma function,
         588–589
      exercises, 590–591
      factorial function, 588
      saddle points, 585–588

step function, 1013–1014, 1014f
Stirling's expansion, 589
Stirling's series
    derivation from Euler-Maclaurin integration
        formula, 623–624
    exercises, 625–626
    Stirling's series, 624
Stirlings formula, 567
Stokes' theorem, 167–168, 167f, 168f, 193–194
    on differential forms, 245–248
STOs, *see* Slater-type orbitals
stream lines, 149
strong interaction, 852
structure constants, 848
student t distribution, 1174–1176, 1177t
student t probability density, 1176f
Sturm-Liouville boundary conditions, 892
Sturm-Liouville equation, 1117
Sturm-Liouville system, 746, 892
Sturm-Liouville theory, 384, 661, 936–937, 1071,
    1073
SU(2)
    and SO(3) homomorphism, 851–852
    isospin and SU(3) symmetry, 852
SU(3) symmetry, 852–861
substitution, 1020
subtraction
    of sets, 1127
    of tensors, 208
successive applications of ∇, 153–154
successive operations, of coordinate
        transformations, 137–138
successive transfer functions, 1002f
successive unitary transformations, 290
sum
    evaluation of, 544–546, 546t
        exercises, 546–547
sum rules, 596
summation of series, 957–958
superposition principle, 402
    for homogenous ODEs, PDEs, 330
surface integrals, 161–162, 161f, 162f
symmetric group, 835, 840–844
    exercises, 844–845
symmetric matrix, 105
symmetric stretching mode, 323
symmetric tensor, 208
symmetrization of kernels, 1069
symmetry, 815, 940–941, 942f
    and physics, 826–830
        exercises, 830
    of equilateral triangle, 817f, 817, 818f
    of solutions, 762–763
    relations, 593–594

T

Taylor expansion, 492–494, 493f
Taylor series, 560
Taylor's expansion, 653
    binomial theorem, relativistic energy, 35–36
    Maclaurin theorem
        exponential function, 27–28
        logarithm, 28–29
tensor analysis, 205–213
    addition and subtraction of, 208
    covariant and contravariant, 206–207
    exercises, 213–215
    isotropic, 209
    symmetric and antisymmetric, 208
tensor derivative operators
    curl, 225
    divergence, 224–225
    gradient, 224
    Laplacian, 225
tensors, *see also* direct product; quotient rule;
        spinors; pseudotensors
    direct product of, 210–211
    in general coordinates
        covariant derivatives, 222–223
        exercises, 226
        metric tensor, 218–219
    second-rank, 207–208
tensors of rank 0, 205
tensors of rank 1, 205
tensors of rank 2, 207–208
three-dimensional (3-D) differential forms, 407
threefold Hermite formula, 883–884
time-independent Schrödinger equation, 300
TM, *see* transverse magnetic
trace matrix, 105, 210
transfer function, 998–999, 998f
    high-pass filter, 999–1000, 999f
    limitations on, 1000–1001
transform, derivative of, 965, 966, *see also*
        Hankel; Laplace; Mellin
transformations
    Gram-Schmidt, 293
    of differential equation into integral equation,
        1049–1050
    of operators, 291
        nonunitary transformations, 293
    of random variables, 1159–1165
    unitary, 287–290
translation, 1022–1023
transpose matrix, 104
transverse magnetic (TM), 651
traveling waves, 435
triangle rule, 788
triangular pulse, Fourier transform of, 976, 977f

triangular symmetry, quantum mechanics of, 829–830

trigonometric form, 904–905

trigonometric functions

exploiting periodicity of, 537–538

trigonometric integrals, 69, 522–524

triple scalar product, 128–130, 129*f*

triple vector product, 130

triplet state, 259

Two and three dimension problems, Green's function, 459–467

two-sided Laplace transforms, 1008

U

ultraspherical polynomials, 388, 899

equation, 903

self-adjoint form, 906

undetermined multipliers, *see* Lagrangian multipliers

uniform convergence, 21–22, 29, 262

uniformly convergent series, properties of, 24

unions, 1127–1130

unique expansion, 494

uniqueness theorem

L'Hôpital's rule, 31

of power series, 30–31

unit cell, 869

unit matrix, 99

unit vectors, 47

unitary matrices, 107

unitary operators

example, 289–290

exercises, 290–291

successive transformations, 290

unitary transformations, 287–288

unitary representation, 821–823, 823*f*

unitary transformation, 297

V

variables

dependent, 1096–1097

Hamilton's Principle, 1097–1098

Laplace's equation, 1101–1102

moving particle–Cartesian coordinates, 1098–1099

moving particle–circular cylindrical coordinates, 1099

independent, 407–408, 411

separation of, 403

variance, 1136–1140

variation, 1081

with constraints, 1111–1112

exercises, 1121–1124

Lagrangian equations, 1112–1113

Schrödinger wave equation, 1116–1117

simple pendulum, 1113–1114, 1113*f*

sliding off a log, 1114–1115, 1114*f*

of linear parameters, 1121

of constant, 338

of parameters, 338, 375–376

variation method, 395–397

exercises, 397

vector analysis

reciprocal lattice, 130

rotation of coordinate transformations, 133–135

vector fields, 46, 143

vector integration

exercises, 163–164

line integrals, 159–160, 160*f*

surface integrals, 161–162, 161*f*, 162*f*

volume integrals, 162–163

vector Laplacian, 155–156

vector model, 786–788

vector potential, 172–175, 175

vector spaces, 253–254, 295

completeness, 255, 262

linear space, 252

vector spherical harmonics

coupling, 810–813

exercises, 813

spherical tensor, 809–810

vector triple product, 130

vectors, 123, 205, *see also* rotations; gradient, ∇; tensors; Stokes' theorem

addition of, 47*f*

angle between two, 798

basic properties of, 124–125

by Gram-Schmidt orthogonalization, 269–275

coefficient, 261

contravariant, 206, 219

contravariant basis, 220–221

covariant, 206

covariant basis, 218, 220–221

cross product, 126–128, 126*f*, 127*f*

differential vector operators, 143

gradient, 143

direct product of, 210–211

dot products, 49–50

exercises, 52–53, 131–133

fields, 123

Gauss' theorem, 164–165, 165*f*

Green's theorem, 165–166

Helmholtz's theorem, 177–180

in function spaces

Dirac notation, 265–266

example, 253–254, 256–263, 265

exercises, 266–269

expansions, 261

Hilbert space, 255–256

orthogonal expansions, 257–258

overview, 251–253
scalar product, 254–255, 260–261
Schwarz inequality, 257
irrotational, 154–155
matrix representation of, 106–107
multiplication of, 252
orthogonality, 51
physical, 272–273
radius vector, 48
Stokes' theorem, 167–168, 167*f*, 168*f*
successive applications of ∇, 153–154
triple product, 130
triple scalar product, 128–130, 129*f*
unit vectors, 47
vibrating string, 382–384
vibration, normal modes of, 322–324
vierergruppe, 820
Volterra equation, 1047, 1048, 1050, 1055, 1067
volume integrals, 162–163
vorticity, 151

W

wave equation, 435, 981–982
d'Alembert's solution of, 436
exercises, 437

wave guides, coaxial, Bessel functions, 671–672
wedge operator, 233
wedge products, 233
Weierstrass, 504
Weierstrass *M* test, 22–23
Weierstrass infinite-product form of, 602
weight diagram, 859*f*, 859, 860*f*
Weyl representation, 121
Whittaker functions, 682, 919
Wigner matrices, 797
WKB expansion, 577
Wronskian determinant, 359–360
Wronskian formulas
Bessel functions, 670–671, 694
confluent hypergeometric functions, 922
linear dependence/independence of functions, 360, 671
solutions of self-adjoint differential equation, 670

Z

zero matrix, 96
zero-point energy, 705, 879
zeros, Bessel function, 648–653

Series and Products

$$f(x) = \sum_{n=0}^{\infty} f^{(n)}(a) \frac{(x-a)^n}{n!}, \quad \frac{1}{1-x} = \sum_{n=0}^{\infty} x^n, \quad (1+x)^\alpha = \sum_{n=0}^{\infty} \binom{\alpha}{n} x^n,$$

$$e^x = \sum_{n=0}^{\infty} \frac{x^n}{n!}, \quad \sin x = \sum_{n=0}^{\infty} \frac{(-1)^n x^{2n+1}}{(2n+1)!}, \quad \cos x = \sum_{n=0}^{\infty} \frac{(-1)^n x^{2n}}{(2n)!},$$

$$\ln(1+x) = \sum_{n=1}^{\infty} \frac{(-1)^{n-1}}{n} x^n, \quad \frac{x}{e^x - 1} = 1 - \frac{x}{2} + \sum_{n=1}^{\infty} B_{2n} \frac{x^{2n}}{(2n)!},$$

$$x \cot x = \sum_{n=0}^{\infty} (-1)^n B_{2n} \frac{(2x)^{2n}}{(2n)!}, \quad \zeta(s) = \sum_{n=1}^{\infty} \frac{1}{n^s}, \quad \zeta(2n) = (-1)^{n-1} \frac{(2\pi)^{2n}}{2(2n)!} B_{2n}.$$

If $f(z)$ has poles at z_n with respective residues b_n,

$$f(z) = f(0) + \sum_n b_n \left(\frac{1}{z - z_n} + \frac{1}{z_n} \right), \quad \cot \pi z = \frac{1}{z} + \sum_{n=1}^{\infty} \left(\frac{1}{z - n} + \frac{1}{z + n} \right),$$

$$\frac{f'(z)}{f(z)} = \frac{f'(0)}{f(0)} + \sum_n \left(\frac{1}{z - z_n} + \frac{1}{z_n} \right), \quad f(z) = f(0) \, e^{z f'(0)/f(0)} \prod_n \left(1 - \frac{z}{z_n} \right) e^{z/z_n},$$

$$\frac{\pi^2}{\sin^2 \pi z} = \sum_{n=-\infty}^{\infty} \frac{1}{(z-n)^2}, \quad \sin \pi z = \pi z \prod_{n=1}^{\infty} \left(1 - \frac{z^2}{n^2} \right),$$

$$\Gamma(z) = \int_0^{\infty} e^{-t} t^{z-1} \, dt, \quad \frac{1}{\Gamma(z)} = z \, e^{\gamma z} \prod_{n=1}^{\infty} \left(1 + \frac{z}{n} \right) e^{-z/n},$$

$$\frac{\Gamma'(z+1)}{\Gamma(z+1)} = -\gamma + \sum_{n=1}^{\infty} \left(\frac{1}{n} - \frac{1}{z+n} \right),$$

$$e^{iz} = e^{-y}(\cos x + i \sin x), \quad \ln z = \ln |z| + i(\arg z + 2\pi n),$$

$$e^{(x/2)(t - 1/t)} = \sum_{n=-\infty}^{\infty} J_n(x) \, t^n, \quad J_\nu(x) = \sum_{n=0}^{\infty} \frac{(-1)^n}{n! \, \Gamma(\nu + n + 1)} \left(\frac{x}{2} \right)^{\nu + 2n},$$

$$(1 - 2xt + t^2)^{-1/2} = \sum_{l=0}^{\infty} P_l(x) \, t^l, \quad P_l(x) = \frac{1}{2^l \, l!} \left(\frac{d}{dx} \right)^l (x^2 - 1)^l,$$

$$\int_{-1}^{1} P_\mu(x) \, P_\nu(x) \, dx = \frac{2\delta_{\mu\nu}}{2\mu + 1},$$

$$e^{i\mathbf{k} \cdot \mathbf{r}} = 4\pi \sum_{l=0}^{\infty} i^l j_l(kr) \sum_{m=-l}^{l} Y_l^m(\theta_k, \varphi_k)^* \, Y_l^m(\theta_r, \varphi_r),$$

$$e^{-t^2+2tx} = \sum_{n=0}^{\infty} H_n(x)\,\frac{t^n}{n!}\,, \qquad H_n(x) = (-1)^n\, e^{x^2}\left(\frac{d}{dx}\right)^n e^{-x^2}\,,$$

$$\frac{e^{-xt/(1-t)}}{1-t} = \sum_{n=0}^{\infty} L_n(x)\,t^n\,, \qquad L_n(x) = \frac{e^x}{n!}\left(\frac{d}{dx}\right)^n (x^n\,e^{-x})\,,$$

$$\int_{-\infty}^{\infty} H_m(x)H_n(x)\,e^{-x^2}\,dx = 2^n\pi^{1/2}n!\,\delta_{mn}\,, \qquad \int_0^{\infty} L_m(x)L_n(x)\,e^{-x}\,dx = \delta_{mn}$$

Fourier Series

$$f(x) = \frac{a_0}{2} + \sum_{n=1}^{\infty}(a_n\cos nx + b_n\sin nx)\,,$$

$$a_n = \frac{1}{\pi}\int_0^{2\pi} f(x)\cos nx\,dx\,, \qquad b_n = \frac{1}{\pi}\int_0^{2\pi} f(x)\sin nx\,dx$$

Integral Transforms

$$F(\omega) = \frac{1}{\sqrt{2\pi}}\int_{-\infty}^{\infty} f(t)e^{i\omega t}dt\,, \qquad f(t) = \frac{1}{\sqrt{2\pi}}\int_{-\infty}^{\infty} F(\omega)e^{-i\omega t}d\omega$$

$$\int_{-\infty}^{\infty} F(\omega)G^*(\omega)\,d\omega = \int_{-\infty}^{\infty} f(t)g^*(t)\,dt\,, \qquad \int_{-\infty}^{\infty} g(y)f(x-y)\,dy = \int_{-\infty}^{\infty} F(\omega)G(\omega)e^{-i\omega x}d\omega$$

$$\frac{1}{4\pi r} = \frac{1}{(2\pi)^3}\int \frac{e^{i\mathbf{k}\cdot\mathbf{r}}}{k^2}\,d^3k\,, \qquad \frac{e^{-mr}}{4\pi r} = \frac{1}{(2\pi)^3}\int \frac{e^{i\mathbf{k}\cdot\mathbf{r}}}{k^2+m^2}\,d^3k$$

Green's Function

$$\nabla^2 V = -\frac{\rho}{\varepsilon_0}\,, \qquad V(\mathbf{r}) = \frac{1}{4\pi\varepsilon_0}\int \frac{\rho(\mathbf{r}')d^3r'}{|\mathbf{r}-\mathbf{r}'|}$$

Greek Alphabet

Alpha	A	α	Nu	N	ν
Beta	B	β	Xi	Ξ	ξ
Gamma	Γ	γ	Omicron	O	o
Delta	Δ	δ	Pi	Π	π
Epsilon	E	ϵ, ε	Rho	P	ρ
Zeta	Z	ζ	Sigma	Σ	σ
Eta	H	η	Tau	T	τ
Theta	Θ	θ	Upsilon	Υ	υ
Iota	I	ι	Phi	Φ	ϕ, φ
Kappa	K	κ	Chi	X	χ
Lambda	Λ	λ	Psi	Ψ	ψ
Mu	M	μ	Omega	Ω	ω